D1361684

Multicultural Projects Index

Multicultural Projects Index

Things to Make and Do to Celebrate Festivals, Cultures, and Holidays Around the World

Second Edition

Mary Anne Pilger

1998
Libraries Unlimited, Inc.
Englewood, Colorado

LIBRARIES UNLIMITED, INC.
P. O. Box 6633
Englewood, CO 80155-6633
1-800-237-6124
www.lu.com

Library of Congress Cataloging-in-Publication Data

Pilger, Mary Anne.
    Multicultural projects index : things to make and do to celebrate
festivals, cultures, and holidays around the world / Mary Anne
Pilger. -- 2nd ed.
        x, 358 p. 22x28 cm.
        Includes bibliographical references and index.
        ISBN 1-56308-524-0
        1. Multicultural education--Activity programs--Indexes.
    2. Festivals--Indexes. 3. Handicrafts--Indexes. 4. Games--Indexes.
    I. Title.
    Z5814.M86P55 1998
    [LC1099]
    016.370117--dc21   89-4445
                                                                          CIP

Contents

Dedication

I dedicate this book to my son, Charles D. Pilger, who gives me his love and care, and appreciation for what I am doing. His marvelous intellect, depth of knowledge, his insistence that one always do their very best, have inspired me and made me better than I am.

Acknowledgements

I thank Mary Ann Still for her marvelous sense of humor, her wonderful mind, her attention to detail, and most of all, her typing and word processing skills that brought the large amount of data in this book together. And my dogs, who love her dearly, thank her too.

Introduction

Crafts or handicrafts, those things we create in our minds and make with our hands, have been the visible proof of humankind's existence on our Earth; the visible demonstrations of cultures, now and in the past; the visible proof of humankind's struggle to find its very reason for being; the visible proof that humans and their cultures are different and unique from others.

The drive to create, to make, is inherent to human interpretation of the world. Human creations, crafts, or handicrafts give us a window to observe lives we cannot live or know. Our fragile existence on this Earth is measured by what we create, what we do with what we have; and these creations leave a historical record for all to observe and interpret.

People, in their uniqueness, in their differences, and in their similarities, are what make the world's peoples so special to one another. Before people can live in peace, there must be understanding, understanding that geography determines how they live and that their culture—their ethnic being—evolves from their need for survival and their need for self-expression. Adaptation to one's environment means providing food, clothing, and shelter. Adaptation to one's personal environment means providing customs for personal growth and creativity. Spiritual and family customs, language and speaking customs, music and dance customs, festival and holiday customs, folklore and games customs—these customs, from the most primitive tribes to our most sophisticated nations, are what make us the same ... and different.

I do not live in a house built on stilts to protect me from wild snakes and animals, maybe you do; I do not drink yak milk for breakfast, maybe you do; I do not go out in a raging blizzard to feed my dogs, maybe you do; I do not pound and grind corn for my dinner, maybe you do; we all do many things in many different ways.

It is my hope that this index to multicultural handicrafts, foods, games, and activities will be used by educators at all levels to assist children and young adults to find the information they need to make something from the cultures of the world. The rewards of learning about the culture of one's own heritage as well as that of others can only result in a world family of peace, love, and true understanding.

Books in this index span the years from the late 1940s to the 1990s. They represent a vast storehouse of knowledge and information about world cultures and their handicrafts. Each author is an artist bringing to their book an intensity and view based on their own personal inspiration to write their book about a particular handicraft from a particular culture or cultures. None of us can duplicate the approach of these authors. They have written from their own intense desire based on their talents or love of someone in their past who shared their love of crafts with them. And these authors come and go over the years, but they give to us and leave with us their special uniqueness in their books.

Books celebrating the Bicentennial of our country were published in the 1970s to give educators and their students access to information about our history, people, and culture. Today, in 1998, we are still using these books, published twenty years ago, as reference works for information we cannot find anywhere else. I urge all of you to hang onto your craft books that represent the cultures of all of us. No craft book is ever out of date, and this information may not pass this way again.

We know not which child will take the spark and ignite the fire of creativity. We can only lead them.

I trust my book will make the task of finding that special item an easier and more fruitful quest.

Key to Index

The Index is arranged in the following order:

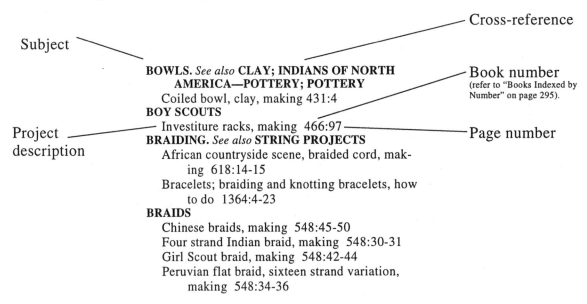

Subject

Cross-reference

Book number
(refer to "Books Indexed by Number" on page 295).

Project description

Page number

BOWLS. *See also* **CLAY; INDIANS OF NORTH AMERICA—POTTERY; POTTERY**
  Coiled bowl, clay, making 431:4
BOY SCOUTS
  Investiture racks, making 466:97
BRAIDING. *See also* **STRING PROJECTS**
  African countryside scene, braided cord, making 618:14-15
  Bracelets; braiding and knotting bracelets, how to do 1364:4-23
BRAIDS
  Chinese braids, making 548:45-50
  Four strand Indian braid, making 548:30-31
  Girl Scout braid, making 548:42-44
  Peruvian flat braid, sixteen strand variation, making 548:34-36

After finding a project of interest, check the book number in "Books Indexed by Number," page 295, to find the author, title, and publication data for the book in which the project is printed.

A

AARON, HENRY
Fun with baseball, activity 1199:32
ABACUS
Abacus beads information 301:63-71
ABORIGINES—BOOMERANGS
Boomerang, cardboard, pattern, making 1213:143
Boomerangs, ruler, making 1320:54
Homemade boomerang that comes back to you, making 1719:72-75
ABORIGINES—HANDICRAFTS
Aboriginal dream maps, paper, watercolors, making 1338:107-108
Computer project: Paint aboriginal dream time picture 1218:68-71
ABORIGINES—MUSICAL INSTRUMENTS
Didgeridoo instrument, long cardboard tube, colored paper, paints, making 1288:34; 1622:9
ABORIGINES—PAINTINGS
Aboriginal bark paintings, paper, colored pencils, making 1338:104-106
Aboriginal painting, brown paper, crayons, making 1478:100-101
ABORIGINES—STRING FIGURES
House 1404:110-114
ACHILLES
Achilles costume, making 213:38-40
ADAMS, ADRIENNE
"Easter Egg Artists," decorating egg activities, how to do 843:31-32
"Woggle of Witches," peanut butter yummies, recipe 843:57-58,129
ADDITIVES. *See also* **FOOD—JUNK FOOD**
List of common food additives 664:172-179
ADINKRA CLOTH. *See* **AFRICA, WEST— HANDICRAFTS**
ADVENT
Advent balloon, making 554:76-77
Advent banner, fabric, felt, and appliqué, making 595:1-7
Advent calendar from Christmas cards, making 669:158-163
Advent calendar, box, candies, making 1477:131
Advent calendar, egg cartons, paper, yarn, making 1568:8-9
Advent calendar, evergreens, making 1080:6-7
Advent calendar, making 273:41-45; 698:97; 795:11; 795:31; 916:83-85
Advent calendar, paper chain loops, making 909:131
Advent calendar, paper, paints, making 1485:19
Advent calendar, patterns, making 134:30; 150:20-29
Advent calendar, posterboard, pictures, making 1717:40-41
Advent candle holder, wooden board, pine cones, making 1301:93
Advent curiosity box, making 1277:26-27
Advent jigsaw puzzle, making 554:72-73
Advent wreath from cereal, food dye, making 1286:104-105
Advent wreath, clay, recipe given, making 595:9-13
Advent wreath, evergreens, making 725:13-14
Advent wreath, making 134:106; 218:68-69; 497:68-69; 672:1-15; 709:78-79; 897:18
Advent wreath, styrofoam base, candles, greenery, how to make 1393:89

Advent, the coming of Jesus Christ, activities and projects for classrooms 1393:82-87
Austrian Advent wreath, evergreens, making 704:79
Calendar, cookie tree, puzzle blocks, treat tree, wooden, making 1049:13
Calendar, making 1023:33
Crown candle wreath, glitter stars, tinsel dome, wood and paper, making 1049:13
History and celebration of Advent 496:102-103
Holly Advent wreath, patterns, felt, making 150:32-33
Sun Advent calendar, paper, making 553:18-19
Swedish Advent calendar, making 795:57
Tree of Life Advent calendar, making 795:82-83
Tree shaped Advent calendar, cardboard, tiny treats, making 1557:4-5
Wreath, Danish cake Advent wreath, recipe 1023:85-88
Wreath, evergreen Advent wreath, Scandinavian, making 795:52-53
Wreath, newspaper, making 1023:25-28
Wreath, Norwegian straw, making 1023:29
Wreath, styrofoam, making 1023:28
Wreath, wire frame, making 1023:29
Wreaths, plastic lids and play dough, making 909:131
AESOP—COOKERY
Aesop's fabled chicken, recipe 365:58
"Town Mouse and the Country Mouse"; Town Mouse's banana split, recipe, make 365:44
AESOP. *See also* **FABLES**
AFGHANISTAN—COOKERY
Abdul's kebabs, recipe 793:60
Bonjan Borani, eggplant and yogurt casserole, recipe 1165:159-160
Eggplant with meat and tomato sauce, recipe 1173:80-81
Pilau, rice casserole, recipe 1165:160
Pudding, Firni cornstarch pudding, recipe 1173:81-82
Rice with carrots and raisins, recipe 1173:79-80
Yakhni pilau, mutton, rice, peppers, tomatoes, yogurt and spices, recipe 1168:121
AFGHANISTAN—COSTUMES
Afghanistan costumes drawing 988:57
AFGHANISTAN—FESTIVALS—COOKERY
Shab-Barat; Chutni Gashneetch (cilantro chutney), recipe 1666:156
Shab-Barat; Pakaura (golden potato coins), recipe 1666:155-156
Shab-Barat; Sheer Payra (cardamom candy), recipe 1666:156
AFGHANISTAN—FESTIVALS—DECORATIONS
Noruz pop-up card, making 1387:50-51
AFGHANISTAN—GAMES
Doorkee per game, how to play 1355:29
Egg jousting game, how to play 956:32-33; 1507:26
Mirbadakan ball game 515:112
Tug of war game, how to play 1507:27
AFRICA
Activities, flags, games, songs, dances, recipes 1381:131-156
AFRICA—ANIMALS
Blown egg animals, hippo, zebra, white rhino, making 677:25
Blown egg animals, mandril, gemsbok, lion, giraffe, elephant, making 677:24
AFRICA—BANTU—STRING FIGURES
String trick 372:14-15

AFRICA—BEADS
African trade-wind beads information 301:21-27
Trade-bead necklace, making 301:87-89
AFRICA—BIRTHDAYS
First birthday celebrations in Africa 472:48
AFRICA—BUSHMEN—GAMES
Stalking game 956:12
AFRICA—CHRISTMAS
Traditional Christmas customs in Africa 218:46-47
AFRICA—CHRISTMAS—HANDICRAFTS
Adinkira stamping, making 795:23
Wrapping paper for Christmas, African Doodle paper, making 795:22
AFRICA—CLOTH
Dashiki cloth, making 1022:21-23
AFRICA—CLOTHING
N'Debele clothing, making 222:56-57
AFRICA—CLOTHING
Dance skirt, making 574:43
Dashiki, making 251:48-49; 574:43
Kente, making 574:43
AFRICA—COOKERY
African meatballs, recipe 1653:99-100
Akara, recipe 622:24
Banana fritters, recipe 1022:47
Bidia, recipe 335:24
Chapatis, recipe 622:18
Chocolate pudding, recipe 574:45
Choroko sauce, recipe 622:30
Coconut millet pudding, recipe 88:211
Egusi soup, recipe 622:29
Fish pepper soup, recipe 622:28
Fish, steamed, recipe 622:32
Fruit salad, recipe 622:25
Fufu, recipe 335:22; 622:18
Ginger beer, recipe 335:42
Ginger root beer, recipe 1694:37
Greens with coconut milk, recipe 622:26
Ground nut sauce, recipe 622:31
History of cookery in 88:201-207
Hot chocolate, recipe 574:45
Joll of rice, recipe 335:39; 622:35; 1694:20
Lemon grass drink, recipe 335:45
Luku, recipe 622:38
Meat curry, recipe 622:40
Meat on a stick, recipe 622:21
Milk and honey, recipe 574:45
Millet cereal, recipe 88:208
Peanut butter soup 384:25
Peanut butter stew, recipe 1694:23
Peanut cookies, recipe 335:36
Peanut soup, recipe 1321:149-150
Peanut stew, recipe 335:27; 574:44
Plantain, baked on the shell, recipe 622:41
Plantain, recipe 622:26
Rice pancakes, recipe 622:20
Sahara fruit shake, recipe 1653:12
Samusas, recipe 622:23
Sesame rice, recipe 1721:26
Spiced red beans, recipe 335:19
Spicy meat cubes, recipe 1694:21
Spinach stew, recipe 622:36
Sweet balls, recipe 622:43
Tapioca fruit soup, recipe 574:44
Ugali millet, recipe 88:210

Upside-down banana gingerbread, recipe 1694:36
Vegetable casserole, recipe 622:34
Vermicelli and raisins, recipe 622:42
Yam balls, recipe 335:31
Yams, recipe 574:55
AFRICA—COSTUMES
African man and woman costumes 213:144-145
Grass skirt, crepe paper, making 7:38-39
Primitive African costumes drawing 988:35
Witch Doctor costume 213:26-28
AFRICA—DESIGNS
Traditional African designs 1022:8-38
AFRICA—DOLLS
Warrior doll, felt, stuffed, patterns, making 487:29
AFRICA—FESTIVALS
Egungun Festival celebration 566:40-41
Harvest May Day celebration 631:76
Independence Day celebrations 566:41
Rain-making festivals 419:89-90
Sowing and harvest celebrations 419:80-90
Yam Festival celebration 566:41
AFRICA—FESTIVALS—PUPPETS
Harvest Festival leopard mask, paper plate, making 1083:172
Harvest Festival puppet projects, patterns, scenes, story starters 1083:172
AFRICA—FOLKLORE
"Ashanti to Zulu"; physical and human geography activities 1458:96-99
Bojabi Tree, Robin Rat, King Leo, Pinky Pig, Giddy Goat, Tommy Tortoise, masks, patterns 1206:6-13
Cendrars, Blaise, "Shadows"; science, reading, art, language activities 1055:174-177
"Fearsome Beast" flannel board Masai tale, patterns, making 1603:105-111
Haley, Gail E., "A Story A Story," reading, writing, thinking activities 1093:172-181
Heart of a monkey fable playlet 1212:49-52
Law of the jungle fable playlet 1212:59-65
Leopard's Drum flannel board patterns, making 910:33,72
Oh, Kojo! How Could You!, River Spirit, dog, cat, Kojo, mother, Anase puppets, patterns 1206:14-19
"Uwungelema" flannel board story, patterns, making 1603:152-157
"Who's in Rabbit's House?," activities, books, crafts, masks, patterns, making 1159:41-47
AFRICA—GAMES
African finger counting game 956:84-85
African Kahla or Wari game 1354:164
African string puzzle game, how to make 1074:267
Beans, stones or marbles, how to play 1534:8-9
Big Snake, Da Ga game 1354:159
Blindman's buff 383:15
Bola game 474:40
Carrying baskets 474:51
Catch the Tail game, how to play 1354:158
Cattle stockade 383:16
Data, making 921:5-6
Game trap 383:18
Go tell Aunt Nancy chanting game 1118:36-38
Handball 383:17
Hen and wildcat 383:16
Hus game, how to make 1074:24-25

Jarabadach 383:18-19
Jumping the Beanbag game 1354:159
Lion and deer tag 383:17
Mancala board game, patterns, making 1541:109-114
Mancala game, how to make and play, tray, paint, stones, dried beans 1256:29
Mancala game, making from egg carton 677:32
Mankala, African board game, egg carton, making 1022:18-20
Match my feet rhythm game 979:20
Mulawbilwa 383:15
Nsikwi 383:16
Oware game, how to make 856:132-134
Simon says 383:17
Spot the lion game 1078:30
Taboo game 474:53
Wari board game, egg carton, glue, how to make 1534:48
Wari game 956:85-87
Wari game, how to make 1074:20-23
Yote game 956:129

AFRICA—HAIRSTYLES
Cornrowing, how to do 251:85
Create hair style called Onigi (sticks), how to thread your hair 1537:39

AFRICA—HAND DECORATIONS
Decorate your hands with mehndi, how to do 1537:30

AFRICA—HANDICRAFTS
African countryside scene, braided cord, making 618:14-15
African figure from paper straws, making 828:81
African lion bank, juice can, paper, patterns, making 1286:29-30
Bookmarks, creepy creatures, buttons and paper, making 1022:28-29
Calabash, papier-mache, African calabash designs given, making 1633:102-105
Gold weights, making 222:18-19
Grigri, African Good Luck charm, cardboard, making 1022:38-39
Walking stick, wooden, making 525:29

AFRICA—HATS
Kufi round hat, paper, patterns, making 1633:94-95

AFRICA—HEADDRESSES
Headdress, making 574:43
Senufo bird headdress, making 222:48-49

AFRICA—HOUSES
African hut from blown egg, making 677:18
Houses from Africa, paper and straw models, making 1094:5
N'Debele house, making 222:20-22

AFRICA—JEWELRY
Anklets, bracelets, necklaces, pasta, string, paints, making 1648:39
Beads, clay dough, making 1022:16
Necklace, African button necklace, patterns, making 1016:155-159
Pendants, Ashanti, Baule, Bapende, making 222:62-63

AFRICA—LANGUAGES
Akan tribal names from days of week for boys and girls 1022:43
Greetings of Africa 601:40-41
Numbers one to ten in Swahili language 390:unp
Swahili words 574:50

AFRICA—MASKS
African lion mask, making 925:59-60

African mask carved wood plaque, making 382:54
African mask for Halloween, pattern, making, 1016:193-198
African masks, paper, decorations, making 204:81-85; 1618:44-46
African wall mask, corrugated cardboard, shoe polish, making 1706:9
Animal head mask, patterns, making 1654:12
Bobo mask, making 222:42-43
Decorative mask from beans and nuts, making 623:9-11
Dogon mask, rabbit and antelope masks, making 222:50-52
Double face mask, making 811:73
Elephant mask, paper bag, gray paint, making 1486:18-19
Foil wall masks, aluminum foil, patterns, making 1633:96-97
History of African masks 204:17-25
Human face mask, patterns, making 1654:11
Lion mask, making 925:59-60
Lion mask, papier-mache, making 1447:6-7
Lion nose mask, paper, tongue depressor, making 1633:100-101
Spirit mini-masks, salt dough, full-size patterns, making 1633:98-99
Tribal masks, newspaper, glue, patterns making 1393:137

AFRICA—MONEY
Money, making 222:16-17

AFRICA—MUSICAL INSTRUMENTS
Baule drum, making 222:30
Drum, making 297:204-205
Lyre, balloon, newspapers, glue, sticks, making 1310:50-51
Thumb piano or sanza piano, wood, varnish, paints, making 1728:22-23
Xylophone, glass bottles, mallets, making 1728:26-27
Zither, tube zither from plastic bottle, strings, making 1514:28

AFRICA—NAMES
Baby names information 695:122
Naming Days information 695:12-23

AFRICA—NEW YEAR'S DAY
Celebration of Now Year's Day in Africa 475:100

AFRICA—PUPPETS
African Plains animal puppets, patterns, making 463:17-26

AFRICA—PYGMIES—GAMES
Catching stars game 956:9

AFRICA—RHYMES
Pao Pao Pao tickling rhyme 780:98

AFRICA—RIDDLES
Selection of African riddles 1161:100

AFRICA—RITUALS
Growing up ritual 695:83-88

AFRICA—SHIELDS
Masai and Zulu shields, making 222:60-61

AFRICA—STORIES USING MUSICAL INSTRUMENTS
Lion on the Path thumb-piano story, how to do 1161:104-106
Rabbit and Hyena Play, the sanza thumb-piano story, how to do 1161:107-110

AFRICA—WEAPONS
Spear, cardboard tubes, patterns, making 1311:134

AFRICA, CENTRAL—CHRISTMAS—COOKERY
Greens and rice, recipe 1666:23
AFRICA, CENTRAL—GAMES
Achi game, patterns, making 1541:37-39
Mankala game, making 519:56-58
Nine Men's Morris game, patterns, making 1541:30-34
Six Men's Morris game, patterns, making 1541:34-36
Three Men's Morris game, patterns, making 1541:34-36
AFRICA, CENTRAL—SCULPTURE
Mangbetu portrait water pot, making 519:53-55
Mintadi sculpture, making 519:51-52
AFRICA, CENTRAL—STRING FIGURES
Camp bed string 372:16-17
AFRICA, EAST—BASKETS
Tutsi basket, woven paper or paper rope, making
1632:34-39
AFRICA, EAST—COOKERY
Baked plantain on the shell, recipe 1198:46
Chapatis, flour, oil, water, recipe 1333:73
Ground nut sauce, recipe 1652:40-41
Meat dish with curry, recipe 1198:38
Railway tea, recipe 1694:39
Steamed papaya, recipe 1452:6
AFRICA, EAST—DYES
Dyes, plant, making 519:16-17
AFRICA, EAST—FANS
Fans, making 519:13
AFRICA, EAST—FLY WHISKS
Fly whisks, making 519:12
AFRICA, EAST—GAMES
Ebenga game 474:44
Mankala game, dried beans, egg carton, how to make
1393:114; 1508:154-156
Ohora game, dried beans, egg carton, how to make
1393:114
Owara game, dried beans, egg carton, how to make
1393:114
AFRICA, EAST—HOUSEHOLD
Calabash kitchen ware, making 519:811
AFRICA, EAST—HOUSES
Bemba huts 469:48-51
Masai huts 469:46-47
AFRICA, EAST—LANGUAGE
Swahili counting book; one to ten with East African cul-
ture explanations 289:unp
Swahili language; 24 words with East African culture ex-
planations 288:unp
AFRICA, EAST—MATS
Nubian mat, making 519:14-15
AFRICA, NORTH—COOKERY
Chicken soup, recipe 446:27-28
Coucous tagine, recipe 88:42-43
Coucous, recipe 88:40-41; 1585:14-15
Date syrup, recipe 1189:47
Hais trail mix, recipe 1350:84-85
Meat roll and egg croquettes, recipe 662:71-75
AFRICA, NORTH—COSTUMES
North African costumes drawing 988:59
AFRICA, NORTH—FESTIVALS—COOKERY
Aid-es-Seghir; Harira Souiria (Ramadan soup), recipe
1666:41
AFRICA, NORTH—GAMES
Dara board game, patterns, making 1541:158-159
Mancala game, making 1507:20-21
Seega board game, patterns, making 1541:161-166

Wari game, how to make and play 1654:15
AFRICA, NORTH—HANDICRAFTS
Leather cushion, making 519:19-21
AFRICA, NORTH—HOUSES
Adobe houses 469:52-53
Desert tents 469:44-45
AFRICA, NORTH—JEWELRY
Grigri amulet, making 519:22-23
Zeriref and Bezima silver jewelry, making 519:24-26
AFRICA, NORTH—OASIS
Oasis from North Africa, paper model, making 1094:45
AFRICA, NORTH—WEAVING
Weaving with palm leaves, making 1189:46
AFRICA, SOUTH. *See also* **SOUTH AFRICA**
AFRICA, SOUTH—COOKERY
Karkelinge, figure eight cookies, recipe 1452:7
AFRICA, SOUTH—GAMES
Mankala game, dried beans, egg carton, how to make
1393:114
Ohora game, dried beans, egg carton, how to make
1393:114
AFRICA, WEST—BASKETS
Basket making, paper cup, raffia, making 1427:289
AFRICA, WEST—BEADS
West African beads information 301:37-43
AFRICA, WEST—CLOTH
Adinkera, the saying Goodbye cloth, making 519:42-44
Adire Eleso, tie-dyed cloth, making 519:45-46
AFRICA, WEST—CLOTHING
Boy's dashiki, making 519:49
Dashiki African shirt, pattern, how to make 1333:85
Dress up clothes, making 519:47-49
Girl's Lapa and Gele, boy's dashiki, making 1427:292
Girl's lapa and gele, making 519:48
Paper dashikis, making 1333:85
AFRICA, WEST—COOKERY. *See also* **GHANA—
COOKERY**
Akara (black-eyed pea fritters), recipe 1427:298-299
Baked plantain on the shell, recipe 1198:46
Banana fritters, recipe 1427:299; 1452:2
Blackberry surprise, recipe 1662:100
Cassava chips, recipe 1427:299
Fried plantain (banana fingers), recipe 1427:299
Fruit salad, recipe 1359:33
Fufu (Cassava balls), recipe 1427:300
Fufu yam dish, recipe 1359:38-39, 1452:3
Ginger fried fish, recipe 1359:42-43
Ground nut stew, recipe 88:208-209; 1359:36-37
Ground nut sauce, recipe 1652:40-41
Joll of rice, recipe 1359:40-41
Kanya sweet meat, recipe 1321:144
Kanyan candy, recipe 1333:85
Kili wili banana or plantain dish, recipe 1359:34-35
Millet porridge, recipe 1359:32
Paw paw and lime, recipe 1359:44
Pick-a-pepper soup, recipe 1198:30; 1650:24
Spiced okra, recipe 1452:4
Sweet potato-peanut butter tarts, recipe 1662:101
West African ginger ale, recipe 1662:98
Yam soup, recipe 659:112
AFRICA, WEST—DOLLS
Akuaba dolls, clay or play dough, making 1427:287
Akuaba doll, making 519:38-39
AFRICA, WEST—FANS
Fans, raffia, straw, sticks, making 1427:292

AFRICA, WEST—FESTIVALS
Harvest Festivals Dogon dancers 826:4-5
AFRICA, WEST—FESTIVALS—COOKERY
Yam Festival, candied yams, recipe 1401:51
AFRICA, WEST—FOLKLORE
"Anansi and the Rock" flannel board story, patterns, making 1604:46-48
"Why Do Monkeys Live in Trees?" flannel board story, patterns, making 1604:111-113
AFRICA, WEST—FOLKLORE—PUPPETS
"All Stories Belong to Anansi" shadow puppets, patterns, making 1602:178-187
"Crocodile and the Hen" shadow puppets, patterns, making 1602:86-91
AFRICA, WEST—GAMES
Haba Gaba game 1146:34-35
Mancala, how to play 1499:35-37
Mankala game, dried beans, egg carton, how to make 1393:114
Ohora game, dried beans, egg carton, how to make 1393:114; 1508:154-156
Oware or Star Play, egg carton, seeds, beans, marbles, making 1427:305-306
Wari board game, patterns, making 1541:115-118
Yote game, how to make 1074:90-91; 1507:23-24
AFRICA, WEST—HANDICRAFTS
Adinkra symbols printed on fabrics, how to do 1654:12-14
Adinkra symbols, making 1427:291
Adire, tie-dye shirt, fabric, dyes, making 1338:56-58
Akan culture Adinkra fabric designs, how to make 1654:12-14
Batik, Adinkra cloth, crayons, making 1427:290
Batik, Adire eleko cloth, flour paste, watercolors, making 1619:40-45
Bowl, papier-mache bowl, paste, recipe, paints, making 1427:297
Computer project: painted walls in houses 1218:40-43
Royal stool, making 519:35-37
AFRICA, WEST—HEADDRESSES
Chi Wara dance headdress, making, 519:33-34
AFRICA, WEST—MASKS
Masks, paper bags, paints, making 1427:295
AFRICA, WEST—MUSICAL INSTRUMENTS
Kora instrument, making 519:28-31
AFRICA, WEST—NAMES
Akan names 519:38-39
Akan names for boys' and girls' stationery, paper, making 1022:42-43
AFRICA, WEST—PUPPET PLAYS
Anansi Finds a Fool 4:41-47
AFRICAN SLAVES—COOKERY
Baked ham, recipe 1449:39
Baked rabbit, recipe 1449:17
Barbecued spareribs, recipe 1449:36
Corn pudding, recipe 1449:14
Creole gumbo, recipe 1449:23
Fried squirrel and tomato sauce, recipe 1449:18
Ham hocks, turnip and mustard greens, recipe 1449:42
Hoecakes, cornmeal, salt, water, recipe 1449:14
Hopping John, peas and rice dish, recipe 1449:42
Sweet potato pie, recipe 1449:39
AFRO-AMERICANS
Culture unit, language, dress, foods, games, bibliographies 574:40-65

Marian Anderson's birthday, sing a spiritual song 1199:49
AFRO-AMERICANS—COOKERY
Ants-on-a-log, celery, raisins, peanut butter, recipe 1198:25
Baked ham, recipe 1449:39
Baked rabbit, recipe 1449:17
Banana pudding, recipe 574:56
Barbecued spareribs, recipe 1449:36
Biscuits, recipe 1414:71
Black-eyed peas, recipe 1414:73
Bread pudding, recipe 1414:76
Buttermilk biscuits, recipe 1162:12-13
Catfish; fried catfish strips, recipe 1414:77
Chicken shortcake, recipe 1162:30-31
Chitt'lins, recipe 574:56
Collard greens, recipe 574:56; 1162:32
Cornbread, recipe 574:57; 1162:33; 1414:72
Corn cobs, roasted, recipe 574:56
Corn pone, recipe 1414:72
Corn pudding, recipe 1162:18-19; 1449:14
Cornmeal and wheat cornbread, recipe 1198:27
Creole gumbo, recipe 1449:23
Deep-fried catfish, recipe 1198:33
Fresh mint tea, recipe 1414:70
Fried apples, recipe 1162:14
Fried fish, recipe 1162:22-23
Fried squirrel and tomato sauce, recipe 1449:18
Ham hocks, turnip and mustard greens, recipe 1449:42
Hoecakes, cornmeal, salt, water, recipe, making 1449:14
Home greens, recipe 1414:74
Hominy grits, recipe 1162:8-9
Hoppin' John, recipe 1162:20-21
Hopping John, black eyed peas, rice, ham, recipe 1198:35
Hopping John, peas and rice dish, recipe 1449:42
Hush puppies, recipe 1162:24-25; 1198:26
Ice cream, recipe 1414:77-78
Lemonade, recipe 1162:35
Peach cobbler, recipe 1162:36-37
Peanut butter and banana sandwich, recipe 1414:75
Peanut butter and vegetable sandwich, recipe 1414:75
Peanut butter, recipe 1414:75
Pork sausage and gravy, recipe 1162:10-11
Potato salad, recipe 1162:34
Pound cake, recipe 1162:38-39
Red beans and rice, recipe 1198:34
Red beans, recipe 574:56
Sassafras tea, recipe 1414:70
Scrambled eggs, recipe 1162:15
Shortbread, recipe 1162:40-41
Short'nin' bread, recipe 574:56
Snackin' cake, recipe 1414:78
Soul food, neck bones and beans, recipe 518:27-29
Sweet potato pie, recipe 1414:76-77; 1449:39
Sweet potato pone, recipe 1162:26-27
AFRO-AMERICANS—FESTIVALS. *See also* **KWANZAA**
Black History Month activity with famous names 1199:28-29
Black History Week finger plays, recipes, games 944:73-75
Kwanzaa celebration, activities, handicrafts, foods, songs 909:149-157
Kwanzaa holiday celebrations 1060:1-31

AFRO-AMERICANS—FOLKLORE

"Great Tug-o-War" flannel board story, patterns, making 1604:73-77

"Gunny Wolf" flannel board story, patterns, making 1201:100-104, 1603:75-79

AFRO-AMERICANS—FOLKLORE—PUPPETS

"Brer Rabbit and the Wonderful Tar-Baby" shadow puppets, patterns, making 1602:158-162

"Wait Till Emmet Comes" shadow puppets, patterns, making 1602:123-129

AFRO-AMERICANS—HANDICRAFTS

Andinkira clay pins, symbols given, making 1414:44-45

Andinkira prints on cloth, making 1414:45-46

Animal chains, paper, patterns, making 1163:16-17

Appliquéd pillow, fabric, stuffing, making 1163:28-29

Changeable pictures, making 1163:36-37

Cross-stitch bookmark, ribbon, cross-stitch canvas, pattern, making 1163:32-33

Drawstring bag, fabric, pattern, making 1163:30-31

Hobbyhorse, dowels, felt, paints, pattern, making 1163:24-25

Hooked rug, rug canvas, yarns, patterns, making 1163:6-7

Jacob's ladder, toy, wood blocks, paints, ribbon, making 1163:22-23

Jump Rope; rope, beads, making 1163:40

Revolving serpent, paper, making 1163:14-15

Shadow puppet, posterboard, paints, making 1163:20-21

Spatterwork picture, paper, paints, making 1163:8-9

Tangram, posterboard, paints, making 1163:38-39

Wallpaper box, box, wallpaper, making 1163:12-13

AFRO-AMERICANS—MUSICAL INSTRUMENTS

Banjo, making 626:74-77

Drum, coffee can, yarn, making 1414:47-48

Rattle, papier-mache, balloon, rice, making 1414:48-50

AFRO-AMERICANS—NEW YEAR'S DAY—COOKERY

Hoppin' John, black-eyed peas and rice, recipe 1716:121-122

AFRO-AMERICANS—PUPPET PLAYS

Brer Fox and Sis Goose 4:48-51

How Rabbit Lost His Fine Bushy Tail 4:52-55

AFRO-AMERICANS—SONGS

Mister Rabbit round song 1115:54

AIRPLANES

Wright Brothers birthday celebration; art, music, foods, games, activities 1104:114-117

AIRPLANES—WARPLANES

Avro Lancaster, English plane, paper model, making 404:26-31

Bell UH-1 Huey, United States plane, paper model, making 404:38-43

British Aerospace Harrier, paper model, making 404:32-37

Fokker Dr 1, German plane, paper model, making 404:8-13

General Dynamics F-111, United States Plane, paper model, making 404:62-64

Lockheed C-130 Hercules, United States plane, paper model, making 404:44-49

Lockheed P-38 Lightning, United States plane, paper model, making 404:21-25

McDonnell Douglas F-15 Eagle, United States plane, paper model, making 404:56-61

Messerschmitt Bf 109, German plane, paper model, making 404:14-16

Mikoyan Gurevich MiG-21, Russian plane, paper model, making 404:51-55

Sopwith Camel, English plane, paper model, making 404:5-7

Spitfire, English plane, paper model, making 404:17-20

ALABAMA—COOKERY

Fig dessert, recipe 654:4

Gumbo soup, recipe 654:3

Peanut-coconut jewels, recipe 654:2

ALABASTER

Imitation alabaster, recipe, making 767:77

ALADDIN AND THE WONDERFUL LAMP

Aladdin's jeweled fruit ambrosia, recipe 569:27-30

ALAMO

Siege of the Alamo, paper folds of story characters, how to cut 406:72-81

ALASKA. *See also* **ESKIMOS; INUIT INDIANS**

ALASKA—CHRISTMAS

Christmas customs in Alaska 1717:30-31

Eskimo Christmas celebration 601:150

ALASKA—COOKERY

Alaskan cranberry relish, recipe 1653:131

Baked Alaska, recipe 666:259

Candied rose hips, recipe 654:8-9

Food products in Alaska 666:257-258

Gold Rush Days in Alaska and the foods people ate 666:252-254

King Crab saute, recipe 666:258-259

Sourdough bread, recipe 492:16-17

Sourdough cookies, recipe 72:150-152

Sourdough pancakes, recipe 654:6-7

Sourdough starter, recipe 492:14-15

ALASKA—FESTIVALS

Eskimo-Indian Olympics, activities, handicrafts, foods, songs, making 909:149-157

ALASKA—GAMES

Ajagaak, how to play 1499:15

Alaskan Aratamiaqutat, how to play 1499:14

Alaskan Hopscotch, hopscotch game 1426:40-41

Eskimo Olympics 376:90

Eskimo sled games 376:91

Muk, silence game 376:91

Silence Muk game, how to play 1355:17

Spinning tops, Kaipsak, game 376:91

ALASKA—THANKSGIVING

Whale Harvest Festival celebration 659:95-96

ALBANIA—CHRISTMAS

Christmas celebration 601:101

ALBANIA—COOKERY

Chicken soup, recipe 895:12

Emator, puff pastry with nuts, recipe 1165:93

Nut cakes (karidopeta), cookies, recipe 72:62-63

Peppers, stuffed green, recipe 895:13-14

Sesame biscuits, recipe 1653:62

Tanabour, barley yogurt soup, recipe 1165:93

ALBANIA—COSTUMES

Albanian costumes drawing 988:43

ALBANIA—FESTIVALS—COOKERY

Eid al-Fitr; yogurt soup, recipe 1666:79

ALBANIA—GAMES

Varra, hopscotch game, how to play 1708:8-9

ALBANIA—LANGUAGE

Numbers 1-9 in Albanian 1708:9

ALCOTT, LOUISA MAY

"Little Women," descriptions and pictures of house 29:Chapter 3

"Little Women"; Jo's New England boiled dinner, recipe 570:45-47

ALCOTT, LOUISA MAY—COOKERY
"Little Women"; Amy's little cheese moons, recipe 365:51
Louisa May Alcott recipes 20:1-81

ALDEN, JOHN
Costume 213:30-32

ALGERIA—COOKERY
Algerian couscous, chicken stew, recipe 1165:49-50
Almond cookies in syrup (makroud el louse), cookies, recipe 72:86-88
Couscous, chicken stew, recipe 1022:44-45

ALGERIA—FESTIVALS—COOKERY
Aid-es-Seghir; chlada fakya (fresh fruit medley), recipe 1666:42
Aid-es-Seghir; fish with cumin, recipe 1666:41-42

ALGERIA—STRING FIGURES
Cock's Feet 1404:22-25

ALGONQUIN INDIANS. See also **WOODLAND INDIANS**

ALGONQUIN INDIANS—BASKETS
Basket, splint type, making 223:28-33

ALGONQUIN INDIANS—BEADWORK
Beadwork, making 223:69-71

ALGONQUIN INDIANS—CANOES
Canoes, birchbark, elm bark, dugout, making 223:22-23

ALGONQUIN INDIANS—CLOTHING
Head coverings, making 223:50

ALGONQUIN INDIANS—COOKERY
Foods eaten by Algonquins, squash recipe 223:24-25
Foods of the Algonquin Indians 666:56-59

ALGONQUIN INDIANS—COSTUMES
Costumes, making 223:48-49

ALGONQUIN INDIANS—FOOTWEAR
Moccasins, making 227:28-29

ALGONQUIN INDIANS—GAMES
Flip and guess sticks, paddle and weighted feathers, bowl toss, making 223:86-88

ALGONQUIN INDIANS—HANDICRAFTS
Health charm, making, 223:82-83
Love fetish, making 223:81-82
Moosehair embroidery, making 223:62-64

ALGONQUIN INDIANS—HOUSEHOLD
Birchbark containers, making 223:33-35
Pots, storage rack, hanging rack, making 223:21

ALGONQUIN INDIANS—HOUSES
Wigwam (wickiup), making 223:16-18

ALGONQUIN INDIANS—MASKS
False Face Society mask, making 223:73-76
Husk Face Society mask, making 223:76-78

ALGONQUIN INDIANS—MUSICAL INSTRUMENTS
Rattles, gourd type, making 223:78-80

ALGONQUIN INDIANS—PEACE PIPES
Peace pipe, miniature, making 223:84-85

ALGONQUIN INDIANS—QUILLWORK
Quillwork, making 223:65-69

ALGONQUIN INDIANS—STENCILS
Birchbark stencils, making 223:36-37

ALGONQUIN INDIANS—TOBOGGANS
Toboggan, Cree Trail, making 467:50

ALGONQUIN INDIANS—WAMPUM
Strings of wampum, macaroni, food coloring, string, making 1699:34-35
Wampum weaving with beads, making 223:58-62

ALGONQUIN INDIANS—WEAVING
Finger weaving a sash, making 223:56-57
Twined bag, woven, making 223:26-28

ALICE IN WONDERLAND
Alice in Wonderland, descriptions and pictures of house 29:Chapter 8
Alice in Wonderland, Mad Hatter, March Hare, Dormouse, fabric, patterns, 484:50-63
Queen of Heart's strawberry tarts, recipe 570:49-52

ALICE IN WONDERLAND—PARTIES
Mad Hatter tea party, menu and recipes, how to plan and give 86:120-127; 86:225-226
Queen of Hearts party, decorations, food, games, costumes, decorations, recipes 74:42-58; 354:32-46

ALIENS—PUPPETS
Alien puppets, dough, making 1372:64

ALIKI
"Corn Is Maize," popcorn, recipe 843:55, 129

ALL FOOLS' DAY. See **APRIL FOOLS' DAY**

ALL SAINTS' DAY
Activities and projects for classrooms 1393:67-68

ALL SOULS' DAY
Activities and projects for classrooms 1393:67-68
Celebrations around the world 504:52-53

ALPHABET
Activities, art, songs, recipes, games 1469:22-23

ALPHABETS—CUNEIFORM
Mysterious tablets, making 173:52-53

AMAZON RIVER. See also **RAIN FOREST**

AMAZON RIVER—DOLLS
Amazonian doll, making 182:74-77

AMAZON RIVER—HOUSES
Amazon River houses 469:32-33

AMAZON RIVER—JEWELRY
Jungle jewelry, pasta, seeds, paints, making 1488:14-15

AMAZON RIVER—PLANTS
Tropical plants, oranges, lemons, pineapples, how to grow 1488:10-11

AMERICAN INDIAN DAY—COSTUMES
Osceola costume, making 272:102-104
Sacagawea costume, making 272:99-102
Tecumseh costume, making 272:96-99

AMERICAN INDIAN DAY—GAMES
Comanche ball and darts 698:75
Feather grab game 698:77
Hand game 698:76
Lotto game 698:76
Omaha plum stone game 698:77
Pueblo squash blossoms game 698:75

AMERICAN INDIAN DAY—POTTERY
Clay pots and jars, making 698:74

AMERICAN INDIAN DAY—SAND PAINTING
Sand painting, making 698:74

AMERICAN INDIAN DAY—TOTEM POLES
Totem poles, making 698:75

AMISH—BUGGIES
Buggy, Amish family buggy, wooden model, making 568:135-144

AMISH—COOKERY
Bachelor hats, recipe 998:66
Baked corn, recipe 1340:62-63
Beef, cream and dried beef, recipe 1340:64-65
Bread soup, cold, recipe 1340:35
Bread, homemade, recipe 1340:18-21
Brown butter, recipe 1340:55

Candied sweet potatoes, recipe 1340:66-67
Caramel frosting, recipe 1340:60
Chicken corn soup, recipe 1340:30-33
Chicken pot pie, recipe 1340:68-69
Chocolate cake, recipe 1340:58-59
Dandelion salad, recipe 998:47
Eggs, sunny side up, recipe 1340:10-11
Fruit salad, recipe 1340:46-47
Ham, potatoes and green beans, recipe 1340:51
Lemonade, recipe 1340:26-27
Lunch pail food, recipes 1340:16-17
Macaroni with cheese and hamburger, recipe 1340:48-50
Mashed potatoes, recipe 1340:54-55
Meat loaf, recipe 1340:44-45
Peanut butter and molasses spread, recipe 1340:76
Pickles, sweet, recipe 1340:56-57
Pretzels, soft, recipe 1340:84-85
Rivels, little dough balls, recipe 1340:32
Roast beef and gravy, recipe 1340:52-53
Root beer, homemade, recipe 1340:82
Salad dressing, recipe 1340:42-43
Schnitz pie, recipe 1340:77-79
School picnics, recipes 1340:70
Shoofly cake, recipe 1340:14-15
Shoofly pie, recipe 998:53-54
Snow ice cream, recipe 1340:83
Strawberry jam, recipe 1340:40-41
Sugar cookies, recipe 1340:80-81
Sunday lunch, recipes 1340:73
Tomato soup, recipe 1340:34
Treats and snacks, recipes 1340:75
Vanilla pudding, recipe 1340:36
Wedding food, recipes 1340:74
Whoopie pies and filling, recipe 1340:22-25
Yeast bread, recipe 1340:18-21

AMISH—GAMES
Rooster fight game 998:76

AMUSEMENT PARKS
History of amusement parks 1153:51-56

ANCIENT CITIES
Compass, making 65:77-78
Imperial agriculture, making 65:79-88
Imperial artist (royal designs), making 65:65-72
Imperial Documents (official seal), making 65:24-28
Imperial odes, making 65:34-36
Law book, making 65:37-40
Legal documents (title deed), making 65:29-31
Maps, making 65:72-77
Peace treaty, making 65:32-34
Towers, making 65:9-15
Walls and buildings, making 65:16-24

ANCIENT NAVY
Flotilla, making 65:41-53

ANDERSEN, HANS CHRISTIAN
"Dance, Thumbelina, Dance," finger puppet, making 753:23
Hans Christian Andersen Fairy Tale Festival 474:27
"Little Mermaid" model, small can, yarn, making 1310:122-123
"Princess and the Pea" banner, making 470:57-61
"Princess and the Pea" glove puppet, making 753:55
"Princess and the Pea," flannel board patterns, making 1201:31-38
"Ugly Duckling," knitted, making 470:62-64
"Ugly Duckling," swan stick puppet, patterns 1206:26-29

ANDERSEN, HANS CHRISTIAN—COOKERY
"Emperor's New Clothes"; Emperor's new pudding, recipe 365:77
"Little Mermaid"; Little Mermaid tuna muffins, recipe 365:34
"Princess and the Pea"; Princess peas, recipe 365:72
"Steadfast Tin Soldier"; Steadfast Tin Soldier filets, recipe 365:68
"Thumbelina"; Thumbelina burgers, recipe 365:70

ANGELS
Floating angels, paper, glue, glitter, patterns, making 1429:44-45

ANGLO-SAXONS—HOUSES
Anglo-Saxon hall building, cardboard, newspaper, making 1183:16-17

ANGOLA
Activities, flags, games, songs, dances, recipes 1381:153-156

ANGOLA—COOKERY
Galina Muamba, Angolan chicken dish, recipe 1165:21

ANGOLA—FESTIVALS
Feast of Kapesi celebration 601:19
Feast of Nganja 601:17-18
Feast of Okambondondo celebration 601:18

ANGOLA—FESTIVALS—COOKERY
Family Day; nyeleng (peanut and beef gumbo), recipe 1666:20

ANGOLA—GAMES
Numbers game 602:21
What Is Big? game 602:18-20
Whistle for Me game 602:20

ANIMALS
Animals Around the World project, making 925:88-89
Songs, finger plays, stories, games, rhythms 1200:65-86

ANIMALS—WOOD CARVING
Hound, Mexican bull, cow, cat, honey bear, wood, carved, making 382:27-36

ANTARCTIC—ANIMALS
Penguin bookend, plastic bottle, sand, paint, making 1484:10-11

ANTARCTICA
Admiral Byrd birthday celebration; art, music, foods, games, activities 1104:10-13

ANTIGUA—SONGS
"Children, Children" 1607:38

ANTLERS—IMPLEMENTS
History of antlers as implements 229:39-42

APACHE INDIANS—COOKERY
Apache pumpkin with sunflower seeds, recipe 1527:25
Pumpkin seeds roasted, recipe 1315:22

APACHE INDIANS—DANCES
Apache Devil dance 465:82-83

APACHE INDIANS—FACE PAINTING
Apache face, making 1046:10-11

APACHE INDIANS—FOOTWEAR
Apache moccasins, making 359:117-124

APACHE INDIANS—GAMES
Hoop and pole game, how to play 1179:246
Moccasin game, how to play 1315:37
Shell dice game, how to play 1699:110
Throw sticks game, how to play 1699:107
Wooden dice game, how to play 1699:108

APACHE INDIANS—MASKS
Apache masks, making 327:45

APACHE INDIANS—MUSICAL INSTRUMENTS

Bull roarer, making 468:114

Dancing bells, making 468:58-59

Water drum, making 468:107

APACHE INDIANS—WAR BONNETS

Warbonnet cases, oatmeal box, making 1699:55

Warbonnets, paper, feathers, making 1699:53

APACHE INDIANS—WEAPONS

Quiver, making 227:45

APARTMENT BUILDINGS

Apartment building model, wood strips, cardboard, making 1512:28-29

APPALACHIA—FOLKLORE—PUPPET PLAYS

Sody Saleratus, puppets and puppet play script, making 1155:45-51

APPALACHIAN MOUNTAINS—DOLLS

Hickory nut clothespin doll, making 298:168-169

APPALACHIAN MOUNTAINS—GNOMES

Pine cone gnome, making 298:160-161

APPALACHIAN MOUNTAINS—LULLABIES

"Hush 'n Bye" 1607:17

APPALACHIAN MOUNTAINS—SONGS

Mocking Bird, lullaby 1220:139

APPLES

Activities and resources to celebrate apple days 592:1-6

Apple dishes, recipes, projects, books, songs 259:93-97

Apple leather, how to make 1482:29

History of apples for Halloween 443:26; 443:26

Johnny Appleseed birthday celebration; art, music, foods, games, activities 1104:6-9

APPLES—COOKERY

American apple pie, recipe 118:152

Apple crisp pie, recipe 172:41

Apple pie, recipe 800:97-98; 1710:last page

Apple yogurt, recipe 1013:52

Applesauce cake, recipe 800:96-97

Applesauce pie, recipe 800:97

Applesauce, apple butter, cookies, and snacks, recipes 376:222-223

Applesauce, recipe 800:95-96

Baked apples, recipe 800:98-99

Butter, apple butter, recipe 800:101-102

Candy apples, recipe 1013:55

Caramel covered apples, recipe 1342:38

Curry from apples, recipe 800:100-101

Jelly, apple jelly, recipe 800:102

Meat loaf, recipe 800:100

Old fashioned taffy, caramel apples, recipe 376:241

Pork chops with jellied apple slices, recipe 800:99

Waldorf salad, recipe 800:94-95

APPLES—DRIED

Dried apple rings, how to make 118:154

Dried apples, how to make 1013:21; 1531:38-39

Sun dried apples, how to do 318:8

APPLES—FINGER PLAYS

Finger plays 1660:37

APPLES—GAMES

A is for apple 1013:56

Apple race 800:84

Apple twirling game 800:82

Bob for apples 1013:56

Ducking for apples 800:79

Fortune telling with apples game 1032:282

Look Ma No Hands game 800:84

Pass the apple 1013:56

APPLES—HEADS

Carved apple head, how to make 1453:29-30

Heads, dried apple heads, making 800:86-87

APPLES—POMANDERS

Apple pomander, cloves, cinnamon, netting, making 1692:22

APPLES—PUPPETS

Apple puppets, dried apple head puppets, making 1285:102-103

APPLES—SONGS

Song, apple song 782:unp

APPLESEED, JOHNNY

Activities and resources to celebrate apple days 592:1-6

Birthday activities, stories, crafts, recipes 558:8-10

Johnny Appleseed Day finger plays and games 944:25-27

APRIL FOOLS' DAY

Activities and projects for classrooms 1393:186-187

Activities, art, crafts, history, stories, songs, recipes, poems, projects, games 128:31-36; 819:60-68; 1469:84-85; 1473:114

Finger plays, recipes, games 944:88-90

First of April Party, making 51:5-11

History and celebration of 496:57-58; 709:149

Letter trick, making 891:48-51

Mirror tableau, making 51:6-8

Noah's Ark peep-show, making 51:8-10

Supper, making 51:10

APRIL FOOLS' DAY—COOKERY

Crazy chocolate popcorn balls, recipe 939:62

Orange custard fool, recipe 1032:201

APRIL FOOLS' DAY—COSTUMES

Ackward person costume, making 272:60-61

Mixed-up costume, making 272:59

APRIL FOOLS' DAY—DECORATIONS

April Fools' Day felt board, what's missing, making 945:175-179

April funnies, making 835:45

Jack in the cup, styrofoam cup, making 835:43

Pig snout, egg carton, elastic, making 1662:48

Silly weather worm, yarn, pattern, making 1393:187

Upside down cards, making 835:44

APRIL FOOLS' DAY—GAMES

April foolers game 698:39

April Fools' Day game 240:22-23

Cows eat brownies game 698:38

Paper puzzle trick, paper, making 1237:91-94

Shoe scramble game 698:38

Silly sentences game 698:38

Wacky art contest game 698:39

APRIL FOOLS' DAY—MAGIC

April Fool again bag trick, activities, foods, handicrafts 31:8-11

April Fool joker cards 31:16-20

April Fools' bets tricks 31:41-45

Fool's card tricks 31:31-40

Foolish shirt trick 31:25-27

Ice in April trick 31:28-30

Magic banana trick, activities, foods, handicrafts 31:12-15

Soggy hat trick 31:21-24

APRIL FOOLS' DAY—PARTIES

April Fools' backwards birthday party, activities, foods, handicrafts 30:123-126

Decorations, snacks, games, making 1266:47-51

Turn-about-party, games, food, how to do 698:37-39

APRIL FOOLS' DAY—PUPPETS
Puppet projects, patterns, scenes, story starters, feature story 1083:63-67

APRIL FOOLS' DAY—SONGS
Songs about April Fools' Day 901:61

ARABIAN NIGHTS—FACE PAINTING
Arabian Night face, how to paint 1533:90-91

ARABIAN NIGHTS—HANDICRAFTS
Fisherman and the Genie, art activities, swirl painting, watercolor, wet chalk game, making 126:54-66

ARABIAN PENINSULA—COOKERY
Almond biscuits, recipe 1165:75
Date bars, recipe 1165:73
Fruit balls, recipe 1165:76
Hoomis, chick pea spread, recipe 1165:72
Limonada, lemonade, recipe 1165:72-73
Mjeddrah, rice with lentils, recipe 1165:74
Shourba Bilsen, thick lentil soup, recipe 1165:72
Stuffed dates, figs, prunes, recipe 1165:75
Tahineh or tahini, sesame seed paste, recipe 1165:74

ARABIAN PENINSULA—FESTIVALS—COOKERY
Eid al-Fitr; apricot squares, recipe 1666:70
Eid al-Fitr; bereshtook nokhochi (chick pea flour squares), recipe 1666:70-71
Eid al-Fitr; hummus bi tahina (chick pea spread), recipe 1666:68-69
Eid al-Fitr; kimaje (Arab flat bread), recipe 1666:69
Eid al-Fitr; lassi (iced yogurt drink), recipe 1666:70
Eid al-Fitr; marinated chick-peas, recipe 1666:69-70
Eid al-Fitr; tahini (sesame paste), recipe 1666:68

ARABIC LANGUAGE
Arabic name designs, how to make 1654:32-33
Arabic words and phrases 671:46
Moslem names for the months of the year 1031:48
Numbers one to ten in Arabic language 399:unp

ARABS—AMULETS
Hand amulet, beads, string, making 1654:29
Seashell amulet, seashells, paints, making 1654:29
Silver amulet, aluminum foil, beads, seeds, string, making 1654:29

ARABS—COOKERY
Apricot and walnut cookies, recipe 1654:34
Arab pocket bread, recipe 88:37-38
Cornbread, recipe 1653:68
Yogurt, recipe 1654:34

ARABS—COSTUMES
Arab woman costume, sheet, making 106:8
Arabian costume drawing 988:58
Harem girl, variety of old clothes, making 1656:189-192
Sheik, variety of old clothes, making 1656:193-196

ARABS—DANCES
Debka dance, how to do 1654:36

ARABS—DOLLS
Arab Sheik doll, making 494:173-185

ARABS—GAMES
Bead game, how to play 1654:35
Fox game, how to play 1654:35

ARABS—HANDICRAFTS
Arabic geometric patterns and designs for stencils, how to make 1654:29-31

ARABS—HOUSES
Arab sheik's tent, making 562:22-23

ARABS—NUMBERS
Numbers one to ten in Arabic language 399:unp

ARABS—TEA
Arabic tea 474:138

ARAPAHO INDIANS—GAMES
Buffalo wheel game 602:166
Hubbub game, how to play 1699:103

ARBOR DAY
Activities and projects for classrooms 1393:190-193
Activities, art, crafts, history, stories, songs, recipes, games, poems 128:45-52; 819:70-74; 1469:88-89
Arbor Day activities, stories, crafts, recipes 558:59-63
Celebration 134:56
Finger plays, games 944:97-98
Plant a tree for Arbor Day, how to do 1208:47-48
Trees for all months 134:60

ARBOR DAY—COSTUMES
Fruit tree costume, making 272:65-66

ARBOR DAY—DECORATIONS
Blossoms from fingerprints, making 1149:103
Rain forest poster of trees and animals, patterns, making 1199:93-97
Tree mobile, paper, patterns, making 1237:97-98
Tree shapes painted from stencils, making 1149:38
Tree, tin cans, paper, patterns, making 1311:162-163

ARBOR DAY—MAGIC
Magic tricks for Arbor Day 1002:7-47

ARBOR DAY—PUPPETS
Puppet projects, patterns, scenes, story starters, feature story 1083:31-37

ARCHEOLOGY
Backyard dig, how to make one 546:39-41
How a pot is reconstructed 1725:61

ARCHITECTURE
30 projects to develop understanding of architecture 220:1-88
Frank Lloyd Wright birthday celebration; music/foods/games/activities 1104:86-89

ARCTIC—FOLKLORE
Joanne the Bear on the Moon, physical and human geography activities 1458:76-79

ARGENTINA
Activities, flags, games, songs, dances, recipes 1381:49-52

ARGENTINA—CHRISTMAS—COOKERY
Carbonada Criolla (meat stew with vegetables), recipe 1666:223
Dulce de leche (milk pudding), recipe 1666:223-224

ARGENTINA—CHRISTMAS—CRECHE
Pesebre creche, clay, how to make 515:14

ARGENTINA—COOKERY
Apple pancake, recipe 793:22; 1381:51
Beef char-broiled with sauce, recipe 1517:33
Beef cook-up 187:15
Beef soup, recipe 1517:21
Breaded beef cutlets, recipe 1517:27
Butter cookies, recipe 1251:46-47
Carbonada, meat and fruit stew, recipe 1165:227
Chicken, marinated, recipe 1517:33
Cookies with filling, recipe 1517:40-41
Cowboy steak, recipe, 1244:129
Dulce de leche, condensed milk pudding, recipe 1123:87
Dulce de leche, sweet milk dessert, recipe 1251:45
Empadas (turnovers), beef, chicken, ham, fruit, recipe 1517:28-29
Empanadas meat pies, recipe 1123:86-87
Filled cookies dessert, recipe 1280:48-49

Finger sandwiches, recipe 1517:38
Fried beef, recipe 895:16
Gaucho sweet potato dish, recipe 1381:51
Gaucho sweet potato, recipe 794:15
Huevos al Nido, eggs in a nest, recipe 1165:228
Meat turnovers, recipe 895:17-18
Milk pudding, flan, recipe 1517:39
Peas and eggs, recipe 1517:34
Petits fours and frosting, recipe 1517:36
Quince crescents (crecientes de membrillo), cookies, recipe 72:174-175
Tamale pie, recipe 662:104-105

ARGENTINA—DANCES
Tango, how to do 1494:221-222

ARGENTINA—DECORATIONS
Gaucho boy pattern, making 1381:52

ARGENTINA—FESTIVALS
Magi Day celebration 601:158

ARGENTINA—FOLKLORE
Gentle beasts, information about guanacos, and llamas 1478:19
"The Gentle People," tales and activities 1478:13-17
Wishful thinking list, how to make 1478:18

ARGENTINA—GAMES
Canasta card game 1132:101-107
Cat and mouse game 967:20
Cat and mouse game, how to play 1355:25
El Hombre, el Tigre, y el Fusil, the man the tiger and the gun, how to play 1494:207-208
El roloj, jump rope game, how to play 1708:10-11
El Tigre, la Persona, y la Camara tiger, the man and the gun 386:49
Fine day to you, your Lordship game 602:133-134
Fisher Martin game 602:135
Man, the tiger and the gun game 602:132-133
Mister Noah had an ark game 602:134-135
Rice pudding game 602:136-137
Ring around a rosy game 602:135

ARGENTINA—HANDICRAFTS
Nature's bounty necklace, paper beads, embroidery floss, making 1478:22-23
Scent-sational flowers from South America, how to grow 1478:21

ARIZONA—COOKERY
Chili con carne with meat, recipe 654:11
Grapefruit and melon salad, recipe 654:12

ARIZONA INDIANS—STORY STICKS
Story stick, stick, yarn, feathers, making 1699:176

ARKANSAS—COOKERY
Ozark pudding, recipe 654:14
Watermelon boat, recipe 654:15

ARKANSAS—HANDICRAFTS
Corncob Hillybilly Yokel Granny, making 298:144-145

ARMED FORCES
Song; Taps 1115:83

ARMENIA—CHRISTMAS
Christmas celebration 601:101-102

ARMENIA—COOKERY
Armenian meat tarts, recipe 1653:101-102
Baklava pastry, recipe 1187:unp
Pilaf, recipe 793:59
Rice-stuffed pumpkin, recipe 1380:23
Sugar cookies, recipe 794:43

ARMENIA—DANCES
Halay, how to do 1494:169-170

ARMENIA—EASTER
Easter egg customs in Armenia 201:28

ARMENIA—EASTER—COOKERY
Lahmajoun (Armenian pizza), recipe 1666:145
Shakarishee (Armenian butter cookies), recipe 1666:146
Topik (potato dumpling), recipe 1666:144-145

ARMOR
Plate armor, making 213:42-43
Shield, spears, axes, cardboard, dowels, paints, making 1181:26-27

ARROWHEADS. See INDIANS OF NORTH AMERICA—ARROWHEADS

ARTISTS—PARTIES
Picasso party, how to plan and give 86:31-37

ARUBA—GAMES
Pele, hopscotch game 1426:8-9

ASANTE (AFRICAN PEOPLE)—HANDICRAFTS
Asante adinkra stamping of cloth, potatoes, stamp pad, fabric, making 1632:18-23
Kente cloth needlepoint wall hanging, canvas, yarn, patterns, making 1716:94-96
Kente pattern needlepoint squares, canvas squares, yarn, making 1716:91-93

ASCENSION THURSDAY
Celebration of facts 496:70

ASH WEDNESDAY
Activities and projects for classrooms 1393:170-171

ASH WEDNESDAY—COOKERY
Pretzels, recipe 1409:21

ASHANTI (AFRICAN PEOPLE)—CLOTHING
Adinkra cloth, how to decorate with potato printed symbols 1179:176-177
Kente cloth shawl, how to make using chromatography 1333:42-46

ASIA—ANIMALS
Blown egg animals, gibbon, tiger, water buffalo, giant panda, making 677:26
Tiger, corrugated cardboard, paints, making 1484:6-7

ASIA—COOKERY
Fruit dessert, recipe 1653:174
Fruit salad, recipe 1653:21

ASIA—DANCES
Folk dance in the East 474:120

ASIA—DRAMA
Side singer and comic retainer 474:101-102

ASIA—GAMES
Asalto board game, patterns, making 1541:174-178
Backgammon board game, patterns, making 1541:219-229
Carrying baskets game 474:51
Chinese Rebel board game, patterns, making 1541:179-182
Egg jousting game 1074:238-239
Fox and Geese board game, patterns, making 1541:167-173
Mancala board game, patterns, making 1541:109-114

ASIA—HANDICRAFTS
Batik, crayon batik, towel, crayons, making 1429:44-45
Batik, how to do 1455:170
Butterfly, paper, patterns, making 1246:34-36
Mehndi design, how to make 1313:46-47
Traditional Asian designs 1246:8-13

ASIA—LANGUAGE
Greetings of Asia words 601:86-87

ASIA—MASKS
Durga mask, cardboard box, dowels, glitter, containers, making 1295:32-33

ASIA—NAMES
  Baby names information 695:123
ASIA—NEW YEAR
  Celebration of New Year 497:154-165
ASIA, EAST
  Activities, flags, games, songs, dances, recipes 1381:59-89
ASIA, EAST—FESTIVALS
  Planting and growing festivals 419:91-106
ASIA, SOUTHEAST. *See also* **SOUTHEAST ASIA**
  Solar New Year, activities and projects for classrooms 1393:194-195
ASIA, SOUTHEAST—COOKERY
  Chopsticks, how to use 1538:38
ASIA, SOUTHEAST—SEALS
  Chop, personal signature seal, how to make 1477:23
ASSINIBOIN INDIANS—MASKS
  Assiniboin masks, making 327:47
ASTROLOGY—PARTIES
  Age of Aquarius party, activities and recipes 809:123-127
ASTRONAUTS. *See also* **SPACE**
  Astronaut, paper, large pattern, making 478:5-9
ASTRONAUTS—CLOTHING
  Astronaut helmet, papier-mache, egg carton, balloon, making 1345:20-21
ASTRONAUTS—COSTUMES
  Astronaut costume 839:3-7, 213:146-147
  Astronaut, costume, paper bag, making 135:6-11
ASTRONAUTS—GAMES
  First Landing on the Moon Anniversary game 240:40
ASTRONAUTS—PUPPETS
  Puppet, paper bag boy or girl astronaut puppet, patterns, making 1107:154-157
ASTRONOMY
  Livingston, Myra Cohn, "Space Songs"; science, reading, art activities 1055:158-166
  Universe sign, making 293:264
ATLANTIC STATES—COOKERY
  Delaware snow cream, recipe 1043:110
  Jewish rye bread, recipe 1043:101
  Maryland crab cakes, recipe 1043:104
  Maryland fried oysters, recipe 1043:103
  Matzoh ball soup, recipe 1043:103
  Minehaha cake, recipe 1043:108
  New York cheesecake, recipe 1043:107
  Pennsylvania Dutch apple meringue, recipe 1043:109
  Pennsylvania Dutch shoo-fly pie, recipe 1043:106
  Snickordoodles, recipe 1043:105
  Soft pretzels, recipe 1043:102
  South Philly cheese steak sandwiches, recipe 1043:104
ATLANTIS
  Dream garden, making 173:64-65
  Enchanted people, making 173:28-29
ATLANTIS—HELMETS
  Atlantis helmets, making 173:22-23
AUDUBON, JOHN J.
  Plant painting, on grid using Audubon's system of painting 1609:85
AUDUBON, JOHN J.—BIRTHDAY
  Birthday celebration; art, music, foods, games, activities 1104:78-81
  Celebrate by making flying birds, cardboard, felt, patterns, making 1199:98-100
  Celebrate; build nesting box, milk cartons, paint, making 1199:100-101

AUSTRALIA
  Activities, flags, games, songs, dances, projects, recipes 282:38-49; 1381:91-94
  Animals, plants and holidays of Australia activities 1378:38-65
  Plants and animals of Australia activities 1378:38-65
  Traditions, customs, economy, ecology, aesthetic awareness units 1378:38-65
AUSTRALIA—ANIMALS
  Kangaroo, crayon kangaroo, patterns, making 1087:51-53
  Kangaroos, great kangaroo race game, cardboard, string, making 1484:14-15
AUSTRALIA—BIRDS
  Cockatoo, cereal box, patterns, making 1087:43-45
  Puppet, paper bag kookaburra puppet, patterns, making 1107:94-104
AUSTRALIA—BOOMERANGS
  Boomerang, cardboard, pattern, making 1213:143
  Boomerangs, ruler, making 1320:54
  Homemade boomerang that comes back to you, making 1719:72-75
AUSTRALIA—CHRISTMAS
  Carols by candlelight tradition 475:55-56
  Celebration of Christmas in Australia 497:103; 601:171; 1049:89
  Christmas customs 149:57
  Christmas customs in Australia 149:57; 473:66-67; 1717:8-9
  Kissing bough, making 497:102-103
  Picnic at beach custom 516:44
AUSTRALIA—CHRISTMAS—COOKERY
  Australian caramel squares, recipe 1666:196
  Pineapple and cabbage salad, recipe 1666:195-196
  Quick bickies (quick biscuits), recipe 1666:196
  Upside down cake, recipe 1666:195-197
AUSTRALIA—COOKERY
  Anzac biscuits, recipe 1076:27; 1244:140-141; 1652:43
  Anzac cookies, recipe 1136:110-111
  Australian oat cakes, recipe 1653:55
  Batter-fried fish and potato scallops, recipes 895:20-21
  Beef curry, recipe 1076:36-37
  Bread and butter custard, recipe 1076:39
  Carpetbag steak, recipe 895:22
  Carpetbagger steak, recipe 1452:15
  Cheese curry biscuits, recipe 1653:62
  Crab and asparagus, recipe 1452:16
  Damper bread, recipe 1244:142-143; 1452:12
  Dampers, recipe 967:21
  Dandenong squares, cookies from the City of Dandenong, recipe 1165:196-197
  Dressing, recipe 1165:195
  Egg and bacon pie, recipe 1076:20-21
  Fish fillets, recipe 1076:30-31
  Fruit muesli, recipe 1076:18-19; 1652:24
  Fruit salad, recipe 1076:19; 1652:25
  Glen Elgin carrot salad, recipe 967:21
  Golden syrup cookies (anzacs), cookies 72:144-145
  Kangaroo soup, recipe 1165:194
  Kangaroo tail soup, recipe 1452:13
  Kiwi tart dessert, recipe 1076:41; 1280:16
  Lamb curry recipe1136:108-109
  Lamingtons, cake and icing dessert, recipe 636:41; 1076:26-27; 1280:18-19
  Leg of lamb, roasted with gravy, recipe 1076:33-35

Lobster and orange salad, recipe 874:60
Mango mayonnaise with ginger, recipe 636:25
Meat pie, recipe 1381:93
Mint sauce, recipe 1076:35
Mussels with herb and tomato dressing, recipe 636:33
Pancakes, recipe 793:69
Pasties, meat pies, recipe 1165:196
Pavlova dessert, recipe 636:31; 1452:17
Pavlova meringue dessert, recipe 1076:42; 1560:38-39
Pineapple and cabbage salad, recipe 1165:194-195
Pineapple cabbage salad, recipe 1452:14
Pineapple fruit cup, recipe 1076:22; 1652:19
Poisson Cru, recipe 636:43
Pumpkin scones, recipe 1544:118
Pumpkin soup, recipe 1076:28-29; 1381:93
Rice, oven baked, recipe 1076:38
Shearer's stew with jumbuck dumplings, recipe 636:30
Simplicity chocolate cake, recipe 967:22
Spider's drink, ice cream, fruit, recipe 1650:19
Sultana loaf, recipe 794:56
Sunshine salad, recipe 1076:30
Tea, recipe 1076:23
Toad-in-the-hole, meat baked in batter, recipe 1165:195
Tomato and mint sandwiches, recipe 1076:24
Tomato pie, recipe 636:28
Whitebait omelette, recipe 636:19

AUSTRALIA—COSTUMES
Paper doll type costume, making 282:48

AUSTRALIA—FESTIVALS
Aborigines Witchetty Grub Festival information 419:2-4
Australia Day National holiday, how to celebrate 1378:59-60
Festivals and celebrations, maps, flags, crafts, making 1305:7-15
Wattle Day celebration 1378:48

AUSTRALIA—FOLKLORE
Aboriginal painting, brown paper, crayons, making 1478:100-101
Lighting the Way folktale and activities 1478:93-96
Reasons for the seasons in Australia 1478:99

AUSTRALIA—GAMES
Bola game 474:40
Bounce eye game 572:26-27
Bounce eye game, how to play 1507:54
Chain Stoop Tag, how to play 1498:9
Conkers game, how to play 1507:55-56
Fill the bottle race 967:20
Forceball, how to play 1497:41
Four square, handball game, how to play 1708:12-13
Gecko Gecko chasing game, how to play 1498:27-29
Kangaroo hop race, how to play 1499:30-32
Kookaburra song and dance game 1114:55
Last couple come game 282:120
Le Herradura or horseshoe quoits, how to play 1499:23
Pass the coconut game 572:42-43
Patrol or six game 967:21
Sheep Do Trails, how to play 1494:194-195

AUSTRALIA—GEOGRAPHY
Where the Forest meets the Sea; physical and human geography activities 1458:24-27

AUSTRALIA—GREAT BARRIER REEF
Great Barrier Reef diorama in box, making 1484:22-23

AUSTRALIA—HANDICRAFTS
Aboriginal bark paintings, paper, colored pencils, making 1338:104-106

Aboriginal dream maps, paper, watercolors, making 1338:107-108
Computer project: Paint aboriginal dreamtime picture 1218:68-71

AUSTRALIA—HEADDRESSES
Feather headdress, corrugated paper, straws, making 1488:12-13

AUSTRALIA—JEWELRY
Jungle jewelry, pasta, seeds, paints, making 1488:14-15

AUSTRALIA—KITES
Trefoil Delta kite, making 1069:243-246
Trefoil Dragon kite, making 1069:247-250

AUSTRALIA—LANGUAGE
Australian slang words 1136:144-145
Meanings of unusual Australian words 1378:61-62
Meanings of words in Waltzing Matilda 1378:61

AUSTRALIA—MAGIC TRICKS
You can't fool me, card trick, how to do 1270:26-27

AUSTRALIA—MUSICAL INSTRUMENTS
Clappers or boomerang clapsticks, cardboard, tongue depressors, making 1646:12-14
Clappers, how to play 1646:21
Didgeridoo instrument, long cardboard tube, paints, making 1622:9

AUSTRALIA—PLANTS
Tropical plants, oranges, lemons, pineapples, how to grow 1488:10-11

AUSTRALIA—PUPPETS
Australian Bush animal puppets, patterns, making 463:27-34
Penguin puppet, making 1305:14

AUSTRALIA—RITUALS
Growing up rituals 695:80-83

AUSTRALIA—SAND STORIES
Sandbox for showing sand stories on overhead projector, how to make 1161:61-63
The Rainbow Snake sand story, how to do 1161:64-69
Why There Is Fire in Wood sand story, how to do 1161:70-74

AUSTRALIA—SCIENCE
How well different strengths of sunscreens work, experiment 1719:70

AUSTRALIA—SONGS
"Kookaburra" 1607:40
Kookaburra round song 1115:15

AUSTRALIA—STRING FIGURES
Dogs on a Leash 1404:22
Throwing a spear figure 423:17-18

AUSTRIA—CHRISTMAS
Celebration of Christmas in Austria 601:102; 661:135; 1049:86
Christmas tree and decorations, how to make 593:10-15
Customs in Austria 425:13-15
Zwetschken Krampus (edible Christmas devil), making 672:16-36

AUSTRIA—CHRISTMAS—COOKERY
Apfelkuchen (Bavarian apple cake), recipe 1666:90
Haselnuss-Kuchlein (hazelnut cookies), recipe 1666:89
Kupferlin (crescent cookies), recipe 1666:89-90
Viennese nut crescents, recipe 704:83

AUSTRIA—CHRISTMAS—DECORATIONS
Nut decorations, making 709:76

AUSTRIA—CHRISTMAS—ORNAMENTS
Foil ornaments, making 1023:50
Stars, double stars, paper, making 1023:138

AUSTRIA—CHRISTMAS—WREATHS
Advent wreath, evergreens, making 704:79
AUSTRIA—COOKERY
Almond crescents (kipferln),cookies, recipe 72:28-29
Apple snow, recipe 661:139
Beef, spiced boiled beef, recipe 1082:24
Broccoli salad with bacon, recipe 1082:32
Chicken, paprika chicken, recipe 1082:22
Chocolate sauce, recipe 1165:104-105
Coffee beans, history of 661:114-117
Cucumber salad, recipe 661:138; 1082:30
Egg custard soup, recipe 1082:21
Ham and noodle casserole, recipe 1082:28
Ham rolls, recipe 895:25-26
Herb-stuffed eggs, recipe 1082:40
Jelly rolls, recipe 1082:19
Linzer cake, recipe 1082:34
Liver dumplings, recipe 661:137
Meat and sauerkraut, recipe 895:24
Morgen Reis (morning rice), recipe 49:253
Pecan crescents, recipe 1477:83
Pork stew, recipe 1082:42
Potato noodles, recipe 1082:24
Potato salad, cooked, recipe 1082:27
Potato soup with hot dogs, recipe 1082:41
Potatoes, bouillon potatoes, recipe 1082:25
Prune fritters, recipe 794:26
Red cabbage salad, recipe 1082:32
Rolls; cinnamon and almond snail rolls, recipe 1082:20
Sacher cake, recipe 1082:36
Sacher torte, chocolate cake, recipe 1165:103-104
Sacher torte, recipe 1280:34-35
Sachertorte, recipe 661:139-140
Salami cones, recipe 1082:40
Salzburg souffle, recipe 858:unp
Salzburger sweet souffle, recipe 1082:33; 1280:32-33
Smoked salmon-stuffed eggs, recipe 1082:40
Strudel dough, history of 661:118
Tomato baskets, recipe 1082:39
Trout Vienna style, recipe 1082:31
Veal, breaded veal (Wiener Schnitzel), recipe 1082:26
Viennese veal cutlets, recipe 895:27
Wiener Schnitzel, history of 661:124-125
Wiener Schnitzel, recipe 661:137-138; 874:50; 967:22
AUSTRIA—COSTUMES
Tyrol costumes drawing 988:44-45
AUSTRIA—DANCES
Waltz dance and costume picture 1000:34-36
AUSTRIA—EASTER
Easter egg customs in Austria 201:24-25
AUSTRIA—FESTIVALS
Epiphany celebration 661:136
Fas Ching Festival celebration 661:133-134
Schemenlauf Festival celebration 661:133
Twelfth Night, history of 709:112-113
AUSTRIA—GAMES
Call ball, how to play 1497:27-28
Numbers game 602:89
Restaurant game 602:89
AUSTRIA—HANDICRAFTS
Bird mobile, walnut shell, making 626:20-22
AUSTRIA—MUSICAL INSTRUMENTS
Sleigh bells, bells, plastic lanyard, beads, making
1646:46-47

AUSTRIA—NEW YEAR'S DAY
Good luck pig, history of 709:97
Merrymaking in Austria 489:16-20
AUSTRIA—NEW YEAR'S DAY—COOKERY
Marzipan animals and vegetables, recipe 709:97-100
AUSTRIA—NEW YEAR'S EVE
New Year's Eve celebration 661:135
AUSTRIA—TOYS
Tumbling man from Austria, history of and how to make
495:24-27
AUTOBIOGRAPHIES
Family survey and family scrapbook, how to make,
1152:179-200
AUTOMOBILES
1930's Roadster, wooden, patterns, making 942:54-55
Ford automobile, first Ford model, wooden, making
567:87-94
Henry Ford birthday celebration; art, music, foods,
games, activities 1104:106-109
MG's ancient and modern, wooden, patterns, making
942:62-67
Old car model, wooden, making 952:76-77
Tin Lizzie, model, wooden, making 923:46-47
Tin Lizzie, nuts and bolts, making 893:109-114
XK 120 Jaguar, wooden, patterns, making 942:56-60
AUTUMN. *See also* **FALL**
Art, cooking, games, dramatics, math, science, music, ac-
tivities 54:1-15
AUTUMN—FESTIVALS
Autumn festivals 419:69-75
AVIATION DAY
Activities, art, songs, recipes, games 1469:124-125
AVOCADO
Avocado pear tree, how to grow 954:126-127
Avocado plant, how to grow 909:122
Grow an avocado from seed 376:98
AZERBAIJAN—FESTIVALS—COOKERY
Eid al-Fitr; Kompot Iz Dyni I Orekhov (melon and wal-
nut compote), recipe 1666:147
Eid al-Fitr; lentil and barley soup, recipe 1666:146-147
AZTECS
Mosaic picture of Aztec design, paper, making 1635:14-
15
AZTECS—CALENDAR
Calendar, day signs and numbers, making 702:8-10
AZTECS—CARVING
Carved relief of Tenochtitlan, making 702:21-23
AZTECS—CLOTHING
Cloak, decorated, making 702:18-20
AZTECS—CODICES
Aztec codex, or picture book, posterboard, making
1633:54-55
Glyphs and codices, making 702:6-7
AZTECS—COOKERY
Avocado dip, recipe 1269:27
Aztec chocolate drink, recipe 1209:70
Chocolate drink, recipe 410:109
Corn or bean soup, recipe 1269:27-28
Mexican hot chocolate, recipe 1269:29
Pumpkin flower tortillas, recipe 659:44
Sweet potato, hot cocoa, recipe 702:14-15
Tomato sauce, cooked, recipe 1269:28-29

AZTECS—FANS

Fan made from layers of feathers, decorations, making 1701:17

Feather fan, paper plate, colored paper, making 1182:23

AZTECS—FESTIVALS

Cinteotl, plant God festival 419:136-138

Corn Festival celebration 659:42-44

Maize corn festivals 419:133-140

Maize plant festivals 419:136-138

Tlaloc, rain God festival 419:138-139

Tosi, ripe maize Goddess festival 419:136-138

Xilonen, plant Goddess festival 419:136-138

Xipe Totec, seed God festival 419:136-138

Xiuhtecuhtli, fire God festival 419:139-140

AZTECS—FOLKLORE

Snake that wriggles, cardboard, making 1447:24-25

AZTECS—GAMES

Palm ball game 956:51

AZTECS—HEADDRESSES

Headdress for ruler, oak tag, gold braid, sequins, making 1635:8-9

AZTECS—HELMETS

Helmet, eagle Knight helmet, making 702:29-31

Helmet, jaguar helmet, oak tag, paints, making 1635:18-19

AZTECS—HOUSEHOLD

Cocoa jug, making 702:27-28

AZTECS—JEWELRY

Jewelry, chest ornament, cardboard, gold paint, making 1635:27

AZTECS—MASKS

Aztec recycled metal face mask, making 1706:21

Mask, gold, papier-mache-covered balloon, gold paint, making 1182:15

Mask, mosaic Sun god, making 702:11-13

Mosaic mask, papier-mache covered balloon, colored paper, glue, making 1182:15

AZTECS—MUSICAL INSTRUMENTS

Drum, making 702:24-26

Whistle from homemade clay, recipe for clay, making 1310:43

AZTECS—SUN GOD

Aztec Sun God, salt dough, paints, patterns, making 1633:50-53

AZTECS—TEMPLES

Aztec temple model, cardboard paints, making 1182:20-21

AZTECS—WEAPONS

Shields for battle, making 702:16-17

B

BABBITT, NATALIE
"Tuck Everlasting," flapjacks, recipe 1216:8

BACH, JOHANN SEBASTIAN
Mister Bach round song 1151:48

BAHAI—FESTIVALS
Ayyam-i-ha, Bahai Days of Generosity holiday, pop-up card, making 1387:12-13

BAHAMAS
Activities, flags, games, songs, dances, recipes 1381:35-38

BAHAMAS—CHRISTMAS—COOKERY
Bullas (Caribbean Christmas cookies), recipe 1666:215-216

BAHAMAS—COOKERY
Banana pudding, recipe 1165:219-220
Conch fritters, recipe 1381:36
Conkies, sweet coconut snack, recipe 1165:220-221
Cracked conch, recipe 1381:35
Curried bananas, recipe 1165:219
Fish Caribbean, tomatoes, onions, peppers, recipe 1381:37

BAHAMAS—FESTIVALS—COOKERY
Boxing Day; Bahamas fish pie, recipe 1666:215
Boxing Day; coconut loaf cake, recipe 1666:215
Boxing Day; corn fritters, recipe 1666:214
Guy Fawkes Day, conkies, coconut cookies, recipe 1165:220-221

BAHAMAS—NEW YEAR'S DAY
Junkanoo Parade celebration 505:29

BAHRAIN—COOKERY
Almond biscuits, recipe 1165:75
Date bars, recipe 1165:73
Fruit balls, recipe 1165:76
Hoomis, chick pea spread, recipe 1165:72
Limonada, lemonade, recipe 1165:72-73
Mjeddrah, rice with lentils, recipe 1165:74
Shourba bilsen, thick lentil soup, recipe 1165:72
Stuffed dates, figs, prunes, recipe 1165:75
Tahineh or tahini, sesame seed paste, recipe 1165:74

BAHRAIN—FESTIVALS—COOKERY
Eid al-Fitr; lamb with dates, recipe 1666:71
Eid al-Fitr; lowzina b'shakar (white sugar candy), recipe 1666:72

BAHRAIN—FESTIVALS—GAMES
Ramadan Festival, hit the shadow game, how to play 1355:33

BALD EAGLE—NATIONAL SYMBOL
History of 333:62-64

BALI. *See also* **INDONESIA**

BALI—HANDICRAFTS
Widyadhari, guardian angels decoration, tag board, making 1338:68-69

BALI—HOUSES
Community housing in Bali 469:36-37

BALI—PUPPETS
Bali shadow puppets, patterns, making 1027:89-94

BALL GAMES
Balls from the Pacific, Ireland and Japan, history of 1497:7
Roman balls, history of 1497:6-7

BALLET
Tutu from netting or fabric, making 1362:48

BALLET—COSTUMES
Ballerina costume, fabric, making 367:18-21; 839:8-11; 1379:23

BALLET—PARTIES
Babes in Toyland birthday party, decorations, games, cake, patterns 1015:54-66
Ballet party, how to plan and give 86:60-65
Ballet party, menu and recipes 86:219-220

BALLOONS
Activities and resources to celebrate balloons day 592:7-12
History of balloons 371:102-107

BALLPOINT PENS
History of 119:188-192

BANANAS
Facts about bananas 616:46-48

BANANAS—COOKERY
Baked bananas, recipe 616:18-19
Banana apple salad, recipe 616:22-23
Banana bran muffins, recipe 616:36-39
Banana fries, recipe 616:20-21
Banana nut bread sandwich, recipe 616:45
Banana nut bread, recipe 616:40-44
Banana shake, recipe 616:27-28
Bananas and berries, recipe 616:14-15
Chocolate banana cookies, recipe 616:31-35
Frozen banana pops, recipe 616:16-17
Triple fruit freeze, recipe 616:24-26

BAND-AIDS
History of 119:103-105

BANGLADESH—CHRISTMAS—CUSTOMS
Christmas customs 149:48

BANGLADESH—COOKERY
Ain Bharta potato and spice dish, recipe 1103:88-89
Bata Ne Tameta, potatoes with gravy, recipe 1165:169
Burfi caramel fudge dessert, recipe 1103:90
Luchis fried bread, recipe 1103:89

BANGLADESH—FESTIVALS—COOKERY
Moharram; Behndi Foogath (stewed okra), recipe 1666:165-166
Moharram; shakkar pongal (rice and lentil pudding), recipe 1666:165
Moharram; zarda (sweet rice), recipe 1666:166

BANNOCK INDIANS—GAMES
Juggling, how to play 1699:126

BARBADOS—COOKERY
Black-eyed peas and rice, recipe 1068:unp
Coconut bread, recipe 1287:unp.
Cornmeal coo-coo dish, recipe 1652:25

BARBADOS—COSTUMES
Banana pudding, recipe, costume 188:6

BARBADOS—HARVEST FESTIVALS—COOKERY
Sugar Cane Festival quick bread, bananas, coconut, honey, recipe 1249:26-27

BARBOUR, KAREN
"Little Nino's Pizzeria," pizza, recipe 1216:25

BARGE—CHINESE
Chinese barge, making 173:40-41

BARK
Bark weaving using tree bark and tree fibers, making 1213:36-37

BARK RUBBINGS. *See also* **RUBBINGS**

BARNUM, P. T.—BIRTHDAY
P.T. Barnum birthday celebration; art, music, foods, games activities 1104:102-105

P.T. Barnum's birthday, be a clown, face-painting, recipe 1199:152-153

P.T. Barnum's birthday, circus stilts, coffee cans, twine, duct tape, making 1199:153-154

BARRETT, JUDI

"Cloudy with a Chance of Meatballs," meatballs, recipe 1216:99

BARRIE, J. M.—BIRTHDAY

Celebrate by conducting "Peter Pan" poll to grow up or stay young 1199:112

BARRIE, J. M.—COOKERY

Little White Bird; bird in the forest, recipe 365:66

"Peter Pan"; Captain Hook's poison cake, recipe 570:65-67

"Peter Pan"; Lost Boys' tofu kebabs, recipe 365:64

"Peter Pan"; Tinker Bell's raspberry buns, recipe 365:76

BARTON, CLARA—BIRTHDAY

Birthday celebration; art, music, foods, games, activities 1104:34-37

Celebrate by making first aid kits, box, medical supplies 1199:285

BASEBALL

Babe Ruth's birthday, activity with song 1199:33

Hank Aaron's birthday, fun with baseball, activity 1199:32

Jackie Robinson's birthday celebration; art, music, foods, games, activities 1104:50-53

Pop-up catcher's mask, making 1388:16-17

BASIN PLATEAU INDIANS—TOYS

Cradle board for doll, milk carton, making 1699:89-90

BASKETBALL

History of basketball 119:118-122

BASKETRY. *See also* **INDIANS OF NORTH AMERICA—BASKETRY**

BASKETS

Balloon basket, yarn, ribbon, balloon, making 1615:14-17

Bark baskets, oatmeal box, glue, making 1421:169

Basket made by weaving or coiling, making 524:22-24

Basket, newspaper, making 1658:19

Beach basket from beach vines and grasses, making 1285:80-83

Cardboard woven basket, cardboard, string, making 1255:37

Cattail basket, making 1421:178

Coiled basket, rope, yarn, making 430:13-15; 1615:14-17

Corn husk coiled basket, making 283:40-41

Cornucopia basket, paper, making 123:34

Easter basket, woven paper, making 123:39-40

Egg basket, making 627:42

Flower basket, artificial flowers, paper, making 1299:28-29

Folded paper baskets, making 438:68

Grass basket, making 337:76-79

Heart basket, paper, patterns, making 1087:85-87

May Day baskets, paper, pattern, making 232:41; 247:14

Openwork basket, yarn, making 430:16

Rag basket, rope, fabric, making 1615:14-17

Reed or willow baskets, making 527:20-21

Ribbon basket, making 430:9-12

Rush and willow baskets, how to make 937:145-146; 1701:18-19

Tub basket, plastic tub, making 430:4-5

Twined basket, plastic tub and yarn, making 430:6-8

Wastebasket, decoupage, making 341:16-18

Willow basket, making 482:38-39

Woven basket from natural materials, making 1531:189-190

Wrought iron basket from soft metal, making 1254:33

Yarn basket, patterns, making 1213:34-35

BASQUE AMERICANS—SONGS

Sleep, Sleep, My Child, lullaby 1220:145

BATHING SUITS—COSTUMES

Bathing suit costume, cl880, making 368:21-26

BATIK

April flowers batik, making 561:100

Armband, making 641:108-109

Batik banner, fabric, dowels, paste, water colors, making 1372:143

Batik, crayon, how to do 805:97

Batik, crayon, paper, making 1067:81-83

Batik, crayon, towel, making 1429:44-45

Batik dyeing, how to do 508:49-53

Batik, fabric, making using crayons 740:63

Batik, imitation, with crayons, making 275:16

Batik painting, how to do 786:43

Batik scarf, fabric, wax, dyes, making 1476:149-150

Batik T-shirt, making 251:42-43

Batik, Adinkra cloth, crayons, making 1427:290

Batik, doing outdoors, making 375:53

Batik, dyed fabric, dyes, wax, patterns, making 525:88-89; 727:12-32; 805:96; 1056:124-125; 1427:200-201

Beach dress, making 641:94-95

Candles as wax for batik, how to do 1505:11

Easter eggs 201:69-91

Eggs, batik decorated eggs, blown eggs, wax, food dyes, making 1505:11

Flour and water paste batik, how to make 1278:12-13

Flour batik, making 461:87

Glue batik, fabric, paints, glue, making 1421:38

Handkerchief, making 641:102-102; 641:96-97

Head scarf, making 641:98-99

Magic batik painting, making 376:175

Pennant, making 641:110-111

Pirate flag, making 641:106-107

Place mat and coasters, making 641:90-91

Quick batik, making 954:114-115

Scarf, making 297:164-165

Step-by-step, how to do 1505:8-9

T-shirt, making 641:92-93

Tablecloth, making 641:100-101

Tie-dyeing, how to do 893:41-45

Tray cloth, making 641:104-105

Wax crayon batik, how to do 1505:10

BATS—PARTIES

Bat cake, recipe 1185:66-67

BAUM, L. FRANK—COOKERY

"Wizard of Oz"; Over the Rainbow milk, recipe 365:55

Dorothy's scrambled eggs, recipe 570:21-22

BAUM, L. FRANK—PUPPETS

"Wizard of Oz" munchkin finger puppets, making 1310:151

BAUM, L. FRANK. *See also* **WIZARD OF OZ**

BAZAARS

Heritage bazaar snacks, recipes 298:278-281

How to run bazaars 298:264-274

Three games of chance for bazaars 298:276-277

BEACH. *See* **SEASHORE—HANDICRAFTS**
BEADS. *See also* **JEWELRY**
Abacus information 301:63-71
Adagio dancers party favors, making 255:64-65
African beads, flour clay, making 1022:16
African trade beads, oven baked clay, making 1556:19
African trade-bead necklace, making 301:87-89
African trade-wind beads information 301:21-27
African, West, beads information 301:37-43
Bead embroidered notebook cover, making 301:119-123
Bead messages information 301:29-35
Bead necklace, decoupage, making 341:40-42
Bead rose, making 301:125-132
Beads as money and documents information 301:13-20
Beads from other countries, making 298:52-74
Beads from paper, how to roll your own, making 1350:70-71
Bow drill, making 301:101-105
Clay beads, how to make 1260:10-11
Clay, rolled paper, cloth, making 1615:42-45
Coffee and tea leaf dough beads, making 1372:71
Cornstarch and dough beads and pendants, making 1372:59-60
Dutch bead garden information 301:45-50
Easter egg from beads, making 255:79-80
Easter rabbit from beads, making 255:78
Embroidery beads information 301:73-82
Halloween pumpkin party pick, making with beads 255:82
Halloween spider, making with beads 255:83
History of beads 255:13-15
Jewels of glass information 301:1-11
Love necklace, making 301:107-112
Macaroni beads, how to paint and string 1446:14-15
Macaroni beads, making 400:20-21
Miniature bead garden, making 301:95-99
Paper beads, making 400:22-23
Prayer beads information 301:51-62
Rose petal beads, dough, recipe, making 531:62; 1372:71
Rose petal beads, flower petals and paste, making 1213:96
Rose petal beads, making 301:91-93
Round and oblong beads, tissue paper, making 1261:20-21
Salt dough beads, recipe, how to make 1278:6-7
Santa from beads, making 255:68-69
Soroban/Analog computer, making 301:113-117
St. Patrick's Day pixie from beads, making 255:77
Tissue paper bead clay, recipe 1455:9
Valentine from beads, making 255:76
Valentine heart from beads, making 255:77
Wise Man from beads, making 255:70-72
BEADWORK. *See also* **INDIANS OF NORTH AMERICA—BEADWORK**
BEANS
History of beans 410:26-32
BEASTS. *See* **MONSTERS**
BEAUTY AND THE BEAST—COOKERY
Lamb chops with currant jelly sauce, recipe 569:46-48
BEDOUINS—AMULETS
Amulet, hajeb, leather purse, making 671:45
Amulet, making 671:45
Amulet, silver, making 671:45
BEDOUINS—CLOTHING
Clothing for man and woman 671:30

BEDOUINS—DOLLS
Arab Sheik doll, making 494:173-185
BEDOUINS—LANGUAGE
Arabic words and phrases 671:46
BEDOUINS—TENTS
Nomad tent, wood dowels, fabric, making 1512:16-17
Tent, Bedouin tent model, making 671:44
BEETHOVEN, LUDWIG—GAMES
Beethoven's birthday game 240:60
BELARUS—HANDICRAFTS
Inlaid box, small box, paint, ribbons, making 1477:57
BELGIUM—BIRTHDAYS
Birthday customs 488:19-21
BELGIUM—CHRISTMAS
St. Nicholas' Day celebration 601:103-104
BELGIUM—CHRISTMAS—COOKERY
Speculaas cookies, recipe 515:18
BELGIUM—COOKERY
Cheesy endive and ham dish, recipe 1518:117
Choux de Bruxelles, Brussels sprouts, recipe 1165:120
Mirrors (speculaas), cookies, recipe 72:30-31
Omelettes at camp, recipes 967:23
Padstools, recipe 188:24
Petits fours for birth celebration, recipe 1220:130-132
Raw vegetable dip, recipe 858:unp
Waterzooi de Poularde, Flemish chicken and vegetable stew, recipe 1165:120
BELGIUM—COSTUMES
Padstools, recipe, costume 188:24
BELGIUM—DANCES
Chimes of Dunkirk, how to do 1494:119-120
Shoes-a-dancing, how to do 1494:127-128
BELGIUM—EASTER
Easter egg customs in Belgium 201:25
BELGIUM—FESTIVALS—COOKERY
Carnival: tarte tatin (apple tart), recipe 1666:104-105
Carnival; stoofperen (stewed pears), recipe 1666:104
BELGIUM—FOLKLORE
"Stone Soup" flannel board story, patterns, making 1604:114-115
BELGIUM—GAMES
Baton Maudit stick game 1119:17
Baton Maudit, the cursed stick, how to play 1494:97
Chenille-assis team game, how to play 1499:30
Le Furet, how to play 1497:24
Le Lettre du Traitre, how to play 1497:40
Passwords game 967:22
Solo Whist card game 1132:50-53
Trip to Rome game 515:18
BELGIUM—NEW YEAR'S DAY
Sylvester's Day and the day after in Belgium 489:21-24
BELGIUM—SONGS
Donkeys and Carrots round song 1115:68
BELL, ALEXANDER GRAHAM
Kite experiment based on early works of Mabel and her husband Alexander 1719:42-45
Tetrahedron kite, making 1069:266-272
BELL, ALEXANDER GRAHAM—BIRTHDAY
Birthday celebration; art, music, foods, games, activities 1104:66-69
Celebrate making tin can telephones, how to do 1199:63-64
BELL, MABEL
Kite experiment based on early works of Mabel and her husband Alexander 1719:42-45

BELTANE FIRE FESTIVAL
Information on celebration 419:65-67
BENIN—GAMES
Cho-Cho-Chuckie, how to play 1494:14
BENIN—HANDICRAFTS
Computer project: Kinglist cloth, create 1218:24-27
Fon story pictures on felt or paper, making 1632:24-27
Ivory leopard of Benin, making 222:38-39
BIBLE—COSTUMES
Assyrian King's robe, making 870:13-16
Crowns, making 870:19-20
Halos, making 870:18-19
Persian King's robe, making 870:12,16-18
BIBLE—HANDICRAFTS
Bible leaf bookmark, making 725:38
Creation wall hanging, making 52:10
Days of creation miniatures, mobiles and a stabile, making 52:8-9
Days of creation puzzle, making 52:4
Dimensional mirrored plaque, making 52:7
Drapery ring miniatures of creation, making 52:6
Flower mosaic to decorate wells, how to do 1467:13
Jonah and the Whale mobile, making 452:58-60
Quilled apple on a Garden of Eden scene, making 52:18-20
Scratch art from scratch, making 52:5
Sponge-towel flowers in a Garden of Eden vase, making 52:18-19
Stuffed pictures of Adam and Eve, making 52:14-15
Vase with clay figures and tissue-paper flowers, making 52:16
Woven story board of the Garden of Eden, making 52:11-13
BIBLE—HANDICRAFTS—ABRAHAM, SARAH AND ISAAC
Fabric-dressed figure of Abraham and Sarah, making 52:48
Mounted picture of Abraham in relief (repousse), making 52:40-41
Styrofoam Abraham and the three angels, making 52:41
Three angels, making 52:42-45
Walnut-head doll of Sarah, making 52:47
Wooden plaque of Sarah and Isaac, making 52:45-46
BIBLE—HANDICRAFTS—DANIEL IN THE LION'S DEN
Daniel in the lion's den slide show, making 52:105-107
No-brush acrylic painting of Daniel in the lion's den, making 52:104
Peek box of Daniel in the lion's den, making 52:103
Rising figure puppet of Daniel in the lion's den, making 52:102
BIBLE—HANDICRAFTS—ISRAELITES ENTER CANAAN
Bread and glue miniatures of temple priests, making 52:90-91
Clay and jute fruit, making 52:89
Cut-outs and drawings of Israelites marching into Canaan, making 52:91-92
Fruit from Canaan painting in plastic, making 52:92
Sculptured soap, making 52:88
BIBLE—HANDICRAFTS—JACOB'S LADDER
Angels climb the Ladder, making 52:54
Dimensional Jacob's Ladder shoe box scenes (1) and (2), making 52:50-51
Jacob's Ladder movie, making 52:52-53

BIBLE—HANDICRAFTS—JONAH AND THE WHALE
Jonah and the Whale beanbag game wall hanging, making 52:110-111
Jonah and the Whale mirror, making 52:112
Mobile of Jonah being swallowed by the whale, making 52:113-114
BIBLE—HANDICRAFTS—JOSEPH AND HIS COAT OF MANY COLORS
Appliqued coat of many colors, making 52:60-62
Batiked coat of many colors, making 52:57-58
Coats of many colors, making 52:56
Cut-out dolls of Joseph and his brothers, making 52:59
BIBLE—HANDICRAFTS—MOSES
Baby Moses in a basket in the River Nile, making 52:71
Crewel painting of Moses and the Burning Bush, making 52:76
Moses and the ten plagues, making 52:74-75
Red Sea parts for Moses and the Israelites, making 52:72-73
Shoe boxes and material Moses, making 52:78-80
Spoon and cup of Moses and the Burning Bush, making 52:70
BIBLE—HANDICRAFTS—NOAH'S ARK. *See also* **NOAH'S ARK**
Colorful feltboard Noah's Ark scene, making 52:24-25
Dimensional Noah's Ark scene, making 52:23
Funny mixed-up Noah's Ark, making 52:22
Hanging Noah's Ark, making 52:25-26
Noah's Ark diorama, making 52:27
Noah's Ark mirrored line drawing, making 52:28
Noah's Ark model, clay for Ark and animals, making 1484:16-17
BIBLE—HANDICRAFTS—THE STORY OF RUTH
Ruth bottle doll, making 52:97-99
Ruth gathering grain in the fields of Boaz, making 52:94-95
Wire figure of Ruth carrying wheat, making 52:96
BIBLE—HANDICRAFTS—THE TEN COMMANDMENTS
Mock stone tablets, making 52:82
"Parchment" window hanging, making 52:84-85
Slate painting, making 52:83
BIBLE—HANDICRAFTS—THE TWELVE TRIBES
Painted eggs of the Twelve Tribes in a carton, making 52:64
Paper mosaic of the Tribes of Israel, making 52:65-66
Silhouette "photograph" of the Twelve Tribes, making 52:67-68
BIBLE—HANDICRAFTS—TOWER OF BABEL
Brick sandpaper Tower, making 52:31
Eraser print Tower, making 52:30
Foreign newspaper Tower, making 52:38
Stacked boxes of Tower of Babel, making 52:33
Textured picture of Tower of Babel, making 52:32
Tin can Tower that rises, making 52:35-36
Tower of Babel storyboard, making 52:37
Tower of Babel in clay relief, making 52:34
BIBLE—PUPPETS
David and Goliath puppet show 756:181-188
Eve stocking puppet, stuffed, making 52:17
Noah's Ark puppet show 756:176-180
BIGFOOT—COSTUMES
Bigfoot monster mask, making 179:40-41
Bigfoot monster tracks, making 179:36-39

BIOGRAPHY—PARTIES

Historical heroes birthday celebration, activities, foods, and handicrafts 30:113-115

BIRD FEEDERS

Milk carton, plastic jugs and pine cone feeders, making 1213:53-54

Scandinavian birdfeed, making 709:81-82

Wooden bird feeder, wood, screws, paint, making 1285:124-126

BIRDS

Bird shooer shoos birds away, paper, styrofoam plates, making 1453:40-42

Cage from Lebanon, cardboard and stick model, making 515:74

John J. Audubon birthday celebration; art, music, foods, games, activities 1104:78-81

Origami birds, how to make 1196:40-41

Songs, finger plays, stories, games, rhythms 1200:65-68

Vulture of the Western Plains model, making 356:12-13

BIRDS—CHRISTMAS

Activities, art, songs, recipes, games 1469:50-51

BIRDS—NESTS

Nesting box, wood, pattern, making 1285:26-27

BIRTHDAYS

Birthdays, history of 190:11-13

Birthstones, history of 660:10-12

Candles, why we light them 660:37

Days of week, meanings of for birthdays 660:9-10

Finger plays and rhymes 1583:131-135

Flowers, history of for birthdays 660:10-12

History of birthdays 660:1-5

Songs, finger plays, stories, games, rhythms 1200:119-120

Spanks and bumps, meaning of 660:40-42

Special birthdays around the world celebrations 660:51-67

Zodiac signs for birthdays 660:14-16

Zodiac signs for China 660:16-17

BIRTHDAYS—COSTUMES

Birthday present costume, cardboard, making 1283:50-53

BIRTHDAYS—DECORATIONS

Nosegays, Victorian, making 670:61-62

BIRTHDAYS—PARTIES

Alphabet theme party, ages 2-4, making 1202:31

Art attack creative art theme party, ages 5-12, making 1202:42-50

Bear theme party, ages 2-4, making 1202:32

Camp-out backyard theme party, ages 7 and u p, making 1202:51-59

Candid camera theme party, ages 10 and up, making 1202:60-65

Carnival theme birthday party, making 896:76-83

Chocolate factory theme party, ages 3-8, making 1202:66-73

Cloud 9, heavenly fantasy theme party, ages 7-10, making 1202:74-79

Club casino theme party, ages 8 and up, making 1202:80-88

Doll shower theme party, ages 5-8, making 1202:89-95

Fire fighter theme party, ages 2-4, making 1202:34

Flower child theme party, ages 9 and up, making 1202:96-107

Foreign Countries theme birthday party, making 896:126-133

Giantland theme party, ages 3-5, making 1202:108-114

Gone fishing theme party, ages 3-6, making 1202:115-120

Grandma's attic theme party, ages 2-4, making 1202:38

Hawaiian Luau theme birthday party, making 896:61-66

Hollywood theme birthday party, making 896:117-125

Horsin' around theme party, ages 7-12, making 1202:121-127

It's a dog's life theme party, ages 3-6, making 1202:128-132

Mermaids theme party, ages 2-4, making 1202:37

Mexican party, making 896:19-25

Mini-chef's theme party, ages 2-4, making 1202:39

Olympic Games theme birthday party, making 896:55-60

Pig-out theme party, ages 5-10, making 1202:140-144

Secret agents theme party, ages 8 and up, making 1202:145-153

Shipwrecked theme party, ages 7-12, making 1202:154-162

So What's vs. The Big Deals theme party, ages 9 and up, making 1202:168-174

Soccer theme party, ages 8 and up, making 1202:163-167

Stargazing theme party, ages 10 and up, making 1202:175-183

Stegosaurus and Friends theme party, ages 4-7, making 1202:184-190

Super heroes theme party, ages 7 and up, making 1202:191-199

Sweepstakes theme party, ages 8 and up, making 1202:200-206

This Is Your Life theme party, ages 13 and up, making 1202:207-213

Trains, cars, airplanes theme party, ages 2-4, making 1202:36

Under the Big Top theme party, ages 5-12, making 1202:214-221

"Wizard of Oz" theme party, ages 2-4, making 1202:40

BIRTHDAYS—TREES

Tree planting birthday custom 488:15-16

BIRTHSTONES

Lucky jewels, magic powers of birthstones 236:46

BLACK HISTORY MONTH

Activities and projects for classrooms 1393:136-138

BLACK HOLES—GAMES

Black hole game, making 1185:94-95

BLACKFOOT INDIANS—CLOTHING

Blackfoot cuff, making 465:36

Blackfoot dress and accessories, making 465:95

Leggings, making 281:26-27

Shirt and dress, fabric, making 281:33-36

BLACKFOOT INDIANS—DESIGNS

Blackfoot designs and symbols 465:69

BLACKFOOT INDIANS—FOOTWEAR

Moccasins, pattern, making 281:27-28

BLACKFOOT INDIANS—GAMES

Hands and feet game 602:167

Stick game, how to make and play 1699:104-105

BLACKFOOT INDIANS—HOUSES

Tepee, making 227:12

BLACKFOOT INDIANS—WAR BONNETS

Warbonnet cases, oatmeal box, making 1699:55

Warbonnet, fabric and feathers, making 281:30-32

Warbonnets, making 1699:52

BLACKFOOT INDIANS—WIGS

Wig, black horse hair, making 281:28-30

BLACKSMITHS

Song; Now the Blacksmith's Arm round song 1115:26

BLIND

Helen Keller, birthday celebration; art, music, foods, games, activities 1104:94-97

BLUE RIDGE MOUNTAINS—COOKERY

Chunky applesauce, recipe 1542:40

BLUEBERRIES

Blueberry Day, activities, art, songs, recipes, games 1469:118-119

Story and fresh blueberries, how to serve 843:64

BLY, NELLIE

Birthday celebration; art, music, foods, games, activities 1104:82-85

BOATS

American cup racer, styrofoam cups, making 556:8-9

Canoe paddles, making 467:66-67

Clermont model, wooden, making 567:49-54

Columbus ships, paper models, making 75:142-144

Diddy port boat, historic, wooden, making 942:40-41

Diddy port boat, making 942:29

Egyptian Felucca boat, wood and styrofoam, making 287:75-78

Inca boat model, making 682:26-27

Jangada boat, wood, making 143:15

Mississippi River boat model, making 356:24-26

Mississippi steamboat, balsa wood, making 925:80-82

Oil tankers, paper, making 1020:73-74

Paddlewheel boat, making 706:23-26; 773:150-151

Philippine Vinta toy boat, paper, making 515:98

Pilgrim boat, paper models, making 75:142-144

Pirate ship, balsa wood, making 925:83-85

Pirate ships, paper models, making 75:142-144

Punt, English, making 467:56-57

River flatboat model, wooden, making 567:46-48

Sampan boat, model, making 494:192-195

Sampan toy boat from Thailand, milk carton, making 515:108

Stern Wheeler model, pattern, making 942:144

Sulu outrigger boat, Philippine wood toy, pattern, making 1027:114-119

Tugboat, cookies, making 1672:89-91

Viking longship, milk carton, making 129:20-21

Whaler boat model, cardboard, patterns, making 942:132-135

BOATS—GAMES

Clipper ship race game, making 942:44-45

Tea clippers game 942:42-43

BODY PAINTS

Recipe for body paints for faces, tattoos, hands, etc. 1372:38-40

BOJAXHIU, AGNES GONXHA—BIRTHDAY

Mother Teresa's birthday; celebrate with friend in need activities 1199:196

BOLIVIA—CHRISTMAS

Christmas celebration 601:159

BOLIVIA—CHRISTMAS—COOKERY

Pastelitos de Almendras (almond cookies), recipe 1666:227

BOLIVIA—COOKERY

Caramel-filled cookies (alfajores), cookies, recipe 72:176-177

Corn packages with husks, recipe 1517:35

Humintas, corn, corn muffin mix, cheese, spices, recipe 1519:118

Little cocoa peaks, recipe 187:17

Papas y Dlotes, potatoes and corn, recipe 1165:230

Saltenas, meat turnovers, recipe 1165:230-231

BOLIVIA—COSTUMES

Girl costume, crepe paper, making 687:26-31

BOLIVIA—FESTIVALS

Carnival celebration 601:159

Fair of the Alacitas eckecko model, making 515:20

Little Things celebration 601:153-154

Ribbons celebration 601:154

BOLIVIA—FESTIVALS—COOKERY

Carnival; empoanadas de queso (chicken turnovers), recipe 1666:227

Carnival; paltas rellenas (stuffed avocados), recipe 1666:226

BOLIVIA—GAMES

Choque game 602:139

Jackstones game 602:138

Juego de panuelo, handkerchief game, how to play 1494:206

Juego del panuelo handkerchief game 383:27

La Palma game 383:28

La Thunkuna, hopscotch game 1426:10-11

Marbles game 602:139

Palma-Palma game 1146:32-33

Paloma Y Gavilan, eagle and pigeon game 383:28

Rirar frijoles, throw the beans game, how to play 1708:14-15

Thieves and guards game 602:138

Throw the beans game 602:137

BOLIVIA—LANGUAGE

Numbers one to ten in Aymara and Quechua 1519:83

BOLIVIA—NEW YEAR'S DAY

Spanish and Indian ceremonials in Bolivia 489:25-30

BOND, MICHAEL

"Bear Called Paddington," marmalade, recipe 1216:36

BONES—GAMES

Knucklebones game, making 229:67

BONES—IMPLEMENTS

History of bones as implements 229:39-42

BONES—MUSICAL INSTRUMENTS

Indian rattle, making 229:73-74

BOOKS

Bible Leaf bookmark, making 725:38

Book Day, activities, art, songs, recipes, games 1469:38-39

Books for children to make for their own writings, how to do 1590:9-73

Books from handmade paper, making 1732:26-27

Family survey and family scrapbook, how to make 1152:179-200

Hornbook, paper, patterns for book and text, making 719:28-29; 1159:130

Hornbooks, gingerbread, recipes 376:271

Thanksgiving bookmark patterns, making 994:15

Under the Big Top book, patterns, making 903:44

Wild West adventure book, making 498:62-63

BOOMERANGS

Boomerang, cardboard, making 152:67; 153:53-57; 310:184; 855:14-19

Homemade boomerang that comes back to you, making 1719:72-75

Paper boomerangs, making 75:128; 996:27

Play boomerangs, making 120:155-157

BOONE, DANIEL
 Costume 213:124-126
BORNEO. *See also* **INDONESIA**
BORNEO—FESTIVALS
 Rice growing festival 419:93-94
BORNEO—HOUSES
 Huts on stilts, dowels, sticks, clay, making 1488:20-21
BOSNIA—HERZEGOVINA. *See* **YUGOSLAVIA**
BOSTON TEA PARTY
 Boston Tea Party play 755:58-64
 Buckram mask, making 755:65-70
BOTSWANA—CHRISTMAS—COOKERY
 Cold beef curry, recipe 1666:18
BOTSWANA—COOKERY
 Dodo, green or yellow plantain chips, recipe 1165:19
BOTSWANA—GAMES
 Stalker game, how to play 1507:10
BOTTLES
 Digging for bottles, information about 118:123-124
 Poison bottles, history of 118:125
BOWLS. *See also* **CLAY; INDIANS OF NORTH**
 AMERICA—POTTERY; POTTERY
 Coiled bowl, clay, making 431:44
BOY SCOUTS
 Investiture racks, making 466:97
BRAIDING. *See also* **STRING FIGURES**
 African countryside scene, braided cord, making
 618:14-15
 Bracelets; braiding and knotting bracelets, how to do
 1364:4-23
BRAIDS
 Chinese braids, making 548:45-50
 Four strand Indian braid, making 548:30-31
 Girl Scout braid, making 548:42-44
 Peruvian flat braid, sixteen strand variation, making
 548:34-36
BRAILLE
 Braille, making 376:137
BRAQUE, GEORGES
 Georges Braque's torn paper mosaics, how to make your
 own 1372:80
BRAZIL
 Activities, flags, games, foods, history, songs, dances,
 recipes 143:1-34; 282:50-63; 1381:45-48
 Festivals, folklore, games, tropical rain forest activities
 1378:198-275
 Traditions, customs, geography, economy, ecology, aes-
 thetic awareness units 1378:198-275
BRAZIL—ACTIVITIES
 Jungle montage, making 143:10
 Rain forest, making 143:11
BRAZIL—BIRDS
 Toucan, paper, paints, patterns, making 1251:36-39
BRAZIL—BIRTHDAYS
 Birthday customs 488:22-25
 Celebrations of birthdays in Brazil 474:83
 Fifteenth cumpleanos birthday party for girls 660:62-63
BRAZIL—BOATS
 Jangada, boat, wood, making 143:15
BRAZIL—CHRISTMAS
 Christmas tree and decorations, how to make 593:150-
 155
 Customs in Brazil 425:20-22

BRAZIL—CHRISTMAS—COOKERY
 Kale greens, shredded, recipe 1223:75
 Manioc meal, toasted, recipe 1223:74
 Pepper and lemon sauce, recipe 1223:75
 Pineapple/lime cooler drink, recipe 1223:76
 Rice with tomatoes and onions, recipe 1223:74
 Smoked and fresh meat with beans and sauce, recipe
 1223:72-73
 Turkey stuffing, recipe 1223:75-76
BRAZIL—CHRISTMAS—DECORATIONS
 Fabric ornament, foam balls, glitter, patterns, making
 1223:69
 Gourd noise maker, gourd, dowel, pebbles, paints, mak-
 ing 1223:67-68
 Reindeer table decoration or hanging ornament, paper,
 ribbon, glitter, making 1223:65-67
 Tinsel-tailed tropical birds, paper, markers, glitter, pat-
 terns, making 1223:70-71
BRAZIL—CHRISTMAS—HANDICRAFTS
 Papai Noel Christmas tree, pattern, making 1305:23
BRAZIL—COOKERY
 Arroz Brasileiro, Brazilian rice, recipe 1165:232-233
 Avocado ice, recipe 1378:262
 Avocado soup, recipe 1058:83-84
 Avocado whip, recipe 1378:262
 Baked bananas, microwave recipe 1211:40
 Bean dish, recipe 1378:262
 Beef barbecue, recipe 1378:263
 Beef char-broiled with sauce, recipe 1517:33
 Beef kabobs, recipe 1265:40-41
 Beijanhos de moca, maidens kisses, candy, recipe 143:32
 Black bean casserole, recipe 1517:30
 Brazil nut sandwiches, docinhos do para, cookies, recipe
 72:178-179
 Brazilian rice, onion, garlic, recipe 1381:47
 Brigadeiro, chocolate candy, recipe 143:27
 Chicken rice soup, recipe 1517:22-23
 Chicken, marinated, recipe 1517:33
 Chocolate balls, brigadeiros, recipe 1324:41
 Chocolate bananas, recipe 143:33
 Chocolate beans 143:28
 Chocolate-dipped Brazil nuts, recipe 282:118
 Chocolate sweet treats, recipe 1517:42
 Chuffasco, grilled steak, recipe 143:31
 Churrasco a gaucha, Brazilian barbecue, recipe 1165:234
 Cocadas, coconut candy, recipe 143:33
 Cocoa, making 143:27
 Coconut candy, recipe 793:27
 Coffee "leftovers" 143:26
 Coffee gelatin dessert, recipe 143:26
 Coffee tasting 143:25
 Couve a mineira, shredded greens, recipe 1165:233
 Dreams pastries, recipe 794:13
 Empadas (turnovers), ham, chicken, beef, fruit, recipe
 1517:28-29
 Farova de ovo, seasoned eggs, recipe 1165:234-235
 Feijoada bean casserole, recipe 143:29
 Feijoada, meat stew with black beans, recipe 1165:232
 Fruited rice, recipe 1265:42
 Fudge balls, recipe 793:28; 1381:47
 Guava toast, recipe 143:28; 188:11
 Hamburger in sauce (picadinho), recipe 662:106
 Iced coffee and chocolate float, recipe 1265:37
 Kale, recipe 1517:34
 Laranjas, orange salad, recipe 1165:233

Milk pudding dessert, recipe 1280:49
Milk pudding, flan dessert, recipe 1517:39
Mocha-flavored cupcakes, recipe 1265:38-39
Molho a campanha, cold sauce to serve with barbecue, recipe 1165:235
Nut cake, recipe 1517:38-39
Pudim de laite condensado (caramel custard), recipe 143:30
Pudim, eggs, sugar and coconut dessert, recipe 1058:85
Pumpkin pudding, recipe 1653:170
Rice, recipe 793:26; 1517:34
Shrimp with corn, recipe 1058:84-85
Sweet treats, light, recipe 1517:42
Tapioca pudding, recipe 1244:134
Tucupi sauce, recipe 143:31

BRAZIL—COSTUMES
Carnival costumes, making 143:18
Gaucho poncho, paper towels, paints, making 1378:250-251
Guava toast, recipe, costume 188:11
Paper doll type costume, making 282:62

BRAZIL—DANCES
Bossa Nova dance, how to do 1494:219-220
Samba dance and costume picture 1000:60-63

BRAZIL—EASTER
Easter celebrations 419:132

BRAZIL—FESTIVALS
Carnavale in Rio de Janeiro, how to celebrate 1378:256-259
Carnival celebration 143:16-19; 419:131; 601:160
Festivals and celebrations, maps, flags, crafts, making 1305:16-26
Midsummer Eve celebrations 419:132
St. John's Day celebration 601:160-162

BRAZIL—FESTIVALS—COOKERY
Carnival; acaraje (black-eyed pea fritters), recipe 1666:229
Carnival; Brasileiras (Brazilian coconut cookies), recipe 1666:230
Carnival; couve a mineira (shredded greens), recipe 1666:229
Carnival; feijoada (Brazilian meat stew), recipe 1666:228-229
Carnival; laranjas (orange salad), recipe 1666:228

BRAZIL—FESTIVALS—HANDICRAFTS
Carnival black cow winding sheet, fabric, paints, making 1516:40-41
Carnival black cow, balloon, newspapers, paints, making 1516:38-39
Carnival Cangaceiro hat, felt, paper, ribbons, making 1516:35-37
Carnival Congo snakes, newspapers, paste, paints, making 1516:46-47
Carnival flag banners, fabrics, sticks, ribbons, making 1516:42-43
Carnival flowers, crepe paper, wire twists, making 1362:146
Carnival Frevo umbrella, paper, sticks, ribbons, making 1516:44-45
Carnival hat or bonnet, paper plate, crepe paper, making 1381:48
Carnival Reisado hat, paper, sequins, beads, making 1516:33-34

BRAZIL—FESTIVALS—MASKS
Carnival mask, paper plate, crepe paper, yarn, making 1305:19; 1381:48; 1574:8-9
Carnival peek-a-boo mask, paper plate, making 1539:102

BRAZIL—GAMES
Bamboo bottle cap bounce game, making 282:120
Cat and rat game, how to play 383:30; 1381:47; 1494:209-210
Catch the broom game 967:23
Chief orders game 602:141
Cinco Marias, jacks game, how to play 1718:10-11
Dancer, little dancer game 602:141-142
Ferol bola (a game for two players) 143:23
Grab bag (Morral) game 1378:242-243
Gude, marbles game 515:22
Hit it off game, how to play 1355:25
Hit the penny game 143:23; 383:31
Marbles games, wooden, making 889:77-84
Morral or grab bag game 383:32
My little boat game 602:139-140
My right side is vacant (Minha Direita Desocupada) game 602:143; 1378:242
Peteca game 602:140-141; 1507:107
Pif Paf card game 1132:99-100
Rabbit in his house (Coelho na Toca) game 1378:241
Samba card game 1132:107-110
Sick cat (Gato Doente) game 602:140; 1378:241
Spoon or domino game 474:38-39
Visit to mom's House game, how to play 1718:10-11
Zoo game 967:23

BRAZIL—HANDICRAFTS
Butterfly, pattern, making 1305:22
Clay figurines, how to make 1378:246-248
Floating city rafts, milk and egg cartons, making 1378:260
Floating stores, milk cartons, making 143:16
Lemanja goddess, combs and mirrors, making 1305:21
Palm tree, pattern, making 1305:22
Paper flowers, making 143:18-19
Parrot, pattern, making 1305:22
Tin-can vehicles, boxes, paints, making 1338:50-51
Waura Indian patapu fish lure, cardboard, paint, making 1378:228

BRAZIL—LANGUAGE
Brazilian language 143:34
Common words and phrases in Portuguese 1324:26
Gaucho words and their meanings 1378:252-253
Numbers one to ten in Portuguese 1711:unp
Portuguese words; numbers, names, school words, colors, months, seasons 1378:263-269

BRAZIL—MASKS
Indian body mask with horns pattern 1378:236
Indian face mask pattern 1378:235
Masks, cardboard, making 143:13

BRAZIL—MUSICAL INSTRUMENTS
Birimbau, making 468:122
Maracas from soda cans, pebbles, making 1378:245
Maracas, cups, dried seeds, making 1715:172
Maracas, papier-mache over light bulbs, making 1378:244
Tambourine, paper plates, bottle caps, making 1378:245

BRAZIL—NEW YEAR'S DAY
Carnival time in Brazil 489:31-35

BRAZIL—POTTERY
Ceramic pots, clay, making 143:13

BRAZIL—RAIN FORESTS

Create miniature rain forest in wide mouth jar, making 1378:209-211

Tropical rain forest in Brazil teaching units 1378:198-275

BRAZIL—TOYS

Ball, felt or Naugahyde, pattern, making 1027:160-162

Toys and dolls, clay, making 143:14

BREAD

Activities, art, songs, recipes, games 259:49-54; 1469:36-37

Baking bread, recipe, how to make 253:125; 6:18-29

Bread around the world 594:53-63

Cuban bread, recipe 594:85-86

DePaola, Tomie, "Strega Nona's Magic Lessons"; science/reading activities 1055:206-210

History of bread 6:6-10; 594:15-26

History of bread in the United States 594:27-35

Modern history of bread in the United States 594:36-49

Pita, Syrian pocket bread, recipe 6:31

Religions and bread 594:67-80

BREMEN TOWN MUSICIANS

Bremen Town Musicians, picture, making 92:25

Cat and donkey masks, paper, patterns, making 92:29-31

Robber masks, paper, patterns, making 92:32-34

Robber's feast of baked beans and frankfurters, recipe 569:37-39

Rooster and dog masks, paper, patterns, making 92:26-28

BRETT, JAN

"Goldilocks and the Three Bears," porridge, recipe 1216:15

BRICKS

Adobe bricks, how to make 182:40-43; 1372:121-122

Clay bricks, making 785:11

BRIDGES

Covered bridge, model, paper sheets given, making 220:54-60

Drawbridge, paper, making 1020:55-57

Inca suspension bridge, making 682:30-31

London Bridge, bridge pictures, toothpick, paper, making 172:16

London Bridge, history of, picture, poem, activities 172:13-17

Suspension bridge, paper, making 1020:51-54

BRITISH COLUMBIA

Activities, projects; recipes, making 282:64-81

BRITISH COLUMBIA—COOKERY

Baked Canadian bacon, recipe 282:119

BRITISH COLUMBIA—COSTUMES

Paper doll type costume, pattern, making 282:80

BRITISH COLUMBIA—FESTIVALS

Indian Potlatch celebration 601:128-129

BRITISH COLUMBIA—GAMES

Fox and Geese game, making 282:121

BRITISH COLUMBIA—STRING FIGURES

Outrigger canoe figure, making 1477:113

BRITISH ISLES. *See also* **ENGLAND; IRELAND; SCOTLAND; WALES**

BRITISH ISLES—HALLOWEEN

Halloween celebrations in the British Isles 474:66-67

BROOMS

Colonial broom, paper, making 877:119

BROWN, MARCIA

"Bun," buns, recipe 1216:41

"Stone Soup," recipe 1216:73

BROWN, MARGARET WISE

"Fish with the Deep Sea Smile" flannel board poem, patterns, making 1603:146-151

BRUNHOFF, JEAN DE—COOKERY

"Story of Babar"; Babar's carob French toast, orange yogurt sauce, recipe 365:18

BUCKAROOS. *See* **COWBOYS**

BUDDHA

Bodhi Day or Buddha's Enlightenment, activities and projects for classrooms 1393:95-96

Large Buddha pattern 1393:214

Nirvana Day or Buddha's Death, activities and projects for classrooms 1393:149-150

Wesak, birthday of the Buddha; history and celebration of 496:69

Wesak, Buddha's birth, enlightenment and death, activities and projects for classrooms 1393:212-214

BUDDHA—BIRTHDAY

Hana Matsuri, activities and projects for classrooms 1393:188-189

Origami flower, origami paper, patterns, making 1199:80-81

BUDDHA—DECORATIONS

Elephant shape decorated cards, making 1313:81

Wesak celebration pop-up card, making 1387:38-39

BUDDHA—FESTIVALS

Elephant Procession Festival celebration 825:26-27

Hana Matsuri, the Birth of Buddha 107:17-21

BUDDHA—FESTIVALS—DECORATIONS

Baisakhi pop-up card, making 1387:52

BUDDHA—FESTIVALS—HAIKU

Nirvana Day or Buddha's Death, haiku poem, how to write 1393:150

BUDDHA—FESTIVALS—LANTERNS

Obon Festivals lanterns, paper, patterns, making 1393:255

Wesak Festival lanterns, paper, ink, patterns, making 1393:255

Wesak lantern, orange or grapefruit, making 1466:25

BUDDHA—HANDICRAFTS

Lotus flowers, paper, pattern, making 1313:80

BUDDHA—STORYTELLING

Hungry Stranger: a Buddhist story from India 1522:126-129

BUDDHA NESTING DOLL STORIES

Why the Years Are Named for Animals nesting doll story, how to do 1161:87-89

BUDDHISM

Buddha, The 810:8

Buddhist Festivals 810:4-5

Meditation information 810:14-15

Spread of Buddhism information 810:6-7

What is Buddhism about information 810:12-13

BUILDINGS

City Hall building, paper, making 1020:33-35

Hollow-block construction, cardboard, cereal boxes, making 1238:63-68

Log construction, paper, making 1238:68-74

Panel construction, cardboard, cereal boxes, making 1238:55-62

Queen Anne House, model, paper sheets given, making 220:38-41

Skyscrapers and tall buildings, paper, making 1020:37-39

Woolworth building, model, paper sheets given, making 220:34-35
BULGARIA—CHRISTMAS
Customs of Christmas in Bulgaria 474:153
BULGARIA—CHRISTMAS—COOKERY
Cookies, yogurt cookies, recipe 704:74-75
BULGARIA—COOKERY
Cucumber and yogurt soup, chilled, recipe 661:227
Green eggplant caviar, recipe 661:226-227
Kisselo mleka, homemade yogurt, recipe 1165:94-95
Lamb, baked and vegetables, recipe 661:228
Lassi, iced yogurt beverage, recipe 1165:95
Meat-eating habits in Bulgaria 662:68-70
Rice pilaf, recipe 661:229
Rice pudding with rose water, recipe 661:229-230
Sarmi with cabbage leaves, veal, pork, rice, yogurt, recipe 1623:120
Walnut tarator soup, walnut yogurt soup, recipe 1165:95
Yogurt-nut cookies (mazni kurabii), cookies, recipe 72:64-65
BULGARIA—COSTUMES
Bulgarian peasants costumes drawing 988:46
BULGARIA—DANCES
Tropanka, how to do 1494:137-138
BULGARIA—EASTER—COOKERY
Khliah Raiska Pititsa (Bird of Paradise bread), recipe 1666:80
Tarator (yogurt walnut soup), recipe 1666:79
BULL ROARERS
Bull roarer, making 495:23
History of bull roarer 495:20-21
Thunderbolt bull roarer, making 495:21-23
BULLFIGHTERS—TOYS
Bullfighter and buff toy, making 182:71-73
BULLS
Mexican bull wood carving, making 382:32
BULULAND—GAMES
Swinging game 474:52
BUNYAN, PAUL
Costume 213:128-130
BURKINA FASO—COOKERY
Akara, black-eyed pea balls, recipe 1165:43
Fo, meat stew, recipe 1165:42-43
BURKINA FASO—FESTIVALS—COOKERY
Bobo Masquerade; African greens in peanut sauce, recipe 1666:37
Bobo Masquerade; ground nut cookies, recipe 1666:37
Bobo Masquerade; ground nut truffles, recipe 1666:37
BURMA—CHRISTMAS
Christmas celebration 601:74
BURMA—COOKERY
Chutney rice, recipe 858:unp
Coconut fritters (mok-si-kyo), cookies, recipe 72:118-119
Stir-fried green beans, recipe 1165:170
Tupa menda, buttered fruit rice, recipe 1165:170-171
BURMA—DANCES
Animal folk dances 474:124
BURMA—FESTIVALS
Birthday celebration 601:45-46

Feast of Lights celebration 601:43-44
Harvest Feast celebration 601:44-45
Water Festival celebration 601:42-43; 826:28-29
BURMA—FESTIVALS—COOKERY
Hta-Ma-Ne; sticky rice with coconut, recipe 1666:167
Thingyan; curried vegetables, recipe 1666:167
BURMA—FESTIVALS—LANTERNS
Wesak lantern, orange or grapefruit, making 1466:25
BURMA—GAMES
Hide and seek game 602:43
Hiding stones game 602:41-42
Hopscotch game 602:42; 984:18
Jumping-seed game 602:42-43
Loo K'Bah Zee game 383:33
Myan Myan musical game 1116:38
Myan, Myan, I pass the shoe from me to you, how to play 1494:50
Rocking game 602:41
Round basket game 602:44
Who has the pebble? game 515:24
BURMA—JEWELRY
Bracelet, making 532:23
BURMA—PUPPETS
Marionette prince, papier-mache, wood, fabric, making 1707:25
BURMA—RITUALS
Buddha growing up ritual 695:93-96
BURROS
Wood carved burro figure, making 382:66-68
BURUNDI—DANCES
Ukwiyereka dance and costume picture 1000:76
BURUNDI—EASTER—COOKERY
Kuku na Nazi (chicken in coconut milk), recipe 1666:22
Split pea and banana porridge, recipe 1666:22
BUSES—PARTIES
Bus cake, recipe 1185:70-71
BUSHMEN—GAMES
Stalking game 956:12
BUSHMEN OF KALAHARI DESERT IN AFRICA—GAMES
Cata and lynx tag, how to play 1498:21-23
Gazelle stalking tag, how to play 1498:21
BUTTER
Butter, Colonial, recipe 831:153-155
Butter, curry, recipe 1147:26
Butter, homemade, recipe 1301:43
Butter, recipe 1531:142-143; 1564:67
Preparation of butter for sale 597:51-52
Shake-and-make butter, recipe 1660:57
BUTTONS
Button collecting; how to classify 625:16-19
Button time table for collecting 734:80-87
Collecting buttons anecdotes 734:1-12; 734:13-25
Collection display, how to do 734:26-34
History of button collecting 625:10-14
History of buttons 625:6-10
Patriotic campaign buttons, making 719:54
BYRD, RICHARD E. ADMIRAL
Birthday celebration; art, music, foods, games, activities 1104:10-13

C

CABLE CARS
Cable car, making 184:32-35
Old street car, paper, making 534:56
CACTI
Miniature cactus garden, how to make 1342:126
CAESAR—COSTUMES
Caesar costume, fabric, pattern, making 367:60-62
CAJUNS—FESTIVALS—COOKERY
Mardi Gras chicken gumbo, recipe 1382:18
CAJUNS—FESTIVALS—DANCES
La danse de Mardi Gras in French and English, music
and score, given 1382:25
CALENDARS
Christmas Calendar, history of 218:6-7
Gregorian Calendar Day family calendar, making 308:45
Sun Advent calendar, paper, making 553:18-19
Window calendar with openings, paper, making 1476:32
Winnebago Indian calendar stick, making 633:129-130
CALIFORNIA. See also INDIANS OF NORTH
AMERICA—CALIFORNIA
CALIFORNIA—COOKERY
Avocado salad (guacamole), recipe 652:112-113
Braised beef with olives, recipe 1347:42
Caesar salad, recipe 343:80-81; 529:139-140
California burgers, recipe 895:148
California Caesar salad, recipe 343:80-81
California smoothie, recipe 1043:160
Cartwheel green salad, dressing, recipe 1347:40
Chili, recipe 1347:38-39
Chinatown's chicken chop suey, recipe 529:144-146
Cioppino, recipe 1043:159
Croutons, recipe 529:140-141
Date and walnut bread, recipe 666:238-239
Date walnut bread, recipe 1043:155
Egg foo yung, recipe 654:19
Figs, masked, recipe 529:146-148
Garlic mashed potatoes, recipe 1347:43-44
Gazpacho soup, recipe 1347:38
Ginger chicken with snow peas, Chinese immigrant rec-
ipe 663:109-110
Grapefruit chiffon pie, recipe 529:148-151
Green goddess salad, history of, recipe 155:16-17
Green salad, recipe 654:18
Lettuce with green Goddess dressing, recipe 529:137-
138
Monte Cristo sandwich, recipe 1165:268-269
Onion and carrots, boiled or steamed, recipe 1347:44
Orange sherbert, recipe 654:17
Pears, blushing pears dessert, recipe 1347:44-45
San Francisco chiopino, recipe 529:142-143
San Francisco sourdough bread, recipe 492:16-17
Scrambled eggs with salmon, recipe 1347:36-37
Tamale pie, recipe 1347:41
Tomato and avocado salsa, recipe 1347:37
CALIFORNIA—FESTIVALS
National Date Festival 474:28
Whale Day; activities, art, songs, recipes, games
1469:80-81
CALIFORNIA—HISTORY
Gold Rush and trail food supply information 663:96-100
San Francisco; Chinese food supply information in Gold
Rush days 663:101-105
CALIFORNIA—HISTORY—COOKERY
Cookery of California information 666:230-234

CAMBODIA—ARCHITECTURE
Bas relief of Apsara, making 532:10
CAMBODIA—COOKERY
Cambodian pineapple compote, recipe 1452:201
Pork balls, recipe 1591:115
Stir-fried squid, recipe 1165:175-176
CAMBODIA—DANCES
Angkar dances, Khmer Civilization 474:121-122
Basic movements of Cambodian classical dance, how to
do 1647:32-33
Royal Khmer Palace dancers 474:122-123
CAMBODIA—FESTIVALS—COOKERY
Visak Bauchea; phaneng kai (chicken stuffed with pea-
nuts), recipe 1666:172-173
CAMBODIA—GAMES
Ang-Konnh, how to play 1494:42
CAMBODIA—HANDICRAFTS
Hmong story cloths, paper, fabric, markers, making
1338:81-83
Paper garland, paper, making 1477:45
CAMBODIA—HATS
Hat, making 532:21
CAMBODIA—LANGUAGE
Khmer language; a few numbers, greetings and basic
words 1591:82
CAMBODIA—POTTERY
Vase, pottery, making 532:18
CAMEROON—COOKERY
Millet and honey balls, recipe 1165:24
CAMEROON—COSTUMES
Prawns, shrimp, costumes 188:16
CAMEROON—EASTER—COOKERY
Fried millet, recipe 1666:25
Poulet au yassa (chicken stew), recipe 1666:24-25
CAMEROON—FESTIVALS—COOKERY
Eid al-Fitr; fried millet, recipe 1666:25
Eid al-Fitr; poulet au yassa (chicken stew), recipe 1666:24-25
CAMEROON—GAMES
Clap ball game 602:22-23
Hen and the leopard game 602:21
Killing the antelope game 474:44; 602:21-22
CAMEROON—MASKS
Dance mask, making 811:74
CAMEROON—POTTERY
Clay cooking pot, making 1070:40-43
CAMEROON—THANKSGIVING
Thanksgiving celebration 601:39
CAMP FIRE PROGRAMS
Awards Camp Fire, making 467:64-65
Ceremonial aids, making 467:63
CAMPAIGN BUTTONS
Patriotic buttons, making 719:54
CAMPING. See also TRAILBLAZING
CAMPING—COOKERY
Bacon and eggs on rocks, making 975:28-29
Bananas in foil, recipe 975:41
Beans, grilled, recipe 975:36
Bread twisters, recipe 975:38-39
Chicken, grilled, recipe 975:32-33
Corn on the coals, recipe 975:37
Fish in foil, recipe 975:34-35
Orange ginger dessert, recipe 975:43
Peaches in foil, recipe 975:40
Roast, underground, recipe 975:44-46
Stew in coffee can, recipe 975:30-31

CANADA

Activities, flags, games, songs, dances, recipes 1381:19-22

CANADA—BIRTHDAYS

Sweet sixteen party for girls 660:64

CANADA—CARNIVALS

Quebec Winter Carnival 474:13-14

CANADA—CHRISTMAS

Celebration of Christmas in Canada 601:140-142; 1049:90

Christmas customs in Canada 1717:10-11

French Canadian Christmas celebration 601:143-144

King of the Cake (Gateau des Rois), how to do 124:171

CANADA—CHRISTMAS—COOKERY

Canadian maple pie, recipe 497:128

Cranberries, candied, recipe 1225:71

Doughnuts, recipe 1225:75

Fruit cake, recipe 1225:73

Fruit fool dessert, recipe 1225:72

Glogg (hot holiday beverage), recipe 1666:261

Hogmanay shortbread, recipe 1128:105

Manchester tart, recipe 1666:261

Maple syrup pie, recipe 1128:104; 1225:74

Meat and potato pie, cipaille, recipe 1225:70

Meat ball stew, recipe 1225:71

Mincemeat pie, recipe 1225:73

Mincemeat, recipe 1225:73

Molasses taffy, recipe 1225:75

Oyster soup, recipe 1225:70

Roast beef, recipe 1666:260

Sugar pie, recipe 1225:74

Tourtiere meat pie, recipe 1128:103

Tourtiere (meat pie), traditional, recipe 497:128; 1666:259-260

Yorkshire pudding, recipe 1666:260

CANADA—CHRISTMAS—HANDICRAFTS

Canada goose ornament, stuffed, felt, stuffing, pattern, making 1225:66-67

Folk art angel, fabric, walnuts, twigs, yarn, patterns, making 1463:20-22

Kissing bough, wire, evergreen, ties, ribbons, making 1225:65

Maple leaf ornament, balsa wood, paints, yarn, pattern, making 1225:68-69

Paper angel, twisted paper, ribbon, lace, yarn, making 1463:23-25

CANADA—COOKERY

Apples, baked, recipe 967:24

Attic char fish dish, recipe 1052:140-141

Bacon, baked Canadian bacon, recipe 874:51

Bannock, native Indian bread, recipe 1515:119

Beef daube, beans, steak, tomato dish, recipe 1452:25

Blizzards drink, fruit juices, cream, recipe 1650:19

Blueberry corn fritters, recipe 1165:260

Blueberry crisp dessert, recipe 1452:27

Bread pudding, recipe 895:31

Canadian apple cake, recipe 1165:261-262

Canadian pastry, recipe 1452:23

Come and get 'em cookies, recipe 1244:136-137

Fish cakes, recipe 794:1

Fish chowder, recipe 793:30

Foil dinner, recipe 967:25

Habitant pea soup, recipe 1165:259-260; 1452:22

Hot apple cider, recipe 1165:262

Ice cream with maple syrup topping, recipe 1381:21

Maple syrup baked beans, recipe 1265:21

Maple syrup pie, recipe 1580:34

Maple syrup short breads, recipe 1165:260-261

Maple-sugaring-time cookies, recipe 72:148-149

Nanaimo bars, recipe 1052:135-136

Open-faced barbecue beef sandwich, recipe 1265:19-20

Popovers, recipe 793:29; 1381:21

Prince Edward Island warm potato salad, recipe 1452:26

Scones, recipe 858:unp

Sloppy Joes, recipe 967:25

Southwestern Ontario fruit salad, recipe 1265:18

Tourtiere pie, pork and veal, recipe 131:27; 1052:139-140

Tourtiere, Canadian pork pie, recipe 1452:24

Vegetable salad, recipe 895:29-30

Wild rice, recipe 1052:141-142

CANADA—COSTUMES

Maple snow, recipe, costume 188:1

Paper doll type costume, pattern, making 282:80

CANADA—DANCES

Las Bastringue, how to do 1494:183-184

CANADA—DOLLS

Potpourri doll, lace, potpourri, stockings, styrofoam ball, making 1463:30-35

CANADA—EASTER

Easter celebration 601:139-140

CANADA—FESTIVALS

Birthday celebration 601:121-122

Canada Day activities, crafts, food 1662:110-113

Canada Day, activities and projects for classrooms 1393:245-247

French Canadian St. Catherine's Day celebration 601:143

French Canadian St. John's Day celebration 601:142-143

Winter Festival celebration 601:124

CANADA—FESTIVALS—COOKERY

Canada Day, maple nut bars, recipe 1662:113

CANADA—FESTIVALS—DECORATIONS

Boxing Day sponge print gift wrap, making 1539:96-97

CANADA—FESTIVALS—HANDICRAFTS

Dominion Day maple leaf art, leaves, paper, paints, patterns, making 1199:146-148

CANADA—FOLKLORE

Chin Chiang and the Dragon's Dance; physical and human geography activities 1458:70-73

Tuk the Hunter folktale and activities 1478:57-61

CANADA—FOLKLORE—CARVING

Inuit soapstone figure, carve from soap, making 1478:66-67

CANADA—FOLKLORE—GAMES

Inuit game, ajaqaq toss and catch game, canning jar rings, stick, making 1478:64

CANADA—FOLKLORE—SNOW GOGGLES

Inuit snow goggles, posterboard, elastic, making 1478:65

CANADA—GAMES

Ajaqaq game 572:32-33

Ajaqaq game, how to play 1507:90

Ball hockey game, how to play 1708:16-17

Camouflage game 967:24

Catch Old Mrs. Winter chasing game, how to play 1498:35

Catch the ball game, how to play 1494:176

Drop the handkerchief game 602:156

Fireflies night game 967:24

French Canada on the bridge of Avignon game 602:162-164

French Canada planting the cabbage game 602:164-165

Here comes a Knight a riding game 602:153-154

Hide the bell game 602:152

Hide the pencil game 602:151

Hoist your sails game 602:152-153

Indian War map game 515:26

International Shopping game 967:24

January game 572:30-31

Muk game, how to play 1507:91

Old Roger game 602:154-155

Pass the broom game 602:151

Slaves of Job passing the shoe game 386:83

Tanuary game 602:151-152

CANADA—HALLOWEEN

Halloween celebration 601:122-123

CANADA—HALLOWEEN—DECORATIONS

Wacky witch, stockings, felt, yarn, twigs, patterns, making 1463:25-29

CANADA—HANDICRAFTS

Eskimos soapstone carvings, clay, making 1338:27-29

CANADA—HOUSES

Log cabin from Canada, cardboard and paper 94:19

CANADA—INDEPENDENCE DAY

Dominion Day celebration, July 1 722:1-4

CANADA—INDIANS. *See also* **KWAKIUTL INDIANS; MICMAC INDIANS**

CANADA—INDIANS—HANDICRAFTS

Sea creature, making 1447:12-13

CANADA—LANGUAGE

Common words and phrases in Canadian English 1580:26

Common words and phrases in French 1580:26

CANADA—LULLABIES

"Comforting Song" 1607:16

CANADA—MAGIC TRICKS

Multiplying fingers, how to do 1270:28-29

CANADA—NEW YEAR

New Year celebration 601:120-121

CANADA—NUMBERS

Numbers one to ten in French language 391:unp

CANADA—RHYMES

"Canoe Song" 1607:20

CANADA—SCIENCE

Gesner's experiment, repeat to compare ways different oils burn 1719:39-41

Kite experiment based on early works of Mabel and her husband Alexander 1719:42-45

CANADA—ST. PATRICK'S DAY

St. Patrick's Day celebration 601:138

CANADA—STRING FIGURES

Casting a Spear, Circle 1404:14-58

CANADA—THANKSGIVING

Thanksgiving celebration 601:142

CANADA—THANKSGIVING—COOKERY

Apple cake, recipe 1249:21-22

CANADA—VALENTINE'S DAY

St. Valentine's Day celebration 601:138

CANAL BOAT ART

Decorating tin can in canal boat tradition, patterns, making 1051:30-34

CANDLES

Candle clock, Colonial Period, making 1043:31

Candle dipping, how to do 1531:98-99

Candleholders, Colonial, clay, making 877:67-70; 877:67-70

Colonial candles, making 673:158-173

Colonial dipped and molded candles, making 1043:30-31

Easter egg candle, making 336:33-34

Fourth of July candle, making 336:25-26

Hanukkah candle, felt appliqué, patterns, making 1016:237-242

Homemade candles, how to make 1421:207

Jack-o-lantern candle, making 336:30-32

Sand candles, how to make 1285:73-74

Sand castle candle, sand, wax, making 1429:56

Snow candles, snow, paraffin, wicking, tin can, making 1285:116-117

Swedish candles, making 955:108-111

Swiss cheese candle, wax, tin can, milk carton, making 297:186-187; 1564:52

Wildflower candles, pressed wild flowers, candles, making 1285:40

World of candles, making 980:32

CANDY

History of candy 762:53-67

Rock candy, recipe 1429:84-85

Vanilla molasses taffy, recipe 118:173

CANNONS

Naval cannon, one that shoots, making 924:54-57

CANOES. *See also* **INDIANS OF NORTH AMERICA—CANOES**

CANYONS

Make your own canyon, making 24:16-17

CARAVANS

Caravan model, making, 16:38-40

CAREERS. *See also individual occupations*

CAREERS—COSTUMES

Astronaut, costume, paper bag, making 135:6-11

Business person, costume, paper bag, making 135:12-16

Chef, costume, paper bag, making 135:46-48

Construction worker, costume, paper bag, making 135:24-26

Fire fighter, costume, paper bag, making 135:27-37

Nurse, costume, paper bag, making 135:42-45

Police officer, costume, paper bag, making 135:38-41

Tennis player, costume, paper bag, making 135:17-23

CARIBBEAN ISLANDS

Activities, flags, games, songs, dances, recipes 1381:23-42

CARIBBEAN ISLANDS—CHRISTMAS

Benne balls, recipe 273:143-145

CARIBBEAN ISLANDS—CHRISTMAS—COOKERY

Caribbean Christmas cake, recipe 1313:195-196

CARIBBEAN ISLANDS—COOKERY

Akkra, recipe 510:26

Asopao, recipe 510:22

Baked plantain, recipe 1468:40-41

Banana bread, recipe 1380:41; 1468:33-35; 1560:35

Banana fritters dessert, recipe 1280:47

Banana fritters, recipe 510:41

Bread, roti bread, recipe 642:42

Bread, sweet cassava bread, recipe 642:37

Callaloo, recipe 510:19

Callaloo, soup, recipe 1198:29

Caribbean style rice, recipe 510:36

Chicken casserole (Fricasee de poulet au coco), recipe 642:30

Chicken, browned down, recipe 510:31

Coconut ice dessert, recipe 510:38; 1280:46
Cornmeal coo-coo, recipe 510:23
Curried lamb, recipe 510:34
Duckunoo, recipe 510:40
Escovitch fish, recipe 510:30
Figues bananes fourrees (bananas), recipe 642:29
Fish, recipe 793:13
Fruit and nut dish, recipe 1487:12-13
Fruit punch, recipe 1251:47
Ginger beer, recipe 510:42
Island smoothies, fruit shakes, recipe 1244:116
Jerk chicken, recipe 1468:37
Johnny cakes, recipe 510:26
Jug jug, recipe 510:36
Jug-a-jug meat dish, recipe 642:32
Keshy yean coe cabarone (shrimp dish), recipe 642:34
Peanut punch, recipe 510:43
Pepperpot soup, recipe 510:18
Pepperpot stew, recipe 510:21
Pineapple drink, recipe 642:40
Pineapple ice cream, recipe 1560:34
Piononos (stuffed plantains), recipe 642:27
Rice and peas or beans, recipe 1468:38-39
Rice and peas, recipe 510:25; 642:22
Sorrel drink, recipe 1468:42-43
Spiced fruit punch, recipe 1468:44
Stamp and go, recipe 510:28
Strawberry freezes, recipe 1244:118
Sweet potato pone, recipe 510:40
CARIBBEAN ISLANDS—GAMES
Bamboula, how to play 1497:32
CARIBBEAN ISLANDS—HANDICRAFTS
Blackbeard jumping jack, oaktag, markers, patterns, making 1251:20-23
Caribbean Village scene, fabric, felt, patterns, making 1251:16-19
Traditional Caribbean designs 1251:8-12
Tropical Island collage, tissue paper, paints, patterns, making 1251:40-42
CARIBBEAN ISLANDS—MUSICAL INSTRUMENTS
Carnival drums, plastic food containers, patterns, making 1051:41-45
Limbo pole, cardboard tubes, juice cans, making 1310:139
Rattle tubo, tin can, making 889:85-89
CARIBBEAN ISLANDS—PATTERNS
Angelfish 1251:38
Blackbeard 1251:20
Palm tree 1251:40
Toucan 1251:36
CARLE, ERIC
"Pancakes, Pancakes," pancakes, recipe 1216:11
CARNEGIE, ANDREW
Birthday celebration; art, music, foods, games, activities 1104:22-25
CARNIVAL
Activities and projects for classrooms 1393:168-169
Fruit hat for Carnival, papier-mache, making 1561:22-23
CARNIVALS. See also **MARDI GRAS**
Activities, art, songs, recipes, games 1469:70-71
Carnival at Nice, France 474:11-12
Carnival celebrations round the world 503:14-15
Mardi Gras carnival in Louisiana 474:11

Mardi Gras celebration 631:36
Summer carnivals 474:14
Traditions of carnivals 566:42-43
Winter carnivals 474:13-14
CAROUSELS. See also **MERRY-GO-ROUNDS**
Merry-Go-Round, paper plates, straws, patterns, making 912:71-72
Plastic bottle carousel, making 955:81
Spoon carousel, making 955:81
CARPENTRY. See **WOODWORKING**
CARROLL, LEWIS
Mad tea party, with paper hats, how to make 1199:25-26
CARS. See **AUTOMOBILES**
CARSON, RACHEL—BIRTHDAY
Celebrate; insects song and game, how to play 1199:113-114
Celebrate; Ladybug bingo game, patterns, how to make and play 1199:114-116
Celebrate; painted butterflies, cardboard, paper, paints, patterns, making 1199:116-117
CARTHAGE
Carthage and Rome, history, stories, maps, puzzles, activities, projects 1041:58-84
CARTOUCHE
Name cartouche, hieroglyphics, how to make 699:14-15
CARVER, GEORGE WASHINGTON—BIRTHDAY
Birthday celebration; art, music, foods, games, activities 1104:122-125
CARVER, GEORGE WASHINGTON—COOKERY
Tuskegee ice cream, recipe 1165:267
CARVING. See also **STONE CARVING; WOOD CARVING**
Carving paste, recipe, making 531:132
Plaster carving, how to do 805:115
Soap carving, making 1376:64-66
Soap stone carving, recipe, making 531:133
CASTLES
Alligators for moat, clothespins, felt, making 1088:106-107
Battering ram, boxes, making 110:24-25
Battle tent, cardboard tube, making 110:14-15
Battlements 214:35
Card castles, making 114:116
Cardboard castle, making 442:11; 562:10-13; 849:28-31
Castle base and moat, papier-mache, making 110:28-29
Castle cake, recipe 449:66
Castle curtain walls, cardboard, paint, making 1682:26
Castle from blown egg, making 677:19
Castle from boxes, making 553:10-11; 634:44-49
Castle from boxes, tissue tubes, and paints, making 1213:120-121
Castle from England model, paper and cans, making 1094:11
Castle from Scotland, paper model, making 1094:43
Castle guard made from spools, making 629:28-29
Castle keep rampart walk, cardboard, paint, making 1682:26
Castle keep tower and roof, cardboard, paint, making 1682:24-25
Castle keep, cardboard, paint, making 1682:24-25
Castle siege tower and wheels, cardboard, paint, making 1682:27

Castle tower, corrugated cardboard, dowels, sticks, making 1512:20-21

Castle with a moat, clay, making 771:38-39

Castle, cardboard, making 731:24-25

Castle, from cereal boxes, making 84:12

Castles, super sand, making 296:180-181

Catapult, boxes, making 110:26-27

Catapult, making 214:37

Church, milk cartons, making 110:12-13

Confectionery castle, recipe 282:89

Cork castles, making 1099:unp

Curtain walls 214:35

Deal castle, sand sculpture, making 723:56-59

Diagram of inside 633:unp

Drawbridge 214:36

Drip castle, sand sculpture, making 723:46-47

Fairy tale castle of food, making 297:240-241

Fairy tale castle, cardboard tubes, paper, patterns, making 1420:60

Gate house and draw bridge, milk carton, making 1100:8-9

Harlech, sand sculpture, making 723:52-55

Henry VIII Castle, Deal Castle, sand sculpture, making 723:56-59

Houses, pattern, cardboard, making 110:22-23

Keep 214:35

Kenmore Castle, cardboard box, large, making 942:78

King Arthur's castle, boxes, tubes, making 1311:84-85

King Arthur's castle, wood, making, 925:22-23

Knight and lady, making 110:18-19

Knight's castle, cardboard tubes, paper, patterns, making 1420:60

Krak des chevaliers, Crusades, sand sculpture, making 723:60-63

Lances, pennants, shields and swords, paper, making 110:20-21

Medieval castles, paper, making 1020:81-94

Miniature castle scene, making 629:142-144

Model from corrugated cardboard, newspapers, making 1679:6-7

Model of castle, towers, moat, cardboard, making 1679:16-21

Motte and Bailey, sand sculpture, making 723:48-51

Norman castle 212:48-59

Paper models, making 75:96-107

People, model for, making 110:16-17

Plaster castle, cardboard and plaster, making 552:20-21

Pop-up castle, making 1388:50-53

Sand castle and keeper, modeling mixture, recipe 531:124-125

Sand castle that lasts, from sand, water, cornstarch, making 1372:125

Sand sculpture castle details, making 723:44-45

Sand, glue and cardboard castle, making 683:43

Shoe box castle, pattern, making 1088:100-102

Shoe box, cardboard tubes and paper castle, making 1105:6-7

Siege tower 214:36

Soldiers and ladies, clothespins, felt, patterns, making 1088:103-105

Stable, shoe box, making 110:14-15

Towers and battlements, milk carton, making 110:10-11

Turret 214:35

Winter sand castles, making 561:73

CASTLES—PARTIES
Castle cake, recipe 1185:58-59

CATAWBA INDIANS—HANDICRAFTS
Plaited placemats, paper, tape, making 1296:102-103

CATSKILL MOUNTAINS REGION—FOLKLORE
"Rip Van Winkle"; physical and human geography activities 1458:80-83

CATTAILS
Cattail fluff pillow, making 1421:146

CAVALIERS—COSTUMES
Captain Crimson costume, fabric, pattern, making 367:14-17

Cavalier costume, fabric, pattern, making 367:89-93

CELTS. *See also* **DRUIDS**

CELTS—COSTUMES
Celtic Queen, costume, cAD50, making 368:85-88

CELTS—FESTIVALS
Beltane May Festival 566:13

New Year, Festival of the Dead and Samhain, harvest festival 419:69-71

CELTS—FESTIVALS—HANDICRAFTS
May Day; Beltane bonfire collage, tissue paper, foil, making 1466:23

Samhain Festival, Samhain lanterns, turnips, candle, string, making 1199:243-244

Samhain Festival; ghostly windsocks, white crepe paper, string, making 1199:242-243

CELTS—SHIELDS
Celtic shield, cardboard, container lids and bottoms, paint, making 1183:6-7

CENTRAL AFRICAN REPUBLIC—COOKERY
Sesame cakes, recipe 1165:23-24

CENTRAL AMERICA. *See also* **LATIN AMERICA**
Activities, flags, games, songs, dances, recipes 1381:23-42

CENTRAL AMERICA—ANIMALS
Jumping Jack monkey toy, oaktag, string, making 1484:12-13

CENTRAL AMERICA—CHRISTMAS
Christmas celebration 601:145

Gourd noisemaker, making 273:141-143

Piñata fish, making 273:132-138

CENTRAL AMERICA—CHRISTMAS—HANDICRAFTS
Angel of clay, making 273:138-140

CENTRAL AMERICA—DANCES
Cheer up dance 697:24-25

CENTRAL AMERICA—DOLLS
Worry dolls, clothes pin, pipe cleaners, popsicle sticks, yarn, making 1219:29; 1633:70-71

CENTRAL AMERICA—FESTIVALS
Feast of the Patron Saint celebration 601:144

CENTRAL AMERICA—FESTIVALS—HANDICRAFTS
Cascarones, decorated eggshells filled with confetti, making 1477:37

Fiesta clay figures, making 1574:28-29

CENTRAL AMERICA—GAMES
Chapete game 956:28-29

Drop the marble game 58:14-15

Piñata game 697:40

CENTRAL AMERICA—HANDICRAFTS
Pollo or chicken made of paper, patterns, making 1633:76-77

Time Line accordion book, paper, ribbons, patterns, making 1332:53-58

Woven wall hanging, cardboard loom, yarn, making 1633:68-69

CENTRAL AMERICA—INDIANS. *See* **CUNA INDIANS**

CENTRAL AMERICA—TOYS

Rattling reptile toy, thin plywood, patterns, making 1051:57-62

CEYLON. *See also* **SRI LANKA**

CEYLON—BIRTHDAYS

Birthday customs 488:26-28

CEYLON—COOKERY

Curried green beans, recipe 793:63

Potato cakes (aardapplen koeken), cookies, recipe 72:120-121

CEYLON—FESTIVALS

Perahera celebration 631:84

CEYLON—GAMES

Leopards and cattle game 383:34

Peralikatuma board game, patterns, making 1074:40; 1541:80-84

CHAD—CHRISTMAS—COOKERY

Mtedza-malawi (peanut vegetable stew), recipe 1666:27

CHAD—COOKERY

Squash with peanuts dessert, recipe 1165:27

Sweet potato salad, recipe 1165:26-27

CHAD—FESTIVALS—COOKERY

Eid al-Fitr; mtedza-malawi (peanut vegetable stew), recipe 1666:27

CHAD—HOUSES

Chad house, making 222:24-25

CHAINS. *See* **PAPER CHAINS**

CHALDEANS—GAMES

Chaldean checkers, making 173:70-71

CHALK

Plaster of Paris sidewalk chalk, recipe 1455:23

CHAN CHAN

Bean bag messages, making 173:48-49

Courtyard houses, making 173:58-59

Games, feather tossers, making 173:68-69

Litter for noble travelers, making 173:38-39

Porter's sling, making 173:34-35

Royal jewels of Chan Chan, making 173:24-25

Shoe box houses, making 173:56-57

Wild animal masks, making 173:76-77

CHANUKAH. *See* **HANUKKAH**

CHAPMAN, JOHN. *See also* **JOHNNY APPLESEED**

CHAPMAN, JOHN—BIRTHDAY

Celebrate by making applesauce, recipe 1199:219-220

Celebrate by making paper trees 1199:220

CHEESE

Camembert cheese, history of 597:64

Cheddar cheese, history of 597:60-64

Cottage cheese, recipe 1564:63

History of cheese 597:55-68

Liederkranz cheese, history of 597:66

Pizza with cheese, recipe 1530:unp

Process cheese, history of 597:66

Roquefort cheese, history of 597:64-65

Swiss cheese, history of 597:58-59

CHEFS

Chef costume, making 839:12-15

Chef costume, paper bag, making 135:46-48

Chef mask, making 846:22-23

Chef's hat, fabric, making 982:24-25

CHEROKEE INDIANS—ALPHABET

Cherokee alphabet 1699:182

CHEROKEE INDIANS—CLOTHING

Cherokee shirt, making 932:51-52

CHEROKEE INDIANS—COOKERY

Bean balls, pinto beans and cornmeal dish, recipe 1527:23

CHEROKEE INDIANS—DREAMS

Dream catcher, paper plate, yarn, beads, making 1633:44-45

CHEROKEE INDIANS—FESTIVALS

Corn Festival celebration 659:54-55

Corn growing festivals 419:146-148

CHEROKEE INDIANS—GAMES

Basket game, how to play 1296:122

Chunkey game, how to play 1608:91

Stickball game, how to play 1444:15

CHEROKEE INDIANS—HANDICRAFTS

Cut-outs from birch bark to decorate objects, patterns, making 1633:40-43

CHEROKEE INDIANS—HOUSEHOLD

Plaited placemats, paper, tape, making 1296:102-103

CHEROKEE INDIANS—LANGUAGE

Sequoyah's Cherokee Syllabary of Cherokee language 1529:last page

CHEROKEE INDIANS—MASKS

Cherokee mask, making 327:45

CHEROKEE INDIANS—MUSICAL INSTRUMENTS

Rattles and noisemakers, gourds, pebbles, shells, beans, how to make 1444:22

CHEROKEE INDIANS—STRING FIGURES

Crow's Feet 1404:22-25

CHERRY BLOSSOM FESTIVAL

Activities, art, songs, recipes, games 1469:86-87

CHESS

History of 127:1-9

CHEYENNE INDIANS—CLOTHING

Cheyenne dress and accessories, making 465:94

CHEYENNE INDIANS—FOLKLORE

Death of the Iron Horse; physical and human geography activities 1458:84-87

CHEYENNE INDIANS—GAMES

Playing bear game 602:167

Running through the line game 602:167

CHEYENNE INDIANS—ROACHES

Roach, making 466:62-63

CHILD, LYDIA MARIA

"Over the River and Through the Woods," pumpkin pie, recipe 1216:52

CHILDREN'S BOOK WEEK

Memory book, making 308:23-24

CHILDREN'S DAY

Children's Day activities, stories, crafts, recipes 558:64-66

History of Children's Day 475:143-144

CHILDREN'S STORIES—DWELLINGS

"Alice in Wonderland," descriptions and pictures of house 299:Chapter 8

"Charlotte's Web," descriptions and pictures of barn 299:Chapter 4

"David Copperfield," descriptions and pictures of house 299:Chapter 5

"Johnny Tremain," descriptions and pictures of house 299:Chapter 6

"Little Women," descriptions and pictures of house 299:Chapter 3

"Robinson Crusoe," descriptions and pictures of island 299:Chapter 7

"Secret Garden," descriptions and pictures of house 299:Chapter 1

"Sword in the Stone," descriptions and pictures of house 299:Chapter 2

CHILE—CHRISTMAS
Christmas celebration 601:162

CHILE—CHRISTMAS—COOKERY
Porotos Granados (vegetabel stew), recipe 1666:222
Sopa de Pescado (fish stew), recipe 1666:221

CHILE—COOKERY
Almond meringues with fresh fruit dessert, recipe 1280:50-51; 1517:43
Beef char-broiled with sauce, recipe 1517:33
Chicken, marinated, recipe 1517:33
Corn packages with husks, recipe 1517:35
Empadas (turnovers), beef, chicken, ham, fruit, recipe 1517:28-29
Empanadas, meat turnovers, recipe 858:unp
Fish soup, recipe 1517:20
Green salads and dressing, recipe 1517:24
Huevos rancheros 187:16
Humitas, recipe 793:20-21
Poor man's steak, recipe 794:12
Porotos granados, beans with vegetables, recipe 1165:226
Salad, mixed green, recipe 1652:26
Seafood salad, recipe 1517:25
Uminatas, corn casserole, recipe 1165:225-226

CHILE—EASTER
Easter celebration 601:162

CHILE—FESTIVALS
Ch'ing Ming, spring festival 419:100-101
Chinese rituals 419:97-104
Chung-Ch'iu, harvest festival 419:101-104
Day of the Cross celebration 601:163-164
La Cueca Chilena celebration 631:86
Mapuche Indians harvest festivals 419:128-130

CHILE—GAMES
Cambio de instrumentos game 383:39
Cat and the mouse game 602:145
Cielo, luna mar, sky, moon, sea game, how to play 1708:18-19
Hen runs game 602:144
Hit the penny game, how to play 1507:108
King's messenger game 383:37
La Barra game 383:36
La Canasta game 383:38
Marbles in Chile 515:28
Quien Es?, Who is it?, how to play 1494:213-214
Sea is rough game 602:144
Va El Tren game 383:37
Who is it? game 602:143

CHILE—MUSICAL INSTRUMENTS
Rain stick, paper tube, plastic lids, sand, birdseed, rice, making 1646:15

CHILE—TEA
Tea in Chile 474:138-139

CHIMES
Elderberry wind chimes, making 1421:88
Seashell chimes, making 1421:89

CHIMU INDIANS. *See also* **PERU**
Bean bag messages, making 173:48-49
Games, feather tossers, making 173:68-69
Litter for noble travelers, making 173:38-39

CHINA
Activities, flags, games, songs, dances, recipes 1381:61-66
Activities, projects, recipes 282:10-23
Culture unit, language, dress, foods, games, bibliographies 574:16-39
Map and food products 986:6-15

CHINA—ANCIENT—CLOCKS
Sand clock to demonstrate Ancient Chinese clock, making 1719:13-15

CHINA—ANCIENT—PAPER MAKING
Make paper to demonstrate Ancient Chinese paper making 1719:10-11

CHINA—ARCHITECTURE
Pagoda, making 532:6

CHINA—BARGES
Chinese barge, making 173:40-41

CHINA—BIRD FEEDERS
Chinese temple bird feeder, making 173:62-63

CHINA—BIRTHDAYS
Birthday customs 488:29-33
Birthday party for one year old child 660:52-54
Celebrations of birthdays in China 474:81-82

CHINA—BRAIDING
Braid, Chinese, making 548:45-50

CHINA—CHOPS
Chinese chop signature, potato printing, making 1179:175
Chops, signatures of people, how to make 1427:126

CHINA—CHOPSTICKS
Chopsticks, how to make from wood and use 1244:39

CHINA—CHRISTMAS
Celebration of Christmas in China 516:18-19
Santa Claus (Dun Che Lao Ren) in China 516:19

CHINA—CHRISTMAS—HANDICRAFTS
Chinese lanterns, used greeting cards, making 1575:12-13
Peacock, making 273:97-101
Straw mosaic cards, making 795:21

CHINA—CLOTHING
Robe, making 173:18-19

CHINA—COOKERY
Almond cakes, recipe 343:132
Almond cookies (hang geen beng), cookies, recipe 72:122-123; 986:40; 1265:113-114; 1427:136
Almond fruit float dessert, recipe 986:38-39; 1280:20-21
Almond milk gelatin, recipe 1274:43-44
Almond milk jelly, Southern cuisine, recipe 797:35
Asparagus or green bean salad, recipe 1695:35
Baked tofu, recipe 1380:33
Barbecued spareribs, recipe 1380:35
Bean curd, recipe 797:17
Bean sprouts with scallions, recipe 986:36-37
Bean sprouts, how to grow 909:23
Beef and broccoli, recipe 895:35
Beef and green pepper, recipe 793:64
Beef and rice stir-fry, recipe 1695:20
Beef slices and snow peas, recipe 1106:56-57
Beef stew, recipe 986:34
Beef with oyster sauce, recipe 853:22

Beef with tomatoes, recipe 853:24
Birthday noodles with peanut sauce, recipe 1244:38
Boiled won tons, recipe 1653:122
Bonbon chicken Sichuan dish, recipe 1690:72
Bows and two fillings for, recipe 88:88-90
Broccoli and carrots with firm tofu, recipe 1165:158
Cabbage with cream sauce, Eastern cuisine, recipe
    797:24
Canton corn soup, recipe 1695:34
Cantonese style barbecued spareribs, recipe 986:30-31
Ch'a Yeh Tan, tea eggs, recipe 1165:158
Ch'ao Hsueh Tou, stir-fried snow peas, recipe 1165:158-
    159
Chi tong, chicken soup, recipe 1653:7
Chicken baked in paper pouch, recipe 1196:17
Chicken flower soup, recipe 50:157
Chicken wings, recipe 895:33
Chicken with dried red chilies, recipe 853:26
Chicken, spiced roast chicken, recipe 986:34
Chicken, stir-fry chicken with vegetables, Southern cui-
    sine, recipe 797:25
Chili beef filling for mandarin pancakes, recipe 1427:137
Chinese cabbage, recipe 986:36-37
Chinese fortune cookies, recipe 1192:472
Chinese menu 986:16-17
Chinese scrambled eggs, recipe 50:157
Chinese spareribs, recipe 343:43
Chinese tea, recipe 874:82
Chop suey soup, recipe 518:16-20
Chopstick-friendly chicken and veggie stir-fry, recipe
    1265:109-110
Chopsticks, how to use 797:44-45; 1538:38
Coconut anise rice cakes, recipe 1452:37
Corn soup, recipe 499:81
Crab omelette, recipe 853:25
Crabmeat puffs, recipe 1452:32
Diem sum, recipe 88:92-93
Egg custard, recipe 1380:10
Egg drop soup, recipe 1081:34; 1106:55; 1204:62;
    1274:38-39; 1452:33; 1735:45-47
Egg flower chicken soup, recipe 986:24-25
Egg flower soup, recipe 188:43; 909:23; 1381:64
Egg foo yung and sauce, recipe 1072:104-105
Egg foo yung, recipe 1152:201; 1653:47-48
Egg rolls, recipe 1265:111-112
Fish baked with sesame seed oil, recipe 853:22
Five spice beef dish, microwave recipe 1211:33
Fluffy white rice, recipe 1695:28
Fortune cakes, using ice cream in cones, recipe
    1178:118-119
Fortune cookies, recipe 282:18; 285:104-105; 498:30-
    32; 513:60-61; 574:20; 986:40-41; 1204:72;
    1454:17-18
Fried ham with rice, recipe 986:26-27
Fried rice, recipe 88:91-92
Fried rice, Southern cuisine, recipe 797:43
Fried won ton, recipe 1427:136
Fu Jung Tan, egg fu jung dish, recipe 1452:34
Green tea, recipe 1072:99-100
History of cookery in China 88:80-88
Honey-glazed chicken wings, recipe 1244:42
Hong Kong cookies, recipe 514:128-129
Hot and sour soup, recipe 853:21
Huo Tui Tan Ch'ao Fan, ham, egg, fried rice, recipe
    1452:36

Jiao-zi, dumpling with meat and vegetable stuffing, rec-
    ipe 1690:70-71
Jook Congee, rice porridge, recipe 1165:156
Lemon chicken wings, recipe 1695:29
Lion-heads casserole, Northern cuisine, recipe 797:28
Mandarin orange-pineapple float, recipe 1265:108
Mandarin pancakes, recipe 1427:137-138
Marbled tea eggs, recipe 1695:30
Meat-eating habits in China 662:93-99
Moon cakes, recipe 1477:109
New Year cake, recipe 797:40
Noodles with meat sauce, recipe 797:22
Onions with beef, recipe 794:52
Orange pudding, recipe 1695:38
Oriental beef kabobs, recipe 343:44
Oriental fried rice, recipe 1321:162
Paper chicken, need parchment paper, recipe 1427:138
Peanut rice faces, recipe 1204:59
Pearl meatballs, microwave recipe 1211:24-25
Pork and walnuts, recipe 1695:23
Pork fried rice, recipe 871:91-92
Pork with green pepper and pineapple, recipe 986:32-33
Pork, twice cooked, Western cuisine, recipe 797:26
Recipe names in Chinese 986:44-45
Red bean popsicles, recipe 1427:139
Rice, fluffy Chinese style, recipe 88:90-91
Rice, recipe 986:20-21
Roast chicken, recipe 1695:21
Sesame noodles, recipe 1380:18
Shao Pi K'u, barbecued ribs, recipe 1165:157-158
Shrimp cakes, recipe 514:130
Shrimp with Hoisin sauce, recipe 986:35
Shrimp with ketchup, recipe 895:34
Shrimp with rice, recipe 858:unp
Silver-wrapped chicken, recipe 1653:115-116
Singing rice, recipe 1427:139
Song dynasty salad, recipe 1721:14
Soy chicken wings, recipe 1560:24
Spareribs with spices, recipe 1274:33-35
Spring rolls, recipe 1427:140
Stir fried beef with sugar peas, recipe 986:28-29
Stir fried green beans with mushrooms, recipe 853:27
Stir fried pork with noodles, recipe 853:28
Stir fried vegetables, recipe 853:23
Stir-fried chicken with peanuts, recipe 1274:40-42
Stir-fried shrimp with garlic, recipe 1381:65
Stir-fried zucchini with garlic, recipe 1410:40
Stir-fry and rice, recipe 1113:50-51
Stir-fry vegetables, recipe 1169:66-67
Sugar glazed walnuts, recipe 1380:42
Supper meat salad and dressing, recipe 1695:24-25
Sweet and pungent pork balls, recipe 662:93-99
Sweet and sour chicken, recipe 874:54
Sweet and sour pork, recipe 1381:65
Sweet bean paste, recipe 1394:20-21
Szechuan pork, recipe 1452:35
Tea eggs with dipping sauce, recipe 1274:36-37
Tea eggs, recipe 853:20
Tea, recipe 986:19
Teem gok, appetizer, recipe 1427:140
Teem gok, dessert, recipe 1653:176
Tofu from soy milk, recipe 1487:26-27
Tofu with vegetables, recipe 1068:unp
Vegetable fried rice, recipe 1380:20
Vegetable stir fry, recipe 1472:25; 1695:31

Vegetables lo mein, recipe 1373:28-29
Vegetables, mixed, stir-fried, recipe 1072:100-101
Vegetables, steamed, recipe 1471:28-29
Watercress soup, recipe 986:24-25
Watermelon ginger dessert, recipe 1695:39
Won ton shrimp, recipe 1653:121
Won ton snacks, recipe 986:22-23
Won ton soup, recipe 187:27
Won ton soup, Southern cuisine, recipe 797:36
Won tons, meat filling, fried, recipe 1204:49

CHINA—COSTUMES
Chinese costumes drawing 988:52
Chinese woman costume, making 417:14-15
Egg flower soup, recipe, costume 188:43
Lion's head or dragon's costume, cardboard box, making 1427:131
Mandarin and wife costumes 213:139-141
Paper doll type costume, pattern, making 282:22
Quick Chinese costume, making 1283:32

CHINA—CRICKETS
Crickets as pets in China 474:59

CHINA—DANCES
Chinese Friendship dance, how to do 1494:53-54

CHINA—DECORATIONS
Twisters from won ton wrappers, making 683:18

CHINA—DESIGNS
Chinese designs to use 167:106-107, 113-116

CHINA—DOLLS
Chinese girl doll, from peanuts, making 623:3-5
Oriental doll, felt, stuffed, pattern, making 487:24-25
Spool doll, making 629:32-33
Tilting doll, making 532:32
Wong Su of China doll, making 494:186-197

CHINA—DRAGONS
Dragon, pop dragon, making 626:25-28
Dragon; Chinese, newspaper, paint, making 1121:20-21
Dragon; Good Luck dragon, papier-mache, patterns, making 1633:142-143
Dragons and color red 167:11
Dragons, Chinese, paper, making 819:29
Paper dragon that moves, making 1447:10-11

CHINA—DRAMA
Chinese theater 474:102-103

CHINA—FACE MAKEUP
Chinese opera face, making using face makeup 380:20-21

CHINA—FANS
Fan of fortune, folding, making 282:21
Fans, tissue paper, glue, making 1427:127

CHINA—FESTIVALS
Birthday of the Moon celebration 631:82
Bun Festival celebration 826:20-21
Chinese New Year 566:36; 574:33
Chung Yang Chieh, kite flying day 474:61-62
Dragon Boat Festival celebration 574:33; 601:48-50
Feast of Lanterns celebration 601:47-48
Full Moon Tea party, recipes, handicrafts 1528:25-27
Kite Flying celebration 601:50-51
Li Chum, spring festival 419:98-100
May Day 574:33
Mid-Autumn Festival, activities and projects for classrooms 1393:38-39
Moon Festival 574:33
Sun Nin, New Year Festival, activities and projects for classrooms 1393:127-129
Winter Festival 574:33

CHINA—FESTIVALS—COOKERY
Birthday of the Moon Festival moon cakes, recipe 1249:45-46
Full Moon Tea party moon scones, recipe 1528:25-26
Harvest Moon Festival cookies, recipe 500:22-23
Ice Festival in Harbin, hot pot food, making 1654:65
Mid-Autumn Festival moon cakes, recipe 1393:39

CHINA—FESTIVALS—GAMES
Harvest Moon Festival circle game, how to play 1401:11

CHINA—FESTIVALS—HANDICRAFTS
Chinese Harvest Moon Festival paper scroll, making 1401:11
Chinese Lantern Festival, paper lantern, making 1313:38
Chinese New Year banner, red paper or felt, cardboard tube, decorations 1179:46-48
Chinese New Year money envelopes, red paper, making 1179:48
Chun Jie or Spring Festival dragon, streamers, making 1477:34
Dragon Boat Festival concertina paper dragon, making 1277:12
Dragon Boat Races, dragon's head pattern 1654:65-66
Full Moon Tea party night sky placemats, foil, making 1528:26-27
Full Moon Tea party telescopes, paper, making 1528:27
Harvest Moon Festival clay rabbit, making 515:30
New Year's Festival Dragon, making 167:41-44

CHINA—FESTIVALS—PUPPETS
Festival of Lanterns, finger plays and puppets, patterns, making 513:59-61

CHINA—FESTIVALS—SCULPTURES
Ice Festival in Harbin, ice sculpture, making 1654:65

CHINA—FISH
Floating paper-cut fish, paper, making 298:222-223

CHINA—FLAGS
Dragon flag, fabric, patterns, making 1246:38-39

CHINA—FLOWERS
Chrysanthemum flower, paper, making 532:54
Peony flower, paper, making 532:50-53

CHINA—FOLKLORE
"Little Fox and the Tiger," flannel board patterns, making 910:7,38
"Monkey and the Tiger," flannel board patterns, making 1201:19-24
"Stonecutter" flannel board story, patterns, making 1604:104-105

CHINA—FOLKLORE—PUPPETS
"Deer, the Fox, and the Tiger" shadow puppets, patterns, making 1602:92-95
Lon Po Po, Shang, Tao, Paotze, Wolf, Mother cylinder puppets, patterns 1206:20-25

CHINA—GAMES
1,2,3 Dragon game, how to play 572:20-21; 1507:28
Beach lame chicken game 383:49
Call the chickens home game 602:50
Cat and mouse game 383:42
Catching seven pieces game 383:46
Catching the dragon's tail game 383:51; 602:44-45
Catching the Dragon's Tail game, how to play 1477:34
Cha Kau Tsz' card game 1132:5-6
Challenge game, how to play 1507:29
Chase the dragon's tail game 58:16-19
Chien-tze style birdie, metal washer, tissue paper, making 1350:82

Chinese Checkers board game, patterns, making 383:40;
    1381:65; 1541:100-108
Chinese chess game, how to make 1074:70-76
Chinese chuck stone game 1354:159
Chinese finger guessing game 282:121
Chinese friends or the sandwich game, making 805:37
Chinese handball 876:80-81
Chinese jump rope 876:48-49; 1244:41
Chinese puzzle game 1078:25
Chinese shuttlecock game 1354:160
Chinese straddle jump rope game, how to play 1501:27-29
Chinese whispers game 1244:41
Chuck stone stick game 1119:17
Clapstick blind man's buff tag, how to play 1498:20
Clasping for seven game 383:45
Da Err game 383:47
Diabolo game, how to make 1074:260-261
Dominoes game, how to play 1507:30-32
Double sixes game, paper, making 1500:24-26
Dragon tag game, how to play 1654:64
Dragon's tail game 979:29
Eagle and chickens game 602:49
Eagle chases chickens game, how to play 1313:92
Fan mier or reverses game 383:52
Fan Tan game, how to play 1507:33
Fingers out game 383:41
First slinging or first matching game 383:44
Five square game, how to play 1688:45-46
Flipball game 1354:160
Forcing the city gates game 383:41
Frying vegetables fruit basket game 383:54
Gat Fei Gei, hopscotch game 1426:32-33
Go game 1074:42-51
Go-bang (tic-tac-toe) game 1074:52
Harvest game, how to play 1507:34
Harvest race game 956:16-17
Hop Scotch 383:48; 602:49-50
Jackstraws game 956:22
Kick the marbles game 383:53
Knucklebones game, how to make and play 1718:38
Lame chicken stick game 383:42; 967:26; 1119:16
Lau chhung game 383:50
Nim game 956:79-81
Nim game, how to play 1507:35
Pickup race game 383:45
Pin the tail on the dragon game 1244:41
Pong Hau K'i game 956:122
Rice bag jacks, fabric squares, rice, string, making
    1427:142
Sampen card game 1132:4
Seeking the gold game 602:45
Selling vegetables game 876:108-109
Shuttlecock game, wire, fabric, feathers, making 383:43;
    602:46; 1427:142
Spellicans game, how to play 956:22; 1507:36
Spreading the fist game 383:47
Stick rhythms game 383:49
Stone, scissors, paper game 602:48
Strike the stick game 602:46-47
T'yow fang zi, hopping house hopscotch game, how to
    play 1708:20-21
Tangram Chinese puzzle, oaktag, patterns, making
    1246:14-17
Tangram puzzle, how to make from black paper 1477:55
Tangram, paper, making 1500:23-24

Tangrams games, making 1507:37-38
Throwing the square game 383:44
Tiger trap game 602:47-48
Tsoo! Tsoo! game 383:41
Water sprite chasing game, how to play 383:53; 602:50;
    1498:36-38
Who crosses the river first? game 1037:20-23
Zhao Lingxiu, find the leader game, how to play 1494:41
Zhua San, pick up three jacks game, how to play
    1718:18-19

CHINA—HALLOWEEN

Hungry Ghosts Festival 504:53

CHINA—HANDICRAFTS

Ball, rolled string yarn, making 298:260
Book of haiku, paper, threads, patterns, making 1332:91-
    100
Bread dough figures, recipe 1427:125
Brush stroke chrysanthemums, paper, patterns, making
    1246:28-29
Burial urn, copy of, papier-mache, paints, making
    1561:34
Butterflies painted on silk, making 298:180-181
Cantonese design appliqued on net, making 298:120-121
Clay bottle, making 1070:44-48
Computer project: draw tiger slippers 1218:36-39
Egg painting, eggs, paints, making 1633:144-145
Hand painted lacquered plate, making 298:190-191
Honeycomb windows, paper, making 298:216-217
Horse made from sculpta mold, making 525:97
Inscrutable Wong, nightdress case, fabric, patterns, mak-
    ing 316:75
Lacquered paper plates, patterns, making 1427:128
Leaf paper-cutouts, making 167:60-65
Math slat book, tongue depressors, yarn, ribbons, mak-
    ing 1332:79-82
Netsuke, Asiatic ram, happy man, sitting horse, making
    167:19-26
Paper-cuts, butterfly, flower, dragon and snowflake, mak-
    ing 1731:end
Paper-cuts, colored tissue paper, patterns, making
    1427:132
Paper-cuts, paper, patterns, making 1633:146-147
Peacocks, paper-cutting, making 1447:22-23
Relief boat relief, making 167:94-95
Relief crane relief, making 167:90-94
Seasons accordion book, paper, yarn, ribbons, patterns,
    making 1332:83-90
Tiger, paper, making 532:59

CHINA—HATS

Coolie hat, paper, making 574:21
Coolie hat, pattern, how to make 1361:72
Hat, Chinese braid hat, paper, patterns, making 823:45
Hat, Chinese traditional hat, paper, pattern, making
    823:46

CHINA—HOUSES

Courtyard houses, making 173:58-59
Sampan boat home model, making 494:192-195

CHINA—KITES

Bow and hoop kite, making 889:90-99
Chinese fan kite, making 1026:71-73
Dragon kite, making 532:41
Golden Dragon kite, making 1026:83-85
Swooping snake kite, bamboo, fabric, string, making
    1219:16-17

CHINA—LANGUAGE
Characters for numbers and months 958:44-45
Characters for words, how to write 935:unp; 958:36-43
Chinese numbers and conversation words 574:27
Common expressions in Chinese 1690:115
Numbers one through seven in Chinese 1708:21
Numbers one to ten in Chinese language 392:unp
Sentence characters, making 958:18-19
Some common words and phrases in Mandarin 1410:22

CHINA—LANTERNS
Chinese lantern, pinpricked paper, making 966:136-137
Lanterns, Chinese paper lantern, making 574:21
Lanterns, oatmeal or salt box, shiny fabric, making 1427:130
Pagoda lanterns, making 282:20

CHINA—MAGIC TRICKS
Chinese hoops, paper trick, how to do 1270:18-19

CHINA—MASKS
Chinese mask from cardboard, crayons, paints, patterns, making 1381:66
Lion mask, making 532:30-31
Masks, miniature, papier-mache, making 167:55-56

CHINA—MUSICAL INSTRUMENTS
Pien chung instrument, how to play 1646:25
Pien chung instrument, paper tube, string, making 1646:23-24

CHINA—NEW YEAR. *See* **CHINESE NEW YEAR**

CHINA—NUMBERS
Numbers one to ten in Chinese language 392:unp

CHINA—PARTIES—BIRTHDAYS
Chinese dragon party, activities, foods, and handicrafts 30:101-104

CHINA—PORCELAIN
Painted porcelain Mandarin egg, making 298:104-105

CHINA—POTTERY
Flower pot, Yuan-Ming, clay, making 1070:50-54
Food jar: Chinese Warring States, clay, making 1070:55-57
Harlequin bowl, clay, making 1070:48-50
Rest pillow, pottery, making 532:17
Sung brush holder, clay, making 1070:58-59

CHINA—PRINTING
Printing blocks, making, 173:46-47

CHINA—PUPPET PLAYS
Why Man Must Harvest His Crops 44:78-81

CHINA—PUPPETS
Chinese puppet, making 483:26
Ku Li Tzu hand puppet, dough, fabric, making 1707:9
Panda puppets, old socks and gloves, making 1484:8-9
Puppets, finger, papier-mache, making 167:52-55

CHINA—RED EGG PARTY
Fortune cookies, making 294:112
Game, tilting scribe, making 294:110-111
Hanging lantern decorations, making 294:102-103
Lantern placemats and invitations, making 294:98
Mask, dancing dragon, making 294:104-105
Noodle drops, making 294:112
Paper blow favors, bing banger noisemaker, making 294:106-109
Red egg souvenir, making 294:99
Slinky cupcake dragon, making 294:100-101

CHINA—RHYMES
Chinese Pat-A-Cake baby clapping rhymes 780:57
Old Chang the Crab tickling rhyme 780:93
Pulling the saw baby lifting rhyme 780:89

This Little Pig tickling rhyme 780:93
Thistle-seed baby lifting rhyme 780:88
Two Little Eyes 780:53

CHINA—RUGS
Rugs, hooked, pillow, making 167:100-105

CHINA—SCREENS
Table screen, small, decoupage paper, making 274:88-91

CHINA—SCROLLS
Scrolls, dowels, rice paper, paints, making 1338:77-80

CHINA—SONGS
"Pulling the Saw" 1607:41
Purple Straight-Grown Bamboo Shoot, lullaby 1220:152-153

CHINA—TANGRAMS
Tangram, making 626:23-25

CHINA—TEA
Chinese Schools of Tea 474:128-130

CHINA—THANKSGIVING
History of Thanksgiving in China 659:16-18

CHINA—TOYS
Cat, making 532:37
Chinese top, helicopter toy, wooden, making 889:14-20
Hobby horse, stick and felt, pattern, making 1027:95-99
Tumbling toy man, posterboard, felt, heavy ball, making 1477:39

CHINA—WRITING
Calligraphy, numbers one to ten, how to do 1244:41

CHINESE. *See* **CHINA—LANGUAGE**

CHINESE AMERICANS—GOLD RUSH
Chinese miners fan tan game, how to play 1214:48

CHINESE IMMIGRANTS—FOLKLORE
Chin Chiang and the Dragon's Dance; physical and human geography activities 1458:70-73

CHINESE NEW YEAR
Activities, patterns, games 50:149-169
Animal horoscope 505:34-35
Celebration of 497:154-165
Chinese New Year 475:97-99
Chinese New Year activities, stories, crafts, recipes 558:39-42
Chinese New Year art and writing activities, patterns, making 1152:100-107
Chinese New Year celebration 499:77; 505:32-33; 566:36; 601:46-47
Chinese New Year finger plays, recipes, games 944:63-64
Chinese New Year program; activities, books, crafts, patterns, making 1159:1-11
Chinese New Year celebration, activities, handicrafts, foods, songs, making 909:19-27
Chinese New Year, history 496:17-19; 513:55
Feast of Lanterns 475:99
Parade, paper lanterns, dragon costumes, making 1266:32-34
San Francisco Festival celebration 826:18-19
Tsao-Chun celebration 505:36-37
Yuan Tan Festival, history of 709:107
Yuan Tan in China 489:44-53

CHINESE NEW YEAR—BULLETIN BOARDS
Lantern, hanging, fan and dragon, making 295:235-236

CHINESE NEW YEAR—CALENDAR
Chinese Calendar, what animal are you, patterns 1199:14-17

CHINESE NEW YEAR—COOKERY
Almond cookies, recipe 1662:18; 1313:211

Barbecued spareribs, recipe 1186:96-97
Ch'a Yeh Tan (tea eggs), recipe 1666:154-155
Chiao-Tzu Wrapper (dumpling wrappers), recipe 1666:152
Chinese spring rolls, recipe 1666:153-154
Egg drop soup, recipe 54:213
Eight treasure rice, recipe 1654:58
Fortune cookies, recipe 1455:151; 1662:19
Fried rice, recipe, how to eat with chopsticks 1199:23-24
Honied walnuts, recipe 1313:211
Jo Pien San Wei (boiled pork slices), recipe 1666:153
Litchi nut fruit mixture, recipe 1666:270
Long life buns, recipe 497:162
New Year's rice, recipe 1666:154
Pastry with coconut, peanuts, sesame seeds, recipe 1654:58
Puffed rice bars, recipe 54:213
Roasted soy bean nuts, recipe 1313:212
Spring rolls, recipe 497:162

CHINESE NEW YEAR—COSTUMES
Chinese dragon, fabric, notions, patterns, making 1435:92-93
Dragon costume, making 272:31-35
Dragon, paper bag, fabric, crepe paper, making 1266:34
Festival costume, making 272:35-36

CHINESE NEW YEAR—DECORATIONS
Chinese wand for waving, ribbon, making 1662:14
Firecrackers, crepe paper, making 1662:17
New Year card, making with pictures of animals 586:26-28
Noisemaker, paper, patterns, making 1237:75-78

CHINESE NEW YEAR—DRAGONS
Chinese dragon, cardboard, paper, sticks, paints, patterns, making 1199:20-22
Dragon from a paper bag, paints, making 1539:86-87
Dragon mask, making 709:111
Dragon toys, making 698:13
Dragon, directions and illustrations for making 1159:4
Dragon, scary, making 698:13
Fire breathing dragon, making 329:8-9

CHINESE NEW YEAR—FANS
New Year fans, paper, patterns, making 1152:104-105

CHINESE NEW YEAR—GAMES
Shuttlecock game, how to make and play 1654:62

CHINESE NEW YEAR—HANDICRAFTS
Banner of Chinese writing, patterns, making 1159:5
Dragon, long tailed, paper, patterns, making 1152:106-107
Fish from tissue paper, pattern, making 1313:204-205
Fortune cookies, paper, patterns, making 1159:7
Good luck money envelope, red paper, decorations, making 1574:4-5
Gung Hay Fat Choy scroll or banner, paper, paints, patterns, making 1393:129
New Year paper-cut outs, making 856:38-45
Pop-up Chinese New Year card, making 1387:47-49
Red envelopes (Li see), gold ink, making 1427:134
Red envelopes, red shiny paper, making 1313:205
Rhymes (couplets) on red paper with Chinese characters, patterns, making 1654:62-63
Tangram puzzle, paper, patterns, making 1159:8

CHINESE NEW YEAR—LANTERNS
Chinese lanterns, making 698:13
Chinese New Year lantern, paper, making 513:59-60
Dragon lantern, making 709:108-111
Lanterns, paper hanging, patterns, making 1159:6; 1199:15-18; 1277:28-29; 1662:15
Lanterns, paper, how to make 1654:64

CHINESE NEW YEAR—MASKS
Chinese New Year masks, paper plates, making 1662:16
Dragon mask, crepe paper, foil, box, making 1706:29
Lion mask, paper, styrofoam trays, sticks, paints, making 1199:19-20

CHINESE NEW YEAR—MUSICAL INSTRUMENTS
Gong, pie tin, box, making 1310:109

CHINESE NEW YEAR—PUPPETS
Chinese dragon, paper bags, making 1083:174-175
Chinese New Year finger plays and puppets, patterns, making 513:56-61
Puppet projects, patterns, scenes, story starters, feature story 1083:173-177
Why Cat Was Left Behind, puppets and puppet play script, making 1155:71-75
You Yuen puppet, tube, broom and puppet, pattern, making 1083:176-177

CHINESE NEW YEAR—ZODIAC CALENDAR
Chinese animals signs dodecahedron, how to make 1654:59-60
Chinese Fortune Zodiac calendar, gives years and characteristics for zodiac animals 1654:58-62
Lunar calendar and horoscope diagram, how to make 1393:128

CHIPPEWA INDIANS. *See also* **OJIBWA INDIANS**
CHIPPEWA INDIANS—BUSTLES
Mide bustle, making 465:56-57

CHIPPEWA INDIANS—CLOTHING
Chippewa finger woven tie sash, making 932:78-81
Chippewa leggings, moccasins, dress, making 223:40
Chippewa man's breechclout, leggings, apron, making 223:46-47
Clothing, making 589:61
Dance dresses, making 589:64-65

CHIPPEWA INDIANS—COOKERY
Chippewa bannock, recipe 305:16
Maple sugar candy, recipe 1699:158-160
Wild rice, recipe 1699:140-141

CHIPPEWA INDIANS—DANCES
Serpentine dance 465:79

CHIPPEWA INDIANS—DREAMS
Dream catcher, paper plate, yarn, beads, making 1633:44-45

CHIPPEWA INDIANS—FOOTWEAR
Moccasins, making 932:92-95

CHIPPEWA INDIANS—GAMES
Corncob darts, how to play 445:26-34
Windigo game 602:168

CHIPPEWA INDIANS—HANDICRAFTS
Birch bark designs, making 1699:178
Cut-outs from birch bark to decorate objects, patterns, making 1633:40-43

CHIPPEWA INDIANS—HATS
Chippewa hat, making 223:54-55

CHIPPEWA INDIANS—HEADDRESSES
Chippewa feather crest, making 589:8-9

CHIPPEWA INDIANS—HOUSEHOLD
Bark containers, paper, making 1699:15
Pots, storage bag, making 223:21

CHIPPEWA INDIANS—HOUSES
Chippewa bed frame, making 633:206-207

CHIPPEWA INDIANS—MUSICAL INSTRUMENTS
Chippewa dance drum, making 465:90
Water drum, making 63:48-49

CHIPPEWA INDIANS—SPEARS
Fish spear, making 466:106
CHOCOLATE
History of 410:48-55
CHOCOLATE CHIP COOKIES
History of 119:106-109
CHOCTAW INDIANS—BEADWORK
Direct beading, how to do 224:28-31
CHOCTAW INDIANS—GAMES
Stealing sticks game 602:168
CHOPSTICKS
How to eat with chopsticks 1199:23-24
CHRISTIAN FESTIVALS
Epiphany celebration 566:26
Pentecost celebration 566:26
Saints Day celebration 566:26
CHRISTMAS. *See also* **SANTA CLAUS** *and* **CHRIST-MAS** *as a subheading under various places, e.g.,*
SWEDEN—CHRISTMAS
Activities, crafts, food 1662:194-207
American Cities celebrate Christmas 475:64-74
Birth of Jesus Christ, activities and projects for class-rooms 1393:106-111
Blessings for Christmas 475:59-60
Cards, history of 425:11-12
Catholic Service 475:49-50
Celebration of Christmas 497:118-131
Celebration of Christmas in the United States 1049:90
Christmas feast celebration, history of 631:114
Christmas in other lands art and writing activities, patterns, making 1152:65-75
Christmas stories, songs, art activities, games, recipes 1135:27-29; 1135:31-33
Christmas story, how to write 498:89-91
Christmas tree in America, history of 475:52-53
Christmas, celebration 133:122-125
Crib for Christmas 475:60-61
Customs of Christmas in the United States 473:20-27
Customs round the world 502:18-19
First Christmas 475:43-47
Flowering branch 475:42
History of Christmas 218:1-5; 513:35; 709:72; 829:41-42
History of Christmas calendar 218:6-7
History of Christmas celebrations 566:28-29
Holly, history of 425:9-10
Learning units, art, language, music, foods, crafts, patterns 1193:15-235
Martin Luther's tree 502:22
Merry Christmas in 37 languages 434:7; 1128:97
Midnight Mass, history of 631:120
Mince pie, history of 425:7-9
Nativity, history and background 726:20-28
Office of the Shepherds 475:63-64
Protestant Service 475:47-48
Songs, finger plays, stories, games, rhythms 1200:39-43
Spirit of Christmas story, paper plate picture, patterns, making 900:37-43
St. Nicholas Day, December 6 475:42
Star of Seven 475:42
Star Singers celebration, history of 631:116
Stockings, history of 425:10
Tree, history of 425:6-7
Twelve Days of Christmas activity, how to do 781:48
Words of Christmas 502:20-21

Yule log lighting, history of 425:7
Yule log, bringing in the Yule log 475:59
CHRISTMAS EVE
History of Christmas Eve celebrations 218:29-32
CHRISTMAS LEGENDS
Christmas Angel 475:74-75
Legend of Christmas Flowers 475:75-76
Legend of the Pine Tree 475:7
Robin Red Breast 475:75
CHRISTMAS TREES
Christmas tree in America 475:52-53
Christmas tree, history of 631:112; 709:75-76,79
Legend of St. Boniface 475:51
Story of St. Winfred 475:51
Winter tree, history of 631:110
CHRISTMAS—BIRDS
Bird's nest legend and nest for tree, making 310:218
Christmas feast tree for the birds 672:215-220
Christmas tree for the animals, pine cones, peanut butter, bird seed, making 1408:15
CHRISTMAS—CANDLES
Candle in the window traditions 475:54
Carols by candlelight information 475:55-56
Christmas candles 475:53-54
White Lightning information 475:54-55
CHRISTMAS—CAROLS
Christmas carols 475:77-91
First New World Carol, Jesous Ahatonhia 631:118
History of Christmas Carols 218:22-26; 425:28-35
Wait's carol 475:78-82
CHRISTMAS—CHILDREN'S PRAYER
Children's Prayer 475:61-62
CHRISTMAS—COLONIAL AMERICA—COOKERY
Beverages, cinnamon tea, recipe 166:2
Beverages, eggnog, recipe 166:2
Beverages, hot mulled cider, recipe 166:2
Breads, angel wing popovers, recipe 166:4
Breads, buttermilk biscuits, recipe 166:3
Breads, cheese recipe 166:5
Breads, cheese sticks, recipe 166:5
Breads, cranberry loaf bread, recipe 166:4
Breads, molasses bread, recipe 166:4
Breads, muffins, recipe 166:5
Breads, orange tea bread, recipe 166:4
Breads, plantation days spoon bread, recipe 166:3
Breads, Sally Lunn breads, recipe 166:3
Breads, southern cornbread, recipe 166:3
Breads, southern short'nin' bread, recipe 166:5
Cakes, applesauce cake, recipe 166:10
Cakes, Betty's best fruit cake, recipe 166:9
Cakes, blackberry cake, recipe 166:10
Cakes, chocolate pound cake, recipe 166:7
Cakes, crumb, coffee cake, recipe 166:7
Cakes, fresh apple cake, recipe 166:10
Cakes, ginger pound cake, recipe 166:7
Cakes, Merry Christmas cake, recipe 166:17
Cakes, old timey raisin spice cake, recipe 166:9
Cakes, old timey seed cake, recipe 166:7
Cakes, perfect pound cake, recipe 166:7
Cakes, rum cake sauce, recipe 166:8
Cakes, whiskey pecan cake, recipe 166:8
Candy, apple leather, recipe 166:19
Candy, cherry creams, recipe 166:17
Candy, crystalized orange peels, recipe 166:19
Candy, fruit balls, recipe 166:17

Candy, fruit candy bars, recipe 166:17
Candy, molasses candy corn balls, recipe 166:19
Candy, molasses taffy, recipe 166:19
Candy, peanut brittle, recipe 166:18
Candy, peanut butter creams, recipe 166:17
Candy, peppermints, recipe 166:18
Candy, pralines, recipe 166:19
Candy, spiced glazed nuts, recipe 166:17
Candy, vanilla creams, recipe 166:17
Candy, vanilla fudge, recipe 166:18
Candy, walnut fudge, recipe 166:18
Cookies, best chocolate brownies, recipe 166:15
Cookies, butter cookies, recipe 166:16
Cookies, caramel bars, recipe 166:14
Cookies, coconut macaroons, recipe 166:16
Cookies, Moravian cookies, recipe 166:15
Cookies, old fashioned gingerbread men, recipe 166:16
Cookies, Scotch shortbread, recipe 166:14
Cookies, soft molasses cookies, recipe 166:14
Cookies, spiced oatmeal cookies, recipe 166:14
Cookies, whiskey balls, recipe 166:15
Lacy pancakes, recipe 166:6
Pies and pastries, chocolate cream pie, recipe 166:11
Pies and pastries, coconut cream pie, recipe 166:11
Pies and pastries, eggnog pie, recipe 166:11
Pies and pastries, grasshopper pie (creme de menthe), recipe 166:12
Pies and pastries, lemon chess pie, recipe 166:13
Pies and pastries, molasses crumb pie, recipe 166:13
Pies and pastries, molasses raisin pie, recipe 166:13
Pies and pastries, old timey egg custard pie, recipe 166:12
Pies and pastries, pecan pie, recipe 166:12
Pies and pastries, pie crust, recipe 166:11
Pies and pastries, pumpkin nut pie, recipe 166:12
Pies and pastries, sugar chess tarts, recipe 166:13
Pies and pastries, sweet potato pie, recipe 166:12
Pies and pastries, vanilla cream pie, recipe 166:11
Relishes, apple relish, recipe 166:24
Relishes, kraut relish, recipe 166:24
Relishes, old fashioned corn relish, recipe 166:24
Relishes, pepper relish, recipe 166:24
Relishes, tomato chili sauce, recipe 166:24
Southern corn meal waffles, recipe 166:6
Sweet pancake topping, recipe 166:6
Treats, ambrosia, recipe 166:21
Treats, baked ham glazes, recipe 166:22
Treats, brandied peaches, recipe, 166:22
Treats, broken glass torte, recipe 166:20
Treats, cherry velvet, recipe 166:21
Treats, Christmas cranberry salad, recipe 166:20
Treats, famous butter mints, recipe 166:22
Treats, Indian pudding, recipe 166:21
Treats, party fruit jubilee, recipe 166:20
Treats, party recipe 166:22
Treats, tipsy cake, recipe 166:21
Treats, tutti frutti, recipe 166:21
CHRISTMAS—COOKERY
Birds Christmas tree, recipe 215:93
Biscochitos, recipe 1043:147
Buche de Noel, recipe 707:56-62
Candy cane cookies, recipe 1193:30
Christmas pudding, recipe 140:96
Church windows, pastry dough, candies, recipe 1080:26-27

Colonial Christmas fruit cake, recipe 191:44-45
Cookies, cut-out cookies, recipe 1186:106-107
Courambiades, cookies, recipe 273:62-64
Cranberry loaf, Early American, recipe 595:37-47
Epiphany orange cake, recipe 703:81-83
Fruit sweetmeats, frosted, recipe 1408:23
Gingerbread Christmas cards 207:108-109
Gingerbread Horn books, recipe 376:271
Gingerbread House, instructions for baking and making 943:7-47
Gingerbread men, recipe 1193:30
Hattie Hoffman's American fruitcake, recipe 497:128
Indian slapjack, recipe 192:47
Moravian Christmas cookies, recipe 1128:117
Moravian Christmas cookies, recipes for light and dark cookies 1232:76
Moravian love feast buns, recipe 1128:157
Mrs. Cratchit's Christmas date pudding, recipe 570:69-72
Mrs. Santa Claus's nut bread, recipe 1178:45
New England bread stuffing, recipe 273:121-123
North Pole cup cake cones, recipe 919:32-33
Paintbrush cookies, recipe 1193:73
Popcorn balls, old fashioned, recipe 434:66
Punch, cranberry juice, raspberry drink mix, recipe 1193:22
Santa Claus eggs, recipe 703:46-47
Santa's cookies, chocolate chip cookies, recipe 1542:110
Soupirs, Sighs cookies, recipe 1128:122
Spice cookies to hang on trees, recipe, how to make 1557:23
St. Lucia buns, recipe 273:79-82; 595:69-75
Sugarplum cake, making 206:62-64
Sugarplums, orange nut sugarplums, recipe 703:79-80
Sugarplums, recipe 1128:40
Sweet potatoes, South Carolina recipe 273:126-128
Taffy candy, recipe 49:288
Taffy pull, recipe 349:20-21
Thomassing cookies, recipe 595:115-119
Truffles, French chocolate truffles, recipe 703:76-78
Turkish delight candy, recipe 215:86-87
Twelfth Night cake, recipe 273:32-35
Wassail bowl, recipe 595:121-123
Wassail Christmas punch, recipe 703:95
Wassail punch, recipe 1193:58
Yule log cake, recipe 449:71
Yule log, chocolate, recipe 595:131-136
Yule log, peanut butter, recipe 502:43
CHRISTMAS—COSTUMES
Biblical boy and girl, variety of old clothes, making 1656:93-100
Christmas cracker costume, fabric, making 1174:131
Christmas fairy costume, fabric, patterns, making 1283:38-41
Christmas pudding costume, fabric, papier-mache, patterns, making 1174:130-131; 1283:42-45
Christmas tree costume, fabric, crepe paper, patterns, making 1174:127-128; 1283:46-49
Christmas tree costume, gold sticky backed plastic, making 1509:74-75
Christmas tree costume, paper bag, making 138:28-32
Father Christmas costume, fabric, patterns, making 1174:128-129
Joseph, costume 272:134-135
King 1, 11, 111, costumes, making 272:137-140
Mary costume 213:58-60

Mary, costume, making 272:133
Santa Claus costume, making 272:140-143
Santa Claus costume, paper bag, making 138:33-38
Santa Claus, paper, making 46:96-98
Shepherd costume, making 272:136
Shepherd's lamb costume, making 272:135-136
Snowman costume, wadding, stuffing, making 1174:132-133
Three Wise Men, variety of old clothes, making 1656:101-112
Wise Man from the East, paper, making 46:102-105

CHRISTMAS—CUSTOMS
Australia 149:57
Bangladesh 149:48
Christmas customs 149:58-64
England 149:34-40
Finland 149:30-31
France 149:40
Germany 149:41-42
Greece 149:45-46
Greenland 149:26-27
Holland 149:31
Hong Kong, 149:52
India 149:49-50
Ireland 149:32
Italy 149:43-44
Japan 149:54
Mexico 149:64-65
New Guinea 149:56
New Zealand 149:57-58
Norway 149:27
Pakistan 149:48
Portugal 149:44-45
Puerto Rico 149:63-64
Scotland 149:33-34
Sicily 149:44
Sweden 149:28-29
United States 149:58-64
USSR 149:46-47
Wales 149:34-40

CHRISTMAS—DECORATIONS
Advent banner, fabric, felt, and applique, making 595:1-7
Advent calendar from Christmas cards, making 669:158-163
Advent calendar, making 273:41-45; 698:97; 795:11; 916:83-85; 1023:33
Advent calendar, patterns, making 150:20-29
Advent calendar, walnuts, egg carton, paint, miniature surprises, making 1203:13
Advent Christmas stocking, felt, yarn, making 1203:16
Angel with horn, paper tube, tinfoil, making 1657:76
Angel, blown egg, pattern, making 1311:174-175
Angel, Madonna or choirboy from glass bottle, making 764:63-65
Angels and bird paper-cutouts for tree, making 1257:42-43
Angels in clusters, felt, wooden beads, pipe cleaners, making 1203:18
Baboushka doll, making 140:182
Bells, macramé Klockstrang, making 595:18-23
Bobeche, making 215:75-76
Card, snowflake Christmas card, paper, making 1524:78
Cards and envelopes, making 1717:36-37
Christmas luminaries, from glass bottle, making 764:61-62

Christmas scene in an egg pattern, making 26:63-65
Christmas stocking, felt, glue, patterns, making 1203:14-15
Chubby cherub from a gourd, making 1304:135
Clay for making decorations, cornstarch, baking soda, water, recipe 1179:25-26
Cookie decorations, patterns, making 1348:unp
Cornucopias and party crackers, making 1717:38-39
Cowboy, foam balls, felt, pattern, making 1360:48-50
Crackers that pop, paper, patterns, making 1320:66-67
Creche from Christmas cards, making 669:171-172; 1023:37-45
Creche from clamshells, making 215:28-30
Creche from natural materials, making 217:103-104
Creche, making 218:69-74; 698:98
Creche, milk carton, making 679:unp
Creche, shoe box, making 140:20-22
Crib from paper straws, making 828:80-82
Dancing girls for tree, paper doilies, pattern, making 1257:40-41
Drummer boy, paper tube, colored paper, making 1657:78
Elf bells, jingle bells, yarn, making 1266:21
Elf collar, tinsel, construction paper, glue, making 1266:21
Father Christmas, paper, making 95:15
Frosty the snowman, paper, making 434:43
Gingerbread man, dough recipe 1203:19
God's eyes, yam, making 595:48-51
Heirloom ornaments, time capsule ornaments holds written thoughts, making 1425:105-106
Jesus and manger, cardboard, making 148:28-29
Lucia crown and robe, making 1023:34-35
Lucia crown, evergreens, making 669:46
Manger, bread dough, recipe 595:95-99
Mary and Joseph, cardboard, making 148:26
Mobile, Twelve Days of Christmas mobile, making 709:122-125
Nativity crib model, paper, making 1678:6-10
Nativity figures, papier-mache, making 641:174-175
Nativity scene and crib in shoe box, clay dough figures, making 273:73-75; 1025:24-26; 1557:14-17
Nativity scene diorama in box, making 1049:42
Nativity scene made from pretzels, doughs, decorations, patterns given for all figures, how to make; 1232:65-75
Nativity scene, clay and fabric, making 553:62-63
Nativity scene, making 448:41
Nativity scene, paper straws, making 828:66
Nativity scene, papier-mache, making 21:80-86; 22:74-81
Nativity, Joseph, Shepherd, Mary, Crib and Babe, paper straws, making 828:81
Nativity, making 629:150-152
North Pole Village, building patterns to photocopy and make 1236:24-34
Origami ornaments, origami paper, paper ribbon, making 1236:47-49
Ornaments, no-bake clay, recipe 1662:202
Paint names, paint, glitter, glue, making 1203:17
Paper chains, paper, foil, making 1348:unp
Partridge in a Pear Tree mobile, making 140:184-185
Partridge in a Pear Tree plaque, making 670:109
Partridge in a Pear Tree, making using peanut sawdust 257:108-110

Plaster of Paris draped cloth for large angels and projects, making 1455:23

Pop-up Christmas card, making 1387:33-35

Pop-up holiday tree, making 1388:48-49

Posadas and pinatas, papier-mache, making 595:87-93

Potpourri sachets, fabric, netting, potpourri, making 1492:14-15

Preserved leaves, leaves, glycerin, making 1257:44

Reindeer magnet, felt, eyes, chenille stems, pattern, making 1360:42-44

Reindeer, red nosed, blown egg, pattern, making 1311:174-175

Rice Krispies Christmas trees, recipe 1203:17

Rudolph, egg carton, making 677:10-11

Rudolph, grocery bag, pattern, making 253:189-191

Santa centerpiece, container, dried materials, making 1257:45

Santa Claus, blown egg, pattern, making 1311:174-175

Santa Claus, paper tube, red paper, making 1657:77

Santa's boot, milk carton, cotton batting, patterns, making 1334:23

Santons of Provence, making 273:22-30

Shepherd and three kings, cardboard, making 148:27

Sleigh, milk carton, patterns, making 1334:24-25

Snow for tree decoration, soap flakes, water, fragrance 1179:24

Snow scene in a jar, making 1179:31

Snow-storm jar, oil, water, confetti, making 1662:194

Snowflakes, German, making 218:80-81

Stable, cardboard, making 148:28-29

Stained glass windows, patterns, making 1203:21

Stars; waxed paper, making 1717:34-35

Stocking, St. Nicholas' Day stocking, fabric, making 595:29-35

Three Kings Crown, cardboard, foil, patterns, making 1492:42-43

Three Kings from glass bottles, making 764:58-60

Three Kings ornaments, making 629:136-137

Three Kings, Blue King, Red King, Green King, paper straws, making 828:81-82

Three Wise Men, felt, pattern, making 867:38-41

Tin soldiers from tooling foil, patterns, making 150:6-9

Tomte figures, making 669:72-73

Toy soldier, felt, pattern, making 867:48-49

Toy soldier, paper, large patterns, making 477:38-44

Twelfth Night crowns, making 273:35-39

Twelve Days of Christmas mobile, making 709:122-125

Up on the housetop, milk carton, making 1334:26

Victorian fan decoration, making 273:18-20

Victorian tree decorations, making 1049:46-47

Village, Christmas Village, buildings, animals, people, Bristol board, making 669:59-73

Village, wooden, making 670:105-106

Wall hanging, Partridge in a Pear Tree, making 768:153-157

We Three Kings, making 297:284-285

Window decorations, plastic wrap and squeeze paint, making 1360:51-53

Wise Man made from beads, making, 255:70-72

Wise Men crowns, making 349:41

Yule log, wooden, making 1049:40

CHRISTMAS—FESTIVALS

History of Christmas Nature Festivals 419:46-49

CHRISTMAS—FINGER PLAYS

Finger plays and rhymes 1583:82-84; 1583:87-93

CHRISTMAS—FOLKLORE—HANDICRAFTS

One Lone Juniper Tree, paper Christmas tree, free-flow string ornaments 125:70-79

CHRISTMAS—GAMES

Christmas ball game, making 329:43

Christmas croquet game, how to play 1557:29

Dressing the tree game, how to play 1557:28

Flip toy into stocking game, making 1568:36-37

Gift game, making 534:96

Hidden card game, how to play 1557:29

Piñata game 329:48

Piñata game, paper bag 829:51

Puzzles and tricks, making 1049:76-77

Santa's sack game, how to play 1557:28

Stockings word game, patterns, making 50:54-55

CHRISTMAS—GIFTS

Giving of gifts traditions 475:56-57

Santa Claus tradition 475:57-58

CHRISTMAS—GREETING CARDS

History of Christmas cards 218:26-28

CHRISTMAS—GREETINGS

Merry Christmas in different languages 1203:11

Merry Christmas in many languages for Christmas cards 1703:16-17

CHRISTMAS—HANDICRAFTS

Advent curiosity box, making 1277:26-27

Angel doll, felt, stuffed, pattern, making 487:34-35

Bells from pears, baked, recipe 1193:36

Crèche and figures, gingerbread recipe, patterns, how to make 1086:116-122

Cut-outs, bow, star, papier-mache, making 1300:62-64

Hand print Christmas card, paper, paints, making 1568:44-45

History and meaning of 149:95-107

Nativity figures dressed in cloth, making 726:32-38

Nativity figures in baker's clay recipe, making 726:39-42

Nativity wall hanging, felt, patterns, making 726:29-31

Pomander, foam ball, potpourri chunks, making 1510:76-77

Reindeer ornament, felt, yarn, paints, making 1568:40-41

Santa Claus mask, paper plate, fiber fill, making 1568:34-35

Stained glass bells cookies, recipe 1193:36

Story of Jesus figures, old Christmas cards, making 1568:18-19

Straw ornaments, Scandinavian, making 453:115-120

Three Kings banner, felt, ribbons, foils, making 1568:12-13

CHRISTMAS—MUSIC

History of Christmas music 149:67-75

CHRISTMAS—PARTIES

Decorations, food, games, making 1266:21-26

Family reunion party, invitations, craft activities, games, recipes, making 1203:73-79

Nativity family, making 294:202-203

Santa's workshop party, invitations, craft activities, gifts to make 1203:34-40

Tannenbaum cake, making 294:192

Tree-trimming party, activities, games, recipes, making 1203:41-52

White Christmas party, invitation, craft activities, games, recipes, making 1203:53-61

CHRISTMAS—PINATAS

Piñata fish, making 273:132-138

Piñata monster, paper bag, making 534:18-19

Piñata, making 329:45-47; 349:24-26

CHRISTMAS—PLANTS

Christmas tree, history of 218:15-19
Evergreen, history of 218:9-10
History of Christmas plants 218:9-20
Holly and ivy, history of 218:12-14
Mistletoe, history of 218:10-12
Poinsettia, history of 218:19-22
Rosemary, history of 218:14-15

CHRISTMAS—PUPPETS

Christmas with the Cratchits puppet show 756:168-176
First Christmas puppet show 756:189-190
King puppet, making 754:208-213
Little Drummer Boy puppet show 756:71-73
Rhythm reindeer, brown paper, cardboard, jingle bells, making 1294:27-28
Santas from Christmas cards, cardboard, wrapping paper, making 1294:29-30
Shepherd's Pipe puppet show 756:159-162
Three Kings puppet play 754:205-208
Three Kings puppet show 756:73-77
Toy soldier, cardboard tube, colored paper, stick, making 1294:31-33
Visit from St. Nicholas puppet show 756:82-86

CHRISTMAS—SAINTS

Christmas saints 149:117-124

CHRISTMAS—WREATHS

Advent wreath, clay, recipe given, making 595:9-13
Advent wreath, evergreens, making 725:13-14
Advent wreath, making 218:68-69; 475:41-42
Advent wreath, newspaper, making 1023:25-28
Advent wreath, Norwegian straw, making 1023:29
Advent wreath, paper and dough, making 897:18
Advent wreath, styrofoam, making 1023:28
Advent wreath, wire frame, making 1023:29
Appalachian braided wreath, fabric, making 273:123-126
Raffia wreath, raffia, ribbons, making 1492:16-17
Salt dough wreath, salt dough, paints, making 1299:46-47
Wreath from dried flowers, making 1455:112
Wreath, Appalachian braided, fabric, making 273:123-126
Wreath, paper plate, pattern, making 1311:172-173
Wreath, pine cones, pattern, making 1360:45-47
Wreath, raffia wreath from raffia, ribbons, ornaments, making 1510:82-83

CINCO DE MAYO. *See also* **MEXICO—FESTIVALS**

Activities, crafts, history and stories for 128:60-68
Hispanic boy costume, paper, making 128:63
Hispanic girl costume, paper, making 128:64
Piñata, balloon, making 128:67

CIPHERS

Ancient Greece scytale device for sending and receiving messages, how to make 1611:33
Julius Caesar's cipher, how to use 1611:9-11

CIRCE—MAGIC TRICKS

Cups and balls, how to do 1270:6-7

CIRCUS

Circus train, paper bags, paints, making 1657:16-17
History of the circus 631:66
Learning units, activities, songs, art, recipes, patterns 1191:1-77
Songs, finger plays, stories, games, rhythms 1200:87

CIRCUS—COSTUMES

Circus tent costume, fabric, patterns, making 1174:82-83

CIRCUS—HANDICRAFTS

Circus tent goody boxes, card stock, cord, feathers, making 1299:24-25
Circus tent, pop-up pattern 1210:8
Clowns from blown eggs, patterns, making 1311:115

CIRCUS—PARADES

Parade for young children, how to do 1266:65-68

CIRCUS—PARTIES

Circus, invitations, decorations, costumes, food, games, recipes 1185:8-9
Clown cake, recipe 1185:56-57
P.T. Barnum birthday celebration; art, music, foods, games, activities 1104:102-105

CIRCUS—RUSSIA

Circus 143:189
Miniature circus 143:189
Real circus 143:190

CITIZENSHIP DAY

Activities and projects for classrooms 1393:29-32

CIVIL WAR. *See also* **UNITED STATES—HISTORY—CIVIL WAR**

CIVIL WAR—COOKERY

Buttermilk biscuits, recipe 1162:12-13
Chicken shortcake, recipe 1162:30-31
Collard greens, recipe 1162:32
Corn pudding, recipe 1162:18-19
Cornbread, recipe 1162:33
Fried apples, recipe 1162:14
Fried fish, recipe 1162:22-23
Hominy grits, recipe 1162:8-9
Hoppin' John, recipe 1162:20-21
Hush puppies, recipe 1162:24-25
Lemonade, recipe 1162:35
Peach cobbler, recipe 1162:36-37
Pork sausage and gravy, recipe 1162:10-11
Potato salad, recipe 1162:34
Pound cake, recipe 1162:38-39
Scrambled eggs, recipe 1162:15
Shortbread, recipe 1162:40-41
Sweet potato pone, recipe 1162:26-27

CIVIL WAR—FLAGS

American flag, 36 states, pattern 1193:391
Confederate flag, pattern 1193:392

CLARK, WILLIAM—GAMES

William Clark's birthday game 240:42

CLAY

Baker's clay, flour and salt, recipe 1213:29; 1350:90
Baker's clay, four and salt, recipe 1305:99
Birds and animals made from clay, how to make 1260:20-21
Bread slice clay, bread, glue, food coloring, recipe 1455:4
Clay from the Earth, how to collect it 1372:114-115
Coffee grounds clay, recipe 1455:6
Finding and forming natural clay 1421:202
Flour clay, recipe 1455:5
Marbelized clay, flour, salt, coffee grounds, making 1286:34-35
Natural clay pots for firing, how to make 1260:44-45
Natural clay, how to gather and prepare 1213:21; 1260:42-43
Pearly clay, salt, cornstarch, water, recipe 1455:2
Quick clay, baking soda, cornstarch, water, food coloring, recipe 1455:5
Sand clay, recipe 1213:45; 1455:9

Soap clay, recipe 1455:4
Soft clay, cornstarch and soda, recipe 1213:29
Tissue paper bead clay, recipe 1455:9

CLAY TABLETS
Clay tablets, dough, recipe, making 1017:47
Cylinder seals, making 173:44-45
Mysterious tablets, making 173:52-53

CLEMENS, SAMUEL—BIRTHDAY
Celebrate with frog jumping contest using tiddlywinks 1199:268-269

CLEMENS, SAMUEL—COOKERY
Cucumber salad, recipe 57:39
Softshell crabs, recipe 57:39
Strawberries and cream, recipe 57:38

CLEOPATRA
Egypt versus Rome, history, stories, maps, puzzles, activities, projects 1041:124-152

CLEOPATRA—COSTUMES
Cap, making 287:51-53
Cleopatra costume, fabric, pattern, making 367:63-66
Costume 213:52-54
Costume, felt, patterns, making 1050:102-105
Costume, making 287:50-53
Decorated headband, making 287:53
Draped cloak dress, making 287:51

CLEOPATRA—HEADDRESSES
Queen's headdress, how to make 699:20-21

CLEOPATRA—WIG
Blue wig, making 287:51

CLOCKS
Big Ben clock, paper, making 295:191
Black Forest cuckoo clock, card board, making 282:86-87
Candle clock, Colonial period, making 1043:31
Cuckoo clock from Switzerland, paper and foil model, making 1094:38-39
Cuckoo clock, cardboard carton, making 679:unp
Cuckoo clock, making 293:203-204
Cuckoo clock, paper plate, making 534:32-33
Water clock, cups, balsa wood, making 1680:7

CLOTHING—HISTORICAL
Literature activities, books, finger plays, games, crafts 480:97-125

CLOWNS
Clown Day, activities, art, songs, recipes, games 1469:122-123
History of clowns 631:68

CLOWNS—COOKERY
Clown cake, recipe 1191:18-19
Ice cream clowns, how to make 1178:154

CLOWNS—COSTUMES
Clown costume, fabric, patterns, making 1283:16-19; 1379:22
Clown costume, red crepe paper, yellow vinyl fabric, making 1509:70-73
Harlequin costume 213:104-106
Pierrot costume 213:106-108

CLOWNS—DECORATIONS
Candy filled clowns, toilet paper tubes, crepe paper, making 1257:24-25

CLOWNS—EGG CLOWNS
Clown's record of his makeup painted on egg clowns, making 1486:16-17

CLOWNS—FACE MAKEUP
Clown face makeup, how to do 1306:38-47; 1314:16; 1320:72-73
Pierrot clown face, how to do 1314:17

CLOWNS—FACE PAINTING
Funny clown, baby clown, card clown, how to paint 1533:45-49

CLOWNS—GAMES
Clown marble roll game, bleach bottle, pattern, making 1311:56-57

CLOWNS—HANDICRAFTS
Clown boxes, plastic tubs, decorations, patterns, making 1286:91-93
Clowns from blown eggs, patterns, making 1311:115

CLOWNS—MASKS
Clown mask, paper plates, yarn, making 1345:6-7
Clown masks from papier-mache, making 1260:34-35

CLOWNS—PARTIES
Clown cake, recipe 1185:56-57

COAT OF ARMS
Coat of arms costume, making 887:76-77
Your coat of arms 118:34-35

COCOA
History of 410:48-55

COCONUTS
Coconut bars, recipe 1487:10-11
Cracking coconut, how to do 1122:26

COINS
Continental coin replicas, making 329:29

COLLAGES
Beatitude collage, making 873:30
Indian corn collage, making 1017:117
Palace princess collage, making 235:46
Paper knight on horseback collage, making 195:113-115

COLLODI, CARLO
Pinocchio's Pannikin poached egg, recipe 570:13-15

COLOMBIA
Activities, flags, games, songs, dances, recipes 1381:53-54

COLOMBIA—COOKERY
Bunuelos, sweet fritters, recipe 1251:44
Dark sugar cookies (cucas), cookies, recipe 72:180-181
Fruit salad, recipe 793:17; 1381:54
Humas Enolla, corn dish, recipe 1165:238-239
Mantequilla de Pobre, poor man's butter, recipe 1165:239
Papas chorreadas, potatoes, tomatoes, onions, cheese, spices dish, recipe 1291:121

COLOMBIA—EASTER—COOKERY
Cocido Bogotano (beef stew), recipe 1666:236-237
Sopa de Maiz (corn soup), recipe 1666:236

COLOMBIA—GAMES
Apostar Aguinaldos game 515:32
El Anillo en la cuerda, the ring on a string game, how to play 1494:215-216
Johnny clap hands game 967:26
Little green stick game 602:147
Ring on the string game 474:42-43; 602:146-147
Toss and catch toy, curtain rings, sticks, string, making 1477:39

COLOMBIA—HANDICRAFTS
Mountain village cloth applique picture 182:18-22

COLOMBIA—HATS
Farmer's hats, how to make 182:26-30

COLOMBIA—WEAVING
Bambulina vest and wall hanging, woven, making 856:92-95

COLORADO—COOKERY
Cantaloupe salad, recipe 654:21
Denver omelet, recipe 1043:153
Denver sandwiches, recipe 652:114-115; 654:22-23
Pikes Peak cooler, recipe 654:22-23
Trout, fresh, recipe 1043:158

COLORS
Songs, finger plays, stories, games, rhythms 1200:11-14

COLORS—CHURCH
Meaning of Church colors 475:159-160

COLUMBUS DAY
Activities and projects for classrooms 1393:51-55
Activities, art, songs, recipes, games 1469:24-25; 1473:38-39
Activities, food, games 1662:152-155
Activities, projects, son 819:10-16
Art, cooking, finger plays, games, drama, math, science and music activities 54:199
Columbus Day finger plays, recipes, games 944:30-31
Columbus Day mural, pattern, making 906:13,65
Columbus Day, celebration 133:119
Latin American celebration of Columbus Day 665:44-52
Learning units, activities, songs, art, recipes, patterns 1191:254-267

COLUMBUS DAY—BOATS
Boats, making 330:unp
Columbus Day ship, paper, pattern, making 232:5; 561:29
Columbus' boats, paper, patterns, making 760:186-187
Columbus' ships from paper and plastic bottle, making 448:24
Columbus' ships mobile, making 448:25
Queen Isabella's Fleet, making 199:51
Santa Maria, making 295:239-240; 648:36-37
Ships and fish felt board, making 945:189-192

COLUMBUS DAY—COMPASS
Compass, how to make 330:unp; 698:79

COLUMBUS DAY—COSTUMES
Queen Isabella costume, making 272:108-109

COLUMBUS DAY—DECORATIONS
Charting the voyage, making 698:78
Columbus picture made from spices, how to do 330:unp
Party decorations, making 134:19-20

COLUMBUS DAY—FINGER PLAYS
Finger plays and rhymes 1583:69

COLUMBUS DAY—FLAGS
Spanish flag, making 295:240

COLUMBUS DAY—GAMES
Big storm game 330:unp
Columbus Day game 240:52
Walk the plank game 330:unp

COLUMBUS DAY—MAGIC
Magic tricks for Columbus Day 1003:7-47

COLUMBUS DAY—PLANTS
Sweet potato plant, how to grow 330:unp

COLUMBUS DAY—PUPPETS
Admiral and the Feathered Pilots puppet play 754:149-153
Christopher Columbus puppet, making 754:153-158
Sea monster puppet, making 330:unp; 330:unp

COLUMBUS DAY—SONGS
Song about Columbus Day 782:unp; 901:8-9; 902:44

COLUMBUS DAY—SPYGLASS
Spyglass, making 698:78

COLUMBUS, CHRISTOPHER
Christopher Columbus, paper plate, pattern, making 413:1-2
Columbus, paper models, making 75:142-144

COLUMBUS, CHRISTOPHER—COSTUMES
Christopher Columbus costume, making 272:105-108

COMANCHE INDIANS—FOLKLORE
"The Legend of the Bluebonnet"; physical and human geography activities 1458:34-37

COMANCHE INDIANS—GAMES
Comanche ball and darts game 698:75

COMICS—HAT
Sun hat from Sunday comic sheets, making 1372:86-87

COMMUNICATION
Teaching activities, art, literature, music, crafts, patterns 1192:467-524

COMMUNITIES
Community, make one from throwaways 834:6-64
Towns, highways and harbors, miniature places, how to make 875:43-44

COMMUNITY HELPERS
Community helpers birthday rally, activities, foods, handicrafts 30:52-54
Songs, finger plays, stories, games, rhythms 1200:47-49
Teaching activities, art, literature, music, crafts, patterns 1192:347-466

COMMUNITY HELPERS—FINGER PLAYS
Finger plays; bakers, carpenters, teachers, firemen, policemen 302:80-81

COMMUNITY HELPERS—PUPPETS
Community helpers puppets, paper bags, patterns, making 940:4-15

COMMUNITY HELPERS—SONGS
Community Helpers song 1150:47

COMPUTERS
Story of 119:80-81

COMPUTERS—PROJECTS
Adinkra cloth, create 1218:60-63
Canciones, songs, write a song 1218:44-47
Cookie stamps, design 1218:64-67
Create a Valentine card 1218:48-51
Design a beaded medallion 1218:76-79
Design a crazy quilt pattern 1218:20-23
Design and build a totem pole 1218:52-55
Design embroider pattern 1218:72-75
Draw tiger slippers 1218:36-39
Kamon family crest, design one 1218:32-35
Kinglist cloth, create 1218:24-27
Masks, design and draw 1218:80-83
Paint Aboriginal dreamtime picture 1218:68-71
Painted walls in houses 1218:40-43
Picture story, Arctic, create 1218:16-19
Pysanky eggs, draw and decorate 1218:56-59
Winter scene, create 1218:28-31

CONGO—CHRISTMAS
Christmas celebration in the Congo 601:27-28; 695:68

CONGO—COOKERY
Coconut macaroons (missikiti), cookies, recipe 72:89-90

CONGO—DOLLS
African jungle boy doll, making 494:231-246

CONGO—FESTIVALS
Harvest Festival celebration 601:20
Leopard Pantomime celebration 601:19-20

CONGO—GAMES

Antelope game 602:24

Antelope in the net game 602:23

Beware the antelope game 58:20-21

Bokwele game 474:51

Cat and the rat game 602:23-24

Rat in his hole game 602:24

Ta Mbele game 602:25

CONGO—HANDICRAFTS

Comb, Congo, making 222:64

CONGO—HOUSES

Hut model, making 494:240-246

CONGO—MUSICAL INSTRUMENTS

Basonge bell, making 222:27

CONGO—NEW YEAR'S DAY

Good time for all in the Democratic Republic of the Congo 489:54-59

CONNECTICUT—BARNS

Barn, Connecticut tobacco barn wooden model, Colonial, making 568:83-88

CONNECTICUT—COOKERY

Brown bread, recipe 654:25

Cucumber salad, recipe 57:39

Pumpkin pie, recipe 654:26

Softshell crabs, recipe 57:39

Strawberries and cream, recipe 57:38

CONNECTICUT—HARRIET BEECHER STOWE HOUSE—COOKERY

Dessert omelet, recipe 57:23

Roast shoulder of lamb, recipe 57:22

CONNECTICUT—MYSTIC SEAPORT—COOKERY

Clam chowder, recipe 57:50

Codfish balls, recipe 57:51

New England boiled dinner, recipe 57:51

CONSTRUCTION WORKERS

Construction worker, costume, paper bag, making 135:24-26

CONTINENTS

Continent puzzle, making 24:6-7

COOKERY—METRIC SYSTEM

Apple crisp, recipe 45:74-75

Banana bread, recipe 45:55-56

Biscuits, recipe 45:57-58

Blueberry muffins, recipe 45:66-67

Brownies, recipe 45:31

Buttermilk pancakes, recipe 45:59-60

Chocolate chip cookies, recipe 45:32-33

Chocolate meringue cookies, recipe 45:34-35

Coffee cake, recipe 45:61-62

Cranberry muffins, recipe 45:68-69

Date bars, recipe 45:36-37

Date-nut meringue cookies, recipe 45:38-39

Dinner menu, recipe 45:83-86

French chocolate, recipe 45:81-82

Fudge, recipe 45:79-80

Ginger cookies, recipe 45:40-41

Granola type cereal, recipe 45:75-76

Grapenut bread, recipe 45:62-63

Hot cocoa, recipe 45:80

Iced tea, recipe 45:82

Meat loaf, recipe 45:83-84

Muffins, recipe 45:64-65

Peanut butter cookies, recipe 45:41-42

Popovers, recipe 45:70-71

Refrigerator date pinwheels, recipe 45:43-45

Refrigerator oatmeal cookies, recipe 45:46-47

Rolled sugar cookies, recipe 45:48-49

Sesame cookies, recipe 45:50-51

Soft sugar cookies, recipe 45:52-53

Uncooked raspberry spread, recipe 45:77

Uncooked strawberry jam, recipe 45:78-79

Whole wheat apricot bread, recipe 45:71-72

COOKIES

Activities and resources to celebrate cookie days 592:25-30

Christmas cookies, recipe 194:20-27

Easter cookies, recipe 194:34-37

Fourth of July cookies, recipe 194:38-41

Half-moon cookies, recipe 194:29

Halloween cookies, recipe 194:42-47

Hanukkah cookies, recipe 194:28-29

Moravian cookie cutters 672:122-139

Shorty shortbread cookies, recipe 194:51

Thanksgiving cookies, recipe 194:48-51

Valentine's Day cookies, recipe 194:30-33

COOPER, SUSAN

"Silver Cow: A Welsh Tale"; butter, recipe 843:61-62

COPERNICUS, NICHOLAUS

Nicholaus Copernicus's birthday, Copernican universe model, making 1199:52

CORN

Grinding corn, how to do 1531:59

History of corn or Indian maize 410:68-87; 659:124

Indian corn collage, making 1017:117

Indian corn pictures, making 440:33

CORN—DOLLS

Corn doll, wheat and rye straw, thread, making 1467:25

Corn husk doll, corn husks, fabric, string making 1213:38-39; 1453:33-37; 1476:74-75

Corn husk Indian doll, making 283:7-10

Scarecrow corn husk doll, making 353:40-41

CORN—FESTIVALS

Maize corn festivals of the Aztecs 419:133-140

CORN—HANDICRAFTS

Corn husk flowers, corn husks, fabric dyes, making 1285:104-105

CORN—JEWELRY

Necklace of corn kernels, how to string 1531:57-58

CORN—WREATHS

Corn husk wreath, wire hanger, dried corn husks, making 1693:22

CORNCOBS

Corn jelly for holiday gifts, recipe 310:216

CORNROWING

Cornrowing, how to do 251:84

CORNWALL—FOLKLORE—HANDICRAFTS

Pixilated!, sunset scene with crayon resist, sunset scene on crumpled paper 125:90-99

COSTA RICA—CHRISTMAS—COOKERY

Arroz con leche (Spanish rice pudding), recipe 1666:242-243

Bunuelos de platano (banana fritters), recipe 1666:243

Capirotada (chocolate bread pudding), recipe 1666:242

Pineapple-coconut smoothie, recipe 1666:244

COSTA RICA—CHRISTMAS—HANDICRAFTS

Ox cart to make, decorated small box, making 515:34

COSTA RICA—COOKERY

Banana bread, recipe 1165:244

Bananas con coco, bananas, coconut, sugar, recipe 1317:120

Baptismal cookies (manon del bautismo), cookies, recipe 72:170-171

Carrot cake, recipe 710:91-95

Pastelillos de carne en parillas, meat and bananas patties, recipe 1165:243-244

Tortilla chips, recipe 1244:124-125

COSTA RICA—GAMES

Forfeits game 697:39

COSTA RICA—HANDICRAFTS

Costa Rican cart, decorated shoe box, patterns, making 1633:72-75

Wooden ox cart model, patterns, making 1633:72-75

COSTUMES

16th Century cape, information on 417:51

17th Century cape, information on 417:51

1800's boys' jacket, information on 417:31

1820's dress, information on 417:35

1860's dress, information on 417:37

Abraham costume 213:18-20

Abraham Lincoln costume, making 272:42-44

Achilles costume 213:38-40

Adam and Eve costume, making 887:66-67

African man and woman costume, making 213:144-145

African witch doctor costume 213:26-28

Anglo Saxon accessories, making 417:88-89

April Fools' Day costumes, making 272:59-61

Arab woman, sheet, making 106:8

Astronaut's main costume, making 839:3-7

Balkan woman costume 213:24-26

Ballerina costume, fabric, making 1174:16

Ballet dress, information on 417:37

Bavarian costume, information on 417:21

Beau Brummell costume 213:112-114

Bedouin, pattern, making 7:56, 94-95

Betsy Ross costume, making 272:81-83

Bishop's cape, information on 417:51

Bodice dress, making 411:32

Bodices and blouses, making 417:40-43

Bodices, making 417:38-39

Bolero jackets, making 417:26-27

Bolivian girl, crepe paper, making 687:26-31

Bonnets, making 417:58-59

Breton blouse, information on 417:43

Britannia costume, fabric, paper, making 1174:11

Bull fighter costume 213:96-98

Caesar costume 213:56-58

Caesar costume, fabric, pattern, making 367:60-62

Capes, making, 417:50-51

Captain Hook costume, making 213:22

Cavalier Captain Crimson costume, fabric, pattern, making 367:14-17

Cavalier costume 213:108-110

Cavalier costume, fabric, pattern, making 367:89-93

Cave man instant costume, making 213:8-10

Cave person's tunic, fabric, making 181:6-9

Celtic accessories, making 417:88-89

Characters costumes, making 417:78-81

Charlemagne costume 213:64-66

Chef costume, making 839:12-15

Chief Powhatan costume 213:35-37

China doll, paper, making 46:23-26

Chinese coolie, making 106:12

Chinese New Year festival costume, making 272:35-36

Chinese woman, making 417:14-15

Civil War soldier costume, making 887:40-41

Cleopatra costume 213:52-54

Cleopatra costume, fabric, pattern, making 287:50-53; 367:63-66

Cleopatra, felt, patterns, making 1050:102-105

Cloaks and coats, making 417:47-49

Coat of arms, making 877:76-77

Coats and cloaks, making 417:47-49

Colonial dress, information on 417:37

Columbus, Christopher, costume, making 272:105-108

Construction Worker costume, making 839:16-19

Count Dracula costume, cape, makeup, making 326:32-34

Count Dracula costume, fabric, pattern, making 367:74-77

Cowboy costume, fabric, making 356:16-17; 1007:18-19

Cowboy Kid costume, fabric, pattern, making 367:35-40

Cowboy, making 7:61; 106:13

Crusader costume, fabric, pattern, making 367:104-105

Cyclops costume, head, tunic, cape, making 326:16-19

Czechoslovakian jacket, information on 417:27

Daisy costume 213:176-177

Daniel Boone costume 213:124-126

Danish peasant costume, information on 417:21

Diamond Jim Brady costume 213:122-124

Dick Turpin costume, fabric, pattern, making 367:56-59

Doctor costume, making 839:20-23

Dress, bodice, making 417:32-37

Dreydl costume, making 272:148-151

Dutch dress, information on 417:35

Dutch jacket, information on 417:29; 417:31

Dutch man and woman costume 213:139

Dwarf costume, information on 417:21

East Indian man, sheet, making 106:9

Egyptian girl, crepe paper, making 687:22-25

Egyptian man, Ancient, costume, making 287:27-31

Egyptian slave instant costume 213:6-8

Ellie Mae costume 213:76-77

European Peasant motifs 417:94-95

Farmer costume, making 839:24-27

Father Time costume, making 213:146-148

Fireman costume, making 839:28-31

Fireworks costume, fabric, cardboard, making 1174:12

Flag costume, making 272:84-85

Flapper costume, fabric, making 585:29

Foreign Legionnaire costume, making 887:26-27

Friar Tuck costume, making 213:70-71; 366:18-19

Friar, making 7:64; 102-103

Frontier Gal costume 213:118

Geisha costume 213:142-145

Gored skirt, information on 417:45

Grass skirt, newspaper, making 1658:73

Greek accessories and ornament, making 417:86-87

Greek couple costumes, making 887:54-55

Greek Lady instant costume 213:8

Greek May Dayr costume 213:136-137

Greek toga, fabric, making 181:20-21

Gypsy costume, information on 417:27

Gypsy dancer costume, fabric, pattern, making 367:109-112

Haman costume, making 272:56-58

Harem girl and sultan, making 213:142-143

Harem girl costume, making 887:1213

Harlequin costume, fabric, patterns, making 213:104-106; 1174:20

Hats and headdresses, making 417:54-55

Hats based on a circle, making 417:60-61
Hawaiian hula dancer, pattern, making 7:68,112-113
Hawaiian princess, posterboard and crepe paper, patterns, making 1050:114-117
Hawaiian Wahini Loa costume, 213:26
Hayley's Comet costume, fabric, cardboard, making 1174:12-13
Hector costume 213:40-46
Helen of Troy costume 213:46-47
Highland May Dayr costume 213:137-139
Highwayman, Dick Turpin costume, fabric, pattern, making 367:56-59
Hillbilly Ellie Mae costume 213:76-77
Hillbilly Toby costume 213:74-76
Hindu lady, sheet, making 106:10
Hula dancer costume from paper bag, making 678:11
Hula dancer, making 106:11
India man and woman costume 213:140-142
Indian boy, crepe paper, making 687:38-41
Indian costume and headdress, paper, making 353:14-15
Indian costume, fabric, patterns, making 1174:24
Indian costume, making 338:84-90
Indian Fakir costume 213:182-184
Indian, pattern, making 7:69, 96-97; 587:19
Irish country lad costume, making 272:51-53
Irish country lass costume, making 272:53-54
Irish Peasant skirt, information on 417:45
Italian blouse, information on 417:41
Jackets, making 417:28-31
Janus Roman God costume, making 272:24-26
Jester costume, fabric, patterns, making 1174:21
Jester costume, making 417:52-53
Jester, pattern, making 7:70,102-103
John Alden costume 213:30-32
John Smith costume 213:32-34
Johnny Appleseed costume, making 272:68-69
Johnny Reb costume 213:120-121
Joseph costume, making 272:134-135
Josephine costume 213:112
Judah Maccabeus costume, making 272:144-146
King I, II, III, costumes, making 272:137-140
King John costume 213:69
King Richard costume, making 213:72-74
King Tut's costume, making 287:31-37
King, making 587:18
Knickerbocker Glory girl costume, fabric, pattern, making 1174:40-41
Knight costume, making 417:53; 417:52-53
Knight in armor costume, paper, making 585:40-41
Knight in shining helmet, making 106:60-63
Knight, making 7:71
Knight, posterboard and felt, patterns, making 1050:106-109
Ladybird costume, fabric, patterns, making 1174:64
Latin American ornaments 417:93
Latin lover costume, fabric, pattern, making 367:86-88
Laurel and Hardy costumes, making 887:32-33
Leprechaun costume, making 272:49-50
Lillian Russell costume 213:122-123
Louis XIV costume 213:110
Madonna costume, making 417:52-53
Maharajah, pattern, making 7:72,94-95
Maid Marian costume 213:72
Mandarin and wife costume 213:139-141
Marie Antoinette costume, making 213:110-112

Mark Antony costume 213:56
Martin Luther King costume, making 272:29-30
Mary costume 213:58-60
Mary costume, making 272:133
Mary Todd Lincoln costume, making 272:45
Medicine man, making 106:64-67
Medieval accessories, making 417:90-91
Medieval tunic, cloth, making 181:30-31
Menorah costume, making 272:147-148
Mexican blouse, information on 417:41
Mexican costume, making 887:72-73
Mexican jacket, information on 417:27
Mexican skirt, information on 417:45
Mexican, making 7:73
Middle Ages princess costume, crepe paper, making 687:44-47
Middle Ages, child costume, crepe paper, making 687:41-43
Miller, crepe paper, making 687:8-9
Miss Charlotte costume, fabric, pattern, making 367:48-55
Monk cape, information on 417:51
Mummy costume, making 887:2-3
Mummy, making 7:73
Napoleon instant costume 213:2-4
Nebuchadnezzar costume 213:48-50
Norman Lady costume 213:66
Norse accessories, making 417:88-89
North American Indian motifs 417:92
Oliver Twist instant costume 213:10-12
Oriental instant costume, making 213:6
Oxford Dictionary costume, cardboard, making 1174:25
Painter costume, making 839:36-39
Palm tree costume, fabric, patterns, making 1174:22-23
Paul Bunyan costume 213:128-130
Peasant, European, motifs 417:94-95
Pharaoh, paper, making 46:82-84
Pierrot clown costume 213:106-108
Pierrot, making 7:75
Pilgrim man, paper, making 353:13
Pilgrim woman costume, paper, making 353:12
Pioneer dress, information on 417:35
Pirate bolero, information on 417:27
Pirate costume, fabric, making 1007:12-13
Pirate costume, fabric, pattern, making 367:102-104
Pirate costume, making 562:17; 887:14-15
Pirate, paper, making 46:85-88
Pirate, pattern, making 7:76; 100-101
Pixie on toadstool, fabric, patterns, making 1174:14-15
Pocahontas costume 213:34-35
Police Officer costume, making 839:40-44
Polish blouse, information on 417:43
Polish jacket, information on 417:31
Polish peasant skirt, information on 417:45
Polynesian girl, fabric, pattern, making 367:11-13
Pop star costume, fabric, pattern, making 367:94-97
Postal Worker costume, making 839:44-48
Prehistoric couple costumes, making 887:28-29
Prince, pattern, making 7:76; 100-101
Princess, making 7:77
Princess, Middle Ages, costume, crepe paper, making 687:44-47
Priscilla Morgan costume, making 213:30
Punk costume, fabric, making 1007:14-15
Puritan costume, information on 417:21

Puritan dress, information on 417:37
Queen Elizabeth costume 213:90-92
Queen Esther costume, making 272:55-56
Queen Guinevere costume, fabric, pattern, making
  367:40-44
Queen Isabella costume, making 272:109-110
Queen Nefertiti's costume, making 287:41-45
Queen, making 587:18
Rameses Il's costume, making 287:37-41
Red Cloud costume 213:132-136
Revolutionary soldier costume 213:116
Rhett Butler costume 213:116-117
Robin Hood costume, fabric, pattern, making 213:66-69;
  366:15-17; 367:22-25
Robin Hood, pattern, making 7:78; 108-109
Roland costume 213:60-62
Russian girl, crepe paper, making 687:33-37
Russian man costume 213:24
Saloon Sal costume, fabric, pattern, making 367:31-34
Sandwich mania costume, fabric, patterns, making
  1174:66
Sarah costume 213:16-18
Scarlett O'Hara costume, making 213:118
Shepherd and lamb costumes, making 272:135-136
Siamese man, sheet, making 106:11
Siegfried costume 213:62-64
Sir Walter Raleigh costume 213:92-94
Skeleton costume, black clothes, reflective tape, making
  1314:41
Skirts, semi circular, making 417:46-47
Skirts, straight, making 417:44-45
Socrates costume 213:47-48
Space Travelers costumes, making 887:56-57
Spanish lady costume 213:94-96
Statue of Liberty costume, making 272:86-88
Stone age boots and leggings, fabric, making 181:14-15
Sultan and Harem girl costume 213:142-143
Swedish blouse, information on 417:41
Swiss peasant skirt, information on 417:45
Tahitian girl, crepe paper, making 687:18-19
Tartan skirt, pleated, newspaper, making 1658:72
Three Kings' Day costumes, making 709:113-115
Totem pole, cardboard carton, making 142:28-29
Toy soldier costume from paper bag, making 678:13
Troll costume, cap, bad, nose, making 326:9-11
Troll, pattern, making 7:83,96-97
Tropical natives costumes, making 887:6-7
Trousers, long and short, making 417:16-21
Tunic, making 272:15-17; 417:8-13
Tunic, one piece, pattern, making 366:10-11
Tunic, square, simple, how to make 15:50
Tyrolean blouse, information on 417:41
Tyrolean jacket, information on 417:29; 417:31
Tyrolean peasant dress, information on 417:35
Ulysses S. Grant costume, making 213:120-121
Uncle Sam costume, making 272:88-91
United Nations blend costume, making 272:113-114
Vests, making 417:22-25
Victorian evening dress cl850, making 368:79-84
Victorian Miss costume, fabric, pattern, making 367:98-
  101
Viking costume, fabric, pattern, making 7:83, 96-97;
  367:106-108
Virginian costume 213:128-129
Vulture Goddess Nekhbet's costume, making 287:45-50

Washington George 213:114-118
Washington, George, costume, making 272:46-47
Washington, Martha, costume, making 272:48
Wellington costume 213:114
Western vest, fabric, making 982:18-19
Wigs and head coverings from plant materials, making
  657:34
Wise Man from the East, paper, making 46:102-105
Witch costume, fabric, making 1007:16-17
Witch costume, pointed hat, cape, making 326:22-24;
  1314:45
Witch dress pattern, making 213:28-29; 252:10-11
Witch gathered skirt pattern, making 7:84,100-101;
  252:18-19
Witch, paper, making 46:106-109
Wizard, making 587:18
Zapata costume 213:130-132

COSTUMES—PATTERNS
Accessories 7:120
Baggy pants or bloomers and top 7:102-103
Barrel 7:106-107
Bodysuit 7:112-113
Bumblebee costume and neck ruffle 7:96-97
Cape 7:100-101
Cloak and bag 7:108-109
Coveralls 7:94-95
Gown or tunic 7:90-91
Headwear and other accessories 7:114-119
Hooded cape 7:104-105
Hooded robe or cloak 7:102-103
Miniskirt and panties 7:98-99
Mittens and gloves 7:118-119
Pull on pants 7:96-97
Robe 7:94-95
Spats 7:120-121
Sweatsuit 7:92-93
Tentacles 7:104-105
Tunic 7:106-107; 7:90-91
Turtleneck 7:98-99
Tutu and slippers 7:112-113
Vest 7:100-101
Wings 7:110-111

COTE D'IVOIRE. *See also* **IVORY COAST**
COTE D'IVOIRE—MASKS
Guro animal mask, posterboard, paints, making 1632:52-
  57
COTE D'IVOIRE—PAINTINGS
Senufo mud painting on clothes, dirt, paint, fabric, mak-
  ing 1632:12-17
COTTON
Eli Whitney birthday celebration; art, music, foods,
  games, activities 1104:30-33
COUNTING—AFRICA
Numbers one to ten in Swahili language 390:unp
COUNTING—ARABS
Numbers one to ten in Arabic language 399:unp
COUNTING—CANADA
Numbers one to ten in French language 391:unp
COUNTING—CHINA
Numbers one to ten in Chinese language 392:unp
COUNTING—GERMANY
Numbers one to ten in German language 393:unp
COUNTING—ITALY
Numbers one to ten in Italian language 394:unp

COUNTING—JAPAN

Numbers one to ten in Japanese language 395:unp

COUNTING—KOREA

Numbers one to ten in Korean language 396:unp

COUNTING—MEXICO

Numbers one to ten in Spanish language 397:unp

COUNTING—RUSSIA

Numbers one to ten in Russian language 398:unp

COWBOYS

Cardboard cowboy, pattern, making 534:50

Cowboy and cowgirl models, paper tubes, making 1310:120-121

Cowboy and cowgirl, paper, large pattern, making 478:17-22; 639:34-35

Cowboys, activities, art, science, songs, recipes 911:102-105

Culture unit, language, dress, foods, games, bibliographies 574:66-83

Gauchos; way of life, clothing, food, language 1378:249-255

Paper cowboys, making 75:30

Sheriff's badge, cardboard, foil, making 1734:17

Sundowner, a cowboy, fabric, patterns, making 316:72-73

Tally to count number of cattle, how to make 1214:139

Wild West playboard, posterboard, making, 534:76

Wood carved cowboy figure, making 382:69-71

COWBOYS—BACKPACK

Bandanna backpack, bandanna or scarf, making 1729:25

COWBOYS—BAGS

Ditty bag, making 574:72

Poke sack to carry valuables, fabric, felt, cord, making 1214:133-134

COWBOYS—BELTS

Braided leather belt, chamois, belt buckle, making 1214:128-129

COWBOYS—BRAIDING

Leather braids, how to make 1734:25

COWBOYS—BRANDING IRONS

Branding irons, making from potatoes 976:30-31

COWBOYS—BRANDS

Brand, potato printed, making 1734:9

COWBOYS—BULLETIN BOARDS

Branding iron, making 295:66-67

Chuck wagon, making 295:66

Cowboy rope sign, making 295:65

Indian symbols and Indian weaving, making 295:68-69

Indian village, making 295:70

Papoose sleeping sack and headband, making 295:69

Ten gallon hat and shoe string tie, making 295:65-66

Totem pole, making 295:67-68

COWBOYS—CLOTHING

Chaps, fabric, felt, making 1734:4

Chaps, making 574:71-72

Cowboy chaparajos, making 870:96-97

Cuffs, making 574:72

Serape, bath towels, fringe, making 1214:125

Slicker, making 574:72

Vest, cowboy vest, leather, making 641:70-71

Western style vest, paper bags, pattern, making 1362:131

COWBOYS—CODE

Code of the West; eight rules 1734:29

COWBOYS—COOKERY

American Cowboy and the Chuckwagon, foods the cowboys ate information 666:200-204

Armadillo rolls, peanut butter, sunflower seeds, recipe 1729:24-25

Bedrolls, tortillas with cream cheese and jelly, recipe 1729:8

Bedrolls, tortillas with ham and cheese, recipe 1729:9

Branding iron biscuits, recipe 1729:16

Butter in a bottle, homemade butter, recipe 1729:15

Campfire fries, potatoes and cheese in foil, recipe 1729:17-18

Chili con carne, recipe 1214:142

Cow chip cookies, no-bake cookies, recipe 1729:23-24

Dried hide, jerky, recipe 1729:10

Get Along Little Doggies, hot dogs and beans, recipe 1729:13

Hoe cake, recipe 574:70

Howlin' coyote toast, recipe 1729:19

MacChili, chili and macaroni, recipe 1729:14

Pinto beans, recipe 574:69

Purple cow, grape juice with ice cream, recipe 1729:7

Rocky mountain mud pie, nuts and brownies, recipe 1729:22

Roundup stew, recipe 574:69

Sidewinder sausages, recipe 1729:12

Sloppy Joes, recipe 1362:131

Son-of-a-gun stew, recipe 1214:143

Sourdough biscuits, recipe 574:70

Spotted pup rice and raisins, recipe 574:69

Spurs and such, munchin' stuff, nuts, cereal, dried fruit, recipe 1729:11

Sun tea, recipe 1729:6

Tall Texas tea, iced tea with fruit juice, recipe 1729:5

Three bean chili, recipe 1734:11

Wild filly frito pie, hamburger casserole, recipe 1729:20-21

COWBOYS—COSTUMES

Cowboy costume, fabric, face makeup, given, making 957:20-25; 1007:18-19

Cowboy Kid costume, fabric, pattern, making 367:35-40

COWBOYS—GAMES

Cattle drive game, how to play 1214:121-122

Know your cans game, canned foods, how to play 1214:137

COWBOYS—HATS

Braided hatband, chamois, making 1214:130

Cowboy hat, carton, making 766:60-61

COWBOYS—LASSOS

Rope spinning and lassoing, how to do 1734:21

COWBOYS—PARTIES

Cowboy party (10 years up) 124:116-122

Cowboys and Indians Party, recipes and games 635:45-48

Home on the Range party, activities and recipes 809:43-48

Western round-up party, menu and recipes, how to plan and give 86:200-207; 86:237

Wild West round-up party, decorations, games, costumes, recipes 74:109-121

COWBOYS—POST OFFICE

Blind post office, how to pick one 1214:138

COWBOYS—PUPPETS

Cowboy puppet, clothespin, making 311:30

Puppet; paper bag cowgirl or cowboy puppet, patterns, making 1107:45-52

COWBOYS—SPURS

Spurs, making 574:72

COWBOYS—WAGONS
Wagon and cowboys from the Far West, paper and wood models, making 1094:6-7

COWBOYS—WEAPONS
Gun case, making 7:120-121

COWS
History of cows in America 597:18-19
Holstein gift boxes, cardboard, paints, making 1564:48

COX, PALMER
"Brownies," paper, patterns, making 1422:27-28

CRACKER JACKS
History of 381:38

CRAYONS
Make from old crayons, how to do 1213:30
Soap crayons, soap flakes, food coloring, water, how to make 1179:54

CREE INDIANS—COOKERY
Pemmican patties, recipe 1296:142

CREEK INDIANS—COOKERY
Hickory nut soup, recipe 1527:xx-xxi

CREEK INDIANS—FESTIVALS
Corn Festival celebration 659:50-51

CREEK INDIANS—THANKSGIVING—DANCES
Creek ribbon dance 624:49-50

CRICKETS
Crickets as pets in China 474:59

CROATIA. *See* **YUGOSLAVIA**

CROCKETT, DAVY
Davy Crockett's pouch, making 719:30-32
Wood carved figure of Davy Crockett, making 382:60-62

CROCKETT, DAVY—GAMES
Davy Crockett's birthday game 240:42

CROCKETT, DAVY—PUPPET PLAYS
Walk Tall,Talk Tall, Davy Crockett 44:93-102

CROSSES
Cross pictures and explanations 475:36-37
Cross, pattern, making 873:59
Cross, toothpicks, pattern, making 254:228-231
Greek Cross, paper, making 545:151-152
Latin Cross, paper, making 545:151-152
Maltese cross information 475:38-39
Maltese Cross, paper, making 545:151-152

CROW INDIANS—BUSTLES
Crow bustle, making 589:43

CROW INDIANS—CLOTHING
Crow cuff, making 465:36

CROW INDIANS—GAMES
Throwing arrows game, making 466:110-111

CROW INDIANS—HEADDRESSES
Crow headdress, making 932:32-34

CROW INDIANS—HOUSES
Tepee, making 227:12

CROW INDIANS—OWNER STICKS
Owner sticks, making 324:42
Owner sticks, making, 445:97-105

CROW INDIANS—RHYMES
"Lullaby of a Dog to Her Pup" 1607:32-33

CROWNS
Carnival accessories, necklace and crown, making 113:42-43
Crown, pattern, making 172:7
Crown, posterboard, making 1096:10
Jeweled crown, paper, foil decals, tinsel, ribbons, patterns, making 1648:13
King's crown, paper, making 214:14; 1105:8-9

King's crown, fabric, patterns, making 1435:17-18
Paper bag crown, making 442:17
Princess crown, making 7:118-119
Queen's crown, paper, making 214:15
Statue of Liberty paper crowns, making 1104:14
Tiara, posterboard, patterns, making 1049:30

CRUSADES—COSTUMES
Crusader costume, fabric, pattern, making 367:104-105

CUBA
Activities, flags, games, songs, dances, recipes 1381:33-34

CUBA—COOKERY
Ajiaco, port and vegetable stew, recipe 1165:218-219
Arroz con pollo, chicken with rice, recipe 1165:217
Avocado salad, recipe 895:39
Black beans and rice, recipe 251:96
Black beans dish, recipe 1380:30
Black beans, recipe 895:38
Cuban bread, recipe 594:85-86
Frijoles negros, black beans, recipe 1165:216
La sopa frijoles negros, black bean soup, recipe 1165:216
Masa real, marmalade tart, recipe 1165:217-218
Matanzas sugar cookies (polvorones matanceros), cookies, recipe 72:161-162
Moros y cristianos, white rice and black beans dish, recipe 1592:117
Orange chicken, recipe 187:11
Pan Cubano yeast bread, recipe 1477:61
Pollo a la pepitoria, chicken and onion dish, recipe 1592:117
Pork, Cuban style, recipe 895:37
Potato omelet, recipe 794:7; 1381:34

CUBA—DANCES
Pepito dance 697:22-23
Rabbit of Hope dance 697:20-21
Tip and heel dance 697:32-33
To get to Heaven dance 697:26-27

CUBA—EASTER—COOKERY
Moros y Cristianos (black beans and rice), recipe 1666:216-217
Orange and onion salad, recipe 1666:217
Orange cake, recipe 1666:217-218
Picadillo Habanera (meat sauce with rice), recipe 1666:217

CUBA—GAMES
Beggar game 697:38
Chocolonga game 383:55
Counting out rhymes game 602:116
Cuba and Spain game, how to play 383:60; 1494:60
Dogs and the chickens game 383:56
Dona Ana No Esta Aqui game 383:58
Excited burro game 474:37
Fans or Los Abanicos game 383:57
Flower garden game 383:55
Fountain game 602:113-115
Hawk game 602:115-116
La Marisola game 383:65
Little dog with a sweet tooth game 697:42
Matandile game 383:67
Matarile game 383:67
My friend has returned from the Orient game 383:58
Nuts game 383:56
Priest's hat game 383:57
San Sereni game 383:60
Shepherdess and the cat game 602:112

CUBA—HANDICRAFTS
Village scene, fabric, felt, oaktag, patterns, making 1251:16-19
CUBA—MUSICAL INSTRUMENTS
Maracas, gourds, making 515:36
Shekere instrument, how to play 1646:54
Shekere instrument, plastic bottle, lanyard, beads, pipe cleaners, making 1646:50-53
CUCKOO CLOCKS—COOKERY
Cuckoo clock cake, recipe 449:55
CUNA INDIANS—COOKERY
San Blas stew, recipe 424:65-66
CUNA INDIANS—MOLAS
Mola cloth rectangle, fabric, felt, pattern, making 1730:50-55
Mola panels, fabric, making 1476:62
CUNEIFORM TABLETS
Mysterious tablets, making 173:52-53
CURACAO—COOKERY
Sponge cookies (panlevi), cookies, recipe 72:163
CYPRUS—COOKERY
Polypikilo, mixed vegetables, recipe 1165:82-83
Village salad, recipe 858:unp
CYPRUS—EASTER—COOKERY
Ma'amoul (filled cookies), recipe 1666:64
Mayeritsa (Greek Easter soup), recipe 1666:63
Simi (Turkish bread rings), recipe 1666:63-64
CZECH REPUBLIC. *See* **CZECHOSLOVAKIA**
CZECHOSLOVAKIA—CHRISTMAS
Christmas celebration 601:104; 661:157-158
Customs of Christmas in Czechoslovakia 473:38-40
CZECHOSLOVAKIA—CHRISTMAS—COOKERY
Cerna Kuba (black barley dish), recipe 1666:88
Houskove Knedliky (bread dumplings), recipe 1666:87
Meringue decorations, recipe 704:70-71
Moravske Vano Ni Kukyse (Moravian Christmas cookies), recipe 1666:88
CZECHOSLOVAKIA—COOKERY
Cabbage, braised, recipe 661:161
Cabbage, red cabbage with fruit, recipe 794:28
Dumplings, history of 661:149-151
Fruit dumplings, recipe 793:43
Hazelnut cake, recipe 858:unp
Ian Hus, carp ponds, and beer breweries, history of 661:151-153
Kolacky, recipe 661:162-163
Liptauer cheese spread, recipe 661:160

Mushrooms, baked, recipe 661:161
Nutroll cookies (kolace), cookies, recipe 72:66-68
Pork loin roast, recipe 661:160
Snadne kolaches, easy kolachese, recipe 1165:102
Zemakove placky, potato pancakes, recipe 1165:102-103
CZECHOSLOVAKIA—DANCES
Ceresnicky dance, how to do 1494:139-140
Polka dance and costume picture 1000:26-29
CZECHOSLOVAKIA—DOLLS
Czechoslovakian doll, making 775:14-17
Doll, balloon sleeve costume doll, yam, making 298:248-249
Dolls, gathered handkerchief, making 298:122-123
CZECHOSLOVAKIA—EASTER
Easter celebration 661:157
CZECHOSLOVAKIA—EASTER—DECORATIONS
Egg designs, making 515:38
CZECHOSLOVAKIA—EASTER—HANDICRAFTS
Easter eggs, making 626:29-30
CZECHOSLOVAKIA—FESTIVALS
Judica Festival egg designs, making 515:38
Lampion Parade celebration 631:54
Winter Scaring Festival celebration 661:156
CZECHOSLOVAKIA—GAMES
Catch Old Mrs. Winter chasing game, how to play 1498:35
Confessions game 602:89-90
Hide the thimble game 602:90
Kritz, hopscotch game 1426:12-13
Zpoved, Confessions game, how to play 1494:114
CZECHOSLOVAKIA—HANDICRAFTS
Chestnut boy, making 298:170
Cut-straw pictures, making 1054:20-21
Eggs, decorated, making 627:90-92
Eggs, painted eggs, patterns, making 1016:57-62
Paperweight, plastic, etched, making 525:62-63
Star and bead jumping jester, making 298:64-65
Textile eggery, making 298:106
CZECHOSLOVAKIA—NEW YEAR'S DAY
New Year's Day celebration 661:158-159
CZECHOSLOVAKIA—PUPPETS
Clown puppet, gourd body, making 298:68-69
CZECHOSLOVAKIA—SONGS
Where Is John? round song 1115:38
CZECHOSLOVAKIA—TOYS
Pecking bird from Czechoslovakia; history of and how to make 495:91-95

D

DAGUERRE, LOUIS-JACQUES-MANDE—BIRTHDAY
Celebrate by taking pictures with instant camera 1199:264-265

DAHOMEY—CHRISTMAS—HANDICRAFTS
Christmas banner, making 795:10

DAIRY DAY
Activities, art, songs, recipes, games 1469:110-111

DAKOTA INDIANS—CLOTHING
Leggings, making 281:26-27
Shirt and dress, fabric, making 281:33-36
Tunic and dress, fabric, making 281:25-26

DAKOTA INDIANS—FOOTWEAR
Moccasins, pattern, making 281:27-28

DAKOTA INDIANS—GAMES
Grizzly bear game 602:169
Snatching places game 602:169

DAKOTA INDIANS—HAIR
Wig, black horse hair, making 281:28-30

DAKOTA INDIANS—MUSICAL INSTRUMENTS
Frame drum mallet, stick, old socks, ribbon, making 1646:57-59
Frame drum, box, paper bag, string, paint, making 1646:57-59
Frame drum, how to play 1646:60

DAKOTA INDIANS—WAR BONNETS
War bonnet, fabric and feathers, making 281:30-32

DAKOTA INDIANS—WINTER COUNT
Winter Count, grocery bags, crayons, making 1332:49-52

DANCERS
Hula dancer costume from paper bag, making 678:11

DANCERS—PUPPETS
Geometric rhythm dancers, box, cardboard, paper, craft sticks, making 1294:23-26

DANCES
Chain dance 474:110-112
Maypole dance 474:115
Round dances 474:113-117
Wind up the apple tree folk dance 474:113-115

DAVID AND GOLIATH
David and Goliath puppet show 756:181-188

DAVID COPPERFIELD
David Copperfield, descriptions and pictures of house 29:chp. 5

DAVIS, JEFFERSON—COOKERY
Chicken a-la-daub, recipe 57:90
Chocolate cream, recipe 57:91
Jelly cake, recipe, making 57:91
Savoury jelly, recipe 57:91
Southern gumbo, recipe 57:90

DAY OF SWINGS
Korean Festival, activities, art, songs, recipes, games 1469:112-113

DAYAK PEOPLE. *See* **RAIN FOREST**

DE ANGELI, MARGUERITE
"Thee, Hannah"; Pennsylvania pretzels, recipe 570:85-87

DE PAOLA, TOMIE
"Merry Christmas Strega Nona," codfish stew, recipe 1216:92-93
"Pancakes for Breakfast," homemade butter, recipe 1216:34
"Strega Nona," homemade pasta, recipe 1216:22
"Strega Nona's Magic Lessons"; science, reading, art, language activities 1055:206-210

"Watch Out for the Chicken Feet in Your Soup," chicken soup, recipe 1216:69
Early American Christmas, pretzels, recipe 1216:27

DECLARATION OF INDEPENDENCE—UNITED STATES. *See also* **UNITED STATES—HISTORY**
History of 333:12-20

DECOUPAGE
Decoupage, papier-mache, how to do 1464:62-63
Japanese table screen, paper, decoupage, making 274:88-91
Oriental pencil holder, decoupage, paper, making 274:91-93

DEFOE, DANIEL
Robinson Crusoe game 1078:82
Robinson Crusoe's homemade oven bread, recipe 570:81-83
Robinson Crusoe, descriptions and pictures of island 29:Chapter 7

DEGEN, BRUCE
"Jamberry," strawberry jam, recipe 1216:37

DELAWARE—COOKERY
Delaware snow cream, recipe 1043:110
Delmarva cheesy chicken, recipe 654:28-29
Jello map of state, recipe 1342:29
Peach melba, recipe 654:28

DELAWARE—WINTERTHUR MUSEUM AND GARDENS—COOKERY
Avocado pears, Florida, recipe 57:95
Cauliflower polonaise, recipe 57:95
Lamb stew with vegetables, recipe 57:94

DELAWARE INDIANS—DOLLS
Odas doll, making 775:50-53

DENMARK
Activities, flags, games, songs, dances, recipes 1381:192
Map, flag, and products 621:6

DENMARK—CHRISTMAS
Celebration of Christmas in Denmark 425:15; 1049:84
Christmas celebration 601:105
Christmas tree and decorations, how to make 593:16-27
Julklapp celebration 51:319-320
Rice pudding and almond custom 516:44

DENMARK—CHRISTMAS—COOKERY
Advent wreath cake, recipe 1023:85-88
Brown Christmas cookies, recipe 1226:75
Chicken with apples, recipe 1666:120
Coffee cake, recipe 1226:74
Cookies, Danish sand cookies, recipe 704:58-59
Danish Kleiner, fried dessert, recipe 1226:73
Dark peppernut cookies, recipe 1226:74
Kransekage, Danish Kransekage, recipe 795:73
Kringle Advent bread, recipe 1128:140
Rice and almond pudding, recipe 1226:73
Rice pudding, recipe 446:47
Ris a L'Amande (Christmas rice pudding), recipe 1128:143
Roddkaal (braised red cabbage), recipe 1666:120-121
Rodgrod Med Flode (raspberry pudding with cream), recipe 1666:121
Scandinavian oat cookies, recipe 703:84-85

DENMARK—CHRISTMAS—DECORATIONS
Basket weave hearts, colored paper, making 1226:65
Christmas garlands, paper, patterns, making 1226:66
Christmas scones, paper, patterns, making 1226:72
Danish Christmas elf, foam balls, paper, paints, making 1226:70

Danish flag garland, paper, patterns, making 1226:67
Three-dimensional star, paper, patterns, making 1226:68-69
Toy soldier, foam balls, paper, paints, making 1226:71
DENMARK—CHRISTMAS—DOLLS
Dolls, yam, making 1023:117-119
Tomte yarn doll, making 1023:119-120
DENMARK—CHRISTMAS—HANDICRAFTS
Angels, paper, making 470:56
Balls, fringed ornament, making 1023:68-69
Christmas hearts, making 470:53-55
Christmas seals, making 795:12-13
Creche, Danish acorn dolls, making 795:58
Danish circles, making 705:20-21
Danish woven baskets, shiny paper, making 1575:14-15
Figures, small stitchery figures, making 795:59
Flags on a string, making 795:2
Heart baskets, Danish woven heart baskets, making 795:68
Hearts woven ornament, making 1023:72-73
Hearts, Danish Christmas hearts, making 704:56; 709:80-81
Reed ornament, making 1023:65
Star ornament, paper, making 1023:77
Star, pleated star ornament, making 1023:64
Wood shaving ornaments, making 795:63
Wreath ornaments, braided, making 795:63
DENMARK—CHRISTMAS—PUPPETS
Nisse finger puppet, making 140:41
DENMARK—COOKERY
Apple dessert, recipe 895:43
Arine Riddere (Poor Knights), recipe 530:20-22
Brune lager, recipe 967:27
Brunede kartofler, sugar-browned potatoes, recipe 1165:136
Coconut dreams (kokosdromme), cookies, recipe 72:32-33
Dapples cookies, recipe 343:131
Ebleskivers donuts, recipe 88:183-185
Flour dumplings, recipe 895:42
Frikadeller veal meatballs, recipe 1113:40-41
Glazed potatoes, recipe 1380:25
Hamburger, recipe 793:37
History of cookery in 88:173-178
Krumkakes, recipe 1381:192
Macaroni salad, recipe 530:15
Meatballs (Frikedeller), recipe 530:18-20
Meatballs, recipe 895:41
Open-faced sandwiches 187:4
Pancake balls (Aebleskive), recipe 525:64
Pickled cucumbers, recipe 621:36
Potato salad, recipe 858:unp
Rice pudding, recipe 621:38-39
Ris a L'Amande, rice pudding, recipe 1165:136
Sandwiches, open-faced, recipe 653:59-60
Smorrebrod, open sandwich, recipe 1165:135
South Jutland meatballs, recipe 1520:117
Tomato and egg open sandwich, recipe 967:27
DENMARK—DANCES
Nixie dance, how to do 1494:147-148
Shoemaker's dance, how to do 1494:153-154
DENMARK—EASTER
Bun Day celebration 973:25-28
DENMARK—EASTER—GAMES
Danish egg rolling game 201:179-180

DENMARK—FESTIVALS
Flag Birthday celebration 973:49-51
Hans Christian Andersen Fairy Tale Festival 474:27
Sankt Hans Aften celebration 973:57
Shrovetide beat the cat out of the barrel game 515:41
DENMARK—FOLKLORE
"Little Mermaid" model, small can, yarn, making 1310:122-123
"Ugly Duckling," swan stick puppet, patterns 1206:26-29
"Wonderful Pot" flannel board story, patterns, making 1604:95-97
DENMARK—GAMES
Baste the bear game 383:71
Bird's alive game 383:71
Danish fish game 979:41
Fish game 602:90-91
Fishing game 383:72
Nimbi game, how to play 1507:62
Ocean is stormy game 1078:32
Robin's Alive game, how to play 1381:192
Snail game 474:95-96
Stykes, sticks game 383:73
Tac tix game 956:81
Third man out game 572:44-45
Troll head game 602:91
Whales game 58:22-23
Whales game, how to play 1494:105
DENMARK—HANDICRAFTS
Angel, making 626:32-34
Chimney sweep, making 470:50-52
Danish bells mobile, making 452:100-101
Danish woven hearts mobile, making 452:107-109
Fairy tale banner, Princess and the Pea, making 470:57-61
Fish; paper strip fish mobile, making 452:112-114
Postman, making 470:47-49
Royal guard, making 470:43-46
Star, interlocking star, making 626:31-32
Ugly Duckling, knitted, making 470:62-64
Weaving paper hearts, how to do 1506:20-21
DENMARK—NEW YEAR'S DAY
Godt Nytaar in Denmark 489:60-63
DENMARK—NEW YEAR'S EVE
New Year's Eve celebration 973:87-89
DENMARK—SONGS
Clocks round song 1115:25
DESERTS
Desert activities, using science, crafts, music 1189:38-51
Desert preservation activities 1189:74-79
DESERTS—ANIMALS
Activities with ants, camels, gila monsters, jack rabbits 1189:54-61
Activities with lizards, ostriches, road runners, snakes, spade foot toads 1189:62-71
DESERTS—CAMEL BAGS
Camel bags, making 173:36-37
DESERTS—FOOTWEAR
Desert sand shoes, making 173:32-33
DESERTS—HANDICRAFTS
Rattlesnake bank, juice can, paper, patterns, making 1286:26-28
DESERTS—HOUSES
Desert tent from blown egg, making 677:18
DESERTS—OASIS
Desert oasis, cork, making 1099:unp

DESERTS—PATTERNS
   Ant 1189:85
   Bactrian camel 1189:87
   Date palm 1189:84
   Dromedary camel 1189:86
   Gila monster 1189:88
   Jack rabbit 1189:90
   Lizard 1189:88
   Ostrich 1189:90
   Prickly pear cactus and flower 1189:82
   Road runner 1189:90
   Saguaro cactus 1189:83
   Snake 1189:89
   Spade foot toad 1189:85
DESERTS—PUPPETS
   Desert animal puppets, beetles, camels, patterns, making
      463:35-42
DEVLIN, WENDE
   "Cranberry Thanksgiving," cranberry bread, recipe
      843:57; 1216:28
DIAMOND JIM BRADY
   Costume 213:122-124
DIARIES
   Diaries, how to write and keep 498:66-68
DICKENS, CHARLES
   "Christmas Carol"; Mrs. Cratchit's Christmas date pud-
      ding, recipe 570:69-72
   "David Copperfield," descriptions and pictures of house
      291:Chapter 5
   Christmas with the Cratchits puppet show 756:168-173
DINOSAURS
   Songs, fingerplays, stories, games, rhythms 1200:84-85
DINOSAURS—PARTIES
   Dinosaur cake, recipe 1185:68-69
DIORAMAS
   African jungle boy setting 494:231-246
   Angelo of Italy setting 494:144-156
   Arab Sheik setting 494:173-185
   Betsy Ross, picture 10:164
   Columbus Day diorama, making 226:38-39
   Desert diorama, making 143:82
   Eskimo and Igloo setting 494:38-49
   Flatboat diorama, making 646:96
   Fort diorama, making 646:89
   French peasant setting 494:119-132
   Hendrik of Holland and the windmill setting 494:95-107
   Hindu lady setting 494:198-210
   Indian Mother and baby setting 494:74-83
   Indian, Desert Indian Village diorama, making 647:78
   Indian, Plains Indian Village diorama, making 647:76
   Indian, Woodlands Indian Village diorama, making
      647:77
   Iranian scenes, making 143:80-81
   Japanese girl setting 494:211-230
   King Arthur, picture 10:160
   Log cabin diorama, making 646:78-85
   Long house, inside and out, making 223:21
   Mexican Pedro goes to market setting 494:50-73
   Nativity scene and crib in shoe box, making 1025:24-26
   Nativity scene diorama in box, making 1049:42
   Nativity scene, picture 10:162-163
   Noah's Ark diorama, making 52:27
   Pancho of Peru setting 494:84-94
   Pied Piper, picture 10:159
   Pioneer half faced camp diorama, making 646:68-71
   Plymouth Village diorama, making 401:30-32
   Rumpelstiltskin, picture 10:162
   School room diorama, making 646:86
   Scotch Highlander setting 494:108-118
   Shingebiss and the North wind, snow scene with crayon
      resist, diorama 125:81-90
   Swedish Greta setting 494:133-143
   Swiss children and their chalet setting 494:157-172
   Wong Su of China setting 494:186-197
DISNEY, WALT—BIRTHDAY
   Birthday celebration; art, music, foods, games, activities
      1104:26-29
   Celebrate with animation activity, how to do 1199:274-
      275
DIXIE CUPS
   History of Dixie cups 119:132-135
DODGE, MARY MAPES. *See also* **HANS BRINKER**
   Hans Brinker; Hans makes waffles, recipe 570:17-19
DOLLHOUSES
   Colonial doll house and doll family, patterns, making
      963:18-173
   Doll house from cardboard carton, making 1213:122-123
DOLLS
   Acorn dolls, making 831:48
   African Akuaba doll, making 519:38-39
   African warrior doll, felt, stuffed, pattern, making 487:29
   Apple dolls, making 831:49
   Apple Granny doll, making 844:28-31
   Apple head doll, apple, spices, fabric, making 1429:94-
      96
   Apple head doll, making 453:103-107; 491:119-125;
      508:42-44; 524:38-39; 527:19; 561:49-50; 587:135;
      604:28-31; 893:22-29; 1013:38-41; 1256:17
   Apple head Granny doll, pattern, making 1027:141-144
   Apple people, making 1017:118
   Barbie dolls, history of 511:83-84, 88
   Befana doll, making 709:117-119
   Carnival doll, papier-mache, pattern, making 1027:165-
      169
   Chinese girl doll from peanuts, making 623:3-5
   Clay dolls from cornstarch clay, recipe, making 1429:79-
      82
   Colonial doll wigs and accessories, patterns, making
      963:163-173
   Corn husk doll, making 217:29-30; 453:107-111;
      491:111-113; 587:134; 604:24-28; 612:unp; 647:36-
      37; 673:218-230; 869:70; 1017:120; 1213:38-39;
      1249:30-32; 1453:33-37
   Corn husk doll, pattern, making 1027:144-149
   Corn husk modern doll, making 283:10-16
   Corncob doll, making 491:41-43
   Dancing paper dolls, paper, making 1256:33
   Daruma dolls, making 497:164
   Daruma dolls, plaster of Paris, paper tubes, patterns, mak-
      ing 1427:202
   Eskimo and Indian dolls, making 491:19-23
   Fairy tale doll, fabric, patterns, making 484:19-21
   G I Joe doll, history of 511:89-95
   Grass doll, making 491:53-55
   Herb dolls, herbs, doll's straw hat, ribbons, making
      1285:66
   History of dolls 491:13-17
   History of dolls in America 491:24-28
   Hula doll, paper bag, making 534:22-23
   Iceland sandbag doll, making 470:76-78

Icelandic doll, fabric, pattern, making 515:62
Indian and Eskimo dolls, making 491:19-23
Ivory Coast grass doll, making 1027:80-81
Kachina doll, making 633:149-150; 673:254-278
Kachina doll, making from wooden spools 629:108-110;
1027:123-127
Kachina dolls, how to make 605:41-48; 605:49-54
Kimono doll, paper, making 480:121-122
Laplander doll, felt stuffed, pattern, making 487:30-31
Maccabee dolls from pipe cleaners, making 448:38
Mannequin doll, French, styrofoam and fabric, making
1027:30-35
Mexican doll, felt, stuffed, pattern, making 487:26-27
Mop doll, mophead, stockings, stuffing, making
1463:36-41
Nesting dolls, styrofoam cups, making 909:12
Newborn baby doll, stockings, stuffing, baby pj's, mak-
ing 1463:42-46
Nutcracker; Clara, Sugar Plum Fairy, Toy Soldier, fabric,
patterns, making 484:65-76
Oriental doll, felt, stuffed, pattern, making 487:21-23
Poke bonnet, making 493:200
Polish peasant doll, wood and fabric, pattern, making
1027:53-61
Potpourri doll, lace, potpourri, stockings, styrofoam ball,
making 1463:30-35
Quaker clothespin doll, making 626:44-46
Rag doll and doll's dress, Pioneer doll, making 646:44-47
Rag doll, early Settlers doll, pattern, making 1027:153-156
Rag doll, T-shirt, fabric, fake fur, stuffing, patterns, mak-
ing 1463:48-57
Raggedy Ann doll, history of 511:85-87
Red Riding Hood cloak for dolls, fabric, making
493:207-210
Red Riding Hood, Hansel, Gretel dolls, fabric, patterns,
making 484:88-92
Roly-poly doll, making 632:18-19
Sleeping Beauty and Prince Florimund dolls, fabric, pat-
terns, making 484:101-106
Soldier bristle dancing doll, patterns, making 1016:147-151
Soldiers and storybook dolls from tin cans, making
680:36-37
South American fruit seller spool doll, making 629:34-35
Straw doll, Colonial Period, making 453:118-120
Swedish wooden doll, making 1027:72-76
Tahitian girl doll, felt, stuffed, pattern, making 487:28
Tiny Tears doll, history of 511:84-85
Tomte yam doll, making 1023:119-120

DOLLS—COSTUMES
Rag doll costume, fabric, ribbons, face paints, making
1509:30-31

DOLLS —FESTIVALS. See JAPAN—FESTIVALS—
DOLLS

DOLLS—FESTIVALS—PUPPETS
Japanese Doll Festival dolls, origami Empress and Emperor, making 1422:23-26

DOMES
Dome fort, tree limbs, branches, material for cover, mak-
ing 1188:30-32
Geodesic dome, straws, clips, ribbons, making 1376:83-86

DOMINICAN REPUBLIC—CHRISTMAS—COOKERY
Banana pudding, recipe 1666:208
Refresco de Coco y Pina (chilled coconut milk and pine-
apple), recipe 1666:208
Sancocho (meat stew), recipe 1666:207-208

DOMINICAN REPUBLIC—COOKERY
Arroz con quandules, peas, coconut milk, rice, recipe
1318:119
Coconut buying, opening, making shredded coconut, rec-
ipe 1165:208
Coconut milk, recipe 1165:208-209
Orange pumpkin soup, recipe 1165:207-208
Sweet potato balls, recipe 1165:209

DOMINICAN REPUBLIC—GAMES
Candelita musical game 1116:19
Moteca game 515:42
Moteca spinning top game, how to play 1499:7-9
Thumper game, how to play 1494:63

DOMINICAN REPUBLIC—HANDICRAFTS
Village scene, fabric, felt, oaktag, patterns, making
1251:16-19

DONKEYS
Donkey, pop-up, paper, pattern 1210:20-21
Prayer of the Donkey, Carmen Bemos de Gasztole
139:67

DONKEYS—SONGS
Tinga Layo!, traditional calypso song 139:68

DOUGHS
Alum dough, recipe 1455:3
Bread dough, recipe 1179:56-57
Clay for making decorations, cornstarch, baking soda,
water, recipe 1179:25-26
Cornmeal dough, recipe 1455:7
Cornstarch-glue dough, recipe 1455:8
Flour, salt and oil dough, recipe 1199:128
Glue-shampoo dough, recipe 1455:6
Oat dough, recipe 1455:10
Playdough, flour and salt, cooked, recipe 1413:70-71
Salad dressing dough, recipe 1455:6
Salt and flour dough., recipe 1277:17; 1633:153
Sculpturing dough from soda, cornstarch, recipe 1251:24
Silly stuff dough, recipe 1455:3
Soap dough, recipe 1455:8

DOUGLASS, BARBARA
"Chocolate Chip Cookie Contest," chocolate chip pizza,
recipe 1216:80

DR. DOLITTLE—COOKERY
Dr. Dolittle's mud puddle drink, recipe 365:81

DR. SEUSS—COOKERY
Green eggs a la Dr. Seuss, recipe 1199:62

DRACULA
Dracula face, making 1046:14-15
Dracula's blood, making 197:25

DRACULA—COOKERY
Batburgers, recipe 1138:32-33

DRACULA—COSTUMES
Count Dracula costume, cape, makeup, making 326:32-
34
Count Dracula costume, fabric, pattern, making 42:33-
39; 367:74-77
Dracula costume, fabric, face makeup given, making
957:88-92

DRACULA—FACE MAKEUP
Dracula and devil face makeup, how to do 1314:42

DRACULA—KITES
Kite; Dracula's bat kit, paper, patterns, making 1138:68-
71

DRACULA—MASKS
Origami Dracula mask, paper, making 1581:20-23

DRAFTS

Snake draft stopper, old necktie, gravel, making 1615:41

DRAG RACERS

Drag racer model, aluminum cans, straws, paper tubes, making 1346:20-21

DRAGONS

Activities and resources to celebrate dragon days 592:37-42

Chinese dragon, paper bags, making 1083:174-175

Chinese dragon, sheet, newspaper, paint, making 1121:20-21

Chinese dragons, paper, making 819:29

Chinese New Year dragon, directions and illustrations for making 1159:4

Dragon flag, fabric, patterns, making 1246:38-39

Dragon, pop-up, paper, pattern 1210:44-45

Fire-breathing dragon, paper towel roll, paper, patterns, making 1286:2-4

Good Luck dragon, papier-mache, patterns, making 1633:142-143

Pop-up dragon that turns into a bird, making 1388:19-21

Pop-up giant dragon for display, making 1388:92

DRAGONS—COOKERY

Dragon's volcano cake, recipe and how to decorate 1415:12-13

DRAGONS—COSTUMES

Dragon costume, fabric, pattern, making 1174:42-43; 1379:23

DRAGONS—MASKS

Dragon mask, hinged lip, cardboard box, egg cartons, making 1345:26-27

DRAGONS—PARTIES

Knights and Dragons party, activities and recipes 809:101-106

DRUIDS—COSTUMES

Picture of Druid costume 313:6

DUTCH COLONISTS—CLOTHING. *See also* **UNITED STATES—HISTORY—COLONIAL PERIOD— DUTCH COLONISTS**

DUTCH WEST INDIES. *See* **CURACAO**

DUTCH—LANGUAGE

Dutch names for the months of the year 1031:46

DWARFS

Dwarf mask, making 840:20-21

DYES

Beet dye, recipe 1455:45

Blackberry and onion skin dyes, recipe, how to do 1284:66-67

Blueberry dye, recipe 1455:44

Coffee dye, recipe 1455:47

Cranberry dye, recipe 1455:43

Dye cloth using dyes you make yourself 1350:66-67

Grape juice dye, recipe 1455:43

Kool-aid dyes, how to do 1421:198

Marigold dye, recipe 1455:46

Mustard dye, recipe 1455:47

Native American natural dyes, how to make 1354:53-54

Natural berry dye, how to do 1421:196

Natural dyes and inks, how to make and use 1421:197; 1429:116-119

Natural dyes, how to make and use 1213:16-17; 1476:147

Natural dyes, how to make and dye socks 1278:10-11

Natural egg dyes, how to do 1421:200

Onion skin dye, recipe 1455:42

Onion skin egg dye, how to do 1421:201

Pioneer dye, onion colored clothes, how to dye T-shirt using onion skins 1349:100-101

Plant dyes and mordants, how to do 1427:118

Purple cabbage dye, recipe 1455:44

Spinach dye, recipe 1455:45

Tea dye, recipe 1455:48

Walnut shell dye, recipe 1455:46

DYES AND DYEING

Ancient dyes, recipes, making 777:70-79

History of dyes 777:70-79

E

EAGLES

Eagle, egg carton, making 378:12-13

Puppet; paper bag eagle puppet, patterns, making 1107:190-197

EARHART, AMELIA—BIRTHDAY

Celebrate by making paper airplanes, patterns 1199:166-167

EARMUFFS

History of earmuffs 119:89-92

EARTH—TEMPERATURE

Hot places and cold places project 24:22-23

EARTH DAY

Activities and projects for classrooms 1393:196-200

At home make dead battery disposal containers, how to do 1199:88

Clean-up walk with gloves and trash bags, how to do 1199:84-85

Reduce, reuse, recycle in classroom, how to do 1199:86-87

EARTH DAY—COSTUMES

Mother or Father Nature costume, making 272:66-67

EARTH DAY—DECORATIONS

Earth Day paper crown or hat, making 1539:8-9

Pop-up Earth day card, making 1387:60-62

EARTH DAY—HANDICRAFTS

Bird's nest supply box, filled with nesting materials, making 1573:34-35

Bus from egg carton, paints, yarn, making 1573:26-27

Cactus from old socks and sand, making 1573:22-23

Changing seasons tree, paper plates, paints, making 1573:38-39

Earth light catcher, plastic lid, food coloring, making 1573:44-45

Galapagos tortoise model, egg carton, old glove, paints, making 1573:32-33

Globe of earth, papier-mache covered balloon, making 1311:178-179

Good Earth necklace, dirt and glue, making 1573:12-13

Hand flower, paper paint, making 1573:14-15

Leaf print, making 1662:68

Nature rubbings, making 1662:68

Oil slick paper, tempera paints, oil, making 1573:30-31

Plastic bag saver box, tissue box, paint, making 1573:18-19

Puzzle tree made from old jigsaw puzzle pieces, making 1573:20-21

Raindrop mobile, paper, twist ties, fiberfill, yarn, making 1573:28-29

Scrap paper scratch pad, making 1573:8-9

Seed sprouting necklace, pill bottle, cotton, yarn, seeds, making 1573:16-17

Summer sun pet rock, rocks, crayons, making 1573:36-37

Talking Earth puppet, paper plates, paper tube, yarn, making 1573:46-47

Track casting, plaster of Paris, making 1662:68

Trash monster, paper bags, making 1573:10-11

Tree rubbings, making 1662:68

Umbrella for spring showers, paper plates, making 1573:42-43

Windsock from recycled materials, making 1573:24-25

Winter snowflakes, tissues, toothpicks, thread, making 1573:40-41

EAST INDIES. *See also* **INDONESIA; NEW GUINEA**

EAST INDIES—COOKERY

Potatoes, spices, recipe 1145:28-29

Raita, yogurt and cucumbers, recipe 1144:27

EAST OF THE SUN AND WEST OF THE MOON

White Bear's baked fillet of sole in cream, recipe 569:40-42

EASTER

Activities, crafts, history and stories for 128:21-30

Activities, finger plays, recipes, crafts 305:24-25

Art, cooking, finger plays, games, drama, math, science, and music, activities 54:107-122

Chickens, history of 44:32

Console! Console! facts 139:35

Customs round the world 503:24-25

Easter animal parade, history of 44:37-39

Easter bells, history of 44:47-49

Easter candlelight, history of 44:18-20

Easter clothes, history of 44:57-60; 139:165

Easter colors, history of 44:44-46; 139:165

Easter customs in other lands 51:33-35

Easter egg customs at the White House 201:29

Easter eggs color stories, songs, rhymes, flannel board patterns 904:134-137

Easter eggs, history of 44:23-31

Easter fire, history of 44:15-17

Easter fireworks, history of 44:21-22

Easter flowers and plants, history of 44:50-53; 139:164

Easter food, facts about 139:155

Easter lamb, history of 44:35-37

Easter rabbit, history of 44:33-35

Easter rabbit, United States, facts about 139:146

Easter stories, songs, art activities, games, recipes 1135:55-57

Easter Sunday; history and celebration of 496:49-53

Easter sunrise, history of 44:11-14

Easter water, history of 44:54-56

Easter, a season and a day, history of 44:6-10

Easter, celebration 133:114-115

Egg activities, math, language, science 992:111-121; 992:96-110

Eggs flannel graph stories and patterns, making 822:43

Eggs in a bag activity, how to do 781:92-94

Eggs, history of 882:4

Fireworks dove 139:106

First Catch Your Hare, England, facts 139:116

Flannel graph stories and patterns, making 822:42

Good Friday; history and celebration of 496:47-48

History of Easter 513:81; 566:30-31; 709:163-166

History of Easter celebrations 566:30-31

History of Easter, Easter bunny and Easter egg 419:58-60

Hot cross buns, history of 44:40-43

In Candle Light, Paschal facts 139:102

Knocking of the eggs at Easter 709:164

Lent, facts about 139:36-37

Mama's baby activity, how to do 781:86-89

Maundy Thursday; history and celebration of 496:45-47

Paschal Lamb facts 139:142

Rabbit robot road relay activity, how to do 781:90-91

Rabbits and Eggs art and writing activities, patterns, making 1152:138-145

Resurrection of Jesus Christ, activities and projects for classrooms 1393:180-183

Songs, finger plays, stories, games, rhythms 1200:96-99

Spring Goddess facts 139:35
Sun dance facts 139:110
Teaching activities, art, literature, music, crafts, patterns
    1192:209-249
Words of Easter 503:26-27
EASTER—ART
Painting with Easter shapes, how to 73:65
EASTER—BULLETIN BOARDS
Easter bulletin board, bunny basket, Easter tree, making
    295:200-202
EASTER—COOKERY
Acorn shaped butter cookies, recipe 1247:46-47
After Easter cookies, recipe 254:76
Baskets, edible, recipe 503:42-43
Bird's nest cupcakes, recipe 1487:18-19
Bunnied eggs, recipe 433:69
Bunny bread, recipe 540:38-39; 555:22-23
Bunny salad, making 164:16-17
Bunny salad, pears, lettuce, recipe 1460:30
Chocolate eggs, recipe 1245:11
Cornish hens with rice stuffing, recipe 871:57-58
Daffodil cake, recipe 206:53-54; 433:71
Dough boys, recipe 254:74-75
Easter basket, popcorn, recipe 939:63-65
Easter cake, recipe 64:61-63
Easter eggs bread, recipe 1032:205-206
Easter nest cake, recipe 449:70
Easter Rabbit salad, recipe 503:42
Egg in a basket, making 433:68
Eggs in a nest, recipe 698:47
Eggs, chocolate eggs, recipe 139:126; 503:43
Eggs, decorating 64:46-49
Frosted grapes, making 433:70
Fudge candy, chocolate and marshmallows, recipe
    1247:45
Gingerbread bunny cookies, recipe 1247:42-44
Holy Saturday Simnel cake, how to decorate 1245:21
Hot cross buns, recipe 1409:27; 1495:128-129
Hot cross cakes, recipe 351:40
Lamb chops, recipe 1111:140
Little lambs cake, recipe and how to decorate 1415:18-19
Marzipan chicks, recipe 1558:25
Mints, recipe 1067:78
Natural dyes for eggs 64:46-47
Naturally dyed Easter eggs, making 433:72
Pancakes, recipe 1247:41
Popcorn balls, Easter eggs, recipe 381:48-49
Pretzels, recipe 1558:22
Rabbit cake, making 139:148
Red Easter eggs, recipe 402:30-33
Stuffed eggs and egg sandwiches, making 64:60-61
Sugar egg frosting, recipe 1178:176
Sugar eggs in egg molds, how to make 1178:174-175
Sunrise sandwiches, recipe 698:46
Sweet Easter bread, recipe 402:30-33
Thumb print nests, recipe 254:77
Tuna burgers, recipe 698:47
EASTER—COSTUMES
Easter Bunny costume, making 272:62-63; 842:45-48
Easter Bunny costume, paper bag, making 138:42-48
Easter egg costume, cardboard, patterns, making
    1283:34-37
Easter Egg costume, making 272:63-64
Easter egg, variety of old clothes, making 1656:17-20

EASTER—DANCES
Easter eggs are rolling 624:27-31
Twelve little rabbits 624:27-31
EASTER—DECORATIONS
Animals, stand up from paper, making 448:17
Apple blossom branch, making 433:52
Baby chick and egg, paper, pattern, making 305:47
Banner, Easter door banner, making 586:33
Basket from plastic berry basket, making 835:47
Basket, carton, making 254:72
Basket, Easter basket from shells, making 216:55-56
Basket, making 196:34-35; 376:188-189
Basket, paper plate, fasteners, making 232:36; 1460:28
Baskets, dough and wax dipped, making 447:28-29
Baskets, egg cartons, making 1067:73-74
Baskets, folded paper, making 438:68
Baskets, paper bunny baskets, making 882:27
Baskets, paper candy baskets, making 555:14-15
Baskets, paper plate, making 609:unp
Baskets, woven, making 882:28-29
Batik eggs, tape, dyes, making 1662:58
Bird nests, recipe 1032:177
Bonbon box, making 51:49-50
Bonnet, paper plate, making 835:48
Bouquet from pipe cleaners, making 835:51
Branch to chase winter away, eggs and paper, making
    555:12-13
Bubbles for Easter, making 433:42
Bunnies from yam, making 891:58-62
Bunnies in a row collage, making 198:62-63
Bunnies, cereal box and paper tubes, making 534:3-4
Bunnies, cotton stuffing on paper, making 1149:61
Bunnies, dough and wax dipped, making 447:26-27
Bunnies, flying bunnies, balloons and cardboard tubes,
    making 555:24-25
Bunnies, newspaper string of bunnies, pattern, making
    1067:69-71
Bunny and snowman, decorated eggs, making 555:6-7
Bunny bag, paper, yarn, pattern, making 253:62-63;
    760:74-75; 1067:64-66
Bunny basket, making 946:70-71
Bunny basket, milk carton, paper bowl, making 1334:8-
    10
Bunny basket, paper bag, pattern, making 275:1
Bunny baskets, paper, patterns, making 1152:143-145
Bunny cards, paper, markers, making 1393:183
Bunny cone model, making 448:17
Bunny ears hat, paper plates, simple, making 1266:54
Bunny ears, bunny nose, bunny tail, making 433:41
Bunny face, paper plate, plastic spoons, making 128:23;
    1460:29
Bunny family, tin cans, paper, patterns, making
    1311:164-165
Bunny from cotton balls, making 835:53
Bunny from egg carton, making 448:19
Bunny from marzipan, making 1245:24-25
Bunny from paper bag, making 448:16
Bunny game for two, making 555:46-47
Bunny hat, paper, making 254:63-64
Bunny hat, paper, pattern, making 232:34-35
Bunny house, cardboard, moss, making 555:60-61
Bunny inside an egg, making 196:32-33
Bunny magnet, felt, pom-poms, patterns, making
    1425:28-29

Bunny poem, paper plate picture, patterns, making 899:21-31

Bunny rabbit from white sock, pink felt, making 1377:28-29

Bunny rabbit, paper plate, pattern, making 233:32

Bunny Trail mural, pattern, making 906:40,76

Bunny with cotton tail, paper, pattern, making 760:76-77

Bunny, cardboard tube and fluff, making 448:18

Bunny, dancing, eggs and string, making 555:10-11

Bunny, fuzzy bunny, making 196:38-39

Bunny, newspaper, pattern, making 253:67-69

Bunny, paper cup and napkin, patterns, making 1067:63-64

Bunny, paper cup, pattern, making 253:60-62

Bunny, paper plates, simple, making 1266:55

Bunny, paper strip, making 253:66-67

Bunny, paper, large pattern, making 477:57-60

Bunny, papier-mache, patterns, making 555:48-49; 1300:69-72

Bunny, pine cone bunny, making 1067:66-67

Bunny, pine cone, pattern, making 253:63-66

Buttercup bunny card, making 351:12

Button buttercups, making 164:28

Candle eggs, eggshell, wax, making 1662:57

Card, Easter bunny cutup card, making 209:19

Card, Easter peek-a-boo egg card, making 209:20-22

Cards decorated with flower petals, making 503:10

Chick in egg, paper, large pattern, making 477:49-52

Chick surprise egg, paper, patterns, making 1393:181-182

Chicken in a nest, making 433:44

Chicken in egg, paper, pattern, making 760:80-81

Chickens, making 139:136

Chicks on the window painting, making 433:36

Chicks, cotton balls, egg carton and paper, making 897:43

Clay egg cup, making 555:42-43

Collages using contact paper, making 1149:84

Collages; Easter shapes and eggs, tissue paper, magazine pictures, making 1149:48,50,52

Collages; egg shaped macaroni collages, making 1149:77

Czechoslovakian painted eggs, patterns, making 1016:57-62

Decorations, eggs, rooster, butterflies, making 113:44-47

Duck and chick, egg carton, making 766:65-66

Duck, swimming duck, cardboard, making 555:30-31

Easter basket pattern 309:57

Easter basket, basket, lace, ribbons, shells, pom-poms, making 1425:32-33

Easter basket, making 164:20-21; 183:34-35

Easter basket, paper, pattern, making 760:72-73

Easter birds, making 139:137

Easter bunnies, paper, making 897:46

Easter Bunny bonnet, paper, patterns, making 823:37-38

Easter Bunny from paper bag, making 678:26

Easter Bunny party favor, balsa wood, making 925:39

Easter Bunny, milk carton, making 79:13

Easter Bunny, paper tubes, making 766:67-68

Easter Bunny, potato, making 433:40

Easter Bunny's house, cardboard, making 891:53-57

Easter cards, making 51:50-52

Easter chicks, making 438:67; 561:94

Easter egg mural, making 906:39

Easter egg shapes painted or finger painted, making 1149:19,32

Easter egg with chick, bread dough, making 816:113-114

Easter egg, papier-mache strips and balloon, making 743:28-29

Easter eggs from shells, making 216:54-55

Easter lamb pop-up card, pattern, making 1006:36

Easter lilies, paper, pattern, making 253:69-70

Easter Parade mural, pattern, making 906:38,74-75

Easter rabbit, styrofoam and paper, pattern, making 912:27-28

Easter straw nests and jellybean eggs, shredded wheat, marshmallows, food coloring, jellybeans, recipe; 1179:88

Egg baskets, making 139:124

Egg cradle, making 698:44

Egg ducks, cardboard, making 555:44-45

Egg dyeing, making 164:6-9

Egg games, making 555:50-51

Egg greeting card, making 946:66-67

Egg head, funny bunny, Humpty Dumpty, patterns, making 1348:unp

Egg necklace, paper, making 835:49

Egg or bunny prints, finger painted, making 1149:107

Egg shapes from sponge prints, making 1149:100-101

Egg sun catcher, making 946:56-57

Egg window decorations, paper, making 374:164-165

Egg, puzzle paper, making 835:52

Egg, woven, making 433:50

Eggheads, eggs and paper-cut characters, patterns, making 1016:63-67

Eggs, basket, bunnies, felt board, making 945:180-184

Eggs, decorated, making 438:66; 1032:203

Eggs, dyed and decorated, making 938:67-68

Eggs, how to paint with poster paints 1446:6-9

Eggs, paper art eggs, making 1149:130

Eggs, papier-mache Easter eggs, making 1017:84

Eggs, storybook characters, making 882:18-23

Eggs, Swiss style Easter eggs, making 897:48

Eggs, tissue paper, making 433:49

Eggs; papier-mache, balloon, paints, making 1558:13

Flour paste, making 139:132

Flower bouquet, making 64:55-56

Flowers, eggshells and crepe paper bouquet, making 894:42-47

Footprint bunny ears, making 433:47

Gelatin Easter eggs, recipe 376:261

Good Friday stained-glass windows, cardboard, colored cellophane, making 1245:19

Grass, growing grass for Easter baskets, how to do 725:31

Greeting cards for Easter, how to make 448:16-19; 837:25-26

Hands activities, bunny, duck, basket of eggs, chick, making 306:46-49

Hen and bunny, yam, making 555:28-29

Hen and chick, paper, pattern, making 254:68-71

Hen and chicks, crepe, paper, making 555:56-57

Hen, papier-mache, making 555:38-39

Jellybean pouch, muslin, ribbon, making 1247:24-25

Jellybean sacks, making 196:36-37

Juggler, cardboard, making 555:52-53

Lacing egg shapes, making 1149:135

Lamb pictures, cotton balls, making 1149:59

Lamb, paper, large pattern, making 477:53-56

Maple-wax Easter eggs, making 51:49

Mice, nest full of mice, eggs, making 555:58-59

Mini-book, making 196:46-51
Mobile for Easter, making 741:34
Mobile, baskets mobile, making 644:38-41
Mobile, Easter eggs mobile, making 772:58
Mobile, Easter symbols, paper, dowels, paint, making 1245:13
Mosaic eggs, paper, tissue paper, making 1149:143
Mural of Easter Egg Parade, making 433:53
Paper dove, making 139:107-108
Peanut decorations, making 257:113
Peek-a-boo Easter egg, decoupage, making 817:83-84
Peter Cottontail, paper, making 164:30-31
Place cards from natural materials, making 217:79
Pop-up Easter card, making 1387:28-29
Pop-up Easter card, patterns, making 1016:68-72
Potato print eggs, making 433:37
Princess and dwarfs, cardboard tubes, making 555:40-41
Rabbit headband, paper, pattern, making 760:78-79
Rabbit's head, making 648:26
Rabbits from clay dough, recipe for dough, making 1247:26-28
Rabbits from clothespins, fabric, paints, making 1247:30-31
Rabbits from eggshells, felt and paper, making 1247:29
Rabbits from white socks, stuffing, felt, fabric, making 1247:32-35
Rabbits, stuffed, fabric, patterns, making 1247:38-40
Rooster, stuffed, cardboard, making 555:8-9
Stand up animals and people, making 698:45
Thumbprint bunnies, making 433:34
Train, Bunny Express, making 226:18-20
Tulip basket, paper, making 374:165-168
Tulips and daffodils, making 297:268-269
Tulips, egg carton, making 835:50
Tulips, paper, pattern, making 760:82-83
Umbrella, paper, pattern, making 760:84-85
Wool bunny, making 433:35
Woven Easter basket, paper, making 123:39-40

EASTER—DOLLS
Bunny doll, felt, stuffed, pattern, making 487:36
Easter egg dolls, making 51:39-42
Little Quakeress, making 51:52-53
Miss Rolly-poly, making 51:45-47

EASTER—DRAWING
Baby chicks, drawing 87:16-17
Basket, drawing 87:5
Cats, drawing 87:18-19
Crocuses, drawing 87:22-23
Daffodils, drawing 87:22-23
Daisy Duck, drawing 87:12-13
Decorating eggs, drawing 87:6-7
Easter bunny, drawing 87:10-11
Lamb, drawing 87:30-31
Tulip, drawing 87:14-15

EASTER—DYES
Natural dyes for eggs 201:46-49; 1179:87

EASTER—FESTIVALS
Ash Wednesday 475:116
Blessing of Easter Fire 475:127
Brotherhood Sunday 475:112-113
Carnival celebrations round the world 503:14-15
Ceremony of Platsenitsis winding sheet 475:124
Easter Mass 475:128-129
Easter parades 475:132-133
Easter Rabbit 475:133

Egg rolling 475:133
God's Acre (Moravians) 475:131-132
Good Friday 475:123-126
Greek Church Easter Vigil 475:129
Holy Saturday 475:126-130
Holy Thursday 475:121-123
Holy Week 475:117
Laetare Sunday 475:116-117
Lent 475:114-115
Lenten foods 475:133-136
Mothering Sunday 475:116
Palm Sunday 475:117-118
Paschal Candle 475:127-128
Protestant celebrations 475:129-130
Stations of the Cross 475:124-126
Sunrise Services 475:131
Symbols of Easter Day 475:136-137
Taking leave of Alleluia 475:114
Tenebrae 475:120-121
World Day of Prayer 475:111-112

EASTER—FINGER PLAYS
Bunny rhymes 698:47
Finger play about the Easter Bunny 260:59
Finger plays about rabbits 302:70-71
Finger plays and rhymes 1583:119-121
Finger plays, games, making 944:91-96

EASTER—GAMES
Bunny games 433:55-65
Bunny hunt game 698:48
Bunny tail game 534:91-92
Easter egg games, making 51:36-39
Easter egg hunt game 1036:263
Easter egg race 164:38-39
Easter games 139:140-141; 240:24-25; 534:93; 1460:30
Egg and spoon race 139:141
Egg gathering and egg relay, how to play 164:13; 503:51
Egg hunt game 698:48; 698:49
Egg rolling, White House, United States 139:140
Egg running contest 698:49
Egg tapping Greece 139:140
Egg toss 139:140
Game for Easter, making 226:17
Good egg, bad egg game 345:43
Greek egg-tapping game, making 64:57-59
Huckle buckle jelly bean game 345:42
Knock eggs and egg toss, how to play 503:50
Nose nudging race game, how to play 1460:30
Pomlazka game, Czechoslavakia 139:141
Spoon race game, how to play 1460:30
Treasure hunt, making 329:24
White House egg roll game 698:49

EASTER—GARDENS
Spring indoor garden, making 164:26-27

EASTER—HANDICRAFTS
Ascension bird from yellow wool, felt, making 1245:29
Baskets for Easter, paper, making 277:49-51
Bunnies, paper bag, making 231:8-9
Bunny bank, plastic tub, making 442:10
Bunny shopping bag, paper, making 351:8
Bunny sock, making 64:53-55
Cake in a basket, making 134:53
Candle making, how to do 139:104-105
Candles, egg shaped, making 1455:99
Chicken in papier-mache egg, wool yam chicken, making 972:unp

Church; gingerbread church, recipe, patterns, assembling, how to do 1086:60-66
Crystal garden, making 134:52
Dinosaur jelly bean bag, making 350:38
Duck and chick, felt, making 628:80-82
Easter basket woven, making 337:86-94
Easter basket, paper, making 351:9
Easter bunny, paper models, patterns, making 640:11-12
Easter chicken, cardboard, making 554:24-25
Easter egg arrangement from dried flowers, making 210:85-86
Easter rabbit, basket and flowers, from cereal boxes, making 84:16
Easter waddle duck, making 183:40-41
Egg cosies, making 449:38
Egg cover, felt, cotton, making 1245:25
Egg made from beads, making 255:79-80
Egg, papier-mache, balloon, paints, making 1561:32
Fabulous jeweled eggs, making 183:30-31
Hats; rabbit, violets and lucky clover, making 351:10-11
Hen from wool yam, making 972:unp
Humpty Dumpty, making 51:42-45
Jeweled display case and stand, making 183:32-33
Lamb to knit, making 139:144
Mandolin, making 51:47
Painted eggs, Poland, making 139:117
Polish rug yarn decorated eggs, making 503:35
Pompom bunny and chick, making 196:58-59
Postage stamp case, paper, making 351:13
Pretty planter, making 183:46-47
Pysanky eggs, Poland, making 139:118-119
Rabbit and hutch from wool yam, making 972:unp
Rabbit made from beads, making 255:78
Seed gifts to give, making 503:10
Stained glass Easter hanging basket, pattern, making 1360:19-21
Sweatshirt, Easter egg decoration, squeeze paint, making 1360:12-14
Ukrainian pysanky eggs, making 503:34-35

EASTER—HATS
Easter basket hat, paper, pattern, making 823:35-36
Easter bonnet, fabric, ribbon, pattern, making 1245:22
Easter bonnet, making 64:52-53; 226:21; 433:48; 698:45
Easter bonnets, paper, making 78:97
Spring bonnet, paper, pattern, making 823:39

EASTER—KITES
Easter kite, making 196:52-57
Kite decorated with bunnies, chicks and eggs, making 1558:28-29

EASTER—MASKS
Easter mask, paper, making 503:46

EASTER—PARTIES
Afternoon tea party 196:13
Beatrix Potter Easter brunch, decorations, games, costumes, recipes 74:71-84
Boy and girl bunny tea party invitations 196:14-15
Bunny biscuits, making 196:19
Bunny butter cookies, making 196:20-21
Decorated eggs, making 294:163
Decorations, snacks, games, making 1266:52-58
Easter brunch, invitations, decorations, food, games 133:130-133
Easter Bunny centerpiece, making 294:166-167
Easter egg cakes and egg float making 294:162
Easter Egg party, how to plan and give 43:65-67

Easter party, recipes and games 635:24-27
Egg bunnies, making 294:168
Egg-dyeing party 201:167-169
Finger sandwiches, making 196:18
Marble swirl cake, making 196:22
Marshmallow bunnies, making 196:17
Teas for Easter 196:16

EASTER—PATTERNS
Peter Cotton Tail, pattern 1192:229

EASTER—POETRY
Bunny poems 433:9-23
Butterfly verse 139:110
Easter blessing verse 139:175
Flower carol verse 139:164
Fly Away, Swallow verse 139:36
Hancucka, traditional rhyme, Poland 139:120
Lamb, William Blake verse 139:143
Moon, William Blake 139:28
Paschal Candle, Joah Mellings, Australia 139:103
Spring, William Blake 139:16
This Bread, Eleanor Farjeon 139:155
Winter Is Past, from the Song of Songs, Solomon 139:16

EASTER—PUPPETS
Bird rod puppet, making 754:144-148
Bunny hand puppet, yarn, making 555:62-63
Bunny puppet, making 433:39
Bunny puppet, styrofoam cup, white card, cotton ball, stick, making 1294:43-45
Easter Bunny puppet, pattern, making 183:36; 1006:38
Easter Bunny, Mr. and Mrs. puppets, paper bags, patterns, making 940:27-28
Easter chick puppet, pattern, making 1006:39
Easter egg finger puppets and rhymes, making 821:34
Easter Egg Hunt, puppets and puppet play script, making 1155:85-89
Easter egg puppets, making 735:58
Easter puppets, paper, making 503:46
Easter rabbit puppets, making 735:57
Easter Rabbit's Basket, puppets and puppet play script, making 1155:90-95
First Easter Eggs puppet play 754:109-117
Five finger puppet bunnies, making 433:38
Goose push puppet, making 754:123-128
Hen push puppet making 754:117-123
Herald push puppet, making 754:139-144
Lion and lamb paper plate puppet, pattern, making 907:31, 72-73
Puppet and story for Easter 1030:101; 1030:47
Puppet projects, patterns, scenes, story starters, feature story 1083:73-83
Rabbit push puppet, making 754:128-134
Springtime puppet play 183:38-39
Turkey push puppet, making 754:134-139

EASTER—SONGS
Bunny Patch song 782:unp
Bunny songs 433:24-32
Did you ever see a Bunny song 782:unp
Down the Bunny Trail song 782:unp
Easter Bunny hippity hop song 782:unp
Easter Bunny song 782:unp
Easter Eggs, traditional song from Russia 139:125
Easter Is Coming, traditional song 139:15
Easter songs for infants and toddlers 908:68
Five songs about Easter bunnies 1150:24-25
Morning Has Broken, traditional Gaelic melody 139:26-27

Old Molly Hare, American Negro Nonsense Song, Easter
eggs 139:114-115
Rabbit Ain't God, traditional Negro nonsense song
139:146-147
Songs about Easter and Easter bunny 901:62-69; 902:31

EASTER—STORIES

Emperor's New Clothes, Hans Christian Anderson
139:166-172
First Easter story 139:10-14
Movable Feast, story 139:28
Secret, traditional tale, Germany, 139:111-113
Selfish Giant, Oscar Wilde 139:18-25

EASTER—SUNRISE

Easter sunrise in pastel chalk, making 433:45

EASTER—TREES

Easter bush, making 648:27
Easter egg plant, tree branch, eggs, ribbon, making
1286:69-70
Easter egg tree, flower pot, branch, decorations, making
1510:34-35
Easter egg trees, making 201:164-166; 503:47; 725:30;
1247:36-37; 1477:47
Easter pyramid tree, making, 555:54-55
Egg tree, branch, paints, making 1245:26-27
Stabile, egg tree, making 741:59-61

EASTER EGGS

Animal egg menagerie, making 351:16-17
Batik teardrop eggs, making 201:81-85
Binsegraas eggs, collage, making 201:93-94
Binsegraas eggs, Polish style, making 201:95-97
Blocked eggs, making 201:63-64
Blown eggs, how to blow, decorate and hang 139:121;
201:43-44; 677:17; 1257:12-13
Candles, Easter egg candles, making 201:153-155
Checked eggs, using dyes, making 201:57
Comic strip eggs, transfer method, making 201:61-62;
201:133-134
Confetti eggs, making 201:150-151
Crayon etched eggs, making 201:146
Crazy quilt eggs, making 201:147
Crepe paper egg dye, making 201:49-50
Cutout eggs, making 201:103-109
Decorated eggs, making 403:25-27
Decorations using dyed eggs, making 201:53-54
Dinosaurus Easter egg, paper glued over balloon, mak-
ing 1377:24-25
Dyes for eggs, making 503:34
Dyes, natural dyes for Easter eggs, making 134:52;
698:42; 709:166; 725:28
Easter birds, making 201:151-152
Easter egg candle, making 336:33-34
Easter egg diorama, making 128:29
Easter egg, decoupage decorated, making 341:36-39
Easter egg, felt, making 628:78-79
Easter egg, paper, pattern, making 760:70-71
Easter eggs painted using stencils, making 1149:38
Easter eggs painted with crumpled paper, making
1149:23
Easter eggs, how to dye and make 351:14; 376:186-187;
1277:6-7
Egg decoration, making 561:93-94
Egg mobiles, making 201:156-158
Egg, pattern, making 128:27
Egg, surprise egg, balloons, papier-mache, making
555:18-19

Eggs dyed with plant imprints, making 725:29
Eggs painted with shaving cream, flour, or shoe polish,
making 1149:8,13,15
Eggs, batik decorated, making 698:41
Eggs, blown out, decorated, pattern for ears, making
253:72-74; 1067:75-77
Eggs, checked, striped, plaid, decorated, making 698:41
Eggs, coloring and dyeing, how to do 698:40; 882:12-13
Eggs, crayon resist decorated, making 698:41
Eggs, decorated fabric scraps, making 226:22-23
Eggs, decorated, making 351:15;448:14-15; 555:34-37;
577:26-27; 882:15-17
Eggs, illustrated eggs, making 196:28-29
Eggs, leaf print decorated, making 698:41
Eggs, shadow box eggs, making 698:44
Eggs, tie-dye decorated, making 698:41
Etched eggs, making 201:69-71
Finger painted eggs, making 201:132-133
Golden eggs, making 201:98-101
Grandpa and Grandma Eggs, making 201:114
Hawaiian Hula dancer egg, making 201:115
Hippie egg, making 201:118
Jeweled Easter eggs, fabric, making 201:102; 1320:88-89
Leaf decorated eggs, making 201:62-63
Lieutenant Flap egg, collage decorated, making 201:119
Lion egg, collage decorated, making 201:126
Madras eggs, making 201:131
Marbled Easter eggs, how to do 1257:14; 1301:99
Marbled eggs, making 1257:14
Moon Men and Moon Maidens eggs, making 201:122-
123
Mr. Rabbit egg, collage decorated, making 201:127
Old Molly Hare, American Negro nonsense song
139:114-115
Pace eggs, how to dye 139:123
Paint an egg, paste an egg, making 139:122
Paint and felt tip pen eggs, making 1257:15
Papier-mache eggs, making 139:131-132
Papier-mache eggs, patterns, making 1300:65-68
Peephole Easter eggs, making 201:134-142
Pigs, egg pigs, collage decorated, making 201:129
Plaid eggs, using dyes, making 201:57-58
Pysanky and Krashanky eggs, making 201:72-80;
201:85-91; 329:20-21; 525:70-71
Rainbow eggs, using dyes, making 201:60-61
Rubber band or tape striped eggs, making 201:56
Scratch carved eggs, making 201:66
Special Child and Easter eggs, making 201:31-32
Special Child and peephole Easter eggs, making 201:143
Striped or banded eggs using dyes, making 201:55-56
Styrofoam eggs, making 201:149
Sugar egg with scene inside, making 1286:71-72
Tie-dyed Easter eggs, making 201:59-60; 329:18-19
Tiffany eggs glace, making 201:144-145
Tweed eggs, making 201:148
Wax crayon eggs, making 1257:15

EASTER EGGS—GAMES

Easter egg roll 201:182
Egg game 201:177-178
Egg race 201:181-182
Egg running contest 201:185-186
Egg-sackly what game 201:178-179
German egg game 201:176-177
German Eierlesen game 201:184-185

Hunts, community hunts, how to do 201:171-173;
201:173-175
Netherlands Eiertikken game 201:180-181
Whither eggshell game 201:183-184

EASTER EGGS—LEGENDS
Celtic folklore 201:17
Chinese legends 201:16
Egyptian legends 201:15
Finland legends 201:16
Hindu mythology about Easter eggs 201:16
Italian legends 201:16
Macedonian legends 201:20
Persian legends 201:18
Russian legends 201:17
Secret, traditional tale, Germany 139:111-113

EASTER RABBIT—TALES
Will You? Won't You?, traditional tale, Africa 139:159-
154

EASTERN WOODLANDS INDIANS. *See also* **ALGON-
QUIN INDIANS; DELAWARE INDIANS;
HURON INDIANS; IROQUOIS INDIANS;
SENECA INDIANS; SHAWNEE INDIANS;
WOODLAND INDIANS**

EASTERN WOODLANDS INDIANS—COOKERY
Pumpkin or squash seeds, toasted, recipe 714:27

ECUADOR—CHRISTMAS
Christmas celebration 601:164; 695:70

ECUADOR—CHRISTMAS—HANDICRAFTS
Creche, bread dough, making 795:36-37

ECUADOR—COOKERY
Black currant muffins, recipe 967:27
Ceviche, shrimp and onion dish, recipe 1319:119
Coconut bars, recipe 1165:237-238
Corn packages with husks, recipe 1517:35
Empadas (turnovers), beef, chicken, ham, fruit, recipe
1517:28-29
Potato soup, recipe 967:28
Quindin, coconut pudding dessert, recipe 1165:238

ECUADOR—EASTER—COOKERY
Llapingachos (Ecuadorian potato cakes), recipe 1666:234
Salsa de Mali (Ecuadorian peanut sauce), recipe
1666:234
Sopa de Crema de Coco (cream of coconut soup), recipe
1666:233-234
South American Capritoda (bread pudding), recipe
1666:235

ECUADOR—FESTIVALS
Day of the Dead celebration 601:165
Old Year celebration 601:154-155

ECUADOR—FESTIVALS—HANDICRAFTS
Fiesta headdresses, paper bags, fabric, making 1338:48-
49

ECUADOR—GAMES
Jacks in Ecuador 515:44

ECUADOR—MASKS
Andean mask, clay, paints, making 1706:23

ECUADOR—NEW YEAR'S EVE
Old Year celebration 665:4

EDISON, THOMAS A.
Birthday celebration; art, music, foods, games, activities
1104:54-57
Song, Who Was Thomas Edison? 902:24

EDWARDS, HAZEL
"There's a Hippopotamus on Our Roof Eating Cake,"
special cake, recipe 1216:56

EGGS. *See also* **EASTER—DECORATIONS**
Batik eggs, how to do 296:126-127
Beliefs about eggs in different countries 1143:20-23
Bisengraas egg, yam wrapped, making 298:100-101
Blowing eggs, how to do 1245:27; 1286:68; 1311:114
Blown egg African animals, elephant, hippo, zebra, white
rhino, making 677:24-25
Blown egg African animals, mandril, gemsbok, lion, gi-
raffe, making 677:24-25
Blown egg Asian animals, gibbon, tiger, water buffalo,
giant panda, make 677:26
Blown egg decorated, making 1253:40-41
Blown egg North American animals, bison, bighorn
sheep, mountain lion, musk ox, making 677:27
Egg and flower Easter cross, making 298:88-89
Egg tucked in dough basket, making 298:102-103
Egg writing in different languages 1081:32
Eggs decorated with pressed flowers and leaves, making
1285:28
Eggs dyed with onion skins, making 1285:30-31
History of eggs 882:4
Mexican cascarones, making 114:92
Ochter-Foggel good luck bird, making 298:90-91
Painted porcelain Mandarin egg; making 298:104-105
Patchwork eggs, making 114:92; 296:128-129
Polish rug yarn decorated eggs, making 503:35
Pysanky egg, geometric design, making 298:82-83
Pysanky eggs, how to make and decorate 525:70-71;
1081:13
Turmeric marbled dyed eggs, making 1673:17
Ukrainian pysanky eggs, making 503:34-35
Wax and dye eggs, making 1640:23

EGGS—HANDICRAFTS. *See also* **EASTER—
HANDICRAFTS**
Czechoslovakian eggs, making 627:90-92
English Pace eggs, making 627:88-89
Heirloom eggs, making 403:82-83
Mexican Cascarones, making 627:97-99
Painted eggs, peasant style, making 627:56
Pennsylvania Dutch patchwork eggs and egg tree, mak-
ing 626:54-57; 627:83-84
Pennsylvania Dutch scratch carved eggs, making 627:85-
87
Polish paper-cut eggs, making 627:93-96

EGGSHELL CRAFTS
Boats, eggshell boats, making 555:26-27
Bunnies, eggshell bunnies, making 196:31
Chick in an eggshell, making 433:4-6
Eggshell flower holder, making 374:164
Eggshell gift using natural materials 217:80
Eggshell mosaics, making 164:42-43; 201:158-160;
374:168-169; 503:47
Eggshell ornament project, making 1032:175-176
Eggshell puppets making 294:164-165
Eggshell vases, making 201:160-163
Eggshells; writing on eggshells, how to do 498:102-105
King and Queen, felt and eggshell puppet, making 26:88-
93
Whale on posterboard covered with eggshells, patterns,
making 1286:74-76

EGYPT
Activities, flags, games, songs, dances, recipes
1381:133-136
Activities, projects, recipes 282:96-112

Discovery of King Tut's tomb; Egyptian hieroglyphics, how to do 1199:252-253

EGYPT—AMULETS

Amulet to bring good luck, baker's clay, paints, making 1350:78-79

EGYPT—BIRTHDAYS

Birthday celebrations in Egypt 695:62

Celebration party for one week old child 660:51-52

EGYPT—BOATS

Felucca boat, wood and styrofoam, making 287:75-78

EGYPT—CHRISTMAS

Christmas celebration in Egypt 601:28

EGYPT—COOKERY

Ancient Day salad, recipe 188:38

Apricot custard, recipe 794:42

Bamia, lamb and okra stew, recipe 1165:58-59

Bassbusa, yogurt and cream of wheat dessert, recipe 1282:89-90

Bread; palace bread from honey and bread crumbs, recipe 1282:90

Charba soup, recipe 287:92

Couscous with lamb stew, recipe 667:262-264

Crepes, recipe 287:93

Cucumber in yogurt, recipe 287:92

Eggeh Bi Betingan, omelet with eggplant, recipe 1165:58

El Belehat stew, recipe 287:92

El Maloria vegetable dish, recipe 287:92-93

Falafel, recipe 1381:135

Ful Mesdames, brown fava beans, recipe 1165:58

Kafta, meat patties, recipe 282:119

Kosheri, lentils, rice and macaroni stew, recipe 1165:59

Lamb, roasted, recipe 667:261-262

Liver and rice, recipe 967:28

Meat patties (kufta), recipe 874:55

Menenas dessert, recipe 287:94

Puffy fritters in syrup (zalabia), cookies, recipe 72:103-105

Spice dip for raw carrots, recipe 1392:unp

Stuffed tomatoes, recipe 858:unp

EGYPT—COSTUMES

Galabiyah adapted to make dress 287:55-56

Girl costume, crepe paper, making 687:22-25

Modem Egyptian costumes, man's shirt, making 287:53-55

Paper doll type costume, pattern, making 282:111

EGYPT—EASTER

Easter celebration 601:28

Palm Sunday celebration 601:29

EGYPT—FACE MAKEUP

Makeup palettes, making 287:64-65

EGYPT—FESTIVALS

Decorated plates, making 287:21-22

Egyptian festival, setting, decorations, foods, making 287:6-22

Embossed metal panel, making 287:17-18

King Tut and God Osiris panel, paper, making 287:20-21

Lotus blossoms, paper, making 287:10-13

Papyrus plant, paper, making 287:13-14

Sham Al-Nessim-the smelling of the spring 474:62-63

Sistrum rattle, wooden, making 287:19-20

Smell the Breezes Day; activities, art, songs, recipes, games 601:21-22; 1469:92-93

White lily, paper, making 287:14-17

EGYPT—FESTIVALS—COOKERY

Maulid al-Nabi; chirkasia (chicken with rice in nut sauce), recipe 1666:50-51

Sham al-Nessim; basboosa (almond cake with lemon syrup), recipe 1666:49-50

Sham al-Nessim; koushry (lentils and rice), recipe 1666:49-50

EGYPT—FESTIVALS—DECORATIONS

Spring cracked egg art, eggshells, food coloring, making 1539:80-81

EGYPT—FOOTWEAR

Sandals, paper, making 282:106

EGYPT—GAMES

Alquerque board game, patterns, making 1541:61-66

Nine Men's Morris game, making 1507:11-12

Seega board game, patterns, making 1541:161-166

Serpent game, clay, making 287:72-73

Silence Is Golden game 282:120

Tug of war game, how to play 1494:23

Wari board game, patterns, making 1507:13-14; 1541:115-118

EGYPT—HANDICRAFTS

Duck, making 287:65-66

Gazelle, making 287:67-68

Hippopotamus ceramic paper weight, making 287:68-69

Mirror with papyrus decoration, making 287:73-75

Name scroll, paper, yarn, hieroglyphs, making 1332:23-28

Obelisk knitting needle holder, making 287:79-82

Perfumed cones, making 287:61-64

Pyramid candy dish, making 287:78-79

EGYPT—HIEROGLYPHICS

Hieroglyphics, making 976:32-33

Scroll place card, making 287:59-60

Table cloth with hieroglyphics, making 287:57-58

Welcome scribe, making 287:58-59

EGYPT—HOUSES

Adobe or Egyptian mud house, pattern, making 1390:78-80

EGYPT—JEWELRY

Beads, paper beads, magazine pages, making 1633:90-91

Bracelet and pendant jewelry, wire, making 889:33-39

Egyptian collar, making 236:34-37

Pendants, making 287:84-85

Scarab necklace, making 287:82-84

EGYPT—LULLABIES

Khod el Bez 780:43

Nahm, Nahm 780:43

EGYPT—MAGIC TRICKS

Cups and balls, how to do 1270:6-7

EGYPT—NEW YEAR'S DAY

Two New Years in Egypt 489:64-69

EGYPT—NILE RIVER

River Nile scene, milk carton, water and seeds, making 515:46

EGYPT—PUPPETS

Egyptian puppet, making 483:19

EGYPT—PYRAMIDS

Pyramids from Egypt, paper and straws, making 1094:15

EGYPT—RHYMES

Adi El Badah tickling rhyme 780:97

Hag Hogaga Wa Bat Allah baby bouncing rhyme 780:72

Tatah Habah Habah baby lifting rhyme 780:87

Wahad Etnen Talatah baby clapping rhyme 780:60

EGYPT—SHABBAT—COOKERY

Tabooli, cracked wheat salad, recipe 1691:27

EGYPT—SUNDIALS
Sundial, bas relief, making 287:69-71
EGYPT—TOYS
Sagat player from Egypt, history of and how to make
495:81-85
EGYPT, ANCIENT. *See also* **CLEOPATRA; HIERO-
GLYPHICS; MUMMIES; PYRAMIDS**
Ancient Egypt Program; activities, books, crafts, pat-
terns, scripts 1159:12-28
Egypt versus Rome, history, stories, maps, puzzles, ac-
tivities, projects 1041:124-152
EGYPT, ANCIENT—ASP
Asp, making 287:25-26
EGYPT, ANCIENT—BOATS
Boats on Nile carrying mummy, how to draw 717:24-25
Boats on Nile, how to draw 717:24-25
Model ancient Egyptian boat, clay, how to make
1351:30-31
Reed boat, thin reeds, balsa wood, making 1367:44-45
EGYPT, ANCIENT—CARTOUCHE
Cartouche, hieroglyphics name, how to make 699:14-15
EGYPT, ANCIENT—CATS
Cats, how to draw 717:11
EGYPT, ANCIENT—CHARIOTEERS
Charioteers, how to draw 717:8-9
EGYPT, ANCIENT—CHARIOTS
Chariot from balsa wood, dowels, wood, making
1367:48-49
Chariot, war machine, how to make 699:28-31
EGYPT, ANCIENT—CLEOPATRA
Cleopatra costume, making 213:52-54; 287:50-53
EGYPT, ANCIENT—CLOCKS
Shadow clock, driftwood, shells, making 1701:29
Water clock, cups, balsa wood, making 1680:7
EGYPT, ANCIENT—CLOTHING
Egypt garment, basic, making 287:23
Tunic, fabric, how to make 1367:10-11
EGYPT, ANCIENT—COOKERY
Cucumber and yogurt dish, recipe 1723:28-29
Dried fruit salad, recipe 1723:29
Fig cakes, recipe 1367:28-29
Foods and cookery in Ancient Egypt 667:237-261
Ful Medames, beans and lentil breakfast dish, recipe
1723:27-28
Honey date cake, recipe 1723:29
Hummus bi tahini, garbanzo beans and sesame dip, rec-
ipe 1723:27
Radish salad, recipe 1723:28
EGYPT, ANCIENT—COSTUMES
Ancient Day salad, recipe, costume 188:38
Ancient Egyptian costume, girl, making 368:39-48
Cloth collars, felt, fabric, velcro, decorations, making
1680:25
Egyptian man, ancient, costume, making 287:27-31
Headbands, making 287:25
Rameses II's costume, making 287:37-41
Vulture Goddess Nekhbet's costume, making 287:45-50
EGYPT, ANCIENT—CROWNS
Crown, double crown of Egypt, making 870:5-6
Crown, King's crown, how to make 699:22
EGYPT, ANCIENT—FACE MAKEUP
Face makeup, making 287:27
EGYPT, ANCIENT—FARMS
Farm girl, how to draw 717:14

EGYPT, ANCIENT—FESTIVALS
Feast of Opet celebration 566:8-9
Festival of Min 566:9
Festival of Nfin celebration 566:9
Nature festivals information 419:13-18
Osiris grain festival information 419:15-18
EGYPT, ANCIENT—FOOTWEAR
Sandals, cardboard, braided raffia, making 1367:11
EGYPT, ANCIENT—GAMES
Dominoes game 956:135-139
Seega game 956:131-133
Senat: ancient board game, how to make 699:26-27
Senet board game, balsa wood, clay, how to make and
play 1367:32-33
Senet game, how to make 1074:53-55
Tahteab stick game 1119:13-14
Tic-tac-toe stone board and counters game, making 1701:14
EGYPT, ANCIENT—GODS
Anubis, God of City of Dead, clay, wire, paint, making
1367:53
EGYPT, ANCIENT—HAIR
Coiffures hairstyles, making 287:24
EGYPT, ANCIENT—HANDICRAFTS
Fish charm to ward off evil, cardboard, clay, making
1680:13
Pen case, reeds, balsa wood, paints, making 1367:41
**EGYPT, ANCIENT—HARVEST FESTIVALS—
DECORATIONS**
Festival of Min harvest scene and hieroglyphs on oaktag,
making 1249:33-35
EGYPT, ANCIENT—HATS
Hat, Ancient Egyptian hat, paper, pattern, making
823:51-52
EGYPT, ANCIENT—HEADDRESSES
Headdress, Queen's headdress, how to make 699:20-21
Medallion headdress, making 870:4-5
Nefertiti headdress, making 870:1-4
Sphinx headdress, making 870:1-4
Vulture headdress, making 870:9-10
EGYPT, ANCIENT—HIEROGLYPHICS
Hieroglyphics patterns, making 1159:18
Hieroglyphics, how to make 699:12
Hieroglyphs, how to make 717:16
EGYPT, ANCIENT—HOUSES
Egyptian villa, cardboard, plywood, plaster of Paris, mak-
ing 1367:19
EGYPT, ANCIENT—HUNTERS
Boy hunter, how to draw 717:13
EGYPT, ANCIENT—INVENTIONS
Sun pole, how to make 1367:43
Water clock, clay pot, water, making 1367:42-43
EGYPT, ANCIENT—JEWELRY
Beads and pendants, clay, making 1070:69-71
Beads, paper, making 1455:174
Egyptian necklace, colored rolled paper, string, making
1254:29
Falcon pectoral, paper, paints, patterns, making 1367:14-15
Jewelry, making 287:26-27
EGYPT, ANCIENT—KING TUT
King Tut death mask, papier-mache, paints, making
1367:54-55
King Tut's costume, making 287:31-37
King Tutankhamen, how to draw 717:28-29
EGYPT, ANCIENT—KING TUT—COSTUMES
Beaded neck-piece, making 287:35-37

False beard, making 287:34-35
Jeweled Pectoral breastplate, how to make 699:18-19
King Tut's costume, making 287:31-37
Pleated apron, making 287:32-33
Red sash, making 287:31-32
Royal symbols, making 287:37
Traditional headpiece, making 287:33-34
EGYPT, ANCIENT—MUMMIES
Coffin and mummy, cardboard, paint, clay, fabric, making 1680:19
Mummification, how to draw 717:20-21
Mummy and mummy case, making 699:9-11
Mummy case pattern, making 1159:22-23
Mummy case, how to draw 717:22-23
Mummy design to enlarge 1159:17
EGYPT, ANCIENT—MUSICAL INSTRUMENTS
Harp, balsa wood, plastic bottle, dowel, making 1367:30
Sistrum rattle, balsa wood, wire, paint, making 1367:31
EGYPT, ANCIENT—PAINTINGS
Frieze paintings, how to make 699:16-17
EGYPT, ANCIENT—PHARAOH
Pectoral, jeweled, making 699:18-19
Pharaoh and crown, how to draw 717:6-7
Pharaoh costume, making 213:54-55; 870:6-7
Pharaoh's Golden mask, papier-mache, gold paint, making 1486:6-7
Pharaoh, paper, making 46:82-84
EGYPT, ANCIENT—POTTERY
Canopic jar, how to draw 717:21
Clay pot, clay, paints, making 1367:36-37
Pottery vase, clay, making 1070:72-74
EGYPT, ANCIENT—PYRAMIDS
Great Pyramid of Cheops, House of the Dead pyramid, how to make 699:6-8
Pyramid, how to draw 717:27
Pyramids, how built, using ramps to move materials, making 1719:5-6
EGYPT, ANCIENT—QUEENS
Queen Nefertiti's costume, making 287:41-45
Queen of Egypt costume, making 870:7-9
Queen's makeup, how to apply 1367:13
Queen, how to draw 717:10
EGYPT, ANCIENT—RAMESES II—COSTUMES
Apron, making 287:37-38; 287:37-38
Blue and green sash, making 287:38-40; 287:38-40
Double crown, making 287:40; 287:40
Loin cloth, making 287:37; 287:37
Red crown, making 287:40; 287:40
White head piece, making 287:40-41; 287:40-41
EGYPT, ANCIENT—SCRIBES
Scribe, how to draw 717:17
EGYPT, ANCIENT—SCROLLS
Scrolls, how to make 699:13-14
EGYPT, ANCIENT—SEALS
Scarab beetle stamp seal, modeling clay, making 1680:11
Scarab seal, clay, making 1070:74-77
EGYPT, ANCIENT—SLAVES
Egyptian slave instant costume 213:6-8
EGYPT, ANCIENT—SOLDIERS
Foot soldier, how to draw 717:8
EGYPT, ANCIENT—SPHINX
Great Sphinx of Giza, how to draw 717:26
Sphinx paper weight, making 287:85-86
EGYPT, ANCIENT—TEMPLES
Temple of Dendur, making 105:48-58

EGYPT, ANCIENT—THANKSGIVING
History of Thanksgiving 659:24-25
EGYPT, ANCIENT—TOMBS
Burial chamber ticket pattern, making 1159:24
Mummy room arrangement, pattern, making 1159:21
Panels for tomb painting, patterns, making 1159:19-20
Pyramid tomb, making 699:6-8
Tomb painters, how to draw 717:19
Tomb painting, how to draw 717:18
Tomb painting, plaster of Paris, paints, making 1367:38
EGYPT, ANCIENT—TOYS
Toy, crocodile, moveable, how to make 699:23-25
EGYPT, ANCIENT—WEAPONS
Battleaxe, cardboard, foil, making 1367:51
Shield, canvas material, paint, making 1367:50
EGYPT, ANCIENT—WEAVING
Loom, balsa wood, dowels, wool, how to build and use 1367:34-35
EGYPT, ANCIENT—WIGS
Egyptian wig, yarn, fabric, felt, making 367:66; 1680:26-27
Wig, black paper, making 1367:12-13
EHLERT, LOIS
"Growing Vegetable Soup," vegetable soup, recipe 1216:70
EL SALVADOR—COOKERY
Frijoles refritos, recipes 1165:248
Guacamole snack, recipe 1038:89
Nogada, pralines, recipe 1165:249
Pupusas bread, recipe 1287:unp.
Refried beans, recipe 1038:89-90
Rice pudding, recipe 794:6; 967:28
Salad, cabbage and vegetables, recipe 1038:91
EL SALVADOR—COSTUMES
Indian costume, making 515:48
EL SALVADOR—FESTIVALS—COOKERY
Salvador del Mundo; biscochitos (anise cookies), recipe 1666:248
Salvador del Mundo; crema de abacate (avocado whip), recipe 1666:248
Salvador del Mundo; nogada (pralines), recipe 1666:249
EL SALVADOR—GAMES
El Gavilan, la coneja, y los conejos, how to play 1494:78-79
Peregrina, hopscotch game 1426:14-15
EL SALVADOR—LANGUAGE
Spanish phrases, adjectives and names 1038:124-125
ELECTION DAY—GAMES
Election Day game 240:56
ELEPHANTS
India sculptured clay elephant, making 1027:99-101
ELIZABETHAN PERIOD—COSTUMES
Ball gown, making 870:76-78
Beret and imbecile sleeves, 1830-1840, making 870:90-92
Canions and slops, making 870:63-64
Day dress, making 870:74-76; 870:80-83
Dutch waist with wheel farthingale, making 870:61-63
Flounced sleeve, mid 1700's, making 870:89-90
Gown with dropped shoulder line, Stuart Restoration, making 870:64-67
Overgown, making 870:58-61
Regency ball gown, making 870:68-74
Virago sleeve, 1600's, making 870:88-89
Walking dress, making 870:79-80
ELLIS, MARY
"Spaghetti Eddie," spaghetti, recipe 1216:23

ENAMELING
  Enamel painting, tin cans, paints, how to do 1181:92-93
ENGLAND
  Activities, flags, games, songs, dances, recipes
    1381:182-184
ENGLAND—APRIL FOOLS' DAY
  Gowk hunt, making 709:152
  History of April Fools' Day 709:152
ENGLAND—BIRTHDAYS
  Birthday customs 488:40-43
  Jolly Old England birthday celebration, activities, foods,
    and handicrafts 30:73-76
  Key to the house twenty-first birthday celebration
    660:65-67
ENGLAND—CASTLES
  Castle from England model, paper and cans, making
    1094:11
ENGLAND—CHRISTMAS
  Boxing Day; history and celebration of 496:111
  Carols, facts about 496:108-109
  Christmas card, facts about 496:105-106
  Christmas customs in England 149:34-40; 497:103;
    1717:16-17
  Christmas, history in the British Isles, 704:17-19
  Christmas tree and decorations, how to make 593:28-35
  Christmas tree information 496:104
  Crib, facts about 496:105
  Customs of Christmas in England 425:19-20; 473:20-27;
    474:151-153
  Evergreens, facts about 496:109-110
  Food and drink, facts about 496:106-108
  Mistletoe ball from fresh greens, making 273:5-8
  Traditional Christmas customs in England 218:41-42
ENGLAND—CHRISTMAS—COOKERY
  Apple yule logs, recipe 1224:77
  Bishop's cup drink, recipe 1128:29
  Bran gift pie, making 51:321
  Brussels sprouts with almonds, recipe 1224:76
  Butter shortbread, recipe 1224:78
  Chestnuts and brussel sprouts, recipe 1666:107-108
  Christmas pudding, carrots and old ale, recipe 149:131
  Christmas pudding, King George I, recipe 149:131
  Christmas pudding, recipe 1224:78; 1666:106
  Coventry Godcakes, recipe 1128:30
  Eggnog, recipe 704:21
  English walnut bread, recipe 218:61-62
  Fruitcake, recipe 1224:79
  Fruitcakes, individual English fruitcakes, recipe 704:22-23
  Hard sauce, recipe 1128:28
  Hot mulled cider, recipe 273:13-14
  Lamb's wool punch, recipe 1128:22-23
  Lemon mint hard sauce, recipe 497:100
  Mincemeat pie, recipe 1224:77
  Mincemeat tartlets, recipe, 497:100
  Mincemeat-filled cookies, recipe 273:8-1 1
  Mincemeat, recipe 1224:76
  Mincemeat, with or without meat, recipe 1128:23-24
  Pavlova, recipe 497:100
  Plum pudding with hard sauce, recipe 704:24-29
  Plum pudding, recipe 497:100; 1128:26-27
  Roast beef, horseradish sauce, recipe 1128:21
  Roast goose with sage and onion stuffing, recipes, mak-
    ing 1128:22
  Roast potatoes, recipe 1224:76
  Roasted and boiled chestnuts, recipe 1666:107

  Trifle, recipe 1224:79
  Twelfth Day cake, recipe 1128:29
  Wassail bowl Christmas punch, recipe 497:101; 703:95;
    1128:25
  Yorkshire pudding, recipe 1128:21
ENGLAND—CHRISTMAS—DECORATIONS
  Butterfly, red foil, paper, pipe cleaner, making 1224:72
  Concertina, paper, making 1224:75
  Robin redbreast, paper, paint, making 1224:73
ENGLAND—CHRISTMAS—HANDICRAFTS
  English crackers, Christmas tree ornaments, making
    795:18
  English holly place cards, paper, making 704:20
  English pomander, orange, cloves, ribbons, making
    273:11-13; 1575:6-7
  Kissing ball, making 672:37-45
  Pearlies, Christmas tree ornaments, making 795:16
  Stockings, Christmas stockings from England, making
    795:3-4
  Victorian fan decoration, making 272:18-20
  Walnut shell cradle, making 273:15-18
ENGLAND—COOKERY
  Afternoon tea, making 437:32
  Apple crumble, recipe 1273:42-43
  Apples, baked with custard, recipe 1620:37
  Boxty on the pan (pancakes), recipe 88:124
  Bread and raisin pudding, recipe 530:32-33
  Browned roast potatoes, recipe 437:24
  Bubble and squeak vegetable dish, recipe 1273:38-39
  Bubble and squeak with a wow-wow sauce, recipe
    1650:26
  Bubble and squeak, recipe 1165:122-123
  Cheese straws treat, recipe 1380:14
  Chops with herbs, English style, recipe 514:132-133
  Christening cake, recipe 1220:128-129
  Cock-a-Leckie soup, recipe 530:28-30
  Coventry Godcakes, cookies, recipe 72:34-36
  Cucumber tea sandwiches, recipe 1165:121-122
  Custard, recipe 437:31
  Egg mornay, recipe 967:50
  Fish and chips, recipe 1380:37; 1452:52
  Fried bread, recipe 437:16
  Frumenty, recipe 659:37
  Gooseberry fool dessert, recipe 1650:38
  Guy Fawkes cake, recipe 88:122-123
  Halibut or haddock, poached, recipe 437:21
  History of cookery in 88:111-119
  Hot cross buns, recipe 492:81-83
  Kedgeree, recipe 437:18; 820:11
  Lamb, roasted, mint sauce, recipe 820:24-25
  Lamb-burgers with bacon, recipe 662:51-53
  Lancashire hot pot, recipe 437:23; 820:35
  Lancashire stew, recipe 1452:53
  Lemon scones, recipe 1361:49
  Lentil and vegetable stew, recipe 1313:140
  Mackerel or trout, baked, recipe 437:41
  Mushrooms on toast recipe 437:17; 1652:25
  Oatmeal bread cottage loaves, recipe 492:27-30
  Old English Wassail drink, recipe 1495:75
  Pancakes, recipe 820:38
  Peanut brittle, recipe 874:80
  Popovers, recipe 514:142
  Queen of puddings, recipe 858:unp; 1165:124
  Roast beef, recipe 437:24
  Royal Tea party cucumber sandwiches, recipe 1528:22

Royal Tea party trifle, recipe 1528:21-22
Royal Tea party, recipes, handicrafts 1528:21-23
Sandwich cake, recipe 1489:22-23
Scones, English baking powder biscuits, recipe 1165:122
Scones, recipe 437:35; 1380:6; 1452:56; 1455:126;
    1628:13
Shepherd's pie, meat and vegetable casserole, recipe
    437:43; 871:28-30; 1165:123; 1273:35-37; 1620:37
Short pastry (bread), recipe 437:31; 437:33; 1452:55
Shrovetide pancakes, recipe 88:121-122
Simnel cake, recipe 364:130-136
Soup, mixed vegetable, recipe 1620:37
Stargazy pie, tuna, eggs, pie crust, recipe 1650:35
Steak and kidney pie, recipe 820:31-32; 1322:119
Steak and mushroom pie, recipe 895:56-57
Steamed pudding, recipe 1472:13-14
Sugar crisps, recipe 1381:183
Summer pudding dessert, recipe 437:27; 820:14;
    1280:40; 1560:7
Sunday noon dinner, recipe 820:24-25
Tea and sugar crisps, recipe 188:21
Tea sandwiches, recipe 793:31
Toad in the hole sausages in batter, recipe 1113:34-35
Toad-in-the-hole, recipe 437:38; 530:30-31
Toast toppers, recipe 1244:69
Treacle tart, recipe 437:29
Trifle dessert, recipe 1452:57
Trifle pudding, recipe 895:58-59
Trifle, recipe 437:30; 557:49; 794:19
Trifle; strawberry and lemon whim-wham, recipe 1273:44
Victoria sandwich, recipe 437:36
Welsh rabbit, recipe 1628:12
Welsh rarebit, recipe 437:41; 820:43; 1273:40-41
Yorkshire parkin, recipe 967:50
Yorkshire pudding, recipe 437:26; 446:29-30; 1381:183;
    1452:54

ENGLAND—COSTUMES
Duke of Wellington hat, making 1174:140
Friar Tuck costume 213:70-71
Henry VIII costume, fabric, patterns, making 1174:30-32
King John costume 213:69
King Richard costume 213:72-74
King, Lady in Waiting, Court Jester, fabric, notions, pat-
    terns, making 1435:17-32
Maid Marian costume 213:72
Merlin the Magician, fabric, notions, patterns, making
    1435:27-28
Occupational costumes, English, pictures of costumes
    313:10-20
Pearlies, making 856:81-83
Pedlar costume, girl, 19th century, making 368:15-20
Queen Elizabeth costume 213:90-92
Queen Elizabeth I costume, fabric, patterns, making
    1174:33-35
Robin Hood and Maid Marion, fabric, notions, patterns,
    making 1435:21-23; 213:66-69
Sir Walter Raleigh costume 213:92-94
St. George costume, fabric, patterns, making 1174:44-46
Tea and sugar crisps, recipe, costume 188:21
Traditional costumes, English, pictures of costumes
    313:21-30
Tudor costume, girl, making 368:59-68

ENGLAND—DANCES
Country dance and costume picture 1000:14-17
Description of English dances 313:31-37

Morris dance bell anklet, how to make 1448:26-27
Pop goes the Weasel, how to do 1494:123-124

ENGLAND—DECORATIONS
Royal Tea party scepters, paper, glitter, making 1528:23

ENGLAND—DOLLS
Billingsgate fishwife (early nineteenth century), making
    59:37-40
Cavalier, laughing, 1645, making 59:31-33
Corn doll, wheat and rye straw, thread, making 1467:25
Fortune telling doll, making 775:88-95
Indian brave wishbone doll, making 298:166-167
Investiture of HRH Prince Charles, Prince of Wales, July
    1, 1969, making 59:80-85
Peddler doll, making 775:58-67
Pikeman, 1660, making 59:34-36
Quaker clothespin doll, making 626:44-46

ENGLAND—DRAMA
Miss Jennie Jones 474:90-92
Punch and Judy show 474:96-98

ENGLAND—EASTER
Beasts' Thorn, traditional tale from England 139:96-99
Easter egg customs in England 201:21-22
First Catch Your Hare 139:116
Ham custom 503:24
Lifting and heaving custom 503:49

ENGLAND—EASTER—GAMES
Nine Men's Morris game, cardboard, wood, paint, mak-
    ing 1245:14-15

ENGLAND—EASTER—HANDICRAFTS
Maundy Thursday maundy purse, felt, soft leather, mak-
    ing 1245:17
Pace eggs, patterned eggs, how to make 1489:20

ENGLAND—EDWARDIAN ERA—COOKERY. See
    MARY POPPINS—COOKERY

ENGLAND—FESTIVALS
Beatrix Potter's birthday; celebrate with rabbit in sign
    language activity 1199:170
Bonfire Day celebration 601:88-89
Corn Festival celebration 659:32-36
Drama festivals in Great Britain 474:17-19
Green Thursday 139:72
Guy Fawkes Day celebration 631:88
Guy Fawkes Day finger plays 54:217
Guy Fawkes Day, history of 709:35
Guy Fawkes Day, Yeoman of the Guard Hunt celebra-
    tion 709:36
Guy Fawkes Day; celebrate by making a stuffed Guy, old
    clothes, stuffing 1199:256-257
Guy Fawkes Night Bonfire Night; history and celebration
    of 496:90-91
Harvest Corn Dolly; corn husks, making 1476:74-75
Harvest Festivals; history and celebration of 496:83-85
Lord Mayor's Show, history and celebration of 496:94-
    96 139:48
Mardi Gras pankace race, and costumes, making 139:48
Maundy Thursday 139:71
May Day celebration, activities, handicrafts, foods,
    songs, making 601:89-90; 909:49-57
May Day crowns 557:48
May Day dance 557:47
May Day Morris Dancers information 419:55-56;
    566:16-17
May Day, crafts, foods, games, making 557:45-51
May Day, Morris Dancers celebrations 826:12-13
Maypole dance celebration 631:32

Maypole, information 566:16-17
Mid-summer Day jump the flame, making 709:179-180
Mid-summer Day, history of 709:179
Mothering Sunday Birth of Simnel cake; story and recipe for cake given, making 364:130-136
Once Every Pancake Day 139:44
Pancake Day or Shrove Tuesday, activities, art, songs, recipes, games 1469:72-73
Pancake race 139:48
Pentecost, Morris Dancers celebrations 826:12-13
Queen's Official Birthday; celebration of 496:72-73
Remembrance Day Veteran's Day; History and celebration of 496:92-93
Sandwich Day; activities, art, songs, recipes, games 1469:34-35
Shakespeare's birthday celebration; make diorama of stage setting 1199:89-90
Shrove Tuesday (Pancake Day); recipe for Shrovetide and fly-off-the-plate pancakes 364:125-129
St. John's Day mazes, making 709:183-184
St. John's Day, history of 709:179
St. Swithin's Day; history and celebration of 496:80
Twelfth Night Festival, history of 709:122
Westminster Greeze 139:45
Whitsuntide celebration 601:106-107

ENGLAND—FESTIVALS—COOKERY
Guy Fawkes Day parkin cake, recipe 384:Nov5
Guy Fawkes Day sweet potato pudding, recipe 54:216
Kings', or Twelfth Night cake, recipe 1643:81
Mardi Gras pancakes, recipe 709:139
May Day trifle, recipe 557:49
Pancakes, recipe 139:46-47
Wassail drink, recipe 1403:31

ENGLAND—FESTIVALS—DANCES
April Fools' Day; there was a man and he was mad 624:20-21

ENGLAND—FESTIVALS—DECORATIONS
May First pressed flower card, making 1539:94-95

ENGLAND—FESTIVALS—GAMES
May Day games 557:49-50

ENGLAND—FESTIVALS—HANDICRAFTS
Guy Fawkes Day Beefeater's medal, making 709:37
Guy Fawkes Day firecracker candies, making 709:37
Harvest Festival Kern maiden, making 709:50
May Day baskets, making 557:46; 626:39-41
May Day flowers, paper, making 557:46
Twelfth Night Festival, Twelve Days of Christmas mobile, making 709:122-125

ENGLAND—FLAG
Pattern for flag 557:51

ENGLAND—FOLKLORE
Boil or Bake a Simnel Cake, traditional tale, Shropshire, England 139:54-57
"Cat and the Mouse" flannel board story, patterns, making 1604:35-39
"Cat and the Mouse," flannel board patterns, making 1201:39-44
"Five Little Chickens" flannel board rhyme, patterns, making 1603:11-13
"Gingerbread Boy," flannel board patterns, making 1201:76-83
"Henny Penny" flannel board, story, patterns, making 1603:56-60
"Johnny-Cake" flannel board story, patterns, making 1603:32-38

King Arthur's castle, boxes, tubes, making 1311:84-85
"Lazy Jack" flannel board story, patterns, making 910:13, 46; 1604:109-110
"Little Red Hen" flannel board story, patterns, making 1603:87-91
"Master of All Masters" flannel board story, patterns, making 1603:112-115
"Old Woman and Her Pig" flannel board story, patterns, making 1603:69-74
"Out! Witch! Out!," traditional tale from England 139:73-76
Robin Hood's quiver and arrows, cardboard tubes, patterns, making 1311:130-131
"Strange Visitor" flannel board story, patterns, making 1201:94-99; 1603:134-139
"Teeny Tiny Woman," flannel board patterns, making 1201:14-18; 1604:57-59
"This Is the House That Jack Built" flannel board story, patterns, making 1603:39-43
"Three Bears" flannel board story, patterns, making 1604:29-34
"Three Little Pigs" flannel board story, patterns, making 1603:80-86
"Travels of a Fox" flannel board story, patterns, making 1604:89-91
"Well of the World's End," flannel board, patterns, making 1201:105-111

ENGLAND—FOLKLORE—COOKERY
Birth of Simnel cake; story and recipe for cake, making 364:130-136
Pancake Day; recipe for Shrovetide and Fly off the Plate pancakes 364:125-129

ENGLAND—FOLKLORE—COSTUMES
Friar Tuck costume, making 366:18-19
Friar Tuck, variety of old clothes, making 1656:137-140
Little Match Girl costume, making 366:87
Merlin, black felt, gold vinyl, gold cord, patterns, making 1656:145-150
Robin Hood costume, fabric, pattern, making 366:15-17; 367:22-25; 1174:107; 1379:15
Robin Hood, variety of old clothes, making 1656:133-136

ENGLAND—FOLKLORE—PUPPETS
Chicken Licken cardboard cut out puppet, making 753:41
Little Red Hen paper wrap around puppet, making 753:34
Robin Hood and Little John puppet show 756:100-107

ENGLAND—GAMES
All Fours (Seven Up) card game 1132:89-91
Allee Allee Oh musical game 1116:20
Arithmetic croquet game, making 1507:63-64
Barley break, last man in hell chasing game, how to play 602:106-107; 1498:40
Blackout card game 1132:81-82
Bowler bash game 1146:42-43
Bowl's game 956:44-45
Brass ring game 956:40-41
British bobby game, how to play 1628:23
British bulldog tag game, how to play 1708:26-27
Bunny hops game, how to play 1499:32-34
Casino card game 1132:85-87
Charades game 956:98-99
Conkers game, how to make 1074:168-169

Conkers, horse chestnut and string game, how to play 1477:108; 1501:31-32
Continental draughts board game, patterns, making 1541:203-207
Cribbage game, how to make 1074:118-123; 1132:82-85
Diagonal draughts board game, patterns, making 1541:202
Dodge ball, how to play 1497:43-44
Dominoes, how to play 1628:21-22
Draughts board game, patterns, making 1541:195-200
Draughts for three board game, patterns, making 1541:208-213
Draw a pail of water chanting game 1118:38-41
Dumb Crambo game 956:100
Fingers and toes rhyming game 1118:6-7
Five Men's Morris game, how to play 1688:42-45
Forceball game, how to play 1497:41
Fox and geese game 383:76; 572:38-39
Fox in the hole game 383:75
Game of goose board game, patterns, making 1541:19-27
Half-ball bowling game, how to play 1651:84-85
Hare and Hounds board game, patterns, making 1541:183-188
Here we go round the mulberry bush chanting game 1118:26
Hide and seek game 557:50
Hit the bucket game 383:75
Jingling tag game, how to play 1498:20
Kickery game 602:107
Leapfrog game, how to play 1507:65
London Bridge game 1074:229
Loser draughts board game, patterns, making 1541:201-202
Ludo board game, patterns, making 1541:49-52
Monday, Tuesday game, how to play 1497:25-26
Muffin Man game 602:107-108
Mulberry bush game 602:108-109
Musical chairs game 557:49
Nap (Napoleon) card game 1132:88-89
Newmarket (Michigan) card game 1063:88-94; 1132:91-92
Nine Holes games, how to play 1688:25-29
Nine Men Morris game 383:77; 805:36; 876:72-73; 1354:165
Nine Men Morris game, board, making 1350:83
Nine Men Morris game, cardboard, wood, paint, making 1245:14-15
Ninepins and Tenpins, how to play 1497:19-21
Parson's cat game 984:37
Pass and catch game, how to play 1497:34-35
Pass the fox game 1078:31
Penny pitch game 1146:28-29
Poor Mary sits a'weeping chanting game 1118:30-32
Prisoner's base game 956:9-10; 1074:217
Queen's Guard board game, patterns, making 1541:129-136
Quoits game, how to make 1074:170-172
Rainbow tag game 967:50
Reversi board game, patterns, making 1541:214-218
Ring a ring a roses chanting game 1118:20
Ring-on-a-string game, how to play 1501:32-33
Ring taw marble game 1119:26-27
Ring the Bull game, how to make 1074:237
Round and Round the Village chanting game 1118:28-29
Royal Casino card game 1132:88

Saxon and dragon rope game, how to play 1501:24
Scotland Yard game 58:24-25
Shove Ha'penny game, how to make 1074:31-37; 1628:23
Sir Tommy game 956:150-151
Sir Tommy game, how to play 1507:66
Snail Whorl game, how to play 1494:110-111
Snakes and Ladders board game, patterns, making 1541:53-60
Snip-snap-snorem game 956:107
Solitaire board game, patterns, making 1541:85-90
Spillikins or pick-up-sticks game, dowels, paints, making 1477:107
Stealing Sticks game, how to play 1381:190
Steeplechase board game, patterns, making 1541:119-127
Stoolball game 956:50
Stroke marble game 1119:32-33
Tiddly winks game, how to play 1628:22-23
Trapball, how to play 1497:18
Tug of war rope game, how to play 1501:21
What's the Time, Mr. Wolf? tag game, how to play 1498:23-27
Whist card game 1132:79-80
Widdy game 979:40

ENGLAND—HALLOWEEN—DANCES
There was an old witch 624:39-42

ENGLAND—HALLOWEEN—GAMES
Apple peel fortune game 709:33
Walnut boat race game, making 709:33-34

ENGLAND—HANDICRAFTS
Beaded posies, making 298:70-71
Bowl of fruit tinsel painting, making 298:184-185
Bracelet, Dorset button bracelet patterns, making 1016:86-91
Crusader design tile, clay, making 1070:78-80
Flowers in pots, paper, making 515:116
Multiplying peep box, making 889:138-143
Pace eggs, making 627:88-89
Primitive cooking pot, clay, making 1070:89-90
Rocking horses, cardboard model, making 1338:86-88
Southern Highlanders' wood pretties, making 626:42-43
Theorum pineapple stencil printing, making 298:178-179
Topiary animal, making 525:18-19
Tudor rose mug clay, making 1070:85-89

ENGLAND—HARVEST FESTIVALS—HANDICRAFTS
Harvest Home or Ingathering Festival corn husk doll, making 1249:30-32

ENGLAND—HISTORY—14TH CENTURY—COSTUMES
Bonnets, plain, making 870:134-136
Calash, soft, making 870:133-134
Collar, plain lace collar and underpropper, making 870:144-146
Dogberry cap, making 870:132-133
Dorothy bag and miser purse, making 870:148-150
Fontange, making 870:136-137
Hennins, making 870:131-132
Mob cap, making 870:137-138
Pouch, making 870:146-148
Ruffs, making 870:140-144
Shoe with long pointed toe, making 870:128-129
Tudor cap, making 870:129-131
Tudor slipper, making 870:128
Victorian maid's cap, making 870:138-140

ENGLAND—HISTORY—16TH CENTURY—COOKERY
Chicken blancmange, recipe 1724:27-28
Fava beans and bacon, recipe 1724:28-29
Pain perdu, French toast, recipe 1724:27
Roasted apples, recipe 1724:29

ENGLAND—HISTORY—20TH CENTURY—COOKERY
Chocolate muffins, recipe 1624:28-29
Kedgeree, fish, rice, eggs, curry, recipe 1624:28

ENGLAND—HOUSES
Devon cottage, clay, making 1070:80-85
English cottage, pattern, making 1390:78-79

ENGLAND—KITES
Roller kite, making 1069:210-215
Triple Yakko Stakk kite, making 1069:207-209

ENGLAND—LENT
Holy Miles, based on a traditional tale from England 139:89-92

ENGLAND—LULLABIES
Rock-a-Bye Baby, Thy Cradle Is Green 780:34

ENGLAND—MUSICAL INSTRUMENTS
Buzz disk instruments, paper plates, string, patterns, making 1646:39-41-42

ENGLAND—NEW YEAR'S DAY
Fun, food in Great Britain 489:36-43

ENGLAND—NEW YEAR'S DAY—DANCES
New Year bells dance 624:5-7

ENGLAND—PARLIAMENT
State opening of Parliament; history and celebration of 496:89

ENGLAND—POETRY
"Old Mother Hubbard" flannel board rhyme, patterns, making 1603:23-28

ENGLAND—PUPPETS
Bailiff's Daughter of Islington puppet show 756:107-110
Golden Glove puppet show 756:119-122
Lady Clare puppet show 756:114-119
Lochinvar puppet show 756:111-114
Moy Castle puppet show 756:123-129
Papier-mache glove puppets, making 1707:11

ENGLAND—RHYMES
Ride a Cock Horse baby bouncing rhyme 780:70
Trot, Trot, Trot baby bouncing rhyme 780:71

ENGLAND—SCIENCE
Demonstrate Newton's law of inertia 1719:31
Mining for crystals 1719:33

ENGLAND—SONGS
Ah, Poor Bird round song 1115:85
Christmas Is Coming round song 1115:87
Come Follow round song 1115:18
Derry Ding Dason round song 1115:30
Ding Dong Bell round song 1115:37
Duchess at Tea round song 1115:75
"Eeny Meeny" 1607:36
Goose round song 1115:32
Great Tom Is Cast round song 1115:37
Hart He Loves the High Wood round song 1115:40
Here Lie the Bones of Lazy Fred round song 1115:52
Hot Cross Buns, traditional English rhyme (song) 139:79
I-Tiddly-I-Ti, traditional song, England 139:163
Let Simon's Beard Alone round song 1115:55
Little Bell at Westminster round song 1115:36
Man with a Wry Nose round song 1115:81
"Ride a Cock Horse" 1607:43
Ride a Cock Horse to Banbury Cross round song 1115:39

Summer Is A-coming In round song 1115:41

ENGLAND—STRING FIGURES
Broom, Candle Caper, Dogs-on-a-Leash, Church Window, Upside Down Cradle 1404:38-123

ENGLAND—TEA
Tea time in England 474:134-137

ENGLAND—TOYS
Alphabet blocks, wooden, pattern, making 1027:26-28
Cup on a stick, wooden, making 1027:28-30
Jack-in-the-Box, cardboard, pattern, making 1027:21-25
Top, making 297:210

ENGLAND—VICTORIAN AGE—COOKERY
Mutton cutlets, recipe 1721:28

ENVIRONMENT
Neighborhood checklist for care of environment 310:233
Personal checklist for care of environment 310:233

EPIPHANY. *See also* **TWELFTH NIGHT**
Celebration of Epiphany or Twelfth Night 496:23-24
Mitten tree, how to make 1199:5

EPIPHANY—COOKERY
Epiphany cake, recipe 635:32-33

EPIPHANY—TWELFTH NIGHT
Adoration of the Magi 475:102-104
Feast of Lights 475:106-107
Feast of the Epiphany at Greek Orthodox Church 475:105-106
Star song, words 475:102-104

EQUATORIAL GUINEA—COOKERY
Fish, grilled, recipe 895:45
Meat stew, recipe 895:46
Pepper soup, recipe 895:47
Pick-a-pepper soup, recipe 1198:30; 1650:24

EQUATORIAL GUINEA—GAMES
Catching stars game, how to play 1507:15

ERECTOR SETS
History of 511:161-164

ERIKSON, LEIF
Leif Erikson Day; celebrate by making Viking helmet and shield 1199:229-232

ESKIMO PIES
History of 119:184-187

ESKIMOS. *See also* **INUIT INDIANS**
Activities, patterns, games 50:89-144
Andrews, Jan, "The Very Last First Day"; science, reading, art activities 1055:144-149
Computer project: picture story, Arctic 1218:16-19
Culture unit, language, dress, foods, games, bibliographies 574:84-101
Eskimo, paper, large pattern, making 478:58-62

ESKIMOS—CARVING
Carving, soapstone, how to do 168:86-98
Carvings, bear and whale soap carvings, making 708:26-27
Soap carving, how to do 524:14-15; 1316:35; 1381:21
Soapstone carving, large cake of soap, making 1296:113
Soapstone carvings, clay, making 1338:27-29

ESKIMOS—CHRISTMAS
Christmas celebration 601:150

ESKIMOS—CLOTHING
Capes, making 574:89
Clothing, man and woman making 307:13
Man's tunic and breeches, pattern, making 281:50-51
Mittens, laced, paper, making 909:151
Mittens, making 482:104-105

71

Parka, making 574:88
Woman's bodice and hood, pattern, making 281:52

ESKIMOS—COOKERY
Agutak ice cream, recipe 424:90-91
Beef jerky, recipe 909:155
Foods of the native Alaskans information 666:247-252
Ice cream (augutak), recipe 574:86
Inuit ice cream, recipe 1527:62
Inupiat food words 424:85-87
Snow ice cream, recipe 574:91

ESKIMOS—COSTUMES
Costumes of Eskimos, making 281:49-53
Eskimos costumes drawing 988:53

ESKIMOS—DESIGNS
Designs for crafts 168:104-109

ESKIMOS—DOG SLED
Dog sled, making 168:66-73

ESKIMOS—DOLLS
Dolls, making 708:28-31
Eskimo doll, and igloo, making 494:38-49
Eskimo dolls, newspaper, glue, fur scraps, making 1338:110-112
Eskimo mother and baby and father, making 59:20-25
Figure dolls, making 168:19-25
Ookpiks, dolls, making 168:12-19

ESKIMOS—EMBROIDERY
Line embroidery, making 168:99-103

ESKIMOS—FESTIVALS
Asking Festival 474:146-147
Eskimo-Indian Olympics, activities, handicrafts, foods, songs, making 909:149-157
Inviting-In-Feast 574:97
North Star Day 574:97
Return of the Sun ceremony celebration 601:124

ESKIMOS—FOOTWEAR
Mukluks, making 574:88
Mukluks, paper bag, making 909:151
Snowshoes; Alaskan Eskimo snowshoes, making 466:126-127; 574:88

ESKIMOS—GAMES
Ajaqaq game 572:32-33
Ajegaung (holes and pin game), making 708:18
Ayagak game, making 307:44
Bilboquet cup and ball game, how to make 1074:252-253
Cat's cradle string game, how to play 1316:30
Catch the bag game 602:171
Eskimo buzz board game, making 445:35-39
Eskimo Olympics 376:90
Follow the leader game 602:170
Football 602:170
Harpoon the seal game, making 631:70-71
Inuit ajaqaq toss and catch game, canning jar rings, stick, making 1478:64
Juggling game, how to play 1699:126
Muk, silence game 376:91
Musk oxen game 602:169-170
Nuglutang game 956:47-48
Rotating balls (yo-yo), making 708:16-17
Sled games 376:91
Snow football game 58:10-11
Spear the whale game 383:20-21
Spinning tops, how to play 1494:178
Spinning tops, Kaipsak game 376 91:
String game magic tricks, how to do 856:135-137

Tingmiujang (images of birds), dice game, making 708:18-19
Toss and catch game, making 445:77-85

ESKIMOS—GOGGLES
Snow goggles, making 466:120-121; 574:89

ESKIMOS—HANDICRAFTS
Engraving, how to do 168:26-37; 708:6-7
Needlecase from bones, making 229:81-83

ESKIMOS—HOUSES
Double decker snow house, making 1312:15
Igloo from blown egg, making 677:18
Igloo from Greenland with Eskimo, kayak and penguin models, clay, making 1094:51-53
Igloo, model, making 307:44
Igloos 469:14-17
Snow house, making 574:86; 708:22-25
Subterranean house, making 574:86

ESKIMOS—HUNTING
Hunting ice scoop, making 708:20-21

ESKIMOS—JEWELRY
Whale tooth necklaces, styrofoam, making 909:151

ESKIMOS—KAYAKS
Kayak, making 168:58-66; 307:45
Kayak, waterproof, making 708:10-13

ESKIMOS—LANGUAGE
Inupiaq Eskimo words 1406:38
Inupiat food words 424:85-87
Language and numbers 307:46

ESKIMOS—LEATHER
Applique patch, making 168:52-54
Applique pen and pencil holder, making 168:54-57

ESKIMOS—MASKS
Alaskan Eskimo mask 204:98-101
Alaskan Eskimo masks, history of 327:36-38
Eighteenth century Alaskan Eskimo mask, carved wood, making 673:239-253
Eskimo bone mask, making 229:75-78
Eskimo mask, finger masks and easy masks, making 327:40-44
Eskimo masks, making 168:38-46; 327:38-44; 708:14-15
Eskimo papier-mache mask, making 755:91-108
Eskimo spirit mask paper plate, making 480:124
Finger masks to act out a story, modeling clay, paints, making 63:24-25; 1486:12-13
Inuit finger masks, posterboard, patterns, making 1633:26-27
Laughing mask, shoebox lid, tongue depressors, patterns, making 1633:28-29
Spirit mask, making 596:41-45

ESKIMOS—MUSICAL INSTRUMENTS
Drum, embroidery hoop, plastic wrap, stick, making 1296:113

ESKIMOS—NETS
Nets, making 574:90

ESKIMOS—ORNAMENTS
Ornaments, sea mammal tooth, necklace, worry hunting hat, making 708:8-9

ESKIMOS—PUPPET PLAYS
Nerrivik, Old Woman of the Sea 4:74-77

ESKIMOS—PUPPETS
Eskimo finger puppet, making 128:41
Eskimo girl puppet, paper bag, patterns, making 940:23

ESKIMOS—SLEDS
Attic hand sled, making 466:122-123
Komatik sled, wooden, making 574:90
Sled or Komatik, making 467:48-49

ESKIMOS—STENCIL PRINTS
Making 168:74-85
ESKIMOS—STORYTELLING
Drawing stories in sand, snow, or mud 1522:119-120
ESKIMOS—STRING FIGURES
Siberian house and two Eskimos running away, making 423:22-23
ESKIMOS—TOOLS
Bow drill, making 466:128-129
ESKIMOS—TOYS
Bull roarer, wood and plastic, pattern, making 1027:120-123
Early bird toy, making 482:74-75
Mouse, animated toy, making 482:74-75
Spear the fish, history of and how to make 495:32-35
ESTONIA—EASTER—COOKERY
Lemon sauce, recipe 1666:134
Potato and apple pudding, recipe 1666:133
Sweet apple bread pudding, recipe 1666:134
ETHIOPIA—CHRISTMAS
Christmas customs in Ethiopia 1717:12-13
Christmas game 601:30-31
ETHIOPIA—COOKERY
Doro wat, chicken stew, recipe 1165:8; 1336:121
Injera, flat bread, recipe 88:38-40; 1022:46
Injera, thin round Ethiopian bread, recipe 1165:8-9
Luku, chicken dish, recipe 1198:37
Meat-eating habits in Ethiopia 662:80-81
Spicy bits (chiko), cookies, recipe 72:91-92
Toasted wheat berries, recipe 1244:90
ETHIOPIA—FESTIVALS
New Year's Day, time of daffodils 489:70-73
New Year's Eve celebration 601:22-23
New Year's Eve celebration street song, Hoya-Hoye 1116:42-43
ETHIOPIA—FESTIVALS—COOKERY
Maskal, alecha (lamb and chicken stew), recipe 1666:7-8
Maskal, injera (Ethiopian flat bread), recipe 1666:8
Maskal, yemiser selatta (lentil salad), recipe 1666:8-9
ETHIOPIA—FOLKLORE—HANDICRAFTS
Jackal's Lawsuit 126:22-25
Jackal's Lawsuit, aluminum foil relief, making 126:26-27
Jackal's Lawsuit, macrame chain, making 126:29-30
Jackal's Lawsuit, stone amulet, making 126:27-29
ETHIOPIA—GAMES
Cock-a-Loo game 515:50
Cock-a-Loo tag, how to play 1498:15
Crow caws game 967:29
Gabata, mancala game, how to make and play 1708:22-23
Hoya-Hoye musical game 1116:42-43
Spear dance game 602:26
ETHIOPIA—HANDICRAFTS
Wish scroll, film containers, pony beads, making 1332:35-38
ETHIOPIA—SONGS
Ushururu, lullaby 1220:149
ETS, MARIE HALL
"Nine Days to Christmas," nachos, recipe 843:66
EUROPE
Activities, flags, games, songs, dances, recipes 1381:157-216

EUROPE—CHRISTMAS
Christmas celebrations 601:100
Christmas greeting words of countries of Europe 601:118-119
EUROPE—EASTER
Easter celebrations 601:97
EUROPE—FESTIVALS
Carnival celebrations 601:94-95
Palm Sunday celebrations 601:96
Saint John's Day celebrations 601:98
Shrove Tuesday celebrations 601:95-96
St. Martin's Day, harvest festival celebration 659:103-105
St. Nicholas Day; celebrate by making shepherd's staffs from food 1199:276
EUROPE—FOLKLORE
Funny Little Bunny Who Just Loved Honey, flannel board patterns, making 910:9,42
EUROPE—GAMES
Accordion card game 1132:76-77
Asalto board game, patterns, making 1074:94-95; 1541:174-178
Authors card game 1132:62-63
Backgammon board game, patterns, making 1541:219-229
Black Lady card game 1132:65
Calculation card game 1132:77-78
Chinese Checkers board game, patterns, making 1541:100-108
Chinese Rebel board game, patterns, making 1541:179-182
Clock card game 1132:73-74
Eights (Crazy Eights) card game 1132:67-68
Fan Tan card game 1132:65-67
Fox and Geese board game, patterns, making 1541:167-173
Game of Goose board game, patterns, making 1541:19-27
Halma board game, patterns, making 1541:91-99
Hearts card game 1132:63-65
Klondike card game 1132:69-71
Klondike for 2 (Double Solitaire) card game 1132:72
La Belle Loucie card game 1132:74-76
Old Maid card game 1132:61-62
War card game 1132:60-61
EUROPE—HANDICRAFTS
Jeweled crown, paper, foil decals, tinsel, ribbons, patterns, making 1648:13
EUROPE—HISTORY—16TH CENTURY—COOKERY
Chicken blancmange, recipe 1724:27-28
Fava beans and bacon, recipe 1724:28-29
Pain perdu, French toast, recipe 1724:27
Roasted apples, recipe 1724:29
EUROPE—HISTORY—HANDICRAFTS
Newsbook, 15th and 16th Century Europe, making 1332:113-118
EUROPE—HOUSES
Early earth lodges 469:56-57
Early farm houses 469:58-59
Stone houses 469:54-55
Timber framed hut, wood, dowels, craft sticks, making 1512:8-9

EUROPE—MASKS
Commedia Del-l'Arte mask, papier-mache, plaster of Paris, paints, making 1706:13
European Festival masks 204:77-80
EUROPE—NAMES
Baby names information 695:123-124
EUROPE—NEW YEAR
Celebration of New Year 601:93
EUROPE—STORYTELLING
Nesting Doll Stories 1522:107-113
EUROPE—STRING FIGURES
Grandmother's Candles string figures story, making 1161:16-21
Lizard and Snake string figures story, making 1161:22-30

EUROPE—THANKSGIVING
Thanksgiving celebrations 601:98-99
EUROPE—VALENTINE'S DAY
Celebration of Valentine's Day 601:94
EUROPE, CENTRAL—COOKERY
Liver spread, recipe 793:8
EWE PEOPLE—HANDICRAFTS
Kente cloth needlepoint wall hanging, canvas, yarn, patterns, making 1716:94-96
Kente pattern needlepoint squares, canvas squares, yarn, making 1716:91-93
EYE OF GOD. *See* **GOD'S EYE**

F

FABERGE EGGS
Emeralds, pearls and scrolls of gold, Russia 139:127
FABIANO, GENTILE DA
Painting of egg and gold done like Gentile da Fabiano, recipe for paint 1372:24-25
FABLES
"Fox and Grapes," fox sculpture, grapes picture, paper, patterns, making 91:12-16
"Lion and the Mouse," lion sculpture, mice pattern, walnut shell and paper making 91:8-11
"Miller, the Boy, and the Donkey" flannel board fable, patterns, making 1603:190-195
"Shepherd's Boy and the Wolf," boy, wolf, sheep, masks, patterns, making 91:21-26
"Tortoise and the Hare," puppets, paper, pattern, making 91:17-20
FABLES—PUPPET PLAYS
"Boy Who Cried Wolf," puppets, play script, making 1155:27-30
"Lion and the Mouse," puppets, play script, making 1155:31-33
"Town Mouse and the Country Mouse," puppets, play script, making 1155:34-40
FABLES—PUPPETS
"Androcles and the Lion," puppets, sets, props, sound effects, making 756:137-139; 1158:83-92
"Blind Men and the Elephant" puppet show 756:37-40
"Crow and the Fox" puppet show 756:35-37
"Fox and the Grapes" puppet show 756:133-134
"Hare and the Tortoise" puppet show 756:131-133
"Lion and the Mouse" puppet show 756:134-137
"Tiger, the Brahman, and the Jackal" puppet show 756:139-144
FABRIC PAINTING
Fabric painting with fabric dyes, making 1261:32-33
FACE MAKEUP
Apache Indian face, making 1046:10-11
China; Chinese opera face, making 380:20-21
Clowns face painting, how to do 380:28-29; 1306:38-47
Count Dracula face painting, how to do 1306:53
Egyptian makeup, making 287:27
Face painting, clowns, monsters, animals, how to do 1619:28-33
Face painting, how to do 1640:28-29
Frankenstein face painting, how to do 1306:51
Halloween face make up, how to do 331:20-21
Halloween grease paint, recipe, making 278:25
India; Kathakali face, making 380:18-19
Indian brave face makeup, how to do 1314:20
Indian face makeup 465:70-71
Indians of North America, faces, making 380:14-15
Japan; Kabuki face, making 380:22-23
Joker face makeup, how to do 1314:23
Masquerade face makeup, how to do 1314:18
Mexico; Huichol face, making 380:16-17
Mummy face makeup 42:73-75
Ninja warrior face painting, how to do 1306:54
Pirate face makeup, how to do 42:65-66; 1306:57; 1314:24
Princess face makeup, how to do 1306:52; 1314:37
Punk face makeup, how to do 1314:39
Skull and monster face makeup, how to do 1314:40-41
Snow Queen face makeup, how to do 1314:19
Sudan; Southeast Nuba face, making 380:24-25
Witch face makeup, how to do 1306:55; 1314:44-45

FACE PAINT
Cornstarch, cream, food coloring, recipe 1413:72
Cornstarch, shortening, and food colors paint, recipe 1199:152
FAIRIES
Christmas Fairy, cardboard, making 1025:29-32
Fairy mask, making 840:15-16
FAIRIES—COOKERY
Fairy cake, recipe 364:25-26; 449:60-61
Fairy cupcakes and icing, recipes 1257:28-29
FAIRIES—COSTUMES
Christmas fairy costume, fabric, patterns, making 1283:38-41
Fairy costume, fabric, face makeup given, making 957:32-37; 1007:20-21
Fairy costume, netting and felt, patterns, making 1050:90-93
Fairy flower costume, fabric, pattern, making 367:67-69
Fairy flower costume, organza fabric, crepe paper, making 1509:34-37
Good fairy costume from paper bag, making 678:12
Gown pattern, making 7:90-91
FAIRIES—PARTIES
Fairy party, invitations, decorations, costumes, food, games, recipes 1185:16-17
FAIRS
History of fairs 631:64
FAIRY PRINCESS
Costume, paper, making 585:44
FAIRY TALES
Castle; fairy tale castle of food, making 297:240-241
Fairy godmother, paper, large pattern, making 478:23-27
Frog Prince, Queen's crown, frog prince, paper, patterns, making 91:27-30
Hansel and Gretel, picture, making 92:36
Jack and the Beanstalk, picture, making 92:53
Literature activities, books, finger plays, games, crafts 480:126-159
Princess, paper, large pattern, making 478:23-27
Rumpelstiltskin, picture, making 92:35
Writing the fairy tale, how to do 290:40-46
FAIRY TALES—COSTUMES
Aladdin, costume, making 366:76-78
Baby Bear costume, making 366:67-69
Cinderella costume, making 366:26-29
Dick Whittington costume, making 366:87
Dwarf costume, making 366:86
Fairy Godmother costume, making 366:30-32
Frog Prince costume, making 366:56-57
Goldilocks costume, making 366:64-66
Little Red Riding Hood costume, making 366:39-41
Prince costume, making 366:86
Princess costume, making 366:58-59
Pumpkin costume, making 366:28-29
Puss in Boots costume, making 366:83-85
Snow White costume, making 366:86
Wolf costume, making 366:42-46
FAIRY TALES—DOLLS
Cinderella paper doll, paper, patterns, making 92:60-61
Doll, fairy tale, fabric, patterns, making 484:19-21
FAIRY TALES—PARTIES
Cinderella's dress up birthday party, activities, foods, handicrafts 30:33-35
FALL. *See also* **AUTUMN; LEAVES; PUMPKINS**
First Day of Fall finger plays and games 944:21-24

Harvest basket, box and paper, making 1089:15
Harvest good luck symbols from dried grasses, making 310:201
Learning units, activities, songs, art, recipes, patterns 1191:186-253
November projects and handicrafts, making 561:41-50
October projects and handicrafts, making 561:29-40
September projects and handicrafts, making 561:19-28
Songs, finger plays, stories, games, rhythms 1200:121-122

FALL—FINGER PLAYS
Finger plays and rhymes 1583:61-69

FALSE FACE SOCIETY. *See also* **FALSE FACE SOCIETY—MASKS; IROQUOIS INDIANS—MASKS**
Eastern Iroquois False Faces, history of 327:6-8

FALSE FACE SOCIETY—MASKS
False Face Society (Iroquois Indians) papier-mache mask, making 223:73-76

FAMILIES
Family or self-portrait collages, making 195:71-79
Family survey and family scrapbook, how to make 1152:179-200
Learning units, activities, songs, art, recipes, patterns 1191:78-127
My family class celebration 134:96-97

FAMILY DAY
Activities, art, songs, recipes, games 1469:40-41

FAMILY TREE
Ancestor chart, making 688:27
Discovering your pedigree 118:26
Fact-finding sheet, making 185:32-33
Family group sheets, making 185:22-25
Family tree 134:98
Family tree bulletin board, making 295:109-112
Family tree chart, making 185:13
Family tree, making 498:18-21; 586:6-7
Family tree, twig, plaster, and circles, making 1089:29
Family Wheel, making 561:28
Genealogy for beginners, how to trace your heritage 1222:1-57
Genealogy, how to do 118:26-30
How to make a family tree 41:54-59; 1715:98-99
How to make your family tree 779:114; 1361:44-46
I'm My Own Grandpaw, poem 118:30
Pattern for family tree 606:203
Sample charts 41:58-59
Time line, making your own 185:8-10
Your Family Tree 199:19-21

FANS
Chinese fans, paper, making 909:21
Japanese fan, making 105:1-3
Mikado fan, making 51:180-181

FARMERS
Farmer Hayseed, fabric, patterns, making 316:66-67
Farmer, paper, large pattern, making 578:54-57

FARMERS—COSTUMES
Farmer costume, making 839:24-27
Farmer costume, paper bag, making 137:23-27
Farmer on tractor costume, paper bag, making 137:40-47
Farmer's wife costume, paper bag, making 137:18-22

FARMERS—PUPPETS
Farmer puppet, paper bag, patterns, making 941:8

FARMS
Alfalfa sprouts, how to grow 1120:31

Animals; activities, games, snacks, making 319:11-12,28
Barn and animals, gingerbread, patterns, recipe, how to make 1086:87-94
Barn and silo, cardboard boxes, paper, crayons, tape, making 1120:20-21
Barn and silo, shoe box, making 442:5
Barn model, making 111:8-9
Buildings, equipment, animals, making 679:unp
Buildings, silo, barn, farmhouse, fence, windmill, dog house, making 670:14-29
Bull, model, making 111:12-13
Chick, model, making 111:24-25
Country play board, posterboard, making 534:74
Duck and pond, model, making 111:22-23
Duckling, model, making 111:26-27
Farm animals, clothespin and paper, making 442:20
Farmyard, model, making 111:28-29
Folding farm, wooden, making 890:26-38
Hen house, model, making 111:8-9
Horse, model, making 111:16-17
Lamb, model, making 111:26-27
Pickup truck paper collage, making 1120:16-17
Pig, model, making 111:14-15
Piglet, model, making 111:26-27
Sheep, model, making 111:18-19
Sheepdog, model, making 111:20-21
Stick fence, craft sticks, making 1120:22-23
Teaching activities, art, literature, music, crafts, patterns 1192:250-346
Tractor and wagon, small boxes, jar lids, buttons, making 1120:14-15
Tractor, model, making 111:10-11
Tractor, model, wooden, making 923:48-52

FARMS—COOKERY
Farm cake, recipe 449:58
Moo-Cow milk shake, recipe 1120:6-7
Stone soup, recipe 1192:258

FARMS—COSTUMES
Barn costume, paper bag, making 137:28-30
Chicken costume, paper bag, making 137:35-40
Cow costume, paper bag, making 137:7-12
Pig costume, paper bag, making 137:31-34
Scarecrow costume, paper bag, making 137:13-17

FARMS—FINGER PLAYS
Finger plays and rhymes 1583:160-169

FARMS—PARTIES
Old MacDonald's barnyard birthday fling, activities, foods, handicrafts 30:58-60
Old MacDonald's Farm party, activities and recipes 809:1-6

FARMS—PUPPETS
Animal puppets, paper bags, patterns, making 941:4-15

FARMS—SONGS
Barnyard songs for infants and toddlers 908:58-59

FAST FOOD. *See* **FOOD—FAST FOOD**

FASTS AND FEASTS. *See the subheading* **FESTIVALS** *under individual countries*

FATHER TIME
New Year's Eve Father Time, cardboard tubes, patterns, making 1311:176-177

FATHER'S DAY
Activities, art, songs, recipes, games 1469:114-115
Activities, crafts, food 1662:92-97
Activities, crafts, history and stories for 128:69-78
Activities, finger plays, recipes, crafts 305:26

Art, cooking, finger plays, games, drama, math, science and music activities 54:196-197

Father's Day art and writing activities, patterns, making 1152:157-166

Father's Day, activities and projects for classrooms 1393:243-244

Father's Day, celebration 133:117

Finger plays, games, making 944:110-112

FATHER'S DAY—COOKERY

Caramel popcorn balls, recipe 939:83-84

Cherry cake, easy, recipe 402:43-46

Mocha chocolate cake, recipe 402:43-46

Necktie cake, making 294:212

Shish kebab, recipe 871:63-65

FATHER'S DAY—DECORATIONS

Card, making 209:28-30; 209:31-32; 561:104

Card, stenciled cut out, patterns, making 1016:127-131

Father's Day cards, making 226:27

Father's Day cards, paper, making 95:27; 95:28; 96:33-35

Pop-up Father's Day card, making 1387:10-11

FATHER'S DAY—GAMES

Father's Day game 240:33-34

FATHER'S DAY—HANDICRAFTS

Badge, tin punch badge, patterns, making 1016:115-120

Best Father Award, making 648:31

DAD plaque, flour and salt dough, wood, making 1067:96-97

Father's gift, decorated rock, making 226:28

Hands down pictures, making 698:59

My Father Likes book, making 698:59

Paperweight, making 561:106

Pencil holder and note pad, making 586:44-45

Table coaster, Hungarian painted flowers, patterns, making 1016:121-126

Workshop organizer, making 294:213

FATHER'S DAY—SONGS

Songs about Father's Day 901:78-82; 902:36

FAWKES, GUY. See also **ENGLAND—FESTIVALS**

Make a stuffed Guy, pantyhose, straw or newspaper, old shirt and pants 1199:256-257

FEAST OF LIGHTS. See also **HANUKKAH**

Ritual of Feast of Lights 419:33-34

FEATHERS

Aztec fan made from layers of feathers, decorations, making 1701:17

Feather necklace, making 1421:155

FEELINGS

Songs, finger plays, stories, games, rhythms 1200:57-60

FEET

Activities and resources to celebrate foot days 592:49-54

FELT

Legend of felt 628:6

FERRIS WHEELS

Big wheel, sticks and wood, moves, making 975:164-169

Ferris Wheel, wood pieces, coat hangers, making 1130:24-25

Story of 119:61

FESTIVAL OF LIGHT. See **SWEDEN—CHRISTMAS**

FESTIVALS. See also the subheading **FESTIVALS** under individual countries

Festa of Birds 474:27

Festival Ring dance 474:19-20

Festival time with children activities 601:173-184

History of Festivals 566:6-7

Little Festivals 474:23-24

FIJI—COOKERY

Ambrosia, recipe 49:253

I'A, steamed fish with sweet potatoes, recipe 1165:200

FIJI—FESTIVALS—COOKERY

Diwali; badam pistaz barfi (Hindu nut candy), recipe 1666:193

Diwali; Coconut milk, recipe 1666:193

FIJI—STRING FIGURES

Basket string 373:21

Fence around the well string 372:38-39

Giant clam string 372:28-29

Lairo or the land crab string 372:18-19

Parakeet's playground string 373:18-23

Well string 372:36-37

FINGER PAINTS

Finger paint, cornstarch, sugar, food coloring, cooked, recipe 1413:73

Homemade finger paint, recipe 1213:26

FINGER PLAYS

John Brown's Baby 104:6-7

London Bridge Is Falling Down, music given 103:18-21

Noble Duke of York 104:12-13

Pawpaw Patch, music given 103:22-23

She'll Be Coming Round the Mountain, music given 103:32-35

Skip to My Lou, music given 103:26-29

FINGER PLAYS—CIRCUS

Circus and zoo finger plays 733:52-55

Circus ponies 735:48

Finger play about the circus 360:100

FINGER PLAYS—CLOWNS

Clown 735:43

FINGER PLAYS—EASTER

Five little bunnies 513:82

FINGER PLAYS—FAMILY

Finger plays about the family 360:40-44

FINGER PLAYS—FARM

Farm animals finger plays 733:16-23

FINGER PLAYS—FARMERS

Farmer in the Dell, music given 103:4-7

FINGER PLAYS—GROUNDHOGS

Five little groundhogs 513:44

FINGER PLAYS—HALLOWEEN

Five little pumpkins 513:20-21

FINGER PLAYS—HANUKKAH

Dreidels 735:68

FINGER PLAYS—INDIANS

Five little Indians finger play 513:12-13

Indian finger plays 292:1-2

FINGER PLAYS—KITES

Kites 735:55

FINGER PLAYS—MEMORIAL DAY

Finger plays about Memorial Day 302:72

FINGER PLAYS—MYTHOLOGY

Finger plays about mythology 302:98-104

FINGER PLAYS—PEOPLE

Finger plays about all kinds of people 360:50-58

FINGER PLAYS—SOLDIERS AND SAILORS

Finger plays about soldiers and sailors 302:84

FINGER PLAYS—SPACE

Finger plays about space 302:52-53

FINGER PLAYS—ST. PATRICK'S DAY

Five little Irishmen 513:72

Five little shamrocks 513:76

Shamrocks 735:56

St. Patrick's Day finger plays 292:6

FINGER PLAYS—THANKSGIVING DAY
Finger plays about Thanksgiving 360:94
Finger plays about turkeys, dinner, Pilgrims 302:62-64
Five fat turkeys 513:30
Thanksgiving children 735:66
Thanksgiving finger plays 292:3
Turkeys 735:67
FINGER PLAYS—TRAINS
Finger plays about trains 360:22-23
Trains 735:16
FINGER PLAYS—TRANSPORTATION
Finger plays about things that go 360:22-28
Finger plays about trains, motorcycles, cars, busses, airplanes 302:85-87
FINGER PLAYS—VALENTINE'S DAY
Finger plays about Valentine's Day 302:9
Five pretty Valentines 513:50; 735:54
Valentine's Day finger plays 292:5; 912:21
FINLAND
Activities, flags, games, map, songs, dances, recipes 621:6; 1381:195-196
FINLAND—CHRISTMAS
Celebration of Christmas in Finland 601:107; 1049:85
Christmas customs 149:30-31
Christmas tree and decorations, how to make 593:138-145
Customs in Finland 425:19
Customs of Christmas in Finland 473:41-43
FINLAND—CHRISTMAS—COOKERY
Pulla yeast coffee bread, recipe 149:127
FINLAND—CHRISTMAS—HANDICRAFTS
Finnish flag garlands, flag pictures, yarn, making 1575:9
FINLAND—COOKERY
Berry shake, recipe 188:29
Bread pudding, recipe 793:36
Bread, homemade, recipe 858:unp
Cheddar bread pudding, recipe 1165:143
Cookie sticks, recipe 621:24
Egg pancakes, recipe 1381:195
Farmer rye bread, recipe 88:180-181
Karelian stew, beef, mutton, pork, kidney, liver, recipe 1428:121
Kesakeitlo soup, recipe 967:29
Pancakes, recipe 794:18
Potatoes, stewed, recipe 621:35
Raspberry mousse, recipe 874:73
Rice-nut steak, recipe 1653:112
Rieska, Finnish rye, recipe 1653:88
Rikkaat ritarit, fried bread dessert, recipe 1165:143-144
Ristinnaulittu Sikka, racked trout, recipe 1165:142-143
Smorrebrod bread, recipe 88:181-182
Sourdough rye bread, recipe 88:182-183
FINLAND—COSTUMES
Berry shake, recipe, costume 188:29
FINLAND—FESTIVALS
Sibelius Festival 474:27
FINLAND—FESTIVALS—COOKERY
May Day; choklad (Finnish chocolate candy), recipe 1666:128
May Day; sima (Finnish lemonade), recipe 1666:128
May Day; tippaleipa (May Day cruller or bird's nests), recipe 1666:127-128
FINLAND—GAMES
Sarvisilla game, how to play 1494:99
FINLAND—HANDICRAFTS
Viking ship in a bottle, making 626:46-48

FINLAND—INDEPENDENCE DAY
Independence Day celebration December 6 722:5-8
FINLAND—TOYS
Prisoner's lock from Finland, history of and how to make 495:64-69
FIRE
Bucket, Colonial, making 877:115-116
Sign, fire sign, Colonial, making 877:116-117
FIRE—FESTIVALS
New fire ceremonies 419:64-67
FIRE DEPARTMENT—PARTIES
Fire Engine #9 party, activities and recipes 809:13-16
FIRE FIGHTERS—FESTIVALS
Dezome-Shiki, the Firemen's Parade 107:67-71
FIREFLIES
Glowworm, paper bags, flashlight, pattern, making 1311:16-17
FIREWORKS
History of fireworks 333:35-40
FIRST NATIONS PEOPLES. *See* **ESKIMOS; HURON INDIANS; INUIT**
FISHES
Carp kite, mini, making 980:42-43
Carp, sparkling, making 486:7-8
Mobile, North African lucky fish mobile, paper, patterns, making 1016:175-180
FISHES—DECORATIONS
Papier-mache fish, balloon covered with papier-mache, making 1253:39
FITZGERALD, JOHN D.
"Great Brain," codfish fillets, recipe 1216:94
FLAG DAY
Activities and projects for classrooms 1393:232-233
Activities, crafts, history and stories for 128:84-93
Finger plays, games, making 944:108-109
Flag patterns, first, second, 25th and today's flag, making 128:87-88
History of Flag Day 199:44
1777 flag, making 272:82-83
FLAG DAY—COOKERY
American flag cake, recipe 43:159
Popcorn poppers, chocolate, recipe 939:80
FLAG DAY—COSTUMES
Betsy Ross costume, making 272:81-83
Flag costume, making 272:84-85
FLAG DAY—DECORATIONS
Ancestral flags, paper, crayons, markers, making 1199:131-132
Design your own flag, magazine pictures, markers, making 1199:130-131
Flag chains, paper, making 1348:unp
Flag picture, making 698:55
Flag sewing card making 698:55
Old Glory banners, making 199:45-47
Star, folded paper, making 586:42
FLAG DAY—PARTIES
All-American Jamboree Party, how to plan and give 43:67-70
FLAG DAY—PUPPETS
Puppet projects, patterns, scenes, story starters, feature story 1083:93-94
FLAG DAY—SONGS
Songs about Flag Day 901:83-87; 902:37

FLAGS. *See also the subheading* **FLAG** *under individual countries*
  Israeli flag, paper, making 543:112
  Jolly Roger flag patterns 1251:22
  1777 flag, making 272:82-83
  Thirteen-star flag, making 186:18-20
  United States, original flag, pattern 157:79
  United States, present flag, pattern 157:80
FLAGS—FINGER PLAYS
  Finger plays and rhymes 1583:129-130
FLATHEAD INDIANS—FOOTWEAR
  Flathead moccasins, making 359:99-103
FLAX
  Finger spinning to make fibers into thread, how to do 1349:98-99
FLIP BOOKS. *See also* **BOOKS**
  Flip book, how to make 1612:28-31
FLOORCLOTHS
  Checkerboard floorcloth, canvas, paints, making 1476:128-129
FLORIDA—CHRISTMAS
  Fort Meyer's singing Christmas tree 475:71
FLORIDA—COOKERY
  Barbecue sauce, recipe 343:106
  Black bean soup, history of, recipe 155:28-29
  Jellied tangerines, recipe 654:31
  Key lime pie, recipe 654:32-33
FLORIDA—EVERGLADES—FOLKLORE
  "Moon of the Alligators"; physical and human geography activities 1458:104-107
FLORIDA—HANDICRAFTS
  Sailor's Valentine and shell box, making 298:156-157
FLORIDA—HISTORY—COOKERY
  Florida cookery and Spanish foods information 666:104-105
FLOWERS
  Chinese lantern, folded paper, making 832:20-21
  Clay flowers, tulips in a bowl, how to make 1260:12-13
  Herb sachets, making 1259:28
  Lavender bundles, making 1259:29
  Multifold flower, paper, making 1238:106-110
  New Amsterdam tulips, making 719:11-13
  Pretty posy, paper, making 1238:103-106
  Tissue paper flowers, how to make 1261:44-45
FLOWERS—COOKERY
  Candied flower heads, making 1467:17
  Candied violets, recipe 1285:44-45
  Chocolate edible petals from flowers, how to make 1259:23
  Edible petals from flowers, how to make 1259:22
FLOWERS—DRIED
  Dried flowers using cornmeal and salt, making 1429:71-73
  Dried leaves and flowers, glycerin, water, making 1259:16-17
  Posy from dried flowers, doily, ribbon, making 1510:50-51
  Sand dried flowers, how to do 1421:208-209
FLOWERS—DYED
  Flowers and grasses dyed, glycerin, cold water dye, making 1259:18-19
FLOWERS—PRESSED
  Card and calendar from pressed flowers, how to make 1259:26-27
  Press flowers, how to do 1419:206-207
  Pressed wild flower gift tags, note cards, bookmarks, paints, making 1285:42-43
FLOWERS—SCENTED. *See* **POTPOURRI**
FLYING SAUCERS
  Flying saucer with launchpad, plastic bottles, paper plates, making 1346:16-17
FOGELSVILLE, PA—MUSICAL INSTRUMENTS
  Boom-bah, stick, things that jingle, making 1361:58
  Boom-bahs, sticks, noise making items, making 1362:77
FOLKLORE
  Adventures of Brer Rabbit, paper folds of story characters, making 406:44-46
  Billy Goats Gruff and the Troll, paper folds of story characters, make 406:82-85
  Bremen Town Musicians, picture, making 92:25
  "Chicken Little" by Steven Kellogg, reading, writing, thinking activities 1093:86-100
  Folktale patterns; reading and writing activities, projects 620:107-124
  Giant tongue pattern for tongue twister telling, making 1159:76
  Gingerbread boy, farmer, fox, old man and old woman, puppets, patterns, making 91:31-40
  Going to St. Ives, paper folds of story characters, making 406:57-60
  Jack and the Beanstalk, paper folds of story characters, making 406:47-56
  John Henry, picture, making 92:11
  Johnny Appleseed, picture 92:8
  Little Red Riding Hood, wolf, mother, grandmother, etc. puppets, making 91:41-50
  Magic Kilt, paper folds of story characters, making 406:67-71
  Paul Bunyan, picture, making 92:14
  Pecos Bill and Slue-Foot Sue, picture, making 92:20
  Pied Piper of Hamelin, paper folds of story characters, making 406:29-32
  Siege of the Alamo, paper folds of story characters, making 406:72-81
  "Stone in the Road" flannel board story, patterns, making 1603:180-183
  Stone Soup, soup, recipe 812:109
  Tall Tales Program; activities, books, crafts, patterns, foods, making 1159:71-81
  Three Bears, Goldilocks, mama, papa, and baby bear puppets, making 91:51-58
  Three Billy Goats Gruff, picture, making 92:40
  Three Little Pigs, paper folds of story characters, making 406:61-66
  Three Little Pigs, pig and wolf masks, patterns, making 91:59-64
FOLKLORE—ART, MUSIC AND COOKING ACTIVITIES
  Hansel and Gretel, making 161:57-62
  Jack and the Beanstalk, making 161:36-39
  Little Red Hen, making 161:40-42
  Little Red Riding Hood, making 161:32-35
  Three little Pigs, making 161:28-31
FOLKLORE—BULLETIN BOARDS
  Alice in Wonderland, making 295:75-76
  Jack and Jill, making 295:74-75
  Jack and the Beanstalk, making 295:73
  King Arthur's castle, making 295:73-74
  Mistress Mary quite contrary, making, 295:75

FOLKLORE—COOKERY. *See also* **MOTHER GOOSE—COOKERY; NURSERY RHYMES—COOKERY;** *and the subheading* **COOKERY** *under titles of works*
Jack and the Beanstalk's green bean casserole, recipe 1215:18
"Little Red Hen," whole wheat bread, recipe 1216:31
Paul Bunyan pancakes, big batch mix, recipe 1159:75
Paul Bunyan's blueberry special cakes, recipe 1159:75
Shady Tree wealthy man's sweet and sour pork, recipe 569:34-36
Twelve Months, Marushka's strawberry chiffon pie, recipe 569:64-67

FOLKLORE—COSTUMES
Gingerbread boy costume, making 338:38-41

FOLKLORE—HANDICRAFTS
Glass Leaves on a Tree?, leaf rubbing, leaf lady 125:50-60
Who Lost the Golden Charm?, floating ghost, ghost mobile, ghost puppet 125:23-30

FOLKLORE—PUPPET PLAYS
Anansi Finds a Fool 4:41-47
Blessing of the Tree 4:37-40
Brer Fox and Sis Goose 4:48-51
How Rabbit Lost His Fine Bushy Tail 4:52-55
How the Spark of Fire Was Saved 4:69-73
Jack and the Northwest Wind 4:60-64
Magic Sarangi 4:82-88
Maui Captures the Sun 4:33-36
Nerrivik, Old Woman of the Sea 4:74-77
Red-Eyed Duck 4:65-68
Robbers 4:56-59
Spirit of the Willow Tree Saves Family Honor 4:89-92
Three Sillies, music given 4:21-32
Two Jack Tales 4:56-64
Walk Tall, Talk Tall, Davy Crockett 4:93-102
Why Man Must Harvest His Crops 4:78-81
Winter of the Blue Snow 4:103-107

FOLKLORE—PUPPETS
City Mouse and the Country Mouse puppets, making 868:49-61
Dumb Wife Cured puppet show 756:90-94
Get Up and Bar the Door puppet show 756:86-90
Johnny-Cake puppet show 756:150-155
Little Red Hen puppets, making 868:80-96
Princess who could not cry puppets, making 868:32-48
Simpleton puppets, making 868:62-79
Tale of the Turnip, finger puppet, patterns, story, making 512:125-129
Youth and the Northwind puppet show 756:40-48

FON PEOPLE—HANDICRAFTS
Fon story pictures on felt or paper, making 1632:24-27

FOOD—FAST FOOD
Automat information 664:65-67
Fast food nutrition information 664:74-75
Fast food school lunch information 664:77-78
History of fast foods 664:64
Hot dogs and hamburgers, history of 664:67-69
McDonald's, history of 664:69-72

FOOD—FOOD BUSINESS
Corporate control of food information 664:119-122
Future foods information 664:122-125
No frills or more frills information 664:127-129
Supermarket traps information 664:125-126
What consumers want information 664:129-133

FOOD—HEALTH FOOD
Information on variety of health food items 664:80-98

FOOD—JUNK FOOD
Additives information 664:50
Butter versus margarine information 664:47-48
Cereals, sugary, information 664:30-31
Chewing gum information 664:34-35
Cholesterol information 664:45-47
Fat facts 664:42-44
FDA information 664:60
Food dyes information 664:55
Hidden fats in foods information 664:48-49
History of junk foods 664:3-20
Ice cream information 664:35-37
Lunch box sugar treats information 664:31-33
Natural additives versus artificial additives information 664:50-60
Popcorn, potato chips information 664:39-41
Saccharin information 664:29-30
Salt in our diet information 664:37-39
Soft drinks information 664:27-29
Sugar in our lives information 664:25-26
Sweet treats and salty snacks information 664:23-41

FOOD—MEAT OR VEGETABLES
Beef, history of 664:99-102
Brown rice information 664:115-116
Dyes in animal feed information 664:105-107
High fiber information 664:112-115
Vegetarian choices information 664:107-112

FOOD—SONGS
Eating Is Fun round song 1115:74
Grains and Beans round song 1115:62
I Want a Chocolate Malted round song 1115:72
Lasagna round song 1115:85
Vegetable Grace round song 1115:90

FOOTBALL—PARTIES
Football Party, recipes and games 635:51-53

FOOTWEAR
Gaiter boot, information on 417:64
Leg shields, information on 417:64
Moccasins, information on 417:63
Sandals, information on 417:63
Stone age boots and leggings, fabric, making 181:14-15

FORBES, ESTHER
"Johnny Tremain," descriptions and pictures of house 29:Chapter 6

FORD, HENRY
Birthday celebration; art, music, foods, games, activities 1104:106-109

FOREMAN, MICHAEL
"War and Peas"; King's royal sandwiches, recipe 843:59, 130

FOREST ANIMALS
Activities with forest animals 1663:56-72

FORESTS
Activities with forest trees, plants, crafts, printing, games, songs 1663:44-53

FORTIFICATION—WORLD WAR I
Maginot Line fortification 212:76-83
Western Front trench system, making 212:60-75

FORTS
Chair indoor fort, making 1188:48-49
Desk indoor fort, making 1188:51
Dome fort, tree limbs, branches, material for cover, making 1188:30-32
Forts of the Wild West models, making 356:28-31
Igloo fort, blocks packed with snow, making 1188:41-44

Lean-to-fort, simple, wood scraps, junk, making 1188:16-17
Log Forts, paper, making 1020:95-107
Pile fort, packing box covered with leaves and tree limbs, making 1188:18
Sand fort, sand, driftwood, old boards, making 1188:33-34
Snow trench fort, making 1188:39-40
Snowball fort, large snowballs, making 1188:37-38
Soldiers of the fort models, making 356:27
Space box indoor fort, making 1188:52-54
Stockade, Treasure Island model, wooden, making 942:92-93
Table indoor fort, making 1188:47-48
Teepee fort, poles, old tarp, making 1188:28-29
Thatched fort, grass or hay bundles, making 1188:26-27
Twin bed indoor fort, making 1188:50
Wattle work fort, tree limbs stuck in ground, thin branches woven in and out, making 1188:21-22
Wild West fort, milk cartons, patterns, making 1311:92-93

FORTS—COOKERY
Fort cake, recipe 449:69

FORTS—FRONTIER
Fort Phil Kearny 212:22-47

FORTS—ITALY
Mount Cassino Fort 212:104-114

FORTS—ROME
Roman fort 212:4-21

FORTS—WORLD WAR II
Mount Cassino Fort 212:104-114

FORTUNE TELLERS
Crystal ball, paper foil ball, making 1105:26-27
Paper fortune teller, making 1429:22-23

FORTUNE TELLERS—COSTUMES
Fortune Teller costume, making 272:92-94

FORTUNE TELLING—GAMES
Fortune telling game 329:34-35

FOURTEENTH CENTURY—COSTUMES.
See ENGLAND—HISTORY—FOURTEENTH CENTURY—COSTUMES

FOURTH OF JULY
Activities, art, crafts, costumes, food, songs, recipes, games 1469:116-117; 1662:114-119
Activities, crafts, history and stories for 128:100-107
Art, cooking, finger plays, games, drama, math, science and music activities 54:197-198
Bicentennial of 1976, history of 333:80-85
Celebration of Independence Day, July 4 722:42-45
Centennial Exhibition of 1876, history of 333:78-79
Fourth of July birthday celebration; art, music, foods, games, activities 133:118; 1104:98-101
Fourth of July, activities and projects for classrooms 1393:248-251
Fourth of July, celebration, flag, band, batons, making 134:57-58
History and celebration of 496:76-77
History of the Fourth of July 199:36; 333:2-12, 21-28
Important events that have taken place on July 4th 333:86-88
Independence Day celebration, invitations, decorations, food, games 133:134-136
Independence Day, history of 513:99
Music and songs, history of 333:48-58
Picnics, history of 333:44-47
Special celebrations, history of 333:75-77
Spirit of '76 painting, history of 333:41-43
United States birthday celebration; art, music, foods, games, activities 1104:98-101

FOURTH OF JULY—BULLETIN BOARDS
Fourth of July bulletin board, making 295:206-211

FOURTH OF JULY—COOKERY
Corn on the cob, recipe 1666:262
Heros punch, recipe 199:42
Ice cream dish, red, white and blue fruits, recipe 1542:90
No-bake patriotic cookies, recipe 698:66
Old Glory cake, recipe 1032:213-214
Patriotic cookies, recipe 199:60-63
Patriotic ice cream parfait, recipe 1032:212
Peanut butter cookies, recipe 1666:262
Pesto and vegetable couscous salad, recipe 1186:102-103
Red, white, and blue cheese pie, recipe 1032:215-216

FOURTH OF JULY—COSTUMES
Firecracker costume, making 338:70-73
Fireworks costume, cardboard, making 1283:78-81
Statue of Liberty costume, making 272:86-88
Statue of Liberty, green fabric, posterboard, crepe paper, patterns, making 1656:21-24
Uncle Sam costume, making 272:88-91
Yankee Doodle Dandy, felt, crepe paper, flag, patterns, making 1656:25-28

FOURTH OF JULY—DECORATIONS
Drum, decorate a red, white and blue oatmeal box, colored paper, making 1179:42-43
Eagle picture from leaves, making 448:23
Firecracker favor, paper tube, tissue paper, stars, ribbon, making 1425:52-53
Firecracker, paper tubes, tissue paper, making 1657:54
Fireworks, paper tube, tissue paper, star stickers, making 1299:40-41
Flag shirt, T-shirt, spray dyes, beads, patterns, making 1425:54-55
Flyer, large plastic bottle bottom, making 1534:22-23
Fountain, soda bottle, clay, straw, making 1534:23
Parade decoration for parade; streamers, balloons, signs, making 1199:150
Patriotic Star hat, paper, pattern, making 823:42
Pop-up Independence Day card, making 1387:16-17
Spinner, clothespin, streamers, making 1534:22
Uncle Sam centerpiece, making 226:34
Yankee Doodle Dandy macaroni hat, making 835:61
Yankee Doodle headband, straws, paper, stars, making 1539:78-79

FOURTH OF JULY—FINGER PLAYS
Finger plays and rhymes 1583:129-130

FOURTH OF JULY—GAMES
Birthday candle squirt game 698:65
Coin game 329:28
Flag tag game, making 329:24
Fourth of July game 240:38
Happy Birthday ring toss game, making 698:64
Independence rhythm game 329:26-27
Liberty Bell beanbag toss game 698:65
States shuffleboard game 698:65
Uncle Sam's fish pond game, making 698:64
Yankee Doodle's pony game 329:25

FOURTH OF JULY—HANDICRAFTS
Candle; Fourth of July, making 336:25-26
Continental coin replicas, making 329:29
T-shirt, patriotic decorations, fabric paints, making 1360:22-24

FOURTH OF JULY—PUPPETS
Uncle Sam puppet, making 448:23

FOURTH OF JULY—SONGS
  Happy Birthday to America song 782:unp
  Songs about Fourth of July 901:88-92
FOX AND HIS TRAVELS
  Finger puppet, patterns, story, making 512:19-27
FRACTUR PAINTING
  Fractur painting, how to do 688:20
FRAGRANCES. *See also* **PERFUMES**
  Homemade perfume, how to make 1421:206
  Special scent gift, making 1616:18-21
FRANCE
  Activities, flags, games, songs, dances, recipes
    1381:169-172
  Activities, history, food, games 143:35-70
FRANCE—APRIL FOOLS' DAY—HANDICRAFTS
  Fish, eraser or potato print fish, making 709:150-151
  Poisson d'Avril (April fish), making 709:149-151
  Stencil, cup or cupcake stencil, making 709:151
FRANCE—ARCHITECTURE
  Skyscrapers from France, cardboard and paper models,
    making 1094:58
FRANCE—ARTISTS
  Georges Braque's torn paper mosaics, how to make your
    own 1372:80
FRANCE—CARNIVALS
  Carnival at Nice 474:11-12
FRANCE—CHRISTMAS
  Celebration of Christmas in France 497:132; 1049:87
  Christmas customs 149:40
  Christmas paper crackers, making 273:30-32
  Christmas tree and decorations, how to make 593:36-41
  Customs of Christmas in France 473:51-55
  History of Christmas in France 704:32
  Paper crackers, making 273:30-32
  Santons of Provence, making 273:22-30
  Shoes in front of fireplace custom 516:45
FRANCE—CHRISTMAS—COOKERY
  Aioli, garlic mayonnaise, recipe 1128:51
  Almond tile cookies, recipe 704:36-37
  Babas au Rhum, recipe 704:38-40
  Ball, French Christmas ball, recipe 704:34-35
  Bread dumplings with mushrooms, recipe 149:129
  Broiled trout, recipe 149:129
  Buche de Noel (Yule log cake), recipe 497:142;
    1128:54; 1666:102
  Chocolate truffles, recipe 1128:55
  Christmas pudding, recipe 149:128
  Galette des Rois, cake of Kings for Epiphany, recipe
    1128:56
  Gratin Dauphinois (potato au gratin), recipe 1666:101
  Mushrooms, French meringue, recipe 497:142
  Nut pudding, recipe 149:129
  Pain D'Epice, spice cake, recipe 1128:53
  Poached filet of dover sole, recipe 149:128-129
  Pompe a L'Huile (Christmas Eve cake), recipe 1128:52
  Red cabbage, baked, recipe 1227:70; 1565:70
  Roast goose with prune and pate stuffing, recipe
    1227:70; 1565:70
  Roast turkey, recipe 149:128
  Terrine d'Anguille (baked eels), recipe 1128:51
  Three Kings' cake, recipe 704:41-42
  Thuringian roast goose, recipe 149:129
  Truffles (chocolate candy), recipe 1666:103
  Twelfth Night cake, recipe 273:32-35

FRANCE—CHRISTMAS—DECORATIONS
  Fruit ornaments, clay recipe, making 1565:74-75
  Noel door hanger, paper, patterns, making 1393:107
  Pere Noel ornament pin, felt, making 1565:73-74
  Star, tri-colored, paper, patterns, making 1565:72-73
  Twelfth Night crowns, making 273:35-39
FRANCE—CHRISTMAS—HANDICRAFTS
  Creche, making 795:14-15
  Epiphany crown, paper, making 704:33
  French stained-glass star, tissue colored papers, making
    1575:16-17
  Kitchen clay fruit ornaments, salt, flour dough, paints,
    making 1227:74-75
  Pere Noel ornament pin, felt, yarn, patterns, making
    1227:73-74
  Tri-colored star, paper, vinyl sheet, metallic cord, mak-
    ing 1227:72-73
FRANCE—CLOWNS—FACE MAKEUP
  Pierrot clown face, how to do 1314:17
FRANCE—COOKERY
  Banana crepes, recipe 909:75
  Baptismal Cake, add French name, recipe 1220:126-127
  Bearnaise sauce, recipe 1438:22
  Beef with bearnaise sauce, recipe 1438:21
  Broccoli crepes, recipe 884:28-29
  Canapes au Roquefort, recipe 536:21
  Carottes Vichy, glazed carrots, recipe 1452:65
  Carrots, glazed, recipe 884:37
  Cassoulet, tomatoes, beans, sausage dish, recipe
    1275:38-39
  Cheese omelet, recipe 1380:11
  Cheese omelette, recipe 1438:28
  Chicken roasted, recipe 530:42-45
  Chicken, sauteed, recipe 884:34-35
  Chocolat drink, recipe 1452:68
  Chocolate bread (pain au chocolate), recipe 49:252
  Chocolate delight dessert, recipe 1560:13
  Chocolate mousse, recipe 884:42-43; 1438:23
  Chocolate pastry recipe 884:30
  Chocolate sauce, recipe 530:47-48
  Chocolate truffles, recipe 1477:119
  Clafouti limousine recipe 536:38
  Clafouti, cherry pudding cake, recipe 1165:118-119
  Cream cheese, sweetened, recipe 1653:54
  Crepe batter, recipe 884:27
  Crepe filling, recipe 88:167-168
  Crepes with strawberries, recipe 884:39
  Crepes, recipe 88:166-167; 143:67; 515:52; 1042:89;
    1301:41; 1380:7; 1381:171; 1438:25; 1653:69
  Croissant sandwiches, recipe 1272:unp
  Croque Monsieur, cheese and ham sandwich, recipe
    1275:40-41
  Croque Monsieur, recipe 188:23; 884:31
  Dessert crepe batter, recipe 884:39
  Dessert crepes with raspberry sauce, recipe 1265:60-61
  Dessert crepes, recipe 793:39
  Egg and rice cakes, recipe 895:50
  Egg; creamed egg, recipe 794:23
  Fondue, recipe 1653:106
  French bread, recipe 492:10-13
  French dressing, recipe 1381:171; 1438:27
  French fries, recipe 1380:27
  French menu 884:14-15
  French onion soup, recipe 1438:20
  French pea soup, recipe 501:83

French toast sandwich, recipe 1542:20-22
French toast, recipe 384:July 14
Garlic mayonnaise (Aioli), recipe 1665:74-75
Green salad, recipe 884:26
Ham and asparagus souffle, recipe 871:30-32
Ham and Swiss cheese toasted sandwich, recipe 1042:90
Ham rolls, recipe 874:21
History of cookery in 88:156-165
Hot chocolate recipe 884:16-17
Hot chocolate, recipe 1275:44-45
Kinds of French cooking and regions 884:7-9
Lemonade, citron presse, recipe 1327:11
Les porc-epics sacres (sweet porcupines), recipe 143:62
Lost bread (French toast), recipe 895:49
Map of food products 884:6
Meat-eating habits of the French 662:54
Meringue shells 143:64
Mixed greens and celery salad, recipe 1265:57
Momay sauce, recipe 884:29; 1438:25
Mousse au chocolat dessert, recipe 1452:67
Mystere medicis drink, recipe 536:17
Omelet aux fines herbs, recipe 874:35
Omelet; sweet souffle omelet, recipe 1143:29
Omelette aux fines herbes, eggs and herbs, recipe 1275:36-37
Onion soup gratinee, recipe 1645:34-35
Onion soup with cheese, microwave recipe 1211:27
Onion soup, recipe 530:40-42; 536:15
Pain perdu, recipe 536:19
Pancakes or crepes, recipe 1113:52-53
Paris-Brest cream puff pastry, recipe 1562:41-42
Pears Helen dessert, recipe 1280:36
Pears Helen, recipe 884:40-41
Pears, stewed, recipe 530:45-46
Peas, green peas, French style, recipe 884:37
Petits fours, recipe 143:63
Pierrot the clown cream puff pastry, recipe 1562:44
Poire Helene, pears, ice cream, jam, recipe 1452:66
Pork chops, Normandy style, recipe 884:32-33
Potato cake, recipe 884:36
Potato gratin, recipe 536:27
Potato pancakes (crepes), recipe 801:107-108
Potato pommes soufflés, recipe 801:104-105
Potatoes and butter, Pommes Anna, recipe 1145:27
Provencale tomatoes, recipe 967:31
Quiche Lorraine, recipe 88:169-171; 143:68; 536:29;
    514:133; 884:20-21; 1113:28-29; 1381:171;
    1438:26; 1645:34-35; 1653:113-114
Quiche, pick-a-filling, recipe 1265:58-59
Quiche, quick, 187:19
Quiche, three cheeses, recipe 1042:90-91
Ratatouille a la nicoise, vegetarian stew, recipe
    1165:117-118
Ratatouille, recipe 536:33
Ratatouille, vegetable stew, recipe 1275:42-43
Salad Nicoise, recipe 884:24-25; 1560:12
Salade mesclun, greens salad, recipe 1275:35
Salade with vinaigrette dressing, recipe 1244:73
Sandwich, croque-monsieur fried sandwich, recipe 1327:10
Sauce bechamel, recipe 88:168-169
Sauce mornay, recipe 88:169
Saute de poulet, sauteed chicken, recipe 1452:63
Seafood crepes, recipe 1438:24
Shell-shaped butter cakes (Madeleines),cookies, recipe
    72:37-38
Souffle au fromage, cheese souffle, recipe 1452:64

Soupe a l'oignon, onion soup, recipe 1165:117
Strawberries Chantilly, recipe 895:51
Strawberry crepes, recipe 1452:62
Tomato quiche, recipe 858:unp
Truffles au chocolat, chocolate candy, recipe 143:63;
    1165:118
Truffles au chocolat, chocolate chip truffles, recipe 1272:unp
Tuna basquaise, recipe 536:35
Tuna fish rice salad, recipe 967:30
Versailles au chocolate recipe 514:134
Vinaigrette dressing, recipe 884:26; 1275:34; 1645:34-35

FRANCE—COSTUMES
Beau Brummell costume 213:112-114
Cavalier costume 213:108-110
Croque Monsieur, recipe, costume 188:23
Josephine costume 213:112
Louis XIV costume 213:110
Marie Antoinette costume, making 213:110-112
Parisian artist, old smock, velvet beret, beard, making
    1509:12-13

FRANCE—DANCES
Chimes of Dunkirk dance, how to do 1494:119-120
Gavotte dance and costume picture 1000:8-10

FRANCE—DOLLS
French peasant doll, making 494:119-132
Madame de Pompadour, making 59:90-93
Mannequin doll, styrofoam and fabric, making 1027:30-35
Pantin (jumping doll), making 105:9-14
Pantin doll, making 775:54-57

FRANCE—DRAMA
Punch and Judy show 474:96-98

FRANCE—EASTER
Easter egg customs in France 201:20

FRANCE—FACE PAINTING
Pierrot clown, how to paint 1533:41-43

FRANCE—FESTIVALS
April Fools' Day 143:40
Bastille Day 143:38
Bastille Day celebration, activities, handicrafts, foods,
    songs, making, 909:69-77
Bastille Day, activities and projects for classrooms
    1393:252-253
Bastille Day, activities, crafts, food 1662:120-122
Bastille Day; history and celebration of 496:78-79
Festival of the Kings celebration 601:108
George Seurat's birthday; celebrate with pointillism
    painting, making 1199:273
Mardi Gras 143:39
Mardi Gras celebration 515:52
Martinmas Day model of St. Martin, clay, making
    1089:25

FRANCE—FESTIVALS—COOKERY
Epiphany bean cake, recipe 709:120

FRANCE—FESTIVALS—GAMES
April Fools' Day fish game, how to play 1473:114

FRANCE—FESTIVALS—HANDICRAFTS
Epiphany crown, making 709:121

FRANCE—FESTIVALS—MASKS
Carnival mask, paper plate, yarn, making 1574:8-9
Carnival mask, papier-mache over clay mold, making
    1327:22-25

FRANCE—FINGER PLAYS
Frere Jacques finger play rhyme 780:110
Les Petites Marionettes finger play rhyme 780:112

FRANCE—FOLKLORE
"Drakes-Tail" flannel board story, patterns, making 1604:106-108
Silly Wishes flannel board patterns, making 910:25,62
So Proud fable playlet 1212:38-39
FRANCE—FOLKLORE—COOKERY
Miller, His Cook and the King; story and menu for King given 364:101-108
FRANCE—FORTIFICATION
Maginot Line fortification 212:76-83
FRANCE—GAMES
Acrostiche game 967:30
Balle Dix Coups game 1078:29
Bon Debarras card game 1063:62-63
Boules or pentanque game, how to play 1327:19
Boxes game 956:114-115
Charlemagne game 143:43
Coinchee card game 1063:75-79
Continental draughts board game, patterns, making 1541:203-207
Diagonal draughts board game, patterns, making 1541:202
Draughts board game, patterns, making 1541:195-200
Draughts for three board game, patterns, making 1541:208-213
Ecarte card game 1132:28-29
Escargot, hopscotch game 1426:16-17
Five Men's Morris game, how to play 1688:42-45
French words picture pairs game, making 1327:30-31
Goose game, paper, making 1500:38-39
Hide, hide game 602:92-93
Jeu de Boules game, how to make 1074:186-191
Lamarelle game 383:79
Le Pouilleux Old Maid card game 1063:49-51
Les billes, marbles game, how to play 1708:24-25
Les boules game, how to play 956:44-45; 1497:36
Les Grelots tag game, how to play 1498:20
London Bridge, heaven and hell game 474:31
Loser draughts board game, patterns, making 1541:201-202
Marble game, making 626:48-49
Marrons (chestnuts) game 143:43
My Great Aunt Lives in Tours game 143:41; 602:91
Old Boy game 956:105
One Little Elephant Went Out One Day game 1126:20
Pipopipette game 956:114-115
Piquet card game 1132:24-28
Prince of Paris game 143:42; 602:92
Quilles game, how to play 956:42-43; 1507:69-70
Reversi board game, patterns, making 1541:214-218
Shut the Box game, how to make 956:89-90; 1074:143-145
Sketch impressions game 967:30
Solitaire board game 956:146-148
Solitaire game, making 1507:67-68
Sur le Pont d'Avignon chanting game 1118:42
Swap chairs by the numbers game, how to play 58:26-27; 1494:115
Vent Frais (Cool Wind) musical game 1116:27
Vingt-et-Une (Blackjack) card game 1132:29-32
FRANCE—HANDICRAFTS
Calvary scene from Brittany model, stones, making 1094:10
Flower transparencies, pressed flowers, making 626:50-51

Head, papier-mache, making 525:39
Interlocking tiles, clay, making 1070:91-93
Jointed Pierrot court jester, paper, making 298:212-213
Lacy snowflake doilies, thread, making 889:8-13
Potato printing, how to do 1278:14-15
Poupard, jester on a stick, making 298:114-115
Silhouettes, paper, making 298:226
Six-sided tiles, clay, making 1070:94-96
FRANCE—HOUSES
Farmhouse from France, paper and fabric model, making 1094:54-56
Peasant house model, making 494:124-130
FRANCE—INDEPENDENCE DAY
Bastille Day celebration July 14 722:9-12
FRANCE—JEWELRY
Perfumed petal beads jewelry, making 1327:15
FRANCE—LANGUAGE
French Language 143:70
Numbers one through ten in French language 391:unp; 1708:17; 1712:unp
Words and expressions in French 1042:128
FRANCE—LANGUAGE—FINGER PLAYS
Finger plays and rhymes 1583:149
FRANCE—LENT
Paper nun, making 139:51
FRANCE—LULLABIES
Fais Dodo Colin 780:44
Une Poule Blanche 780:32
FRANCE—MAGIC TRICKS
Magic tree, paper trick, how to do 1270:22-23
FRANCE—NAMES
Naming Days information 695:30
FRANCE—PLAYS
Moliere, a Doctor in Spite of Himself 159:34-38
FRANCE—PUPPET SHOWS
Chinese Shadow Show (Ombres Chinoises) 143:47
Guignol 143:45
Polichinelle 143:44
Puppets, making 143:46
FRANCE—PUPPETS
French puppet, making 483:27
Pantins, cardboard, patterns, making 1422:17
FRANCE—RHYMES
Cheval baby bouncing rhyme 780:77
French Peek-A-Boo 780:48
Paris baby bouncing rhyme 780:73
Petit Pouce tickling rhyme 780:98
Tape Tape Petites Mains baby clapping rhyme 780:58
Une Poule sur un Mur tickling rhyme 780:102
Where Is Thumbkin? Finger play rhyme 780:110
FRANCE—SONGS
French cathedrals round song 1115:36
Frere Jacques round song 1115:12; 1607:42
Frere Jacques, lullaby 1220:146
Round song of names of French cathedrals, music, words 1477:62
Sur le Pont d'Avignon round song 1115:46
Vent Frais (Cool Wind) round song 1115:33
FRANCE—STRING FIGURES
Eiffel Tower figure, making 423:21
Saw, Scissors 1404:115-118
FRANKENSTEIN—COSTUMES
Frankenstein costume and make up 617:57-61
Frankenstein monster costume, neck electrodes, makeup, making 326:35-37

Frankenstein monster mask, making 179:42-43
Instant Frankenstein costume 213:2
FRANKENSTEIN—FACE PAINTING
Face painting, how to do 1306:51
FRANKFURTERS. *See* **HOT DOGS**
FRANKLIN, BENJAMIN
Franklin's postal system, it's fun to get mail, making
1199:9-20
Poor Richard's memory game 719:20
FRANKLIN, BENJAMIN—BIRTHDAY
Birthday celebration; art, music, foods, games, activities
1104:46-49
Franklin's birthday celebration, electrifying experiment,
how to do 1199:8-9
FRANKLIN, BENJAMIN—COOKERY
Mayz and broiled steak, recipe 57:26-27
FRANKS—COSTUMES
Charlemagne costume 213:64-66
FRENCH ACADIENNES—COOKERY
Mardi Gras chicken gumbo, recipe 1382:18
FRENCH ACADIENNES—DANCES
La danse de Mardi Gras in French and English, music
and score, given 1382:25
FRENCH CANADIANS—DANCES
Las Bastringue dance, how to do 1494:183-184
FRESCOES
Plaster of Paris fresco painting, making 1455:26
FRIEDMAN, INA R.
"How My Parents Learned to Eat," white rice, recipe
1216:19
FRIENDS
Make a Friend Day, activities, stories, crafts, recipes
558:5-7
FRIENDSHIP
Bracelets; braiding, and knotting bracelets, how to do
1364:4-23
FRIENDSHIP BRACELETS. *See* **GUATEMALA—**
HANDICRAFTS
FRIEZES
Frieze, paper, making 966:114-115
Sting frieze, making 830:66-67
Wall frieze, making 235:60
FRISBEES
History of Frisbees 119:97-102
FROG PRINCE
Frog Prince toy, making 346:30
FROGS
Champion jumping frog paper toy, making 1238:77-80
Frog jumping contest 118:111
Frog jumping, information about 118:110
How to catch 118:111-113
FRONTIER AND PIONEER LIFE. *See also* **WILDER,**
LAURA INGALLS
FRONTIER AND PIONEER LIFE—BASKETS
Harvest basket, making 1727:11
FRONTIER AND PIONEER LIFE—BEADWORK
Beaded bracelet and ring, making 1243:106-107
FRONTIER AND PIONEER LIFE—BOATS
Diorama, flatboat, how to make 646:96
Flatboat model, making 646:94-96
FRONTIER AND PIONEER LIFE—CANDLES
Candle dipping, how to do 1349:226
Candles, beeswax, candlewick, making 1214:59
FRONTIER AND PIONEER LIFE—CHRISTMAS
Christmas tree and decorations, how to make 593:76-83

FRONTIER AND PIONEER LIFE—CHRISTMAS—
DECORATIONS
Scented cinnamon ornaments, making 1727:13
FRONTIER AND PIONEER LIFE—CLOCKS
Sand clock, glasses, skewer, sand, how to make
1349:119
FRONTIER AND PIONEER LIFE—CLOTHING
Beaver skin hat mold, using felt and liquid starch, mak-
ing 1214:24
Possibles bag to hold mountain men's valuables, cham-
ois, leather laces, making 1214:28-30
Schoolmarm or housewife costume, making 870:103-104
Sunbonnet hat, cloth, ribbon, thread, pattern 870:100-
102; 1214:65-67
FRONTIER AND PIONEER LIFE—COOKERY
Apple Brown Betty, recipe 529:167-169
Apple cider punch, recipe 501:84
Apple core vinegar, recipe 885:132-133
Apple pie, recipe 885:124-125
Apple turnovers, recipe 885:122-123
Apples and onions, fried, recipe 885:127-128
Apples, dried and raisin pie, recipe 885:130-131
Apples, dried, recipe 885:128-129
Applesauce, recipe 1417:34-35; 1727:12
Baked beans with pork, recipe 501:36-37
Baked beans, recipe 1043:60
Baked ham slice, recipe 1417:22
Bean porridge, recipe 885:28-29
Bean soup, Capitol Hill Senate recipe 663:137-138
Bean soup, recipe 885:27-28
Beans, baked, recipe 885:26-27
Beans, chuckwagon, Oklahoman Indian recipe 663:82-83
Beef enchiladas, recipe 663:81-82
Beef jerky, recipe 1165:267-268
Beet pickles, recipe 885:136-137
Birds nest pudding, recipe 885:126-127
Biscuits, baking soda, recipe 1043:59
Biscuits, light, recipe 885:72-73
Biscuits, sour dough, recipe 885:80-81
Biscuits, sour milk, recipe 885:73-75
Blackbird pie, recipe 885:41-43
Blueberry pie, recipe 501:21
Blueberry pudding and sauce, recipe 885:49-51
Boston brown bread, recipe 885:86-87
Bread pudding, recipe 501:43
Bread, Graham bread, recipe 885:81-82
Bread, Long Winter bread, recipe 885:83-85
Bread, recipe 885:68-70
Bread, salt rising, recipe 885:75-77
Bread, white, recipe, making 501:38-41
Breakfast menu, recipes 18:7-23
Breakfast sausage balls, recipe 1670:8-9
Bubble and squeak, recipe 501:37
Buckwheat pancakes, recipe 1243:84-85
Burgoo pot luck, recipe 663:25-26
Butter and jam sandwiches, recipe 1670:16-17
Butter, homemade, recipe 18:20-21; 501:44-46; 885:166-
169; 1349:83; 1670:14-15
Buttermilk cornbread, recipe 1670:20-21
Cabbage and apple salad, recipe 1417:24
Cakes, heart shaped, recipe 885:200-201
Cambric tea, recipe 885:186-187
Camping bread, recipe 529:166-167
Candy, molasses on snow, recipe 885:192-193
Candy, pulled, recipe 885:190-191

Carrots, creamed, recipe 885:107
Cheese, hard cheese, recipe 885:172-176
Cheese, how to make 1349:85
Cheyenne gingerbread, recipe 529:170-171
Chicken pie, recipe 885:160-161
Chicken, fried, recipe 501:35; 885:158-159
Chicken, ginger with snow peas, California Chinese recipe 663:109-110
Chicken, roasted, recipe with stuffing 501:35; 885:162-163
Clam chowder, recipe 501:9
Codfish balls, recipe 885:31-32
Corn crackling, recipe 885:25
Corn dodgers, recipe 885:23
Corn fritters, recipe 1043:59
Corn pudding, recipe 663:27
Corn stew, recipe 501:28-29
Corn, creamed, recipe 885:108-109
Corn, dried, recipe 885:108
Corn, hulled, recipe 885:96-97
Corn, parched, recipe 885:212
Cornbread, recipe 885:24-25
Cornmeal mush, fried, recipe 885:21
Cottage cheese balls, recipe 885:170-171
Cowboy pie, recipe 1043:60
Crackers, Swedish, recipe 885:90-91
Cranberry apple punch, recipe 501:87
Cranberry jelly, recipe 885:48-49; 1043:61
Creamy oatmeal, recipe 1670:10-11
Cucumber pickles, green, recipe 885:138-139
Custard pie, recipe 885:198-199
Custard, soft, recipe 501:33
Date and walnut bars, recipe from Golden West 663:111
Doughnuts, recipe 885:88-89
Dried apple slices, how to make 1349:179
Dried apples, recipe 1214:64
Dried-apple sauce, recipe 1243:71
Duck, wild roasted, recipe 885:39-41
Dumplings, white flour, recipe 885:73-74
Eggnog, recipe 885:184-185
Eggs, stuffed, recipe 501:33
Fish, fried, recipe 885:44-45
Flap jacks, recipe 501:43
Fried apples and onions, recipe 1243:46
Fruit leather, recipe 1455:160
Fruit soup, recipe 1417:25
Fruit, dried and stewed, recipe 885:54-55
Fruit, sun dried, recipe 885:53-54; 1043:57
Ginger cookies, recipe 18:22-23; 1417:18-19
Ginger water, recipe 885:185-186
Gingerbread, recipe 1243:131
Goose, roasted, recipe 885:164-165
Hailstone ice cream, recipe 1243:120-121
Hamantaschen, Jewish New York City recipe 663:139-140
Hangtown fry, recipe 1214:50
Hard-boiled eggs, recipe 1417:9
Hardtack, recipe 885:98
Hasty pudding, recipe 885:20
Heart-shaped cakes, recipe 1243:36-37
Hollandsche apple Koek, Dutch Michigan recipe 663:58-59
Homemade butter, recipe 1243:47; 1417:16-17
Homémade crackers, recipe 1214:62—63
Honey and butter snack, recipe 1349:65

Hot slaw, recipe 501:31
Hotcakes, recipe 1653:87
Huckleberry pie, recipe 885:52-53
Ice cream, cheap, recipe 1214:98
Ice cream, recipe 501:79; 885:209-211
Indian fry bread, recipe 1214:34-35
Irish soda bread, Boston immigrant recipe 663:138-139
Irish stew, recipe 501:37
Jack rabbit stew, recipe 885:37-39
Jelly, crab apple, recipe 885:38-39
Johnny cake, recipe 501:29; 885:21-22
Johnny cakes, recipe 529:164-166; 1214:74
Journey cakes (also called Johnny cakes), recipe 1455:129
Kartoffelpuffer meat and potatoes, German Ohio recipe 663:57-58
Lard and cracklings, recipe 885:146-147
Laura Ingalls Wilder's little maple cakes, recipe 1670:2
Lemonade, recipe 885:188-189; 1670:30-31
Lettuce leaves with vinegar and sugar, recipe 885:112
Ma's best butter cookies, recipe 1670:26-29
Meat pie, three layered, recipe 529:161-163
Milk toast, recipe 501:43
Mince pie without meat, recipe 501:87
Mincemeat pie, recipe 885:154-155
Mock apple pie, recipe 1214:113-114
Mock oysters, recipe 1214:97
Molasses on snow candy, recipe 1243:22-23
Oyster soup, recipe 885:29-30
Pancake men, recipe 885:92-93
Pancakes buckwheat, recipe 885:94-95
Pancakes, recipe 1670:4-7
Parsnips, fried, recipe 885:110
Pecan pie, recipe 663:27-29
Pepparkakor cookies, recipe 1417:40-41
Pickles and pickle making, recipe 885:133-134
Pie crust, family paste for pies, recipe 885:194-195
Pie crust, fine for company recipe 885:196-197
Pig, roasted, recipe 885:151-153
Plum preserves, recipe 885:60
Plum pudding, recipe 501:90-91
Popcorn and milk, recipe 885:217; 1670:18-19
Popcorn balls, recipe 885:216-217; 1214:112; 1243:108-109
Popcorn, recipe 885:213-215
Pork sausage patties, recipe 1417:8
Portable soup, recipe 1214:11
Pot roast of ox, recipe 885:177-179
Potato soup, recipe 501:31; 1417:30-31
Potatoes, mashed, cakes, fried, hashed brown, recipes 885:102-106
Pots de creme, Jefferson White House French recipe 663:136-137
Pound cake, recipe 885:204-205
Pulled molasses candy, recipe 1243:48-49
Pumpkin marmalade, recipe 501:43; 1727:12
Pumpkin pie, recipe 501:84
Pumpkin stewed and pies, recipes 885:117-121
Raspberry quencher drink, recipe 501:19
Root beer, recipe 1214:110-111
Round rye bread, recipe 1417:12-15
Rye bread, recipe 18:16-19
Rye n' Injun bread, recipe 885:86-87
Salmon croquettes, recipe 501:8

Salt pork with gravy, fried, recipe 885:18-19
Sausage, homemade, recipe 885:149-150
Shrimp gumbo from Louisiana, recipe 663:29-30
Sopa de albondigas soup, Spanish Texas recipe 663:80-81
Sourdough biscuits and twists, recipe 1653:89-90
Sourdough biscuits, recipe 1043:58
Sourdough chocolate cake, recipe 528:19
Sourdough flapjacks, recipe 1214:46
Sourdough pancakes, recipe 88:229-230; 1043:58
Sourdough starter, recipe 88:230; 528:18; 885:77-79; 1043:57; 1214:45; 1455:119-120
Spareribs, baked, recipe 885:148
Spotted pup, recipe 663:83-84
Spritz cookies, Swedish Great Plains recipe 663:60-61
Squash, Hubbard, baked, recipe 885:114-115
St. Lucia buns, recipe 1417:38-39
Stewed celery, recipe 501:31
Strawberry jam, recipe 501:21; 885:62-63; 1670:12-13
Stuffed tomatoes, recipe 501:31
Succotash, recipe 529:163-164; 885:111
Summer pudding, Oregon Trail recipe 663:108
Swedish almond rusks, recipe 1417:26-27
Swedish meatballs, recipe 1417:32-33
Swedish pancakes, recipe 1417:36-37
Swedish potatoes, recipe 1417:23
Swedish rice porridge, recipe 18:14-15; 1417:10-11
Swiss cheese and onion pie, Wisconsin dairylands recipe 663:59-60
Tacos, recipe 1043:61
Taffy, plain and molasses, recipes, making 501:80-81
Thanksgiving pumpkin pie, recipe 1243:95-96
Tomato green pickles, recipe 885:139-140
Tomato preserves, recipe 885:135; 885:61-62
Tomatoes with sugar and cream, recipe 885:113
Town party lemonade, recipe 1243:61
Turkey, wild roasted, recipe 885:46-48
Turnip snacks and turnips mashed, recipes, making 885:115-116
Vanity cakes, recipe 885:202-203
Vinegar pie, recipe 885:197-198
Welsh rarebit, recipe 501:43
Zucchini parmesan, Western Italian recipe 663:112

FRONTIER AND PIONEER LIFE—COSTUMES
Apron, making 646:20-21
Bonnet, making 646:22-23
Coonskin hat, making 646:26-27
Fringed shirt, making 646:24-25
Frontier Gal costume, making 213:118
Pioneer costume, making 646:18-20
Virginian costume, making 213:128-129

FRONTIER AND PIONEER LIFE—CRADLES
Cradle model, making 646:39-40

FRONTIER AND PIONEER LIFE—DANCES
Polka and the waltz dances, how to do 1243:72-73
Square dance, how to do 1214:107-109

FRONTIER AND PIONEER LIFE—DIARIES
Travel diary, paper, cardboard, fabric, making 1214:60-61

FRONTIER AND PIONEER LIFE—DOLLS
Applehead Granny doll, pattern, making 1027:141-144
Corn husk doll, making 1027:144-149; 1727:8-9
Corn husk dolls, cornhusks, cloth, yarn, how to make 1419:192-193
Doll's dress, making 646:46-47

Hester Hollyhock and Fanny Fuchia pioneer dolls, making 415:25-27
Rag doll, pattern, making 646:44-45; 1027:153-156
Yarn doll, yarn, ribbon, making 1418:22-23

FRONTIER AND PIONEER LIFE—DYES
Dyeing costumes or cloth, how to do 646:63
Dyes, making 646:61-62
Dyes, onion colored clothes, how to dye T-shirt using onion skins 1349:100-101
Onion-skin dye, making 1418:9-11

FRONTIER AND PIONEER LIFE—FLOWERS—DRIED
Dried flower frame, making 1727:11

FRONTIER AND PIONEER LIFE—FOLKLORE
"Sarah, Plain and Tall"; physical and human geography activities 1458:92-95
"Three Names"; physical and human geography activities 1458:62-65

FRONTIER AND PIONEER LIFE—FOOTWEAR
Moccasins made by Indians for Lewis and Clark, chamois, thread, fabric paints, making 1214:17-19

FRONTIER AND PIONEER LIFE—FORTS
Diorama of fort, how to make 646:89
Fort Phil Kearny model, making 212:22-47
Fort, how to make 646:87-88
Wild West fort, milk cartons, patterns, making 1311:92-93

FRONTIER AND PIONEER LIFE—GAMES
Button, Button game, how to play 1214:115
Cabinet game, how to make and play 1609:27
Do You Trust Me? game, how to play 1609:56
Fox and Geese game, how to play 1349:45
Hide the Thimble game, how to play 1243:33
Knucklebones game, how to play 1349:133
Pioneer Apple games, how to play 1419:7
Shuffling the Brogue game, how to play 1609:55
Stealing stick game, how to play 1214:76-77

FRONTIER AND PIONEER LIFE—GOLD RUSH
Balance to weigh gold and silver, soda bottle, clothespin, paper cup, making 1214:43-44
Gold brick, paper bag, making 1214:51-53
Pan for gold, how to do 1214:39-41
Stream in a plastic bottle to demonstrate sediment in water 1214:42

FRONTIER AND PIONEER LIFE—HAIR
Rag curls, how to make 1214:106

FRONTIER AND PIONEER LIFE—HANDICRAFTS
Autograph book, making 1243:93-94
Block and sponge printing projects, making 1727:24-25
Bullwhacker, rope, stick, making 1214:75
Bunny pincushion, fabric, felt, patterns, making 1418:16-17
Button decorated box, making 1727:18
Button decorated frame, making 1727:28
Clove apple, making 1243:21
Decoupage box, making 1727:29
Geraniums in decorated tin cans, making 1243:119
Magic wallet, paints, making 1418:24-25
Name cards, making 1243:97
Noggin, making 892:29-32
Pillow hearts, stuffed fabric, making 1727:14
Pioneers and covered wagon, pipe cleaners, fabric, making 1376:56-57
Potpourri pot rest, stuffed fabric, making 1727:16
Red and white striped gift wrap paper, making 1243:83

Rocking animals, making 482:44-45
Star-edged shelf paper, making 1243:60
Story square, stitched fabrics, making 1727:17
Thimble pictures, making 1243:59

FRONTIER AND PIONEER LIFE—HERBS
Dried herbs and flowers, making 1418:8

FRONTIER AND PIONEER LIFE—HOME LIFE
Home life, display ideas, patterns, making 1159:143

FRONTIER AND PIONEER LIFE—HOUSEHOLD
Beds models, making 646:84
Braided mat, fabric, making 1418:6-7
Broom, making 646:48-49
Cache of supplies buried in ground, how to do, with can of pop 1214:27
Clothing rack model, making 646:81
Cooking rack, making 646:66-67
Fireplace model, making 646:82-83
Pioneer water carrier, paper model, how to make 1349:117
Table and bench model, making 646:80
Trencher, making 646:57

FRONTIER AND PIONEER LIFE—HOUSES
Diorama, log cabin, making 646:78-85
Half-faced shelter, making 646:64-65; 646:68
Sod house, making 1312:17

FRONTIER AND PIONEER LIFE—INKS
Walnut ink, how to make 1349:157

FRONTIER AND PIONEER LIFE—JEWELRY
Heart brooch, fabric, pin, making 1727:14-15

FRONTIER AND PIONEER LIFE—JOURNALS
Journals kept by trappers, cardboard, felt, paper, making 1214:32-33

FRONTIER AND PIONEER LIFE—LANTERNS
Tin-punch lantern, Wild West cowboy patterns, making 1051:110-114

FRONTIER AND PIONEER LIFE—LOG CABINS
Log cabin, how to build 646:72-74; 719:40-41
Log cabin, paper rolls, making 101:25; 1017:25

FRONTIER AND PIONEER LIFE—MILLS
Quern mill model, making 646:75

FRONTIER AND PIONEER LIFE—MUSICAL IN-STRUMENTS
Fiddle, homemade, can, string, pencil, making 1349:177

FRONTIER AND PIONEER LIFE—NEWSPAPERS
Print an engraving for newspaper illustrations, making 1214:95
Set a page of type and print it, how to do 1214:93-94

FRONTIER AND PIONEER LIFE—PATCHWORK
Patchwork pillow, fabric, stuffing, making 297:188-189; 1418:14-15

FRONTIER AND PIONEER LIFE—PEOPLE
Pom pom pioneer man and woman, paper tubes and cups, patterns, making 912:95-98
Sunbonnet Sue, or Pioneer lady from glass bottle, making 764:53-55

FRONTIER AND PIONEER LIFE—POUCHES
Davy Crockett's pouch, making 719:30-32

FRONTIER AND PIONEER LIFE—PUPPETS
Shadow puppets, wood, cardboard, wire, dowels, making 1349:192-193

FRONTIER AND PIONEER LIFE—QUILTING
Bear's paw quilt block greeting card made from paper, patterns, making 1240:42-43
Broken dishes quilt puzzle made from paper, patterns, making 1240:26-27

Corn and beans quilt block recipe folder made from paper, patterns, making 1240:48-49
Dresden plate quilt block made from paper, patterns, making 1240:53
Hanging windmill star quilt block made from paper, patterns, making 1240:60-61
House on a hill and pine tree quilt blocks made from paper, patterns, making 1240:32-33
Nine patch quilt squares, fabric, making 1243:34-35
Patchwork quilt, making 646:42-43
Quilt patterns; nine patch, schoolhouse, making 1159:140-142
Quilted potholder, fabric, patterns, making 1418:18-19
Quilted tissue bag, making 297:190-191
Quilts, a simple nine-patch collage made from paper, patterns, making 1240:12-13
Saying good-bye quilt block bookmark made from paper, patterns, making 1240:16-17
Shoofly quilt block made from paper, patterns, making 1240:36-37
Sunshine and shadows quilt block weather diary made from paper, patterns, making 1240:56-57

FRONTIER AND PIONEER LIFE—ROPING
How to spin a rope 1609:84

FRONTIER AND PIONEER LIFE—RUGS
Braided rug, fabric, making 1727:6-7
Hooked rug, fabric strips, making 1727:6-7
Rag rug, fabric, crochet needle, making 1214:103-104
Rug, braided, making 646:41

FRONTIER AND PIONEER LIFE—SCHOOLS
Diorama of school room, how to make 646:86
Dunce cap, making 646:53
Hornbook, making 646:50-51
Quill pen, making 646:52
Sampler, ABC, making 646:54-55

FRONTIER AND PIONEER LIFE—SPINNING
Finger spinning to make fibers into thread, how to do 1349:98-99
Spinning wheel, making 646:58-60

FRONTIER AND PIONEER LIFE—STENCILING
Stencil designs, how to make 1349:216-217
Stenciled box, wood, paints, making 1418:32-33

FRONTIER AND PIONEER LIFE—STOREKEEPERS
Balance scale for pioneer storekeepers, how to make 1349:153

FRONTIER AND PIONEER LIFE—TINWORK
Punch tin picture, aluminum foil, pie plate, how to do 1349:116-117

FRONTIER AND PIONEER LIFE—TOWNS
Frontier Town, making 942:146-147; 942:146-147

FRONTIER AND PIONEER LIFE—TOYS
Checkerboard, stenciled wood, making 1727:26-27
Drum, tin drum, pattern, making 1027:156-159
Jacob's ladder toy, wood, ribbon, making 1727:21-23
Jumping jack, cardboard, brass fasteners, string, making 1349:236-237
Whirligig toy, string, button, making 1727:20

FRONTIER AND PIONEER LIFE—TRANSPORTA-TION
Buckboard, balsa wood, making 925:77-79; 925:77-79

FRONTIER AND PIONEER LIFE—WAGONS
Covered wagon model, making 646:90-93
Covered wagon, cardboard box, large, making 539:19; 539:19
Covered wagon, paper, making 1017:27; 1017:27

Wagon and cowboys from the Far West, paper and wood models, making 1094:6-7

FRONTIER AND PIONEER LIFE—WATER
Dowsing for water, how to do 1214:88-89
Windlass to wind rope in well, making 1214:90
Windmill model, pin wheel from paper, making 1214:91-92

FRONTIER AND PIONEER LIFE—WEAPONS
Flintlock pistol, making 719:34-38
Hunting knife, making 646:36-37
Powder horn, making 646:33-35
Rifle, making 646:28-30
Sheath, making 646:37-38
Shot pouch, making 646:31-33

FRONTIER AND PIONEER LIFE—WELLS
Well and sweep model making 646:76-77

FRONTIER AND PIONEER LIFE—WINDOWS
Oiled paper windows, making 1214:87

FRONTIER AND PIONEER LIFE—WREATHS
Wreath, natural materials, making 1727:10

FRUIT LEATHER
Fruit leather, recipe 1477:53; 1653:182; 1660:30

FRUITS
Orange and lemon chutney, recipe 1655:28-29

FULLER, BUCKMINSTER R.
Tetrahedron kite, making 1069:266-272

FUNGI
Bracket fungi painting, how to do 1421:41

FUR TRAPPERS
Beaver skin hat mold, using felt and liquid starch, making 1214:24
Cache of supplies buried in ground, how to do, with can of pop 1214:27
Journals kept by trappers, cardboard, felt, paper, making 1214:32-33
"Possibles" bag to hold mountain men's valuables, chamois, leather laces, making 1214:28-30

FUR TRAPPERS—COOKERY
Indian fry bread, recipe 1214:34-35

FUTURE—COSTUMES
Costume from bubble pack, making 1174:39

G

GABON—GAMES
Gathering stars chasing game, how to play 1498:33-34
GABON—HANDICRAFTS
Naja basket, making 222:40-41
GABON—MASKS
Gabon, Africa mask, making 811:61
GAG, WANDA
"Millions of Cats," activities and questions 758:47-53
Vegetable cats, recipe 758:53
GAG, WANDA—PUPPETS
"Millions of Cats" puppets, paper bag, making 838:25
GALDONE, PAUL
"Gingerbread Boy"; gingerbread cookies, recipe 843:59-50, 130
"Gingerbread Boy"; tree ornaments, dough, recipe 843:60
"Gingerbread Man," gingerbread men, recipe 1216:76
"Three Little Pigs"; flannel board story, patterns, making 843:76,135-136
GAMBIA—GAMES
Crick-crack crocodile rope game, how to play 1501:23
GAMBIA—HANDICRAFTS
Tie-dye T-shirt with spider web pattern, making 1448:20-21
GAMBIA—MUSICAL INSTRUMENTS
Kundiand Kasso harps, making 222:32-35
GAMES. *See also the subheading* **GAMES** *under individual topics*
A-Wuni-Kuni 386:24
Acorn toss Pilgrim game 436:59
Across the Amazon 732:271
Aesop's Mission 1036:25
African finger counting game 956:84-85
Alquerque 1037:27-28
American Eagle 732:20
Appalachia; bluebird, bluebird game 602:184-185
Appalachia; booger man game 602:186
Appalachia; here we go over the mountain two by two game 602:183-184
Appalachia; sheep-nanny game 602:184
Arches game 602:157-158
Barnyard Bedlam game 967:51
Bat the balloon game 602:159-160
Battle for the Sahara 732:238
Battledore and shuttlecock game 362:23
Bean bag toss game, fabric, beans, making 1213:135
Botticelli 791:125-126; 1036:34
Boules, les 956:44-45
Box puzzles, small boxes, pictures, making 1213:139
Brooklyn Bridge 1036:120
Brownies and Fairies game 809:133
Bum, Bum, Here We Come game 602:156-157
Bunny games for Easter 433:55-65
Card Stock Market card game 1132:142-146
Carnival frisbee throw, making 375:111
Cat's Cradle game and history of game 791:86-91; 1036:37; 1074:254-259
Charlie Chaplin relay 375:34
Charlie Chaplin went to France 1126:85
Checkerboards, wood or cardboard, how to make 1615:34-37
Checkers game, big pizza box, making 1213:138
Chicago game 572:24-25; 572:24-25
Chinese checkers, how to make 1074:88-89

Chinese friends or the Sandwich game, making 805:37
Chinese get up game 984:25
Chinese handball game 876:80-81
Chinese hop game 737:3
Chinese jump rope 876:48-49
Chinese ping pong 732:109
Chinese tag 876:13-14
Chinese volleyball game 732:44
Chinesenspiel, Pachisi game, how to make 1074:32-33
Christmas bag game 362:12
Cinderella 732:109
Clipper ship race game, making 942:44-45
Clown target game, making 1185:84-85
Computers and Tic-Tac-Toe, computer game, how to play 1688:77-83
Concentration game 572:34-35
Cowboy and Indian obstacle race 635:47
Cowboy roundup game 534:81
Cowboys and Indians 876:119; 1036:127
Creative Olympics 1131:86-89
Danish Fish game 979:41
Danish rounders 1036:202
Declaration of Independence 51:117
Discovery of Little America 1078:81
Dom dom malayas 1126:58
Dreidels 956:101-102
Easter Bunny tail game 534:91-92
Easter egg fun game 534:93
Easter egg hunt 905:26; 1036:263
Eskimo Ayagak game, making 307:44
Eskimo games 376:91
Eskinose 732:114
Father Christmas' treasure store 635:21
Foreign shopping 1078:31
Foreign stamps 1078:26
Fourth of July Jackstraws 51:119
French and English game 362:49
French cricket game 449:116
French Le Pouilleux Old Maid card game 1063:49-51
Frog in the Lea game 967:51
Fruit basket game 602:159
German game 1036:209
German whist game 114:115
Girl Scout baseball 1078:44
Girl Scout Promise & Law 1078:64
Going to Boston 956:89; 1036:58
Going to Jerusalem game 602:158
Good Morning, Your Majesty 1126:94
Greek ball game 1036:212
Grunt, Pig, Grunt game 602:157
He Can Do Little game 602:160
Hide the Thimble Pilgrim game 436:57
Hiding the thimble game 362:54
History of games 791:2
Hopscotch International 984:18-19
Hopscotch, history of game 791:77-78
Horse and Indians game, felt, cork, making 1099:unp
How Many Miles to Babylon? 1126:111
How Many Miles to Burnham Bright? game 602:185-186
How Many Miles to London? 1078:22
I'm a Pretty Little Dutch Girl 1126:55
Indian and Rabbits, making 118:282
Indian ball game 720:89
Indian bowl game 984:6-7
Indian dart throw game, making 375:111

Indian game 956:95
Indian hoop tag game 564:154
Indian kickball game 956:14
Indian wrestling 956:35
International Kim's game 967:54
Ish-Kabibble 833:unp
Jacks game and history of game 791:25-26
Jan-Kem-Po 956:19-20
Japanese tag 249:21
Japanese tag 1249 21:
Jousting 635:65
Jousting games, wooden, making 942:74-76
Jump rope game and history of game 791:27-33
Jump the beanbag game 602:160-161
Kalah, egg carton 984:42-43
Kalah, making 120:46-49
Kaling 51:194
Kamikaze 732:250
Kendo 386:61
Khanhoo card game 1132:7-9
Kickball, Indian style 375:41
Klondike solitaire card game 1037:40-42
Klondike, or seven card solitaire card game 720:222-223
Knight of the Whistle Castle 362:52
Knucklebones game, dice, modeling dough, making 1320:26-27
Lemme sticks 386:63
London 1036:222
London Bridge 474:30-32; 956:53-55; 1036:151
London Bridge game and history of game 791:16-19
Marbles game and history of game 791:81-83
Marco Polo 1036:245
May-Day combat 51:75-77
Maypole 1036:152
Michigan card game 1063:94
Nim, ancient math game, how to play 1715:31
Nine Men Around the Square, making 948:38-39
Nine Men Morris 1037:12-13
Nine Men Morris, making 805:36
Nine Men's Morris 876:72-73; 956:134-135
Nine Men's Morris board game, pattern, making 1477:106
Nine Men's Morris game, history of 1688:51-53
Nine Men's Morris game, how to make 921:12; 1074:59-61
Nine pins 876:92-93
Noah's Ark 905:68
Norwegian ball game 275:128
O'Leary 1036:227
Ojiisan-Obaasan 386:70
Oklahoma gin card game 1063:44-45; 1132:132
Oliver, Oliver, Oliver Twist 1126:85
Olympics backyard games, making 1121:12-13
Origami game and history of game 791:65-71
Pachisi 1037:16-19
Pike's Peak 732:252
Pilgrim spoonball, making 180:44-47
Piñata game 1036:268
Pirate chase 564:144-145
Pirates treasure hunt board, making 295:166
Pony Express 1078:69
Prince Charles, Princess Diana, and their carriage game 449:106
Proverbs 386:76

Proverbs game 362:31
Pyramid building 876:122
Pyramid clumps 732:90
Pyramid marble game 1119:28
Pyramid play offs 732:91
Pyramid puzzle, making 805:39
Pyramid races 732:130; 1131:88
Queen Anne and her maids game 362:60-61
Quilles game, how to make 1074:192-195
Quoits game, making 877:105
Railway carriages 449:110
Russian Scandal game 362:39
Sea lion game 602:161-162
Shape game 967:51
Shepherdess and the wolf game 362:14
Ships on the Ocean 635:51
Shove Winter out 956:35-36
Siamese softball 732:35
Spade Oklahoma card game 1063:45
St. Patrick's Day game 534:90-91
Stool of Repentance game 362:42
Tangram game, how to make 1074:274-275
Tangrams 956:155-156
Tangrams, burlap, making 818:54-56
Tea Clippers game 942:42-43
Ten Little Indians 720:83
Tenpins with decorated bodies and heads, cardboard tubes, paper, paints, making 1260:30-31
Three Steps to Germany game 833:unp
Three-in-a-row games played around the world, how to play 1688:85
Tic-tac-toe game, history of 1688:38-42
Tic-tac-toe game, wood, paint, making 1465:67-69
Tigre, la Persona y la Camara, (Tiger, the Man and the Gun) 386:49
Tom Sawyer's fishing game, making 719:44-45
Tom-tom dance 905:38
Treasure hunt games, making 1185:86-87
U.S. Cities, going for distance game, making 655:60
U.S.A. game 1078:46
U.S.A. game, making 655:24-25
Uncle Sam 876:33-34
Valentine candy charades 732:204
Valentine game 534:89
Wells Fargo 732:259
Western Union 1036:105
When I Go to California 386:96
Which Am I? game 602:159
Wild Wild West 732:260
Yankee Doodle cracker 737:21
Zimba game 474:34-35
GAMES—JUMP ROPE
Chants for jumping rope 1501:12-18
GAMES—MUSICAL
Cinderella musical jump rope game 1116:71
Come Follow musical game 1116:26
Counting Rhymes musical games 1116:61
Down the Mississippi musical jump rope game 1116:71
John Brown's Baby musical game 1116:24
Lady Round the Lady musical game 1116:46-47
My Mother Was Born in England musical game 1116:67
Peruvian Wolf musical game 1116:17
Tarantella musical game 1116:57-59
GAMES—TRAVELERS
Botticelli 1034:28-31; 1044:20-22

Dance daringly in Denmark 1044:52-53
Eagle eye 1044:32-33

GARDENS
For potatoes and tomatoes, thank you, Thomas Jefferson! 118:100
Victorian garden plan pattern 220:24-25

GARDENS—BIBLICAL
Herb gardens 475:151-153
Mary garden 475:153-155
Peace gardens 475:155

GARDENS OF ADONIS
Information on 474:28

GARGOYLES
Monster face, dough, recipe for dough, making 1486:22-23

GARLANDS
Evergreen garland, evergreen branches, wire, making 1285:91

GAUCHOS
Gauchos; way of life, clothing, food, language 1378:249-255

GAUCHOS—COSTUMES
Gaucho poncho, paper towels, paints, making 1378:250-251

GEISEL, THEODOR
"Green Eggs and Ham," green eggs and ham, recipe 1216:115
"Scrambled Eggs Super!," scrambled eggs, recipe 1216:114

GEISEL, THEODOR—COOKERY
Green eggs a la Dr. Seuss, recipe 1199:62

GENEALOGY. *See* **FAMILY TREE**

GENGHIS KHAN
Royal Pavilion, making 173:60-61

GEORGE, JEAN
"My Side of the Mountain," rabbit stew, recipe 1216:96

GEORGIA—COOKERY
Ambrosia, recipe 654:36
Country Captain chicken, history of, recipe 155:32-33
Green peanuts, boiled, recipe 654:37
Peach cobbler, recipe 1342:49
Turnip greens, recipe 654:35

GERMANIC PEOPLE. *See* **NORSEMEN**

GERMANY
Activities, flags, games, songs, dances, recipes 1381:177-180
Activities, projects, recipes 282:82-95

GERMANY—BIRTHDAYS
Birthday celebrations in Germany 695:64-65
Birthday customs 488:34-36
Celebrations of birthdays in Germany 474:85

GERMANY—CHRISTMAS
Advent celebration 497:60-69
Celebration of Christmas in Germany 601:109; 1049:86
Christmas customs in Germany 149:41-42; 473:28-31; 661:86-88; 1717:14-15
Christmas Eve ceremony 474:149-150
Christmas tree and decorations, how to make 593:42-49
German celebration, activities, handicrafts, foods, songs, making 909:129-137
Star of Seven 475:42
Traditional Christmas customs in Germany 218:38-39

GERMANY—CHRISTMAS—COOKERY
Braised red cabbage, recipe 497:66
Braised sweet and sour cabbage, recipe 1128:64
Chocolate macaroons, recipe 1234:70
Chocolate shells cookies (schokolademuscheln), recipe 1234:73
Christollen (Christmas bread), recipe 1128:62-63
Cinnamon star cookies, recipe 1234:70
Cookies, German spice cookies, recipe 704:80-81
Custard apple tort (schwarz walder apfelkuchen), recipe 1234:74
Fruit bread (schnitz-oder hutzelbrot), recipe 1234:75
German ginger cookies, recipe 218:55-57
Ginger cookies (lebkuchen), recipe 1234:72
Gingerbread house, recipe 1023:100-103; 1080:20-21
Gingerbread people or animal cookies, recipe 1666:117
Honey cookies (braune kuchen), recipe 1234:70
Honey spice cookies, recipe 273:51-54
Lebkuchen (German honey cakes), recipe 1128:116
Lebkuchen (spice bars), recipe 1666:117-118
Linzertorte, recipe 1234:75
Marzipan stuffed prunes, recipe 704:82
Marzipan, recipe 1234:71; 1305:32
Nurnburg star cookies, recipe 1023:103-105
Pfeffernusse (German pepper nuts cookies), recipe 1128:123; 1234:71; 1666:116
Potato dumplings, recipe 497:66
Roast goose, recipe 497:66; 1128:63
"S" butter cookies, recipe 1234:73
Speculaas cookies, recipe 1234:73
Spice cookies (pfefferkuchenpuppen), recipe 1234:72
Spicy cakes (lebkuchen) on trees custom 516:45
Springerle bars, recipe 1234:71
Springerle cookies, recipe 1128:114, 121
Springerle, recipe 1023:96-98
Stollen, easy, recipe 54:219
Stollen, recipe 497:66; 1234:74

GERMANY—CHRISTMAS—DECORATIONS
Advent calendar, making 273:41-45
Advent calendar, paper, cardboard, paints, making 1234:68-69
Advent wreath decorations, making 497:68-69; 672:1-15
Angels, tiny, from fabric and beads, making 273:45-47
Bell, fringed bell, colored paper, making 1228:51
Bell, modern, gilt paper, making 1228:52
Bell, traditional, silver, gold paper, making 1228:54
Christmas trees from Germany, paper, tissue paper, patterns, making 1393:109
Cornucopia, square top, making 273:48-51
Cornucopias, paper, making 672:166-177
Dove of peace, paper, making 1228:53
Gingerbread house, dough and candies, making 1234:65-67
Stars, pleated stars, paper or foil, making 1228:50
Stars, ribbon star, ribbon, making 1228:55
Stars, spikey Christmas stars, foil, making 1228:48

GERMANY—CHRISTMAS—HANDICRAFTS
Advent calendar, paper, paints, making 1485:19
Advent calendar, pattern, making 1305:30-31
German Advent calendar, felt, dowel, paints, making 1575:28-29
Sheep, woolly, made from wool on cardboard tubes 273:54-60
Star ornament, making 1023:51-53

GERMANY—CLOCKS
Grandfather clock, wooden miniature, how to make 525:58-59

GERMANY—COOKERY

Anise drops, recipe 343:132

Apfel strudel, apple strudel, recipe 1452:78

Apfelpfannekuchen, apple pancakes, sour cream, apple-sauce, recipe 1244:62-64

Apple cake, recipe 650:41; 1280:38-39

Apple crumb cake, recipe 661:99-100

Apple torte, recipe 1124:121

Aufschnitt, cold meat platter, recipe 269:19

Baked apples, recipe 1439:23

Bavarian dumplings, recipe 1560:10

Bavarian pork roast, recipe 1439:26

Beef broth, recipe 650:18

Beef rolls in cream sauce, recipe 650:25

Beer brewing and sausage making in the Middle Ages 661:52-59

Berlin cream pancakes, recipe 1439:25

Berliner Pfannkuchen, Berlin doughnuts, recipe 1452:72

Black Forest torte, recipe 650:42

Blitzkuchen, lightning spice cake, recipe 1477:72

Bockwurst, veal sausage, recipe 1452:75

Bologna with rutabagas, recipe 650:35

Butter cookies, recipe 650:40

Cherry soup, cold, recipe 661:96

Chocolate drink, recipe 269:36

Chocolate torte, recipe 188:26

Cinnamon stars (zimtsteme), cookies, recipe 72:39-40

Cod and potatoes, recipe 501:83

Cod with mustard sauce, recipe 650:28

Cookies, soft, recipe 874:74

Creamed herring, recipe 1439:21

Creamed spinach, recipe 650:30

Cucumber and sour cream salad, recipe 1439:21

Deerback cake, recipe 650:38

Deutsches beefsteak (hamburger), recipe 662:45-46

Eggs, pickled eggs, recipe 794:25

Fried fish, recipe 874:42

Fruit pudding, recipe 269:32

Frumenty, recipe 88:106-107

Green beans, recipe 650:31

Hamburger, history of 661:64-66

Hamburgers, recipe 269:30; 661:96-97

Heaven and earth, apples, potatoes, frankfurters, recipe 1650:36

Herb quark with potatoes and cucumber salad, recipe 269:40

Himmel und Erde, heaven and earth potatoes, apples, bacon, recipe 1452:76

Himmel und Erde, heaven and earth potatoes and apple, recipe 1165:134

Himmel und Erde, recipe 967:31

History of cookery in 88:94-106

Honey spice cookies (Nurnbergers), recipe 88:107-108

Hunter's cabbage, recipe 1439:27

Jam cookies, recipe 858:unp

Kartoffelklosse, potato dumplings, recipe 1452:77

Liver dumplings, recipe 650:20

Marble cake, recipe 269:21

Marinated roast, recipe 650:24

Marzipan balls, recipe 269:44

Meat dumplings, recipe 793:40

Muesli cereal, recipe 1487:6-7

Mushrooms, recipe 874:36

Noodle salad, recipe 650:34-35

One-pot meal, recipe 650:32

Open-face sandwiches, recipe 650:36

Pancakes, filled, recipe 895:53

Pancakes; egg pancakes, recipe 1081:35

Paprika Schnitzel, veal with paprika, recipe 1452:74

Pork roast, recipe 650:26

Potato apple saute, recipe 1380:26

Potato cakes, kartoffel puffer, recipe 1485:9

Potato dumplings (pflaumen knodel), recipe 650:27; 801:108-109; 871:34; 1439:26

Potato pancakes, recipe 269:18; 661:99

Potato salad, hot, with bacon, recipe 895:54

Potato salad, recipe 269:31

Potato soup, recipe 650:36; 1439:20

Potatoes, history of 661:66-68

Potatoes, parsley, recipe 650:28

Pretzel A B C's 187:23

Pretzel initials, recipe 282:119

Pretzels, giant, recipe 909:134

Pretzels, recipe 1278:4-5

Quark fruit cream, recipe 269:20

Red cabbage, recipe 650:30

Rindergulasch, beef goulash, recipe 1452:73

Roasted sauerkraut and pork, recipe 1439:28

Rolladen beef dish, recipe 1439:22

Rotkraut mit apfeln, red cabbage with apples, recipe 1165:133-134

Rye and ham sandwiches, recipe 1124:120

Salad with sweet and sour dressing, recipe 650:21

Sauerbraten, recipe 661:97-99; 871:32-33; 1265:67-68; 1439:24

Sauerkraut, history of 661:62-64

Semolina dumplings, recipe 650:20

Spaetzle (German noodle), recipe 88:110; 650:23

Spiced cookies, recipe 1265:69-70

Stollen, recipe 88:108-109

Sweet-and-sour red cabbage, recipe 1265:66

Veal cutlets, recipe 874:46

Veal scallopini, recipe 514:135

Wiener Schnitzel, veal cutlet, recipe 269:26; 1381:179

GERMANY—COSTUMES

Chocolate torte, recipe, costume 188:26

Paper doll type costume, pattern, making 282:94

Pied Piper costume, fabric, making 1174:50

Tyrolean, variety of old clothes, making 1656:29-32

GERMANY—DANCES

Ach Yah! song and dance game 1114:30-31

Atlantic mixer dance, how to do 1494:133-134

Eins Zwei Drei dance, how to do 1494:149-150

GERMANY—DOLLS

Peasant girl from Bavaria, fabric, ping pong ball, cork, making 1094:42

GERMANY—EASTER

Easter egg customs in Germany 201:20

Easter, celebration of 661:90

Pretzel hearts 139:85

GERMANY—EASTER—COOKERY

Pretzel bake, recipe 139:86-87

GERMANY—EASTER—GAMES

Eierlesen egg game 201:184-185

German egg game 201:176-177

GERMANY—EASTER—HANDICRAFTS

Egg tree, making 64:49-50

Egg with picture, papier-mache, making 274:119-123

GERMANY—EASTER—SONGS

Steeple Bells, traditional song, Germany 139:109

GERMANY—FESTIVALS

Carnival before Lent celebration 826:14-15

Corn Festival celebration 659:27

Festivals and celebrations, maps, flags, crafts, making 1305:27-37

First day of school, Schultute, making 1305:35

Munich Beer Festival celebration 566:21

Oktoberfest celebration 661:92-94

Oktoberfest Festival, activities and projects for classrooms 1393:49-50

Shrove Tuesday, celebration of 661:90

St. John's Day flaming wheel contest, making 709:181-182

St. John's Day, history of 709:181

St. Martin's Festival celebration 661:94

Walpurgis Night celebration 661:90-91

GERMANY—FESTIVALS—COOKERY

Jelly filled doughnuts, easy, recipe 54:219

GERMANY—FESTIVALS—HANDICRAFTS

First day of school cone, paper, making 1381:180

First day of school paper cone, crepe paper, candies, making 1398:37

Schultute first day of school gift, making 1477:100

GERMANY—FOLKLORE

"Bremen Town Musicians" flannel board story, patterns, making 1603:122-127

Clever, eh? fable play 1212:84-90

Goldilocks and the Three Bears toy, cardboard and felt, making 346:15-17

Hansel and Gretel Walk with bread 1199:3

"Three Wishes" flannel board story, patterns, making 1603:158-163

GERMANY—FOLKLORE—COOKERY

Clever Gretel; story and recipe for roast chicken, making 364:109-116

Dwarf Long Nose; story and recipe for chocolate potato cake and icing 364:56-89

Hansel and Gretel spare ribs, recipe 1264:39

Old Woman and the Tramp; story and hearty soup recipe 364:145-154

GERMANY—FOLKLORE—COSTUMES

Red Riding Hood and her Granny costume, patterns, making 1174:106

GERMANY—FOLKLORE—HANDICRAFTS

Candy house, recipe 1216:84

Hansel and Gretel and gingerbread house models, milk cartons, making 1311:94-95

Hansel and Gretel gingerbread house and village, recipe, patterns, making 1278:1278

Shoemaker and the Elves, flannel board, patterns, making 1201:133-138

GERMANY—FOLKLORE—MUSICAL INSTRUMENTS

Pied Piper and rats music from juice cans, making 1310:96-97

GERMANY—FOLKLORE—PUPPETS

"Elves and the Shoemaker," shoemaker, wife and elf puppets, patterns 1206:30-33

"Frog Prince" shadow puppets, patterns, making 1602:144-150

"Red Riding Hood" shadow puppets, patterns, making 1602:115-122

GERMANY—GAMES

Adam Had Seven Sons game 602:93

Asalto game, making 1507:71-72

Baste the Bear game 282:120; 383:81

Bell and hammer game, how to make 1074:138-139

Broom croquet game 386:33

Chinesenspiel game, making 1507:73-74

Counting out game 474:36

Dog collar game 383:81

Gluckshaus game, how to make 1074:140-141

Hopscotch, hinkspiel game, how to play 1355:36

How Deep Is the Water? game, how to play 1355:14

How Will It End? drawing game 967:31

Little Hans game 602:94-95

Paradies Hupfen, hopscotch game 1426:18-19

Plate, potato, broom relay 386:71

Poch game, how to make 1074:124-126

Ringel, Ringel game 602:95

Sechs and Sechzig (Sixty-Six) card game 1132:38-40

Skat card game 1132:32-38

Solitaire board game, patterns, making 1541:85-90

Unwrap the chocolate game 58:28-29

Unwrap the chocolate game, how to play 1494:102-103

Voelkerball game, how to play 1497:37

GERMANY—HANDICRAFTS

Black Forest cuckoo clock, cardboard, making 282:86-87

Carnival clown shoes and wig, making 1485:20-21

Eggs; Pennsylvania Dutch patchwork eggs and egg tree, making 626:54-57

German snowflakes mobile, making 452:92-94

Gingerbread house, cardboard, patterns, gingerbread recipe, making 1485:25-27

Mirror, rose bordered, making 298:54-55

Ochter-Foggel good luck bird, making 298:90-91

Ribbon wrapped wax flower egg, making 298:84-85

Scherenschnitte lacy heart, paper, making 298:202-203

Tulip eggs on tree, making 298:98-99

Walnut head prune peasants, making 298:150-151

Wild turkey with colorful tail, making 298:158-159

GERMANY—LANGUAGE

Common words and phrases in German 1175:24

Finger plays and rhymes in German language 1583:150

Numbers one to ten in German language 393:unp

GERMANY—LULLABIES

"Schlaf, Kindlein, Schlaf" 1607 11:

GERMANY—MAGIC TRICKS

Vanishing key, how to do 1270:24-25

GERMANY—MUSIC—PUPPETS

Hansel and Gretel opera puppets, and stage, patterns, making 1310:154-159

GERMANY—MUSICAL INSTRUMENTS

Sleigh bells, bells, plastic lanyard, beads, making 1646:46-47

GERMANY—NEW YEAR'S DAY

Onion custom 505:21

Time of new beginnings in Germany 489:74-78

GERMANY—NEW YEAR'S EVE

New Year's Eve, celebration of 661:89

GERMANY—NUMBERS

Numbers one to ten in German language 393:unp

GERMANY—OKTOBERFEST

Burgomaster decoration, making 294:40-41

Gingerbread house and cake, making 294:36-37

Harvest cask centerpiece, making 294:42-43

Hats, making 294:44-45

Ring toss game, horse and rider game, pretzel game, making 294:46-48

Stein favors, making 294:38-39

Stein placemats, making 294:34-35

Weiner decorations, making 294:35

GERMANY—RHYMES

Hoppa, Hoppa Reiter baby bouncing rhyme 780:72

GERMANY—SCHOOLS

First Day of School cone, making 856:20-23

GERMANY—SCIENCE

Von Guericke's experiment showing strength of vacuum 1719:25-26

GERMANY—SONGS

Ach Du Lieber Augustin round song 1115:84

C-O-F-F-E-E round song 1115:65

Music Alone Shall Live round song 1115:61

Oh, How Lovely Is the Evening round song 1115:16

Schlaf, Kindlein, and Schalf lullabies 780:39

GERMANY—TOYS

Jumping Jack toy, making 626:52-54

Noah's Ark wooden toy, pattern, making 1027:36-44

GERSHWIN, GEORGE—BIRTHDAY

Celebrate by making watercolor pictures of Big Apple 1199:221-222

GESNER, ABRAHAM, DR.

Gesner's experiment, repeat to compare ways different oils burn 1719:39-41

GHANA—BIRTHDAYS

Birthday customs 488:37-39

GHANA—CHRISTMAS

Christmas celebration 601:31-32

GHANA—CLOTHING

Adinkra cloth, how to decorate with potato printed symbols 1179:176-177

Asante people Adinkra cloth, fabric, patterns, black paint, making 1633:112-115

Asante people kente cloth weaving made from paper, making 1633:110-111

Kente cloth shawl, how to make using chromatography 1333:42-46

Kente paper weaving, paper, yarn, dowel, making 1633:110-111

GHANA—COOKERY

African doughnuts, recipe 1508:144-147

Akla, bean balls, recipe 1508:120-123

Akwadu, banana-coconut bake, recipe 1165:32

Ampesi (boiled starchy vegetables), recipe 1508:87-90

Avocado spread, recipe 1508:126-127

Baked plantains, recipe 1265:147

Banku cornmeal dish, recipe 1508:93-96

Bean stew, recipe 1508:74-77

Boiled corn, recipe 1508:104-105

Cabbage salad, recipe 1265:146

Cakes, twisted cakes, recipe 794:38

Chichinga (grilled pieces of meat), recipe 1508:107-110

Corned beef stew, recipe 1508:64-67

Egg curry, recipe 1508:71-73

Fish and gravy, recipe 1508:68-71

Fish turnovers, recipe 1508:110-114

Fresh coconut, recipe 1508:116-120

Fresh fruit with coconut dip 187:40

Fried red plantain slices, recipe 1508:99-101

Fufu, mashed vegetables, recipe 188:13

Fufu, plantain, yam, or sweet potato balls, recipe 1165:30-31

Fufu, potato type dish, recipe 1508:85-87

Gari Foto, fried rice, recipe 1508:61-64

Gari, cassava dish, recipe 1508:83-84

Ghana cakes, recipe 1427:301

Ginger beer drink, recipe 1508:32-34

Ground nut soup (Ghana peanut soup), recipe 1427:301

Ground nut paste, recipe 1508:128-129

Ground nut toffee (or peanut cakes), recipe 1508:147-149

Hkatenkwan, one-pot meal with ginger chicken and okra, recipe 1165:31

Homemade peanut butter, recipe 1244:97

Joffof Ghana, chicken and rice Ghana, recipe 1165:31-32

Joll of rice, recipe 1508:44-47

Kelewele (fried plantain cubes), recipe 1508:114-116

Kenkey cornmeal dish, recipe 1508:90-93

Lemon squash drink, recipe 1508:29-30

Lemongrass tea drink, recipe 1508:37-39

Light or pepper soup, recipe 1508:54-57

Meat stew, recipe 1508:77-79

Orange slices, recipe 1508:141-144

Palaver stew, recipe 1508:47-50

Palmnut soup, recipe 1508:50-54

Papaya jam (pawpaw jam), recipe 1508:130-131

Pawpaw with lime, recipe 1508:133-134

Peanut butter soup, recipe 1244:98-99

Peanut butter stew or soup with chicken, recipe 1508:41-43

Plantain chips, recipe 1508:124-126

Rice and beans, recipe 1508:96-99

Rice balls, recipe 1508:81-83

Roasted corn, recipe 1508:106

Roasted ripe plantain, recipe 1508:101-102

Sugar bread (asikyire paano), cookies, recipe 72:93-94

Sweet balls dessert, recipe, making 1280:14

Sweet balls, doughnuts, recipe 1198:47

Twisted cakes, recipe 1508:134-137

Vegetable stew, recipe 1265:144-145

Vegetarian ground nut soup, recipe 1508:57-61

West African peanut soup, recipe 1265:142-143

Yams, candied, recipe 384:Sept 12

GHANA—COSTUMES

Fufu, mashed vegetables, recipe, costume 188:13

GHANA—DANCES

Clapping dance, how to do 1494:26-27

Kye Kye Kule dance, how to do 1494:28-29

GHANA—DOLLS

Asante people Akua-ba doll, paper or fabric, full-size patterns, making 1633:106-109

Ashanti doll, cardboard, pattern, making 1022:40-41

Ashanti doll, making 222:8-9

GHANA—FANTI TRIBE—SONGS

"Kye Kye Kule" 1607:37

GHANA—FESTIVALS

Children's Day celebration 601:33

Durbar celebration 631:44

First Fruits celebration 631:80

Harvest Festival celebrations 659:108

Yam Festival celebration 601:23-24

GHANA—FESTIVALS—COOKERY

Harvest Festival; fufu (yam or sweet potato loaf), recipe 1666:30-31

Homowo Festival; fufu (yam or sweet potato loaf), recipe 1666:30-31

Homowo Festival; hkatenkwan (ginger chicken and okra), recipe 1666:31

New Year, Odwira, Akuapim tribe fufu yam dish, recipe 1574:22-23

GHANA—FESTIVALS—MASKS

Yam Harvest Celebration spirit mask, papier-mache, making 1467:28-29

GHANA—FOLKLORE

"Why Hare Is Always on the Run" folktale and activities 1478:47-50

Collecting water from plants for drinking, how to do 1478:53

Proverbs of Africa 1478:52

GHANA—FOLKLORE—MASKS

Animal masks, cardboard, dowel, paints, making 1478:54-55

GHANA—GAMES

A-fishing game 602:26-27

A-fishing rope game, how to play 1501:19

Achi game 956:123

Ampe game, how to play 1507:16

Ampe' (1-2-3-Shoot-African Style) musical game 1116:15

Big snake game 1078:29

Big snake game, how to play 1507:17

Blind crow game 967:32

Boa constrictor game 602:28-29

Che Che Koole (African Chant) song and dance game 1114:64-65

Fishermen game 58:30-31

Hawk game 602:27-28

Oware game, how to play 1494:15

Oware, or capture the seeds game, how to play 1508:154-156

Two friends game 602:29

GHANA—HANDICRAFTS

Adinkra cloth signs and symbols on T-shirt, making 1448:18-19

Adinkra cloth, paper cloth, yarns, making 1332:39-44

Adinkra designs for fabric or paper, making 1477:120

Adinkra symbols; patterns for symbols with meanings given 1332:39-44

Andinkira clay pins, symbols giving, making 1414:44-45

Andinkira prints on cloth, making 1414:45-46

Asante adinkra stamping of cloth, potatoes, stamp pad, fabric, making 1632:18-23

Ashanti gold weights, flour clay, making 1022:34-37

Batik, Adinkra cloth, crayons, making 1427:290

Belt, woven, making 856:88-91

Computer project: Adinkra cloth, create 1218:60-63

Kente cloth needlepoint wall hanging, canvas, yarn, patterns, making 1716:94-96

Kente pattern needlepoint squares, canvas squares, yarn, making 1716:91-93

Linguists staffs, tall wooden staffs, dowels, clay, paints, making 1338:59-60

Money bag, paper, yarn, beads, making 1427:296

GHANA—HARVEST FESTIVALS—COOKERY

Yam or "To Hoot at Famine" Festival yam muffins, recipe 1249:41-42

GHANA—SONGS

Movement song and hat to make, directions given 376:71

GHANA—STRING FIGURES

The Mosquito string figures story, making 1161:5-8

GHOULS. *See* **MONSTERS**

GIBBONS, GAIL

"Happy Birthday," lemon birthday cake, recipe 1216:58

GIFF, PATRICIA REILLY

"The Beast in Ms. Rooney's Room," reading, writing, thinking activities 1093:41-51

GILBERT ISLANDS—STRING FIGURES

Four stars of Itai leaves and their well string 373:62-66

GILSON, JAMIE

"Thirteen Ways to Sink a Sub"; reading and writing activities, projects 606:107-119

GINGERBREAD

Church, patterns, assembling, decorating, how to do 1086:60-66

Colonial House, patterns, assembling, decorating, how to do 1086:46-51

Crèche and figures, recipe, patterns, assembling, decorating, how to do 1086:116-122

Gothic house, patterns, assembling, decorating, how to do 1086:53-59

Hansel and Gretel cottage, patterns, assembly and decorations, making 1086:23-28

Hansel and Gretel gingerbread candy house, making 1017:142-143

Irish gingerbread cake, recipe 1128:28

Noah's Ark and animals, patterns, assembly instructions, how to make 1086:95-103

Southampton Victorian house, patterns, assembling, decorating, how to do 1086:67-79

GINGERBREAD BOY

Puppets, costumes, masks, cooking, science, math, music activities 1358:158-178

GINGERBREAD MEN

Gingerbread man, dough recipe 1203:19

Little old woman's gingerbread man cookies, recipe 1215:24

GINSBURG, MIRRA

"Chick and the Duckling"; flannel board figures, patterns, making 843:76, 137

GIRL SCOUTS—HANDICRAFTS

Girl Scout braid, making 548:42-44

GLACIERS

Glacier, pop-up, pattern 1210:9

GLAZER, TOM

"On Top of Spaghetti," meatballs, recipe 1216:98

GLUES

Colored glues, recipe 1455:32

Cornstarch glue, recipe 1213:24

Decoupage and collage glue, recipe 1455:30

Milk glue, recipe, how to make 1564:19

Non-paper glue, recipe 1455:32

GNOMES

Cardboard tube gnomes, making 534:70

Felt or wool fabric gnomes, patterns, making 1531:82-83

Gnome costume, fabric, face makeup given, making 957:38-43

Stone gnome, painted, making 310:34

GOATS

Goat cheese, recipe 1014:132-142

GOBI DESERT—HANDICRAFTS

Appliqued mural, felt, dowel, making 1716:97-101

GOD'S EYE

Eye of God mobile, making 452:115-117; 749:61

Eye of God weaving, making 120:61-63; 126:74-75; 251:5; 432:22-23; 595:48-51; 795:43; 877:52-53; 991:95-98; 1277:20-21

Eye of God, making 526:41-42; 1262:18-19

God's Eye, miniature made from craft sticks, yarn, making 1715:56-57

God's Eye sailboats, yam, making 770:44-45

God's Eye (Ojo de Dios), yarn, twigs, making 275:80; 720:14-15; 1476:87-88; 1567:71; 1605:16

Pueblo and Navaho weaving, making 324:30

Shape of tree, making 501:32

Yarn star, making 1262:18-19

GODZILLA. See MONSTERS—COOKERY

GOFFSTEIN, M. B.

"Fish for Supper," fried fish, recipe 1216:91

"Laughing Latkes," recipe for latkes 1216:7

GOLD RUSH

Balance to weigh gold and silver, soda bottle, clothespin, paper cup, making 1214:43-44

Gold brick, paper bag, making 1214:51-53

Gold Rush Days in Alaska and the foods people ate 666:252-254

Pan for gold, how to do 1214:39-41

Stream in a plastic bottle to demonstrate sediment in water 1214:42

GOLD RUSH—COOKERY

California Gold Rush Days and the Hangtown Fry information 666:225-229

Hangtown fry, recipe 1214:50

Sourdough bread and starter, recipe 1455:119-120

Sourdough flapjacks, recipe 1214:46

Sourdough starter, recipe 1214:45

GOLD RUSH—GAMES

Chinese miners fan tan game, how to play 1214:48

GOLDILOCKS AND THE THREE BEARS

Baby Bear's cradle bed, cardboard, fabric, patterns, making 484:113-115

Baby Bear's little chair, cardboard, fabric, patterns, making 484:123-124

Bear's Victorian table, cardboard, fabric, patterns, making 484:116

Father Bear's big winged armchair, cardboard, fabric, patterns, making 484:120-122

Finger puppet, patterns, story, making 512:41-48

Goldilocks and the Three Bears dolls, fabric, patterns, making 484:31-46

Goldilocks and the three bears toy, cardboard and felt, making 346:15-17

Mother Bear's comfortable armchair, cardboard, fabric, patterns, making 484:116-119

Mother Bear's cushioned footstool, cardboard, fabric, patterns, making 484:116-119

Puppets, costumes, masks, cooking, science, math, music activities 1358:25-41

GOURDS

Decorated gourd, making 991:166-167

Gourd dipper, gourd, shoe polish, sandpaper, making 1284:90-91

Gourd drum, chamois leather, wire, shoe polish, making 1284:92-93

Gourds to shake, making 527:23

Hat rack from gourds, making 527:22

Musical gourd guitar, making 1421:173

Musical gourd shaker, making 1421:172

Planters and bird houses from gourds, making 310:28-29

GOURDS—HANDICRAFTS

Things to make with gourds 1304:5-57

GRAHAME, KENNETH

One hundred easy recipes from the book "Wind in the Willows" 77:1-117

GRAINS

History of use in world, with recipes 88:1-261

GRANDMA MOSES—BIRTHDAY

Celebrate by painting primitive scene, how to do 1199:201

GRANDPARENTS

"Happy Birthday Sam," activities, art, science, music cooking, drama 716:66-67

GRANDPARENTS' DAY

Activities and projects for classrooms 1393:24-26

Activities, art, songs, recipes, games 1469:12-13

Activities, crafts 1662:144-147

Activities, finger plays, recipes, crafts 305:26

Interview your grandparents, questions to ask 1715:90-91

GRANDPARENTS' DAY—FINGER PLAYS

Finger plays and games 944:17-18

GRANDPARENTS' DAY—GAMES

Grandparents' Day game 240:47

GRASSES

Bundled grass figures, making 526:45-54

Grass figures, making 861:28

Grass handle, how to make 937:63-64

Tassel doll, grass, making 937:66

GRASSES—DRIED

Dragonfly from grass, making 14:42-43

GRASSES—DYED

Dyeing grasses, how to 14:6-7

GRASSLANDS

Miniature grasslands, how to make 875:56-57

GRAVES

Origami grave with headstone, paper, making 1581:28-31

GREAT BRITAIN. See ENGLAND; IRELAND; SCOTLAND; WALES

GREAT BRITAIN—ANCIENT

Anglo-Saxon hall building, cardboard, newspaper, making 1183:16-17

Celtic shield, cardboard, container lids and bottoms, paint, making 1183:6-7

Illuminated manuscript, cream paper, tea, felt-tipped pens, making 1183:21

William I the Conqueror's crown, cardboard, gold paint, making 1183:27

GREAT BRITAIN—FESTIVALS

Festivals and celebrations, maps, flags, crafts, making 1305:38-45

GREAT BRITAIN—GAMES

Hop-round and Scotch-Hoppers, hopscotch games 1426:20-23

GREAT BRITAIN—MAGIC TRICKS

One-way street, card trick, how to do 1270:12-13

GREECE

Activities, flags, games, songs, dances, recipes 1381:197-200

GREECE—BIRTHDAYS

Birthday customs 488:44-47

GREECE—CHRISTMAS

Celebration of 497:132-133

Christmas celebration 601:109-110

Christmas customs 149:45

Christmas customs in Greece 1717:18-19

Customs of Christmas in Greece 473:58-59

GREECE—CHRISTMAS—COOKERY

Butter cookies, recipe 446:39-40
Christopsomo, Christ bread, recipe 1128:70
Cookies, Greek nut cookies, recipe 704:76-77
Courambiades cookies, recipe 273:62-64
Diples cookies, recipe 1128:69
Kourabiedes shortbread, recipe 1128:68
Kourabiedes, recipe 497:142
Vasilopita, St. Basil bread, recipe 1128:71

GREECE—COINS

Coins of Greece, posterboard, foil, yarn, patterns, making 1427:146

GREECE—COOKERY

Arni psito, leg of lamb, recipe 1452:84
Avgolemono soup, recipe 1440:21
Baked fish, microwave recipe 1211:35
Baklava pastry, recipe 1452:87
Baklava, dessert, filo pastry, recipe 1427:158-159
Baklava, recipe 514:136-137
Beef and onion stew, recipe 880:34
Butter cookies, recipe 880:40
Candy balls, recipe 874:79
Celery marinated, recipe 1440:24
Chicken roasted, recipe 880:32
Chicken soup, recipe 530:55-56
Clove cookies (kourabiedes), cookies, recipe 72:69-70; 667:172
Cookies, kourabiedes, recipe 854:4
Country salad, vegetables and feta cheese, recipe 1440:22
Crema karamela, egg custard, recipe 1381:199
Cucumber and yogurt dip, recipe 880:24
Cucumber salad, recipe 858:unp
Dolmades, stuffed grape leaves with lemon sauce, recipe 1440:20
Drachma fried potatoes, recipe 1427:159
Egg and lemon sauce, avgolemono, recipe 1427:160
Egg and lemon soup, recipe 880:31; 1292:120
Egg lemon soup with meatballs, recipe 871:43-45
Eggplant salad, recipe 880:25
Fava, split pea soup, recipe 1452:86
Fish baked, recipe 880:34
Fish soup, recipe 1440:25
Fish, psariplaki, recipe 854:24
Fruit and yogurt, recipe 880:41
Greek salad, recipe 794:33; 880:23; 895:62; 1427:160; 1452:82
Halva farina cake, recipe 1691:42
Halvah, cereal dish, recipe 1427:161
Halvah, recipe 88:55-56
Honey cheese pie, recipe 880:44
Keftedes, meatballs, recipe 1440:27
Koulourakia, shortbread cookie, recipe 1427:161-162
Kourabiedes cookies, recipe 88:56-57
Lamb chops, baked with feta cheese, recipe 1440:23
Lamb in a bag, recipe 1427:162
Lamb kebabs, recipe 874:49; 1560:18
Lamb stew with eggplant puree, recipe 530:57-59
Lamb with rice, recipe 895:61
Lamb, skewered, recipe 880:18
Lemon soup, soupa avgolemono, recipe 1427:162-163
Lentil soup and fassoulada soup, recipe 1427:163
Lentil soup, recipe 793:45; 880:29
Little shoes, lamb, eggplant, cheese, recipe 1650:32-33
Marinated mushrooms, microwave recipe 1211:23
Meat, Souvlakia, recipe 854:26
Melomacrons, honey cake, recipe 1165:91-92
Mezethes, Taramosalata, recipe 854:18-19
Moussaka recipe 662:64-68
Moussaka sauce, white sauce for casserole, recipe 1165:91
Moussaka, baked meat and eggplant, recipe 667:170-171
Moussaka, recipe 1452:85
Okra, stewed, recipe 854:29
Orange yogurt cake, recipe 880:42
Pasta with browned butter sauce, recipe 880:36
Pastry, Baklava, recipe 854:36
Patate moussaka, potato casserole, recipe 1165:90
Patatokeftehes, potato pancakes, recipe 1427:164-165
Phyllo leaves spinach pie, recipe 88:58-59
Pitas stuffed with beef, recipe 1440:28
Poor Man's cake, recipe 1122:70
Potatoes, baked potatoes oregano, recipe 880:36
Psari Plaki, fish plaki, recipe 1452:83
Rice pilaf, recipe 880:37; 1380:23
Rice pudding with cinnamon, recipe 530:60-61
Rice pudding, recipe 880:43; 1440:27
Salad, Horiatiki salata, recipe 854:31
Salata, Greek salad with dressing, recipe 1165:91
Shortbread cookies, recipe 895:63-64
Soup, Avgolemono, recipe 854:20-22; 1165:89-90
Spinach pie, recipe 188:33; 880:20
Spinach triangles, recipe 1204:75
Stuffed grape leaves, recipe 880:26
Stuffed tomatoes, recipe 1440:23
Stuffed vine leaves, recipe 667:169-170
Summer salad, recipe 1440:26
Tiropetes, pies, recipe 1427:165
Tomatoes stuffed with feta cheese, recipe 880:39; 1652:30
Tzatziki, cucumber, yogurt and garlic sauce, recipe 1244:83
Walnut honey pastry, recipe 880:44
Walnut-honey pastry, recipe 1280:30-31
Yogurt pie, recipe 530:62-63
Zucchini, fried, recipe 880:37

GREECE—COSTUMES

Chiton, information on 417:11-13
Chiton, simple from sheet, making 384:May 27
Greek costumes drawing 988:39
Greek couple costumes, making 887:54-55
Greek dancer costume 213:136-137
Greek lady instant costume 213:8
Greek peasants drawing 988:25
Greek toga, fabric, making 181:20-21
Jewelry, Greek, cardboard, making 181:28-29
Laurel wreath, paper, making 181:26-27
Mask, Grecian soldier shadow mask, making 969:41-43
Poet's lyre, cardboard, pattern given, making 181:22-25
Spinach pie, recipe, costume 188:33

GREECE—DANCES

Kalamatianos dance and costume picture 1000:4-47
Never on a Sunday dance, how to do 1494:145-146

GREECE—EASTER

Customs of Easter 503:24

GREECE—EASTER—COOKERY

Baklava (nut and honey pastry), recipe 1666:76-77
Easter bread, easy, recipe 54:221
Koulourakia Easter cookies, recipe 1495:138-139

Lambrotsomo (Greek Easter bread), recipe 1666:76
Mayeritsa (Easter soup), recipe 1666:75-76
Melopitta (honey pie), recipe 1666:78
GREECE—FESTIVALS
Epiphany or Twelfth Day celebration 626:57
Foods for Festivals 854:40-44
Greek Festival Year and Greek celebrations 667:165-168
GREECE—FOLKLORE
"Lion and the Mouse" flannel board story, patterns, making 1604:87-88
Greek fable, Rain or Shine fable skit 1212:30-36
GREECE—FOLKLORE—PUPPETS
"Dog and His Bone" shadow puppets, patterns, making 1602:69-70
"Fox and the Grapes" shadow puppets, patterns, making 1602:67-69
GREECE—GAMES
Birds, giants, dwarfs, game 967:32
Circle Ball, Hide, Krifto, Odd and Even, Pebble, Rider Ball, how to play 383:84; 572:10-11; 1427:167-168
Flipball game 1354:160
Greek ball street game, how to play 1477:105
Greek Olympic Ball game 1078:28
Hook the driftwood stick game 1119:9
Hoops game, how to play 1507:75
Krotalias stick game 1119:19-21
Pebble chase game 383:83
Pebble game 602:96
Rider ball game 383:83
Ring around the rosie game 474:31-33
Syllables game, how to play 1494:116
Throwing pottery pieces game 515:54
GREECE—HANDICRAFTS
Colored straw classical scene, making 298:146-147
Computer project: design embroidery pattern 1218:72-75
Embroidered cloth, fabric, thread, patterns, making 1427:147-148
Horn of plenty, making 626:59-61
Peasant bag, burlap embroidered, making 889:67-71
Sponge printing, making 626:57-59
Straw painting, drinking straws, paper, patterns, making 1427:155-156
GREECE—KITES
Hexafringe six-sided kite, dowels, brown paper, string, patterns, making 1475:35-39
GREECE—LANGUAGE
Numbers one to ten in Greek language 1713:unp
GREECE—LENT—COOKERY
Potato kurkaras, making 139:50
GREECE—MAGIC TRICKS
Greek marbles, how to do 1270:8-9
GREECE—MASKS
Greek Tragedy Mask 204:73-75
Play masks, paper, egg cartons, string, making 1427:152-153
GREECE—MUSICAL INSTRUMENTS
Panpipes, plastic tubing, tape, clay, making 1728:20-21
GREECE—MYTHOLOGY—PUPPETS
"Perseus and Medusa" shadow puppets, patterns, making 1602:212-221
GREECE—MYTHOLOGY. *See also* **MYTHOLOGY**
GREECE—NEW YEAR'S DAY
Saint Basil's Day in Greece 489:79-84

GREECE—POTTERY
Amphorae urns or vases, clay, paints, making 1338:98-101
Painted earthenware, clay, paints, patterns, making 1427:154
GREECE—PUPPETS
Karagiosi puppets, tag board, paper fasteners, patterns, making 1427:149-150
Karagos puppet, making 856:104-109
Karagos puppet, posterboard, dowel, patterns, making 1381:199-200
GREECE—SHABBAT—COOKERY
Sopa de avas, bean soup, recipe 1691:26-27
GREECE—THANKSGIVING
History of Thanksgiving 659:19-21
GREECE—TOYS
Yo-yo, coat buttons, paper clip, string, making 1427:157
Yo-yo, making 495:18-19
GREECE—WORRY BEADS
Komboloi, worry beads, beads, yarn, filament, making 1427:151
Worry beads, making 298:74
GREECE, ANCIENT
Abacus, balsa wood and dowels, clay, making 1681:21
Enchanted people, making 173:28-29
Greece versus Rome, history, stories, maps, puzzles, activities, projects 1041:30-57
Persia versus Greece, history, stories, maps, puzzles, activities, projects 1041:5-29
GREECE, ANCIENT—ARCHITECTURE
Classic column, making 700:8-10
Parthenon from Greece, paper and macaroni model, making 1094:30
Parthenon, how to draw 1548:15
Temple, cardboard, shoe box, making 1681:14-15
GREECE, ANCIENT—ARMOR
Crested helmet, how to draw 1548:10
Shield with Trojan horse design, how to draw 1548:9
Spartan warrior in full armor, how to draw 1548:22-23
GREECE, ANCIENT—ART
Terra-cotta figure art, making 700:6-7
GREECE, ANCIENT—BOATS
Athenian trireme ship, how to draw 1548:24-25
GREECE, ANCIENT—CLOTHING
Chiton, Doric style, patterns, making 1041:23
Greek tunic, making 700:23-24
Ladies robe, how to draw 1548:4-5
Man's robe, how to draw 1548:20
Scarf with printed borders, making 700:18-19
GREECE, ANCIENT—CODES
Scytale device for sending and receiving messages, how to make 1611:33
GREECE, ANCIENT—COINS
Athenian Drachma coin, making 700:16-17
GREECE, ANCIENT—COOKERY
Foods and cookery in Ancient Greece 667:150-161
Greek salad, making 700:20
History of cookery in 881:45-49
Horta, green leafy vegetables, recipe 1267:29
Savoro, pickled fish, recipe 1267:27-28
Souvlaki, meat on skewers, recipe 1267:28
Tzatzibi, yogurt and garlic dip, recipe 1267:26-27
Yogurt with honey and nuts, recipe 1267:29
GREECE, ANCIENT—COSTUMES
Achilles costume 213:38-40

Aiquiuettes, making 870:124-126
Armlets, making 870:121-123
Buskins, making 870:123-124
Doric chiton, making 870:23-25
Grecian costume, girl's, 5th Century BC, making 368:11-14
Greek costume, fabric, patterns, making 1174:27
Greek warrior costume, making 870:25-26
Hector costume 213:40-46
Helen of Troy costume 213:46-47
Ionic chiton, making 870:21-23
Socrates costume 213:47-48
Stephane (diadem), making 870:120-121

GREECE, ANCIENT—DOLLS
Toy doll with movable arms and legs, making 700:21-22

GREECE, ANCIENT—DRAMA
Tragic and comedy masks, how to draw 1548:19

GREECE, ANCIENT—FESTIVALS
Dionysius Drama Festival celebration 566:10-il
Dionysius Spring Festival 566:10
Greek nature myths and rituals 419:23-27
Olympic Games 566:11

GREECE, ANCIENT—GAMES
Five stones or knucklebones game 956:22-24
Knucklebones game, a game of skill 700:25-26
Knucklebones game, how to play 1681:22

GREECE, ANCIENT—GODDESSES
Artemis portrait, how to draw 1548:4-5

GREECE, ANCIENT—GODS
Pan, playing reed pipes, how to draw 1548:13
Zeus portrait, how to draw 1548:7

GREECE, ANCIENT—HANDICRAFTS
Grecian vase, bottle, clay, paint, making 1681:8
Greek urn, copy of, papier-mache, paints, making 1561:12-13
Owl cup, clay, making 1070:97-100
Vase, how to draw 1548:17

GREECE, ANCIENT—HATS
Spartan hat, paper, pattern, making 923:50

GREECE, ANCIENT—HELMETS
Atlantis helmets, making 173:22-23

GREECE, ANCIENT—KINGS
Alexander the great portrait, how to draw 1548:28-29

GREECE, ANCIENT—MASKS
Happy face, sad face masks, cardboard, paints, making 1486:24-25
Medusa's mask, cardboard, felt, patterns, making 1681:17-19

GREECE, ANCIENT—MUSICAL INSTRUMENTS
Lyre stringed instrument, making 700:14-15
Panpipes, drinking draws, cardboard, making 1681:23
Panpipes, paper plate, straws, making 1310:92-93

GREECE, ANCIENT—MYTHOLOGY
Snakes and serpents, making 1447:24-25

GREECE, ANCIENT—OLYMPICS
Olympic runner, how to draw 1548:26-27

GREECE, ANCIENT—PUPPETS
Grecian puppet, making 483:19

GREECE, ANCIENT—SCROLLS
Alphabet scroll, making 700:31

GREECE, ANCIENT—STATUES
Statues of Gods and Goddesses, making 700:11-13

GREECE, ANCIENT—WEAPONS
Catapult, weapon in miniature, making 700:27-30

GREEK ORTHODOX CHURCH—EASTER—DECORATIONS
Pop-up Orthodox Easter card, making 1387:40

GREENHOUSES
Greenhouse, wood, windows, plastic, making 1312:41

GREENLAND—CHRISTMAS—CUSTOMS
Christmas customs 149:26-27

GREENLAND—DOLLS
Eskimo dolls, newspaper, glue, fur scraps, making 1338:110-112

GREENLAND—IGLOOS
Igloo from Greenland, with Eskimo, kayak, penguin models, clay, making 1094:51-53

GREENLAND—LULLABIES
"Comforting Song" 1607:16

GREETING CARDS
Game cards, paper, paints, making 1613:18-19
Game cards, Trickster, paper, paints, making 1613:30-33
Hidden message cards, paper, paints, making 1613:43
Jigsaw puzzle cards, paper, paints, making 1613:42
Maze cards, paper, paints, making 1613:45
Puzzle cards, paper, paints, making 1613:42-45
Toy cards, paper, paints, making 1613:16-17
Yarn cards, paper, paints, making 1613:34-37

GREGORIAN CALENDAR DAY
Calendar, special family one, making 308:45

GRENADA—CHRISTMAS—COOKERY
Caribbean spice cake, recipe 1666:206
Coconut spinach, recipe 1666:206
Tropical smoothie, recipe 1666:207

GRENADA—COOKERY
Callaloo, vegetable stew with greens, recipe 1165:205-206
Nutmeg ice cream, recipe 1165:206-207
Spice squares, cookies, recipe 1165:206

GRIMM, JACOB
Hansel and Gretal walk with bread 1199:3

GROS VENTRE INDIANS—TOYS
Spinning top, cardboard, nail, making 1699:99

GROTESQUES
Dough monster face, recipe for dough, making 1486:22-23

GROUNDHOG DAY
Activities and projects for classrooms 1393:139-140
Activities, art, songs, recipes, games 1469:62-63
Activities, crafts, songs 1473:92-93
Activities, patterns, games 50:147-148
Art, cooking, finger plays, games, drama, math, science and music activities 54:185
Finger plays, recipes, games, making 944:65-66
Groundhog poem, paper plate picture, patterns, making 900:61-67
Groundhog shadows, making 310:188
Groundhog, yawning, paper, making 99:16
Groundhogs, activities, art, science, songs, recipes 911:130-133
History of Groundhog Day 513:43
Learning units, art, language, music, foods, crafts, patterns 1193:323-341
Paper bag groundhog, how to make 1199:30-31
Pop-up Groundhog Day card, making 1387:58-59
Shadow silhouettes, how to make 1199:31
Show Groundhog in his hole, cup, paper, popsicle stick, how to make 448:47

GROUNDHOG DAY—COOKERY
Lemon popcorn, recipe 939:34-35
GROUNDHOG DAY—DANCES
Out with winter 624:8-9
GROUNDHOG DAY—FINGER PLAYS
Finger plays and rhymes 1583:105-106
GROUNDHOG DAY—GAMES
Shadow tag, how to play 1664:unp
GROUNDHOG DAY—PATTERNS
Groundhog and shadow, pattern 1193:338
Groundhog, pattern 1193:335, 337, 338, 340
GROUNDHOG DAY—PUPPETS
Finger plays and puppets, patterns, making 513:44-47
Groundhog finger puppet, making 1083:41
Groundhog pop-up puppet, making 907:27
Groundhog puppet, paper cup, stick, making 1664:unp
Groundhog puppet, pattern, making 1014:96
Groundhog shadow puppet, paper, stick, flashlight, making 1664:unp
Puppet projects, patterns, scenes, story starters, feature story 1083:39-42
GROUNDHOG DAY—SHADOWS
Artwork from outdoor shadows, how to do 1664:unp
Sun art, sun makes shadow designs, how to do 1664:unp
GROUNDHOG DAY—SONGS
Five Groundhog Day song 1664:unp
Mr. Groundhog song 782:unp
See My Shadow song 782:unp
Songs about Groundhog Day 901:43; 902:22
GROUNDHOG DAY—WEATHER
Sundial, cardboard, thread spool, making 1664:unp
Weather wheel, posterboard, markers, making 1664:unp
GROUNDHOGS. *See* **WOODCHUCKS**
GUAM—FOLKLORE—HANDICRAFTS
Juan Malo and His Magic Rod 126:98-105
Juan Malo and His Magic Rod, art activities, decorated box, making 126:109
Juan Malo and His Magic Rod, art activities, shell pictures, making 126:108-109
Juan Malo and His Magic Rod, art activities, slot sculpture, making 126:106-107
GUATEMALA—CHRISTMAS
Christmas customs in Guatemala 1717:20-21
GUATEMALA—CHRISTMAS—COOKERY
Arroz Guatemalteco (Guatemalan-style rice), recipe 1666:250-251
Carne en Jocon (beef casserole), recipe 1666:250
GUATEMALA—COOKERY
Arroz Guatemalteo (Guatemalan-style rice), recipe 1165:250
Baked bananas, recipe 858:unp
Liquado sandia, watermelon smoothie, drink, recipe 1165:250
Tortillas, recipe 1666:249-250
GUATEMALA—DOLLS
Worry dolls, thread, wire twists, colored paper, making 1730:43-49
GUATEMALA—EASTER
Holy Week colored sawdust celebration 665:28-30
GUATEMALA—FESTIVALS
St. Thomas Day celebration (Flying Pole dance) 665:66-72
GUATEMALA—GAMES
Andares-Andares game, how to play 1494:73-74
Catch the cap game 58:32-33
Disconnect game 602:123

El Reloj (the clock) game 572:40-41
El Reloj game, how to play 1507:92
Pin game 956:45-46; 1494:77
GUATEMALA—HANDICRAFTS
Animalitos, little animals, paper, felt, stuffing, patterns, making 1633:80-81
Animalitos, woven yarn small animals, making 1219:13
Bird puppets, clay, feathers, making 1338:32-34
Friendship bracelets, embroidery threads, patterns, how to make 1352:5-48
Green toad bank, papier-mache, paints, making 1633:84-85
Plate (glazed pottery), Guatemalan design patterns, paper plates, making 1633:82-83
Village scene, fabric, felt, oaktag, patterns, making 1251:16-19
Wild jungle cat, felt, yarn, patterns, making 1633:78-79
Woven belt, yarn, straws, making 1730:22-27
GUATEMALA—MUSICAL INSTRUMENTS
Marimba, toy, fruit crate wood, making 515:56
GUATEMALA—NESTING DOLL STORIES
Nothing But Trouble nesting doll story, how to do 1161:85-86
GUERICKE, OTTO VON
Otto Von Guericke's experiment showing strength of vacuum 1719:26-26
GUINEA—COOKERY
Ground nut chicken, recipe 1165:40
Peanut balls, recipe 1165:39-40
GUINEA—FESTIVALS—COOKERY
Eid al-Fitr; elele (bean cakes), recipe 1666:35
GUNDERHEIMER, KAREN
"Happy Winter," hot cocoa, recipe 1216:67
GUNNIWOLF
Finger puppet, patterns, story, making 512:49-53
GURO PEOPLE—MASKS
Guro animal mask, posterboard, paints, making 1632:52-57
GUYANA—CHRISTMAS—COOKERY
Curried zucchini soup, recipe 1666:239-240
GUYANA—COOKERY
Channa bean snack, recipe 1380:32
Fish pie, recipe 967:33 19
Fish, steamed, recipe 967:32-33
GUYANA—FESTIVALS—COOKERY
Diwali; curried zucchini soup, recipe 1666:239-240
GUYANA—GAMES
Ring on a string game, how to play 1501:32-33
GUYANA—STRING FIGURES
The Mosquito string figures story, how to make 1161:5-8
GYPSIES
Finger puppet, fabric, pattern, making 573:117-126
Gypsy encampment from Hungary, matchboxes paper model, making 1094:31
Hungarian Gypsy life and Festival celebrations 661:181-182
GYPSIES—COSTUMES
Gypsy dancer costume, fabric, pattern, making 367:109-112
Gypsy, variety of old clothes, making 1656:183-184
GYPSIES—DOLLS
Gypsy doll and clothes, patterns, making 3:75-79
GYPSIES—MUSICAL INSTRUMENTS
Flamenco castanets, clam shells, cord, making 1310:136

H

HAIDA INDIANS—COOKERY
Salmon patties, recipe 1194:18
HAIDA INDIANS—GAMES
Haida game using two sticks and wide elastic, making 1194:25
HAIDA INDIANS—HANDICRAFTS
Haida raven pictures from jigsaw shapes, making 1447:18
HAIDA INDIANS—HOUSES
Haida house, making 171:20-26
HAIDA INDIANS—MASKS
Haida mask, cardboard, patterns, making 1051:99-103
HAIDA INDIANS—MUSICAL INSTRUMENTS
Rattles, whale rattle, cardboard, making 1699:81-82
HAIDA INDIANS—TOTEM POLES
Thunderbird mask totem pole, making 1486:14-15
HAITI
Activities, flags, games, songs, dances, recipes 1381:25-28
HAITI—CHRISTMAS—COOKERY
Run down mackerel, recipe 1666:210
HAITI—COOKERY
Accra or calas, black-eyed pea patties, recipe 1165:211-212
Avocado salad with pineapple, recipe 858:unp
Melongene, eggplant and tomato, recipe 1381:27
Plat national dried beans and rice, recipe 1381:27
Pois et Ris, kidney beans and rice, recipe 1165:210-211
Rice and beans, recipe 1068:unp
Sauce ti-malice, spicy tomatoes, onions and hot peppers, recipe 1221:119
Sweet potato pudding cake, recipe 1165:211
Sweet red pepper soup, recipe 1165:210
HAITI—FESTIVALS—COOKERY
Carnival; callaloo (spinach stew), recipe 1666:210
Carnival; plantain soup, recipe 1666:203
Day of the Dead; coconut almond tart, recipe 1666:211
HAITI—FESTIVALS—MASKS
Carnival mask, paper plate, yarn, making 1574:8-9
HAITI—GAMES
Ainsi Font, Font, Font des Zami game, how to play 1494:58-59
Opselets, jacks game played with goat knuckles, how to play 1708:28-29
HAITI—HANDICRAFTS
Sculptures of fish, making 856:112-115
Steel drum cutouts, paints, paper, making 1338:40-42
HALEY, ALEX PALMER—BIRTHDAY
Celebrate by making explore your roots family tree, pattern 1199:183-185
Celebrate by making family portrait, paper, markers 1199:185
HALEY, GAIL E.
"A Story, A Story," reading, writing, thinking activities 1093:172-181
"A Story, A Story," Ananse's baked yams and peaches, recipe 569:31
HALLOWEEN
Activities and projects for classrooms 1393:60-66
Activities, food, costumes 1662:158-170
Activities, songs, fingerplays for Halloween, simple to do 1166:28-32
Halloween celebrations in the United States 474:66-67
History and celebration of 496:86-88

History of Halloween 252:2-3; 400:9-12; 426:1-13; 426:23-27; 435:4-5; 443:4-7; 513:19; 566:22-23; 709:23; 829:17-18
Learning units, activities, songs, art, recipes, patterns 1191:268-337
Songs, fingerplays, stories, games, rhythms 1200:14-21
HALLOWEEN—COOKERY
Apples decorated with horror faces, recipe 1487:17
Apples, soothsayer's sliced apples, chocolate, caramel recipe 1353:14
Banana dessert, witch's froth, recipe 1257:36-37
Black cats, cookies, recipe 1179:224
Cakes decorated with horror faces, recipe 1487:16-17
Candy from cereal, recipe 1248:46
Chocolate cookies, recipe 1248:43-44
Creepy-crawlies, small cakes, licorice legs, making 1299:74-75
Crunchy bones cookies, recipe 1353:8
Devil's cake with tombstones, recipe 1353:10-11
Devil's hot fudge sauce, recipe 1248:42
Goblin's float drink, recipe 1248:44
Jack-o-lantern cookies, store cookies and orange frosting 1248:47
Magic broomstick punch, recipe 1179:224
Main dishes, desserts, punches, recipes 1667:14-58
Monster mash cookies, recipe 1248:41-42
Pumpkin mousse, Ichabod Crane's baked pumpkin mousse, recipe 1353:18
Pumpkin muffins, recipe 1495:36
Pumpkin pudding, recipe 1495:36
Punch, witches' blood punch, juices, cloves, recipe 1186:104
Spiders, chocolate, recipe 1353:17
Witches brew fruit drink, recipe 1248:45
Witches brew punch, recipe 1353:13
Witches brew, decorated fish bowl cauldron 1299:76-77
Worms, orange jelatin worms, recipe 1186:105
HALLOWEEN—COSTUMES
Baby ghost costume, fabric, making 1174:113
Baby witch costume, fabric, pattern, making 1174:111
Bat costume, fabric, making 1174:110
Bat costume, garbage bag, paper, making 1248:40
Cape, black, felt, fabric, ribbon, making 1248:38
Davy Jones' ghostly parrot puppet, making 179:16-19
Devil costume, red satin and ribbons, making 1509:16-17
Dracula costume, making 42:33-39
Dracula's blood, making 197:25
Executioner, variety of old clothes, making 1656:41-44
Fangs, styrofoam cup, patterns, making 1248:36
Frankenstein's monster mask, making 179:42-43
Frankenstern's blood, recipe 1248:36
Grim reaper, variety of old clothes, making 1656:33-38
Headless ghost costume, fabric, making 1174:112
Headless man, variety of old clothes, making 1656:51-54
Judge costume, fabric, toilet paper rolls, making 1174:124-125
Mask, African mask for Halloween, pattern, making 1016:193-198
Mummy costume, toilet paper, making 1174:124-125
Nightmare costume, fabric, patterns, making 1174:114
Pirate costume, making 42:61-69; 426:44
Pirate ghost of Davy Jones, making 179:10-11
Pirate tattoos, making 179:12-13
Pirate's eye patch, making 179:14-15
Scars, how to make 1248:37

Spider web T-shirt, pattern, making 1248:39
Witch costume, fabric, patterns, making 1174:115
Witch costume, purple fabric, felt, making 1509:50-51
Zombie hands, gloves, gauze, red paint, making 1248:35

HALLOWEEN—DECORATIONS
Aliens, panty hose, paper, making 1667:30-31
Bat party favors, toilet paper tubes, paper cups, patterns, making 1266:11
Cat card design, oaktag, pattern, making 1248:18-19
Demons from paper, patterns, making 1248:30-31
Frankenstein model, boxes, paper tubes, paper, making 1667:46-51
Frieze with black paper Halloween shapes, making 1486:20-21
Ghosts and projects, Plaster of Paris draped cloth, making 1455:23
Ghosts from tissue paper, making 1248:28-29
Ghosts, figures to hang, white fabric, cotton, yarn, making 1179:222
Jack-o-lantern candle, jar, paper, candle, making 1667:59-61
Jack-Light lantern, milk carton, patterns, making 1334:18-19
Jack-o-lantern pumpkin with four different faces to carve, patterns 1248:26-27
Jack-o-lantern, make your own 1335:28-30
Large size patterns and carving instructions for over 30 pumpkin faces 1363:1-107
Mobile, foam sheet, paints, patterns, making 1360:25-27
Pop-up Halloween card, making 1387:56-57
Pumpkin painting; faces on pumpkins, how to paint 1335:24-25
Pumpkin tureen, how to make 1335:36
Pumpkins from tin cans, glass jars, boxes, making 1311:166-167
Rutabaga lantern, rutabaga, candle, making 1284:99-100
Sock pumpkin, old sock, stuffing, paints, making 1569:8-9
Spider web place mats, black paper, white paint, making 1179:222
Spiders, buttons, ribbons, paper, making 1667:38-39
Spooky napkin rings, card stock, paper tubes, paints, making 1299:18-19
Tree branch Halloween tree, making 1286:94-96
Trick or treat bags from five different designs, patterns, making 1248:20-25
Witch silhouette for window, paper, making 1257:38
Witch's necklace, shrink plastic, paints, pattern, making 1360:28-31
Witch, cardboard, yarn, patterns, making 1667:19-23
Witch, paper cup, blown egg, pattern, making 1311:168-169

HALLOWEEN—FACE PAINTING
Devil, pumpkin, skull, witch, bat, Dracula, how to paint 1533:51-69
Witch face painting, how to do 1306:55

HALLOWEEN—FINGER PLAYS
Finger plays and rhymes 1583:70-75

HALLOWEEN—GAMES
Apple bobbing 51:196; 829:26; 426:32-35; 1524:68
Apple games, how to play 504:47-48
Pumpkin numbers game, bottle caps, paper, how to make and play 1569:10-11
Tic-Tac-Toe game, magnetic sheeting, paint, making 1360:32-34

Trick or treat, and reverse trick or treat, how to play 1667:28-29

HALLOWEEN—MASKS
Monster mask, oaktag, patterns, making 1248:32-33
Monster masks, paper, stickers, making 1299:48-49
Skeleton, pattern, making 1191:330

HALLOWEEN—MUSICAL INSTRUMENTS
Clatter stick noisemaker, metal washers, bells, string, making 1310:113

HALLOWEEN—PARTIES
Decorations, food, games, parade, play, how to do 1266:7-19

HALLOWEEN—PATTERNS
Black Cat 1248:24
Devil 1248:25
Moon face 1248:25
Owl 1248:22
Pumpkin 1248:20
Witch 1248:23

HALLOWEEN—PLAYS
Scarecrow and the Sleepy Pumpkin Patch play, script, easy 1266:14-19

HALLOWEEN—PUPPETS
Pumpkin head, polyfoam, craft sticks, orange paper, making 1294:11-14
Skeleton bag puppet, pattern, making 1191:331
Talking pumpkin puppet, tennis ball, paints, making 1569:12-13
Ten Little Jack-o-lanterns, finger puppets, black gloves, making 1294:8-10
Witch, black cloth, black paper, making 1294:15-18

HAMBURGERS
Best burgers, recipe 118:158
Hamburgers in McDonald's in foreign countries 662:124-125
History of hamburger 662:18-20
History of hamburger in the United States 662:21-24

HAND PUPPETS. See PUPPETS—HAND

HANDS
Hand painting patterns 1253:11
Hand print Christmas card, paper, paints, making 1568:44-45
Hand reindeer ornament, felt, yarn, paints, making 1568:40-41
Handprint Indian, bunny, goose, ghost, turkey, tree, making 254:204-207
Hands, activities, art, science, songs, recipes 911:134-137
Plaster casting of hands, plaster of Paris, clay, paints, making 1181:32-33

HANNIBAL
Carthage versus Rome, history, stories, maps, activities, puzzles, projects 1041:58-84

HANS BRINKER
Han's waffles, recipe 570:17-19

HANSEL AND GRETEL
Bookmark, paper, patterns, making 92:52
Candy house, recipe 1216:84
Gingerbread cottage, patterns, assembling, decorating, how to do 1017:142-143; 1086:23-28
Hansel and Gretel picture, making 92:46

HANSEL AND GRETEL—COOKERY
Hansel and Gretel oatmeal cookies, recipe 738:unp
Healthy children's cookie houses, graham crackers, recipe 1215:38
Witch gingerbread house cookies, recipe 569:53-58

HANSEL AND GRETEL—PUPPETS

Finger puppet, patterns, story, making 512:55-66

Hansel and Gretel puppets, paper, patterns, making 92:47-49

Witch puppet, paper, patterns, making 92:50-51

Witch, Hansel and Gretel wooden spoon puppets, making 238:24-35

HANUKKAH

Activities and projects for classrooms 1393:90-92

Activities, finger plays, recipes, crafts 305:20-21

Activities, food, crafts 1662:188-193

Activities, projects, song 819:18-22

Babylonians turn to the moon 115:48-50

Candle, Hanukkah, How to light 115:28

Candle blessings 369:25

Candles, more about 115:34

Candles, who lights? 115:32

Celebration of candles 115:27-45

Celebration of Hanukkah 134:107; 497:30-39; 499:77-78; 601:126

Chanukah celebration 566:25

Chanukah party, invitations, decorations, food, games 133:141-143

Christmas for Jewish families 115:105-107

Gregorian calendar 115:53-54

Hanukkah 134:28

Hanukkah connection 115:51-52

Hanukkah festival 474:148-149

Hanukkah menorah 115:40

Hanukkah stories, songs, art activities, games, recipes 115:5-25; 1135:35-37

Hanukkah, history of 369:5-22; 496:100-101; 709:90-91; 829:53-54

Hanukkah, when does it come this year? 115:47-54

Jewish celebration, activities, handicrafts, foods, songs, making 909:99-107

Learning units, art, language, music, foods, crafts, patterns 1193:1-14

Meaning of Hanukkah 711:55; 712:31-32

Nineteen-year cycle 115:50-51

Songs, fingerplays, stories, games, rhythms 1200:44-45

Why the moon and not the sun? 115:54

HANUKKAH—BULLETIN BOARDS

Dreidel Piñata, making 295:225-227

Dreidel, spinning, making 295:227

Menorah, making 295:225

HANUKKAH—CANDLES

Candle box for Hanukkah candles, making 115:87-93

Candle felt appliqué picture, patterns, making 1016:237-242

Candles, dipped, making 53:25-26; 115:35-36

HANUKKAH—COOKERY

Alef-bet pretzels, recipe 370:46

Almond cookies, recipe 1180:24-25

Apple chutney, recipe 1685:43

Applesauce, recipe 115:62-63; 262:46-47; 370:21-22; 497:36; 1112:62-63; 1685:41

Bagels, pizza, recipe 370:29

Bimuelos or loukomades, fried treats, recipe 1691:109

Brownies, recipe 1112:65-66

Butter cookies, recipe 262:30; 1112:63-65

Cake with chocolate coins in center, recipe 1180:20-21

Candle salad, recipe 133:142; 370:27

Candy Dreidels, recipe 370:42

Carob brownies, recipe 1179:18-19

Chanu-Cookies, recipe 370:48

Cheese coins and cheese puff, recipes 370:26,28

Cheese latkes and sour cream topping, recipe 497:36

Chicken soup, recipe 370:10-11

Chocolate balls, recipe 1704:41

Cookies for Hanukkah, recipe 434:68

Cookies, cut-out, recipe 1186:106-107

Cookies, rolled, cut-out holiday symbols, recipe 1704:44-45

Cornflake chicken, recipe 370:36

Doughnut holes, recipe 1685:44

Doughnuts (sufganiyot), recipe 769:26

Dreidel cookies, recipe 1685:45

Dreidel sandwich, recipe 370:24

Dreidel, edible, making 1112:58-59

Dreidels, health food, recipe 370:30

Drinks; hot cocoa, mulled cider, punch, recipes for 370:52-54

Egg cream, recipe 370:51

Falouris (Indian latkes), recipe 1685:42

Foods of the Maccabees 115:68-69

Fruit and nut salad, recipe 370:31

Fruit shake, recipe 370:50

Fudge brownies, recipe 116:54-55

Hanukkah cookies, recipe 376:199

Hanukkah desserts, sugar cookies, recipe 115:64-67

Hanukkah menorah centerpiece, recipe 116:56

Hot dog kebabs, recipe 370:35

Kugel noodle pudding, recipe 279:90

Latkes (potato pancakes), recipe 1666:54-55

Latkes pancakes, recipe 1399:30-31

Latkes sandwich, easy, recipe 370:34

Latkes, blender, potato, cheese, apple and cinnamon, recipes 370:16-19

Latkes, carrot, recipe 370:20

Latkes, Grandma's latkes, recipe 1290:unp. Last page

Latkes, no peel, recipe 769:26

Latkes, non-potato, recipe 1502:23

Latkes, potato pancakes, recipe 434:69; 1193:7; 1451:92

Latkes, recipe 54:208; 262:46; 819:19; 829:59; 916:78-79; 993:last page; 1197:30-31; 1289:60; 1502:22; 1685:40

Latkes, sweet cheese, recipe 1180:23

Latkes, sweet potatoes, recipe 1502:23

Laughing latkes, recipe 1216:7

Maccabee hero sandwich, recipe 370:32

Mamaliga, recipe 711:58-59

Meatballs, recipe 370:39

Meat loaf, recipe 370:40

Menorah or Dreidel cake, recipe 370:47

Menorah salad, recipe 1399:31

Menorah sandwich, recipe 370:25

Menorah, edible, making 1112:59-61

Minted tea and cardamon coffee, recipes 497:36

Noodle kugel, recipe 1399:31

Noodle pudding 206:59-61

Onion soup, recipe 370:12

Pot roast, recipe 370:37

Potato latkes, recipe 115:57-62; 116:50; 133:142; 207:110-112; 279:91; 305:21; 310:208; 369:31; 384:Dec 8; 543:76-77; 580:unp; 698:96; 711:56-57; 769:26; 989:unp; 1032:222; 1179:15-16; 1180:22-23; 1266:30; 1305:48; 1313:185; 1357:42-43; 1380:24; 1495:64; 1523:unp; 1660:36; 1704:42-43

Potato pancakes, raisins and almond candy, recipes 402:73-76

Potato pancakes, recipe 1391:134

Potato vegetable latkes, recipe 1112:61-62

Pudding, steamed, recipe 1313:186

Punch, recipe 279:92

Rugelach, half-moon shaped cookies, recipe 1704:46-47

Sesame seed candy (Sephardic nut brittle), recipe 711:59-60

Six Dreidel sandwiches, recipe 116:48-49

Snow cream, recipe 370:43

Star of David cake, recipe 829:59

Stick snow icing, recipe 116:55

Sufganiyot donuts, recipes 116:52; 262:48-49; 369:31; 370:44-45

Sufganiyot jelly donuts, recipe 1112:66-67

Sufganiyot, Israeli doughnuts, recipe 1691:110

Sugar cookies, molded, recipe 279:93

Two syrups for soofganiyot, recipe 116:53

Winter stew, recipe 370:38

HANUKKAH—COSTUMES

Dreydl costume, making 272:148-151

Judah Maccabeus costume, making 272:144-146

Menorah costume, making 272:147-148

HANUKKAH—DANCES

Chanukah dance, how to do 279:80

Dances for Hanukkah 542:10-21

Hanukkah O Hanukkah 624:56-60

Hora dance, how to do 279:84; 1357:28-29

HANUKKAH—DECORATIONS

Ancient city greeting card, making 1704:32

Blown egg decoration, making 677:20

Candles, crayon, multi-colored candles, white candles, making 1180:10

Candles, painted candles, acrylic paints, making 1180:11

Candy dish, papier mache, recipe, making 1180:19

Card 209:9

Cards, potato designs, paper, making 1399:43

Chanukah mobile, making 279:78

Chanukiah candle holder, clay, varnish, paints, making 1626:27

Designs for Hanukkah crafts 262:60

Dreidel box and games, making 712:37-38

Dreidel box, milk carton, making 679:unp

Dreidel centerpiece, making 279:74

Dreidel decoration, milk container, making 1301:97

Dreidel from pencil, making 835:17

Dreidel from potato, making 310:206

Dreidel game, making 363:58-60

Dreidel place card, making 279:79

Dreidel shaped menorah, making 134:29

Dreidel story, paper plate picture, patterns, making 900:13-19

Dreidel top, making 709:91

Dreidel, cardboard tube, making 115:77-80

Dreidel, cardboard, making 916:79-80

Dreidel, cardboard, markers, making 1462:29

Dreidel, clay, making 53:28; 279:73

Dreidel, egg carton, making 53:28; 434:46; 1502:13

Dreidel, milk carton, pattern, making 1311:170-171

Dreidel, mock pomander, making 53:34-35

Dreidel, oaktag, patterns, making 1477:134

Dreidel, paper, pattern, making 819:21-22

Dreidel, ping pong ball, making 53:28

Dreidel, posterboard, making 53:30; 1495:61

Dreidel, quick and easy, making 115:76

Dreidel, ringing Dreidel, felt, bell, dowel, making 1180:14-15

Dreidel, salt dough, baked, recipe 1180:12-13

Dreidel, standing, making 53:32

Dreidel, stapled cardboard, making 53:29

Dreidel, stuffed, making 115:95-97

Dreidel, toothpick and button, making 53:28

Dreidel, wheel, making 53:28

Dreidel, wooden, making 115:81-82

Dreidels, making and painting with 698:96; 909:111

Dreidels, milk carton, making 438:63

Dreidels, paper, paper cups, making 1399:38-39

Five Maccabees on parade, glove fingers, making 53:39

Gelt (money) coins, clay, gold, silver paint, making 1704:33

Gelt, party favors, making 1266:29

Gift wrap, making 279:77

Greeting card, Menorah card, making 837:19

Hanukkah card, paper, paint, candle pattern, making 95:7; 1393:92

Hanukkah mobile, making 586:22

Hanukkah mobiles, paper, making 448:38

Hanukkah mural, making 906:20

Hanukkah symbols felt board, making 945:208-210

Hanukkah wall hanging, pattern, making 96:102-104

Hat, Hanukkah candle hat, paper plate, paper, making 1266:27

Hebrew letter patterns for Hanukkah 1180:32

Helmet, papier mache, balloon, cardboard, recipe, making 1180:16-17

Holiday creative drawing activities 1337:20-25

Kippah, hand paint, making 53:85

Kippah, hand sewn, making 53:86-87

Kippah, paper, making 53:84

Mat, embroidered, making 53:36

Mats, table, fabric, making 53:45

Mats, table, tie-dyed, fabric, making 53:46

Menorah banner, felt, dowel, gold cord and fringe, making 1360:38-41

Menorah design mosaic tray, making 53:50

Menorah from bottle caps or acorns, making 262:58-59

Menorah from pinecones and seeds, making 1067:219-220

Menorah from potatoes, making 310:209

Menorah made of mud dauber nests, making 310:205

Menorah, bread dough, making 816:115-116

Menorah, car distributor cap, making 262:57

Menorah, cardboard and dough, making 897:18

Menorah, cardboard box, foil, making 1356:9

Menorah, clay, making 53:13; 712:32-36; 1017:137; 1203:92

Menorah, clay, paint, candles, making 1180:6-7

Menorah, clothespin, making 53:22

Menorah, copper pipe, making 1203:93

Menorah, decorated, making 279:76

Menorah, dough, recipe given, making 1356:7

Menorah, egg carton, decorations, making 53:15; 279:75; 1266:28

Menorah, egg carton, foil, making 1356:8

Menorah, eggshells, making 53:19-20

Menorah, flameless, egg cartons, paper, crayons, making 1502:10

Menorah, gum drop candy, making 53:16

Menorah, hand prints, paper, making 1502:11

Menorah, making 297:276-277; 648:48-49; 698:95
Menorah, oil in glasses, making 53:21
Menorah, paper cup, making 53:12
Menorah, paper, making 95:6; 645:54-56; 819:19
Menorah, paper, pattern, making 305:43; 1305:49
Menorah, plaster cast, making 53:18-19
Menorah, play dough, making 909:111
Menorah, sand cast, making 53:38
Menorah, small cans, foil, sand, making 1356:9
Menorah, spool, making 53:23
Menorah, test tube, making 53:24
Menorah, thimbles, making 53:14
Menorah, wood and bolts, making 1203:91
Menorah, wood, metal nuts, candles, making 1357:16-17
Menorah, wooden spools, making 1203:92
Menorah, wooden, making 53:17
Mezuzah from shell, making 262:69
Mezuzah, bead and wood, making 53:80
Mezuzah, clay, making 53:83
Mezuzah, matchbox, making 53:80
Mezuzah, papier-mache, making 53:81
Mezuzah, plastic bottle, making 53:80
Mezuzah, seashell, making 53:82-83
Mezuzah, spool, making 53:80
Mezuzah, wood, making 53:82
Mizrahim, bright crayon, paper, making 53:90
Mizrahim, circle, paper, making 53:90
Mizrahim, collage, paper, making 53:89
Mizrahim, crayon rubbing, paper, making 53:89
Mizrahim, embroidered, fabric, pattern, making 53:91-92
Mizrahim, mock stained glass, paper, making 53:90
Mizrahim, mosaic, egg shell, making 53:90
Mizrahim, pencil painted, paper, making 53:89
Mizrahim, watercolor, paper, making 53:89
Mizrahim, window, paper, making 53:90
Mobiles, light-ups, chains, how to make 1356:17-21
Mural, making 698:95
Napkin holder, cardboard, making 53:47
Napkin rings, cardboard, making 53:48
Paper chains, making 262:59-61
Paper menorah, paper, tissue paper, making 1399:19
Picture, pipe cleaner, making 53:37
Pop-up Hanukkah card, making 1387:30-32
Potato print gift wrap, making 310:207
Recipe tray, glass and cardboard, making 53:48-49
Scented lamp, clay, yogurt cartons, paints, candle, making 1180:28-29
Shield, cardboard, paper, varnish, paints, making 1180:18
Spinning stars from paper and string, making 1502:19
Star box, decorated, patterns, making 1016:227-231
Star card, patterns, making 1016:232-236
Star of David from soda straws, making 448:38
Star of David mobile, cardboard, making 448:39
Star of David mobile, pipe cleaners, making 1462:30
Star of David ornament, making 835:19
Star of David ornament, popsicle sticks, making 1425:98
Star of David pendant, cardboard, foil, string, making 1502:18
Star of David, cardboard, making 115:98-99
Star of David, craft foil, making 1080:18
Star of David, macaroni, making 53:33-34
Star of David, making 648:50-51
Star of David, paper, making 94:16

Stencils; Star of David, sun, tree and dove, making 1704:34-36
Symbol, cardboard, making 53:33
Tablecloth, bleached design, making 53:43-44
Tablecloth, paper-cutout, making 53:42
Tablecloth, runner, making 53:44
Thimble menorah, thimble, styrofoam, candles, making 1399:18-19
Torah card, making 835:18
Tree menorah, clay, paint, making 1180:8-9
Wine decanter label, aluminum, making 53:88
Wine decanter, simple, making 53:87
Wine decanter, textured bottle, making 53:88

HANUKKAH—DOLLS
Doll, plastic bottle, making 53:40
Maccabee dolls from pipe, cleaners, making 448:38

HANUKKAH—FINGER PLAYS
Candles and latkes fingerplay 1654:122
Finger plays about Hanukkah 302:65; 1583:84-86
Finger plays, recipes, games, making 944:44-45
Five Little Pieces of Hanukkah, fingerplay 1357:35
Have you ever seen a Dreidel fingerplay? 1654:122

HANUKKAH—GAMES
Ball in the Dreidel cup game, making 53:66
Be my shadow game, how to play 1399:53
Bingo game, making 769:25
Candle and menorah game 279:87
Doughnuts for two game 279:88
Dreidel and put-and-take game, making 329:40-41
Dreidel from egg carton, dowel, making 1179:14-15
Dreidel game 115:74-75; 369:28-29; 434:55; 474:46; 769:24; 956:101-102; 1704:29
Dreidel game, cardboard, pattern, how to make 1393:90-91
Dreidel game, construction paper, making 1356:11-13
Dreidel game, dough Dreidel, recipe given, making 1356:11-13
Dreidel game, how to make 1074:142; 1462:28
Dreidel game, how to make and play 448:39; 543:75; 580:unp; 626:74; 1179:13-14; 1357:46-47; 1399:34-35
Dreidel game, pencil, cardboard, making 1356:11-13
Dreidel games 370:60-61; 1289:41
Dreidel nut toss game, making 53:65
Dreidel spinner game 53:68
Dreidel spinning game, making 909:112; 1266:31
Dreidel, cardboard, pencil, making 1704:26-27
Eight candles match-up game, cardboard, making 1356:14
Flip the latke game, paper plates, sticks, making 1356:15
Get latkes in the oven game, making 53:62
Gift box game 279:87
Hanukkah bingo game 370:62
Hanukkah gelt treasure hunt 370:64
Hanukkah number game 53:70
Hanukkah word game 53:69
Hop game, making 53:64
Judah Maccabee line up game, making 543:63
Latke toss game, how to play 1502:25
Light-the-menorah game, making 53:63
Maccabee bowling game, how to make 1502:24
Maccabees and Syrians game 279:89
Number game, kattoves game, how to play 1399:33
Pancakes in the frying pan game 279:88

Pin the candle on the menorah game, paper, making 1356:16

Pin the shield on Judah Maccabee game, making 53:63

Puzzle, cut and paste, making 53:66-67

Scramble game 279:89

Spin the Dreidel game, how to make box 829:60

Star of David number game, making 909:113

Sufganiyot on a string game 370:63

To the Temple board game, how to make 1502:14-15

Word and puzzle games 262:80-85

HANUKKAH—HANDICRAFTS

Acorn menorah, making 1691:107

Apron for Hanukkah, paper bag, making 1083:142

Ashtray, photo, glass, making 53:119

Bell pull, fabric, making 53:98

Bibs for baby, making 543:74

Book covers, paper, making 53:95

Bookends, baskets, making 53:96

Bookmarks, paper, making 53:94

Bookplates, paper, making 53:96

Bottle cap menorah, making 1691:106

Bulletin board, cork, making 53:116

Candles, Chanukah decorated, making 1277:19

Candlestick, making 1313:184

Cards, how to make 1356:22-24

Cobbler apron, making 543:72-73

Coin pouch, velvet, gold cord, pattern, making 1180:30-31

Cookie container, tin box, decorated, making 53:100

Dreidel charm necklace, paper, yarn, making 1654:123

Dreidel game, making 54:209

Dreidel spinning game, paper, making 298:210-211

Dreidel top, making 626:71-73

Dreidel, cardboard, making 384:Dec 4

Dreidel, egg carton, making 133:142

Dreidel, making 376:197; 497:38-39; 1691:107-108

Dreidels, flower, paper, making 53:130

Dreidels, sit up, paper, making 53:130

Fold dye papers, making 543:66-67

Gelt holder, detergent bottle, paper, making 1356:25

Gift boxes, decorated, making 53:127

Gifts, note pad, jigsaw puzzle, frame, place mats, making 1356:26-28

Greeting cards, buttons and paper, making 53:132-133

Greeting cards, crayon lift off, paper, making 53:133-134

Greeting cards, hole punch, paper, making 53:134-135

Greeting cards, linoleum block printed, paper, making 53:137-138

Greeting cards, potato prints, making 308:31

Greeting cards, relief printed, paper, making 53:136

Greeting cards, simple, making 53:132

Greeting cards, wood block printed, paper, making 53:138-139

Hanukkah traditions book, making 498:88-89

Herbal oil, recipe, making 1180:26

Jewelry boxes, egg cartons, making 53:109

Jewelry boxes, styrofoam egg, making 53:110

Jewelry holder, wire, making 53:111

Jewelry, nuts, making 53:108

Judah Maccabee model, making 543:62

Key holder, shrink plastic, making 53:107

Magnetic put-ons, Hanukkah symbols, felt, making 53:98-99

Matzo bag, making 376:198

Menorah candleholder, making 856:58-65

Menorah mobile, making 452:85-88

Menorah, clay, paints, making 1704:17-19

Menorah, making 376:196

Menorah, paper, making 54:208

Menorah, wooden, making 891:117-121

Menorahs, paper and wood, making 543:64-65

Necklace, craft plaster, making 53:108

Paperweight, making 53:120

Paperweights, rock, making 543:70

Pencil holder, making 543:71

Pictures, framed, making 543:68-69

Pin cushion, basket, making 53:118

Planter shoe, old shoe, making 53:103

Planter, sand, colored, making 53:104-105

Pot holder, fabric, making 53:101

Reuben's Tale picture book, making 1704:40

Scented soap, soap flakes, food coloring, scent, making 1179:17

Soap, hand painted, making 53:117

Spinning Dreidel, making 1313:185

Sport patches, fabric, making 53:114-115

Star of David, 3-D, paper, making 53:130

Sweet scented oil, recipe, making 1180:27

Towel, decorated, making 53:112-113

Wrapping paper, simple 53:122- 126,128-129

HANUKKAH—HANDS ART ACTIVITIES

Hands activities for Hanukkah, making 306:24

HANUKKAH—KITES

Star of David kite, pattern, making 1427:178-179

HANUKKAH—PARTIES

Candle menorah, making 294:188-189

Candlelight dinner, how to do 370:56

Chanukah party invitations, decorations, menus and games, making 2:29-36

Decorations, food, games, making 1266:27-31

Dreidel cake, making 294:186

Dreidel game, making 204:187

Dreidel grab bag centerpiece or decorated spinning Dreidel, making 370:57-58

Dreidel napkin rings, paper, making 829:56

Dreidels, miniature, cardboard, making 829:58

Festival of Lights party, invitations, craft activities, games, recipes, making 1203:89-95

Hanukkah candy holders, balloon, making 53:58

Hanukkah candy holders, Maccabbee, cardboard, making 53:60

Hanukkah candy holders, making 53:58-59

Hanukkah house shaped invitations, paper, making 53:53.

Hanukkah invitations, styrofoam, making 53:52

Hanukkah party favors, bean bag, making 53:57

Hanukkah party favors, Dreidel game, making 53:56

Hanukkah place cards, paper, making 53:54-55; 829:57

Hanukkah place mats and star napkin rings, paper, making 829:56

Happy Hanukkah party, invitations, craft activities, games, recipes, making 1203:80-88

Menorah centerpiece, styrofoam, making 829:57

Menorah invitations, paper, making 829:55

Menorah or shield invitation, making 370:56-57

Mobile, Hanukkah mobile, cardboard, making 829:58

Open house party, how to give 370:57

Pajama party, how to give 370:58

Paper chain decorations, making 370:56

Star of David invitations, paper, making 829:55

Star of David, making 294:190

HANUKKAH—PATTERNS
Menorah pattern 309:35
HANUKKAH—PLAYS
Antiochus costume, picture of 53:72
Child, pictures of 53:73
Farmer costume, picture of 53:72
Hellenist, pictures of 53:73
Judah Maccabee, pictures of 53:72
Syrian soldier, pictures of 53:73
Woman, pictures of 53:73
HANUKKAH—PUPPETS
Candle puppets, toilet tissue tubes, making 1135:36
Dreidel puppets, making 735:68
Hanukkah candle puppet, paper tube, making 907:22
Puppet projects, patterns, scenes, story starters, feature
story 1083:139-142
Puppet theaters, box, making 53:78
Puppets, finger, Hannah, paper, making 53:77
Puppets, finger, Mattathias, paper, making 53:77
Puppets, making 53:74-75
Shadow box and stick puppets, making 1399:42
Swallowing box puppet, box, making 1083:142
HANUKKAH—SONGS
Dreidel song 115:83
Dreidel song words 1462:31
Songs about Hanukkah 901:24-28
HARVEST FESTIVALS—COOKERY
Rice ring, recipe 1401:50
HARVEST FESTIVALS—GAMES
Harvest game 240:46
HARVEST FESTIVALS—HANDICRAFTS
Corn dollies 566:20
Corn dollies from wheat, making 1531:28-29
Corn husk flowers, corn husks, fabric, dyes, making
1285:104-105
Harvest basket, box and paper, making 1089:15
Leaf window decoration, leaves, waxed paper, making
1401:30
Patchwork wall hanging, fabric, paper, making 1401:31
Salt-dough models of harvest fruits and vegetables, rec-
ipe 1277:17
Turnip lanterns, turnips, small candles, string, making
1285:106-107
Wheat weaving decorations, making 1531:28-29
HARVEST FESTIVALS—HATS
Harvest hats, papier-mache in fruit and vegetable shapes,
making 1610:48
HARVEST FESTIVALS—PUPPETS
Apple puppets, dried apple head puppets, making
1285:102-103
HATCH CHILI FESTIVAL, HATCH, N.M.—
COOKERY
Green chile roll-ups, recipe 1416:unp
Measuring chili pepper heat of different types of peppers
by Scoville heat units 1416:unp
HATS
Aladdin hat, making 366:77
Babushka, fabric, making 889:106-112
Balaclava hat, making 1174:140
Beret, crocheted wool, making 690:24-25
Betsy Ross hat, making 272:82
Bishop's mitre, newspaper, making 736:51
Bonnet from newspaper, making 271:61
Bonnets, simple, 14th century English, making 870:134-
136

Buccaneer hats, paper, making 74:126-127
Cap liner from newspaper, making 271:63
Cap or tam from newspaper, making 271:62
Captain Hook's hat, paper, making 250:unp
Captain's hat, paper, making 297:252-253
Cavalier hat, making 366:85; 367:90
Chinese braid hat, paper, pattern, making 823:45
Chinese coolie hat, cardboard, making 106:12
Chinese hat, making 142:35; 294:99
Chinese traditional hat, paper, pattern, making 823:46
Clown hat, old felt hat, yarn, making 1314:16
Colonial cap, making 118:143
Colonial hat, making 448:46
Colonial Mother Hubbard-style, paper, making 480:120
Columbus hat, making 272:105-107
Coolie hat 417:61; 574:21
Coonskin hat, making 646:26-27
Court jester hat, making 774:101-102
Crown, making 142:34; 872:19
Crown, paper bag, making 442:17
Crown, paper straws, making 828:91-92
Crown, paper, making 123:32-34
Crown, posterboard, making 1096:10
Crown, shiny paper, making 966:146-147
Crowns and hats (bobby, chef, space helmet), making
857:52-53
Crowns, king or queen, pasta, paper, paints, making
1299:8-9
Duke of Wellington hat, making 1174:140
Dutch cap 417:59
Dutch girl hat, paper, pattern, making 823:47
Dutchess headdress, paper, making 809:150
Egyptian hat, ancient, paper, pattern, making 823:51-52
Fez from paper bag, making, 678:23
Fiesta pom pom hat, paper, pattern, making 823:48-49
Fourth of July hats from paper bag, cardboard, and plas-
tic jug, making 448:22
Franklin, Benjamin Franklin's hat, making 670:72-73
French maid cap 417:55
George Washington hat 50:218
George Washington hat, paper, making 878:88
George Washington's General hat, paper, pattern, mak-
ing 823:31-32
George Washington three-cornered hat, paper, pattern,
making 186:21-22; 823:30
German feathered hat, making 294:44-45
Haman hat, making 272:57
Haman hat, paper bag, making 543:98
Hanukkah candle hat, paper plate, paper, making
1266:27
Hat Day, activities, art, songs, recipes, games 1469:58-
59
Headband from newspaper, making 271:63
Hula skirt hat, paper, pattern, making 823:76
Indian feather band, paper, pattern, making 823:17
Indian headdress 417:57
Indian headdress from paper bags, making 678:22
Indian headdress, making 142:34
Irish country lad's hat, making 272:51-52
Italian feathered hat, making 294:120
Japanese hat, making 272:114
Jester cap, making 142:37
Jester hat, egg carton, paper, making 1345:24-25
Jester hat, paper, pattern, making 823:68-69
King's crown, paper foil, making 214:14; 449:25

Kippah, hand painted, making 53:85
Kippah, paper, making 53:84
Knight helmet with plume, cardboard, paper, making 1682:11
Knight helmet, cardboard, making 588:12-13
Knight helmet, making 142:37
Laurel wreath, paper, making 181:26-27
Leprechaun hat, making 272:49-50; 1689:30
Lincoln hat, making 648:14-15; 670:68
Lincoln hat, paper, pattern, making 823:33
Lincoln, Mary Todd, hat, making 272:45
Marine hat, making 272:80
Masquerade hat, cardboard, paint, patterns, making 1314:18
Medieval hat, fabric, making 1174:29
Medieval Hennin 417:61
Medieval lady's hat, paper, making 449:29
Merlin's magic hat, paper, making 809:150
Mexican sombrero, making 282:31
Moon hat, metallic paper, ribbon, making 1299:20-21
Multipurpose cap, paper, making 1238:13-16
Napoleon's hat, making 670:71
Norse helmet 417:61
Nurse hat, making 272:78-79
Paper strip hats, making 267:20-21
Party hat, paper, making 1238:24-28
Pharaoh (headdress), paper, making 46:83-84
Pied Piper hat, making 1174:140
Pierrot hat, cardboard, felt, making 1314:17
Pilgrim bonnet, making, 295:222
Pilgrim fedora, paper, making 436:43
Pilgrim hat, boy, paper, pattern, making 823:18-19
Pilgrim hat, girl, paper, pattern, making 823:20
Pilgrim hat, making 142:35; 294:184; 295:221-222; 648:44-46
Pilgrim hat, paper, pattern, making 305:39; 436:42; 760:218-219
Pilgrim man's hat, making 272:126-127
Pilgrim woman's hat, making 272:130
Pirate hat from paper bags, making 678:21
Pirate hat, cardboard, patterns, making 1314:24
Pirate hat, making 367:102
Pirate hat, paper and felt, making 1096:11
Pirate hat, paper, making 75:26; 133:39; 232:25; 878:96
Pirate hat, plastic carton, making 766:56-57
Pleated hat, from newspaper, making 271:64
Poke bonnet 417:61
Printing press special, newspaper, making 1238:17-20
Puritan hat 417:57
Queen Esther hat, making 272:55-56
Queen paper plate crown, making 231:38
Queen's crown, paper, making 214:15
Red Cross hat, paper, pattern, making 823:63
Robin Hood hat, fabric, making 449:26
Robin Hood hat, making 7:118-119; 367:24; 774:103; 1174:140
Royal crown, egg carton, making 766:62
Royal crown, patterns, paper, making 1016:166-171
Russian fur hat, paper, making 909:11
Safari hat, cookies, making 1672:130
Safari hat, paper, pattern, making 1088:116-119
Saxon helmet 417:61
Sentry, making 142:36
Sombrero from paper straws, making 828:88-89
St. Lucia crown, paper, making 1080:10-11

St. Patrick's Day crown, making 448:13
St. Patrick's Day hats, paper plates, making 909:41
Star Boy hat, paper, making 1080:11
Star of David hat, paper, pattern, making 823:22
Statue of Liberty crown, paper, making 558:11
Steamship hat, cardboard box, paper tubes, making 1345:16-17
Stovepipe hat, making 272:42-43
Sun hat, metallic paper, ribbon, making 1299:20-21
Sunglasses hat from newspaper, making 271:65
Three-cornered hat from newspaper, making 271:47
Three-cornered hat, paper, pattern, making 275:23-24; 480:184-185
Three-cornered hat, tricorn, paper, making 607:unp
Tiara crown, paper, making 809:152
Tiara, cardboard, tinfoil, patterns, making 1314:37
Tri-corner Colonial hat, making 877:118
Tricorn hats, oaktag, paper, patterns, making 1199:53
Tricorne hat, pattern, making 281:101
Turban, paper, pattern, making 823:44
Turkish Fez, paper, making 1238:21-24
Twenties man's hat, cardboard, pattern, making 1174:38
Uncle Sam hat 199:58
Uncle Sam hat, making 272:89-90
Uncle Sam hat, soup can and felt, making 374:131-132
Victorian maid cap, making 870:138-140
Vienna top hat, making 295:190
Viking hat, paper, making 1238:9-12
Wise Man from the East (turban), paper, making 46:105
Witch hat, cardboard, tape, pattern, making 1314:45
Witch hat, patterns, making 1435:73-75

HAVASUPAI INDIANS—COOKERY

Corn and pumpkin stew, recipe 1699:139

HAWAII

Clothing, food, language, music, crafts, folklore activities 1378:1-37
Traditions, customs, geography, economy, ecology, activities 1378:1-37

HAWAII—BIRTHDAYS

Birthday customs 488:48-52
Celebrations of birthdays in Hawaii 474:85
Hawaiian Luau theme birthday party, making 896:61-66

HAWAII—CHRISTMAS—COOKERY

Merry Christmas salad, recipe 874:62

HAWAII—CHRISTMAS—DANCES

Christmas Luau dance 624:62-69

HAWAII—CHRISTMAS—DECORATIONS

Kini popo, making 709:76-78

HAWAII—CLOTHING

Hula skirt, crepe paper, making 1310:140; 1378:24-25
Hula skirt, making 251:50; 1017:97
Hula skirt, paper, making 878:96
Hula skirt, simple, leaves, paper bag strips, making 1477:97

HAWAII—COOKERY

Ambrosia, recipe 1296:144
Apple Waldorf salad, recipe 1653:20
Cheese spread, recipe 1378:32
Feasts and Festivals in Hawaii and the foods they eat 666:281-283
Flower lei soup, recipe 1378:31
Fruit salad, recipe 1378:31
Hawaiian hamburgers, recipe 653:62-64,118
Hawaiian muffins, recipe 1653:58
Hawaiian popcorn bars, recipe 381:53

Hawaiian punch bowl, recipe, making 654:40
Lomi salmon, recipe 794:57
Macadamia nut, coconut bars, cookies, recipe 72:136-137
Menehune punch, recipe 1378:31
Pancakes, recipe 1653:94
Pineapple chicken, recipe, making 666:283-284
Pork chops Waikiki, recipe 654:39

HAWAII—COOKERY—HISTORY
Foods and cookery of the first Hawaiians 666:265-272

HAWAII—COSTUMES
Hawaiian costumes drawing 988:60
Wahini Loa costume 213:26

HAWAII—DANCES
Hukilau dance, how to do 1494:200-202

HAWAII—DOLLS
Hula doll, paper bag, making 534:22-23

HAWAII—FESTIVALS
Aloha Week celebration 601:134-135
Lei Day celebration, activities, handicrafts, foods, songs, making 909:59-67
Mele Kalikimaka Festival, how to celebrate 1378:29-31

HAWAII—FESTIVALS—GAMES
Makahiki, New Year celebration games, how to play 1296:128

HAWAII—FESTIVALS—LEIS
Lei Day lei, tissue flowers, making 308:61
Lei Day, tissue paper leis, patterns, how to make 1393:204

HAWAII—GAMES
Hawaiian Statehood game 240:43
Kimo jacks game, how to play 1718:32-33
Loulou game 383:87
Noa game 383:85
Pa-pohene game 383:86
Pa-pohene game, how to play 1494:197
Pahee gamae 383:85
Puhenehene game 383:86

HAWAII—HATS
Hula skirt hat, paper, pattern, making 823:76

HAWAII—LANGUAGE
Hawaiian everyday words 384:June 11
Hawaiian names, numbers, colors, phrases and others 1378:32-34
Sound of Hawaiian language and some of its words 1378:13-14

HAWAII—LEIS
Flower lei, patterns, making 1083:86-87
Flower leis, making 1017:97
Hawaiian lei, paper, making 857:60-61
Lei bag pig, paper bag, making 1083:89
Lei, paper, making 275:86
Lei, tissue paper, making 765:93; 909:61
Leis, making 217:70-71
Leis, newspaper, making 1658:73
Leis, paper, yarn and straws, making 897:37

HAWAII—LUAU PARTY
Aloha grass skirt and flowery lei, making 294:138-139
Basket of flowers favors and fruit centerpiece, making 294:134-137
Dancing poles and drums, making 294:142
Flower basket cake, making 294:132-133
Lei invitations and flower place mats, making 294:130
Sleeping volcano game, making 294:140-141
Tiki masks, making 294:139

Vine decorations, making 294:131

HAWAII—MUSICAL INSTRUMENTS
Uli-Uli, making 468:47

HAWAII—PLANTS
Pineapple plant, how to grow 909:62

HAWAII—PRINCESSES—CLOTHING
Hawaiian princess costume, posterboard and crepe paper, patterns, making 1050:114-117

HAWAII—PUPPET PLAYS
Maui Captures the Sun 4:33-36

HAWAII—PUPPETS
Hula hand puppets, paper, making 909:64

HAWAII—QUILTING
Appliquéd pineapple quilt, making 298:118-119
Quilt with Hawaiian designs, fabric, making 1378:26-27

HAWAII—SONGS
I Hold Thee, My Baby, lullaby 1220:142

HAWAII—STRING FIGURES
Cat's Cradle and variations of strings 372:66-73
House of a Chief string 373:14-15
Maui's lasso string 372:40-43
Open the Gate string 372:22-23
Salt Cave string 372:62-65

HAWAII—THANKSGIVING
Makahiki Festival celebration 659:93-95

HAWAII—VOLCANOES
Hawaiian eruption, model volcano demonstrates 1455:77

HAYES, HELEN—BIRTHDAY
Celebrate by acting out different emotions activity 1199:233

HEADBANDS
Laurel wreath, paper, making 181:26-27

HEART DAY
Activities, art, songs, recipes, games 1469:66-67

HEBREW CALENDAR
Information about Hebrew Calendar 712:12,14

HEBREW LANGUAGE
Numbers one through ten in Hebrew 1366:unp

HEBREWS—THANKSGIVING
History of Thanksgiving 659:22-24

HEDGEHOGS
Mrs. Teasel hedgehog, fabric, decorations, patterns, making 1510:32-33
Potato hedgehog, making 23:16-17
Toy stuffed hedgehog, fabric, making 971:unp
Walking hedgehog, yarn, making 770:51-51
Wool hedgehog, making 1012:58

HEDGEHOGS—COOKERY
Hedgehog cake, recipe 449:51
Hedgehog family cake, recipe and how to decorate 1415:28-29

HEIDI
Heidi's toasted cheese sandwiches, recipe 570:27-29

HELEN OF TROY
Helen of Troy costume 213:46-47

HELMETS
Atlantis helmets, making 173:22-23
Balloon mold papier-mache helmet, making 7:41-42
Egg container helmet, making 7:45-46
Helmet, making 213:44-46
Helmet, paper bag, paints, patterns, making 1657:56-57
Knight helmet, cardboard, making 588:12-13
Paper helmet, pattern, making 1348:unp
Papier-mache helmet, paints, making 1181:24-26

Silver helmet, papier-mache, paint, making 1561:24-25
Warrior helmet, decorated bristol board, how to make 1350:74-75

HENNING, DOUG
Multiplying fingers, how to do 1270:28-29

HENRY, MARGUERITE
"Misty of Chincoteague" pot pie, recipe 570:37-39

HERALDRY
Book-plates, making 51:377
Colors 51:369-371
Design in decorative language, how to make 51:371-376
Divisions 51:367-368
Field and the points of heraldry 51:366
Floral vocabulary 51:377-379

HERBS
Cure-alls using herbs, making 798:37-49
Drying herbs, how to do 798:75
Herb vinegar, recipe 1213:98

HERBS—BATH BAGS
Bath bags, fabric, dried herbs, making 1285:67

HERBS—BUNDLES
Lavender bundles, making 1259:29

HERBS—DOLLS
Herb dolls, herbs, doll's straw hat, ribbons, making 1285:66

HERBS—PET COLLARS
Pennyroyal pet collars, fabric, herbs, making 1285:68-69

HERBS—PILLOWS
Sweet dreams pillow, flower petals, herbs, pattern, making 1213:99

HERBS—SACHETS
Herb sachets, making 1259:28

HERBS—WREATHS
Wreath from herbs on coat hanger, how to make 1419:213

HERMANN, CARL
Vanishing key, how to do 1270:24-25

HEROES
Heroes and Heroines; reading and writing activities, projects 620:158-171

HEX SIGNS
Hex sign, making 118:78
Hex signs for your home 118:77
Hex signs, paper, making 877:40

HIDATSA INDIANS—GAMES
Feathered darts game, how to play 1699:118

HIEROGLYPHICS
Hieroglyphics, how to make 699:12
Name Cartouche, hieroglyphics, how to make 699:14-15
Scroll place card, making 287:59-60
Scrolls, how to make 699:12-14
Welcome scribe, making 287:58-59

HILLBILLIES
Ellie Mae costume 213:76-77
Toby costume 213:74-76

HINDUS—BIRTHDAYS
Hindu birthday celebrations 695:57-60

HINDUS—COOKERY
Carrot halva, recipe 1709:9

HINDUS—COSTUMES
Hindu lady, sheet, making 106:10

HINDUS—DOLLS
Hindu lady doll, making 494:198-210

HINDUS—FESTIVALS
Car Festivals celebrations 566:35

Divali, the Hindu New Year, activities and projects for classrooms 1393:71-72
Diwali Festival celebration 566:34
Dusshera Festival celebration 566:35
Ganesh Chaturthi Festival celebration 826:24-25
Holi celebration 566:35
Marriage celebration 631:40
Raksha Bandhan Festival celebration 566:34

HINDUS—FESTIVALS—COOKERY
Baisakhi Festival, cereal dessert, recipe 1313:77
Baisakhi Festival, chappati, recipe 1313:77

HINDUS—FESTIVALS—DECORATIONS
Baisakhi Festival pop-up card, making 1387:52
Diwali Festival of Lights pop-up card, making 1387:24
Raksah Bandhan (Hindu family holiday), pop-up card, making 1387:14

HINDUS—FESTIVALS—HANDICRAFTS
Diwali; Hindu floor painting, paper, glue, grains, beans, making 1393:72
Raksha Bandhan Celebration, brothers and sisters bracelets, making 1610:21
Raksha Bandhan Festival plaited rakhi bracelets, making 1277:14-15
Raksha Bandhan Rakhi; bracelet, ribbon, making 1709:27
Rangoli patterns, making 1278:22-23

HINDUS—FLOWERS
Marigold garland flowers, thread, making 1709:17

HINDUS—HAND DECORATIONS
Mehndi hand patterns, how to apply 1709:31

HINDUS—HOUSES
Home with walled in garden, model, making 494:206-210

HINDUS—LANGUAGE
Hindi names for the months of the year 1031:47
Numbers one through ten in Hindi language 1365:unp.

HINDUS—MASKS
Ganesh elephant mask, cardboard, paint, making 1709:13

HINDUS—NATURE FESTIVALS
Diwali, Festival of lights 419:110-111
Hindu rituals 419:107-121

HIPPIES
Hippy family, paper models, making 966:170-171

HISPANIC AMERICANS—FESTIVALS
Three Kings Day celebration 499:77

HISPANIC AMERICANS—FOLKLORE
"Family Pictures"; physical and human geography activities 1458:88-91

HISPANIC AMERICANS—GAMES
Cobra game 602:187
Key of Rome and Take It game 602:188
Little Blind Chicken game 602:187-188

HOBAN, LILLIAN
"Arthur's Christmas Cookies," salt dough cookies, recipe 1216:81

HOBAN, RUSSELL
"Bread and Jam for Frances," bread and jam, recipe 1216:35

HOBOS
Hobo stove, making 590:90-91

HOBOS—LANGUAGE
Hobo signs, making 976:40-41

HOBOS—PARTIES
Come as a bum birthday party, activities, food, handicrafts 30:30-32

Hobo Heaven party, activities and recipes 809:107-110
Hobo Hobnob party, how to plan and give 43:50-53

HODGKIN, DOROTHY
Mining for crystals 1719:33

HOLLAND. *See* **NETHERLANDS**

HOLY THURSDAY
Holy Thursday, William Blake 139:72

HOME REMEDIES
Athlete's foot 118:63
Bangs and bruises 118:63
Common cold 118:63
Coughing 118:63
Earache 118:63
Freckles 118:62
Hiccups 118:62
Insect bites, stings, and itches 118:62
Lotions, potions and strange notions 118:61
Nosebleed 118:63
Pains and sprains 118:63
Poison ivy 118:63
Small cuts 118:63
Sneezing 118:63
Sore throat 118:63
Splinters and thorns 118:63
Sunburn 118:62
Toothache 118:63
Warts 118:62

HOMES
All around the house; literature, activities, crafts, games 1390:1-28
Castles in the Air; literature, activities, crafts, games 1390:184-216
Cave, coops and cages; literature, activities, crafts, games 1390:156-183
City homes, country homes; literature, activities, crafts, games 1390:29-55
Clean and tidy; literature, activities, crafts, games 1390:84-111
Hideaways; literature, activities, crafts, games 1390:136-155
Moving and building; literature, activities, crafts, games 1390:112-135
Pyramids and pagodas, literature, activities, crafts, games 1390:56-83

HOMESTEADERS. *See* **FRONTIER AND PIONEER LIFE**

HONDURAS—CHRISTMAS—COOKERY
Refresco de Lechosa (milk and papaya drink), recipe 1666:247
Sapa de Aguacate (chilled avocado), recipe 1666:246
Torrijas (fried cake dessert), recipe 1666:246-247

HONDURAS—COOKERY
Calabacitas con jitomate, zucchini with tomatoes, recipe 1165:247
Chiles rellenos, stuffed chili peppers, recipe 1165:247

HONDURAS—GAMES
Lay Rayuela, hopscotch game 1426:24-25

HONDURAS—HANDICRAFTS
Pollo or chicken made of paper, patterns, making 1633:76-77

HONDURAS—KITES
Kite to make 515:60

HONG KONG—CHRISTMAS—CUSTOMS
Christmas customs 149:52

HONG KONG—COOKERY
Cold noodles with peanut sauce, recipe 1392:unp

HONG KONG—GAMES
Chung Tou The Tou, plant beans, reap beans, how to play 1494:39
Cut the Bean Curd game, how to play 1499:24-25
Plant beans, reap beans game 602:51

HONG KONG—HANDICRAFTS
Pinwheel; straw and cardboard pinwheel, making 1256:25

HOPI INDIANS—CLOTHING
Hopi dress, making 224:90-91
Hopi vest, woven, making 224:122-123
Pueblo dress, bath towels, making 1699:50
Shirts, fringed, fabric, making 281:41-43
Tunic, fabric, pattern, making 281:43
Woman's dress, pattern, making 281:45

HOPI INDIANS—COOKERY
Beef jerky, recipe 1380:36
Blue fry bread, recipe 574:134
Blue marbles cornmeal balls, recipe 1527:14
Corn cakes, boiled, recipe 1368:28
Fried corn cakes, recipe 1599:18
Fried Pinyon nut cakes, recipe 1599:18
Thumbprint bread, kolatquvil, recipe 1527:13

HOPI INDIANS—COSTUMES
Snake dance costume, making 467:42-43

HOPI INDIANS—DANCES
Hopi snake dance 574:146

HOPI INDIANS—DOLLS
Hopi Kachina Tihus dolls, making 466:98-99
Hopi Kachinas, making 445:111-126
Kachina butterfly maiden doll, making 775:80-83
Kachina cradle doll, paper tube, papier-mache, patterns, making 1633:36-37
Kachina doll wood carved figure, making 382:78-80
Kachina doll, cardboard, feathers, paints, making 1699:97
Kachina doll, how to draw 591:30-31
Kachina doll, making 171:56-64; 227:54-55; 467:44-45; 586:10; 605:41-48; 605:49-54; 633:149-150; 673:254-278; 714:29-31
Kachina doll, making from spools 629:108-110
Kachina doll, styrofoam block, paints, yarn, making 1368:54
Kachina doll, wooden, pattern, making 1027:123-127
Kachina dolls, clay, fabric scraps, making 1092:110-111

HOPI INDIANS—FESTIVALS—DOLLS
Corn dance dolls, oaktag, markers, patterns, making 1249:19-20

HOPI INDIANS—GAMES
Alquerque board game, patterns, making 1541:61-66
Indian kickball game 1074:214-216

HOPI INDIANS—HANDICRAFTS
Friendship stick, making from spools 629:102-104
Friendship sticks, making 482:126-127

HOPI INDIANS—HOUSES
Adobe, making 574:131

HOPI INDIANS—JEWELRY
Hopi necklace, making 227:31

HOPI INDIANS—LULLABIES
Hopi lullaby 780:33

HOPI INDIANS—MASKS
Kachina mask, making 63:26-27; 204:106-109
Kachina mask, round carton, feathers, making 1699:74

HOPI INDIANS—NATURE FESTIVALS
Kachina Dolls Festival 419:152-153
Planting and growing festivals 419:151-155
Snake Ceremony Festival 419:153-155

HOPI INDIANS—WOOD CARVING
Eagle Kachina wood carved figure, making, 382:75-76

HORNBOOK
Bread dough hornbooks, recipe 1193:451
Hornbook model, wooden, making 567:126-127
Hornbook, making 436:30; 877:113-114
Hornbook, paper, patterns for book and text, making 1159:130
Pattern for making hornbook 1191:453
Wooden hornbook, making 493:221-225

HORNS—CARVING
Bank from horn, making 229:85-86
Clean, cut and shape horns for carving, how to do 229:54-56
Decorating horns, how to do 229:57
Horn specimen decoration, making 229:84-85
Pencil holder, making 229:87
Suncatcher, making 229:88
Wall plaque, making 229:90-91
Window ornament, making 229:89-90

HORNS—IMPLEMENTS
History of animal horns as implements 229:43-47

HORNS—JEWELRY
Necklaces from horns, making 229:62-63
Pendants from horns, making 229:59-61

HORSES
Bucking bronco, cardboard carton, toy, making 1348:unp

HOSHANAH RABBAH
Meaning of Hoshanah Rabbah 712:26

HOT CROSS BUNS
Make a batch of buns, hot cross buns, recipe 139:80-81

HOT DOGS
History of hot dogs 303:9-20
How they are made 303:29-35
Making hot dogs or frankfurters at home, recipe, 303:36-47
Records and facts about hot dogs 303:57-62

HOT DOGS—COOKERY
Barbecue coated franks, recipe 303:53
Camper's Wiener stew, recipe 303:52
Cheese dogs, recipe 303:50-51
Corn dogs, hush puppies, recipe 303:54-56
Hot dogs and beans, recipe 303:49
Little dogs, recipe 303:51
Round dogs, recipe 303:53-54

HOT PEPPERS—NEW MEXICO—HATCH REGION—COOKERY
Green chile roll-ups, recipe 1416:unp
Measuring chili pepper heat of different types of peppers by Scoville heat units 1416:unp

HOUDIN, JEAN-EUGENE ROBERT
Magic tree, paper trick, how to do 1270:22-23

HOUDINI, HARRY
Great escape, Houdini ring trick, how to do 1270:14-15
National Magic Day; celebrate by learning magic tricks 1199:240-241

HOUDINI, HARRY—BIRTHDAY
Birthday celebration; art, music, foods, games, activities 1104:74-77

HOUSES
Clay cottages, miniature, making 1260:22-23
Courtyard houses, making 173:58-59
Dome, dowels, garden hose, making 1312:10-11

Double decker snow house, making 1312:15
Greenhouse, wood, windows, plastic, making 1312:41
Miniature house, cardboard boxes, fabrics, paper, paints, making 1181:16-19
Newspaper log cabin, making 1312:13
Palm hut, palm branches, making 1312:14
Queen Anne Victorian house, gingerbread, recipe, patterns, making 1086:67-79
Saltbox house, gingerbread, recipe, patterns, assembling, how to do 1086:36-45
San Francisco row house, paper, patterns, making 1152:161-166
Sod house, making 1312:17
Solar heating for house, making 1312:44
Stone and concrete house, making 1312:26-32
Tetrahedron, inflatable, plastic, making 1312:8-9
Town house, gingerbread, recipe, assembly instructions, how to do 1086:80-86
Town house, wooden, making 922:56-71
Windmill, plywood, bicycle wheel, making 1312:38-39

HOWARD JOHNSON'S RESTAURANTS
History of 119:142-146

HUICHOL INDIANS—GOD'S EYE
God's eye, making 63:42-43
God's eye, miniature, craft sticks, yarn, making 1715:56-57

HUICHOL INDIANS—YARN PAINTING
Huichol yarn paintings, colored pencil version, making 1338:24-26
Yarn and beeswax paintings, cardboard, yarn, making 1476:56
Yarn art bowl and picture, Huichol Indian designs given, making 1633:56-59
Yarn painting, making 63:40-41

HUNGARY—CHRISTMAS
Christmas celebration 601:110

HUNGARY—COOKERY
Apricot pastries, recipe 895:67
Baklava, recipe 88:78-79
Betusutemeny, letter cookies, recipe, making 858:unp
Bogracs gulyas, Hungarian goulash, recipe 1165:100
Cabbage and noodles, recipe 794:27
Cherry filling, recipe 385:39
Chicken paprikash, recipe 661:183-184; 1165:100-101
Cherry soup, cold, recipe 385:24; 1560:20
Cold plate, recipe 385:18
Cottage cheese filling, recipe 385:38
Creamed spinach with fried rolls, recipe 385:40
Cucumber salad, recipe 385:29
Dessert crepes, recipe 661:187
Dessert pancake and filling (palacsinta), recipe 88:77-78
Dry bean soup with smoked sausage, recipe 385:23
Dumplings, recipe 661:185-186
Egg noodles, Galuska, recipe 1380:19
Eggs Casino, recipe 385:21
Evening fairies (estike), cookies, recipe 72:71-72
Fried, breaded pork or veal, recipe 385:34
Galuska, recipe 385:31
Goulash, recipe 385:24; 661:183-184
Green pepper salad, recipe 385:27
History of cookery in 88:76-77
Hungarian goulash soup, recipe 1303:115
Hungarian goulash, recipe 895:66
Korozot dip, recipe 499:81-82
Liptoi cheese, recipe 188:31

Noodles with cottage cheese, recipe 385:35
Paprika cheese sticks, recipe 1244:78
Paprika chicken, recipe 385:30
Paprika potatoes, recipe 385:29
Plum cake, recipe 711:34-35
Poppy seed filling, recipe 385:38
Roux, recipe 385:40
Salad dressing, recipe 385:27
Scrambled eggs, recipe 385:19
Squash in sour cream, recipe 661:186
Strudel, recipe 385:37
Stuffed green peppers in tomato sauce, recipe 385:33
Tomato salad, recipe, making 385:27
Ujhazi chicken soup, recipe 385:43

HUNGARY—COSTUMES
Hungarian costumes drawing 988:40-41
Hungarian man and girl costumes, drawing 988:40-41
Liptoi cheese, recipe, costume 188:31

HUNGARY—DANCES
Csardas dance and costume picture 1000:30-33
Cshebogar dance, how to do 1494:129-130

HUNGARY—EASTER
Easter egg customs in Hungary 201:28

HUNGARY—EASTER—COOKERY
Csipetke (dumplings), recipe 1666:85-86
Csirke Paprikas Galuskaval (chicken paprika), recipe 1666:85-86
Pogacsa (Hungarian butter cookies), recipe 1666:86-87

HUNGARY—FESTIVALS—HANDICRAFTS
Wedding Dance Pole, making 856:46-49

HUNGARY—GYPSIES
Gypsy encampment from Hungary, matchboxes model, making 1094:31
Hungarian Gypsy life and festival celebrations 661:181-182

HUNGARY—HANDICRAFTS
Smocking, how to do 955:34-35
Table coaster, Hungarian painted flowers, patterns, making 1016:121-126

HUNGARY—VALENTINE'S DAY
History of Valentine's Day in Hungary 709:133

HUNGARY—VALENTINE'S DAY—COOKERY
Mezeskalacs (Hungarian cookie), recipe 709:133-135

HURON INDIANS—CHRISTMAS—SONGS
Huron Christmas carol, music 1225:78-79
Huron Christmas carol, words 1225:55

HURON INDIANS—GAMES
Guess how many game 602:171
Tipcat game 602:171

HUTCHINS, PAT
"Don't Forget the Bacon," bacon, recipe 1216:101
"Doorbell Ran," chocolate chip cookies, recipe 1216:77

HYMAN, TRINA SCHART
"Little Red Riding Hood," bread and sweet butter, recipe 1216:33

I

ICE CREAM
Baked Alaska, history of 597:82-83
Baked Alaska, recipe 1564:74-75
Colonial ice cream, recipe 831:151-152
Freezer, history of 597:75
History of ice cream 597:73-77; 762:39-51
Homemade ice cream with recycled tin cans, recipe 1301:44-45
Homemade ice cream, recipe 1660:60
Ice cream soda, history of 597:76
Preparation of ice cream for market 597:77-79
Use of ice cream in the world 597:81-82

ICE CREAM—GAMES
Invention of the ice cream cone game 240:41

ICELAND—BIRTHDAYS
Birthday customs 488:53-55

ICELAND—CHRISTMAS—COOKERY
Cheddar cheese soup, recipe 1666:129

ICELAND—COOKERY
Baked Atlantic fish, recipe 188:19
Half moons (halfmanar), cookies, recipe 72:41-42
Herring salad, recipe 1669:121

ICELAND—COSTUMES
Baked Atlantic fish, recipe, costume 188:19

ICELAND—DOLLS
Doll, sandbag, making 470:76-78
Icelandic doll, fabric, pattern, making 515:62

ICELAND—FESTIVALS—COOKERY
First Day of Summer; poached dried fruit, recipe 1666:129

ICELAND—FESTIVALS—HANDICRAFTS
Bun Day; Bolladagur sticks, making 1477:31

ICELAND—GAMES
Egg game 967:33
In-and-out-the-windows game, how to play 1494:96
Name game 470:71

ICELAND—HANDICRAFTS
Fish, paper, making 470:82-83
Fishermen in oilskins, making 470:66-70
Sheep, woolly, making 470:79-81
Walrus, knitted, making 470:75
Witch, pipe cleaners, making 470:72-74

ICELAND—NEW YEAR'S DAY
Flaming festival fires in Iceland 489:85-88

IDAHO—COOKERY
Lentil loaf, recipe 654:43
Potatoes, baked, recipe 654:42
Potatoes, stuffed, recipe 666:237-238
Steak and potatoes, history of, recipe 155:8-9

IDOMA PEOPLE—MASKS
African elephant mask, paper bag, gray paint, making 1486:18-19

IGLOOS
Igloo fort, blocks packed with snow, making 1188:41-44
Snow mound cave, making: 562:51-52
Snowball cave, making 562:50-51

IGLOOS—COOKERY
Igloo cake, recipe 449:71

ILLINOIS—COOKERY
Cornmeal crisps, recipe, making 793:5
German scrambled egg, recipe 654:47
Kielbasa sausage, recipe 654:46
Rice pudding, baked, recipe 654:45

ILLINOIS—GAMES
Chicago game 572:24-25

IMMIGRANTS
Irish immigrants in Boston; foods they ate 663:122-126
Jewish immigrants in New York City; foods they ate 663:126-135

INCAS
Maps, raised, making 682:6-7

INCAS—ASTRONOMY
Recording sunsets, how to do 682:8-9

INCAS—BOATS
Inca boat, making 682:26-27

INCAS—BRIDGES
Bridges, suspension, making 682:30-31

INCAS—CITIES
City model, making 682:20-21

INCAS—FESTIVALS
Festival of the Sun celebration 665:74-76; 826:16-17
Sun Gods of Peru 566:18-19

INCAS—GAMES
Tying the sun to the hitching post chasing game, how to play 1498:29-30

INCAS—HANDICRAFTS
Black cats poster and pin, oaktag, dough, patterns, making 1251:29-31

INCAS—HARVEST FESTIVALS—HANDICRAFTS
Aymurray Sun T-shirt, fabric, paint, pattern 1249:23-25

INCAS—HARVEST FESTIVALS—SYMBOLS
Cornucopia pattern 1249:8
Inca Sun God pattern 1249:8
Sunflower pattern 1249:9

INCAS—IRRIGATION
Irrigation lines, demonstrate 682:14-15

INCAS—MUSICAL INSTRUMENTS
Clay pan pipes, making 482:62-63
Whistle from homemade clay, recipe for clay, making 1310:43

INCAS—NATURE FESTIVALS
Festival of the Sun; Inca winter solstice festival 419:124-125
Inca rituals 419:122-127
Invention of the Cross, harvest festival of the Incas 419:126-127
Kapaj Raymi, great festival ritual 419:123-124

INCAS—PLANTS
Fertilization of plants, demonstrate how Incas did it 682:16-17

INCAS—QUIPUS
Quipu number record, making 682:10-11
Quipu, making and using 976:34-35

INCAS—RAMPS
Ramps, observing ramps information 682:12-13

INCAS—ROADS
Roads, paved, making 682:28-29

INCAS—SCULPTURES
Ancient Peruvian idol sculpture, dough, paints, patterns, making 1251:27-28

INCAS—WEAVING
Andean weavings, making 182:58-61
Weaving, woven mat, making 682:22-23

INDIA
Activities, flags, games, songs, dances, recipes 1381:101-106

INDIA—BATIK
Batik violet cushion, making 813:56-57

INDIA—BIRTHDAYS

Birthday customs 488:56-60
Celebrations of birthdays in India 474:85-86
Hindu birthday celebrations 695:57-60
Moslem birthday celebrations 695:61

INDIA—CHRISTMAS

Christmas customs in India 149:49-50; 473:64
Christmas lights celebration 601:75
Kerala, Christmas celebration 601:77-78
South Central India; Christmas celebration 601:79

INDIA—CHRISTMAS—DOLLS

Dolls and animals, stuffed, making 795:17

INDIA—CLOTHING

Paisley bandanna, butta motif, handkerchief, fabric crayons, patterns, making 1586:40-41
Sari from slip and T-shirt, making 1328:14

INDIA—COOKERY

Almond laddous, recipe 813:93
Am Ki Chatni, fresh mango and coconut chutney, recipe 1165:165
Baked fish topped with coconut-tomato chutney, recipe 1265:98-99
Banana and orange shake, recipe 1239:38
Banana chapati, recipe 967:34
Banana milk, recipe 813:93
Banana raitha, recipe 1313:43; 1560:23
Bhapa Doi, recipe 514:137
Biryani rice, recipe 1068:unp
Bread, deep-fried whole wheat bread, recipe 576:45
Bread, unleavened whole wheat bread, recipe 576:44
Burfi candy, recipe 515:64
Carrots with grated coconut and raisins, recipe 1265:96
Carrots with grated coconut, recipe 576:31
Channa dal, curried chickpeas, recipe 1452:90
Chapatis bread, recipe 909:105; 1142:29
Chapatis flat bread, recipe 1165:164; 1265:100-101; 1380:7
Chapatis flat wheat bread, recipe 1452:92
Chapatis, Indian fried bread, recipe 1122:85
Chapatis, recipe 88:4-6; 507:28; 1090:29; 1244:34-35; 1287:unp.; 1405:27; 1579:113-114; 1653:56
Chapatis, wheat cakes, recipe 813:92
Chicken curry and rice, recipe 1405:28
Chicken curry, recipe 1244:32-33; 1381:104
Chickpeas, spicy, recipe 1405:22-23
Chicken tikka, recipe 1405:20
Chutney relish from oranges and lemons, recipe 1490:20
Chutney, apple, recipe 576:43
Chutney, fresh coriander, recipe 576:42
Coconut delight, coconut, peanuts, recipe 813:93; 1381:104
Coconut macaroons, recipe 1244:30
Cucumber chutney, recipe 507:32; 1405:23
Cucumber raita, recipe 1313:43
Curried chickpeas Dal, recipe 576:38; 1652:37
Curry, fish, Southern style, recipe 1405:24
Curry, fruit 187:32
Dahi Murghi, chicken and yogurt dish, recipe 1452:93
Dal lentil spread, recipe 1380:33
Drink, salty yogurt, recipe 576:47
Eating utensils used by people in India 507:44
Eggs pulusu, recipe 1489:24
Eggs; spicy scrambled eggs, recipe 1143:28
Fish, spicy fried, recipe 576:28
Gajar halva, carrot halva, recipe 1452:95

Gajar halva, sweet carrot pudding, recipe 1165:166
Garam masala, recipe 576:24
Geeli khichri mung beans, recipe 1721:27
Ghee, Indian butter, recipe 1165:163-164
Ginger parkin, recipe 813:93
History of cookery in 88:60-68
Ice cream, recipe 1090:29
Indian meal, how to set up room 813:23-24
Indian meal, what to serve 813:22-24
Kaji, cashew snack, recipe 188:39
Kari, chicken curry, recipe 1165:164-165
Keema curry, recipe 662:88-92
Kitchiri, rice and lentils dish, recipe 1276:34-35
Kulfi, Indian ice cream, recipe 1313:121
Lamb and basmati rice, recipe 1276:42-43
Lamb curry with almonds, recipe 1405:26
Lamb curry, recipe 507:20
Lamb kebabs, recipe 576:25
Lamb or chicken curry, recipe 1343:51
Lentil and noodle soup, recipe 1265:97
Lentils with garlic and onion, recipe 576:37
Mango lassi drink, recipe 1380:13
Mango with yogurt dressing, recipe 1265:102
Masala rice, recipe 507:19
Meat-eating habits in India 662:88-92
Meat, spiced ground, recipe 576:23
Mushroom curry, recipe 1405:22
Naan, yeast bread, recipe 1276:36-37
Nimbu Chatni, date and lemon chutney, recipe 1165:166
Onion fritters, recipe 507:32
Pastries, deep fried, recipe 576:20
Peanut chutney relish, recipe 1380:43
Peanut chutney, recipe 909:105
Peanut dip, recipe 1204:58
Potato and cauliflower curry, recipe 1328:10-11
Potato cakes, recipe 794:50
Potato, tomato, and ginger savory, recipe 507:22
Potatoes and peas, recipe 576:33
Pumpkin curry, recipe 576:34
Purees, recipe 507:18
Puri puffs, recipe 1660:44
Puris, flat, round whole wheat bread, recipe 1381:104
Railway tea, recipe 1694:39
Raita sauce, cucumbers, yogurt, recipe 1276:44
Raita, cucumber, yogurt, recipe 1579:115
Rice with peas, recipe 1405:25
Rice, boiled, recipe 507:30
Rice, spiced, recipe 576:29
Royal kulfi, recipe 1313:122
Saffron rice, recipe 1452:94
Samosas, pasty filled with vegetables, recipe 1313:43-44
Sesame sweets, sesame chikkis, cookies, recipe 72:124-125
Sheb Ki Chatni, apple chutney, recipe 1452:91
Shrimp curry, recipe 813:92
Shrimp with mint, recipe 1405:21
Spiced tea, recipe 576:46
Spinach dal, recipe 507:31
Stuffed parathas, bread and vegetable curry, recipe 1560:22-23
Tandoori chicken drumsticks, recipe 1276:40-41
Tea, recipe 507:15
Tomato and onion chutney, recipe 507:18
Upma, recipe 793:62
Vadai, recipe 967:34

Vermicelli pudding, recipe 1276:38-39
Whole wheat bread, unleavened, recipe 1652:20-21
Whole wheat cakes, deep-fried, recipe 1652:21
Yogurt and bananas, recipe 576:39; 1652:38
Yogurt chicken, recipe 576:27
Yogurt drink, lassi, recipe 1564:59
Yogurt with cucumber and mint, recipe 576:41
Yogurt with cucumber and raisins, recipe 1392:unp
Yogurt with cucumber and tomato, recipe 576:41;
    1652:39

INDIA—COSTUMES
Dancer from Poroja, fabric, making 813:35-36
East Indian man, sheet, making 106:9
Fakir costume 213:182-184
Folk dancer, male costume, fabric, making 813:40-42
Gaur folk dance costume, fabric, making 813:38-40
Girl from Maharashtra costume, fabric, making 813:42-
    44
Hindu lady, sheet, making 106:10
Indian costumes drawing 988:54-56
Kaju, cashew snack, recipe, costume 188:39
Man and woman of India costumes 213:140-142
Palace Guard costume, pattern, paper, making 813:49-51
Prince, legendary, pattern, fabric, making 813:46-49
Princess costume, fabric, making 813:36-38
Sari, fabric, pattern, making 813:33-35
Village artisan, pattern, fabric, making 813:44-46

INDIA—COUNTING
Numbers one through ten in Hindi language 1365:unp.

INDIA—DANCES
Kathak dance and costume picture 1000:68-71
Kolattam, the stick folk dance 474:126-127

INDIA—DOLLS
Doll, paper cup, yarn, patterns, making 1311:66-69
Hindu lady doll, making 494:198-210

INDIA—DRAMA
Mime 474:100
String holders 474:100-101

INDIA—EASTER
Kerala; Easter celebration 601:78-79
South Central India; Easter celebration 601:80

INDIA—FACE MAKEUP
Kathakali face, making with makeup 380:18-19

INDIA—FESTIVALS
Bengal; Big Day celebration 601:75-76
Brother and Sister Day celebration 601:53-54
Christian celebrations 913:71
Diwali 134:106
Diwali celebration 497:8-17; 631:96
Diwali Festival, food, games, making 557:19-25
Diwali or Deepavali, Festival of Lights celebration
    913:59-60
Diwali, Festival of Light 474:65-66
Diwali, history of 709:41
Diwali, the Hindu New Year, activities and projects for
    classrooms 1393:71-72
Diwali, the Hindu New Year; celebration of 496:21-22
Festival of Lights celebration 601:52-53
Ganesh Chaturthi Festival celebration 826:24-25
Harvest Festival, Hindu women honor Gauri 659:108-
    110
Hindu Brothers' Day, Raksha Bandhan celebration
    913:62
Hindu Durga Puja at Amber celebration 913:55-56
Hindu Durga Puja in Bengal celebration 913:56-57

Hindu Dussehna, Ten Nights celebration 913:42-45
Hindu Dussehra at Mysore celebration 913:46-47
Hindu Dussehra in Jaipur celebration 913:47-48
Hindu Dussehra in Kulu celebration 913:48-54
Hindu Holi in Bombay celebration 913:18
Hindu Holi in Orissa celebration 913:19-20
Hindu Holi, Festival of Spring celebration 913:14-18
Hindu Janmastami, Krishna's Birthday celebration
    913:37-41
Hindu Kali, Dark Mother celebration 913:62-65
Hindu Lakshmi Puja for Goddess of Prosperity celebra-
    tion 913:60-61
Hindu Marriage of Meenakshi celebration 913:21-26
Hindu Nawarati in South India celebration 913:54
Hindu Rath Yatra, Temple Chariot of Puri celebration
    913:27-34
Hindu Shivratri, Night of Shwa celebration 913:9-13
Hindu Sun Festival at Konarak celebration 913:35-36
Holi celebration 631:26
Holi, Indian Spring Festival; projects with fingerpaint,
    making 1393:179
Holi, Spring Festival, activities and projects for class-
    rooms 1393:178-179
Jains Festival celebrations 913:71
Kalpa Vruksha celebration 631:30
Kerala; Onam celebration 601:54
Makra Sankrant celebration 601:51
Moslem Holy Days celebration 913:67-70
Mother Teresa's birthday; celebrate with friend in need
    activities, how to do 1199:196
North India, Baswant; Thread Ceremony celebration
    601:55
Onam in Kerala celebration 913:89-93
Pongal, Rice Harvest Festival celebration 913:79-82
Pongal, Rice Harvest Festival, activities and projects for
    classrooms 1393:123-124
Rain celebration 913:87-88
Republic Day celebration 913:74-78
Ring dance celebration 631:22
Sikh celebrations 913:70-71
South India Doll Festival celebration 601:57
South India, Pongal celebration 601:56-57
Spring and the New Year celebrations 913:83-86

INDIA—FESTIVALS—COOKERY
Baisakhi Festival, cereal dessert, recipe 1313:77
Baisakhi Festival, chappati, recipe 1313:77
Burfi, sweet meat, recipe 1313:168
Diwali Feast foods; almond Halvah, carrot halva, recipes
    497:12-14
Diwali Feast foods; Gulab Jaman, Badam Pistaz Barfi,
    Ghee; recipes given 497:12-14
Diwali Festival Barfi, recipe 1089:27
Diwali Festival chapati bread, recipe 557:22
Diwali; Ghee (Indian clarified butter), recipe 1666:160
Diwali; Halvah (dessert), recipe 1666:162
Diwali; Massoor Dal (orange lentils), recipe 1666:160
Diwali; Paratha (flat bread), recipe 1666:160
Diwali; Roshmalay (sweet cheese balls), recipe 1666:161
Diwali; Savia (sweet noodle dessert), recipe 1666:162
Holi or Hola Mohalla, coconut candy, recipe 1466:11
Jalebis, sweet meat, recipe 1313:168-169
Janmash Tami Festival, sweet butters, recipe 1313:118-
    199
Pakoras, pieces of vegetables fried in batter, recipe
    1313:168

117

INDIA—FESTIVALS—DECORATIONS

Diwali Festival of Lights pop-up card, making 1387:24

Diwali floating candles, paper tubes, paper, making 1539:90-91

Holi Fire Festival Sun, yellow paper, ribbon, making 1179:74-75

Pongol, Rice Harvest Festival, miniature pictures, how to make 1393:124

INDIA—FESTIVALS—GAMES

Diwali Festival games 557:25

INDIA—FESTIVALS—HANDICRAFTS

Bengal horse, pattern, clay, making 813:75-76

Bengal lady container, plastic bottle, making 813:72-75

Bookmark, paper, making 813:64

Curtain of Jasmine flowers, paper, making 813:13-14

Diva lamp, making 1313:165

Divali Festival of Lights card, making 1313:159

Divali, diva clay lanterns, making 1313:19-20

Diwali clay lamps for Diwali Festival, making 813:66-67

Diwali Festival Alpana (good luck designs), making 709:42

Diwali Festival banana leaf 557:23-24

Diwali Festival diyas lights, making 557:21

Diwali Festival lamp, clay, making 813:66-67; 856:66-69

Diwali Festival rangoli patterns, how to make 1278:22-23

Diwali Festival rangoli pictures, making 557:21

Diwali Festival, floor designs, making 909:101

Diwali Festival, lamps, floating, making; 909:103

Diwali Festival, lamps, play dough, recipe 909:101

Diwali Festival, spice books, making 909:103

Diwali gifts; papier-mache turtle, making 497:16-17

Diwali; Hindu floor painting, paper, glue, grains, beans, making 1393:72

Elephant note pad and pencil holder, cardboard, patterns, making 813:62-64

Festival of Lights oil burning lamp, clay, wick, making 1477:122

Flowerpots, metallic, making 813:17-18

Holi Festival flower garland, splatter painting, making 1277:10-11

Incense burner, clay, making 813:19-20

Lantern, paper, making 813:9-11

Lanterns, glowing, acetate film, making 813:20-22

Lotus programs, paper, making 813:7-8

Mask, festive, pattern, paper, making 813:18-19

Peacock from Bengal, paper, pattern, making 813:67-70

Peacocks, standing, paper, making 813:14-15

Placemats, felt, making 813:27-28

Raksha Bandhan Festival cards, making 1313:109

Rangoli patterns, making 1313:160-162

Saffron or spice jars, decorated, making 813:65-66

Tray, painted, cardboard, making 813:25-26

Wall hanging, felt, making 813:12-13

INDIA—FESTIVALS—PUPPETS

Diwali Festival, shadow puppets, styrofoam, making 909:102

Diwali Hindu New Year Festival puppet projects, patterns, scenes, story 1083:180-181

Diwali Hindu New Year Ravana puppet, pattern, making 1083:180-181

Holi Festival of Spring puppet patterns, scenes, story 1083:178-179

Shadow puppet for overhead projector, patterns, making 1083:178-179

INDIA—FLAG

Pattern of flag 557:26

INDIA—FOLKLORE

"A Drum," folktale and activities 1478:37-40

"Cat and the Parrot" flannel board story, patterns, making 1603:140-145

"How Little Frog Tricked the Lion" flannel board patterns, making 910:31,70

"Monkey and the Crocodile" flannel board fable, patterns, making 1603:196-201

"Monkey and the Crocodile," monkey and crocodile jointed puppets, patterns 1206:34-38

"See for Yourself" flannel board story, patterns, making 1604:68-72

"Tiger, the Brahman, and the Jackal" fable play 1212:78-83

INDIA—FOLKLORE—COOKERY

Chapati bread, recipe 1478:43

INDIA—FOLKLORE—HANDICRAFTS

Enty Merchants, Erith Robbers 126:11-15

Enty Merchants, Erith Robbers, art activities, baker's clay ornaments, making 126:18-21

Enty Merchants, Erith Robbers, art activities, exotic forest, making 126:16-17

Waisted drum, flower pots, bag, paints, making 1478:44-45

INDIA—FOLKLORE—PUPPETS

"Blue Jackal" shadow puppets, patterns, making 1602:196-203

"Brahman, the Tiger and the Jackal" shadow puppets, patterns, making 1602:151-157

"Monkey and the Crocodile," puppets and puppet play script, making 1155:63-66

INDIA—GAMES

Bagh-Bandi game, how to play 1507:39

Balancing toys game 58:38-39

Camel Rush game 1074:240-241

Chausar game, how to make 1074:29-31

Cheetah, cheetal game 572:14-15

Cheetah, Cheetal game, how to play 1507:40

Chilly, hopscotch game 1426:26-27

Deer and leopard game 602:51-52

Diwali walk game 557:25

Flower game 515:64

Gooli danda game 383:96

Gora game 602:59

Guards of the treasure room game 813:53-54

Gulli Danda stick game 1119:18-19

Hopscotch, Ekerid Dukaria, how to play 1355:36

Jackal hit wood game 383:95

Kabaddi # 1 game 383:88

Kabaddi # 2 game 383:89

Kabaddi, tag game, how to play 1708:30-31

Kabbaddi game, how to play 1494:44

Kabbaddi, a village game 1239:45

Kae danda game 383:92

Kho-kho chasing game, how to play 1498:38

Kho-kho game 383:93

Lalamlali game 602:54-55

Little stick, big stick game 602:53-54

Needles for sale game 602:58-59

Pachisi board game, patterns, making 1541:41-48

Pachisi game 1074:26-31

Pachisi game, making 1507:41-43

Pachisi, an Indian game, paper, clothespins, patterns, making 1246:44-45
Pass on game 967:34
Raah, alina and the bandits game 813:52-53
Scorpion's sting game 383:92
Sia Mar Danda game 383:95
Snakes and ladders game, how to make 1074:131-133
Snakes and ladders game, making 1507:44-45
Stick dance game 602:57-58
Tag and circle tag game 602:52-53
Talisman game 813:54-55
Tiger and the goat game 602:55
Tiger tag game 557:25
Water pots game 602:55-56
Waxbill hunt game 813:52
Who is it? game 602:56-57
Wifti Dandu stick game 1119:11-13

INDIA—HAND DECORATIONS
Decorate your hands with mehndi, how to do 1537:30
Hand painting patterns 1253:11
Mehndi hand patterns, how to make and apply 1448:22-23; 1709:31

INDIA—HANDICRAFTS
Flowered tile, clay, making 1070:102-105

INDIA—HANDICRAFTS
Block printing on fabric, how to make printing block 1254:9
Block printing with eraser stamps, fabric, making 889:113-118
Fish candle holder, clay, making 1070:106-110
Miniature painting, paper, patterns, making 1246:40-43
Miniature paintings, paper, watercolors, making 1338:70-72
Mural; green mural panel, making 813:57
Palm leaf sequence book, paper, ribbons, pony beads, patterns, making 1332:75-78
Papier-mache horse, cardboard tubes, paint, making 1447:28-29
Peacock, national bird of India, paper plate, paints, patterns, making 1633:128-131
Safari, potato safari, making 925:24-25
Snake-charmer from India, pipe cleaners and paper, making 1094:14
Talisman, to ward off bad luck, shells, paint, string, making 1648:31
Teacloth, turquoise fabric decorated, making 813:59-61

INDIA—HARVEST FESTIVALS—COOKERY
Rice Harvest Festival yogurt sweet treat, recipe 1249:47-48

INDIA—HARVEST FESTIVALS—HANDICRAFTS
Rice Harvest Festival water buffalo model, clay, paints, making 1249:47-48

INDIA—HOUSES
Farm houses 469:38-39
Hindu home with walled in garden, model, making 494:206-210

INDIA—JEWELRY
Bracelets, making 813:29-30
Jewelry box, beaded, cardboard, making 813:71-72
Kashmir pendant, making 813:32
Necklace, making 813:30
Pendant, buckskin, making 813:78
Pendant, elephant leather pendant, making 813:78-79
Pendant, enamel bead clay pendant, making 813:81-82
Pendant, felt pendant, making 813:79-80

Pendant, mirrored clay pendant, making 813:80-81
Sandal jewelry clay holder, making 813:82-83

INDIA—LAMPS
Diwali gifts; dipa lamp, making 497:16

INDIA—LANGUAGE
Numbers one through ten in Hindi language 1365:unp.

INDIA—LULLABIES
Hati Jhulare 780:34

INDIA—MAGIC TRICKS
Ribbon trick, Indian rope trick, how to do 1270:16-17

INDIA—MASKS
Krishna legend replica mask, plastic modeling material, plaster of Paris, making 1706:11

INDIA—MOSAICS
Mosaic, making 499:80

INDIA—MUSIC
Snake charmed by music model, felt, horn, making 1310:150

INDIA—MUSICAL INSTRUMENTS
Wood scraper instrument, cardboard tube, tongue depressors, paint, making 1646:28-29

INDIA—NAMES
Naming Days information 695:38-41

INDIA—NATURE FESTIVALS
Hindus; Diwali, Festival of Lights 419:110-111
Hindus; Ganges River; Makara Sankranti festival 419:112
Hindus; Gauri, harvest festival 419:109-110
Hindus; Holi rituals 419:108-109
Hindus; Makara Sankranti; coming of spring festival 419:111-112
Rituals of the Saora people 419:112-117
Rogonadur-Saoras, harvest of red gram bean festival 419:116-117
Saoras, Jammolpur, blessing of seeds festival 419:113-116

INDIA—NEW YEAR'S DAY
Bengal; New Year celebration 601:76-77
Diwali (Festival of Lights) celebration 475:99-100; 505:44-55
Procession of New Year's in India 489:89-97

INDIA—NUMBERS
Numbers one to ten 557:20

INDIA—PUPPET PLAYS
Magic Sarangi 4:82-88

INDIA—PUPPETS
Horse and rider string puppets, fabric, wood, making 1707:27
Indian pop-up puppet, cardboard, foil, making 1707:6
Kathputli marionette string puppet, wood, fabric, making 1707:23
Shadow puppet, cardboard, paints, flashlight, patterns, making 1381:104-105
Shadow show with puppets, how to make 1328:19-21
Twirling palm puppet, posterboard, straws, patterns, making 1633:124-127

INDIA—RHYMES
"Little Bird" Hindi speaking people 1607:34
"Little Elephant Swaying" Hindi speaking people 1607:30
Chai Aar Peek-A-Boo rhyme 780:49
Hindi Peek-A-Boo 780:49
Namo Ganesha baby clapping rhyme 780:64
Ta Ta Ta Lie baby clapping rhyme 780:63

INDIA—RITUALS
Hindu growing up ritual 695:88-92
INDIA—RUGS
Rag rugs, rags, thread, making 1219:22-23
INDIA—STORYTELLING
Hungry Stranger: A Buddhist Story from India 1522:126-129
INDIA—TIE-DYE
Handkerchiefs, tie-dye, making 1328:25-27
Scarves; tie-dye (Schiboris) scarves, fabric, making 813:57-59
INDIA—TOYS
Elephant, sculptured clay, pattern, making 1027:99-101
INDIANA—COOKERY
Black walnut cookies, recipe 654:50-51
Herb cornbread, recipe 343:111
Persimmon pudding, recipe 654:49-50
INDIANS OF NORTH AMERICA. *See also groups of Indians, e.g.,* **EASTERN WOODLAND INDIANS** *and individual nations and tribes*
Activities, flags, games, songs, dances, recipes 1381:7-12
Buffalo, how to draw 591:21
Corn, how to draw 591:32
Culture unit, language, dress, foods, games, bibliographies 574:128-160
Golden Eagle, history of 465:12-13
Hand Indian head, paper, making 94:7
Indian accessories, from cereal boxes, making 84:19
Indian boy, paper plate, pattern, making 233:9
Indian chief from tissue paper, making 747:25-26
Indian face, paper-cutting, how to do 742:44
Indian from North America, fabric, felt and paper model, making 1094:59-60
Indian, milk carton, making 79:5
Indian, paper models, patterns, making 639:15-16
Indian, paper, pattern, making 253:166-168; 761:31-32; 1067:190-192
Indians, paper plate, pattern, making 413:3-4
Learning units, activities, songs, art, recipes, patterns 1191:338-400
INDIANS OF NORTH AMERICA—AMULETS
Warrior's Eye of God amulet, sticks, yarn, making 1427:272
INDIANS OF NORTH AMERICA—ANIMALS
Learn respect for animals as the Indians did 1297:74
INDIANS OF NORTH AMERICA—ANKLEBANDS
Ankleband, paper, feathers, making 1170:13
INDIANS OF NORTH AMERICA—ANKLETS
Ankle wrap, making 224:80
Anklets and leg bands, making 589:46-47
Anklets, yarn, shoelaces, making 1699:47
INDIANS OF NORTH AMERICA—ARMBANDS
Arm bands and anklets, making 465:48-49; 589:50
Arm bands, beaded and feather, making 466:158
Arm band, paper, feathers, making 1170:13
Arm bands, plastic bottles, fabric, making 1699:45
Caddo medallion armband, making 932:61-63
Ceremonial bands, making 633:25-27
Wrist wrapping, making 224:141
INDIANS OF NORTH AMERICA—ARROWHEADS
Arrowhead, carve from soap, patterns of different kinds, making 1170:17
Arrowheads, how to mount 467:16-17
INDIANS OF NORTH AMERICA—BAGS
Bag, making 224:168
Bags and pouches, making 465:52-53
Bandolier bag, making 224:161-164
Burlap bag, woven, making 482:102-103
Dance bag, making 8:76-77
Hunting bag, Apache beaded, making 298:56-57
Hunting or medicine bag, making 8:78
Leather bag, making 224:150-156
Leather pouch, making 63:8-9
Medicine pouch, making 633:141-143
Net market bag, cotton cord or yarn, making 1296:94-95
Pouch, making 633:79-81
Sauk carrying case, making 932:103-107
Tobacco pouch, making 8:76-77
Wampum pouch, felt, making 628:52-54
INDIANS OF NORTH AMERICA—BASKETRY
Basket weaving, making 224:206-212; 633:90-93
Basket woven from newspaper, making 1699:17-18
Basket, coiled, making 63:10-11; 959:26-33
Basket, twine, raffia, making 1368:34
Basket; birch bark basket, making 466:134-135
Basketry, making 324:31-33
Baskets, birchbark, making 633:178
Baskets, how to draw 591:22-23
Baskets; lazy squaw coiled grass basket, making 466:132-133
Plaited mat, making 959:33-35
Plants for weaving baskets 959:23-26
Twined basket, making 959:26-29
Willow basket, making 482:38-39
Woven baskets from vines, making 1376:4-6
INDIANS OF NORTH AMERICA—BEADWORK
Arm bands, beaded, making 776:18
Bead band, woven on beading loom, making 1477:109
Bead designs, making 444:118-122
Bead loom, making 444:15-21
Bead necklaces, making 467:36-37
Bead weaving, how to do on cardboard loom 1254:31
Bead weaving, how to make loom from cardboard box 1254:31
Belts, beaded, making 444:22-30; 776:27-30
Belts, woven beads, making 776:43-44
Beaded book covers, making 444:85-91
Beaded bracelets, making 444:47-49
Beaded coin purses, making 444:50-56
Beaded hat band, making 776:40
Beaded headbands, making 444:39-46
Beaded knife sheaths, making 444:73-84
Beaded necklaces, making 444:31-37
Beaded rosettes, making 444:110-117
Beading bands, making 589:102-103
Beadwork and beadwork designs, making 465:58-61
Beadwork, history of 444:9-12
Beadwork, making 227:26; 633:73-77
Belt bags, making 444:67-72
Bracelets, beadwork, making 776:18-19
Computer project: design a beaded medallion 1218:76-79
Earrings, beaded, making 776:30
Indian beadwork, making 466:54-55
Lazy stitch, making 444:57-64
Loom from milk carton, making 679:unp
Napkin rings, beaded, making 776:20
Neckbands and headbands, beaded, making 776:15-17
Neckbands, woven, making 776:41
Necklaces with pendants, beaded, making 776:24-27
Neckties, beaded, making 776:18
Northern Plains moccasins, making 444:92-100

Pendants, woven, making 776:45
Purses and handbags, beaded, making 776:22-23
Rings, beaded, making 776:31
Table mats, beaded, making 776:10-14
Thunderbird designs and other designs and symbols 465:66-67
Weaving frame, styrofoam, making 776:34-35
Weaving with beads, how to do 776:32-51
Woodland moccasins, making 444:101-109

INDIANS OF NORTH AMERICA—BELTS
Belt, concho, cardboard, tin foil, pattern, making 1170:10
Belt, leather and bead combo, making 224:134-136
Belt, patchwork leather, making 224:137-139
Belts, making 633:67-68
Concha belts, making 466:41-45
Conchas, making 466:46-47
Stick weave belt or band, yam, making 298:254-255

INDIANS OF NORTH AMERICA—BIRD HOUSES
Bird houses, hollow log, making 466:144-145

INDIANS OF NORTH AMERICA—BIRTHDAYS
Celebrations of birthdays in Indian tribes 474:84-85

INDIANS OF NORTH AMERICA—BODY PAINT
Body paint, making 63:34-35

INDIANS OF NORTH AMERICA—BRAIDS
Four strand Indian braid, making 548:30-31

INDIANS OF NORTH AMERICA—BREASTPLATES
Bone breastplate, making 466:78-79; 960:100-102
Bone breastplates, chokers and ties, making 465:41-43
Bone breastplates, tag board, yarn, making 1699:57
Breastplate, making 69:30-31
Indian breastplate, papier-mache, making 765:74-78
Quill breastplates and otters, making 589:57
Thunderbird chest plate, making 69:16-17

**INDIANS OF NORTH AMERICA—BURDEN BAS-
KETS**
Burden basket and tumpline, making 647:32-33
Burden basket and tumpline, paper bags, fabric, paints, making 1427:259

INDIANS OF NORTH AMERICA—BUSTLES
Bustles, hair, feather, Sioux, Oklahoma and bustle tricks, making 589:28-39
Bustles; butterflies, U-shaped, sunbursts, Crow bustle, bustle styles 589:40-45
Dance bustle, cardboard, fabric sash, making 1699:48
Dancing bustle, making 69:21
Sunburst bustles, making 465:54-55

INDIANS OF NORTH AMERICA—CALENDAR
Calendar stick, making 63:13
Calendar stick, popsicle sticks, making 1170:7
Native American Moon calendar and symbols 1249:13-18
Winnebago calendar stick, making 633:129-130

INDIANS OF NORTH AMERICA—CALIFORNIA. *See
also individual nations, e.g.,* **MAIDU INDIANS**
Tools and ornaments 960:9-16

**INDIANS OF NORTH AMERICA—CALIFORNIA—
BASKETRY**
Basketry of California Indians 959:5-7

**INDIANS OF NORTH AMERICA—CALIFORNIA—
HEADDRESSES**
Headdress, jumping dance, making 63:30-31

**INDIANS OF NORTH AMERICA—CALIFORNIA—
MUSICAL INSTRUMENTS**
Clapper, Maidu and Miwak tribes PakPapa instrument, making 468:37

INDIANS OF NORTH AMERICA—CANOES
Birch bark canoe model, balsa wood, paints, making 1368:42-43
Canoe model, styrofoam, yarn, making 1699:27
Canoe, birch bark canoe, making 227:20
Canoe, cardboard, string, making 1170:40
Canoe, making 647:63-64
Canoes, how to draw 591:16-17
Hunters in canoe toy, making 355:10-11

INDIANS OF NORTH AMERICA—CLOTHING
American Indian costume, making 870:94-96
Apron, making 69:22
Breechcloth and apron, leggings, making 465:28-29;
466:36-39; 589:51-53; 633:36-39; 633:40-42;
1699:42
Buckskin shirts, making 466:31-33
Buckskin, making 589:78-79
Capes, beaded, making 467:34-35
Capes, yokes, vests, cuffs and gauntlets, making 465:32-
37
Chief's neckpieces, toy, making 355:22-23
Eye shade, making 63:21-22
Fur poncho, making 224:101-106
Girl's dress and boy's pants, making 324:12-13
History of Indian clothing 227:21
Lakes Indian capelet, making 932:47-48
Leather vest, making 224:86-89
Leggings, old jeans, leather boot laces, making 1699:43-
44
Loin cloth, making 224:92-95
Pueblo dress, bath towels, making 1699:50
Quiver muff, making 224:157-160
Robes and blankets, making 633:43-47
Sash, woven with beads, making 224:129-133
Scarf, potato print, making 224:142-144
Shirt and leggings, making 482:68-69
Shirt, paper costume, making 585:37
Shirts, making 633:32-35
Vest from brown bag, Native American designs given, making 1633:16-17
Vest, paper bag, paints, yarn, making 1699:41
Vests, making 633:28-31
Vests; beaded vests, and rodeo vests, making 466:56-59
War shirts, making 465:30-31
Woman's dress, making 482:70-71; 633:53-58
Women and girls' cape, paper, making 1699:49
Yoke dress, making 224:95-100

INDIANS OF NORTH AMERICA—CLUBS
Ceremonial club, making 227:53

INDIANS OF NORTH AMERICA—COOKERY
Acorn mush and acorn mush soup, recipe 1043:5
Atole, acorn meal, recipe 1427:274
Baked beans with maple sugar, recipe 1527:72-73
Baked fish, recipe 1381:10
Baked potatoes, making 8:85
Baked pumpkin, recipe 1699:137-138
Baked squash, recipe 1699:145-146
Bean-hole beans from DownEast Maine, recipe 410:106
Beans, cooked, recipe 1043:6
Beef jerky, recipe 1699:153
Beef jerky, recipe 1380:36; 1427:274
Blue pinole cornmeal drink, recipe 1527:12
Blueberry roll-ups, recipe 1380:39
Boiled eggs, recipe 1699:150
Boiled rabbit with dumplings, recipe 1527:70-71

Candied sweet potatoes, recipe 410:104
Chicken stew, recipe 410:110
Clover, steamed, recipe 1699:144
Cocoa and chocolate, recipe 410:108
Cocoa shells, recipe 410:108-109
Corn and pumpkin stew, recipe 1699:139
Corn cakes, boiled, recipe 63:78-79
Corn chowder, recipe 410:111
Corn fritters, recipe 410:111-112
Corn mush, recipe 1170:27
Corn pudding from fresh corn, recipe 410:111
Corn pudding, recipe 499:81
Corn soup, recipe 1606:54; 1699:142
Corn stew, recipe 410:110
Corn, dried, recipe 1043:8
Corn, parched, recipe 1043:8
Corn, popped, homemade, making 652:102-103;
    1699:151
Cornmeal biscuits, recipe 1296:140
Cornmeal bread, recipe 1427:275
Cornmeal crisps, recipe 1427:275
Crab apple jelly, recipe 1043:10
Dried fruit, making 63:76
Fireplace, making 8:83
Fish baked in clay, recipe 1296:133
Fish soup, recipe 1699:148-149
Foods of the Indians of the West 666:213-218
Foods of the New England Indians 666:16-20
Foods of the Southern Indians 666:100-104
Fried green tomatoes, recipe 410:107
Fried squash blossoms, recipe 1699:147
Fried squash blossoms, recipe 1527:56
Fried sweet and sour tomatoes, recipe 410:108
Fruit leather, recipe 1427:276; 1699:154-155
Fry bread, recipe 574:134; 1381:10; 1606:54-55;
    1660:48-49; 1699:134-135
Green tomato pie, recipe 410:107-108
Hominy cakes, recipe 1170:28
Hominy, recipe 1043:7; 1699:143
Indian cake, recipe 410:113
Indian corn pudding, recipe 1666:263-264
Indian fry bread, recipe 909:85; 1214:34-35
Indian hash browns, recipe 410:104
Indian pudding, recipe 410:113; 1381:10; 1495:17
Indian villages of the Southwest and foods they ate
    666:190-193
Jerky, fish, recipe 424:75
Jerky, meat, recipe 424:74
Johnny cakes, cornmeal pancakes, recipe 1170:28;
    1455:129; 1621:32-33
Kneel down bread, recipe 1699:136
Maple sugar candy, recipe 1699:158-160
Maple sugar drink, recipe 1527:59
Mississippi mud pie, recipe 1296:141
Mouse cache soup, recipe 1527:48
Mushrooms cooked in oil, recipe 1527:50
Nut butter, making 63:82; 1043:5
Nuts, roasted, ground, ground nut cakes, recipes, making
    1043:4
Paper bread, making 8:84
Peanut butter, recipe 410:105; 1699:157
Peanut soup, recipe 410:105-106
Peanuts, roasted, recipe 410:105
Pekee bread or paper bread, recipe 1427:277
Pemmican cakes, recipe 1527:57

Pemmican, dried foods, recipe 1427:277
Pemmican, recipe 63:77; 424:76-77; 1043:6
Piki, recipe 1043:9
Popcorn balls, recipe 1043:11
Potato baked in hot coals, recipe 410:103-104
Pumpkin pudding, recipe 1170:27
Pumpkin shell soup, recipe 1527:78-79
Raisins, how to make 1699:156
Roasted corn on the cob, recipe 1527:11
Roasted pumpkin seeds, recipe 1699:152
Seafood chowder, recipe 410:109
Soffkee corn soup or cereal, recipe 1296:140
Spit roasts, making 8:84
Spoon bread, recipe 1191:358
Squash pudding, boiled, recipe 1043:10
Squash, baked, recipe 1043:7
Strawberry cornbread, recipe 1252:40-41
Strawberry juice, recipe 63:83
Succotash, recipe 410:106-107; 1191:351; 1495:53;
    1527:xxiii
Sweet potatoes, drying, how to do 410:104-105
Sweet southern popcorn, recipe 1296:133
Tse Aste (bread cooked on a stone), recipe 1427:278
Turtle stew, recipe 466:148
Venison and hominy stew, recipe 1527:38-39
Wild grape dumplings, recipe 1527:60-61
Wild green salad, recipe 63:81
Wild rice casserole, recipe 1170:27
Wild rice with blueberries, recipe 1043:8
Wild rice, recipe 1699:140-141
Zuni succotash, recipe 1043:9
INDIANS OF NORTH AMERICA—COSTUMES
Buffalo dance costume, making 465:74-75
Chief Massasoit costume, making 272:131-132
Costume and headdress, paper, making 353:14-15
Costume, making 647:21-23
Devil dance costume, making 465:72-73
Eagle dance costume, making 465:76-77
Indian boy, crepe paper, making 687:38-41
Indian costume, fabric, patterns, making 338:84-90;
    842:19-24; 1283:20-23; 1379:41
Osceola costume, making 272:102-104
Sacagawea costume, making 272:99-102
Tecumseh costume, making 272:96-99
INDIANS OF NORTH AMERICA—COUP STICKS
Coup stick, branch or dowel, feathers, pattern, making
    1170:16
Coup stick, making 633:144-145
INDIANS OF NORTH AMERICA—CRADLE BOARDS
Cradleboards, making 574:135; 633:152
INDIANS OF NORTH AMERICA—DANCES
Basic body movements for dances 692:23-29
Basic Indian dance steps 465:80-81; 692:30-35
Buffalo dance 465:86; 692:84-87
Costuming for dances, how to do 692:103-113
Eagle dance 465:87
Fancy dancing, how to do 692:42-55
Flag dance, how to do 692:75-77
Hoop dance and dance hoops, how to make 465:84-85
Hoop dance, how to do 692:96-102
Old-time dancing 692:36-41
Rain dance 1114:62-63
Round dance, how to do 692:63-67
Scout dance, how to do 692:72-74
Shield dance, how to do 692:78-80

Snake dance, how to do 692:81-83
Stomp dance, how to do 692:88-95
Two-step dance, how to do 692:68-71
War dance, how to do 692:56-62

INDIANS OF NORTH AMERICA—DESIGNS
Indian designs and symbols 466:49-53
Indian designs, making 482:64-65
Native designs and colors 63:86-90
Symbols, designs, motifs, making 633:99-104

INDIANS OF NORTH AMERICA—DOGS
Dog harnesses, making 466:162-163

INDIANS OF NORTH AMERICA—DOLLS
Applehead doll, making 298:148-149
Corn cob doll, corn cob, fabric, yarn, making 633:151;
    1699:92-93
Corn husk dolls, making 296:242-243; 482:76-77;
    647:36-37; 775:42-53; 1296:90; 1621:34-35
Indian and her papoose, toy, making 355:26-27
Kachina doll, cardboard, feathers, paints, making
    1699:97
Micmac corn husk dolls, making 1606:56-58

INDIANS OF NORTH AMERICA—DREAMS
Dream catcher, for babies, grapevines, yarn, wax, beads,
    shells, making 1296:17
Dream catcher, twigs, yarn, making 1429:18-19
Dream Journal, how to keep 1296:18

INDIANS OF NORTH AMERICA—DYES
Dyeing fabric with natural dyes, how to do 1368:36
Dyes and paints, making 633:94-97
Dyes, natural 63:12; 1170:37

INDIANS OF NORTH AMERICA—FACE MAKEUP
Indian brave face makeup, how to do 1314:20
Indian makeup 465:70-71
Indians of North America, faces, making 380:14-15

INDIANS OF NORTH AMERICA—FACE PAINTING
Indian face painting, how to do 39:54-55; 1533:85

INDIANS OF NORTH AMERICA—FANS
Fans, birchbark, making 633:179
Feather fans, making 63:33; 467:38-39

INDIANS OF NORTH AMERICA—FEATHERS
Feathers, felt, making 628:44-46
Feathers, how to prepare 63:32; 465:14-15

INDIANS OF NORTH AMERICA—FESTIVALS
All American Indian Day 574:146
American Indian Day 574:146
American Indian Day, finger plays and puppets, patterns,
    making 513:12-16
American Indian Day, history of 513:11
Bunny dance Feast celebration 601:135-136
Green Corn Festival celebration 601:136
Indian Day of Glory 574:146
Inter-tribal celebration, activities, handicrafts, songs,
    foods 909:79-87
Inter-tribal Indian Ceremonial 574:146
Karok Indians Harvest Festival celebration 659:56
Maple Festival celebration 601:136-137
Native American ceremonial dances; activities and pro-
    jects for classrooms 1393:227-231
Native American Pow Wow, activities and projects for
    classrooms 1393:33-37
Potlatch celebration, list of foods to try 1170:29
Rain dance Festival celebration 601:137-138
Salish Indians Harvest Festival celebration 659:56

**INDIANS OF NORTH AMERICA—FESTIVALS—
    HANDICRAFTS**
American Indian Day sand clay beads, making 1495:13

**INDIANS OF NORTH AMERICA—FESTIVALS—
    MUSICAL INSTRUMENTS**
Pow Wow tribal ceremony, drum, oatmeal box, paper,
    making 1574:30-31

INDIANS OF NORTH AMERICA—FIRE
Fire coloration 589:98
Fire without matches, roasting and stewing fire, making
    633:157-159
Pumpbore (making fire), making 8:83; 466:172-173

INDIANS OF NORTH AMERICA—FISHING
Fishing lures, making 1699:28

INDIANS OF NORTH AMERICA—FOLKLORE
Celebration flannel board patterns, making 910:17,52
Mother Nature's Gift flannel board patterns, making
    910:21,56

**INDIANS OF NORTH AMERICA—FOLKLORE—
    HANDICRAFTS**
Why Wild Rabbit Stopped Hunting Game, string-rubbing
    net, rabbit puppet 125:31-40

INDIANS OF NORTH AMERICA—FOODS
Berries, history of 410:98
Corn, grinding corn, how to do 959:88-90
Jerusalem artichokes, history of 410:97
Maple sugar, history of 410:91-92
Nuts, history of 410:99-100
Plums, history of 410:99
Squash and pumpkin, history of 410:96-97
Strawberries, history of 410:88-89
Sunflower seeds, history of 410:97-98
Wild cherries, history of 410:99
Wild rice, history of 410:92-94

INDIANS OF NORTH AMERICA—FOOTWEAR
Corn husk sandals, making 482:78-79
Eastern, Western, Southwestern moccasins, mock, mak-
    ing 224:173-174
Moccasins made by Indians for Lewis and Clark, cham-
    ois, thread, fabric paints, making 1214:17-19
Moccasins, felt, leather thongs, patterns, making 1393:34
Moccasins, felt, suede, shoe laces, beads, making
    1621:26-28
Moccasins, leather, pattern, making 641:80-83; 892:118-
    123
Moccasins, Lenape, making 482:72-73
Moccasins, making 465:44-47; 466:40-41; 589:48-49;
    633:48-51; 647:24-26; 870:126-127
Moccasins, socks, yarn, beads, patterns, making
    1427:263
Sandals, rawhide, making 466:24-25
Sandals, woven, making 224:178-181
Shawnee moccasins, making 114:151
Snowshoes, wooden, making 466:124-125

INDIANS OF NORTH AMERICA—GAMES
Arrow game 383:24
Arrow toss game 69:14
Asalto board game, patterns, making 1541:174-178
Atl-atl contests 934:28
Ball court games 934:12
Ball equipment, making 934:58-60
Ball race game 27:51; 383:22; 1699:125
Battledore and shuttlecock game 383:26
Bow and arrow contests 934:25-28
Bowl game 984:6-7

Bowl game, making 324:40; 445:15-19
Bowl games, how to play 1699:106
Breath holding contests 934:22
Buckskin ball game 383:24
Bull roarer or moaning stick, making 445:59-65
Buzz, whirling toy, making 1699:121
Canoe sports 934:38
Canoe tilting contest 831:22
Cat's cradle string game, how to play 1699:129
Cherry stones game, flat box, cherry pits, making 647:80; 1427:280
Chinese Rebel board game, patterns, making 1541:179-182
Chuke board game, how to play 1499:21-23
Chunkey game, how to play 934:44; 1296:115
Corn cob dart and ball game 633:187
Corn cob darts, making and playing 63:66-67; 227:40; 445:26-34
Cup on stick game, paper cup, stick, making 1427:281
Cup-on-a-stick game, making 647:84
Dice games 27:51
Diving for gold nuggets game 831:22
Dodge ball game 934:10
Double ball and stick games, making 445:66-76; 934:8-9
Double relay game 565:180
Eskimo buzz board, making 445:35-39
Feathered darts game, how to play 1699:118
Fighting serpents gaming equipment 934:70-71
Five stone toss game 831:21-22
Floating log games 934:40
Foot catch game 934:9
Foot races, how to play 1699:131
Fox and Geese board game, patterns, making 1541:167-173
Fruit and nut toss game, coffee can, fruits, nuts, making 1427:282
Guessing game 27:50
Guessing game, making 445:914; 647:83
Hand game 69:11
Hand games 934:49-50; 1699:116
Hawk fighting game 934:21
Hidden ball game, making 63:64-65; 633:189
Hidden object game, how to play 1170:34
Hidden stick game, how to play 1699:115
History of Indian games 934:1-3
Hoop and arrow game 633:189
Hoop and darts game, how to make and play 1699:120
Hoop and lances game, how to make and play 1699:119
Hoop and pole equipment, making 934:62-63
Hoop and pole games 466:112-113; 934:30-31
Hopi darts equipment, making 934:68-69
Horseback tilting game 934:20-21
Hubbub game, how to play 1699:103
Humming toy game, button, string, cardboard, making 1427:283
Ice game 831:22
Ice shinny game 934:42-43
Indian pebble games, making 296:146-147
Indian wrestling 956:35
Jackrabbits hit game, making 63:68-69
Juggling game 934:11
Juggling game, how to play 934:11; 1699:126
Jumping frog equipment, making 934:64-65
Kainsish game, how to make and play 1699:113
Kick ball game 934:10
Kick the stick game 633:188; 977:41

Kick the stick relay game 383:26
Kick-stick race, making 63:60-61
Kickapoo, hand game 474:41
Kickball game 956:14
Kuntasso gaming equipment, making 934:65-66
Lacross stick and ball game, broomstick, burlap, ball, making 1368:30-31
Lacrosse game 934:6-7
Lacrosse sticks game, making 466:108-109; 934:74-75
Leaf contest game 831:23
Log racing game 831:22
Making squash blossoms string game, how to play 1501:35
Moccasin game, sticks, cups, pebbles, making 1606:62-64
Moccasins game, how to make and play 934:48-49; 1699:117
Native American bean game, how to play 1419:13
Nut game and stone toss game 714:22-23
Obstacle race game 831:21
Papago game, four cups, sand, rocks, making 1427:284
Papago game, how to play 383:25; 1507:101
Peachstone game 659:57
Pebble game, how to play 1361:78
Pima sticks game 383:23; 1146:12-13
Pin and target game, how to make and play 1699:122
Plum-stone basket gamble, making 63:62-63
Poie flying game 934:18
Pokean game, how to make and play 1699:127
Racket ball (lacrosse), how to make and play 1699:123
Rattler game, how to play 1494:177
Retrieving stones game 831:22
Ring and arrow game 383:25
Ring and pin equipment, making 934:61
Ring and pin games 934:28-29; 1354:161
Ring and pin toss game, making 63:72-74
Ring it game 633:190
Ring stick game, hula hoop, sticks, making 1427:284
Ring toss game, how to make and play 1699:130
Rooster balance game, how to play 1361:78
Shell dice game, how to play 1699:110
Shinny (ice game) 831:22
"Shinny" game, playing 69:24; 934:8; 1699:124
Simba game 633:191
Snow snake equipment, making 934:60-61
Snow snake game, making 445:46-58; 633:188; 934:43
Snowshoe and toboggan racing 934:44-46
Spear it game, cardboard, bone or stick, string, making 1170:35
Standing cob game, how to make and play 1699:128
Stick counting game, how to play 1699:114
Stick dice equipment, making 934:67-68
Stick dice game, how to play 1699:111
Stick dice games 934:52-53
Stick game 27:50
Stick game, how to make and play 1699:104-105
Stick game, how to play 1170:35
Stick game, making 69:6-7
Stick games 633:187; 934:50
Stick guessing game, sticks or bones, making 1427:284
Stick passing game, sticks, making 1427:285
Stick target games 934:31-34
Stick-in-a-hoop game, making 647:82
Stilt racing game 934:18
Stone dice games 934:54-56

Symbols memory game, symbol patterns, how to make and play 1381:11-12
Target ring game, making 934:71-72
There game 831:21
Throw sticks game, how to play 1699:107
Toe-throw slide game 831:21
Tokinawas game 383:25
Top spinning contests 934:34
Tops game 27:51
Tortoise and hare race, making 482:50-51
Toss and catch game, making 445:77-85
Toss ball game, making 324:40-41; 445:40-45
Toss up game, twigs, how to play 1170:35
Tossing contents game 934:17-18
Tossing game, making 647:81
Trap ball game 934:12-13
Trick the Dancers game 58:12-13
Tug of war contests 934:22-23
Turnabout game 633:190-191
Walnut shell games, how to play 1699:112
Water games 831:22
Where is the stick? game 383:22
Where's the chief? game, making 719:50-51
Whip top equipment, making 934:72-73
Wooden dice game, how to play 1699:108
Wooden dice game, making 69:19
Wrestling 633:192; 934:23-24
Zuni kick stick game, making 445:20-25

INDIANS OF NORTH AMERICA—GOD'S EYE
God's eye, woven, making 63:42-43

INDIANS OF NORTH AMERICA—GREAT BASIN
Tools and ornaments 960:17-24

INDIANS OF NORTH AMERICA—GREAT PLAINS— FOLKLORE
"The Gift of the Sacred Dog"; physical and human geography activities 1458:58-61

INDIANS OF NORTH AMERICA—HAIR
Hair ornaments, making 467:30-31

INDIANS OF NORTH AMERICA—HANDICRAFTS
Birch bark belt board, making 224:202-205
Burnt etching, making 589:99
Doorstop, wooden Indian doorstop, making 892:16-21
Felt hanging, making 224:188-191
Flower pots, making 482:50-51
Gourd Indian, styrofoam and paper, pattern, making 912:43-44
Haida raven pictures from jigsaw shapes, making 1447:18
Lucky rabbit's foot, making 482:48-49
Milk carton Indian, making 534:44
Mimbres mirror, stenciling, making 224:197-201
Neckerchief slides, making 466:90-91
Tennessee grasshopper tent, plant stems, paper straws, sting, making 1296:104
Thunderbird, paper, glue, making 1170:5
Wall hanging, making 69:9; 224:184-188

INDIANS OF NORTH AMERICA—HARVEST FESTIVALS—COOKERY
Green Corn Dance Harvest Festival cornbread, recipe 1574:18-19

INDIANS OF NORTH AMERICA—HATS
Turbans and hair feathers, making 589:18-19

INDIANS OF NORTH AMERICA—HEADBANDS
Headband, feathered, making 180:18-19
Headband, felt or fabric, making 1476:150-151
Headband, making 297:172-173; 355:30-31; 633:21-24; 647:20; 649:50-51; 1699:51
Headband, paper, feather, making 760:220-221; 809:150; 878:94; 1170:12
Headband, tapestry cloth, yarn, patterns, making 1586:19
Headbands and hair bands, making 8:63
Headbands, beaded, making 589:12-13
Headbands, wristbands and armbands, fabric, paints, making 1361:75
Headbands, yarn, feathers, beads, making 1427:261

INDIANS OF NORTH AMERICA—HEADDRESSES
Chief's headdress, toy, making 355:19-21
Headdress, Acoma Indian, making 482:66-67
Headdress, canvas and felt, making 830:108-109
Headdress, feather, how to draw 591:9
Headdress, feather, making 8:64-68; 14:22-23; 466:65
Headdress, horn, making 589:10
Headdress, making 7:39-40; 574:135
Headdress, paper, making 123:57-58; 534:9; 634:22-23; 878:95
Headdress, with wool braids, making 690:9
Indian Chief headdress, making 670:69
Indian maiden headdress, making 670:70
Roach headdress, making 465:26-27

INDIANS OF NORTH AMERICA—HORSES
Horse trading game to learn colors and names of horse breeds, making 1214:6-7
How many hands high is a horse? 1214:5

INDIANS OF NORTH AMERICA—HOUSEHOLD
Bed, willow branches, making 590:26-27
Boxes for storage, paper, yarn, making 1699:23
Cooking basket, paper, string, making 1170:25
Cooking rack, making 647:59
Corn husk mat, making 647:34-35
Drying rack, making 647:58
Gourd bowl, dried gourd, paints, making 1213:81
History of household items 227:32
Ladles, bowls, and drinking cups, making 466:138-139
Metate stone, making 647:71
Mortar and pestle, making 647:65
Rustic furniture, making 466:176-179
Utensils, shells, sticks, foil, string, making 1170:26
Woven mat, paper, bark, twigs, leaves, making 1170:2

INDIANS OF NORTH AMERICA—HOUSES
Adobe house, making 647:67-69
Chickee, paper, straws, pattern, making 1170:22
Dens, making 633:204
Five-pole, two-kid teepee, making 118:87-88
Great Plains Indian teepee, information on 118:85-87
History of Indian homes 227:6
Hogan, paper, popsicle sticks, pattern, making 1170:19
Longhouse, paper, crepe paper, pattern, making 1170:21
Longhouses 469:18-19
Longhouses, how to draw 591:6-7
Pueblo, boxes, sticks, making 1170:23
Shelter, kinds of 324:8
Teepee toy, making 355:12
Teepee, brown paper bag, paints, patterns, making 1427:268
Teepee, cloth, making 8:24-31
Teepee, designs, dew-cloth, making 465:96-101
Teepee, from boxes, making 634:18-22
Teepee, how to draw 591:3
Teepee, making 212:43-45; 296:72-73; 324:9-10; 466:164-165; 633:198-200; 647:53-55

Teepee, paper cup, making 180:34-35
Teepee, paper plates, making 1017:26
Tipi, paper, patterns, making 1393:37
Tipi, plastic tub, paper, sticks, pattern, making 1170:20
Tipis 469:20-23
Tipis, history, structure and use of 987:3-77
Wickiup, making 647:61-62
Wickiup, plastic tub, masking tape, making 1170:18
Wigwam, making 466:166-167; 633:202-203
Wigwam, paper, making 123:30
Wigwams, how to draw 591:4-5
Wigwams, paper, making 1017:26
Wigwams, small paper model, making 1699:13-14

INDIANS OF NORTH AMERICA—HUNTING
Duck decoy, cattail leaves, string, making 1699:29

INDIANS OF NORTH AMERICA—JEWELRY
Beads, homemade, clay, making 1699:69
Bracelets and necklaces, beads, pasta, pipe cleaners, making 1067:199-2OO
Bracelet from shells, how to make 960:77-78
Bracelet, silver, plastic bottles, alum foil, making 1699:67
Bracelets, tongue depressors, making 878:94
Copper pendant, embossed, making 224:52-54
Copper shapes, linked, making 224:55-62
Earring loops, yarn, bottle caps, making 1699:68
Earrings, bead dangles, making 224:76-79
Indian beads, baker's clay, making 980:10
Jewelry from salt clay, macaroni, corn, making 647:27-29
Jewelry, bone, making 224:63-67; 960:103-104
Necklace, bead and seed, making 224:74-75
Necklace, bear claw, making 465:40; 466:71
Necklace, bear claw, plastic claws and salt dough claws, making 1699:58-59
Necklace, bone and shell, making 466:77
Necklace, dried seeds, fishing line, making 1170:9
Necklace, feather and thong, making 224:70-73 making
Necklace, fetish, Iroquois, felt bag, making 1699:65
Necklace, fetish, soap, making 1699:64
Necklace, macaroni, making 878:94
Necklace, maize, making 424:25
Necklace, making 69:27; 633:70-72
Necklace, seed and corn, making 1699:66
Necklace, shell, macaroni, food coloring, making 1699:60
Necklaces and dew claws, making 589:66-68
Salish owl pendant, making 932:69-71
Shell fragments for neckwear, making 224:40-41
Shell jewelry, how to make 960:79-81
Shells with beaded tops, making 224:35-37
Wrist band, making 224:49-51

INDIANS OF NORTH AMERICA—LEATHER
Leather rawhide, how to make 466:20-21; 589:76-77
Leather, sewing, how to do 224:84-86
Tanning method for leather, how to do 466:26-28

INDIANS OF NORTH AMERICA—LEG BANDS
Leg bands, sleigh bells, and tin cone ankle bands, making 466:158

INDIANS OF NORTH AMERICA—MAPS
Map of Indian tribes from 1700 to 1800 227:front, back book
Map of tribes 8:8-9

INDIANS OF NORTH AMERICA—MASKS
History of North American Indian masks 204:44-56
Mask, corn husk, making 811:78
Mask, Haida, making 204:102-105
Mask, Kachina, tag board, yarn, feathers, making 324:44; 1427:262
Mask, shaman, paper, yarn, cornhusks, pattern, making 1170:11
Mask, spirit, papier-mache, raffia, making 1368:52
Masks and shields, toy, making 355:24-25
Masks, how to draw 591:28-29
Masks, making 482:80-81; 633:153-154; 647:49; 846:34-35
Solid faces, body paint, and wigs, making 589:112-116

INDIANS OF NORTH AMERICA—MEDICINE BAG
Medicine bag, leather or fabric, making 1296:20

INDIANS OF NORTH AMERICA—MEDICINE POUCH
Medicine pouch, fabric, leather, yarn, making 1361:77

INDIANS OF NORTH AMERICA—MOTIFS
Mimbres motifs 224:198

INDIANS OF NORTH AMERICA—MUSIC
Curing sickness with songs 299:33-36
Death songs 299:51-54
Good hunting and bountiful crops songs 299:37-42
Love songs 299:47-50
Lullabies 299:43-46
Nature of Indian music 299:9-18
Songs of joy and sorrow 299:19-26
War songs 299:27-32

INDIANS OF NORTH AMERICA—MUSICAL INSTRUMENTS
Bells for knee band, making 8:81
Bells, dancing bells, making 589:70-71
Bells, making 324:39
Bullroarer, making 299:70-75
Bullroarer, paint stick, leather boot lace, making 1699:85
Bullroarer, wood, twine, making 1608:10
Bullroarers and moraches, making 589:74
Bullroarers, wood, string, making 1296:93
Buzzing toy, making 63:56
Carving guide 299:56-57
Clapper, making 299:64-65
Clapper, Pak Papa California Indian instrument, making 468:37
Dance rattles and bell strips, making 714:16-19
Dancing bells, making 468:57-60
Designs for decorating instruments 299:100-109
Drum and drumstick, canvas fabric, dowels, raffia, making 1368:32-33
Drum and drumsticks, making 324:37; 589:80-83
Drum, coffee can, making 253:171-172; 878:93
Drum, double head, making 299:80-87
Drum, making 633:107-109; 647:47
Drum, oatmeal box, milk jugs, making 1699:83-84
Drum, tom-tom drum, felt, making 628:47-48
Drum, water, making 8:80; 63:48-49
Drums and tom-toms, making 227:56-57; 324:36-37; 465:89
Drums, quick and easy, coffee cans, decorated, making 1393:228-229
Drumsticks, making 299:88-91
Flageolet, or love flute, making 466:151-153
Flute, bamboo, making 299:92-99
Gourd rattle, making 63:52-53; 466:156-157
Gourd rattles, pebbles, felt, feathers, making 1427:260-261
Groaning stick, making 63:57-58

Indian musical instruments, making 482:90-91
Indian rattles, making 445:86-96
Jingler anklets, making 299:76-79
Jingles, tin cone, making 589:69
Love flute, making 468:150-151
Mouth bow, making 156:40-41
Musical bow, making 63:50-51
Pow Wow bells, felt, jingle bells, making 1310:137
Rasp, musical, making 299:66-69
Rasp, traditional rasp, two dowels, making 1393:231
Rattle and drum, yogurt cup, pebbles, stick, making 1649:21
Rattle, ankle rattle bracelet from ping pong balls and rice 623:15
Rattle, detergent bottle, stick, decorations, making 1310:44-45
Rattle, dried beans, ball, paint, making 1368:32
Rattle, making 8:81; 227:59; 647:48
Rattle, soda pop can, making 1393:230
Rattle, stick, shells, rocks, making 1170:33
Rattles and noise makers, making 633:110-112
Rattles, dance and turtle, making 589:72-73
Rattles, gourd, making 299:58-63
Rattles, gourd, tin can and plastic, making 324:38-39
Rattles, turtle shell, making 467:40-41
Rattles, whale rattle, cardboard, making 1699:81-82
Shaker, paper plates, making 878:93
Skin drum, fruit juice can, paper, making 1310:40-41
Tom-Tom drum, making 466:154-155
Whelk Indian rattles, making 418:41-42

INDIANS OF NORTH AMERICA—MYTHS
Indian myths and legends art and writing activities, patterns, making 1152:42-48

INDIANS OF NORTH AMERICA—NAMES
Boys' and girls' names and their meanings 633:233-235
How an Indian was named 27:38-40

INDIANS OF NORTH AMERICA—NATIVE AMERICAN DESIGNS
Bear 1252:14
Beaver 1252:14
Bee 1252:12
Bird 1252:14
Deer 1252:14
Dragonfly 1252:12
Fish 1252:12
Frog 1252:12
Goat 1252:15
Grasshopper 1252:14
Lightning bolt 1252:15
Moon 1252:15
Rabbit 1252:15
Sheep 1252:15
Sun 1252:15
Turtle 1252:12

INDIANS OF NORTH AMERICA—NATURE FESTIVALS
Planting and harvesting festivals 419:143-155

INDIANS OF NORTH AMERICA—NORTHEAST. *See* **WOODLAND INDIANS**

INDIANS OF NORTH AMERICA—NORTHWEST COAST INDIANS—BOXES
Indian birchbark box, birch bark, patterns, making 1422:33-34

INDIANS OF NORTH AMERICA—NORTHWEST COAST INDIANS—COOKERY
Buckskin bread, recipe 1380:8
Salmon cakes, recipe 1380:37

INDIANS OF NORTH AMERICA—NORTHWEST COAST INDIANS—FESTIVALS—COOKERY
Salmon barbecue celebration, recipes 1331:42-45

INDIANS OF NORTH AMERICA—NORTHWEST COAST INDIANS—HOUSES
Plank house, wood crates, balsa wood, paint, making 1368:25

INDIANS OF NORTH AMERICA—NORTHWEST COAST INDIANS—TOTEM POLES
Balsa wood totem pole, decorated, making 1368:24
Computer project: design and build a totem pole 1218:52-55
Totem pole, boxes, paint, making 1170:24

INDIANS OF NORTH AMERICA—NORTHWEST COAST INDIANS—TRAPPING
Salmon trap, plywood, grasses, stones, making 1368:26

INDIANS OF NORTH AMERICA—ORNAMENTS
Ornaments, making 8:69-73; 633:65-66
Tassels, fur and yarn pompoms, making 589:100-101

INDIANS OF NORTH AMERICA—OWNER STICKS
Owner stick, dowels, twine, feathers, making 1699:177
Ownership staffs, ceremonial lances and coup sticks, making 466:82-83
Possession stick, making 63:16
Round sticks, decorated, making 589:110-111

INDIANS OF NORTH AMERICA—PACK RACK
Pack rack, making 466:136-137
Sled pack rack, making 467:53-54

INDIANS OF NORTH AMERICA—PACK SADDLES
Packsaddles, making 466:159-161

INDIANS OF NORTH AMERICA—PAPOOSES
Papoose carrier, making 227:38
Papoose holder, making 272:101

INDIANS OF NORTH AMERICA—PARFLECHE
Gross Venture parfleche, making 932:106-109
Parfleche, making 8:79; 465:38-39; 633:82-83

INDIANS OF NORTH AMERICA—PARTIES
Arrow place mats and invitations, making 294:82
Bird masks, making 294:88-89
Games; canoe race, bean race, corn toss, sticks and stones, making 294:92-93
Headband, feathered, and quiver and arrows, making 294:90-91
Indian Pow Wow (7 years up) 124:150-157
Indian snacks, making 294:94-95
Pow Wow Party, how to plan and give 43:21-24
Shield decorations, making 294:86
Totem pole cakes and favors, making 294:83-85
Totem pole, making 294:87
Warrior medallion, making 294:94-95

INDIANS OF NORTH AMERICA—PEACE PIPES
Calumets, pipes, making 589:93
Peace pipe bag, making 633:141-143
Peace pipe, feathered, making 296:236-237
Peace pipe, how to draw 591:10-11
Peace pipe, making from spools 629:105
Peace pipe, paper tube, feathers, yarn, beads, making 1699:36
Peace pipes, making 227:49; 465:50-51; 466:92-93

INDIANS OF NORTH AMERICA—PECTORAL
Pectoral, leather and bone pectoral, making 224:68-69

INDIANS OF NORTH AMERICA—PEOPLE
Models of people from pipe cleaners, making 647:74-75
INDIANS OF NORTH AMERICA—PETROGLYPHS
Petroglyphs, designs, plaster of Paris, making 1699:164-165
INDIANS OF NORTH AMERICA—PICTOGRAPHS
Glossary of Native American pictographs 1427:258
Indian pictographs, making 714:14-15
Indian picture writing 8:87; 27:41-46; 131:44-46
Pictographs, making 524:9-11
Pictographs, paper, paints, making 1699:166
Picture dictionary 1152:44
INDIANS OF NORTH AMERICA—PIPES
Pipe stems, pipe bowls, pipe tomahawks, making 589:94-97
Pipes, making 482:58-59; 633:136-140
INDIANS OF NORTH AMERICA—POTTERY
Bowl, clay or dough, making 1699:20-22
Bowl, rolled clay, paints, making 1427:264-265
Clay coiled pot, making 63:14-15; 959:56-60; 1170:31
Clay pot, paint, making 1368:36
Clay pottery and kiln, making 633:180-184
Clay, how to find, clean and prepare 959:52-56
Direct-fire pottery, how to make 959:64-67
Dollhouse dishes, making 647:38-39
Pots, how to finish and decorate 959:62-64
Pots, model and mold, how to make 959:60-62
Pottery, how to draw 591:24-25
Pottery, recipes for clay doughs, making 324:34-35
INDIANS OF NORTH AMERICA—POWWOW
How to run a Pow Wow 692:114-119
INDIANS OF NORTH AMERICA—PRINTING
Stamp printing, decorations, patterns, making 1170:32
INDIANS OF NORTH AMERICA—PUPPET PLAYS
How the Spark of Fire Was Saved 4:69-73
Red-Eyed Duck 4:65-68
INDIANS OF NORTH AMERICA—PUPPETS
American Indian jointed shadow puppet, making 757:112-119
American Indian puppet, making 483:26
Indian boy puppet, paper bag, patterns, making 941:38-39
Indian finger puppet, making 745:18
Indian man and woman puppets, patterns, making 1006:17-18
Indian puppet, paper bag, patterns, making 940:20
Puppets, made with peanuts 647:90-96
Samoset and Chief Massasoit, sock puppets, making 353:19
INDIANS OF NORTH AMERICA—QUILLWORK
Quilled box, porcupine quills, food coloring, making 1606:59-60
INDIANS OF NORTH AMERICA—ROACHES
Roaches, hair roach, top feathers, and feather roach, making 589:20-27
INDIANS OF NORTH AMERICA—ROSETTES
Forehead rosettes, making 589:14-17
Rosettes, dancers' forehead rosettes, making 714:9-11
INDIANS OF NORTH AMERICA—RUGS
Rug, from rags, making 224:182-183
INDIANS OF NORTH AMERICA—SAND PAINTING
Plaque, sandpainting, making 224:192-196
Sandpainting without sand, making 69:12
Sandpainting, colored, making 1699:172

Sandpainting, simple version of sandpainting using Indian designs, colored sand, sandpaper, making; 1179:166-167
Sandpainting; T'hunderbird in sand, making 298:154-155
Sandpainting, how to do 63:38-39; 227:58; 633:132-133; 647:86-87
INDIANS OF NORTH AMERICA—SHIELDS
Indian shield, balsa wood, making 925:55-56
Shield model, fabric, feathers, raffia, paint, making 1368:47
Shield, making 324:46; 633:146-148; 647:45-46
Shield, paper plates, paints, making 1699:31-32
Shields and coup sticks, making 589:84-87
Warrior shield, making 297:132-133
INDIANS OF NORTH AMERICA—SIGN LANGUAGE
Indian sign language, how to do 8:89-92; 27:24-36; 976:28-29
Sign language, hand movements, pictures 1170:38-39
INDIANS OF NORTH AMERICA—SIGNALS
Blanket signal, making 633:115
Smoke signals for day and night, making 8:88; 633:113-116
Trail and warning signs, making 633:117-118
INDIANS OF NORTH AMERICA—SLEDS
Sled, making 633:215-216
INDIANS OF NORTH AMERICA—SOUTHEAST—BASKETRY
Basketry of Southeast Indians 959:15-18
INDIANS OF NORTH AMERICA—SOUTHEAST—JEWELRY
Mound Builders pendants, styrofoam, clay, yarn, making 1699:61-62
INDIANS OF NORTH AMERICA—SOUTHEAST—POTTERY
Pottery of the Southeast Indians 959:46-49
INDIANS OF NORTH AMERICA—SOUTHEAST—TOOLS
Tools and ornaments 960:44-48
INDIANS OF NORTH AMERICA—SOUTHEAST—WOODWORKING
Woodworking of the Southeast Indians 959:73-76
INDIANS OF NORTH AMERICA—SOUTHWEST—AMULETS
Eye of God warrior amulet, yarn, making 298:240-241
INDIANS OF NORTH AMERICA—SOUTHWEST—BASKETRY
Basketry of Southwest Indians 959:12-14
Baskets, making 227:36
INDIANS OF NORTH AMERICA—SOUTHWEST—BURDEN BASKETS
Burden baskets to carry food, wood, paper, yarn, making 1699:19
INDIANS OF NORTH AMERICA—SOUTHWEST—COOKERY
A-Maizeing corn, roasted corn, recipe 1729:68
Cactus cooler, sherbet soda, recipe 1729:59
Chaco tacos, recipe 1729:70-71
Full moon pudding, cornmeal pudding, recipe 1729:72-73
Indian Diamonds, cookies, recipe 1729:74-75
Leapin' lizard leather, fruit leather, recipe 1729:65
Papago pumpkin, pumpkin dessert, recipe 1729:60
Pow Wow Posole, pork and hominy stew, recipe 1729:69
Powerful pinons, spiced pinon nuts, recipe 1729:64

Prairie dog pumpkin muffins, recipe 1729:61-62
Pueblo "Horno" bread, recipe 1729:66-67
Roadrunner roasted pinon nuts, recipe 1729:62-63
Sandpainted suns, cookies, recipe 1729:76

**INDIANS OF NORTH AMERICA—SOUTHWEST—
FOLKLORE—HANDICRAFTS**

How Napai Made the Animals, clay animals, sandpaper
drawing 125:102-107

**INDIANS OF NORTH AMERICA—SOUTHWEST—
FOOTWEAR**

Southwest type moccasins, how to make 359:111-124

**INDIANS OF NORTH AMERICA—SOUTHWEST—
GAMES**

Ball juggle race 565:176
Ball race game, how to play 1699:125
Ball toss race 565:42
Bird flight game 565:172
Blanket basket, ball game 565:125
Bowl catch game 565:105
Bowl toss game 565:107
Boy-beat-girl game 565:50
Clown ball game 565:136
Corncob ring toss game 565:127
Dart and rings game 565:182
Five stones toss game 565:108
Flying feather game 565:134
Foot cast ball game 565:148
Four stick game 565:200
Guess stick game 565:203
Hand game 565:272
Hidden ball game 565:204
Hoop and lance game 565:269
Horserace game 565:264
Kick stick race 565:56
Kickball races 565:51
Knotty game 565:206
Moose stalk game 565:74
Over and over game 565:158
Pine cone hoop toss game 565:123
Pony ride game 565:119
Rattler game 565:70
Ring in a ring game 565:179
Stalking game 565:68
Straight path ball game 565:258
Three throw ball game 565:138
Toe throw stick game 565:148
Toes corncob toss game 565:130
Toss a ring game 565:41

**INDIANS OF NORTH AMERICA—SOUTHWEST—
HANDICRAFTS**

Bola tie, making 525:84
Flame design tie-dyed fabric, making 298:134-135

**INDIANS OF NORTH AMERICA—SOUTHWEST—
HOUSES**

Pueblo village houses, boxes, paints, making 1699:15-16

**INDIANS OF NORTH AMERICA—SOUTHWEST—
JEWELRY**

Bracelet, silver, plastic bottles, aluminum foil, making
1699:67
Bracelet, silver, turquoise, paper, foil, making 1017:30

**INDIANS OF NORTH AMERICA—SOUTHWEST—
MASKS**

Kachina mask and miniature mask, making 327:22-25
Kachina masks, shapes, colors, features, making 327:19-
21

Southwest Kachina masks, history of 327:16-18

**INDIANS OF NORTH AMERICA—SOUTHWEST—
MUSICAL INSTRUMENTS**

Gourd dance rattles, gourds, paints, making 1729:77

**INDIANS OF NORTH AMERICA—SOUTHWEST—
PAINTS**

Stem paint brush and clay paint, making 1213:20

**INDIANS OF NORTH AMERICA—SOUTHWEST—
POTTERY**

Indian coil pottery, flour and salt clay, making 1729:78-
79
Mimbres pottery, clay, paints, making 1338:14-16
Pottery of Southwest Indians 959:38-46
Pottery, how to make Southwestern Indian pottery
605:87-107
Southwest-Indian bowl, clay, making 1070:140-142

**INDIANS OF NORTH AMERICA—SOUTHWEST—
TOOLS**

Tools and ornaments 960:25-32

**INDIANS OF NORTH AMERICA—SOUTHWEST—
VILLAGES**

Desert Indian Village diorama, making 647:78

INDIANS OF NORTH AMERICA—SPIRITS

Spirit plate, dessert plate, ink or markers, making
1296:19

INDIANS OF NORTH AMERICA—STORY BEADS

Story bead, paper, yarn, glue, paints, making 1296:104-
105

INDIANS OF NORTH AMERICA—STORY STICKS

Story stick, stick, yarn, feathers, making 1699:176

INDIANS OF NORTH AMERICA—STORYTELLING

Storytelling bag, paper bag, crayons, making 1699:181

**INDIANS OF NORTH AMERICA—TALKING
FEATHER**

Talking feather, feather, beads, laces, making 1699:179

INDIANS OF NORTH AMERICA—TOBOGGANS

Toboggan, how to draw 591:18-19

INDIANS OF NORTH AMERICA—TOOLS

Bone awl, making 960:91-92
Bone fish hook, making 960:93-96
Bone hoe, making 960:96-99
Bone scraper, making 960:89-90
Bones, how to locate and clean 960:82-88
Fish hooks from shells, how to make 960:71-73
Knife and ax sheaths, leather, making 466:22-23
Knives, shell knives, how to make 960:65-67
Needle case, bone, making 63:18-19
Pump drill, making 445:106-110; 466:74
Shell containers, how to make 960:68-70
Tools from shells, how to make 960:74-76

INDIANS OF NORTH AMERICA—TOTEM POLES

Coffee can Totem poles, making 1361:76
Thunderbird mask Totem pole, making 1486:14-15
Totem pole, cardboard, clay, paints, making 1393:35
Totem poles, how to draw 591:26-27

INDIANS OF NORTH AMERICA—TOYS

Buffalo toy, making 227:41
Cradleboard for doll, milk carton, making 1699:89-90
Cradle charms, clay or cardboard, making 1699:91
Deer hat for hunting, paper, making 1699:94
Dog travois toy, sticks, string, making 1699:98
Humming toy, making 227:42
Indian people toys, making 355:3-7
Indian ponies and riders, toy, making 355:17-18

Koshare tumbling toy, posterboard, marbles, making 1296:21

Papoose in a cradle, toy, making 355:15-16

Spear, cardboard, feathers, making 1699:95-96

Spinning top, cardboard, nail, making 1699:99

Toy canoe, making 180:22-23

War dance toy, paper model, making 545:94

INDIANS OF NORTH AMERICA—TRANSPORTATION

History of Indian transportation 227:16

INDIANS OF NORTH AMERICA—TRAVOIS

Travois model, twigs, fabric, paint, making 1368:44-45

Travois, making 227:17; 355:18; 647:56-57; 1427:270

INDIANS OF NORTH AMERICA—TRIBES

Major Indian tribes of North America map and list 934:VI-IX

Major Indian tribes of the North American continent 299:IX-XI

INDIANS OF NORTH AMERICA—TWIG ANIMALS

Twig animals from little twigs, making 1213:47

INDIANS OF NORTH AMERICA—VILLAGES

Indian Village, teepee, Chiefs, Council fire, canoe, Totem Pole, making 670:52-57

Village from yarn and sticks, making 770:36-37

INDIANS OF NORTH AMERICA—WAMPUM

Wampum beads, making 688:9

Wampum belt, macaroni, yarn, making 1170:8

Wampum, how to draw 591:20

Wampum, making 647:50; 719:10

Weaving macaroni wampum, making 482:98-99

INDIANS OF NORTH AMERICA—WAR BONNETS

War bonnets, double-tailed, horned, and storage case, making 465:18-23

War bonnets, making 465:16-17; 466:69; 589:2-7; 633:59-64; 714:24-25

INDIANS OF NORTH AMERICA—WEAPONS

Bow and arrow, making 296:78; 647:40-42

Bow and arrow, wood, feathers, paint, string, making 1368:46-47

Bow and arrows, ceremonial, making 466:94-95

Bows and arrows, arrowheads, how to draw 591:12-13

Bows, flat, and arrows, making 633:222-226

Bullet pouches, making 8:76-77

Clubs, making 227:44

Gauntlet, making 224:139-140

Lance, making 633:145

Quiver, making 647:43

Tomahawk, making 296:66-67; 647:44

Tomahawks, how to draw 591:14-15

Tomahawks, pipe, cardboard, twine, pattern, making 1170:15

Tomahawks, spiked-club, cardboard, feathers, making 1170:14

War clubs, making 466:104-105; 589:75

INDIANS OF NORTH AMERICA—WEAVING

Cigar box loom, making 633:88-89

Loom, basic, making 224:113-121

Outdoor looms, making 633:85-88

Shadow box weaving, how to do 1152:47-48

Weaving frame, wood, nails, bodkin, making 1368:38

INDIANS OF NORTH AMERICA—WHISTLES

Turkey leg whistle, turkey leg, making 1427:271

INDIANS OF NORTH AMERICA—WINTER COUNT

Winter Count model, paper, pattern, making 1170:6

Winter Count, old sheet, paints, making 1699:173-174

Winter Count, paper, making 1017:28

Winter counter, making 633:119-121; 633:119-121

INDIANS OF NORTH AMERICA—WOOD CARVING

Carved figure, comic Indian, wood, making 382:72-74

Wood, carved, Indian chief, making 382:23

Wood plaque, buffalo skull, carved, making~?382:56

Wood plaque, carved, making 382:55

Wood plaque, carved, Thunderbird, making 382:50-51

INDIANS OF NORTH AMERICA—WOODWORKING

Bark, bark cordage, making 959:93-95

Birch bark containers, making 959:91-93

Mortar, how to burn and scrape 959:88-90

Spoon carved from wood, making 959:95-99

Woodworking materials 959:84-88

INDIANS OF NORTH AMERICA—WREATHS

Corn husk wreath, wire hanger, corn husks, making 1427:260

INDIANS OF NORTH AMERICA—WRITING

Picture writing, symbols used, patterns, making 1170:3-4

INDIANS OF NORTH AMERICA—YARN PAINTINGS

Yam painting, making 63:40-41

INDONESIA

Activities, flags, games, songs, dances, recipes 1381:95-98

INDONESIA—BIRTHDAYS

Birthday celebrations in Indonesia 695:62

INDONESIA—COOKERY

Atjar ketimoen, cucumber relish, recipe 188:41

Bird's nest soup, recipe 1650:22-23

Chicken satay, recipe 1560:26

Coconut chicken, recipe 187:26

Corn fritters, recipe 710:52-53

Es Campur dessert, ice with toppings, recipe 1085:89

Fried rice, recipe 794:55; 1085:86-87; 1381:97

Gado gado snack, vegetables with peanut sauce, recipe 1650:20-21

Gado gado, cooked vegetable salad, recipe 1165:189

Katjang saos, peanut sauce, recipe 1165:189

Lontong, Indonesian rice rolls, recipe 1165:191

Nasi goreng (rice, pork and vegetables), recipe 1165:190; 874:56-57

Ox-eye eggs, fried eggs, recipe 1244:18

Potatoes, spices, recipe 1145:28-29

Raita, yogurt and cucumbers, recipe 1144:27

Sate ajam, skewered chicken, recipe 1165:190-191

Sate, marinated meat dish, sate peanut sauce, recipes 1085:88

Scrambled eggs with tomato, recipe 858:unp

Sweet banana crisps (rempah pisang manis), cookies, recipe 72:138-139

Timor achar, pepper salad with sesame seeds, recipe 1165:188

INDONESIA—COSTUMES

Atjar ketimoen, cucumber relish, recipe, costume 188:41

INDONESIA—DANCES

Three Indonesian folk dances 474:124-125

INDONESIA—DOLLS

Bamboo leaf doll, making 532:34-35

INDONESIA—FESTIVALS

Children's Day, dragon song and game 1398:39

Feast of Rice celebration 601:58-59

Horse Festival celebration 826:30

INDONESIA—FESTIVALS—COOKERY

Salamatan; goda goda (vegetable salad), recipe 1666:190

Salamatan; gotuk (sweet potato balls with coconut), recipe 1666:191

Salamatan; kueh prol nanas (Indonesian bread pudding), recipe 1666:192

Salamatan; rudjak (fruit salad), recipe 1666:191

INDONESIA—FOLKLORE

"Counting Crocodiles" flannel board story, patterns, making 1603:176-179

INDONESIA—GAMES

Elephant, man and ant game 602:59-60

Kowah card game 1132:10

Kulit K'rang game, how to play 1507:46

Kulit K'rang shell game 1119:21

Main karet gelang, rubber band game, how to play 1708:32-33

Totit card game 1132:11-12

Wora-Wora Tjintjin, ring and loose string game, how to play 1494:47

INDONESIA—HANDICRAFTS

Ikat weaving using dyed threads, making 1506:22-23

Palm leaf sequence book, paper, ribbons, pony beads, patterns, making 1332:75-78

Tangram, paper, patterns, making 1244:19

INDONESIA—HOUSES

Huts on stilts, dowels, sticks, clay, making 1488:20-21

INDONESIA—MASKS

Rangda mask, making 532:28

INDONESIA—MUSICAL INSTRUMENTS

Prayer drum, round box, paper, dowel, making 1631:119

INDONESIA—PUPPETS

Menak rod puppet, cardboard, dough, making 1707:19

Paper bag Indonesian hand puppet, patterns, making 1381:98

Shadow puppet from Indonesia, history of and how to make 495:70-74

INDONESIA—SHADOW PUPPETS

Wayang Kulit shadow play figures, paper, making 515:66

Wayang Kulit shadow puppet, cardboard, sticks, making 1707:15

INKS

Berry ink, Colonial recipe 1043:28

Berry ink, recipe 1196:11; 1476:24

Colonial berry ink, recipe, making 1309:8

Colonial walnut ink, recipe, making 1309:9

Natural dyes and inks, how to make and use 1429:116-119

Nut ink, Colonial recipe 1043:29

Nut ink, recipe 1196:11

Nut ink, walnut, pioneer, how to make 1349:157

Tree bark ink, recipe 1196:11

INSECTS

Songs, fingerplays, stories, games, rhythms 1200:101-103

INTERNATIONAL WOMEN'S DAY

Activities and projects for classrooms 1393:166-167

INUIT INDIANS. *See also* **ESKIMOS**

INUIT INDIANS—COOKERY

Inuit ice cream, recipe 1527:62

INUIT INDIANS—GAMES

Nauktak game 1121:14

Silence (Muk) game, how to play 1355:17

Tiliraginik Qiriqtagtut game 1121:15

Tu Nu Miu game 1121:14

INUIT INDIANS—LULLABIES

"Comforting Song" 1607:16

INUIT INDIANS—PUPPETS

Inuit finger puppet, paper, making 1448:24-25

INUIT INDIANS—STRING FIGURES

Caribou string 373:28-29

Kayak string 373:54-57

Little dog with big ears string 373:76-80

Porcupine string 373:44-46

Seagull or man carrying a kayak string 372:58-61

Two brown bears and their caves string 372:34-35

IOWA—COOKERY

Amana cookies, recipe 654:54-55

Corn on the cob, recipe 654:53

Cornmeal crisps, recipe 793:5

Popcorn, easy baked caramel popcorn, recipe 1342:93

IRAN

Activities, flags, games, songs, dances, recipes 1381:111-114

Activities, history, foods, games 143:71-108

IRAN—BIRTHDAYS

Birthday customs 488:61-65

Celebrations of birthdays in Iran 474:85

IRAN—CHRISTMAS

Celebration of Christmas in Iran 516:14-17

IRAN—COFFEE

Coffee in Iran 474:138

IRAN—COOKERY

Brittled almonds, recipe 143:96

Chelo, recipe 143:106

Cherry rice, recipe 794:48

Coucou-ye sabzi, omelet of greens and herbs, recipe 1165:79

Dough yogurt drink, recipe 1381:113

Khorak-e mahi sefid, pan-fried fish, recipe 1165:80-81

Khoresht-e fesenjan, chicken in pomegranate sauce, recipe 1165:78-79

Marzipan, recipe 143:107

Nan-e shirini, Persian cookies, recipe 1165:80

Orange apricot balls, recipe 143:106

Persian cookies (nane shirini), cookies, recipe 72:106-107

Sabzi pollo, green herb rice, recipe 1165:81

Sharbat-e toot-farangi, strawberry syrup, recipe 1165:79-80

Yogurt honey cake, recipe 143:104-105

Yogurt soup, cold, recipe 1381:113

Yogurt, recipe 143:103-104

IRAN—DANCERS

Dancer from Iran, paper and foil model, making 1094:22-23

IRAN—FESTIVALS

Chahar Shanbeh Sori (Last Wednesday of the Year) 143:97

Cizdah-Bedar (The Thirteenth Day) 143:98

No-Ruz (New Year's Day) 143:96

No-Ruz dinner 143:97

Sabzeh (Symbol of Spring) 143:97

Wedding celebration 143:99-100

IRAN—FESTIVALS—COOKERY

Noruz, New Year, Sabzih sprouts, wheat seeds of lentils, recipe 1654:149

Nou Ruz; kateh (golden rice cake), recipe 1666:61

Nou Ruz; salata (mixed vegetable salad), recipe 1666:62

Nou Ruz; taratoor (salad dressing), recipe 1666:62

IRAN—FESTIVALS—HANDICRAFTS

Noruz Festival sabzeh pot of growing seeds, making 1574:12-13

Noruz pop-up card, making 1387:50-51

Noruz sprouting seeds, to welcome spring, how to do 1179:80-81

Noruz, New Year, eggs, colored, making 1654:149

IRAN—GAMES

Alak do lak game 143:101

As Nas card game 1132:13-15

Ashukh (knucklebones) game 143:102

Board game 143:77

Cat and mouse chasing game, how to play 1498:43-44

Ear and nose game 602:61; 967:34

Goosh va damagh, ear and nose game, how to play 143:102; 1494:156

Haft sang, seven stories tag game, how to play 1708:34-35

Knuckle bones game 602:60

Nomads and Settlers stick game 1119:14-16

Puck and handle game 602:63

Tap, tap, paste game 602:61-62

Who was it? game 602:62

Wolf and flock game 602:62-63

IRAN—JEWELRY

Lucky hand charm, making 856:110-111

IRAN—LANGUAGE

Iran Language 143:108

IRAN—MOSAICS

Mosaic designs, cardboard, colored paper, making 1654:152

IRAN—NATURE FESTIVALS

No-ruz New Year Festival 419:120-121

No-ruz Spring Festival 419:120-121

IRAN—NEW YEAR'S DAY

New Year celebration 601:59-61

Norooz, celebration of New Year's Day in Iran 475:100

Noruz Festival, history of 709:101

Noruz in Iran 489:98-106

IRAN—NEW YEAR'S DAY—HANDICRAFTS

Sabzeh, making 709:102

IRAN—RUGS

Persian rug to make, cardboard weaving, making 515:68

Persian rug, cardboard, paper, yarn, making 1381:114

IRAQ

Activities, flags, games, songs, dances, recipes 1381:115-118

IRAQ—CHRISTMAS

Celebration of Christmas in Iraq 516:24-29

IRAQ—COOKERY

Compot-e aloo, prune compote, recipe 1165:77

Cucumber salad, recipe 1381:117

Date cakes (tamriah), cookies, recipe 72:112-113

Hummus be Tahini, chickpeas with sesame paste, recipe 1381:116-117

Ma'mounia dessert, recipe 1369:119

Nan-e lavash, flat bread, recipe 1165:77

Yogurt and cucumber salad, recipe, making 794:47

Yogurt soup, making 187:34

IRAQ—EASTER

Easter egg customs in Iraq 201:28

IRAQ—FESTIVALS

Breaking of the Fast celebration 601:61-62

IRAQ—FESTIVALS—COOKERY

Eid al-Fitr; shirini (Kurdish pumpkin dessert), recipe 1666:60

Eid al-Fitr; tamur ou rashi (tahina with dates), recipe 1666:60

IRAQ—FESTIVALS—HANDICRAFTS

Noruz pop-up card, making 1387:50-51

IRAQ—GAMES

Backgammon board game, patterns, making 1541:219-229

Magura, Pecan Hole game, how to play 1494:161-162

Tawlie game 1037:24-26

There was a man who had six girls games 602:64

IRAQ—HOUSES

Reed houses of the Marsh Arabs, straw, cardboard, making 1512:12-13

IRAQ—KITES

Fanus kite, making 515:70

IRELAND

Activities, flags, games, songs, dances, recipes 1381:188-189

IRELAND—CHRISTMAS

Christmas customs 149:32

Customs of Christmas in Ireland 474:151

IRELAND—CHRISTMAS—COOKERY

Almond paste or marzipan, recipe 1229:71

Apple and bread dressing, recipe 1229:74

Broiled Irish ham, recipe 1229:74

Carrageen moss jelly, recipe 1229:73

Christmas pudding, recipe 1229:70; 1452:103

Cookies, candied citron, raisins, almonds, recipe 1229:70

Irish gingerbread cake, recipe 1128:28

Irish soda bread, recipe 1229:74

Minanollag fruitcake, recipe 1726:31

Mince tartlets, recipe 1229:71

Salmon, dressed whole, recipe 1229:73

Soda scones, recipe 1229:72

Spiced beef, recipe 1128:25; 1229:73

IRELAND—CHRISTMAS—DECORATIONS

Stephen's Day wren, paper, paints, pipe cleaners, making 1229:66-67

Thatched cottages decorations, match boxes, paper, fabric, making 1229:68-69

Turnip candle holder, turnip, plate, holly, greens, making 1229:65

IRELAND—CHRISTMAS—HANDICRAFTS

Irish candles, beeswax, wicks, making 1575:10-11

IRELAND—COOKERY

Bangers, potatoes and sausages, recipe 1244:61

Boxty bread, potato bread, recipe 1726:42

Bread and butter pudding, recipe 1165:129-130

Broonie, Irish gingerbread, recipe 188:22

Buttermilk oaten bread, recipe 793:32-33; 1381:189

Champ, potatoes, onion, recipe 1726:39

Champs, potato and butter dish, recipe 1244:60

Chicken and leek pie, recipe 1726:33

Chicory salad with buttermilk-egg dressing, recipe 1726:43

Colcannon, mashed potatoes with cabbage, recipe 1165:128

Colcannon, potatoes and cabbage dish, recipe 1244:61

Corned beef and cabbage, recipe 1452:100; 1726:41

Dublin coddle, potatoes, ham, onions, recipe 1726:22

Dublin coddle, recipe 895:69

Iced beet salad, recipe 1726:23

Irish candy, recipe 1381:189
Irish coffee for kids, recipe 895:71
Irish coffee sauce, recipe 1452:104
Irish moss pudding, recipe 1644:15
Irish soda bread, American version, recipe 133:113-114
Irish soda bread, recipes 492:53-55; 501:82; 895:70; 909:45; 1455:123; 1495:123
Irish soda bread, traditional, recipe 133:113
Irish stew, recipe 794:20; 1165:128-129; 1192:10; 1381:189; 1452:101; 1726:24
Limerick ham with sweet-and-sour Brussels sprouts, recipe 1726:34-35
Nore salmon cakes with lemon parsley sauce, recipe 1726:36
Oatcakes, cookies, recipe 72:43-44
Oatmeal bread, recipe 1165:129
One-skillet farmhouse-style fry, bacon, eggs, tomatoes, recipe 1726:21
Potato cakes, recipe 1452:102
Potatoes and peas, recipe 1244:61
Pratie oaten, small fried cakes, recipe 1726:20
Rumpled e thumps, potatoes, leeks and cheese dish, recipe 1244:61
Soda bread, recipe 1380:6; 1430:118; 1474:94-95; 1653:76; 1726:19
Spiced apple tarts, recipe 1726:28-29
Watercress soup, recipe 1726:32
Wheaten rhubarb crumble, recipe 1726:26-27
IRELAND—COSTUMES
Broonie, Irish gingerbread, recipe, costume 188:22
Description and pictures of Irish costumes 313:57-61
IRELAND—DANCES
Irish trot 624:15-17
Jig dance and costume picture 1000:18-21
Little Irish dance, how to do 1494:121-122
IRELAND—EASTER
Easter egg customs in Ireland 201:21
IRELAND—FESTIVALS
Puck Fair and Pattern 474:25
St. Patrick's Day celebration, activities, handicrafts, songs, foods 601:105; 909:39-47
IRELAND—FESTIVALS—COOKERY
Halloween; colcannon (potato casserole), recipe 1666:112
National Day Irish potato candy, recipe 1199:66-67
National Day Irish soda bread, recipe 1199:67
St. Patrick's Day cakes, recipe 874:75
Wren Day; boiled fruitcake, recipe 1666:113
IRELAND—FESTIVALS—DANCES
St. Patrick's potato race dance 624:18-19
IRELAND—FOLKLORE
"Field of Boliauns," flannel board, patterns, making 1201:126-128
Little Old Lady and the Leprechaun flannel board patterns, making 910:19,54
IRELAND—FOLKLORE—COOKERY
Clever Oonagh; story and recipe for griddle bread, making 364:41-55
IRELAND—FOLKLORE—HANDICRAFTS
Bread for a Fighting Giant 126:31-39
Bread for a Fighting Giant art activities, giant papier mache mask, making 126:40-42
Bread for a Fighting Giant, art activities, cut paper designs, making 126:42-44

Bread for a Fighting Giant, art activities, 18th century greeting card, making 126:45
Bread for a Fighting Giant, art activities, mounted and painted designs, making 126:45
IRELAND—GAMES
Ball in the decker game, how to play 1497:30-31
Jackstones jacks game 1119:41
Pass the orange game, how to play 58:40-41; 1494:109
Soldier's game, how to play 1507:76
Spoil Five card game 1132:92-94
Spy for riders tag game, how to play 1498:15
IRELAND—HALLOWEEN
Halloween celebrations in Ireland 474:66-67
IRELAND—HALLOWEEN—COOKERY
Colcannon, potatoes, cabbage, recipe 1726:38
IRELAND—HALLOWEEN—DECORATIONS
Lantern from turnips, called bogies, making 1453:74-75
IRELAND—HALLOWEEN—HANDICRAFTS
Jack-o-lantern, making 626:62-64
IRELAND—HANDICRAFTS
Hills and dales felt painting, making 298:110-111
Pressed flower nosegay, making 298:162-163
St. Brigid's cross, weave from grass or straws, making 1477:28
IRELAND—JEWELRY
Brooch, cardboard, decorations, making 1448:16-17
Shamrock pin, making 626:61-62
IRELAND—LACE MAKING
Knotted fringe fancy lace, yam, making 298:238-239
IRELAND—LANGUAGE
Numbers one to ten in Gaelic 1714:unp
IRELAND—LENT
Calvary Robin, traditional tale from Ireland 139:95
IRELAND—LULLABIES
Ballad of Downal Baun 780:33
IRELAND—NEW YEAR'S DAY
Fun, food in Ireland 489:36-43
IRELAND—PUPPETS
Molly Malone puppet show 756:94-96
IRELAND—RHYMES
"Clap Handies" 1607:24
"Gee Up a Chapaillin" 1607:25
IRELAND—STRING FIGURES
Duck's Feet 1404:22-25
IRELAND—TOYS
Irish wobble tumbler toy, patterns, making 1016:49-54
IROQUOIS INDIANS—BAGS
Twined bag, woven, making 223:26-28
IROQUOIS INDIANS—BASKETRY
Basket, splint type, making 223:28-33
IROQUOIS INDIANS—BEADWORK
Beadwork, making 223:69-71
IROQUOIS INDIANS—BELTS
Beaded belt, buckskin or canvas, making 1323:22
IROQUOIS INDIANS—CANOES
Canoes, birchbark, dugout, making 223:22-23
IROQUOIS INDIANS—CLOTHING
Breech cloth, making 281:6
Iroquois girl's leggings, moccasins and dress, making 223:43-44
Iroquois man's breechclout, leggings, kilt, making 223:44-45
Man's shirt, fabric, making 1323:9
Man's tunic, fabric, making 281:6-7
Mohawk neck bib, fabric, making 1323:9

Warrior's breech-clout, fabric, making 1323:11
Warrior's kilt, fabric, making 1323:11
Warrior's leggings, fabric, making 1323:10
Woman's dress, fabric, making 1323:12
Woman's leggings, fabric, making 1323:17
Woman's skirt, fabric, making 281:8; 1323:17
Woman's tunic, fabric, making 281:7-8
Yarn sash, fabric, making 1323:20

IROQUOIS INDIANS—COOKERY
Cornbread, recipe 1271:287
Corn grinding, how to do 1271:145
Corn pone, recipe 1271:289
Foods eaten by Iroquois, squash recipe 223:24-25
Foods of the Iroquois Indians 666:56-59
Iroquois leaf bread, recipe 410:112
Squash, baked, recipe 1676:30
Strawberry drink, recipe 1527:49
Succotash, corn, beans, recipe 1676:30
Succotash, recipe, making 659:58; 1296:135

IROQUOIS INDIANS—COSTUMES
Costumes, making 223:48-49

IROQUOIS INDIANS—DOLLS
Apple head dolls and figures, how to make 1179:208-209
Corn husk doll, making 775:44-49

IROQUOIS INDIANS—FACE PAINTING
Paint your face like the Iroquois, how to do 1537:21

IROQUOIS INDIANS—FALSE FACE SOCIETY
Eastern Iroquois False Faces, history of 327:6-8

IROQUOIS INDIANS—FESTIVALS
Corn Festival celebration 659:55
Three Sisters Harvest Day celebration, how to do 1271:65-70

IROQUOIS INDIANS—FESTIVALS—DOLLS
Three Sisters Harvest corn husk dolls, making 1271:100

IROQUOIS INDIANS—FESTIVALS—JEWELRY
Three Sisters Harvest necklaces, corn, bean and squash seeds 1271:98-99

IROQUOIS INDIANS—FESTIVALS—MASKS
Three Sisters Harvest corn husk mask, making 1271:100

IROQUOIS INDIANS—FOOTWEAR
Moccasins, leather, making 1323:18
Moccasins, making 8:61
Moccasins, pattern, making 281:9-13; 1476:148-149

IROQUOIS INDIANS—GAMES
Bowl game, how to play 1608:84; 1676:19
Dart game 602:171-172
Double ball and stick game, making 445:66-76
Flip and guess sticks, paddle and weighted feathers, bowl toss, making 223:86-88
Sacred bowl game, how to play 1296:119
Snow snake game, making 445:46-58
Snow snake, painted designs, how to make and play 1476:64-65
Snow snake, tree branch, metal washers, making 1477:30
Three Sisters corncob dart game, how to play 1271:99
Three Sisters knots game, how to play 1271:61-62
Three Sisters lap circle game, how to play 1271:59
Three Sisters trust walk game, how to play 1271:61
Three Sisters workers of Jobe game, how to play 1271:59-60

IROQUOIS INDIANS—GARDENS
Compost pile, how to make 1271:96-97
How to grow Three Sisters garden of corn, beans and squash 1271:49-51

Three Sisters bean seed plantings, how to do 1271:132-136
Three Sisters garden designs, in the round, in a barrel, trellis, how to make 1271:53-57

IROQUOIS INDIANS—GARDENS—BAGS
Three Sisters seed bag, leather, fabric, making 1271:190

IROQUOIS INDIANS—GARDENS—BASKETRY
Three Sisters birch basket for seeds, birch bark, raffia, corn husks, making 1271:189-190

IROQUOIS INDIANS—GARDENS—HANDICRAFTS
Three Sisters digging stick, how to make 1271:313

IROQUOIS INDIANS—GARDENS—POUCHES
Three Sisters seed-saving pouches, felt, leather, yarn, how to make 1271:80-82

IROQUOIS INDIANS—GARDENS—SEEDS
Three Sisters seed bank of heirloom seeds, how to do 1271:83-86

IROQUOIS INDIANS—HANDICRAFTS
Birchbark stencils, making 223:36-37
Health charm, making 223:82-83
Love fetish, making 223:81-82
Moosehair embroidery, making 223:62-64
Three Sisters bean-bottled soup gifts, how to make 1271:43
Three Sisters cookbook, how to make 1271:108-109

IROQUOIS INDIANS—HATS
Iroquois hat, making 223:51-53

IROQUOIS INDIANS—HEADBANDS
Woman's headband, fabric, making 1323:19

IROQUOIS INDIANS—HEADDRESSES
Headdress, feathers, making 1323:6-7
Headdress, paper, feathers, making 1699:56
Warrior's headdress, skull cap type, leather, wood, fabric, making 1323:6-8

IROQUOIS INDIANS—HOUSEHOLD
Birchbark containers, making 223:33-35
Pots, hanging rack, storage bag, making 223:21
Three Sisters birchbark cup, how to make 1271:314

IROQUOIS INDIANS—HOUSES
Longhouse, making 223:14-16; 227:8-9; 574:131
Longhouse, paper, crepe paper, pattern, making 1170:21
Longhouse, wood, twigs, fabric, leather, making 1368:20-21
Longhouses, how to draw 591:6-7
Three Sisters wigwam, poles, cord, making 1271:181-184
Wigwam (wickiup), making 223:16-18

IROQUOIS INDIANS—JEWELRY
Fetish necklaces, felt bag, making 1699:65
Silver brooches and silver gorget, making 1323:21
Woman's bead necklace, making 1323:19

IROQUOIS INDIANS—MASKS
Bushy head mask, making 327:48
Corn husk mask, making 227:64; 324:45; 204:110-113
False Face mask, making 482:84-85; 596:32-35
False Face mask, cardboard, paints, making 1699:73
False Face Society mask 462:28-29
False Face Society papier-mache mask, making 223:73-76
False Face style mask, mold method, mache method, miniature, easy 327:12-15
False Faces and masks, carved and whittled, making 466:87-89
Feathers for False Face mask, crepe paper, making 327:15

Husk Face Society corn husk mask, making 63:28-29
Husk Face Society mask, making 223:76-78
Shaman mask, paper, yarn, cornhusks, pattern, making 1170:11

IROQUOIS INDIANS—MUSICAL INSTRUMENTS
Rattles, gourd type, making 223:78-80

IROQUOIS INDIANS—NATURE FESTIVALS
Corn growing festivals 419:148-149

IROQUOIS INDIANS—OWNER STICKS
Three Sisters possession stick, how to make 1271:314

IROQUOIS INDIANS—PEACE PIPES
Peace pipe, miniature, making 223:84-85

IROQUOIS INDIANS—POUCHES
Beaded pouch, buckskin or canvas, making 1323:23

IROQUOIS INDIANS—QUILL WORK
Quill work, making 223:65-69

IROQUOIS INDIANS—ROACHES
Roach, making 281:14-15

IROQUOIS INDIANS—STORYTELLING
Storytelling bag, paper bag, crayons, making 1699:181

IROQUOIS INDIANS—WAMPUM
Strings of wampum, macaroni, food coloring, string, making 1699:34-35
Wampum weaving with bead, making 223:58-62

IROQUOIS INDIANS—WEAPONS
Tomahawk and war club, making 1323:23
Tomahawk, making 714:25

IROQUOIS INDIANS—WEAVING
Finger weaving a sash, making 223:56-57

IRVING, WASHINGTON—COOKERY
Apple pie, recipe 57:75
Gingersnaps, recipe 57:75
Ichabod Crane's baked pumpkin mousse, recipe 1353:18
Speculaas, recipe 57:74

ISLAM—ART—HANDICRAFTS
Islamic pattern decorated shoe or gift box, how to do 1632:46-47

ISLAM—FESTIVALS
Historical events of Islam celebrations, activities and projects for classrooms 1393:275-278

ISRAEL
Activities, flags, games, songs, dances, recipes 1381:121-124

ISRAEL—BIRTHDAYS
Bar Mitzvah for boy's celebration 660:58-60
Bas Mitzvah for girl's celebration 660:60-61
Birthday customs 488:66-69
Celebrations of birthdays in Israel 474:82-83

ISRAEL—CITRUS GROVES
Citrus grove planting, making 117:140

ISRAEL—COOKERY
Apple burger meatballs, recipe 662:83-87
Apple cake, recipe 1380:38
Apple noodle kugel, recipe 1380:17
Applesauce, recipe 909:115
Avocado with honey sauce, recipe 643:12
Bagel cookies, ka'achei sumsum, recipe 1427:185-186
Bean soup, recipe 1001:33
Beef casserole, cholent, recipe 643:32
Birth celebration, chick peas and parsley salad, recipe 1220:135
Blintzes from Romania, recipe 117:162-163
Blintzes, recipe 1653:70
Blueberry filling for blintzes, recipe 1441:27
Carrot kugle, recipe 1660:34

Carrot, sweet potato, apple tzimmes, recipe 1244:104-105
Challah bread, recipe 88:28-29; 492:86-89; 1427:186-187
Charoses, apple and nut paste, recipe 1380:42
Cheese blintzes, recipe 1001:30; 1265:87-88
Chicken soup with knaidlach, matzo ball dumplings in chicken soup, recipe 1165:60-61; 1441:20
Chicken soup, recipe 518:21-24; 1139:108-109
Chicken stuffed with oranges, recipe 446:34-35; 1001:43
Chicken with oranges, microwave recipe 1211:34-35
Chocolate chip cookies from United States, recipe 117:167
Cream cheese labneh, recipe 1653:54
Date and nut pudding recipe 643:39
Dessert shish kebab, recipe 1441:22
Doughnuts, recipe 1001:23
Egg and tomato scramble, recipe 100:120
Eggplant salad, recipe 1139:107-108
Eggplant, recipe 793:56
Falafel balls, recipe 1204:78-79
Falafel croquettes, recipe 667:227
Falafel in pita, recipe 1001:21
Falafel, chick pea balls in pita bread, recipe 1427:187
Falafel, chick pea patties, recipe 1477:116
Falafel, chick peas, recipe 1441:28
Falafel, recipe 117:159; 967:35; 1653:107-108
Fish, baked, recipe 1001:27
Fruit fritters, recipe 1427:188
Fruit soup, recipe 895:73-74; 1001:29
Ground meat with sesame sauce, recipe 1001:26
Haman's pockets (hamantaschen), cookies, recipe 72:108-109
Hamantaschen Purim cakes, recipe 667:229-230
Holiday date bits, recipe 188:37
Honey clusters, recipe 794:46; 1381:122-123
Hummus and tehima, recipe 117:160
Hummus bi tahina, recipe 1653:82
Hummus, chick peas, recipe 1139:105-106
Hummus, recipe 1204:79
Ilana yeast cake, recipe 643:14
Israel map cookies, recipe, making 117:28
Israeli menu 1001:16
Israeli salad, recipe 1001:19
Kibbutz carrot salad, recipe 1001:25
Kichels, biscuits, recipe 1165:62
Kipferln cookies from Austria, recipe 117:166
Kishuim, squash and tomato dish, recipe 874:63
Latkes (potato pancakes), recipe 801:106-107; 1427:191
Latkes, cheese, recipe 909:115
Latkes, potato, recipe 643:42; 1380:24; 1653:125
Latkes, recipe, making 187:35; 1455:158
Lemony coconut cookies, recipe 1265:89
Lukshen kugel, noodle pudding, recipe 1165:61-62
Mandelbrot, almond cookies, recipe 1165:61
Marak perot, fruit soup from Russia, recipe 117:156
Matzo ball soup, recipe 1380:34
Matzo balls, recipe 1381:123
Matzo layer cake, recipe 1001:45
Matzo meal pancakes, recipe, making 88:26-28
Meatballs, recipe 667:228
Meat-eating habits in Israel 662:83-87
Melon dessert, recipe 1001:46; 1280:22-23
Moroccan salad, recipe 643:15
Noodle pudding, recipe 667:229

Noodle pudding, sweet, recipe 895:75
North African chicken soup, recipe 1001:40
Pita sandwiches, recipe 117:158
Pita, flat bread, recipes 1427:191; 1653:81
Plavah sponge cake, recipe 643:28
Poppy seed cake, recipe 1001:36; 1280:24-25
Poppy seed candy, recipe 1427:192
Potato knishes, recipe 1380:27
Potato pancakes, recipe 1265:85-86
Recipe names in the Hebrew Alphabet 1001:48
Russian salad, recipe 1001:32
Sabbath stew, recipe 1001:38
Salat hatzulecm, eggplant salad from Greece, recipe 117:157
Scnecken buns, recipe 117:164-165
Sesame bars, recipe 1204:71
Shakshooka egg and tomato dish, recipe 117:161
Tehima sauce, recipe 117:159
Turkey schnitzel, recipe 1001:35
Tzimmes fleishig, stewed carrots with meat, recipe 1165:63
Tzimmes milchig, stewed carrots, recipe 1165:63

ISRAEL—COSTUMES

Abraham costume 213:18-20
Holiday date bits, recipe, costume 188:37
Sarah costume 213:16-18

ISRAEL—DANCES

Around We Go dance, how to do 1494:163-164
Brotherhood dances 542:34-47
Hora chain dance 474:110-112
Hora dance and costume picture 1000:48-51
Hora dance, how to do 1362:145; 1381:123
Hora, circle folk dance, how to do 1477:96
Hora, how to do 117:177
Israel Independence Day dances 542:82-102
Mayim Mayim dance, how to do 1494:169-170
Sheep shearing dances 542:142-144
Sulam Yaakov dance, how to do 1494:171-172
Tzadik Katamar Yifrach dance, how to do 1494:167-168
Wine Festival dances 542:106-109
Ya Tsa Tsa, Via La La song and dance game 1114:50-51

ISRAEL—DOLLS

Dolls, coming home paper dolls, patterns, making 117:72-73

ISRAEL—FESTIVALS

Birthday chair raising in place of spanking 660:42
Festivals and celebrations, maps, flags, crafts, making 1305:46-55
Hamish Asar Bishvat, the New Year of the trees 474:63-64
Hanukkah celebration 631:102
Independence Day flowers of Israel, embroidered, making 543:116-117
Independence Day Israeli flag, paper, making 543:112
Independence Day pebble art, making 543:114-115
Independence Day Star of David, making 543:113
Independence Day wall hanging, burlap pictures, making 543:120-121
Rosh Hashanah to Yom Kippur, activities and projects for classrooms 1393:44-46
Simhat Torah celebration 631:78
Sukkot Harvest Festival, activities and projects for classrooms 1393:47-48
Tree planting festival 566:38
Tree planting festival celebration 566:38

Tu Bishvat celebration, crafts, foods, games, making 557:39-44
Tu Bishvat dance 557:40
Yom Kippur celebration 601:62-63

ISRAEL—FESTIVALS—COOKERY

Israel Independence Day falafel, recipe 543:118

ISRAEL—FESTIVALS—GAMES

Lag B'Omer game, tuna fish cans, paper, patterns, making 1427:195
Tu Bishvat games 557:43

ISRAEL—FESTIVALS—HANDICRAFTS

Tu B'Shevat beginning of spring drawing activities 1337:26-29
Tu Bishvat forest trees, paper, making 557:42
Tu Bishvat window boxes, paper, making 557:41
Yom Ha'Atzma'ut, Israeli Independence Day drawing activities 1337:40-41

ISRAEL—FLAG

Pattern of flag 557:44

ISRAEL—FOLKLORE

Crowded fable play 1212:68-73
"Peace and Quiet" flannel board story, patterns, making 1603:184-189
Problems! Problems! fable playlet 1212:53-58

ISRAEL—GAMES

Adjuim, the square and jar game, how to play 1708:36-37
Adras, Israeli tic tac toe game 117:53
Bli Yadayim, without hands game, how to play 1494:158
Dreidle game, gift box lid, dreidle, making 1427:194
Flyaway birds game 557:43
Hamesh Avanim, five stones game, how to play 1718:12-13
Helpless hands game 557:43
Hold the rope game 58:42-43
Ice cream train (Yesh Li Gleeda) musical game 1116:23
Leg relay game, how to play 1497:39-40
Sabra (bom in Israel) games 117:52-53
Tea and rice musical game 1116:51
Tiger's ball game, how to play 1497:38
Without hands hat game, how to play 1477:69

ISRAEL—HANDICRAFTS

Ceramic tile tray, making 117:150
Door Mezuzah and pendants, wood and wire, making 889:50-56
Glass glue decorations, making 117:147
Hiker's stick, wooden, making 117:151
Magen David decorations, chain, pin wheel, hanging, star, making 117:144-145
Mizrah hanging, fabric, making 117:143
Paper-cutting, making 117:146
Stained glass window, black paper, tissue paper, tape, making 1381:124
Stitchery, embroidery, patterns 1427:183

ISRAEL—HARVEST FESTIVALS—HANDICRAFTS

Succot, gazebo, leaves, sticks, glue, shoe box, making 1427:171
Succoth Festival of the Booths miniature succah in shoe box, making 1249:33-35

ISRAEL—HISTORY—COOKERY

History of foods and cookery in Israel 667:210-221

ISRAEL—INDEPENDENCE DAY—COOKERY

Aliyah fleet center- piece, recipe 116:87
Eggplant frisbees, recipe 116:89
Eggplant salad, recipe 116:88

Falafel chick pea patties, recipe 1112:107-109
Falafel fried balls, recipe 1289:155
Falafel, recipe 116:91
Fruit soup, recipe 116:86
Golda Meir's chocolate chip cookies, recipe 1112:109-110
Jaffa orange sorbet, recipe 1112:110-111
Kibbutz vegetable salad, recipe 1112:105-107
Pita sandwiches, recipe 116:90
Tehina sauce, recipe 116:92
Trifle from England and Israel, recipe 116:93-94

ISRAEL—INDEPENDENCE DAY—PARTIES
Invitations, decorations, menus, and games, making 2:58-65
ISRAEL—LANGUAGE
Jewish names for the months of the year 1031:50
Numbers one through ten in Hebrew 1366:unp.
ISRAEL—LULLABIES
Numi Nim 780:45
ISRAEL—MAPS
Map of Israel, bread dough, recipe 117:29
ISRAEL—MOSAICS
Mosaic tile, making 117:148-149
ISRAEL—MUSICAL INSTRUMENTS
Instruments made of plants, making 1427:180
ISRAEL—NATURE FESTIVALS
Nature festivals and rituals 419:28-38
ISRAEL—NEW YEAR'S DAY
Holy days in Israel 489:107-113
ISRAEL—NEW YEAR—COOKERY
Honey clusters, recipe 1427:190
ISRAEL—NUMBERS
Negev numbers 557:40
ISRAEL—OASIS
Palm tree oasis, planting, making 117:138-139
ISRAEL—PARTIES
Israel Independence Day party, ideas for 117:141
ISRAEL—PUPPET PLAYS
Blessing of the Tree 4:37-40
ISRAEL—PUPPETS
Solomon and the Bees puppet show 756:48
ISRAEL—RHYMES
Potche Potche baby clapping rhyme 780:60
ISRAEL—RITUALS
Growing up ritual 695:97-100
ISRAEL—SEALS
Seals, making from sculpta mold 525:43
ISRAEL—SOLAR COOKERS
Solar cooker, making 117:262
ISRAEL—SONGS
Haida, Haida round song 1115:89
Night Has Descended, lullaby 1220:154
Shalom round song 1115:88
ISRAEL—SYMBOLS
Symbols for crafts, patterns, making 117:152-153
ISRAEL—TEMPLES
Herod's temple, patterns, build of cardboard 117:200-207
ISRAEL—TOYS
Dreidel of Israel, wooden, making 889:46-49
Haman knocker from Israel; history of and how to make 495:40-44
ISWA INDIANS—COOKERY
Prince Albert pumpkin bread, recipe 424:57

ITALY
Activities, flags, games, songs, dances, recipes 1381:163-166
Folklore, foods, games, music, festivals, activities 1378:102-146
Traditions, customs, geography, ecology, aesthetic awareness units 1378:102-146
ITALY—BIRTHDAYS
Birthday customs 488:70-72
ITALY—CHRISTMAS
Celebration of Christmas in Italy
Christmas customs 149:43-44; 218:43-45; 425:15-17; 473:56-57; 474:151; 601:111; 1049:88; 1717:22-23
Christmas tree and decorations, how to make 593:56-63
History of Christmas in Italy 704:43
Natale celebration 497:82-91
ITALY—CHRISTMAS—COOKERY
Almond macaroons, recipe 1230:69; 1566:69
Anguille in Umido Al Vino Bianco (stewed eel), recipe 1128:76
Artichokes with garlic and oil, recipe 497:88
Baccala alla Romana (codfish Roman style), recipe 1128:80
Baccala Italian salt cod, recipe 497:88
Baked cod fish, recipe 1230:66
Bread, Italian Christmas bread, recipe 704:50-53
Candy, Sienese nougat candy, recipe 704:48-49
Cannoli, recipe 1230:68; 1566:68
Cassata alla Siciliana (Sicilian cake), recipe 1666:95-96
Cod, recipe 1566:66
Eel, fried, recipe 1566:67
Fried eel, recipe 1230:67
Frittata (pancake omelet), recipe 703:29-31
Fritto misto di pesci fish fry, recipe 1128:79
Fritto misto, recipe 497:88
Lenticchie in umido (stewed lentils), recipe 1666:93-94
Lentils with hot and sweet sausage, recipe 497:88
Lentils with sausage, recipe 1230:66; 1566:66
Linguine con funghi (linguini with mushrooms), recipe 1666:94
Mixed fry of vegetables, recipe 1230:67
Orange and onion salad, recipe, making 1128:80
Panettone (Italian Christmas bread), recipe 1128:82; 1666:95
Panettone, recipe 497:88
Ricotta cheese pie, recipe, making 704:45-47
Risotto con frutti di marc (rice with shellfish), recipe 1128:77
Spaghetti with tuna and anchovies, recipe 1128:78
Spaghetti with tuna, recipe 1230:67; 1566:67
Strufoli dessert, recipe 1230:69
Strufoli, recipe 1566:69
Uova tonnate (tuna stuffed eggs), recipe 1666:94
Vegetable fry, recipe 1566:67
Vongole oreganate (stuffed baked clams), recipe 1128:76
Zuppa di cozze (mussel soup), recipe 1128:78
ITALY—CHRISTMAS—DECORATIONS
Modern ceppo, making 497:90-91
Nativity scene figures from clay, making 273:73-75
Quilled star, colored paper, pattern, making 1230:73
Quilled star, paper, patterns, making 1566:72-73
Stained glass window, paper, tissue paper, pattern, making 1230:70-71; 1566:70-71

ITALY—CHRISTMAS—FOLKLORE

"Legend of Befana" Christmas tree decorations, patterns, making 1378:124-126

ITALY—CHRISTMAS—HANDICRAFTS

Flower chain, making 705:54-55

Napkin holder, Christmas tree napkin holder, making 704:44

Nativity scene, felt, pipe cleaners, beads, paints, making 1575:24-27

Nutshell babies, Christmas tree ornaments, making 795:16

Presepio Nativity scene, paper, patterns, making 1305:61

Tree chain, making 705:50-53

ITALY—COOKERY

Almond ice cream, recipe 321:23

Almond macaroons (amaretti), cookies, recipe 72:45-46

Amaretti cookies, recipe 1378:135

Anise cookies, recipe 1452:111

Antipasto platter, recipe 188:32

Antipasto salad, recipe 1265:51

Antipasto, before the food, recipe 1165:108

Bean and tuna fish salad, recipe 1551:34-35

Biscotti ai pignoli (pine nut cookies), recipe 1378:137

Biscuit Tortoni dessert, recipe 1280:37

Biscuit Tortoni, recipe 1009:42

Bisignano spinach, recipe 1009:36

Blueberry spumoni dessert, recipe 1452:113

Bread, recipe 1055:208

Bruschetta open sandwich, bread, basil, tomatoes, recipe 1392:unp

Calzone, recipe 1665:101

Cannoli a la Siciliana, recipe 88:139

Cannoli, recipe 1265:52

Cappuccino coffee, recipe 66:19

Caramel oranges, recipe 66:39

Cassata, Siciliana dessert, recipe 1378:136

Cauliflower, Italian style, recipe 1009:38

Chicken broth with beaten egg, recipe 530:86-87

Chicken risotto, recipe 321:22

Chicken, fried, recipe 895:77-78

Chicken, hunter's style, recipe 1009:34

Chinese pasta, recipe 1009:28

Chocolate cream, recipe 530:89-90

Colored peppers pizza, recipe 1665:100

Cucumber raita, recipe 1665:59

Eggplant and vegetable relish, recipe 667:144-145

Fettuccine Alfredo, recipe 1452:110

Fettucine Alfredo, parmesan sauce with pasta 1165:111

Fettucine, egg noodles with butter and cheese, recipe 874:22

Fetuccine with mushrooms and cream, recipe 1373:27

Focaccia flat bread with sun-dried tomatoes, recipe 1265:49-50

Frittata egg dish, recipe 1380:10

Frittata, omelet, recipe 1165:108

Gnocchi (potato dumplings), recipe 801:108-109

Granita di limone, lemon water ice, recipe 1551:40-41

Green salad, recipe 321:27

Halibut with tomato, recipe 321:27

Ham and melon dish, recipe 1380:35

Herbed zucchini, recipe 895:81

Hero sandwiches 187:2

History of foods and cookery in Italy 88:125-132; 667:93-136

Italian bread, recipe 1287:unp.

Italian chicken and spaghetti, microwave recipe 1263:90-91

Italian ice, recipe 1378:135

Italian menu 1009:18

Italian pizza, recipe 794:34-35

Italian popcorn, microwave recipe 1263:22

Italian salad dressing, recipe 1009:23

Lasagna, baked, recipe 874:53; 1381:165

Lazy lasagne, microwave recipe 1263:100

Lemon ice dessert, microwave recipe 1211:40-41

Lemon ice, recipe 1452:112

Marinara sauce, recipe 1244:59

Meatballs, broiled, recipe 1169:52-53

Minestrone soup, recipe 518:10-14; 874:30; 1551:32-33

Minestrone vegetable soup, recipe 66:21

Minestrone, recipe 1009:24

Mozzarella in a carriage, recipe 667:4

Neapolitan lasagna, recipe 662:58-63

Neapolitan pizza, recipe 1551:42-44

Noodles and beans, recipe 1122:51

Osso buco, veal dish, recipe 321:25

Pane unatata, garlic bread, recipe 1165:112

Pasta dough, recipe 1378:134

Pasta e fagioli, noodle and bean soup, recipe 1165:109

Pasta with ham and leek, recipe 1551:36-37

Pasta, homemade, recipe 1244:54-55; 1373:18-19

Pasta, how to cook 1373:22-23

Pasta, recipe 88:133-134

Pasta, with soft cheese, recipe 66:32

Pesto Genovese, recipe 667:142

Pesto, recipe 1244:58

Pizza dough, recipe 1665:98

Pizza muffins, recipe 1413:22-23; 1660:18

Pizza Napolitana, recipe 321:26

Pizza sauce, no-cook, recipe 1009:41

Pizza sticks, microwave recipe 1263:54

Pizza topping, hamburger seasoned, recipe 1009:41

Pizza, cool rise, recipe 88:138-139

Pizza, dough and toppings, recipe 1560:16-17

Pizza, history of 1423:unp

Pizza, Margherita pizza, recipe 1195:12-13

Pizza, Neopolitan, recipe 66:23

Pizza, dough and sauce, recipe 871:85-88; 1009:40; 1113:6-7; 1423:unp

Polenta cornmeal dish, recipe 1380:28

Polenta, recipe 88:134; 1665:65

Pollo alla cacciatore, chicken cacciatore, recipe 1452:108

Pork chops, Italian style, recipe 1009:33

Primavera sauce, fresh vegetable pasta sauce, recipe 1165:110

Rice with seafood, recipe 530:87-88

Rice with zucchini, microwave recipe 1211:28-29

Rice, Milan style, recipe 667:142-143

Risi e bisi, recipe 88:136-137; 1068:unp

Risotto con scampi, recipe 967:36

Risotto Milanese style, recipe 858:unp

Risotto rice dish, recipe 1009:25; 1380:22

Risotto with sausage, recipe 1551:38-39

Risotto, rice and chicken dish, recipe 1665:114-115

Rosemary sauce, recipe 1244:59

Sage sauce, recipe 1244:59

Salad dressing, recipe 874:67

Salsa al limone, lemon cream sauce for pasta, recipe 1165:110-111

Sauce Bolognese, recipe 88:135-136

Spaghetti and sauce, recipe 1169:50-51
Spaghetti Bolognese, recipe 321:28; 1113:46-47;
    1373:26
Spaghetti sauce, recipe 874:66-67
Spaghetti with broccoli, recipe 66:37
Spaghetti with garlic and oil, recipe 793:46
Spaghetti with marinara sauce, recipe 1380:16
Spaghetti with meatballs, recipe 871:40-42
Spaghetti with meat sauce, recipe 1009:31
Spaghetti with tomato sauce, recipe 895:79-80
Spaghetti, recipe 1381:165; 1413:36-37
Spaghetti/pizza pie, microwave recipe 1263:96-97
Spinach Bisignano, recipe 1652:28-29
Spinaci, olio e limone, spinach, oil, lemon, recipe 1452:109
Stracciatella, Italian chicken soup, recipe 1653:8
Stracciatella, recipe 321:21
Straw and hay noodles, recipe 1009:27
Strawberry frullato drink, recipe 1380:12
Strawberry ice cream, recipe 66:27
Tagliatelle with Bolognese sauce, recipe 66:34
Tomato sauce and meatballs, recipe 1378:135
Tomato sauce and mozzarella cheese pizza, recipe
    1665:100
Tomato sauce, recipe 514:138-139
Tuna and bean salad, recipe 321:20
Vegetable risotto, recipe 321:25
Wine custard, recipe 667:145
Zucchina with parrnigiano, recipe 321:22

ITALY—COSTUMES
Antipasto platter, recipe, costume 188:32
Italian Tyroleans costumes drawing 988:31
Tyrol costumes drawing 988:44-45

ITALY—DANCES
La Monferrina: the Corrente dance, how to do 1378:115-116
Tarantella dance and costume picture 1000:4-7
Tarantella dance, how to do 1362:143

ITALY—DOLLS
Angelo of Italy doll, making 494:144-156

ITALY—DRAMA
Punch and Judy show 474:96-98

ITALY—EASTER
Easter egg customs in Italy 201:25

ITALY—EASTER—COOKERY
Egg tucked in dough basket, recipe 1378:128-131

ITALY—FACE PAINTING
Venetian mask, how to paint 1533:92-93

ITALY—FESTIVALS
Cricket Festival celebration 566:16-17; 601:90
Epiphany; Befana, history of 709:116
Festa del Grillo, the Cricket 474:58-59
Festival of Las Fallas-Valencia 474:16-17
Festival of Piedigrotto (foot of the grotto) 474:20-21
Festival of the Alban Hills 474:59-60
Festivals and celebrations, maps, flags, crafts, making
    1305:56-66
Italian Feast Days celebrations 667:136-138
Leonardo da Vinci's birthday; paint portrait of self, making 1199:82-83
Maria Montessori's birthday; celebrate with fraction fun math activity, how to do 1199:197
Santa Lucia's Day, how to celebrate 1378:122-123

ITALY—FESTIVALS—COOKERY
Epiphany bean cake, recipe 709:120
Santa Lucia's cereal, recipe 1378:136

ITALY—FESTIVALS—DECORATIONS
Cricket Festival cricket house, berry basket, making
    1539:98-99

ITALY—FESTIVALS—DOLLS
Epiphany; Befana doll, making 709:117-119

ITALY—FESTIVALS—MASKS
Carnival mask, paper plate, yarn, making 1574:8-9
Carnival mask, papier-mache over clay mold, making
    1195:26-27
Venetian Carnival mask, papier-mache, paints, making
    1295:13

ITALY—FOLKLORE
A Twist of Dough, based on a traditional tale from Italy
    139:83-84
"Buchettino" flannel board story, patterns, making
    1604:98-100
Panettone, based on a traditional Italian tale 139:158-162
Pinocchio toy, making 346:30
Pinocchio's nose grew, pop-up, making 1388:54-56
"The Story of Campriano" folktale and activities
    1478:69-75

ITALY—FOLKLORE—COOKERY
Minestrone soup, recipe 1478:79
Pinocchio cookies, recipe 346:48
Pinto Smalto story and recipe for marzipan and coconut
    kisses, making 364:90-100

ITALY—FOLKLORE—GAMES
Game of Goose board game, posterboard, paints, making
    1478:78

ITALY—FORTS
Mount Cassino Fort 212:104-114

ITALY—GAMES
Balito game 383:100
Bocce game 1074:191; 1146:38-39
Briscola card games 1132:20-21
Campana, hopscotch game 1426:28-29
Cencio Mollo (the wet handkerchief) game 1378:114
Chicken Market game 383:99; 602:96-97
Croatia game 383:100
Five Men's Morris game, how to play 1688:42-45
Follow-chase game 602:97
Follow-through tag game 383:99
Hopscotch game, how to play 1507:77-79
Il Cucuzzaro, pumpkin planter game, how to play
    1378:114; 1494:108
Italian wall marbles game 1119:32
Le Bocce game 383:100
Lotto (lottery) game, cardboard, pictures, making
    1378:113-114
Mora game, how to play 1507:80
Morra game 383:102; 572:46-47; 956:102-103
Morra, how many fingers game 474:45-46
Palm ball game, how to play 1507:81
Scopa card game 1132:22-23
Tarantella musical game 1116:57-59
Tombola game, how to make and play 1195:25

ITALY—HANDICRAFTS
Bookbinding, how to bind a book 856:124-127
Byzantine plate, clay, making 1070:60-62
Corsage pin purse, leather and felt, making 889:21-26
Cross stitch sailing boat, yarn, making 298:256-257
Egg tucked in dough basket, making 298:102-103
Pugillares notebooks, wax paper, brown yarn, making
    1332:109-112

139

St. Francis of Assisi pine cone bird feeders, making 1378:111

St. Francis of Assisi animal mobile, patterns, making 1378:109-110

ITALY—HOUSES

Small house model, making 494:150-155

ITALY—LANGUAGE

Finger plays and rhymes in Italian 1583:149

Italian names, numbers, colors, days of week 1378:137-138

Italian seasons, months, phrases, everyday words 1378:138-140

Numbers one to ten in Italian 394:unp

ITALY—MAGIC TRICKS

Quick Italian coin trick, how to do 1270:10-11

ITALY—MASKS

Masked ball half mask, making 1486:10-11

ITALY—MOSAICS

Mosaic, ceramic tiles, how to make 525:54-55

ITALY—MUSICAL INSTRUMENTS

Tarantella tambourine, paper plates, bells, making 1310:142

ITALY—NAMES

Naming Days information 695:26-28

ITALY—NUMBERS

Numbers one to ten in Italian language 394:unp

ITALY—PAINTERS

Painting of egg and gold like Gentile da Fabiano, recipe for paint 1372:24-25

ITALY—PUPPET PARTY

Feathered hat and headband, making 294:120

Folk art window banners, making 294:121

Pinocchio centerpiece, making 294:122-123

Puppet invitations and place mats, making 294:114-115

Puppet theater, making 294:124-125

Tambourine favors, making 294:118-119

Theater cake and puppets, making 294:116-117

Theater puppets, making 294:126-127

ITALY—PUPPETS

Marionettes, wire, newspaper, yarn, making 1338:89-92

Puppets, glove, making 626:64-66

Rain in the face hand puppet, making 298:112-113

ITALY—SONGS

Dona Nobis Pacem round song 1115:90

Ego Sum Pauper round song 1115:86

Hush-a-bye, My Lovely Child, lullaby 1220:148

Michael's Rooster, traditional song, Italy 139:136

ITALY—TOYS

Ancient bead rattle toy, making 1027:44-46

Piggy in the Pen toy, making 297:208-209

ITALY—VOLCANOES

Vulcanian eruption, model volcano demonstrates 1455:78

ITALY—WEAVING

Rag weaving, making 298:136

ITALY, ANCIENT—COSTUMES

Caesar, white fabric, gold spray paint, glitter, making 1656:155-158

Cleopatra, white, black and gold fabric, gold vinyl and braid, making 1656:159-162

IVORY COAST. *See also* **COTE D' IVOIRE**

IVORY COAST—CHRISTMAS—COOKERY

Avocat Epice (avocado boat), recipe 1666:32

IVORY COAST—CLOTHING

Fabric painting with mud, making 856:84-87

Korhogo people mud cloth, fabric, mud, designs given, making 1633:116-119

IVORY COAST—COOKERY

Calalou, eggplant and okra stew, recipe 1165:33-34

Chicken a la n'gatietro, fried chicken in peanut sauce, recipe 1165:34

Kyekyire paano, toasted cornmeal cookies, recipe 1165:35

Tiba yoka, baked bananas, recipe 1165:35

IVORY COAST—DOLLS

Grass doll, making 1027:80-81

IVORY COAST—FESTIVALS—COOKERY

Eid al-Fitr; aloca (fried plantain slices), recipe 1666:32

IVORY COAST—HANDICRAFTS

Andinkira clay pins, symbols giving, making 1414:44-45

Andinkira prints on cloth, making 1414:45-46

Baule gold weights, flour clay, making 1022:34-37

IVORY COAST—MASKS

Baule mask, papier-mache, pattern, making 1022:30-32

Elephant mask, making 856:75

IVORY COAST—PAINTINGS

Senufo Tribe mud painting, duck cloth, fabric dyes, making 1716:88-89

IVORY COAST—RHYMES

Ivory Coast bouncing rhyme 780:79

J

JACK AND THE BEANSTALK

Giant, mother, boy masks, paper, patterns, making 92:54-57

Hen that Laid the Golden Egg, paper, patterns, making 92:58-59

Jack and the Beanstalk, picture, making 93:93

Puppets, costumes, masks, cooking, science, math, music activities 1358:104-121

Puppets, paper bags, patterns, making 940:56-60

JACOB'S LADDER

Jacob's ladder, making 120:143-145

JACOBS, JOSEPH

"Johnny-Cake," recipe 1216:13

JAINS—FESTIVALS—DECORATIONS

Baisakhi pop-up card, making 1387:52

Diwali Festival of Lights pop-up card, making 1387:24

JAMAICA

Activities, flags, games, songs, dances, recipes 1381:29-32

JAMAICA—CHRISTMAS

Christmas in Jamaica customs 510:11

JAMAICA—CHRISTMAS—COOKERY

Caribbean banana bread, recipe 1666:212

Curried meat, recipe 1666:212

Jamaica Coat of Arms (rice and peas), recipe 1666:213

Jerk pork and chicken, recipe 1666:213

JAMAICA—COOKERY

Akkra, fried black-eyed peas, recipe 1652:31

Arrowroot biscuits, cookies, recipe 72:164-165

Banana fritters, recipe 1380:40

Bananas, baked, recipe 1381:31

Beef patties, recipe 510:32

Coconut rice and peas, recipe 895:84

Coconut sherbet, making 187:12

Curried goat, recipe 895:83; 1593:118

Escovitch, fried fish in marinade, recipe 1165:212-213

Fish stew, recipe 1381:31

Fried plantains (bananas), recipe 895:85

Ham banana roll, recipe 1381:31

Jamaica pepperpot, recipe 967:37

Jamaican patties, ground beef, recipe 1660:70

Jerked pork and chicken, recipe 1165:213-214

Johnny cakes or bakes, recipe 1652:34

Mango clown, recipe 858:unp

Plantain fritters, recipe 1593:118

Rice and beans, recipe 1538:26-27

Rice and peas dish, recipe 1652:32; 1165:215

Stamp and go, codfish snacks, recipe 1165:214

JAMAICA—GAMES

Ring tunes game 474:88-90

Sally Water game, how to play 1494:56

JAMAICA—PUPPETS

Jamaican girl finger puppet, making 128:41

JANICE

"Little Bear Learns to Read the Cookbook," chocolate cake, recipe 1216:59

JAPAN

Activities, flags, games, songs, dances, recipes 1381:71-76

Crafts, folklore, holidays, clothing, food activities 1378:66-101

Culture unit, language, dress, foods, games, bibliographies 574:16-39

Japan, activities, history, foods, games 143:109-140

Japan; reading and writing activities, projects 620:125-144

Traditions, customs, geography, aesthetic awareness units 1378:66-101

JAPAN—BANNER FESTIVAL

Fish kite place mats, invitations, making 294:50

House kite and fish kite, making 294:60-63

Karate belts, making 294:64

Lushea tassels, making 294:64

Wind toys, pinwheels, making 294:58-59

JAPAN—BATIK

Batik, dyed fabric, dyes, wax, patterns, making 1427:200-201

JAPAN—BIRTHDAYS

Birthday celebrations in Japan 695:52-53

Birthday customs 488:73-79

Birthday party for one year old child 660:52-54

Birthday traditions in Japan 472:44

Celebrations of birthdays in Japan 474:83; 474:85

Seven-five-three celebration party 660:55-56

JAPAN—BOATS

Boat from sheeet of paper, making 1477:38

JAPAN—BOOKBINDING

Bookbinding; traditional Japanese way, how to do 1476:27-28

JAPAN—BOOKS

Book, making 70:41

Scrapbook, accordion style, heavy paper, cloth, ribbon, making 1477:25

Seasons accordion book, paper, yarn, ribbons, patterns, making 1332:83-90

JAPAN—CALENDARS

Japanese calendar 574:31

JAPAN—CHERRY BLOSSOMS

Cherry blossom tree, branch and tissue paper blossoms, making 1091:30

Cherry blossom, paper, making 532:58

Cherry blossoms, tissue paper, making 909:31

JAPAN—CHRISTMAS

Christmas customs 149:54; 218:43; 473:65

Christmas tree and decorations, how to make 593:170-173

JAPAN—CHRISTMAS—HANDICRAFTS

Dip and dye paper, making 795:22

Japanese origami ornaments, making 1575:18-19

Tanabata decorations, making 795:6

Thread balls, Christmas tree ornaments, making 795:16-17

JAPAN—CLOTHING

Getas slippers, making 574:23

Kimono decorations, patterns, making 814:68-70

Kimono information 417:13

Kimono, decorated paper, making 1091:31

Kimono, pattern, making 814:51-55

Kimono, short, pattern, making 814:55

Kimonos and fans, making 143:121-122

Kimonos, simple, fabric, paint, making 1378:75-76

Obi belt, pattern, making 814:62-63

Trousers, pattern, making 814:60-62

Yukata jacket, pattern, making 814:58-59

JAPAN—COMPUTERS

Soroban/Analog computer, making 301:113-117

JAPAN—COOKERY

Almond cookies, recipe 1378:93

Almond cubes with fruit, recipe 1378:93

Avocados Fukushima, recipe 814:93
Bean paste soup, recipe 724:23
Bean sprout salad, recipe 814:93-94
Beef sukiyaki, recipe 1378:92
Beef teriyaki, recipe 1265:121-122
Beef, simmered with vegetables (sukiyaki), recipe
    724:28
Broccoli, steamed with sesame dressing, recipe 1265:120
Carved fruit, recipe 1552:40-41
Chawan mushi, eggs steamed in cups, recipe 1452:118
Chicken and egg over rice, recipe 1064:81-82
Chicken and egg soup, recipe 1165:180
Chicken baked in foil (tori no gingami yaki), recipe
    1427:215
Chicken in a pot, recipe 724:32
Chicken rice, recipe 852:28
Chicken teriyaki, recipe 852:20
Chicken wings teriyaki, recipe 1178:54
Chicken, broiled (teriyaki), recipe 724:32
Chopsticks, how to use 1538:38
Cucumber with crab, recipe 724:24
Dashi (seaweed stock), recipe 261:25
Egg roll, recipe 1427:215-216
Egg soup, recipe 1427:216
Egg soup, beaten, microwave recipe 1211:26
Egg-drop soup, recipe 724:23
Eggplant with sesame seeds, recipe 852:22
Eggs steamed in cups, (chawan mushi), recipe 724:38
Fish, broiled with shoyu, recipe 852:26
Fish, salt broiled (shioyaki), recipe 724:37
Fox noodles, recipe 261:28
Fresh pineapple with almond cream, recipe 143:139
Fried fish and vegetables, recipe 895:87-89
Fried rice, recipe 1378:92; 1381:74
Fried squid, recipe 1721:15
Gohan, boiled rice, recipe 1165:181
Golden chestnuts, recipe 261:42
Green tea Bavarian cream, recipe 1452:122
Green tea ice cream, recipe 143:140
Grilled chicken (yakitori), recipe 1552:38-39
Japanese salad, recipe 1427:216-217
Kappa rolls, recipe 261:35
Kushiyaki, shrimp and vegetables on skewers, recipe
    1452:119
Meat-eating habits in Japan 662:93-99
Miso soup, recipe 261:25; 1552:34-35
Mushrooms grilled, recipe 852:22
Noodle pancake, baked, recipe 1380:17
Noodles with lemon ginger sauce, cold, recipe 1380:16
Omlette with peas, rolled, recipe 1552:36-37
Oyako domburi, chicken omelet over rice, recipe
    1165:181
Pickled cabbage salad, recipe 852:26
Prawn and watercress soup, recipe 852:20
Radish flowers, recipe 1629:13
Ramen noodle soup, recipe 1244:46
Rice balls, recipe 1660:42
Rice dumplings, recipe 1093:127
Rice with chicken and vegetables, recipe 530:100-102
Rice, boiled Japanese style, recipe 530:99
Rice, recipe 261:30
Sakura salad, recipe 814:94
Savory steamed custard, recipe 1552:42-44
Seafood with oranges, recipe 814:93
Sesame seed dressing with broccoli, recipe 724:26

Shrimp and vegetables broiled (kushiyaki), recipe 724:35
Shrimp, scrambled egg and vegetables, recipe 1629:12
Soba noodles in broth, recipe 1265:123
Spinach, boiled, recipe 724:27
Steamed broth with chicken, egg and vegetables, recipe
    530:96-98
Strawberries with meringue, recipe 530:102-103
Sukiyaki, recipe 261:31; 794:53; 1427:217
Sukiyaki, simmered beef and vegetables, recipe
    1452:120
Sunomono salad, cucumber or zucchini dressing, recipe
    1660:32
Sunomono, cucumber and shrimp salad, recipe
    1165:180-181
Sunomono, recipe 143:137
Sushi rice, recipe 261:34
Sushi, recipe 1427:218; 1452:121
Sweet and pungent pork balls, recipe 662:93-99
Sweet azuki squares (yokan), cookies, recipe 72:140-141
Sweet bean paste, recipe 1394:20-21
Tempura fried vegetables, recipe 1064:85-87
Tempura, recipe 143:138; 793:67; 871:45-47; 1427:219;
    1653:126
Tentsuyu sauce, recipe 852:25
Teriyaki chicken, recipe 1381:74
Teriyaki, marinated beef, recipe 1165:181
Teriyaki, recipe 143:139
Tofu from soy milk, recipe 1487:26-27
Tofu toss, recipe 188:44
Tofu, recipe 143:137
Tsukemono, Japanese pickles, recipe 1427:220
Tuna fish salad, recipe 852:22
Vegetable pancakes, recipe 1064:83-84
Vegetable rice, recipe 1560:25
Vegetable tempura, recipe 187:28; 852:24
White salad with tofu, recipe 261:19

JAPAN—COSTUMES
Chignon pins, pattern, making 814:63-64
Fan, wood and paper, patterns, making 814:86-87
Furoshiki bundle carrier costume, pattern, making
    814:81-82
Geisha costume 213:142-145
Headpiece, girl's Flower Festival headpiece, pattern,
    making 814:66-67
Japanese kimono costume drawing 988:50-51
Kimono, simple, paper, making 480:121
Samurai costume, fabric, post cards, making 1174:84-85
Tofu toss, recipe, costume 188:44

JAPAN—CREWEL
Crewel, basics and how to make chair cushion 70:44-45

JAPAN—DANCES
Mai dance and costume picture 1000:72-75
Tanko Bushi dance, how to do 1494:51-52

JAPAN—DOLL FESTIVAL
Daruma doll favors, making 294:54
Dolls; Hina, Kokeshi, puppet, making 294:56-57
Fans, making 294:55
Flower tower centerpiece, making 294:52-53
Teahouse cake, making 294:51

JAPAN—DOLLS
Cloth doll, pattern, making 1027:101-104
Daruma doll, papier-mache, balloon, paints, making
    1477:43
Daruma dolls from Japan, history of and how to make
    495:59-63; 497:164

Daruma dolls, plaster of Paris, paper tubes, patterns, making 1427:202; 1427:202
Doll, paper cup, yarn, patterns, making 1311:66-69
Japanese girl doll, making 494:211-230
Japanese lady, 59:10-12
Japanese lady, from tea strainer, fabric, paper, making 1094:50
Japanese paper dolls, making 105:44-47
Kani Ningyo origami doll, paper, making 298:208-209
Kiku doll, pattern, making 814:78-81
Kokeshi doll, cardboard tube, papier-mache, full-size patterns, making 1633:134-135
Kokeshi doll, pattern, making 143:133; 532:33; 814:77-78
Kokeshi dolls, making 167:29-36
Kokeshi string-box doll, pattern, making 814:75-76

JAPAN—DRAGONS
Paper dragon that moves, making 1447:10-11

JAPAN—DRAMA
Drama in Japan 474:103

JAPAN—EARTHQUAKES
Japanese "shaking table" to test how buildings would stand up during earthquake, making 1719:48-51

JAPAN—EATING
Rules for eating with chopsticks 1325:39

JAPAN—FACE MAKEUP
Kabuki face, making using makeup 380:22-23

JAPAN—FACE PAINTING
Ninja warrior face painting, how to do 1306:54

JAPAN—FANS
Fan dance costume, pattern, making 814:64-65
Fan, making 105:1-3
Fan, wood and paper, patterns, making 814:86-87
Fans, posterboard, tongue depressors, making 1427:207
Mikado fan, making 51:180-181
Uchiwa fan, posterboard, tongue depressor, Japanese designs given, making 1633:136-137

JAPAN—FESTIVALS
Anniversaries of the Buddha celebrations 810:38-40
Aoi Matsuri, the Emperor Pays Homage 107:41-45
Bon Festival 280:59-64
Bonten Festival 280:29-30
Boy's Day 574:33
Boys' Festival 280:50-54
Boys' Festival celebration 601:65
Child festivals: Shichi-Go-San, Child Day and Hina Matsuri, Doll's Fest 107:46-55
Children's Day, activities and projects for classrooms 1393:207-208
Dance of the Golden Dragon, a special Matsuri 107:28-30
Dezome-Shiki, the Firemen's Parade 107:67-71
Doll Festival 574:32-33
Doll's Day and Boy's Day, activities, handicrafts, songs, making 909:29-37
Doll's Day party, making 909:31
Festival of the Dead celebration 601:66
Festivals to honor the gods 280:10-12
Fire Festival 280:25-28
First Days Festival 280:91-93
Flower festival, how to celebrate 54:222
Gion celebration 631:58
Gion Festival 280:32-40
Gion Matsuri, the Gods Stop a Plague 107:36-40
Girl's Doll Festival (lena Matsuri) celebration 566:38
Girl's Doll Festival, how to celebrate 54:222

Girls' Day Festival 280:55-58
Girl's Festival celebration 601:64-65
Great Last Day Festival 280:87-88
Hana Matsure American Festival 574:33
Hari-Kuyo, Final Rest for Broken Needles 107:72-75
Harvest Festival celebrations 659:106-107; 826:22-23
Health and Sports Day, foods, games, making 557:12-18
Higan Festival celebration 810:41
Hina Matsuri (Girl's Doll Festival) celebration 566:38
Hina-Matsuri, Doll's Festival 107:53-55; 143:1118; 474:60-61
Hiroshima Day, activities and projects for classrooms 1393:256-258
Hounen-Odori celebration 631:74
Kamaktira Festival 280:69-70
Kanto Matsuri, Harvest Festivals 107:56-58
Matsuri, the Neighborhood Festival 107:11-16
Moon viewing celebration 601:66-67
New Year's Day 280:88-91; 566:36-37; 574:32
Obon Festival celebration 810:42,43
Obon, Buddhist respect for the dead, activities and projects for classrooms 1393:254-255
Okunchi Festival in Nagasaki 280:43-49
One Thousand Person Procession Festival 280:40-43
Peace Festival 280:49
Rice planting and harvesting festivals 280:75-78
Roughhouse Festival 280:13-25
Sapporo Snow Festival 280:65-69
Setsubun Festival celebration 810:43; 280:70-71
Setsubun, Cast Out the Devils 107:59-62
Shichi-Go-San Festival 280:58-59
Shogatsu (New Year's Holiday) 143:117
Snow Festival, sculptures instead of snowmen 107:63-66
Spring Hina-Matsuri Festival, history of 709:147
Spring, Summer, and Fall festivals 280:72-75
Star Festival, Tanabata 143:119; 280:78-80; 574:33; 631:62
Tanabata, a Legend of the Heavens 107:76-78
Tango-No Sekku celebration 631:34
Tango-No-Sekku, Boy's festivals 474:61
Tea ceremony song from Aizu district 1362:140
Tea ceremony, how to celebrate 1378:90-91
Tea ceremony, how to do 1362:140-141
Tonge-no Sekku (Boy's Festival) 143:118
Year End fairs 280:81-86

JAPAN—FESTIVALS—COOKERY
Health and Sports Day lunch, noodles and vegetables, recipe 557:16
Health and Sports Day tea, recipe 557:16-17
Shichi Go San Festival treats, cereal, marshmallows, on skewers, making 1199:263

JAPAN—FESTIVALS—COSTUMES
Kimonos and stars, paper hospital gowns decorated, making 1266:70

JAPAN—FESTIVALS—DECORATIONS
Children's Day carp streamer, paper, paints, making 1629:19
Children's Day stuffed paper fish, making 1539:84-85
Tanabata, Star Festival, poems hung on bamboo branch, making 1629:27

JAPAN—FESTIVALS—DOLLS
Balloon seller doll, tennis balls, paper, making 814:31-32
Doll's Day stand for dolls, making 909:32
Doll, paper, making 814:16-19
Hina-Matsuri, Doll's Festival 107:53-55

Japanese Doll Festival dolls, origami Empress and Emperor, making 1422:23-26

JAPAN—FESTIVALS—FLOWER ARRANGING

Ikebana flower arrangement, making 814:47-50

JAPAN—FESTIVALS—GAMES

Health and Sports Day games 557:17

Ring around the river game, making 1266:76

JAPAN—FESTIVALS—HAIKU

Tanabata Star Festival haiku; branches decorated with haiku, making 1199:155-156

JAPAN—FESTIVALS—HANDICRAFTS

Boy's Festival carp wind sock pattern, fabric, coat hanger, material, making 1219:14-15

Boys' Festival carp windsock, tissue paper, making 1477:60

Children's Day egg figurine, paper, yarn, patterns, making 1633:132-133

Children's Day wind fish, fabric, wire hanger, making 1615:33

Children's Festival, Kodomo-No-Hi, carp, paper, dowels, making 1574:14-15

Doll's Festival, or Hinamatsuri pop-up card, making 1387:26

Flying fish, paper, making 814:36-38

Folding screen, wood and paper, making 814:33-36

Kakemono panel, plastic, making 814:22-23

Kimono party favors, paper, tissue paper, markers, making 1266:74

Magpie bridge and shaped decorations, paper, glue, crayons, making 1266:73

Menu, large paper, making 814:15

Mobile, Mukado-tako, paper, making 814:38-40

Moon viewing class festival, making 134:104

Shichi Go San Festival; treat bags, white freezer wrap, markers, making 1199:261-262

Star cup party favors, paper cups, stickers, making 1266:74

Sticker poem decorations, construction paper, stickers, making 1266:71

Tablecloth and napkin, decorated fabric, making 814:11-14

Tanabata paper decorations, making 856:24-31

Tanabata Star Festival star-gazers; cardboard tubes with tracing paper patterns, making 1199:157-158

Tanabata Star Festival streamers, paper, sticks, making 1477:83

Zabuton cushion, fabric, making 814:27-30

JAPAN—FESTIVALS—KITES

Boy's Day carp kite, making 909:33

Boy's Day Festival carp bag kite, paper bag, making 1083:182

Boy's Festival, carp kite, making 54:223

Children's Day carp kite, making 105:15-16

Children's Day carp kite, paper cup, paper, string, making 1393:208

Children's Day, carp kite, making 1447:14

Kite Festival carp kite, making 709:153-156

JAPAN—FESTIVALS—LANTERNS

Lanterns, paper and balloon lanterns, making 814:23-26

Tanabata hanging lantern, making 298:62-63

JAPAN—FESTIVALS—MASKS

Dragon mask, papier-mache,, making 814:26-27

JAPAN—FESTIVALS—ORIGAMI

Health and Sports Day origami sailboat, making 557:15

JAPAN—FESTIVALS—PARTIES

Tanabata Star Festival, legend, kimonos, poems, decorations, games, play, making 1266:69-78

JAPAN—FESTIVALS—PLAYS

Star Festival, mini-play, script, how to do 1266:77-78

JAPAN—FESTIVALS—PUPPETS

Boy's Day Festival puppet projects, patterns 1083:182

Girl's Day Festival puppet projects, patterns 1083:183-184

Girl's Day Festival tube doll puppet, pattern, making 1083:183-184

Health and Sports Day cup puppets, making 557:14

Spring Hina-Matsuri Festival eggshell puppet, making 709:147-148

JAPAN—FESTIVALS—SCROLLS

Scrolls, paper scrolls, making 814:20-21

JAPAN—FLAG

Pattern of flag 557:18

JAPAN—FLOWER ARRANGING

Ikebana flower arrangement and planter, making 889:57-65

JAPAN—FOLKLORE

Accordion folded tiny book, paper, ribbon, making 1478:110-111

"Crane Wife," Yohei, wife and crane stick puppets, patterns 1206:39-43

Japanese fable, Think twice skit 1212:18-20

Little Bunny and Crocodile flannel board patterns, making 910:15,50

Mask; The Funny Little Woman mask, patterns, making 1093:130

Mask; The Funny Little Woman Oni mask, pattern, making 1093:131

Mosel, Arlene, "The Funny Little Woman," reading/writing/think/activities 1093:122-132

Origami paper people, kimono pattern, making 1478:112-113

"Rat's Daughter" flannel board story, patterns, making 1603:128-133

"Roly-Poly Rice Ball" flannel board story, patterns, making 1604:92-94

Street Storyteller 474:145

Tongue-cut sparrow, cards for story show, making 1422:36

Turtle birthday cards, paper, crayons, making 1478:109

Urashima the Fisherman folktale and activities 1478:103-107

JAPAN—FOLKLORE—COOKERY

Old Woman who lost her Dumpling; story and recipe, for Dumplings, making 364:32-40

JAPAN—FOLKLORE—HANDICRAFTS

Biggest Fool 126:46-49

Biggest Fool, art activities, origami, scroll, making 126:50; 126:51-53

Stolen Charm, string painting of flowers and weeds, ogre paper bag mask 125:61-69

JAPAN—FOLKLORE—PUPPETS

"Rabbit of Inaba" shadow puppets, patterns, making 1602:96-99

"Silly Jellyfish" shadow puppets, patterns, making 1602:136-143

JAPAN—GAMES

Badger the Sun chasing game, how to play 1498:31-33

Ball in the hole game 814:45-46

Beads game 814:46-47

Bean go game 1146:26-27
Big lantern, little lantern game 383:109; 602:64-65
Bivalve shell game, kai-awase, painted shells, making 1256:30-31
Bounce the ball game 383:106
Cat and mice game 602:65-66
Clap game 602:66-67
Crab race game 143:131
Devil and the frog game 602:66
Faces game, how to play 1507:47
Fisherman game 814:41; 1378:81
Five eyes game 383:109
Foreigner game 383:112
Fuku Warai game, pattern for face given, making 1378:80; 1427:221
Fuku Warai, pin the parts on the face game, how to play 143:129; 1501:29-30
Furoshiki Mawaski, scarf passing game, how to play 1494:48
Go game 1074:42-51
Go-bang board game, patterns, making 1541:147-152
Go-bang game, making 921:7
Go-bang, tic-tac-toe game 1074:52
Hana, hana, hana, kuchi game 383:105
Hanakago game 383:118
Hanetsuki game 383:104
Hasami Shogi board game, patterns, making 1541:153-157
Hasami Shogi game 383:107
Hunting the treasure game 383:107
Images of Buddha game, how to play 1078:24; 1507:48
Jan Ken Po game 143:131; 383:110; 474:37-38; 557:17; 574:30; 602:68; 956:19-20; 967:37; 1355:32; 1507:49
Janken finger game, how to play 1499:16-18
Japanese tag game 1378:81
Kabu card game 1132:12-13
Kage-Bohi-Onigo tag, how to play 1498:13
Kagome-Kagome game 383:116
Kai-Awase bivalve shell game, how to make and play 1701:15
Kai-Awase, shells game, making 1320:70-71
Karuta game 143:129
Karutatori game 383:113
Kazuken finger game, how to play 1499:16
Kendo game 386:61
Kick the can game 383:109
Nekki stick game 1119:19
Ninuki-Renju game 956:142-144
Nose, nose, nose, mouth game 602:67
Observation puzzle, making 814:41-44
Ojiisan-Obaasan, grandfather-grandmother, Reuben and Rachel game 386:70
Oki Chochin, Chrissi Chochia game 383:109
Old man and old woman game 602:69-70
Old woman, the lion, and the warrior game 602:69
Otedama game 383:117
Otedama jack bean bag game 736:35-37
Otedama, hand ball game, how to play 1718:14-15
Poem card playing game 383:114
Poem cards game, poems given, making 1427:224-230
Portrait painter game 602:67
Portrait painting games 572:18-19
Rakan san game 143:130; 383:111; 1378:80
Removing the dice game 814:45

Rock-paper-scissors game, how to play 383:110; 1355:32
Scissors chess game 383:107
Scissors game, paper, and stone 1378:79
Shogi game, how to make 1074:77-83
Skillful carriers game 814:44; 1378:81
Slap hand game 383:110
Squirrels want a hole game 602:70
Sugoroku game 383:115
Table speeches game 474:39
Tag 383:104
Takara-Sagashi game 383:107
Takaratori game 383:117
Yemari game 383:106
Zui Zui Zukorobashi game 557:17

JAPAN—GARDENS

Tabletop garden in tray, metal tray, how to make 1629:24-25
Tray gardens, gift box, small plants, making 1427:212

JAPAN—HAIKU

Book of haiku, paper, threads, patterns, making 1332:91-100
Haiku poetry 143:120
Haiku poetry, how to write 1715:132

JAPAN—HANDICRAFTS

Box decorated with eggshells, patterns, making 814:85-86
Brush stroke chrysanthemums, paper, patterns, making 1246:28-29
Computer project: Kamon family crest, design one 1218:32-35
Duck, folded paper, making 525:92
Embroidered flowers and leaves, yarn, making 298:258-259
Faces, Japanese paper faces, making 545:92
Family crest, mon-kiri craft, paper-cutting, patterns, making 1427:205
Fold and dye wrapping paper called Itajime-shibori, making 1476:48
Folding and tying paper and dying it, how to do 1638:93-94
Inro boxes, making 814:84-85
Japanese flower crests, paper, patterns, making 1246:22-25
Japanese Shibori designs, dying cloth with designs, making 1354:52
Kimono doll bookmark, paper, making 1629:21
Mizuhiki gift wrap cords, making 1477:132
Mobile, flying fish, making 691:12-13
Mobile, Japanese, lanterns mobile, making 772:76-77
Moni-Kiri family crests, paper, making 298:196-197
Nightingale of Japan wall hanging, making 814:83
Plum blossom flower, paper, making 532:55-56
Porcelain plaque, making 532:13-14
Star, pierced paper, family crest, making 857:46-47
Star, silver paper folded, making 525:92
Stencil, flower, making 167:69-72
Stencils designs, use of 167:73-79
Tatamis, paper, making 574:24
Textile printing, repeated emblem, making 298:174-175
Wood cuts, potatoes or wood, paint, making 1427:213
Woodblock prints, foam trays, paper, inks, making 1338:73-76

JAPAN—HARVEST FESTIVALS—HANDICRAFTS

Hounen-Odori Festival origami flowers, paper, making 1249:43-44

JAPAN—HELMETS

Helmet, making 532:22

JAPAN—HOUSES

Paper window house model, making 494:219-230

JAPAN—KITES

Carp kite, tissue paper, tag board, pattern, making 105:15-16; 532:43-44; 1427:202

Fighter kites, the Sanjo Rokkaku, Szilagi, and Nagasaki Hata, making 1069:218-232

Fish balloon kites, making 532:48-49

Fish kite, making 626:69-71

Japanese fish kite, making 274:20-23; 809:152

Nagasaki Fighting kite, making 1026:75-77

Origami bug kites, making 1069:217

Tiger kite, paper, bamboo sticks, patterns, making 1427:208

JAPAN—LAMPS

Japanese lamp from toothpicks, making 952:112-113

JAPAN—LANGUAGE

Common words and phrases in Japanese 1325:27

Finger plays and rhymes in Japanese 1583:150

Japanese conversational words 1378:95-96

Japanese Hiragana symbols 1064:130

Japanese language 143:140

Japanese numbers and conversation words 574:27

Japanese words, everyday words 1378:93-95

Numbers one to ten in Japanese language 395:unp

JAPAN—LANTERNS

Lantern, paper, making 966:118-119

Lantern, small paper lantern, making 966:142-143

Lanterns (chochin), construction paper, tissue paper, making 1427:211

Lantern, paper, easy, how to make 274:44-47; 1093:127-129

Lantern, Tanabanta hanging lantern, making 298:62-63

JAPAN—MAGIC TRICKS

Magic swan, origami trick, how to do 1270:20-21

JAPAN—MASKS

Carved wooden mask, making 856:73

Geisha mask, making 846:38-39

Masks for NO theater, aluminum foil, marker, making 1427:209-210

Masks, theater, making 167:48-51

JAPAN—NAMES

Naming Days information 695:43-45

JAPAN—NATURE FESTIVALS

Bean Throwing Night, bye to winter, welcome spring festival 419:105-106

Festival of Spring, national holiday festival 419:106

Japanese rice growing rituals 419:104-106

JAPAN—NESTING DOLL STORIES

Why the Years Are Named for Animals nesting doll story, how to do 1161:87-89

JAPAN—NEW YEAR'S DAY

Celebration of New Year's Day in Japan 54:222; 497:158-159; 475:97; 505:40-41; 566:36-37; 601:63

Charms on tree custom 505:21

Gan-Tan in Japan 489:114-122

JAPAN—NEW YEAR'S DAY—COOKERY

Cucumber slices, recipe 1666:181

Dashi, recipe 497:162

Mizutaki (tabletop cooking in broth), recipe 1666:182-183

Ozoni (New Year's soup with rice cake), recipe 1666:180-181

Plum blossom eggs, recipe 1666:181

Sliced carrots, recipe 1666:181

Soba noodles in broth, recipe 497:162

Toshi Koshi Soba (buckwheat noodles in broth), recipe 1666:180

Tsukemono (picked vegetables), recipe 1666:182

JAPAN—NEW YEAR'S DAY—DOLLS

Daruma dolls, making 497:164

JAPAN—NEW YEAR'S DAY—GAMES

Fuku Wari game, how to play 505:43

Hanetsuki game, how to play 505:42

Kakizome game, how to play 505:42

Karuta game, how to play 505:42

JAPAN—NEW YEAR'S EVE

Oshoogatsu Festival, history of 709:103

JAPAN—NEW YEAR'S EVE—HANDICRAFTS

Gohei, making 709:105-106

Shimekazari, making 709:103-105

JAPAN—NUMBERS

Numbers one to ten in Japanese 395:unp; 557:13

JAPAN—ORIGAMI

Origami boat, paper, making 1500:12-16

Origami cygnet, making 1447:20-21

Origami dog, sailboat, fish, swan, patterns, making 1378:83-88

Origami flower, patterns, making 1016:75-79

Origami hat, paper, making 1381:75

Origami helmet, making 1629:13

Origami rocking bird, making 297:202-203

Origami, making 143:134

Origami, tissue paper, making 1427:210

JAPAN—PAPER

Rice paper, making 143:120

JAPAN—PICTURE DRAWING STORIES

Bo ga Ippon (What Will It Be?) picture drawing story, how to do 1161:56-57

Number Story picture drawing story, how to do 1161:58-59

The Black Cat picture drawing story, how to do 1161:48-51

The Wild Bird picture drawing story, how to do 1161:52-55

JAPAN—PUPPETS

Bunraku life-like puppet, papier-mache, fabric, wood, dowels, making 1707:21

Japanese Bunraku puppet, cardboard, making 480:123

Samurai Warrior puppets, paper and fabric, patterns, making 1027:105-113

String puppet, fabric, cord, buttons, decorations, making 1219:20-21

JAPAN—RHYMES

"Above the Rooftops" 1607:29

Agari Me 780:53

Ha Ke Yoi baby lifting rhyme 780:87

Japanese Peek-A-Boo 780:48

Kai Kuri tickling rhyme 780:98

Luntaro's Ride baby bouncing rhyme 780:78

Musun-De 780:54

JAPAN—SAMURAI

Nikko Grand Festival, the March of the Samurai 107:31-35

JAPAN—SCIENCE
Repeat Matuyama's experiment with magnetic fields 1719:52-54

JAPAN—SCREENS
Folding screen, posterboard, markers, making 1633:138-139
Shoji screens, making 78:96
Table screen, small, paper decoupage, making 274:88-91

JAPAN—SCROLLS
Scroll painting, wall scroll, fabric, making 889:131-137

JAPAN—SONGS
Bento-Uri street vendor round song 1115:35
Usagi Usagi!, traditional song, Japan 139:34

JAPAN—STORYTELLING
Origami (paper folding) stories 1522:74-84
Storyteller box, cardboard box, making 1093:126

JAPAN—STRING FIGURES
Cat's cradle and variation strings 372:66-73
Elastic band string 373:23
Japanese butterfly string 372:24-25

JAPAN—TABLES
Serving table, wood, measurements given, making 1361:160
Tables, low Japanese table, cardboard box, pattern, making 1378:74

JAPAN—TEA CEREMONY
Kanten, recipe 143:124
Tea ceremony (Chanoyu), how to do 143:122; 474:130-133
Tea party, activities and recipes 809:117-121
Tea party, Japanese fans, paper, making 1528:19
Tea party, recipes 1528:17-19
Tea party noodle soup, recipe 1528:17
Tea party sweet rice cakes, recipe 1528:18

JAPAN—TEA HOUSE
Tea house, model, cardboard box, pellon, patterns, making 1378:71-73

JAPAN—THEATER—MASKS
NO actors and masks for them, and box stage, making 1486:8-9
NO character theater mask, papier-mache, balloon, paints, making 1706:13

JAPAN—TOYS
Daruma toy, making 143:133
Hare, making 532:37-38
Roly-Poly egg doll toy, making 626:67-69

JAPAN—WIND CHIMES
Furins, wind chimes, making 143:135

JAPAN—WOODWORKING
Horse, wooden lacquered horse, making 814:72-74
Lacquer boxes, making 167:86-87
Lacquerware tray, making 167:81-85
Lacquered box, patterns, making 1320:78-79
Wooden lacquered box, making 814:71-72

JAVA. *See also* **INDONESIA**

JAVA—BATIK
Batik scarf, fabric, wax, dyes, making 1476:149-150
Batik, how to make 525:88-89

JAVA—GAMES
Dragon (Ular Naga) musical game 1116:35

JAVA—MASKS
Javanese Theatrical mask, making 204:90-93

JAVA—NATURE FESTIVALS
Rice growing festival 419:94

JAVA—PUPPETS
Javanese puppet, making 483:27
Wayang kulit, shadow puppets, dowels, paper, markers, making 1338:65-67

JEFFERSON, THOMAS
French food in the Jefferson White House 663:116-121

JEFFERSON, THOMAS—COOKERY
Ice cream, recipe 57:42-43
Noodles a la macaroni, recipe 57:43
Sorrel soup, recipe 1733:71

JEFFERSON, THOMAS—GAMES
Thomas Jefferson's birthday game 240:23
Thomas Jefferson nickel race game 719:26

JERKY
Jerky, strips of seasoned meat, recipe 1660:69

JESSE TREE
Christmas tree and decorations, how to make 593:126-131
History and background of Jesse Tree 726:4-8

JESSE TREE—HANDICRAFTS
Figures and symbols, baker's clay, recipe, patterns, making 726:9-12
Jesse Tree, stand up tree, patterns, making 726:13-15
Sewing cards, making 726:16
Stained glass window Jesse Tree, making 726:16-18
Star of David, paper, how to make 726:18-19

JESTERS—COSTUMES
Neck ruffle, making 7:116-117

JESTERS—PUPPETS
Wooden spoon jester puppet, felt, fabric, bells, pens, making 1181:10-11

JESUS CHRIST
Advent, the coming of Jesus Christ, activities and projects for classrooms 1393:88-89
Christmas, birth of Jesus Christ, activities and projects for classrooms 1393:106-111
Cross facts 139:93
Crown of Roses, Peter Tshaikovsky 139:100-101
Easter, resurrection of Jesus Christ, activities and projects for classrooms 1393:180-183

JESUS CHRIST—NATIVITY. *See also* **NATIVITY**
Nativity shadow puppet presentation, stage, angels, baby Jesus, Joseph, Mary, animals, Three Wise Men, patterns for puppets; 1236:86-94

JEWELRY. *See also* **BEADS**
Arab belt, making 236:22-23
Bangle, jeweled, twisted tissue paper, making 1261:16-17
Beads; rose petal beads, flower petals and paste, making 1213:96
Bird brooch, twisted tissue paper, making 1261:18-19
Bracelets; braiding and knotting bracelets, how to do 1364:4-23
Brooch from clay, how to make 1260:14-15
Egyptian collar, making 236:34-37
Necklace, African button, patterns, making 1016:155-159
Necklace, pebble, making 1421:156
Necklace, seed, making 1421:157
Papier-mache jewelry, making 1253:42-43
Seed jewelry, seeds, elastic, making 1510:66-67
Stone Age jewelry, plastic lids, making 442:52
Stones from tissue paper, making 1261:14
Strings from tissue paper, making 1261:15

JEWISH COOKERY
    Chango bars, chocolate chip and nut bars, recipe
      1674:unp
    Jalapeno bagels, recipe 1674:unp
JEWISH HOLIDAYS
    Chanukah 566:25
    Chanukah party, candlelight dinner 81:19-26
    Dreidel, cardboard, making 54:208
    Feast of Purim 566:24-25
    Four Questions 475:26
    Haggadah 475:25
    Hamishah Asar Bishvat 475:19-22
    Hanukkah 475:11-19
    Jewish prayer for peace 475:4
    Lag Ba'Omer party, cookout 81:53-58
    Menorah made from spool, how to make 275:97
    Papier mache fruit, making 363:58-61
    Passover or Pesach 475:24-25; 566:24
    Pesach party, birthday party 81:41-46
    Pilgrim Festivals 475:22-23
    Purim 475:8-10
    Purim party, progressive dinner 81:33-40
    Rosh Hashanah 566:24
    Rosh Hashanah party, Tashlich tea 81:7-12
    Sabbath 475:5-7
    Seder service 475:27-28
    Seder symbols 475:25-26
    Shabbat party, open house 81:65-71
    Shavuot 475:28-30
    Shavuot party, brunch 81:59-64
    Star of David mobile, making 403:29-30
    Sukkah, making 134:21
    Sukkot 475:30-34
    Sukkot party, snacks 81:13-18
    Tree planting 475:19-22
    Tu B'Shevat party, fruit-tasting party 81:27-32
    Yom Ha'Atzmaut party, picnic 81:
    Yom Kippur 475:10-11
JEWISH SABBATH. *See also* **SABBATH**
    Meaning of Sabbath 711:15; 712:15-16
JEWISH SABBATH—COOKERY
    Avacado and fruit salad, recipe 1441:25
    Beet borscht, recipe 711:24-25
    Challah bread, recipe 1287:unp
    Chicken soup, recipe 711:22-23
    Cholent, beef, beans, grains, recipe 1441:24
    Chopped liver, recipe 711:20-21
    Company stuffing, recipe 116:9
    Fancy dress chicken 116:3
    Fruit compote, recipe 711:28
    Grandma's chicken soup, recipe 116:2-3
    Heavenly hallah, recipe 116:4-6
    Potato kugel, recipe 711:26-27
    Sabbath mousse, recipe 116:10-11
    Sabbath queen's crown, recipe 116:6-7
    Sparkling salad, recipe 116:8-9
JEWISH SABBATH—HANDICRAFTS
    Candleholders for Sabbath, dough, recipe, making 1376:75-76
    Candlestick, making 712:16-17
    Challah, making 711:16-19
JEWISH SABBATH—PARTIES
    Oneg Shabat, invitations, decorations, menus, and games,
      making 2:78-84

JOHN HENRY
    John Henry, picture, making 92:11
    Pop-up, paper, making 92:12-13
JOHNNY APPLESEED. *See also* **APPLES; CHAPMAN,**
    JOHN
    Apple tree, paper, making 92:10; 843:37-38
    Art, music and cooking activities 161:53-56
    Baked apple treats, recipe 384:Sept 26
    Fan apple, paper, making 92:9
    Johnny Appleseed Day finger plays, recipes, games
      944:25-27
    Johnny Appleseed, picture, making 92:8
JOHNNY APPLESEED—BIRTHDAY
    Activities, art, songs, recipes, games 1469:14-15
    Birthday celebration; art, music, foods, games, activities
      1104:6-9
JOHNNY APPLESEED—COSTUMES
    Johnny Appleseed costume, making 272:68-69
JOHNNY APPLESEED—PUPPETS
    Apple-Seed John puppet show 756:59-65
JOHNNY TREMAIN
    Johnny Tremain, descriptions and pictures of house
      29:Chapter 6
JOHNSON, TONY
    "Vanishing Pumpkin," cooked pumpkin, recipe 1216:120
JOHNSON, WILLIAM H.
    Sunday going to church collage, paper, making 298:220-
      221
JONES, CASEY
    Birthday celebration; art, music, foods, games, activities
      1104:70-73
JORDAN—COOKERY
    Cucumber laban salad, yogurt, cucumbers, garlic, mint,
      recipe 1241:120
    Date and nut fingers, recipe 1165:67-68
    Date cakes (tamriah), cookies, recipe 72:112-113
    Ful mesdames, brown fava beans, recipe 1165:67-68
    Hoomis, chickpea spread, recipe 1165:72
JORDAN—FESTIVALS—COOKERY
    Eid al-Fitr; yalanchi (filling for stuffed vegetables), rec-
      ipe 1666:57
JOSSE, BARBARA
    "Jam Day," biscuits, recipe 1216:39
JUDAISM
    Ten commandments for today, cardboard, paint, making
      1626:9
JUG BANDS
    Bottle organ, boing box, maracas, bells, making 1310:76-
      80
    Pie tin cymbals, balloon bassoon, making 1310:87-88
    Tap-a-taps, spoon clappers, chimes, utensils, making
      1310:81-83
    Tube kazoo, comb kazoo, knot popper, making 1310:84-
      86
JUMPING JACKS. *See also* **PANTINS—FRANCE**
JUNETEENTH DAY
    Activities, crafts, history and stories for 128:94-99
JUNGLES
    Jungle animals from blown eggs, patterns, making
      1311:116-117
    Jungle collage frieze, paper, making 1092:74-76
    King or Queen of the Beasts, writing, art activities, pat-
      terns, making 1152:5-18
    Miniature jungle, how to make 875:56-57

JUNGLES—COSTUMES

Tarzan and Jane costumes, fabric, patterns, making 1174:78

JUNGLES—FOLKLORE

Law of the jungle fable playlet 1212:59-65

JUNGLES—PARTIES

Jungle safari party, decorations, games, cake, patterns 1015:103-119

Jungle, invitations, decorations, costumes, food, games, recipes 1185:10-11

Safari party (7 years up) 124:61-69

JUNGLES—PUPPETS

Jungle animals puppets, patterns, making 463:49-56

JUNK FOOD. *See* **FOOD—JUNK FOOD**

K

KACHINA DOLLS

Hopi Kachina doll, styrofoam block, paints, making 1368:54

Hopi Kachina, making 445:111-126

Hopi Tihus dolls, making 466:98-99

Kachina dolls, clay, fabric scraps, making 1092:110-111

Kachina dolls, making 171:56-64; 467:44-45; 586:10

Kachina figure, cardboard tubes, fabric, feathers, paint, making 1476:75-76

Kachina mask, making 63:26-27

KACHINA MASKS

Kachina-style mask, and miniature Kachina mask, making 327:22-25

Southwest Kachina masks, history of 327:16-18

KAHL, VIRGINIA

"Dutchess Bakes a Cake," light and lovely cake, recipe 1216:60

KANGAROOS

Kangaroo, pop-up, paper, pattern 1210:40-41

KANSAS—COOKERY

Roast tenderloin of beef, recipe 654:59

Swedish rusk, recipe, making 654:57-58

KELLER, HELEN—BIRTHDAY

Birthday celebration; art, music, foods, games, activities 1104:94-97

Celebrate by playing hearing, whispering game 1199:140

Celebrate by playing sight, I spy game 1199:140

Celebrate by signing your name, manual alphabet given 1199:138

Celebrate by taste test activity 1199:141

Celebrate by touching textures activity 1199:142

Celebrate with cupcake flowers, baking, fragrances, making 1199:143

KELLOGG'S CORN FLAKES

History of 119:136-141

KENTUCKY—CELEBRATIONS—BURGOO

A burgoo celebration 51:132-133

Burgoo stew, recipe 51:133-134

Corn roast 51:134-137

KENTUCKY—COOKERY

Burgoo pot luck Frontier recipe 663:25-26

Crispy fried chicken, history of, recipe 155:18-19

Kentucky fried chicken, recipe 654:61

Mint tea, iced, recipe 654:62

KENTUCKY—HISTORY

Potluck on the Kentucky Frontier; food supply information 663:6-13

KENYA

Activities, flags, games, songs, dances, recipes 1381:141-144

Crafts, foods, folklore, tribal customs activities 1378:147-197

Traditions, customs, geography, economy, ecology, aesthetic awareness units 1378:147-197

KENYA—CHRISTMAS—COOKERY

Fillet of beef with pineapple, recipe 1666:5

Peach chutney, recipe 1666:5-6

KENYA—CLOTHING

Masai clothing, making 222:58-59

KENYA—COOKERY

Banana smoothie, making 187:42

Chapatis, fried bread, recipe 1198:28

Chicken and bread, recipe 793:54

Fried cookies (maandazi), cookies, recipe 72:95-96

Fufu cassava dish, recipe 1521:121

Green bananas, recipe 967:37

Irio, corn, potatoes, chick peas, recipe 1381:143

Mango snow dessert, recipe 1207:92-93

Plantains in coconut mile, recipe 1207:92

Rice pancakes, recipe 1652:22

Samosas pastry snacks, meat, peppers, onions, recipe 1381:143

Sukuma wiki, collard greens, recipe 1165:5-6

Three-in-one vegetable, recipe 1694:26

Ugali, cornmeal porridge, recipe 1165:5

Vermicelli and raisins dessert, recipe 1280:15

Vermicelli with fruit and nuts dessert, recipe 1380:19

Whole wheat bread, unleavened, recipe 1652:20-21

KENYA—DOLLS

Doll, paper cup, yarn, patterns, making 1311:66-69

KENYA—FESTIVALS

Festivals and celebrations, maps, flags, crafts, making 1305:67-74

KENYA—FOLKLORE

"Bringing the Rain to Kapiti Plain"; physical and human geography activities 1458:38-41

KENYA—GAMES

Animal keepers game, how to play 1494:18

Hunting the leopard game 602:31

Kigogo board game, how to make and play 1632:40-45

Our work is done like this game 602:29-30

Shisima game, how to play 1688:33-34

KENYA—HOUSES

Yikuyu house, making 222:26

KENYA—LANGUAGE

African names 1378:191

Swahili words; people, numbers, animals, common words and phrases 1378:191-192

KICKAPOO INDIANS—GAMES

Hand game 602:172

KING, MARTIN LUTHER, JR.

Activities, crafts, songs 1473:76-78

Flag of Freedom, fabric, dowels, making 1662:11

History of Martin Luther King 199:18

I Have a Dream art and writing activities, patterns, making 1152:93-99

Learning units, art, language, music, foods, crafts, patterns 1193:307-322

Martin Luther King Day activities and projects for classrooms 1393:133-135

Martin Luther King Day, celebration 133:111

Nobel Peace Prize ribbon, felt board, making 945:162-163

Portrait, make life-size figures 1662:12

KING, MARTIN LUTHER, JR.—BIRTHDAY

Activities, art, songs, recipes, games 1469:56-67

Birthday activities, projects, poems 819:32-42

Birthday activities, stories, crafts, recipes, making 558:35-38

Birthday celebration; art, music, foods, games, activities 1104:42-45

Birthday finger plays, recipes, games, making 944:60-62

KING, MARTIN LUTHER, JR.—COSTUMES

Martin Luther King costume, making 272:29-30

KING, MARTIN LUTHER, JR.—DECORATIONS

"I Have a Dream" join hands poster, making 1461:29

Pop-up Martin Luther King Day card, making 1387:63

KING, MARTIN LUTHER, JR.—GAMES

Concentrate on King game 698:17

March to Washington game 698:16
Martin Luther King, Jr. birthday game 240:10

KING, MARTIN LUTHER, JR.—PUPPETS

Martin Luther King puppet, stuffed paper bag, basic body pattern, making 1083:28-30
Puppet projects, patterns, scenes, story starters, feature story 1083:28-30

KING, MARTIN LUTHER, JR.—SONGS

Songs for Martin Luther King's birthday 901:41-42
"We Shall Overcome," words 1662:10

KING TUT. *See* **EGYPT, ANCIENT—KING TUT**

KINGS

Carnival accessories, necklace and crown, making 113:42-43
Crown and scepter, from cereal boxes, making 84:13-14
Crown and sword, newspaper, making 1658:77-78
Crown from paper straws, making 828:91-92
Crown, paper, making 123:32-34; 384:Jan6
Crown, pattern 157:10
Crown, shiny paper, making 966:146-147
Crown, throne, scepter, paper, making 698:22
King's crown, making 670:74
King's crown, paper foil, making 449:25
Paper and photography King figure, making 231:27
Regal robes, fabric, fur, ribbon, making 1671:28-29
Royal crown, egg carton, making 766:62
Royal crown, paper, making 1105:8-9
Royal crown, patterns, paper 1016:166-171
Royal sandwiches, recipe 843:59,130
Scepter, paper making 1096:10
Three Kings, plastic bottles, making 553:30-31

KINGS—MASKS

King mask, making 840:3-4; 846:10-13
King mask, paper, simple, making 966:20-21

KINGS—PUPPETS

Fat old King wooden spoon puppet, making 238:39

KIOWA INDIANS—FOOTWEAR

Kiowa moccasins, making 359:87-93
Moccasins, making 932:96-100

KIPLING, RUDYARD—COOKERY

Auntie Em's famous fudgy frosting, recipe 365:83
"Jungle Book"; Baloo's mint brownies, recipe 365:85
"Jungle Book"; Mowgli's tiger milk, recipe 365:53
"Just So Stories"; best beloved cracker bites, recipe 365:46
"Just So Stories"; lions and tigers and bears, oh my!, recipe 365:82

KITES

Australian Trefoil Delta kite, making 1069:243-246
Australian Trefoil Dragon kite, making 1069:247-250
Ballookites from Thailand, making 532:45
Benjamin Franklin birthday celebration; art, music, foods, games, activities 1104:46-49
Bluebird kite, paper, sticks, making 1313:32
Box kite, Tumbling Star, fabric, dowels, patterns, making 1483:73-75
Carp kite from Japan, making 532:43-44
Carp kite, making 709:153-156
Carp kite, tissue paper, tag board, pattern, making 1427:202
Carp kites, tissue paper, sequins, pattern, making 1285:24
Carp mini-kite, making 980:42-43
Chinese fan kite, making 1026:71-73
Chinese Golden Dragon kite, making 1026:83-85
Della Porte kite, fabric, dowels, patterns, making 1483:68-69
Dragon kite from China, making 532:41
Dragon kite, paper, sticks, making 1313:141-142
Easter kite 196:52-57
Honduras kite, making 515:60
Japanese carp bag kite, paper bag, making 1083:182
Japanese carp kite, making 105:15-16; 909:33
Japanese fighter kites, making 1069:218-232
Japanese fish kite, making 274:20-23; 809:152; 1055:95
Japanese Nagasaki Fighting kite, making 1026:75-77
Korean kite, making 1026:67-69
Lag B'Omer kite, making 712:78-82
Malay bow kite, making 889:93-95
Malayan bow kite, making 1026:79-81
Malaysian kite, making 532:42
Oriental kite from paper bag, making 678:36-37
Paper bag kite, pattern, making 1213:136
Six-pack sled design kite, fabric, patterns, making 1483:70-72
Sled kite, fabric, dowels, patterns, making 1483:66-67
Stunt kite, fabric, dowels, patterns, making 1483:76-77
Tiger kite, paper, bamboo sticks, patterns, making 1427:208
United States Star Streaker kite, making 1026:87-89
Vietnamese kitchen kite, making 792:16-19
Vietnamese Rabbit ballookites, making 532:46-47
War Lord face kite, making 1026:31-33

KLAMATH INDIANS

Rabbit string game 372:54-57

KLAMATH INDIANS—STRING FIGURES

Rabbit, Rising and Setting Sun, Six-Pointed Star 1404:81-109

KLEENEX

History of Kleenex 119:128-131

KNIGHTS

Frieze of day in the life of a knight, fabric, cardboard, making 1682:28
Goblet, making 731:32
Knight bank from plastic bottle and seeds, making 623:22-24
Knight funny face from paper bag, making 678:9
Knight, paper, large patterns, making 478:28-33
Knockout boxes, making 731:30-31
Paper knight on horseback collage, making 195:113-115
Paper knights, making 75:35
Throne, making 731:30-31

KNIGHTS—ARMOR

Armor, making 731:28-29
Plate armor, patterns, making 942:71-73

KNIGHTS—BREASTPLATES

Breastplate, cardboard, aluminum foil, making 1671:32-33

KNIGHTS—CASTLES

Castle, cardboard, making 731:24-25

KNIGHTS—CHAIN MAIL

Chain mail, making 731:29; 942:70

KNIGHTS—COAT OF ARMS

Stained glass coat of arms, window, paper, crayons, making 1682:13

KNIGHTS—COSTUMES

Costume, posterboard and felt, patterns, making 1050:106-109

Dragonslayer, fabric, notions, patterns, making 1435:24-26

Knight costume with sword, helmet, fabric, foil, making 1509:18-19

Knight costume, fabric, face makeup given, making 957:54-59

Knight in armor, costume, paper, making 585:40-41

Knight in shining helmet making 106:60-63

Roland costume 213:60-62

KNIGHTS—FLAGS

Flags and banner, making 731:31

KNIGHTS—HELMETS

Helmet, cardboard, aluminum foil, making 1671:33

Helmet, carton cylinder, making 480:119

Knight helmet with plume, cardboard, paper, making 1682:11

Knight helmet, cardboard, making 588:12-13

Knight's helmet, gray tag board, making 1486:26-27

KNIGHTS—JOUSTING

Joust for fun jousting games, wooden, making 942:74-76

Jousting stage with moveable figures, cardboard, paint, making 1682:18-19

KNIGHTS—MASKS

Masks, Knight mask, making 846:14-15

KNIGHTS—PARTIES

Knights and Dragons party, activities and recipes 809:101-106

Knights around the table party, decorations, games, costumes, recipes 74:150-166

KNIGHTS—RINGS

Ring, ribbon ring, making 731:32

KNIGHTS—ROBES

Royal robes, making 731:28-29

KNIGHTS—SHIELDS

Shield, cardboard, paper, making 1671:33

Shield, making 731:29

KNIGHTS—WEAPONS

Gauntlet, dagger and sword, cardboard, aluminum foil, making 1671:34

Knight's shield, sword and helmet from boxes, making 634:50-53

Sword, making 731:28

Sword, shield, helmet, cardboard, making 562:13-14

KNITTING

Bobbin knitting, yarn, thread spool, nails, how to do 1255:29

French knitting, how to do 690:10

KNOTS

Lashing, clove hitch knot, how to tie 1188:23

Shear knot, how to tie 1188:25

Square-lashing, how to tie 1188:24

KNOTTING

Bracelets; braiding and knotting bracelets, how to do 1364:4-23

KNOTTING—ORIENTAL

Rya tufting, making 954:106

KODACHROME COLOR FILM

History of 119:197-201

KOOKABURRAS

Puppet; paper bag kookaburra puppet, patterns, making 1107:94-104

KOREA

Activities, flags, games, songs, dances, recipes 1381:67-70

KOREA—BIRTHDAYS

Birthday celebrations 695:54-55

Birthday customs 488:80-81

Birthday party for one year old child 660:52-54

KOREA—COOKERY

Barbecued beef, recipe 1019:36

Bean sprout salad, microwave recipe 1211:30

Bean sprout salad, recipe 1019:22; 1442:22

Beef patties, recipe 1071:98

Beef short rib soup, recipe 1019:26

Beef short ribs, simmered, recipe 1019:37

Beef soup, recipe 1442:21

Beef spinach soup, recipe 1452:128

Bintaetok, filled mung bean pancakes, recipe 1452:129

Bul Ko Kee, barbecued beef, recipe 1165:178-179; 1452:132

Bulgo-ki, recipe 793:65

Bulgogi grilled beef strips, recipe 1293:119

Chestnut balls, recipe 1442:22-23

Chicken wings, deep fried, recipe 1019:28

Chicken, pear, and pine nut salad with sesame dressing, recipe 1452:133

Chicken, simmered, recipe 1019:40

Chicken, stir-fried, recipe 1442:26

Chicken, steamed with tofu, recipe 1019:40

Cho Kanjang, Korean dipping sauce, recipe 1452:130

Cinnamon foldovers, mils-sam, cookies, recipe 72:126-127

Cucumber pickles, recipe 1071:97-98

Cucumber soup, cold, recipe 1019:25

Dumplings, recipe 1019:30

Egg custard with meatballs, recipe 1019:42

Fish patties, recipe 1019:27

Fried egg roll, recipe 1071:96

Fried shrimp, recipe 1442:20

Grilled beef with vegetables, recipe 1019:34

Kimchi Chinese cabbage dish, recipe 1442:23

Kimchi, pickled cabbage, recipe 1019:20; 1165:179

Kimchi, vegetable pickle, recipe 1452:131

Korean menu 1019:16

Manduguk, meat and vegetable filled wontons, recipe 1442:28

Naeng Yon, cold noodle soup, recipe 1442:27

Noodles, recipe 1019:19

Peppers, stuffed, steamed, recipe 1019:41

Pork, simmered, recipe 1019:39

Potato soup, recipe 1019:26

Pulgogi, spiced meat dish, recipe 1442:24-25

Rice omelet, recipe 1071:95

Rice, recipe 1019:19

Salad, mixed vegetable, recipe 1019:22

Sesame beef, making 187:29

Sesame seeds, toasted, recipe 1019:18

Simmered beef short ribs, recipe 446:35-36

Spinach salad, cooked, recipe 1442:25

Spinach salad, recipe 1019:23

Vegetables, mixed, with cellophane noodles, recipe 1019:32

Vinegar soy sauce, recipe 1019:18

White rice, recipe 1442:22

KOREA—FESTIVALS

Alphabet Day; activities, art, songs, recipes, games 1469:22-23

Buddha's birthday celebration 1160:20-21

Cherry Blossom Festival celebration 1160:18-19

Children's Day celebration 1160:22-23
Christmas celebration 1160:30-31
Chu-Sok, Korean Harvest Moon Festival, activities and projects for classrooms 1393:40-41
Day of Swings; activities, art, songs, recipes, games 1469:112-113
Great Moon Festival (Tae-Bo-Rum) cerebration 1160:16-17
Harvest Moon Festival celebration 1160:26-27
Lunar New Year's Day (Sol-Nal) celebration 1160:8-15
Sol-Nal, New Year Festival, activities and projects for classrooms 1393:125-126
Swing Day (Tan-O-Day) celebration 601:68; 1160:24-25
Winter Solstice Day celebration 1160:28-29

KOREA—FESTIVALS—COOKERY
Sol; bulgogi (Korean barbecued beef), recipe 1666:177-178
Sol; kimchi (pickled cabbage), recipe 1666:178
Sol; naing kuk (cold cucumber soup), recipe 1666:179

KOREA—FESTIVALS—GAMES
Children's Day Festival, Yut board game, making 1574:16-17

KOREA—FESTIVALS—HANDICRAFTS
Chu-Sok Harvest Moon Festival fan, paper, feathers, making 1393:41
Sol-Nal, Korean New Year, family tree pattern, making 1393:126

KOREA—FOLKLORE
"Don't Let the Tiger Get You" flannel board story, patterns, making 1604:101-103

KOREA—GAMES
Four field kono game 383:120
Go-oot-Kyung-ju, flower relay game 474:48
Man, gun, tiger game 383:119
Nyout board game, patterns, making 1541:189-194
Nyout game 956:126-127
Putung Putung game, how to play 1494:46
Shuttlecock game, how to play 1507:50
Tug o' war game 581:44-45
Well kono game 383:119
Yoot game 383:121

KOREA—HAIKU
Book of haiku, paper, threads, patterns, making 1332:91-100

KOREA—HANDICRAFTS
Crown, making 532:24
Seasons accordion book, paper, yarn, ribbons, patterns, making 1332:83-90

KOREA—KITES
Korean kite, making 1026:67-69

KOREA—LANGUAGE
Korean alphabet symbols 1071:137
Numbers one to ten in Korean language 396:unp

KOREA—MASKS
Shaman's mask, making 532:29

KOREA—NEW YEAR
New Year celebration 601:67

KOREA—NEW YEAR—GAMES
Yut game, how to make and play 1654:71

KOREA—NUMBERS
Numbers one to ten in Korean language 396:unp

KOREA—POTTERY
Lotus pot, pottery, making 532:16

KOREA—PUPPETS
Dragon puppet, paper bag, patterns, making 1633:140-141

KOREA—STRING FIGURES
Candles, Cat's Cradle, Cow's Eyeball, Cradle, Chessboard 1404:115-123

KOREA, SOUTH—GAMES
Ball rolling game 602:72-73
Flower relay game 602:71-72
Mek Konk game 602:71
Pangic Chang Man game 602:72
Seesaw game 602:73-74
Token giving game 602:73

KROLL, STEVEN
"If I Could Be My Grandmother," cookies, recipe 1216:14
"Loose Tooth," muffins, recipe 1216:43

KUBLAI KHAN
Astonishing acrobats, making 173:74-75
Chinese barge, making 173:40-41
Robe, making 173:18-19
Royal Pavilion, making 173:60-61

KUWAIT
Activities, flags, games, songs, dances, recipes 1381:119-120

KUWAIT—COOKERY
Almond biscuits, recipe 1165:75
Date bars, recipe 1165:73
Fruit balls, recipe 1165:76
Hoomis, chick pea spread, recipe 1165:72
Limonada, lemonade, recipe 1165:72-73
Mjeddrah, rice with lentils, recipe 1165:74
Shourba Bilsen, thick lentil soup, recipe 1165:72
Stuffed dates, figs, prunes, recipe 1165:75
Tahineh or tahini, sesame seed paste, recipe 1165:74

KWAKIUTL INDIANS—COOKERY
Salmon cakes, recipe 1296:143-144

KWAKIUTL INDIANS—MASKS
Transformation mask, paper, paints, making 1448:12-13

KWAKIUTL INDIANS—STRING FIGURES
Threading a closed loop figure, making 423:37-39

KWANZAA
Activities and projects for classrooms 1393:112-115
Afro-American celebration, activities, handicrafts, foods, songs, making 909:139-147
Afrocentric Women Hairstyles information 560:17-21
Celebration of Kwanzaa 134:107; 497:138; 499:77; 560:27-29; 1060:1-31
Celebration program, Kwanzaa, how to do 1654:17
Finger plays, recipes, games, making 944:56-57
Information about Kwanzaa 560:1-2
Karamu feast, information 560:9-10
Kwanzaa fashion suggestions, head wrapping 560:23-25
Kwanzaa symbols 560:5-8
Nguzo Saba, The Seven Principles, information 560:3-4
Principle #1 Umoja, activities for children 1634:3-4
Principle #2 Kujichagulia, activities for children 1634:5-6
Principle #3 Ujima, activities for children 1634:7-8
Principle #4 Ujamma, activities for children 1634:9-10
Principle #5 Nia, activities for children 1634:11-12
Principle #6 Kuumba, activities for children 1634:13-14
Principle #7 Imani, activities for children 1634:15-16
Seven days special ideas for 384:Dec27
Zawadi (Gifts) 560:31

KWANZAA—CLOTHING

Boy's sleeveless Dashiki, fabric, patterns, making 1344:61

Girl's full-length buba, fabric, patterns, making 1344:62

KWANZAA—COOKERY

Ambrosia, recipe 1659:89; 1716:130

Banana boat, recipe 1032:223

Banana loaf, recipe 1344:64-65

Banana pudding, recipe 1556:32

Beef roast, recipe 1716:123-234

Benne wafer, recipe 1659:86-87

Candied sweet potatoes, recipe 1344:63-64; 1556:29; 1716:127

Chicken from Sierra Leone, recipe 1344:64

Chocolate almond cookies, recipe 1716:132-133

Chocolate chip cookies, recipe 1250:37-38

Cod strips, recipe 1634:20

Colored salad, recipe 1556:31

Corn muffins, recipe 1250:39

Cornbread, recipe 1716:128-129; 1179:37; 1556:32

Cornmeal mush, recipe 1666:264

Finger delights from various fruits, recipe 1556:28

Fruit salad, seasonal fruits, recipe 1716:120

Ginger beer, recipe 1556:28

Gracie's green beans with almonds, recipe 1716:126

Green salad, recipe 1716:120-121

Ground nut stew, recipe 1716:125-236

Honey-glazed sweet potatoes, recipe 1198:42

Hoppin' John, black-eyed peas and rice, recipe 1716:121-122

Hot apple cider, recipe 1716:133

Jamaican carrot juice, recipe 1344:66

Jambalaya (one-pot stew), recipe 1666:265

Karamu feast tabbouleh, recipe 1662:208

Karamu feast, corn fritters, recipe 1199:288-289

Kuumba salad, red, black and green ingredients, recipe 1344:65-66

Kwanzaa menu recipes 560:11-15

Latino Kwanzaa beans and rice, recipe 1344:65

Mixed salad greens with orange-lemon dressing, recipe 1198:41

Nutty bananas, recipe 909:145

Nutty muffins, recipe 1634:20

Obe efo, vegetable soup, recipe 1634:20

Peach cobbler, recipe 1198:45

Peanut and rice pudding, recipe 1659:84-85

Peanut butter and jelly cookies, recipe 1666:266

Peanut butter cookies, recipe 1250:40-41

Peanut butter fudge, recipe 1250:42

Peanut butter stew, recipe 1556:30

Peanut butter, recipe 1634:20

Pineapple sunrise punch, recipe 1716:133-134

Plantain delights, recipe 1634:20

Steamed kale, recipe 1198:43

Stewed chicken and dumplings, recipe 1344:63

Sugar cookies, recipe 1716:131-132

Sweet fruit dressing, recipe 1344:66

Sweet potato dessert, recipe 54:211

Sweet potato pie, recipe 909:145; 1393:115

Tropical fruit punch, recipe 1556:31

Tuna-sesame salad, recipe 1716:123

Uncle Herbert's spiced baked apples, recipe 1716:129-130

Yam chips, recipe 1659:88

Yams in a jacket, recipe 1634:20

Zucchini muffins, recipe 1716:127-128

KWANZAA—DECORATIONS

African animals parade on paper, patterns, making 1250:43-47

African mask, balloon, newspaper, flour, water, paints, making 1556:16

African masks, paper plate, zebra, elephant, leopard, making 909:141

African rain stick, cardboard tube, split peas, paint, making 1556:23

African trade beads, oven baked clay, making 1556:19

Afrocentric vest, brown paper bag, fabric, markers, making 1556:13

Bendera paper flag, paper, paints, making 1570:34-35

Book holder, cereal box, paper, paint, making 1556:20

Bush tree for Christmas, making 909:141

Calendar, 7 principles, felt, ribbon, gold cord, making 1360:54-57

Candles card and favors, paper, paper tubes, yarn, making 1570:20-23

Children's hand print, making 1634:223

Clay gifts or decorations, making 1716:83-84

Elephant bank, glass jars, cardboard, patterns, making 1250:32-33

Family tree, muslin, fabric paint, dowel, making 1556:8

Flag table decoration, index cards, straws, making 1654:16

Garvey's bendera, Marcus Garvey's flag, fabric, dowel, making 1659:54-56

Harvest banner, paper, prints with fruits and vegetables, making 1570:12-13

Horn, plastic bottle with mouthpiece, making 1556:22

Jigsaw puzzle, cereal box, magazines, making 1556:14

Kikombe cha umoja, big cup, foil, paper tube, making 1570:10-11

Kinara candleholder and Mishuma Saba candle flames, making 1556:7

Kinara, bread dough clay, candles, making 1659:50-53

Kufi paper hat, paper, paints, making 1570:44-45

Kwanzaa candles, cans, candles, paint, making 1662:210

Kwanzaa cards, paper, decorations, fabric scraps, making 1344:58

Kwanzaa memory book, paper, making 1556:24

Mkeka mat, grocery bags, fabric, making 1556:15

Mkeka woven mat, black, red and green paper, making 1179:37-39

Mkeka woven mat, newspaper, paints, making 1477:140

Mkeka woven table mat, red, black, green paper, making 1199:286-287

Mkeka, paper mat, paper, making 1570:8-9

Mkeka, woven mat, ribbon, glue, making 1659:57-61

Muhindi decoration, dried peas and beans, magnet, glue, making 1199:288

Nguzo Saba mobile, paper plate, cardboard, paint, making 1556:17

Nia scroll, fabric, paper, ribbon, making 1556:20

Place mats, paper, making 909:142

Pop-up Kwanzaa card, making 1387:21-23

Savings bank, paper tube, paper, plastic wrap, making 1556:18

Scrapper, sandpaper, wood blocks, making 1556:23

Spirit people, felt, fabric, markers, patterns, making 1250:28-29

Swahili words for decorations, paper, crayons, paints, making 1250:26

Tambourine, aluminum pie pans, ribbons, bells, making 1556:22
Terrarium jar, pebbles, foil, small plants, making 1556:21
Treasure box, shoe box, fabric, decorations, making 1556:25
Tribal pouch, felt, button, yarn, making 1556:11
Unity cup, plastic cup, beads, making 1556:10
Unity dolls, brown paper, yarn, fabric, making 1556:12
Vegetable garden in jars of water, making 1250:34-35
Welcome banner, felt, ribbon, paint, making 1556:9

KWANZAA—DOLLS
Handmade doll, muslin, African design fabric, pattern, making 1716:116-118

KWANZAA—GAMES
African map word game, how to play 1634:24
Candles game, how to make 1570:24-25
I got the spirit game 1344:59-60
Kalahor mancala or awari, egg cartons, making 1659:64-65
Kwanzaa board game, how to play 1634:26
Kwanzaa game, how to play 1634:22
Mankala game, dried beans, egg carton, how to make 1393:114
Owara game, dried beans, egg carton, how to make 1393:114
Star game, pennies, paper, pencil, making 1250:36

KWANZAA—HANDICRAFTS
Accordian book, paper, making 1716:109-111
African bead necklace, cord, beads, making 1716:80
African bowl or mask, papier-mache, making 1198:55-57
African headdress and skirt, African fabric, making 1198:58-59
African patterns for projects 1250:20-25
African proverb scroll, cardboard tube, fabric, making 1250:30-31
Appliqued mural, felt, dowel, making 1716:97-101
Beaded necklace or bracelet cord, beads, making 1716:78-79
Beeswax candles, making 1716:63-64
Bendera y taifa unity flag, black, red and green fabric, making 1716:73-74
Bracelet, papier-mache, making 1716:76-77
Children's block kinara, wood, shellac, making 1716:58-59
Drilled children's block kinara, wood, shellac, making 1716:60
Family history book and tape, how to make 1659:70-72
Handmade book with fabric cover, making 1659:73-76
Handprint, plaster of Paris, making 1554:30
Idnara (candleholder), making 497:139
Kente cloth needlepoint wall hanging, canvas, yarn, patterns, making 1716:94-96
Kente pattern needlepoint squares, canvas squares, yarn, making 1716:91-93
Kikombe Cha Umoja: family Kwanzaa cup, felt, making 1250:17
Kinara tapestry, colored felt, patterns, making 1198:52-54

Kinara, candleholder, wool, bottle caps, paints, making 1250:13; 1554:29; 1634:19
Kinara, large wooden block kinara, wood, shellac, making 1716:61
Kinara, sculptural assemblage kinara, bag of turned cored wood, making 1716:62
Kitchen clay, flour, salt, oil, recipe 1250:19
"Light the world candles" gift, plaster of Paris, how to make 1634:21
Marbled paper, liquid starch, oil paints, making 1716:104-105
Mazao: miniature fruits and vegetables, clay and paints, making 1250:11
Mazoa bowl, bowl, papier-mache, paints, making 1716:70-71
Mishumaa Saba: candles, felt, foil, making 1250:18
Mkeka cloth mat, fabric, making 1716:65
Mkeka mat, felt, burlap, straw, how to make 1634:19
Mkeka mat, woven paper strips, making 1554:28
Mkeka woven yarn mat, yarn, drinking straws, making 1716:66-67
Mkeka, red, green, black paper placemat, making 1574:26-27
Mkeka, woven mat, colored paper, making 1198:50-51
Mkeka: place mat, muslin, markers, patterns, making 1250:12
Noodle necklace gift, ziti noodles, how to make 1634:21
Pop-up cards, paper, markers, making 1716:107-018
Quilt, fabric, batting, pattern, making 1659:77-81
Sekere (shake-a-ray), papier-mache, pulp recipe, making 1634:21
Vibunzi: miniature ears of corn, clay, paints, making 1250:14
Wrapping paper, styrofoam shapes, ,paints, making 1716:102-103
Zawadi necklace, making 1277:24-25
Zawadi: African trade beads, clay, paints, making 1250:15-16

KWANZAA—MASKS
African mask, papier-mache, balloon, making 1659:66-69
Papier-mache mask, paints, making 1716:81-82

KWANZAA—MUSICAL INSTRUMENTS
Rain sticks, cardboard tubes, rice, paints, making 1716:85-86
Rattles, papier-mache over balloons, seeds, making 1716:87

KWANZAA—PAINTINGS
Senufo Tribe mud painting, duck cloth, fabric dyes, making 1716:88-89

KWANZAA—PARTIES—DECORATIONS
Coasters, container tops, yarn, making 1556:27
Napkin rings, cardboard tubes, fabric, making 1556:26

KWANZAA—PUPPETS
Hand puppets, felt, paper, patterns, making 1716:112-116

KWANZAA—SONGS
It's Kwanzaa Time 1344:68-69
This Little Light 1344:67
We Are Pulling Together 1344:67

L

LABOR DAY
Activities and projects for classrooms 1393:22-23
Activities, art, food, songs, recipes, games 1469:10-11; 1662:134-137
Celebrate with job charades game, how to play 1199:200
History and celebration of Labor Day 199:48; 496:68

LABOR DAY—COOKERY
Campfire stew, recipe 698:72

LABOR DAY—DECORATIONS
Decorations for your bicycle 199:49
Hats, tools, workers, felt board, making 945:186-188

LABOR DAY—FINGER PLAYS
Finger plays and games 944:14-16

LABOR DAY—GAMES
Cup toss game 698:72
Labor Day charades game 698:72
Labor Day game 240:45
Paper plate discus throw game 698:72
Rope and clothespin games and relays 698:72
Tag games 698:73

LABOR DAY—PARTIES
Games, foods, celebration, how to do 698:71-73

LABOR DAY—PUPPETS
Puppet projects, patterns, scenes, story starters, feature story 1083:103-105
Worker puppet, paper plate, making 1083:104

LAG B'OMER
Meaning of Lag B'Omer 711:79; 712:75-76

LAG B'OMER—COOKERY
Apricot bars, recipe 1691:232
Bagels, recipe 711:80-83
Baked salmon, recipe 1691:230-231
Coleslaw, recipe 1685:79; 1691:231-232
Cucumber salad, recipe 1685:78
Peanut butter cookies, recipe 116:98
Potato salad, recipe 1685:79
S'mores, recipe 81:56
Sandwich cookies, making 80:67
Shish kabob, recipe 81:56
Tabooli salad from Egypt, recipe 116:97
Tabouleh wheat salad, recipe 1685:78
Yohai sandwich, recipe 116:96

LAG B'OMER—DANCES
Dance for Lag B'Omer 542:74-78

LAG B'OMER—DECORATIONS
Bookmark, making 81:58
Holiday creative drawing activities 1337:42-43
Rebus invitation, making 81:54
Star of David pinwheel, making 82:66
Team ribbons, making 81:55
Trail snack pack, making 81:55

LAG B'OMER—GAMES
Action relay game, making 543:125
Bubbles, colores, making 82:68
Lag B'Omer aim game 712:76-77
Rainbow treasure hung game 81:57
Relays 81:57
Target toss game, making 543:126

LAG B'OMER—HANDICRAFTS
Boats or barges, making 543:124
Golf course, making 82:64
Lunch box, decorated, making 543:127
Lunch tote, making 80:66
Picnic pocket, making 82:67

Sun hat, making 80:68
Woven picnic basket, making 1691:228-229

LAG B'OMER—KITES
Lag B'Omer kite, making 712:78-82

LAG B'OMER—PARTIES
Lag B'Omer picnic party, invitations, decorations, menus and games, making 2:66-71

LAG B'OMER—PUPPETS
Shoe puppet, making 82:65

LAMBS. *See* **SHEEP**

LAMPS
Oil lamps, Portuguese, making 955:106-107

LANGUAGES
Hobo signs, making 976:40-41
Pig Latin, making 976:24-25

LANTERNS
Chinese lantern decorations, paper, making 750:6-7
Chinese lantern, paper, making 275:37
Chinese lantern, pin-pricked paper, making 966:136-137
Chinese New Year's lantern, paper, making 513:59-60
Chinese paper lanterns, making 574:21
Colonial metal lantern, making 673:137-157
Colonial tin-punch lantern, tin can, pattern, making 1429:86-87
Japanese lamp from toothpicks, making 952:112-113
Japanese lantern, paper, easy, making 274:44-47; 966:118-119; 966:142-143
Luminaries, large jar, paper, glue, making 1421:142
Mobile, Japanese lanterns mobile, making 772:76-77
Oriental lantern, paper, making 123:34-35
Paper lanterns, colored paper, paints, making 1253:33
Paper lanterns, traditional Chinese, paper, yarn, making 1266:33
Paul Revere's lantern, making 831:125-126
Pierced metal lantern, tin can, candle, making 1477:123
Pierced tin can lantern, making 1476:135-136
Pioneer tin-punch lantern, Wild West cowboy patterns, making 1051:110-114
Squash-o-lantern, squash, candle, making 1421:170

LAOS—ARCHITECTURE
Stupa, making 532:7

LAOS—COOKERY
Kay Patkhin Ginger, chicken dish, recipe 1165:174-175
Khao Poon with chicken, recipe 1165:174
Or lam, quail stew, recipe 1452:199

LAOS—DANCES
Folk dance in Laos 474:123

LAOS—FESTIVALS
Baci Good Luck Festival string around wrist 1477:73

LAOS—FESTIVALS—COOKERY
Pli Mai Festival, keng kalampi (Laotian cabbage soup), recipe 1666:173-174

LAOS—FOLKLORE
Nine-in-one Grr! Grr!; physical and human geography activities 1458:20-23

LAOS—GAMES
Chopsticks Jack game, how to play 1494:43
Pick up sticks 602:74

LAPLAND—BIRTHDAYS
Celebrations of birthdays in Lapland 474:82

LAPLAND—DOLLS
Laplander doll, felt, stuffed, pattern, making 487:30-31

LAPP, ELEANOR
"Blueberry Bears," pancakes, recipe 1216:9

LATIN AMERICA—CHRISTMAS
Christmas Day celebration 665:86-88
Christmas Eve celebration 665:84-86
Las Posadas, celebration of 497:104-117
Noche buena celebration 665:84-86
Posada celebration 665:78-82
Three King's Day celebration 665:16-18
LATIN AMERICA—CHRISTMAS—COOKERY
Bunuelos, recipe 497:112; 795:49
Ensalada de noche buena, recipe 497:112
Pasteles, recipe 497:112
Quesadilla, recipe 795:49
Raisin white sauce, recipe 497:112
Tembleque, recipe 497:112
LATIN AMERICA—CHRISTMAS—HANDICRAFTS
Advent calendar, making 795:31
Banners, paper, making 795:26
Cards, yam and beeswax card, making 795:46-47
Creche, making 795:34-35
Doll, papier-mache doll tree ornament, making 795:40
Flowers, paper, making 795:27
God's Eye, making 795:43
Molas, Christmas cards, paper and cloth Molas, making 795:44-45
Ornaments, clay and yarn, making 795:41
Piñata ball and mini-piñatas, making 795:39
Piñatas, making 795:28-30
Pompon and tassel, yarn, making 795:42
Sampler, needlepoint or cross stitch, making 497:116-117
Suns, tiny clay sun tree ornaments, making 795:40
Tin ornaments, making 795:38
Tree of Life, paper, making 795:32-33
LATIN AMERICA—COOKERY
Meat-eating habits in Latin America 662:100-107
LATIN AMERICA—EASTER
Judas Iscariot Festival celebration 665:30-32
LATIN AMERICA—FESTIVALS
All Saints' Day celebration 665:60-66
All Souls' Day celebration 665:60-66
Carnival celebrations 665:22-26
Columbus Day celebration 665:44-52
LATIN AMERICA—GAMES
London Bridge game 474:31-32
LATIN AMERICA—HALLOWEEN
Halloween celebration 665:54-66
LATIN AMERICA—HANDICRAFTS
Bark painting, making 169:108
Cast brass and silver, making 169:91-93
Computer project: Canciones, songs, write a song 1218:44-47
Cut through appliqué, making 169:64-67
Designs to use for projects 169:109-113
Incised designs in wood, making 169:57-58
Line embroidery, making 169:96-100
Needlepoint making 169:74-75
Pre-Columbian king figure sculpture, dough, paints, patterns, making 1251:25-26
Raised line designs, making 169:87-90
Sculpture, laminated cardboard, making 169:31-34
Sculpture, laminated relief, cardboard, making 169:34-35
Sculpture, papier-mache, making 169:51-53
Wax carving, making 169:44-45
Wool pictures, making 169:82

LATIN AMERICA—JEWELRY
Jewelry, laminated, making 169:38-41
LATIN AMERICA—MASKS
History of Latin American masks 204:37-43
Masks, sheet metal relief design, making 169:20-23
Repousse masks, metal relief design, making 169:20-23
LATIN AMERICA—MUSICAL INSTRUMENTS
Calabash, making 468:48-49
Gourd Scraper, balloon, paper, glue, cord, making 1310:48-49
Maracas, cans, lentils, rice, paper, making 1310:78-79
Maracas, yogurt containers, tape, dry peas, beans, foil, making 1728:8-9
Tambourine, papier-mache, metal washers and rings, making 1728:6-7
LATIN AMERICA—NAMES
Baby names information 695:124
LATIN AMERICA—PATTERNS
Angelfish 1251:38
Blackbeard 1251:20
Palm tree 1251:40
Toucan 1251:36
LATIN AMERICA—SONGS
Fray Martin round song 1115:13
LATVIA—COOKERY
Sour cream bowknots (tokorzvarhitjas), cookies, recipe 72:73-74
LATVIA—EASTER—COOKERY
Lemon sauce, recipe 1666:134
Potato and apple pudding, recipe 1666:133
Sweet apple bread pudding, recipe 1666:134
LAWSON, ROBERT
"Rabbit Hill"; Sulphronia's Southern fried chicken, recipe 570:41-42
LAZARUS, EMMA—GAMES
Emma Lazarus' birthday game 240:40
LAZYBONES DAY. See **NETHERLANDS—FESTIVALS**
LEAP YEAR DAY
Activities and projects for classrooms 1393:155-156
LEAR, EDWARD
"Owl and the Pussycat" flannel board poem, patterns, making 1603:116-121
"Owl and the Pussycat," puppets, costumes, masks, cooking, science, math, music activities 1358:122-140
Owl's and the Pussycat's pea-green squash boats, zucchini, peas, recipe 1215:16
LEATHER
Key fob, barrette, and wristband of leather, making 525:100-103
Paper leather, making 897:12
Rawhide and buckskin, making 467:6-7
Tanning a hide, how to do 937:153-154
Tool and lace leather, how to do 937:149-150
LEATHER—HANDICRAFTS
Bracelets, decorated, making 427:7
Change purse, making 427:4-9
Medallions, leather, making 1615:46-47
Neckerchief slides from leather scraps, making 978:22-23
Sun visor, making 427:14-16
Tooled belt and pouch, making 427:8-11
Wallet, making 427:12-13
LEAVES
Leaf calendar, leaves, cardboard, glue, making 1258:10-11

Leaf prints and patterns, paper, paints, making 1196:57; 1258:12-13

Leaves change color and fall off tree flip book, making 1453:10-11

LEBANON—BIRTHDAYS

Birthday celebrations in Lebanon 695:64

LEBANON—COOKERY

Arab pizza, recipe 997:37

Baba Ghannooj, eggplant dip, recipe 1165:65

Baked kibbih, lamb or beef, bulgar, onions, spices, recipe 1594:118

Chard and yogurt soup, recipe 997:26

Chick peas, recipe 794:45

Chick pea dip, recipe 1654:33

Chicken, garlic chicken, recipe 997:41

Cracked wheat pilaf, recipe 997:25

Cracked wheat salad, recipe 997:39

Cucumber and yogurt salad, recipe 895:93

Eggplant dip, recipe 997:35

Eggs and beans, recipe 446:24-25; 997:38

Fish and rice stew, recipe 997:28

Ghuryyebeh, holiday cookie, recipe 1246:47

Hummus and tahini dip, recipe 997:22

Kabobs, recipe 997:36

Kibbeh balls in yogurt, recipe 997:34

Kibbeh bil sanieh, stuffed meat loaf, recipe 1165:64

Kibbeh, baked, recipe 997:19

Kibbeh, fried hamburger, recipe 1165:65-66

Lamb, ground lamb mixture, recipe 997:18

Lebanese menu 997:16

Lemonade, recipe 997:29

Lentils and rice, recipe 1244:109

Ma'mounia, dessert, recipe 1165:66-67

Meat loaf, cold, recipe 997:42

Meat with green peas, recipe 895:91

Milk pudding, recipe 997:31

Pancakes, stuffed, recipe 997:32; 1280:26-27

Peasant salad, recipe 997:21

Pocket bread, recipe 1287:unp.

Rice pilaf, recipe 895:92

Semolina cookies (ma'amoul), recipe 72:110-111

Shishkebab, recipe 667:201-202

Squash omelet, recipe 793:57

Stuffed pita pockets, making 187:1

Swordfish, broiled, recipe 667:202

Tabbouleh, cracked wheat and parsley salad, recipe 667:203; 858:unp; 1165:66

Tomatoes, stuffed, recipe 997:24

Yogurt soup, recipe 667:202

LEBANON—EASTER—COOKERY

Kak bi halvib (Easter milk cookies), recipe 1666:56

Ma'amoul, dates and nuts pastry, recipe 1245:23

LEBANON—FESTIVALS—COOKERY

Eid al-Adha; teen mihshee (stuffed figs), recipe 1666:56

LEBANON—GAMES

Pebble toss game, how to play 1494:157

Stone toss game 979:28

LEBANON—HISTORY—COOKERY

History of foods and cookery in Lebanon 667:188-200

LEBANON—NAMES

Naming Days information 695:25-26

LEBANON—NEW YEAR'S DAY

Celebration of New Year's Day in Lebanon 475:100

LEBANON—TOYS

Bird cage, cardboard and stick model, making 515:74

LEE, ROBERT E.—COOKERY

"Robert E Lee" cake, recipe 57:10

LENT

Activities and projects for classrooms 1393:170-171

Appreciation award, pattern, making 873:55

Ash Wednesday 139:49

Ash Wednesday; celebration of 496:40

Beatitude collage, making 873:30

Boaster poster, making 873:49

Celebrate with children's balloons, making 873:32

Chain of hearts, paper, making 873:4

Cross, pattern, making 873:59

Egg-shell boat, making 139:77

Family collage, making 873:17

Family parable, making 873:27

Family puzzle, making 873:20

Flowers, planting 873:13

Gift tags, making 873:18

Lenten calendar, making 873:6-7

Lenten grab bag, making 873:14

Mothering Sunday; celebration of 496:42

Nine Tailors 139:78

Palm Sunday; celebration of 496:43-44

Passion Sunday, Carlin Sunday, celebration of 496:43

Place mats, making 873:36

Prayer tree, paper, making 873:8-9

Procession with cross, making 873:58-59

Sheep maze, making 873:23-25

Sundays of Lent; celebration of 496:41-42

LENT—COOKERY

Pancakes, recipe 1032:194

Pretzels, recipe 1409:21

Seder meal, making 873:56-57

Unleavened bread, recipe 873:57

LEPRECHAUNS

Card, making 209:17-18; 209:17-18

Leprechaun stories, songs, art activities, games, recipes 1135:47-49

Leprechaun, milk carton, making 79:12

Leprechaun, paper models, patterns, making 639:30-31

Leprechaun, paper plate, pattern, making 413:13-14

Leprechaun, paper, large pattern, making 477:45-48

Leprechaun, pattern, making 128:7; 208:8; 1192:14

Shamrock leprechaun, paper, pattern, making 254:48-51

LEPRECHAUNS—COSTUMES

Leprechaun costume, making 842:37-39

LEPRECHAUNS—FINGER PLAYS

Finger plays and rhymes 1583:195

LEPRECHAUNS—HATS

Leprechaun hat, paper, pattern making 128:11; 254:46-47

LEPRECHAUNS—MASKS

Leprechaun mask, pattern, making 275:54

LEPRECHAUNS—PUPPETS

Leprechaun styrofoam ball puppet, making 907:32

Puppet, paper bag mouth puppets, patterns, making 1155:197-198

LEPRECHAUNS—SONGS

Songs about leprechauns 901:58-60; 902:30

LESOTHO—COOKERY

Cornmeal flatbread, recipe 1165:17

Fried ripe plantains, recipe 1165:16-17

Setjetsa, vegetable and cereal dish, recipe 1165:16

LESOTHO—FESTIVALS—COOKERY
Moshoeshoe Day; cabbage and bacon, recipe 1666:15
Moshoeshoe Day; mealie-meal (cornmeal cakes), recipe 1666:16

LESOTHO—GAMES
Murabaraba game (Twelve Men's Morris), how to play 1688:67-70

LEVANTE, LES
You can't fool me, card trick, how to do 1270:26-27

LEVI'S
History of Levi's 119:114-117

LEVITIN, SONIA
"Journey to America," porridge, recipe 1216:18
"Nobody Stole the Pie," cherry pie, recipe 1216:53

LEWIS AND CLARK
Captain Lewis's field book with sketches of plants and animals, how to make with chamois, paper, yarn; 1214:13-14
Journal kept by Lewis and Clark, red paper, notebook, glue, making 1214:15-16
Lewis and Clark Expedition food supply information 663:87-90
Moccasins made by Indians for Lewis and Clark, chamois, thread, fabric paints, making 1214:17-19

LEWIS AND CLARK—COOKERY
Portable soup, recipe 1214:11

LEWIS, C. S.
"Lion, the Witch and the Wardrobe," Turkish delight, recipe 1216:86

LEWIS, THOMAS P.
"Hill of Fire"; science, reading, art, language arts activities 1055:123-128

LIBERIA—COOKERY
Abala, savory steamed rice, recipe 1165:37-38
Dried seeds for snacking, recipe 1165:36-37
Ginger cookies, recipe 1165:38-39
Kanya, peanut bars, recipe 1165:38
Liberian rice bread, recipe 1427:302
Real ginger ale, recipe 1244:101
Rice bread, recipe 1165:36
Sweet potato puffs, recipe 1380:25

LIBERIA—FESTIVALS—COOKERY
Agrarian Tribal Festival, black beauty and ponki rice (eggplant and pumpkin rice), recipe 1666:33-34
Agrarian Tribal Festival, rice with chicken, recipe 1666:34

LIBERIA—FOLKLORE—PUPPETS
"Who Is Strongest?" shadow puppets, patterns, making 1602:163-169

LIBERIA—GAMES
Hop-sing game, how to play 1494:20
Hopping fun game 515:76
Jumping game 602:32

LIBERIA—INDEPENDENCE DAY
Independence Day celebration July 26 722:13-17

LIBERIA—MASKS
Poro mask, making 222:44-46

LIBERIA—NEW YEAR'S DAY
Time of singing in Liberia 489:123-126

LIBERIA—PROVERBS
Proverbs of Africa 1478:52

LIBERTY BELL
History of Liberty Bell 333:65-74

LIBYA
Activities, flags, games, songs, dances, recipes 1381:137-140

LIBYA—COOKERY
Al Batheeth, date candy, recipe 1165:53
Couscous, chicken and vegetable dish, recipe 1381:139
Lamb couscous, recipe 1450:120
Lamb soup, recipe 1381:139

LIBYA—FESTIVALS—COOKERY
Eid al-Fitr, semesmyah (sesame candy), recipe 1666:40
Eid al-Fitr, stuffed tomatoes, recipe 1666:39-40

LIBYA—GAMES
Hopscotch, Neggeza game, how to play 1355:36

LIFE SAVERS CANDY
History of Life Savers 119:147-151

LIGHTHOUSES
Lighthouse, cardboard carton, making 679:unp
Lighthouse, cookies, making 1672:87-88
Paper plate lighthouse, making 534:36
Roop, Peter, "Keep the Lights Burning, Abby"; science, reading, art activities 1055:139-143

LINCOLN, ABRAHAM
Abraham Lincoln, paper models, patterns, making 639:24-25
Abraham Lincoln, paper plate, pattern, making 413:12,19
History of Lincoln's birthday celebration 199:22
Learning units, art, language, music, foods, crafts, patterns 1193:342-395

LINCOLN, ABRAHAM—BIRTHDAY
Abe, cut-and-paste, paper, making 95:20
Accordion-pleated paper Lincoln, making 50:214
Activities and projects for classrooms 1393:141-145
Activities, art, crafts, patterns, songs, recipes, games 50:205-215; 1469:64-65; 1473:97, 101-102
Art, cooking, finger plays, games, drama, math, science, and music, activities 54:186-187
Birthday celebration; art, music, foods, games, activities 1104:58-61
Lincoln/Washington, milk carton, making 79:11
Penny rubbings, pennies, paper, pencil, making 1199:45

LINCOLN, ABRAHAM—COOKERY
Apple pan dowdy, Abe's favorite, recipe 1193:351
Gingerbread with lemon sauce, recipe 871:54-55
Lincoln log cake, recipe 698:25
Vanilla almond cake (Mary Lincoln's white cake), recipe 57:31
Vanilla pecan pie, recipe 57:30

LINCOLN, ABRAHAM—COSTUMES
Abraham Lincoln costume, making 272:42-44
Mary Todd Lincoln costume, making 272:45

LINCOLN, ABRAHAM—DECORATIONS
Log cabin mural, making 906:19

LINCOLN, ABRAHAM—GAMES
Abraham Lincoln's birthday game 240:1,4
Birthday celebration, pitching pennies game 1199:44
Milkie, Abe's marble game, how to play 1651:46-47
Presidents' Day game 240:14-15

LINCOLN, ABRAHAM—HANDICRAFTS
Abe's log cabin, making 561:78
Edible log cabin, milk carton, pretzels, making 1662:32
Lincoln's log cabin, making 199:23-25; 698:24
Log cabin popcorn centerpiece, making 939:36-40
Log cabin, cardboard, making 891:15-20
Log cabin, making 648:14-15
Log cabin, milk carton, making 607:unp

Log cabin, paper logs, how to make 1342:87
Log cabin, paper rolls, making 916:100-101
Place cards, candy dish, coaster, making 226:14-16
Top hat pin, paper, making 448:47

LINCOLN, ABRAHAM—HANDS ART ACTIVITIES
Hands activities, Mr. Lincoln, making 306:35

LINCOLN, ABRAHAM—HATS
Abraham Lincoln's hat, paper, pattern, making 648:14-15; 823:33
Stove pipe hat, paper, making 1662:33

LINCOLN, ABRAHAM—PATTERNS
Lincoln silhouette, pattern 1193:388
Log cabin pattern, how to make 1393:142-143
Silhouette head pattern, making 1393:145
Silhouette, paper plate, making 374:154-156

LINCOLN, ABRAHAM—PUPPETS
Abe Lincoln tongue depressor puppet, making 907:29
Abraham Lincoln puppet, pattern, making 754:33-40; 1006:31
Lincoln rod puppet, paper, making 384:Feb 12
Puppet Play; Young Abe Wrestles Armstrong 754:30-33

LINCOLN, ABRAHAM—SONGS
Honest Abe song 792:unp; 1150:15
Songs for Abraham Lincoln's birthday 901:53-54

LINCOLN LOGS
History of Lincoln Logs 511:160-161

LINDBERGH, CHARLES—COSTUMES
Lucky Lindy, fabric, notions, patterns, making 1435:108-111

LINDGREN, ASTRID
Pippi Longstocking doll, cardboard tube, paper, making 1420:36

LIONS
Lion, pop-up, paper, pattern 1210:42-43

LITHUANIA—CHRISTMAS
Christmas tree and decorations, how to make 593:64-75

LITHUANIA—DANCES
Kalvelis dance, how to do 1494:141-142

LITHUANIA—EASTER—COOKERY
Lemon sauce, recipe 1666:134
Potato and apple pudding, recipe 1666:133
Sweet apple bread pudding, recipe 1666:134

LITHUANIA—HANDICRAFTS
Lithuanian straw construction mobile, making 452:89-91

LITTER
Green messages using litter, making 1701:26-27

LITTERBAG DAY
Activities, art, songs, recipes, games 1469:90-91

LITTLE FEAST. *See* **IRAN—CHRISTMAS**

LITTLE RED HEN
Puppets, costumes, masks, cooking, science, math, music activities 1358:58-83

LITTLE RED HEN—COOKERY
Quick grain of wheat bread, recipe 1215:12

LITTLE RED RIDING HOOD
Puppets, costumes, masks, cooking, science, math, music activities 1358:1-24

LITTLE RED RIDING HOOD—COOKERY
Grandmother's chocolate cupcakes, recipe 569:49-52
Granny's custard, recipe 1215:26
Little Red Riding Hood sugar cookies, recipe 738:unp

LITTLE RED RIDING HOOD—DOLLS
Double doll, Little Red Riding Hood and Wolf, fabric, felt, stuffing, patterns, making 1463:58-69

Red Riding Hood cloak for dolls, fabric, making 493:207-210
Red Riding Hood, Hansel and Gretel dolls, fabric, patterns, making 484:88-92

LITTLE RED RIDING HOOD—PUPPETS
Finger puppet, patterns, story, making 512:83-88
Granny and wolf puppets, fabric, felt, making 830:164-167
Little Red Riding Hood, puppets and puppet play script, making 1155:52-57
Puppets, paper bag, patterns, making 940:40-44
Red Riding Hood fabric and felt puppet, making 830:160-161

LITTLE WOMEN
Jo's New England boiled dinner, recipe 570:45-47
Little Women, descriptions and pictures of house 29:Chapter 3

LOBEL, ANITA
"The Pancake," pancakes, recipe 1216:10

LOBEL, ARNOLD
Cookies from "Frog and Toad Together," no bake chocolate chip cookies, recipe 1216:79

LOG CABINS. *See also* **LINCOLN, ABRAHAM**
Abe's log cabin, making 561:78
Gingerbread log cabin, dough recipe, patterns, making 1203:20
Lincoln log cabin, making 698:24
Log cabin from Canada, cardboard and paper model, making 1094:19
Newspaper log cabin, making 1312:13
Pioneer log cabin, paper rolls, making 1017:25
Pretzel log cabin on paper, pattern, making 1390:76-77

LONGFELLOW, HENRY WADSWORTH
Three Kings puppet show 756:73-76

LONGFELLOW, HENRY WADSWORTH—COOKERY
Double veal chops, recipe 57:34
Sons of Hiawatha; Hiawatha's custardy cornbread, recipe 365:67
Vegetable soup, recipe 57:35

LOOFAHS
Loofah, how to grow 1259:30-31

LORD, JOHN VERNON
"Giant Jam Sandwich," bread, recipe 1216:30

LOS POSADOS. *See also* **MEXICO—FESTIVALS**
Celebration 134:107

LOUISIANA—CARNIVALS
Mardi Gras carnival 474:11

LOUISIANA—COLONIAL PERIOD—CHRISTMAS—COOKERY
New Orleans sweet potato pie, recipe 1733:73

LOUISIANA—COOKERY
Bananas, baked, recipe 654:65-66
Chicken, sautéed a la Creole, recipe 529:104-105
Creole cookery of Louisiana in pioneer days 663:16-22
Jambalaya, recipe 654:64-65
Lost bread (Pain Perdu), recipe 529:106-107
Pecan pie, recipe 529:107-108
Rice, boiled, recipe 529:103-104
Shrimp gumbo, Creole recipe 663:29-30
Shrimp gumbo, recipe 529:101-103
Shrimp Jambalaya, history of, recipe 155:4-5

LOUISIANA—HISTORY—COOKERY
Creole cookery of Louisiana information 666:132-137

M

MACEDONIA—FESTIVALS—DECORATIONS
Prvi Mart (Macedonian Spring Festival), pop-up card, making 1387:14

MACEDONIA. *See also* **YUGOSLAVIA**

MAD HATTER—PARTIES
Mad Hatter Party, recipes and games 635:37-40
Mad Hatter Tea party, how to plan and give 86:120-127

MADAGASCAR—COOKERY
Soupe a la Malgache, soup of the Malagasies, recipe 1165:13
Tomatoes rougaille, tomato sauce, recipe 1165:13

MADAGASCAR—EASTER—COOKERY
Curried rice with raisin and nuts, recipe 1666:12
Shrimp in coconut milk, recipe 1666:12

MADAGASCAR—FESTIVALS—COOKERY
Famadihana; curried rice with raisin and nuts, recipe 1666:12
Famadihana; shrimp in coconut milk, recipe 1666:12

MADISON, DOLLY
Dolly doll, fabric, making 493:88-100

MAGAZINES
How to create and make 1630:5-46

MAGIC
Tomie dePaola's "Strega Nona's Magic Lessons," science, reading activities 1055:206-210

MAGIC—PARTIES
Harry Houdini birthday celebration, art, music, foods, games, activities 1104:74-77

MAGICIANS
Magician's cape, felt, pattern, making 1015:130

MAIDU INDIANS—FOLKLORE—PUPPETS
"How the Sun and Moon Came to Live in the Sky" shadow puppets, patterns, making 1602:170-177

MAIDU INDIANS—GAMES
There are no "Maidu" game, how to do 1608:27

MAIDU INDIANS—MUSICAL INSTRUMENTS
Musical bow, making 63:50-51

MAINE—COOKERY
Bread pudding, recipe 654:69
Cod, poached, recipe 654:68

MAINE—PASSAMAQUODDY INDIANS—GAMES
All-tes-teg-enuk bowl game, how to play 1507:96

MAIZE
Maize necklace, making 424:25

MAIZE—NATURE FESTIVALS
Maize corn festivals of the Aztecs 419:133-140

MAKAH INDIANS—COOKERY
Buckskin bread, recipe 1380:8

MAKEUP. *See* **FACE MAKEUP**

MALAGASY REPUBLIC—GAMES
Fanorona board game, patterns, making 1541:67-74

MALAITA—MUSICAL INSTRUMENTS
Stamping tubes, bamboo sticks, rocks, making 1649:45

MALAWI—CHRISTMAS—COOKERY
Chicken, ground nut, mtedza malawi, recipe 497:142
Cornmeal porridge, nsima, recipe 497:142

MALAWI—COOKERY
Steamed greens, recipe 1694:227

MALAYSIA
Activities, flags, games, songs, dances, recipes 1381:85-89

MALAYSIA—CHRISTMAS
Christmas celebration 601:84-85

MALAYSIA—COOKERY
Begedil, potato cutlet, recipe 1491:117
Biryani rice, recipe 1165:187
Biryani, lamb in yogurt, recipe 1165:187
Coconut rice, recipe 1380:21
Lemon rice, recipe 1165:186
Pengat pisang, banana porridge, recipe 1165:186

MALAYSIA—FESTIVALS—COOKERY
New Year; ayer batu bandong (rose cooler), recipe 1666:189
New Year; nasi mlinyak (Malaysian yellow rice), recipe 1666:188
New Year; sevian (rice vermicelli dessert pudding), recipe 1666:188
New Year; sothi (coconut shrimp soup), recipe 1666:187

MALAYSIA—GAMES
Bamboo long game 383:124
Blind quasar game 383:125
Calah panjang game 383:124
Football 602:74-75
Gasing, spinning tops game, how to play 1708:38-39
Grinding stone game 383:126
Kulit K'rang shell game 1119:21
Memutar pinggan, plate spinning game, how to play 1494:45
Turtle's nest game 383:125

MALAYSIA—HANDICRAFTS
Eggplant pottery, making 532:15
Malaysian mouse, paper, patterns, making 1246:36-37

MALAYSIA—HOUSES
Huts on stilts, dowels, sticks, clay, making 1488:20-21

MALAYSIA—KITES
Malayan Bow kite, making 1026:79-81
Malayasian kite, making 532:42

MALAYSIA—NATURE FESTIVALS
Rice growing festivals 419:94

MALI
Emperor's trousers, making 173:20-21

MALI—CLOTHING
Bamana people mud cloth, fabric, mud, designs given, making 1633:116-119

MALI—COOKERY
Peanut and meat stew, recipe 1165:45
Spinach and peanut stew, recipe 1165:44
Veggie rice, making 187:39

MALI—FESTIVALS
Chi Wara, making 222:36-37

MALI—FESTIVALS—COOKERY
Eid al-Fitr; lamb stew, recipe 1666:38
Eid al-Fitr; sweet couscous, recipe 1666:38-39

MALI—GAMES
Sey game 956:128-129; 1074:161
Sey, pebble hiding and guessing game, how to play 1708:40-41

MALI—HANDICRAFTS
Bambara spoon, making 222:12

MALI—TOYS
Horse, sculpted salt dough, making 1027:82-84

MALTA—COOKERY
Omelet, recipe 967:38

MALTA—FESTIVALS
Good Friday celebration 826:10-11

MANDAN INDIANS
Legends 344:24
Songs and stories of the Mandan Indians 344:24-33

MANDAN INDIANS—GAMES
Feathered darts, how to play 1699:118

MANDAN INDIANS—HOUSES
Mandan earth lodge, making 227:10-11

MANUSCRIPTS
Illuminated manuscript, cream paper, tea, felt-tipped pens, making 1183:21

MAORIS—COOKERY
Paraoa parai bread, recipe 1244:148-149

MAORIS—GAMES
Hipitoi game, similar to Simon Says, how to play 1355:44
Hurippa, jacks game, how to play 1718:16-17
Mu Torere game, how to play 956:130-131; 1688:35-37

MAPLE SUGAR
History of maple sugar 410:91-92

MAPLE SUGAR—COOKERY
Maple people, recipe 71:104-105

MAPLE SYRUP
Maple candy, recipe 285:92
Maple syrup candy, recipe 453:125-127

MAPS
Animals around the world, making 925:88-89
Pirate map, making 1683:21
Salt map mixtures for making maps, recipes 1455:11-13

MAPUCHE INDIANS—NATURE FESTIVALS
Harvest festivals of the Mapuche Indians of Chile 419:128-130

MARDI GRAS
Activities and projects for classrooms 1393:168-169
Finest and Fattest, traditional tale, France 139:38-43
King of the Carnival, New Orleans 139:44
Mardi Gras celebration 631:36
Mardi Gras masks, art and writing activities, patterns, making 1152:108-122
Meaning of the carnival 419:57-58
New Orleans' Mardi Gras, history of 709:138; 709:140

MARDI GRAS—COOKERY
Chicken gumbo, recipe 1382:18
King cake, recipe 1666:268
New orange pancakes, recipe 54:217
Raspberry lemonade, recipe 54:217
Red beans and rice, recipe 1666:269

MARDI GRAS—DANCES
La danse de Mardi Gras in French and English, music and score provided 1382:25

MARDI GRAS—ENGLAND
Pancake race celebration 709:139
Pancake race costumes, making 709:139

MARDI GRAS—ENGLAND—COOKERY
Pancakes, recipe 709:139

MARDI GRAS—MASKS
Carnival heads made from coasters, making 1420:8
Carnival masks, sun, clown, cat, paper plates, patterns 1199:37-39; 1420:8
Mask, giant box mask, pattern, making 361:76-77

MARDI GRAS—MUSICAL INSTRUMENTS
Maracas, papier-mache, making 1277:4-5

MARDI GRAS—PUPPETS
Puppet projects, patterns, scenes, story starters, feature story 1083:59-61

MARDI GRAS—SWITZERLAND—MASKS
Basle double mask, making 709:140-141

MARINES—COSTUMES
Marine costume, making 272:79-80

MARIONETTES
Angel marionette, fabric, making 553:20-21
Butterfly marionette, paper, straws, string, patterns, making 1138:20-23
Cardboard marionettes, making 729:18-19
Clown spool marionette, making 757:162-183
Fish marionettes, paper, making 291:66-71
Five-string marionettes, making 745:56-57
Girl marionette, making 681:36-39
Leprechaun marionette, making 754:72-97
Marionette magic, paper, making 311:50
Marionettes, making 70:34; 483:16-25; 585:8
Nutcracker tube marionette, making 757:139-161
Paper napkin marionettes, making 545:86-87
People marionettes, making 745:58-59
Pinocchio paper tube puppet, making 384:Nov.24
Robot marionette, wood, making 926:72-75
Simple marionettes, making 745:52-53
Spacemen marionettes, making 361:36-45
Spooky the Ghost scarf marionette, making 757:133-138
Three-string marionettes, making 745:54-55
Tissue marionette, making 831:62-64

MARK TWAIN. *See* **CLEMENS, SAMUEL**

MARSHALL, JAMES
"George and Martha," split pea soup, recipe 1216:68
"Yummers!" banana split bar, recipe 1216:87

MARTINIQUE—HANDICRAFTS
Pierced-pattern candle holders, clay, making 1070:111-113

MARTINQUE—VOLCANOES
Pelean eruption, model volcano demonstrates 1455:79

MARY POPPINS. *See also* **TRAVERS, P. L.**

MARY POPPINS—COOKERY
Angel cake, recipe 1643:39
Apple Brown Betty, recipe 1643:39
Apple Charlotte, recipe 1643:39
Apple crumble, recipe 1643:40-41
Apricot puree, recipe 1643:42
Arrowroot drink, recipe 1643:43
Baked custard, recipe 1643:44
Beef patties or small hamburgers, recipe 1643:45
Blackberry and apple puree, recipe 1643:46
Bread and butter pudding, recipe 1643:47
Bread sauce for roast chicken, recipe 1643:48
Candy kisses, recipe 1643:118
Carrots, recipe 1643:49
Ceiling cake, recipe 1643:50
Cheese on toast, recipe 1643:51
Cherry pie, recipe 1643:52-53
Chocolate fudge, recipe 1643:54
Date bread, recipe 1643:55
Dumplings, recipe 1643:57
Dundee cake, recipe 1643:58-59
Easter cake, recipe 1643:60-61
Fish cakes, recipe 1643:64-65
French toast, recipe 1643:66
Fruit salad, recipe 1643:67
Gingerbread stars, recipe 1643:68
Gooseberry fool dessert, recipe 1643:69
Ham scallop, recipe 1643:72-73
Honey and bananas, recipe 1643:74
Honey bread, recipe 1643:75
Irish stew, recipe 1643:76
Jam tarts, recipe 1643:77
Kedgeree fish dish, recipe 1643:80
Kings or Twelfth Night cake, recipe 1643:81

Ladies' cookies, recipe 1643:82
Lancashire hot pot stew, recipe 1643:83
Lemon pudding, recipe 1643:85
Lemon souffle, recipe 1643:86-87
Macaroni and cheese, recipe 1643:88
Meat loaf, recipe 1643:89
Nut loaf, recipe 1643:92
Oatmeal cookies, recipe 1643:93
Onion tart, recipe 1643:94
Orange pudding, recipe 1643:95
Pancakes, recipe 1643:96
Pineapple fritters, recipe 1643:97
Queen of puddings, recipe 1643:98-99
Rice and raisin pudding, recipe 1643:100
Roast chicken, recipe 1643:102
Rock cake, recipe 1643:103
Salad dressing, recipe 1643:56
Shepherd's pie, recipe 1643:105
Shortbread, recipe 1643:106
Trifle, recipe 1643:108-109
Upside down cake, recipe 1643:111
Very plain cake, recipe 1643:114
Walnut cake, recipe 1643:115
Welsh rarebit, recipe 1643:117
Yorkshire pudding, recipe 1643:119
Zodiac cake, recipe 1643:120

MARYLAND—COOKERY
Chicken Maryland, recipe 529:57-59
Crab cakes, recipe 1043:104
Crab, deviled, Baltimore recipe 529:55-57
Fried oysters, recipe 1043:103
Maryland fried chicken, history of, recipe 155:12-13
Maryland stuffed ham, recipe 654:71
Strawberry fool, recipe 654:72

MARYLAND—HISTORY—COOKERY
Maryland Eastern Shore and Nation's Capital foods information 666:82-87

MASAI—BIRTHDAYS
Coming of age ceremonies 660:56-58

MASKS. *See also* **HALLOWEEN—MASKS**
Africa double face mask, making 811:73
African ceremonial mask, papier-mache, making 1027:85-88
African decorative mask from beans and nuts, making 623:9-11
African mask carved wood plaque, making 382:54
African mask for Halloween, pattern, making 1016:193-198
Aluminum foil mask of your own face, how to make 1350:76-77
Brazil Waura Indian patapu mask, making 143:13
Cameroun dance mask, making 811:74
Carnival masks, history of 596:47-51
Chinese dragon mask, making 709:111
Clown masks from papier-mache, making 1260:34-35
Computer project: design and draw 1218:80-83
Currier and Ives, "Favorite Cat" mask, making 105:66-67
Dragon head mask, papier-mache, making 596:64-68
Dragon mask, making 840:13-14; 846:16-19
Dragon mask, paper, making 290:27-33
Dwarf mask, making 840:20-21
Eagle mask, making 811:85
Egyptian, paper, making 480:119
Eskimo bone mask, making 229:75-78
Eskimo mask, carved wood, making 673:239-253

Eskimo papier-mache mask, making 755:91-108
Eskimo spirit mask, paper plate, making 480:124
Eskimo spirit totem masks, making 596:41-45
European Festival masks 204:77-80
False Face Society masks 462:28-29
Far Eastern masks 204:26-31
Gabon Africa mask, making 811:61
Geisha mask, making 846:38-39
Grecian soldier shadow mask, making 969:41-43
Greek Tragedy mask 204:73-76
Haida Indian mask, cardboard, patterns, making 1051:99-103
Harriet Tubman paper mask, making 755:78-82
History of European masks 204:10-16
History of masks 204:1-9; 596:1-8,27-32; 755:13-28
Indian corn husk mask, making 811:78
Indian Kacina mask, making 324:44
Indian mask, making 355:24; 846:34-35
Indian masks, cardboard, making 482:80-81
Indian masks, how to draw 591:28-29
Iroquois corn husk mask, making 324:45
Iroquois False Face, making 596:32-35
Ivory Coast Baule mask, papier-mache, making 1022:30-32
Janus head mask, papier-mache, making 596:62-63
Janus mask, pattern 1193:246
Kachina mask, making 63:26-27; 596:35-39
King mask, making 811:48; 840:3-4; 846:10-13
King mask, paper, making 290:14-21; 966:20-21
Knight face from paper bag, making 678:9
Knight mask, making 846:14-15
Leprechaun, pattern, making 275:54
Lion mask from China, making 532:30-31
Mardi Gras Basle double mask, making 709:140-141
Mardi Gras giant mask, pattern, making 361:76-77
Mardi Gras King and Queen head masks, papier-mache, making 596:64
Mardi Gras masks, paper plates, patterns, making 1152:113-117
Micronesia mask, making 811:71
Moon mask, cardboard, patterns, making 1051:68-73
Paul Bunyan mask, paper, patterns, making 92:17-19
Pirate mask, making 846:36-37
Pocahontas paper bag mask, making 755:51-57
Prince mask, making 840:7-8
Princess mask, making 811:49; 840:9-10; 846:20-21
Queen mask, making 811:44; 811:48; 840:5-6
Queen mask, paper, making 290:22-26
Rangdas mask from Indonesia, making 532:28
Santa Claus mask, making 848:12-13
Santa Claus mask, paper plate, fiber fill, making 1568:34-35
Shaman mask from Korea, making 532:29
South Pacific masks 204:32-36
Spring masks, history of 596:69-71
St. Nicholas mask, making 709:62-64
Sun God head mask, papier-mache, making 596:59-61
Three-dimensional masks, waste paper, making 1732:19
Totem masks, making 596:41-46
Troll King mask, making 811:75
Troll mask, making 840:20-21
Tuscarora Harvest mask, making 596:39-41
Venetian mask, making 295:190
Waura Indians patapu mask, making 143:13
Winnie the Pooh masks, paper, making 277:95-96
Witch doctor mask, wool, making 690:45

Wizard mask, making 811:70
Wizard mask, paper, making 290:33-35
MASKS—INDIANS. *See* **INDIANS OF NORTH AMERICA—MASKS**
MASSACHUSETTS—CHRISTMAS
Boston candle in the window tradition 475:54
MASSACHUSETTS—COOKERY
Boston baked beans, history of, recipe 155:22-23
Candied cranberries, recipe 654:75
Double veal chops, recipe 57:34
Irish soda bread recipe from Boston Irish immigrants, making 663:138-139
Tollhouse cookies, recipe 654:74-75
Vegetable soup, recipe 57:35
MASSACHUSETTS—HISTORY—COOKERY
Baked beans, codfish cakes and clam chowder information 666:25
Fish fries, clambakes, and sugarin-off parties information 666:42-46
New England desserts information 666:39-42
New England fireplace cookery information 666:30-36
New England foods and people today information 666:46-48
Puritan family at the table information 666:36-38
MASSACHUSETTS—OLD STURBRIDGE VILLAGE—COOKERY
Roast turkey and stuffing, recipe 57:54-55
MASSACHUSETTS—PLYMOUTH PLANTATION—COOKERY
Cambridge pudding, recipe 57:63
Poached bass or cod, recipe 57:62
MASSASOIT, CHIEF
Sock puppet, making 353:19
MATUYAMA, MOTONORI
Repeat Matuyama's experiment with magnetic fields 1719:52-54
MAURITANIA—FESTIVALS—COOKERY
Eid al-Fitr; lamb stew, recipe 1666:38
Eid al-Fitr; sweet couscous, recipe 1666:38-39
MAY DAY
Activities and projects for classrooms 1393:201-203
Activities, art, songs, recipes, games 1469:94-95
Activities, crafts, history and stories for 128:53-59; 819:76-82; 1473:131-136
Art, cooking, finger plays, games, drama, math, science and music activities 54:192-193
English celebration, activities, handicrafts, songs, foods, making 909:49-57
Finger plays, games, making 944:99-100
History and celebration of in Denmark, England, United States 419:61-64
History and celebration of in Switzerland, Burma and Japan 419:61-64
History and celebration of May Day 496:62-68; 709:157-159
May Day combat 51:75-77
May Day sports 51:72-73
MAY DAY—COOKERY
Sunshine oatmeal cookies, recipe 1735:65-57
MAY DAY—COSTUMES
Green Man, fabric, leaves, twigs, making 1466:23
Maypole costume, making 272:73-75
Queen of the May costume, making 272:70-73
MAY DAY—DANCES
Maypole dance 51:79-80; 698:53; 819:80-81

Maypole dance, how to do 909:53; 1473:134
Wind Up the May Tree dance 624:32-33
MAY DAY—DECORATIONS
Baldrics or sashes, fabric, ribbon, crepe paper, making 1266:59
Basket of dried flowers, making 210:88
Baskets and cones, making 447:70-75
Basket, circle, posterboard, patterns, making 1179:91-92
Basket, colored paper, patterns 909:51; 1237:101-110
Basket, from plastic tub and paper, making 891:69-72
Basket, from toothpicks, making 448:20
Basket, making 51:74-75; 217:65-66; 498:105-108; 648:29; 698:52; 883:23-25
Basket, mobile, making 448:20
Basket, paper, pattern, making 232:41; 351:9; 384:Apr30; 545:58; 760:94-95; 766:69-70; 819:77-78; 1393:203
Basket, paper bag, making 247:14
Basket, plastic bottle and ribbon, making 894:61-65
Basket, plastic container, old magazines, making 1377:6-7
Basket, plastic, with ribbons, making 310:197; 1393:202
Bracelet, button bracelet, patterns, making 1016:86-91
Cardboard roll ups, making 447:68-69
Crown of paper flowers, Tahitian coronet, making 1016:80-85
Daffodil, paper, making 835:55
Doily basket, making 835:57
Doily nosegay, making 835:58
Eggshell spring bouquet, making 448:21
Flora doll, making 709:157-158
Flower chain, making 648:28
Flower toss, making 709:160
Flower vases, hanging, from plastic tumblers and jars, making 894:66-69
Flowers, dried, making 698:52
Flowers, paper, making 698:51
Japanese origami flower, patterns, making 1016:75-79
May cone, paper, making 1179:92
May Day crowns, paper, making 909:51
May Day hat, paper, pattern, making 823:40
Maypole hats, flowers, ribbon, simple, making 1266:59
Maypole mobile, making 644:42-44
Maypole tree from beach umbrella, how to do 1266:60
Maypole, cans, paper plate, streamers, making 1310:134-135
Maypole, making 51:77-79; 698:52; 909:53; 1179:93; 1473:133
Maypole, straws and paper, making 835:59
Mayflowers, tissue paper, making 1473:132
Old fashioned nosegays, making 698:52
Party favors from cardboard tubes, making 448:20
Pom-poms, making 698:51
Roses and carnations, making 698:51
Silver daisy, making 698:51
Tissue flowers, making 835:56
Tulips or daffodils, egg carton, making 698:51
MAY DAY—FINGER PLAYS
Finger plays and rhymes 1583:113
MAY DAY—GAMES
Flower archery game, pattern, making 1473:134-135
May Day game 240:28
Nuts in May game, how to play 1031:26-28
Ring around the Maypole game, how to play 1266:63

MAY DAY—HANDICRAFTS
Maypole, majstang, sticks, rope, flowers, ribbons, making 1477:77

MAY DAY—HANDS
Hands activities, May basket, making 306:54

MAY DAY—PARTIES
Decorations, snacks, games, making 1266:59-63

MAY DAY—PUPPETS
Five May basket puppets, making 735:59
Puppet projects, patterns, scenes, story starters, feature story 1083:85-91

MAY DAY—SONGS
May Day song 782:unp; 1150:30
Maypole song 1477:59
Songs about May Day 901:70

MAYANS—BRIDGES
Build a bridge to demonstrate ancient Mayan suspension bridge, making 1719:18

MAYANS—COOKERY
Chocolate drink, recipe 659:45

MAYANS—FESTIVALS
Corn Festival celebration 659:42
St. Thomas Day celebration, Flying Pole dance 665:66-72

MAYANS—GAMES
Tlachtli game 1074:200-201

MAYANS—HANDICRAFTS
Mayan figure, clay, making 1070:115-117
Pollo or chicken made of paper, patterns, making 1633:76-77

MAYANS—LANGUAGE
Mayan numbers 1589:44-45

MAYANS—MYTHOLOGY—PUPPETS
"Hunahpu and Xbalanque" shadow puppets, patterns, making 1602:222-232

MAYANS—RITUALS
Growing up ritual 695:104-106

MAYFLOWER
Cut and paste picture, patterns, making 254:164-167
Mayflower centerpiece, miniature, paper, making 829:34
Mayflower ship in a walnut shell, making 436:32
Mayflower Thanksgiving tile, flour clay, clay recipe, pattern, making 1252:20-22
Mayflower wall hanging, felt, paper, yarn, making 1571:8-9
Mayflower, paper, making 94:12
Miniature Mayflower, making 180:24-27
Walnut Mayflower place cards, making 401:28-29

MAYFLOWER—COOKERY
Mayflower potato boats, recipe 1097:unp

MAYFLOWER—GAMES
I Sailed on the Mayflower game 1097:unp

MBUTI PYGMIES. *See also* **RAIN FOREST**
MBUTI PYGMIES—HEADDRESSES
Feather headdress, corrugated paper, straws, making 1488:12-13

MBUTI PYGMIES—JEWELRY
Jungle jewelry, pasta, seeds, paints, making 1488:14-15

MBUTI PYGMIES—PLANTS
Tropical plants, oranges, lemons, pineapples, how to grow 1488:10-11

MCCLOSKEY, ROBERT
"Blueberries for Sal," blueberry jam, recipe 1216:38
"Homer Price," doughnuts, recipe 1216:46

MCPHAIL, DAVID
"The Cereal Box," activities 1216:14

MEDALLIONS
Leather medallions, leather, making 1615:46-47
Punched metal medallions, making 1615:48

MEDICINE MAN. *See* **NAVAHO INDIANS—SAND PAINTING**
MEDIEVAL PERIOD. *See* **MIDDLE AGES**
MEGAPHONES
Megaphone, paper or cardboard, making 1622:17

MELVILLE, HERMAN—BIRTHDAY
Celebrate by making sailing ships from plastic bottles 1199:172-173
Celebrate by making sailor's knots, twine, dowel, beads, patterns 1199:175-177
Celebrate by making undersea art, paper, tissue paper, shells, glue 1199:178-179
Celebrate by making whale scrimshaw from soap, black tempera paint 1199:174

MEMORIAL DAY
Activities and projects for classrooms 1393:215-216
Activities, crafts, history and stories for 128:79-83
History of Memorial Day 199:32

MEMORIAL DAY—COSTUMES
Marine costume, making 272:79-80
Nurse costume, making 272:78-79
Parade costume, making 272:76-77

MEMORIAL DAY—DECORATIONS
Happy memory written by each student for display, making 1199:119
Memorial Day soldier, paper bag, patterns, making 234:44-45
Memorial Day soldier, paper, pattern, making 232:45
Patriotic windsock, nylon fabric, felt, making 1662:90
Poppies, red crepe paper, green pipe cleaners, making 1524:37
Tissue poppies, red tissue paper, pipe cleaners, making 1199:118-119

MEMORIAL DAY—FINGER PLAYS
Finger plays and games about Memorial Day 302:72; 944:106-107

MEMORIAL DAY—GAMES
Memorial Day game 240:30-32

MEMORIAL DAY—HANDICRAFTS
Parade stilts, making 199:34-35
Victory friendship pins, making 199:33

MEMORIAL DAY—WREATHS
Memorial Day wreath, posterboard, stars, glue, making 1662:89

MENNONITES—COOKERY
Popcorn cake, recipe 659:128

MERLIN
One-way street, card trick, how to do 1270:12-13

MERLIN—COSTUMES
Merlin, black felt, gold vinyl, gold cord, patterns, making 1656:145-150

MERMAIDS
Mermaids, papier-mache, making 1338:21-23

MERMAIDS—COSTUMES
Mermaid costume, fabric, making 1379:22

MERRY-GO-ROUNDS. *See also* **CAROUSELS**
Carousel and carousel animals, paper tubes, paints, making 1338:17-20
Merry-go-round cake, how to decorate 1178:122-123
Merry-go-round, cardboard, making 554:12-13

Merry-go-round, cheesebox and scraps, making 1130:26-27

Merry-go-round, cookies, making 1672:182-186

Mobile, Merry-go-round mobile, making 644:13

Paper folds, cut to make Merry-go-round, how to do 406:23-25

MERRY-GO-ROUNDS—COOKERY

Merry-go-round cake, recipe 449:57

MESOPOTAMIA—NATURE FESTIVALS

Tammuz God Nature Festival 419:19-22

METRIC SYSTEM—COOKERY

Apple crisp, recipe 45:74-75

Banana bread, recipe 45:55-56

Biscuits, recipe 45:57-58

Blueberry muffins, recipe 45:66-67

Brownies, recipe 45:31

Buttermilk pancakes, recipe 45:59-60

Chocolate chip cookies, recipe 45:32-33

Chocolate meringue cookies, recipe 45:34-35

Coffee cake, recipe 45:61-62

Cranberry muffins, recipe 45:68-69

Date bars, recipe 45:36-37

Date-nut meringue cookies, recipe 45:38-39

Dinner menu, recipe 45:83-86

French chocolate, recipe 45:81-82

Fudge, recipe 45:79-80

Ginger cookies, recipe 45:40-41

Granola type cereal, recipe 45:75-76

Grapenut bread, recipe 45:62-63

Hot cocoa, recipe 45:80

Iced tea, recipe 45:82

Meat loaf, recipe 45:83-84

Muffins, recipe 45:64-65

Peanut butter cookies, recipe 45:41-42

Popovers, recipe 45:70-71

Refrigerator date pinwheels, recipe 45:43-45

Refrigerator oatmeal cookies, recipe 45:46-47

Rolled sugar cookies, recipe 45:48-49

Sesame cookies, recipe 45:50-51

Soft sugar cookies, recipe 45:52-53

Uncooked raspberry spread, recipe 45:77

Uncooked strawberry jam, recipe 45:78-79

Whole wheat apricot bread, recipe 45:71-72

MEXICAN AMERICANS—COOKERY

Chango bars, chocolate chip and nut bars, recipe 1674:unp

Jalapeno bagels, recipe 1674:unp

MEXICO

Activities, flags, games, songs, dances, recipes 282:24-37; 1381:13-18

Culture unit, language, dress, foods, games, bibliographies 574:102-127

Lewis, Thomas P, "Hill of Fire"; science, reading, art activities 1055:123-128

Map and food products 189:6-11

MEXICO—BIRTHDAYS

Birthday customs 488:82-89

MEXICO—BIRTHDAYS—PARTIES

Fifteenth cumpleanos birthday party for girls 660:62-63

Mexican birthday party, making 896:19-25

MEXICO—BRIDGES

Build a bridge to demonstrate ancient Mayan suspension bridge, making 1719:18

MEXICO—CHRISTMAS

Celebration of Christmas in Mexico 497:104-106, 111; 516:8-13; 695:71-76; 1049:89

Christmas customs 149:64-65; 218:42-43; 473:60-63; 1717:24-25

Customs in Mexico 425:22

History of Christmas in Mexico 709:85-86

Mexican celebration, activities, handicrafts, foods, songs, making 909:119-127

MEXICO—CHRISTMAS—COOKERY

Apricot-filled pastries, recipe 1567:68

Bunuelos (fried pastry), recipe 1666:252

Bunuelos, donuts, recipe 1128:87

Candied pumpkin, recipe 1567:69

Capirotado, fuit and cheeses dish, recipe 1567:69

Chestnut cake, recipe 1567:68

Chocolate Mexicano (Mexican hot chocolate), recipe 1666:254-255

Christmas Eve salad, recipe 704:87

Cookies, Mexican nut cookies, recipe 704:91

Eggnog, recipe 1567:69

Empanadas, meat pastry patties, recipe 1567:66-67

Empanadas, recipe 704:88-90

Ensalada de noche buena (Christmas salad), recipe 1666:253

Ensalada de noche buena, Christmas Eve salad, recipe 1128:86

French toast, Mexican style, recipe 1567:67-68

Fried pastry, recipe 446:45-46

Nachos, recipe, making 843:66

Nut cookies, recipe 1567:68

Posada treats, recipe 1152:201

Pozole soup, recipe 1567:66

Red snapper Veracruz style, recipe 1567:66

Tamales, sweet, recipe 1567:67

MEXICO—CHRISTMAS—DECORATIONS

Christmas tree and decorations, how to make 593:156-163

Christmas, greeting cards, how to make 70:104

La Navidad Christmas pop-up card, making 1387:40

Papel picado pierced paper banner, tissue paper, making 1477:136

MEXICO—CHRISTMAS—FINGER PLAYS

Finger plays and rhymes 1583:82-83

MEXICO—CHRISTMAS—GOD'S EYE

Ojo de Dios, God's Eye, sticks, yarn, making 1567:71

MEXICO—CHRISTMAS—HANDICRAFTS

Angel luminaries, patterns, making 1152:70-75

Animals, wrapped yarn animals, papier-mache, yarn, making 1567:70

Christmas, candle holders, making 70:106

Christmas, greeting cards, making 70:104

Christmas, seals, holiday, making 70:107

Christmas, tree decorations, pompoms, mosaic ornaments, making 70:111

Christmas, Twelve Days of Christmas ornaments, making 70:109

Napkin rings, Mexican flowered napkin rings, making 704:84-85

Posada clay figures, making 856:50-57

Posadas, Christmas Pageants of Mexico, making 1589:10

Serapes, blankets, paper, making 909:121

Tin ornaments, Mexican painted tin ornaments, making 672:178-191

Wrapping paper, rainbow wrapping paper, making 70:108

MEXICO—CHRISTMAS—LANTERNS
Lanterns, making 1023:54-55

MEXICO—CHRISTMAS—PIÑATAS
Christmas spider piñata, balloon, paper, paste, patterns, making 1051:152-157

Donkey piñata, making 709:86-89

Mexican piñata, papier-mache, balloon, making 1575:30-32

Piñata games and songs 1589:14

Piñatas, balloon and newspaper, making 1023:58-61

Piñata, balloon, papier-mache, making 1393:102

Piñata, brown bag, making 54:225; 1083:190; 1459:31

Piñata, making 70:105; 497:114-115; 593:160; 698:102; 909:123

Piñata, papier-mache, making 473:62-63; 672:81-116

Star piñata, papier-mache, tissue paper, making 1567:72-73

MEXICO—CHRISTMAS—PUPPETS
La Posada and Procession puppet projects, patterns 1083:190

MEXICO—CHRISTMAS—SONGS
Christmas Cradle song 474:154

MEXICO—CLOTHING
Charro, suit, making 574:109

Poblana, skirt, making 574:109

Poncho, fabric, making 574:108; 1329:15-17

Rebozo, shawl, making 574:108

Serape from brown kraft paper, paints, making 1381:16

Serapes, blankets, making 574:108

MEXICO—COOKERY
Apple soup, recipe 1339:26

Arroz a la Mexicana, Mexican rice, recipe 1165:254

Avocado dip, recipe 189:26-27

Avocado salad, recipe 895:96

Avocado soup, recipe 1452:136

Avocado, recipe 1244:122

Bananas, grilled bananas, recipe 815:90-93

Bean burritos, microwave recipe 1263:56

Bean burritos, recipe 1542:66

Bean soup, recipe 1339:20

Bean tostados, recipe 895:95

Bean-pepper salad, recipe 1696:35

Beef stew, recipe 874:52

Beef-filled tortillas, recipe 1452:138

Blended fruit drinks, recipe 1696:40

Brown sugar candy (dulce de piloncillo), recipe 794:5; 1381:16; 1427:243-244

Bunuelos, recipe 1653:59

Burrito, recipe 54:225; 88:11; 1413:34-35

Burritos, making 187:3

Butter cakes (manticados), recipe 1427:244

Chango bars, chocolate chip and nut bars, recipe 1674:unp

Chayotes rellenos, squash, peppers, tomatoes, cheese, recipe 1452:139

Cheese cookies, tapabocas, cookies, recipe 72:159-160

Cheese nachos, simple, recipe 909:125

Cheesy quesadillas, recipe 1244:120

Chicken enchiladas, recipe 1339:28; 1605:41

Chicken fajitas, recipe 1265:26-27

Chicken with mole sauce, recipe 1339:27

Chile, recipe 574:107

Chili con came, recipe 652:48-49; 1113:24-25; 1413:40-41

Chili dip, microwave recipe 1263:27

Chimichangas (deep fried filled tortillas), recipe 1427:244-245

Chocolate caliente Mexicano, hot chocolate 17:36; 1589:34-35

Cocoa balls, recipe 1251:43

Confetti rice, recipe 1265:28-29

Corn and wheat tortillas, recipe 88:8-10

Corn cake, recipe 967:40

Corn chips, recipe 909:125

Corn tortillas, recipe 1455:128; 1589:30-31

Cornbread, fast and easy, recipe 1265:30

Cowabunga casserole, microwave recipe 1263:99

Crisp tortillas with beef, recipe 189:42-43

Donkey ears, fried puffed pastries, recipe 1650:42

Empanadas, recipe 1032:262-263

Enchilada and sauce, recipe 189:22-23

Enchilada sauce, recipe 251:90

Enchilada with salsa de jitomate, recipe 17:25-26

Enchiladas, recipe 574:107; 858:unp; 1536:last

Estofado, beef and vegetable dish, recipe 1339:22

Fiesta fajitas, beef or chicken salsa tortillas, recipe 1696:21

Flan (Mexican custard), recipe 1427:245-246

Fresh salsa, recipe 1244:121

Fried pastry, recipe 189:36-37

Fried potatoes, recipe 1696:31

Fried tortillas with cheese, recipe 189:38-39

Frijoles refritos, recipe 17:22

Frijoles, bean dish, recipe 574:106; 1452:140

Fruit snack, recipe 1385:44

Guacamole dip, recipe 17:30; 189:26-27; 574:113; 815:90-93; 967:39; 1165:252-253; 1178:102; 1329:10-11; 1339:20; 1385:42-43; 1413:24-25; 1542:98; 1543:69; 1560:33; 1605:55; 1665:94

Guacamole salad, recipe 514:140

Guacamole soup, recipe, making 909:125

Guacamole tacos, recipe 1204:78

Hamburger hash, recipe 189:32-33

Hot chocolate, microwave recipe 1211:20

Hot chocolate, recipe 523:28; 574:107; 1244:123; 1380:12; 1605:44; 1652:18; 1696:38

Huevos rancheros, ranch-style Mexican eggs, recipe 1165:253-254

Jalapeno bagels, recipe 1674:unp

Kidney bean salad, recipe 189:40-41

Mango with cinnamon dessert, recipe 1280:45

Mango with cinnamon, recipe 189:25

Meat and potato tacos, recipe 1696:23

Meat, skewered meat, recipe 815:90-93

Meatballs, recipe 1696:25

Mexi dip ole, recipe 1169:20-21

Mexican bean salad, recipe 1265:25

Mexican chicken, microwave recipe 1263:89

Mexican chocolate drink, recipe 189:18-19; 1427:246; 1666:254

Mexican cornbread, recipe 1380:29

Mexican meal, decorations and foods to serve 815:11-13

Mexican menus 189:16-17

Mexican-mix casserole, recipe 540:32-33

Mexican rice, recipe 189:28-29; 1696:29

Mexican sauce, recipe 1339:25

Mexican smoothie drink, recipe 1385:39

Mexican tamale pie, recipe 653:65,120-121
Mole poblano de guajolote (fowl in chocolate chili sauce), recipe 17:43; 1666:254
Nachos, microwave recipe 1263:29
Nachos, recipe 189:38-39; 384:Sept 16; 1381:16; 1660:19
Nachos, tortilla chips, refried beans, recipe 1542:99
Naquis (doughnuts), recipe 1427:247
No-fry tortilla chips, recipe 1696:30
Nut brittle, recipe 1477:108
Pan dulce, sweet bread, recipe 574:107
Pastelitos de boda (wedding cake), recipe 1427:247
Peppers and egg, recipe 815:90-93
Peppers stuffed with shrimp, recipe 1339:21
Picadillo, spiced ground meat, recipe 1165:255
Pinapple sorbet, recipe 1339:22-23
Pollo pibil, recipe 17:34
Polvorones, Mexican wedding cookies, recipe 1165:255
Polvorones, sugar cookies, recipe 1605:44
Polvorones, tea cakes, recipe 1452:141
Quesadillas, cheese snack, recipe 812:113; 1427:248
Quesadillas, refried beans, cheese on tortilla, recipe 1715:106
Quesadillas, tortillas with cheese, recipe 1589:32-33; 1665:66
Quesadillas, wheat tortillas and cheese, recipe 1385:21-22
Red snapper with lime juice, recipe 189:30-3 1
Refried beans, recipe 189:24; 793:12; 1380:30; 1560:33
Rice delight, recipe 523:27
Rice pudding, recipe 895:97; 1265:31
Rice with milk, recipe 189:44
Salsa cruda, recipe 17:20; 1477:93
Salsa, sauce, recipe 1385:31; 1542:100-101; 1560:33
Salsa, red tomato sauce, recipe 189:35; 1165:253; 1665:93
Salted pepitas, pumpkin seeds, recipe 1427:248
Sauce, Mexican, recipe 815:90-93
Skillet pasta, recipe 1696:28
Sopaipillas, recipe 282:118; 1653:60; 1660:45
Stew, recipe 514:139
Taco salad, making 523:26
Taco salad, microwave recipe 1263:114-115
Tacos, beans, cheese, lettuce, tomatoes, recipe 1392:unp
Tacos, microwave recipe 1263:62
Tacos, recipe 189:34; 282:35; 343:60-61; 523:24-25; 574:107; 1178:68-69; 1381:15; 1427:249; 1536:last; 1605:22; 1653:92
Tacos, soft, recipe 1055:126
Tamale beef squares, recipe 1169:47-49
Tamale pie, recipe 662:106-107
Tamales, recipe 1666:251-252
Toasted cheese sandwiches, recipe 1696:24
Tortilla crisps, recipe 1169:18-19
Tortilla faces and twins, making 683:12-13
Tortilla roll-up, microwave recipe 1263:28
Tortilla soup, recipe 1696:34
Tortillas, corn, recipe 1660:44
Tortillas, hot chocolate tortillas, recipe 815:90-93
Tortillas, Mexican flat bread, recipe 1165:252
Tortillas, recipe 17:21; 251:94; 574:106; 1380:8; 1427:249; 1452:137; 1560:32; 1653:91; 1660:43
Tortillas, wheat, recipe 1385:19-20
Tortillas, with chicken, making 189:22-23
Tostados, microwave recipe 1263:68

Turkey baked with salsa and cheese, Mexican sombreros, recipe 1169:40-42
Two-cheese enchiladas, recipe 1696:20
Veracruz style fish, recipe 1339:25
Vermicelli soup, recipe 189:20-21
Wedding cakes, recipe 1696:39
Xochimilco salad, recipe 815:90-93
Zucchini and corn, recipe 189:32-33

MEXICO—COSTUMES
Boy's everyday outfit, making 815:33-34
Girl's dresses, making 815:40-45
Girl's everyday outfit, making 815:32-33
Guacamole, recipe, costume 188:4
Indian dancer costume, making 815:45-47
Jewelry and headdress, making 815:47-48
Man's traditional outfit, making 815:34-36
Mexican costume, drawing 988:27
Mexican costume, making 887:72-73
Mexican costumes drawing 988:37
Mexican Indian costumes drawing 988:63
Paper doll-type costume, pattern, making 282:36
Sombrero, making 815:35-36
Tunic, making 815:47
Zapata costume 213:130-132

MEXICO—DANCES
Chicken dance 697:30-31
El mosquito dance, how to do 1494:89-90
Handkerchief game dance 697:18-19
Hat dance, how to do 1362:144
Huapango dance and costume picture 1000:56-59
La Cucaracha dance, how to do 1494:82-83
La Raspa dance, how to do 1494:91-92
Let's Cha Cha, how to do 1494:87-88
Linda Mujer dance, how to do 1494:84-86
Mexican (Hat) clap dance song and dance game 1114:44-45; 1494:80-81
Mexican Hat dance hat, papier-mache, making 1310:141
Mexican Hat dance, music given, how to dance instructions 1381:17
Mexican National Folk Dance, Jarabe Tapatio 474:119-120
Raspa dance 815:55-57
Turkey game dance 697:34-35
Two and two are four dance 697:36-37

MEXICO—DOLLS
Amatl witchcraft dolls, brown paper, paint, making 1427:233
Colima clay doll, making 775:30-33
Doll, paper cup, yarn, patterns, making 1311:66-69
Mexican doll, felt, stuffed, patterns, making 487:26-27
Pedro doll goes to market, making 494:50-73

MEXICO—FACE MAKEUP
Huichol face, making with makeup 380:16-17

MEXICO—FESTIVALS
Activities, crafts, history and stories for 128:60-68
Cinco de Mayo art and writing activities, patterns, making 1152:146-151
Cinco de Mayo Festival finger plays, recipes, games, making 944:101-102
Cinco de Mayo, activities and projects for classrooms 1393:205-206
Cinco de Mayo; activities, art, songs, recipes, games 1469:98-99
Corpus Christi Day celebration (Flying Pole dancers) 665:72-74

Day of the Dead sugar skulls, marzipan, sugar, icing, making 1329:22
Day of the Dead, activities and projects for classrooms 1393:69-70
Day of the Holy Kings celebration 601:147-148
Decorations, characters, costumes and action ceremony 815:6-11
Festival of Independence, costumes, food, piñata, making 557:5-11
Festivals and celebrations, maps, flags, crafts, making 1305:75-84
Fiesta celebration 601:131-132
Fiestas in Mexico 474:25-27
Green Squash Festival celebration 709:55
Independence Day activities and projects for classrooms 1393:27-28
Independence Day finger plays and games 944:19-20
Las Posadas, Mary and Joseph's search for shelter, activities and projects for classrooms 1393:101-102
Piñata celebration 601:32-133
Posadas celebration 601:146; 631:106

MEXICO—FESTIVALS—CLOTHING
Independence Day serape and rebozo, making 557:7

MEXICO—FESTIVALS—COOKERY
Cinco de Mayo burritos, recipe 1662:79
Cinco de Mayo salsa dip, recipe 1662:81
Cinco de Mayo sangria drink, recipe 1199:111
Cinco de Mayo tacos, recipe 1553:31
Cinco de Mayo tortilla crispies, recipe 1662:80
Cinco de Mayo, chicken and tortilla casserole, recipe 1186:100-101; 1186:100-101
Day of the Dead, skull cookies, recipe 1477:121
Day of the Dead (Pan de los Muertos), Bread of the Dead, recipe 1424:last pg.; 1589:18-19; 1666:255-256
Independence Day chocolate drink, recipe 557:8-9
Independence Day taco salad, recipe 557:8

MEXICO—FESTIVALS—COSTUMES
Cinco de Mayo serape costume, paper bag, paints, patterns, making 1199:109
Hispanic boy costume, paper, making 128:63
Hispanic girl costume, paper, making 128:64

MEXICO—FESTIVALS—DECORATIONS
Cascarones, eggs, making 574:111
Flowers, tissue paper, making 574:110
Independence Day mural, paper, paint, making 1589:22-23
Placemats, paper, making 574:111

MEXICO—FESTIVALS—FLAGS
Flag, paper, making 857:36-37
Flags, making 574:111

MEXICO—FESTIVALS—GOD'S EYE
God's Eye, making 574:112

MEXICO—FESTIVALS—HANDICRAFTS
All Souls' Day Festival sugar-icing skulls, making 1277:22-23
Cinco de Mayo paper flowers, tissue paper, making 1553:30
Corpus Christi Festival; corncob donkey, making 495:46-49
Day of the Dead papel picado, tissue paper skeleton, pattern, making 1654:101
Day of the Dead paper skull, pattern, making 1393:70
Day of the Dead skeleton, patterns, cardboard, glitter, making 1730:32-37

Fiesta clay figures, making 1574:28-29
Independence Day noisemakers, making 557:6
Indian Idol statuette, making 815:67-68
Indoor Festival; decorative panels, flowering tree, mural panel, making 815:14-31
Indoor Festival; piñatas, jars, vases, place cards, programs, making 815:14-31
Tree of Life clay candleholders, clay, paints, making 1730:38-43

MEXICO—FESTIVALS—KITES
Cinco de Mayo fish kite, tag board, patterns, making 1152:150-151

MEXICO—FESTIVALS—LANTERNS
Cinco de Mayo paper lanterns, paper, making 1553:31

MEXICO—FESTIVALS—MASKS
Day of the Dead; skull mask, papier-mache, paints, making 1706:7
Indoor Festival celebration; metal mask, spotted pigeons, garlands, make 815:14-31

MEXICO—FESTIVALS—MUSICAL INSTRUMENTS
Cinco de Mayo maracas, paper plates, crepe paper, dried beans, making 1199:110
Fiesta seed shaker maracas, paper cups, beans, making 1539:100-101

MEXICO—FESTIVALS—PIÑATAS
Cinco de Mayo piñata, balloons, tissue paper, paste, making 1199:107-108
Independence Day Piñata, making 557:9-10
Piñata, balloon, making 128:67

MEXICO—FESTIVALS—PUPPETS
Day of the Dead Festival puppet projects, patterns, scenes, story starters 1083:189
Day of the Dead string skeleton puppet, making 1083:189
Mexican Fiesta puppet projects, patterns, scenes, story starters 1083:185-188

MEXICO—FISH
Angelfish, paper, paints, patterns, making 1251:36-39

MEXICO—FLAGS
Aztec emblem on Mexican flag model, cardboard, yarn, felt, glue, how to make 1182:28
Mexican flag, paper or fabric, making 1605:38
Pattern of flag 557:11

MEXICO—FOLKLORE
"La Hormiguita" flannel board story, patterns, making 1604:49-56
"Rattlesnake, Mouse and Coyote" flannel board story, patterns, making 1603:167-171
Three Sillies flannel board patterns, making 910:11,44

MEXICO—FOLKLORE—HANDICRAFTS
Burro's Load 126:67-70
Burro's Load, art activities, Eye of God weaving, making 126:74-75
Burro's Load, art activities, paper bag burro piñata, making 126:71-73

MEXICO—GAMES
A La Vibora de la Mar, Sea Serpent game, how to play 1589:40-41
Angel and the Devil game 876:50-51
Animal tracks game 474:33
Bread and cheese game 602:126
Chapete game, how to play 1507:93
Conquian card game 1132:97-99
Coyote and sheep game 282:121; 383:129

Dona Blanca circle game, how to play 602:128-129; 1589:38-39

El Periquito, the little parrot game, how to play 1494:75-76

Eye of the Great Maya game 815:53-54

Finger game 474:158

Flipball game 1354:160

Fruits game 383:129

Godparents game 602:129

House party game 815:49

Indian kickball game, how to play 1507:94

Indian kickball game, how to set up and play 1589:36-37

Kickball game 572:36-37

La Pelota game 383:128

Little ball game 383:128

Little clown game 383:127

Little parrot game 602:125

Los hoyos (the holes tag ball game), how to play 1708:42-43

Maitre d' Hotel Rodeo game 815:52

Maracas tag game, learn to say colors in Spanish, how to play 1646:9

Oranges and lemons chanting game 1118:33-35

Piñata and song, making 967:38-39

Piñata game, how to make 474:46-47; 697:40; 815:50-52; 1074:234-236; 1355:26-27

Ribbons game 602:124-125

Rompiendo La Piñata game 383:130

Salazar's obelisks game, how to play 1497:22

Singing game, naranja dulce or sweet orange, words 1477:63

Spot tag, how to play 1498:9

Spotted bird game 602:127-128

Street of the Tompeate game 602:125-126

Three gentle raps game 602:124

Tlachtli and bumpball game, how to play 1497:33

Tlachtli game, making 1074:200-201

Treasure of Rafael game 815:52-53

Treasure of the Aztecs game 815:50

MEXICO—GEOGRAPHY

"Hill of Fire"; physical and human geography activities 1458:42-45

MEXICO—GOD'S EYE

Eye of God, making 139:94; 296:68-69; 709:55-57

Eye of God, Ojo de Dios, birthday marker, yarn, making 298:242-243

God's Eye, how to weave using sticks and yarn, making 1605:16

God's Eye, mobile, making 452:115-117

God's Eye, yarn, twigs, making 1476:87-88; 1477:79

God's Eye, yarn, ice cream sticks, making 1427:236

MEXICO—HAIRSTYLES

Girl's festive hairstyles, making 815:37-40

MEXICO—HANDICRAFTS

Aztec codex, or picture book, posterboard, making 1633:54-55

Aztec Sun God, salt dough, paints, patterns, making 1633:50-53

Aztec warrior wall panel, making 815:74-77

Bark painting, brown paper, paints, patterns, making 1427:234

Bark paintings, plywood, paints, patterns, making 1251:32-35

Beaded dish, making 298:52-53

Burro, making 494:54-64

Candles, making 815:69-70

Candlestick, metallic, making 815:68-69

Cascarones, eggs decorated, making 627:97-99

Curandero healing books, brown bags, ribbons, making 1332:63-68

Ebony floral dish, making 298:192

Egg cascarones, making 114:92

Fiesta string, gourds and string, making 889:72-76

Fish net knotted lace, yarn, making 298:236-237

Flowers, tissue paper, pipe cleaners, making 1633:66-67

Knife sheath, making 467:78-79

Mermaids, papier-mache, making 1338:21-23

Papel Picado, pierced paper, making 1017:93

Papel Picado, pierced paper, tissue paper, string, making 173:18-21

Papeles cortados, paper-cutouts, patterns, making 1422:38

Paper figures, brown paper, making 1730:28-31

Pom-pom donkey pull, yam, making 298:234-235

Rooster, metal rooster, making 815:65-66

Time line accordion book, paper, ribbons, patterns, making 1332:53-58

Tissue paper flowers, tissue paper, wire, making 1427:240-241

Tree of Life, papier-mache, paper tube, paints, making 1633:62-65

Wall hanging, appliqued cloth, how to make 1278:18-19

MEXICO—HATS

Fiesta pom-pom hat, paper, pattern, making 823:48-49

Hat, Mexican hat tray, making 815:70-71

Sombrero from paper straws, making 828:88-89

MEXICO—HOUSES

Little house, making 494:68-73

MEXICO—INDEPENDENCE DAY

Independence Day celebration September 16 722:18-23

MEXICO—JEWELRY

Clay beads, making 574:109

Necklace, beaded, and loom, making 815:71-74

Necklace, tin and bead, making 298:72-73

MEXICO—LANGUAGE

Common words and phrases in Spanish 1411:27

Spanish words and numbers 574:115-116

Write like the Aztecs 1589:42-43

MEXICO—LANTERNS

Tin lanterns, making 70:102

MEXICO—MARKETS

Market stall, making 494:64-68

MEXICO—MASKS

Aztec recycled metal face mask, making 1706:21

God Quetzalcoatl mosaic mask, paper, patterns, making 1329:25-27

Masks from paper bags or cardboard, making 1605:53

Masks, paper plates, patterns, making 1427:236

MEXICO—MUSICAL INSTRUMENTS

Castanets, walnut or bone, making 468:40-41

Easy musical instruments, making 1662:76

Gourd guiro, making 468:32

Maraca, pantyhose container, dried beans, making 1088:52

Maracas from dried beans in plastic bottle, making 1394:25

Maracas from plastic containers, making 1361:54

Maracas, how to play 1646:8

Maracas, miniature, walnut shells, making 1429:88-89

Maracas, papier-mache, making 1427:234; 1455:17; 1662:77

Maracas, plastic bottles, rice, beans, corn, making 1646:6-7

Water drum, making 468:91

MEXICO—NAMES

Naming Days information 695:32-34

MEXICO—NATURE FESTIVALS

Planting festivals 419:140-142

MEXICO—NEW YEAR'S DAY

Fiesta time in Mexico 489:127-131

MEXICO—NEW YEAR'S EVE

Castillo celebration 665:8

MEXICO—NUMBERS

Numbers one to ten in Spanish language 397:unp

MEXICO—PAINTERS

Diego Rivera fresco painting, making 1455:26

MEXICO—PAINTING

Birds of a feather yarn painting, making 298:230-231

Huichol yarn paintings, colored pencil version, making 1338:24-26

Painted ebony paper plate, paper plates, paints, making 1427:237

String painting, vegetables, making, 297:70-71

Yarn and beeswax paintings, cardboard, yarn, making 1476:56

Yarn art bowl and picture, Huichol Indian designs given, making 1633:56-59

Yarn painting 70:98

Yarn painting, cardboard, yarn, making 1427:242

MEXICO—PIÑATA PARTY

Eye of God decorations, making 294:68

Fiesta flags, making 294:72-73

Flowers, pot of, making 294:69

Hat dance mat, making 294:80

Maracas, shaking, making 294:78-79

Mission bell toss game, making 294:74-75

Piñata party, piñata, paper bag, tissue paper, making 1178:170-171

Piñata, hanging, making 294:76-77

Senorita centerpiece, making 294:70-71

Serape placemats and invitations, making 294:66-67

Sol cake, making 294:67

MEXICO—PIÑATAS

Angel piñata, paper, making 1299:60-61

Piñata from papier-mache covered balloon, making 1278:24-25

Piñata, balloon, making 43:126-127

Piñata; bumblebee piñata, paper bag, making 1088:121-122

Piñata, making 297:198-199; 815:28-29

Piñata, paper bag, crepe and tissue paper, making 384:Dec12; 1017:94; 1427:238

Piñata, wooden frame, making 525:106-107

Piñatas, papier-mache, patterns, making 1455:19; 1654:99-100

MEXICO—PLAYS

Legend of Two Volcanoes play 815:58-64

MEXICO—POTTERY

Mayan figure, clay, making 1070:115-117

Metepec, Sun, plate-size pottery, dough, recipe, making 1372:67

Piggy bank, clay or papier-mache, making 515:80

Pottery from clay, pinch and coil pots, making 1605:50

Pottery, papier-mache bowls, paste, recipe, making 1427:239

Pre-Columbian pitcher, clay, making 1070:118-121

MEXICO—QUILTING

Yo-yo quilting, making 70:99

MEXICO—RITUALS

Growing up rituals 695:102-104

MEXICO—SONGS

Curate Won't Go to Church, Ma'am, nonsense song from Mexico 139:173-174

MEXICO—STENCILING

Basics and six patterns, making 70:100-101

MEXICO—TEA

Hot chocolate in Mexico 474:138

MEXICO—TIN WORK

Tin animals, making 482:112-113

Tin ornaments, aluminum trays, punch, patterns, making 1730:12-17

Tin rooster, aluminum pie plate, patterns, making 1633:60-61

MEXICO—TOYS

Secret bird box, papier-mache, pattern, making 1027:127-130

MEXICO—VILLAGES

Mexican village, clay houses, how to make 1351:32-33

MEXICO—WOOD CARVING

Mexican bull wood carving, making 382:32

MICE

Piñata mouse, making 122:67

MICHELANGELO

Fresco painting, making 1455:26

MICHIGAN—CHRISTMAS

Christmas gift to the people, Lansing, Michigan 475:67

MICHIGAN—COOKERY

Cornish pasties, recipe 654:77-78

Hollandsche Apple Koek, recipe 663:58-59

Rhubarb parfait, recipe 654:78-79

MICHIGAN—HISTORY

Dutch food on the Appleseed Trail in pioneer days 663:46-49

MICKEY MOUSE—PUPPETS

Mickey Mouse puppet, making 250:unp

MICMAC INDIANS OF CANADA—DOLLS

Corn husk dolls, making 1606:56-58

MICRONESIA—MASKS

Micronesia mask, making 811:71

MIDDLE AGES

Medieval-style meal of bread plates with food, how to serve to your friends 1350:88

Middle Ages program, activities, books, crafts, patterns, making 1159:148-160

MIDDLE AGES—BOOKS

Medieval book, paper, foil, thread, making 1332:119-130

MIDDLE AGES—CASTLES

Castle curtain walls, cardboard, paint, making 1682:26

Castle keep rampart walk, cardboard, paint, making 1682:26

Castle keep tower and roof, cardboard, paint, making 1682:24-25

Castle keep, cardboard, paint, making 1682:24-25

Castle siege tower and wheels, cardboard, paint, making 1682:27

Medieval castle theater, cardboard box, making 1386:87-89

Norman castle 212:48-59

Pop-up castle, making 1388:50-53

MIDDLE AGES—CHRISTMAS

Boar's head procession 202:95-96
Christmas celebrations in the Middle Ages 202:90-103
Christmas Customs and the Winter World 202:97-98
Democratic customs 202:100
Evergreenery in the Hall 202:91-92
First foot 202:93-94
Frumenty and Posset 202:95
Humble pie 202:100-101
Mistletoe and the kissing bush 202:92
Play of the Three Shepherds 202:101-103
Wassailing with the Milly 202:96
Yule candle 202:94
Yule log 202:95

MIDDLE AGES—CHRISTMAS—GAMES

Bee in the Middle game 202:98
Hunt the Slipper game 202:99-100
Meanings of Christmas games and Blind Man's Bluff 202:98-99

MIDDLE AGES—CLOTHING

Adornments, bells, buttons, fur, embroidered ribbon, making 774:70-71
Belt buckle, making 774:81
Bishop's alb, chasuble, cope, making 774:32-35
Bishop's crosier, making 774:110
Bishop's miter, making 774:96-97
Circle for cape, cope, cloak, mantle, how to make 774:2-9
Circlet, making 774:101
Court jester suit and hat making 774:47-48; 774:101-102
Craftsman gown, making 774:42-43
Crown, making 774:83-85
Designs, geometric, border, animal and flower designs, making 774:53-57
Fool's head, making 774:111
Hennin, making 774:98-99
Herald, tabard, making 774:40
Heraldic designs, making 774:59-61
Hood, making, 774:88
King's gown, robe, lining and collar, how to make 774:22-24
King's scepter, making 774:108-109
Knight breastplate and backplate, making 774:74-77
Knight shirt and tunic, making 774:38-39
Man's hat, making 774:86-88
Medallion, making 774:82
Merchant gown, and tunic, making 774:40-41
Minstrel suit and collar, making 774:48-49
Monk habit and cowl collar, making 774:36-38
Nobleman gown, making 774:30-31
Noblewoman gown and cape, making 774:26-29
Peasant gown and tunic, making 774:44-45
Pouches, making 774:106-107
Queen's gown, cape and collar, how to make 774:24-26
Robin Hood hat, making 774:103
Sorcerer gown, making 774:46
Sorcerer wand, making 774:109
T-shaped gown, how to make 774:10-15
Tunic, how to make 774:16-19

MIDDLE AGES—COAT OF ARMS

Stained glass coat of arms, window, paper, crayons, making 1682:13

MIDDLE AGES—COOKERY

Almoundyn Eyroun, recipe 202:127
Bacon and pea soup, recipe 1721:19

Bread, payn pur-dew, recipe 202:118
Bread, rose petal bread, recipe 202:119-120
Cake, circletes, almond cardamon cake, recipe 202:121-122
Cameline sauce, recipe 1268:10
Canel cucumber, recipe 202:128
Capon, sweet capon, recipe 202:122-123
Caraway seed shortbread, recipe 202:118-119
Chardwardon, recipe 202:128
Destiny cake, recipe 202:120-121
Dukess Wynges, recipe 202:123
Fruit beef, recipe 202:122
Fruyte Fritours, recipe 202:127-128
Green fish sauce, recipe 1268:11
Green salad, recipe 1268:9
Jusselle Date, recipe 202:126
Lamb stew, recipe 1268:29
Lamb's wool cider, recipe 202:130-131
Leek soup, recipe 1268:28
May Sallat, recipe 202:129
Mulled apple or pear cider, recipe 202:130
Mutton stew, recipe 1268:8
Pasta and apricot butter, recipe 202:125
"Pease porridge," dried green peas, milk, recipe 1268:28-29
Peppermint rice, recipe 202:124-125
Pokerounce, honey toast with pine nuts, recipe 1268:29
Swete f ysshe en doucette, recipe 202:123-124
Swithin cream, recipe 202:126
Wassail bowl, recipe 595:121-123

MIDDLE AGES—COSTUMES

Child's costume, crepe paper, making 687:41-43
Gowns and tunics, making 870:29-57
Knight costume with sword, helmet, fabric, foil, making 1379:27; 1509:18-19
Medieval costume, fabric, patterns, making 1174:28
Medieval tunic, cloth, making 181:30-31
Page costume, king costume, queen costume, peasant costume, information 417:11-19
Patterns 202:111-115
Princess costume, crepe paper, making 687:44-47
Robin Hood, Maid Marian, Friar Tuck, Little John, Sheriff costumes, making 774:50-51

MIDDLE AGES—DOLLS

Medieval dolls and clothes, patterns, making 3:102-107

MIDDLE AGES—EASTER

Easter celebrations 202:42-47
Morris Dancers 202:46
Mystery Play of Noah's Flood 202:46-47
Pace egging 202:43

MIDDLE AGES—FEASTS

Arranging the tables 202:107-108
Ceremonial objects on the High Table 202:109-110
Costumes 202:111-115
Costumes and Rotation robes 202:110-111
Decorating the Hall with banners and wall hangings 202:106-107
Decorations for the table 202:108-109
Lighting the Hall 202:107
Rotation 202:104-105

MIDDLE AGES—FESTIVALS

All Fools' Day celebrations 202:48-50
April Fools' Day April Revelry Revealed 202:50
April Fools' Day Feast of Fools and the Boy Bishop 202:49-50

April Fools' Day Lord of Misrule, Motley, and Whidder-
shins 202:48-49
April Fools' Day Mirror of Fools and Brunellus the Ass
202:50
Cuckoo song 202:60-61
December Hunt the Slipper and January Play of St.
George 202:83-84
Divination of February Valentines 202:84
Diviner eggs and Destiny cakes 202:62
Festival banner and coats-of-arms, patterns, making
1159:153
Festival costume pictures 1159:155
Goose Procession 202:78-80
June Mid-summer 202:84
Lamma Day bringing home the bacon 202:75-76
Lamma Day celebrations 202:73-76
Lamma Day High Summer Finale 202:76
Lamma feasts 202:75
Lamma Lands 202:73-74
May Day Maypole costume, making 272:73-75
May Day Queen of the May costume, making 272:70-73
May Day celebrations 202:51-56
May Day Spring Green Foods and Jack-in-the-Green
202:53-54
May Day wreaths and Baldrics for May guests 202:52
May Day wreaths and Hoops in the Hall 202:52
Maying-Round-the-Merry-Maypole 202:54
Maypoles 202:51-52
Medieval Feast 202:11-13; 202:13-15
Medieval Feast description 202:4-5
Medieval Feast Invitation to Ingenuity 202:15
Michaelmass celebrations 202:77-80
Michaelmass Glove 202:77-78
Mid-summer Eve celebrations 202:57-69
Mid-summer Eve crowns and boughs 202:59
Mid-summer Eve Cuckoo-Foot Ale 202:60
Mid-summer Eve Farewell Rogation and threading of the
needle 202:68-69
Mid-summer Eve Festival Fires 202:58-59
Mid-summer Eve First Rogation 202:59
Mid-summer Eve Play of St. George 202:65-68
Mid-summer Eve Rose 202:62
Mid-summer Eve St. John's Wort and Hemp Seed
202:62-63
Mid-summer Eve Wet Fire 202:63
Mid-summer Mumming Plays 202:65
Old Pagan Customs and New Medieval Uses 202:63-64
Peddler booth, sketch to copy 1159:154
Queen of the May 202:52
Souling and Soul cakes 202:84
St. Catherine's Day Catherine Cakes and Wiggs 202:88
St. Catherine's Day circles, candle jumps and fireworks
202:89
St. Catherine's Day Lamb's wool and the Catherine
bowl 202:88
St. Catherine's Day or Catherning celebrations 202:87-89
St. Johns Fern 202:65
St. Johns Humney 202:59-60
St. Swithin's Day apples for eating and bobbing 202:72
St. Swithin's Day celebrations 202:70-72
St. Swithin's Legend 202:70-72
Twelfth Night disguises 202:17
Twelfth Night fires 202:21-22
Twelfth Night Guise Procession 202:17
Twelfth Night Hobby Horse 202:23

Twelfth Night January celebrations 202:16-29
Twelfth Night Lamb's wool 202:20
Twelfth Night Mummers Mummings 202:23-24
Twelfth Night oranges and lemons 202:26-27
Twelfth Night Oxhorn cake and dance 202:22-23
Twelfth Night Play of St. George 202:24-26
Twelfth Night Three King's Star 202:28-29
Wassailing the Trees 202:19-20

MIDDLE AGES—FESTIVALS—GAMES
May Day backgammon game 202:55
May Day Nine Mans Morris game 202:55-56
May Day Superlative games 202:55

MIDDLE AGES—FOLKLORE—COOKERY
Pinto Smalto story and recipe for marzipan and coconut
kisses, making 364:90-100

MIDDLE AGES—FOOTWEAR
Mediaeval footwear, making 870:127-128
Shoes, making 774:104-106

MIDDLE AGES—GAMES
Apple bobbing 202:72
Backgammon 202:55
Bee in the middle 202:98
Billiards 202:55
Blind man's buff 202:99
Catherine candle jump 202:89
Chess 202:55
Egg rolling 202:43
Hoop rolling 202:52
Hunt the slipper 202:99-100
King William 202:37
Lady Anne 202:36-37
Lovers by Lot 202:34-35
Maying 202:54
Nine Mans Morris 202:55-56
Oranges and lemons 202:26-27
St. John's Humney 202:59-60

MIDDLE AGES—GARDENS
Plants for a Mary Garden, list given 725:12

MIDDLE AGES—HALLOWEEN
Apple Candlelight Procession 202:86
Apple Parings and Apple Bobbing 202:86
Crowdie 202:86
Halloween celebrations 202:81-86
Jack-o-lanterns and Bonfire in the Hall 202:83
King Crispin and the Revelers Boot Baldrics 202:83
Nutcrack Night 202:84-86

MIDDLE AGES—HATS
Jester's hat, egg carton, paper, making 1345:24-25
Medieval lady's hat, cone hat, ribbons, scarf, making
1671:16-17

MIDDLE AGES—HELMETS
Helmet, making 774:89-95

MIDDLE AGES—JEWELRY
Jewelry brooch, making 774:81

MIDDLE AGES—JOUSTING
Jousting stage with moveable figures, cardboard, paint,
making 1682:18-19

MIDDLE AGES—KNIGHTS
Frieze of day in life of a knight, fabric, cardboard, mak-
ing 1682:28
Knight's helmet, gray tag board, making 1486:26-27

MIDDLE AGES—KNIGHTS—PARTIES
Knights around the table party, decorations, games, costumes, recipes 74:150-166

MIDDLE AGES—NATURE FESTIVALS
  Spring rites and celebrations 419:56-57
  Winter and spring celebrations 419:53-56
MIDDLE AGES—PUPPETS
  Medieval puppet, making 483:18
MIDDLE AGES—TAPESTRY
  Tapestry, woven on cardboard loom, yarn, fabric, making 1679:12-13
MIDDLE AGES—VALENTINE'S DAY
  Country Superstition and Grand Idea 202:39
  Divining by Hemp Seed 202:39
  Love Divinations 202:38
  Night Yarrow 202:40
  Valentine Conversations and Rebus Writing 202:40-41
  Valentine's Day celebrations 202:30-41
  Yarrow 202:39-40
MIDDLE AGES—WEAPONS
  Catapult model, wooden trebuchet, balsa wood, dowels, string, making 1679:24-25
  Shield, making 774:79
  Sword, making 774:78
MIDDLE ATLANTIC STATES. *See also* **DELAWARE; MARYLAND; NEW JERSEY, NEW YORK; PENNSYLVANIA**
MIDDLE ATLANTIC STATES—COOKERY
  Apple pie, recipe 1576:45
  Brussels sprouts with parmesan cheese, recipe 1576:41
  Crab salad, recipe 1576:37
  Garlic bread, recipe 1576:40
  Hoecake rolls, recipe 1576:38
  Hot potato salad, recipe 1576:43-44
  Soul food barbecue sauce, recipe 1576:42
  Spaghetti with tomato sauce, recipe 1576:39
  Succotash, recipe 1576:43
  Three bean salad, recipe 1576:37
MIDDLE EAST. *See also* **ARABIAN PENINSULA**
  Activities, flags, games, songs, dances, recipes 1381:109-130
MIDDLE EAST—COFFEE
  Tafaddul, come and eat 474:137-138
MIDDLE EAST—COOKERY
  Almond soup, recipe 1452:146
  Apple burger meatballs, recipe 662:83-87
  Baba ghanouj, eggplant and spice dish, recipe 1244:113
  Borek, pastry and cheese dish, recipe 1560:40
  Burghul, recipe 1452:150
  Curried chicken, recipe 1452:149
  Date syrup, recipe 1189:47
  Falafel, chick pea snack, recipe 1313:57
  Fish, cold fish with rice, recipe 637:30
  Hummus, chick peas, tahini, recipe 1542:42
  Hummus, garbanzo bean paste, recipe 1380:32
  Hummus, chick peas, recipe 637:27; 1110:26; 1244:113
  Kebabs, ground meat, recipe 637:29
  Kebabs, recipe 1113:18-19
  Lamb stew, recipe 1452:147
  Lentil bake, recipe 1110:28-29
  Limoonada drink, recipe 637:36
  Matzo balls, recipe 1452:148
  Muhallabia, ground rice pudding, recipe 637:34
  Persian chicken, recipe 637:32
  Pilaf, recipe 1108:26
  Pita flat bread, recipe 1122:104; 1380:9
  Pita, recipe 1452:152
  Rice pilaf, recipe 1452:151
  Rice salad with pork, recipe 1108:28-29
  Salata arabieh,, recipe 637:31
  Spanish rice, recipe 1108:27
  Sweet figs, recipe 1452:153
  Tabbouleh, bulgar wheat dish, recipe 207:94-95; 1472:11
  Tobbouli, dressing, recipe 1653:35-36
  Turkish coffee, recipe 637:38
  Yogurt drink, laban, recipe 1564:59
MIDDLE EAST—COSTUMES
  Eastern costume, girl, making 368:73-78
MIDDLE EAST—FESTIVALS
  Noruz to Sizdar-Bedah, New Year, activities and projects for classrooms 1393:176-177
MIDDLE EAST—FESTIVALS—GAMES
  Ramadan Festival, hit the shadow game, how to play 1355:33
MIDDLE EAST—HAND DECORATIONS
  Decorate your hands with mehndi, how to do 1537:30
MIDDLE EAST—HANDICRAFTS
  Hand of Fatima, good luck charm, wire, ribbon, making 1477:43
MIDDLE EAST—NAMES
  Baby names information 695:122-123
MIDDLE EAST—WEAVING
  Weaving with palm leaves, making 1189:46
MIDSUMMER—COOKERY
  Grapefruit or orange baskets, recipe 1313:97
MIDSUMMER—FESTIVALS
  Sun fire circle dance, how to do 1313:93
MIDSUMMER—GAMES
  Oranges and lemons game, how to play 1313:98
MIDSUMMER DAY
  History and celebration of 496:74-75
MIDSUMMER EVE
  Solstice festivals 419:67-68
MIDSUMMER EVE—PARTIES
  Mid-summer Feast Party, recipes and games 635:53-56
MIDWEST—COOKERY
  American Indian wild rice cakes, cookies, recipe 72:153-154
  Angel food cake, recipe 1043:134
  Chicago deep dish pizza, recipe 1043:131
  Chicken with herbed dumplings, recipe, making 871:19-20
  Cinnamon rolls, recipe 1043:129
  Coneys, recipe 1043:133
  Dutch apple kuchen, recipe 1043:135
  Dutch cookery in the Midwest information 666:166-168
  Fish balls, recipe 1043:133
  Food Festivals of the Midwest and Great Plains information 666:180-181
  German cookery in the Midwest information 666:168-171
  Hoosier coleslaw, recipe 343:82
  Indiana herb cornbread, recipe 343:111
  Lemon chess pie, recipe 895:142
  Meat loaf, recipe 662:112-114
  Missouri dumplings, recipe 343:114
  Oven barbecued brisket, recipe 895:140
  Pasties, recipe 1043:132
  Potato salad, recipe 666:184
  Scalloped corn, recipe 895:141
  Scandinavian cookery in the Midwest 666:172-174
  Spritz cookies, recipe 1043:135
  Strawberry shortcake, recipe 666:185; 1043:134
  Swiss fondue, recipe 1043:130
  Wisconsin cabbage soup, recipe 343:95

MILITARY UNIFORMS
  Early American soldier model, making 719:18-19
MILK
  Animals giving milk 597:9-17
  Cream cheese, making 597:17
  Foreign language words for milk 1564:76
  History of milk 597:9-17
  History of milk in America 597:18-25
  Milk activities, art, science, songs, recipes 911:164-167
  Milk as food 597:39-40
  Preparation of milk for sale 597:28-34
  Use of milk in the world 597:41-42
MILK BOTTLES
  History of milk bottles 119:152-157
MILLS
  Finger plays and music for the Mill 689:65-68
MILLS—DOLLS
  Mill doll, fabric, patterns, making 1609:78
MILNE, A. A.
  Pooh Bear picnic, decorations, games, costumes, recipe 74:28-41
  Winnie the Pooh activities and recipes from Pooh books 1028:1-81
  Winnie the Pooh activities, math, language, science 92:142-153
  Winnie the Pooh and his friends, tracing patterns 1028:74-81
  Winnie the Pooh program, activities, books, crafts, patterns, scripts, making 1159:100-113
MILNE, A. A.—COOKERY
  Honey graham crackers, recipe 1495:82
  Winnie the Pooh's honey bears cookies, recipe 1199:12
MIMBRES INDIANS—POTTERY
  Mimbres pottery, clay, paints, making 1338:14-16
  Southwest Indian bowl, clay, making 1070:140-146
MINNESOTA—COOKERY
  Danish dessert, recipe 654:81
  Norwegian meatballs, recipe 654:82-83
MINNESOTA—COOKERY—GERMANY.
  See WISCONSIN—COOKERY—GERMAN
MINNESOTA—COOKERY—SWEDISH.
  See WISCONSIN—COOKERY—SWEDISH
MISS PIGGY
  Miss Piggy Day class celebration, making 1134:92-93
MISSISSIPPI—COOKERY
  Custard, recipe 654:85
  Fish stew, recipe 654:86
MISSOURI—CHRISTMAS
  Christmas Carols Are for Everyone, St. Louis, Missouri 475:67-68
MISSOURI—COOKERY
  Biscuits and gravy, recipe 654:88-89
  Dumplings, recipe 343:114
  Wigwam pudding, recipe 654:90
MISTLETOE
  History of mistletoe 709:73
MISTY OF CHINCOTEAGUE
  Chincoteague pot pie, recipe 570:37-39
MITTEN, THE
  Finger puppet, patterns, story, making 512:89-103
MOBILES. *See also* **STABILES**
  Angel choir mobile, making 452:95-97
  Angel mobile, making 669:138-139
  Bird mobile, stuffed birds, making 586:38
  Chad Gadya mobile, making 709:174-177

  Chanukah mobile, making 279:78
  Christmas ball mobile in circle, making 669:150-152
  Christmas ball mobile, making 669:144-145
  Christmas card mobile, making 669:170
  Christmas stockings mobile, making 644:24-25
  Christmas tree mobiles, making 644:28-30; 669:142-143
  Coat hanger mobile, making 1258:22
  Columbus' ships mobile, making 448:25
  Danish bells mobile, making 452:100-101
  Danish woven hearts mobile, making 452:107-109
  Easter egg mobile, making 201:156-158
  Easter eggs mobile, empty, making 772:58
  Easter mobile, making 741:34
  Eye of God mobile, making 452:115-117
  Eye of God mobile, woven, making 749:61
  German snowflakes mobile, making 452:92-94
  Hanukkah menorah mobile, making 452:85-88
  Hanukkah mobile, cardboard, making 829:58
  Hanukkah mobile, making 586:22
  Hanukkah mobile, paper, making 448:38
  Japanese lanterns, making 772:76-77
  Jewish star mobile, paper, making 81:9
  Jonah and the Whale mobile, making 452:58-60
  Lithuanian straw construction mobile, making 452:89-91
  May basket mobile, making 448:20
  Maypole mobile, making 644:42-44
  Merry Christmas mobile, making 942:27
  Partridge in a Pear Tree mobile, making 140:184-185
  Santa Claus mobile, paper, patterns, making 253:194-199
  Santa face mobile, making 452:68-70
  Shavuot mobile, making 543:134-135
  Shoji screens, making 78:96
  St. Patrick's Day mobile, paper, making 95:22
  Star of David mobile, cardboard, making 448:39
  Star of David mobile, making 403:29-30
  Sukkot mobile, making 543:48-49
  Thanksgiving mobile, making 180:10-11
  Tunisian lucky fish mobile, paper, patterns, making 1016:175-180
  Twelve Days of Christmas mobile, making 709:122-125
  Twig mobile, twigs, pine cones, string, making 1258:23
  Valentine hearts mobile, making 452:75-78
  Valentine mobile, making 648:18-19
  Valentine mobile, paper, pattern, making 99:17; 232:26-27
  Windmills mobile, making 691:8-9
  Winnie the Pooh mobile, making 277:130-131
MOCCASINS
  How to make moccasins 359:22-55
MOHAWK INDIANS—COOKERY
  Hominy, recipe 1699:143
MOHAWK INDIANS—SPIRITUAL OBJECTS
  Akwesasne star, tissue paper, oak tag, thread, making 1296:100
MOLDAVIA—TALES
  Guguze's Gift, a Moldavian tale, Spiridon Vangheli 139:60-63
MOLUCCAS. *See* **INDONESIA**
MONASTERIES
  Illuminated manuscript, cream paper, tea, felt-tipped pens, making 1183:21
MONDRIAN
  Painting; hardboard abstract painting, making 812:36
MONGOLIA—COOKERY
  Shaptak, lamb in spices, recipe 1165:155

MONGOLS
    Astonishing acrobats, making 173:74-75
    Chinese barge, making 173:40-41
    Robe, making 173:18-19
    Royal Pavilion, making 173:60-61
MONKEY AND THE CROCODILE—PUPPETS
    "Monkey and the Crocodile," puppets and puppet play
        script, making 1155:63-66
MONKEYS
    Victorian monkey counterbalance toy, cardboard, pat-
        terns, making 1051:129-133
MONKS
    Monk doll, stuffed, making 830:30-31
MONSTERS. *See also* **DRACULA; FRANKENSTEIN**
    Activities and resources to celebrate monster days
        592:79-84
    Balloon monster model, making 248:18-21
    Monster program, activities, books, crafts, patterns,
        scripts, making 1159:29-53
    Mud monsters, how to make 875:58-60
    Space monster model, making 248:22-23
    "Where the Wild Things Are" book; make your own mon-
        sters 286:88
MONSTERS—COOKERY
    Cookie monsters, making 683:9
    Vanilla Godzilla food model, making 1057:138-139
MONSTERS—COSTUMES. *See also* **HALLOWEEN—**
    COSTUMES
    Count Dracula costume, cape, make-up, making 326:32-
        34
    Cyclops costume, head, tunic, cape, making 326:9-11
    Draculita costume and make-up, making 617:44-50
    Frankenstein's monster costume, neck electrodes, make-
        up, making 326:35-37
    Monster costume, paper bag, making 1096:11
    Monster mask, making 840:26-27
    Science fiction monsters, ideas for costumes 326:43-47
    Vampire costume, fingernails and make-up, making
        326:29-31
    Werewolf costume, making 617:51-56
    Werewolf or Wolfman costume, mask, making 326:38-40
MONSTERS—DECORATIONS
    Black light decorations, making 617:64-65
    Floating ghost, making 617:73-74
    Ghost's coffin, making 617:71-72
    Giant monster, paper, making 1096:14
    Monster mobile, making 617:66-67
    Monster sounds, making 617:62-63
    Skeleton, dancing, making 617:67-70
    Spiders and bats, making 617:65-66
MONSTERS—HANDICRAFTS
    Gourd monsters, making 683:32
MONSTERS—MAKEUP
    Beards, making 617:33-34
    Blood, making 617:32-33
    Draculita monster makeup, how to put on 617:44-50
    Greasepaint and shadowing, how to put on 617:41-43
    Scar, rubber cement, making 617:30
    Scars, gelatin, making 617:30-31
MONSTERS—MASKS
    Monster papier-mache masks, making 617:19-26
MONSTERS—PARTIES
    Monster party, how to plan 617:75-90
    Monster Rumpus birthday party, decorations, games,
        cake, patterns 1015:41-53

Monster, invitations, decorations, costumes, food, games,
    recipes 1185:14-15
MONSTERS—PUPPETS
    Finger puppet, fabric, pattern, making 573:94-98
    Mouth puppets, box, making 681:16-17
    Monster puppet, old glove, making 325:12-15
    Ogre puppet, paper bag, patterns, making 1107:207-213
    Pom-pom puppet, pattern, making 1030:120-121
    Puppet, paper bag mouth puppets, patterns, making
        1155:199-200
MONTAGUE, JOHN, THE FOURTH EARL OF
    SANDWICH
    Sandwich Day celebration; invent new sandwiches, mak-
        ing 1199:250-251
MONTANA—COOKERY
    Carrots, scalloped, recipe 654:92-94
    Meat stew, recipe 343:54
    Senate bean soup, recipe 654:92-93
MONTENEGRO. *See* **YUGOSLAVIA**
MONTESSORI, MARIA—BIRTHDAY
    Celebrate with fraction fun math activity, how to do
        1199:197
MONTGOMERY, LUCY MAUD
    "Anne of Green Gables," afternoon ruby tea biscuits, rec-
        ipe 563:22-23
    "Anne of Green Gables," butterscotch pudding, recipe
        563:43
    "Anne of Green Gables," caramel pudding sauce, recipe
        563:48
    "Anne of Green Gables," chicken saucy, recipe 563:15
    "Anne of Green Gables," chocolate Goblin's Food cake,
        recipe 563:36
    "Anne of Green Gables," coconut macaroons, recipe
        563:25
    "Anne of Green Gables," cookbook, recipes 563:1-48
    "Anne of Green Gables," cowcumber boats, recipe 563:9
    "Anne of Green Gables," liniment cake, recipe 563:38-39
    "Anne of Green Gables," Marill's plum pudding, recipe
        563:46-47
    "Anne of Green Gables," Maritime gingersnaps, recipe
        563:26-27
    "Anne of Green Gables," Miss Ellen's pound cake, rec-
        ipe 563:24
    "Anne of Green Gables," Mrs. Irving's shortbread, rec-
        ipe 563:32
    "Anne of Green Gables," orange angel cake and glaze,
        recipe 563:30-31
    "Anne of Green Gables," raspberry cordial, recipe
        563:16-17
    "Anne of Green Gables," raspberry tarts, recipe 563:28-
        29
    "Anne of Green Gables," vanilla ice cream, recipe
        563:34-35
    "Anne of Green Gables," vegetable soup, recipe 563:12-
        13
    Egg salad sandwiches, recipe 563:18
    Lemonade, old-fashioned, recipe 563:19-21
    Lettuce salad and Thousand Island dressing, recipes
        563:10-11
MONTHS
    Dutch names for the months of the year 1031:46
    Hindi names for months of the year 1031:47
    Jewish names for months of the year 1031:50
    Moslem names for months of the year 1031:48
    Names of months around the world, chart 1031:44-45

MOON
 Usagi! Usagi!, traditional song, Japan 139:34
MOON DAY
 First Moon Landing, 1969; activities, art, songs, recipes, games 1469:120-121
MOON DAY—GAMES
 First Landing on the Moon anniversary game 240:40
MOORE, CLEMENT CLARKE
 Celebrate anniversary of "The Night Before Christmas" with read-aloud activity 1199:284
 Visit from St. Nicholas puppet show 756:82
MORAVIA—CHRISTMAS
 Christmas tree and decorations, making 593:106-113
MORAVIA—CHRISTMAS—COOKERY
 Christmas cookies, recipe, make cutters 672:117-142
 Molasses spice cookies, recipe 672:141
 Moravske vano ni kukyse (Moravian Christmas cookies), recipe 1666:88
 Vanilla sugar cookies, recipe 672:140-141
MORAVIAN CHURCH—HANDICRAFTS
 Christingle, lighted orange, candle, making 1313:187
MORMONS—COOKERY
 Quilters potato salad, history of, recipe 155:6-7
MOROCCO—COOKERY
 Almond and honey pastries, recipe 1265:135-136
 Beef tajine with almonds and prunes, recipe 1587:121
 Birth celebration sweets, recipe 1220:133
 Cocoa cookies, recipe 793:50-51
 Couscous, stew, vegetables, meat, recipe 1265:137-138
 Mantecados, cinnamon cookies, recipe 858:unp
 Mint tea, microwave recipe 1211:22
 Quick Moroccan bread, recipe 1165:47
 Sesame cornes de gazelles, almond crescent cookies, recipe 1165:48
 Sweet couscous with raisins dessert, recipe 1380:18
 Tagine de poulet aux pruneaux et miel, chicken with prunes and honey, recipe 1165:46-47
 Zeilook, eggplant salad, recipe 1165:46
MOROCCO—COSTUMES
 Summer salads, recipe, costume 188:12
MOROCCO—FESTIVALS—COOKERY
 Aid-es-Seghir; bisteeya (chicken pie), recipe 1666:43
 Aid-es-Seghir; mescouta (date bars), recipe 1666:44
 Aid-es-Seghir; mint tea, recipe 1666:43-44
MOROCCO—GAMES
 Hyena chase game, making 1507:18-19
MOROCCO—HANDICRAFTS
 Calabash with base, papier-mache, Moroccan bowl designs given, making 1633:102-105
 Key fob, barrette and wristband of leather, making 525:100-103
 Khamsas (Good Luck Hands), foil, charms, making 1338:54-55
MOROCCO—SONGS
 Ram Sam Sam round song 1115:51
MOSAICS
 Flower mosaic to decorate wells, how to do 1467:13
 Iran mosaic, making 143:83
 Jewish star bean mosaic, making 81:18
 Menorah design mosaic tray, making 53:50
 Pebble mosaic, making 1701:10-11
 Plaster of Paris mosaics with shells, beans, pine cones, making 1455:27
 Roman art mosaic, eggshells, poster paints, making 1184:13

 Rosh Hashanah New Year mosaic, making 279:36-37
 Seed mosaic, beans and seeds, making 1213:69
 Seed mosaic, seeds, cardboard, glue, making 1285:96
MOSAICS—ROME—ANCIENT
 Rabbit mosaic, making 105:61-63
MOSEL, ARLENE
 "Funny Little Woman," reading, writing, thinking activities 1093:122-132
 "Funny Little Woman," rice dumplings, recipe 1216:20
MOSES. *See* BIBLE—HANDICRAFTS—MOSES
MOTHER GOOSE. *See also* NURSERY RHYMES
MOTHER GOOSE—COOKERY
 Adventures of Simple Simon, cherry pie cup cakes, recipe 1216:51
 Bat, Bat, Come Under My Hat, raspberry cake, recipe 1216:54
 Clever Hen, bread, recipe 1216:32
 Davy Dumpling, dumplings, recipe 1216:21
 Fishy, Fishy in the Brook, fish sticks, recipe 1216:92
 Handy Pandy, sugar candy, recipe 1216:88
 Hot Cross Buns, recipe 1216:40
 Little Jack Horner, Jack's Christmas plum pie, recipe 1216:49
 Little Miss Muffet, curds and whey, recipe 1216:118
 Little Tommy Tucker, bread and butter, recipe 1216:32
 Mother Goose Day pat-a-cakes, recipe 1199:105
 Muffin Man, muffins, recipe 1216:42
 Old Woman Who Lived Under a Hill, baked apples, recipe 1216:109
 Pease Porridge Hot, porridge, recipe 1216:17
 Queen of Hearts, tarts, recipe 1216:47
 Three Little Kittens, chocolate cream pie, recipe 1216:50
MOTHER GOOSE—PARTIES
 Mother Goose Party, decorations, games, costumes, recipes 74:12-27
MOTHER TERESA—BIRTHDAY
 Friend in need activities for shut ins, charitable agencies, how to do 1199:196
MOTHERS—FESTIVALS
 Mothering Sunday 139:52
MOTHER'S DAY
 Activities and projects for classrooms 1393:209-211
 Activities, art, songs, recipes, games, writing activities 1469:104-105; 1152:152-156
 Activities, crafts, food 1662:82-87
 Activities, crafts, history and stories for 128:69-78
 Activities, finger plays, recipes, crafts 305:26
 Activities, projects, song 819:84-96
 Art, cooking, finger plays, games, drama, math, science and music activities 54:193-194
 Boil or Bake a Simnel Cake, traditional tale, Shropshire, England 139:54-57
 Finger plays, games, making 944:103-105
 History of 475:142-143
 Mother's Day celebration 133:116-117
 Party, lunch 134:54-55
 Violets in the Lane facts 139:57
MOTHER'S DAY—COOKERY
 Chicken cordon bleu, recipe 871:61-63
 French toast, recipe 1032:208
 Main dishes, desserts, punches, recipes 1668:14-58
 May basket cake, making 294:210
 Mother's Day cake and frosting, recipes 874:77-78
 Mother's Day fruit cake, recipe 402:39-42

Pancakes for breakfast, recipe 1257:18-19
Strawberries deluxe, recipe 402:39-42
MOTHER'S DAY—DECORATIONS
Paper flowers, crepe paper, making 1558:6-7
Pop-up Mother's Day card, making 1387:10-11
Popcorn flowerpots for table decorations, making
939:70-72
MOTHER'S DAY—GAMES
Mother's Day game 240:29
MOTHER'S DAY—HANDICRAFTS
Apron, paper napkins and ribbon, making 894:58-60
Basket of love, paper twist, ribbons, fruit basket, making
1668:28-31
Basket, paper, pattern, making 254:79-81
Book weight, metal washers, paper, decorations, making
1668:49-51
Bookmark, felt, patterns, making 1257:20
Bouquets, felt, yarn, patterns, making 1257:21
Candy mold magnets, plaster of Paris, making 254:85
Card, carved wood design, printed, making 674:104-
106
Card, helpful bouquet, making 209:25-27
Card, helping hands, making 648:30Card, my loves
keeps growing, making 209:23-24
Card, Swiss paper-cuts, patterns, making 1016:100-105
Corsage, making 891:74-80
Coupon book of promises, making 308:63
Dyed noodle and wooden bead jewelry, making 1668:18-
19
Fish net soap present, making 308:62
Flower necklace, paper, simple, making 611:11
Flowerpot, paper, making 534:51-52
Flowerpot, styrofoam, decorated, making 611:25
Garden posy, making 139:53
Hands down pictures, making 698:56
Helping hands recipe holder, paper, clothespin, magnets,
making 1668:59-61
Homemade bubble bath, making 1662:85
I remember Mama collage, making 698:57
Lacy trinket box, making 294:211
Mother's bouquet, making 226:26
Mother's card, making 226:24
Mother's Day cards, paper, pattern, making 95:26;
232:42
Mother's Day cards, patterns, making 96:31-32
Mother's gift, making 226:25
Paperweight, glass and feathers, patterns, making
1016:95-99
Plate of promises gift, paper plate, making 1067:80-81
Plate of promises, paper plate, making 253:76-77
Pot holder, patterns, making 1016:106-111
Pressed flower projects, making 447:96-105
Silhouettes, making 698:58
Soap balls, colored and scented, making 1455:90
Soap shapes, Ivory Snow, making 1149:140
MOTHER'S DAY—PUPPETS
Puppet and story for Mother's Day 1030:20
MOTHER'S DAY—SONGS
Mothering Sunday, traditional carol 139:58-59
Songs about Mother's Day 901:71-76
MOTION PICTURES. *See* **MOVIES**
MOUND BUILDERS—JEWELRY
Pendants, styrofoam, clay, yarn, making 1699:61-62
MOUNTAIN CLIMBERS
Bivouac tent, making 562:27-28

Frame tent, making 562:29
Tube tent, making 562:30
MOUNTAIN MEN
Beaver skin hat mold, using felt and liquid starch, mak-
ing 1214:24
Cache of supplies buried in ground, how to do with can
of pop 1214:27
Journals kept by trappers, cardboard, felt, paper, making
1214:32-33
Possibles bag to hold mountain men's valuables, cham-
ois, leather laces, making 1214:28-30
MOUNTAIN MEN—COOKERY
Indian fry bread, recipe 1214:34-35
MOUSE TRAPS
History of mouse traps 511:68-69
MOVEMENT
Songs, fingerplays, stories, games, rhythms 1200:104-
117
MOVIES
Hall of Fame hand prints, making 834:36
MOVIES—DRIVE IN
History of drive in movies 119:93-96
MOVIES—PARTIES
Hollywood theme birthday party, making 896:117-125
MOZAMBIQUE—COOKERY
Arroz de coco, coconut milk rice, recipe 1165:10-11
Bolo polana, potato and nut cake, recipe 1165:11
Chum-chum, recipe 793:52-53
Fish and shrimp stew, recipe 1452:5
Ovos moles de mango, mango and egg pudding, recipe
1165:11
MOZAMBIQUE—EASTER—COOKERY
Bolo polana (nuts and potato cake), recipe 1666:10-11
Easter; camarao grelhado piri piri (garlic shrimp), recipe
1666:10
MOZAMBIQUE—FESTIVALS
Blessing of seeds and tools celebration 601:35-36
MOZAMBIQUE—FESTIVALS—COOKERY
Eid al-Fitr; bolo polana (nuts and potato cake), recipe
1666:10-11
Eid al-Fitr; camarao grelhado piri piri (garlic shrimp),
recipe 1666:10
MUHAMMAD, PROPHET. *See also* **MUSLIMS**
MUHAMMAD, PROPHET—BIRTHDAY
Milad-an-Nabi, activities and projects for classrooms
1393:273-274
MUMMER'S PLAYS AND SWORD DANCES
Information about 419:52
MUMMIES. *See also* **EGYPT, ANCIENT—MUMMIES**
Mummy case pattern, making 1159:22-23
Mummy design to enlarge, making 1159:17
Mummy room arrangement, pattern 1159:21
MUMMIES—COSTUMES
Mummy costume, make-up, making 42:70-75; 326:41-42
MUNCH, EDVARD
Copy Munch's painting style with fingerpaint, making
1372:41-43
MUNROE, ROXIE
Christmas time in New York; Christmas ornaments, mak-
ing 843:43
MUSIC—BULLETIN BOARDS
Cymbals, drum, maracas, guitar, noisemaker, making
295:276-278

MUSIC DAY

Music Day activities, stories, crafts, recipes, making 558:48-51

MUSICAL INSTRUMENTS

Aeolian harp, making 888:54; 890:97-107

African drum, making 297:204-205

African instruments, making 953:48-49

Appalachian dulcimer, making 468:132-134

Bagpipe model, making 494:114

Banjo, Afro American, making 626:74-77

Banjo, plastic container, wood, fishing line, paints, making 1288:18-19

Banjo, wood, nails, rubber bands, making 1610:59

Beaters for playing instruments, simple to make 1288:18-19

Bells, flowerpot hand bell or set of hanging bells, making 1288:26-29

Bullroarer, wood, making 1465:139-141; 1622:41

Chinese wood block, making 578:13

Cymbals, pot lids, making 1361:54

Didgeridoo (instrument), long cardboard tube, colored papers, paints, making 1288:34; 1622:9

Drum beater heads, sticks and soft materials, making 1513:11

Drum from mixing bowl or can, waxed paper, cloth, making 1513:5

Drum from yogurt cup, making 1513:21

Drum, rawhide tom-tom, making 468:102-103

Drum, tin baking ring, paper, balloon, cord, making 1288:14-17

Drum, tin, early settlers, pattern, making 1027:156-159

French horn from rubber hose, funnel and mouthpiece, making 1622:21

Gourd guitar, making 1421:173

Gourd shaker, making 1421:172

Guitar, box guitar, paper, tape, rubber bands, making 1288:38-41

Guitar, make from wood, nails, rubber bands, making 1361:57

Harp, box, tape, rubber bands, making 1288:38-41; 1514:5

Harp, the storyteller's harp, making 173:10-11

Harp, wooden, from Paraguay, making 515:94

Horn pipes, cardboard tubes, rubber hose, funnel, making 1288:34-37

Horn, garden hose, funnel, colored tape, cord, making 1288:34-37

Imbria, cigar box, making 953:50

Indian rattle from bones, making 229:73-74

Kaffir, coconut, making 953:50

Kalimba, sardine can, making 953:51

Kazoo, cardboard tube, cellophane, making 1429:20

Kazoo, paper tubes, rubber bands, paint, making 1728:16-17

Lagerphon, making 953:30-31

Maracas, miniature, walnut shells, making 1429:88-89

Maracas, plastic bottle, beans, paints, making 1610:59

Maracas, plastic container, wooden beads, making 1288:9

Maracas, soda can, paper clips, making 1288:8

Morache, American Indian, making 578:14-15

Mouth bow, Indian, making 156:40-41

Mouth bow, yardstick, fishing line, making 1310:42

Organ, bubble organ, bottles, straws, colored water, making 1288:32-33

Pan pipes, straws, card board, paints, making 1610:59

Panpipes from plastic tubing, making 1622:7

Panpipes, bamboo sticks, dowels, making 1285:64-65

Panpipes, bamboo, making 1702:28

Panpipes, small plastic pipe, clay, tape, making 1288:31

Papoose pipe, making 578:109-110

Pipes of Pan (syrinx), making 890:93-96

Poet's lyre, cardboard, pattern given, making 181:22-25

Psaltry, simple, making 156:60

Rattle, tin box, plastic buttons, making 1288:9

Rattles and rasps, walnut shells, wood, stick, making 1702:29

Shakers, soda can, plastic containers, boxes and fillings, making 1288:6-9

Shepherd's pipe, making 521:24-28; 526:78-80; 954:135

Shepherd's pipe, recorder type, making 468:149

Shepherd's pipes, making 953:41

Slit drum, wood, making 1465:152-154

Swanee whistle, making 571:26-27

Syrinx, Pipes of Pan, making 890:93-96

Tambourine from aluminum pie plates and pumpkin seeds, making 1698:22

Tambourine, baking ring, metal washers, paints, ribbons, making 1288:10-13

Tambourine, paper or plastic plate, making 1513:39

Tambourines, aluminum pie plates, jingle items, making 1361:54

Thumb piano; ice cream stick, tuned, tin can, coconut, making 468:83-88

Thumb piano, Kafir, making 954:134

Thumb piano, making 888:80

Thumb piano, Uganda, making 495:75-80

Tom-tom drum, flower pots, fabric, cord, making 1288:14-17

Tom-tom drum, making 937:42

Triangle and striker, metal bolts, cord, ribbons, making 1288:22-23

Whistle, whoosing whistle, plastic pipe, making 1288:30-31

Whistle, wood, making 1465:147-149

Whistles, whizz-it whistle, plastic pipe, making 1288:30

Xylophone, driftwood, making 1702:29

Xylophone, pencil xylophone, making 1288:24-25

Zither, box zither, box, tape, rubber bands, making 1288:38-41

Zither, tube zither, plastic bottle, strings, making 1514:28

MUSLIMS

Moslem Creed: Fasts and Festivals 667:178-181

MUSLIMS—ART—HANDICRAFTS

Islamic pattern decorated shoe or gift box, how to do 1632:46-47

MUSLIMS—BIRTHDAYS

Celebration party for one week old child 660:51-52

Moslem birthday celebrations 695:61

MUSLIMS—COOKERY

Fruit drink, recipe 1722:26

Sweet rice or pilaf, recipe 1637:25

MUSLIMS—FESTIVALS

Bairam, Moslem Festival celebration 914:69-70

Birthday of the Prophet Muhammad; history and celebration of 496:28-29

Eid al-Adha Festival activities and projects for classrooms 1393:266-268; 1393:269

Eid al-Fitr Festival stylized designs, how to make 1393:267-268

Historical events of Islam celebrations, activities and projects for classrooms 1393:275-278

Id-al-Fitr celebration 631:98

Id-al-Fitr Festival 566:32

Milad-an-Nabi, Prophet Muhammad's birthday, activities and projects for classrooms 1393:273-274

Muharram celebration 631:46

New Year, Hari Raya Ruasa, Merlin face mask, pattern, making 1654:73-74

Pilgrimage to Mecca celebration 566:33

Ramadan and Id-al-Fitr; history and celebration of 496:81-82

Ramadan Festival 566:32

Ramadan Festival decorative script, how to do 1393:265

Ramadan Festival, activities and projects for classrooms 1393:264-265

Stoning the Devils celebration 631:100

MUSLIMS—FESTIVALS—DECORATIONS

Eid al-Fitr Festival pop-up card, making 1387:36-37

Eid al-Fitr Festival printed greeting cards, making 1277:8-9

MUSLIMS—HANDICRAFTS

Book cover for special book, cardboard, trims, making 1722:11

Islamic art star, paper plates, making 1722:31

MUSLIMS—LANGUAGE

Moslem names for the months of the year 1031:48

MUSLIMS—MOSQUE

Mosque model, shoe box, paints, making 1722:16-17

MUSLIMS—NATURE FESTIVALS

Death of Husain festival 419:118-119

Moslem rituals 419:107-121; 419:117-121

MUSLIMS—TEA

Moslem tea and recipe for rice cakes 474:139

MYANMAR. *See* **BURMA**

MYTHICAL BEASTS

Gryphons and other beasts, draw and print, making 1092:63-65

MYTHOLOGY. *See also* **GREECE—MYTHOLOGY**

Jason and the Golden Fleece, paper folds of story characters, making 406:33-43

Labyrinth from egg carton, making 677:33

Mythical creatures, jointed paper creature, making 1447:8-9

MYTHOLOGY—COSTUMES

Cyclops costume, head, tunic, cape, making 326:16-19

MYTHOLOGY—FINGER PLAYS

Finger plays about mythology 302:98-104

N

NAMES

History of and some meanings of names 660:20-35

How an Indian was named 27:38-40

Paint names, puffy paint, glitter, glue, making 1203:17

Surnames A-Z 118:31

What's in a name? 118:30-34

NAMIBIA—CHRISTMAS—COOKERY

Kejenou (chicken and shrimp stew), recipe 1666:19-20

NAMIBIA—COOKERY

Thick millet porridge, recipe 1165:20

NAPOLEON

Costume, making 213:2-4

NARRAGANSETT INDIANS—COOKERY. *See also*
SHINNECOCK INDIANS—COOKERY

Native American Clambake, recipe 1296:138

NASKAPI INDIANS—MASKS

Naskapi mask, making 327:45

NATCHEZ INDIANS—NATURE FESTIVALS

Growing and planting festivals 419:146

NATIVE AMERICAN DAY—PUPPETS

Puppet projects, patterns, scenes, story starters, feature
story 1083:107-109

NATIVITY. *See also* **JESUS CHRIST**

Nativity scene with clay figures, recipes for clays, making 1717:33

NATURAL MATERIALS

Nature notebook, paper, lino roller, inks, making
1258:14-15

NATURE CRAFTS

Simple projects using branches, leaves and seeds based
on world traditions 1702:4-32

NAVAHO INDIANS—BELTS

Belt, concho, cardboard, tin foil, pattern, making 1170:10

Concho belt, making 227:27

NAVAHO INDIANS—CANOES

Canoes, stiff paper, markers, making 1199:212

NAVAHO INDIANS—CLOTHING

Blouse, making 932:44

Clothing, making 281:37-41

Dress, two piece dress, making 932:40-43

Woman's blouse, pattern, making 281:39-40

NAVAHO INDIANS—CODE

Navaho code talkers of WWII 1296:117-118

NAVAHO INDIANS—COOKERY

Blue cornbread, recipe 1321:114

Cornbread, recipe 1199:215

Fruit leather, recipe 1342:165

Fry bread, recipe 1427:276; 1653:60

Navaho fry bread, recipe 720:192; 793:2; 1342:143

NAVAHO INDIANS—FOOTWEAR

Navaho moccasins, making 359:111-117

NAVAHO INDIANS—GAMES

Bouncing sticks game 602:172-173

Coyote and the father game 602:173-174

Ring game 602:174

NAVAHO INDIANS—HANDICRAFTS

Big Long Man and the Giant 126:89-92

Big Long Man and the Giant, art activities, nature weaving, making 126:94-97

Big Long Man and the Giant, art activities, sand painting,
making 126:93-94

NAVAHO INDIANS—HOUSEHOLD

Mat; sweet selling grass mat, sticks, twine, grasses, making 1284:12-14

NAVAHO INDIANS—HOUSES

Earth lodge, wood base, moss, leaves, soil, making
1368:21

Hogan, oak tag, markers, patterns, making 1296:96-97

Hogan, paper, popsicle sticks, pattern, making 1170:19

Navaho summer shelter, making 804:52-54

Tepees and hogans, oaktag, egg carton, twigs, paints,
making 1199:210-211

NAVAHO INDIANS—JEWELRY

Concha belts, making 605:35-39

Concha buttons, making 605:31-33

Navaho jewelry, how to make 605:11-17

Silver rings with stones, how to make 605:23-26

Silver rings without settings, how to make 605:19-22

Turquoise, how to cut and polish 605:27-30

NAVAHO INDIANS—MASKS

Navaho masks, making 327:45

NAVAHO INDIANS—MUSICAL INSTRUMENTS

Drum rattle, making 468:54-55

Groaning stick, making 63:57-58

NAVAHO INDIANS—RITUALS

Growing up ritual 695:107-111

NAVAHO INDIANS—SAND PAINTING

Colored sand, rice, and salt, making 1372:126-127

Navaho sand painting, colored sand, cardboard, glue,
making 1199:214

Navaho symbols in sand painting, making 1372:128-129

Sand painting, colored sand, glue, patterns, making
1427:265-267

Sand painting, how to make 63:38-39; 714:6-8856:116-
119

Sand paintings, dyes, glue, making 1296:95

Sand paintings, powder paints, glue, making 1368:56-57

Sun medallion in style of Navaho sand painting, cardboard, sand, making 1477:53

NAVAHO INDIANS—STRING FIGURES

Apache Door, Big Star, Bow, Lizard, Tent, Two Coyotes
1404:36-88

Butterfly string 373:36-39

Hogan figure, making 423:27-29

Many stars string 372:51-53

NAVAHO INDIANS—TOTEM POLES

Totem poles, cardboard tubes, paper, paints, making
1199:208-209

NAVAHO INDIANS—VILLAGES

Village from shoebox, paper, clay, decorations, making
1199:212

NAVAHO INDIANS—WEAVING

Blankets, making 227:34-35

Chief's woven hanging, yarn, making 298:250-251

Cloth weaving, making 324:26-29

Eye of God weaving, making 324:30

Navaho rugs, how to weave 605:79-86

Navaho rugs, patterns, how to make 605:59-77

NAVIGATION INSTRUMENTS—ANCIENT

Astrolabe, cardboard, paint, making 1182:9

Compass, jar lid, cardboard, felt-tip pens, making 1182:9

Hourglass, plastic bottles, foil, cardboard, making 1182:8

NAVY—ANCIENT

Flotilla, making 65:41-53

NAVY—WEAPONS

Naval cannon, one that shoots, making 924:54-57

NDEBELE PEOPLE—JEWELRY

Ndebele bead bracelet, beads, wire, making 1632:28-32

NEAR EAST—COOKERY
Bulgur with vegetables, recipe 88:22-24
Carrots and peas with spice, recipe 88:25-26
Fruit kabobs, recipe 514:131-132
Ground lamb with bulgur, kibbi nayya, recipe 88:24-25
NEBRASKA—COOKERY
Crackers, crispy, recipe 1342:113
Porcupine meatballs, recipe 654:97
Raisin sour cream pie, recipe 654:96
NEBUCHADNEZZAR
Costume 213:48-50
NEGRITOS PEOPLE. *See* **RAIN FOREST**
NEPAL—COOKERY
Sherpa popcorn, recipe 1244:44-45
NEPAL—FESTIVALS
Gunla Festival celebration 810:44-45
NEPAL—MASKS
Durga mask, cardboard box, dowels, glitter, containers,
making 1295:32-33
NETHERLANDS
Activities, flags, games, songs, dances, recipes 1381:173-
176
NETHERLANDS—BEADS
Dutch bead gardens information 301:45-50
NETHERLANDS—BIRTHDAYS
Birthday celebrations 695:65
Birthday customs 488:90-93
NETHERLANDS—CHRISTMAS
Black Pete, history of 709:68
Christmas customs 149:31; 473:32-37
Customs and Sinterklaas surprises 856:16-19
Sinter Klaas party picture 473:36-37
Sinter Klaas, history of 709:68
Sinterklaas and Zwarte Piet, black and white line draw-
ing 515:82
Sinterklaas celebration 497:40-49
NETHERLANDS—CHRISTMAS—COOKERY
Cookies, initial letter, recipe 273:69-71
Leterbankets, recipe 497:46
Letter cake, recipe 473:35
Marzipan carrots, recipe 497:46
Marzipan, recipe 497:46
Olie bollen (Dutch-fried pastries), recipe 497:46;
1080:12-13; 1128:112; 1452:163; 1666:114-115
Speculaas, Dutch Christmas cookies, recipe 497:46;
1165:132; 1437:101
Spritz (Dutch sugar cookies), recipe 1666:114
NETHERLANDS—CHRISTMAS—DECORATIONS
Beaded Christmas garland, making 497:49
Christmas tree and decorations, how to make 593:50-55
Pinwheel decorations, making 497:48
Shoe, wooden, cardboard, making 273:65-69
NETHERLANDS—COOKERY
Alphabet chocolates, recipe 1244:79
Apple pancakes, recipe 1560:6
Apple pudding, recipe 501:83
Boerenkass soup, recipe 1452:159
Cocoa, making 874:83
Coleslaw salad, recipe 1113:12-13
Cream pudding, recipe 530:77-79
Curried kool sla au gratin, curried cabbage cheese casse-
role, recipe 1165:131-132
Diebollen, donuts, recipe 88:196-197

Dutch Hodgepodge, recipe 659:92
Dutch pancake, recipe 874:26; 1380:9
Dutch pea soup, recipe 1588:119
Dutch split pea soup, Erwtensoep, recipe 1452:160
Dutch vegetable mix, recipe 794:22
Eggs stuffed with cheese, recipe 530:71-72
Fish fillets, recipe 1452:162
Gossip heads (kletskoppen), cookies, recipe 72:47-48
Green pea soup, recipe 967:40
Groentesoep, vegetable soup with barley, recipe 88:195-196
History of cookery in 88:188-194
Hutspot met klapstuck, meat and vegetable stew, recipe
1165:130-131
Hutspot stew, recipe 1452:161
Hutspot, boiled beef, recipe 858:unp
Hutspot, recipe 874:47
Jan Hagel cookies, recipe 1122:57
Koek, breakfast cake, recipe 88:194-195
Ont bijt, Dutch breakfast, recipe 188:25
Pancakes, recipe 88:198-199; 1122:80-81
Potatoes, mashed, recipe 530:75-76
Raisin pancake, drie in de pan, recipe 1653:94
Roast beef snack, recipe 874:20
Rolled rib of pork with apples, recipe 530:72-74
Tomato soup with meatballs, recipe 793:38; 1381:175
Waffles, recipe 88:199-200
Watergruel cereal, recipe 88:198
NETHERLANDS—COSTUMES
Dutch man and woman costumes 213:139
Holland costumes drawing 988:29; 988:49
Ont bijt, Dutch breakfast, recipe, costume 188:25
NETHERLANDS—DANCES
Rijpe gerst dance, how to do 1494:151-152
NETHERLANDS—DOLLS
Hendrik of Holland doll and windmill, making 494:95-
107
NETHERLANDS—EASTER
Easter egg customs in Holland 201:25
NETHERLANDS—EASTER—DANCES
Winging ceremony for Easter folk dance 474:112-113
NETHERLANDS—EASTER—GAMES
Eiertikken egg game 201:180-181
NETHERLANDS—EASTER—HANDICRAFTS
Easter trees, making 139:128-130
Palm Sunday Dutch palmpaas, decorated stick, making
1245:7
NETHERLANDS—FESTIVALS
Lazybones Day jump rope rhymes 557:55-56
Lazybones Day, crafts, foods, games, making 557:52-59
Lazybones Day; activities, art, songs, recipes, games
1469:106-107
St. Nicholas Day; activities, art, songs, recipes, games
1469:44-45
Van Gogh's birthday celebration; cardboard, dried seeds
sunflower mosaic, making 1199:74
Windmill Day; activities, art, songs, recipes, games
1469:102-103
NETHERLANDS—FESTIVALS—COOKERY
Lazybones Day cakes, recipe 557:57
NETHERLANDS—FESTIVALS—GAMES
Lazybones Day games 557:57-58
NETHERLANDS—FESTIVALS—HANDICRAFTS
Lazybones Day flowers, paper, making 557:56-57
Lazybones Day Jingle Jangles, pie tins, making 557:53

NETHERLANDS—FLAG
Pattern for flag 557:59
NETHERLANDS—GAMES
All the Birds Fly game 557:58; 602:99-100
Alle Vogels Vliegen, All the Birds Fly game, how to
play 1494:94-95
Captured game 602:97-98
Days of the week hopscotch, how to play 1708:45
In Holland Stands a House game 602:98-99
Kinder Kaatsen game 557:57
Klabbejass card game 1132:48-50
Prooi, sardines game 386:75
Windmill game 58:34-37
NETHERLANDS—HANDICRAFTS
Delft blue tiles, making 626:35-36
Dutch girl hat, paper, pattern, making 823:47
Jeweled, monogrammed, ribboned egg, making 298:86-87
Tulips, making 626:37-39
Windmill from Holland, paper and straw model, making
1094:34-35
Wooden shoe and tulip, paper, pattern, making 760:62-63
NETHERLANDS—LANGUAGE
Dutch names for the months of the year 1031:46
NETHERLANDS—MUSICAL INSTRUMENTS
Dutch jug drum, Rommel Pot, making 468:111
NETHERLANDS—NEW YEAR'S DAY—COOKERY
Oliebol, New Year's doughnuts, recipe 1452:158
NETHERLANDS—NUMBERS
One to ten in Dutch language 557:53
NETHERLANDS—PUPPETS
Leak in the Dike puppet show 756:51-59
NETHERLANDS—SONGS
I've a Wagon Full of Chickens, traditional song, the
Netherlands 139:138-139
NETHERLANDS—STORYTELLING
Handkerchief stories 1522:62-73
Paper-cutting or tearing stories 1522:85-101
NETHERLANDS ANTILLES. *See* **CURACAO**
NETTLES
Nettle soup, recipe 1010:27
NEVADA—COOKERY
Bean casserole, recipe 654:100-101
Pinon nut sunflower cakes, recipe 654:99
NEVADA—JEWELRY
Turquoise and silver bracelets, paper, aluminum foil,
macaroni, how to make 1342:140
NEW AMSTERDAM
Tulips, how to make 719:11-13
NEW BRITAIN—MASKS
Bird mask, fabric, wood, paints, making 1706:25
NEW CALEDONIA—STRING FIGURES
The Mosquito string figures story, make 1161:5-8
NEW ENGLAND—CHRISTMAS—COOKERY
Maple bars, recipe 1128:125
NEW ENGLAND—COLONIAL PERIOD—COOKERY
Acorn squash baked with apples, recipe 130:71
Apples and bacon, recipe 130:69
Applesauce, making 130:119
Appones, recipe 130:99
Batter dipped squash blossoms, recipe 130:89
Berry pie filling, recipe 130:115
Bluefish, recipe 130:15
Boysenberry slump, recipe 130:117
Bread pudding, recipe 130:113
Chestnut cakes, recipe 130:101

Chicken corn chowder, recipe 130:57
Clam cakes, recipe 130:25
"The" clam chowder, recipe 130:19-21
Clambake, recipe 130:37-39
Codfish balls, recipe 130:17
Corn fritters, recipe 130:91
Cranberry relish, recipe 130:121
Dandelion wine, recipe 130:133
Dill-bean salad, recipe 130:65
Elderberry wine, recipe 130:135
Fish stock, recipe 130:35
Fricassee of chicken, recipe 130:45
Gingerbread, recipe 130:109
Great oyster soup, recipe 130:11-13
Green potato soup, recipe 130:85
Herbed wild rice, recipe 130:77
Hot mustard, recipe 130:123
Indian pudding, recipe 130:111
Indian vegetables, recipe 130:53-55
Iroquois soup, recipe 130:29-31
Lobster salad, recipe 130:27
Maple beer, recipe 130:139
Mint vinegar, recipe 130:125
Mohawk corn, recipe 130:93
Mulled cider, recipe 130:131
Mushroom soup, recipe 130:79
Mustard greens with bacon, recipe 130:87
Oatmeal bread, recipe 130:105
Passamaquoddy sardines, recipe 130:23
Pheasant with chestnut stuffing, recipe 130:49
Pickled Jerusalem artichokes, recipe 130:75
Popcorn, recipe 130:95
Pumpkin bread, recipe 130:107
Pumpkin, recipe 130:73
Rich oyster dressing, recipe 130:33
Roast venison, recipe 130:51
Roasted peppers, recipe 130:67
Salad of wild greens, recipe 130:61
Salmon fluff, recipe 130:7-9
Sauces for fish, recipe, 130:127
Scallop of turkey, recipe 130:43
Sliced squash, recipe 130:83
Spoon bread, recipe 130:103
Squaw bread, recipe 130:97
Stuffed squash, recipe 130:81
Succotash, recipe 130:59
Sumac-ade, recipe 130:137
Thanksgiving, menu 130:40-41
Watercress salad, recipe 130:63
"Wild and wonderful" duck, recipe 130:47
NEW ENGLAND—COOKERY
Apple pie, recipe 1496:45
Baked acorn squash, recipe 1496:44
Baked bean soup, recipe 343:95
Baked beans, recipe 652:118-119; 1496:42-43
Blueberry cake, recipe 1496:40
Blueberry pie, recipe 529:19-20
Boston baked beans, recipe 529:12-14
Chicken vegetable pie with crust, recipe 1496:41-42
Clam chowder, recipe 518:30-32; 529:9-11; 895:137
Cornbread, Yankee, recipe 88:225-226
Griddle cakes with maple syrup, recipe 1496:35
Hot mulled cider, recipe 895:136
Indian cress salad, recipe 1496:37
Indian pudding, baked, recipe 1496:44-45

Indian pudding, recipe 529:17-18
Lobster salad, recipe 1496:44
Louisa May Alcott recipes 20:1-81
Maine style clam chowder, recipe 1496:36
Maple pumpkin pie, recipe 895:138
Meatloaf, recipe 1496:38-39
Molasses pumpkin pie, recipe 88:232-233
New England boiled dinner, recipe 529:14-16
New England bortsch, recipe 343:96
New England clam chowder, recipe 343:97
New England Johnnycake, recipe 343:110
Pie crust, recipe 88:231
Red flannel hash dinner, recipe 653:74-76
Rye and Indian bread, recipe 88:234-235
Scalloped potatoes, recipe 1496:39-40
Sour milk pie, recipe 793:6-7
Yankee meat pie, recipe 662:111-112

NEW ENGLAND—DOLLS
Mill doll, fabric, patterns, making 1609:78

NEW GUINEA. *See also* **INDONESIA**

NEW GUINEA—CHRISTMAS—COOKERY
Roast pork with plantains and sweet potatoes, recipe
1666:194-195

NEW GUINEA—CHRISTMAS—CUSTOMS
Christmas customs 149:56

NEW GUINEA—COSTUMES
Cone-shaped costume, making 856:78

NEW GUINEA—GAMES
Mailong Sera game 602:76-77
Stepping on the dog game 602:75-76
Taking Coconuts or Ver Ver Aras Lamas game, how to
play 1477:105
Ver Ver Aras Lama, how to play 1494:196

NEW GUINEA—HEADDRESSES
Feather headdress, corrugated paper, straws, making
1488:12-13

NEW GUINEA—HOUSES
Huts on stilts, dowels, sticks, clay, making 1488:20-21
New Guinea stilt houses 469:34-35

NEW GUINEA—JEWELRY
Jungle jewelry, pasta, seeds, paints, making 1488:14-15

NEW GUINEA—MASKS
Rope and shell mask, making 1701:20-21

NEW GUINEA—NATURE FESTIVALS
Planting and growing festivals 419:91-93

NEW GUINEA—PLANTS
Tropical plants, oranges, lemons, pineapples, how to
grow 1488:10-11

NEW GUINEA—STRING FIGURES
Fire string 372:26-27
Ghost dance string 372:32-33
Trick string 373:69

NEW HAMPSHIRE—COOKERY
Dandelion salad, recipe 654:104
Red flannel hash, recipe 654:103

NEW HAMPSHIRE—FOLKLORE
"Ox-Cart Man"; physical and human geography activities 1458:28-31

**NEW HAMPSHIRE—STRAWBERY BANKE—
COOKERY**
Corn pudding, recipe 57:71
New England fish chowder, recipe 571:70
Twelfth Night cookies, recipe 571:71

NEW HEBRIDES—STRING FIGURES
Laia flower string 372:44-47

NEW IRELAND—MASKS
New Ireland mask 204:86-89

NEW JERSEY—COOKERY
Blueberry sauce, recipe 654:106
Fried tomato slices, recipe 654:107
Garden State fruit cup, recipe 1576:36
Hero sandwiches, recipe 654:108

NEW JERSEY—FESTIVALS
Baby parade, Ocean City, baby pictures made from plastic lids, pictures 1199:186-187

NEW JERSEY—FOLKLORE—HANDICRAFTS
Which a Witch story 126:76-81
Which a Witch, art activities, corn husk dolls, making
126:82-85
Which a Witch, art activities, stenciled name plaque,
making 126:86-88
Which a Witch, art activities, stenciled paper, making
126:88

NEW MEXICO—CHRISTMAS
Modem Bethlehem celebration 475:65-66

NEW MEXICO—COOKERY
Biscochitos, recipe 1043:147
Bunch o' muncho nachos, recipe 1729:36
Burros, bean burritos, recipe 1729:38-39
Chihuahua cheese crisps, New Mexican pizzas, recipe
1729:44
Day of the Dead bread, recipe 1729:49-50
Eggs, ranch style eggs, recipe 654:111
Feast Day cookies, recipe 1729:46-47
Fiesta fondue, dessert nachos, recipe 1729:48
Fruit leather, recipe 1342:165
Green chile roll-ups, recipe 1416:unp
Green chile stew, history of, recipe 155:26-27
Holy Moly Guacamole, recipe 1729:41
Homemade corn tortillas, recipe 1729:32-33
Homemade flour tortillas, recipe 1729:34-35
Hotter than you-know-what salsa, recipe 1729:40
Measuring heat of chili peppers of different types of pep-
pers by Scoville heat units 1416:unp
Navajo fry bread, recipe 1342:143
New Mexican Moo Juice, hot chocolate 1729:31
Peppy Pepitas, roasted pumpkin seeds, recipe 1729:45
Roasted pumpkin seeds, recipe 654:110
Sizzlin' sombreros, beef empanadas, recipe 1729:37-38
Whole lotta tostada salad, recipe 1729:42
Zigzag Jicama, recipe 1729:43

NEW MEXICO—DOLLS
Corn husk doll, corn husks, yarn, making 1729:52-53

NEW MEXICO—PIÑATAS
Piñata, paper bag, crepe paper, yarn, making 1729:51-52

NEW YEAR'S DAY
Activities and projects for classrooms 1393:118-119
Activities, art, songs, recipes, games 1469:52-53
Activities, crafts, food, songs 1473:74-75; 1662:2-9
Activities, projects, poetry 819:24-30
Art, cooking, finger plays, games, drama, math, science
and music activities 54:183-184
Belgium celebration 134:108
Bulgaria celebration 134:108
Customs around the world 505:50-51
Finger plays, recipes, games, making 944:58-59
Following the New Year across the United States
489:152-161
Greece celebration 134:108
Happy New Year in seven languages 916:90

Happy New Year in sign language 1199:2
History of New Year celebrations 489:9-15; 496:15-16;
631:122
History of New Year's Day 709:92,94-97
Learning units, art, language, music, foods, crafts, patterns 1193:236-248
Mummers parade 505:27
New Year celebration 133:110-111; 601:120-121
Parades around the world 505:26-27
Tournament of Roses parade 505:27
Words to welcome New Year from other countries
505:12-13

NEW YEAR'S DAY—COOKERY
Dundee cake, recipe 402:9-12
Good luck foods around the world 505:38
Good luck shortbread, recipe 402:9-12
Hoppin' John, pork and black-eyed peas, recipe 1524:56
New Year's honey cake, recipe 505:39
Popcorn recipes, making 939:26-31
Stamps for New Year's cookies, air-hardening clay, making 1477:19

NEW YEAR'S DAY—COSTUMES
Cuckoo clock costume, making 272:26-28
Janus, Roman God, costume, making 272:24-26

NEW YEAR'S DAY—DECORATIONS
Collages, New Year's collages and confetti collage, making 1149:67
Floating art confetti pictures, colored chalks and water, making 1149:152
Greeting card, New Year's resolutions card, making 837:41
Hat, making 226:6
Lantern, paper, patterns, making 1016:3-7
New Year and birthday cards, from colored metal foil, making 113:40
New Year calendar, from colored metal foil, making 113:41
Noisemaker, crackers, making 134:43; 226:7
Noisemaker, felt board, making 945:160-161
Party decorations, making 134:42
Rattlers, tin plate, making 134:43
Scrapbook, making 226:5

NEW YEAR'S DAY—GAMES
Happy New Year game, making 894:9-10
New Year's Day game 240:6
New Year's games, making 376:182
Road builder game, making 894:11-12

NEW YEAR'S DAY—HANDICRAFTS
Janus pin, making 709:93-94

NEW YEAR'S DAY—HANDS ART ACTIVITIES
Hands activities, noisemaker, cap gloves, snowflake, penguin, making 306:28-31

NEW YEAR'S DAY—MAGIC
Calendar mind reading 35:23-26
Chinese New Year paper trick 35:20-22
Happy New Year card trick 35:8-12
Magical calendar trick 35:35-37
Magical New Year card trick 35:32-34
New Year passes trick 35:42-45
New Year penny trick 35:17-19
Noise makers trick 35:38-41
Ring's predictions trick 35:13-16
Seven important dates card trick 35:27-31

NEW YEAR'S DAY—MASKS
Janus mask, pattern 1193:246

NEW YEAR'S DAY—NATURE FESTIVALS
History of New Year's Day nature festivals 419:49-52

NEW YEAR'S DAY—PARTIES
Cook's brunch, invitations, games, recipes, making 1203:96-103
End of the year party, 9 years and up 124:175-187

NEW YEAR'S DAY—PUPPETS
Baby New Year puppet, patterns, making 1006:27
Bear finger puppet, cardboard, patterns, making 1016:8-12
Father Time puppet, patterns, making 1006:28
Father Time's baby puppet, paper plates, making 1083:24
Old Mrs. Weather puppet, patterns, making 1083:25-26
Puppet projects, patterns, scenes, story starters, feature story 1083:20-27
Tiny Tina time traveler puppet, making 1083:24

NEW YEAR'S DAY—SONGS
Songs about New Year 901:38-40

NEW YEAR'S EVE
Activities and projects for classrooms 1393:116-117
Noise making, history of 709:97

NEW YEAR'S EVE—BULLETIN BOARDS
New Year's Eve bulletin board, making 295:188-193

NEW YEAR'S EVE—COOKERY
Chicken tetrazzini, recipe 871:50-51
Marzipan lucky charms, recipe and how to decorate 1415:44-45
Midnight popcorn clocks, recipe 939:146-147

NEW YEAR'S EVE—COSTUMES
Father Time costume 213:146-148

NEW YEAR'S EVE—DECORATIONS
Bell noisemaker, bells, chenille stems, ribbon, making 1425:7-8
Father Time, cardboard tubes, patterns, making 1311:176-177
Favors, candy sacks, nylon net, ribbon, making 1425:5-6
Horn, making 329:7
New Year party hat, making 254:1-2; 297:278; 448:47; 835:29; 1425:2-4
Noisemaker, making 329:6; 648:13
Noisemaker, paper plate, making 835:31
Noisemaker, ruboff letters, stick on stars, making 1425:9-10
Noisemaker, styrofoam cup, making 835:30
Noisemakers, juice cans, making 308:40
Pop-up New Year's Eve card, making 1387:44-46
Yearbook, scrapbook, making 329:10-11

NEW YEAR'S EVE—GAMES
New Year's Eve game 240:64
Scrambled headlines, game, making 329:5

NEW YEAR'S EVE—MUSICAL INSTRUMENTS
Party horn from colored paper, making 1310:108

NEW YORK—COOKERY
Cabin raisin' raisin pie, recipe 1456:5-6
Cheesecake, recipe 654:114; 1043:107
Coleslaw, recipe 654:115
Cornbread, recipe 1456:10
Eggs Benedict, history of, recipe 155:20-21
Ichabod Crane's baked pumpkin mousse, recipe 1353:18
Lockport granola, recipe 1456:34
New York fortune cookies, recipe 1456:26
New York mud cookies, recipe 1456:33
Peekskill mud cheese sandwich, recipe 1456:34
Pizza, recipe 1456:14-16
Seneca Indian stew, recipe 654:113

Snake snack trail mix, recipe 1456:11
Troy peanut butter logs, recipe 1456:34
Watermelon bucket of fruit, recipe 1456:28

NEW YORK—FESTIVALS—COOKERY
Little Italy - Festival of San Gennaro; fruitcake pizza cookies, recipe 1666:271
Little Italy - Festival of San Gennaro; tort mandorla (almond torte), recipe 1666:271

NEW YORK —FESTIVALS—WOODSTOCK
Woodstock anniversary; love beads, macaroni, yarn, food coloring, making 1199:190
Woodstock anniversary; sign of the sixties, peace hand sign, how to do 1199:191
Woodstock anniversary; sixties snack, granola bars, recipe 1199:190-191
Woodstock anniversary; tie-dyeing T-shirt, how to do 1199:188-190

NEW YORK —FOLKLORE
Rip Van Winkle; physical and human geography activities 1458:80-83

NEW YORK—HANDICRAFTS
German walnut head prune peasant doll, making 298:150-15 1
Mosaic yam Shaker rug, making 298:232-233
Wild turkey with colorful tail, making 298:158-159

NEW YORK—HISTORY—COOKERY
Dutch festivals and observances information 666:69-71
Dutch kitchen information 666:67-69
Dutch settle New Netherlands; foods information 666:59-63

NEW YORK —PIRATES—COOKERY
Blackbeard's gunpowder punch, recipe 1456:29
Saturnalia pirates stew, recipe 1456:29

NEW YORK—SLEEPY HOLLOW—COOKERY
Apple butter, recipe 57:79
Apple pie, recipe 57:75
Cheshire pork, recipe 57:79
Gingersnaps, recipe 57:75
Shrewsbury cake, recipe 57:78
Speculaas, recipe 57:74
Standing rib roast, recipe 57:59
Stone ground cornbread, recipe 57:58

NEW YORK CITY
Song, Thirty Purple Birds round song 1115:44

NEW YORK CITY—COOKERY
Hamantaschen, Jewish recipe from New York City, making 663:139-140
Pretzels, recipe 1542:108-109

NEW YORK CITY—GAMES
Chun-Gum, Chewing Gum, musical game 1116:54-55

NEW ZEALAND—CHRISTMAS
Christmas celebration 601:171
Christmas customs 149:57-58
Picnic at beach custom 516:44

NEW ZEALAND—CHRISTMAS—COOKERY
Canterbury lamb with honey, recipe 1666:198
Cauliflower with peanut sauce, recipe 1666:198-199
Plum pudding ice cream cake, recipe 1666:199
Toheroa soup (clam chowder), recipe 1666:197

NEW ZEALAND—COOKERY
Kiwi cup, recipe 1244:146
Kiwi fruit smoothie drink, recipe 1412:74
Kiwi sorbet, recipe 1165:198-199

Kumara and apple casserole, sweet potato and apple casserole, recipe 1165:197-198
Lamingtons, recipe 636:41
Mango mayonnaise with ginger, recipe 636:25
Mussels, with herb and tomato dressing, recipe 636:33
Oaty bars, recipe 1244:147
Paraoa parai, Maori bread, recipe 1244:148-149
Pavlova, meringue fruit dessert, recipe 636:31; 1165:199
Pikelets pancakes, recipe 1412:74-75
Poisson Cru, recipe 636:43
Pumpkin soup, recipe 1412:72-73
Rock cakes, recipe 1165:198
Samoan baked fish, recipe 1412:72
Shearer's stew with jumbuck dumplings, recipe 636:30
Tomato pie, recipe 636:28
Whitebait omelet, recipe 636:19

NEW ZEALAND—FESTIVALS
Maori Poi Ceremony celebration 601:168

NEW ZEALAND—GAMES
Fire's on Mount Cook game 967:40-41
Folding arms game, how to play 1497:29
Hipitoi Maori game, similar to Simon Says, how to play 1355:44
Hokoparepare Maori musical game 1116:56-57
Hurippa, jacks game, how to play 1718:16-17
Jump the Ladder and Patty put the kettle on, how to play 1718:16-17
Knucklebones, how to make and play 1718:38
Maori lemme sticks game 386:63
Mu Torere game, making, how to play 956:130-131; 1507:57-58; 1688:35-37
New Zealand game 1078:30
Queenie game, how to play 1494:193
Rounders game 515:84
Shopping basket game 967:41
Stick games 58:46-47
Walking tall game, how to play 1507:59
Wet day in camp game 967:41

NEW ZEALAND—KITES
Tri-D box kite, making 1069:138-143

NEW ZEALAND—STRING FIGURES
Maoris two diamonds figure, making 423:30-32

NEWSPAPERS
Nellie Bly birthday celebration; art, music, foods, games, activities 1104:82-85

NEWSPAPERS—HANDICRAFTS
Christmas tree decorations from newspaper, making 271:38
Crown and sword, newspaper, making 1658:77-78
Grass skirt, newspaper, making 1658:73
Jester, newspaper, making 1658:36
Kinara, plaster of Paris, milk cartons, candles, making 1659:46-50
Kindling bricks, Nantucket kindling and carrier from newspaper, making 271:68-69
King, newspaper, making 1658:36-37
Leis, newspaper, making 1658:73
Piñata from newspaper, making 271:85
Princess, newspaper, making 1658:36

NEWTON, SIR ISAAC
Demonstrate Newton's law of inertia 1719:31

NEZ PERCE INDIANS—BEADWORK
Beadwork, beaded rosette, canvas, beads, thread, making 1296:111

NEZ PERCE INDIANS—GAMES

Pine cone tossing games, how to play 1601:25

NICARAGUA—CHRISTMAS—COOKERY

Calabaza enmielada (honeyed squash), recipe 1666:244

Sopapillas (fried pastries), recipe 1666:245

NICARAGUA—COOKERY

Banana milkshake, recipe 1039:109

Cheesies, quesillos, recipe 1039:109

Ejotes envueltos en huevo, string beans with egg, recipe 1165:246

Gallo pinto rice and bean dish, recipe, making 1039:108

Horchata rice and milk punch, recipe 1380:22

Maduro en gloria, heavenly bananas, recipe 1165:245-246

NICARAGUA—GAMES

Martinillo game 602:130-131

Piñata game 602:131-132

Senor Caracol game 602:129-130

NICARAGUA—LANGUAGE

Spanish words and phrases 1039:138

NICARAGUA—PIÑATAS

Piñata bird, paper bag, making 515:86

NIGER—FESTIVALS—COOKERY

Eid al-Fitr; joloff (rice with lamb), recipe 1666:27-28

NIGER—GAMES

Dara game (Twelve Men's Morris), how to play 1688:71-74

NIGER—HANDICRAFTS

Wodaabe people mirror pouch, posterboard, yarn, making 1633:92-93

NIGERIA

Activities, flags, games, songs, dances, recipes 1381:145-148

Activities, history, foods, games 143:141-172

NIGERIA—BIRTHDAYS

Birthday customs 488:94-98

NIGERIA—CHRISTMAS

Christmas in Wurkumland celebration 601:34-35

NIGERIA—CLOTHING

Dashike, fabric 143:148

Lapa, fabric skirt, making 143:149

NIGERIA—COOKERY

Baked bananas, recipe 143:158

Chin chin, recipe 143:154

Fried yams, recipe 143:157

Fufu, boiled yam dish, recipe 1381:146

Ground nut chop, recipe 143:156

Ground nut soup, recipe 143:155

Ground nut (peanut) soup, recipe 1381:146

Mango and banana sundae, recipe 858:unp

Masah pancake, recipe 1431:118

Meat and potatoes, recipe 794:39

Ogede sise, boiled bananas, recipe 1165:29-30

Peanut cookies, kulikuli, cookies, recipe 72:97-98

Pepper soup, recipe 1165:28-29

Pineapple punch, recipe 143:158

Rice foo foo, recipe 143:157

Toasted corn and peanuts, recipe 1165:29

NIGERIA—COSTUMES

Ground nut soup, recipe, costume 188:15

NIGERIA—DANCES

Mowrah Cawkah dance, how to do 1494:30-32

NIGERIA—EASTER

Easter celebration 601:35

NIGERIA—FESTIVALS

Festivals and celebrations, maps, flags, crafts, making 1305:85-92

Fishing festival celebration 826:6-7

Sallah Festival celebration 826:8-9

Zolla Festival celebration 601:24-25

NIGERIA—FESTIVALS—COOKERY

Eid al-Fitr; boiled brown beans or chick-pea salad, recipe 1666:28-29

Eid al-Fitr; kuli kuli (ground nut patties), recipe 1666:28-29

Yam Harvest Festival; futari (yams and squash), recipe 1666:29-30

NIGERIA—FESTIVALS—MASKS

Yam Harvest Celebration, spirit mask, papier mache, making 1467:28-29

NIGERIA—FESTIVALS—MUSICAL INSTRUMENTS

Zolla Harvest Festival drum, oatmeal box, paints, making 1539:88-89

NIGERIA—GAMES

Ayo, or capture the seeds game, how to play 143:171-172; 1508:154-156

Catch your tail game 143:169

Da ga, the big snake game 143:169

Dara game (Twelve Men's Morris), how to play 1688:71-74

Derrah, tic-tac-toe, paper, making 1500:32

Hide oh! hide oh! game 602:33

Jump over the bag game 979:19

Jumping the beanbag game 143:170

Moonshine baby game 143:170

Nte-too, playing with seeds game 143:170

Onide comes game 602:32-33

Pinching the foot game 602:34

Ta Galagala, hopscotch game 1426:30-31

Trapping tigers game, how to play 1494:16

War canoe contest game, how to play 1499:28-29

Who has feathers? game 602:33-34

NIGERIA—HANDICRAFTS

Adire elaso, tie-dyeing, making 143:146-147

Batik fabric, fabric, wax, dye, how to do 1381:147

Benin leopard, pattern, making 1022:21-23

Calabashes, making 143:145

Elephant applique picture, fabric, felt, making 1254:15

Ibo Ikenga, making 222:47

Nigerian cloth, dyed, making 1022:24-26

Tie dye fabric, making 222:11

Tie dye T-shirt, making 499:79

NIGERIA—HARVEST FESTIVALS—MASKS

Harvest mask, oaktag, pattern given, making 1249:39-40

NIGERIA—HOUSES

Kano house, making 222:23

NIGERIA—LANGUAGE

Nigeria language 143:172

Nigerian proverbs 1164:37

Some words in English, Fulani, Hausa, Ibo, and Yoruba 1164:25

NIGERIA—MASKS

African elephant mask, paper bag, gray paint, making 1486:18-19

African tribal mask, cardboard, pattern, making 1305:89

Mask, pattern for face, making 1381:147-148

Papier-mâché ceremonial masks, making 143:146

Yoruba ancestor mask, chicken wire, papier mache, making 1706:27

188

NIGERIA—MUSICAL INSTRUMENTS

Aerophones, woodwinds, making 143:162

Chordophones, making 143:162

Cornstalk or bamboo fiddle, making 468:123

Double drum, making 222:31

Drumbeats, how to do 143:162

Drums, making 143:160

Idiophones, making 143:161

Nigerian drum, making 222:28-29

Shekere instrument, how to play 1646:54

Shekere instrument, plastic bottle, lanyard, beads, pipe cleaners, making 1646:50-53

NIGERIA—NEW YEAR'S DAY

Happy New Year in Nigeria 489:132-134

NIGERIA—RHYMES

"Ekin, Ekeji, Eketa" 1607:19

NOAH'S ARK. *See also* **BIBLE—HANDICRAFTS—NOAH'S ARK**

Ark and animals, gingerbread, recipe, patterns, how to make 1086:95-103

Ark matchbox animals, cardboard, patterns, making 1051:15-19

Model of Noah's Ark, making 279:96

Noah's animals, wooden, making 389:42

Noah's Ark model, clay for Ark and animals, making 1484:16-17

Noah's Ark model, milk carton, patterns, making 1311:96-97

Noah's Ark wooden toy, pattern, making 1027:36-44

Noah's Ark, making 670:41-43

Noah's Ark, paper plate, pattern, making 233:38-39

Noah's Ark, wooden, making 389:40-41

NOAH'S ARK—COOKERY

Noah's Ark cake, recipe 449:66-67

NOAH'S ARK—PUPPETS

Noah's Ark puppet show 756:176-180

NOISEMAKERS

Party noisemakers, paper, making 1299:30-31

NORMANS—CASTLES

Norman castle 212:48-59

NORMANS—COSTUMES

Norman lady costume 213:66

NORSEMEN. *See also* **VIKINGS**

NORSEMEN—NATURE FESTIVALS

Nature rites of Northern people 419:39-41

NORTH AFRICA. *See* **AFRICA, NORTH**

NORTH AMERICA—ANIMALS

Blown egg bison, big horn sheep, musk, mountain lion, making 677:27

NORTH AMERICA—LANGUAGE

Greetings of North America 601:152

NORTH CAROLINA—CHRISTMAS

Largest living Christmas tree in Wilmington 475:71

Singing Christmas tree in Charlotte, North Carolina 475:72-74

NORTH CAROLINA—COOKERY

Apple muffins, recipe 654:117-118

Barbecued ribs, history of, recipe 155:14-15

Honeybee candy, recipe 1342:53

Sausage balls, recipe 654:118

Whole wheat bread, recipe 343:115

NORTH CAROLINA—GAMES

How many miles to Babylon? game, how to play 1355:16

Molly Bright game, how to play 1355:16

NORTH DAKOTA—COOKERY

Bannock, recipe 654:122

Berry butter, recipe 654:120

Honey salad dressing, recipe 654:121

NORTH POLE—GAMES

Spiral quest for the North Pole game, how to make and play 1296:126-127

NORTHEAST—COOKERY

Apple pandowdy, recipe 1043:94

Blueberry muffins, recipe 1043:87

Clams, steamed and fried, recipes 1043:90

Corn oysters, recipe 1043:91

Cranberry sauce, recipe 1043:93

Doughnuts, raised, recipe 1043:89

Fried dough, recipe 1043:88

Harvard beets, recipe 1043:93

Joe froggers, cookies, recipe 72:155-156

New England clam chowder, recipe 1043:92

Pears in chocolate sauce, recipe 794:4

Pumpkin pie, recipe 1043:95

Red flannel hash, recipe 1043:91

Sourdough cookies, recipe 72:150-152

Split pea soup, recipe 871:81-82

NORTHEAST INDIANS. *See* **DELAWARE INDIANS; HURON INDIANS; SHAWNEE INDIANS; SHINNECOCK INDIANS; TUSCARORA INDIANS; WOODLAND INDIANS; WINNEBAGO INDIANS**

NORTHERN HEMISPHERE—SOLSTICE

Summer Solstice postcards, wish I were here, making 1199:133-134

Summer Solstice watermelon craft, seeds, paper, glue, making 1199:134-135

Winter Solstice, celebrate by making pine cone bird feeders 1199:283

Winter Solstice; celebrate by making vegetable soup, recipe 1199:281

NORTHERN PEOPLE. *See* **NORSEMEN; VIKINGS**

NORTHMEN. *See* **NORSEMEN; VIKINGS**

NORTHWEST COAST—COOKERY

Apple cake, recipe 1331:41

Blackberry cobbler, recipe 1331:44-45

Clam chowder, recipe 1331:39

Green salad with blue cheese and Oregon hazel nuts, recipe 1331:40-41

Indian bread, baked, recipe 1331:44

Pancakes, recipe 1331:35-36

Salmon, oven-broiled corn on cob, recipe 1331:43

Scrambled eggs, recipe 1331:34

Smoked ham slices, fried, recipe 1331:34-35

Smorrebrod (bread) with shrimp, recipe 1331:37

Smorrebrod (bread) with roast beef, recipe 1331:37-38

Smorrebrod (bread) with turkey, recipe 1331:38

Tomato salad, recipe 1331:43-44

NORTHWEST COAST—FESTIVALS—COOKERY

Salmon barbecue celebration, recipes given 1331:42-45

NORTHWEST COAST INDIANS. *See also* **FLATHEAD INDIANS; HAIDA INDIANS; KLAMATH INDIANS; KWAKIUTL INDIANS; MAIDU INDIANS; PAIUTE INDIANS; TLINGIT INDIANS; YUMA INDIANS**

NORTHWEST COAST INDIANS—BAGS

Tote bag, button bird, making 224:145-149

NORTHWEST COAST INDIANS—BASKETRY

Basket, twigs, weaving supplies, making 1608:34

NORTHWEST COAST INDIANS—BOXES
Boxes, making 171:102-107
NORTHWEST COAST INDIANS—CANOES
Canoe, ceremonial canoe, making 227:18-19
NORTHWEST COAST INDIANS—COOKERY
Broiled salmon steaks with juniper berries, recipe
1527:69
Caribou stew, silver and red salmon, rice supper, recipes
424:82-83
Raspberries and honey ice cream, recipe 1608:19
NORTHWEST COAST INDIANS—FOLKLORE
Whale in the Sky, totem pole, patterns 1206:44-47
NORTHWEST COAST INDIANS—FOOTWEAR
Mukluk moccasins, making 359:104-110
NORTHWEST COAST INDIANS—GAMES
Back game 565:235
Ball drop game 565:178
Ball in air game 565:174
Ball relay 565:31
Bead in hand game 565:262
Bear cave chief game 565:209
Bear race game 565:44
Beaver lodge game 565:179
Big hurry pole game 565:218
Bird flight game 565:172
Bird notes game 565:76
Bowl catch game 565:105; 565:107
Bowl game 565:236
Breath hold pebble contest 565:81
Breath hold tag 565:25
Bump ball game 565:144
Captive ball game 565:175
Captive of war game 565:89
Catamount game 565:242
Circle break game 565:222
Clatawa game 565:250
Come back ball game 565:111
Crab race game 565:45
Crooked path game 565:165
Cross country relay game 565:27
Danger signal game 565:63
Dark walk game 565:85
Disk roll game 565:149
Double relay game 565:33
Drop stick game 565:177
Find the chief game 565:255
Fish trap game 565:23
Fishing game 565:97
Flying feather game 565:134
Foot pull game 565:237
Four stick game 565:200
Fox and geese game 565:109
Frog race game, how to play 565:46; 1296:125
Grizzly guard game 565:226
Guard the chief game 565:66
Guess stick game 565:203
Hand game 565:272
Handicap ball toss 565:112
Harpoon Chief game 565:94
Hidden ball game 565:204
Hit the stone game 565:139
Hole ball game 565:152
Hoop and lance game 565:269
Hop between game 565:162
Hop game 565:161

Hop, jump game 565:162
Indian darts game 565:141
Jump race game 565:163
Kiwa trail game 565:21
Lance chief game 565:240
Lance hold game 565:215
Log chief game 565:239
Moose stalk game 565:74
Obstacle race 565:43
One pebble game 565:202
Over and over game 565:158
Pebble patterns game 565:65
Pine cone hoop toss game 565:123
Pole pull game 565:246
Pole push game 565:248
Raiders game 565:101
Rattler game 565:70
Rebound game 565:116
Ring around game 565:156
Sit pole pull game 565:217
Sit wrestle game 565:233
Slip stick game 565:248
Stalking game 565:68
Star ball game 565:150
Stick and ring game 565:183
Stick in the sand game, how to play 1608:19
Stick relay game 565:32
Stop game 565:213
Straight path ball game 565:258
Strong arm game 565:232
Strong badger game 565:245
Tender of the fire game 565:72
There and back game 565:212
There are no "maidu" game, how to do 1608:27
There game 565:75
Tillikum game 565:168
Touch and go game 565:154
Tracks game 565:86
Trail of silence game 565:98
Trapped game 565:243
Trophy snatch game 565:238
Turn stick game 565:187
Turnabout game 565:166
Turtle keeper game 565:158
Twin tag game 565:24
What do I hold? game 565:201
Whirl and catch game 565:110
Wind hoop game 565:25
NORTHWEST COAST INDIANS—HATS
Hats, making 224:164-168
NORTHWEST COAST INDIANS—HEADBANDS
Headbands, making 224:169-172
NORTHWEST COAST INDIANS—HOUSES
Cedar houses 469:24-27
Haida house, making 171:20-26
Northwest Coast Indian house, balsa wood, making
925:92-93
Plank house, making 804:19-22
Totem plank lodge, making 227:14-15
NORTHWEST COAST INDIANS—MASKS
Kwakiutl, bird mask, cardboard box, ribbon, feathers,
making 1295:19
Large snout and beak masks, making 327:34-35
Northwest Coast mask, shapes, colors, features, making
327:28-29

Single faced and doubled faced masks, making 327:30-33

Symmetrical design mask, paper, making 1092:90-92

NORTHWEST COAST INDIANS—MUSICAL INSTRUMENTS

Bullroarer, wood, twine, making 1608:10

Clapper rattle, bamboo pole, making 1608:31

Drum, ice cream tub, rawhide, making 1608:21

Flute, PVC pipe, bamboo, making 1608:39

Square hand drum, making 468:104

NORTHWEST COAST INDIANS—STRING FIGURES

Fastenings of the raven's plumage string 373:47-49

NORTHWEST COAST INDIANS—TOOLS

Tools and ornaments 960:1-8

NORTHWEST COAST INDIANS—TOTEM POLES

Animal Totem pole, paper tubes, posterboard, patterns, making 1633:30-33

Miniature Totem poles, making 633:124-127

Totem pole wall hanging, making 925:57-58

Totem pole, paper, making 845:40-43

Totem pole, small or large boxes, making 1699:169-171

Totem poles, how to draw 591:26-27

Totem poles, making 171:27-34; 227:60-61; 324:47; 465:102-103; 466:118-119; 629:106-107; 714:12-13; 924:24-27

Totem toys, making 482:42-43

NORTHWEST COAST INDIANS—WOODWORKING

Woodworking of Northwest Coast Indians 959:70-72

NORWAY

Activities, flags, games, songs, dances, recipes 1381:194

Map, flag and products 621:6

NORWAY—CHRISTMAS

Celebration of Christmas 1049:85

Christmas customs 149:27; 473:44-45; 474:150-151

Witches custom 516:38-40

NORWAY—CHRISTMAS—COOKERY

Berlin wreath cookies, recipe 1023:98-100

Christmas bread, recipe 446:42-45

Christmas Eve meal; rice pudding and almond, recipe 621:11

Cookies, Norwegian Cassandra cookies, recipe 707:30-31

Dill shrimp sauce for fish balls, recipe 1666:122

Fiskeboller (Norwegian fish balls), recipe 1666:122

Gingerbread house cookies recipe 473:44-45

Julebrod, Christmas bread, recipe 621:17-19

Mor Monsen's Kaker (Mother Monsen's cake), recipe 1666:123

Ris A L'Amande, Christmas rice pudding, recipe 1128:143

Stuede Poteter (creamed potatoes), recipe 1666:122-123

NORWAY—CHRISTMAS—DOLLS

Dolls, yarn, making 1023:117-119

Tomte yam doll, making 1023:119-120

NORWAY—CHRISTMAS—HANDICRAFTS

Norwegian reindeer wood clothes pegs, felt, decorations, Tools, making 1575:8

Rosemaling, Norwegian Rosemaling, making 795:69

NORWAY—COOKERY

Apple cake, recipe 794:16

Arendal cakes, recipe 1395:119

Baked cod, recipe 621:30-31

Berry pudding, recipe 1122:101

Fish loaf, recipe 967:42

Flarn cookies, recipe 1381:194

Flatbread, recipe 621:26-27

Flois grod, recipe 50:18

Fruit soup dessert, recipe 1280:43

Fruit soup, fruktsuppe, recipe 621:40-41

Krokan ice cream, recipe 1264:27

Lefse flat bread, recipe 1380:24

Lefse, fried potato bread, recipe 1165:137

Meatballs, recipe 621:32-33

Menu, Norwegian, ideas for 621:14-15

Oatmeal raisin soup, recipe 1122:42

Open-faced sandwiches, recipe 621:22-24

Peas, boiled, recipe 621:36

Polar fish, recipe 858:unp

Potato dumplings, kumpe, recipe 1122:43

Potato soup, recipe 621:20-21; 1380:26

Potatoes, boiled, recipe 621:35

Raspberry soup, recipe 1380:39

Rice porridge, recipe 621:16

Rice pudding, recipe 621:37

Smorgasbord, history of 621:9-10

Sunday breakfast, recipe 793:34

Toskakake, almond caramel topped cake, recipe 1165:138

Whole wheat rusks, recipe 621:28-29

NORWAY—DANCES

Courting dances 474:117

Halling dance and costume picture 1000:37-39

NORWAY—DOLLS

Hardanger bride doll, making 59:13-15

Troll doll, good fortune doll, yam, making 298:246-247

NORWAY—FESTIVALS

Constitution Day celebration 973:44-48

Feeding of the Birds celebration 601:116-117

Holmenkollen Day celebration 973:15-18

Jonsok celebration 973:54-57

Sun Day or Soldag, activities, art, songs, recipes, games 1469:60-61

Sun Pageant celebration 973:19-23

NORWAY—FOLKLORE

"Goat in the Turnip Field" flannel board story, patterns, making 1603:64-68

"House in the Woods" flannel board story, patterns, making 1603:14-18

"Hungry Cat" flannel board story, patterns, making 1604:60-67

"Lad and the North Wind," ram, wind, Peter, mother, innkeeper puppets, patterns 1206:48-56

"Three Billy Goats Gruff," flannel board patterns, making 1201:66-70

"Three Billy Goats Gruff," puppets, costumes, masks, cooking, science, math, music activities 1358:84-103

"Three Billy Goats" flannel board story, patterns, making 1603:44-49

"Why Mr. Bear Has a Short Tail" flannel board patterns, making 910:23,60

NORWAY—FOODS

Customs and foods eaten in Norway 621:9-11

NORWAY—GAMES

Cut the oats game 602:100-101

Fox and geese game, making 1507:82-83
Hoppe-strikk, jump rope game, how to play 1708:46-47
Landing in Paradise, hopscotch game 984:18
Stick and stones game 572:8-9
Waves game, how to play 967:42; 1355:13

NORWAY—HANDICRAFTS
Brikke Band, making 470:28-29; 626:79-80
Hot plate mat, making 298:58-59
Lapp baby carry cot, making 470:38-39
Needle book, national costume, making 470:24-25
Reindeer, pipe cleaner, making 470:40-41
Sea serpents, making 470:21

NORWAY—INDEPENDENCE DAY
Independence Day celebration May 17 722:24-28

NORWAY—KNITTING
Puffin, knitted, making 470:37
Sea-whips, knitted, making 470:22-23
Seals, knitted, making 470:26-27

NORWAY—NEW YEAR'S EVE
New Year's Eve celebration 973:89

NORWAY—PAINTERS
Munch, Edvard; copy Munch's painting style with finger-paint, making 1372:41-43

NORWAY—PUPPETS
Three Billy Goats Gruff puppet show 756:156-159

NORWAY—RHYMES
"Kella Bukk" 1607:35

NORWAY—ROSEMALING
Rosemaling serving tray, how to do 626:77-79
Rosemaling decorated utensils, making 298:188-189

NORWAY—SONGS
Sleep Gently Now My Little Friend, lullaby 1220:147

NORWAY—TOYS
Balancing potato man and his dog, making 298:152-153

NORWAY—TROLLS
Troll, felt, making 470:30-36

NOVA SCOTIA—CHRISTMAS
Celebration of Christmas in Nova Scotia 1049:90

NOVA SCOTIA—DANCES
Flowers of May dance, how to do 1494:187-188

NOVA SCOTIA—FESTIVALS
Apple Blossom Festival celebration 601:126-127
Highland Games celebration 601:127-128

NUMBERS. *See* **COUNTING**

NUMEROFF, LAURA JOFFE
"If You Give a Mouse a Cookie," chocolate chip cookies, recipe 1216:78

NURSERY RHYMES
Baa, Baa Black Sheep, history of, picture, poem, activities 172:59-65
Curly Locks, history of, picture, poem, activities 172:107-11
Daffy Down Dilly, history of, picture, poem, activities 172:89-92
Doctor Foster, history of, picture, poem, activities 172:19-22
Georgie Porgie, history of, picture, poem, activities 172:131-134
Hark, Hark, history of, picture, poem, activities 172:127-129
Hey Diddle Diddle, history of, picture, poem, activities 172:71-74
Hickory, Dickory, Dock, history of, picture, poem, activities 172:139-145

Humpty Dumpty egg head on brick wall, pattern, making 1348:unp
Humpty Dumpty, history of, picture, poem, activities 172:23-28
Jack and Jill, history of, picture, poem, activities 172:47-50
Jack Be Nimble, history of, picture, poem, activities 172:29-32
Jack Spratt, history of, picture, poem, activities 172:103-106
Lady Bird, Lady Bird, history of, poem, picture, activities 172:111-115
Little Bo-Peep, history of, picture, poem, activities 172:85-88
Little Boy Blue, history of, picture, poem, activities 172:51-54
Little Jack Horner, history of, picture, poem, activities 172:33-36
Little Miss Muffet shadow puppet play, making 1177:26-27
Little Miss Muffet, history of, picture, poem, activities 172:81-84
London Bridge, history of, picture, poem, activities 172:13-17
Mary Had a Little Lamb, history of, picture, poem, activities 172:167-170
Mistress Mary, history of, picture, poem, activities 172:75-79
Needles and Pins, history of, picture, poem, activities 172:43-46
Old King Cole, history of, picture, poem, activities 172:5-8
Pat A Cake, history of, picture, poem, activities 172:123-126
Peter Peter Pumpkin Eater, history of, picture, poem, activities 172:161-166
Peter Piper, history of, picture, poem, activities 172:171-174
Polly Put the Kettle On, history of, picture, poem, activities 172:135-137
Pussy Cat, Pussy Cat, history of, picture, poem, activities 172:55-58
Rain, Rain Go Away, history of, picture, poem, activities 172:9-12
Ride a Cock Horse, history of, picture, poem, activities 172:67-70
Ring Around a Rosie, history of, picture, poem, activities 172:93-96
See-Saw, Margery Daw, history of, picture, poem, activities 172:59-65
Sing a Song of Sixpence, history of, picture, poem, activities 172:37-41
There was an Old Woman, history of, picture, poem, activities 172:97-101
Three Blind Mice, puppets, costumes, masks, cooking, science, math, music activities 1358:141-157
Three Little Kittens, history of, picture, poem, activities 172:175-179
Three Little Kittens, puppets, costumes, masks, cooking, science, math, music activities 1358:179-193
Twinkle Twinkle Little Star, history of, picture, poem, activities 172:151-160
Wee Willie Winkie, history of, picture, poem, activities 172:117-121

NURSERY RHYMES—COOKERY
Baker's man sunshine orange pat-a-cake, recipe 1215:40
Bunman's quick and easy hot cross buns, recipe 1215:34
Cow that jumped over the moon's moooo shake, recipe 1215:22
Humpty Dumpty's off the wall toast, bread, eggs, recipe 1215:10
Little Jack Horner's plum cobbler pie, recipe 1215:44
Little Miss Muffet's curd and whey with fruit and nuts, recipe 1215:28
Little Miss Muffet's curds and whey, recipe 1564:18
Queen of Hearts' jam and honey filled meringue tarts, recipe 1215:30
Simple Simon's frozen yogurt pie, recipe 1215:42

NURSERY RHYMES—COSTUMES
Curly Locks, Curly Locks costume, making 841:16
Hickety, Pickety, my black hen costume, making 841:38
Hot Cross Buns boy costume, making 366:34-37
Humpty Dumpty costume, making 841:39-42
I Love Little Pussy costume, making 841:28-32
Jack and Jill costume, making 366:86
Jack be Nimble costume, making 841:26
Knave of Hearts costume, making 366:52-54
Little Bo-Peep costume, making 366:71-74; 841:3-11
Little Boy Blue and cow costumes, making 841:17-25
Little Boy Blue costume, making 366:86
Little Jack Horner costume, making 841:27
Little Miss Muffet costume, making 366:21-24
Little Miss Muffet, spider, curds and whey costumes, making 841:13-15
Little Robin Redbreast costume, making 841:33-35
Mary Had a Little Lamb and sheep costumes, making 841:3-11
Mary Mary Quite Contrary costume, making 366:80-81; 841:12
Milkmaid, Alice, Bo-Peep, and Miss Muffet costume, fabric, making 1174:97
Old King Cole costume, making 366:87
Old Mother Hubbard costume, making 841:43-48
Once I Saw a Little Bird costume, making 841:33-35
Pat A Cake costume, making 366:87
Polly Put the Kettle On costume, making 841:16
Queen of Hearts costume, making 366:48-51
There Once Were Two Cats of Kilkenny costume, making 841:28-32
There Was a Little Girl costume, making 841:16
There Was an Old Woman Who Lived in a Shoe costume, making 841:43-48
Wee Willie Winkie costume, making 366:61-62
Wise Old Owl Sat in an Oak costume, making 841:36-37

NURSERY RHYMES—FACE MAKEUP
Little Miss Muffet face makeup, how to do 1314:36

NURSERY RHYMES—FLANNEL BOARDS
"Old Mother Hubbard" flannel board rhyme, patterns, making 1603:23-28

NURSERY RHYMES—GAMES
Change hands clap game 1118:12

Draw a pail of water game 1118:38-41
Eensy weensy spider game 1118:14
Farmer's in the Dell game 1118:21-23
Finger names game 1118:6
Fly away Peter game 1118:13
Foot names game 1118:7
Go tell Aunt Nancy game 1118:36-38
Here we go round the mulberry bush 1118:26
Here's my lady game 1118:17
Here's the church game 1118:10
In and out the dusty bluebells game 1118:32-33
King of the castle game 1118:17
Little piggy game 1118:6
London Bridge game 1118:42-43
Lucy Locket game 1118:20
Oats and beans and barley grows game 1118:23
One potato game 1118:15-16
Oranges and lemons game 1118:33-35
Pat-a-cake game 1118:9
Piling hands game 1118:13
Poor Mary sits a'weeping game 1118:30-32
Ring a ring a roses game 1118:20
Round and round the garden game 1118:8
Round and round the Village game 1118:28-29
See-saw, Marjorie Daw game 1118:17
Sur le Pont d'Avignon game 1118:42
The big ship sails on the Ally-Ally O game 1118:24-26

NURSERY RHYMES—PARTIES
Mother Goose party, activities and recipes 809:7-11
Nursery Rhymes theme party, making 896:93-98

NURSERY RHYMES—PUPPETS
Hickory Dickory Dock shadow puppets, patterns, music, making 1602:47-48
Little Miss Muffet shadow puppets, patterns, music, making 1602:45-47
Old MacDonald shadow puppets, patterns, music, making 1602:43-45

NUTCRACKER
Clara doll, fabric, patterns, making 484:65-69
Nutcracker toy soldier prince doll, fabric, patterns, making 484:72-76
Pralines from the Fortress of Sweets, recipe 569:73-75
Puppet, Nutcracker tube marionette, making 757:139-161
Sugar Plum Fairy doll, fabric, patterns, making 484:69-72

NUTRITION
Activities, art, songs, recipes, games 1469:82-83
Songs, finger plays, stories, games, rhythms 1200:23-25

NUTS—HANDICRAFTS
Chinese girl, little one, made from peanuts, making 623:3-5
Nut stenciled bandanna, fabric, nuts, ink pad, making 1285:100-101
Things to make with nuts 1304:69-89
Totem pole match holders from tubes and acorns, making 623:12-13

O

OCEAN
Coral, pattern, making 1190:84
Crab, pattern, making 1190:87
Fish, pattern, making 1190:86
Jelly fish, pattern, making 1190:86
Octopus, pattern, making 1190:85
Scuba diver, pattern, making 1190:83
Sea horse, pattern, making 1190:84
Seaweed, pattern, making 1190:82
Shark, pattern, making 1190:88
Whale, pattern, making 1190:89

OCEAN—PUPPETS
Ocean animal puppets, patterns, making 463:57-63
Roland and Celia under the Ocean, puppets, sets, props, sound effects, making 1158:117-125

ODOR EATERS
Russian scientist discovers chemical that eats odors 1719:65-67

OGALA SIOUX INDIANS—DANCES
Sundance, how to do 1362:51

OGRES—COSTUMES
Ogre costume, making 42:46-52

OHIO—CHRISTMAS
International Christmas in Dayton, Ohio 475:69

OHIO—COOKERY
Apple brown betty, recipe 652:116-117
Apples, fried, recipe 654:125
Germans of Ohio meat and potatoes eating customs in pioneer days 663:40-45
Hamburger, history of, recipe 155:30-31
Honey nut bars, recipe 654:124
Kartoffelpuffer, German recipe 663:57-58

OJIBWA INDIANS. *See also* **CHIPPEWA INDIANS**

OJIBWA INDIANS—COOKERY
Baked pumpkin, recipe 1699:137-138
Popped wild rice, recipe 1527:26
Wild rice, recipe 1445:29

OJIBWA INDIANS—FOLKLORE—HANDICRAFTS
Shingebiss and the North Wind, snow scene with crayon resist, diorama 125:80-89

OJIBWA INDIANS—HANDICRAFTS
Birchbark container, stencil, how to make 1445:24

OJIBWA INDIANS—SONGS
Hush Little Baby, lullaby 1220:144

OJIBWA INDIANS—WEAVING
Weaving, how to do 482:92-93

OJO-DE-DIOS. *See* **GOD'S EYE**

O'KEEFFE, GEORGIA—BIRTHDAY
Celebrate by painting watercolor flowers 1199:260

OKINAWA—DANCES
Okinawan Home Sweet Home Folk Dance 474:125-126

OKLAHOMA—COOKERY
Chuckwagon beans, Indian recipe, 663:82-83
Custard, baked fudge custard, recipe 654:127
Nasturtium, recipe 654:128

OKLAHOMA—HISTORY
Oklahoma chuckwagon food supply information 663:73-79

OKTOBERFEST. *See* **GERMANY—FESTIVALS**

OLYMPICS
Backyard Olympics games, making 1121:12-13
Barefoot marble race 977:14
Bicycle Olympics 114:71-74
Can can walk 977:26
Discus throw 977:9

Eskimo Olympic games 376:90
Fifty yard dash 977:10
Fifty yard swim 977:11
Fish on a string 977:12
Gold Medal, paper, making 1017:24
Hammer throw 977:8
High hurdles 977:27
High jump 977:3 1
Indoor Olympics 977:6-7
Javelin throw 977:9
Jumping the stream 977:29
Junior Olympics, how to have an event 375:30-31
Kid croquet 977:13
Low hurdles 977:9
Obstacle course 977:24-25
Right on throw 977:20
Shoe launch 977:22
Shot put 977:21
Shot put on 977:8
Slalom 977:31
Standing broad jump 977:23
Swim medley 977:11
Torch, paper, making 1017:24
Tunnel game 977:28

OLYMPICS—COOKERY
Olympiad cake, making 43:166-167

OLYMPICS—PARTIES
Olympiad Party, how to plan and give 43:45-49
Olympic Games theme birthday party, making 896:55-60
Olympic party, 7 years up 124:122-130
Olympics party, how to plan and give 86:142-151
Olympics party, menu and recipes 86:229-230

OMAHA INDIANS—NAMES
Naming Days information 695:45-49

OMAN. *See also* **ARABIAN PENINSULA**

OMAN—COOKERY
Almond biscuits, recipe 1165:75
Date bars, recipe 1165:73
Fruit balls, recipe 1165:76
Hoomis, chick pea spread, recipe 1165:72
Limonada, lemonade, recipe 1165:72-73
Mjeddrah, rice with lentils, recipe 1165:74
Shourba Bilsen, thick lentil soup, recipe 1165:72
Stuffed dates, figs, prunes, recipe 1165:75
Tahineh or tahini, sesame seed paste, recipe 1165:74

ONEIDA INDIANS—COOKERY
Corn soup, recipe 1699:142

ONONDAGA INDIANS—MUSICAL INSTRUMENTS
Rattle, gourd, making 1699:78-79

ONONDAGA INDIANS—STRING FIGURES
Crow's Feet, 1404:22-25

ORBACH, RUTH
"Apple Pigs," apple pan dowdy, recipe 1216:48
"Apple Pigs," applesauce and baked apples, recipe 843:64-65, 131

ORCHESTRAS—COSTUMES
Conductor model, ping pong ball, fabrics, dowels, felt, making 1728:18-19

ORCHESTRAS—PARTIES
Orchestra party, how to plan and give 86:152-159

OREGON—COOKERY
Filbert cheese wafers, recipe 654:130
Strawberry shortcake, recipe 654:131
Tillamook soup from the great Northwest, history of, recipe 155:10-11

OREGON—HISTORY
Oregon Homesteaders and Mountain men food supply information 663:90-95

ORGAN GRINDERS
Organ grinder monkey, milk cartons, colored paper, making 1310:148-149

ORIENTAL FESTIVALS—PARTIES
Oriental festival party, how to plan and give 86:160-167
Oriental festival party, menu and recipes 86:231-232

ORIENTAL HANDICRAFTS
Oriental Pavilion, cardboard carton, making 679:unp

ORIGAMI. *See also* **JAPAN—ORIGAMI**
Hydrangea plant, making 893:95-101
Origami, making 126:50

ORIGAMI—MASKS
Monster origami mask, making 322:8-9

OSAGE INDIANS—COOKERY
Osage Indian bread, recipe 410:112-113

OSAGE INDIANS—FOOTWEAR
Osage moccasins, making 359:94-98

OSAGE INDIANS—GAMES
Hiding the thimble game 602:175

OSAGE INDIANS—STRING FIGURES
House, Jacob's Ladder 1404:26-110
Thumb catch figure, making 423:18-19

OTOMI INDIANS—HANDICRAFTS
Curandero healing books, brown bags, ribbons, making 1332:63-68
Paper figures, brown paper, making 1730:28-31

OWL AND THE PUSSYCAT
Puppets, costumes, masks, cooking, science, math, music activities 1358:122-140

P

PACIFIC ISLANDS—COOKERY
South Sea fruit shake, recipe 1653:12
PACIFIC ISLANDS—JEWELRY
Necklace from recycled materials, paper tubes, foil, paints, making 1648:45
PACIFIC ISLANDS—MUSICAL INSTRUMENTS
Stamping tubes, bamboo sticks, rocks, making 1649:45
PACIFIC ISLANDS—NAMES
Baby names information 695:123
PACIFIC NORTHWEST. *See* **NORTHWEST COAST**
PAGODAS
Literature, activities, crafts, games 1390:56-83
Paper pagodas, making 996:45
PAINTING
Bracket fungi painting, how to do 1421:41
China painting, how to do 51:272-294
Glass painting on glass, how to do 1640:24-25
Pointillism, dots of color, making 1619:16-19
Sand painting, how to do 1421:29
Sponge painting, papier-mache, how to do 1464:61
Stone painting, how to do 1421:25
PAINTING—AMERICAN FOLK ART
Reverse glass painting, how to do 524:55
Reverse glass painting, making 70:26
PAINTING—THEOREM
Theorem painting, stencil and color, making 673:279-304
PAINTS
Black and white opaque window paint, recipe 1455:39
Egg tempera paint, recipe 1455:37
Glue paint, recipe 1455:37
Milk paint, recipe 1455:36
Milk paint, recipe, how to do 1278:8-9
Opaque finger paint, recipe 1455:35
Opaque window paint, recipe 1455:39
Pan paints, watercolor paints, recipe 1455:38
Somewhat opaque finger paint, recipe 1455:35
Thick paint for cardboard boxes, recipe 1455:38
Transparent finger paint, recipe 1455:34
Transparent window paint, recipe 1455:40
PAIUTE INDIANS—CLOTHING
Paiute vest, making 932:55-58
PAIUTE INDIANS—GAMES
Hoop and darts, how to make and play 1699:120
Rock jacks game 602:175-176
PAIUTE INDIANS—HOUSES
Wikiup, making 804:37-39
PAKISTAN
Activities, flags, games, songs, dances, recipes 1381:107-108
PAKISTAN—CHRISTMAS
Christmas celebration 601:80-81
Christmas customs 149:48
PAKISTAN—COOKERY
Chana dahl, chickpeas, recipe 1165:162
Chapli kabab, meat patties, recipe 1165:161-162
Coconut almond candy, recipe 895:100
Deram fiti, making 187:33
Kachoomber, salad, recipe 1165:162
Keema matter pilau, rice and beef dish, recipe 1595:119
Kheema mattar curry, ground beef dish, recipe 1156:87-88
Khoa cottage cheese dish, recipe 1380:15
Kima, recipe 794:49

Pakistani kima, ground beef, tomato, curry, recipe 1381:108
Shahi tukra dessert, recipe 1156:90-91
Sheer khorma vermicelli dessert, recipe 1156:89-90
Tandoor rotis bread, recipe 1156:86-87
Yogurt chicken, recipe 895:99
PAKISTAN—FESTIVALS
Feast of the Gift celebration 601:68-69
Festival of Basanth, kite flying day 474:62
PAKISTAN—FESTIVALS—COOKERY
Eid al-Fitr; murgh tikha lahori (Tandoori chicken), recipe 1666:157-158
Eid al-Fitr; pulao arasta (Pakistani rice), recipe 1666:158
Eid al-Fitr; shahi tukra (Pakistani sweet bread), recipe 1666:158-159
Eid al-Fitr; yakhni (Pakistani broth), recipe 1666:157
PAKISTAN—GAMES
Gulli Danda game 515:90
Gulli Danda stick game 1119:18-19
Jackstones game 602:77
Kokla-chaupakee game, how to play 1355:28-29
Mazdoori game 967:42-43
Old woman game 602:78
Sathi Khoj, lost a couple game, how to play 1494:37
PAKISTAN—HANDICRAFTS
Lucky animals, Sathia floor decoration, shoebox lid, paint, making 1447:26-27
PAKISTAN—NATURE FESTIVALS
Moslem Hunza seed sowing ritual 419:118
Moslem spring kite flying contest 419:119-120
PALACE GUARDS
Palace guard, tin cans, colored paper, pattern, making 1311:30-31
PALM SUNDAY
Palm branch, paper, making 1409:22
Palm Sunday 139:65-66
PALM SUNDAY—GERMANY
Oberammergau celebration 139:70
PALMS
Plaiting palms, how to do 725:25
PAN AMERICAN DAY
Activities, crafts, history and stories for 128:37-44
PAN AMERICAN DAY—PUPPETS
Chilean boy finger puppet, making 128:40
Cowgirl finger puppet, making 128:40
Eskimo finger puppet, making 128:41
Jamaican girl finger puppet, making 128:41
PANAMA
Activities, flags, games, songs, dances, recipes 1381:39-42
PANAMA—CHRISTMAS—COOKERY
Flan Almendra (almond pudding), recipe 1666:241
Sancocho (beef and vegetable soup), recipe 1666:240-241
PANAMA—COOKERY
Blade's black beans, recipe 1370:121
Citrus squares, recipe 1165:242
Guacamole, recipe 1381:41
Picadillo, meat and rice dish, recipe 1381:41
Sighs, suspiros, cookies, recipe 72:172-173
Toasted cashew nuts, recipe 1244:126
PANAMA—COSTUMES
Pollera costume, making 856:78
PANAMA—GAMES
Baseball in Panama 515:92

PANAMA—MOLAS

Mola cloth rectangle, fabric, felt, pattern, making 1730:50-55

Mola design to appique with yarn, making 1381:41-42

Molas, fabric panels made from paper, making 1338:35-37

Monster molas, fabric, felt, patterns, making 1251:12-15

PANAMA—RHYMES

Tortita, Tortita baby clapping rhyme 780:62

PANCAKE DAY

Celebration and history of, pancake recipe given 496:35-40

PANCAKE TUESDAY. *See also* **SHROVE TUESDAY**

Customs round the world 503:16-17

Pancake race game 503:16-17

Pancakes, recipe 503:17

PANCAKES

Activities, art, songs, recipes, games 1469:72-73

PANCAKES—PARTIES

Pancake Party, recipes and games 635:43-45

PANDAS

Giant panda bank, juice can, paper, patterns, making 1286:22-23

PANTINS

Pantins, cardboard, patterns, making 1422:17

PANTINS—FRANCE

Pantin jumping doll, making 105:9-14

PANTOMIMING

History of pantomiming 755:29-32

PAPAGO INDIANS

Legends 344:56

Songs and stories of the Papago Indians 344:56-61

PAPER AIRPLANES

First international paper airplane competition 114:55

Have your own neighborhood paper airplane Olympics 114:56

PAPER CHAINS

Chain of hearts, paper, making 873:4

Chanukah paper chains, making 81:21

Decorative chains, paper, making 1238:98-103

Hanukkah paper chains, making 262:59-61

Polish paper chains, making 626:83-84

PAPER-CUTTING

Indian face, paper, making 742:44

Pilgrim faces, paper, making 742:44

Santa face, paper, making 742:44

PAPER POP-UPS. *See* **POP-UPS**

PAPERMAKING

Aged paper, making 1455:166

Handmade paper, old paper, flowers, leaves, grass, blender, making 1616:12-15

Homemade paper with inlaid leaves, old paper, leaves, screen, making 1285:92-95

Homemade recycled paper, making 1213:18-19

Make your own from scrap paper using mold and deckle 1372:90-93

Make your own paper, how to do 1196:26-27

Marbeling paper, how to do 1181:82-83

Marbelized paper ; marble paint your own paper, how to do 1254:41

Marbling, marbled paper, how to make 1640:30-31

Parchment paper from tissue paper, making 747:47

Parchment paper, making 308:75-76

Rice paper from tissue paper, making 747:46

Rice paper, making 143:120; 499:142

Stained glass paper, making 428:45-46

Wrapping paper, marbled, how to make 1196:62-63

PAPERWEIGHTS

Flower paperweights, making 1510:64-65

PAPIER MACHE

Blue and water recipe, making 1633:152

Flour and water recipe, making 1633:152

How to do it, recipe 1464:10

Large papier-mache objects, how to make 1455:18

Oriental hollow gourd, making 274:115-119

Papier-mache dough for shaping into objects, recipe 1455:20

Papier-mache paste, recipe 1455:30

Papier-mache pulp, recipe 1455:15

Piñata, papier-mache, making 759:27-29

Very soft papier-mache, recipe 1455:16

PAPUA NEW GUINEA. *See also* **NEW GUINEA**

PAPUA NEW GUINEA—COOKERY

Banana baki baki, recipe 967:43

Boiled shrimp, recipe 1165:192

Grilled fish, recipe 1165:192-193

Vegetables cooked in bamboo, recipe 967:43

PAPUA NEW GUINEA—MASKS

Bird mask, fabric, wood, paints, making 1706:25

Koveve tribe bush and sea spirits mask, plastic bottle, cardboard tubes, raffia, making 1706:17

PAPUA NEW GUINEA—STRING FIGURES

Eel or catching crabs string 372:20-21

Lizard and Snake string figures story, making 1161:22-30

Trick string 373:69

PARAGUAY—COOKERY

Cornmeal muffins, chepa, recipe 1653:68

PARAGUAY—COSTUMES

Cornbread, recipe, costume 188:10

PARAGUAY—EASTER—COOKERY

Sopa Paraguaya (Paraguayan cornbread), recipe 1666:231

PARAGUAY—GAMES

Maravilla, Maravilla game, how to play 1494:218

PARAGUAY—MUSICAL INSTRUMENTS

Harp, wooden, making 515:94

PARTIES

Animal safari birthday party, activities, foods, and handicrafts 30:77-82

April Fools' backwards birthday party, activities, foods, handicrafts 30:123-126

Beatrix Potter Easter brunch, decorations, games, costumes, recipes 74:71-84

Beyond the Stars party, activities, recipes 809:79-84

Big Top birthday party, invitations, decorations, foods, games 133:16-20

Carnival, come to a carnival party, invitations, decorations, foods 133:96-100

CB truckers birthday rally party, activities, foods, handicrafts 30:55-57

Chanukah party, invitations, decorations, food, games 133:141-143

Chinese dragon party, activities, foods, and handicrafts 30:101-104

Christmas cookie factory party, decorations, games, costumes, recipes 74:167-180

Christmas party, 7 year and up 124:164-174

Christmas party, how to plan and give 43:72-76

Christmas party, invitations, decorations, food games 133:144-147

Christmas party, recipes and games 635:18-20

Cinderella dress up birthday party, activities, foods, handicrafts 30:33-35

Circus birthday party, decorations, foods, games, patterns 1011:71-91

Circus party, invitations, decorations, costumes, food, games, recipes 1185:8-9

Clown birthday party, activities, foods, handicrafts 30:16-18

Clown party, how to plan and give 43:16-20

Cowboy party, 10 years up 124:116-122

Cowboys and Indians party, recipes and games 635:45-48

Easter brunch, invitations, decorations, food, games 133:130-133

Easter Egg party, how to plan and give 43:65-67

Easter party, recipes and games 635:24-27

Fairy party, invitations, decorations, costumes, food, games, recipes 1185:16-17

Farm party; Old MacDonald farm party, activities, recipes 809:1-6

Fire Engine #9 party, activities and recipes 809:13-16

Footballers Feast party, recipes and games 635:51-53

Fourth of July party, recipes and games 635:59-61

Globe-trotting party, activities and recipes 809:93-96

Go West party, 7 years up 124:87-98

Goin' Fishin' party, activities, foods, handicrafts 30:131-134

Green Eggs and Ham breakfast, ideas for 133:159

Halloween Happening party, activities, foods, handicrafts 30:143-146

Halloween party, 6 years and up 124:138-149

Halloween party, how to plan and give 43:70-72

Halloween party, invitations, decorations, food, games 133:137-140

Harvest Birthday party, activities, foods, handicrafts 30:147-150

Hawaiian luau birthday party, activities, foods, and handicrafts 30:105-107

Hearts Galore party, how to plan and give 43:25-29

Historical heroes birthday celebration party, activities, foods, and handicrafts 30:113-115

Hobo Heaven party, activities, recipes 809:107-110

Hobo Hobnob party, how to plan and give 43:50-53

Home on the Range party, activities and recipes 809:43-48

Independence Day party celebrations, invitations, decorations, food, games 133:134-136

Indian Pow-Wow party, 7 years up 124:150-157

Japanese birthday tea party, activities, foods, and handicrafts 30:91-95

Japanese Tea party, activities and recipes 809:117-121

Jolly Old England birthday celebration party, activities, foods, handicrafts 30:73-76

Jolly Roger birthday party, invitations, decorations, food, games 133:38-40

Jungle breakfast party, ideas for 133:159

Jungle party, invitations, decorations, costumes, food, games, recipes 1185:10-11

Jungle Safari birthday party, decorations, games, cake, patterns 1015:103-119

Knights and dragons party, activities and recipes 809:101-106

Knights around the table party, decorations, games, costumes, recipes 741:150-166

Leprechaun hideaway birthday party, activities, food, handicrafts 30:70-72

Mad Hatter party, recipes and games 635:37-40

Mad Hatter tea party, how to plan and give 86:120-127

Mad Hatter tea party, menu and recipes 86:225-226

Mexican patio party, activities, foods, and handicrafts 30:96-100

Mid-Summer Eve party, recipes and games 635:53-56

Monster party, invitations, decorations, costumes, food, games, recipes 1185:14-15

Mother Goose party, activities, recipes 809:7-11

Mother Goose party, decorations, games, costumes, recipes 74:12-27

Old MacDonald barnyard birthday fling party, activities, foods, handicrafts 30:58-60

Olympiad party, how to plan and give 43:45-49

Olympics party, 7 years up 124:122-130

Olympics party, how to plan and give 86:142-151

Olympics party, invitations, decorations, foods, games 133:101-104

Olympics party, menu and recipes 86:229-230

Oriental festival party, how to plan and give 86:160-167

Oriental festival party, menu and recipes 86:231-232

Picasso party, how to plan and give 86:31-37

Picasso party, menu and recipes 86:216

Pirate birthday bash party, activities, foods, and handicrafts 30:61-64

Pirate party, invitations, decorations, costumes, food, games, recipes 1185:20-21

Pirate party, recipes, and games 635:48-5 1

Pirate plunder party, decorations, games, costumes, recipes, making 74:122-139

Pirate treasure hunt party, menu and recipes 86:233-234

Pirate treasure hunt party,, how to plan and give 86:168-177

Pirate treasure party, activities and recipes 809:61-65

Pizza birthday festival party, activities, foods, and handicrafts 30:83-85

Pooh Bear picnic party, decorations, games, costumes, recipes 74:28-41

Pow-Wow party, how to plan and give 43:21-24

Rodeo roundup birthday party, invitations, decorations, foods, games, etc. 133:45-48

Safari party, 7 years up 124:61-69

Safari party, how to plan and give 86:178-185

Safari party, recipe and menus 86:235

Sea life birthday party, decorations, games, whale cake, patterns 1015:79-92

Space adventure birthday party, decorations, foods, games, patterns 1011:17-33

Space Blast-Off party, how to plan and give 43:35-38

Space fantasy party, how to plan and give 86:186-193

Space party, invitations, decorations, costumes, food, games, recipes 1185:18-19

Space station party, decorations, games, costumes, recipes 74:98-108

Space voyage birthday party, invitations, decorations, foods, games, etc. 133:49-53

Space wars birthday party, activities, foods, handicrafts 30:48-51

Spots party, invitations, decorations, costumes, food, games, recipes 1185:22-23

Spring party, 4 years and up 124:78-87

St. Patrick's Day party, 7 years and up 124:47-54
St. Patrick's Day party, how to plan and give 43:63-64
Tea party formal luncheon, how to plan and give 43:58-61
Tea party, making 1032:241-242
Teddy picnic, invitations, decorations, costumes, food, games, recipes 1185:12-13
Twelfth Night party, recipes and games 635:30-34
Under the Big Top party, activities, recipes 809:55-60
Valentine party, 5 years and up 124:39-46
Valentine's Day party, invitations, decorations, food, games 133:127-129
Water Carnival birthday party, activities, foods, handicrafts 30:135-138
Western round-up party, how to plan and give 86:200-207; 86:237
Wild west round-up party, decorations, games, costumes, recipes, making 74:109-121
Winter celebration, ideas 133:156-157
Wizard of Oz party, activities and recipes 809:49-53

PARTIES—COOKERY
Birthday stew, recipe 30:38-42
Butterfly cake, recipe 1185:66-67
Castle cake, recipe 449:66; 1185:58-59
Clown cake, recipe 1185:56-57
Cuckoo clock cake, recipe 449:55
Drum decorated cake, pattern, recipe 1073:100-101
Farm cake, recipe 449:58
Fort cake, recipe 449:69
Galleon ship cake, recipe 449:67
Hedgehog cake, recipe 449:51
Humpty Dumpty cake, recipe 449:54-55
Humpty Dumpty decorated cake, patterns, recipe 1073:15-17
Igloo cake, recipe 449:71
Merry-Go-Round cake, recipe 449:71
Noah's Ark cake, recipe 449:66-67
Noah's Ark decorated cake, patterns, recipe 1073:69-72
Pirate ship cake, recipe 449:67
Rabbit cake, recipe 1185:60-61
Rocket cake, recipe 1185:64-65
Space ship cake, recipe 449:62
Teddy Bear cake, recipe 1185:62-63
UFO cake, recipe 449:69
Village cake, recipe 449:59

PARTIES—DECORATIONS
Chinese lantern decorations, paper, making 750:6-7
Circus tent centerpiece, making 713:38-39
Hanukkah place cards, paper, making 53:54-55

PARTIES—PRE-TEEN
Halloween party, recipes, games 635:75-77

PARTIES—WINNIE THE POOH
Christmas party, foods, games, activities 277:105-135
Eeyore birthday party, food, activities 277:7-34
Honey tasting party for Pooh, foods, games, activities 277:81-102
Picnic, swimming and exposition party, foods, games, activities 277:57-78
Woozle-Wizzle snow party, foods, games, activities 277:105-135

PASSAMAQUODDY INDIANS
Indians birchbark box, birch bark, patterns, making 1422:33-34

PASSAMAQUODDY INDIANS—GAMES
All-tes-teg-enuk bowl game, how to play 1507:96
Bowl games, how to play 1699:106

PASSOVER. *See also* PESACH
Activities, crafts, history and stories for 128:15-20
Festival of Freedom, activities and projects for classrooms 1393:184-185
Finger plays, games, making 944:86-87
History and celebration of 496:54-56
History of Passover 709:171-172
Meaning of Passover 711:69; 712:60-62
Passover or Pesach celebration 566:24
Passover ritual 419:31

PASSOVER—COOKERY
Albondigas de matzah brei, fried matzah dish, recipe 1691:184
Almond macaroons, recipe 263:66
Apple and walnut haroset, recipe 1685:64
Apple cake, recipe 851:61
Applesauce, recipe 851:39
Babonatza, Passover raisin pudding, recipe 1691:182
Baby Moses salad, recipe 851:34; 1112:95-96
Beef tzimmes, recipe 116:76
Beet horseradish, recipe 1685:66
Bimuelos de matzah, fried matzah pancakes, recipe 1691:183
Blender potato latkes, recipe 851:41
Boobelach (fried matzo cakes), recipe 1666:53
Brownies, recipe 1685:74
Charoses, apple and nut paste, recipe 1380:42
Charoses, Ashkenazic and Sephardic, recipe 711:73-74
Charoses, recipe 49:131; 128:19; 308:55; 1032:199; 1111:235; 1495:128
Charoset (Passover chopped nuts and apples), recipe 1666:52
Charoset, recipe 496:56
Chicken soup, recipe 851:16-17; 1666:52-53
Chicken stuffed with oranges, recipe 1001:43
Chocolate chip kisses, recipe 1112:98
Chocolate covered matzahs, recipe 1112:101-102
Chocolate matzah sandwiches, recipe 116:83
Chocolate nut and raisin clusters, recipe 851:68
Cookies, easy, no flour, recipe 363:56
Date and almond haroset, recipe 1685:65
Farfel and cheese, recipe 1112:99-100
Fish, baked, recipe 279:154
Fried matzos, recipe 279:150
Fruit pies, recipe 116:82
Gefilte fish, recipe 279:153; 1685:67
Gelfilte fish kabobs, recipe 851:19
Golden spinach layers from Turkey, recipe 116:77
Haroset, Eastern European style, recipe 799:unp
Haroset, Israeli style, recipe 799:unp
Haroset, recipe 116:74; 263:67; 698:36; 1112:95; 1179:83; 1391:135; 1691:180-181
Haroset, sweet spread, recipe 1662:52
Imberlach, Passover jaw breakers, recipe 116:81
Jam cookies, recipe 116:80
Jam puffs, recipe 543:109
Knaidlach (matzo balls), recipe 1666:53
Knaidlach, matzah balls, recipe 116:79
Macaroons, recipe 279:152; 698:36; 851:59; 1685:72; 1691:183-184
Matzah ball dumplings, recipe 263:65
Matzah balls, recipe 851:18; 1451:94
Matzah brei, recipe 116:78; 263:62-63; 851:26; 1112:100-101
Matzah meal latkes, recipe 851:23

Matzah pizza, recipe 851:50
Matzo bread, recipe 1662:53
Matzo layer cake, recipe 446:40-41; 1001:45
Matzo, recipe 698:36
Matzoh ball soup, recipe 1043:103
Matzoh balls, recipe 711:71-72
Matzoh brei, recipe 711:70-71; 1685:75
Matzoh, recipe 1685:62
Matzohs, recipe 351:39
Matzos (unleavened bread), recipe 1666:52
Melon dessert, recipe 1001:46
Meringues, recipe 1685:73
North African chicken soup, recipe 1001:40
Nut torte, recipe 711:75-76
Orange sponge cake, recipe 1685:70
Passover lemon sponge cake, recipe 1666:54
Passover rolls, recipe 279:151
Passover sponge cake, recipe 1662:55
Pesach rolls, recipe 263:63-64
Potato latkes, recipe 49:132
Potatonik, potato and egg dish, recipe 1685:68
Raspberry sauce, recipe 1685:71
Salami latkes, recipe 851:48
Seder plate, how to prepare 1687:unp
Seder plate, recipe 116:75
Sponge cake and chocolate nut cake, recipes 402:26-29
Sponge cake, recipe 711:77-78
Tostado, recipe 851:51
Tsimmes, recipe 851:42
Vegetable and fruit kugel cupcakes, recipe 1112:96-97
Vegetable kugel, recipe 1685:69
Zweibel matzah, recipe 263:62

PASSOVER—DECORATIONS
Afikomen bag, making 279:141
Afikomen cover, paper, decorations, making 1179:82-83
An only kid picture, making 543:107
Blown egg decoration, making 677:20
Bookmarks for Haggadah, making 543:105
Camera-less photograph, making 279:134
Chad Gadya mobile, making 709:174-177
Coasters, cardboard, making 448:46
Elijah's cup, decorated, making 263:70
Elijah's goblet, making 648:24-25
Feel and tell box, making 543:108
Haggadah cover, paper, making 263:74
Hebrew plaque, making 279:140
Holiday creative drawing activities 1337:34-39
Kiddush cup, making 851:14
Matzah cover, fabric, making 263:72-73
Matzah cover, making 279:138; 851:14
Matzah holder, making 279:135
Matzo cover, making 543:104
Passover place setting, paper, making 351:19
Pillow cover, making 851:14
Pillowcase, fabric, making 263:73-74
Place cards, making 263:75; 851:14
Seder and Seder plate, how to do 799:unp
Seder food, Afikoman, felt board, making 945:171-174
Seder place cards, making 712:63
Seder plate, decorated, making 263:71-72
Seder plate, making 648:25; 851:14
Seder plate, paper, pattern, making 1393:185
Seder table centerpiece, making 712:64-66
Symbols of Passover for crafts 263:68

Watercress hedgehog, egg decorated, cress seeds, making 1466:17
Window ornament, making 279:139
Wine coasters, making 279:137
Woven placemats, making 279:136

PASSOVER—FINGER PLAYS
Matzah ball fingerplay 1654:124
Visiting Israel fingerplay 1654:124

PASSOVER—GAMES
Charoses game 279:149
Compote game 279:148
Golf game, how to play 1305:52
Logging nuts game, how to play 1305:52
Passover lotto game, how to play 1179:81-82
Pharoah's hop game 279:147
Polo game, how to play 1305:52
Treasure hunt: Afikomon game, making 698:36
What am I? game, making 543:106
Where's the Afikomen? game 279:148
Word games 263:77-81

PASSOVER—HANDICRAFTS
Chad Gadya mobile, folk song, paper, patterns, making 1427:172-175
Elijah's cup, making 1691:177
Matzah cover, fabric, making 1691:179

PASSOVER—PARTIES
Passover Family Seder, invitations, decorations, menus and games, making 2:53-57

PASSOVER—PUPPETS
Puppet projects, patterns, scenes, story starters, feature story 1083:69-72
Swallowing animal puppets, patterns, making 1083:71-72

PASSOVER—SONGS
Chad Gadya song, words given 709:173
Dayenu, Song of Thanksgiving 799:unp

PASSPORT
Application form pattern, making 282:1-2
Visas, pattern 282:3

PASTA
Activities, art, songs, recipes, games 1469:32-33

PASTES
Bookbinder's paste, recipe 1213:25
Crazy paste, recipe 1213:25
Emergency paste, recipe 1455:31
Flour and water paste, recipe 1213:24
Homemade rice paste, how to make 1421:190
Japanese rice paste, transparent paste, recipe 767:19
Library paste, recipe 1213:24
Paper paste, recipe 1455:31
Papier-mache paste, recipe 1455:30

PASTILLAGE
Modeling objects from sugar paste, making 70:55

PATCHWORK. *See also* **QUILTING**
Appliqué hand cutouts, making 145:32-33
Basics and three patterns 70:82-83
Child's building block, making 145:54-55
Curtain trim, making 145:43
Friendship wall hanging, making 145:56-59
Guitar strap, making 145:48-49
Head scarf, making 145:30
Napkins, making 145:53
Patchwork cushion, fabric, patterns, ribbons, making 1320:64-65
Patchwork pictures, making 721:22; 721:22
Patchwork pot holders, making 561:62

Pillows, appliqué, making 145:46-47
Pillows, making 145:44-45
Placemats, making 145:51-52
Rug, making 145:36-37
Skirt, making 145:24-27
Sneakers, making 145:31
Table runner, making 145:50
Table, making 145:40-42
Tote bag, making 145:22-23
Towels, making 145:60-61
Tray, making 145:38-39
Vest, making 145:28-29
Wall hanging, picture, making 145:62-63

PATTERNS

American flag, 36 states 1193:391
Angel luminaria 1152:70-75
Ant 1189:85
Bactrian camel 1189:87
Bald eagle 282:69
Benin leopard of Nigeria pattern 1022:23
Cherry tree 760:36-37
Christopher Robin pattern 277:138
Circus tent, pop-up, pattern 1210:8
Columbus Day ship 232:5
Columbus' boats 760:186-187
Confederate flag 1193:392
Coral, making 1190:84
Cowboy and cowgirl, large 478:17-22
Crab, making 1190:87
Cross, pattern 873:59
Crown 122:230; 1083:167
Crown, kings 157:10
Crown, pattern, making 172:7
Date palm 1189:84
Dog house, pop-up, pattern 1210:7
Dove in wreath 1152:92
Dragon 592:38
Dragon, large 478:34-39
Dromedary camel 1189:86
Duck, large 476:41-46
Easter basket 309:57; 760:72-73
Easter basket pattern 1083:78
Easter egg 760:70-71
Eeyore, Winnie the Pooh, pattern 277:144
Eskimo face, pattern 1193:304
Eskimo pie 50:92
Eskimo, large 478:58-62
Family tree pattern 1193:317
Fish, making 1190:86
Gila monster 1189:88
Gingerbread man 1011:67
Glacier, pop-up, pattern 1210:9
Groundhog, pattern 1193:335, 337, 338, 340
Halloween cat 760:190-191
Hannah 53:77
Honey Pot 992:144
Humpty Dumpty 232:4
Igloo 50:101
Indian headband 760:220-221
Ivory Coast Baule mask 1022:30,33
Jack rabbit 1189:90
Jelly fish, pattern, making 1190:86
Kangaroo, Winnie the Pooh, pattern 277:145
King Cole 122:228
Knight, large 478:28-33

Leprechaun and mushroom 309:43
Leprechaun, making 128:7
Liberty Bell 50:235-236
Lincoln silhouette 50:211
Little Boy Blue 122:109
Lizard 1189:88
Log cabin 760:34-35
Mary, Mary, Quite Contrary 122:211
Mattathias 53:77
May Basket 760:94-95
May Day basket, making 128:57
Menorah 309:35
Octopus, making 1190:85
Ostrich 1189:90
Owl, Winnie the Pooh, pattern 277:140
Palm tree 1152:7
Patriot hat 760:135-136
Piglet, Winnie the Pooh, pattern 277:141
Pilgrim clothes pattern 1152:58-64
Pilgrim figure and face pattern 1152:56-57
Pilgrim hat 760:218-219
Pooh pattern 277:139
Prickly pear cactus and flower 1189:82
Princess, large 478:23-27
Rabbit, Winnie the Pooh, pattern 277:142
Road runner 1189:90
Rudolph head 232:17
Saguaro cactus 1189:83
Santa Claus 309:33
Santa face mask 1083:147
Scarecrow 309:19; 592:110
Scuba diver, making 1190:83
Sea horse, making 1190:84
Seaweed, making 1190:82
Shamrock 309:41; 992:15,18
Shamrock patterns 760:55-56
Shamrock tree 760:55-56
Shamrocks and tulips 779:189
Shark, making 1190:88
Snake 1189:89
Spade foot toad 1189:85
Tetrahedron 157:37
Thunderbird Totem 282:72
Tigger, Winnie the Pooh, pattern 277:143
Tulip 309:49
Tulip and wooden shoe 760:62-63
Tulips 760:82-83
Washington's cherry tree 760:36-37
Wee Willie Winkie 122:187
Whale, making 1190:89
Windmill 232:31-32; 760:59-61
Winnie the Pooh 992:142
Wooden shoe and tulip 760:62-63

PAUL BUNYAN

Blue ox mask, paper, patterns, making 92:15-16
Paul Bunyan mask, paper, patterns, making 92:17-19
Paul Bunyan, picture, making 92:14

PAUL BUNYAN—PUPPET PLAYS

Winter of the Blue Snow 4:103-107

PAULING, LINUS

How much vitamin C is in common beverage, experiment 1719:59-61

PAULSEN, GARY

"The Island," camp food, canned food, recipe 1216:95

PAVILIONS
Royal Pavilion, making 173:60-61
PAWNEE INDIANS
Legends 344:46-47
Songs and stories of the Pawnee Indians 344:47-54
PAWNEE INDIANS—CLOTHING
Pawnee headpiece, making 932:29-32
PAWNEE INDIANS—GAMES
Hands game 602:176
PAWNEE INDIANS—NATURE FESTIVALS
Corn growing festivals 419:150
PEACE
Peace on Earth art and writing activities, patterns, making 1152:86
PEACE DAY. *See* **UNITED STATES—FESTIVALS**
PEANUTS
Activities, art, science, songs, recipe 911:172-177
Activities, art, songs, recipes, games 1469:78-79
George Washington Carver birthday celebration; art, music, foods, games 1104:122-125
History of peanuts 410:17-25; 762:9-23
How to make peanut butter, recipe 1178:83
Information about peanuts 257:7-13
Peanut butter, recipe 1453:38
Peanuts, information about 118:103
PEANUTS—DOLLS
Dolls, bedded dolls, making using peanuts 257:103-104
Figure dolls, making using peanuts 257:76-77
Folk dolls, making using peanuts 257:73-74
Gingerbread dolls, making using peanuts 257:102-103
Old man doll, making using peanuts 257:77-78
Peanut shell doll, making 257:75-76
Pop-off head dolls, making using peanuts 257:78-80
PEANUTS—HANDICRAFTS
Circus clowns, making using peanuts 257:85-86
Partridge in a Pear Tree, making using peanut sawdust 257:108-110
Poinsettia, peanut petal flowers, making using peanuts 257:97-98
Santa star, making using peanut sawdust 257:107-108
PEARY, ROBERT E.
Eskimo papier-mache mask, making 755:91-108
Where there is North story for masks and pantomime 755:83-90
PEBBLES. *See* **ROCKS**
PECOS BILL
Pecos Bill and Slue-Foot Sue, picture, making 92:20
PECOS BILL—PUPPETS
Pecos Bill puppet, paper, patterns, making 92:21-22
Slue-Foot Sue puppet paper, patterns, making 92:23-24
PEEP SHOWS
Victorian peep-show box, shoe box, patterns, making 1051:190-194
PENGUINS
Penguin, pop-up, paper, pattern 1210:34-35
PENNSYLVANIA—CHRISTMAS
Largest Nativity scene in Bethlehem, Pennsylvania 475:70-71
Moravian Love Feast 475:82-91
PENNSYLVANIA—COOKERY
Apple butter, recipe 659:100
Chicken-corn soup from the Pennsylvania Dutch, history of, recipe 155:24-25
Chocolate velvet dessert, recipe 654:134

Dutch funnel cakes, recipe 652:120-121
Hoagie, hero, submarine or poor boy, recipe 793:9
Pancakes with berries, recipe 1576:35
Pennsylvania Dutch apple meringue, recipe 1043:109
Pennsylvania Dutch apples and bacon, recipe 1576:35
Pennsylvania Dutch funnel cakes, recipe 654:133
Pennsylvania Dutch shoo-fly pie, recipe 1043:106
Pennsylvania potato soup, recipe 343:94
Pennsylvania pretzels, recipe 570:85-87
Philadelphia soft pretzels, recipe 1455:122
Potato soup, recipe 343:94
Rivel soup, Pennsylvania Dutch recipe 343:93
Snickerdoodles, recipe 1043:105
South Philly cheese steak sandwiches, recipe 1043:104
PENNSYLVANIA—FESTIVALS—COOKERY
Mother Goose Day pat-a-cakes, recipe 1199:105
PENNSYLVANIA—HISTORY—COOKERY
Food of the Pennsylvania Dutch 666:76-82
Pennsylvania Dutch shoo-fly pie, recipe 666:94-95
Quakers and Germans in Pennsylvania; foods they ate 666:72-76
PENNSYLVANIA—INDEPENDENCE NATIONAL HISTORICAL PARK—COOKERY
Mayz and broiled steak, recipe 57:26-27
PENNSYLVANIA—MUSICAL INSTRUMENTS
Fogelsville boom-bahs, sticks, noise making items, making; 1361:58; 1362:77
PENNSYLVANIA—PHILADELPHIA—CITY TAVERN—COOKERY
Chicken marinade, recipe 57:15
Stuffed crabs, recipe 57:14
PENNSYLVANIA—SONGS
Here Take this Lovely Flower, lullaby 1220:144
Sleep, My Baby, Sleep, lullaby 1220:140-141
PENNSYLVANIA—THANKSGIVING
Schwenkfelder Festival celebration 659:97
PENNSYLVANIA—VALENTINE'S DAY—HANDICRAFTS
Pennsylvania German Valentines, making 709:129-132
PENNSYLVANIA DUTCH—COOKERY
Apples, dried, ham and dumplings, recipe 871:11-12
Boova Shenkel, recipe 529:34-37
Chicken corn chowder, recipe 871:82-83
Chicken corn soup with noodles, recipe 529:29-31
Corn Dodgers, recipe 659:127
Ebell tart, recipe 529:39-40
Green corn soup, recipe 659:127
Milk pie, recipe 794:2
Molasses pie, Neversink, recipe 659:101
Moravian Christmas cookies, recipes for light and dark cookies 1232:76
Pie pastry, recipe 529:37-39
Shoofly pie, recipe 529:41-43; 1600:68-69
Shredded carrot mold, recipe 793:10
Sweet mit sour tongue, recipe 529:34-37
PENNSYLVANIA DUTCH—HANDICRAFTS
Babushka, fabric, making 889:106-112
Bisengraas egg, yarn wrapped, making 298:100-101
Egg tree stabile, making 741:59-61
Folk art dish, making 297:184-185
Folk art hearts and flowers box, making 298:186-187
Hex barn sign, making 298:176-177
Hex sign, wooden, making 525:33
Hex signs, paper, making 877:40

Ochter-Foggel good luck bird, making 298:90-91
Patchwork eggs and egg tree, making 626:54-57
Patchwork eggs, making 627:83-84
Pennsylvania Dutch design apron, fabric stenciled, making 889:100-105
Pig and girl two way doll, making 298:132-133
Pinpricked dot Valentine, making 298:198-199
Scratch carved eggs, making 627:85-87
Star sign, pattern, making 220:46-47

PENNSYLVANIA DUTCH—THANKSGIVING
Amkarch (Harvest Home) Festival celebration 659:99

PENOBSCOT INDIANS—FOOTWEAR
Penobscot moccasins, making 359:69-79

PENS
Quill pen, making 1196:10; 1213:15
Reed or quill pens, making 1476:24-25

PENTECOST—FESTIVALS
Holy Trinity 475:140
Pentecost celebration 475:138-139

PEOPLE
Balloon people with feet, making 1017:18
Body parts, paper, how to make 787:17-18
Cone 3D people, paper, making 10:79-83
Face, paper plate saucer face, patterns, making 1067:152-154
Head from paper, making 787:15-16
Heads, cardboard tubes, making 965:76-77
Kid clone, large models, newspaper, making 1658:24
Paper people, large figures, paper, making 1092:47-49
Paper people, making 534:15
Paper tube people, making 214:20-21
Papier-mache people, making from strips on newspaper shapes 743:57
People, cardboard tube, making 534:66-67
Plank people, wood, making 926:66-67
Portraits, paper, how to make 787:20-23
Puppets, babies, girls, making 735:41-44
Self, paper plate self, patterns, making 1067:154-155
Stick figures, wood, making 926:68-69

PEOPLE—FINGER PLAYS
Finger plays about all kinds of people 360:50-58

PEOPLE—SONGS
Songs about Me 1150:55-58

PERFUMES. *See also* **FRAGRANCES**
Flower perfume, making 1259:21

PERSIA
Astronomer's tunic, making 173:16-17
Clay folk from Ur, making 173:26-27
Cylinder seals, making 173:44-45
Mysterious tablets, making 173:52-53

PERSIA—GAMES
Games, Chaldean checkers, making 173:70-71
Solemn action game 383:131

PERSIA—HANDICRAFTS
Ancient vase, clay, making 1070:122-125

PERSIA—HOUSES
Courtyard houses, making 173:58-59
Shoe box houses, making 173:56-57

PERSIA—MASKS
Wild animal masks, making 173:76-77

PERU. *See also* **INCAS**
Activities, flags, games, songs, dances, recipes 1381:55-58

PERU—CHRISTMAS
Painted Christmas saints from Cuzco, making 672:46-66

PERU—COOKERY
Beef stew, recipe 1517:23
Ceviche, fish marinated in lime juice, recipe 1307:121
Choclos, corn ears, recipe 188:9
Egg, filled egg, recipe 794:11
Llapingachos, potato cakes, recipe 1165:236
Peruvian popcorn, recipe 381:19
Pie of the Sierra, potatoes, tomatoes, cheese, recipe 1381:57
Pie of the Sierra, recipe 793:18-19
Potatoes a la Huancaina, recipe 858:unp
Potatoes, recipe 1244:132
Salsa de mali, South American peanut sauce, recipe 1165:236-237
Sweet egg squares, hucvos chimbos, cookies, recipe 72:182-183

PERU—COSTUMES
Choclos, corn ears, recipe, costume 188:9
Peruvian Indians costume drawing 988:62

PERU—DIORAMAS
Hatmaker's shop, how to make 182:31-35

PERU—DOLLS
Pancho of Peru doll, making 494:84-94
Peruvian doll, making 775:68-73

PERU—FESTIVALS
Festival of the Sun celebration 665:74-76
Harvest Festival celebration 601:155
Lord of the Earthquakes Festival 182:86
Market Day celebration 601:155-156
Sun Festival celebration 826:16-17
Sun Gods of Peru 566:18-19

PERU—FESTIVALS—COOKERY
Carnival; papas a la huancaina (yellow potatoes), recipe 1666:232
Carnival; papas rellenas (pototoes stuffed with meat), recipe 1666:232-233

PERU—GAMES
Blind hen game 383:133
Calabaza game 383:132
Calabaza musical game 1116:19
Clock game 602:148-149
Echunga Para La Yunga musical game 1116:39
El Reloj (the clock) game 515:96
El Reloj, the clock game, how to play 1494:217
Gallinita Ciega (blind chicken) musical game 1116:11
Games, feather tossers, making 173:68-69
Help game 383:132
King may pass 602:149
Peruvian Wolf musical game 1116:17
Tying the sun to the hitching post chasing game, how to play 1498:29-30
Wolf game 383:133
Wolf game, how to play 1381:57
Wolf, are you ready? game 602:148

PERU—HANDICRAFTS
Ancient Peruvian idol sculpture, dough, paints, patterns, making 1251:27-28
Bean bag messages, making 173:48-49
Black cats poster and pin, oaktag, dough, patterns, making 1251:29-31
Braid; Peruvian flat braid, making 548:34-36
Clay beads, clay, paints, making 1381:58
Dance capes, fabric, decorations, making 1338:46-47

Lamb, padded, making 494:90-94
Litter for noble travelers, making 173:38-39
Porter's sling, making 173:34-35
Raised design on cardboard, cord, glue, making 1381:58
Royal jewels of Chan Chan, making 173:24-25

PERU—HOUSES
Courtyard houses, making 173:58-59
Hut from cardboard, making 494:87-90
Shoe box houses, making 173:56-57

PERU—INDEPENDENCE DAY
Independence Day celebration July 28 722:29-33

PERU—LANGUAGE
Basic words in Spanish and Quechua 1307:85

PERU—LULLABIES
"Cradlesong of the Sparrows" 1607:15

PERU—MASKS
Andean mask, clay, paints, making 1706:23
Negrito mask, making 182:87-89
Wild animal masks, making 173:76-77

PERU—NATURE FESTIVALS
Crop festivals 419:130-131

PERU—TOYS
Bullfighter and bull toy, making 182:71-73
Flippy acrobat toy, making 182:68-70
Llama, stuffed fabric, pattern, making 1027:162-164

PESACH. *See also* **PASSOVER**

PESACH—COOKERY
Charoset, recipe 1720:32
Haroset drink, recipe 1289:119
Latkes, recipe 1720:32
Nut and raisin cookies, recipe 1720:32
Pesach pizza, recipe 81:44
Pesachip cake, recipe 81:44
Vegetables and dips, recipe 81:44

PESACH—DANCES
Dances for Pesach 542:62-68

PESACH—DECORATIONS
Alphabet pyramid centerpiece, making 81:43
Balloon invitation, making 81:42
Charoset, making 80:61
Eggshell plaque, making 81:46
Flowers for spring, making 80:59
Matzah cover, making 80:58
Pillow placecards, felt, rickrack, sequins, stuffing, making 1289:118
Seder plate, decorated paper plate, recipe 1720:10
Seder plate, making 80:56
Seder table flowers, making 82:50
Silver goblet for Elijah, making 80:57
Wine sipper place cards, making 81:43

PESACH—GAMES
Cross the Red Sea game 81:45
Find the Afikomen game 81:45
Seder game "no hands," making 82:57
What's missing game 81:45

PESACH—HANDICRAFTS
Afikomen cloth, tie dye, making 80:60
Four cup counter, making 82:55
Haggadah bookmark, making 82:56
Kippah, colorful, making 82:51
Matzah tray, making 82:53
Moses in the basket, making 82:58
Seder pillow, making 82:54
Tambourine, making 80:62
Wine tray, making 82:52

PETER AND THE WOLF
Finger puppet, patterns, story, making 512:109-123

PETER PAN
Art, music and cooking activities, making 161:44-47
Captain Hook bank, making 250:unp
Captain Hook costume, making 213:22
Captain Hook's head, hat and hair, paper, making 250:unp
Captain Hook's poison cake, recipe 570:65-67
Conduct Peter Pan poll; grow up or stay children forever 1199:112
Peter Pan and Wendy dolls, fabric, patterns, making 484:96-99
Peter Pan birthday party, making 896:1-5
Peter Pan costume, making 213:20
Peter Pan, green tights, green felt, dagger, making 1656:151-153
Tinker Bell costume, making 213:20-22

PETER PIPER—COOKERY
Pita pizzas, recipe 365:31

PETER RABBIT—COOKERY
Currant buns, recipe 285:83
Mr. McGregor's garden salad, recipe 1215:20

PETS
Pet Day; activities, art, songs, recipes, games 1469:96-97

PETS—HANDICRAFTS
Pennyroyal pet collars, fabric, herbs, making 1285:68-69

PHILADELPHIA—PENNSYLVANIA—COOKERY
Soft pretzels, recipe 1455:122

PHILIPPINES—ARCHITECTURE
Bulol, making 532:11

PHILIPPINES—BIRTHDAYS
Birthday customs 488:99-102

PHILIPPINES—BOATS
Vinta toy boat, paper, making 515:98

PHILIPPINES—CHRISTMAS
Celebration of Christmas 497:135-136
Christmas celebration 601:83-84
Christmas customs in the Philippines 1717:26-27
Christmas star from wooden sticks and paper, making 273:103-107
Customs of Christmas in the Philippines 474:154

PHILIPPINES—CHRISTMAS—COOKERY
Banana fritters, recipe 1233:72
Chicken rice soup, recipe 1233:70
Churros, crullers, recipe 1233:73
Flan, caramel custard, recipe 497:142
Kare-Kare, oxtail stew in peanut butter sauce, recipe 1233:71
Kari Kari (oxtail stew), recipe 1666:186
Lumpia sauce, recipe 1233:70
Lumpiang uboi (Filipino spring rolls), recipe 1666:185
Meat turnovers, recipe 1233:71
Rellenong manok, baked stuffed chicken, recipe 1233:72
Roast pork, pan fried, recipe 1233:71
Salabat (ginger tea), recipe 1666:184
Salabat, ginger tea, recipe 1233:73
Sinangag (garlic rice), recipe 1666:186
Tsokolate, chocolate, egg and milk dessert, recipe 1233:73
Ukoy, shrimp snacks, recipe 1233:70

PHILIPPINES—CHRISTMAS—DECORATIONS
Christmas star, making 497:136-137

PHILIPPINES—CHRISTMAS—HANDICRAFTS

Star lantern (parol), kiteribs, tissue paper, making 1654:77-78

Star lanterns, balsa wood strips, tissue paper, wire, patterns, making 1233:65-59

PHILIPPINES—COOKERY

Adabo, chick and pork stew, recipe 1165:183

Adobo, recipe 967:44

Banana nibbles, making 187:31

Champarado, rice, cocoa and honey dish, recipe 1627:92

Chicken adobo, recipe 793:68; 895:102

Maja blanca, coconut cake, recipe 1165:184

Meat soup, recipe 794:54

Meatballs and mochi rice, recipe 895:103

Peanut squares, pastillas de mani, cookies, recipe 72:142-143

Philippine fruit salad, recipe 1165:184-185

Picadillo, pork, tomatoes and potatoes, recipe 874:48

PHILIPPINES—DANCES

A La Hoy dance, how to do 1494:203-204

Apat Apat dance, how to do 1494:198-199

Philippine Folk Dance 474:127

PHILIPPINES—DOLLS

Visayan doll, making 532:36

PHILIPPINES—EASTER

Palm Sunday in the Philippines 475:118

PHILIPPINES—FESTIVALS

Baptism celebration 601:81-82

Fiesta celebration 601:82-83

Nationalground nut celebration 631:56

PHILIPPINES—FESTIVALS—COOKERY

Avocado pear ice cream, recipe 1313:175

Chicken adobo, recipe 1313:175

Rellenong bangus or stuffed milk fish, recipe 1313:175

PHILIPPINES—FESTIVALS—HANDICRAFTS

Fiesta tin can lantern, making 1313:174

PHILIPPINES—FOLKLORE—PUPPETS

"Why Mosquitos Buzz in Our Ears" shadow puppets, patterns, making 1602:130-135

PHILIPPINES—GAMES

Cat and dog game 602:78

Cat and mice game 58:48-49

Day and night game 602:79

Eggshell relay game 967:44

Hide and seek game 602:81

Ilocano ball game 602:80

Lame duck game 383:137

Pantaluntun game 602:81

Pip, pap, pong game 602:82

Potato joust game 383:136

Presohan chasing game, how to play 1498:42

Pusa at aso game, how to play 1507:51

Pusa, cat and dog game, how to play 1494:192

Puss in the circle game 383:137

San Pedro and San Pablo game 383:135

Sipa Sipa game 383:137

Sticks game 602:80

Stoop tag game 383:136

Sungka, Conglak or Ddkon game, how to play 1313:198-199

Tag 602:79

Tapatan game, how to play 1688:29-33

Touch pole tag chasing game, how to play 1498:41

PHILIPPINES—HOUSES

Huts on stilts, dowels, sticks, clay, making 1488:20-21

PHILIPPINES—INDEPENDENCE DAY

Independence Day celebration June 12 722:34-37

PHILIPPINES—MUSICAL INSTRUMENTS

Tinakling poles, making 468:39

Tinikling poles, long poles, wood blocks, making 1310:138

PHILIPPINES—NEW YEAR'S DAY

Mingling of old and new in the Philippines 489:135-140

PHILIPPINES—STRING FIGURES

Noose figure, making 423:26-27

PHILIPPINES—TOYS

Sulu outrigger boat, wooden toy, pattern, making 1027:114-119

PHOENIX—COSTUMES

Firebird, fabric, notions, patterns, making 1435:45-47

PICASSO, PABLO—PARTIES

Picasso party, how to plan and give 86:31-37

Picasso party, menu and recipe 86:216

PICKLES

Activities, art, songs, recipes, games 1469:16-17

Pickle activities, patterns, making 992:37-50

Pickle Day activities, stories, crafts, recipes, making 558:67-69

PICTURE WRITING

Indian picture writing 131:44-46

PIED PIPER—COSTUMES

Pied Piper costume, fabric, making 1174:50

PIEGAN INDIANS—GAMES

Stick counting game, how to play 1699:114

PIES

Activities, art, songs, recipes, games 1469:30-31

PIGS

Books, activities, patterns, projects 927:69-76

PIGS—FESTIVALS

National Pig Day, history of 513:63

Pig Day, activities, art, songs, recipes, games 1469:76-77

PILGRIMS

Boy and girl Pilgrim, paper, large pattern, making 477:25-32

Learning units, activities, songs, art, recipes, patterns 1191:401-459

Mr. and Mrs. Pilgrim, paper plate, pattern, making 413:5-8

Mr. and Mrs. Pilgrim, paper, pattern, making 411:11-14

Paper-cutting, Pilgrim faces, how to do 742:44

Pilgrim and Indian Village, milk cartons, paper, making 1017:128-129

Pilgrim boy, cardboard, making 766:81-83

Pilgrim boy, paper and paper roll, making 99:7

Pilgrim girl, cardboard, making 766:84-86

Pilgrim girl, paper and paper roll, making 99:8

Pilgrim head, making 648:44-46

Pilgrim man, paper, pattern, making 253:168-169

Pilgrim man, paper, patterns, making 1067:192-194

Pilgrim woman, paper plates, making 1067:195-196

Pilgrim woman, paper, pattern, making 253:169-171

Pilgrim, paper models, making 75:142-144

Pilgrim, paper models, patterns, making 639:12-13

Pilgrims, art and writing activities, patterns, making 1152:49-64

Pilgrims, people, Indians, canoes, horses, decorations, making 561:43-46

Sculptures, paper, patterns for figures and clothes, making 1152:54-64

PILGRIMS—CLOTHING

Pilgrim boy and girl hats, paper, pattern, making 823:18-20

Pilgrim buckle belt, making 180:20-21

Pilgrim collar, making 436:48

Pilgrim hat, paper, pattern, making 760:218-219

PILGRIMS—COOKERY

Apple doughnuts, Plymouth recipe 436:63

Applesauce, recipe 436:70

Bannock cakes, recipe 1525:100

Bearberry jelly, recipe 1525:103-104

Boiled salad, recipe 1666:263

Cambridge pudding, recipe 57:63

Corn on the cob, recipe 436:65

Corn soup, recipe 1525:91-93

Cranberries, cooked, recipe 436:69

Cranberry relish, recipe 1666:263

Cranberry sauce with orange, recipe 1621:40-41

Frumenty, recipe 1437:100-101

Fry bread, Navaho recipe 436:67

Hot nuts, recipe 1525:105

Indian pudding, recipe 436:66; 1525:95-96

Pilgrim Settlers foods 666:21-24

Poached bass or cod, recipe 57:62

Pumpkin pie, Colonial recipe 436:62

Red pickled eggs, recipe 1525:93-94

Spice cucumber catsup, recipe 1525:98-99

Succotash stew, recipe 1525:96-98

Swizzle drink, recipe 1525:104

Whole baked pumpkin stuffed with apples, recipe 1525:101-102

PILGRIMS—COSTUMES

Bonnet, paper, making 878:90

Captain John Smith costume 213:32-34

Chief Powhatan costume 213:35-37

Collar, paper, making 878:89

John Alden costume 213:30-32

Pilgrim boy and girl, variety of old clothes, making 1656:71-78

Pilgrim boy costume, making 842:13-16

Pilgrim girl costume, making 842:17-18

Pilgrim man costume, making 272:126-129

Pilgrim man costume, paper, making 353:13

Pilgrim woman costume, making 272:129-130

Pilgrim woman costume, paper, making 353:12

Pocahontas costume 213:34-35

Priscilla Morgan costume, making 213:30

PILGRIMS—DOLLS

Corn husk dolls, making 1621:34-35

Pilgrim boy and girl paper dolls with paper Pilgrim clothing, making 1252:24-29

Priscilla doll, 1620, making, fabric 493:55-69

PILGRIMS—GAMES

Acorn toss game 436:59

Bird, beast or fish game 39:49-50

Corn game 39:51

Even/odd game 39:50

Hide the thimble game 436:57

Pilgrim spoonball, making 180:44-47

Pumpkin roll game 39:52

Stool ball game 39:51

Twenty questions game 39:50

PILGRIMS—HANDICRAFTS

Pilgrim face mats, making 447:134-139

Pilgrim hat favor, glass jar, making 374:172-173

Pilgrim hat party favors, paper, making 829:35

Pilgrim, milk carton, making 79:6

Ship; Pilgrim ship, paper bags, making 1083:137

PILGRIMS—PUPPETS

Pilgrim boy and girl puppet, paper bags, patterns, making 941:40-41

Pilgrim men, Miles Standish and John Hopkins, sock puppets, making 353:18

Pilgrim woman and man puppets, patterns, making 1006:15-16

Pilgrim women, Priscilla and Mary, sock puppets, making 353:17

Puppet, finger, making 745:18

Puppet; Pilgrim giant puppet, paper bags, making, 1083:138

Puppet; Pilgrim string puppet making 1083:137

Puppets; Pilgrim finger puppets, patterns, making 1083:134

PILGRIMS—THANKSGIVING

First Thanksgiving celebration 659:78-84

History of Pilgrims Thanksgiving 659:59-67

Squanto, information about 659:69-79

Thanksgiving Festival 419:74-75

PILLOWS

Bandanna pillow, making 251:46

Paper pillow figures, stuffed, making 10:148-154

PIMA INDIANS—GAMES

Pima relay race game, how to play 1651:39-40

Vaputta game 602:177

PIMA INDIANS—LULLABIES

Pima Wind Song 780:33

PIMA INDIANS—STORY STICKS

Story stick, stick, yarn, feathers, making 1699:176

PIÑATAS. *See also* **MEXICO—CHRISTMAS; MEXICO—FESTIVALS**

Balloon and newspaper piñata, making 1196:70-71

Balloon and newspaper, making 1658:32-33

Balloon piñata, making 128:67

Bumblebee piñata, paper bag, making 1088:121-122

Christmas piñata, making 329:45-47

Christmas piñata, paper bag, making 308:32-33

Christmas spider piñata, balloon, paper, paste, patterns, making 1051:152-157

Clown face piñata, making 134:91

Dinosaur piñata, making 133:28

Donkey piñata, making 709:86-89

Dreidel piñata, making 295:225-227

Easy piñata, making 278:16

Flag, United States, piñata, making 128:92

History of pinatas 83:9-17

How to make 83:56-69; 295:189-190; 297:198-199

How to use a piñata 83:49-55

Latin American piñata ball and mini-piñata, making 795:39

Latin American piñata, making 795:28-30

Mexican papier-mache, making 672:81-116

Mini piñata bat, paper, treats, patterns, making 1138:18-19

Paper bag burro piñata, making 126:71-73

Paper bag piñata, making 124:174; 254:25-26; 384:Dec 12; 574:110; 829:51; 1017:94; 1083:190

Paper bag piñata, paint, making 1662:78

Papier-mache covered balloon piñata, making 1278:24-25

Papier-mache over balloon piñata, making 1237:63-67
Papier-mache piñata, balloon, making 1067:83-84
Papier-mache piñata, making 251:78-79; 473:62-63;
    595:87-93; 1455:19
Piñata bird, paper bag, making 515:86
Piñata fish, making 273:132-138
Piñata from newspaper, making 271:85
Piñata from paper bag, making 678:24
Piñata game 329:48; 474:46-47; 1036:268
Piñata game, how to make and play 1355:26-27
Piñata games and songs 1589:14
Piñata mouse, making 122:67
Piñata party, how to make piñata, paper bag, tissue pa-
    per, making 1178:170-171
Piñata pig, making 896:24-25
Piñata song 665:82
Piñata, balloon, making 43:126-127
Piñata, balloon, papier-mache, making 743:32-33;
    1393:102
Piñata, making 332:10-12,16-17; 349:24-26; 557:9-10;
    593:160; 713:30-32; 1074:234-236
Piñata, monster, paper bag, making 534:18-19
Piñata, paper bag, making 909:123; 1550:76
Piñata, paper, making 554:74-75
Piñata, papier-mache, making 759:27-29
Piñatas, balloon and newspaper, making 1023:58-61
Piñatas, making 497:114-115; 815:28-29
Pumpkin piñata, paper bag, making 441:45
Rites of Spring piñata, balloon and newspaper, making
    310:192
Star piñata, balloon, papier-mache, making 1476:84-85;
    1605:26-27
Star piñata, papier-mache over balloon, making 1589:12-
    13
Star piñata, papier-mache, tissue paper, making 1567:72-
    73
Stories, Five Gold Chains, the Huarache Makers, Pebbles
    of Sal Agua 83:18-48
Tortoise piñata, papier-mache, green paint, making
    1484:18-19
Valentine's Day piñata, making 309:40
Wooden frame piñata, making 525:106-107

PIÑATAS—FINGER PLAYS
Finger plays and rhymes 1583:84

PINE CONES
Christmas decorations from pine cones, making 685:20-
    23
Christmas tree, making from pine cones 848:40-41
Christmas tree, pine cones and pompoms, making 912:85
Christmas tree, pine cones, making 1149:35
Menorah from pine cones and seeds, making 1067:219-
    221
Turkey from pine cones, making 891:113-116; 1067:206-
    207
Turkey, pine cones, making 217:88-89; 226:48; 253:182-
    185
Turkey, pine cones, paper, making 912:87
Turkeys, styrofoam and pine cones, making 709:52-54
Wreath from cones, making 217:99-100
Wreath, pine cone and nuts, making 916:86-87
Wreath, table wreath from pine cones, nuts, seed, mak-
    ing 673:201-212

PINEAPPLES
History of pineapples 410:40-47

PINOCCHIO
Art, music and cooking activities, making 161:48-52
Pinocchio centerpiece, making 294:122-123
Pinocchio cookies, recipe 346:48
Pinocchio paper tube puppet, making 384:Nov.24
Pinocchio toy, making 246:28-29
Pinocchio's Pannikin poached egg, recipe 570:13-15
Pop-up Pinocchio nose, making 1388:54-56

PINPRICK PICTURES
Pinprick pictures, making 524:63

PINPRICKING
Pinpricking and tearing, how to do 966:18-19
Pinpricking, how to do 966:28-29

PIONEERS. *See* FRONTIER AND PIONEER LIFE
PIPPI LONGSTOCKING
Pippi doll, cardboard tube, paper, making 1420:36

PIRATES
Bake a pirate Island, dough, paints, making 1683:22-23
Code of conduct, how to write 1736:11
Paper pirates, making 75:28-29
Pirate from paper straws, making 828:82
Pirates, paper models, making 75:142-144

PIRATES—BULLETIN BOARDS
Parrot, making 295:169-170
Peg leg and hook, pirate flag, making 295:168-169
Sword, eye patch and mustache, making 295:170-171

PIRATES—COINS
Golden dubloons and silver pieces of eight, making
    1736:23

PIRATES—COOKERY
Blackbeard's gunpowder punch, recipe 1456:29
Cannonballs, cream cheese, nuts, cocoa, recipe 1559:30-31
Necklaces, fruits on a string, recipe 1559:30
Pirate ship cake, recipe 449:67
Saturnalia pirates stew, recipe 1456:29
Ship's biscuits, recipe 1736:7
Treasure chests, chocolate mini-roll and candies, recipe
    1559:30
Tropical boats, oranges and gelatin, recipe 1559:31

PIRATES—COSTUMES
Pirate boy and girl, shirts, variety of old clothes, making
    1656:175-181
Pirate costume and hat, cardboard, making 1683:8-9
Pirate costume, fabric, making 1007:12-13; 1379:40
Pirate costume, fabric, pattern, making 367:102-104
Pirate costume, making 42:61-69; 562:17; 887:14-15
Pirate costume, striped T-shirt, scarf, eye patch, making
    1509:38-39
Pirate ghost of Davy Jones, making 179:10-11
Pirate, paper, making 46:85-88
Quick pirate costume, making 1283:32
Shoe buckles, cardboard, foil, ribbons, making 1736:4

PIRATES—EYE PATCH
Eyepatch, black paper, elastic, making 1559:9
Pirate eye patch, making 179:14-15

PIRATES—FACE MAKEUP
Pirate face makeup, how to do 1314:24

PIRATES—FACE PAINTING
Face painting for pirates, how to do 1306:57
Pirate face, how to paint 1533:86-87

PIRATES—FLAGS
Jolly Roger flag pattern 1251:22

Jolly Roger flag, pattern, making 1683:16-17
Jolly Roger or Black jack flag, cardboard, felt, stick, making 1559:21
Pirate flag, tie dyed, making 641:106-107
Skull and crossbones flag, making 1736:19
PIRATES—GAMES
Battleship game, how to make and play 1559:32
Black spot game, how to do 1559:28-29
Fishing game, how to do 1559:28-29
Pirate pictures game, how to do 1559:28-29
Treasure hunting game 1559:16-17
Treasure Island game, how to do 1559:28-29
PIRATES—HANDICRAFTS
Blackbeard jumping jack, oaktag, patterns, making 1251:20-23
PIRATES—HATS
Captain hat, black cardboard, making 1559:10
Pirate hat and eye patch, paper and felt, making 1096:11
Pirate hat, making 678:21
Pirate hat, paper, pattern, making 232:25
Pirate hat, plastic carton, making 766:56-57
PIRATES—HOOK
Hook, plastic bottle, plastic coat hanger, making 1559:9
PIRATES—LANGUAGE
Phrases that seamen and pirates used 1736:26-27
PIRATES—LOGBOOKS
Logbook, notebook, making 1559:14-15
PIRATES—MAPS
Map, paper, tea bag, making 1559:14-15
Pirate map, making 1683:21
Treasure map, how to make 1736:15
PIRATES—MASKS
Mask, pirate mask, making 846:36-37
PIRATES—PARROTS
Parrots, cardboard, paint, patterns, making 1559:26
PIRATES—PARTIES
Pirate birthday bash, activities, foods, and handicrafts 30:61-64
Pirate party, invitations, decorations, costumes, food, games, recipes 1185:20-21
Pirate Party, recipes and games 635:48-51
Pirate plunder party, decorations, games, costumes, recipes, making 74:122-139
Pirate Treasure hunt party, how to plan and give 86:168-177
Pirate Treasure hunt party, menu and recipes 86:233-234
Pirate Treasure party, activities and recipes 809:61-65
Skull and crossbones party, decorations, recipes, games 1559:26-31
PIRATES—PUPPETS
Captain Plunder Bones stick puppet, making 681:24-25
Davy Jones ghostly parrot puppet, making 179:16-19
Pirate Pete finger puppet, making 757:26-31
Pirate puppet, papier-mache, balloon, paints, making 1561:28-29
PIRATES—SHIPS
Figurehead for ship, modeling clay, making 1683:15
Pirate ship, balsa wood, making 925:83-85
Pirate ship, cereal box, newspaper, paints, making 1559:18-19
Pirate Ship, wooden, patterns for boat and crew, making 942:84-87
Porthole, cardboard, making 1559:14-15
Ship, cardboard, making 562:15-16

PIRATES—TATTOOS
Pirate tattoos, making 179:12-13
PIRATES—TELESCOPES
Telescope, paper, making 1559:14-15
PIRATES—TREASURE CHESTS
Treasure chest from paper bag, making 678:27
Treasure chest, cardboard box, paints, making 1559:23
Treasure chest, cardboard, patterns, making 1683:24-25
Treasure chest, wooden, pattern, making 942:95
PIRATES—WEAPONS
Dagger and cutlass weapons, cardboard, making 1559:11
Sword, cardboard, foil, making 1736:21
Weapons, wooden, making 942:94
PIZZA
Activities, art, songs, recipes, games 1469:20-21
Pizza, activities, art, science, songs, recipes 911:178-181
PIZZA PARLORS
Chef apron and hat, making 293:110-112, 117-118
Hero sandwich, making 293:116-117
Pizza and spaghetti, making 293:112-113
Pizza cutter and oven, making 293:113-115
Smiling pizza sign, making 293:110
PLAINS INDIANS
Tools and ornaments 960:33-43
PLAINS INDIANS—AMULETS
Amulet, door, making 298:60-61
PLAINS INDIANS—BAGS
Bags and pouches, making 589:108
Lakota - Sioux charm bag, felt, yarn, beads, patterns, making 1633:20-23
PLAINS INDIANS—BASKETRY
Basketry of Plains Indians 959:8-12
PLAINS INDIANS—BEADWORK
Beading, how to do 224:23-26
Beadwork loom, making 224:22-23
Beadwork, beads, threads, patterns, making 1636:20-21
Bracelets, making 224:26-27
Plains beading, making 589:106-107
PLAINS INDIANS—BELTS
Belt, concho, cardboard, tin foil, pattern, making 1170:10
Link belt, making 932:82-84
PLAINS INDIANS—BREASTPLATE
Breastplate, papier-mache, making 765:74-78
PLAINS INDIANS—CALENDAR
Calendar stick, leather, paints, making 1418:40
PLAINS INDIANS—CLOTHING
Breech clouts, aprons, and leggings, making 465:28-29
Cuffs and gauntlets, making 465:36-37
Dresses and leggings, making 589:62-63
Leggings and breechcloths, making 589:52
Leggings, making 932:87-89
Man's outfit, tunic, leggings, decorations, making 1368:10-11
Plains Indian dress, making 932:38-40
Shirts, making 589:54
Vests and cuffs, making 589:56
Vests, making 465:35
War shirt, making 465:30
Woman's outfit, tunic, decorations, making 1368:10-13
Yoke dress, making 224:95-100
PLAINS INDIANS—COOKERY
Boiled eggs, recipe 1699:150
Broiled buffalo steaks, recipe 1527:36-37
Meat-eating habits of the Plains Indians 662:108-110

PLAINS INDIANS—COSTUMES
 Girl's costume, making 465:94-95
 Prairie costumes, leggings, making 8:46-47
 Prairie costumes, loin cloth, making 8:46
 Prairie costumes, moccasins, making 8:58-59
 Prairie costumes, shirt, making 8:48-49
 Prairie costumes, woman's belt, making 8:51
 Prairie costumes, woman's cape, making 8:51
PLAINS INDIANS—DANCES
 Sundance, how to do 1362:51
PLAINS INDIANS—DOLLS
 Corn cob doll, corn cob, fabric, yarn, making 1699:92-93
PLAINS INDIANS—FESTIVALS—HANDICRAFTS
 Sioux Sunground nut skull, papier-mache, paints, yarn,
  making 1633:22-25
PLAINS INDIANS—FOOTWEAR
 Moccasin designs, making 465:47
 Moccasins, burlap fabric, cardboard, string, paints, mak-
  ing 1368:11
 Moccasins, fabric, thread, making 1608:66
 Moccasins, felt, patterns, making 1636:18-19
 Northern Plains moccasins, making 444:92-100
 Plains type moccasins, how to make 359:80-103
PLAINS INDIANS—GAMES
 All in air game 565:133
 Ball in air game 565:174
 Ball juggle race 565:176
 Ball relay 565:31
 Ball toss race 565:42
 Bead in hand game 565:262
 Beaver lodge game 565:179
 Bird flight game 565:172
 Bowl catch game 565:105
 Bowl game 565:236
 Bowl toss game 565:107
 Buffalo corral game 565:90
 Buffalo hide game 565:223
 Buffalo robe name 565:224
 Bump ball game 565:144
 Copperhead game 565:244
 Corncob darts game, how to play 1296:122
 Corncob ring toss game 565:127
 Coup game 565:100
 Coup stick game 565:231
 Crooked path game 565:165
 Cross country relay 565:27
 Crow arrow throw game 565:140
 Danger signal game 565:63
 Dark walk game 565:85
 Double ball game 565:180
 Double relay game 565:33
 Dual game 565:82
 Eleven stick game 565:199
 Find the chief game 565:255
 Flying feather game 565:134
 Going on a hunt game 565:96
 Guess stick game 565:203
 Hand game 565:272
 Hidden ball game 565:204
 Hoop and lance game 565:269
 Hoop toss game 565:121
 Hop between game 565:162
 Hop game 565:161
 Hop, jump game 565:162
 Indian darts game 565:141

 Indian foot race game 565:48
 Jump race game 565:163
 Keen eye game 565:78
 Lance Chief game 565:240
 Lance hold game 565:215
 Lancehead game 565:34
 Medicine drum game 565:229
 Medicine lodge game 565:227
 Moose stalk game 565:74
 Okotoks game 565:143
 Over and over game 565:158
 Pebble patterns game 565:65
 Pebble pictures game 565:171
 Pine cone hoop toss game 565:123
 Pole pull game 565:246
 Pole push game 565:248
 Racket ball game 565:184
 Raiders game 565:101
 Rattler game 565:70
 Shield and ball game 565:113
 Shield on shield game 565:115
 Sit wrestle game 565:233
 Sky Okotoks game 565:144
 Stalking game 565:68
 Star groups game 565:83
 Stick and ring game 565:183
 Stick relay game 565:32
 Stop game 565:213
 Straight path ball game 565:258
 Strong arm game 565:232
 Strong badger game 565:245
 Tender of the fire game 565:72
 There game 565:75
 Three throw ball game 565:138
 Tipi race 565:36
 Tracks game 565:86
 Trail of Silence game 565:98
 Whirl and catch game 565:110
 Wolf chase game 565:93
PLAINS INDIANS—HOUSEHOLD
 Drying and cooking racks, making 647:58-59
PLAINS INDIANS—HOUSES
 Teepee, making 647:53-55
 Teepee, Naugahyde, pattern, making 1027:136-140
 Teepee, old blankets, stakes, paints, making 1368:16-17
 Teepee, paper or fabric, patterns, making 1636:12-13
 Teepee, patterns, making 1390:78-80
 Teepees, how to draw 591:3
 Tipi, bamboo poles, blankets, making 1608:62
 Tipi, making 804:64-70
 Tipi, plastic tub, paper, sticks, pattern, making 1170:20
 Tipis, sticks, yarn, paper, felt, how to make 1296:110
 Wickiup, plastic tub, masking tape, making 1170:18
PLAINS INDIANS—JEWELRY
 Chest piece, interwoven, making 224:32-34
 Clay bead necklace, clay, paints, making 1418:38-39
PLAINS INDIANS—MASKS
 Plains Indians masks, making 327:47
PLAINS INDIANS—MUSICAL INSTRUMENTS
 Rasp, wooden stick, making 1699:77
 Rattle, gourd, making 1699:78-79
PLAINS INDIANS—OWNER STICKS
 Owner stick, dowels, feathers, paints, making 1418:41
PLAINS INDIANS—PARFLECHE
 Parfleche or pouch, making 714:20-21

Parfleche pocketbook, making 482:106-107
Parfleche to store clothing, paper, yarn, making 1699:24
Parfleche, making 227:37; 589:90

PLAINS INDIANS—POUCH
Leather pouch, leather, paints, making 1418:36-37
Pouch, chamois, felt, trims, making 1699:26

PLAINS INDIANS—SHIELDS
Plains Indian shields, making 466:101-103
Shield, Plains Indians designs given, posterboard, making 1633:18-19
Shields, making 227:46

PLAINS INDIANS—SIGN LANGUAGE
Action, signs for 317:33-36
Body and senses, signs for 317:10-11
Body paint, war paint, signs for 317:76-77
Counting, signs for 317:8-9
Dress and adornment, signs for 317:52-53
Family and daily life, signs for 317:30-32
Feelings and emotions, signs for 317:22-25
Hand signs 1636:26-27
History of war, signs for 317:70
Indian Nations, signs for 317:16-17
Life in the tribe, signs for 317:12-15
Nature and animals, signs for 317:38-47
Objects, signs for 317:48-51
On the trail and on the warpath, signs for 317:54-60
Picture writing, signs for 317:68-69
Plains Indians sign language 1368:48
Qualities and faults, signs for 317:26-29
Signals, signs for 317:73
Time, signs for 317:18-20
Trading and palavering, signs for 317:62-67
Trail and exploit marks, signs for 317:71-72
Where?, signs for 317:20-21

PLAINS INDIANS—SMOKE SIGNALS
Smoke signals, how to send 1636:29

PLAINS INDIANS—TOYS
Shield for boys, Naugahyde, pattern, making 1027:131-136

PLAINS INDIANS—TRAVOIS
Travois, making 647:56-57

PLAINS INDIANS—VILLAGES
Plains Indian Village diorama, making 647:76

PLAINS INDIANS—WAR BONNETS
Bonnet case, oatmeal box, making 1699:55
Plains bonnet, paper bag, making 1699:54
War bonnet, paper, felt, patterns, making 1636:24-25

PLAINS INDIANS—WEAPONS
Coup stick, fur, felt, feathers, yarn, making 1699:33

PLAINS INDIANS—WINTER COUNT
Winter count on buffalo hide, fabric, paints, making 1368:51

PLANTS—DOLLS
Dolls to make from plant materials, making 657:68-73

PLASTER CASTS
Sand casting with plaster of Paris, how to do 1213:51

PLAYS—ELIZABETHAN
Merlin Plays Minstrel play 159:13-17

PLAYS—FRANCE—MOLIERE
A Doctor in Spite of himself 159:34-38

PLOW MONDAY FESTIVAL
Information about 419:51-52

PLYMOUTH COLONY. *See* **PILGRIMS**

PLYMOUTH VILLAGE
Plymouth Village Diorama, making 401:30-32

POCAHONTAS—COSTUMES
Chief Powhatan costume, making 213:35-37
Pocahontas costume, making 213:34-35

POCAHONTAS—HEADBANDS
Indian headbands, brown and colored papers, patterns, making 1199:60-61

POINSETTIAS
Poinsettia Day; activities, art, songs, recipes, games 1469:46-47

POLAND
Activities, flags, games, songs, dances, recipes 1381:201-204

POLAND—CHRISTMAS
Christmas Supper celebration 601:112-113
Customs of Christmas in Poland 473:38-40
Polish Christmas traditions 451:18-19
Wigilia; celebration of 497:70-81

POLAND—CHRISTMAS—COOKERY
Almond soup, recipe 704:75
Barsz with mushroom Uszki soup, recipe 1128:97
Christmas carp, recipe 1128:92
Karp smozony (fried carp), recipe 1666:130
Kisiel zurawinowi (cranberry pudding), recipe 1666:131
Kluski z makiem (poppy seed noodles), recipe 1666:132
Kutya (wheat berry pudding), recipe 1666:131
Kutya, wheat berry pudding, recipe 497:76
Mazurkas, recipe 704:72-73
Mushroom uszki, dumplings, recipe 1128:94
Noodles with poppy seeds and butter, recipe 1128:92
Pierozhki, potato cheese dumplings, recipe 497:76
Podkovy, sweet horseshoe shaped rolls, recipe 1128:96
Polish stuffed cabbage, recipe 497:76
Poppy seed cake, recipe 497:76
Poppy seed cookies, recipe 1666:132
Twelve fruit compote, recipe 1128:95
Vegetarian barszcz soup, recipe 497:76

POLAND—CHRISTMAS—DECORATIONS
Angel, making 497:80-81
Christmas tree and decorations, how to make 593:90-97
Egg ornament decoration, making 497:78-79

POLAND—CHRISTMAS—HANDICRAFTS
Christmas tree ornaments, making 451:20-23
Heart ornament, paper, making 1023:77-80
Moon, paper, making 1023:135
Mushroom, paper, making 1023:136-137
Polish star, making 705:28-31
Riband, Christmas tree ornament, making 795:19
Star ornament, making 1023:63-64
Swiat, the World, paper, making 1023:139-140
Treetop angel, paper, making 1023:81-84
Wycinanki, paper-cutouts, making 795:20

POLAND—CHRISTMAS—PLAYS
Christmas spider puppet play 451:29-31
Christmas Szopka play 451:25-31
Christmas Szopka theater, making 451:25

POLAND—COOKERY
Apple dessert, recipe 1532:100
Apple soup, recipe 1381:203
Apples; fried apple dessert, recipe 1125:112
Barley soup, recipe 990:16-17
Bigos, pork and sauerkraut dish, recipe 1532:98-99
Bigos, sauerkraut and meat dish, recipe 1374:119
Bread, semi-short bread with plums or apricots, recipe 990:39
Carrot gingerbread, recipe 990:47

Cauliflower with Polish sauce, recipe 990:32
Chicken, Polish style, recipe 990:35
Chrusciki deep fried pastries, recipe 1381:203
Cucumbers in sour cream, recipe 1381:203
Dilled cucumber salad, recipe, making 895:107
Eggs stuffed with ham, recipe 990:22
Fish, roasted stuffed fish, recipe 990:36-37
Food and customs 990:8-11
Green bean soup, recipe 895:105
Grzyby w smietanie, mushrooms in sour cream, recipe 1165:145-146
Herring paste, recipe 990:19
Holiday cookies, recipe 187:22
Hunter's stew, recipe 990:18-19
Kluski z kapusta po Polski, Polish noodles and cabbage, recipe 1165:144-145
Map with food products 990:6
Mazurek with chocolate glaze, recipe 990:45
Mushrooms in vinegar, recipe 990:20
Noodles with poppy seed, recipe 446:30
Noodles with poppy seeds, recipe 990:38
Pan-fried mushrooms, recipe 1165:145
Pierozki, recipe 990:24-25
Pigeons in tomato sauce, recipe 990:42-44
Plum and rhubarb soup, recipe 990:27; 1652:42
Polish menu 990:14-15
Poppy seed cake, recipe 895:108
Pork roast, recipe 895:106
Potato pancakes, recipe 794:29
Potatoes with cheese jackets, recipe 874:63
Red cabbage and apple salad, recipe 1125:111-112; 1532:98
Rutabagas and carrots, recipe 990:30
Salad, recipe 793:41
Semi-shortbread with plums or apricots dessert, recipe 1280:41
Sour cream and cottage cheese snacks, recipe 1125:111
Spring vegetable soup, recipe 990:25
Tomato and onion salad, recipe 990:30
Vegetable garni, recipe 990:40
Vegetable salad, recipe 990:29
Zupa nic, nothing soup, recipe 188:30

POLAND—COSTUMES
Zupa nic, nothing soup, recipe, costume 188:30

POLAND—DOLLS
Peasant doll, wood and fabric, pattern, making 1027:53-61

POLAND—EASTER
Easter egg customs in Poland 201:25-26
Hancucka, traditional rhyme, Poland 139:120
History of Easter in Poland 709:167

POLAND—EASTER—COOKERY
Easter cakes, mazurek wielka- nocny, cookies, recipe 72:75-76
Royal mazurek shortbread cake with glaze sauce, recipe 1176:34

POLAND—EASTER—GAMES
Easter games 451:14

POLAND—EASTER—HANDICRAFTS
Easter eggs, making 451:15
Easter yam eggs, making 451:16
Egg pitchers, making 451:17
Eggs decorated with rug yarns, making 503:35
Folk paper-cutouts, cocks in tree, tulip, making 709:167-170
Wax design batik eggs, making 1277:6-7

POLAND—FESTIVALS
Corn Festival celebration 659:30-31

POLAND—FESTIVALS—COOKERY
New Year's Day: bigos (Polish hunter's stew), recipe 1666:132-133

POLAND—FINGER PLAYS
The Crab finger play story, how to do 1161:97

POLAND—GAMES
Dzien Dobry, Howdy Neighbor game 386:46
Gry game 451:12
Jak Sie Masz game, how to play 1494:100
Klass, hopscotch game 1426:34-35
Polish Bezique card game 1132:44
Running fox game 451:12
Witch and the angels game 451:13

POLAND—HANDICRAFTS
Decorated egg water pitcher, making 298:94-95
Kaleidoscope collage, making 297:206-207
Ribands, paper, making 996:38-39
Scallop edged ribands, paper, making 298:204-205
Snow and pine branch stenciled egg, making 298:80-81

POLAND—LANGUAGE
Polish phrases, titles and adjectives 1125:41
Some words and numbers in Polish 1176:21

POLAND—NESTING DOLL STORIES
Naughty Marysia nesting doll story, how to do 1161:80-83

POLAND—PAPER-CUTTING
Greeting cards, papercut, making 626:80-83
Paper chain, making 626:83-84
Paper-cut eggs, making 627:93-96
Paper-cutting, how to do 515:100
Paper designs, making 451:6-1 1
Traditional Polish paper-cut, patterns, making 1381:203-204
Wycinanki cut paper designs, making 1476:21-22; 1477:125
Wycinanki rooster in a fir tree, paper, making 298:224-225
Wycinanki, kurpie-style, paper, patterns, making 1422:31-32
Wycinanki, paper-cutouts, paper, making 1338:93-95

POLAND—PUPPETS
Stick puppet toy, making 1027:46-52

POLAND—SCIENTISTS
Nicholaus Copernicus's birthday, Copernican universe model, making 1199:52

POLAND—STORYTELLING
Captain from Krakow story 1522:92-101

POLAND—TOYS
Pecking bird from Poland; history of and how to make 495:91-95

POLAND—VALENTINE'S DAY—HANDICRAFTS
Hearts and flowers Valentine, Polish paper-cuts, patterns, making 1016:27-3 1

POLAR REGIONS—PUPPETS
Polar Regions animal puppets, patterns, making 463:65-71

POLISH AMERICANS—FESTIVALS
Pulaski Day; celebrate by saying Polish greeting 1199:235

POLITICAL PARTIES
Democratic donkey pattern 199:63
Republican elephant pattern 199:63

POLYNESIA—COOKERY

Beef and tomatoes, recipe 895:111
Fried rice, recipe 895:110
Pineapple shrimp, recipe 895:112-113
Pineapple-banana boats, recipe 1380:41
Punch, recipe 514:141-142

POMANDERS

Apple pomander, cloves, cinnamon, netting, making 1692:22
Colonial pomander ball, orange, spices, making 1309:40-41
Fruit pomanders, oranges, cloves, making 1510:24-25
Old-fashioned Colonial pomanders, making 1455:116
Orange and clove pomander, how to make and decorate 1259:24-25
Orange and clove, making 1673:19
Orange and spice pomander, making 1213:97
Orange pomander, how to make 1655:24-25
Orange spice pomander, making 1320:10-11
Orange-clove pomander, recipe 1542:111
Pomander ball from fruits and spices, how to make 1419:202-203
Pomander ball, oranges, spices, making 1348:unp
Pomander balls, fruit, spices, ribbons, making 1531:92-93
Pomander, orange, cloves, ribbon, making 1285:140

POMO INDIANS—GAMES

Stick dice, how to play 1699:111

POOH BEAR. *See* **MILNE, A. A.**

POP-UPS

Basset hound, pop-up, paper, pattern 1210:12-13
Bear, pop-up, paper, pattern 1210:36-37
Bunny, pop-up, paper, pattern 1210:18-19
Card, Christmas tree card, paper, making 1141:23
Carnival pop-up card, pattern, making 1006:44
Cat, pop-up, paper, pattern 1210:16-17
Christmas card pop-up, paper, making 1025:14-16
Christmas tree pop-up card, making 209:7
Christmas tree pop-up card, patterns, making 1016:245-249
Cow, pop-up, paper, pattern 1210:22-23
Donkey, pop-up, paper, pattern 1210:20-21
Dragon, pop-up, paper, pattern 1210:44-45
Duck, pop-up, paper, pattern 1210:28-29
Easter egg pop-up, paper plates, making 1083:80
Easter lamb pop-up card, pattern, making 1006:36
Frog, pop-up, paper, pattern 1210:24-25
Ghost pop-up card, paper, making 214:8
Hen, pop-up, paper, pattern 1210:32-33
Kangaroo, pop-up, paper, pattern 1210:40-41
Lion, pop-up, paper, pattern 1210:42-43
Mutt, pop-up, paper, pattern 1210:14-15
Owl, pop-up, paper, pattern 1210:30-31
Penguin, pop-up, paper, pattern 1210:34-35
Reindeer, pop-up, paper, pattern 1210:38-39
Rhino, pop-up, paper, pattern 1210:46-48
Sheep, pop-up, paper, pattern 1210:26-27
Terrier, pop-up, paper, pattern 1210:10-11
Valentines Day peek and pop-up card, paper, making 209:12-14
Vampire pop-up card, paper, making 197:50-53
Witch pop-up card, paper, making 214:9

POPCORN

Activities, art, songs, recipes, games 1469:26-27
Castle centerpiece for St. Patrick's Day, recipe 939:52-56
Chop suey popcorn, recipe 964:70
Christmas wreaths, popcorn, making 939:140
Cracker Jack history 964:20-22
Easter basket from popcorn, making 939:63-65
First automatic popcorn popper 964:15-18
Green popcorn shamrocks, making 939:57-58
Hawaiian popcorn bars, recipe 381:53
Hickory smoked popcorn, recipe 939:128
History of our gift from the Indians 939:13-16
History of popcorn 659:125-126; 762:25-37
History of popcorn through the ages 964:3-53
Homemade Indian popcorn, making 652:102-103
Indians, popcorn experts, how they did it 964:10-11
Log cabin popcorn centerpiece, making 939:36-40
New Year's Eve midnight popcorn clocks, making 939:146-147
Peruvian popcorn, recipe 381:19
Pizza popcorn, recipe 381:35
Popcorn balls, old fashioned for Christmas, recipe, making 434:66
Popcorn chili, recipe 964:69
Popcorn Day activities, stories, crafts, recipes, making 558:21-23
Popcorn filled chuck wagons, recipe and how to make chuck wagons 939:100-102
Popcorn Taiglach, recipe 939:111-112
Thanksgiving First Feast and popcorn 964:12
Toppings for popcorn, recipe 1401:27

PORTRAITS

People portraits, paper, making 787:20-23

PORTUGAL—CHRISTMAS

Christmas customs 149:44-45

PORTUGAL—CHRISTMAS—COOKERY

Bomboms de figo (fig bonbons), recipe 1666:98

PORTUGAL—COOKERY

Bread pudding, recipe 667:86-87
Codfish balls, recipe 1375:119
Cookies, Portuguese sighs cookies, recipe 794:37
Eggs and onions, coimbra, recipe 895:115
Fish with sauce, recipe 874:41
Green cabbage soup, recipe 667:86
History of cookery in Portugal 88:148-150
History of foods and cooking in Portugal 667:37-87
Meat-eating habits in Portugal 662:55-57
Noodles and tuna, recipe 895:116
Orange cake, recipe 858:unp
Pao, country bread, recipe 1165:113-114
Rabanados, sweet toast, recipe 188:20
Sopa de pedra, stone soup, recipe 1165:113
Sponge cake, pao de lao, recipe 88:153-154
Sponge cakes, pao de lo, cookies, recipe 72:49-50
Sweet bread, recipe 88:152-153

PORTUGAL—EASTER—COOKERY

Easter; bolo de amendoa (almond cake), recipe 1666:98
Porco assado (stuffed roast pork), recipe 1666:97
Spinach with pine nuts and raisins, recipe 1666:97-98

PORTUGAL—FESTIVALS

Feast of Trays Festival, Festa dos Tabuleiros, collect, give things to the poor activities 1574:20-21
Festivals of Iberia celebrations 667:72-78

PORTUGAL—FOLKLORE—HANDICRAFTS

John and the Twin Giants, giant paper-bag stick puppet, folded paper picture 125:118-130

PORTUGAL—GAMES

Game of the stone 602:101
Hit the stones game 58:50-51
Newspaper walk game 967:44

PORTUGAL—HANDICRAFTS
Goblet, clay, making 1070:126-129
Moorish plate, clay, making 1070:129-133
Oil lamps, making 955:106-107
Red Rooster of Barcelos, clay, making 1070:133-136

PORTUGAL—LANGUAGE
Numbers one to ten in Portuguese 1711:unp
Portegese common words, school words, names 1378:264-269
Portegese words; numbers, colors, months, seasons 1378:263-264

PORTUGAL—TOYS
Balancing fisherman from Portugal; history of and how to make 495:36-39
Windmill, wood and cardboard, pattern, making 1027:62-71

POSADAS. *See* **MEXICO—CHRISTMAS**

POST OFFICE
Dance game; Postman, Postman, song and dance game 1114:15
Mailbag, paper, making 1033:21
Post Office Eagle emblem pattern 1083:46
U.S. mail box, box and paper bag, making 442:58

POST OFFICE—BULLETIN BOARDS
Mail chart and mail sticker poster, making 295:103-104
Mail pouch and mail box, making 295:104-105
Mail truck making 295:103
Stamp showcase, making 295:105-106

POSTCARD DAY
Activities, art, songs, recipes, games 1469:100-101

POTATO CHIPS
How potato chips are made 1197:8-9

POTATOES
Burlap sack potato invitations, making 1197:58
Grow a potato 376:97
Growing potatoes for the future 801:58-68
History of potatoes 410:6-13; 801:5-29
Life story of potatoes 801:30-41
Potato activities, patterns, making 992:34-36
Potatoes for home garden 801:44-53
Potatoes for the market place 801:53-57
Potatoes, activities, art, science, songs, recipes 911:186-189

POTATOES—COOKERY
Baked potatoes, recipe 1145:26
Pigs in blankets, recipe 801:105-106
Pommes soufflés, recipe 801:104-105
Potato crepes, recipe, making 801:107-108
Potato dumplings, recipe 801:108-109
Potato hash, recipe 801:101-102
Potato pancakes, latkes, recipe 801:106-107
Potato salad, recipe 801:100-101
Shepherd's pie, recipe 801:102-103
Ways to cook potatoes 801:93-110

POTATOES—GAMES
Hot potato game 1197:61
Hot potato, how to play 801:80-81
Pass the potato game 1197:61
Potato roll game, how to play 801:82-83
Potato sack race game 1197:60
Potato sack race, how to play 801:81-82
Potato spoon race, how to play 801:83
Steal the potato game 1197:60

POTATOES—HANDICRAFTS
Potato and peanut people, making 553:48-49
Potato head that grows hair, making 801:85

POTATOES—PRINTING
Potato print Easter eggs, making 433:37
Potato print wrapping paper for Thanksgiving, making 401:36-38

POTPOURRI
Citrus potpourri, recipe 1455:114
Colonial potpourri, flower petals, recipe, making 1309:38
Covers for potpourri jar lids, pressed flowers, ribbons, paper, making 1284:59
Flower petals, borax, cornmeal, making 1284:57-58
Flower potpourri, making 1259:20
Heirloom dress box sachet, recipe 1220:111-112
Lavender-rose potpourri, recipe 1455:115
Peppermint potpourri, recipe 1455:114
Potpourri and sachet, recipe, making 1213:92-93
Potpourri baskets, potpourri, recipe, making 1510:62-63
Potpourri, how to make 1421:212
Spice potpourri, recipe 1455:115
Strawberry potpourri, recipe 1455:113
Sweet nursery potpourri, recipe 1220:14-15

POTTER, BEATRIX
Beatrix Potter Easter brunch, decorations, games, costumes, recipes 74:71-84

POTTER, BEATRIX—BIRTHDAY
Celebrate with rabbit in sign language activity 1199:170

POTTER, BEATRIX—COOKERY
"Tale of Mrs. Tiggy-Winkle"; her pineapple right-side-up muffins, recipe 365:21
"Tale of Peter Rabbit"; Peter and Benjamin's bunny cake, recipe 365:49
"Tale of Two Bad Mice"; Hunca Munca's fresh squeezed muffins, recipe 365:22
Mr. McGregor's garden salad, recipe 1215:20
Peter Rabbit carrot bars, recipe 738:unp
Peter Rabbit currant buns, recipe 285:83

POTTERY
Basic natural kiln 1421:204
Bowl, making 524:19
Bowls and cups, how to make 694:33-43
Clay pinch pot, making 1421:203
Clay pot on potter's wheel, how to make 1254:42-43
Clay pots from Earth's clay, making 1372:116-117
Coil clay pot, making 1255:7
Kiln using sawdust in garbage can, making 1285:37-39
Kiln, outdoor, bricks, how to construct 1129:28-29
Map of people and places that make pots 694:60-61
Pinch pots from clay, making 1260:16-17
Pinch pots, clay, making 1285:34-35
Pots to hold fire, how to make 694:44-49
Pots to hold water, how to make 694:51-59
Pottery kiln, making 293:173-174
Pottery wheel, spinning, making 293:170-171

POWHATAN
Chief Powhatan costume, making 213:35-37

PRAIRIE. *See* **FRONTIER AND PIONEER LIFE**

PRAIRIES—FOLKLORE
"Three Names"; physical and human geography activities 1458:62-65

PREHISTORIC ART
Mud paint for cave paintings, recipe, how to do 1372:112

PREHISTORIC PAINTINGS
Cave paintings, brown paper, paints, how to do 1296:90
Prehistoric wall painting; paints made from soils, wood ashes, lard, making 1284:131-132

PREHISTORIC PEOPLE—CLOTHING

Cave person tunic, fabric, making 181:6-9

PREHISTORIC PEOPLE—COSTUMES

Prehistoric couple costumes, making 887:28-29

Stone Age costume, fabric, patterns, making 1174:26

PREHISTORIC PEOPLE—FOOTWEAR

Stone age boots and leggings, fabric, making 181:14-15

PREHISTORIC PEOPLE—MASKS

Wild animal masks, paper, patterns given, making
181:16-19

PREHISTORIC PEOPLE—MUSICAL INSTRUMENTS

Buzz disc bullroarer, making 1310:30-31

Gourd rattles, balloon, newspapers, glue, making
1310:34-35

Log drum, fruit juice cans, paper, making 1310:26-27

Rib bone clappers, rib bones, making 1310:28

PREHISTORIC PEOPLE—NATURE FESTIVALS

Nature festivals information 419:5-12

PREHISTORIC PEOPLE—TOOLS

Stone age tools, cardboard, making 181:10-13

PRESIDENTS—UNITED STATES

President's birthdays, celebration 133:112

Presidential Press Conference activity, how to do 781:64-
66

PRESIDENTS—UNITED STATES—MAGIC

Abe versus George trick 36:27-29

Drop of a hand card trick 36:34-37

Hopscotch game, magic 36:8-11

Lincoln penny trick 36:20-22

Pick a President trick 36:38-41

Prediction magic game 36:12-15

Presidential coins trick 36:42-44

Professor Phantom trick 36:16-19

Washington dollar trick 36:23-26

Which President trick 36:30-33

PRESIDENTS' DAY

Finger plays, recipes, games, making 944:76-77

Presidents' Day art patterns, making 9:18-19

Presidents' Day master word list, making 9:24-26

Presidents' Day, activities, making 9:6

Student playing cards for Presidents' Day lingo, making
9:27-76

PRESIDENTS' DAY—DECORATIONS

Collages; Presidents' Day collage and star collage, making 1149:41, 43

Star cookie cutter prints, making 1149:88

PRESIDENTS' DAY—PUPPETS

Puppet projects, patterns, scenes, story starters, feature
story 1083:51-54

PRETZELS

Philadelphia soft pretzels, recipe 118:170

PRINCES—COSTUMES

Tunic pattern, making 7:90-91

PRINCES—MASKS

Prince mask, making 840:7-8

PRINCESSES

Princess funny face from paper bag, making 678:8

PRINCESSES—COSTUMES

Gown pattern, making 7:90-91

Princess costume, fabric, face makeup given, making
957:48-53

Princess costume, fabric, patterns, making 1174:42

PRINCESSES—FACE MAKEUP

Princess face makeup, how to do 1314:37

PRINCESSES—FACE PAINTING

Face painting for Princess, how to do 1306:52

PRINCESSES—MASKS

Princess mask, making 840:9-10; 846:20-21

PRINCESSES—PUPPETS

Princess stick puppet, making 681:26-27

PRINTING. *See also* **POTATOES—PRINTING**

Block prints, how to make and use 1446:20-23

Potato printing, papier-mache, how to do 1464:54-65

Potato prints on paper and fabric, how to do 1197:44;
1446:10-13

String and block of wood printing, how to do 1196:24

PRINTS

Techniques for block, stencil and monoprinting, how to
do 1641:8-23

PRODUCE MARKETS

Bananas, making 293:153-154

Berry basket, making 293:157

Fruit basket, making 293:155-156

Fruits and vegetables, making 293:152-153

Hanging fruit scale, making 293:155

Red tomato sign, making 293:151-152

PROKOFIEV, SERGEI

Peter and the Wolf puppet show 756:163-165

PROSPECTORS

Wood carved prospector figure, making 382:63-65

PUEBLO INDIANS—BASKETRY

Baskets, coiled basket from cord and paper, making
889:27-32

PUEBLO INDIANS—COOKERY

Corn chile bread, recipe 1296:131-132

Kneel down bread, recipe 1699:136

Peach crisp, recipe 1527:xxv

Pumpkin pie pockets, recipe 1296:132

Trail snack, apple leather, recipe 1296:131

PUEBLO INDIANS—DOLLS

Clay storyteller dolls, clay, paints, making 1296:93

Indian Mother and baby dolls, making 494:74-83

Kachina doll, how to draw 591:30-31

Kachina figure, cardboard tubes, fabric, feathers, paint,
making 1476:75-76

PUEBLO INDIANS—FESTIVALS

Corn Festival celebration 659:53

PUEBLO INDIANS—GAMES

Coyote and the sheep game 602:178

Dodge ball game 602:177-178

Hidden ball game 602:178-179

Pa-tol sticks game 474:45

Picaria game, how to play 1688:46-50

Pueblo squash blossoms game 698:75

PUEBLO INDIANS—HANDICRAFTS

Pueblo Yucca or cattail tray, making 482:40-41

Tree of Life clay symbol, making 815:82-83

PUEBLO INDIANS—HOUSEHOLD

Metate stone, making 647:71

PUEBLO INDIANS—HOUSES

Adobe house, making 647:67-69

Adobe, making 574:131

Oven, brick, making 647:70

Pueblo dwellings, making 227:13

Pueblo house from boxes, making 494:80-83

Pueblo house, boxes, sticks, making 1170:23

Pueblo villages and houses 469:28-31

PUEBLO INDIANS—JEWELRY
    Concha belts, making 605:35-39
    Concha buttons, making 605:31-33
    Pueblo jewelry, how to make 605:11-17
    Silver rings with stones, how to make 605:23-26
    Silver rings without settings, how to make 605:19-22
    Turquoise, how to cut and polish 605:27-30
PUEBLO INDIANS—MASKS
    Kachina mask, making 596:35-39
    Pueblo mask, making 227:62-63
PUEBLO INDIANS—NATURE FESTIVALS
    Corn growing festivals 419:150-151
PUEBLO INDIANS—POTTERY
    Animals, pottery, how to make 482:52-57
    Clay coil ceremonial bowl, making 298:164-165
    Pottery, how to draw 591:24-25
PUEBLO INDIANS—STRING FIGURES
    Hut 1404:103-108
PUEBLO INDIANS—WEAVING
    Eye-of-God weaving, making 324:30
PUERTO RICO—BIRTHDAYS
    Fifteenth cumpleanos birthday party for girls 660:62-63
PUERTO RICO—CHRISTMAS
    Christmas and the Three Kings Day celebration 601:151-152
    Christmas customs 149:63-64
    Customs in Puerto Rico 425:23
    Three Kings Day celebration 665:12-16
PUERTO RICO—COOKERY
    Banana cake, recipe 895:118-119
    Beans and rice, recipe 794:9
    Butter cookies, recipe 793:16
    Citrus pops, recipe 188:3
    Orange pudding, recipe 895:120
    Rum lard cookies, mantecados con ron, cookies, recipe 72:166-167
    Surullitos, cheese and cornmeal fritters, recipe 1432:119
    Surullitos, cornmeal fritters, recipe 1380:28
    Turmeric rice with pigeon peas, recipe 1068:unp
PUERTO RICO—COSTUMES
    Citrus pops, recipe, costume 188:3
PUERTO RICO—FESTIVALS
    Feast of the Cross celebration 601:151
    St. John the Baptist Day celebration 665:36-42
PUERTO RICO—FESTIVALS—HANDICRAFTS
    Three Kings, making 626:84-86
PUERTO RICO—FESTIVALS—PUPPETS
    Mid-Autumn Festival story lantern, paper plate, making 1083:194
    Three Kings Day King and camel puppet, patterns, making 1083:191-192
    Three Kings Day puppet projects, patterns, scenes, story 1083:191-192
PUERTO RICO—FOLKLORE
    "Little Cockroach Martina" flannel board story, patterns, making 1603:95-102
PUERTO RICO—GAMES
    Big flower game 615:21-22
    Cat and the mouse game 602:118
    Colored ribbons game 602:120; 615:17-18
    Give me a light game 602:119-120
    Jump over the little board game 615:11-12
    Matatiru-tiru-la musical game 1116:60
    Onions for Mother game 602:117-118; 615:15-16
    Rice with milk game 615:9-10

    Rumble to the bottom musical game 1116:34
    Somebody game 615:27-28
    Stick game 602:119
    Stones game 602:120-121
    Stones game, how to play 1494:61-62
    There's fire over here game 615:26
    Two by two game 615:7-8
    Viper of the sea game 615:29-30
    You fib game 615:25; 697:41
    Your sewing machine game 615:23-24
PUERTO RICO—HANDICRAFTS
    Gourd bowls, papier-mache paints, making 1338:43-44
PUERTO RICO—LULLABIES
    "El Coqui" 1607:13
PUERTO RICO—NEW YEAR'S EVE
    New Year's Eve celebration 665:8-10
PULASKI, COUNT KAZIMIERZ
    Pulaski Day; celebrate by saying Polish greeting 1199:235
PUMPKINS
    History of pumpkins 219:11-21; 252:102
    How to grow, harvest, decorate and save seeds 1335:2-12
    Large size patterns and carving instructions for over 30 pumpkin faces 1363:1-107
    Pumpkin growing contest, how to do 310:101
    Pumpkin stories, songs, art activities, games, recipes 1135:11-13
    Pumpkins, activities, art, science, songs, recipes 911:190-195
    Seeds, plant pumpkin seeds, how to do 435:33
PUMPKINS—COOKERY. See also **HALLOWEEN—COOKERY**
    Fried pumpkin flowers, recipe 1335:38-39
    Maple pumpkin cookies, recipe 1335:52-53
    Pumpkin bread, recipe 1335:56
    Pumpkin butter, recipe 1335:57
    Pumpkin pie, recipe 1335:44-45
    Pumpkin rolls, recipe 1335:46-48
    Pumpkin seeds, roasted and fried, recipes 1335:54
    Pumpkin snack chips, recipe 1335:42
    Pumpkin soup, recipe 1335:35; 1660:34
    Pumpkin waffles, recipe 1335:40
    Raisin-pumpkin cookies, recipe 1335:50-51
    Roasted pumpkin seeds, making 1453:78-79
    Seeds, fried pumpkin seeds, recipe 435:56
    Toasted pumpkin seeds, recipe 1660:34
PUMPKINS—FINGER PLAYS
    Fingerplays 1660:37
PUMPKINS—GAMES
    Pumpkin and Halloween games 435:46-53
PUMPKINS—HANDICRAFTS
    Pumpkin seed necklace, making 1335:22
    Tambourine from aluminum pie plates and pumpkin seeds, making 1698:22
    Totem pole, pumpkin, making 219:80-81
PUNK
    Punk theme birthday party, making 896:40-46
PUNK—COSTUMES
    Punk costume, making 1174:39
PUPPETS. See also **ITALY—PUPPET PARTY**
    Abraham Lincoln puppet, pattern, making 1006:31
    African Plains animal puppets, patterns, making 463:17-26
    American Indian puppet, making 483:26

215

Apple puppets, dried apple head puppets, making 1285:102-103

Australian Bush animal puppets, patterns, making 463:27-34

Bag head puppet from paper bag, pattern, making 1212:105-106

Bunraku Japanese puppets, making 143:128

Chinese puppet, making 483:26

Columbus puppet, making 754:153-158

Corn husk puppets, making 448:34

Cowboy puppets, clothespin, making 311:30

Crown for puppet, making 981:17

Crown pattern for basic puppet, making 1083:20

Cupid puppet, pattern, making 1006:29

Desert animal puppets, patterns, making 463:35-42

Easter Bunny puppet, making 183:36

Easter Bunny puppet, pattern, making 1006:38

Easter chick puppet, pattern, making 1006:39

Egyptian puppet, making 483:19

Endangered Species puppets, patterns, making 463:73-77

Father Time puppet, patterns, making 1006:28

Forest animal puppets, patterns, making 463:43-48

French Fry holder marching band puppet, making 907:56

French puppet, making 483:27

George Washington puppet, pattern, making 1006:30

Glove puppets, fabric, buttons, beads, making 1219:18-19

Goldilocks folded paper puppet, making 907:59

Granny, Red Riding Hood, puppet, fabric and felt, making 830:164-165

Grecian puppet, making 483:19

Greek Karagos puppet, making 856:104-109

Groundhog pop-up puppet, making 907:27

Guignol French puppet, making 143:45

Gypsy Rose pencil puppet, making 311:47

Hansel and Gretel puppets, paper, patterns, making 92:47-49

Hanukkah candle puppet, paper tube, making 907:22

Hanukkah candle puppets, toilet tissue tubes, making 1135:36

Herald push puppet, making 754:139-144

History of puppets 459:4-9; 756:9-16; 757:9-11

Hula dancer whisk broom puppet, making 907:47

Indian family peanut puppets, making 647:90-96

Indian man and woman puppets, patterns, making 1006:17-18

Japanese Bunraku puppet, cardboard, making 480:123

Japanese eggshell puppet, making 709:147-148

Japanese Festival cup puppets, making 557:14

Javanese puppet, making 483:27

Jungle animal puppets, patterns, making 463:49-56

Keystone Kop puppet, making 588:26-27

King and Queen puppets, felt, eggshells, making 26:88

King or Queen puppet, patterns, paper, making 1083:164-165

King puppet, making 754:208-213

Leprechaun puppet, making 754:72-97

Leprechaun puppets, pattern, making 1006:37

Lincoln puppet, making 754:33-40

Little Red Hen puppets, making 868:80-96

Little Red Riding Hood and wolf puppets, patterns, making 91:43-46

Little Red Riding Hood, felt and fabric puppet, making 830:160

Little Red Riding Hood, mother, grandmother, etc., patterns, making 91:47-50

Medieval puppet, making 483:18

Mickey Mouse puppet, making 250:unp

Neighborhood buildings and table top puppets, making 838:28-30

Neighborhood people table top puppets, making 838:31-34

New Year baby puppet, pattern, making 1006:27

Ocean animal puppets, patterns, making 463:57-63

Papier-mache head puppet, patterns, making 1212:114-118

Pecos Bill puppet, paper, patterns, making 92:21-22

Pilgrim man and woman puppets, patterns, making 1006:15-16

Pinocchio paper tube puppet, making 384:Nov24

Polar Regions animal puppets, patterns, making 463:65-71

Polichinelle French puppet, making 143:44

Prince and Princess puppets, yarn, making 770:16-17

Princess who could not cry puppets, making 868:32-48

Punch and Judy puppets, making 681:9

Punch and Judy puppets, paper, patterns, making 1422:18

Punch and Judy show 756:19-20

Punch and Toby puppets, making 159:20-22

Puppet, cereal box, making 1238:35-43

Queen, King, Rumpelstiltskin puppets, paper, patterns, making 92:36-39

Samurai Warrior puppets, paper and fabric, patterns, making 1027:105-113

Sicilian puppet, making 483:27

Stone Age puppet, making 483:18

Theater for glove puppets, box, fabric, trims, making 1219:19

Three Bears, Baby and Papa Bear puppets, patterns, making 91:56-58

Three Bears, Goldilocks and Mama Bear puppets, patterns, making 91:53-55

Three Billy Goats Gruff puppets, making 868:20-31

Tortoise and Hare puppets, paper, patterns, making 91:18-20

Troll puppet, felt, making 352:15

Troll puppet, paper, patterns, making 92:43-45

Turkish puppet, making 483:26

Uncle Sam hat pattern for basic puppet, making 1083:20

Uncle Sam puppet, making 448:23

Uncle Sam puppet, pattern, making 1006:45

Vietnamese water puppet show, how to make stage, puppets, rods 792:33-44

Wadded paper puppet, pattern, making 1212:110-112

Washington puppet, making 754:59-69

Winnie the Pooh pencil puppets, making 277:17-18

Wolf, Red Riding Hood, felt and fabric puppet, making 830:166-167

Woodchuck puppet, pattern, making 1014:96

Yahlmulka pattern for basic puppet, making 1083:20

PUPPETS—FINGER

Chicken Licken cardboard cut-out puppet, making 753:41

Chilean boy finger puppet, making 128:40

Christmas glove finger puppets, making 706:15

Christmas trees, making 735:71

Circus ponies, making 735:48

Clown puppet from blown egg, making 677:23

Clown puppets, making 735:43

Desperado puppet, fabric, pattern, making 573:45-48
Dreidels, making 735:68
Ducklings, five yellow ducklings, making 735:30
Easter egg finger puppets and rhymes, making 821:34
Easter eggs, making 735:58
Easter rabbits, making 735:57
Eskimo finger puppet, making 128:41
Family, mother, father, baby, felt, patterns, making
    1262:32-33
Fox and his travels, finger puppet, patterns, story, mak-
    ing 512:19-27
Goldilocks and the Three Bears, finger puppet, patterns,
    story, making 512:41-48
Groundhog finger puppet, making 1083:41
Gunniwolf, finger puppet, patterns, story, making
    512:49-53
Hannah, paper, making 53:77
Hansel and Gretel, finger puppet, patterns, story, making
    512:55-66
Henny Penny, finger puppet, patterns, story, making
    512:67-76
Indian, pattern, making 745:18
Jamaican girl finger puppet, making 128:41
Little Red Hen paper wrap around puppet, making
    753:34
Little Red Hen, finger puppet, patterns, story, making
    512:34
Little Red Riding Hood, finger puppet, patterns, story,
    making 512:83-88
Martians, egg carton, making 603:26-27
Mattathias, paper, making 53:77
May baskets, five May baskets, making 735:59
Nisse finger puppet, making 140:41
Peter and the Wolf, finger puppet, patterns, story, mak-
    ing 512:109-123
Peter Piper thumb and fist finger puppet, making 753:17
Pilgrim finger puppets, patterns, making 1083:134
Pilgrim, pattern, making 745:18
Pirate finger puppet from blown egg, making 677:21;
    677:23
Pirate Pete finger puppet, making 757:26-31; 757:26-31
Princess and the Pea glove puppet, making 753:55
Purim finger puppets, making 712:51-56
Scarecrow puppet, fabric, pattern, making 573:60-61
Shamrocks, making 735:56
Tale of the Turnip, finger puppet, patterns, story, mak-
    ing 512:125-129
Thanksgiving children, making 735:66
Theater, paper plate finger puppet theater, pattern, mak-
    ing 907:62,77
Troll puppet, fabric, pattern, making 573:58
Unicorn puppet, fabric, pattern, making 573:49-53
Valentine fairy goblins puppets, making 354:21
Valentine fairy puppets, making 354:20
Valentine finger puppets, paper, patterns, making 760:29
Valentine red finger puppets and rhymes, making
    821:42-43
Valentines, five Valentines, making 735:54

PUPPETS—FOLKLORE PLAYS
Anansi Finds a Fool 4:41-47
Blessing of the tree 4:37-40
Brer Fox and Sis Goose 4:48-51
How Rabbit Lost His Fine Bushy Tail 4:52-55
How the Spark of Fire Was Saved 4:69-73
Jack and the Northwest Wind 4:60-64

Johnny-cake, puppets and puppet play scripts, making
    1155:41-44
Lion and the Mouse, puppets and puppet play scripts,
    making 1155:31-33
Little Red Riding Hood, puppets and puppet play scripts,
    making 1155:52-57
Magic Sarangi 4:82-88
Maui Captures the Sun 4:33-36
Monkey and the Crocodile, puppets and puppet play
    scripts, making 1155:63-66
Nerrivik, Old Woman of the Sea 4:74-77
Red-Eyed Duck 4:65-68
Robbers 4:56-59
Spirit of the Willow Tree Saves Family Honor 4:89-92
Three Billy Goats Gruff, puppets and puppet play scripts,
    making 1155:58-62
Three Sillies, music given 4:21-32
Town Mouse and the Country Mouse, puppets and pup-
    pet play scripts, making 1155:34-40
Two Jack Tales 4:56-64
Walk Tall, Talk Tall, Davy Crockett 4:93-102
Why Man Must Harvest His Crops 4:78-81
Winter of the Blue Snow 4:103-107

PUPPETS—GLOVE
Italian glove puppets, making 626:64-66

PUPPETS—HAND
Cat's meow puppet, paper, making 1238:43-46
Clay head puppet, pattern, making 1212:112-114
Hawaiian Hula hand puppets, paper, making 909:64
Indian puppets, patterns, making 513:13-16
Irishmen and shamrocks puppets, patterns, making
    513:72-79
Jester, newspaper, making 1658:36
King, newspaper, making 1658:36-37
Mitt puppet, fabric, pattern, making 1212:108-110
Princess, newspaper, making 1658:36
Royal Court puppets, styrofoam ball, handkerchief, mak-
    ing 311:48-49
Stuffed head puppets, fabric, pattern, making 1212:120-
    123
Uncle Sam puppet, patterns, making 513:102-108
Valentine puppets, patterns, making 513:53-54

PUPPETS—HATS
Robin Hood Hat, making 949:120-121

PUPPETS—MOUTH
Gypsy puppet, fabric, pattern, making 573:117-126

PUPPETS—NURSERY RHYMES. *See* **NURSERY
    RHYMES—PUPPETS**

PUPPETS—PAPER BAG
Eagle paper bag puppet, patterns, making 1107:190-197
Easter Bunny, Mr. and Mrs., paper bags, patterns, mak-
    ing 940:27-28
Eskimo girl, paper bag, patterns, making 940:23
Gingerbread Man, old Man and Woman, paper bags, pat-
    terns, making 941:48-53
Goldilocks and the Three Bears, paper bags, patterns,
    making 941:43-46
Indian boy and girl, paper bags, patterns, making 941:38-
    39
Indian, paper bag, patterns, making 940:20
Kookaburra paper bag puppet, patterns, making 1107:94-
    104
Little Red Hen, paper bag, patterns, making 939:51
Little Red Riding Hood, paper bags, patterns, making
    940:40

M.L. King, Jr. puppet, stuffed paper bag, basic body pattern, making 1083:28-30

Pilgrim boy and girl, paper bags, patterns, making 941:40-41

Queen of Hearts paper bag puppet, making 907:28

Queen paper bag puppet, patterns, making 1107:110-117

Scarecrow paper bag puppet, patterns, making 1107:12-20

Thanksgiving paper bag puppets, making 401:18-20

Three Little Pigs, and Wolf, paper bags, patterns, making 941:55-58

Totem pole puppet from paper bag, making 678:16-17

Troll, paper bag, patterns, making 940:49

Uncle Sam paper bag puppet, patterns, making 1107:177-182

Unicorn paper bag puppet, patterns, making 1107:214-222

Viking paper bag puppet, patterns, making 1107:118-125

Yak paper bag puppet, patterns, making 1107:140-146

PUPPETS—PLAYS

Androcles and the Lion, puppets, sets, props, sound effects making 1158:83-92

Three Sillies, music given 4:21-32

Walk Tall, Talk Tall, Davy Crockett 4:93-102

PUPPETS—ROD

Dragon rod puppet, making 757:70-82

Lincoln rod puppet, paper, making 384:Feb 12

Princess rod puppet, making 757:83-100

PUPPETS—SHADOW

American Indian jointed shadow puppet, making 757:112-119

Bali shadow puppets, patterns, making 1027:89-94

Chinese shadow show, making 143:47

Circus shadow, posterboard, pattern, making 907:14, 66-67

Colored puppets, cellophane and cardboard, making 1177:20-21

Hand shadows with props, how to make 1177:8-12

Hand shadows, how to make 1177:4-7

Jointed colored puppets, cellophane, cardboard, patterns, making 1177:22-23

Jointed puppets, cardboard, patterns, making 1177:16-19

Shadow puppets, simple, cardboard, making 1177:14-15

Shadow theater, cardboard box, old picture frame, making 1177:12

PUPPETS—SOCK

Indians, Samoset and Chief Massasoit, sock puppets, making 353:19

Martian puppet, old sock, making 325:37-40

Pilgrim men, Miles Standish and John Hopkins, sock puppets, making 353:18

Pilgrim women, Priscilla and Mary, sock puppets, making 353:17

PUPPETS—SPACEMEN

Astronaut boy or girl paper bag puppet, patterns, making 1107:154-157

Spaceman puppet, sponge, making 311:31

PUPPETS—SPOON

Hansel, Gretel, Witch wooden spoon puppets, making 238:24-35

King wooden spoon puppet, making 238:39-42

Pop singer wooden spoon puppet, making 238:48-53

Queen wooden spoon puppet, making 238:43-46

PUPPETS—STAGES

Elizabethan stage, cardboard, making 159:6-10

Palace for puppets, cardboard, making 938:109-110

Punch and Judy theatre book, making 159:18-20

Stage from sheet and box, making 1212:123

PUPPETS—STICK

Clown stick puppet, making 588:22-23; 629:67-68

Goldilocks stick puppet, pattern, making 1088:24

Johnny Cake stick puppet, pattern, making 1155:211

Lincoln tongue depressor puppet, making 907:29

Pirate, Captain Plunder Bones puppet, making 681:24-25; 681:24-25

Polish stick puppet toy, making 1027:46-52

Princess puppet, making 681:26-27

Stick puppet from cardboard and paper, patterns, making 1212:105

The Mitten stick puppets, patterns, making 480:85

Three Bears stick puppets, patterns, making 1088:23-24

PUPPETS—STRING

Prince, paper wads, making 75:58-61

Snow White puppet, milk carton, making 679:unp

PURIM

Feast of Purim celebration 566:24-25

Finger plays, recipes, games, making 944:78-79

Jewish Feast of Lots, activities and projects for classrooms 1393:157-158

Meaning of Purim 711:63; 712:48-50

Purim celebration, making 134:45

Purim, celebration 133:114

PURIM—COOKERY

Adloyada punch, recipe 116:72

Baklava, recipe 1685:57

Carrot ginger candy, recipe 711:66-67

Chickpeas, recipe 1685:56

Chocolate fudge, recipe 116:71

Fish chowder, recipe 279:113

Halvah, recipe 1112:86-87

Haman's hats, recipe 1032:197

Hamantaschen cookies, recipe 1289:89

Hamantaschen pastries, recipe 363:54-56; 1157:unp; 1199:58-59; 1495:104

Hamantaschen Purim cakes, recipe 667:229-230

Hamantaschen, cookies, recipe 1427:189; 1691:155-156

Hamantashen, Haman's whatsis, recipe 116:66-67

Hamantashen, recipe 54:204; 64:13; 81:37; 279:110; 402:19-21; 543:94-95; 711:64-65; 712:58-59; 1079:unp; 1112:84-86; 1313:56; 1451:93; 1685:54

Harmless Haman, making 81:37

Hummus, recipe 1112:83-84

King Ahasuerus's crown, recipe 116:64-65

Kooky cake, recipe 116:68-69

Kooky Purim centerpiece, recipe 116:70

Marshmallow cookies, no bake, recipe 1112:87-88

Oznej Haman, recipe 1313:57

Poppy seed candy, recipe 712:57-58

Poppy seed cookies, recipe 711:68; 1305:53

Potato puffs, recipe 279:112

Purim hero, recipe 81:36

Queen Esther and Haman gingerbread cookies, making 543:96-99

Salad bar, recipe 81:36

Shirley Temple's drink, recipe 81:37

Stewed prunes, recipe 1685:56

Sweet and sour meatballs, recipe 279:111

PURIM—COSTUMES

Costume, flat paper, making 82:48
Crowns, headresses, hats, making 1691:152-153
Haman costume, making 272:56-58
Haman, fabric, making 1691:152
King Ahasuerus, fabric, cardboard, making 1691:151
Mordecai, cardboard box, fabric, making 1691:151
Queen Esther and Haman costumes, making 543:96-99
Queen Esther costume, making 272:55-56
Queen Esther, cardboard, crepe paper, making 1691:150-151
Robe, quick and easy, making 82:44
Robe, royal, making 82:45

PURIM—DANCES

Dances for Purim 542:50-57
Purim dance, how to do 279:105
Purim's here again dance, how to do 279:103

PURIM—DECORATIONS

Balloon face, making 81:35
Blown egg decoration, making 677:20
Box grogger, making 279:98
Circle of friends, making 81:35
Funny face bean bags, making 81:40
Grogger, noisy, making 80:49
Haman plate rattle, making 80:48
Holiday creative drawing activities 1337:30-33
Hoot Haman, making 82:42
Horse for morde car, making 80:53
King's Purim crown, making 279:101
Megillah scroll, paper, markers, patterns for characters, making 1654:126
Noah's Ark, making 279:96
Noisemaker, giant, making 279:97
Paper doll invitation, making 81:34
Purim grogger noisemaker, making 363:61
Purim mask, making 279:95
Purim paraders, making 80:52
Queen Esther's crown, making 279:100
Rattle from baking powder can, making 891:43-47
Shalach Manot basket, making 80:54; 81:35
Wax print, making 279:99

PURIM—FINGER PLAYS

My hat is has three corners finger play 1654:125

PURIM—GAMES

Can you listen? game 279:107
Give Haman a toothache game 81:39
Haman on the gallows game 279:108
Hamantashen game 279:107
Hit Haman game, making 543:93
Mumble jumble game, making 543:91
Pass the hat game 81:38
Pin the crown on Esther game 279:109
Pin the tail on Haman's horse game 279:109
Purim parade game 78:39
Put the crown on Queen Esther game 81:38
Who am I? game 279:108

PURIM—HANDICRAFTS

Greggor, how to make 1313:56
Grogger from matchbox, making 448:46
Groggers, making 543:92
Masks for Megillah's tale play, making 543:100-101
Megillah, paper, how to make 1313:55
Noisemakers, making 1691:154-155
Purim balloons, making 543:90

Purim treats basket, making 82:47
Queen Esther's crown, making 543:99
Shalach manot basket, making 82:46

PURIM—JEWELRY

Queen Esther jewelry, making 82:43

PURIM—MASKS

Mask, paper plate, making 80:51

PURIM—MUSICAL INSTRUMENTS

Gragger noisemaker, box, dried beans, making 1310:112
Graggers, noisemakers, paper plates, tin cans, making 1179:76-77

PURIM—PARTIES

Purim costume party, invitations, decorations, menus and games, making 2:44-52

PURIM—PUPPETS

Festival of Lots Purim puppets, making 298:126-127
Glove puppets of Esther, Mordecai, Ahazuerus, felt, patterns, making 1466:6-7
Mask for Queen Esther puppet, making 754:101-108
Puppet show, how to make puppets and present 1179:77-79
Puppet, paper plate, making 80:50
Purim finger puppets, making 712:51-56
Purim puppets, paper tubes, colored paper, patterns, making 1427:181-182
Queen Esther Saves Her People puppet play 754:98-101

PURIM—SONGS

Story of Esther, felt board song, making 1654:125

PURITANS. *See also* UNITED STATES—HISTORY—COLONIAL PERIOD—PURITANS

PURITANS—COSTUMES

Puritan costume, girl, cl655, making 368:31-38

PURITANS—DOLLS

Puritan woman of the seventeenth century, making 59:28-30

PUSS IN BOOTS

Marquis of Carabas's rabbit, recipe, making 569:16-17
Puss in Boots toy, cardboard and felt, making 346:18-19

PUZZLES

Advent jigsaw puzzle, making 554:72-73
American Jigsaw puzzle, making 719:48
Heart and clevis puzzle, making 773:84-85; 773:84-85
Ox-yoke puzzle, making 118:266-267; 773:82-83
Photograph puzzle, picture, cardboard, making 1196:74
Pizza puzzles, making 163:71
Pyramid puzzle, making 773:86-87
Valentine puzzle, making 648:20
Victorian puzzle, how to make 1074:272

PYGMIES. *See also* RAIN FOREST

PYGMIES—GAMES

Catching stars game 956:9
Gathering stars chasing game, how to play 1498:33-34

PYRAMIDS

Great Pyramid of Cheops, House of the Dead Pyramid, how to make 699:6-8
Literature, activities, crafts, games 1390:56-83
Pyramid of straws, glue and thread, making 828:17-18
Pyramid, from blown egg, making 677:18
Pyramids built, using ramps to move materials, making 1719:5-6
Pyramids from Egypt, paper and straws, making 1094:15

PYSANKY EGGS

Computer project: Pysanky eggs, draw and decorate 1218:56-59

Q

QATAR. *See also* **ARABIAN PENINSULA**
QATAR—COOKERY
    Almond biscuits, recipe 1165:75
    Date bars, recipe 1165:73
    Fruit balls, recipe 1165:76
    Hoomis, chick pea spread, recipe 1165:72
    Limonada, lemonade, recipe 1165:72-73
    Mjeddrah, rice with lentils, recipe 1165:74
    Shourba bilsen, thick lentil soup, recipe 1165:72
    Stuffed dates, figs, prunes, recipe 1165:75
    Tahineh or tahini, sesame seed paste, recipe 1165:74
QUAKERS—CLOTHING. *See* **UNITED STATES—HIS-**
    TORY—COLONIAL PERIOD—QUAKERS—
    CLOTHING
QUAKERS—DOLLS
    Quaker clothespin doll, making 626:44-46
QUAKERS—GAMES
    Road to freedom board game, how to make and play
    1297:48-49
QUEEN NEFERTITI—COSTUME
    Felt necklace, making 287:42-43
    Gold lame neckpiece, making 287:43-45
    Red head piece, making 287:41-42
QUEENS
    Crown, queen crown, making, 670:75
    Paper plate crown, making 231:38
    Queen crown, paper, patterns, making 91:28
    Queen mask, making 840:5-6
    Scepter, dowel and styrofoam ball, making 231:38
QUEENS—COSTUMES
    Queen costume, fabric, making 1379:41
    Queen Guinevere costume, fabric, pattern, making
    367:40-44
    Regal robes, fabric, fur, ribbon, making 1671:28-29
QUEENS—PUPPETS
    Fat old Queen wooden spoon puppet, making 238:43-46

    Puppet; paper bag Queen puppet, patterns, making
    1107:110-117
QUILLING
    How to do and how to color 75:16-19
    Paper quilling, how to do 877:13-15
    Paper quilling, making 172:109
QUILLS
    Quills, pens, feathers, making 1320:60-61
QUILTING. *See also* **PATCHWORK**
    Appliqué pictures, making 15:38-40
    Applique, fabric, thread, how to do 1181:50-51
    Apron, patchwork, making 706:89-90
    Bib apron, patchwork, making 706:90-91
    Collector's quilt, making 15:34-36
    Colonial patchwork quilt square or pot holder, making
    673:85-114; 673:85-114
    Computer project: design a crazy quilt pattern 1218:20-23
    Crib quilt, patchwork, making 673:115-136
    Doll's bed cover, how to make and quilt 598:44-48
    Eyeglass case, fabric, patterns, making 1320:44-45
    Fabric quilting, making 499:80
    Patchwork pillow, fabric, making 938:92
    Patchwork pillow, making 598:39-43
    Patchwork pockets, making 15:32-33
    Patchwork quilt mural, paper, making 1092:115-116
    Patchwork quilt, making 688:11
    Patchwork square pattern, fabric, patterns, how to do
    1181:46-49
    Pencil case, quilted, making 1062:28-29
    Pillow, patchwork, making 706:89
    Pot holders, appliqué and quilted, making 706:84-85
    Quilt, fabric, how to make 916:14-17
    Quilt, making 706:86
    Simple patchwork, making 877:58-60
    Wall hanging from fabric scraps glued down, making 231:39
    Yo-yo quilting, making 70:99

R

RABBITS

Bunny, pop-up, paper, pattern 1210:18-19

Songs, finger plays, stories, games, rhythms 1200:96-99

RABBITS—PARTIES

Rabbit cake, recipe 1185:60-61

RACERS. *See also* **SKATEBOARDS**

RACERS

Pedal-powered raceabout, wooden, making 481:68-78

Soapbox racer, wooden, making 481:59-67

Sport roadster, wooden, making 481:41-49

Two-man sidewalk handcar, wooden, making 48:79-87

RACES

Marathon for everyone, how to do 310:56-57

RACES—COOKERY

Race track cake, recipe 449:68

RACING CARS

Drag racer model, aluminum cans, straws, paper tubes, making 1346:20-21

RACING CARS—GAMES

Road-race game, making 176:26-29

RAGS

Placemats from rags, braided, making 1262:30-31

RAILROADS. *See also* **UNITED STATES—RAILROADS—HISTORY**

Casey Jones birthday celebration; art, music, foods, games, activities 1104:70-73

Death of the Iron Horse; physical and human geography activities 1458:84-87

RAIN

Rain May Day 1114:64-65

RAIN—FESTIVALS

African rain-making festivals 419:89-90

RAIN—FINGER PLAYS

Finger plays and rhymes 1583:107-111

RAIN FOREST

Bird of Paradise, crepe paper, crayons, making 1488:8-9

Creepy crawlies, worms, snakes, others, clay, paints, making 1488:18-19

Feather headdress, corrugated paper, straws, making 1488:12-13

Flying toucan bird model, balloon, papier-mache, making 1488:26-27

Forest Festival people, life-size flat paper models, making 1488:24-25

Huts on stilts, sticks, dowels, clay, making 1488:20-21

Jaguar disguise, paper bag, felt, paints, making 1488:16-17

Jungle jewelry, pasta, seeds, ribbons, paints, making 1488:14-15

Miniature tropical garden in plastic bottle, making 1488:22-23

Poster of rain forest animals and trees, patterns, making 1199:93-97

Rain forest tropical animals, decorated, plants, display, making 1484:20-21

Rain forest village with huts, trees, vines, fruits, making 1488:6-7

Rain forest, miniature rain forest in wide mouth jar, making 1378:209-211

Rain forest, tropical, in Brazil, teaching units 1378:198-275

Tropical plants, oranges, lemons, pineapples, how to grow 1488:10-11

RAIN FOREST—DOLLS

Amazonian doll, making 182:74-77

RAIN FOREST—GEOGRAPHY

Where the Forest Meets the Sea; physical and human geography activities 1458:24-27

RALEIGH, SIR WALTER

Costume, making 213:92-94

RALLY DAY

History of Rally Day 475:144

REBUS

Rebus dictionary 118:192

RECYCLING. *See also* **NEWSPAPERS—HANDICRAFTS; PAPERMAKING**

Animals and fish, stuffed, waste paper, making 1732:20-21

Baskets bound from rags, making 15:84-86

Baskets crocheted from rags, making 15:82-83

De-inker, lifts magazine or newspaper picture, making 1196:62-63

Earth-friendly shopping bag, how to make 1301:76-77

Film-can trolls, making 978:15

Furoshiki to use instead of paper bag, fabric, making 15:87

Handmade paper from waste paper, making 1732:24-25

Paper portraits, three-dimensional, waste paper, making 1732:11

Waste paper, from trash bags, making 1732:14-15

Things to make and do from throw aways with children 1301:25-32

RECYCLING—BOTTLES

Christmas luminaries from glass bottles, making 764:61-62

Sunbonnet Sue or pioneer lady from glass bottle, making 764:53-55

Three Kings from glass bottles, making 764:58-60

RED CROSS

Clara Barton birthday celebration; art, music, foods, games, activities 1104:34-37

REINDEER

Reindeer, activities, art, science, songs, recipes 911:202-205

Reindeer, pop-up, paper, pattern 1210:38-39

RELIGION—ANCIENT EMPIRE

Prayers and chants, making 65:59-64

Ziggurat, making 65:54-58

RELIGION—BEADS

Prayer beads information 301:51-62

RELIGIOUS CLOTHING

Chausuble, making 870:113-115

Cope and mitre, making 870:115-117

Square cap, biretta and skull cap, making 870:117-119

REPUBLIC OF SOUTH AFRICA—JEWELRY

Ndebele bead bracelet, beads, wire, making 1632:28-32

REVERE, PAUL

Paul Revere candleholder, making 719:24-25

REY, H. A.

"Curious George and the Pizza," pizza, recipe 1216:26

"Curious George Takes a Job," spaghetti, recipe 1216:24

RHINOCEROS

Rhino, pop-up, paper, pattern 1210:46-48

RHODE ISLAND—COOKERY

Cranberry-orange punch, recipe 654:137

Johnny cakes, recipe 654:136

Rhode Island Johnny cake, recipe 594:34-35; 1297:55

RHODE ISLAND—WANTON-LYMAN-HAZARD HOUSE—COOKERY
Cobblestones, recipe 57:82
Plum cake, recipe 57:82
Seafood casserole, recipe 57:83
RHODESIA—CHRISTMAS
Christmas celebration 601:37-38
RHODESIA—GAMES
Poison game 602:34-35
Thumping sticks game 602:35-36
RICE, EVE
"Benny Bakes a Cake," chocolate birthday cake, recipe 1216:57
"Oh, Lewis," hot tea, chocolate cake, recipe 1216:60
RICE
Chopsticks, how to eat rice with 1637:19
Colored rice pictures, making 461:44
Different flavors added to bowls of rice, how to do and taste 1637:20-21
Grow your own rice plants 1637:10-11
Orange rice, recipe 1655:27
Rice, carrot and cheese loaf, recipe 1637:22-23
Rice, how to boil 1637:6-7
Rice, recipe 1068:unp
Wild rice, history of 410:92-94
RICE—FESTIVALS
Japanese rice growing rituals 419:104-106
Rice growing festivals 419:92-97
RIVERA, DIEGO
Fresco painting, making 1455:26
RIVERBOATS
Decorating tin can in the canal boat tradition, patterns, making 1051:30-34
ROADS
Road system from masking tape, making 24:24-25
ROBERTSON, ANNA MARY—BIRTHDAY
Grandma Moses birthday; celebrate by doing primitive painting 1199:201
ROBIN HOOD—COSTUMES
Costume, making 213:66-69
Friar Tuck costume, making 213:70-71
Friar Tuck costume, variety of old clothes, making 1656:137-140
King John costume, making 213:69
King Richard costume, making 213:72-74
Maid Marian costume, making 213:72
Robin Hood costume, variety of old clothes, making 1656:133-136
ROBINS—FOLKLORE
Calvary Robin, traditional tale from Ireland 139:95
ROBINSON CRUSOE
Descriptions and pictures of island 29:Chapter 7
Robinson Crusoe birthday party, making 896:12-18
ROBINSON CRUSOE—COOKERY
Crusoe's South Seas Smoothy, recipe 365:24
Robinson Crusoe's homemade oven bread, recipe 570:81-83
ROBINSON, JACKIE—BIRTHDAY
Birthday celebration; art, music, foods, games, activities 1104:50-53
ROBOTS
Pop-up noisy robot, making 1388:76-78
Retro-rocket robot model, boxes, foil, patterns, making 1311:82-83

Space robot, blown egg robot, pattern, making 1311:120-121
ROBOTS—COSTUMES
Robot costume, cardboard boxes, patterns, making 1283:74-77
Robot costume, fabric, making 1379:22
ROBOTS—MASKS
Robot mask, paper, decorations, making 1618:44-48
ROCKETS
Space rocket model, plastic bottle, egg carton, straw, making 1346:10-11
ROCKETS—PARTIES
Rocket cake, recipe 1185:64-65
ROCKS
Pebble painting, how to do 1258:16-17
Rocks, activities, art, science, songs, recipes 911:206-209
ROCKWELL, HARLOW
"My Kitchen," soup and sandwich, recipe 1216:75
RODEOS—COSTUMES
Cowboy costume, fabric, face makeup given, making 957:20-25
RODEOS—JAPAN
Namaoi Matsuri and Yabusame, Japanese Rodeo 107:22-27
ROGERS, WILLIAM PENN—BIRTHDAY
Celebrate by making rope lassos 1199:254-255
ROLLER SKATES
History of roller skates 119:179-183
ROMANIA—COOKERY
Beans with olive oil, recipe 661:247-248
Beef sausages, grilled, recipe 661:247
Ciorba of veal soup, recipe 1596:119
Cornmeal mush with cheese, recipe 661:248-249
Mammaliga, cornmeal porridge bread, recipe 1165:96
Meat-eating habits in Romania 662:68-70
Nut pastries, recipe 661:249-250
Sour soup with meatballs, recipe 661:246
Tokana, shepherd's stew, recipe 1165:97
ROMANIA—EASTER—COOKERY
Mamaliga de aur (Romanian Bread of Gold), recipe 1666:81
Mamaliga umpluta (cornmeal-mushroom balls), recipe 1666:81-82
Vegetable lentil soup, recipe 1666:81
ROMANIA—FESTIVALS
Simbra Oilor Festival celebration 661:243
Young Girl Fair Festival celebration 661:244
ROMANIA—FOLKLORE
Little Rabbit and Tiny Bug with Golden Wings flannel board patterns, make 910:29,68
ROMANIA—GAMES
Cat and mouse game, how to play 1355:25
ROME, ANCIENT
Carthage and Rome, history, stories, maps, puzzles, activities, projects 1041:58-84
Egypt versus Rome, history, stories, maps, puzzles, activities, projects 1041:124-152
Gaul versus Rome, history, stories, maps, puzzles, activities, projects 1041:85-113
Greece versus Rome, history, stories, maps, puzzles, activities, projects 1041:30-57
ROME, ANCIENT—ARCHITECTURE
Aqueduct arch, how to draw 1549:10
Arch, how to build 701:12-14

Colosseum, how to draw 1549:16-17

ROME, ANCIENT—ARMOR

Armor and chain mail, scale, making 701:8-10

Gladiator's helmet, how to draw 1549:21

ROME, ANCIENT—ARMY

Roman standard and wreath, cardboard, cloth, dowel, making 1183:11

ROME, ANCIENT—CAESAR

Caesar costume, making 213:56-58

ROME, ANCIENT—CHARIOTEERS

Charioteer, cart and horse, how to draw 1549:18-19

ROME, ANCIENT—CHRISTMAS—HANDICRAFTS

Ancient Roman wreath, clothes hanger, fabrics, making 1575:22-23

ROME, ANCIENT—CLOTHING

Palla, simple shawl, bed sheet, string, making 1184:23

Stephane, diadem, making 870:120-121

Stola, simple dress, bed sheets, string, cardboard, brooches, making 1184:22

Toga, how to draw 1549:8

Toga, patterns, making 1041:24

Tunic, large T-shirt, bed sheets, string, making 1184:23

Tunics, togas and pallas, making 701:15-16

ROME, ANCIENT—CODES

Julius Caesar's cipher, how to use 1611:9-11

ROME, ANCIENT—COINS

Coins of the realm, making 701:25-26

ROME, ANCIENT—COOKERY

Celery and leeks in honey sauce, recipe 1625:26

Chicken boiled with spices, recipe 1625:27

Dates with almonds, recipe 1625:28

Foods and cookery in Ancient Rome 667:93-113

History of cookery in 88:49-55

Nutty omelet, recipe 1625:28

Pumpkin and apple dessert dish, recipe 1625:27

Roman custard, recipe 1625:29

Roman dinner set up, menu, recipes, making 1041:144-147

Roman toast, recipe 1625:28

Sesame honey candy, recipe 1122:29

Sweet wine cakes, recipe 1625:29

ROME, ANCIENT—COSTUMES

Aiquillettes, making 870:124-126

Armlets, making 870:121-123

Buskins, making 870:123-124

ROME, ANCIENT—EMPERORS

Augustus, first Emperor of Rome portrait, how to draw 1549:7

Emperor wreath, headband, making 1671:16

ROME, ANCIENT—FESTIVALS

Apples for Pomona Festival 504:46

Festivals of the Roman people celebrations 667:104-105

Lemuria celebration 1041:78

Saturnalia Harvest Festival celebration 566:11

Terminalia celebration 1041:76-77

ROME, ANCIENT—FESTIVALS—COOKERY

Saturnalia Festival upside-down pineapple cake, recipe 1403:14

ROME, ANCIENT—FORTIFICATION

Assault tower, making 701:27-31

Battering ram, making 701:17-19

Drawbridge, making 701:30-31

Roman fort, making 212:4-21

ROME, ANCIENT—GAMES

Game of robbers, Ludus Latruneulorum 701:20-21

Hopscotch game 956:30-32

King Caesar tag game, how to play 1498:13-14

Palm ball game 956:51

ROME, ANCIENT—GENERALS

Constantino the Great portrait, how to draw 1549:28

ROME, ANCIENT—HAIR

Hairstyles of wealthy Roman women, how to draw 1549:25

ROME, ANCIENT—HALLOWEEN—DECORATIONS

Balancing apple, making 709:32-33

ROME, ANCIENT—HANDICRAFTS

Laurel wreath for games or races winner, paper, pipe cleaners, paints, making 1184:15

Pugillares notebooks, wax paper, brown yarn, making 1332:109-112

ROME, ANCIENT—MARK ANTONY

Mark Antony costume, making 213:56

ROME, ANCIENT—MASKS

Masks for Roman theater plays, papier-mache on cardboard, paints, making 1184:17

ROME, ANCIENT—MOSAICS

Mosaic designs, colored paper, making 1326:13

Mosaic tile, how to draw 1549:27

Mosaics, making 701:22-24

Rabbit mosaic, making 105:61-63

Roman art mosaic, eggshells, poster paints, making 1184:13

ROME, ANCIENT—NATURE FESTIVALS

Ceres Festival information 419:36-37

Floralia Festival information 419:7

Roman Nature Festivals information 419:35-38

Saturnalia Festival information 419:37-38

ROME, ANCIENT—NEW YEAR'S DAY

Janus pin, making 701:6-7

ROME, ANCIENT—NUMBERS

Roman numeral tablet, making 701:11

ROME, ANCIENT—SOLDIERS

Roman soldier costume, making 870:26-27

ROME, ANCIENT—STATUES

Statue of a Roman, wire, wallpaper paste, fabric strips, poster paints, making 1184:27

ROME, ANCIENT—THANKSGIVING

History of Thanksgiving in ancient Rome 659:19-21

ROME, ANCIENT—TOGAS

Roman toga, towels, making 1671:23

Toga, bed sheet, making 1184:23

ROME, ANCIENT—VILLAS

Roman villa, boxes, cardboard, paints, making 1184:8

ROME, ANCIENT—WARFARE

Julius Caesar's siegeworks at Alesia, boxes, making 1041:104-106

Marching camp, boxes, making 1041:47-50

ROME, ANCIENT—WRITING

Wax writing table, wax, tray, making 1326:25

Writing tablet, cardboard box, clay, poster paints, making 1184:21

ROOSEVELT, ELEANOR—BIRTHDAY

Celebrate by making a declaration of human rights 1199:234

ROPE

Coiled mats and containers, rope, glue, making 1262:36-37

Rope critters, fiber art, making 1615:8-9

Rope pads and mats; animals hot pads, making 182:52-57

Rope work, making mat and Jacob's latter, how to do
825:48-53
Rope, making 118:53
Valuable rope 118:52
ROSEMALING. *See also* **NORWAY—HANDICRAFTS**
Norwegian rosemaling, making 795:69
Utensils decorated with rosemaling, making 298:188-189
ROSH CHODESH—PARTIES
Invitations, decorations, menus, games, making 2:85-92
New Moon party; invitations, decorations, menus, games,
making 2:85-92
ROSH HASHANAH
Celebration of Rosh Hashanah 133:118; 505:46-47;
566:24
History of 496:19-21; 709:43
Meaning of 711:29; 712:18-19
ROSH HASHANAH—COOKERY
Apple and honey treat, recipe 1662:148
Apple cup and honey, recipe 543:28
Apple kuchen, Hungarian plum cake, recipe 711:34-35
Apples and honey, recipe 712:19; 1111:97
Baked apples, recipe 1112:29-30
Brisket of beef, recipe 1685:15
Carrot coins, recipe 1032:217
Carrot tsimmes, recipe 279:49; 1112:27-28; 1691:43
Challah bread, recipe 363:57; 1686:last
Chunky honey carrots, recipe 116:17
Conglomerates, recipe 116:18
Frosted grapes and honeyed apples, recipes 402:53-56
Hallah braided bread, recipe 1289:17
Hallah bread, recipe 264:60-62
Halva farina cake, recipe 1691:42
Halva, recipe 1691:42
Holiday fruit pizza, recipe 1662:150
Honey baked apples, recipe 264:59-60
Honey cake, recipe 116:19; 264:62-64; 402:53-56;
711:32-33; 1289:16, 173; 1685:17; 1691:43-44
Honey fruit cake, recipe 543:29
Invitations, decorations, menus, and games, making 2:9-
14
Kayek biscuits, recipe 264:65
New moon cookies, recipe 81:10
No-bake cookies, recipe 279:51
Orange chicken, recipe 1112:28-29
Parve honey cake, recipe 1111:254
Pear strudel, recipe 1112:31-32
Pescado al la greca, recipe 116:14
Pineapple tea cooler, recipe 81:10
Popcorn taiglach, recipe 939:111-112
Potato knishes, recipe 116:16-17
Raisin cake, recipe 1691:44
Raisin challah bread, recipe 1685:12-13
Round hallah, recipe 116:4-6
Rugelach, dough cake with filling, recipe 1685:16
Shofar on the mountain centerpiece, recipe 116:22
Sponge cake, recipe 279:50
String beans fountainbleau, recipe 279:48
Surprise sandwich, recipe 81:10
Sweet potato pudding, recipe 1685:14
Taiglach, honey candy, recipe 116:20-21; 1451:90
Tsimmes, recipe 711:30
Tzimmes carrots, recipe 264:64
Yam and carrot tzimmes, recipe 116:15
ROSH HASHANAH—DANCES
Rosh Hashanah dance, how to do 279:42

ROSH HASHANAH—DECORATIONS
Calendar invitation, making, 81:8
Calendar, making 1691:39-41
Challah cover, round, making 80:16
Greeting card, cardboard, gold markers, making 1626:24
Holiday collage, cardboard, making 264:72-73
Holiday creative drawing activities 1337:10-15
Holiday table centerpiece, making 80:17
Magen David, Star of David, popsicle sticks, making
279:38
Mizrah, making 264:75-77
New Year card, making 80:14; 1691:41; 543:22-23
New Year cards, spatter, making 279:35
New Year greeting card holder, making 279:33
New Year mosaic, making 279:36-37
Pop-up Rosh Hashanah card, making 1387:42-43
Puzzle New Year cards, making 279:34
Shanah Tovah card, making 709:44; 712:20-21
Shofar place cards, making 81:9
Shofar to sew, making 80:15
Shofar, making 648:34-35
Star mobile, paper, making 81:9
Wheel of time, Hebrew months, paper plate, making
81:12
Yom Tov fruit or nut bowl, papier-mache, making
279:32
ROSH HASHANAH—GAMES
Apple relay game 81:11
Beanbag playmates game 279:45
Fight the candles game, making 279:46
Jewish symbol concentration game, making 279:44
New Year bingo game, making 543:24
Number scramble game 81:11
Traveling through Israel game 279:46
Word games 264:79-84
ROSH HASHANAH—HANDICRAFTS
Hallah cover, fabric, making 264:71-72
Jewish calendar, making 264:68-71
Placemats, making 543:26-27
Pomander balls, making 264:74
Pop-up greeting card, paper, making 1662:149
Trivet wooden, making 543:25
ROSH HASHANAH—PARTIES
Invitations, decorations, menus and games, making 2:9-
14
ROSH HASHANAH—PUPPETS
Puppet projects, patterns, scenes, story starters, feature
story 1083:111-113
ROSH HASHANAH—YOM KIPPUR
Picture album, hanging, making 82:16
Raisins, make your own, making 82:17
Shanah Tovah mailbag, making 82:14
Shanah Tovah mosaic, making 82:15
Singing Yom Tov Chazan, making 81:18
ROSH HODESH
Information about Rosh Hodesh 712:13
ROSH HODESH—COOKERY
Moon crescent cookies, recipe 1691:8
ROSS, BETSY
1777 Flag, making 272:82-83
Birthday celebration; art, music, foods, games, activities
1104:38-41
ROSS, BETSY—COSTUMES
Betsy Ross costume, making 272:81-83
Flag costume, making 272:84-85

ROUND-UPS—PARTIES

Western round-up party, menu and recipes, how to plan and give 86:200-207; 86:237

RUBBINGS

City rubbings, making 310:287

Colonial gravestone rubbings, making 831:135

Gravestone rubbing, making 118:224

Historic rubbings, making 70:61

Horse brass rubbings, making 806:42-43

Manhole cover rubbings, making 428:27-29; 806:55-56

Textures and impressions, paper, crayons, making 1617:34-35

Tombstone rubbing, making 806:40-41; 806:40-41

Wax rubbings using crayons, how to do 1261:30-31

RUDOLPH, WILMA—BIRTHDAY

Celebrate with Rudolph relays, outdoor activity 1199:136

RUG HOOKING

Basics and four designs for rugs, making 70:92-93

RUGS

Rag mat, prodded, burlap, fabric, making 1255:31

Rug, braided, fabric, making 1017:121

Rug, braided, making 297:152-153

Rug, hooked, miniature, yarn, making 1320:24-25

Rug, rag, making 554:6-7

Rug, scatter, woven, making 916:12-14

RUMANIA—COOKERY

Corn meal squares, recipe 794:31

RUMANIA—COSTUMES

Rumanian costumes drawing 988:48

RUMPELSTILTSKIN

Banana bread, recipe 569:76-78

Queen, king, Rumpelstiltskin puppets, paper, patterns, making 92:36-39

Rumpelstiltskin, picture, making 92:35

RUSSELL, LILLLAN

Costume, making 213:122-123

RUSSIA

Activities, flags, games, songs, dances, recipes 1381:207-216

Soviet Union, activities, history, foods, games 143:173-206

RUSSIA—ARCHITECTURE

Kremlin in Russia, matchbox, foil and paper model, making 1094:46-47

Red Square, miniature, making 143:183

RUSSIA—BIRTHDAYS

Birthday customs in Russia 488:112-117

RUSSIA—CHRISTMAS

Celebration of Christmas 218:45-46; 497:144-153; 661:273-274; 914:90-93

Christmas customs 149:46-47; 425:27-28; 473:50

Christmas tree and decorations, how to make 593:84-89

St. Nicholas Day finger plays, recipes, games, making 944:42-43

RUSSIA—CHRISTMAS—COOKERY

Bliny, recipe 497:150

Borsch, recipe 497:150

Cabbage pierozhki, recipe 497:150

Cabbage soup, (shchi), recipe 1231:72-73

Kasha stuffing for roast chicken, recipe 1231:72

Kissel, cranberry dessert, recipe 1128:133

Kutya, traditional, recipe 1128:130

Kutya, wheat berries, honey, poppy seeds, recipe 1231:74

Pelmeni, recipe 497:150

Piroshki, meatballs in pastries, recipe 703:59-63

Rice and raisin kutya, recipe 1128:133

Rombaba cake, recipe 1231:75

Siberian meat dumplings, (pelmeni), recipe 1231:73-74

RUSSIA—CHRISTMAS—DECORATIONS

Grandfather Frost tree-topper, paper, cotton balls, glitter, stars, patterns, making 1231:68-69

Laquer box gift wrap, boxes, tissue paper, making 1231:70-71

Matrioshka doll hanging ornament, colored paper, yarn, patterns, making 1231:65-67

RUSSIA—CHRISTMAS—HANDICRAFTS

Grandfather Frost, appliqué and embroidery, making 497:152-153

RUSSIA—CIRCUS

Circus in Russia 143:189

Circus in Russia, miniature 143:189

Circus in Russia, real 143:190

RUSSIA—COOKERY

Almond cookies, recipe 999:23

Apple potato salad, recipe 1697:35

Beef casserole, recipe 999:26

Beef stroganoff, recipe 661:277-278; 999:22; 1535:35; 1555:36

Beet borscht soup, recipe 1077:105-106

Bitki, hamburger cakes, recipe 662:49-50

Blini pancakes, recipe 88:74-75; 1452:42

Blini, recipe 541:43; 1535:18-19

Boiled potatoes, recipe 1535:21

Borsch, beet soup, recipe 661:275-276; 1535:26

Borsch, pork and vegetable soup, recipe 1407:35

Borsch, Ukrainian, recipe 541:34

Borscht, beetroot soup, recipe 1555:36

Borscht, cabbage, recipe 143:201

Borscht, cold vegetarian beet soup, recipe 999:28; 1165:147; 1381:214; 1697:34

Buckwheat kasha, recipe 661:278

Cabbage filled turnovers, recipe 1697:20

Cabbage pie, recipe 1642:121

Cabbage soup, simple, recipe 909:15

Cabbage stir-fry, recipe 1697:21

Cherry vareniki, recipe 794:30

Chicken baked in sour cream, recipe 1697:24

Chicken Kiev, recipe 1535:32-33

Chicken Satsivi, recipe 541:29

Cookies, sugar, recipe 1381:214

Cotletki, meat patties, recipe 1165:147-148

Cranberry dessert pudding, recipe 661:279-280

Cucumber salad with sour cream, recipe 999:20

Cucumber salad, recipe 1452:46

Easter cake, recipe 88:71-72

Egg and sausage sandwich, recipe 1244:76-77

Egg salad, recipe 999:20

Fruit-sweetened beef, recipe 1697:23

Georgian cheese pie, recipe 999:24

Gogel-mogel, recipe 143:205

Grechnevaia kash, buckwheat groats, recipe 1165:148

Hamburger cutlets with sauce, recipe 1077:106

Herring in mustard sauce, recipe 999:21

History of cookery in 88:68-71

Honey spice cake (dessert), recipe 1280:44; 1535:43

Hot borscht soup, recipe 1452:45

Indian tea, recipe 1535:23
Kasha, beef broth and buckwheat groats, recipe 1697:29
Kasha, buckwheat, chicken broth, egg dish, recipe 1452:43
Kisel apple pudding, recipe 1452:47
Kompot, fruit drink, recipe 1535:36
Koulich, recipe 143:185
Kugel potato dish, recipe 1077:107-108
Lamb kebabs, recipe 999:24
Lukshena kugel, noodle pudding, recipe 143:203
Meat bouillon soup, recipe 1535:28
Mint cookies, miatniye prianiki, cookies, recipe 72:77-78
Noodle and cheese casserole, recipe 187:24
Noodle kigel, recipe 793:42; 1381:214
Omelet smetanoi, omelet with sour cream, recipe 1165:149
Pancakes, thin, recipe 1697:31
Paskha, recipe 541:41
Pirog apple dessert, recipe 1407:35
Pirozhki, dough covered meat mixture, recipe 446:31-
    33; 1452:44
Pirozhki, savory filled pastries, recipe 661:276-277;
    1535:28-29
Poppy seed cake, recipe 1697:39
Pot cheese croquettes, recipe 661:278-279
Potato babka, recipe 874:61
Potato pancakes, easy, recipe 1697:30
Potato piroshki, recipe 1204:77
Pretzels, recipe 143:190
Raspberry kisel, fruit drink, recipe 1535:36-37
Rice and spice dish, recipe 88:73-74
Russian salad, recipe 1148:26
Russian sweet treats, cookies, recipe 1246:46
Russian tea cakes, making 206:90-91
Russki salat, recipe 1165:148-149
Rye bread, recipe 1535:22; 1652:23
Salad Olivier, chicken and potato salad, recipe 1535:40
Salad Stolichnij, recipe 541:14
Sausage, recipe 1535:23
Scalloped potatoes, recipe 1535:32
Sharlotka, apple Charlotte dessert, recipe 1165:150-151
Shchi with sauerkraut, recipe 541:23
Sibierskie pelmenia, Siberian meat dumplings, recipe
    1165:149-150
Sirniki, cheese pancakes, recipe 1535:39
Sirniki, recipe 143:204
Sirnini, bite-size pancakes, recipe 188:34
Smetana mushrooms, recipe 1560:21
Solyarika, sauerkraut, recipe 143:203
Straw potatoes, fried potatoes, recipe 1535:31
Strawberry kissel, recipe 999:22
Studen, chicken dish, recipe 1535:42
Uzbek plov, recipe 541:32
Varenyky, sweet dumplings filled with cherries, recipe
    1555:36
Vatrushky, cheese tarts, recipe 143:205
Vegetable salad vesna, recipe 1535:31
Vegetable salad, recipe 999:27
Vinegret, cooked vegetables with vinegar and oil, recipe
    1535:41
Zakuska appetizer, recipe 1535:25
RUSSIA—COSTUMES
Balkan woman costume, making 213:24-26
Girl costume, crepe paper, making 687:33-37
Russian man costume, making 213:24
Russian peasant's costume drawing 988:47
Sirniki, bite-size pancakes, recipe, costume 188:34

RUSSIA—DANCES
Korobushka dance, how to do 1494:143-144
Kozachok dance and costume picture 1000:22-25
Troika dance, how to do 1362:142; 1494:131-132
RUSSIA—DOLLS
Flax dolls, straw, twigs, yarn, making 1338:96-97
Matroyshka doll, paper tubes, paint, glue, making
    1381:215-216
Nesting dolls, Russian, cans, paper, patterns, making
    1246:18-21
RUSSIA—EASTER
Blessing the food custom 503:24
Easter celebration 143:185; 661:271-273; 914:21-27
Easter egg customs in Russia 201:25-27
RUSSIA—EASTER—COOKERY
Candied citrus fruit peel, recipe 1666:137-138
Easter sweet bread, recipe 1697:38
Khachapuri (Georgian cheese bread), recipe 1666:143
Koulich Easter cake, recipe 1305:95
Koulitchey Resurrection bread, recipe 1495:139
Kulich (Easter cake), recipe 1666:135-136
Pashka (Russian Easter cheese dessert), recipe 1653:175;
    1666:137
Rice pilaf with dried fruits and almonds, recipe
    1666:142-143
Shashlik (pork shish-kebabs), recipe 1666:142
Walnut honey candy, recipe 1666:143-144
Yaitsa po russki (stuffed eggs), recipe 1666:135
RUSSIA—EASTER—DECORATIONS
Decorate Easter eggs using spinach, beets and onion skin
    dyes, how to do 1538:15
RUSSIA—EASTER—HANDICRAFTS
Easter eggs, colored paper, paint, paste, making
    1178:169
RUSSIA—FABLES
Great Yellow Yo-yo Yolk, traditional fable from Russia
    139:133-135
Three Bread Rolls, Russian fable told by Tolstoy 139:88
RUSSIA—FESTIVALS
Anniversary of the Revolution celebration 914:86-90
Anniversary of Victory celebration 914:40-41
Army Day celebration 914:16
Bairam, Moslem Festival celebration 914:69-70
Baltic Holiday of Song celebration 914:75-77
Birthday celebration 143:187
Boy's Day celebration 914:16
Butter Week Festival celebration 661:274
Children's Book Festival celebration 914:29
Cosmonaut's Day celebration 914:31-33
Cotton Harvest Festival celebration in Uzbekistan
    914:80-81
Festivals and celebrations, maps, flags, crafts, making
    1305:93-100
Grape Harvest Festival celebration in the Caucasus
    914:81-84
Holidays of Soviet Regions 914:54-59
Lenin's birthday, Subbotnik, celebration 914:29-31
May Day celebration 143:185; 914:34-39
May Day festival celebration 661:273
Mid-Summer Eve celebration 914:51-53
Mushroom Harvest Festival celebration in Byelorussia
    914:84-85
National Sports Day celebration 914:77-78
New Year's celebration 143:187
Pancake Day celebration 914:19-20

Revolution Day celebration 143:182
School Graduation Day celebration 914:48-51
Sports Day celebration in Central Asia 914:66-69
Subbotnik (Lenin's birthday) celebration 914:29-31
Tatar Festival of the Plow celebration 914:59-62
Wedding celebration 143:188
Wedding Day celebration in Central Asia 914:71-75
Wheat Harvest Festival celebration 914:79-80
Winter Festival celebration, activities, songs 909:9-17
Women's Day celebration 914:17-18
Young Pioneer's Festival celebration 914:41-47
Ysyakh, a Yakutsk Festival celebration 914:62-66

RUSSIA—FESTIVALS—HANDICRAFTS
St. Nicholas Day felt board, making 945:203-207

RUSSIA—FINGER PLAYS
Pal'chik-Mal'chik finger play rhyme 780:108

RUSSIA—FOLKLORE
Answer me this riddles 1478:30
Bean puzzle, making 1478:31
Chick and the Duckling; flannel board figures, patterns, making 843:76, 137
"The Clever Maiden," folktale and activities 1478:25-29
Half of the reward fable play 1212:96-101
Jeweled egg like Faberge egg, clay, papier-mache, making 1478:34-35
Palace, miniature palace from boxes, ice, making 1478:32-33
"Stone Soup," flannel board patterns, making 1201:90-93
"Straw Ox," ox, man, woman, bear, rabbit, wolf, fox puppets, patterns 1206:57-64
"Turnip" flannel board story, patterns, making 1603:50-55
Very Important Field Mouse flannel board patterns, making 910:27,64

RUSSIA—FOLKLORE—HANDICRAFTS
Magic Lifesaving Stick, fingerprint animals, cotton bunny, making 125:14-22
Owl, Old Friend, owl seed mosaic, felt mouse wall hanging, making 125:108-117

RUSSIA—FOLKLORE—PUPPETS
"Mr. Bear Squash You All Flat" shadow puppets, patterns, making 1602:79-84

RUSSIA—GAMES
Bear game 602:104-105
Bell in the steeple game 58:52-55
Cat and mouse game, how to play 1355:25
Egg jousting game, how to play 956:32-33; 1507:26
Garontki bowling game, how to play 1651:80-81
Gorelki game 602:104; 1078:28
Gorelki tag game, how to play 1498:23
Gorelki, widower or last couple out game 383:139
Grandfather Panas game 602:195
Gypsy game 602:105-106
Hole ball game, how to play 1497:23
Karavai, the round loaf, game 143:187
Klassiki, hopscotch game 1426:38-39
Korobushka song and dance game 1114:60-61
Lapkta baseball game, how to play 1651:72-74
Red light, green light game 984:19
Troika musical game 1116:52-53

Tskhenburti game, how to play 1497:42-43
Tyzicha card game 1132:58-59
Vint card game 1132:53-57
Zeros game, how to play 1494:112-113

RUSSIA—HANDICRAFTS
Faberge eggs, how to make with sequins, glitter and beads 1489:19
Jeweled crown, paper, foil decals, tinsel, ribbons, patterns, making 1648:13
Pysanky, making 143:186
Rooster, strutting, crested egg rooster, making 298:92-93

RUSSIA—LANGUAGE
Common words and phrases in Russian 1582:26
Numbers one to ten in Russian language 398:unp
Russian alphabet 1077:149-150; 1407:36
Russian words 1407:37
Soviet Union language 143:106

RUSSIA—LULLABIES
Baiu-Baiushki-Baiu 780:42
Liuli, Liuli, Liuli 780:43

RUSSIA—NEW YEAR'S DAY
Grandpa Frost and Yolka in the USSR 489:162-166
New Year's Day celebration 914:9-14

RUSSIA—NUMBERS
Numbers one to ten in Russian language 398:unp

RUSSIA—PUPPETS
Babushka puppet show 756:78-82
Peter and the Wolf puppet show 756:163-167

RUSSIA—RHYMES
Bliny baby clapping rhyme 780:57
Edu-Edu baby bouncing rhyme 780:70
Ladushki baby clapping rhyme 780:61
"Little White Rabbit" 1607:21
"Liuli, Liuli, Liuli" 1607:28
Soroka tickling rhyme 780:95
Zaika Belen'kii Sidit baby lifting rhyme 780:85

RUSSIA—SCIENCE
Russian scientist discovers chemical that eats odors 1719:65-67

RUSSIA—SONGS
Bai, Bai, Bai, Bai, lullaby 1220:150
Tumba, Tumba round song 1115:28-29

RUSSIA—TEA
Tea in Russia 474:133-134

RUSSIA—TOYS
Matryoshka disappearing toy, making 856:100-103
Pecking birds moving toy, cardboard, patterns, making 1051:124-128
Russian bear from Russia; history of and how to make 495:86-90

RUTH, BABE—GAMES
Babe Ruth Baseball Anniversary game 240:50

RUTH, GEORGE HERMAN—BIRTHDAY
Babe Ruth's birthday, activity with song 1199:33

RWANDA—EASTER—COOKERY
Kuku na nazi (chicken in coconut milk), recipe 1666:22
Split pea and banana porridge, recipe 1666:22

RWANDA—GAMES
Igisoro or capture the seeds game, how to play 1508:154-156

S

SABBATH. *See also* **JEWISH SABBATH; SHABBAT**
SABBATH—COOKERY
Burckas, cream cheese on spinach, recipe 1112:16-18
Chicken soup, recipe 1112:12-13
Cholent, children's, recipe 1112:18-20
Friday night pot roast, recipe 1112:14-15
Grape juice, recipe 1112:6
Mandelbrot, recipe 1112:20-22
Matzah balls, recipe 1112:13-14
Vegetarian chopped liver from eggplant, recipe 1112:10-11
SACAJAWEA
Birthday celebration; art, music, foods, games, activities 1104:118-121
SACHETS
Coffee filter sachets, making 1286:44-45
Colonial sachet, fabric, potpourri, making 1309:32-33
Herb bath fragrances, fabric, herb mixtures, making 1510:74-75
Herbal sachets, fabric, sachet mix, making 1531:88-90
Lavender bags, fabric, dried lavender, making 1510:22-23
Potpourri hearts, fabric, potpourri, making 1510:42-43
SAFARI
Backpack, paper bag, making 1088:120
Binoculars, cardboard tube, making 1088:115
Safari hat, paper, pattern, making 1088:116-119
Telescope, cardboard tube, making 1088:115
SAFARI—PARTIES
Safari party, how to plan and give 86:178-185
Safari party, recipe and menus 86:235
SAFARI PARKS
Animal models for wildlife parks, paper tubes, cardboard, making 1467:26-27
SAFETY
Safety on the streets projects to do 763:10,14,18; 763:22, 26, 28
SAILORS
Nautical Bill, fabric, patterns, making 316:75
SAILORS—COOKERY
Hardtack bread, recipe 1455:127
Ship's biscuits, recipe 6:31; 825:22-25
Tavern biscuits, recipe 1321:130
SAILORS—COSTUMES
Sindbad the Sailor costume, fabric, face make-up given, making 957:44-47
SAILORS—FINGER PLAYS
Finger plays about sailors and soldiers 302:84
SAILORS—HANDICRAFTS
Sailor samplers, making 825:14-21
Ship in a bottle, making 825:26-33
Straw boxes, making 825:40-49
SAILORS—HATS
Sailor hat, paper folded, making 1348:unp
Sailor hat, paper, pattern, making 823:58
SAILORS—ROPES
Rope work, making mat and Jacob's Ladder with rope 825:48-53
SAILORS—SCRIMSHAW
Scrimshaw, making 825:34-39
SAILORS—VALENTINES
Sailor Valentines, making 825:8-13

SAINT. *See listings under* **ST.**
SAINT-EXUPERY, ANTOINE DE—COOKERY
"Little Prince," Little Prince love notes, recipe 365:79
SAMHAIN FESTIVAL. *See* **CELTS—FESTIVALS**
SAMOA—DANCES
Siva dance, how to do 1647:45
SAMOA—FESTIVALS
Greeting ceremony celebration 601:169
SAMOA—FINGER PLAYS
Ulu, Uauau finger play rhyme 780:106
SAMOA—LULLABIES
Samoan Rock-a-Bye 780:34
SAMOA—RHYMES
Samoan baby bouncing rhyme 780:76
SAMOSET
Sock puppet, making 353:19
SAMURAI—JAPAN
Nikko Grand Festival, the March of the Samurai 107:31-35
SAMURAI—PUPPETS
Samurai warrior puppets, paper and fabric, patterns, making 1027:105-113
SAN FRANCISCO—HOUSES
San Francisco row house, paper, patterns, making 1152:161-166
SAND
Activities with sand, using science, crafts, music 1189:3-35
Colored sand, making 438:86; 720:16-17
Colored sand, layered in jar, making 1372:130
Sand castles, making 1149:112
Sand clay, recipe 1213:45
Sand play dough, making 1189:21
White Sands and Gray Sands, round song 1115:35
SAND CASTLES
How to build using history of real castles 5:3-29
Sand castles, how to make 56:22-27
Sand castles, miniature, how to do 875:29-32
SAND PAINTING
Cross or ram's horn sand painting, patterns, making 1286:79-82
Indian sand painting, how to do 647:86-87
Navaho sand paintings, sand, powder paints, glue, making 714:6-8; 1368:56-57
Sand painting in jars, sand, powdered tempera paints, making 1285:78-79; 1421:111
Thunderbird in sand, Indian sand painting, making 298:154-155
SAND SCULPTURES
Castle details, making 723:44-45
Castles; Krak des Chevaliers, Crusades, making 723:60-63
Deal castle, making 723:56-59
Drip castle, making 723:46-47
Harlech castle, making 723:52-55
Henry VIII Castle, Deal Castle, making 723:56-59
Motte and Bailey, making 723:48-51
Pyramids, making 723:34-35
Sand cities, castles, forts, houses, making 310:23
Sphinx, making 723:34-35
SANDWICHES
Activities, art, songs, recipes, games 1469:34-35
SANTA CLAUS
History of Santa Claus 218:33-37; 709:68
History of Santa Claus in several countries 917:unp

Old-fashioned Santa card, posterboard, making 1703:18-19
Saint Nicholas, history of 631:108
SANTA CLAUS—HANDICRAFTS
Cylinder Santa Claus, potato chip can, patterns, making 1286:97-100
Mammoth Santa, cardboard shapes, making 1203:21
SANTEE DAKOTA INDIANS—GAMES
Moccasins, how to make and play 1699:117
SAUDI ARABIA—COOKERY
Basbousa, recipe 793:55
Blehat lahma, lamb loaves with apricots and egg, recipe 1165:69
Date cakes, tamriah, cookies, recipe 72:112-113
Masala tea, recipe 1673:19
Tabbouli salad, recipe 1102:69-70
Yalanchi, stuffed tomatoes, recipe 1165:68-69
SAUDI ARABIA—FESTIVALS—COOKERY
Hajj; shorabat bazeela (vegetable and lentil), recipe 1666:58
Hajj; tabbouleh (cracked wheat salad), recipe 1666:59
SAUDI ARABIA—GAMES
Airplane game 602:82
Hit the holes game 58:56-57
Kaab game 515:102
Marbles game 602:83
Shadow tag game, how to play 1477:52
SAUDI ARABIA—LANGUAGE
Arabic symbols of written Arabic language 1102:118
SAWYER, RUTH
"Journey Cake, Ho," journey cake, recipe 1216:12
SAXONS—COSTUMES
Saxon warrior costume, information on 417:11
SCABBARDS
Scabbard, making 7:120-121
SCANDINAVIA. *See also* **DENMARK; FINLAND; NORWAY; SWEDEN**
SCANDINAVIA—CHRISTMAS
Christmas in the country 973:84-85
Christmas season in 973:65-86
Christmas tree information 973:77
History of Christmas in 704:54-55
SCANDINAVIA—CHRISTMAS—BIRDS
Scandinavian bird feed, making 709:81-82
SCANDINAVIA—CHRISTMAS—COOKERY
Cookie stamps and dough, recipe 795:71
Cookies, spritz cookies, recipe 704:62-63
Herring salad, recipe 1128:142
Lucia buns, recipe 704:64-66
Marzipan candy sculpture, making 795:70
Potatoes, caramelized potatoes, recipe 704:57-58
Rice porridge, recipe 795:72
Rice pudding recipe 1666:119
Sandkake (Scandinavian pound cake), recipe 1666:118
Shortbread, recipe 795:71
St. Lucia buns, recipe 273:79-82; 795:72
SCANDINAVIA—CHRISTMAS—HANDICRAFTS
Advent wreath, evergreens, making 795:52-53
Angels, Bjorn Wiinblad angels, making 795:67
Apples and toadstools, papier-mache, making 795:66
Father Christmas, making 470:85-86
Gnomes, yarn, making 470:88-89
Heart chains, paper, making 795:65
Kraemmerhus, paper cornucopias, making 795:65

Sheaves of grain, making 795:52
Stars, flat stars, making 795:64
Straw ornaments for Christmas tree, making 453:115-120
Wheat bundles, making 795:64
Wheat wreath, making 273:87-89
Wooden candle tree, making 273:82-86
Wooden cutouts for the tree, making 273:77-79
Wreaths, paper flower wreaths, making 795:68
SCANDINAVIA—COOKERY
Baked cod, recipe 1452:167
Fattigmands bakkels, fried cookies, recipe 1452:170
Fruktsuppe, fruit soup, recipe 1452:172
Gingersnaps, recipe 1560:5
Hot iron cookies, recipe 1495:76
Kottbullar, meatballs, recipe, making 662:46-48
Potato soup, recipe 1452:166
Sardine sandwiches, recipe 1452:169
Scandinavian rye bread, recipe 492:31-33
Scandinavian salad, recipe 1653:33
Smorrebrod, little open sandwiches, recipe 1560:4
Spritz, recipe 1452:171
Swedish meatballs, recipe 1452:168
SCANDINAVIA—EASTER
Easter Day celebration 973:33-35
Easter eggs customs 973:30-33
Easter witches 973:29-30
Lenten season celebrations 973:24-35
SCANDINAVIA—FESTIVALS
Mid-summer celebration 601:91
Mid-summer in the land of the Midnight Sun celebration 973:52-54
SCANDINAVIA—FOLKLORE
Stone Soup flannel board patterns, making 910:35,76
SCANDINAVIA—GAMES
Carousel game 474:50
Windspel game, how to play 1497:18
SCANDINAVIA—HANDICRAFTS
Grass stars, making 527:26
Polar bears, knitted, making 470:90-92
Skier from Scandinavia, pipe cleaners and paper model, making 1094:26-27
Viking Rune stone, rocks, Rune alphabet given, making 1332:105-108
SCANDINAVIA—TOYS
Horse, wooden toy, making 1027:77-79
SCARECROWS
Activities and resources to celebrate scarecrow days 592:109-114
Happy scarecrow mobile, making 452:64-65
History of scarecrows around the world 1436:8-29
How to make from old clothes, two sticks and stuffing 1543:84-87
Popcorn scarecrows, recipe, making 939:122-126
Scarecrow centerpiece, making 376:191
Scarecrow garden guard, sticks, yarn, paints, making 1377:12-13
Scarecrow, broom and paper, making 35127:
Scarecrow, detergent bottle, yarn, patterns, making 1311:60-61
Scarecrow, garden, making 252:82-83
Scarecrow, how to make 118:101-103; 310:93
Scarecrow, paper, large pattern, making 477:5-10
Scarecrow, porch, making 252:84
Scarecrow, straw, tin can, pebbles, old clothes, how to make 1436:28-29

Scarecrow, stuffed clothing, how to make 334:48-51
Scarecrow, wood, rope, fabrics, making 869:76-77;
    1121:4-5
Three-square scarecrow, paper, making 94:4
SCARECROWS—COSTUMES
Costume, making 252:22-23; 338:10-12; 842:4-8
Costume, old clothes, fabric, straw, making 1509:28-29
Costume, paper, making 585:36
SCARECROWS—DOLLS
Scarecrow corn husk doll, making 353:40-41
SCARECROWS—PUPPETS
Puppet, paper bag scarecrow puppet, patterns, making
    1006:12; 1107:12-20
SCENTS. *See* **FRAGRANCES; PERFUMES**
SCHEER, JULIAN
"Rain Makes Applesauce," applesauce, recipe 1216:108
SCHWEITZER, BYRD BAYLOR
"Amigo"; reading, writing, thinking activities 1093:23-
    30
"Everybody Needs a Rock"; science, reading, art, lan-
    guage arts activities 1055:129-132
SCOOTERS. *See* **SKATEBOARDS**
SCOTCH TAPE
History of Scotch tape 119:170-173
SCOTLAND
Activities, flags, games, songs, dances, recipes 1381:185-
    186
SCOTLAND—CASTLES
Castle from Scotland, paper model, making 1094:43
SCOTLAND—CHRISTMAS
Christmas celebration 601:113-114
Christmas customs 149:33-34
SCOTLAND—CHRISTMAS—COOKERY
Hogmanay shortbread, recipe 704:30-31; 1128:105
SCOTLAND—CLOTHING
Paisley bandanna, butta motif, handkerchief, fabric cray-
    ons, patterns, making 1586:40-41
SCOTLAND—COOKERY
Bannocks, recipe 88:6-7
Cullen skink, fish soup, recipe 1452:180
Feather fowlie, Scottish chicken soup, recipe 1165:124-
    125
Haggis, pudding sausage, recipe 1452:183
Honey butter, recipe 1478:91
Oat cookies, recipe 1560:8
Oatcakes, recipe 1452:179
Scones, recipe 88:120; 1452:178; 1653:61-62
Scotch broth, recipe 874:31
Scotch eggs, recipe 501:82
Scotch eggs, sausage covered eggs, recipe 1165:125
Shortbread cookies, recipe 72:51-52; 1032:254
Shortbread, recipe 384:Jan25; 557:36; 1381:186
Skirlie, fried oatmeal, recipe 1452:181
Stargazy pie, tuna, eggs, pie crust, recipe 1650:35
Stovies, potatoes and meat, recipe 1452:182
Sweet scones, recipe 1244:66-67
Trifle, recipe 523:42
SCOTLAND—COSTUMES
Description and pictures of Scottish costumes 313:38-50
Highland May Dayr costume, making 213:137-139
Loch Ness Monster costume, bubble pack, making
    1174:47
Scotland costumes drawing 988:38
SCOTLAND—DANCES
Highland Fling dance and costume picture 1000:11-13

SCOTLAND—DOLLS
Scotch Highlander doll, making 494:108-118
SCOTLAND—EASTER
Easter celebration 601:114
Easter egg customs 201:22
SCOTLAND—FESTIVALS
Hogmanay Day, crafts, foods, games, making 557:33-38
Kern maiden or corn dolly 626:87
Sir James Barrie's birthday; celebrate; conduct Peter Pan
    poll 1199:112
SCOTLAND—FESTIVALS—COOKERY
Hogmanay Day shortbread, recipe 557:36
New Year's berry oatmeal shortbread, recipe 1666:109-110
New Year's Hogmanay (Scottish New Year's bun), rec-
    ipe 1666:109
SCOTLAND—FESTIVALS—GAMES
Hogmanay Day First Foot game 557:35
SCOTLAND—FESTIVALS—HANDICRAFTS
Hogmanay Day kilt, paper, making 557:36
Hogmanay pop-up card, making 1387:52
SCOTLAND—FLAG
Pattern of flag 557:38
SCOTLAND—FOLKLORE
"The Blue Eyed Hare" folktale and activities 1478:81-86
SCOTLAND—FOLKLORE—COOKERY
Witches brew drink, apple cider, cinnamon, recipe
    1478:88
SCOTLAND—FOLKLORE—COSTUMES
Peter Pan, green tights, green felt, dagger, making
    1656:151-153
SCOTLAND—FOLKLORE—HANDICRAFTS
Beeswax candles, sheet of beeswax, wicking, making
    1478:89
SCOTLAND—FOLKLORE—PUPPETS
Hare puppets, paper, making 1478:90
SCOTLAND—GAMES
Barley break, last man in hell chasing game, how to play
    1498:40
Charlie over the Water game, how to play 1381:190
How many miles to Babylon? game 383:142
Kick the can game 602:109
Magic ball game 1078:32
Scotch Whist, catch the ten, card game 1132:94-96
Scotland's burning musical game 1116:27
Smuggle the geg game 383:143
Spanish Knight game 602:110
Stealing sticks game, how to play 1381:190
Wee Bologna man game, how to play 383:141; 1494:104
SCOTLAND—HALLOWEEN
Halloween celebration 601:91-92
SCOTLAND—HALLOWEEN—COOKERY
Witches brew drink, apple cider, cinnamon, recipe 1478:88
SCOTLAND—HALLOWEEN—GAMES
Walnut boat race, making 709:33-34
SCOTLAND—HALLOWEEN—HANDICRAFTS
Beeswax candles, sheet of beeswax, wicking, making
    1478:89
Lantern from turnips, called bogies, making 1453:74-75
SCOTLAND—HANDICRAFTS
Angus from Aberdeen, fabric, patterns, making 316:68-71
Corn dolly, making 626:87-89
Plaid sash, woven, making 525:46-47
Scotsman, bottle covered, make to look like Scotsman,
    making 830:152-153

SCOTLAND—HOUSES

Wee house model, making 494:115-116

SCOTLAND—MUSICAL INSTRUMENTS

Bagpipe, plastic bag, party horn, making 1310:46

SCOTLAND—NEW YEAR'S DAY

First footing custom 505:19

Hogmanay customs 505:19

Hogmanay Festival celebration 566:14

Wassail custom 709:96

SCOTLAND—NEW YEAR'S DAY—COOKERY

Hogmanay shortbread, recipe 709:95

SCOTLAND—SONGS

Sandy McNab round song 1115:48

Scotland's burning round song 1115:33

SCOTLAND—STRING FIGURES

Leashing of Lochiel's dogs string 372:30-31

Tying Dogs' Feet 1404:22-25

SCOTLAND—TEA

Scottish tea and tea table 474:137

SCOTT, SIR WALTER

Lochinvar puppet show 756:111-112

SCOUTING

Bone and horn ornaments, making 467:86-87

Neckerchief slides, making 467:82-85

Vest for emblems and awards, making 467:80-81

SCRIMSHAW

Scrimshaw, making 376:172; 524:59; 688:31; 825:34-39

Scrimshaw, paraffin and plastic bottle, making 877:90-92

Scrimshaw, plaster, making 282:78; 954:130

Scrimshaw, plastic, how to make 118:235; 1421:20

SCUBA DIVERS

Diver's masks and oxygen tanks, oatmeal boxes and bleach bottles, making 1190:50

SCULPTURE. *See also* **SAND SCULPTURES; SLATE—SCULPTURE**

Ancient Peruvian idol sculpture, dough, paints, patterns, making 1251:27-28

Animal from wood branch, how to make 1258:24-25

Clay critter pots, sculpting dough, recipe, making 1618:30-33

Fast food, giant food sculpture, paper, fabric, making 1618:26-29

Pre-Columbian king figure, dough, paints, patterns, making 1251:25-26

Sculpting dough, soda, cornstarch, recipe 1251:24

Soft sculptures, paper or fabric, paints, stuffing, making 1618:10-15

Statue of snow and ice, how to carve 525:78-79

Stone sculpture, styrofoam, papier-mache, sand, making 1658:50

SEA—PARTIES

Under the Sea birthday party, decorations, foods, games 1011:107-125

SEALS—WAXED

King's seal, making 980:18

Ring seal, plaster of Paris, making 1350:80-81

SEASHELLS. *See* **SHELLS**

SEASHORE. *See also* **SAND**

SEASHORE—HANDICRAFTS

Sand castles, how to make 1285:73-74

Seashell wind chime, seashells, dowel, string, ribbon, making 1284:31

Seaside scene, cardboard, seashore items, making 1467:18

Whelk Indian rattles, making 418:41-42

SEASONS

Songs, finger plays, stories, games, rhythms 1200:121-130

SEASONS—FALL. *See* **FALL**

SEASONS—SPRING. *See* **SPRING**

SEASONS—SUMMER. *See* **SUMMER**

SEASONS—WINTER. *See* **WINTER**

SEAWEED—COOKERY

Irish Moss pudding, recipe 1153:72

SEEDS

Necklaces, seeds, making 1278:16-17

Seed mosaic, beans and seeds, making 1213:69

SEEDS—HANDICRAFTS

Totem pole from seeds, making 844:18-19

SEMINOLE INDIANS—CLOTHING

Dress, two-piece dress, making 932:45-47

Fabric, decorative, making 227:30

Man's coat, fabric, making 281:17-19

Skirt, Seminole piecework, making 224:107-112

Woman's blouse, fabric, making 281:20-21

SEMINOLE INDIANS—COOKERY

Fruit and fish Seminole style, recipe 424:60

Hominy, recipe 1172:22

Seminole drink, recipe 424:61

SEMINOLE INDIANS—COSTUMES

Osceola costume, making 272:102-104

SEMINOLE INDIANS—DOLLS

Corn cob doll, corn cob, fabric, yarn, making 1699:92-93

Patchwork skirt Seminole doll, making 298:128-129

SEMINOLE INDIANS—FESTIVALS

Corn Festival celebration 659:51-53

SEMINOLE INDIANS—GAMES

Pole ball game, how to play 1172:14

SEMINOLE INDIANS—HOUSES

Chickee, paper, straws, pattern, making 1170:22

Seminole grass house, making 227:7

Seminole shelter, making 804:80-82

SEMINOLE INDIANS—PATCHWORK

Seminole patchwork bag, making 15:30

Seminole patchwork, making 15:27-30; 70:36-37

SENDAK, MAURICE

"Chicken Soup with Rice," recipe 1216:72

"In the Night Kitchen," morning coffee cake, recipe 1216:45

SENDAK, MAURICE—BIRTHDAY

Celebrate; make prehistoric clay dough Wild Things 1199:127-128

Celebrate; make Wild Things world in box, magazine pictures, paints 1199:128

SENECA INDIANS

Stone reading, how to do 1296:98-99

SENECA INDIANS—FOOTWEAR

Moccasins, making 227:28-29

SENECA INDIANS—GAMES

Hoop and pole game, branches, twine, making 1608:82

SENECA INDIANS—HATS

Seneca cap, making 482:66-67

SENEGAL—COOKERY

Couscous, making 187:38

Papaya, fresh, recipe 1392:unp

Tiebou dienn or ceeb u jen, fish stew, recipe 1165:41-42

SENEGAL—FESTIVALS—COOKERY

Eid al-Fitr; mafe of Senegal (stew of lamb), recipe 1666:35-36

Eid al-Fitr; peanut butter, recipe 1666:36

SENEGAL—GAMES

Lagan Buri game 967:45

SENSES

Songs, finger plays, stories, games, rhythms 1200:61-64

SENUFO PEOPLE—PAINTINGS

Mud painting on clothes, dirt, paint, fabric, making 1632:12-17

SERBIA. See YUGOSLAVIA

SEURAT, GEORGE—BIRTHDAY

Celebrate by making pointillism painting 1199:273

SEUSS, DR.

"Green Eggs and Ham," green eggs and ham, recipe 1216:115

"Scrambled Eggs Super!," scrambled eggs, recipe 1216:114

SHABBAT. See also SABBATH

SHABBAT—COOKERY

Apple cake, recipe 1380:38

Bean soup, recipe 1691:27

Braided challah, bread, recipe 1685:4

Carrot pudding, recipe 279:29

Challah bread, recipe 1626:19

Challah, recipe 543:16-18

Challe, recipe 279:25-26

Chicken roasted, recipe 279:28

Chicken soup, recipe 279:27; 1685:6; 1691:26

Cholent stew, recipe 265:69

Cholent, meat and vegetable dish, recipe 1691:29

Fruit kugel, recipe 265:70-71

Gedempte chicken, recipe 1685:8

Gefilte fishkabobs, recipe 81:68

Hallah bread, recipe 265:65-67; 1289:173; 1451:96; 1691:28

Hummus, recipe 265:69-70

Mandelbrot, almond bread, recipe 1685:9

Matzoh balls, recipe 1685:7

Sopa de avas, recipe 1691:26

Strudel pudding, recipe 279:30

Super split, recipe 81:68

Tabooli, cracked wheat salad, recipe 1691:27

Vegetarian chopped liver, recipe 1685:5

Waldorf salad, recipe 81:68

SHABBAT—DANCES

Dances for Shabbat 542:2-6

Shabbat dance, how to do 279:20

SHABBAT—DECORATIONS

Candleholders, clay, making 279:11

Candles, making 265:75-76

Candlesticks, Shabbat, making 279:17

Candlesticks, stones, making 265:77

Challe cover, simple, making 279:12

Counter for Shabbat, making 82:6

Eternal light, making 279:15

Flower centerpiece, making 81:67

Havdalah candle, making 265:76; 279:13

Holiday creative drawing activities 1337:6-9

Horseradish holder, crepe paper clay, making 279:16

Open House invitations, making 81:66

Origami nut cups, making 81:67

Ring of flowers for table, making 82:7

Salt and pepper shakers, making 279:14

Shabbat picture centerpiece, making 82:10

Wine coaster, making 81:71

SHABBAT—GAMES

Add a letter game 279:24

I am Shabbat game 279:23

Progressive story game 81:69

Puzzles and word games 265:79-83

Shabbat charades 81:70

Shabbat ponder game 81:69

Tea pot game 81:70

What is missing? game 279:23

Who has the candle? game 279:24

SHABBAT—HANDICRAFTS

Besamim box, making 543:19

Besamin box, raisin boxes, adhesive paper, making 1691:24-25

Candlesticks, making 543:12

Challah cover, making 82:8; 543:13

Havdallah spice box, making 82:12

Napkin rings, making 543:14

Pushke, metal container, making 265:73-74

Pushke charity box, metal containers, paint, candle sticks, stones, making 1691:22-23

Salt shaker, making 82:9

Shine-through kiddush cup, making 82:11

Spice box, making 265:78

SHADOW PUPPETS. See also PUPPETS—SHADOW

Theater, stage and figures, cardboard box, paint, flashlight, making 1678:39-44

SHADOWS

Cendrars, Blaise, "Shadows"; science, reading, art, language activities 1055:174-177

Shadow portraits, paper for portrait and background, making 1261:28-29

Shadow show, cardboard box, light, making 1257:39

Shadows, activities, art, science, songs, recipes 911:214-217

SHAKERS—CHRISTMAS—DECORATIONS

Woven Christmas ornaments, red and green paper, making 1639:83

SHAKERS—COOKERY

Apple dumplings, recipe 1639:64-65

Berry jam, recipe 1639:61-62

Canterbury applesauce, recipe 1639:63

Caramel candy, recipe 1639:67

Lemonade, recipe 1639:56

Roasted chestnuts and popcorn, recipe 1639:68

Yeast bread, recipe 1639:57-59

SHAKERS—GAMES

Bag of marbles and jacks, how to make 1639:87

Jacks, how to play 1639:86

Jump rope, how to make rope, piece of garden hose 1639:90

Marbles game, how to play 1639:85

SHAKERS—HALLOWEEN—DECORATIONS

Paper lanterns, , tissue paper, black paper, flashlight, making 1639:81

SHAKERS—HANDICRAFTS

Cross-stitch pincushion , making 1639:108-109

Cross-stitch sampler, pattern, making 1639:110-111

Cross-stitch vocabulary, making 1639:106-107

Dorothy opera cloak, doll-sized, patterns, making 1639:112-113

Fir balsam pillows, making 1639:114

Jam labels and seed packets, how to make 1639:80

Knitted headband, yarn, needles, making 1639:101

Knitted spool doll rug, yarn, needles, making 1639:103-104

Knitted tube headband, yarn, needles, making 1639:102
May baskets, paper, paper fasteners, flowers, making
    1639:79
Potpourri, how to make 1639:70-71
Rug, mosaic-yarn, making 298:232-233
Valentine, how to make 1639:78

SHAKERS—THANKSGIVING—DECORATIONS
Place cards, paper, making 1639:82

SHAKERS—WOODWORKING
Boy's ruler, molding, making 1639:93
Broom, long stick, pine needles, making 1639:98
Candleholder, pine wood, nails, making 1639:94

SHAKESPEARE, WILLIAM—BIRTHDAY
Celebrate birthday by making diorama of stage setting
    1199:89-90
Shakespeare's birthday; celebration of facts 496:61

SHAKESPEARE, WILLIAM—COOKERY
Shakespeare's breakfast sandwiches, recipe 365:17

SHAPES
Songs, finger plays, stories, games, rhythms 1200:11-14

SHARMAT, MITCHELL
"Gregory the Terrible Eater," scrambled eggs, recipe
    1216:117

SHAVUOT
Meaning of Shavuot 711:84; 712:83-84
Ritual of Shavuot 419:31-32

SHAVUOT—COOKERY
Apple and cream cheese spread, recipe 1112:116
Bagels, recipe 1112:116-118
Beet borsht, quick, recipe 279:168
Blintzes, recipe 711:88-89; 1685:82; 1691:255
Borsht, beet soup from Russia, recipe 116:102
Burekas, dough with potato, egg and cheese filling, rec-
    ipe 1691:254
Butter, how to make 1112:115
Cheese blintzes, recipe 402:34-38; 1112:119-120;
    1451:95
Cheese soufflé sandwiches, recipe 81:62
Cheese squares, recipe 543:138
Cheesecake, recipe 711:90-91; 1685:87; 1691:256
Easy cheesy blintzes, recipe 116:103
Eggs and tsibeles, recipe 711:85
First Spring salad, recipe 116:101
French toast, recipe 1112:120-121
Fruit pizza, recipe 81:62
Fruit shake, recipe 81:62
Granola, recipe 116:106
Lemon cream sherbet, recipe 711:92
Lime mold, recipe 279:172
Lox, eggs and onions, recipe 1685:86
Mama Ligga from Romania, recipe 116:105
Melon bowls, recipe 116:100
Milk and honey cookies, making 80:72
Noodle cheese pudding, recipe 279:170
Noodle kugel, recipe 402:34-38; 1685:85
Noodle pudding, recipe 116:104-105; 711:86-87
Pineapple surprise salad, recipe 279:171
Pizza, mock, recipe 279:169
Samosas, recipe 1685:84
Sembussak pastries, recipes 363:53-54
Ten commandments cake, recipe 116:107
Yogurt salad, recipe 1112:118-119

SHAVUOT—DANCES
Dances for Shavuot 542:116-122

SHAVUOT—DECORATIONS
Alphabet and Torah mural, making 81:61
Basket for Shavuot greens, making 82:71
Flower favor, making 712:85
Flower magnet, making 81:64
Flowers for Shavuot, making 80:70
Framed finger painting, making 279:160
Fruit mountain, making 712:84
Holiday creative drawing activities 1337:44-45
Mezuzah, making 279:158
Nut cup, making 279:156
Party straws, making 279:157
Self frame picture, making 279:161
Shavuot paper-cut, making 82:70
Ten Commandments plaque, making 279:159
Ten Commandments, making 80:71
Torah scroll invitation, making 81:60
Torah, miniature, making 279:162

SHAVUOT—DOLLS
Corn husk doll: Biblical Ruth, making 1691:250-251

SHAVUOT—GAMES
Catch Goliath game 279:166
Memory lotto game, making 543:137
Shamos game 279:167
Shavuot bingo 81:63
When Moses climbed Mt. Sinai game 81:63
Who do? game 279:166

SHAVUOT—HANDICRAFTS
Confirmation cap, making 82:72
Egg carton flowers, making 1691:253
Eggshell basket, making 543:132
Flower fancies, making 543:130-131
Flower pot from cheese carton, making 543:133
Mobile for Shavuot, making 543:134-135
Moses and the Ten Commandments model, making 543:136
Seven fruits of Israel in mock stained glass, making
    1691:251-252

SHAVUOT—PARTIES
Shavuot party, invitations, decorations, menus and
    games, making 2:72-77

SHAWNEE INDIANS
Tecumseh costume, making 272:96-99

SHAWNEE INDIANS—COOKERY
Johnnycake or Shawnee cake, recipe 1504:27

SHAWNEE INDIANS—FOOTWEAR
Shawnee moccasins, making 359:56-61

SHAWNEE INDIANS—LANGUAGE
Shawnee words, ten in list 1504:53

SHEEP
Lambs, activities, art, science, songs, recipes 911:16-163
Sheep, pop-up, paper, pattern 1210:26-27

SHELLS
Decorating with shells, boxes, paper, glue, making 1258:18
Garden of shells and plants in a jar of water, making
    1258:19

SHELLS—HANDICRAFTS
Crèche from clamshells, making 215:28-30
Doves, Victorian shell sculpture, patterns, making
    1016:135-139
Easter basket from shells, making 216:55-56
Easter eggs from shells, making 216:54-55
Shellfish Christmas ornament, making 215:32
Shell magnets for Christmas, making 215:31
Snowman Christmas tree ornament from starfish, mak-
    ing 216:51-52

SHEMINI AZERET
Meaning of Shemini Azeret 712:26
SHERLOCK HOLMES—COSTUMES
Sherlock Holmes, variety of old clothes, making 1656:141-144
SHINNECOCK INDIANS—COOKERY
Bread dessert and sweet stuff, recipes, making 424:52
Carol's candy, recipe 424:51
Cattail biscuits, recipe 424:50-51
Shinnecock succotash, recipe 424:48
SHIPS
Figurehead for ship, modeling clay, making 1683:15
Navy ship, wooden, making 942:87
Pirate ship crew, clothespins, making 942:86-87
Pirate ship, cereal box, newspaper, paints, making 1559:18-19
Pirate ship, wooden, patterns, making 942:84-85
SHIPS—COOKERY
Galleon or pirate ship cake, recipe 449:67
SHIRTS
Dashiki, making 251:48-49
SHOES
Moccasin pattern, leather, making 955:92-95
SHOSHONE INDIANS
Sacagawea costume, making 272:99-102
SHOSHONE INDIANS—COOKERY
Steamed clover, recipe 1699:144
SHOSHONE INDIANS—FOOTWEAR
Shoshone moccasins, making 359:80-86
SHOSHONE INDIANS—GAMES
Juggling, how to play 1699:126
SHOSHONE INDIANS—JEWELRY
Shoshone necklace, making 932:71-74
SHROVE TUESDAY. See also **PANCAKE TUESDAY**
Celebration and history of, and pancake recipe 496:35-40
Once Every Pancake Day, England, festivals 139:44
SHROVE TUESDAY—PARTIES
Pancake party, recipes and games 635:43-45
SIAM. See **THAILAND**
SICILY—CHRISTMAS—CUSTOMS
Christmas customs 149:44
SICILY—COOKERY
Apple fritters, recipe 895:124-125
Beefsteak, recipe 895:123
Tomato salad, recipe 895:122
SICILY—GAMES
Pignalla game 474:47
SICILY—PUPPETS
Sicilian puppet, making 483:27
SICILY—VOLCANOES
Strombolian eruption, model volcano demonstrates 1455:76
SIDE SHOWS
History of side shows 631:70
SIERRA LEONE—COOKERY
Abala, savory steamed rice, recipe 1165:37-38
Chicken from Sierra Leone, recipe 1344:64
Dried seeds for snacking, recipe 1165:36-37
Ginger cookies, recipe 1165:38-39
Kanya, peanut bars, recipe 1165:38
Peanut bars, kanya, cookies, recipe 72:99
Rice bread, recipe 1165:36
Rice, roll, recipe 967:46

SIERRA LEONE—FESTIVALS
New Year Festival celebration 601:26-27
SIERRA LEONE—FESTIVALS—COOKERY
Eid al-Fitr; black beauty and ponkie rice (eggplant and pumpkin rice), recipe 1666:33-34
Eid al-Fitr; rice with chicken, recipe 1666:34
SIERRA LEONE—GAMES
Haba Gaba game, how to play 1494:22
Mankala game, making 222:13-15
SIKHISM
Chauri or whish to wave over scriptures, making 1700:19
Decorations in the Harimander (temple), papier-mache shapes on foil-covered cardboard, making 1700:12
Sikh flag, fabric, rod, making 1700:31
SIKHISM—COOKERY
Karah parsad sweet mixture, recipe 1700:23
SIKHS—FESTIVALS—COOKERY
Baisakhi Festival, cereal dessert, recipe 1313:77
Baisakhi Festival, chappati, recipe 1313:77
SIKHS—FESTIVALS—DECORATIONS
Baisakhi Festival, pop-up card, making 1387:52
Diwali Festival of Lights pop-up card, making 1387:24
SIKHS—FESTIVALS—HANDICRAFTS
Raksha Bandhan Festival plaited rakhi bracelets, making 1277:14-15
SIKHS—HANDICRAFTS
Garland with characters from Sikh prayer, the Mool Mantra, making 1313:78
Saffron yellow flag with black khanda, Sikh symbol, making 1313:78
SILHOUETTES
Lincoln and Washington silhouettes, paper plate, making 374:154-156
Shadow portraits, paper for portrait and background, making 1261:28-29
SILK
Game; Silk Road board game; silk merchant's travels in ancient times, making 1279:20, 25
SILK SCREENING
Screen and squeegee, wood, mesh, making 1476:43
Tempera silk screens, embroidery hoop, cloth, stencils, making 1617:44-48
SILKWORMS
Raising and growing silkworms, how to do 574:25
SILVER
Silver work, history of 605:7-10
SILVER JEWELRY. See **NAVAHO INDIANS— JEWELRY; PUEBLO INDIANS—JEWELRY**
SILVERSTEIN, SHEL
Eighteen flavors from "Where the Sidewalk Ends," pumpkin, lemon ice cream, recipe 1216:82-83
SIMHATH TORAH
Meaning of Simhath Torah 712:26
SIMHATH TORAH—COOKERY
Caramel-nut apples and chocolate-coconut apples, recipe 1685:34-35
Etrog, citron, marmalade, recipe 116:46
Fruit float, recipe 116:42
Giggling fruit float centerpiece, recipe 116:43
Harvest fry, recipe 116:41
Jelly apples, recipe 1685:36
Mundel bread, recipe 279:71
Salmon loaf, recipe 279:70

Soomsoom bars from Israel, recipe 116:44-45
Sweet potato delight, recipe 279:69
Yom Tov roly-poly from the USA, recipe 116:40
SIMHATH TORAH—DECORATIONS
Holiday creative drawing activities 1337:18-19
Israel's flag, making 80:32
Simhath Torah decorations, making 712:30
Simhath Torah flag, making 279:60
Yarn and pin picture, making 279:61
SIMHATH TORAH—GAMES
Etrog game 279:67
Mix-up game 279:67
Scrambled eggs game 279:68
SIMHATH TORAH—HANDICRAFTS
Papier-mache fruit, making 712:28-29
SIMHATH TORAH—PARTIES
Simhath Torah party, invitations, decorations, menus and
games, making 2:23-28
SINBAD THE SAILOR—COSTUMES
Sinbad the Sailor costume, fabric, face makeup given,
making 957:44-47
SINGAPORE
Activities, flags, games, songs, dances, recipes 1381:85-
89
SINGAPORE—COOKERY
Benkang pisang, banana cake, recipe 1381:87
Fried kway teow, recipe 967:47
IIkan bilis with spinach soup, recipe 967:46
SINGAPORE—GAMES
Arbus tree seed game, how to play 1355:32
Five stones jacks game, how to play 1718:20-21
Rubber bands game, how to play 1355:31
SIOUX INDIANS
Songs and stories of the Sioux 344:34-45
SIOUX INDIANS—BUSTLES
Bustles, Sioux bustle, making 589:32-33
SIOUX INDIANS—CLOTHING
Clothing, making 589:59
Men's clothing, making 227:24-25
Sioux cuff, making 465:36
Sioux dress and leggings, making 465:95
Sioux ghost shirts, making 466:34-35
Sioux jingler anklet, making 932:64-66
Women's clothes, making 227:22-23
SIOUX INDIANS—COOKERY
Plum butter, recipe 1296:142-143
Plum raisin bread, recipe 1296:142-143
Wa-Ha-Pi Papa Sa-Ka La-Ko-Ta, recipe 424:78-79
Wagmiza washa sweet berry snack, recipe 1527:16
Wo-Japi, recipe 1043:146
Wojabi fruit pudding, recipe 1527:63
SIOUX INDIANS—COSTUMES
Ghost dance shirt, making 63:36-37
Red Cloud costume, making 213:132-136
SIOUX INDIANS—DESIGNS
Sioux designs and symbols 465:69
SIOUX INDIANS—GAMES
Moccasin game 602:179
SIOUX INDIANS—HEADDRESSES
Feather hair decoration, feathers, paint, making 1648:19
Headdress, fabric or canvas, feathers, paints, making
1368:8-9
Sioux turban headdress, making 466:66

SIOUX INDIANS—HOUSES
Sioux teepee, making 227:12; 562:34-37; 574:131
SIOUX INDIANS—JEWELRY
Ornaments, jewelry, and bead weaving, making 324:20-
25
SIOUX INDIANS—LANGUAGE
Sioux names glossary 466:181-182
SIOUX INDIANS—MUSICAL INSTRUMENTS
Bone whistle, making 468:145
Frame drum mallet, stick, old socks, ribbon, making
1646:57-59
Frame drum, cardboard box, paper bag, sting, paint, mak-
ing 1646:57-59
Frame drum, how to play 1646:60
Rasp, making 468:29
SIOUX INDIANS—PARFLECHE
Parfleche, canvas, laces, paints, making 1296:112
SIOUX INDIANS—WAR BONNETS
War bonnet, making 227:50-51; 324:17-19
SIXTIES. *See* **NEW YORK—FESTIVALS—
WOODSTOCK**
SKATEBOARDS
Skateboarding games, how to do 258:36-44
SKELETONS—COSTUMES
Skeleton costume, black clothes, reflective tape, making
1314:41
SKELETONS—FACE MAKEUP
Skull and monster face makeup, how to do 1314:40-41
SKIING
Skier from Scandinavia, pipe cleaners and paper model,
making 1094:26-27
SKULL AND CROSSBONES
Paper folds, cut and made into skull and crossbones, how
to do 406:13-15
SKYSCRAPERS
Gingerbread skyscraper, patterns, assembling, decorat-
ing, how to do 1086:80-86
SLATE—SCULPTURE
Bird carving on slate, making 584:19-23
Carving on slate, how to do 584:16-37
Horse carving on slate, making 584:25-27
Sailboat carving on slate, making 584:23-24
Whale carving on slate, making 584:29-33
SLAVERY
Activities, crafts, history and stories for 128:94-99
SLEEPING BEAUTY
Awakening celebration of roasted spice chicken, recipe
569:43-45
Sleeping Beauty's royal bed, cardboard, fabric, patterns,
making 484:125-128
SLEEPING BEAUTY—DOLLS
Sleeping Beauty and Prince Florimund dolls, fabric, pat-
terns, making 484:101-106
SLEPIAN, JAN
"Hungry Thing," gollipops, recipe 1216:85
SLINGSHOTS
Slingshot, making 118:279-280; 310:42
SLOVAC REPUBLIC. *See* **CZECHOSLOVAKIA**
SLOVENIA. *See* **YUGOSLAVIA**
SMITH, CAPTAIN JOHN
Captain John Smith costume, making 213:32-34
SMOKEY BEAR
Birthday celebration, art, music, foods, games, activities
1104:110-113

SNAKES

Slinky snake paper toy, making 1238:31-34

Snake charmer from India, pipe cleaners and paper, making 1094:14

SNAKES—GAMES

Rattlesnake musical game 1116:21

SNEAKERS

History of sneakers 119:174-178

SNOW

Blizzard scene in a jar, jar, glitter, moth flakes, making 1429:21

Snow candles, snow, paraffin, wicking, tin can, making 1285:116-117

Snow globes from jelly jars, making 1203:37

Snow King and Queen, foam cups, patterns, making 1311:70-71

Snow sculpture, making 526:89-90

Snow sculpture, outdoors, making 916:42-44

Snow trench fort, making 1188:39-40

Snowball fort, large snowballs, making 1188:37-38

Snowstorm in a jar, jar, oil, water, confetti, making 1662:194

Soap clay, laundry soap, recipe 1455:4

Statue of snow and ice, how to carve 525:78-79

SNOW WHITE AND THE SEVEN DWARFS

Wicked Queen's poison baked apples, recipe 569:7-9

SNOWFLAKES

German snowflakes mobile, making 452:92-94

German snowflakes, making 218:80-81

SNOWMEN

3-D Scotch snowman, paper, fabric, pattern, making 912:133-134

SOAP

Hand soap, Colonial recipe 1043:29

Ivory, the soap that floats, history of 118:47

Scented soap, soap, fragrant oil, food coloring, making 1285:141-143

Soap balls, handmade, recipe, making 438:50

Soap carving, making 1376:64-66

Soft soap carving, how to do 1354:44

SOAP BOX RACERS

Wooden racers, how to make 1074:196-199

SOAP DERBY

Story of Soap Derby 119:69

SOCRATES

Socrates costume, making 213:47-48

SOFT DRINKS

America's sweet tooth 118:171

History of soda pop 762:69-80

SOFT SHOE DANCING

Top hat for dancer, black posterboard, making 1362:55

SOLAR COOKERS

Reflector oven, making 937:13

SOLDIERS

American soldier, War of Independence costume, making 870:104-109

British soldier, War of Independence costume, making 870:104-109

Civil War soldier costume, making 887:40-41

Doll, bristle soldier doll, patterns, making 1016:147-151

Memorial Day soldier, paper bag, patterns, making 234:44-45

Memorial soldier, paper, pattern, making 232:45

Royal guard soldier, clothespin, making 442:46

Sergeant Gruff, fabric, patterns, making 316:73-74

Soldier boy mask, paper, making 862:30-31

Soldier hat, paper, pattern, making 823:57

Soldier, paper cup, making 965:12

Toy soldier, cylinder, paper tube, making 442:18

Toy soldier, felt, pattern, making 867:48-49

Toy soldier, paper models, patterns, making 75:34; 639:20-21

Union and Confederate soldiers costumes, making 870:109-112

SOLDIERS—FINGER PLAYS

Finger plays about soldiers and sailors 302:84

SOLSTICE

Inca Winter Solstice Festival 419:124-125

Solstice festivals 419:67-68

Summer Solstice activities and projects for classrooms 1393:241-242

Summer Solstice postcards, wish I were here, making 1199:133-134

Summer Solstice watermelon craft, seeds, paper, glue, making 1199:134-135

Winter Solstice activities and projects for classrooms 1393:103-105

Winter Solstice, celebrate by making pine cone bird feeders 1199:283

Winter Solstice, celebrate by making vegetable soup, recipe 1199:281

SOMALIA—COOKERY

Curry in a hurry dish, recipe 1165:6-7

Liver and onions, recipe 1371:121

SOMALIA—FESTIVALS—COOKERY

Eid al-Adha; skudahkharis (lamb and rice), recipe 1666:6

Eid al-Fitr; skudahkharis (lamb and rice), recipe 1666:6

SOMALIA—GAMES

Gariir, jacks game, how to play 1718:22-23

Hyena race game, how to play 1355:38-39

SOMALIA—LANGUAGE

Common Somali words 1371:81

SONGS

Victorian round song 1115:56

SOUP

Activities, art, songs, recipes, games 1469:54-55

SOUSA, JOHN PHILIP—BIRTHDAY

Birthday celebration; art, music, foods, games, activities 1104:18-21

Celebrate by making simple musical instruments 1199:258-259

SOUTH AFRICA. *See also* **AFRICA, SOUTH**

Activities, flags, games, songs, dances, recipes 1381:149-152

SOUTH AFRICA—BEADWORK

Neckband and pendant, heavy paper, yarn, pony beads, patterns, making 1332:29-34

SOUTH AFRICA—CHRISTMAS

Natal Christmas celebration 601:33-34

SOUTH AFRICA—CHRISTMAS—COOKERY

Baked mealies and tomatoes, recipe 1666:13-14

Karringmelkbeskuit (buttermilk rusk), recipe 1666:14-15

Krakelinge (figure-eight cookies), recipe 1666:14

SOUTH AFRICA—COOKERY

Baked bananas, recipe 1560:37

Bobotie, beef dish, recipe 1560:36-37

Bobotie, meat curry casserole with custard topping, recipe 1165:14-15

Bobotie, stew, recipe 635:52

Clams, baked, recipe 967:47

236

Coconut barfi candy, recipe 1563:122
Corn soup with tomato, recipe 1694:32
Engelegte, curry pickled fish, recipe 1165:15-16
Fruit salad, recipe 1694:33
Lamb stew, recipe 895:127
Mealie meal bread, recipe 1244:95
Milk tart, recipe 895:128-129
Paxview special pudding, recipe 967:48
Soetkoekies, cookies, recipe 515:112
SOUTH AFRICA—DANCES
Pata Pata dance, how to do 1494:33-34
SOUTH AFRICA—GAMES
African hop scotch 602:36-37
Drie blikkies, three tins game, how to play 1708:50-52
Feather game 602:36
Poison game, how to play 572:22-23; 1507:22
Robot game 967:47
What's the Time, Mr. Wolf? tag game, how to play
1498:23-27
SOUTH AFRICA—HANDICRAFTS
Umcamelo, headrest, making 519:64
SOUTH AFRICA—HOUSES
Bushmen huts 469:42-43
Rest house, paper, making 515:112
SOUTH AFRICA—JEWELRY
Beaded necklaces and bangles, Ubuhlali and Umnaka,
making 519:60-63
SOUTH AMERICA
Activities, flags, games, songs, dances, recipes 1381:43-
58
SOUTH AMERICA—ANIMALS
Jumping Jack monkey toy, oaktag, string, making
1484:12-13
SOUTH AMERICA—BIRTHDAYS—HANDICRAFTS
God's Eye, woven, making 1277:20-21
SOUTH AMERICA—CHRISTMAS
Christmas ornaments, making 182:94-96
SOUTH AMERICA—COOKERY
Caramel pudding, recipe 597:38
Creme de abacate, cream of avocado dessert, recipe
1452:191
Empanadas, meat filled turnovers, recipe 1452:188
Rice and tomatoes, recipe 1452:190
Seviche of striped bass, recipe 1452:187
Stuffed avocados, recipe 1452:186
Sweet squash, recipe 1452:189
SOUTH AMERICA—DIORAMAS
Hatmaker's shop, how to make 182:31-35
SOUTH AMERICA—DOLLS
Amazonian doll, making 182:74-77
Fruit seller spool doll, making 629:34-35
SOUTH AMERICA—FESTIVALS
St. John's Day love superstitions 709:182
SOUTH AMERICA—FESTIVALS—HANDICRAFTS
Cascarones, decorated eggshells filled with confetti, mak-
ing 1477:37
Fiesta clay figures, making 1574:28-29
SOUTH AMERICA—FURNITURE
Leather triangle stool, how to make 182:44-51
SOUTH AMERICA—GAMES
Angel and Devil musical game 1116:22
Chapete game 956:28-29
Chuke board game, how to play 1499:21-23
El-Reloj, the clock game 474:48
Foot beanball, how to play 1651:120-121

Frijoles game 1146:24-25
Matatiru-tiru-la musical game 1116:60
Ring on a string game, how to play 1501:32-33
SOUTH AMERICA—HANDICRAFTS
Clay turtle bank, making 182:65-67
Leather goatskin on wood picture, making 182:23-25
SOUTH AMERICA—HOUSES
Adobe bricks, how to make 182:40-43
Farmer's huts, how to make 182:26-30
Stilt house, balsa wood, making 925:90-91
SOUTH AMERICA—LANGUAGE
Greeting words of South American countries 601:167
SOUTH AMERICA—MASKS
South American mask, making 204:94-97
SOUTH AMERICA—MUSICAL INSTRUMENTS
Guiros, bottle or bead guiro, making 1288:20-21
Rainmaker, cardboard tube, craft sticks, dried peas, mak-
ing 1278:20-21
Wooden drums, making 182:90-93
SOUTH AMERICA—NATURE FESTIVALS
Inca and Indian rituals 419:122-132
SOUTH AMERICA—ROPE—HANDICRAFTS
Rope pads and mats, animal hot pads, making 182:52-57
SOUTH AMERICA—STRING FIGURES
Fish trap string 373:12-13
SOUTH AMERICA—TOYS
Bullfighter and bull toy, making 182:71-73
Flippy acrobat toy, making 182:68-70
Street racers, making 182:78-83
SOUTH AMERICA—WEAVING
Andean weavings, making 182:58-61
SOUTH AMERICAN INDIANS—STRING FIGURES
Fly figure, making 423:24-25
SOUTH CAROLINA—COOKERY
Cornbread, recipe 1287:unp.
Hopping John, rice and peas, recipe 654:140
Hush puppies, recipe 343:112
Sesame bar cookies, recipe 654:139-140
SOUTH CAROLINA—HISTORY—COOKERY
Charleston and the Carolina Rice Plantations information
on foods 666:117-121
SOUTH CAROLINA—LULLABIES
Hush 'n Bye 780:37
Sweet Water Rolling 780:31
SOUTH DAKOTA—COOKERY
Rodeo hamburgers, recipe 654:144
Wheat garden salad, recipe 654:142-143
SOUTH KOREA—GAMES
Kong-Keui jacks game, how to play 1718:24-25
SOUTH PACIFIC—COOKERY
Tropical fruit dish, recipe 1244:150-151
SOUTH PACIFIC—MASKS
History of South Pacific masks 204:32-36
New Ireland mask 204:86-89
SOUTH PACIFIC—STRING FIGURES
King fish string 372:48-50
Little fishes string 373:67-68
Lizard string 373:16-17
Looper caterpillar string 373:26-27
Palm tree figure 423:20-21
Porker the Pig string 373:70-74
Sardines string 373:36-39
Sea snake string 373:24-25
Setting sun string 373:30-32
Taro patch/Hawaiian stars string 373:40-43

SOUTHEAST ASIA. *See also* **ASIA, SOUTHEAST**
SOUTHEAST ASIA—COOKERY
Banana, fried banana cakes, recipe 638:28
Chicken simmered in coconut milk, recipe 638:11
Nasi goreng, recipe 638:24
Oyster omelet, recipe 638:30
Peanut sauce, hot, recipe 638:26
Pork chili, hot marinated pork, recipe 638:18
Prawn soup with lemon-grass, recipe 638:21
Prawns, sweet and sour, recipe 638:33
SOUTHEAST ASIA—GAMES
Kulit K'Rang game 956:33
SOUTHEAST ASIA—HANDICRAFTS
Palm leaf sequence book, ribbons, beads, patterns, making 1332:75-78
SOUTHEAST ASIA—NEW YEAR—HANDICRAFTS
Solar New Year stick figure dolls in traditional clothing, making 1393:195
SOUTHERN HEMISPHERE—SUMMER
Celebrate first day of summer with pictures, shells, sand collage, making 1199:272
SOUTHERN STATES—COOKERY
Awendaw, baked hominy, recipe 88:226-227
Baked cheese grits, recipe 1205:43-44
Barbecued spare ribs, recipe 1205:42
Buttered grits party brunch, recipe 653:77-78
Buttermilk biscuits, recipe 1205:34-35
Chicken, gravy and dumplings, recipe 1043:119
Coleslaw with sugar, oil and vinegar dressing, recipe 1205:44
Confederate soldier cake, recipe 1043:122
Corn pudding, recipe 529:85-86; 794:3; 1205:39-40
Crab chowder, recipe 1205:36-37
Cucumber and onions with sliced tomatoes, recipe 1205:41
Florida barbecue sauce, recipe 343:106
Fried ham and apples, recipe 1205:34
Green beans and pork, recipe 1205:39
Grits and fried grits, recipes 1043:115
Ham and candied sweet potatoes, recipe 529:79-81
Hominy grits, recipe 652:122-123
Hush puppies, recipe 492:59-61; 666:142; 1043:116
Jambalaya, recipe 662:114-117
Massie stack cake, recipe 1043:118
Minted iced tea, recipe 1205:41
North Carolina whole wheat bread, recipe 343:115
Oven-fried chicken, recipe 1205:38
Peach pie, deep dish, recipe 529:87-90
Peanut butter soup, creamy, recipe 529:77-78
Peanut cake, recipe 1043:121
Pecan pie, recipe 666:142-143; 1043:122
Persimmon cookies, recipe 88:228-229
Popovers with bacon, recipe 529:81-82
Seafood gumbo, recipe 1043:117
Shortnin' bread, recipe 529:77-78; 1043:116
Skillet cornbread, recipe 1205:37
Sorghum molasses raisin bread, recipe 88:227-228
South Carolina hush puppies, recipe 343:112
Southern corn pudding, recipe 1381:5
String beans, Carolina, recipe 529:83-85
Sweet potato pie, recipe 1043:120; 1205:45
Sweet potato pudding, recipe 793:11
Tavern biscuits, cookies, recipe 72:157-158
Virginia spoon bread, recipe 343:110

SOUTHERN STATES—DOLLS
Topsy-Eva, two dolls in one, making 298:130-131
SOUTHERN STATES—HANDICRAFTS
Knotted corn husk throw ball, making 298:140-141
SOUTHERN STATES—PUPPET PLAYS
Jack and the Northwest Wind puppet play 4:60-64
Robber's puppet play 4:56-59
Two Jack Tales puppet plays 4:56-64
SOUTHWEST
Schweitzer, Byrd Baylor, "Amigo"; reading, writing, thinking activities 1093:23-30
SOUTHWEST—COOKERY. *See also* **COWBOYS—COOKERY**
Bean soup, recipe 529:117-118
Biscochitos, recipe 1043:147
Burritos, recipe 1043:143
Capirotada, recipe 1043:146
Chili con carne, recipe 529:118-120; 662:117-120; 666:207; 1043:144
Chili with meat, recipe 895:144
Hearty Southwestern pan bread, recipe 1495:174
Mexican cooking in the Southwest, information 666:196-199
Mexican corn, recipe 529:123-124
Pecan pie, recipe 895:146
Pinole, recipe 1043:148
Refried beans, recipe 1043:144
Scrambled eggs, salsa, cheese, recipe 1542:17
Sopaipillas, recipe 1043:147
Southwest salad bowl, recipe 343:81
Spanish caramel custard, recipe 529:124-126
Tamale pie, recipe 88:233-234; 529:120-122; 1043:145
Three bean salad, recipe 895:145
Tortillas, recipe 1043:143
Tostados, recipe 871:22-23
Trapper's fruit, recipe 1043:145
Wo-Japi, recipe 1043:146
SOUTHWEST AFRICA. *See* **NAMIBIA**
SOUTHWEST COAST INDIANS—GAMES
Ring and pin game, wooden stick, rawhide, plastic baseball, making 1608:56
SOUTHWEST COAST INDIANS—HANDICRAFTS
Spirit figure, paper tube, milk carton, dowel, making 1608:43
SOUTHWEST COAST INDIANS—MUSICAL INSTRUMENTS
Flute, PVC pipe, bamboo, making 1608:39
Morache, branch, basket or metal bowl, making 1608:56
SOUTHWESTERN STATES—COOKERY
Breakfast burrito, recipe 1384:36-37
Chorizo, sausage and chilies, recipe 1384:37
Enchiladas, recipe 1384:40-41
Flan with caramel sauce, recipe 1384:44-45
Green salad and dressing, recipe 1384:42
Posole, one dish stew, meat, hominy, chilies, recipe 1384:43-44
Refried beans, recipe 1384:38-39
Salsa, recipe 1384:37
Spanish rice, recipe 1384:41
Tacos, recipe 1384:38
SOVIET UNION. *See* **RUSSIA**
SPACE
Mobile of space, making 691:44-45
Moonscape, potato printed, making 379:62-63
Satellite, yogurt container, making 684:10-11
Space walk mobile, making 100:42-43

SPACE—BULLETIN BOARDS

Flying saucer, making 295:92
Moon lands, making 295:94
Ricky Robot, making 295:93-94
Shooting star, making 295:91-92
Solar system, making 295:91
Three-stage rocket, making 295:92-93

SPACE—CLOTHING

Space helmets, cardboard, making 897:55
Walkie-talkie space helmets from boxes, making 634:36-39

SPACE—COOKERY

Space ship cake, recipe 449:62

SPACE—COSTUMES

Space hero costume, boy or girl, leotard, leggings, silver boots, making 1509:42-43
Space Invader costume, fabric, face makeup given, making 957:82-87
Spaceman costume, making 338:19-22

SPACE—FINGER PLAYS

Finger plays about space 302:52-53

SPACE—PARTIES

Beyond the Stars party, activities, recipes 809:79-84
Black hole game, making 1185:94-95
Outer space class party 134:94-95
Space Adventure birthday, decorations, foods, games, patterns 1011:17-33
Space Blast-Off party, how to plan and give 43:35-38
Space fantasy party, how to plan and give 86:186-193
Space fantasy party, menu and recipes 86:235-236
Space party, 6 years and up 124:30-38
Space wars birthday, activities, foods, handicrafts 30:48-51
Space, invitations, decorations, costumes, food, games, recipes 1185:18-19
Star Invaders theme birthday party, making 896:47-54

SPACE—PUPPETS

Bodies for puppets, fabric hands, making 752:22-23
Chomper, paper plate puppet, making 752:11
Creature puppet, milk carton, making 752:14-15
Finger space puppets, making 752:8-9
Heads for puppets, papier-mache, making 752:20-21
Monster puppet, mitten cosmic monster, making 752:18
Moon crawler puppet, five-legged, glove, making 752:19
Moving puppet, cardboard, making 752:26-27
Planet, crazy planet stick puppet, making 752:12-13
Snake, space snake sock puppet, making 752:24-25
Space cadet puppet, paper bag, making 752:16-17
Theater, cardboard box, making 752:28-29
Walking hand robot, making 752:10

SPACE AGE TOYS

Al-Lek creature, making 931:18-22
Cylindrical glider, making 931:68-70
Dancing top, making 931:52-55
Gi-Lek creature, making 931:42-45
Jo-Lek creature, making 931:23-27
Large eyed mini-creature, making 931:60-63
Mini-creature, making 931:56-59
Mini-Lek, creature making 931:46-51
Monster, making 931:71-74
One-Lek creature, making 931:28-31
Rustling monster, making 931:80-83
Spiky monster, making 931:75-79
Tu-Lek creature, making 931:32-36
Wide mouthed mini-creature, making 931:64-67
Wy-Aut creature, making 931:36-40
Yo-Lek creature, making 931:18-22

SPACE COMMUNITY

Future fashions, paper, making 834:64
Galaxy flags, paper, making 834:61
Interplanetary passport, paper, making 834:60
Plants, planet plants, paper, making 834:63
Space helmet, ice cream carton, making 834:59
Spaceship, rubber inner tubes, making 834:58
Zoo animals, paper, making 834:62

SPACE PEOPLE

Alien, blown egg alien, pattern, making 1311:120-121
Bionic bag friends, paper bags, making 728:36-39
Harding, Lee, "The Fallen Spaceman," reading, writing, thinking activities 1093:110-121
Martian from cans, making 965:136-137
Moon people, plastic egg, making 422:35
Space traveler, gear and suit, cardboard, making 181:42-45

SPACE PEOPLE—COSTUMES

Moon maiden costume, making 205:74-83
Space man costume, making 205:84-95

SPACE PEOPLE—DOLLS

Man on the moon, making 59:86-89

SPACE PEOPLE—MARIONETTES

Spacemen marionettes, making 361:36-45

SPACE PEOPLE—MASKS

Alien from outer space mask, egg carton, paper tubes, making 1345:10-11
Curly, droopy, Jake and Kate masks, cardboard, balloons, patterns, make 361:50-57
Devil mask, straw board, pattern, making 361:58-59
Extraterrestrial mask, styrofoam, pipe cleaners, making 181:46-47
Large spaceman mask, making 361:78-80
Spaceman clown mask, balloon, pattern, making 361:66-67
Spaceman foil man mask, pattern, making 361:60-61
Spaceman professor mask, balloon, pattern, making 361:70-71

SPACE PEOPLE—PUPPETS

Alien puppets, dough, making 1372:64
Martian puppet, old sock, making 325:37-40
Puppet, paper bag mouth puppet, patterns, making 1155:203-204
Space lady rod puppet, making 361:24-25
Spaceman box puppet, making 361:20-21
Spaceman Charlie puppet, balloon, pattern, making 361:64-65
Spaceman hand puppet, making 361:18-19
Spaceman puppet, sponge, making 311:31
Spaceman rod puppet, making 361:16-17; 361:22-23
Winnie and Bouncy Man stick puppets, making 361:30-34

SPACE ROBOTS

Space robot, blown egg, patterns, making 1311:120-121

SPACE SHIPS

Balloon spaceship, making 872:51
Flying Saucer spaceship from boxes, making 634:32-35
Or-bits, astronaut, making 68:29
Or-bits, cupnik 2, making 68:31
Or-bits, cupnik, making 68:30
Or-bits, mach mite, making 68:19
Or-bits, nip ship, making 68:22
Or-bits, or-bit parts, making 68:12-18
Or-bits, petal ship, making 68:21
Or-bits, ring racer, making 68:24
Or-bits, spinnerator 2, making 68:27

Or-bits, spinnerator, making 68:26
Or-bits, sprinter, making 68:24-25
Or-bits, tri-fly, making 68:23
Or-bits, tri-mite, making 68:20
Or-bits, trimaran, making 68:32-33
Or-bits, wobbler, making 68:34
Or-bits, X-plorer, making 68:28
Platter ships, alley-n ship, making 68:38
Platter ships, flat brat, making 68:40
Platter ships, hoop-la, making 68:45-46
Platter ships, hoopship, making 68:43-44
Platter ships, hurla hoop, making 68:47
Platter ships, plain old platter ship, making 68:35
Platter ships, rim spinner, making 68:36
Platter ships, rim spinner 2, making 68:37
Platter ships, rope-a-lope 68:39
Platter ships, super flatship, making 68:41-42
Rocket ship, cardboard, making 134:94
Shuttle, soda bottle, making 684:28-29
Space rocket model, plastic bottle, egg carton, straw,
    making 1346:10-11
Spaceship, cardboard, making 562:8-10
Star Truck, carpet tube and wood, making 942:152-153

SPACE STATIONS
Bleep and Peep models, making 929:46-47
Cosmic centipede model, making 929:33-35
Cosmic ray bombarder model, making 929:57-59
Lunar colony computer model, making 929:27-31
Meteor man life-support stand model, making 929:20-21
Meteor man model, making 929:17-19
Meteor models, making 929:69-71
Orbital be-bobs models, making 929:43-45
Orbital ray detector model, making 929:53-55
Planetary plants models, making 929:65-67
Saucerettes models, making 929:41-42
Solar saucer model, making 929:37-40
Space box indoor fort, making 1188:52-54
Space colony, paper, making 112:10-11
Space cruiser shuttle, paper, making 112:22-23
Space cruisers, paper, making 112:16-21
Space people, paper, making 112:24-25
Space station buildings, paper, making 112:26-29
Space station party, decorations, games, costumes, reci-
    pes 74:98-108
Space station, plastic container, making 684:18-19
Spaceship, paper, making 112:8-9
Triangle transistor model, making 929:23-26
Walking factory, paper, making 112:12-15

SPACE TRAVEL—PUPPETS
Jody's Journey, puppets, sets, props, sound effects, mak-
    ing 1158:107-115

SPACE VEHICLES
Astro Shuttle model, making 929:13-15
Elastic-powered moon buggy, cardboard, spools, pat-
    terns, making 1051:201-205
Hot rod transporter model, making 929:9-11
Interplanetary Rover model, making 929:49-51
Moon buggy, egg carton, paper tubes, making 684:26-
    27; 719:55-57; 1346:26-27
Space ship, making 184:24-25
Supersonic Space Patroller model, making 929:61-63

SPACE WEEK. *See* **UNITED STATES—FESTIVALS**

SPAIN
Activities, flags, games, songs, dances, recipes 1381:159-
    162
Map and food products 147:6-15

SPAIN—CHRISTMAS
Celebration of Christmas 516:30-35; 601:114-115;
    1049:88
Swinging in the Sun custom 516:32-33
Twelfth Night custom 516:34-35

SPAIN—CHRISTMAS—COOKERY
Almond cookies, recipe 1470:66
Almond soup, recipe 1128:149
Andalusian rice salad, recipe 1470:68
Apple compote, recipe 1470:66
Besugo A La Madrilena, baked whole porgy, recipe
    1128:149
Candy, turron, honey and almonds, recipe 1217:10-11
Caramel custard, recipe 1470:67
Cochinillo Asado, roast suckling pig, recipe 1128:150
Fried pastry, recipe 1470:68
Green beans in tomato sauce, recipe 1470:65
Hot chocolate, recipe 1470:66
Marzipan, recipe 1470:67
Nut crescents, recipe 1470:65
Nut cups, recipe 1470:66
Paella, recipe 1666:100
Pear compote, recipe 1470:67
Queso Frito (fried cheese), recipe 1666:99
Roscon de Reyes, Mee Yings bread, recipe 1128:151

SPAIN—CHRISTMAS—DECORATIONS
Creche, nacimiento, and figures, patterns, making
    1470:69-73
Drum, zambomba drum tree ornament, paper, making
    1470:75
Guitar tree ornament, buttons, pipe cleaners, making
    1470:74

SPAIN—COOKERY
Beef stew, recipe 530:113-115
Café con leche, coffee with milk, recipe 1452:209
Caramel custard, recipe 147:32-33
Chicken shells with mayonnaise, recipe 530:110-112
Chicken with rice, recipe 147:28-29; 871:39
Churros, recipe 656:21
Coffee with milk, recipe 147:20-21
Cold fresh vegetable soup, recipe 147:38-39
Cucumber, tomato and green pepper, recipe 147:37
Custard with strawberry preserves, recipe 530:115-117
Eggplant and rice, recipe 1443:25
Empanada gallega, Galician turnover, tuna, egg, onion,
    recipe 1341:42-44
Empanadas, recipe 1032:262-263
Ensaladilla rusa salad, tuna, eggs, peppers, carrots, pota-
    toes, recipe 1341:36-37
Flan and caramel sauce, recipe 1443:23
Flan, caramel custard dessert, recipe 1154:104-105;
    1477:47; 1265:75-76
Fruit and sour cream, recipe 874:72
Fruit dish, recipe 874:70
Fruit punch, recipe 147:34-35
Galician tuna salad, recipe 793:48
Gazpacho cold soup, recipe 1341:34; 147:38-39; 871:37-
    38; 1154:100-101; 1443:24
Gazpacho, chilled tomato soup with vegetables, recipe
    1165:115-116
Gazpacho, cold vegetable soup, recipe 1452:205

Gazpacho, recipe 187:20; 667:83-84
Green bean salad, recipe 1443:26
History of cookery in 88:143-148
History of foods and cookery 667:37-87
Horchata, tiger nuts, sugar and water drink, recipe
  1341:40-41
Hot chocolate, recipe 1154:106
Iced coffee, recipe 656:30
Leche frita, dried custard squares, recipe 1381:161
Lentil soup, Madrid style, recipe 1652:26
Lentil soup, recipe 147:22-23
Little cakes, recipe 530:117-120
Mantecadas de astorga, Spanish cupcakes, recipe
  1452:208
Meat-eating habits of Spain 662:55-57
Mejillones a la vinagreta, marinated mussels, recipe
  1452:207
Milk, fried milk (leche frita) dessert, recipe 1564:55
Paella, one pot, meat and vegetable dish, recipe 1265:77-
  78
Paella, recipe 88:154-155; 147:26-27; 446:36-37;
  656:24; 1443:22; 1452:206; 1560:14-15
Paella, rice and fish dish, recipe 1381:161
Pan con tomate y jamon, bread with tomatoes, recipe
  1244:81; 1341:38-39
Pimiento drop biscuits, recipe 1265:79-80
Potato omelet, recipe 656:26; 667:84; 1380:11
Rice with chicken, recipe 667:85
Rosquillas pastries, recipe 88:150-151
Salad, recipe 147:24-25
Sangria custard, recipe 147:34-35
Sangria drink, recipe 1443:24
Seville bread puffs, recipe 793:49; 1381:161
Shrimp cocktail and sauce, recipe 1443:20
Spanish chocolate drink, recipe 1209:70
Spanish meatballs, recipe 147:36
Spanish menu 147:19
Spanish old clothes, leftovers, recipe 794:36
Spanish omelette, recipe 147:40-41; 1443:28; 1452:204
Spanish rice, recipe 1380:21
Spinach a la Manchega, recipe 858:unp
St. Joseph's wood shavings, Virutillas de San Jose, cook-
  ies, recipe 72:53-55
Stewed vegetables, recipe 147:30-31
Tiger nut milk, recipe 656:29
Tomato and vegetable soup, cold, recipe 656:34
Tortilla a la Espanola, Spanish omelet, recipe 1165:115
Tortilla Espanola, recipe 1154:101-102
Turron de Jijona, recipe 656:44
Turrones, sweet almond dessert, recipe 1443:27
Valencian salad recipe 1443:21
Vegetable and meat stew, recipe 1443:26

SPAIN—COSTUMES
Bullfighter costume, making 213:96-98
Christopher Columbus costume, making 272:105-108
Queen Isabella costume, making 272:109-110
Sailor costume, making 272:108-109
Spanish dance costume, crepe paper, making 1174:91
Spanish girl costume, making 368:27-30
Spanish lady costume, making 213:94-96

SPAIN—DANCES
Castanets for flamenco dance, walnut shells or wooden
  spoons, making 1362:57
Dancers from Spain, clay models, making 1094:18
Fandango dance and costume picture 1000:40-43

Flamenco dance steps, how to do 1362:57
Flamenco dancers, wire form, papier-mache, paints, mak-
  ing 1217:22-25
I Have a Little Doll dance 697:28-29
Religious dance in Seville 474:119
Seven Jump folk dance 474:118-119
Tip and heel dance 697:32-33
Wedding folk dance 474:118

SPAIN—DRAMA
Saeta 474:98-100

SPAIN—EASTER
Easter egg customs in Spain 201:21

SPAIN—EASTER—HANDICRAFTS
Egg and flower Easter cross, making 298:88-89

SPAIN—FESTIVALS
Festivals and celebrations, maps, flags, crafts, making
  1305:101-109
Festivals of Iberia celebrations 667:72-78

SPAIN—FOLKLORE
"Elegant Rooster" flannel board story (with Spanish), patterns, making 1604:21-28

SPAIN—GAMES
Alquerque board game, patterns, making 1074:38-40;
  1507:84-85; 1541:61-66
Alquerque board game, posterboard, checkers, making
  1477:46
Bullfight game 697:43
Charrada game, how to play 1507:86
La luna y las estrellas de la manana, the moon and morn-
  ing stars tag game, how to play 1708:54-55
La Malilla card game 1132:16-18
La Mosca card game 1132:18-19
Moon and morning stars game 602:101-102
Moon and morning stars shadow tag game, how to play
  1477:52
Pelele game, how to play 1507:87
Pelele tossing strawman game, how to make 1074:230-232
Salazar's Obelisks game, how to play 1497:22
Spanish musical jump rope game 1116:71
Spanish words picture pairs game, how to make 1217:30-31
Tag, how to play 1494:101

SPAIN—HANDICRAFTS
Pomander from orange, cloves, ribbon, making 1217:16
Soldier, stuffed fabric pillow, making 830:82-83
Sun, hammered gold-look foil, making 525:14-15
Tin lantern, how to make 856:120-123
Wrapped-yarn star pin winding, making 298:244-245

SPAIN—HATS
Matador hat, making 1671:17

SPAIN—LANGUAGE
Finger plays and rhymes 1583:145-151
Hours from one o'clock to twelve o'clock in Spanish
  1708:11
Numbers one to ten in Spanish language 397:unp
Spanish words and numbers 574:115-116

SPAIN—MUSICAL INSTRUMENTS
Castanets, corrugated cardboard, bottle caps, patterns,
  making 1646:33-34
Castanets, how to play 1646:35
Castanets, walnut or bone, making 468:40-41
Guitar, shoe box, rubber bands, making 1728:10-11
Maracas, yogurt containers, tape, dry peas, beans, foil,
  making 1728:8-9
Tambourine, papier-mache, metal washers and rings,
  making 1728:6-7

SPAIN—NEW YEAR'S EVE
New Year's Eve dance 624:70-71
SPAIN—RHYMES
Aserrin, Aserran baby bouncing rhyme 780:75
Ay Mama tickling rhyme 780:101
SPAIN—SONGS
"Al Corro de la Patata" 1607:39
Fray Felipe round song 1115:12
Martinello, Martinello round song 1115:12
Sleep, My Little Babe, lullaby 1220:146
SPANISH AMERICANS—COOKERY
Enchiladas, recipe 1536:last
Tacos, recipe 1536:last
SPATS
Pattern, making 7:120-121
SPEARE, ELIZABETH GEORGE
"Sign of the Beaver," corn cake, recipe 1216:29
SPICES
Grinding spices 1673:12
Heating spices 1673:13
Spice ring, embroidery hoop and spices, making
1109:93-96
Spices forest in a jar, making 310:135
Turmeric marbled dyed eggs, making 1673:17
SPIES
Fat and old disguises, making 718:38-41
Hair changes, making 718:50
Hand and nails, how to change appearance 718:47
Hats, making 718:52
Make-up, how to put on 718:30-33
Mustaches, making 718:48
Quick disguise collection, making 718:26-27
Scarves, making 718:53
Secret hiding places in clothes, making 718:42-45
Special effects makeup, how to do 718:34-35
Spot the spies game, making 718:22-23
Spy challenge game, making 718:20-21
Wigs, making 718:51
SPINNING
Finger spinning to make fibers into thread, how to do
1349:98-99
Spindle to spin wool thread from wool, making 1095:6-8
SPONGES
Loofah, how to grow 1259:30-31
SPOOLCRAFT
Spool castle guard, making 629:28-29
SPORTS
Babe Didrikson Zaharias birthday celebration, art, music,
foods, games, activities 1104:90-93
Big sport sculptures, life-size figures, cardboard, making
855:118-121
SPOTS—PARTIES
Spots, invitations, decorations, costumes, food, games,
recipes 1185:22-23
SPRING
April projects, handicrafts, making 561:93-102
Art, cooking, finger plays, games, drama, math, science
and music activities 54:141-162
Celebration of Spring 134:66
Finger plays and rhymes 1583:107-108
March projects, handicrafts, making 561:83-92
May projects, handicrafts, making 561:103-112
Songs, finger plays, stories, games, rhythms 1200:125-129
Teaching activities, art, literature, music, crafts, patterns
1192:21-208

SPRING—DECORATIONS. *See also* **EASTER; EGGS;
EGGSHELL CRAFTS**
Wooden shoe and tulip, paper, pattern, making 760:62-63
SPRING—FESTIVALS
History of Spring festivals 709:142
SPRING—FINGER PLAYS
First Day of Spring finger plays, games, making 944:82-85
SPRING—HANDICRAFTS
Fabulous jeweled eggs, making 183:30-31
Jeweled display case and stand, making 183:32-33
Rites of Spring piñata, balloon and newspaper, making
310:192
SPRING—MUSIC
Hoop rolling 134:68
May pole dance 134:68
Morris dance 134:68
Waltz of the Flowers, simple flower costumes, making
134:68
SPRING—NATURE FESTIVALS
Spring and winter festivals 419:53-56
Spring festivals 419:53-60
SPRING—WEATHER
Art, cooking, finger plays, games, drama, math, science
and music activities 54:123-140
SPYRI, JOHANNA
Heidi's toasted cheese sandwiches, recipe 570:27-29
SRI LANKA. *See also* **CEYLON**
SRI LANKA—COOKERY
Dal, spiced lentils, recipe 1165:168
Kiribath, rice squares, recipe, costume 188:40
Meen molee, fish coconut curry, recipe 1165:167
Red lentil curry, microwave recipe 1211:30-31
SRI LANKA—FESTIVALS
Elephant Procession Festival celebration 826:26-27
New Year celebration 810:29
Peraheras Festival celebration 810:27-28
Sri Lanka festivals celebration 810:24-25
Wesak Festival celebration 810:26
SRI LANKA—FESTIVALS—COOKERY
Sangamitta Day: ghee rice, recipe 1666:164
Sangamitta Day: gingered bananas, recipe 1666:164
Sangamitta Day: rotis (Sri Lankan coconut flat bread),
recipe 1666:163
SRI LANKA—FESTIVALS—DECORATIONS
Wesak lantern, orange or grapefruit, making 1466:25
SRI LANKA—GAMES
Nerenchi game (Twelve Men's Morris), how to play
1688:63-67
Stations game, how to play 1494:40
SRI LANKA—HANDICRAFTS
Sri Lanka spiky caterpillar, paper, patterns, making
1246:26-27
SRI LANKA—LULLABIES
"Lullaby" 1607:12
SRI LANKA—MASKS
Sanni curing illnesses wooden mask, making 1706:19
ST. ANDREW'S DAY. *See also* **SCOTLAND—FESTIVALS**
History and celebration of 49:99
ST. DAVID'S DAY. *See* **WALES—FESTIVALS**
ST. FRANCIS OF ASSISI
St. Francis of Assisi pine cone bird feeders, making
1378:111
St. Francis of Assisi animal mobile, patterns, making
1378:109-110

ST. GEORGE'S DAY
History and celebration of 496:59-61

ST. LUCIA'S DAY. *See also* SWEDEN—CHRISTMAS
Activities, art, songs, recipes, games 1469:48-49
St. Lucia's Day 134:106

ST. LUCIA'S DAY—COOKERY
Pepparkakor cookies, recipe 1218:67

ST. MARTIN'S DAY
Harvest Festival in Europe 659:103-105

ST. NICHOLAS. *See* SANTA CLAUS

ST. NICHOLAS DAY
Activities and projects for classrooms 1393:93-94
History of St. Nicholas Day 709:61-62,67-68

ST. NICHOLAS DAY—HANDICRAFTS
St. Nicholas mask and headdress, making 709:62-67

ST. PATRICK'S DAY. *See also* IRELAND—FESTIVALS
Activities and projects for classrooms 1393:172-175
Activities crafts, history and stories for 128:4-14
Activities famous sayings activity, how to do 781:74-75
Activities, games, making 992:12-36
Activities, projects, poems 819:44-58
Activity, catch the lie, how to do 781:79
Art, cooking, finger plays, games, drama, math, science, and music, activities 54:189-190
Flannel graph stories and patterns, making 822:14-15
Green color activities, art, games, science, music, recipes 904:31-38
History and celebration of 496:32-34; 513:71
Irish celebration, activities, handicrafts, foods, songs, making 909:39-47
Leprechaun stories, songs, art activities, games, recipes 1135:47-49
St. Patrick's Day activities, stories, crafts, recipes 558:52-55
St. Patrick's Day, celebration 133:113-114
Teaching activities, art, literature, music, crafts, patterns 1192:1-20

ST. PATRICK'S DAY—ACTIVITIES
St. Patrick's dictionary hunt activity, how to do 781:84
St. Patrick's memory game activity, how to do 781:76-78

ST. PATRICK'S DAY—BULLETIN BOARDS
Clay pipe and shillelagh, making 295:237-238
Leprechaun family, making 295:238

ST. PATRICK'S DAY—COOKERY
Emerald Isle pie, recipe 402:22-25
Green Castle centerpiece, popcorn, recipe 939:52-56
Green popcorn shamrocks, recipe 939:57-58
Irish soda bread, recipe 49:190; 376:260; 402:22-25; 871:60-61; 1455:123
Irish stew, recipe 1111:141
Mulligan stew, recipe 376:260; 698:32
Pepper Leprechaun, recipe 698:32
St. Patrick's Day cakes, recipe 874:75
St. Patrick's Day pie, recipe 308:51
St. Patrick's day surprises, baked potatoes with cream, recipe 1178:76

ST. PATRICK'S DAY—COSTUMES
Irish country lad costume, making 272:51-53
Irish country lass costume, making 272:53-54
Leprechaun costume, making 272:49-50; 842:37-39
Leprechaun, variety of old clothes, making 1656:13-16

ST. PATRICK'S DAY—DANCES
Irish jig 698:30

ST. PATRICK'S DAY—DECORATIONS
Candy dish, making 561:88
Card with moveable tabs, making 374:159
Collage for St. Patrick's Day, paper, making 835:41
Collages; shamrock collages from tissue paper, contact paper, making 1149:43,46,57,84
Cross and chapel windows card, making 374:162-163
Crown, making 448:13
Elf, making 448:13
Gold, shamrocks, leprechaun, felt board, making 945:167-170
Greeting card for St. Patrick's Day, making 837:46
Greeting cards, making 448:11-12
Hands activities, lucky shamrock, making 306:43
Harp, posterboard, making 1310:111
Hats, paper plate, making 909:41
Irish hat, cookies, making 1672:82-83
Leprechaun boy, paper, making 95:23
Leprechaun girl, paper, making 95:24
Leprechaun hats, paper, patterns, making 1689:30
Leprechaun ladders, paper and straws, making 897:40; 909:41
Leprechaun shadow boxes and picture, making 448:10
Leprechaun, milk carton, making 79:12
Leprechaun, paper models, patterns, making 639:30-31
Leprechaun, paper, large pattern, making 477:45-48
Leprechauns, Mr. and Mrs., paper cups, yarn , patterns, making 1311:160-161
Leprechauns, paper patterns, making 1689:26-27
Luck-o-the-Irish card, paper, markers, confetti, making 1425:24-25
Magic green crystal garden, making 1662:37
Pop-up St. Patrick's day card, making 1387:54-55
Pot of Gold mural, making 906:34
Potato press pictures, green, making 835:40
Rainbow gold, paper, making 819:45
Shamrock button, dimensional paints, buttons, making 1425:23
Shamrock face, pattern, making 128:8
Shamrock hat, paper, pattern, making 823:34
Shamrock mosaics, paper, making 128:12
Shamrock paint sticker, dimensional paints, making 1425:22
Shamrock patterns, paper, making 760:55-56
Shamrock pin, bread dough, making 816:110
Shamrock pins, paper, safety pins, patterns, making 1689:13
Shamrock puzzle mural, making 906:35
Shamrock rice pictures, making 1149:73
Shamrock shadows, paper, making 819:45
Shamrock shape sponge prints, making 1149:100-101
Shamrock shapes laced, making 1149:135
Shamrock shapes painted, making 1149:32
Shamrock swag, paper, patterns, making 1016:41-48
Shamrock tree, making 448:13
Shamrock tree, paper, pattern, making 760:53-54
Shamrock wand, paper, making 835:39
Shamrock, making 648:23
Shamrocks painted with shaving cream or corn syrup, making 1149:8,17
Shamrocks, fancy, making 448:11
Shamrocks, paper, pattern, making 208:9
Shamrocks; finger-painting shamrock shapes or prints, making 1149:19,107

Shamrocks; paper art shamrocks, making 1149:130
Snake, making 648:22
Sprout shamrocks, how to grow 909:42
St. Patrick's Day leprechaun card, paper, making 209:17-18
St. Patrick's Day rainbow card, paper, making 209:15-16
St. Patrick's mobile, paper, making 95:22
ST. PATRICK'S DAY—DOLLS
　　Dolls, lucky charm dolls, yarn, patterns, making
　　　　1016:39-43
ST. PATRICK'S DAY—FINGER PLAYS
　　Finger plays and rhymes 1583:118; 1583:195-196
　　Finger plays, games, making 944:80-81
ST. PATRICK'S DAY—GAMES
　　Find the shamrock game, making 534:90-91
　　Shamrock hunt game 698:30
　　St. Patrick's Day game 240:18-19
ST. PATRICK'S DAY—HANDICRAFTS
　　Four leaf clover lucky charm, how to make 310:189
　　Pixie made from beads, making 255:77
　　Shamrocks paper-cutting, making 384:Mar13
ST. PATRICK'S DAY—MAGIC
　　Magic tricks for St. Patrick's Day 1005:8-46
ST. PATRICK'S DAY—PARTIES
　　Erin pipe favors, making 294:155
　　Games, decorations, songs, and food, how to do 698:30
　　Party and decorations 134:50-51
　　Shamrock cakes and limeade, making 294:154
　　St. Bridget's cross, making 294:156-157
　　St. Patrick's boat, making 294:160
　　St. Patrick's Day party, 7 years up 124:47-54
　　St. Patrick's Day party, how to plan and give 43:63-64
ST. PATRICK'S DAY—PATTERNS
　　Leprechaun and mushroom pattern 309:43
　　Shamrock pattern 309:41
ST. PATRICK'S DAY—PUPPETS
　　Finger plays and puppets, patterns, making 513:72-79
　　Lazy Leprechaun puppet play 754:70-71
　　Leprechaun Marionette, making 754:72-97
　　Leprechaun marionette, paper, string, patterns, making
　　　　1393:173-175
　　Leprechaun puppet, pattern, making 1006:37
　　Leprechaun puppet, pot of gold and rainbow theater, pat-
　　　　terns, making 1083:58
　　Leprechaun styrofoam hall puppet, making 907:32
　　Leprechaun's Gold, puppets and puppet play script, mak-
　　　　ing 1155:80-84
　　Puppet projects, patterns, scenes, story starters, feature
　　　　story 1083:55-58
　　Shamrock puppets, making 735:56
ST. PATRICK'S DAY—SONGS
　　I'm a Little Leprechaun song 782:unp
　　Leprechaun's March song 782:unp
　　Leprechauns song 782:unp
　　Songs about St. Patrick's Day 902:29-30; 1150:21
　　Songs for St. Patrick's Day 901:58-60
ST. PATRICK'S DAY—SYMBOLS
　　Bodhrans and bones, drawing 490:20-21
　　Fairy's harp, drawing 490:16-17
　　Irish country cottage, drawing 490:4-5
　　Irish jig, drawing 490:24-25
　　Leprechauns, drawing 490:6-9
　　Pipers and fiddlers, drawing 490:18-19
　　Pot o' Gold, drawing 490:10-11
　　Shamrock, Irish, drawing 490:12-13

Shillelagh, drawing 490:14-15
St. Patrick and the Serpent, drawing 490:26-27
St. Patrick, drawing 490:28-29
Sweet Molly Malone, drawing 490:22-23
ST. PATRICK'S DAY—TOYS
　　Irish wobble tumbler toy, patterns, making 1016:49-54
ST. SYLVESTER'S DAY
　　How celebrated 505:22-23
ST. VALENTINE'S DAY. *See also* **VALENTINE'S DAY**
ST. VALENTINE'S DAY—DECORATIONS
　　Pop-up heart card, paper, making 1477:32
STABILES. *See also* **MOBILES**
　　Butterflies, batik butterflies, making 741:62
　　Tirol swallow tree, making 741:63
STADIUMS
　　Stadium, paper, making 1020:111-121
STAINED GLASS
　　Good Friday stained glass windows, cardboard, colored
　　　　cellophane, making 1245:19
　　Gothic windows, paper crayon, pattern, making
　　　　1152:155-156
　　Jesse Tree stained glass window, making 726:16-18
　　Picture, stained glass design on paper, crayons, making
　　　　1254:23
　　Stained glass coat of arms, window, paper, crayons, mak-
　　　　ing 1682:13
　　Stained glass, paper, paints, making 1619:20
　　Triptych, tissue paper, making 1531:93-94
STAMPS
　　Plaster of Paris initial stamps, making 1260:40-41
STANDISH, MILES
　　Miles Standish sock puppet, making 353:18
STAR OF DAVID
　　Milk carton Star of David, making 679:unp
　　Paper straws Star of David, making 645:52-53
　　Star of David hat, paper, pattern, making 823:22
　　Star of David picture frame, popsicle sticks, making
　　　　1017:139
　　Star of David, making 648:50-51
　　Star of David, paper, making 726:18-19
　　Star of David, toothpicks, pattern, making 254:232-233
STARS
　　Wishing stars, paper, pattern, making 414:12
STATUE OF LIBERTY
　　Birthday activities, stories, crafts, recipes, making
　　　　558:11-14
　　Birthday celebration; art, music, foods, games, activities
　　　　1104:14-17
　　Crowns; Statue of Liberty paper crowns, making 558:11;
　　　　1104:14
　　Liberty torch, paper, making 558:12
　　Paper plate, pattern, making likeness of 413:15
STATUE OF LIBERTY—COSTUMES
　　Statue of Liberty costume, making 272:86-88
STATUE OF LIBERTY—GAMES
　　Emma Lazarus birthday game 240:40
STATUES
　　Big sport sculptures, life-size figures, cardboard, making
　　　　855:118-121
　　Photo statues, foam coreboards, making 1017:22
STEIG, WILLIAM
　　"Sylvester and the Magic Pebble," alfalfa sandwiches,
　　　　recipe 1216:122

STENCILING

How to do using ready-made stencils, patterns 1261:26-27

STENCILS

Christmas tree, pattern, making 761:18

Colonial stenciling, how to do 831:135-136

How to cut out and use for stenciling 1446:16-19

Nut-stenciled bandanna, fabric, nuts, ink pad, making 1285:100-101

Pennsylvania Dutch design apron, fabric, making 889:100-105

Stationary, stenciled notes, paper, paint, making 1476:39-40

Stenciling fabric frieze, how to cut stencils and apply color 1181:74-77

Theorem paintings, stencils and color, making 673:279-304

STEVENSON, ROBERT LOUIS

Treasure Island; sailor's chipped beef, recipe 570:35-36

STEVENSON, ROBERT LOUIS—GAMES

Robert Louis Stevenson birthday game 240:57

STICKERS

Custom-designed stickers; lick-it-later gums, making 1372:74-76

STILTS

Can walkers, cans, rope, making 1213:137

History of stilts 439:1-41

Juice cans, rope stilts, shoes, how to make 1350:69

STONE AGE PEOPLE—CLOTHING

Patterned purse, cloth, string, making 1725:26

Tunic and trousers, fur fabric, twine, making 1725:24-25

STONE AGE PEOPLE—COOKERY

Wild fruit compote, recipe 1725:34

STONE AGE PEOPLE—FOOTWEAR

Boots, fur fabric, twine, making 1725:25

STONE AGE PEOPLE—HANDICRAFTS

Coil pot, clay, making 1725:38-39

STONE AGE PEOPLE—HEADDRESSES

Reindeer headdress, fur fabric, chicken wire, papier-mache, making 1725:50-51

STONE AGE PEOPLE—HOUSES

Longhouse, twigs, cardboard, hay, making 1725:21

Mammoth bone hut, fur fabric, twigs, string, cardboard strips, making 1725:18-20

STONE AGE PEOPLE—JEWELRY

Necklace, clay, string, making 1725:27

STONE AGE PEOPLE—MUSICAL INSTRUMENTS

Gourd rattle, balloon, papier-mache, making 1725:40

Neolithic drum, cotton fabric, clay, twine, pot, making 17125:40

STONE AGE PEOPLE—PAINTINGS

Painted cave wall, chicken wire, papier-mache, how to make 1725:42-43

STONE AGE PEOPLE—PUPPETS

Stone Age puppet, making 483:18

STONE AGE PEOPLE—RELIGION

Shrine, clay, paints, corrugated cardboard, making 1725:53

STONE AGE PEOPLE—TOOLS

Bow-drill, dowels, wood, twig, string, making 1725:33

Hand axe, stone, how to make 1725:13

STONE AGE PEOPLE—TRANSPORTATION

Reed boat, cotton fabric, caning, string, making 1725:45

Wagon, cup model, clay, making 1725:46

STONE AGE PEOPLE—WEAPONS

Harpoon and throwing stick, sticks, twine, making 1725:15

Spear and spear thrower, papier-mache, making 1725:28

STONE CARVING

Carve plaster and vermiculite rock, how to do 1618:18-21

Soap stone carving stone, recipe, making 696:53

Turtle stone carving, making 920:66

STONE SOUP

French soldiers' beef stew, recipe 569:21-23

Stone Soup, recipe 540:26-27; 812:109

STONE WALLS

Stone wall activities 1014:52-58

STONECRAFT

Clown, making 670:86-87

Duke and the Dutchess, making 670:90-91

Flintstone characters, making 670:91-92

Owl and the pussy cat, making 670:88-89

Painting rock faces, how to do 310:31

Pebble painting, how to do 14:4-5

Rabbit and ducklings, making 670:89

Stone animals, making 670:89

Stone gnome, painted, making 310:34

Turtles, making 670:92-93

STORYTELLING

Adventures of Brer Rabbit, paper folds of story characters, making 406:44-46

Billy Goats Gruff and the Troll, paper folds of story characters, making 406:82-85

Going to St. Ives, paper folds of story characters, making 406:57-60

Jack and the Beanstalk, paper folds of story characters, making 406:47-56

Jason and the Golden Fleece, paper folds of story characters, making 406:33-43

Magic Kilt, paper folds of story characters, how to cut 406:67-71

Pied Piper of Hamelin, paper folds of story characters, making 406:29-32

Siege of the Alamo, paper folds of story characters, how to cut 406:72-81

Storyteller's harp, making 173:10-11

Three Little Pigs, paper folds of story character s, making 406:61-66

STOVES

Hobo stove, making 590:90-91

STOWE, HARRIET BEECHER—COOKERY

Dessert omelet, recipe 57:23

Roast shoulder of lamb, recipe 57:22

STREGA NONA

Strega Nona's magic pasta, recipe 569:18-20

STRING

Activities and resources to celebrate string days 592:121-126

String art picture, cardboard, making 1612:10-11

STRING FIGURES

Cat's cradle, how to make and play 423:39-41; 1501:35-39

Cat's eye figure, making 423:44-45

Eiffel Tower figure, making 423:21

Fish in a dish figure, making 423:46-47

Parachute, how to make and play 1501:40-42

String figures, making 118:275-277

Strings for use in telling stories, how to make 1161:4-5

Whirrer, how to make and play 1501:43-44

STRING FIGURES—ABORIGINES
    House 1404:110-114
STRING FIGURES—AFRICA—BANTU
    Moth or spectacles string, making 372:12-13
    String trick, making 372:14-15
STRING FIGURES—AFRICA—CENTRAL
    Camp bed string, making 372:16-17
STRING FIGURES—AFRICA—ZULU
    Zulu moth figure, making 423:29-30
STRING FIGURES—ALGERIA
    Cock's Feet 1404:22-25
STRING FIGURES—AUSTRALIA
    Australian throwing a spear figure, making 423:17-18
    Dogs on a Leash 1404:22
STRING FIGURES—CANADA
    Casting a Spear, Circle 1404:14-58
STRING FIGURES—CHEROKEE INDIANS
    Crow's Feet 1404:22-25
STRING FIGURES—ENGLAND
    Broom, Candle Caper, Dogs on a Leash, Church Window, Upside Down Cradle 1404:38-123
STRING FIGURES—ESKIMOS
    Siberian House and two Eskimos running away figure, making 423:22-23
STRING FIGURES—EUROPE
    Lizard and Snake string story, string figures, how to make 1161:22-30
STRING FIGURES—FIJI
    Basket string, making 373:21
    Fence around the well string, making 372:38-39
    Giant clam string, making 372:28-29
    Lairo or the land crab string, making 372:18-19
    Parakeet's playground string, making 373:18-20
    Well string, making 372:36-37
STRING FIGURES—FRANCE
    Saw, Scissors 1404:115-118
STRING FIGURES—GHANA
    The Mosquito string story, string figures, how to make 1161:5-8
STRING FIGURES—GILBERT ISLANDS
    Four stars of Itai leaves and their well string 373:62-66
STRING FIGURES—GUYANA
    The Mosquito string story, string figures, how to make 1161:5-8
STRING FIGURES—HAWAII
    Cat's cradle and variations of string, making 372:66-73
    House of a chief string, making 373:14-15
    Maui's lasso string, making 372:40-43
    Open the gate string, making 372:22-23
    Salt cave string, making 372:62-65
STRING FIGURES—INUIT INDIANS
    Caribou string, making 373:28-29
    Kayak string, making 373:54-57
    Little dog with big ears string, making 373:76-80
    Porcupine string, making 373:44-46
    Seagull or man carrying a kayak string, making 372:58-61
    Two brown bears and their caves string, making 372:34-35
STRING FIGURES—IRELAND
    Duck's Feet 1404:22-25
STRING FIGURES—JAPAN
    Cat's cradle and variations of string, making 372:66-73
    Elastic band string, making 373:23
    Japanese butterfly string, making 372:24-25

STRING FIGURES—KLAMATH INDIANS
    Rabbit, Rising and Setting Sun, Six-Pointed Star 1404:81-109
STRING FIGURES—KOREA
    Candles, Cat's Cradle, Cow's Eyeball, Cradle, Chessboard 1404:115-123
STRING FIGURES—KWAKIUTL INDIANS
    Threading a closed-loop figure, making 423:37-39
STRING FIGURES—MAORI
    Maoris two-diamond figure, making 423:30-32
STRING FIGURES—NAVAHO INDIANS
    Apache Door, Big Star, Bow, Lizard, Tent, Two Coyotes 1404:36-88
    Butterfly string, making 373:33-35
    Many stars string, making 372:51-53
    Navaho hogan figure, making 423:27-29
STRING FIGURES—NEW CALEDONIA
    The Mosquito string story, string figures, how to make 1161:5-8
STRING FIGURES—NEW GUINEA
    Fire string, making 372:26-27
    Ghost dance string, making 372:32-33
    Trick string, making 373:69
STRING FIGURES—NEW HEBRIDES
    Laia flower string, making 372:44-47
STRING FIGURES—NORTHWEST COAST INDIANS
    Fastenings of the raven's plumage string, making 373:47-49
STRING FIGURES—ONONDAGA INDIANS
    Crow's Feet, 1404:22-25
STRING FIGURES—OSAGE INDIANS
    House, Jacob's Ladder 1404:26-110
    Osage Indians thumb catch figure, making 423:18-19
STRING FIGURES—PAPUA NEW GUINEA
    Eel or catching crabs string, making 372:20-21
    Lizard and Snake string story, string figures, how to make 1161:22-30
    Trick string, making 373:69
STRING FIGURES—PHILIPPINES
    Philippines noose figure, making 423:26-27
STRING FIGURES—PUEBLO INDIANS
    Hut 1404:103-108
STRING FIGURES—SCOTLAND
    Leashing of Lochiel's dogs string, making 372:30-31
    Tying Dogs' Feet 1404:22-25
STRING FIGURES—SOUTH AMERICA
    Fish trap string, making 373:12-13
    South American Indians fly figure, making 423:24-25
STRING FIGURES—SOUTH PACIFIC
    King fish string, making 372:48-50
    Little fishes string, making 373:67-68
    Lizard string, making 373:16-17
    Looper caterpillar string, making 373:26-27
    Porker the Pig string, making 373:70-74
    Sardines string, making 373:36-39
    Sea snake string, making 373:24-25
    Setting sun string, making 373:30-32
    South Pacific palm tree figure, making 423:20-21
    Tarao patch, Hawaiian stars string, making 373:40-43
STRING FIGURES—STORIES
    Cat's cradle string story, two versions, string figures, how to make 1161:32-44
    Grandmother's Candles string story, string figures, how to make 1161:16-21

Lizard and Snake string story, string figures, how to make 1161:22-30

The Farmer and His Yams string story, string figures, how to make 1161:9-15

STRING FIGURES—TLINGIT INDIANS

Salmon River string, making 373:58-61

STRING FIGURES—TONGA

Fanene's skipping rope string, making 373:50-53

STRING FIGURES—TORRES STRAIT

Torres Strait man on a bed figure, making 423:36-37

Torres Strait yam thief figure, making 423:32-35

STRING FIGURES—TORRES STRAITS

Casting a Spear, Man on a Bed, Palm Tree, Slithering Serpent, Three Diamonds 1404:50-100

STRING FIGURES—UNITED STATES

Apache Door, Big Star, Bow, Dogs on a Leash, House, Hut, Jacob's Ladder, Lizard, Magic Carpet, Six-pointed Star, Rabbit, Tent, Two Coyotes; 1404:26-120

STRING FIGURES—ZUNI INDIANS

Hut, Magic Carpet 1404:19-103

STRING GAMES

Breastbone and ribs game, how to make 1074:259

Fighting headhunter's game, how to make 1074:258

Fish spear game, how to make 1074:255

Mouse game, how to make 1074:256

Outrigger canoe game, how to make 1074:255

SUBMARINES—COSTUMES

Submarine commander costume, fabric, making 1174:86

SUDAN—COOKERY

Chicken and potatoes, recipe 1165:25-26

Fatayer bil-leban, yogurt pancakes, recipe 1165:25

Ful-Sudani, peanut macaroons, recipe 858:unp

Shorba, puree of lamb soup, recipe 1433:118

SUDAN—DOLLS

Sudanese bride doll, making 775:84-87

SUDAN—FACE MAKEUP

Southeast Nuba face, making using makeup 380:24-25

SUDAN—FESTIVALS—COOKERY

Eid al-Adha; eggplant and peanut salad, recipe 1666:26

SUDAN—GAMES

Don-Don Ba Ji game, how to play 1494:19

Leopard trap game, how to play 967:48; 1355:36

Safragat game 956:133

Unlock the door for me game 602:37-38

SUDAN—HOUSES

Nuba house, making 222:26

SUDS

Pictures made with suds, paper, glue, varnish, making 1258:20-21

Soap bubbles, recipe 1413:74-75

SUKKOT

Activities, art, songs, recipes, games 1469:18-19

Celebration of Succoth 601:125

Friendly Sukkah bee 82:21

History of Succot 709:58-59

Meaning of Succot 711:44; 712:26

Ritual of Sukkoth 419:32-33

Succot finger plays, recipes, games, making 944:28-29

Succot, celebration 133:120-121

SUKKOT—COOKERY

Apple candy, recipe 1313:152

Apple crunch, recipe 116:38

Apple snack, making 80:28

Apple strudel, recipe 1451:91

Apricot walnut pie and crust, recipes 711:52-54

Artichokes, stuffed, recipe 266:76-77

Aunt Betty's stuffed cabbage, recipe 116:32-33

Bull's eye sandwiches, recipe 266:78

Cabbage or peppers, stuffed, recipe 711:45-47

Carrot raisin salad, recipe 543:44

Cookie paint, recipe 543:58-59

Cranberry apple bread, recipe 1685:29

Date bread, recipe 266:79

Flag cookies, recipe 543:56-57

Fruit punch, recipe 266:80

Golden harvest tsimmes, recipe 1112:51-53

Hallah, cranberry, recipe 266:74-75

Mandlebrot, recipe 711:48-49

Pecan apple pudding, recipe 711:50-51

Pineapple-banana squoosh, recipe 116:36

Pumpkin-banana bread, recipe 1685:31

Pumpkin cookies, recipe 81:16

Pumpkin popovers, recipe 1685:30

Pumpkin pot centerpiece, recipe 116:34

Pumpkin tzimmes, recipe 116:35

Pumpkin, stuffed, recipe 266:72-73

Roasted pumpkin seeds, recipe 116:37

Stuffed cabbage, recipe 1313:152; 1685:28

Succhini bread, recipe 1112:53-54

Three blender shakes, recipe 116:36-37

Tieglach Harvest purple plum cake, recipe 402:57-61

Tuna cornucopias, recipe 81:16

Vegetables stuffed, recipe 1112:49-51

SUKKOT—DANCES

Dances for Sukkot 542:126-136

SUKKOT—DECORATIONS

Bean mosaic, making 81:18

Bird for the Sukkah, making 80:27

Birds from blown eggs, decorated, making 266:62-63

Carrot plant, making 279:57

Centerpiece of fruits, making 279:58

Cloud, paper, making 266:65

Cornucopia collage, paper, making 81:15

Etrog, panty hose containers, making 266:68-69

Flag for Simhat Torah, fabric, dowel, apple, making 1289:41

Fruit and vegetable chains, making 266:61-62

Fruit animals, making 709:58-59

Fruit mobile, making 80:30

Fruit mosaic, making 80:25

Fruit, paper bag, making 80:26

Holiday creative drawing activities 1337:16-17

Holy Ark model, making 279:59

Pretzels decorations, making 279:55-56

Pumpkin centerpiece, making 81:15

Simhat Torah flag, making 266:69

Star invitation, paper, making 81:14

Star of David, making 279:54

Succah decorations, making 279:53

Sukkah, 8x8 ft. wood Sukkah, how to build 1289:37-38

Sukkah hut, shoe box, paper, string, making 1539:82-83

Sukkah, miniature, Lincoln logs, making 266:67

Sukkah, miniature, shoe box, making 266:66

Sukkah, table top, making 80:24

Sukkot designs for crafts 266:70

SUKKOT—GAMES

Flag game, making, 543:55
Look for the etrog 81:17
Mish mash 81:17
Word games 266:81-86

SUKKOT—HANDICRAFTS

Flags, plain and fancy, making 543:54
Fruit basket, clay dough, recipe, making 543:42-43
Fruit box, making 82:23
God's Eye, yarn, making 266:64
Hand broom for the Sukkah, making 82:24
Harvest basket, making 80:29
Harvest cart, making 543:41
Mobile, musical 82:20
Mobile, Sukkot, making 543:48-49
Picture collage, making 543:53
Seed mosaics, making 543:45-47
Simhat Torah, making 543:50-51
Simhat Torah flags, making 1691:84-89
Succoth centerpiece, milk carton, making 54:207
Succoth party, invitations, decorations, menus, and games, making 2:15-22
Sukkah booth, twigs, leaves, flowers, making 1574:24-25
Sukkah, miniature, making 543:40
Sukkah, wooden, how to build 266:56-60
Torah scroll, paper, making 54:207
Torah, paper, making 543:52

SULAWESI. *See* **INDONESIA**

SUMATRA. *See* **INDONESIA**

SUMERIANS—GAMES

Royal Game of Ur, how to make 1074:56-58

SUMMER

First day of Summer activities 1662:102-108
First Day of Summer, finger plays, recipes, games 944:113-116
Songs, finger plays, stories, games, rhythms 1200:129-130

SUMMER SOLSTICE

Tissue paper flowers, how to make 1393:242

SUMMER—FESTIVALS

History of Summer festivals 709:178,181,182-183

SUMMER—FINGER PLAYS

Finger plays and rhymes 1583:122-130

SUMMER—GAMES

Early Summer game 240:35-36
Indian Summer game 240:53
Summer vacations game 240:44
Summertime shadows game 240:39

SUMMER—NATURE FESTIVALS

Summer festivals 419:61-68

SUN

Activities, art, songs, recipes, games 1469:60-61
Clay sun wall plaque, how to make 1351:12-13
Use Sun to find directions project 25:20-21

SUNDAY SCHOOL—BULLETIN BOARDS

David's sling, making 295:79
Holy Village, making 295:81-82
Pharaoh's Pyramid, making 295:80
Stained glass window, making 295:79-80
Story boards, inspirational sayings, making 295:80-81
Ten Commandments tablets, making 295:81

SUNDIALS

Egyptian bas relief sundial, making 287:69-71
Equatorial sundial, making 937:129-130
Pebble and sand sundial, making 1701:28

SUNSCREENS

How well different strengths of sunscreens work, experiment 1719:70

SUPERMARKETS. *See* **FOOD; FOOD—FOOD BUSINESS**

SUPERSTITIONS

Athlete's foot 118:63
Bangs and bruises 118:63
Common cold 118:63
Coughing 118:63
Earache 118:63
Freckles 118:62
Hiccups 118:62
Insect bites, stings and itches 118:62
Lotions, potions and strange notions 118:61
Nosebleed 118:63
Pains and sprains 118:63
Poison ivy 118:63
Small cuts 118:63
Sore throat 118:63
Splinters and thorns 118:63
Sunburn 118:62
Toothache 118:63
Warts 118:62

SWAHILI LANGUAGE

Numbers one to ten in Swahili language 390:unp
Swahili counting book; one to ten with East African culture explanations 289:unp
Swahili language; 24 words with East African culture explanations 288:unp
Swahili words 1250:26-27
Swahili words and phrases used for Kwanzaa 1659:92-93
Swahili words; people, numbers, animals, common words and phrases 1378:191-192

SWEDEN

Activities, flags, games, songs, dances, recipes 1381:193
Map, flag, and products 621:6

SWEDEN—CHRISTMAS

Advent celebration 973:66-67
Celebration of Christmas 218:39-41; 516:20-23; 1049:84
Christmas customs 149:28-29; 473:46-49; 1717:28-29
Christmas Eve, Julafton, celebration 973:78-84
Christmas preparations 973:73-76
Christmas tree and decorations, how to make 593:114-125
Customs in Sweden 425:18-19
Jultomten, history of 709:67-68
Lucia Day celebration 497:50-59; 973:67-73
Saint Knut's Day celebration 973:91-93
Santa Claus in Sweden 973:80-83
Swedish Christmas program; activities, books, crafts, patterns, making 1159:162-168

SWEDEN—CHRISTMAS—COOKERY

Cookies, Swedish finger cookies, recipe 707:24-25
Glogg, recipe 497:56
Janssons Frestelse (Jansson's Temptation), recipe 1666:125-126
Julekaka Christmas bread, recipe 1503:90
Julskinka (mustard-glazed ham), recipe 1666:125
Klenater (Swedish Christmas bow-knots), recipe 1666:126
Lucia buns, recipe 1023:88-93
Lucia buns, simple, recipe 1023:93-96
Luciapepperkakor, Lucia gingersnaps, with fancy sugar icing, recipe 1128:120
Lussekator, Lucia buns, recipe 1128:139

Lussekatter, Lucia buns, recipe 497:56
Pancakes, Swedish pancakes, recipe 795:72
Red cabbage salad, recipe 1128:142
Red cabbage with apples, recipe 497:56
Rice porridge, recipe 704:60-61
Rice pudding with one almond, recipe 1459:32
Roast loin of pork, recipe 497:56
Rutabagas, buttered, recipe 497:56
Santa Lucia buns, recipe 856:37
Santa Lucia saffron buns and bread, recipes 703:32-41
Scandinavian Yule red cabbage, recipe 703:44-45
Spareribs, recipe 1128:142
Vanilla cookie shapes, cross, star, priest's hair, church
    door, recipe 709:82-85

SWEDEN—CHRISTMAS—DECORATIONS
Dalarna, horses, paper, pattern, making 1305:116
Holiday decorations made with wheat 1301:96
Julbrock, goat, straw, yarn, making 1305:116
Tomten, clay, making 1305:116

SWEDEN—CHRISTMAS—HANDICRAFTS
Advent calendar, making 795:57
Advent calendar, posterboard, pictures, making 1717:40-
    41
Bird ornament, paper, making 1023:69-72
Candles, hand-dipped, making 497:58-59
Chip-cuckoo ornament, making 672:204-214
Harlequin angel, paper, making 669:128
Heart baskets, making 473:49; 551:12
Horses, Swedish horses, making 795:60
Julbrock goat, making 795:62
Lucia crown and robe, making 1023:34-35
Peace tree, making 795:56
Pig card, paper, pattern, making 1159:164
Pig, paper, making 1023:138
Santa Lucia Crown, making 856:32-37
Santa with sack, making 551:14
Santa's elves, making 551:13
Snowflakes, making 551:13
Snowman and skiing Lapp, making 551:16-17
St. Lucy crown, paper, making 1159:166
Stars, making 551:12
Straw stars, making 473:48
Swedish dowel Christmas tree, pine board, dowels, pat-
    terns, making 1159:163,167
Swedish star, making 705:32-33
Swedish star, yarn, straws, pattern, making 1159:164
Tissue paper ball, making 669:78-80
Tomte card, paper, pattern, making 1159:165
Tomte figures, making 669:72-73
Tomte paper strip decoration, pattern, making 1159:165
Tomten elf, making 795:54-55
Tree, angel and figures, making 551:15-16
Woven heart basket, paper or felt, making 1476:31
Yulemen, cardboard, making 795:61

SWEDEN—COOKERY
Applecake with vanilla sauce, recipe 1165:141
Chocolate oatmeal cookies, recipe 874:73
Frozen lemon mousse, recipe 858:unp
Fruit salad, recipe 1381:193
Fruit soup, recipe 794:17
Ginger snaps, recipe 525:67
Gingerbread cookies, and gingerbread house, recipe
    551:10-11
Kjottboller, Swedish meatballs, recipe 1165:140-141
Lucia buns, recipe 88:178-179

Lucia cats, cookies, recipe 557:30
Meatballs, kottbullar, recipe 1503:89
Meatballs, recipe 188:27; 621:32-33
Molasses gingersnaps, sirapspepparkakor, cookies, rec-
    ipe 72:56-57
Pancake torte, recipe 895:133-134
Pancakes, jack pannkaka, egg pancake, recipes 1503:88
Pea soup with pork, recipe 895:132
Pepparkakor cookies, recipe 1218:67
Poor man's cake, recipe 525:66
Prune pudding, recipe 793:35
Pudding, rommegrot cream pudding, recipe 1503:91
Rice pudding dessert, recipe 621:37; 1380:20
Rye cookies, recipe 88:187
Saffron buns, recipe 551:9
Sailor's beef, recipe 895:131
Sausage pate, recipe 1165:139-140
Schmorr gurken, cucumbers with bacon, recipe 1165:139
Surprise rice pudding, making 187:21
Swedish meatballs, recipe 343:61; 525:66; 871:35-37;
    1244:80; 1380:36; 1381:193; 1452:168
Swedish pancakes, recipe 88:185-186
Vanilla sauce, recipe 1165:141-142

SWEDEN—COSTUMES
Meatballs, recipe, costume 188:27

SWEDEN—DANCES
Bleking dance, how to do 1494:125-126
Child Is Down dance, how to do 1494:117-118

SWEDEN—DOLLS
Doll, rope, making 470:16-18
Swedish Greta doll, making 494:133-143
Wooden doll, making 1027:72-76

SWEDEN—EASTER
Bun Day celebration 973:28-29
Catch a Witch! 139:108
Easter witches custom 503:25

SWEDEN—EASTER—HANDICRAFTS
Easter eggs, making 551:19
Easter rooster, making 551:21
Easter tree decorations, making 551:18-19
Easter twigs, making 64:50
Easter witch, making 551:20
Palm Sunday decoration of branches and feathers, mak-
    ing 1245:6

SWEDEN—FESTIVALS
Corn Festival celebration 659:30
Day of St. Lucia Queen of Lights 474:64-65
Feeding of the Birds celebration 601:116-117
Festivals and celebrations, maps, flags, crafts, making
    1305:110-118
Lucia Day, crafts, foods, games, making 557:27-32
May Day, history of 709:160
Mid-sommar (Mid-summer) celebration 973:57-64
Mid-summer Day celebration 631:60
Mid-summer Day Maypole celebration 709:182
Saint Lucia celebration 631:104
Saint Lucia Day celebration 601:115-116
Spring Capping at Uppsala celebration 973:39-43
Spring Festivals, history of 709:146
St. Lucia Day celebration 566:14
St. Lucia Day, activities and projects for classrooms
    1393:97-100
St. Lucia Day, history of 709:69
St. Lucia Day; activities, art, songs, recipes, games
    1469:48-49

St. Lucia Day; celebrate by making girls' crowns and boys' hats 1199:277-279

Twelfth Night, history of 709:112-113

Vasalopp, Swedish National Ski Festival celebration 973:7-14

Walpurgis Eve celebration 631:28

Walpurgis Eve celebration 973:36-39

SWEDEN—FESTIVALS—COOKERY

Lucia Day cats, cookies, recipe 557:30

St. Lucia Day buns, recipe 1381:196

St. Lucia Day, Lucia buns, lily, boys, Lucia cats, crown shapes, recipe 709:70-71

St. Lucia Day, sweet buns, recipe 1305:113

St. Lucia Day; Lussekatter (Lucia buns), recipe 1666:124-125

SWEDEN—FESTIVALS—DECORATIONS

St. Lucia Day crown, paper, markers, making 1381:196

St. Lucia Day; boys' star hat, paper, patterns, making 1393:100

St. Lucia Day; girls' crown, paper, patterns, making 1393:98-99

SWEDEN—FESTIVALS—GAMES

Lucia Day games 557:31

SWEDEN—FESTIVALS—HANDICRAFTS

Lucia Day crowns, paper, making 557:29

Lucia Day Star Boy hats, paper, making 557:30

Lucia Day wooden plaque, making 557:29

May Day muguets des bois, lilies of the valley, making 709:161-162

Maypole, majstang, sticks, rope, flowers, ribbons, making 1477:77

Spring festivals, Pask Ris, Easter twigs, making 709:146

St. Lucia crown, paper, making 1080:10-11

St. Lucia Day clothespin candle, paper, pattern, making 1305:114

Star Boy hat, paper, making 1080:11

SWEDEN—FLAG

Pattern of flag 557:32

SWEDEN—FOLKLORE

"Soup from a Nail" flannel board story, patterns, making 1603:172-175

Country mouse and city mouse fable playlet 1212:44-48

SWEDEN—FOLKLORE—HANDICRAFTS

Troll and the Unearthly Noise, troll collage, pine cone troll 125:41-49

SWEDEN—FOLKLORE—PUPPETS

"Runaway Pancake" shadow puppets, patterns, making 1602:101-107

SWEDEN—GAMES

Bezique card game 1132:40-43

Bow and curtsy tag 602:102

Carousel musical game 1116:40-41

Color chase game 557:31

Drop the stone game 557:31

Gooddag game, how to play 1507:88

Handshake race game 572:28-29

North wind and the South wind game, how to play 1494:98

Number game 602:101-102

SWEDEN—HANDICRAFTS

Advent calendar, making 551:8

Angel, pleated, making 470:15

Animas of Skansen, making 551:25

Archipelago steamship, making 551:29

Battling rams all in a row, paper, making 298:206-207

Brown bears, knitted, making 470:13

Candles, making 955:108-111

Computer project: cookie stamps, design 1218:64-67

Corn husk sweeper maid doll, making 298:142-143

Cross stitch on Binca cloth, making 470:11-12

Dala horse, clay, paints, making 551:30; 1418:31

Doves, paper, making 470:14

Fir cone creatures, making 470:9

Fish bookmark, making 470:10

Heart basket, paper, making 1010:58

Hobbyhorse, making 551:27

Holiday bird, paper, making 515:104

Jumping Jack, making 551:22

Log cabin bank, making 626:89-91

Mid-summer wreath, reeds, dried flowers, making 1418:28

Nils Holgersson, making 551:24

Snowball pyramids, making 470:19

Stenciled box, wooden box, paints, making 1418:32-33

Straw star, making 626:92-93

Trolls, making 551:26-27

Viking ship, making 551:28-29

Witch tree, making 139:129

Wool pictures, simple, making 470:7-9

Woven tulip tapestry, yam, making 298:252-253

SWEDEN—HOUSES

Sod roofed home model, making 494:138-142

SWEDEN—NEW YEAR'S EVE

New Year's Eve celebration 973:90-91

SWEDEN—NUMBERS

Numbers one to ten in Swedish 557:28

SWEDEN—PUPPETS

Hand puppet, making 551:22-23

SWEDEN—RHYMES

"Come Harvest" 1607:22-23

SWEDEN—SONGS

Glad and Good round song 1115:82

SWEET POTATOES

History of sweet potatoes 410:13-16

Plant, how to grow 471:71

Sprouting sweet potatoes, how to do 1024:20-21

Sweet potato plant, how to grow 721:43

Vines from sweet potatoes, growing 217:42

SWEET POTATOES—SONGS

Sweet Potato round song 1115:80

SWISS FAMILY ROBINSON

Family Robinson chicken salad, recipe 365:35

Swiss Family Robinson lobster bisque, recipe 570:31-33

SWITZERLAND

Activities, flags, games, songs, dances, recipes 1381:167-168

SWITZERLAND—BIRTHDAYS

Celebrations of birthdays in Switzerland 474:87

SWITZERLAND—CHRISTMAS

Celebration of Christmas 1049:87

SWITZERLAND—CHRISTMAS—COOKERY

Baseler Leckerli, Basel Treats, cookies with white sugar icing, recipe 1128:115

Swiss almond drops, recipe 218:54-55

SWITZERLAND—COOKERY

Alpine omelet, recipe 1383:22-23

Apres ski fondue, recipe 1244:51

Baked chicken and vegetables, recipe 1383:26-27

Bircher muesli recipe 858:unp

Birchermusli cereal, recipe 1133:92

Bundner gerstensuppe, grison barley soup, recipe
1165:106
Cabbage soup, recipe 1383:25
Cereal bircher-benner style, recipe 1383:22
Cheese fondue, recipe 1244:53; 1380:14; 1434:119
Cherry bread pudding, recipe 1383:37
Chocolate fondue, microwave recipe 1211:43
Chocolate fondue, recipe 1244:53; 1381:168; 1383:40
Chocolate icing, recipe 1165:107
Cookies from the city of Basel, recipe 1383:38-39
Cookies, leckerli, recipe 72:58-59
Double chocolate cake, recipe 1165:106-107
Fondue dips, recipe 1244:52
Fondue, recipe 1165:105-106; 1560:11
Fried apples and bread slices, recipe 1383:21
Fried potatoes, recipe 1383:29
Garden-style vegetable salad, recipe 1383:33
Gruyere pie, recipe 874:27
Hiker's cheese slices, recipe 967:48
Kartoffelrosti, fried potato cake, recipe 1133:94-95
Muesli cereal, recipe 1487:6-7
Noodles with saffron, recipe 1383:34-35
Onion salad, recipe 1383:30
Peek-in-the-oven casserole, recipe 1383:35
Poached perch fillets, recipe 1383:32
Potatoes, grated potatoes, recipe 794:24
Raclette dish, potatoes, gherkins, onions, raclette or
Swiss cheese, microwave recipe 1211:36-37
Swiss apple cake, recipe 530:130-133
Swiss birchermuesli cereal, recipe 1653:42
Swiss cheese fontina, recipe 530:126-127
Swiss cutlets in butter, recipe 530:128
Swiss pancakes, recipe 71:38-39
Swiss tea, cheese and bread, recipe 653:68-73
Tomatoes Fribourg style, recipe 1383:30-31
Valais-style fondue, recipe 1383:42

SWITZERLAND—DANCES
Courting dances 474:117

SWITZERLAND—DOLLS
Swiss children dolls and their chalet, making 494:157-172

SWITZERLAND—EASTER
Easter egg customs 201:24

SWITZERLAND—EASTER—COOKERY
Festival bread, zopf, recipe 1313:67

SWITZERLAND—EASTER—HANDICRAFTS
Easter egg cracking and how to decorate eggs 856:128-
131

SWITZERLAND—FESTIVALS
Chalanda Matz to welcome spring 49:206
Festivals and celebrations, maps, flags, crafts, making
1305:119-126
Spring festivals, history of 709:143
Twelfth Night, history of 709:112-113

SWITZERLAND—FESTIVALS—COOKERY
Fastnacht; mehlsuppe (browned-flour soup), recipe
1666:91-92
Fastnacht; risotto in bianco (white rice), recipe 1666:91
Fastnacht; rosti (crusty potato cake), recipe 1666:92-93
Fastnacht; zwiebelwahe (onion tart), recipe 1666:92

SWITZERLAND—FESTIVALS—HANDICRAFTS
Spring festivals Boogg, Old Man Winter, snowmen, and
ice cream, making 709:143-144

SWITZERLAND—GAMES
Drei-mann hoch, Three-man deep game, how to play
1494:107

Drummer contest game 474:51
Eagle and goats game 602:103
Goatherd game 602:103
Jass card game 1132:45-48
Name the animal game 58:58-59

SWITZERLAND—HANDICRAFTS
Computer project: winter scene, create 1218:28-31
Cuckoo clock from Switzerland, paper and foil model,
making 1094:38-39
Fingerknotted key cord, string, making 1477:57
Swiss paper-cuts greeting card, patterns, making
1051:90-94
Swiss turnip light, making 659:111

SWITZERLAND—HARVEST FESTIVALS—COOKERY
Onion Festival onion soup, recipe 1249:28-29

SWITZERLAND—HOUSES
Chalet from blown egg, making 677:18
Chalet model home, making 494:168-171

SWITZERLAND—LANGUAGE
Phrases and words in German, French and Italian
1133:130

SWITZERLAND—MARDI GRAS—MASKS
Basle double mask, making 709:140-141

SWITZERLAND—MOTHER'S DAY
Mother's Day card, Swiss paper-cuts, patterns, making
1016:100-105

SWITZERLAND—THANKSGIVING—HANDICRAFTS
Turnip lights, Rabenlichter, making 709:49

SWORD IN THE STONE
Sword in the Stone, descriptions and pictures of house
29:Chapter2

SWORDS
Making 7:120-121

SYRIA
Activities, flags, games, songs, dances, recipes 1381:125-126

SYRIA—CHRISTMAS
Customs of Christmas 474:150

SYRIA—COOKERY
Artichokes with ground meat, recipe 1242:120
Baba ghannooj, eggplant dip, recipe 1165:65
Fried kibbeh, hamburger, recipe 1165:65-66
History of foods and cookery in Syria 667:188-200
Kibbeh bil sanieh, stuffed meat loaf, recipe 1165:64
Ma'mounia, dessert, recipe 1165:66-67
Pita, Syrian pocket bread, recipe 6:31; 1244:110-111
Rendered butter cookies, ghoraybeh, cookies, recipe
72:114-115
Shishkebab, recipe 667:201-202
Swordfish, broiled, recipe 667:202
Tabbouleh, cracked wheat and parsley salad, recipe
667:203; 1165:66

SYRIA—FESTIVALS
Harvest Feast celebration 601:69

SYRIA—FESTIVALS—COOKERY
Eid al-Adha; labna (yogurt cheese), recipe 1666:55

SYRIA—GAMES
Ball game 602:84
Choosing it game 602:83
Hat tag game 602:83-84
Marbles game 602:84

SYRIA—HANDICRAFTS
Water wheel, wood and cans, making 515:106

SYRIA—NEW YEAR'S DAY
Celebration of New Year's Day in 475:100

T

T-SHIRTS
Painting T-shirts, how to do 1614:10-17
T-shirt transfers, fabric, crayons, making 1421:39
Tie-dye T-shirts, how to do 1614:44-48

TAFFY
Taffy pull, recipe 1067:57-58

TAHITI—COSTUMES
Girl costume, crepe paper, making 687:18-19

TAHITI—DOLLS
Girl doll, felt, stuffed, patterns, making 487:28

TAHITI—HANDICRAFTS
Crown or garland of paper flowers, patterns, making 1016:80-85

TAIWAN—CHRISTMAS
Formosa; Christmas celebration 601:85

TAIWAN—COOKERY
Chinese tea, how to prepare 1479:119
Rice soup or congee, recipe 1479:121

TAIWAN—FESTIVALS
Dragon Boat Festival boat race 557:61
Dragon Boat Festival, crafts, foods, games, making 557:60-65
Festivals and celebrations, maps, flags, crafts, making 1305:127-136

TAIWAN—FESTIVALS—COOKERY
Dragon Boat Festival treats, recipes, making 557:63

TAIWAN—FESTIVALS—GAMES
Dragon Boat Festival games 557:63

TAIWAN—FESTIVALS—HANDICRAFTS
Chinese Valentine's Day card, pattern, making 1305:135
Dragon Boat Festival dragon boats, milk cartons, making 557:62
Dragon Boat Festival drums, oatmeal box, making 557:62
Lantern, lucky fish lantern, paper, making 1305:130

TAIWAN—FLAG
Pattern for flag 557:65

TAIWAN—GAMES
Beanbags game 557:64
Chien-tze style birdie, metal washer, tissue paper, making 1350:82
Chinese chopsticks 557:64
Clapstick blind man's bluff game, how to play 1494:36
Gentze game 557:63
Growing rice game 602:85

TAIWAN—HANDICRAFTS
Sachet, netting, potpourri, spices, making 1305:132

TAIWAN—MUSICAL INSTRUMENTS
Friction drum, paper version, making 468:112

TAIWAN—NEW YEAR'S DAY
Kiong-Lee at New Year's celebration 475:101-102

TAIWAN—NUMBERS
One to ten 557:61

TANGANYIKA—GAMES
Moto game 1078:35

TANKS
Cotton spool tank, making 129:22-23

TANKS—COOKERY
Tank cake, recipe 449:63

TANNING
How to tan a hide 937:153-154

TANZANIA—CHRISTMAS—COOKERY
Kashata (coconut balls), recipe 1666:4
Supa ya ndizi (East African plantain soup), recipe 1666:3
Wali na samaki (rice with fish), recipe 1666:3-4

TANZANIA—COOKERY
Chapatis, fried bread, recipe 1198:28
Chopped steak and bananas, recipe 662:76-82
Coconut milk, recipe 1694:31
Fried cookies, maandazi, recipe 72:95-96
Ground nut crunch, making 187:41
Kidney bean and coconut milk soup, recipe 1694:30
Meat-eating habits in Tanzania 662:76-82
Meatcakes, recipe 1165:4
Plantain chips, recipe 1380:40
Spiced papaya, recipe 1165:3
Whole wheat bread, unleavened, recipe 1652:20-21

TANZANIA—FESTIVALS—COOKERY
Eid al-Fitr; kashata (coconut balls), recipe 1666:4
Eid al-Fitr; supa ya ndizi (East African plantain soup), recipe 1666:3
Eid al-Fitr; wali na samaki (rice with fish), recipe 1666:3-4

TANZANIA—GAMES
Chikincha game, how to play 1494:24-25
Giants house game 967:49

TAP DANCING
Top hat for dancer, black posterboard, making 1362:55

TAPESTRY
Rag tapestry, making 251:108

TAYLOR, SYDNEY
"All of a Kind Family" soup, recipe 1032:245-246

TEA BAGS
History of tea bags 119:167-169

TEAS
Dandelion tea, recipe 375:85
Sun tea, recipe 384:July 3; 1032:295

TEDDY BEARS
Activities, art, songs, recipes, games 1469:28-29
"Corduroy"; book; activities, art, science, music, cooking, dramatics 716:144-145
Finger play, Teddy Bears 918:23
"Jamberry"; book; activities, art, science, music, cooking, dramatics 716:150-151
"Jesse Bear, What Will You Wear?"; book; activities, art, science, music, 716:148-149
Legend of the Teddy Bear, history of 890:117
Papier-mache bear, making 198:42-43
Teddy Bear book, making 903:7
Teddy Bear picnic and berry basket, making 442:53
Teddy Bear picnic mural, patterns, making 906:47,78
Teddy Bear picnic, activities, foods, and handicrafts 30:26-29
Teddy Bear picnic; book; activities, art, science, music, cooking, drama 716:152-153
Teddy Bear print, making 1017:58
Teddy Bear tea party 134:89
Teddy Bear, paper bag, patterns, making 234:17
Teddy Bear, paper, pattern, making 760:21-22
"This Is the Bear"; book; activities, art, science, music, cooking, drama 716:146-147

TEDDY BEARS—COOKERY
Teddy Bear cake, recipe 449:50

TEDDY BEARS—FESTIVALS
Teddy Bear Day, history of 513:91

TEDDY BEARS—PARTIES
Teddy Bear birthday, decorations, foods, games, patterns 1011:1-16
Teddy Bear cake, recipe 1185:62-63
Teddy Bear picnic, invitations, decorations, costumes, food, games, recipes 1185:12-13

TEDDY BEARS—PUPPETS
Finger plays and puppets, patterns, making 513:91-96
Puppets, five Teddy Bears, making 735:21
Teddy Bear puppet, stuffed, making 907:13

TEDDY BEARS—SONGS
Teddy Bear song 902:79
Teddy Bear songs for infants and toddlers 908:77

TEENY TINY DAYS
Activities and resources to celebrate Teeny Tiny Days 592:127-132

TEEPEES
Back rest, paper, making 1699:12
Card, teepee shaped card, patterns, making 1016:216-219
Carpet, rug and cardboard tube teepee, how to make 1361:74
Five-pole, two-kid teepee, making 118:87-88
Great Plains Indian teepee, information on 118:85-87
History, structure and use of teepees 987:3-77
Indian teepee from boxes, making 634:18-22
Indian teepee, teepee designs, teepee dew-cloth, making 465:96-101
Newspaper and poles teepee, making 310:53
Paper bag teepee, making 1083:137
Paper teepee, patterns, making 254:198-201
Paper-cup teepee, making 180:34-35
Plains Indian teepee, paper or fabric, patterns, making 1390:78-80; 1636:12-13
Pole bean teepee, making 869:72
Sioux teepee, making 562:34-37
Teepee bookends, making 482:88-89
Teepee fort, poles, old tarp, making 1188:28-29
Teepee toy, making 355:12-14
Teepee, canvas, making 590:36-39
Teepee, cardboard box, large, making 539:26-27
Teepee, making 296:72-73; 324:9-10; 466:164-165; 647:53-55; 670:52
Teepee, Naugahyde, pattern, making 1027:136-140
Teepee, old blankets, stakes, paints, making 1368:16-17
Teepee, paper plates, making 1017:26
Toy teepee, paper, paint, making 1699:11

TEETH
First Lost Tooth, class play 134:80

TELEPHONES
Alexander Graham Bell birthday celebration; music, foods, games, activities 1104:66-69

TEMPLES
Chinese temple bird feeder, making 173:62-63

TEN COMMANDMENTS. *See* BIBLE—HANDICRAFTS— THE TEN COMMANDMENTS

TENNESSEE—COOKERY
Apples, dried, recipe 654:146-147
Hominy grits, recipe 654:148

TENNESSEE—RHYMES
"Singing Bird" 1607:26-27

TENNIS
Lawn tennis net, making 51:55-69
Tennis tote, making 70:69

TENNIS PLAYERS
Tennis player costume, paper bag, making 135:17-23

TENNIS—COOKERY
Tennis cake, recipe 449:59

TENTS
Arab Sheiks tent, making 562:22-23
Bivouac tent, making 562:27-28

TEPEES. *See* TEEPEES
TERESA, MOTHER. *See* BOJAXHIU, AGNES GONXHA
TERMITES
Model of termites nest (termitarium), dough, paints, making 1484:26-27

TETA—MAGIC TRICKS
Cups and balls, how to do 1270:6-7

TETON DAKOTA INDIANS—GAMES
Hidden stick game, how to play 1699:115

TETON SIOUX INDIANS—GAMES
Seven Lakota council fires game, how to do 1296:123
Shooting the buffalo, hoop rolling game, how to play 1677:28

TEXAS—BRANDS
Cowboy alphabet and brands, making 1550:30
Create a personal brand, making 1550:31

TEXAS—CATTLE DRIVERS—CLOTHING
Braided hatband, chamois, making 1214:130
Braided leather belt, chamois, belt buckle, making 1214:128-129
Poke sack to carry valuables, fabric, felt, cord, making 1214:133-134
Serape, bath towels, fringe, making 1214:125

TEXAS—CATTLE DRIVERS—GAMES
Cattle drive game, how to play 1214:121-122

TEXAS—CATTLE DRIVES
Blind post office, how to pick one 1214:138
Tally to count number of cattle, how to make 1214:139

TEXAS—CATTLE DRIVES—COOKERY
Chili con carne, recipe 1214:142
Son-of-a-gun stew, recipe 1214:143

TEXAS—CATTLE DRIVES—GAMES
Know your cans game, canned foods, how to play 1214:137

TEXAS—CHRISTMAS
Birds Christmas tree, Fort Worth, Texas 475:66-67
Christmas Candelabra, Fort Worth, Texas 475:69

TEXAS—COOKERY
Barbecue sauce, recipe 652:124-125; 654:150
Chili con carne, recipe 793:1; 1381:5; 1413:40-41
Chili from the Rio Grande Valley, history of, recipe 155:2-3
Cowboy beans, recipe 1550:45
Empanadas, recipe 1032:262-263
Pecan brittle, recipe 654:152
Scalloped sweet potatoes, recipe 654:151
Sopa de Albondigas soup, Spanish recipe 663:80-81
Vinegar pie, recipe 1550:45

TEXAS—FESTIVALS
Juneteenth, emancipation of slaves in Texas, activities and projects for classrooms 1393:234-240

TEXAS—FESTIVALS—COOKERY
Cinco de Mayo; quesadillas (tortilla sandwiches), recipe 1666:267
Cinco de Mayo; sopa de tortilla (tortilla soup), recipe 1666:266

TEXAS—FOLKLORE
"Charge This to the Cap" masks, making 1550:89-91
"Coyote Tries to Steal the Sun" rod masks, making 1550:87-88
"El Pajaro Cu" paper plate puppets, making 1550:91-93
"Family Pictures"; physical and human geography activities 1458:88-91
"Ghost of Jean Lafitte" plastic bottle puppets, making 1550:100

"The Legend of the Bluebonnet"; physical and human geography activities 1458:34-37

"Rattlesnake's Dispute" rattlesnake sock puppet, making 1550:94-95

"Young Moon Chief" overhead shadow puppets, making 1550:108-114

TEXAS—GAMES

Bees in the hive, how to play 1718:34-35

Pigs in the pen, how to play 1718:34-35

Sheep over the fence, how to play 1718:34-35

Texan hopscotch game 1426:44-45

TEXAS—HANDICRAFTS

Texas longhorn bank, juice can, paper, patterns, making 1286:24-25

TEXAS—MEXICAN FESTIVALS

Marketplace, boxes, paper, making 1550:72-73

TEXAS—MEXICAN FESTIVALS—COOKERY

Avocado dip, recipe 1550:75

Hot chocolate, recipe 1550:75

Nachos, recipe 1550:75

Tacos, recipe 1550:74

TEXAS—MEXICAN FESTIVALS—HANDICRAFTS

Mexican mask, box, making 1550:78

Mock tin work toys, aluminum foil, making 1550:77-78

Papier-mache and plastic bottle animals, making 1550:79

Tinwork ornaments, aluminum foil, making 1550:78

Yarn painting, yarn, making 1550:77

TEXAS—PUPPETS

Clothesline puppet, making 1550:36

Cowboy and cowgirl puppets, making 1550:47

Exaggerated expression character puppet, making 1550:33

Famous Texans rod bag puppets, making 1550:23-24

Milamo bird puppet, envelope, making 1550:51

Pecos Bill boat prop puppet, patterns, making 1550:54

Sock earthworm and earth bag, making 1550:51

Texas eyes puppet, making 1550:35

Whiffle pooffle, paper plate puppet, making 1550:53

TEXAS—RANCHES

Build a table-top ranch, boxes, making 1550:28-29

TEXAS—TRANSPORTATION

Chuckwagon, build a wagon, paper, making 1550:44

TEXAS—WILDLIFE

Build a wildlife habitat, making 1550:20-21

THAILAND

Activities, flags, games, songs, dances, recipes 1381:77-80

THAILAND—ARCHITECTURE

Phi's house, making 532:8-9

THAILAND—BIRTHDAYS

Birthday celebrations in Thailand 474:87; 695:55-56

Birthday customs 488:108-111

THAILAND—BOATS

Sampan toy boat, milk carton, making 515:108-96

THAILAND—COOKERY

Banana-nut dessert, recipe 1265:130

Beef noodles, recipe 388:22

Chicken kabobs, recipe 1585:65

Chicken masman curry, recipe 388:29

Chicken satay with peanut sauce, recipe 1380:34

Chicken soup with lemon, recipe 388:26

Coconut custard, recipe 388:42

Coconut dessert, recipe 794:51

Coconut milk cookies, tong ek, recipe 72:128-129

Corn fritters, recipe 1560:27

Cucumber salad, recipe 388:23

Fried rice, golden, recipe 188:42

Fried rice with chicken and curry, recipe 1477:36

Fried rice with chicken, recipe 1265:128-129

Galloping horses, pork, pineapple, peanuts, recipe 1650:37

Hilltribe rice, recipe 1244:20

Holiday feasts in Thailand 388:12

Kaeng chued, shrimp soup, recipe 1452:196

Khao phat, rice and pork, recipe 1452:200

Limeade drink, microwave recipe 1211:21

Lumpia, pancake type food with meat, recipe 1381:79

Marinated chicken, recipe 388:38

Martabak, ground beef omelet, recipe 1165:171-172

Meat satay, recipe 1165:172

Panaeng beef curry, recipe 388:30

Peanut dipping sauce, recipe 1165:173

Peanut sauce, recipe 1381:79

Pineapple-fish noodles, recipe 388:21

Satay, marinated meat broiled on skewers, recipe 1381:79

Satay, recipe 388:39

Shrimp and mushroom soup, recipe 388:27

Spinach salad, recipe 388:25

Staples in Thailand, nam pla prig, rice and noodles 388:18-19

Steamed fish, recipe 388:40

Steamed tofu, recipe 388:41

Stewed bananas in syrup, recipe 388:43

Stir-fried meat with sweet basil, recipe 388:33

Stir-fried vegetables, recipe 388:31

Thai chicken pizza, recipe 1545:42-44

Thai egg rolls, recipe 388:34; 446:22-24

Thai fried rice, recipe 388:37

Thai salad with bean sprouts, recipe 1265:127

Tom kar gai, coconut chicken soup, recipe 1244:212

THAILAND—COSTUMES

Golden fried rice, recipe, costume 188:42

Siamese dancer drawing 988:21

THAILAND—FESTIVALS

Loy Krathong Festival, green paper banana leaf boats, making 1654:75

Loy Krathong Festival, spirit house, cardboard, making 1654:75

Loy Krathong; celebration of 497:18-29

Pujas celebration 810:19

Songkran celebration 601:71

Songkran, Thai New Year celebration 810:23

Thai Festivals celebrations 810:16-17

Vaisakha celebration 810:18

Vassa and Kathina celebration 810:19-22

THAILAND—FESTIVALS—COOKERY

Loi Krathong; tam taeng (cucumber salad), recipe 1666:171

Loy Krathong Feast foods; coconut milk, chicken curry, recipes 497:24

Loy Krathong Feast Foods; golden silk, recipe 497:24

Loy Krathong Feast foods; pineapple chutney, barbecued chicken, recipes 497:24

Songkran; foit'on rum (golden threads around meat bundles), recipe 1666:168-169

Songkran; kai yang (Thai grilled chicken), recipe 1666:170

Songkran; moo thod katiem prik (sliced pork with hot sauces), recipe 1666:169-170

Songkran; peanut sauce, recipe 1666:169

Songkran; sangkaya (Thai custard), recipe 1666:171

THAILAND—FESTIVALS—DECORATIONS
Wesak lantern, orange or grapefruit, making 1466:25
THAILAND—FESTIVALS—HANDICRAFTS
Loy Krathong gifts, woven fish, making 497:28-29
Loy Krathong gifts; lotus blossom, making 497:26-27
THAILAND—GAMES
Hit the coin game 602:85
Maakgep jacks game, how to play 1718:26-27
Mah kha diew, horse with one leg tag game, how to play 1708:56-57
O-O-Oh-Soom game, how to play 1494:38
Takram game 602:86; 967:49
THAILAND—HANDICRAFTS
Royal Thailand elephant and tiger, paper, patterns, making 1246:30-33
THAILAND—JEWELRY
Necklace, making 532:23
Swan pendant, making 532:20
THAILAND—KITES
Elephant balloon kites, making 532:45
Owl kite, paper, string, clothespins, patterns, making 1633:148-149
THAILAND—NAMES
Naming Days information 695:35-38
THAILAND—NATURE FESTIVALS
Rice growing festivals 419:94-97
THAILAND—NEW YEAR'S DAY
Festivals of fun in Thailand 489:141-147
New Year celebration 601:70-71
THAILAND—RITUALS
Growing up rituals 695:96-97
THANKSGIVING. *See also* **PILGRIMS; TURKEYS**
Activities and projects for classrooms 1393:75-80
Activities, finger plays, recipes, crafts 305:15-16; 558:24-26; 1662:174-186
Art, cooking, finger plays, games, drama, math, science and music activities 54:33-50
Flannel graph stories and patterns, making 822:38
Historical Thanksgiving, making 498:82-83
History of Thanksgiving 401:9-10; 496:97-98; 513:29; 631:90; 659:9-14; 709:48-49,51,54; 783:15-19; 829:29-30
History of Thanksgiving customs 783:19-26
Songs, finger plays, stories, games, rhythms 1200:35-37
THANKSGIVING—ART
Painting with Thanksgiving shapes, how to 73:61-62
THANKSGIVING—BULLETIN BOARDS
Thanksgiving bulletin board, making 295:222
THANKSGIVING—COOKERY. *See also* **PILGRIMS— COOKERY**
Apple pandowdy, recipe 1252:38-39
Boiled salad, recipe 1666:263
Candy corn cupcakes, recipe 1546:15
Chocolate fudge, recipe 1252:47
Corn chips, recipe 1313:146
Corn chowder, recipe 1735:28-30
Corn scones, recipe 1252:46
Crackerjacks, popcorn, recipe 1313:145
Cranberry apples, baked, recipe 1401:51
Cranberry punch, recipe 1546:14
Cranberry relish, recipe 1546:15; 1666:263
Cranberry-applesauce bread, recipe 1252:42-43
Cranberry-orange muffins, recipe 1660:45

Gingerbread cookies, recipe 1546:17
Ice cream turkey, recipe 1662:184
Indian corn pudding, recipe 1666:263-264
Indian cornbread, recipe 180:40-41
Indian pudding pie, pumpkin, recipe 206:57-58
Indian pudding, recipe 39:58; 131:19-21; 134:27; 401:50-52
Maple-nut berry popcorn balls, making 180:38-39
Molasses chewies and taffy for pulling, recipes 783:243
Native American strawberry cornbread, recipe 1252:40-41
Old English "sallet," making 180:36-37
Pilgrim cornbread, recipe 353:27
Pilgrim pumpkin cookies, recipe 402:67-72
Pilgrim punch, recipe 1097:unp
Pilgrim stuffing, recipe 659:120
Popcorn balls, recipe 1313:145
Pumpkin bread, recipe 1178:46; 1252:37; 1735:25-27
Pumpkin butter, making 134:25
Pumpkin cookies, recipe 1662:186
Pumpkin custards a la mode, recipe 1169:189-191
Pumpkin ice cream, recipe 1662:185
Pumpkin pie, recipe 1313:146; 1546:16; 1666:264
Pumpkin seeds, roasted, recipe 659:136
Pumpkin soup, baked, recipe 207:106-107
Sugar cookies, patterns for cutting, recipe 1252:44-45
Turkey, 1881 recipe 39:57
THANKSGIVING—COSTUMES
Chief Massasoit costume, making 272:131-132
Indian boy and girl, variety of old clothes, making 1656:79-88
Indian costume, paper bag, making 138:12-16
Mayflower costume, paper bag, making 138:21-27
Pilgrim boy and girl, variety of old clothes, making 1656:71-78
Pilgrim costume, paper bag, making 138:17-20
Pilgrim man costume, making 272:126-129
Pilgrim woman costume, making 272:129-130
Pumpkin costume, paper bag, making 138:8-11
THANKSGIVING—DECORATIONS
Apple turkeys, making 1167:30
Ball of Thanks, circles from cardboard, making 1237:49-54
Banner of Thanksgiving pictures on fabric, crayon drawings, making 1621:11-15
Candy or fruit box, patterns, making 1237:37-42
Corn projects, making 447:136
Gourds, varnished table decorations, making 1257:34-35
Hand Indian head, paper, making 94:7
Harvest collage, cardboard, leaves, seeds, making 1546:8
Indian and Pilgrim flip dolls, making 698:90
Indian bowl from salt box, making 448:37
Indian corn pictures, paper scraps, making 1149:45
Indian dance mask, making 436:45
Indian drum, coffee can, making 1067:195-196
Indian head, making 648:47
Indian headdress, making 436:50
Indian shield, paper plate, making 436:35
Indian vest, paper, making 436:43
Indian, paper, pattern, making 253:166-168; 1067:190-192
Indians and Pilgrims, paper cups, simple, making 612:unp
Mayflower wall hanging, felt, paper, yarn, making 1571:8-9

Mayflower, paper, making 94:12
Pilgrim and Indian eggs, making 401:21-24
Pilgrim and Indian, cookies, making 1672:148-150
Pilgrim boy and girl hat favors, paper cup, paper, yarn, making 1571:28-31
Pilgrim collar, making 436:48
Pilgrim egg carton heads, making 448:35
Pilgrim face mats, making 447:134-139
Pilgrim fedora, paper, making 436:43
Pilgrim hat favor, making 448:37
Pilgrim hat, collar and bonnet, cardboard, paper, how to make 1546:22-23
Pilgrim hat, paper, making 436:42
Pilgrim hat, paper, pattern, making 305:39
Pilgrim head, making 648:44-46
Pilgrim man, paper, patterns, making 1067:192-194
Pilgrim woman, paper plates, making 1067:194-195
Pilgrims from paper bags, making 448:36
Plymouth Village diorama, making 401:30-32
Plymouth Village, boxes, making 698:88
Pop-up Thanksgiving card, making 1387:18-20
Table favor, turkey, wooden balls, felt, pattern, making 1360:35-37
Teepee, tall, making 436:29
Thankful hands Pilgrim boy and girl, paper plate, paper, yarn, making 1571:12-15
Turkey dangling coin saver, cardboard, making 1237:42-46
Turkey or leaf streamers, crepe paper, making 1546:9
Turkey, milk carton, patterns, making 1334:20-22
Turkeys from apples, making 1167:30
Turnip lights, Rabenlichter, making 709:49
Wampanoag Indian girl place card, patterns, making 1237:46-48

THANKSGIVING—DOLLS
Corn husk doll, simple, making 612:unp

THANKSGIVING—DRAWING
Indians, men and women, how to draw and color 1547:unp
Mayflower male passenger, how to draw and color 1547:unp
Pilgrims, young and old, men and women, how to draw and color 1547:unp

THANKSGIVING—FICTION
"Three Names"; physical and human geography activities 1458:62-65

THANKSGIVING—FINGER PLAYS
Finger plays about turkeys, dinner, Pilgrims 302:62-64
Finger plays and rhymes 1583:76-81
Funny turkey and Thanksgiving friends finger plays 1167:32

THANKSGIVING—GAMES
Dance with the Indian game 783:219
Egg race, old English game, how to play 1524:72
Hide the Indian corn game 1167:31
I Sailed on the Mayflower game 1097:unp
Indian bowl game 132:34-35
Indian Chief Says game 783:221
Indian nut game 709:51-52
Indian toss and catch game 132:36-38
Match up game with Thanksgiving symbols, how to make 1546:28-29
Priscilla, where art thou? 783:221
Race game to get to grandma's or grandpa's house, making 1546:26-27

THANKSGIVING—HANDICRAFTS
Birch-bark eagles, paper, making 180:4-5
Corn wreath, corn cobs, wire, making 1546:18
Cross stitch sampler, making 436:33
Hand activities, leaves, turkeys, Native Americans, making 306:16-19
Indian basket, making 180:14-15
Indian beads, making 436:31
Indian feathered headband, making 180:18-19
Indian placemats, making 180:12-13
Leaf printing, how to do 1546:21
Mayflower ship in walnut shell, making 436:32
Mayflower Thanksgiving tile, flour clay , clay recipe, pattern, making 1252:20-22
Miniature Mayflower, making 180:24-27
More Indian cutouts, making 180:6-9
Patchwork placemats, making 401:25-27
Patchwork quilt, making 436:44
Pilgrim buckle belt, making 180:20-21
Pilgrim-Indian chain, making 180:28-31
Thanksgiving quilt mural, making 906:17
Turkey centerpiece, flour clay model, clay recipe, making 1252:19
Wampum belts, making 132:26-27

THANKSGIVING—MAGIC
Pilgrim hat trick, making 37:22-25

THANKSGIVING—PARTIES
Indian corn decorations, making 294:182-183
Mayflower cake and Pilgrim pies, making 294:178
Mayflower centerpiece, miniature, paper, making 829:34
Pilgrim hat favors, paper, making 294:184; 829:35
Plymouth Rock game, making 294:179
Pow-Wow party, how to plan and give 43:21-24

THANKSGIVING—PLAYS
Thanksgiving at Plymouth and five other plays 783:91-186

THANKSGIVING—PUPPETS
Corn husk puppets, making 448:34
Pilgrim lady puppet, making 754:188-192
Pilgrim man puppet, making 754:192-204
Sailing ship puppet, felt, paper, yarn, making 1571:10-11
Turkey stick puppet, tongue depressor, colored paper, egg carton, making 1294:20-22

THANKSGIVING—SONGS
Song, I'm a Little Indian song 782:unp

THAUMATROPES
Cardboard, making 114:63
How to make a thaumatrope 587:181
Victorian thaumatrope toy, cardboard, patterns, making 1051:10-14

THEATERS. *See also* **PUPPETS—STAGES**

THEE, HANNAH
Pennsylvania pretzels, recipe 570:85-87

THEMES—COOKERY
Apple dishes, recipes, projects, books, songs 259:93-97
Bread dishes, recipes, projects, books, songs 259:49-54
Candy dishes, recipes, projects, books, songs 259:115-119
Cheese dishes, recipes, projects, books, songs 259:23-25
Chicken dishes, recipes, projects, books, songs 259:15-20
Cookie recipes, projects, books, songs 259:123-129
Corn dishes, recipes, projects, books, songs 259:81-84

Dessert dishes, recipes, projects, books, songs 259:107-111
Egg dishes, recipes, projects, books, songs 259:29-33
Fruit dishes, recipes, projects, books, songs 259:87-89
Meat dishes, recipes, projects, books, songs 259:7-12
Noodle dishes, recipes, projects, books, songs 259:43-46
Pancake dishes, recipes, projects, books, songs 259:101-104
Pumpkin dishes, recipes, projects, books, songs 259:11-77
Sandwich dishes, recipes, projects, books, songs 259:57-62
Soup dishes, recipes, projects, books, songs 259:37-39
Vegetable dishes, recipes, projects, books, songs 259:65-68

THOR
Thor Festival celebration 631:94

THREE BEARS
Goldilocks and bears puppets, paper bags, patterns, making 941:43-46
Goldilocks and the Three Bears stick puppets, patterns, making 1088:23-25
Goldilocks and the Three Bears storybook door, patterns, making 1087:30-31
Goldilocks puppet, folded paper puppet, making 907:59
Three Bears brownies, recipe 738:unp
Three Bears puppet show 756:145-150
Wee Bear's special porridge, recipe 569:1-3

THREE BEARS—COOKERY
Hot and yummy breakfast porridge, recipe 1215:8

THREE BILLY GOATS GRUFF
Goat puppets, paper, patterns, making 92:41-42
Puppets, costumes, masks, cooking, science, math, music activities 1358:84-103
Puppets, paper bags, patterns, making 940:46-49
Puppets; paper bag mouth puppets, patterns, making 1155:185-190
Three Billy Goats Gruff puppet show 756:156-159
Three Billy Goats Gruff puppets, making 868:20-31
Three Billy Goats Gruff, picture, making 92:40
Three Billy Goats Gruff, puppets and puppet play script, making 1155:58-62
Troll puppet, paper, patterns, making 92:43-45

THREE BILLY GOATS GRUFF—COOKERY
Banana-peanut butter Troll cookies, recipe 1215:36
Goats Gruff meadow salad, recipe 569:10-12

THREE BLIND MICE
Puppets, costumes, masks, cooking, science, math, music activities 1358:141-157

THREE KING'S DAY—COOKERY
Bean cake or King's cake, recipe 1495:80

THREE LITTLE KITTENS
Puppets, costumes, masks, cooking, science, math, music activities 1358:179-193

THREE LITTLE PIGS
Finger puppet, patterns, story, making 512:131-135
Flannel board story, patterns, making 843:76, 135-136
Paper-cutting story, making 49:156-159
Puppets play, stages, scenery, puppets, refreshments 915:8-28
Puppets, costumes, masks, cooking, science, math, music activities 1358:42-57
Puppets, paper bags, patterns, making 941:55-58
Puppets, Three Little Pigs paper bag puppets, making 838:24
Three Little Pigs pillows, fabric, stuffed, making 284:83

THREE LITTLE PIGS—COOKERY
Big Bad Wolf's little pigs in blanket, biscuit, hot dogs, recipe 1215:14
Cinnamony, jinnamony baked apples, recipe 1215:32

THREE MUSKETEERS
Cavalier costume, making 213:108-110

THUMBELINA
Thumbelina honey ice cream, recipe 569:61-63

TIBET—COOKERY
Chapati, recipe 793:61
Fried barley cookies, shabale, recipe 72:130-132

TIBET—FESTIVALS
Dalai Lama birthday celebration 810:37
Gutor Festival celebration 810:31
Losar Festival celebration 810:31-33
Monlam Chemno Festival celebration 810:34-36
Nga Cho Chenmo Festival celebration 810:37
Prayer Days Festival celebrations 810:34-36

TIBET—FOLKLORE
"See for Yourself" flannel board story, patterns, making 1604:68-72

TIBET—GAMES
Abhadho jacks game, how to play 1718:28-29
Samba (bridge), how to play 1718:28-29
Szima (hooks), how to play 1718:28-29
Tibetan memory trick game 956:96-97

TIE-DYE
Step-by-step, how to do 1505:14-17
T-shirt and tights tie-dyed, how to do 1181:54-55
T-shirt tie-dyed, how to do 1377:16-18
T-shirt, how to dye, making 1505:22-23
Tie-dye, fabric, dyes, how to do 1421:199
Wall-hanging, fabric, dyes, making 1505:25

TIERRA DEL FUEGO—GAMES
Shove Winter out game 956:35-36
Shove Winter out game, how to play 1507:109

TIMBUKTU
Camel bags, making 173:36-37
Courtyard houses, making 173:58-59
Dancers rings and tambourines, making 173:72-73
Shoe box houses, making 173:56-57
Trading beads, making 173:50-5 1

TIME CAPSULES
How to make a time capsule from a box 1350:53
Large glass jar, treasures, pattern, making 1311:54
Plastic cup time capsule, collages, making 1618:16-17

TIME ZONES
What time is it where you live project 25:26-27

TIN
Tin-punch pictures, tin, hammer, nails, making 1429:68-70

TIN CANS. See **RECYCLING**

TINKER TOYS
History of Tinker Toys 511:158-160

TINSEL PORTRAITS
Tinsel portraits, metallic paper, paints, sequins, making 1678:20-22

TIPI. See **TEEPEES**

TISHAH B'AV
Israeli coat of arms 712:72-74
Israeli flag 712:70-71
Meaning of Tisha B'av 712:69

TISHAH B'AV—COOKERY
Carrot-apple-raisin-salad, recipe 116:60
Chunky tomato and lettuce salad, recipe 116:61
Cucumber tree centerpiece, recipe 116:59
Date patties from Iraq, recipe 116:62
Pre-fast eggs, recipe 116:110
Salad sprouts, recipe 116:58
Shamir pastries, recipe 116:111

TLINGIT INDIANS—GAMES
Come here game 602:180
TLINGIT INDIANS—HANDICRAFTS
Ladle, making 227:39
TLINGIT INDIANS—HATS
Tlingit hat, making 227:52
TLINGIT INDIANS—STRING FIGURES
Salmon River string 373:58-61
TLINGIT INDIANS—TOTEM POLES
Thunderbird mask totem pole, making 1486:14-15
TLINGIT INDIANS—WEAPONS
Armor, making 227:47
TOBAGO—COOKERY
Arima, almond chicken, recipe 1165:204
Bammy, pan fried bread, recipe 1165:204-205
Browned-down chicken, recipe 1198:39
Fungi, cornmeal cake, recipe 1165:203
Ginger beer, recipe 446:20
Johnny cakes or bakes, recipe 1652:34
Rice and peas dish, recipe 1652:32
TOBAGO—GAMES
Triei jacks game, how to play 1718:30-31
TOGO—COOKERY
Fruit salad, recipe 967:49
TOGO—GAMES
A-Fishing game 602:26-27
Boa constrictor game 602:28-29
Hawk game 602:27-28
Two friends game 602:29
TOGO—HANDICRAFTS
Kente cloth needlepoint wall hanging, canvas, yarn, patterns, making 1716:94-96
Kente pattern needlepoint squares, canvas squares, yarn, making 1716:91-93
TOLKIEN, J.R.R.—COOKERY
"Hobbit"; supercalciumpoweristicextra-berrydocious shake, recipe 365:25
TOM SAWYER
Tom's fried fish, recipe 570:43-44
TOM THUMB
Tom Thumb bread and butter pudding with candied fruit, recipe 569:58-60
TOMATOES
History of tomatoes 410:33-39
Tomato stories, songs, art activities, games, recipes 1135:71-73
TOMBOUCTOU. *See* TIMBUKTU
TONGA—FESTIVALS
Sunday School Day celebration 601:171-172
TONGA—NEW YEAR
New Year celebration 601:170
TONGA—STRING FIGURES
Fanene's skipping rope string, making 373:50-53
TOOLS
Stone Age tools, cardboard, making 181:10-13
TOOLS—PUPPETS
Long time ago tools, puppet stories, activities and patterns, making 357:10-13
TOOTH FAIRY
Tooth fairy pillow, felt, polyfil, making 1301:78-79
TOOTHPASTE
Story of toothpaste 119:35
TOOTHPICKS
Japanese lamp from toothpicks, making 952:112-113

TOPS
Simple spool and pencil top, making 152:101-102
TORAH
Torah mobile, making 82:26
TORRES STRAITS—STRING FIGURES
Casting a Spear, Man on a Bed, Palm Tree, Slithering Serpent, Three Diamonds 1404:50-100
Man on a Bed figure, making 423:36-37
Yam Thief figure, making 423:32-35
TOTEM—MASKS
Totem masks, making 596:41-46
TOTEM POLES
Animal totem pole, paper tubes, posterboard, patterns, making 1633:30-33
Balsa wood totem pole, decorated, making 1368:26
Cardboard roll totem pole, Indian design patterns, making 897:12; 253:172-175; 1067:196-198
Carved wood totem pole, making 524:32-33; 920:53-55
Clay model totem pole, making 1253:5; 1419:211
Coffee can totem pole, making 297:130-131; 1361:76
Computer project: design and build a totem pole 1218:52-55
Cut-paper totems, making 1092:79-80
Egg carton totem pole, making 376:27; 561:41; 677:36; 766:22; 878:94
Milk carton totem pole, making 534:45
Miniature totem poles, making 633:124-127
Paper totem pole, making 845:40-43
Papier-mache totem poles, making 376:159; 788:54; 1260:39
Pumpkin totem pole, making 435:32
Seed totem pole, making 844:18-19
Totem match holders from tubes and acorns, making 623:12-13
Totem pole wall hanging, making 925:57-58
Totem pole, log, paints, making 1421:91
Totem pole, making from spools 629:106-107
Totem pole, paper bags and tubes, colored paper, patterns, making 282:72-73; 678:16-17; 1311:14-15; 1657:70-71
Totem pole, tin cans, making 965:122-123
Totem poles, how to draw 591:26-27
Totem poles, making 171:27-34; 227:60-61; 342:20; 355:8-9; 436:38; 465:102-103; 466:117-119; 670:56-57; 698:75; 714:12-13
Totem toys, making 482:42-43
Turtle shell totem pole, making 466:149
Valentine totem pole, paper, making 94:24
West Coast Indians totem poles, making 324:47
Whale in the Sky, totem pole, patterns 1206:44-47
Wind spinner, making 67:27
TOTEM POLES—COOKERY
Totem pole cake, making 43:169
TOTEM POLES—COSTUMES
Costume, cardboard box, making 142:28-29
TOWER OF BABEL. *See* BIBLE—HANDICRAFTS—TOWER OF BABEL
TOWERS
Tower, wooden model, making 952:20-21, 46-47, 90-91
Towers of cork and toothpicks, making 952:12-13
Watch tower, corrugated cardboard, making 881:24-26
TOWNS. *See* VILLAGES
TOY SOLDIERS—COSTUMES
Toy soldier costume from paper bag, making 678:13
Tunic pattern, making 7:90-91

TOY SOLDIERS—PARTIES

Babes in Toyland birthday party, decorations, games, cake, patterns 1015:54-66

TOYS

Balancing acrobat, making 856:96-99

Balancing parrot, wood, making 925:18

Balancing toy, paper, making 250:unp

Ball and cup toy, making 773:20

Beaky paper toy, making 1238:88-92

Buzz saw, button on a string, making 773:18-19

Chickens pecking toy, making 773:48-49

Climbing bear toy, making 773:32-33

Climbing pull toy, making 954:138

Do-nothing machine, smoke grinder, making 773:24-25

Erector Set, history of 511:161-164

Falling wonder paper toy, making 1238:116-117

Finger top, Whirley Top toy, making 773:34-35

Flipper paper toy, making 1238:84-88

Flipperdinger, Appalachian Mountain toy, making 376:156; 495:54-58; 773:12-13

Frisbee, history of 511:105-107

Gabby paper mouth toy, making 1238:46-52

Goldilocks and the Three Bears toy, cardboard and felt, making 346:15-17

History of toy business 511:13-17

History of toys and games 511:19-25

Hoop roll toy, making 773:21

Hula Hoop, history of 511:107-110

Hummer two, paper, making 151:37-38

Jack-in-the-Box toy, milk cartons, tubes, patterns, making 1311:124-125

Jacob's Ladder toy, making 773:22-23

Jumping Jack, cardboard, crayons, making 1256:23

Kineograph, cardboard, patterns, making 1422:10

Lazy tongs toy, paper, fabric, sticks, patterns, making 1422:29-30

Lego, history of 511:155-158

Lincoln Logs, history of 511:160-161

Lionel trains, history of 511:27-33

Lopper ball, papier-mache, balloon, making 1238:118-124

Matchbox cars, history of 511:43-49

Mountain bolo, Eskimo Yo yo, making 773:30-31

Mouse trap, history of 511:68-69

One puff does it paper toy, making 1238:124-127

Origami water-bomb, paper, patterns, making 1051:134-138

Phenakistoscope, cardboard, patterns, making 1422:8

Pillars of Solomon trick toy, making 773:60-61

Pinocchio toy, making 346:28-29

Puss in Boots toy, cardboard and felt, making 346:18-19

Russian pecking-birds moving toy, cardboard, patterns, making 1051:124-128

Silly Putty, history of 511:71-79

Smoke grinder toy, making 773:28-29

Spindle top toy, making 773:38-39

Spinner paper toy, making 1238:113-116

Spinning top toy, making 773:36-37

Spinning toy, 1800's, making 719:42-43

Spinning toy, paper, making 1348:unp

Stand-up sort of guy paper toy, making 1238:80-83

Stick horse toy, making 773:26-27

Taleidoscope, making 121:33-35

Thaumatrope, cardboard, patterns, making 1422:7

Thaumatrope, cardboard, pencils, string, how to make 1397:30

Tin Woodman toy, making 346:36

Tinkertoys, history of 511:158-160

Tube hummer, paper, making 151:41

Twister, history of 511:97-102

Victorian monkey counterbalance toy, cardboard, patterns, making 1051:129-133

Victorian peep-show box, shoe box, patterns, making 1051:190-194

Victorian thaumatrope toy, cardboard, patterns, making 1051:10-14

Whimmy Diddle, carved wood, making 673:25-33

Whimmy Diddle, making 773:16-17

Whimmy Diddle, tree branch, how to make 1285:138-139

Whimmy Diddle, wooden, making 375:52

Whirligig toy, carved wood, making 673:34-66

Whirligig, double, making 773:15

Whirligig, making 773:14-15

Whirly-twirly paper toy, making 1238:95-98

Wrestler's, dancer's toy, making 773:40

Yahtzee, history of 511:56-59

Zoetrope, cardboard, patterns, making 1422:9-10

TRACTOR TRAILERS

Tanker cab, boxes, making 129:14-15

Tanker trailer, boxes, making 129:16-17

TRACTOR TRAILERS—COOKERY

Tractor trailer cake, recipe 449:65

TRACTORS—COOKERY

Tractor cake, recipe 449:65

TRADE

Trading beads, making 173:50-51

TRAFFIC SIGNALS

Songs, finger plays, stories, games, rhythms 1200:47-49

TRAILBLAZING. See also CAMPING

Trailblazing, how to do 546:7-8

TRAILBLAZING—GAMES

Fugitive and the hunters game, how to do 546:8

TRAINS

Burton, Virginia Lee, "Choo Choo," science, reading, art, language activities 1055:188-192

Steam locomotive, old-fashioned model, making 924:18-23

Toy train, wooden, making 389:36-37

Train, wooden model, making 952:52-53

TRAINS—COOKERY

Train cake, recipe 449:64

TRAINS—FINGER PLAYS

Finger plays about trains 360:22-23

TRAINS—SONGS

Train songs for infants and toddlers 908:50-5 1

TRAMPOLINES

History of trampolines 119:123-127

TRANSPORTATION

Airplanes, balloons, helicopters; literature, activities, crafts, games 1389:135-164

Automobiles; literature, activities, crafts, games 1389:53-77

Dream machines and Merry-go-rounds, literature, activities, crafts, games 1389:165-195

Feet and flippers; literature, activities, crafts, games 1389:1-31

Land and water; literature, activities, crafts, games 1389:78-103

Skates and swings; literature, activities, crafts, games 1389:32-52

Songs, finger plays, stories, games, rhythms 1200:50-54

Trolley cars and rickshaws; literature, activities, crafts, games 1389:196-217

Trucks and tractors; literature, activities, crafts, games 1389:104-134

TRANSYLVANIA—GAMES

Counting out game 474:36

TRAVEL—PARTIES

Globe-trotting party, activities and recipes 809:93-96

TRAVEL—SONGS

Traveling songs for infants and toddlers 908:45-47

TRAVERS, P. L. *See also* **MARY POPPINS**

TRAVERS, P. L.—COOKERY

Mary Poppins; Mary Poppins amazing peach pie, recipe 365:84

TRAVOIS

Pole and blanket travois, making 937:36

TREASURE ISLAND

Sailor's chipped beef, recipe 570:35-36

TREES

Activities with trees and leaves, crafts, printing, puppets, games, songs 1663:24-41

Prayer tree, paper, making 873:8-9

TREES—BIRTHDAYS

Tree planting birthday custom 488:15-16

TRESSELT, ALVIN

"The Mitten" stick puppet patterns, making 480:85

"The Mitten," finger puppet, patterns, story, making 512:89-103

"The Mitten"; mittens, paper, making 843:49-50

"White Snow, Bright Snow"; cupcake snowmen, recipe 843:68-69, 132

TRINIDAD—COOKERY

Arima, almond chicken, recipe 1165:204

Bammy, pan fried bread, recipe 1165:204-205

Banana muffins, recipe 187:13

Browned-down chicken, recipe 1198:39

Channa bean snack, recipe 1380:32

Fungi, cornmeal cake, recipe 1165:203

Johnny cakes or bakes, recipe 1652:34

Peanut flip drink, recipe 1380:43

Peanut punch, recipe 446:21

Rice and peas dish, recipe 1652:32

TRINIDAD—DOLLS

Carnival doll, papier-mache, pattern, making 1027:165-169

TRINIDAD—FESTIVALS

Carnival celebration 601:148-149

Divali celebration 601:130

TRINIDAD—FESTIVALS—COOKERY

Carnival; baked plantains, recipe 1666:203-204

Carnival; double stuffed potatoes, recipe 1666:204

Carnival; mariquitas (fried banana chips), recipe 1666:203

Holi; bammies (sweet potato fried bread), recipe 1666:204-205

Holi; sweet potato cookies, recipe 1666:205

TRINIDAD—FESTIVALS—MASKS

Carnival mask, paper plate, yarn, making 1574:8-9

TRINIDAD—GAMES

Counting out game, how to play 602:121; 1494:57

Jumby, hopscotch game 1426:36-37

Triei jacks game, how to play 1718:30-31

Trier game, how to play 572:16-17; 1507:95

TRINIDAD—RHYMES

"Clap Hands" 1607:24

TRINIDAD—SONGS

"Brown Girl in the Ring" 1607:45

"Mangoes" 1607:44

TRINIDAD—VALENTINE'S DAY—DANCES

Gypsy in da moonlight 624:10-11

TROLLS

Film-can trolls, making 978:15

Troll, felt, making 470:30-36

Trolls, making 551:26-27

Trolls, making using peanuts 257:115-116

TROLLS—COSTUMES

Troll costume, cap, beard, nose, making 326:9-11

TROLLS—MASKS

Troll mask, making 840:20-21

TROLLS—PUPPETS

Puppet; paper bag mouth puppet, patterns, making 1155:205-206

Troll puppet, felt, making 352:15

TROPICS. *See also* **RAIN FOREST**

TROPICS—HOUSES

Palm hut, palm branches, making 1312:14

TROPICS—TREES

Palm tree, life size, tin cans, poster paper, pattern, making 1311:26-27

TRUCKERS

CB truckers birthday rally, activities, foods, handicrafts 30:55-57

TRUCKS

Trailer truck model, wooden, making 923:38-43

Truck model, wooden, making 923:30-37

Wood truck, making 926:42-44

TRUCKS—PARTIES

Car and truck party, 3 years and up 124:158-163

TU B'SHEVAT

Alfalfa sprouts, how to grow 1691:123

Avocado plant, how to grow 1691:126

Feed winter birds, making 82:40

Meaning of Tu Bishvat 711:61; 712:40-41

Pineapple-top plant, how to grow 1691:128-129

Plants to grow, bean sprouts, making 80:43

Plants to grow, sweet potato vine, carrot and turnip tops, making 80:42

Seed plants, how to grow 1691:123-124

Sweet potato vine, how to grow 1691:124

Upside-down garden, how to grow 1691:127-128

Vegetable-top plant, how to grow 1691:126

TU B'SHEVAT—COOKERY

Carob chip cookies, recipe 1685:49

Carrot-apple-raisin-salad, recipe 116:60

Chocolate fondue, recipe 81:30

Chunky tomato and lettuce salad, recipe 116:61

Cucumber tree centerpiece, recipe 116:59

Date-nut balls, recipe 711:62

Date-nut bread, recipe 1685:48

Date patties from Iraq, recipe 116:62

Dates, stuffed, recipe 543:85

French toast, recipe 279:130

Fruit kugel, recipe 1112:74-75

Fruit salad, recipe 1685:51

Fruitful salad, recipe 1112:73-74

Graham square delights, recipe 279:132

Kofyas, wheat pudding, recipe 1691:130

Mushroom-barley soup, recipe 1685:50
Pre-fast eggs, recipe 116:110
Salad sprouts, recipe 116:58
Shamir pastries, recipe 116:111
Stuffed figs and dates, recipe 1112:75-77
Tea sandwich, recipe 279:131

TU B'SHEVAT—DANCES
Creative movement dance 279:124
Dances for Tu B'Shevat 542:26-30

TU B'SHEVAT—DECORATIONS
Almond tree, blooming, making 279:120
Almond tree, making 82:38
Centerpiece, making 80:44
Everything prize tree, twigs, making 81:32
Felt bean bags, making 279:122
Garden marker place cards, paper, making 81:29
Holiday creative drawing activities 1337:26-29
Napkin rings from cans, making 279:121
Orange tree, making 82:39
Palm tree, making 80:45
Plants grown from fruit and vegetable seeds, how to do 543:80-84
Potato initial print, making 279:118
Scrabble invitation, making 81:28
Seed grab-bag centerpiece, making 81:29
Sponge painting, making 279:116
Terrarium, parsley seeds, making 363:62
Tree for Tu B'Shevat, making 712:42-47
Tree planter, making 279:115
Tree poster, making 712:41-42
Tree, orange, making 80:46
Trees from different media, making 279:117
Weed and tissue collage, making 279:119

TU B'SHEVAT—GAMES
Ball pass game 279:127
Blintze game 279:127
Find Aleph game 279:129
Focus game 81:31
Fruit tag game 279:128
Trees game, making 543:87
When I plant a tree in Israel I will take game 81:31

TU B'SHEVAT—HANDICRAFTS
Tree certificate, frame, making 82:37
Tree plaque, making 543:86
Watering can bank, making 82:36

TU B'SHEVAT—PARTIES
Tu B'Shevat party, Arbor Day, invitations, decorations, menus and games 2:37-43

TUAREGS
Desert sand shoes, making 173:32-33

TUBMAN, HARRIET
Harriet Tubman paper mask, making 755:71-77
Harriet Tubman, Conductor of the Freedom Train story for masks, pantomime 755:71-77

TUDOR TIMES—COOKERY
Chicken blancmange, recipe 1724:27-28
Fava beans and bacon, recipe 1724:28-29
Pain perdu, French toast, recipe 1724:27
Roasted apples, recipe 1724:29

TUNIC
Astronomers tunic, making 173:16-17

TUNISIA—COOKERY
Chakchouka, recipe 858:unp
Flaky nut triangles, samsa, cookies, recipe 72:100-102
Ghoriba sablee au beurre, butter cookies, recipe 1165:52

Honey-dipped doughnuts, recipe 187:37
Salata de zaalouk, cooked vegetable salad, recipe 1165:50-51
Salata meshwiya, tuna fish salad, recipe 1165:51
Sweet couscous, cereal grain dish, recipe 1244:86
Tunisian t'chat-tchouka, baked eggs casserole, recipe 1165:51-52

TUNISIA—FESTIVALS—COOKERY
Aid-es-Seghir; mhalbya (Tunisian rice pudding), recipe 1666:45
Aid-es-Seghir; sables (sand cookies), recipe 1666:45
Aid-es-Seghir; stuffed dates with fondant, recipe 1666:45-46
Ras el Am; mhalbya (Tunisian rice pudding), recipe 1666:45
Ras el Am; sables (sand cookies), recipe 1666:45
Ras el Am; stuffed dates with fondant, recipe 1666:45-46

TUNISIA—HANDICRAFTS
Mobile, North African lucky fish mobile, paper, patterns, making 1016:175-180

TUNISIA—PUPPETS
African warrior carved wooden puppet, making 1707:13

TUNISIA—STRING GAMES
Banana string game, how to do 1244:88-89

TURKEY
Activities, flags, games, songs, dances, recipes 1381:127-130

TURKEY—CHRISTMAS—DECORATIONS
Stocking for Christmas, paper, yarn, pattern, making 1393:108

TURKEY—COOKERY
Almond cookies, recipe 1381:129
Apples with whipped cream, recipe 874:71
Bean flatterer, beans, egg, tomato, recipe 1381:129
Bean flatterer, recipe 793:58
Cacik, cucumber and yogurt salad, recipe 1165:84-85
Cookies, recipe 515:110
Dalmatian fish stew, recipe 1305:145
Fried eggplant with yogurt sauce, recipe 1597:120
History of foods and cookery in Turkey 667:178-183
Hummus, recipe 1560:19
Imam bayildi, vegetarian stuffed eggplant, recipe 1165:83-84
Lamb kebabs, recipe 188:35; 1021:27
Moussaka recipe 662:64-68
Pilaf, recipe 794:44
Pilav, rice, raisins, nuts, recipe 1381:129
Sesame brittle, recipe 384:Oct8
Shish kabob, meat grilled on a skewer, recipe 1165:85
Shish kebabs, recipe 515:110; 1244:107-108
Simple halva, recipe 1165:86
Sweet cooked apples, microwave recipe 1211:39
Thick yogurt, recipe 1165:84
Turkish Ayran yogurt beverage, recipe 1653:18
Turkish coffee, making 874:83
Turkish coffee, recipe 1597:123
Turkish delights, gelatin and fruit juice dessert, recipe 1597:122
Yogurt cheese spread, recipe 1380:15
Yogurt with garlic, recipe 1597:120

TURKEY—COSTUMES
Lamb kebabs, recipe, costume 188:35
Sultan and Harem girl costumes 213:142-143
Turkish peasants costumes drawing 988:42

TURKEY—DANCES
Ali Pasa dance, how to do 1494:173-174
Halay dance and costume picture 1000:52-55

TURKEY—DOLLS

Turkish sock doll, making 775:34-41

TURKEY—FESTIVALS

Candy Holiday celebration 601:72-73

Festivals and celebrations, maps, flags, crafts, making 1305:137-141

Seker Bayrami Candy Holiday, recipe for sesame brittle, making 384:Oct8

Sheker Bairam Candy Festival 474:57

TURKEY—FESTIVALS—COOKERY

Kurban Bayrami; bulgur pilavi (cracked wheat pilaf), recipe 1666:65

Kurban Bayrami; cacik (cucumber salad), recipe 1666:65-66

Kurban Bayrami; domatesli mercimek corbasi (Turkish lentil soup), recipe 1666:65

Kurban Bayrami; locum (Turkish delight), recipe 1666:66

TURKEY—FOLKLORE

The Most Wonderful Gift folktale and activities 1478:115-118

TURKEY—FOLKLORE—COOKERY

Lemonade, recipe 1478:123

TURKEY—FOLKLORE—HANDICRAFTS

Most Wonderful Gift; decorated carpet, rug or mat, fabric paints, making 1478:122

Most Wonderful Gift; mirror decorated with Turkish designs, papier-mache, paints, making 1478:120-121

One Man's Horse 126:110-115

One Man's Horse, art activities, costumed stick puppets, making 126:118-120

One Man's Horse, art activities, felt wall hanging, pillow cover, making 126:121-123

One Man's Horse, art activities, shadow puppets and theater, making 126:116-117

TURKEY—GAMES

Blind Man's Bluff tag, how to play 1498:18-20

Fox and hen game 602:86

Fukla game 58:60-61

Kukla game, how to play 1494:159-160

Presents and punishments game 602:87

TURKEY—HANDICRAFTS

Brass hammering, brass or copper foil, plywood, paints, making 1381:130

Kilims, flat woven rugs, cardboard, yarn, making 1338:62-64

Oil lamp, clay, making 1070:62

Rooster plate, Anatolia, clay, making 1070:65-68

TURKEY—INDEPENDENCE DAY

Republic Day celebration October 29 722:38-41

TURKEY—LANGUAGE

Finger plays and rhymes 1583:147-148

TURKEY—MUSICAL INSTRUMENTS

Crescent or Johnny jingle, making 468:70-72

TURKEY—NEW YEAR'S DAY

Time of feasting in Turkey 489:148-151

TURKEY—PUPPETS

Karaghoiz, the Turkish hero comic shadow puppet, making 1707:17

Turkish puppet, making 483:26

TURKEY—TOYS

Firildak toy, making 251:4

TURKEYS. *See also* **THANKSGIVING— DECORATIONS**

Songs, finger plays, stories, games, rhythms 1200:35-37

Turkeys, activities, art, science songs, recipe 911:246-251

TURKEYS—TURKEY CALLER

Paper, making 152:53-54

Turkey call instrument, making 773:134-136

TUSCARORA INDIANS—MASKS

Harvest mask, making 596:39-41

TUTANKHAMEN. *See also* **EGYPT, ANCIENT—KING TUT**

Egyptian hieroglyphics, how to do 1199:252-253

TUTSI PEOPLE—BASKETS

Tutsi basket, woven paper or paper rope, making 1632:34-39

TWAIN, MARK

Adventures of Tom Sawyer; Tom Sawyer fishing game, making 719:44-45

Huck Finn's log raft, making 297:54-55

TWAIN, MARK—COOKERY

Cucumber salad, recipe 57:39

Soft-shell crabs, recipe 57:39

Strawberries and cream, recipe 57:38

Tom Sawyer; Tom's fried fish, recipe 570:43-44

TWELFTH NIGHT. *See also* **EPIPHANY**

Twelfth Night cake, recipe 273:32-35

Twelfth Night crowns, making 273:35-39

Twelfth Night, Epiphany, the coming of the Magi, activities and projects for classrooms 1393:120-122

TWELFTH NIGHT—COOKERY

Bombe drink, recipe 1203:123

Chili cheese turnovers, recipe 1203:121-122

Guacamole, recipe 1203:123

King cake, recipe 1203:123-124

Nachos with sausage, recipe 1203:122

Refried bean dip, recipe 1203:122

Taquitos, recipe 1203:123

TWELFTH NIGHT—PARTIES

Twelfth Night party, recipes and games 635:30-34

Twelfth Night, invitations, activities, games, recipes, making 1203:104-110

TWENTIES—COSTUMES

1920 evening dress, girl, making 368:55-58

Boy and girl costumes, fabric, patterns, making 1174:37-38

U

UDRY, JANICE
"A Tree Is Nice"; leaf skeletons, making 843:39
"A Tree Is Nice"; science, reading, art, language arts activities 1055:49-54

UFO'S
Flying saucer with launchpad, plastic bottles, paper plates, making 1346:16-17

UFO'S—COOKERY
UFO cake, recipe 449:69

UGANDA—CHRISTMAS—COOKERY
Engege Apolo (Ugandan-style fried fish), recipe 1666:9-10

UGANDA—COOKERY
Bananas, cooked, recipe 794:40
Chapatis, fried bread, recipe 1198:28
Choroko sauce, recipe 1652:40
Fried cookies, maandazi, recipe 72:95-96
Fruit platter, recipe 188:18
Whole wheat bread, unleavened, recipe 1652:20-21

UGANDA—COSTUMES
Fruit platter, recipe, costume 188:18

UGANDA—GAMES
Bottle Relay game, how to play 1494:17
Hurly Burly game, how to play 1497:42

UGANDA—MUSICAL INSTRUMENTS
Thumb piano, Uganda, making 495:76-80

UGANDA—RHYMES
"Kaleeba!" 1607:31

UGLY DUCKLING
Children's cornbread for the swan, recipe 569:79-81

UKRAINE—CHRISTMAS
Christmas celebration 601:117-118
Christmas tree and decorations, how to make 593:132-137

UKRAINE—CHRISTMAS—COOKERY
Medivnyk, Ukrainian honey loaf, recipe 1128:132
Pampushky (filled doughnuts), recipe 1666:141
Ukrainian Christmas kalach bread, recipe 1128:131

UKRAINE—COOKERY
Cabbage rolls, recipe 501:83
Holiday nut cookies, rohlichky, recipe 72:79-80

UKRAINE—EASTER—COOKERY
Borshch Ukrainsky (Ukrainian-style beet soup, recipe 1666:139
Chereshyanyk (cherry bars), recipe 1666:140
Hard-cooked eggs, recipe 1666:139
Ukrainian spinach and noodles, recipe 1666:140

UKRAINE—EASTER—HANDICRAFTS
Egg painting, making 70:54
Pysanky egg, making 297:200-201
Ukrainian pysanky eggs, making 503:34-35

UKRAINE—HANDICRAFTS
Computer project: Pysanky eggs, draw and decorate 1218:56-59
Glass painting; night in the woods, making 298:182-183
Pysanka eggs, geometric design, making 298:82-83
Pysanky eggs, how to make and decorate 525:70-71; 1081:13

UNCLE SAM
History of Uncle Sam 333:59-61
Uncle Sam centerpiece, making 226:34
Uncle Sam Day; history of 384:Mar13
Uncle Sam flag standard, making 629:128-129
Uncle Sam, paper models, patterns, making 639:37-38
Uncle Sam, paper plate, pattern, making 413:18-19

UNCLE SAM—COSTUMES
Uncle Sam costume, making 272:88-91

UNCLE SAM—GAMES
Uncle Sam fish pond game 698:64

UNCLE SAM—HAT
Uncle Sam hat, soup can and felt making 374:131-132

UNCLE SAM—PUPPETS
Puppet; paper bag Uncle Sam puppet, patterns, making 1107:177-182
Uncle Sam puppet, pattern, making 448:23; 1006:45

UNDERGROUND RAILROAD—FICTION
"The Drinking Gourd," physical and human geography activities 1458:54-57

UNICORNS
Unicorn costume, fabric, pattern, making 1174:85

UNITED ARAB EMIRATES. *See also* **ARABIAN PENINSULA**

UNITED ARAB EMIRATES—COOKERY
Almond biscuits, recipe 1165:75
Date bars, recipe 1165:73
Fruit balls, recipe 1165:76
Hoomis, chick pea spread, recipe 1165:72
Limonada, lemonade, recipe 1165:72-73
Mjeddrah, rice with lentils, recipe 1165:74
Shourba bilsen, thick lentil soup, recipe 1165:72
Stuffed dates, figs, prunes, recipe 1165:75
Tahineh or tahini, sesame seed paste, recipe 1165:74

UNITED KINGDOM OF GREAT BRITAIN. *See* **ENGLAND; IRELAND; SCOTLAND; WALES**

UNITED NATIONS
United Nations party 474:140-141

UNITED NATIONS—COSTUMES
Peaceful Planet costume, making 272:111-113

UNITED NATIONS DAY
Activities 1662:156-157
Activities and projects for classrooms 1393:56-59
History of United Nations Day 199:52-53
United Nations Day, celebration 133:119

UNITED NATIONS DAY—COSTUMES
United Nations blend costume, making 272:113-114

UNITED NATIONS DAY—DECORATIONS
Patriotic glue prints, making 199:56-59
Peace dove, making 199:54-55

UNITED NATIONS DAY—FESTIVALS
International Literacy Day; word read in seven languages activity 1199:202
United Nations Day; celebrate by acting as representative of foreign country 1199:238-239

UNITED NATIONS DAY—HANDICRAFTS
Doll cut-outs from 9 cultures, paper, patterns, making 1393:57-59

UNITED STATES
Activities, flags, games, songs, dances, recipes 1381:3-12

UNITED STATES—ASTRONAUTS
Rocket thrusters allow astronauts to maneuver in space, making 1719:56-58

UNITED STATES—CHRISTMAS
Customs in United States 425:23

UNITED STATES—CHRISTMAS—COOKERY
Ambrosia, recipe 273:128-129
New England bread stuffing, recipe 273:121-123
Puffed rice-molasses balls, recipe 273:116-117
South Carolina orange sweet potatoes, recipe 273:126-128

UNITED STATES—CHRISTMAS—DECORATIONS
Card for Christmas, making 273:109-112
Rudolph the red-nosed reindeer head, paper, patterns, making 1393:110

UNITED STATES—CHRISTMAS—HANDICRAFTS
Angel, twisted paper, ribbon, lace, yarn, making 1463:23-25
Appalachian braided wreath, fabric, making 273:123-126
Ball from ribbon, making 273:117-121
Folk art angel, fabric, walnuts, twigs, yarn, patterns, making 1463:20-22
Stocking, felt, making 273:112-115

UNITED STATES—COOKERY
Acorns, recipe 118:178
All American hamburger, recipe 794:3
Ant on a log, peanut butter, raisins, recipe 1302:40
Ants-on-a-log, celery, raisins, peanut butter, recipe 1650:21
Apple brown Betty dessert, recipe 1380:38
Apple pie using ingredients from around the world, recipe 1540:last
Apple pie, recipe 1165:264; 1710:last
Baked beans, recipe 1380:81; 1394:18-19
Batter-dipped corn dogs, recipe 118:159
Beef jerky, recipe 1165:267-268
Boston baked beans, recipe 131:35; 187:7
Boston brown bread, recipe 1165:263
Brownies, chocolate, recipe 131:30
Cajun breakfast special, recipe 1560:31
Cattails, pancakes, recipe 118:178
Chocolate drop cookies, recipe 967:52
Corn beef hash, recipe 1560:28
Corn popper, making 118:165
Corn popping, how to 118:166
Cornbread, recipe 1287:unp.; 1401:26
Crab clambake, recipe 967:52
Crepes, recipe 858:unp
Crispy potato chips, recipe 118:163-164
Dandelions, recipe 118:178
Day lilies, recipe 118:177-178
Early American graham cracker cake, recipe 188:2
Egg salad on sesame seed rolls, making 131:24
Eggnog, recipe 131:38
Foraging 118:177
Fried dough, recipe 118:167-168
Granola, homemade, recipe 88:241-242
Hamburgers, recipe 1257:26-27
History of cookery in United States 88:212-225
Hollywood salad bowl, recipe 1560:30
Hominy, recipe 1380:29
Hoppin' John bean dish, recipe 1380:31
Hopping John, peas, ham and rice dish, recipe 1165:265-266
Hopping John, ham, black eyed peas, recipe 1650:31
Hush puppies, cornmeal, recipe 1650:29
Indian corn pudding, recipe 187:5
Luau punch, recipe 187:10
Meat-eating habits in the United States 662:108-125
Millet and ground round casserole, recipe 88:243
Monte Cristo sandwich, recipe 1165:268-269
Olive Halloween buns, recipe 967:52
Pancakes, silver dollar, recipe 131:21
Peanut brittle, recipe 1165:266
Peanut butter apple sandwich, recipe 1302:41
Peanut butter banana shake, recipe 1302:41
Peanut butter crunch balls, recipe 1302:40
Peanut butter orange sandwich, recipe 1302:39
Peanut butter raisin delight, recipe 1302:39
Peanut butter, homemade, recipe 1302:37
Pecan pralines, recipe 1165:267
Pie crust, 3-minute goof-proof pie crust, recipe 1165:265
Pie crust, recipe 1165:264-265
Popcorn balls, recipe 118:166
Posole, recipe 967:53
Pumpkin pie, recipe 131:42; 1560:29
Rio Grande chili, recipe 187:6
Rivel soup, recipe 343:93
Roasted corn, recipe 1244:135
Rose petals recipe 118:179
S'mores, recipe 118:169
Shoofly pie, recipe 1650:41
Skillet quick bread, recipe 88:245
Snickerdoodles, recipe 187:9
South Carolina orange sweet potatoes, recipe 273:126-128
Southern pecan pie, recipe 187:8
Spicy ketchup, recipe 118:162-163
Submarine sandwich, recipe 118:160-162
Surfer's shake, recipe 1560:30
Triticale raisin muffins, recipe 88:242
Tuskegee ice cream, George Washington Carver recipe 1165:267
Vanilla milkshake, recipe 1380:13
Whole wheat rolls, recipe 88:244

UNITED STATES—COSTUMES
Minnie Mouse costume, fabric, patterns, making 1174:100-101
Pop Star drummer, plastic bottle, fabric, yarn, making 1728:12-13

UNITED STATES—DANCES
Amos Moses dance, how to do 1494:185-186
Circle Virginia reel, how to do 1494:179-180
Elvira dance, how to do 1494:181-182
Tennessee Saturday Night dance, how to do 1494:189-190

UNITED STATES—ELECTION DAY
Celebrate with mock election activity 1199:248-249

UNITED STATES—FESTIVALS
Alex Haley's birthday, family portrait, paper and markers, making 1199:185
Alex Haley's birthday; explore your roots family tree, pattern, making 1199:183-185
Amelia Earhart's birthday; celebrate by making paper airplanes, patterns 1199:166-167
Audubon's birthday; celebrate by making flying birds, patterns 1199:98-100
Audubon's birthday; celebrate; build nesting box, milk cartons, paint 1199:100-101
Babe Didrikson Zaharias' birthday; celebrate practice putting golf balls 1199:137
Birthday celebrations 601:121-122
Black History Month, activities and projects for classrooms 1393:136-138
Citizenship Day, activities and projects for classrooms 1393:29-32
Clara Barton's birthday; celebrate by making first aid kits 1199:285
Columbus Day, activities and projects for classrooms 1393:51-55

Eleanor Roosevelt's birthday; celebrate making declaration of human rights 1199:234

Flag Day ancestral flags, paper, crayons, markers, making 1199:131-132

Flag Day, activities and projects for classrooms 1393:232-233

Flag Day, Betsy Ross birthday celebration; art, music, foods, games, activities 1104:38-41

Flag Day; design your own flag, magazine pictures, markers, making 1199:130-131

Frank Lloyd Wright's birthday, celebrate by designing playhouses on paper 1199:125

George Gershwin's birthday; watercolor pictures of Big Apple, making 1199:221-222

George M. Cohan's birthday; celebrate with Yankee Doodle Sing-along 1199:149

Georgia O'Keeffe's birthday; celebrate by painting watercolor flowers 1199:260

Good Neighborhood Day; gingerbread to give neighbors as treat, recipe 1199:224

Grandma Moses's birthday; celebrate by painting primitive scene, how to do 1199:201

Grandparent's Day; interview your grandparents, questions to ask 1715:90-91

Grandparents' Day, activities and projects for classrooms 1393:24-26

Groundhog Day, activities and projects for classrooms 1393:139-140

Groundhog Day, paper bag groundhog, making 1199:30-31

"Happy New Year" in sign language 1199:2

Harry Houdini, National Magic Day; celebrate by doing magic tricks 1199:240-241

Helen Hayes's birthday; act out different emotions activity 1199:233

Helen Keller's birthday; celebrate by hearing, whispering game, making 1199:140

Helen Keller's birthday; celebrate by signing your name, manual alphabet given 1199:138-139

Helen Keller's birthday; celebrate by taste test activity 1199:141

Helen Keller's birthday; celebrate by touching textures activity 1199:142

Helen Keller's birthday; celebrate with cupcake flowers, baking cups, fragrances 1199:143

Helen Keller's birthday; celebrated by sight, I spy game, making 1199:140

Herman Melville's birthday; undersea art, paper, tissue paper, shells, making 1199:178-179

Herman Melville's birthday; sailing ships from plastic bottles, making 1199:172-173

Herman Melville's birthday; sailor's knots, twine, dowel, beads, patterns, making 1199:175-177

Herman Melville's birthday; whale scrimshaw from soap, black tempera paint, making 1199:174

Hot Dog and Baked Beans Month cookout, baked beans, recipe 1199:168-169

Ice Cream Month, homemade ice cream, recipe 1199:169

John Philip Sousa's birthday; celebrate by making simple musical instruments 1199:258-259

Johnny Appleseed's birthday, apple trees, colored papers, glue, making 1199:220

Johnny Appleseed's birthday, applesauce, recipe 1199:219-220

Labor Day, activities and projects for classrooms 1393:22-23

Labor Day; celebrate with job charades game, how to play 1199:200

Maurice Sendak's birthday; make prehistoric clay dough Wild Things 1199:127-128

Maurice Sendak's birthday; make Wild Things world, box, magazine pictures, paint 1199:128

May Baskets celebration 601:133-134

Memorial Day, activities and projects for classrooms 1393:215-216

Moon Day finger plays, games, making 944:120-121

National Adoption Week; celebrate by learning about adoption 1199:266-267

National Dairy Month, large cow head, tail with udder to milk, large patterns, making 1199:122

National Dairy Month, milkshakes, recipe 1199:124

National Popcorn Poppin' Month; cinnamon or peanut buttery popcorn, recipes 1199:245-246

National Recreation and Parks Month camping out small tent activity, making 1199:168

Native American Powwow, activities and projects for classrooms 1393:33-37

Noah Webster's birthday; celebrate by doing different dictionary activities 1199:236-237

P.T. Barnum's birthday, be a clown, face-painting, recipe 1199:152-153

P.T. Barnum's birthday, circus stilts, coffee cans, twine, duct tape, making 1199:153-154

Peace Day, modern peace symbol, plastic lid and yarn, making 1199:182

Peace Day; doves for peace, cardboard, felt, fiberfill, pattern, making 1199:180-181

Pulaski Day; celebrate with Polish greeting, how to say 1199:235

Samuel Clemens's (Mark Twain) birthday; celebrate with frog (plastic chips) jumping contest 1199:268-269

Sandwich Day; celebrate by inventing new sandwich, breads, fillings, making 1199:250-251

Space Week; astronaut mission patch, round plastic lid, glitter, paper, making 1199:163-164

Space Week; celestial mobile, wire hangers, string, foil, making 1199:164-165

Space Week; lunar art using finger paints, making 1199:159-160

Space Week; model of relative sizes of planets, making 1199:161-163

Space Week; sun prints, light sensitive paper, objects, making 1199:160-161

Thanksgiving, activities and projects for classrooms 1393:75-80

United Nations Day, activities and projects for classrooms 1393:56-59

Veterans Day/Remembrance Day, activities and projects for classrooms 1393:73-74

Walt Disney's birthday; celebrate with animation activity, how to do 1199:274-275

Will Rogers' birthday; celebrate by making rope lassos 1199:254-255

Wilma Rudolph's birthday, celebrate with Rudolph relays, outdoor activity 1199:136

UNITED STATES—FESTIVALS—DECORATIONS

Memorial Day tissue poppies, red tissue paper, pipe cleaners, making 1199:118-119

Memorial Day; happy memory written by each student for display, making 1199:119

UNITED STATES—FESTIVALS—HANDICRAFTS
Shadow silhouettes, how to make 1199:31

UNITED STATES—FESTIVALS—MASKS
Carnival mask, paper plate, yarn, making 1574:8-9

UNITED STATES—FESTIVALS—VETERANS DAY
Activities 1662:172-173
History of Veterans Day 199:32

UNITED STATES—FESTIVALS—VETERANS DAY— COOKERY
Popcorn, hickory smoked recipe 939:128

UNITED STATES—FESTIVALS—VETERANS DAY— DECORATIONS
Pop-up Veterans Day card, making 1387:63

UNITED STATES—FESTIVALS—VETERANS DAY— GAMES
Veterans Day game 240:57

UNITED STATES—FESTIVALS—VETERANS DAY— HANDICRAFTS
Victory friendship pins, making 199:32

UNITED STATES—FESTIVALS—VETERANS DAY— PARTIES
All-American Jamboree Party, how to plan and give 43:67-70

UNITED STATES—FOLKLORE
"Anna Mariah" flannel board story, patterns, making 1604:16-20
"Goat in the Chile Patch" flannel board story (with Spanish), patterns, making 1604:40-45
"In a Dark, Dark Wood" flannel board story, patterns, making 1604:83
"Three Little Kittens" flannel board story, making 1604:13-15
"Wizard of Oz" munchkin finger puppets, making 1310:151

UNITED STATES—FOLKLORE—PUPPETS
"Hungry Monster" shadow puppets, patterns, making 1602:72-77

UNITED STATES—GAMES
Alaskan Hopscotch, Texan Hopscotch, Potsy, hopscotch games 1426:40-45
All the fish in the sea game, how to play 1499:25-26
Asalto board game, patterns, making 1541:174-178
Blackberry chasing game, how to play 1498:34
Blind Man's Buff tag, how to play 1498:18-20
Cat and mouse game, how to play 1355:25
Chinese Checkers board game, patterns, making 1541:100-108
Chinese Rebel board game, patterns, making 1541:179-182
Chivalry board game, patterns, making 1541:137-146
Choosing sides, how to play 1507:99
Consequences, paper, making 1500:40-42
Continental draughts board game, patterns, making 1541:203-207
Diagonal draughts board game, patterns, making 1541:202
Dodge ball game, how to play 1497:43-44
Dominoes, how to play 1499:38-43
Doubling board game, patterns, making 1541:230-231
Draughts board game, patterns, making 1541:195-200
Draughts for three board game, patterns, making 1541:208-213
Fox and Geese board game, patterns, making 1541:167-173
Go-bang board game, patterns, making 1541:147-152
Going to Boston game, how to play 1507:100
Grandmother's footsteps tag, how to play 1498:27
Halma board game, patterns, making 1541:91-99
Hide and seek tag, how to play 1498:15
How many miles to Babylon? game, how to play 1355:16
Hula hoop games, how to play 1499:11
Jacks, how to play 1718:34-35
Kick the can, how to play 1708:58-59
Kim's memory game, how to play 1499:20
Le Herradura or horseshoe quoits game, how to play 1499:23
Leapfrog, how to play 1499:12-13
Loser draughts board game, patterns, making 1541:201-202
Ludo board game, patterns, making 1541:49-52
Man overboard game, how to play 1499:26-27
Molly Bright game, how to play 1355:16
Ninepins and tenpins game, how to play 1497:19-21
Nyout board game, patterns, making 1541:189-194
Pass and catch game, how to play 1497:34-35
Picture consequences, paper, making 1500:43
Pitchball game, how to play 1497:31
Queen's Guard board game, patterns, making 1541:129-136
Reversi board game, patterns, making 1541:214-218
Sam Loyd's game, making 1507:102-103
Sardines tag, how to play 1498:15
Shadow tag game, how to play 1498:13
Simon Says game, how to play 1499:19
Snakes and ladders board game, patterns, making 1541:53-60
Stoolball game, how to play 1497:33-34

UNITED STATES—GEOGRAPHY
"The Drinking Gourd"; physical and human geography activities 1458:54-57
"Katy and the Big Snow"; physical and human geography activities 1458:8-11
"Legend of the Bluebonnet"; physical and human geography activities 1458:34-37
"The Little House"; physical and human geography activities 1458:16-19
"Ox-Cart Man"; physical and human geography activities 1458:28-31

UNITED STATES—HANDICRAFTS
Carousel and carousel animals, paper tubes, paints, making 1338:17-20
Comic book, paper, markers, making 1332:59-62
Computer project: design a crazy quilt pattern 1218:20-23

UNITED STATES—HISTORY—COLONIAL PERIOD
Ducking stool model, wooden, making 567:153-156
Pillory model, wooden, making 567:150-152
Stocks model, wooden, making 567:148-149
Tom Thumb model, wooden, making 567:66-74

UNITED STATES—HISTORY—COLONIAL PERIOD— BARNS
Barn, Connecticut tobacco barn, wooden, making 568:83-88
Barn, old stone and wood, making 568:79-82

UNITED STATES—HISTORY—COLONIAL PERIOD— BASKETRY
Basketry, making 831:127-129
Basketry, paper, making 688:8

UNITED STATES—HISTORY—COLONIAL PERIOD—BOOKS

Country diary, making 193:28-29

UNITED STATES—HISTORY—COLONIAL PERIOD—BRIDGES

Bridge, King-Post truss covered bridge, wooden, making 568:103-110

Bridge, lattice truss covered bridge, wooden, making 568:110-119

Bridge, open King-Post bridge, wooden, making 568:101-102

UNITED STATES—HISTORY—COLONIAL PERIOD—CANALS

Canal packet model, wooden, making 567:55-59

UNITED STATES—HISTORY—COLONIAL PERIOD—CANDLES

Candle clock, making 1043:31

Candle dipping, how to do 688:10

Candleholder, clay, making 877:67-70; 1070:137-139

Candleholder, making 225:29

Candleholder, Paul Revere's candleholder, making 719:24-25

Candle making, hand dipped, making 831:123-124

Candle making, how to do 893:30-40

Candle making, petaled candles, making 831:124-125

Candle stick, making 893:121-124

Candles, Colonial, making 673:158-173

Candles, dipped and molded, making 118:48-50; 877:61-66; 1043:30-31

Candles, making 225:30; 453:55-59

Candlestick, silver, making 225:30

UNITED STATES—HISTORY—COLONIAL PERIOD—CANOES

Log canoe or pirogue, model, wooden, making 567:10-11

UNITED STATES—HISTORY—COLONIAL PERIOD—CAROLINIANS—CLOTHING

Costumes of the Colonists of the Carolinas, making 281:64-72

Man's coat, pattern for Carolina Colonist, making 281:66-68

Woman's bodice, sleeves and Bertha, pattern, making 281:70-71

UNITED STATES—HISTORY—COLONIAL PERIOD—CHRISTMAS

Christmas tree and decorations, how to make 593:98-105

UNITED STATES—HISTORY—COLONIAL PERIOD—CHRISTMAS—COOKERY

Baked ham and maple syrup, recipe 1733:72

Baked stuffed fillets with creole sauce, recipe 1733:72

Beverages, cinnamon tea, recipe 166:2

Beverages, eggnog, recipe 166:2

Beverages, hot mulled cider, recipe 166:2

Breads, angel wing popovers, recipe 166:4

Breads, buttermilk biscuits, recipe 166:3

Breads, cheese biscuits, recipe 166:5

Breads, cheese sticks, recipe 166:5

Breads, cranberry loaf bread, recipe 166:4

Breads, molasses bread, recipe 166:4

Breads, muffins, recipe 166:5

Breads, orange tea bread, recipe 166:4

Breads, plantation days spoon bread, recipe 166:3

Breads, Sally Lunn breads, recipe 166:3

Breads, southern cornbread, recipe 166:3

Breads, southern short'n bread, recipe 166:5

Cakes, applesauce cake, recipe 166:10

Cakes, Betty's best fruit cake, recipe, making 166:9

Cakes, blackberry cake, recipe 166:10

Cakes, chocolate pound cake, recipe 166:7

Cakes, crumb coffee cake, recipe 166:8

Cakes, fresh apple cake, recipe 166:10

Cakes, ginger pound cake, recipe 166:7

Cakes, Merry Christmas cake, recipe, making 166:7

Cakes, old timey raisin spice cake, recipe 166:9

Cakes, old timey seed cake, recipe 166:7

Cakes, perfect pound cake, recipe 166:7

Cakes, rum cake sauce, recipe 166:8

Cakes, whiskey pecan cake, recipe 166:8

Candied cranberries, recipe 1733:73

Candy, apple leather, recipe 166:19

Candy, cherry creams, recipe 166:17

Candy, crystallized orange peels, recipe 166:19

Candy, fruit balls, recipe 166:17

Candy, fruit candy bars, recipe 166:17

Candy, molasses candy corn balls, recipe 166:19

Candy, molasses taffy, recipe 166:19

Candy, peanut brittle, recipe 166:18

Candy, peanut butter creams, recipe 166:17

Candy, peppermints, recipe 166:18

Candy, pralines, recipe 166:19

Candy, spiced glazed nuts, recipe 166:17

Candy, vanilla creams, recipe 166:17

Candy, vanilla fudge, recipe 166:18

Candy, walnut fudge, recipe 166:18

Cookies, best chocolate brownies 166:15

Cookies, butter cookies, recipe 166:16

Cookies, caramel bars, recipe 166:14

Cookies, coconut macaroons, recipe 166:16

Cookies, Moravian cookies, recipe 166:15

Cookies, old fashioned gingerbread men, recipe 166:16

Cookies, scotch shortbread cookies, recipe, making 166:14

Cookies, soft molasses cookies, recipe 166:14

Cookies, spiced oatmeal cookies, recipe 166:14

Cookies, sugar cookies, recipe 795:95

Cookies, whiskey balls, recipe 166:15

George Washington's eggnog, recipe 1733:71

Gingerbread cookies, recipe 192:42-44

Johnny cakes, recipe 795:95

Lacy pancakes, recipe 166:6

Moravian Christmas cookies, recipe 1733:73

New Orleans sweet potato pie, recipe 1733:73

Pies and pastries pie crust recipe 166:11

Pies and pastries, chocolate cream pie, recipe 166:11

Pies and pastries, coconut cream pie, recipe 166:11

Pies and pastries, eggnog pie, recipe 166:11

Pies and pastries, grasshopper pie, creme de menthe, recipe 166:12

Pies and pastries, lemon chess pie, recipe 166:13

Pies and pastries, molasses crumb pie, recipe 166:13

Pies and pastries, molasses raisin pie, recipe 166:13

Pies and pastries, old timey egg custard pie, recipe 166:12

Pies and pastries, pecan pie, recipe 166:12

Pies and pastries, pumpkin nut pie, recipe 166:12

Pies and pastries, sugar chess tarts, recipe 166:13

Pies and pastries, sweet potato pie, recipe 166:12

Pies and pastries, vanilla cream pie, recipe 166:11

Plum pudding, suet plum pudding, recipe 795:95

Relishes, apple relish, recipe 166:24

Relishes, kraut relish, recipe 166:24

Relishes, old fashioned corn relish, recipe 166:24
Relishes, pepper relish, recipe 166:24
Relishes, tomato chili sauce, recipe 166:24
Sorrel soup, recipe 1733:71
Southern corn meal waffles, recipe 166:6
Sugarplums, recipe, making 795:94
Sweet pancake topping, recipe, making 166:6
Treats, ambrosia, recipe 166:21
Treats, baked ham glazes, recipe, making 166:22
Treats, brandied peaches, recipe 166:22
Treats, broken-glass torte, recipe, making 166:20
Treats, cherry velvet recipe 166:21
Treats, Christmas cranberry salad, recipe 166:20
Treats, famous butter mints, recipe 166:22
Treats, Indian pudding, recipe 166:21
Treats, party cheese logs, recipe 166:22
Treats, party fruit jubilee, recipe 166:20
Treats, tipsy cake, recipe 166:21
Treats, tutti fruitti, recipe 166:21

**UNITED STATES—HISTORY—COLONIAL PERIOD—
CHRISTMAS—DECORATIONS**
Advent Calendar, Tree of Life Advent Calendar, making
   795:82-83
Apple fan, making 831:141
Cards, cooked Christmas cards, making 795:106
Cards, cut-paper and watercolor cards, making 795:92
Cards, gumdrop cards, making 795:107
Christmas cookies for tree, making 453:120-123
Christmas stars, straw, making 453:116-117
Creche, Christmas cookie creche, making 795:98-99
Della Robbia wreath, making 831:144
Flying angel, fabric, making 1733:68
Fractur painting card, making 795:93
Garland and fruit swag, making 831:144
Garlands of popcorn and cranberries, making 672:143-
   152
Gingerbread sculpture cookies, recipe, making 795:100
Hex sign barn decorations, ornaments, making 795:89
Kissing ball, making 831:142
Mini tree, making 831:143
Mural, primitive Christmas mural, making 795:80-81
Paper chains for Christmas tree, making 672:153-165
Pomander balls, orange, cloves, making 1733:69
Popcorn balls and wreaths, making 795:104
Pretzel ornaments, making 795:102
Quilt paper decorations, making 795:78
Quilt wall hanging, paper, making 795:76-77
Quilted balls, ornaments, making 795:88
Quilted Christmas stocking, fabric, making 1733:68
Quilted decorations, making 795:79
Quilted ornaments, making 795:91
Sachets, fabric, fragrant wood, making 1733:69
Stained glass cookies, ornaments, making 795:100-101
Sugar balls with tiny scenes, ornaments, making 795:103
Wax ball and figures, making 795:87
Weather vanes, miniature, ornaments, making 795:90
Whirligig, cardboard, making 795:86
Wood turnings, ornaments, making 795:91
Wrapping paper, cookie cutter and vegetable prints, mak-
   ing 795:105
Wreath, straw, making 831:143
Yule log, making 831:143

**UNITED STATES—HISTORY—COLONIAL PERIOD—
CHRISTMAS—DOLLS**
Corn husk dolls, making 1733:66-67

Creche, rag dolls, apple dolls, rag doll animals, making
   795:83-85
Doll from straw, making 453:118-120

**UNITED STATES—HISTORY—COLONIAL PERIOD—
CHRISTMAS—GAMES**
Christmas dancing game 831:73

**UNITED STATES—HISTORY—COLONIAL PERIOD—
CLOTHING**
School clothes, making 228:22-31

**UNITED STATES—HISTORY—COLONIAL PERIOD—
COOKERY**
Apple Brown Betty, recipe 1600:70
Apple butter, recipe 57:79; 1308:8-9; 1455:159
Apple Charlotte, recipe 594:51
Apple crisp, recipe 57:66
Apple fritters, recipe 453:8-9
Apple muffins, recipe 57:66
Apple pandowdy, recipe and history of apple pandowdy
   668:51-56
Apple pie, recipe 57:75
Apple rings, fried, recipe 1600:69
Applesauce, recipe 1600:71
Avocado pears Florida, recipe 57:95
Baked pumpkin pudding, recipe 1308:34
Beef stew, recipe 831:150
Beefsteak pie, recipe 1308:32-33
Black bean soup, recipe 1043:26
Blackberry shrub, raspberry leaf tea, whipped syllabub,
   recipe 658:114-115
Blueberry jam, recipe 191:46
Blueberry slump, rose honey strawberry fool, pie crust,
   making 658:101-104
Boston baked beans, recipe 831:149-150; 871:6-7
Boston brown bread, recipe 871:123-124
Bountiful bread, recipe 191:36-37
Brandied fresh peaches, recipe 57:18
Bread pudding, recipe 871:100-101
Bread, recipe 831:153-155
Breakfast puffs, recipe 1308:12-13
Brunswick stew, recipe 831:149
Butter, making, recipe 118:43-44; 453:15; 831:152-153;
   1035:88; 1043:25
Cambridge pudding, recipe 57:63
Candied orange peel, recipe 193:47
Candy, Yankee molasses, recipe 1342:23
Cauliflower polonaise, recipe 57:95
Cheese, recipe 831:152
Cheshire pork, recipe 57:79
Chicken a-la-daub, recipe 57:90
Chicken marinade, recipe 57:15
Chicken pudding, recipe 658:55; 1308:20-21
Chipmonk pie, recipe 57:67
Chocolate cream, recipe 57:91
Christmas fruit cake, recipe 191:44-45; 191:44-45
Cider, hot spiced, recipe 453:7-8
Clam chowder, recipe 57:50; 871:8-9
Cobblestones, recipe 57:82
Codfish balls, recipe 57:51
Codfish cakes, recipe 871:9-10
Cookbook for a history of your family's favorite food,
   how to start and keep 1297:83
Corn chowder, recipe 831:150
Corn custard, recipe 1600:71
Corn oysters; recipe and history of corn oysters 668:41-
   44

Corn pone, recipe 57:87
Corn pudding, recipe 57:71
Corn sticks, recipe 1043:25
Cornbread, recipe 453:5-6; 1455:119
Cornmeal pudding, recipe 1043:24
Country Captain, Brunswick stew, recipes 658:56-59
Crabs, soft-shell, recipe 57:39
Crab stew, codfish cakes, scalloped oysters, recipes 658:63-66
Crab, stuffed, recipe 57:14
Cranberry muffins, recipe 193:44-45
Cranberry-apple pie, recipe 57:67
Cucumber salad, recipe 57:39
Dessert omelet, recipe 57:23
Dressed eggs, recipe 1308:16-17
Dried fruit and vegetables, recipe 453:24-27
Drying corn, drying herbs, drying marigold petals, how to do 658:76-78
Fish chowder, recipe 831:150; 1043:27
Flummery, recipe 225:31
French pancakes, recipe 57:19
Fried ham with gravy, recipe 1308:14-15
Fruit cake, recipe 57:46-47
Fruit and raisins, oven-dried, recipe 1455:161
Fruit leather, recipe 916:64-65
Frumenty, recipe 1437:100-101
Ginger cakes, recipe 57:86
Gingerbread, recipe 1600:69-70
Gingersnaps, recipe 57:75; 193:43
Grape ketchup, cranberry sauce, corn relish, apple butter, recipes, make 658:94-96
Green beans, recipe 1308:28
Ham, fried with red eyed gravy, recipe 658:48-49
Hasty pudding, Indian pudding, carrot pudding, recipes 658:80-86
Hasty pudding, recipe 376:195; 1043:23; 1661:60
Herb teas, recipes, making 1035:89
Herbs, bunching herbs, how to do 225:27-28
History of Colonial cooking 658:8-36
Hoe cakes, recipe 492:65
Hopping John, sweet potatoes and apples, recipes, making 658:71-73
Ice cream, recipe 57:42-43; 831:151-152
Indian pudding, recipe 193:42; 597:27; 871:98-99; 916:65; 1032:271
Indian pudding, recipe and history 668:35-40
Irish soda bread, recipe 453:9-10
Jelly cake, recipe 57:91
Jerky, recipe 916:65-67
Johnny cake, recipe 1032:269; 1600:67
Johnny cake, recipe and history 668:29-34
Johnny cakes or Journey cakes, recipe 191:41; 453:6-7; 1043:24; 1308:10-11
Lamb, roast shoulder, recipe 57:22
Lamb stew with vegetables, recipe 57:94
Leather britches, recipe 658:72-76
Liberty tea, recipe 1308:41
Maple sugar on snow, recipe 1600:67-68
Maple syrup, recipe 916:67-71
Maple treat, sugar on snow, how to make 1437:100
Mayz and broiled steak, recipe 57:26-27
Mid-Atlantic Colonies; shoo-fly pie, recipe and history of shoo-fly pie 668:74-78
Mid-Atlantic Colonies; snickerdoodles, recipe and history of snickerdoodles 668:68-73

Mulled cider, recipe 1735:31-33
Mulligan stew, recipe 831:149
New England apple pie, recipe 1035:87
New England boiled dinner, recipe 57:51
New England clam chowder, recipe 597:26-27; 666:48-49
New England corn oysters, recipe 666:49-50
New England fish chowder, recipe 57:70
New England hoe cake, recipe 1035:88
New England Indian pudding, recipe 666:50-51
New England pumpkin pie, recipe 1035:86
Noodles a la macaroni, recipe 57:43
Nut pie, spiced nuts, candied rose petals, recipes, making 658:101-104
Nuts, roasted, making 453:27-28
Nuts, spiced, recipe 1308:40
Pease porridge, pumpkin soup, hotch-potch, recipes 658:39-42; 1661:60
Philadelphia Pepperpot soup, recipe 658:39-42
Pilgrim's cake, recipe 1661:60
Pilgrim's dessert, stewed pumpkin, recipe 1043:28
Plum cake, recipe 57:82
Poached bass or cod, recipe 57:62
Poet and peasant, recipe 831:149
Popped corn, making 453:33-34
Porridge, recipe 1043:23
Pumpkin pudding, cranberry pudding, recipes 658:80-86
Queen's cake, recipe 191:42-43; 1308:38
Raisin cakes, recipe 710:75-77
Raspberry flummery, recipe 1308:35; 1437:102
Red flannel hash, New England boiled dinner, succotash stew, recipes 658:47-50
Red flannel hash, recipe, and history of 668:45-50
Rhode Island Johnny cake, recipe 594:34-35
Rice pudding, recipe 57:11
Roast turkey and stuffing, recipe 57:54-55
Robert E. Lee cake, recipe 57:10
Ryaninjun Colonial Yankee bread, recipe 492:37-39
Sallet with egg yolk dressing, Boston baked beans, recipes 658:72-76
Sally Lunn bread, recipe 1308:26-27
Savoury jelly, recipe 57:91
Seafood casserole, recipe 57:83
Shoo-fly pie, raspberry flummery, marchpane, lemon sucket, recipe 658:101-104
Shoo-fly pie, recipe 1600:68-69
Shrewsbury cake, recipe 57:78; 191:38-39
Southern Colonies; chicken from the Indies; recipe and history of 668:101-106
Southern Colonies; hush puppies, recipe and history of hush puppies 668:90-95
Southern Colonies; shortnin' bread, recipe and history of shortnin' bread 668:107-112
Southern Colonies; spoon bread, recipe and history of spoon bread 668:96-100
Southern gumbo, recipe 57:90
Southern spoon bread, recipe 57:10-11
Speculaas, Dutch Christmas cookies, recipe 57:74; 1437:101
Spiced punch from Williamsburg, Virginia, recipe 652:88-89
Spoon bread, Boston brown bread, Johnny cakes, recipes, making 658:89-92
Spoon bread, recipe 1600:66-67
Squash soup, recipe 1043:26

Standing rib roast, recipe 57:59
Stirabout stew, recipe 191:40
Stoneground cornbread, recipe 57:58
Strawberries and cream, recipe 57:38
Strawberry jam, recipe 191:47
Succotash, recipe 1043:27
Succotash, recipe and history of succotash 668:24-28
Sweet potato pie, recipe 57:87
Sweet potatoes and apples, recipe 1308:24-25
Taffy, recipe 916:71-73; 1067:57-58
Tarts, almond, recipe 1308:36-37
Trifle from Britain, recipe and history of 668:113-119;
    871:6-7
Twelfth Night cookies, recipe 57:71
Vanilla almond cake, Mary Lincoln's white cake, recipe
    57:31
Vanilla pecan pie, recipe 57:30
Veal balls, recipe 1308:22-23
Veal chops, recipe 57:34
Vegetable soup, recipe 57:35
Whipped Syllabub, recipe 1308:29
Yeast bread, recipe 1455:118

**UNITED STATES—HISTORY—COLONIAL PERIOD—
    DANCES**
Baptist dancing game 831:79
Betsy liner dancing game 831:76
Bow Bow Bow Belinda, Virginia Reel, song and dance
    game 1114:52-54
Coffee grows on white oak trees dancing game 831:74-75
Frog pond dancing game 831:71
Lazy Mary dancing game 831:69
Muffin Man dancing game 831:72
Oranges and lemons dancing game 831:68
Soldier, soldier, will you marry me? dancing game 831:70
Yankee Doodle dancing game 831:77-78

**UNITED STATES—HISTORY—COLONIAL PERIOD—
    DOLLS**
Acorn dolls, making 831:48
Apple dolls, making 831:49
Applehead doll, making 453:103-107
Bottle dolls, making 831:49
Colonial dollhouse, furniture, doll family, patterns, mak-
    ing 963:18-173
Colonial dolls, crepe paper, making 123:46-47
Corn husk doll, making 453:107-111
Corncob dolls, how to make 1419:190-191
Corncob dolls, making 228:23-25
Dolls clothing for Schoolmaster, boy and girl, making
    228:25-31
Dolls dress, making 225:55-57
George and Martha paper dolls, making 191:24-29
Rag doll, making 453:100-103; 831:47-48
Sock Sam doll, making 415:20-24
Stuffed doll, making 225:50-53

**UNITED STATES—HISTORY—COLONIAL PERIOD—
    DUTCH COLONISTS—CLOTHING**
Costumes of Dutch Colonists, making 281:82-87
Samare of Dutch woman, pattern, making 281:85-86

**UNITED STATES—HISTORY—COLONIAL PERIOD—
    DUTCH COLONISTS—COOKERY**
Anise sugar koekjes, cookies, recipe 1297:44

**UNITED STATES—HISTORY—COLONIAL PERIOD—
    DYES**
Natural dyes to color yarn, how to make and use 1297:71

**UNITED STATES—HISTORY—COLONIAL PERIOD—
    FARMS**
Flail model, wooden, making 567:113-114
Grain cradle model, wooden, making 567:110-112
Harrow model, wooden, making 567:107-109
Neck yoke, wooden, making 567:xixxx
Ox cart, model, wooden, making 567:12-15
Ox yoke, wooden, making 567:xviii
Plow model, wooden, making 567:103-106
Tobacco roller model, wooden, making 567:16-18
Whipple trees, wooden, making 567:xix

**UNITED STATES—HISTORY—COLONIAL PERIOD—
    FIRES**
Camp fire, winter, making 831:159
How to start a fire 831:157-158
Hunter's fire, making 831:159
Log Cabin fire, making 831:158-159
Teepee fire, making 831:158
Trench fire, making 831:159

**UNITED STATES—HISTORY—COLONIAL PERIOD—
    FLAGS**
British Union Jack, fabric, making 193:24-27
Colonial banners, fabric 193:24-27
Dutch East India Flag, fabric, making 193:26-27
Flag ceremonies 831:115-120
French Fleur-de-Lis Flag, fabric, making 193:27
Grand Union Flag, fabric, making 193:24-27
Viking Raven Flag, fabric, making 193:26-27

**UNITED STATES—HISTORY—COLONIAL PERIOD—
    FURNITURE**
Bed, bundling bed, wooden, making 568:29-31
Bed, tester bed, wooden, making 568:31-34
Bed, trundle bed, wooden, making 568:34-35
Bench model, making 225:18
Chest six board chest wooden, making 568:50
Cradle model, making 225:21-23
Cradle model, wooden, making 567:123-125
Cradle, making 171:87-91
Cradle, rocking cradle, wooden, making 568:38
Cradle, swinging cradle, wooden, making 568:36-37
Cupboard model, making 225:20-21
Cupboard, pine cupboard, wooden, making 568:39-42
Fan rocker and fly chaser, Ben Franklin chair 118:84
Four poster canopy bed, making 118:82-83
Making 568:48-49
Rocking chairs, history of 118:84
Settle model, wooden, making 567:131-133
Table, hutch table, settle, and chest, wooden, making
    568:25-27
Table, trestle table and benches, wooden, making 568:23-
    25
Trestle table, making 171:81-86
Trestle table, making model 225:17-18
Windsor chair model, making 225:19-20

**UNITED STATES—HISTORY—COLONIAL PERIOD—
    GAMES**
Backgammon game 831:30
Basket or tin can bowling 831:20
Bird, beast or fish game 831:27
Blindmans bluff game 831:27
Bowling games 831:19
Bowls game 831:18
Call ball game 831:14
Catching a greased pig game 831:15
Checkers board, making 877:75-76

Chess 831:29-30

Chip stone game 831:18

Chip stones, game with top, how to play 1437:100

Chuck a farthing game 831:18

Climbing a greased pole game 831:16

Colonial categories game 831:31

Colonial charades, word charades, art charades, proverbs for charades 831:25-26

Compliments game 831:28

Corn darts game, making 193:35

Cricket game 831:20-21

Cup and ball game, wooden cup and ball, making 1309:16

Dominoes game 831:31

Draughts, checkers 831:30

Duck and drake game 831:13

Even odd game 831:29

Fan tan game 831:29

Fox and geese game, how to play 1297:81

Fox and geese, outdoor tag game, how to play 1437:99-100

Game of graces, catch a hoop game, making 1309:14-15

Go bang game 831:31

Haley-over ball game, how to play 1651:58-59

Hide the thimble game 831:27

Hit the ball game 831:19-20

Hoop rolling and hoop diving 831:20

Hop, step and jump game 831:13-14

Hopscotch 831:16

Huntsman game 831:28

Indian games 831:21-23

Indian jumbled words game 831:31

Jousting 831:16

Keep at it game 831:19

Kite flying, paper, dowels, paints, making 1309:17-19

Leap frog relay 831:15

Losing game 831:30-31

Marble games, making 228:46

Peg a farthing game 831:18

Poison sticks game 831:21

Poses and imitations game 831:28-29

Prisoner's base game 831:14-15

Puss in the corner game 831:13

Quoits game, making 877:105

Red, white and blue game 831:31-32

Riddles to perform game 831:28

Ringer, marbles, tournament play 831:17-18

Roll-ball game, how to play 1651:88

Round and Round the Village game chanting game 1118:28-29

Seesaw string game, making 877:83-85

Skin the snake relay game 831:15

Skipping stones game 831:13

Speeches and recitations game 831:28

Squat, tag 831:18

Stick games 831:20

Stilts game 831:16

Stool ball 831:19

Strike or spare it game 831:19

Tag 831:18

Tangrams game 831:32-33

Thread the needle game 831:13

Tongue twisters game 831:28

Trap ball game 831:18-19

Tug of war game 831:14

Twenty questions game 831:27

Up Jenkins game 831:27

Word games 831:32

UNITED STATES—HISTORY—COLONIAL PERIOD— HANDICRAFTS

Ancestor chart, making 688:27

Battledore and shuttlecock, making 228:36

Bread dough sculptures, making 893:73-81

Buckets, making 228:38-40

Candles, dipped and molded, making 1455:94-95

Chessmen, nuts and bolts, making 893:61-66

Chest treasure box, cardboard, making 191:34-35

Compass, cork, pin in bowl of water, how to make 1297:15

Corn husk flower arrangement making 893:91-94

Corn husk pads, mats, baskets, making 453:34-37

Corn shuck table mats and doormat, braided, making 673:231-238

Cross-stitch sampler, fabric, threads, making 1309:30-31

Decoupage, making 893:47-51

Decoy, making 688:14

Dried materials, making 893:83-89

Eagle, carved wood, making 225:62-64

Embroidery, pinpunch embroidery, making 877:54-58

Fan, folding, posterboard, paints, pattern, making 1309:22-23

Fire bucket, making 877:115-116

Fire sign, making 877:116-117

Flowers, everlasting bouquets, making 453:89-97

Flowers, pressed, making 453:90-92

Folded paper boxes, making 877:26-27

Four leaf cuts all in a square, paper, making 298:200-201

Frames, folded paper frames, making 877:24-25

Friendship pillow, fabric, stuffed, making 191:30-31

Friendship pincushion, fabric, embroidery thread, making 1309:34-35

Fruit pyramid, fruit, styrofoam cup, making 1309:26-27

Gravestone rubbings, making 831:135

Hex signs, making 688:19

Hooking, hand hooking, how to do 831:127

Hornbook, how to make 719:28-29

Hornbook, making 228:35; 688:15; 877:113-114

Ice lights, making 831:125

Kaleidoscope, making 893:67-71

Lantern, Colonial metal lantern, making 673:137-157

Lantern, tin can lantern, making 877:67-68

Lantern, tin can, making 482:114-115

Paper-cutting, paper chains, and snowflakes, making 453:73

Paper, making 225:59

Papier-mache, making 893:52-59

Papyrotamia, making 453:73-79

Paul Revere lantern, making 831:125-126

Pinprick picture, making 688:29

Pomander ball, orange, spices, ribbon, making 1309:40-41; 1437:102

Pomander balls, making 193:41; 225:61; 453:81-84; 831:137

Pomander, old-fashioned, making 1455:116

Pomanders and sachets, making 70:27

Portraiture, making 688:25

Potichomania, picture pasting, making 225:59-60

Potpourri and sachets, making 831:138-139

Potpourri, flower petals, making 1309:38

Potpourri, scented, making 453:96-97

Pressed flowers, making 193:40
Pricked paper work, making 228:49-50
Quill pen, making 228:32-33; 877:114-115; 1309:6
Quill pen, mock-type, making 719:16-17
Rose beads, making 831:137-138
Rug, braided, miniature, making 225:43-45
Rugmaking, how to do 225:43-45; 453:61-67
Rugs, braided, making 70:46
Sachet, fabric, potpourri, making 453:84-85; 1309:32-33
Sampler, embroidery stitches, making 453:39-43; 688:7; 432:44-46; 831:129-132
Sampler, how to embroider 1297:79
Sampler, little houses, making 191:20-23
Scrimshaw, making 688:31
Scrimshaw, paraffin and plastic bottle, making 877:90-92
Sign board, making 688:12
Silhouettes, making 453:69-71; 688:23; 831:126-127
Snowflakes, paper-cutting, making 877:20-23
Spinning, dyeing, and weaving, how to do 225:32-37
Spinning, information on 453:47-53
Spray spatter, making 688:35
Stenciling, how to do 831:135-136
Stenciling, making 688:22
Tanning, poke bag, making 228:44-45
Theorem pineapple stencil printing, making 298:178-179
Tie dyeing, how to do 893:41-45
Tin lanterns, making 831:125
Tin-punch lantern, Colonial lantern, tin can, pattern, making 1429:86-87
Tinsel painting, making 877:29-31
Tinware and tole painting, making 228:41-43
Tinware, ornamented, making 688:16
Trinket box, making 688:21
Tussie-mussie bouquet, flowers, doily, making 1309:39
Tussy mussy, herbal bouquet, how to make 1419:189
Wall sconce model, making 225:30
Wax fruit, making 688:32
Wax seal and signet, making 1309:10
Welcome pineapple, making 698:14
Whirligigs, paper, patterns, making 1320:32-33

**UNITED STATES—HISTORY—COLONIAL PERIOD—
HATS**

Hat, fancy straw hat, flowers, ribbon, making 1309:24-25
Tri-corner hat, making 877:118

**UNITED STATES—HISTORY—COLONIAL PERIOD—
HERBS**

Growing, harvesting, and decorating with herbs 831:161-163
Herb garden, making 453:85-86
Herbs, drying, how to do 453:86-87

**UNITED STATES—HISTORY—COLONIAL PERIOD—
HOUSEHOLD ITEMS**

Andirons models, making 225:26-27
Broom, paper, making 877:119
Butter churn model, wooden, making 567:134-136
Butter churn, making 118:43
Churn, paddle churn, wooden, making 568:44-47
Churn, rocker chum, wooden, making 568:43-45
Crockery models, making 225:28
Foot stove model, wooden, making 567:128-130
Pewter dishes models, making 225:24-25
Pots and trivets models, making 225:25-26
Stoneware storage jar, clay, making 1070:143-146
Tin lantern, making 118:51-52

Utensils and other household items for model home, making 225:23-28
Wool wheel model, wooden, making 567:137-140

**UNITED STATES—HISTORY—COLONIAL PERIOD—
HOUSES**

Colonial barn, making 171:40-45
Colonial furniture for model home, making 225:17-23
Colonial village mural, how to make 193:16-21
Gingerbread Colonial house, recipe, assembling, decorating, how to do 1086:46-51
Lighting for Colonial home model, making 225:29-30
Log cabin model, wooden, making 567:141-144
Log cabin, making 296:74-75
Model room with fireplace, making 225:11-16
New England Colonial home model, making 225:9-10
Saltbox house, making 171:35-39

**UNITED STATES—HISTORY—COLONIAL PERIOD—
HUSKING BEE**

Husking Bee, information on 453:31-37

**UNITED STATES—HISTORY—COLONIAL PERIOD—
INKS**

Berry ink, recipe, making 1043:28; 1309:8
Nut ink, recipe 1043:29
Walnut ink, recipe, making 1309:9

**UNITED STATES—HISTORY—COLONIAL PERIOD—
KITES**

Kite activities 831:42-43
Kites, making 688:17
Kites, paper, making 877:99-103

**UNITED STATES—HISTORY—COLONIAL PERIOD—
KNITTING**

Spool knitting, how to do 877:49-51

**UNITED STATES—HISTORY—COLONIAL PERIOD—
LACEMAKING**

Tambour, lacemaking, making 228:57-60

**UNITED STATES—HISTORY—COLONIAL PERIOD—
MANNERS**

Prepare a manners book based on children's behavior and manners in 1700's, how to do 1297:80

**UNITED STATES—HISTORY—COLONIAL PERIOD—
MASKS**

Pocahontas paper bag mask, making 755:51-57

**UNITED STATES—HISTORY—COLONIAL PERIOD—
MEETING HOUSE**

Meeting house, wooden, making 568:53-57
Pew for the meeting house, wooden, making 568:59
Pulpit and platform, wooden, making 568:57-58

**UNITED STATES—HISTORY—COLONIAL PERIOD—
MILLS**

Grist mill model, wooden, making 567:117-122
Samp mill model, wooden, making 567:115-116
Water wheel model, wooden, making 567:117-122

**UNITED STATES—HISTORY—COLONIAL PERIOD—
MONEY**

Wampum beads, making 688:9

**UNITED STATES—HISTORY—COLONIAL PERIOD—
MUSICAL INSTRUMENTS**

Drum and bank, making 719:21-23
Drum, coffee can, making 877:106
Drums, marching drum, coffee can drum, kettle drum, making 831:107-108
Fife, making 831:108
Glassy cord, making 831:107
Guitar, shoe box, making 877:107
Noisemakers, making 831:109

Ringing glasses, making 831:107
Strummers, slingshot and shoe box banjo, making
    831:110
Whistles, straw, making 877:108
Willow whistle, making 831:108

**UNITED STATES—HISTORY—COLONIAL PERIOD—
    PAINTING**
Fractur painting, making 688:20
Glass painting, making 688:30
Landscape painting, making 688:26
Reverse glass painting, making 70:26; 228:55-56
Still-life picture, making 688:28

**UNITED STATES—HISTORY—COLONIAL PERIOD—
    PAINTS**
Milk paint, recipe, how to make 1278:8-9; 1455:36

**UNITED STATES—HISTORY—COLONIAL PERIOD—
    PLAYS**
Pocahontas and Captain John Smith masks and pantomime
    for play 755:47-50

**UNITED STATES—HISTORY—COLONIAL PERIOD—
    PUPPETS**
Marionette, tissue, making 831:62-64
Marionettes, making 70:34
Punch and Judy, making 831:62
Puppets, hand, making 70:35

**UNITED STATES—HISTORY—COLONIAL PERIOD—
    PURITANS—CLOTHING**
Cloak and hat, fabric, pattern, making 281:76-77
Costumes of the Puritans, making 281:74-81
Man's doublet, collar, fabric, pattern, making 281:75-76
Woman's costume, fabric, pattern, making 281:78
Woman's hat, fabric, pattern, making 281:79

**UNITED STATES—HISTORY—COLONIAL PERIOD—
    QUAKERS—CLOTHING**
Costumes of the Quakers, making 281:88-92
Woman's bodice and sleeve for Quaker dress, pattern, mak-
    ing 281:90-91

**UNITED STATES—HISTORY—COLONIAL PERIOD—
    QUILTING**
Patchwork and quilting, how to do 225:37-42; 688:11,
    33; 831:132-134; 877:13-15; 877:58-60
Patchwork pillow, making 225:40-42; 453:18-21
Quilted butterfly, making 228:51-54
Quilted patchwork square or potholder, making 225:38-
    39; 673:85-114
Quilting, paper filigree, making 228:51

**UNITED STATES—HISTORY—COLONIAL PERIOD—
    RECREATIONS**
Bon fires 831:114
Corn Husking Bee 831:113
Greased watermelon battle and feast 831:114
Quilting Bee 831:113
Spelling Bee 831:113-114

**UNITED STATES—HISTORY—COLONIAL PERIOD—
    ROADS**
Road, plank, wooden, making 568:99
Tollhouse and Pike, wooden, making 568:120-125

**UNITED STATES—HISTORY—COLONIAL PERIOD—
    SCHOOLS**
Hornbook model, wooden, making 567:126-127
Old District Schoolhouse, wooden, making 568:60-63
Pen, inkwell, writing materials, making 228:31-33
Pupils' desks and dunce stool, wooden, making 568:68-
    70
School bench for older pupils, wooden, making 568:71

School bench for younger children, wooden, making
    568:70-71
School clothes, making 228:22-31
School desk with a drawer, wooden, making 568:66-68
Schoolmaster's desk and platform, wooden, making
    568:64-65
Schoolroom furniture, making 228:17-21
Schoolroom model, making 228:14-17
Wood-burning stove, wooden, making 568:72-73

**UNITED STATES—HISTORY—COLONIAL PERIOD—
    SCHOOLS—BIRD FEEDERS**
Bird feeder, wooden, making 192:32-33

**UNITED STATES—HISTORY—COLONIAL PERIOD—
    SCHOOLS—DOLLS**
Rag doll, making 192:24-27

**UNITED STATES—HISTORY—COLONIAL PERIOD—
    SCHOOLS—GAMES**
Puzzle, sponges, red, white and blue, making 192:28-29
Tricks, missing number trick, making 192:30-31

**UNITED STATES—HISTORY—COLONIAL PERIOD—
    SCHOOLS—HANDICRAFTS**
Paper-cuttings, making 192:20-23

**UNITED STATES—HISTORY—COLONIAL PERIOD—
    SCHOOLS—INKS**
Cranberry ink, making 192:19
Walnut shell ink, making 192:18

**UNITED STATES—HISTORY—COLONIAL PERIOD—
    SCHOOLS—PENS**
Quill pen, making 192:16-17

**UNITED STATES—HISTORY—COLONIAL PERIOD—
    SHIPS**
Clermont model, wooden, making 567:49-54
Merrimac model, wooden, making 567:75-78
Monitor model, wooden, making 567:79-81
River flatboat model, making 567:46-48

**UNITED STATES—HISTORY—COLONIAL PERIOD—
    SOAP**
Colonial soaps, recipes 1455:88-91
Grandma's Lye Soap, poem 118:46
Soap, hand soap, recipe 1043:29
Soap, making 118:46-48; 831:134

**UNITED STATES—HISTORY—COLONIAL PERIOD—
    SONGS**
Popular songs 831:81-105

**UNITED STATES—HISTORY—COLONIAL PERIOD—
    SOUTH—COOKERY**
Brunswick stew, recipe 871:15-16
Ham hocks and collard greens, recipe 871:13-15
Jambalaya, recipe 871:17-18
Lemon chess pie, recipe 871:111-112
Ozark pudding, recipe 871:101

**UNITED STATES—HISTORY—COLONIAL PERIOD—
    STORES**
Miniature general store, making 70:38-39

**UNITED STATES—HISTORY—COLONIAL PERIOD—
    STORIES**
Children's stories 831:53-56

**UNITED STATES—HISTORY—COLONIAL PERIOD—
    SUGARING**
Maple syrup candy, making 453:125-127

**UNITED STATES—HISTORY—COLONIAL PERIOD—
    THEATER**
American theater, 1750-1800, history of 831:57-60

UNITED STATES—HISTORY—COLONIAL PERIOD—TOYS

Ball and cup, making 831:38
Buzz saw, making 831:38
Corn husk dolls, making 193:36-39
Flipperdinger, making 831:39
Horse toy, stick horse, making 228:61-63
Humming toy, cardboard, making 193:33-34
Jointed figure toy, making 688:24
Log animals, making 831:37
Mountain bolo, making 831:38
Play mouse, making 831:38
Rocking horse, making 171:76-80
Spinners, button and string, making 877:82-83
Tops, simple, making 877:77-78
Whirligig, making 225:46-49

UNITED STATES—HISTORY—COLONIAL PERIOD—TRANSPORTATION

Bicycle, early model, wooden, making 567:82-86
Buggy, Amish family buggy, wooden, making 568:135-144
Cart, making 171:93-97
Concord Coach model, wooden, making 567:34-45
Conestoga wagon model, wooden, making 567:28-33
Covered wagon, making 171:98-101
Horse-car model, wooden, making 567:60-65
One-horse shay model, wooden, making 567:23-27
Sleigh, Dutch, wooden, making 568:96-98
Sleigh, early American, wooden, making 568:93-95
Sleigh, early model, wooden, making 567:19-22
Surrey, fringed-top surrey, wooden, making 568:126-134
Travois, model, wooden, making 567:8-9
Wheels, making 568:10-12
Wheels, wooden, making 567:xvi-xvii

UNITED STATES—HISTORY—COLONIAL PERIOD—TREATIES

Peace treaty, create one of your own, how to do 1297:39

UNITED STATES—HISTORY—COLONIAL PERIOD—VIRGINIANS—CLOTHING

Breeches, fabric, pattern, making 281:59-60
Costumes of Colonists of Virginia, making 281:56-63
Doublet, fabric, pattern, making 281:58-59
Woman's bodice and sleeve, pattern, fabric, making 281:61-62
Woman's cap, pattern, making 281:63

UNITED STATES—HISTORY—COLONIAL PERIOD—WEATHER VANES

Colonial mural of weather lore, making 193:30-31
Weather vane, aluminum and stick, making 877:108-111
Weathervane, making 688:13
Weathervanes, wooden, making 568:89-90

UNITED STATES—HISTORY—COLONIAL PERIOD—WEAVING

Loom for weaving, making 453:49-50
Weaving, information on 453:47-53
Weaving, loom from cardboard box and how to weave 877:45-49

UNITED STATES—HISTORY—COLONIAL PERIOD—WELLS

Well sweep model, wooden, making 567:145-147
Well, making 171:50-55

UNITED STATES—HISTORY—1770—CLOTHING

Colonial costumes, 1770, making 281:94-109
Costumes of early Republic, making 281:118-129
Man's breeches, pattern, making 281:100
Man's coat and waistcoat pattern, making 281:97-100

Tricome hat, pattern, making 281:101
Watteau gown, patterns, making 281:102-109
Woman's dress, patterns, making 281:124-128

UNITED STATES—HISTORY—REVOLUTIONARY WAR

Independence Day noisemakers, tissue roll, dry beans, making 1298:67

UNITED STATES—HISTORY—REVOLUTIONARY WAR—COOKERY

Apple butter, recipe 1043:47
Chess pie, recipe 1043:43
Cornmeal spoon bread, recipe 1043:42
Cottage cheese, recipe 1043:45
Fruit jelly, recipe 1043:46
Indian pudding, recipe 1043:43
Maple syrup candy, how to make 1043:41
Old Glory ice cream, recipe 1298:66
Sweet potato cake, recipe 1043:41
Sweet potato pudding, recipe 1043:42
Virginia pound cake, recipe 1043:44

UNITED STATES—HISTORY—REVOLUTIONARY WAR—COSTUMES

Revolutionary soldier costume, making 213:116

UNITED STATES—HISTORY—REVOLUTIONARY WAR—GAMES

British spy, a board game, how to play 1298:40-41
Brother Benjamin, a game 1298:60
Catch a tea smuggler game, how to play 1298:22
Revolutionary body parts, a game, how to do 1298:15
Tax and be taxed, two games, how to play 1298:24
Yankee Doodle game, making 719:15

UNITED STATES—HISTORY—REVOLUTIONARY WAR—PLAYS

Boston Massacre, a play 1298:28-31

UNITED STATES—HISTORY—REVOLUTIONARY WAR—QUILTING

Paper quilt, paper, crayons, making 1298:19

UNITED STATES—HISTORY—REVOLUTIONARY WAR—SOLDIERS

Early American soldier model, making 719:18-19

UNITED STATES—HISTORY—REVOLUTIONARY WAR—UNIFORMS

Jacket and gaiters, pattern, making 281:113
Overalls, pattern, making 281:115
Uniform, pattern, making 281:116
Uniforms of the Revolutionary War, making 281:110-116

UNITED STATES—HISTORY—1783-1865—GAMES

Mississippi Trist, board game of Ohio and Mississippi rivers, making 1609:14-15

UNITED STATES—HISTORY—1783-1865—TRANSPORTATION

Flatboat, wood scraps, nails, twine, making 1609:13

UNITED STATES—HISTORY—19TH CENTURY—BARNS

Barn, gingerbread, recipe, patterns, assembly instructions, how to make 1086:87-94

UNITED STATES—HISTORY—19TH CENTURY—COOKERY

Applesauce, recipe 1417:34-35
Baked ham slice, recipe 1417:22
Buttermilk biscuits, recipe 1162:12-13
Cabbage and apple salad, recipe 1417:24
Chicken shortcake, recipe 1162:30-31
Collard greens, recipe 1162:32
Corn pudding, recipe 1162:18-19

Cornbread, recipe 1162:33
Fried apples, recipe 1162:14
Fried fish, recipe 1162:22-23
Fruit soup, recipe 1417:25
Ginger cookies, recipe 1417:18-19
Hard-boiled eggs, recipe 1417:9
Homemade butter, recipe 1417:16-17
Hominy grits, recipe 1162:8-9
Hoppin' John, recipe 1162:20-21
Hush puppies, recipe 1162:24-25
Lemonade, recipe 1162:35
Peach cobbler, recipe 1162:36-37
Pepparkakor cookies, recipe 1417:40-41
Pork sausage and gravy, recipe 1162:10-11
Pork sausage patties, recipe 1417:8
Potato salad, recipe 1162:34
Potato soup, recipe 1417:30-31
Pound cake, recipe 1162:38-39
Round rye bread, recipe 1417:12-15
Scrambled eggs, recipe 1162:15
Shortbread, recipe 1162:40-41
St. Lucia buns, recipe 1417:38-39
Swedish almond rusks, recipe 1417:26-27
Swedish meatballs, recipe 1417:32-33
Swedish pancakes, recipe 1417:36-37
Swedish potatoes, recipe 1417:23
Swedish rice porridge, recipe 1417:10-11
Sweet potato pone, recipe 1162:26-27

**UNITED STATES—HISTORY—19TH CENTURY—
     HANDICRAFTS**
Animal chains, paper, patterns, making 1163:16-17
Appliquéd pillow, fabric, stuffing, making 1163:28-29
Braided mat, fabric, making 1418:6-7
Bunny pincushion, fabric, felt, patterns, making 1418:16-
     17
Changeable pictures, making 1163:36-37
Chromatrope toy, posterboard, paints, patterns, making
     1418:24-25
Cross-stitch bookmark, ribbon, cross-stitch canvas, pat-
     tern, making 1163:32-33
Drawstring bag, fabric, pattern, making 1163:30-31
Dried herbs and flowers, making 1418:8
Hobbyhorse, dowels, felt, paints, pattern, making
     1163:24-25
Hooked rug, rug canvas, yarns, patterns, making 1163:6-
     7
Jacob's Ladder, toy, wood blocks, paints, ribbon, mak-
     ing 1163:22-23
Jump rope, rope, beads, making 1163:40
Magic wallet, wood, paints, making 1418:32-33
Onion-skin dye, making 1418:9-11
Patchwork pillow, fabric, stuffing, making 1418:14-15
Quilted potholder, fabric, patterns, making 1418:18-19
Revolving serpent, paper, making 1163:14-15
Shadow puppet, posterboard, paints, making 1163:20-21
Spatterwork picture, paper, paints, making 1163:8-9
Tangram, posterboard, paints, making 1163:38-39
Wallpaper box, box, wallpaper, making 1163:12-13
Yarn doll, yard, ribbon, making 1418:22-23

**UNITED STATES—HISTORY—19TH CENTURY—
     HOUSES**
Gothic house, gingerbread, recipe, assembly instructions,
     how to do 1086:53-59

UNITED STATES—HISTORY—1804—CLOTHING
Man's coat, 1804, pattern, making 281:120-122

UNITED STATES—HISTORY—1815—COSTUMES
Empire costume, girl, c1815, making 368:89-95
UNITED STATES—HISTORY—1820-1840—CLOTHING
Costumes worn in 1835, making 281:130-138
Costumes worn in 1847, making 281:139-145
Man's coat and waistcoat, pattern, making 281:142
Man's coat, 1828, pattern, making 281:132-134
Woman's bodice and sleeve, pattern, making 281:134-
     138
Woman's sleeve and bodice, making 281:143
**UNITED STATES—HISTORY—VICTORIAN AGE.
     See VICTORIAN AMERICA**
UNITED STATES—HISTORY—1850-1870—CLOTHING
Costumes worn in 1860's, making 281:146-152
Man's coat and waistcoat, 1860, pattern, making
     281:148-149
Woman's costume, bodice, sleeve and yoke, pattern, mak-
     ing 281:150-152
**UNITED STATES—HISTORY—CIVIL WAR—
     COOKERY**
Appleade, recipe 1043:77
Barley water, recipe 1043:78
Biscuits, beaten, recipe 1043:74
Buttermilk pancakes, recipe 1043:72
Chicken pie, recipe 1043:75
Doughnuts, recipe 1043:72
Fried potatoes, recipe 1043:73
Gingerbread, recipe 1043:76
Hardtack bread, recipe 1043:73; 1455:127
Hot chocolate, recipe 1043:77
Sponge cake, recipe 1043:76
**UNITED STATES—HISTORY—CIVIL WAR—
     COSTUMES**
Civil War soldier costume, making 887:40-41
Johnny Reb costume, making 213:120-121
Rhett Butler costume, making 213:116-117
Scarlett O'Hara costume, making 213:118
Ulysses S. Grant costume, making 213:120-121
UNITED STATES—HISTORY—CIVIL WAR—DOLLS
Colonel in the Confederate Army, 1861, making 59:77-79
Colonel in the Union army, 1861, making 59:73-76
**UNITED STATES—HISTORY—CIVIL WAR—
     UNIFORMS**
Officer and Private uniforms, making 281:153-157
Officer's coat, pattern, making 281:155
Private's tunic, pattern, making 281:156
**UNITED STATES—HISTORY—20TH CENTURY—
     COOKERY**
Apple brown betty, recipe 1577:32-33
Blueberry muffins, recipe 1577:14-15
Cheese omelet, recipe 1577:10-11
Chicken salad sandwiches, recipe 1577:37
Corn oysters, recipe 18:40-41; 1577:24-25
Country hotpot, leeks, potatoes, cheese, milk, butter, rec-
     ipe 1624:27
Cream cheese and walnut sandwiches, recipe 1577:36
Cream of carrot soup, recipe 18:32-33; 1577:18-19
Dinner menu, recipes 18:25-45
French salad and dressing, recipe 1577:26-27
French salad, recipe 18:42-43
Fresh green beans, recipe 1577:23
Gingerbread, recipe 1577:38-39
Green beans, recipe 18:39
Ham slice, recipe 1577:9
Ice cream snowballs, recipe 18:44-45; 1577:28-29

Jelly biscuits, recipe 1577:34-35
Lemon ice, recipe 1577:40-41
Lemonade, recipe 1624:27
Mashed potatoes, recipe 1577:22
Peanut cookies, recipe 1624:26-27
Potatoes, mashed, recipe 18:38
Roasted beef tenderloin, recipe 18:36-37; 1577:20-21
Salmon with lemon butter, recipe 18:34--35
Saratoga potatoes, recipe 1577:12-13
Strawberries with cream, recipe 1577:8
Waldorf salad, recipe 1624:29

**UNITED STATES—HISTORY—20TH CENTURY—
GAMES**
Hoop and stick, making 1578:32

**UNITED STATES—HISTORY—20TH CENTURY—
HANDICRAFTS**
Candy crystals, making 1578:23
Embroidered handkerchief, making 1578:16-17
Fancy fan, gift wrap, paints, making 1578:8-9
Glass paperweight, felt, small objects, making 1578:10-11
Heart-shaped sachet, fabric, potpourri, making 1578:14-15
Leaf-print wrapping paper, making 1578:38-39
May basket, posterboard, ribbon, flowers, making
1578:30-31
Paper snowflakes, making 1578:22
Pressed-flower bookmark, making 1578:36-37
Seashell picture frame, making 1578:40
Silhouettes, paper, making 1578:24-25
Soap bubbles, recipe, making 1578:33
Toss pillow, fabric, stuffing, making 1578:18-19
Trinket box, wooden box, paints, making 1578:6-7
Walnut-shell surprises, felt, foil, making 1578:28-29

UNITED STATES—HISTORY—1920s—COSTUMES
1920 evening dress, girl, making 368:55-58

UNITED STATES—HISTORY—1940s—COOKERY
Applesauce cupcakes, recipe 1480:28-29
Carrot curls and celery fans, recipe 1480:21
Deviled eggs, recipe 1480:20
French toast, recipe 1480:32
Fried bacon, recipe 1480:10-11
Fried potatoes, recipe 1480:8
Frozen fruit cups, recipe 1480:14-15
Fruit bars, recipe 1480:40-41
Jelly flags, peanut butter, jelly, bread, recipe 1480:35
Nut and raisin bread, recipe 1480:38-39
Parsley biscuits, recipe 1480:24-25
PBJ roll-ups, peanut butter, jelly, recipe 1480:34
Quick coffee cake, recipe 1480:12-13
Toad-in-a-Hole, recipe 1480:9
Victory garden soup, recipe 1480:36-37
Vitality meat loaf, recipe 1480:22-23
Vitamin A salad, lemon gelatin, recipe 1480:18-19
Volcano potatoes, recipe 1480:26-27
Waldorf salad, recipe 1480:33

UNITED STATES—HISTORY—1940s—GAMES
Handshake game, posterboard, paints, making 1481:32-
33

UNITED STATES—HISTORY—1940s—HANDICRAFTS
Apple potholder, felt, patterns, making 1481:22-23
Button collage, picture, buttons, making 1481:41-42
Corral bookends, wood, paints, making 1481:34-35
Leather topped box, leather, paints, making 1481:38-39
Patriotic pinwheel, paper, pencils, making 1481:8-9
Pot holder, felt, plastic, pattern, making 1481:26-27

Scottie bookmark, felt, ribbon, pattern, making 1481:24-
25
Scrap paper jar, making 1481:40-41
Soap fish, pattern, making 1481:30-31
Star whirler, dowel, ribbons, making 1481:6-7
Star-stamp stationery, stamp pad, paper, making
1481:10-11
V-J Day parachute, fabric, string, making 1481:18-19
V-stitch handkerchief, thread, making 1481:16-17
Victory garden in a jar, making 1481:14-15

UNITED STATES—HISTORY—COSTUMES
Pre-1914 suit with hobble skirt, making 870:84-86

UNITED STATES—HISTORY—GAMES
Anagrams, how to play 1396:11
Apple games, how to play 1396:18
Bag and stick game, how to play 1396:20
Buzz game, how to play 1396:30
Charades, how to play 1396:8
Cobweb game, how to play 1396:21
Cudgel game, how to play 1396:6
Cupid's leaving game, how to play 1396:10
Dominoes, how to play 1396:12
Duck, Duck, Goose game, how to play 1396:23
Dumb crambo game, how to play 1396:9
Famous romances game, how to play 1396:20
Gossip game, how to play 1396:17
Graces game, how to play 1396:24
I have a basket game, how to play 1396:10
Pick-up sticks game, how to play 1396:13
Pinch no smiling game, how to play 1396:7
Post Office game, how to play 1396:22
Ring taw game, how to play 1396:24
Shinny game, how to play 1396:27
Spelling game, how to play 1396:30
Spin the trencher game, how to play 1396:22
Taboo game, how to play 1396:11
Tiddly winks game, how to play 1396:13
Tug-of-war game, how to play 1396:26
Twenty questions, how to play 1396:8

UNITED STATES—HOUSES
Apartment building model, wood strips, cardboard, making 1512:28-29

UNITED STATES—MAGIC TRICKS
Great escape, Houdini ring trick, how to do 1270:14-15

UNITED STATES—MUSICAL INSTRUMENTS
Kettledrum, cookie tin, cellophane, felt, making 1728:14-15

UNITED STATES—NEW YEAR'S DAY—COOKERY
Hoppin' John bean dish, recipe 1380:31

UNITED STATES—NEW YEAR'S EVE
Noisemakers from soda cans, stickers, foil, making
1199:291

UNITED STATES—PUPPET PLAYS
Winter of the Blue Snow 4:103-107

UNITED STATES—RAILROADS—HISTORY
Transcontinental railroad completed freight train mural,
making 1199:193-195
Transcontinental railroad completed game, how to play
1199:192-193

UNITED STATES—SCHOOLS
Traffic light game, how to play 1199:207
Traffic light made from egg cartons, colored paper, mak-
ing 1199:205

UNITED STATES—SCIENTISTS
How much vitamin C is in common beverage, experiment 1719:59-61

UNITED STATES—SONGS
"Bingo" flannel board folk song, patterns, making 1603:61-63
"Hush, Little Baby" flannel board song, patterns, making 1603:19-22
"I Got Me a Cat" flannel board song, patterns, making 1603:92-94
Rock-a-bye Baby, lullaby 1220:138

UNITED STATES—SOUTH—COSTUMES
Southern belle, green plastic trash bags, ribbons, making 1509:22-25

UNITED STATES—SPACE SHUTTLES
Rocket thrusters allow astronauts to maneuver in space, making 1719:56-58

UNITED STATES—SPORTS—COSTUMES
American footballer costume, fabric, patterns, making 1283:28-31

UNITED STATES—STRING FIGURES
Apache Door, Big Star, Bow, Dogs on a Leash, House, Hut, Jacob's Ladder, Lizard, Magic Carpet, Six-pointed Star, Rabbit, Tent, Two Coyotes; 1404:26-120

UNITED STATES—SYMBOLS
American eagle posterboard stand up model, patterns, making 1286:108-112
Symbols of America 199:12-17

UNITED STATES—TOYS. *See also* **TOYS**
Lazy tongs toy, paper, fabric, sticks, patterns, making 1422:29-30

UNITED STATES SENATE—COOKERY
Bean soup, recipe 871:80-81

UPPER VOLTA. *See* **BURKINA FASO**

UR
Astronomer's tunic, making 173:16-17
Clay folk from Ur, making 173:26-27

Courtyard houses, making 173:58-59
Cylinder seals, making 173:44-45
Games, Chaldean checkers, making 173:70-71
Mysterious tablets, making 173:52-53
Shoebox houses, making 173:56-57
Wild animal masks, making 173:76-77

URUGUAY—COOKERY
Caramel custard, recipe 794:14
Dulce de leche, milk sweets, recipe 1165:229
Gaucho torta frita, recipe 793:24
Grilled steak, recipe 793:23

URUGUAY—DANCES
Huffy little horsey dance 624:61-62

URUGUAY—EASTER—COOKERY
Asado (Uruguay roasted beef), recipe 1666:224-225
Chaja (cream filled sponge cake), recipe 1666:225

URUGUAY—GAMES
Blind hen game 383:146
Canasta card game 1132:101-107
Color market game 383:145
Mantantirulirula game 515:120
Mantantirulirula game, how to play 1494:211-212
Squirrel up a tree chasing game, how to play 1498:44
Wolf game 383:146

UTAH—CHRISTMAS
Christmas Cheer week in Salt Lake City, Utah 475:70

UTAH—COOKERY
Ice box cake, recipe 654:155-156
Potato soup, recipe 654:154
Quilter's potato salad, history of, recipe 155:6-7

UTE INDIANS—GAMES
Juggling, how to play 1699:126
Sticks game 602:181

UTE INDIANS—MUSICAL INSTRUMENTS
Morache, branch, basket or metal bowl, making 1608:56

V

VALENTINE'S DAY

Activities and projects for classrooms 1393:146-148

Activities, crafts, stories, recipes, making 558:43-47

Activities, patterns, games 50:171-204

Activities, Valentine's Day, making 9:5

Art and writing activities, patterns, making 1152:123-130

Art, cooking, finger plays, games, drama, math, science and music activities 54:91-106

Color stories, songs, rhymes with flannel board patterns 904:128-129

Crafts for Valentine's day, making 1662:20-29

Flannel graph stories and patterns, making 822:14-15

History and celebration of 496:25-27

History of American Valentines 89:21-37

History of cards in the United States 709:129

History of Valentine symbols 89:42-47

History of Valentine's Day 89:1-4; 513:49; 709:126-127; 715:6-7; 829:5-6; 916:94-96

History of Valentines 354:6

Learning units, art, language, music, foods, crafts, patterns 1193:396-446

Paper Valentines in England 89:10-19

Songs, finger plays, stories, games, rhythms 1200:55-56

Superstitions and customs 715:43-46

Valentine customs of long ago 89:5-9

VALENTINE'S DAY—COOKERY

Cherry cheesecake cupcakes, recipe 1705:47

Chocolate kiss oatmeal cookies, recipe 1705:46

Gingerbread heart cookie, how to decorate 1301:49

Heart cakes, cake mix, recipe 1178:120

Heart cookies, recipe 1735:51-53

Linzor heart cookies, recipe 206:50-52

Queen of Hearts cookies, recipe 1193:412

Red raspberries thumbprint cookies, recipe 1705:44

Scones, recipe 1705:42-43

Sweetheart cake, icing, recipe 1186:98-99

Sweetheart fudge, recipe 1705:45

Taffy pull, recipe and how to do 1402:19

VALENTINE'S DAY—COSTUMES

Cupid costume, making 842:40-44

Cupid, variety of old clothes, making 1656:9-12

Heart costume, posterboard and doilies, patterns, making 1050:164-166

Heart costume, satin fabric, cardboard, patterns, making 1174:17

King or Queen of Hearts costume, making 272:38-39

Knave of Hearts costume, making 272:39-41

Valentine card costume, making 272:37

Valentine costume, making 338:52-56

Valentine costume, paper bag, making 138:39-41

VALENTINE'S DAY—DECORATIONS

1800's puzzle pocket Valentine, making 1705:25

Cards, paper, making 1402:38-39

Fold-and-cut Valentines, paper, making 1237:81-84

Guest soaps, soap flakes, food coloring, yarn, plastic wrap, making 1572:38-39

Hanger heart sachets, old Valentines, yarn, scented powder, making 1572:36-37

Heart basket, paper or felt, patterns, making 1179:50-51

Heart mobiles, paper, making 1237:84-88

Heart placemats, paper, doilies, yarn, making 1266:37

Heart-shaped book, paper, ribbon, making 1610:11

Heart-shaped candy holder, doilies, yarn, making 1425:17-18

Heart, paper plate, card, pattern, making 1311:158-159

Love bug party favors, clothespins, felt, pompoms, eyes, making 1266:37

Lute Valentine, paper, making 1310:110

Magnet, candy magnet, moldable plastic decorated, making 1360:6-8

Old-fashioned cut-out hearts, paper, making 1705:13

Old-fashioned Valentines, making 698:19

Origami gift container, paper, patterns, making 1016:32-36

Piñata for Valentine's Day, making 309:40

Polish paper-cut hearts and flowers, patterns, making 1016:27-31

Pop-up hearts card,, colored paper, making 1393:147

Potpourri hearts, fabric, ribbons, potpourri, making 1425:12-13

Rebus, Valentine rebus, making 1705:30-31

Sachet heart pillows, making 310:190

Sachet, heart, felt, making 628:76-77

Stained glass suncatcher, frame, liquid leading, making 1425:19-20

Sweets box, milk cartons, paper bowl, making 1334:6-7

Treasure box, sticks, doilies, beads, making 1425:14-16

Treat bags, brown paper bags, paints, making 1657:55

Valentine totem pole, paper, making 94:23

Valentine wreath, making 586:31

Victorian style card, making 1253:35

VALENTINE'S DAY—DOLLS

Lucky rag doll, boy and girl model, fabric, yarn, making 1705:18-21

Valentine rag doll, making 354:28-29

VALENTINE'S DAY—FINGER PLAYS

Finger plays and rhymes 1583:104-105

VALENTINE'S DAY—GAMES

Heart game, making 534:89

Heart relay race, making 241:33-37

Heartbeat game, making 241:38-40

Hearts all in a row game, making 1705:40-41

VALENTINE'S DAY—HANDICRAFTS

Computer project: create a Valentine card 1218:48-51

Flowers, fabric, how to make 715:16-19

Heart pin, cardboard, buttons, making 1705:28-29

Heart pouch, felt, making 1262:35

Heart-shaped box, papier-mache, making 1300:48-51

Heart-shaped frame, papier-mache, making 1300:53-57

Heart, fabric, stuffed, how to make 40:14-23

Hearts and sweethearts jewelry, clay dough, recipe, making 200:42-45

Lace paper Valentines, easy, making 274:60-62

Legend of St. Valentine poem on decorated dove, making 1705:14-15

Necklace, Victorian heart, fabric, making 40:45-46

Nosegay, dried flowers, making 310:191

Pennsylvania German Valentines, making 709:129-132

Pincushion heart, fabric, making 598:66-67

Pincushion, cross-stitch, making 447:44-45

Pincushion, heart-shaped , fabric, stuffing, making 1376:14-16

Potpourri heart sachets, fabric, potpourri, making 1510:42-43

Pouches, heart-shaped, felt, patterns, making 1257:10-11

Sachet heart pillows, making 310:190

Sachet, heart, felt, making 628:76-77

Sachet; sweetheart sachet, felt, lace, potpourri, making 1360:9-11

Scarf with wood heart, making 1376:41-42

Tussie mussie, making 709:127-128
Valentines, pop-up cards, paper, patterns, making
1320:42-43
VALENTINE'S DAY—PARTIES
Decorations, food, games, play, making 1266:35-45
Heart invitations, placemats, and fold out hearts, paper,
making 829:7-8
Heart lollipops, heart butterflies, heart wreath, paper,
making 829:11
Heart streamer, ruffled Valentine, paper, making 829:12
Invitations, decorations, gifts, games, recipes 1402:42-47
Queen of Hearts party, decorations, games, costumes,
recipes 74:42-58
Tea party, sandwiches, pudding, recipes 1528:9
VALENTINE'S DAY—PATTERNS
Hearts patterns 309:39
VALENTINE'S DAY—PLAYS
Every Bunny Needs Some Bunny, play, script, easy
1266:40-45
VALENTINE'S DAY—PUPPETS
Cupid puppet, pattern, making 1006:29
Dancing Valentine puppet, sponge, straws, paper, mak-
ing 1294:37-39
Finger plays and puppets, patterns, making 513:50-54
Mailman puppet, making 754:44-54
Puppets, five Valentines, making 735:54
Queen of Hearts paper bag puppet, making 907:28
Red Valentine finger puppets and rhymes, making
821:42-43
Valentine finger puppet, paper, patterns, making 760:29
Valentine heart puppet, paper, rubber band, making
1572:12-13
Witch Valentine, puppets and puppet play script, making
1155:76-79
VAMPIRELLA—COSTUMES
Vampirella costume, making 42:40-45
VAMPIRES
Vampire pop-up card, making 197:50-53
VAMPIRES—COSTUMES
Vampire costume, fingernails, make-up, making 326:29-
31
VAN GOGH, VINCENT—BIRTHDAY
Copy van Gogh's sunflower mosaic using dried seeds on
cardboard, making 1199:74
VAN WOERHOM, DOROTHY O.
"Meat Pies and Sausage," meat pies, recipe 1216:100
VANILLA
History of vanilla 410:95
VEGETABLES—HANDICRAFTS
Things to make with gourds 1304:5-57
VEGETARIANS. *See also* **FOOD**
VEGETARIANS—COOKERY
Recipes for vegetarians for a variety of foods, making
664:139-171
VENEZUELA—BIRTHDAYS
Birthday customs 488:118-122
VENEZUELA—CHRISTMAS
Celebration of Christmas 497:106,111; 601:166; 695:76-
77
VENEZUELA—CHRISTMAS—COOKERY
Bien Me Sabe de Coco (cake with cream of coconut), rec-
ipe 1666:238-239
Hallacas Centrales (filled cornmeal patties), recipe
1666:237

VENEZUELA—COOKERY
Breakfast cocoa, recipe 188:7
Brown and white sandwiches, recipe 967:53
Caviar criollo, black beans dish, recipe 1675:119
Fried bananas, recipe 794:10
Pabellon criollo, sliced steak with rice and black beans,
recipe 1165:240-241
VENEZUELA—COSTUMES
Breakfast cocoa, recipe, costume 188:7
VENEZUELA—DOLLS
Carnival doll, papier-mache, pattern, making 1027:165-
169
VENEZUELA—FESTIVALS
Birthday Piñata celebration 601:156-157
VENEZUELA—HANDICRAFTS
Clay turtle bank, making 182:65-67
VENEZUELA—INDEPENDENCE DAY
Independence Day celebration July 5 722:46-48
VENEZUELA—TOYS
Corncob donkey, making 495:46-49
Street racers, making 182:78-83
VERMONT—COOKERY
Fish roll ups, recipe 874:43
Maple bars, recipe 654:158
Maple snow, milk, maple syrup, condensed milk, recipe
1179:8
Maple syrup candy, recipe 1179:8-9
New England boiled dinner, recipe 654:159
VERMONT—SHELBURNE MUSEUM—COOKERY
Apple crisp, recipe 57:66
Apple muffins, recipe 57:66
Chip monk pie, recipe 57:67
Cranberry-apple pie, recipe 57:67
VERNAL EQUINOX—DECORATIONS
Lion and lamb brown bag puppets, making 1199:69-71
Wind streamers, crepe paper, craft sticks, making
1199:71
VETERANS DAY. *See* **ENGLAND—FESTIVALS;
UNITED STATES—FESTIVALS—VETERANS
DAY**
VICTORIAN AGE
Victorian lady from paper straws, making 828:78-79
VICTORIAN AGE—CHRISTMAS—HANDICRAFTS
Cornucopia, paper doily, ribbon, making 1400:30
Dried fruit decorations, making 1400:30
Hearts, lacy hearts, fabric, wallpaper, stuffing, making
1400:30
Victorian decorations, garlands, popcorn strings, and
more, making 1575:20-21
VICTORIAN AGE—COSTUMES
Victorian man and lady costumes, fabric, patterns, mak-
ing 1174:35-36
VICTORIAN AGE—TOYS
Spinning thaumatrope of Jonah and the whale, cardboard,
making 1447:16-17
Thaumatrope, cardboard, pencils, string, how to make
1397:30
Thaumatrope, cardboard, patterns, making 1320:76-77
VICTORIAN AMERICA—COOKERY
Cucumber boats, recipe 1526:29
Egg fingers, recipe 1526:28-29
French bonbons, recipe 1526:10
Nut sandwiches, recipe 1526:28
Raspberry jam tarts, recipe 1526:29

VICTORIAN AMERICA—GAMES

Charades, how to play 1526:34
Grandmother's trunk, how to play 1526:33-34
Hunt the slipper, how to play 1526:35
Rigmarole, how to play 1526:33
Truth, how to play 1526:35

VICTORIAN AMERICA—HANDICRAFTS

Friendship pillow, fabric, batting, making 1526:14
Handkerchief doll, making 1526:18
Hot-house flowers, tissue paper, making 1526:11
Pressed flowers in a frame, making 1526:16
Sewing basket, basket, fabric, flowers, ribbon, making 1526:21
Silhouette portrait, making 1526:15
Tassel doll, yarn, felt, making 1526:20

VIENNA—CHRISTMAS. *See also* AUSTRIA— CHRISTMAS

Candy tree, star topped Viennese candy tree, making 672:67-80

VIETNAM

Activities, flags, games, songs, dances, recipes 1381:81-84
Cricket, catch a cricket, how to do 792:20
Vietnam National Flag entertainment 474:141-145

VIETNAM—COOKERY

Asparagus soup, recipe 446:25-26; 630:26
Batter fried cauliflower, recipe 895:152
Beef noodle soup (pho bo), recipe 1584:121
Beef, grilled lemon grass beef, recipe 630:35
Beef, stir-fried with green beans, making 630:29
Carrot salad, recipe 630:19
Cauliflower, stir-fried, recipe 630:27; 1075:93-94
Cha gio, spring rolls, recipe 1452:197
Chao, chicken and long rice soup, recipe 792:26-27
Chicken cabbage salad, recipe 630:21
Chicken, braised, recipe 630:37
Chicken, long rice soup, recipe 187:30
Fish, steamed, recipe 630:42
Goi cuon, meat and vegetable roll, recipe 1075:90-91
Meat and eggs, steamed, recipe 630:42
Meatballs, recipe 630:36
Moon cakes, playdough, recipe 909:92
Moon cakes, recipe 792:28-29
Nem nuong, grilled meatballs, recipe 1165:177-178
Nuoc cham sauce for goi cuon, recipe 1075:92
Nuoc cham, fish sauce spice, recipe 1452:198
Nuoc cham, fish sauce, recipe 630:19; 1068:unp; 1165:177; 1584:121
Princess cakes, banh cong chua, cookies, recipe 72:133-135
Rice noodle salad, recipe 630:22
Rice noodles, recipe 630:18
Rice, recipe 630:18
Rice, fried, recipe 630:30; 895:151; 1068:unp
Rice, fried with egg, recipe 1075:93
Rice, sticky with corn and coconut, recipe 630:39
Shrimp salad, recipe 630:23
Spring rolls, vegetables and meat in rice paper, recipe 630:32; 1381:83
Steamed tofu, recipe 630:40
Sweet and sour soup, recipe 630:25
Sweet potatoes with peanuts, recipe 630:40
Sweet soup, green beans, coconut, recipe 1381:83
Vietnamese salad, recipe 858:unp

VIETNAM—DRAMA

Hat Bo theater in Vietnam 474:105

VIETNAM—FESTIVALS

Mid-Autumn Festival, activities, handicrafts, foods, songs, making 909:89-97
Tet celebration 631:24
Tet Nguyen-den, the New Year celebration 792:8-11
Tet Trung-Thu, Autumn Moon festivals, activities and projects for classrooms 1393:42-43
Tet Trung-Thu, the Mid-Autumn Festival celebration 792:12-13
Tet, New Year Festival, activities and projects for classrooms 1393:130-132
Trung Thu, Feast of the Children 474:57-58

VIETNAM—FESTIVALS—COOKERY

Tet Nguyen-den, bo nuong (beef meatballs), recipe 1666:175
Tet Nguyen-den, goi (salad), recipe 1666:175-176
Tet Nguyen; nuoc cham (Vietnamese dipping sauce), recipe 1666:176

VIETNAM—FESTIVALS—DRAGONS

Tet; New Year festival dragon, paper cup, straws, paper, patterns, making 1633:150-151

VIETNAM—FESTIVALS—GAMES

New Year, Tet beanbag game, how to play 1574:6-7

VIETNAM—FESTIVALS—HANDICRAFTS

Tet Trung-Thu, Autumn Moon Festival story cloth, fabric, making 1393:43

VIETNAM—FESTIVALS—LANTERNS

Tet Trung-Thu Festival lantern, making 709:38-40; 792:14-15
Tet, Vietnam New Year swinging lanterns, paper, making 1539:92-93

VIETNAM—FESTIVALS—PUPPETS

Mid-Autumn Festival puppet projects, patterns, scenes, story starters 1083:193-194

VIETNAM—FOLK TALES

Why the Monsoon Comes Every Year tale 792:30-31

VIETNAM—FOLKLORE—PUPPETS

"Toad Visits the Emperor" shadow puppets, patterns, making 1602:188-195

VIETNAM—GAMES

Bite the carp's tail game, making 792:24
Hopscotch 984:19
Kick swing game, how to play 1494:49
O-Lang game, making 792:22-23
Pick up sticks game 984:12
Tower of Hanoi game, how to play 1507:52

VIETNAM—HAIKU

Book of haiku, paper, threads, patterns, making 1332:91-100

VIETNAM—HANDICRAFTS

Moon book, making 909:92
Phoenix, paper, making 532:57

VIETNAM—KITES

Kite, kitchen kite, making 792:16-19
Rabbit balloon kites, making 532:46-47

VIETNAM—LANGUAGE

Few phrases in Vietnamese language 792:45

VIETNAM—LANTERNS

Lanterns, Festival, paper, making 909:91

VIETNAM—NEW YEAR—PUPPETS

Tet dragon puppet, paper bag, patterns, making 1393:131-132

VIETNAM—NEW YEAR'S DAY
Animals predict your coming custom 505:21
Tet Nguyen-den, Vietnam New Year 474:21-23; 601:73
VIETNAM—PUPPETS
Water puppet show play, Under the Carambola Tree 792:40-44
Water puppet show puppets, making 792:34-39
Water puppet show rods, making 792:34
Water puppet show stage, making 792:33
VIETNAM, SOUTH—BIRTHDAYS
Celebrations of birthdays in South Vietnam 474:86-87; 488:103-107
VIKINGS
Leif Ericson Day; celebrate by making Viking helmet and shield 1199:229-232
Viking man model, making 470:2-5
VIKINGS—COOKERY
Baked trout stuffed with onions and mushrooms, recipe 1457:29
Broiled salmon, recipe 1457:27-28
Parsley butter, recipe 1457:27
Pork and leak stew, recipe 1457:28-29
Porridege, recipe 1457:27
VIKINGS—COSTUMES
Siegfried costume, making 213:62-64
Tunic pattern, making 87:90-91
Viking boy and girl, variety of old clothes, making 1656:209-215
Viking costume, fabric, pattern, making 367:106-108
VIKINGS—FESTIVALS
Festival of Yule celebration 566:12
VIKINGS—GAMES
Fox and geese game 956:124-125
VIKINGS—HANDICRAFTS
Viking ship in a bottle, making 626:46-48
VIKINGS—HELMETS
Helmet, chicken wire, papier-mache, making 1684:22
Helmet, papier-mache, egg carton, making 1345:22-23
Helmet, papier-mache, making 1330:11
VIKINGS—JEWELRY
Jewelry from modeling clay, making 1684:16-17
VIKINGS—LANGUAGE
Rune stone, paper, rocks, Rune alphabet given, making 1332:105-108
Runic alphabet secret message, how to write, Runic alphabet given 1330:22-23
VIKINGS—PUPPETS
Puppet, paper bag Viking puppet, patterns, making 1107:118-125
VIKINGS—SHIELDS
Shield, cardboard, pasted newspaper, making 1684:23
VIKINGS—SHIPS
Longboat, cardboard, fabric, making 1684:8-11
Viking longboat model, plastic bottle, paper tubes, making 1346:8-9
Viking longship, milk carton, making 129:20-21
Viking ship model, wooden, making 567:3-7
Viking ship, making 551:28-29
VIKINGS—VILLAGES
Viking village, clay, making 771:42-43
VIKINGS—WEAPONS
Battle axe, chicken wire, papier-mache, making 1684:20-21
Battle axe, folded origami, paper, making 1581:13-15
VILLAGES
3-D lift-up village and city, paper, making 954:22-23

Buildings, church, stores, townhouse, bakery, RR station, school, making 670:21-40
Indian village, chiefs, Council fire, teepee, canoe, totem pole, making 670:52-57
Little town, buildings from boxes, colored paper and paints, making 1213:124-125
Paper bag buildings, making 440:12
Toy village, paper boxes, making 123:86-87
Village, cardboard box, making 965:26-27
VILLAGES—COOKERY
Village cake, recipe 449:59
VINCI, LEONARDO DA—BIRTHDAY
Celebrate by painting portrait of self, making 1199:82-83
VIOLETS
Violet butter, recipe 1014:189
VIRGIN ISLANDS—THANKSGIVING
Hurricane Thanksgiving Day celebration 659:99
VIRGIN MARY
Paper model Virgin Mary, making 966:152-153
VIRGINIA—APPOMATTOX COURT HOUSE—COOKERY
"Robert E. Lee" cake, recipe 57:10
Rice pudding, recipe 57:11
Southern spoon bread, recipe 57:10-11
VIRGINIA—BOOKER T. WASHINGTON NATIONAL MONUMENT—COOKERY
Corn pone, recipe 57:87
Ginger cakes, recipe 57:86
Sweet potato pie, recipe 57:87
VIRGINIA—CHRISTMAS
White Lightning celebration 475:54-55
VIRGINIA—COLONIAL PERIOD—COOKERY
Apple butter, recipe 1308:8-9
Beefsteak pie, recipe 1308:32-33
Breakfast puffs, recipe 1308:12-13
Chicken pudding, recipe 1308:20-21
Dressed eggs, recipe 1308:16-17
Fried ham with gravy, recipe 1308:14-15
Green beans, recipe 1308:28
Johnny cake, recipe 1308:10-11
Liberty tea, recipe 1308:41
Nuts, spiced, recipe 1308:40
Pumpkin pudding, baked, recipe 1308:34
Queen cakes, recipe 1308:38
Raspberry flummery, recipe 1308:35
Sally Lunn bread, recipe 1308:26-27
Sweet potatoes and apples, recipe 1308:24-25
Tarts, almond, recipe 1308:36-37
Veal balls, recipe 1308:22-23
Whipped Syllabub, recipe 1308:29
VIRGINIA—COLONIAL WILLIAMSBURG—COOKERY
Brandied fresh peaches, recipe 57:18
Corn fritters, recipe 529:59-60
French pancakes, recipe 57:19
Spiced punch from Williamsburg, Virginia, recipe 652:88-89
VIRGINIA—COOKERY
Fried tomatoes, recipe 529:62-63
Pecan waffles, recipe 654:161-162
Spiced punch, recipe 654:163
Spoon bread, recipe 343:110; 529:61-62
Strawberry shortcake, recipe 529:64-66
Tapioca pudding, creamy, recipe 529:67-68

VIRGINIA—DOLLS
Blue Ridge Mountain roll doll, making 298:124-125
VIRGINIA—HISTORY—COOKERY
From the Starving Time to Virginia Tidewater cookery information 666:105-117
VIRGINIA—JAMESTOWN
1600's broadside advertisement encouraging people to move to VA, create 1297:29
VIRGINIA—MONTICELLO—COOKERY
Ice cream, recipe 57:42-43
Noodles a la macaroni, recipe 57:43
VIRGINIA—MOUNT VERNON—COOKERY
Fruit cake, recipe, making 57:46-47
VIRGINIA—WHITE HOUSE OF THE CONFEDERACY—COOKERY
Chicken a-la-daub, recipe 57:90

Chocolate cream, recipe 57:91
Gumbo, recipe 57:90
Jelly cake, recipe 57:91
Savory jelly, recipe 57:91
VOLCANOES
Diorama; clay diorama with erupting volcano, making 1286:36-37
Lewis, Thomas P., "Hill of Fire"; science, reading, art, language activities 1055:123-128
Volcano, how to make 1378:7-8
VOLCANOES—COOKERY
Dragon volcano cake, recipe and how to decorate 1415:12-13

W

WAGONS
Buckboard wagon, wooden, making 481:36-40
Circus wagon, paper, making 123:92
Covered wagon, cardboard box, large, making 539:19
Covered wagon, posterboard, patterns, making 912:15-16
Wagon, wooden, making 481:11-17; 833:unp

WALES
Activities, flags, games, songs, dances, recipes 1381:187

WALES—CHRISTMAS
Christmas Customs 149:34-40

WALES—CHRISTMAS—HANDICRAFTS
Welsh border fan, oat, wheat, rye straws, patterns, making 1224:74

WALES—COOKERY
Bara brith bread, recipe 967:50-51
Caws pobi, Welsh rabbit or rarebit, recipe 1165:126-127
Girdle scones, cacen-gri, cookies, recipe 72:60-61
Sticky Welsh gingerbread, recipe 1165:126
Welsh cakes cooked on top of stove in skillet, recipe 1381:187
Welsh cakes, recipe 794:21
Welsh rarebit, recipe 1560:9

WALES—COSTUMES
Description and pictures of Welsh costumes 313:51-55
Welsh costume, girl, making 368:69-72

WALES—FESTIVALS
St. David's Day; history and celebration of 496:30-31

WALES—FESTIVALS—COOKERY
St. David's Day leek and chicken pot pie, recipe 1666:111
St. David's Day leek soup, recipe 1666:110
St. David's Day Welsh rarebit, recipe 384:Mar.1

WALES—VALENTINE'S DAY
History of Valentine's Day in Wales 709:135-136

WALES—VALENTINE'S DAY—HANDICRAFTS
Welsh love spoons, clay, making 709:136-137

WALPURGIS NIGHT
Information on celebration 419:65

WAMPANOAG INDIANS
Wampanoag Indian girl place card, patterns, making 1237:46-48

WAMPANOAG INDIANS—COOKERY
Native American clambake, recipe 1296:138
Potato bargain, recipe 1296:139

WAMPUM. See also IROQUOIS INDIANS; WOOD-LAND INDIANS
Wampum weaving with beads, making 223:58-62

WARD, SALLY G.
"Molly and Grandpa," blueberry muffins, recipe 1216:44

WARPLANES. See AIRPLANES—WARPLANES

WASHINGTON (STATE)—CHRISTMAS
Seattle's Christmas Ship 475:68-69

WASHINGTON (STATE)—CHRISTMAS—COOKERY
Fruit snacks, recipe 654:167

WASHINGTON (STATE)—COOKERY
Nut loaf, recipe 654:165-166
Oatmeal bread, recipe 343:114-115
Raspberry apples, recipe 793:4
Washington State oatmeal bread, recipe 343:114-115

WASHINGTON MONUMENT
Washington Monument, model, making 186:14-16

WASHINGTON, BOOKER T.—COOKERY
Corn pone, recipe, making 57:87
Ginger cakes, recipe, making 57:86
Sweet potato pie, recipe, making 57:87

WASHINGTON, D.C.—CHRISTMAS—COOKERY
Andrew Jackson's spoon bread, recipe 1235:72
Andrew Jackson's turkey hash, recipe 1235:73
Cumin flavored spring peas, recipe 1235:75
Dolly Madison's frying herbs, recipe 1235:74
Martha Washington's fruited white cake, recipe 1235:75
Martha Washington's spiced gyngerbread, recipe 1235:72
Mrs. Harry Truman's Ozark pudding, recipe 1235:75
Mrs. Lyndon B. Johnson's popovers, recipe 1235:72
Mrs. Theodore Roosevelt's Indian pudding, recipe 1235:76
Pheasant with spaetzle, recipe 1235:74
Plantation pound cake, recipe 1235:76
Roast lamb with elderberry sauce, recipe 1235:73
Spaetzle, recipe 1235:74
Teddy Roosevelt's Christmas turkey, recipe 1235:73
Teddy Roosevelt's Philadelphia sand tarts, recipe 1235:75
Wild rice casserole, recipe 1235:74

WASHINGTON, D.C.—CHRISTMAS—DECORATIONS
Door decorations, paper, ribbon, patterns, making 1235:71
Garland paper chain, paper, tape, making 1235:70
Star mobile, cardboard, yarn, patterns, making 1235:68-69
Uncle Sam hat ornament, cardboard tube, paper, patterns 1235:66-67

WASHINGTON, D.C.—FESTIVALS
Cherry Blossom Festival; activities, art, songs, recipes, games 1469:86-87

WASHINGTON, D.C.—HISTORY—COOKERY
U.S. Senate bean soup, recipe 666:93-94

WASHINGTON, GEORGE
Design your own dollar, making 1199:54
Learning units, art, language, music, foods, crafts, patterns 1193:447-515
Your Presidential proclamation, pattern 1199:54-55

WASHINGTON, GEORGE—BIRTHDAY
Activities, art, songs, recipes, games 1469:68-69
Activities, crafts, songs 1473:97-100
Activities, patterns, games 50:216-236
Art, cooking, finger plays, games, drama, math, science, and music, activities 54:187-188
Birthday celebration; art, music, foods, games, activities 1104:62-65
Collage of Washington's life, making 186:46-47
History of Washington's birthday celebration 199:26
Lincoln, Washington, milk carton, making 79:11
Map puzzle, thirteen states, making 186:41-43
Planting, Martha Washington geranium, making 186:44-45
Washington's birthday, activities and projects for classrooms 1393:151-154

WASHINGTON, GEORGE—BIRTHDAY—SONGS
Songs for George Washington's birthday 901:55-56

WASHINGTON, GEORGE—COOKERY
Cherry cobbler, recipe 199:27; 871:56-57
Cherry delights, recipe 186:12-13
Cherry popcorn balls, recipe 939:47-48
Cherry tree cake, recipe 206:131-134
Four-layer cherry pie, recipe 1193:465
Fruit cake, recipe 57:46-47
George Washington's eggnog, recipe 1733:71
George Washington's fruit cake, recipe 1495:103

Hoe cakes, recipe 871:124-125
Martha Washington's tea cakes, recipe 1193:470
Oatmeal, Valley Forge, recipe 186:28-31
Philadelphia pepper pot soup, recipe 871:78-80

WASHINGTON, GEORGE—COSTUMES
Costume, making 213:114-116; 213:117-118
George Washington costume, making 272:46-47
Martha Washington costume, making 272:48

WASHINGTON, GEORGE—DECORATIONS
Birthday card, making 186:10-11
Cherries, paper, patterns, making 1067:36-38
Cherries, paper, pattern, making 253:36-37
Cherry tree centerpiece, making 916:102-103
Cherry tree, making 297:266-267
Cherry tree, paper, pattern, making 760:36-37
Cherry trees, fingerprints, making 1149:102
Cherry trees, paper, twigs, red circles, making 1149:53
George Washington, cut-and-paste, paper, making 95:21
George Washington, paper plate, pattern, making 413:10-11
George Washington, paper, models, patterns, making 639:26-27
Hatchet, paper, popsicle stick, pattern, making 253:34-35; 1067:34-36
Mount Vernon, home of George Washington, patterns 1473:100
Place cards, candy dish and coaster, making 226:14-16
Washington's head, hatchet and cherries, making 648:21

WASHINGTON, GEORGE—FLAGS
Flag, thirteen star, making 186:18-20

WASHINGTON, GEORGE—GAMES
Cabinet game, how to make and play 1609:27
Games for Washington's birthday, making 891:32-37
George Washington's birthday game 240:15
Name game, making 186:23
Washington crosses the Delaware game 1078:38

WASHINGTON, GEORGE—HANDICRAFTS
Cherry magnet, felt, pom poms, wire, patterns, making 1067:38-39
Cherry refrigerator magnet, making 253:37-38
Cherry tree, paper, tissue paper, making 1393:154
George and Martha paper dolls, making 191:24-29
Quill pen, making 186:36-37
Silhouette head pattern, making 1393:153
Silhouette, paper plates, making 374:154-156
Stars and Stripes sampler, making 199:28-31
Washington's peek box, making 698:25

WASHINGTON, GEORGE—HATS
George Washington General hat, paper pattern, making 823:31-32
George Washington three cornered hat, paper, pattern, making 823:30
Hat, paper, making 50:218
Hat, three-cornered, making 186:21-22
Tricorn hats, oaktag, paper, patterns, making 1199:53

WASHINGTON, GEORGE—PATTERNS
Washington silhouette, pattern 1193:504

WASHINGTON, GEORGE—PUPPETS
George Washington puppet, pattern, making 1006:30
Washington and the First Flight in America puppet play 754:55-59
Washington puppet, making 754:59-69

WASHINGTON, GEORGE—SONGS
Song about George Washington 902:24

WASHINGTON, MARTHA
Martha Washington, paper plate, pattern, making 413:9

WASHINGTON, MARTHA—COOKERY
Vanilla creams, Martha Washington Jets, recipe 166:17

WATER
Dowsing for water, information about 118:126-127

WATER DIVINERS
Divining rod, making 310:43

WATER SKIS
History of water skis 119:110-113

WATER WHEELS
Paddle wheels, simple to demonstrate early water power 318:17

WATERMELONS
Watermelons, activities, art, songs, science, recipes 911:258-261

WAURA INDIANS—HANDICRAFTS
Waura Indian patapu fish lure, cardboard, paint, making 1378:228

WEATHER
Weather folklore information 118:54

WEATHER VANES
Colonial, aluminum and stick, making 877:108-111
Fish weather vane, styrofoam, making 67:28-29
Goose wind vane, making 526:64-65
Papier-mache model, making 1615:10-13
Weather vane, making 105:24-25; 310:256; 376:117; 688:13
Weather vane mobile, making 691:18-19
Weather vane information 118:55

WEAVERS
Weaver's cloak, making 173:14-15

WEAVING
Andean weavings, making 182:58-61
Backstrap loom weaving, how to do 720:10-11
Basket weaving table mat, making 337:72-75
Basket weaving with crepe paper, making 275:83
Basket, weaving or coiling, making 524:22-24
Basket, woven wool, making 690:39
Berry basket weaving, making 93:107
Birdhouse, basket weaving, making 337:80-85
Bookmark, woven, making 337:19-20
Branch weaving, how to do 1421:130
Burlap beach weavings, making 418:51-53
Butter tub basket, woven, making 1109:85-88
Cages and webs, weaving, how to do 526:33-42
Card weaving, how to do 720:12-13
Card weaving, wool, making 690:38
Cardboard loom pillow, making 337:56-59
Cardboard loom potholder, making 337:52-55
Cardboard loom weaving, how to do 10:20-24; 275:84
Cardboard loom woven coat hanger, making 337:60-65
Cardboard loom woven scarf, making 337:66-71
Cardboard weaving painted hanging, making 1506:18-19
Cardboard weaving, how to do 482:94-95
Cattail weaving, how to do 1421:180
Christmas garland, finger woven, making 337:44-45
Clutch bag, woven, making 337:26-30
Curtains, finger woven, making 337:46-48
Cut-paper weaving, cut and paste, paper, making 97:32
Danish paper hearts, how to weave 1506:20-21
Doll purse, woven, how to make 586:24-25
Fabric on paper weaving, making 10:14-17
Face wall hanging, woven, making 337:21-25

Fence weaving, how to do 1421:131
Finger weaving, bookmark, yarn, making 1262:22-23
Finger weaving, making 70:48
Finger-woven belt, making 337:42-43
Fish mobile, woven, making 337:15-18
Fruit basket weaving, how to do 1421:133
God's Eye weaving, yam, making 432:22-23; 749:59-61; 991:95-98
God's Eye, stick weaving, making 720:14-15
Grass basket, basket weaving, making 337:76-79
Heart basket, fabric, making 1615:24-29
Heddle, making 954:91
Ikat weaving from Indonesia using dyed threads, making 1506:22-23
Inkle loom weaving, how to do 955:10-13
Inkle loom, wooden, making 955:8-9
Loom for weaving from newspaper, making 271:74
Loom from box top, making 480:59
Loom from drinking straws, making 275:82
Loom from plastic or paper cup, making 275:77
Loom from shoebox lid, making 1350:64-65
Loom weaving, making 120:20-21
Loom, belt loom from plastic straw, making 954:92
Loom, cardboard loom, making 805:86; 877:45-49; 1062:7; 1095:10-12
Loom, frame loom, how to make 805:88
Loom, heddle loom from popsicle sticks, making 954:93
Loom, homemade, making 561:22
Loom, inkle loom from box and stick, making 954:94-95
Loom, making 358:49; 924:14
Loom, milk carton loom, making 805:85
Loom, picture frame, making 1062:6
Loom, popsicle stick loom, how to make 805:90-91
Loom, portable, making 225:33-37
Loom, rectangular, circular, making 293:180-182
Loom, shoe box loom, making 805:84-85; 1062:6
Loom, simple loom, wood, dowels, cardboard, making 937:141-143; 1511:12-13
Loom, soda straw loom, making 996:56-57
Loom, styrofoam dishes, making 1062:6
Loom, wooden loom, making 749:52
Looms; burlap, branch and basket, simple, making 286:76
Macaroni weaving, how to do 482:96-97
Mat woven on cardboard loom, yarn, making 1255:27
Mat, rectangular, woven on cardboard, making 749:30
Mat, round, woven on cardboard, making 749:38
Mat, table, woven on frame, making 749:54
Mat, woven, wool, making 690:38
Navaho rug, how to weave 605:79-86
Necklace, spool weaving, making 337:31-33
Outdoor weavings, making 310:39
Over and under weaving, making 954:90
Paper loom, making 10:8-13
Paper plate picture, making 440:42
Paper straw braids and plaits, how to make 828:48-55
Paper straws and different ways to weave them 828:32-45
Paper weaving with strips of paper, making 10:6-19; 172:63; 805:83; 966:112-113; 991:193-195; 1506:12-13
Party placemat, woven, making 337:9-11
Pencil case, woven wool, making 690:39
Pendant, finger weaving, making 337:49-5 1
Persian rug, cardboard weaving, making 515:68
Placemat, woven, how to make 924:14-17

Placemat, woven paper, making 438:5
Plaid sash, woven, how to make 525:46-47
Plant holder, woven, making 337:12-14
Raffia, woven, making 830:16-17
Reweaving burlap, how to do 314:17-23
Round mat, woven, making 587:39
Rug, woven, making 337:38-41; 561:22; 916:12-14
Shadow box weaving, how to do 1152:47-48
Shoulder bag woven around book as loom, yarn, making 1262:42-43
Simple weaving, how to do 70:91
Snake, garden, spool weaving, making 337:34-37
Soda straw loom weaving with yarn, how to make 1614:24-27
Spaghetti weaving, making 683:38-39
Spool weaving on a frame, making 749:57
Star ornament, fabric, making 1615:24-27
Straw woven belt, making 251:104
String tie, woven, making 587:39
Strings and straws weaving, how to do 805:89
Striped belt, making 432:19-21
Tapestry frame, how to set up 1506:14-15
Tapestry weaving on frame, making 749:56
Tapestry weaving, how to make 1506:16-17
Tapestry, woven on cardboard loom, yarn, fabric, making 1679:12-13
Thrumming loom, making 955:34-35
Tree loom, making 251:106
Twig weaving, twigs, grasses, yarn, making 1285:136-137
Twig weavings, yarn, fabric, pipe cleaners, making 1618:42-43
Twining on frame, how to do 955:14-17
Wall hanging, making 105:31-34
Wall hanging, woven wire weaving, making 991:108-111
Wastebaskets, cardboard, woven, making 10:18-19
Weave a picture, how to do 1017:23
Weaving into burlap, how to do 749:50
Weaving into cotton mesh, how to do 749:48
Weaving into scrim, how to do 749:46
Weaving into wire, how to do 749:49
Weaving loom and loops, how to do 1213:28
Weaving on a branch, how to do 749:64
Weaving on a coat hanger, how to do 749:63
Weaving on cardboard, how to do 376:179; 749:29-44
Weaving spool, making 120:193-196
Weaving trays, styrofoam trays, making 1421:132
Weaving using grasses, how to do 358:48-50
Weaving with drinking straws, how to do 376:176; 749:62; 828:27-31
Weaving with paper, how to do 267:22-23; 553:34-35; 749:19-28
Weaving, easy, how to do 70:9; 461:66; 877:45-49
Weed weaving, how to do 954:98-99
Wild weavings, fabric, making 996:66
Winter scarf, making 432:23-25
Woven blanket sign, making 293:179-180
Woven creations, making 293:182-185
Woven mat, leather, making 641:68-69
Woven pendant, making 432:26-28
Woven tapestry with a message, how to make 1506:24-26
Woven tapestry, making 432:29-32
Yarn weaving decoration on two sticks, making 1348:unp

WEAVING—SONGS

Derry Ding Dason round song 1115:30

WEBSTER, NOAH—BIRTHDAY

Celebrate by doing different dictionary activities 1199:236-237

WEDDINGS—HANDICRAFTS

Wedding crown, posterboard, paints, making 1477:81

WELLS

Well, clay, making 771:10-11

WELLS—DECORATIONS

Flower mosaic to decorate wells, how to do 1467:13

WEREWOLVES—COSTUMES

Werewolf costume and mask, making 42:53-60; 248:14-15; 326:38-40; 617:51-56

Wolfman costume, mask, making 326:38-40

WEST BENGAL—MASKS

Durga mask, box, dowels, glitter, containers, making 1295:32-33

WEST INDIES

King Who Wanted to Touch the Moon, traditional tale from the West Indies 140:29-33

WEST INDIES—COOKERY

Rice pudding, molded, recipe 793:15

Salad, recipe 514:143

WEST INDIES—COSTUMES

West Indian costumes drawing 988:61

WEST INDIES—DANCES

Limbo Rock dance, how to do 1494:64-65

Manee Gogo dance, how to do 1494:68-69

WEST INDIES—TOYS

Twirling Yo-yo from the West Indies; history of and how to make 495:28-31

WEST VIRGINIA—COOKERY

Hominy, recipe 654:170

Molasses cookies, recipe 654:169

Southern cornbread, recipe 654:171

WEST VIRGINIA—HANDICRAFTS

Bean bag toss and catch man, making 298:116-117

WESTWARD MOVEMENT

California Trail and Gold Rush food supply information 663:96-100

Great Plains; Buffalo Hunters and Sod Busters food supply information 663:51-56

Indian foods of the Southwest in pioneer days 663:67-68

Kentucky potluck on the Kentucky frontier; food supply information 663:6-13

Lewis and Clark Expedition food supply information 663:87-90

Michigan; Dutch food on the Appleseed Trail information 663:46-49

Ohio, Germans of Ohio meat and potatoes eating information 663:40-45

Oklahoma chuckwagon foods in pioneer days 663:73-79

Oregon Homesteaders and Mountain men food supply information 663:90-95

Sacajawea birthday celebration, art, music, foods, games, activities 1104:118-121

San Francisco, Chinese immigrants food supply information 663:101-105

Slave and Indian food supplies in pioneer days 663:22-24

Spanish foods in pioneer days 663:68-73

Town folk models, making 356:10-11

Wild West play board, posterboard, making 534:76

Wisconsin; Swiss, Cornish and Scandinavian foods in pioneer days 663:49-50

WESTWARD MOVEMENT—BIRDS

Vulture of the Western Plains model, making 356:12-13

WESTWARD MOVEMENT—BISON

Bison model, making 356:22

WESTWARD MOVEMENT—BOATS

Mississippi River boat model, making 356:24-26

WESTWARD MOVEMENT—CITIES

Oklahoma City model, making 356:8-9

WESTWARD MOVEMENT—CLOTHING

Frontiersman wamus, making 870:97-100

WESTWARD MOVEMENT—COOKERY

California date-nut walnut bread, recipe 1043:155

California smoothie, recipe 1043:160

Cioppino, recipe 871:24-26; 1043:159

Cobb salad, recipe 1043:156

Colorado trout, recipe 1043:158

Crab and grapefruit cocktail, recipe 895:149

Crab Louis, recipe 1043:157

Denver omelet, recipe 1043:153

Filbert crescents, recipe 1043:160

Fruit soup, recipe 1043:156

Montana meat stew, recipe 343:54

Pecan waffles, recipe 1043:154

Salmon loaf, recipe 1043:157

Spareribs, baked spareribs dinner, recipe 653:79-82

Western steak and eggs, recipe 1043:153

WESTWARD MOVEMENT—COSTUMES

Sheriff or cowboy suit costume, making 356:16-17

WESTWARD MOVEMENT—FORTS

Forts of the Wild West models, making 356:28-31

WESTWARD MOVEMENT—GAMES

Billiards model, making 356:14-15

WESTWARD MOVEMENT—PARTIES

Go West party, 7 years up 124:87-98

Wild West round-up party, decorations, games, costumes, recipes, making 74:109-121

WESTWARD MOVEMENT—PONIES

Cow ponies models, making 356:6-7

WESTWARD MOVEMENT—SOLDIERS

Soldiers of the fort models, making 356:27

WESTWARD MOVEMENT—STAGECOACHES

Stagecoach model, making 356:3-5

WESTWARD MOVEMENT—TRAINS

Iron Horse locomotive model, making 356:18-21

WESTWARD MOVEMENT—WAGON TRAINS

Wagon train model, making 356:23

WESTWARD MOVEMENT—WAGONS

Covered wagon, from cereal boxes, making 84:35-36

Covered wagon, paper boxes, making 123:91-92

WHALES

Activities, art, songs, recipes, games 1469:80-81

WHEAT

History of wheat in cultures 88:12-29

History of wheat in Egypt 88:31-36

Threshing and grinding wheat, how to do 1531:46-49

Wheat sunburst, making 296:240-241

Whole wheat muffins, recipe 614:30

WHISTLES

Grass-blade whistles, making 118:109

Paper whistle, making 310:74

Warbler whistle, thin cardboard, patterns, making 1051:80-84

Wild beast whistles, making 120:184-186

Willow whistle, making 954:72

WHITE, E. B.
  "Charlotte's Web," descriptions and pictures of barn 29:Chapter 4
WHITE, T. H.
  "Sword in the Stone," descriptions and pictures of house 29:Chapter 2
WHITNEY, ELI
  Birthday celebration; art, music, foods, games, activities 1104:30-33
WHITSUNTIDE
  History and celebration of Whitsuntide 496:71
WHITTLING
  3-D forms from balsa wood, making 789:35
  Fish carved mobile, making 789:37
  Hardwood sculpture, making 789:38-43
  How to whittle 118:227-228; 789:30-31
  Softwood sculpture, making 789:32-34
  Stack sculpture, making 789:36
WIGS
  African dancer wig, making 7:35
  Egyptian wig, yarn, fabric, felt, making 367:66; 1680:26-27
  Judge wig, painters, cap, index cards, making 1656:220
  Troll wig, making 7:34
WIGWAMS. *See also* **WOODLAND INDIANS**
  Wigwam, paper, making 123:30
WILD WEST. *See* **COWBOYS; WESTWARD MOVEMENT**
WILDE, OSCAR—COOKERY
  "Selfish Giant"; Selfish Giant cookies, recipe 365:86
WILDER, LAURA INGALLS
  Laura Ingalls Wilder program, activities, books, crafts, patterns, making 1159:136-147
  Pioneer home life, display ideas, patterns, making 1159:143
WILDER, LAURA INGALLS—BIRTHDAY
  Laura Ingalls Wilder birthday, activity with bread and butter 1199:34-36
WILDER, LAURA INGALLS—COOKERY. *See also* **FRONTIER AND PIONEER LIFE—COOKERY**
  Laura's wedding cake, recipe 885:206-207
  Ma's pumpkin pie, recipe. "Little House in the Big Woods" 570:73-75
WILDER, LAURA INGALLS—QUILTING
  Nine-patch quilt pattern, making 1159:141
  Quilt patterns, making 1159:140-142
  Schoolhouse quilt pattern, making 1159:142
WILDLIFE PARKS
  Animal models for wildlife parks, paper tubes, cardboard, making 1467:26-27
WILLIAMS, BARBARA
  "Kevin's Grandma," peanut butter soup, recipe 1216:71
WILLIAMS, MARGERY—COOKERY
  "Velveteen Rabbit," rabbit soup, recipe 365:71
WILLIAMS, VERA B.
  "Cherrie and Cherry Pits," reading, writing, thinking activities 1093:62-70
WIND CHIMES
  Japanese furins, glass pendants, making 143:135
  Oriental tin can lids chimes, making 680:10-11
  Shell chimes, making 864:30
WIND IN THE WILLOWS
  100 easy recipes from the book "Wind in the Willows" 77:1-117
  Rat's baked ham, recipe 570:89-91

WIND RACERS
  Wind racer land-yacht toy, spools, dowel, cardboard, patterns, making 1051:1-4
WIND SOCKS
  Independence Day wind socks, paper, making 133:135-136
  Windsock, fabric, ribbons, making 15:134-135; 1376:24-26
WINDMILLS
  Dutch mill model from oats cereal box, making 494:103-107
  Milk carton windmill, paper plate, making 556:46-47
  Mobile of windmills, making 691:8-9
  Model windmill, papier-mache, making 641:126-127
  Paper windmill, simple, making 966:40-41
  Portuguese wooden toy windmill, pattern, making 1027:62-71
  Tissue roll windmill, making 374:142-143
  Windmill Day; activities, art, songs, recipes, games 1469:102-103
  Windmill from blown egg, making 677:19
  Windmill from cardboard, making 461:66; 554:50-51; 877:45-49
  Windmill from colored metal foil 113:53
  Windmill, cookies, making 1672:84-86
  Windmill, from cereal boxes, making 84:31
  Windmill, paper, pattern, making 151:96-98; 232:31-32; 760:59-61
  Windmill, plywood, bicycle wheel, making 1312:38-39
WINNEBAGO INDIANS—FOOTWEAR
  Winnebago moccasins, making 359:62-69
WINNEBAGO INDIANS—GAMES
  Plum pits game 602:181-182
WINNIE THE POOH
  Pooh Bear picnic, decorations, games, costumes, recipes 74:28-41
WINNIE THE POOH—COOKERY
  Eeyore's birthday cake with pink icing, recipe 277:11
  Honey-nut bread sandwiches, recipe 277:10
  Honey recipes, making 276:19-115
  Pink honey lemonade, recipe 277:12
  Thistle snow ice cream soda, recipe 277:13
  Winnie the Pooh's honey bears cookies, recipe 1199:12
WINNIE THE POOH—GAMES
  Musical Pooh pillows game 277:33-34
  Picking thistles game 277:14-15
  Piglet tag game 277:32
  Pin the tail on Eeyore game 277:30
  What's the time, Eeyore, game 277:31
WINNIE THE POOH—HANDICRAFTS
  Bear button, paper, pattern, making 1159:107
  Bear shapes for hums or poems, patterns, making 1159:108
  Eeyore memo tail, paper, pattern, making 1159:107
  Eeyore stuffed animal, making 315:14-17
  Felt pictures, making 315:40-45
  Hunny Pot, making 315:46-51
  Kanga and Roo, stuffed animals, making 315:22-25
  Owl stuffed animal, making 315:34-37
  Piglet stuffed animal, making 315:30-33
  Rabbit stuffed animal, making 315:10-13
  Tiddely-Pom snow scene, making 315:52-53
  Tigger stuffed animal, making 315:26-29
  Winnie the Pooh stuffed animals, making 315:18-21

WINNIE THE POOH—PARTIES
   Bear party hat, paper, pattern, making 1159:109
   Christmas party; foods, games and activities 277:105-135
   Eeyore birthday party with foods, games and activities
      277:7-34
   Honey tasting party for Pooh; foods, games and activities 277:81-102
   Picnic, swimming and expatiation party; foods, games
      and activities 277:57-78
   Spring party with foods, games and activities 277:37-54
   Woozle-wizzle snow party; foods, games and activities
      277:105-135
WINNIE THE POOH—PATTERNS
   Pooh and his friends; patterns for tracing 277:138-145
WINTER. *See also* **SNOW; SNOWFLAKES; SNOWMEN**
   Activities, finger plays, recipes, crafts 305:6-7
   Art, cooking, finger plays, games, drama, math science,
      music, activities 54:73-90
   December projects and handicrafts, making 561:51-62
   February projects and handicrafts, making 561:73-82
   First day of winter finger plays, recipes, games, making
      944:46-49
   Flannel graph stories and patterns, making 822:33
   January projects and handicrafts, making 561:63-72
   Learning units, art, language, music, foods, crafts, pat-
      terns 1193:249-306
   Songs, fingerplays, stories, games, rhythms 1200:122-125
   Welcome Winter activities, crafts, stories, recipes, mak-
      ing 558:30-32
WINTER—CLOTHES
   Literature activities, books, finger plays, games, crafts
      480:81-96
WINTER—COOKERY
   Snowman snacks, making 134:65
WINTER—FESTIVALS
   History of winter festivals 709:60
WINTER—FINGER PLAYS
   Finger plays and rhymes 1583:97-103
WINTER—FOLKLORE—HANDICRAFTS
   Shingebiss and the North Wind, snow scene with crayon
      resist, diorama 125:80-89
WINTER—HOLIDAYS
   Winter Holidays Program; activities, books, crafts, pat-
      terns, scripts, making 816:161-181
WINTER—NATURE FESTIVALS
   Winter and spring celebrations 419:53-56
WINTER—SONGS
   Build a Little Snowman 782:unp
   It Is Snowing 782:unp
   Sing a Song of Winter 782:unp
   Sliding Song 782:unp
   Snowman Ran and Ran 782:unp
   Songs about winter 1150:11-18
   Winter songs for infants and toddlers 908:65-67
WISCONSIN—COOKERY
   Cabbage soup, recipe 343:95
   Cheese snack tray, recipe 654:173
   Summer squash, recipe 654:174
   Swiss cheese and onion pie, recipe 663:60-61
WISCONSIN—COOKERY—GERMAN
   Cheesecake, recipe 529:203-205
   Frankfurters with hot potato salad, recipe 529:201-203
   Kartoffel Kuklein, recipe 529:200
   Pot roast, braised, recipe 529:195-197
   Potato pancakes, recipe 529:198-199

   Red cabbage, recipe 529:198
WISCONSIN—COOKERY—SWEDISH
   Christmas gingersnaps and icing, recipe 529:188-190
   Cucumber salad, recipe 529:183
   Macaroni party salad, recipe 529:184-185
   Scandinavian calla lillies, recipe 529:186-187
   Swedish meatballs, recipe 529:181-182
WISCONSIN—FESTIVALS—COOKERY
   Octoberfest; bratwurst (German sausage), recipe
      1666:269-270
WISCONSIN—HISTORY
   Swiss, Cornish and Scandinavian foods in pioneer days
      663:49-50
WISCONSIN—HISTORY—COOKERY
   Swiss and Cornish foods in Wisconsin information
      666:174-176
WISCONSIN—SONGS
   Hush Little Baby, lullaby 1220:144
WISHING WELLS
   Wishing well, bread dough, making 816:39-41
WITCH DOCTORS
   Mask, witch doctor mask, wool, making 690:45
WITCHCRAFT—FOLKLORE—HANDICRAFTS
   Which a Witch, art activities, corn husk dolls, making
      126:82-85
   Which a Witch, art activities, stenciled name plaque,
      making 126:86-88
   Which a Witch, art activities, stenciled paper, making
      126:88
   Which a Witch, story 126:76-81
WITCHES. *See also* **HALLOWEEN**
   October witches art and writing activities, patterns, mak-
      ing 1152:25-35
WITCHES—COSTUMES
   Witch costume, fabric, patterns, making 1283:12-15
WITCHES—FACE MAKEUP
   Witch face makeup, how to do 1314:44-45
WIZARD OF OZ
   Tin Woodman toy, making 346:36
WIZARD OF OZ—PARTIES
   Wizard of Oz party, activities, recipes 809:49-53
WIZARDS
   Collar for wizard, making 252:32
   Pumpkin head wizard, baker's dough, recipe, patterns,
      making 1152:39-41
   Wizard, paper, large pattern, making 478:40-44
WIZARDS—COSTUMES
   Wizard costume, fabric, making 1379:14
WIZARDS—HATS
   Hat, paper bag, making 1105:12-13
   Wizard hat, making 1096:10
WIZARDS—PUPPETS
   Wizard puppet, pattern, making 1006:14
WOOD CARVING
   African Mask carved wood wall plaque, making 382:54
   Bowls and candlesticks, how to make 454:26-27
   Bowls and noggins, making 467:90-91
   Buffalo skull carved wood wall plaque, making 382:56
   Burro carved wood figure, making 382:66-68
   Comic Indian carved wood figure, making 382:72-74
   Davy Crockett carved wood figure, making 382:60-62
   Decoy duck, wood, carved, making 382:28
   Decoy, wood, making 920:25
   Eagle carving, wood, making 920:32-35
   Eagle Kachina carved wood figure, making 382:75-77

Eskimo mask, carved wood, making 673:239-253
Indian carved wood wall plaque, making 382:55
Kachina doll carved wood figure, making 382:78-80
Mask carving, wood, making 920:50-52
Mexican bull, wood, carved, making 382:32
Prospector carved wood figure, making 382:63-65
Roadrunner bird, wood, carved, making 382:31
Thunderbird carved wood wall plaque, making 382:50-51
Totem poles carving, wood, making 524:32-33; 920:53-55
Whimmy Diddle, carved wood, making 673:25-33
Whirligig, carved wood, making 673:34-66
Wind vane, goose, making 526:64-65
Wooden spoons, making 382:43

WOODCHUCKS. *See also* **GROUNDHOGS**
Woodchuck puppet, pattern, making 1014:96

WOODLAND INDIANS. *See also* **ALGONQUIN INDI-
ANS; DELAWARE INDIANS; HURON INDIANS;
IROQUOIS INDIANS; SENECA INDIANS;
SHAWNEE INDIANS**
Designs and symbols 465:69
Tools and ornaments 960:49-58

WOODLAND INDIANS—BAGS
Bags and pouches, making 589:109

WOODLAND INDIANS—BASKETRY
Basketry of Northeast Indians 959:18-22; 959:2-4

WOODLAND INDIANS—BEADWORK
Bead weaving, making 8:34-39
Woodland beading, making 589:104-104

WOODLAND INDIANS—CANOES
Canoe, making 647:63-64

WOODLAND INDIANS—CLOTHING
Breech clouths, aprons, leggings, making 465:28-29
Capes and yokes, making 465:32-34
Leggins and aprons, making 589:53
Moccasins, bags, pouches, and headdress, making 324:14-17
Ribbon shirts, old shirts, ribbons, patterns, making
1493:161-162
Vests, making 589:60
War shirts, making 465:31

WOODLAND INDIANS—COOKERY
Acorn squash baked with apples, recipe 130:71
Apples and bacon, recipe 130:69
Applesauce, recipe 130:119
Appones, recipe 130:99
Batter-dipped squash blossoms, recipe 130:89
Berry pie filling, recipe 130:115
Bluefish, recipe 130:15
Boysenberry slump, recipe 130:117
Bread pudding, recipe 130:113
Chestnut cakes, recipe 130:101
Chicken corn chowder, recipe 130:57
Children's tea, recipe 424:44
Clam (Quahog) chowder, recipe 1296:136-137
Clam cakes, recipe 130:25
"The" clam chowder, recipe 130:19-21
Clambake, recipe 130:37-39
Codfish balls, recipe 130:17
Colonial New England recipes based on Indian foods
130:7-139
Corn and nut pudding, recipe 714:27
Corn fritters, recipe 130:91
Cranberry relish, recipe 130:121
Dandelion wine, recipe 130:133
Dill-bean salad, recipe 130:65
Elderberry wine, recipe 130:135

Fish stock, recipe 130:35
Fricassee of chicken, recipe 130:45
Fry bread, recipe 424:43
Gingerbread, recipe 130:109
Hassanamisco fruit bars or spread, recipe 424:31
Hot mustard, recipe 130:123
Indian pudding, recipe 130:111
Indian vegetables, recipe 130:53-55
Lobster salad, recipe 130:27
Maple beer, recipe 130:139
Mint vinegar, recipe 130:125
Mohawk corn, recipe 130:93
Mulled cider, recipe 130:131
Mustard greens with bacon, recipe 130:87
Nipnuic Indians winter stew and dumplings, recipe
424:28-29
Nut butter, recipe 714:27-28
Oatmeal bread, recipe 130:105
Okra, corn and tomato stew, recipe 424:30
Oyster dressing, recipe 130:33
Passamaquoddy sardines, recipe 130:23
Pheasant with chestnut stuffing, recipe 130:49
Pickled Jerusalem artichokes, recipe 130:75
Popcorn, making 130:95
Pumpkin bread, recipe 130:107
Pumpkin soup, recipe 1493:108
Pumpkin, recipe 130:73
Rice, herbed wild, recipe 130:77
Rice, wild rice and cranberry stuffing, recipe 1493:108
Roast venison, recipe 130:51
Roasted poppers, recipe 130:67
Salad, watercress, recipe 130:63
Salad, wild greens, recipe 130:61
Salmon fluff, recipe 130:7-9
Sauces for fish, recipe 130:127
Sliced squash, recipe 130:83
Soup, corn or maize, recipe 424:21-23
Soup, dried corn, recipe 1608:81
Soup, green potato, recipe 130:85
Soup, Iroquois, recipe 130:29-31
Soup, mushroom, recipe 130:79
Soup, oyster, recipe 130:11-13
Spoon bread, recipe 130:103
Squaw bread, recipe 130:97
Stuffed squash, recipe 130:81
Succotash, recipe 130:59; 1493:108
Sumac-ade, recipe 130:137
Sunflower cakes, recipe 1493:108
Thanksgiving, menu 130:40-41
Tsaragi peanut butter stew, recipe 424:33
Tsaragi yellow maize pudding, recipe 424:24
Turkey with wild rice stuffing, recipe 424:36-39
Turkey, scallop of, recipe 130:43
"Wild and wonderful" duck, recipe 130:47

WOODLAND INDIANS—COSTUMES
Forest costumes, cape, making 8:53-54
Forest costumes, leggings, making 8:52
Forest costumes, moccasins, making 8:60-61
Forest costumes, shirts, making 8:53-54
Forest costumes, vest, making 8:56
Girl costume, making 465:92-93

WOODLAND INDIANS—FOOTWEAR
Eastern Woodland-type moccasins, making 359:56-79
Iroquois moccasins, making 8:61
Moccasin designs, making 465:46-47; 467:32-33

Moccasins, old socks, embroidery thread, beads, patterns, making 1493:165
Woodland moccasins, making 444:101-109

WOODLAND INDIANS—GAMES
Back game 565:235
Bead in hand game 565:262
Bear hunt game 436:56
Beaver lodge game 565:179
Bird flight game 565:172
Bird notes game 565:76
Bowl catch game 565:105
Bowl toss game 565:107
Circle break game 565:222
Copperhead game 565:244
Corncob ring toss game 565:127
Crooked path game 565:165
Cross country relay 565:127
Danger signal game 565:63
Dark walk game 565:85
Flying feather game 565:134
Guard the chief game 565:66
Guess stick game 565:203
Hand game 565:272
Hidden ball game 565:204
Hit the tree game 565:146
Hoop and lance game 565:269
Hop between game 565:162
Hop game 565:161
Hop, jump game 565:162
Indian blindfold game 436:52
Indian darts game 565:141
Jump race game 565:163
Kick stick game 565:58
Kiwa trail game 565:21
Log Chief game 565:239
Log sit game 565:167
Menominee foot race 565:47
Moose stalk game 565:74
Obstacle race 565:43
Pebble patterns game 565:65
Pine cone hoop toss game 565:123
Pole pull game 565:246
Racket ball game 565:184
Raiders game 565:101
Rattler game 565:70
Ring and pin game, pipe cleaners, straws, feathers, making 1493:134-139
Ring on a stick game 436:54
Seneca hoop and pole game, branches, twine, making 1608:82
Skunk game 565:234
Snow boat game 565:173
Stalking game 565:68
Star groups game 565:83
Stick and ring game 565:183
Straight path ball game 565:258
Strong arm games 565:232
Strong badger game 565:245
Tender of the fire game 565:72
There game 565:75
Tracks game 565:86
Trail of Silence game 565:98
Turn stick game 565:187
Whirl and catch game 565:110
Woodpecker game 565:124

WOODLAND INDIANS—HANDICRAFTS
Bark scraping designs, how to do 482:86-87
Cut-outs from birch bark to decorate objects, patterns, making 1633:40-43
Dream catcher, paper plate, yarn, beads, making 1633:44-45

WOODLAND INDIANS—HATS
Woodland hat, making 589:11

WOODLAND INDIANS—HOUSEHOLD
Mortar and pestle, making 647:65

WOODLAND INDIANS—HOUSES
Dome house, cardboard, paint, patterns, making 1493:128-129
Longhouse, cardboard, paint, patterns, making 1493:126-127
Wigwam, making 804:91-94
Wigwams, how to draw 591:4-5

WOODLAND INDIANS—POTTERY
Pottery of Northeast Indians 959:49-52
Pottery pot, coil method, clay, making 1493:46
Pottery pot, pinch method, clay, making 1493:45

WOODLAND INDIANS—TRACKING
Animals tracks, plaster, making 1493:77

WOODLAND INDIANS—VILLAGES
Villages from cartons, paper, making 1017:128-129
Woodland Indian village diorama, making 647:77
Woodland village diorama, longhouse, dome houses, cardboard, patterns, making 1493:126-133

WOODLAND INDIANS—WAMPUM
Wampum belt, weaving method, macaroni, cardboard, patterns, making 1493:172-174

WOODLAND INDIANS—WEAVING
Weaving; bag weaving, making 466:140-143

WOODLAND INDIANS—WICKIUP
Wickiup, making 647:61-62

WOODLAND INDIANS—WOODWORKING
Woodworking of the Northeast Indians 959:76-83

WOODSTOCK. *See* **NEW YORK—FESTIVALS—WOODSTOCK**

WOODWORKING
Noah's animals, making 389:42

WOODWORKING—BOATS
Paddle boat, wooden, making 431:21-23

WOODWORKING—GAMES
Noughts and crosses, tic tac toe, wooden, making 803:14-16
Ring toss game, wood, making 926:51-52
Skittle bowl game, wooden, making 431:30-32
Solitaire board, wooden, making 803:26-28

WOODWORKING—MUSICAL INSTRUMENTS
Xylophone, making 389:46-47

WOODWORKING—NOAH'S ARK
Noah's Ark, making 389:40-41

WOODWORKING—PUPPETS
Puppet theater, wooden, making 803:44-48

WOOL
Lamb, woolly, simple, how to make 796:30-31
Spin raw wool, how to do 937:138
Washing, carding, spinning and weaving with wool 1531:144-149

WORLD
Around the world poster, making 24:8-9

WORLD—HANDICRAFTS
World Friendship tree, making 856:12-15

WORLD ENVIRONMENT DAY
Reusable drawstring carrying bag, fabric, cord, making 1477:70
WORLD ENVIRONMENT DAY—HANDICRAFTS
Clean up lady, plastic bottle, making 308:68-69
WORLD HEALTH DAY—DECORATIONS
Hand covers nose and mouth with tissue on paper face, making 1199:79
WORLD WAR I—AIRPLANES
Biplane with flying ace model, plastic bottle, how to make and fly 1346:22-25
WORLD WAR I—FORTIFICATION
Maginot Line fortification 212:76-83
Western Front trench system 212:60-75
WORLD WAR II—COOKERY
Applesauce cupcakes, recipe 18:60-61
Cream cheese frosting, recipe 18:62
Deviled eggs, recipe 18:53
Lunch menu, recipe 18:48-62
Victory Garden vegetable soup, recipe 18:54-55
WORLD WAR II—FORTS
Mount Cassino Fort 212:104-114
WORTHINGTON, PHOEBE
"Teddy Bear Baker," Teddy bear cake, recipe 1216:55
WRAPPING PAPER
Dipped and dyed papers, paper, paints, making 1281:42-43
Marbled papers, marbling inks, paper, making 1281:38-41
Paste and paint papers, recipe, making 1281:6-9
Print your own with poster or powder paints, how to do 1259:36-37
Roller-patterned papers, paper, paints, making 1281:14-16
Screen-printed papers, screen printing frame, paints, making 1281:30-33
Splatter designed papers, paints, paper, making 1281:24-29
Sponge-printed papers, paper, sponges, paints, making 1281:34-37
Stenciled papers, paper, paints, stencil, making 1281:17-23
Vinegar and sugar paste papers, recipe, making 1281:10-13
WREATHS
Advent wreath from cereal, food dye, making 1286:104-105
Advent wreath, making 497:68-69
Colonial Della Robbia wreath, making 831:144
Colonial straw wreath, making 831:143
Cone and twig wreath, coat hanger, twigs, cones, making 1285:98-99
Corn husk wreath, wire hanger, dried corn husks, making 1213:70; 1693:22
Dried apple wreath, making 1213:71
Dried flower wreath, making 1455:112
German Advent wreath, making 672:1-15
Gift wreath, miniature toys, gifts, glue, making 1203:23
Grapevine wreath, making 1213:67; 1421:148
Pine cone wreath, making 1213:68
Popcorn wreath, making 1213:72
Pretzel wreath, ribbon, glue, making 1203:22
Raffia wreath from raffia, ribbons, ornaments, making 1510:82-83
Ribbon wreath, ribbons, glue, making 1203:23
Seed mosaic wreath, making 1213:69
Sunflower seed wreath, making 1421:147
Wreath from herbs on coat hanger, how to make 1419:213

WRIGHT BROTHERS
Aviation Day; activities, art, songs, recipes, games 1469:124-125
WRIGHT BROTHERS—BIRTHDAY
Birthday celebration, art, music, foods, games, activities 1104:114-117
WRIGHT BROTHERS—GAMES
Anniversary of the Wrights flight game 240:60
Paper airplane game, how to make 1342:52
WRIGHT, FRANK LLOYD—ACTIVITIES
Interviewing long-time residents of your neighborhood re: house changes 1638:80
Origami paper tulip, made from geometric shapes 1638:88-92
Searching for clues to history of old houses, how to do 1638:81-82
Stained glass window design, how to do 1638:73
WRIGHT, FRANK LLOYD—BIRTHDAY
Birthday celebration; art, music, foods, games, activities 1104:86-89
Celebrate by designing playhouses on paper 1199:125
WRIGHT, FRANK LLOYD—COOKERY
Favorite breakfast, steel-cut oatmeal, recipe 1638:65
WRIGHT, FRANK LLOYD—HOLLYHOCK HOUSE—ACTIVITIES
Designing a city, how to do 1638:104-106
Finding hexagons in nature, how to do 1638:107-109
Model textile block from plaster, how to make 1638:98-100
WRIGHT, FRANK LLOYD—TALIESIN FESTIVALS—ACTIVITIES
How to prepare for, music, poetry, food, crafts 1638:110-134
WRIGHT, FRANK LLOYD—TALIESIN FESTIVALS—COOKERY
Cinnamon muffins, recipe 1638:126-127
Cream puffs with whipped cream, recipe 1638:120-121
Geometric shape cookies, recipe 1638:131-132
Hot spiced apple cider, recipe 1638:127
Hot white chocolate, recipe 1638:133
Orange spice tea with milk and sugar, recipe 1638:114
Strawberry swirl, recipe 1638:113
WRIGHT, FRANK LLOYD—TALIESIN FESTIVALS—DECORATIONS
Basket of Spring grass, wheat seeds, soil, basket, making 1638:115
Building a cantilever and model of Falling water with graham cracker and icing 1638:95-97
Dried autumn leaves, making 1638:128
Origami pin wheel, making 1638:122-123
Paper snowflakes, making 1638:134
Spring party hat, old hat, ribbons, flowers, making 1638:116
WYOMING—COOKERY
Beef burgers, recipe 654:178
Glazed nuts, recipe 793:3
Potatoes, fried, recipe 654:177
WYOMING—FOLKLORE
"Stone Fox"; physical and human geography activities 1458:100-103
WYSS, JOHANN DAVID
Swiss Family Robinson lobster bisque, recipe 570:31-33

X

XEROX MACHINES

History of Xerox machines 119:193-196

Y

YAFFE, ALAN

"Magic Meatballs"; meatballs, recipe 1216:97

YAK

Puppet, paper bag yak puppet, patterns, making
1107:140-146

YAQUI INDIANS—MUSICAL INSTRUMENTS

Raspador, making 468:30

YARN

Yarn activities, art, science, songs, recipes 911:268-271

YEMEN. *See also* **ARABIAN PENINSULA**

YEMEN—COOKERY

Almond biscuits, recipe 1165:75

Date bars, recipe 1165:73

Fruit balls, recipe 1165:76

Hoomis, chick pea spread, recipe 1165:72

Limonada, lemonade, recipe 1165:72-73

Mjeddrah, rice with lentils, recipe 1165:74

Shourba bilsen, thick lentil soup, recipe 1165:72

Stuffed dates, figs, prunes, recipe 1165:75

Tahineh or tahini, sesame seed paste, recipe 1165:74

YEMEN—GAMES

Caroms game, how to make 1074:98-99

Name Tag game, how to play 1498:15

Snapping disks 602:87

YEMEN—HANDICRAFTS

Jambiya, paper, making 515:124

YO-YO

History of Yo-yo 495:16-18

YOGURT

Homemade yogurt, recipe 1660:60

YOKUTS INDIANS—GAMES

Kainsish game, how to make and play 1699:113

Walnut shell games, how to play 1699:112

YOLEN, JANE

Stout's candy from "The Giant's Farm," recipe 1216:88

YOM HA'ATZMAUT

Meaning of Yom Ha'azmaut 711:79

Meaning of Yom Ha'azmaut (Israeli Independence Day)
712:67-68

YOM HA'ATZMAUT—COOKERY

Birthday cake for Israel, making 80:64

Cottage cheese filling, recipe 81:50

Fruity milkshake, making 82:62

Israeli Independence Day falafel fried balls, recipe
1289:155

Milk and honey treat, recipe 81:50

Sandwich cone, recipe 81:50

YOM HA'ATZMAUT—DECORATIONS

Birthday fan for Israel, making 82:61

Holiday creative drawing activities 1337:40-41

Jigsaw invitation, paper, making 81:48

Potato print picnic bags, making 81:49

Sand scapes, making 81:52

YOM HA'ATZMAUT—GAMES

Balloon basketball game 81:51

Eggshell race game 81:51

Nut race 81:51

YOM HA'ATZMAUT—HANDICRAFTS

Walk-a-thon backsack, making 82:60

YOM KIPPUR

History of Yom Kippur 709:45

Meaning of Yom Kippur 711:36; 712:22-23

YOM KIPPUR—COOKERY

Apple and honey dish, making 80:20

Apple compote, recipe 543:37

Apple embalmed with cloves, recipe 1112:39

Apple-honey cupcakes, recipe 1112:42-43

Babaganoush, eggplant salad, recipe 1685:20

Bagels, recipe 1685:24

Butter cookies, recipe 711:42-43

Challah bread, recipe 1455:121

Chocolate mandelbrot, recipe 116:28-29

Falafel, chickpea patties, recipe 1685:21

Greek lemonade, recipe 1112:39-40

Hallah ladder centerpiece, recipe 116:30

Kasha varnishkas, noodles and buckwheat, recipe
1685:22

Knishes, recipe 1685:23

Kreplach, Jewish wonton, recipe 1112:41-42

Kreplach, recipe 711:37-39

Kubbanah, recipe 1112:36-37

Meat kreplach, recipe 116:24-25

Rugalach, recipe 711:40-41

Sukkot vegetable soup, recipe 1691:72

Super supper scramble, recipe 116:27

Sweets to eat, making 80:21

Toasted top tuna, recipe 116:26

Walnut and raisin spread, recipe 1685:25

Yemenite High Holy Day soup, recipe 1112:36-39

YOM KIPPUR—DECORATIONS

Holiday creative drawing activities 1337:14-15

Jonah and the Whale, making 709:46-47

New Year cards, making 80:22

YOM KIPPUR—HANDICRAFTS

Candlesticks for Yom Tov, making 80:19

Clouds of glory, making 1691:69

Flowers, white paper flowers, making 712:23-24

Hanging birds, making 1691:67-68

Kidduschcup, silver, making 80:18

Placemat, woven, making 543:32-33

Spice ball, making 1691:71

Sukkah in a Sukkah, making 1691:70-71

Sukkot chain, making 1691:67

Temple from boxes, making 543:34-35

Tooled prayer book cover, making 1691:56-57

Vase for flowers, making 543:36

YOM KIPPUR—PUPPETS

Puppet projects, patterns, scenes, story starters, feature
story 1083:111-113

YORUBA TRIBE—RHYMES

"Ekin, Ekeji, Eketa" 1607:19

YOUNG, MERIAM

"Jelly Beans for Breakfast," jelly beans, recipe 1216:89

YUGOSLAVIA—COOKERY

Cabbage leaves, stuffed, recipe 661:210-211

Creveni kupus, stewed red cabbage, recipe 1165:98

Green salad with yogurt dressing, recipe 661:211

History of cooking in Yugoslavia 661:193-199

Kisel zelje, pickled or fresh cabbage salad, recipe
1165:98

Meat-eating habits in Yugoslavia 662:68-70

Meat stew, recipe 793:44

Pogaca, peasant bread, recipe 1165:99

Pork kebabs, broiled, recipe 661:210

Serbian cheese pie, recipe 661:209
Slovenian nut roll, recipe 661:211-213
String bean soup, recipe 794:32
Walnut-filled cookies, kifli, recipe 72:81-83

YUGOSLAVIA—COSTUMES
Yugoslavs costume drawing 988:23

YUGOSLAVIA—DANCES
I planted watermelons kolo dance 624:36-38
Kola chain dance 474:110-112
Savila se bela loza dance, how to do 1494:135-136

YUGOSLAVIA—DOLLS
Martian Medicine Man doll, making 495:14-15
Newspaper boy doll, making 495:10-1 1
Pestle doll, making 495:9-10
Wooden spoon dolls, making 495:11-14

YUGOSLAVIA—EASTER—COOKERY
Dubrovnik fish stew, recipe 1666:83
Prebanac (baked lima beans), recipe 1666:84
Servian Musaka (eggplant casserole), recipe 1666:83-84
Slovenian almond bars, recipe 1666:85

YUGOSLAVIA—FESTIVALS
Festivals and celebrations, maps, flags, crafts, making 1305:142-146
Krsna Slava Festival celebration 661:207-208

YUGOSLAVIA—GAMES
Crushed Peppers, Vibersko, musical game 1116:30-31
Zmirke game, how to play 1494:106

YUGOSLAVIA—HANDICRAFTS
Wreath, cheese cloth and flowers, making 515:126

YUGOSLAVIA—NAMES
Naming Days information 695:28-29

YULE LOGS
History of Yule logs 709:75

YUMA INDIANS
Legends 344:10
Life in the tribe 344:10-11
Songs and stories of the Yuma Indians 344:11-22

YURTS—HOUSES
Yurts and Kazak people houses 469:40-41

Z

ZAHARIAS, BABE DIDRIKSON
Birthday celebration; art, music, foods, games, activities 1104:90-93

ZAHARIAS, BABE DIDRIKSON—BIRTHDAY
Celebrate by practicing putting golf balls 1199:137

ZAIRE—COOKERY
Chicken moambe, chicken stew, recipe 1165:22-23
Fish and greens, recipe 1165:22
Stew, simple African, recipe 188:17

ZAIRE—COSTUMES
Costume 188:17

ZAIRE—EASTER—COOKERY
Pinto beans with potatoes, recipe 1666:21

ZAIRE—GAMES
Catching stars game, how to play 1507:15

ZAIRE—HEADDRESSES
Feather headdress, corrugated paper, straws, making 1488:12-13

ZAIRE—JEWELRY
Jungle jewelry, pasta, seeds, paints, making 1488:14-15

ZAIRE—MASKS
African ceremonial mask, papier-mache, making 1027:85-88

ZAIRE—PLANTS
Tropical plants, oranges, lemons, pineapples, how to grow 1488:10-11

ZAIRE—STORIES USING MUSICAL INSTRUMENTS
Rabbit and Hyena Play the Sanza thumb piano story, how to do 1161:107-110

ZAMBIA—COOKERY
Chicken moambe, chicken stew, recipe 1165:22-23
Fish and greens, recipe 1165:22
Mushrooms with peanut sauce, recipe 794:41

ZAMBIA—EASTER—COOKERY
Pinto beans with potatoes, recipe 1666:21

ZAMBIA—GAMES
Crocodile, may I cross the river? game 967:53
Hand clapping game 602:39
Kuomboka Lozi tribe ceremony keep the ball afloat game, making 1574:10-11
Snakes game 602:38-39

ZAMBIA—HANDICRAFTS
Barotse bowl, making 222:10

ZANZIBAR—FOLKLORE
Heart of a monkey fable playlet 1212:49-52

ZEMACH, HARVE
"Nail Soup," recipe 1216:74

ZIMBABWE—COOKERY
Breedie, beef stew, recipe 1165:18
Cornmeal cake, recipe 1165:18-19
Flapjacks, recipe 967:45
Green mealie pudding, recipe 1137:121-122
Sweet potato cookies, recipe 1244:92-93; 1598:120
Trifle dessert, recipe 1137:123-124

ZIMBABWE—FESTIVALS—COOKERY
Agrarian Tribal Festival; huku ne dovi (chicken and ground nut stew), recipe 1666:17
Agrarian Tribal Festival; sadza (corn meal mush, fried)), recipe 1666:17-18

ZIMBABWE—GAMES
Iguni jacks game, how to play 1718:36-37
Lost shoe relay game 967:45
Tsoro Yematatu game, how to play 1688:34-35

ZIMBABWE—JEWELRY
Ndebele bead bracelet, beads, wire, making 1632:28-32

ZIMBABWE—LANGUAGE
Phrases of the Shona and Ndebele peoples 1137:150

ZIPPERS
History of zippers 119:162-166

ZODIAC—COSTUMES
Aquarius costume, fabric, patterns, making 1174:63
Aries costume, fabric, patterns, making 1174:54
Cancer costume, fabric, patterns, making 1174:56-57
Capricorn costume, fabric, patterns, making 1174:62
Gemini costume, fabric, patterns, making 1174:55-56
Leo costume, fabric, patterns, making 1174:58-59
Libra costume, fabric, patterns, making 1174:59
Pisces costume, fabric, patterns, making 1174:63
Sagittarius costume, fabric, patterns, making 1174:61
Scorpio costume, fabric, patterns, making 1174:60-61
Taurus costume, fabric, patterns, making 1174:55
Virgo costume, fabric, patterns, making 1174:59

ZOETROPES
Zoetrope, making 105:39-42

ZOO
Songs, finger plays, stories, games, rhythms 1200:88

ZOOS—COOKERY
Zoo cake, recipe 449:58

ZOOS—FINGER PLAYS

Finger plays about giraffes, elephants, kangaroos 302:76-79

Finger plays; tigers, seals, bears, monkeys 302:76-79

ZOOS—SONGS

Zoo songs for infants and toddlers 908:60-61

ZULUS—BEADWORK

Neckband and pendant, heavy paper, yarn, pony beads, patterns, making 1332:29-34

Necklace based on Zulu beadwork, how to make 1448:14-15

ZULUS—CLOTHING

Zulu clothing, making 222:53-55

ZULUS—COOKERY

Oxtail soup, recipe 1321:145

ZULUS—DOLLS

Zulu doll, making 775:74-79

ZULUS—STRING FIGURES

Moth figure, making 423:29-30

Moth or spectacles string 372:12-13

ZUNI INDIANS

Animal effigy, making 63:46

ZUNI INDIANS—COOKERY

Green chili stew, recipe 1527:28-29

Stuffed squash blossom, baked and stuffed squash, recipe 424:70-72

Succotash, recipe 1043:9

ZUNI INDIANS—DOLLS

Hooped skirt charm doll, making 298:66-67

Kachina cradle doll, paper tube, papier-mache, patterns, making 1633:36-37

ZUNI INDIANS—FOLKLORE—PUPPETS

"Turkey Maiden" shadow puppets, patterns, making 1602:204-211

ZUNI INDIANS—GAMES

Awithlaknannai game, making 1074:41; 1507:97-98

Fighting Serpents board game, patterns, making 1541:74-79

Jack rabbits hit game, making 63:68-69

Kick stick race game, making 63:60-61

Pokean, how to make and play 1699:127

Ring toss game, how to make and play 1699:130

Shuttlecock game 602:182

Standing cob game, how to make and play 1699:128

Zuni kick stick game, making 445:20-25

ZUNI INDIANS—HANDICRAFTS

Animal fetishes from tea leaf and flour dough, recipe, making 1372:72

ZUNI INDIANS—MASKS

Hand masks, paper, patterns, making 1633:38-39

Yoyemshi, clown or mudhead mask, paper bag, feathers, making 1699:72

Zuni Shalakos masks, making 327:46

ZUNI INDIANS—POTTERY

Pottery, making 227:33

ZUNI INDIANS—STRING FIGURES

Hut, Magic Carpet 1404:19-103

ZUNI INDIANS—TOYS

Bird toy, making 482:72-73

Books Indexed by Number

See "Books Indexed by Author" for an alphabetical list of books by author.

1. Abisch, Roz. *The Make-It, Play-It Game Book.* New York: Walker and Co., 1975.
2. Abramson, Lillian S. *Jewish Holiday Party Book.* New York: Bloch Publishing Co., 1966.
3. Ackley, Edith Flack. *Dolls to Make for Fun and Profit.* New York: J. B. Lippincott Co., 1951.
4. Adair, Margaret *Weeks. Folk Puppet Plays for the Social Studies.* New York: John Day, 1972.
5. Adkins, Jan. *The Art and Industry of Sandcastles.* New York: Walker and Co., 1971.
6. Adkins, Jan. *The Bakers.* New York: Charles Scribner's Sons, 1975.
7. Albala, Leila. *Easy Halloween Costumes for Children.* Quebec, Canada: Alpel, Chambly, 1987.
8. Albrechtsen, Lis. *Tepee and Moccasin, Indian Crafts for Young People.* New York: Van Nostrand Reinhold Co., 1970.
9. Alexandre, Stella V. *Winter Days Holiday Lingo.* Belmont, Calif.: David S. Lake Publishers, 1987.
10. Alkema, Chester Jay. *Creative Paper Crafts.* New York: Sterling Publishing Co., 1967.
11. Alkema, Chester Jay. *Masks.* New York: Sterling Publishing Co., 1971.
12. Alkema, Chester Jay. *Monster Masks.* New York: Sterling Publishing Co., 1973.
13. Alkema, Chester Jay. *Puppet Making.* New York: Sterling Publishing Co., 1971.
14. Allen, Judy. *Exciting Things to Do with Nature Materials.* New York: J. B. Lippincott Co., 1977.
15. Allison, Linda. *Rags: Making a Little Something out of Almost Nothing.* New York: Clarkson N. Porter, 1979.
16. Alton, Walter G. *Making Models from Paper and Card.* New York: Taplinger Publishing Co., 1974.
17. Alvarado, Manuel. *Mexican Food and Drink.* New York: Bookwright Press, 1988.
18. *American Girls Cookbook.* Middleton, Wisc.: Pleasant Co., 1990.
19. Amery, Heather. *The Knowhow Book of Print and Paint.* New York: Sterling Publishing Co., 1976.
20. Anderson, Gretchen. *The Louisa May Alcott Cookbook.* Boston: Little, Brown and Co., 1985.
21. Anderson, Mildred. *Papier Mache and How to Use It.* New York: Sterling Publishing Co., 1971.
22. Anderson, Mildred. *Papier Mache Crafts.* New York: Sterling Publishing Co., 1975.
23. *Animals.* Caroline Pitcher, Consultant. New York: Franklin Watts, 1983.
24. Arnold, Caroline. *Land Masses, Fun, Facts and Activities.* New York: Franklin Watts, 1985.
25. Arnold, Caroline. *Maps and Globes, Fun, Facts and Activities.* New York: Franklin Watts, 1984.
26. Arnold, Susan Riser. *Eggshells to Objects, a New Approach to Egg Crafts.* New York: Holt, Rinehart and Winston, 1979.
27. Artman, John. *Indians: An Activity Book.* Carthage, Ill.: Good Apple, 1987.
28. Arvois, Edmond. *Making Mosaics.* New York: Sterling Publishing Co., 1964.

29. Ashe, Rosalind. *Children's Literary Houses.* New York: Facts on File Publications, 1984.
30. Atyeo, Marilyn. *Birthdays, a Celebration.* Atlanta, Ga.: Humanics Limited, 1984.
31. Baker, James W. *April Fools' Day Magic.* Minneapolis, Minn.: Lerner Publications Co., 1989.
32. Baker, James W. *Birthday Magic.* Minneapolis, Minn.: Lerner Publications Co., 1988.
33. Baker, James W. *Christmas Magic.* Minneapolis, Minn.: Lerner Publications Co., 1988.
34. Baker, James W. *Halloween Magic.* Minneapolis, Minn.: Lerner Publications Co., 1988.
35. Baker, James W. *New Year's Magic.* Minneapolis, Minn.: Lerner Publications Co., 1989.
36. Baker, James W. *Presidents' Day Magic.* Minneapolis, Minn.: Lerner Publications Co., 1989.
37. Baker, James W. *Thanksgiving Magic.* Minneapolis, Minn.: Lerner Publications Co., 1989.
38. Baker, James W. *Valentine Magic.* Minneapolis, Minn.: Lerner Publications Co., 1988.
39. Baldwin, Margaret. *Thanksgiving.* New York: Franklin Watts, 1983.
40. Barkin, Carol. *Happy Valentine's Day.* New York: Lothrop, Lee and Shepard Books, 1988.
41. Barkin, Carol. *Happy Thanksgiving.* New York: Lothrop, Lee and Shepard Books, 1987.
42. Barkin, Carol. *The Scary Halloween Costume Book.* New York: Lothrop, Lee and Shepard Books, 1983.
43. Barron, Cheryl Carter. *Great Parties for Young Children.* New York: Walker and Co., 1981.
44. Barth, Edna. *Lilies, Rabbits, and Painted Eggs, The Story of the Easter Symbols.* New York: The Seabury Press, 1970.
45. Barta, Ginevera. *Metric Cooking for Beginners.* Short Hills, N.J.: Enslow Publishers, 1978.
46. Barwell, Eve. *Disguises You Can Make.* New York: Lothrop, Lee and Shepard Co., 1977.
47. Barwell, Eve. *Make Your Pet a Present.* New York: Lothrop, Lee and Shepard Co., 1977.
48. Batho, Margot. *Sandcasting.* Minneapolis, Minn.: Lerner Publications Co., 1973.
49. Bauer, Caroline Feller. *Celebrations.* New York: H. W. Wilson Co., 1985.
50. Bauman, Toni. *Winter Wonders.* Carthage, Ill.: Good Apple, 1986.
51. Beard, Lina. *The American Girls Handy Book.* Boston: David R. Godine, 1987.
52. Becker, Joyce. *Bible Crafts.* New York: Holiday House, 1982.
53. Becker, Joyce. *Hanukkah Crafts.* New York: Bonim Books, 1978.
54. Beckman, Carol. *Channels to Children, Early Childhood Activities.* Colorado Springs, Colo.: Channels to Children, 1982.
55. Beetschen, Louis. *Country Treasures.* New York: Pantheon Books, 1971.
56. Beetschen, Louis. *Seaside Treasures.* New York: Pantheon Books, 1971.

57. Beilenson, Evelyn L. *Early American Cooking, Recipes from America's Historic Sites.* White Plains, N.Y.: Peter Pauper Press, 1985.

58. Benarde, Anita. *Games from Many Lands.* New York: Sayre Publishing, 1970.

59. Benbow, Mary. *Dolls, Traditional and Topical, and How to Make Them.* Boston: Plays, 1970.

60. Bender, Lionel. *Crocodiles and Alligators.* New York: Gloucester Press, 1988.

61. Bender, Lionel. *Lizards and Dragons.* New York: Gloucester Press, 1988.

62. Berenstain, Michael. *The Castle Book.* New York: David McKay Co., 1977.

63. Bernstein, Bonnie. *Native American Crafts Workshop.* Fearon Teacher Aids. Belmont, Calif.: Pitman Learning, 1982.

64. Berger, Gilda. *Easter and Other Spring Holidays.* New York: Franklin Watts, 1983.

65. Berman, Paul. *Make-Believe Empire, a How-To Book.* New York: Atheneum, 1982.

66. Biucchi, Edwina. *Italian Food and Drink.* New York: The Bookwright Press, 1987.

67. Blocksma, Mary. *Action Contraptions.* New York: Prentice Hall Books, Simon and Schuster, 1987.

68. Blocksma, Mary. *Space-Crafting, Invent Your Own Flying Spaceships.* New York: Simon and Schuster, 1986.

69. Blood, Charles L. *American Indian Games and Crafts.* New York: Franklin Watts, 1981.

70. Bodger, Lorraine. *Crafts for All Seasons.* New York: Universe Books, 1980.

71. Borghese, Anita. *The Down to Earth Cookbook.* New York: Charles Scribner's Sons, 1973.

72. Borghese, Anita. *The International Cookie Jar Cookbook.* New York: Charles Scribner's Sons, 1975.

73. Bos, Bev. *Don't Move the Muffin Tins.* Roseville, Calif.: Turn the Page Press, 1978.

74. Boteler, Alison. *The Children's Party Handbook.* Woodbury, N.Y.: Barron's, 1986.

75. Bottomley, Jim. *Paper Projects for Creative Kids of All Ages.* Boston: Little, Brown and Co., 1983.

76. Bowman, Bruce. *Toothpick Sculpture & Ice-Cream Stick Art.* New York: Sterling Publishing Co., 1976.

77. Boxer, Arabella. *The Wind in the Willows Cookbook.* New York: Charles Scribner's Sons, 1983.

78. Brashears, Deya. *Dribble Drabble, Art Experiences for Young Children.* Fort Collins, Colo.: DMC Publications, 1985.

79. Breznau, Claudia. *Container Crafts.* Minneapolis, Minn.: Judy/Instructo, 1981.

80. Brinn, Ruth Esrig. *Let's Celebrate, 57 Jewish Holiday Crafts for Young Children.* Rockville, Md.: Kar-Ben Copies, 1977.

81. Brinn, Ruth Esrig. *Let's Have a Party.* Rockville, Md.: Kar-Ben Copies, 1981.

82. Brinn, Ruth Esrig. *More Let's Celebrate, Fifty-Seven All New...* Rockville, Md.: Kar-Ben Copies, 1984.

83. Brock, Virginia. *Pinatas.* New York: Abingdon Press, 1966.

84. Brokamp, Marilyn. *Once upon a Cereal Box.* Minneapolis, Minn.: T. S. Denison and Co., 1982.

85. Brockway, Maureen. *Clay Projects.* Minneapolis, Minn.: Lerner Publications Co., 1973.

86. Brokaw, Meredith. *The Penny Whistle Party Planner.* New York: Weidenfeld and Nicolson, 1987.

87. Brook, Bonnie. *Let's Celebrate Easter, a Book of Drawing Fun.* Mahwah, N.J. Watermill Press, 1988.

88. Brown, Elizabeth Burton. *Grains, An Illustrated History with Recipes.* Englewood Cliffs, N.J.: Prentice-Hall, 1977.

89. Brown, Fern G. *Valentine's Day.* New York: Franklin Watts, 1983.

90. Brown, Jerome C. *The Dinosaur Color and Pattern Book.* Belmont, Calif.: David S. Lake Publishers, 1989.

91. Brown, Jerome C. *Fables and Tales Papercrafts.* Belmont, Calif.: Fearon Teacher Aids, 1989.

92. Brown, Jerome C. *Folk Tale Papercrafts.* Belmont, Calif.: David S. Lake Publishers, 1989.

93. Brown, Jerome C. *Great Gifts for All Occasions.* Belmont, Calif.: Fearon Teacher Aids, 1986.

94. Brown, Jerome C. *Holiday Art Projects.* Belmont, Calif.: Fearon Teacher Aids, 1984.

95. Brown, Jerome C. *Holiday Crafts and Greeting Cards.* Belmont, Calif.: Fearon Teacher Aids, 1983.

96. Brown, Jerome C. *Holiday Gifts and Decorations.* Belmont, Calif.: David S. Lake Publishers, 1986.

97. Brown, Jerome C. *Paper Designs.* Belmont, Calif.: David S. Lake Publishers, 1983.

98. Brown, Jerome C. *Paper Menagerie.* Belmont, Calif.: David S. Lake Publishers, 1984.

99. Brown, Jerome C. *Papercrafts for All Seasons.* Belmont, Calif.: David S. Lake Publishers, 1984.

100. Brown, Jerome C. *Puppets and Mobiles.* Belmont, Calif.: Fearon Teacher Aids, 1983.

101. Brown, Marc. *Finger Rhymes.* New York: E. P. Dutton, 1980.

102. Brown, Marc. *Hand Rhymes.* New York: E. P. Dutton, 1985.

103. Brown, Marc. *Party Rhymes.* New York: E. P. Dutton, 1988.

104. Brown, Marc. *Play Rhymes.* New York: E. P. Dutton, 1987.

105. Brown, Osa. *The Metropolitan Museum of Art Activity Book.* New York: Random House, 1983.

106. Bruun-Rasmussen, Jens Ole. *Make-Up, Costumes and Masks.* New York: Sterling Publishing Co., 1976.

107. Buell, Hal. *Festivals of Japan.* New York: Dodd, Mead and Co., 1965.

108. *Build Your Own Airport.* Caroline Pitcher, Consultant. New York: Franklin Watts, 1985.

109. Number not used.

110. *Build Your Own Castle.* Caroline Pitcher, Consultant. New York: Franklin Watts, 1985.

111. *Build Your Own Farm Yard.* Caroline Pitcher, Consultant. New York: Franklin Watts, 1985.

112. *Build Your Own Space Station.* Caroline Pitcher, Consultant. New York: Franklin Watts, 1985.

113. Burggraf, Manfred. *Fun with Colored Foil.* New York: Watson-Guptill Publications, 1968.

114. Burns, Marilyn. *Good Times. Every Kid's Book of Things to Do.* New York: Bantam Books, 1979.

115. Burns, Marilyn. *The Hanukkah Book.* New York: Four Winds Press, 1981.

116. Burstein, Chaya M. *A First Jewish Holiday Cookbook.* New York: Bonim Books, 1979.

117. Burstein, Chaya M. *A Kid's Catalog of Israel.* New York: Jewish Publications Society, 1988.

118. Caney, Steven. *Kids' America.* New York: Workman Publishing, 1978.

119. Caney, Steven. *Steven Caney's Invention Book.* New York: Workman Publishing Co., 1985.

120. Caney, Steven. *Steve Caney's Playbook.* New York: Workman Publishing Co., 1975.

121. Caney, Steven. *Steven Caney's Toy Book.* New York: Workman Publishing Co., 1972.

122. Carlisle, Jody. *Classroom Nursery Rhymes Activity Kit.* West Nyack, N.Y.: The Center for Applied Research in Education, 1983.

123. Carlson, Bernice Wells. *Make It Yourself.* New York: Abingdon Press, 1950.

124. Carlson, Bernice Wells. *The Party Books for Boys and Girls.* New York: Abingdon Press, 1963.

125. Carlson, Bernice Wells. *Picture That!* Nashville, Tenn.: Abingdon Press, 1977.

126. Carlson, Bernice Wells. *Quick Wits and Nimble Fingers.* Nashville, Tenn.: Abingdon Press, 1979.

127. Carroll, David. *Make Your Own Chess Set.* Englewood Cliffs, N.J.: Prentice-Hall, 1974.

128. Carroll, Jeri A. *Learning About Spring and Summer Holidays.* Carthage, Ill.: Good Apple, 1988.

129. *Cars and Boats.* Caroline Pitcher, Consultant. New York: Franklin Watts, 1983.

130. Carson, Dale. *Native New England Cooking.* Old Saybrook, Conn.: Peregrine Press, Publishers, 1980.

131. Cary, Pam. *North American Food and Drink.* New York: The Bookwright Press, 1988.

132. Cauley, Lorinda Bryan. *Things to Make and Do for Thanksgiving.* New York: Franklin Watts, 1977.

133. *Celebrate.* First United Nursery School. Oak Park, Ill.: Rainbow Publishing Co., 1987.

134. *Celebrate Everyday, Hundreds of Celebrations.* Edited by Lisa Lyons Durkin. Bridgeport, Conn.: First Teacher Press, 1987.

135. Chacon, Rick. *Grocery Bag Art, Careers.* Huntington Beach, Calif.: Teacher Created Materials, 1985.

136. Chacon, Rick. *Grocery Bag Art, Circus.* Huntington Beach, Calif.: Teacher Created Materials, 1985.

137. Chacon, Rick. *Grocery Bag Art, Farm.* Huntington Beach, Calif.: Teacher Created Materials, 1985.

138. Chacon, Rick. *Grocery Bag Art, Holidays.* Huntington Beach, Calif.: Teacher Created Materials, 1985.

139. Chapman, Jean. *Pancakes and Painted Eggs, a Book for Easter and All the Days of...* Chicago, Ill.: Childrens Press, 1983.

140. Chapman, Jean. *The Sugar-Plum Christmas Book.* Chicago, Ill.: Childrens Press, 1977.

141. Chernoff, Goldie Taub. *Clay-Dough, Play-Dough.* New York: Walker and Co., 1974.

142. Chernoff, Goldie Taub. *Easy Costumes You Don't Have to Sew.* New York: Four Winds Press, 1975.

143. *Children Are Children Are Children.* Ann Cole et al. Boston: Little, Brown and Co., 1978.

144. Chivers, David. *Gorillas and Chimpanzees.* New York: Gloucester Press, 1987.

145. Choate, Judith. *Patchwork.* Garden City, N.Y.: Doubleday and Co., 1976.

146. Choate, Judith. *Scrapcraft.* Garden City, N.Y.: Doubleday and Co., 1973.

147. Christian, Rebecca. *Cooking the Spanish Way.* Minneapolis, Minn.: Lerner Publications Co., 1982.

148. *Christmas.* Caroline Pitcher, Consultant. New York: Franklin Watts, 1983.

149. *Christmas Around the World: A Celebration.* Dorset, England: New Orchards Editions Ltd., Sterling Publishing Co., 1978.

150. *Christmas Trims Kids Can Make.* Des Moines, Iowa: Meredith Corporation, 1988.

151. Churchill, E. Richard. *Fast and Funny Paper Toys You Can Make.* New York: Sterling Publishing Co., 1989.

152. Churchill, E. Richard. *Instant Paper Toys.* New York: Sterling Publishing Co., 1986.

153. Churchill, E. Richard. *Paper Toys That Fly, Soar, Zoom & Whistle.* New York: Sterling Publishing Co., 1989.

154. Civardi, Anne. *The Knowhow Book of Action Games.* New York: Sterling Publishing Co., 1976.

155. *16 Classic American Recipes and the Stories of How They Began.* Avery Island, La.: McIlhenny Co., [198-].

156. Cline, Dallas. *Cornstalk Fiddle and Other Homemade Instruments.* New York: Oak Publications, Div. of Embassy Music Corp., 1976.

157. Cobb, Mary. *Practical Patterns.* Belmont, Calif.: Fearon Teacher Aids, 1989.

158. Cobb, Vicki. *The Secret Life of School Supplies.* New York: J. B. Lippincott Co., 1981.

159. Cochrane, Louise. *Tabletop Theatres and Plays.* Boston: Plays, 1974.

160. Number not used.

161. Cohen, Lynn. *Fairy Tale World.* Palo Alto, Calif.: Monday Morning Books, 1986.

162. Colbridge, A. M. *Scale Models in Balsa.* New York: Taplinger Publishing Co., 1971.

163. Cole, Ann. *Purple Cow to the Rescue.* Boston: Little, Brown and Co., 1982.

164. Cole, Marion. *Things to Make and Do for Easter.* New York: Franklin Watts, 1979.

165. Collier, James Lincoln. *Jugbands and Handmade Music.* New York: Grosset and Dunlap, 1973.

166. *Colonial Holiday Treats.* High Point, N.C.: Hutcraft, 1971.

167. Comins, Jeremy. *Chinese and Japanese Crafts and Their Cultural Backgrounds.* New York: Lothrop, Lee and Shepard Co., 1978.

168. Comins, Jeremy. *Eskimo Crafts and Their Cultural Backgrounds.* New York: Lothrop, Lee and Shepard Co., 1975.

169. Comins, Jeremy. *Latin American Crafts and Their Cultural Backgrounds.* New York: Lothrop, Lee and Shepard Co., 1974.

170. Comins, Jeremy. *Slotted Sculpture from Cardboard.* New York: Lothrop, Lee and Shepard Co., 1977.

171. Comins, Jeremy. *Totems, Decoys and Covered Wagons.* New York: Lothrop, Lee and Shepard Co., 1976.

172. Commins, Elaine. *Lessons from Mother Goose.* Atlanta, Ga.: Humanics Learning, 1989.

173. Conaway, Judith. *City Crafts from Secret Cities.* Chicago, Ill.: Follett Publishing Co., 1978.

174. Conaway, Judith. *Dollhouse Fun, Furniture You Can Make.* Mahwah, N.J.: Troll Associates, 1987.

175. Conaway, Judith. *Easy-to-Make Christmas Crafts.* Mahwah, N.J.: Troll Associates, 1986.

176. Conaway, Judith. *Great Gifts to Make.* Mahwah, N.J.: Troll Associates, 1986.

177. Conaway, Judith. *Great Indoor Games from Trash and Other Things.* Milwaukee, Wisc.: Raintree Publishers Limited, 1977.

178. Conaway, Judith. *Happy Day! Things to Make and Do.* Mahwah, N.J.: Troll Associates, 1987.

179. Conaway, Judith. *Happy Haunting, Halloween Costumes You Can Make.* Mahwah, N.J.: Troll Associates, 1986.

180. Conaway, Judith. *Happy Thanksgiving, Things to Make and Do.* Mahwah, N.J.: Troll Associates, 1986.

181. Conaway, Judith. *Make Your Own Costumes and Disguises.* Mahwah, N.J.: Troll Associates, 1987.

182. Conaway, Judith. *Manos, South American Crafts for Children.* Chicago, Ill.: Follett Publishing Co., 1978.

183. Conaway, Judith. *Springtime Surprises! Things to Make and Do.* Mahwah, N.J.: Troll Associates, 1986.

184. Conaway, Judith. *Things That Go, How to Make Toy Boats, Cars, and Planes.* Mahwah, N.J.: Troll Associates, 1987.

185. Cooper, Kay. *Where Did You Get Those Eyes.* New York: Walker and Co., 1988.

186. Cooper, Michael. *Things to Make and Do for George Washington's Birthday.* New York: Franklin Watts, 1979.

187. Cooper, Terry Touff. *Many Friends Cooking, An International Cookbook for Boys and Girls.* New York: Philomel Books, 1980.

188. Cooper, Terry Touff. *Many Hands Cooking.* New York: Thomas Y. Crowell Co., 1974.

189. Coronado, Rosa. *Cooking the Mexican Way.* Minneapolis, Minn.: Lerner Publications Co., 1982.

190. Corwin, Judith Hoffman. *Birthday Fun.* New York: Julian Messner, 1986.

191. Corwin, Judith Hoffman. *Colonial American Crafts, the Home.* New York: Franklin Watts, 1989.

192. Corwin, Judith Hoffman. *Colonial American Crafts, the School.* New York: Franklin Watts, 1989.

193. Corwin, Judith Hoffman. *Colonial American Crafts, The Village.* New York: Franklin Watts, 1989.

194. Corwin, Judith Hoffman. *Cookie Fun.* New York: Julian Messner, 1985.

195. Corwin, Judith Hoffman. *Creative Collage.* New York: David McKay Co., 1980.

196. Corwin, Judith Hoffman. *Easter Fun.* New York: Julian Messner, 1984.

197. Corwin, Judith Hoffman. *Halloween Fun.* New York: Julian Messner, 1983.

198. Corwin, Judith Hoffman. *Papercrafts, Origami, Papier-Mache, and Collage.* New York: Franklin Watts, 1988.

199. Corwin, Judith Hoffman. *Patriotic Fun.* New York: Julian Messner, 1985.

200. Corwin, Judith Hoffman. *Valentine Fun.* New York: Julian Messner, 1982.

201. Coskey, Evelyn. *Easter Eggs for Everyone.* New York: Abingdon Press, 1973.

202. Cosman, Madeline Pelner. *Medieval Holidays and Festivals.* New York: Charles Scribner's Sons, 1981.

203. Number not used.

204. Cosner, Shaaron. *Masks Around the World and How to Make Them.* New York: David McKay Co., 1979.

205. Cox, Marcia Lynn. *Creature Costumes.* New York: Grosset and Dunlap, 1977.

206. Coyle, Rena. *My First Baking Book.* New York: Workman Publishing Co., 1988.

207. Coyle, Rena. *My First Cookbook.* New York: Workman Publishing Co., 1985.

208. Cracchiolo, Rachelle. *Calendar Activities.* Sunset Beach, Calif.: Teacher Created Materials, 1980.

209. Cracchiolo, Rachelle. *Holiday Cards.* Sunset Beach, Calif.: Teacher Created Materials, 1982.

210. Cramblit, Joella. *Flowers Are for Keeping.* New York: Julian Messner, 1979.

211. Cross, Jeanne. *Simple Printing Methods.* New York: S. G. Phillips, 1972.

212. Cummings, Richard. *Make Your Own Model Forts and Castles.* New York: David McKay Co., 1977.

213. Cummings, Richard. *101 Costumes for All Ages, All Occasions.* Boston: Plays, 1987.

214. Curtis, Annabelle. *Knowhow Book of Paper Fun.* New York: Sterling Publishing Co., 1976.

215. Cutler, Katherine N. *Crafts for Christmas.* New York: Lothrop, Lee and Shepard Co., 1974.

216. Cutler, Katherine N. *Creative Shellcraft.* New York: Lothrop, Lee and Shepard Co., 1971.

217. Cutler, Katherine N. *From Petals to Pinecones.* New York: Lothrop, Lee and Shepard Co., 1969.

218. Cuyler, Margery. *The All-Around Christmas Book.* New York: Holt, Rinehart and Winston, 1982.

219. Cuyler, Margery. *The All-Around Pumpkin Book.* New York: Holt, Rinehart and Winston, 1980.
220. D'Alelio, Jane. *I Know That Building.* Washington, D.C.: The Preservation Press, 1989.
221. Number not used.
222. D'Amato, Janet, and Alex. *African Crafts for You to Make.* New York: Julian Messner, 1969.
223. D'Amato, Janet, and Alex. *Algonquian and Iroquois, Crafts for You to Make.* New York: Julian Messner, 1979.
224. D'Amato, Janet, and Alex. *American Indian Craft Inspirations.* New York: M. Evans and Co., 1972.
225. D'Amato, Janet, and Alex. *Colonial Crafts for You to Make.* New York: Julian Messner, 1975.
226. D'Amato, Janet, and Alex. *Handicrafts for Holidays.* New York: Lion Press, 1967.
227. D'Amato, Janet, and Alex. *Indian Crafts.* New York: Sayre Publishing, 1968.
228. D'Amato, Janet, and Alex. *More Colonial Crafts for You to Make.* New York: Julian Messner, 1977.
229. D'Amato, Jane Potter. *Who's a Horn? What's an Antler? Crafts of Bone and Horn.* New York: Julian Messner, 1982.
230. *Dandy Dinosaurs.* Better Homes and Gardens. Des Moines, Iowa: Meredith Corporation, 1989.
231. Darling, Kathy. *Alphabet Crafts.* Palo Alto, Calif.: Monday Morning Books, 1985.
232. Dawson, Jean Elizabeth. *Frog's Legs and Scrambled Eggs.* Bloomfield, Conn.: Junior Arts and Crafts House, 1981.
233. Dawson, Jean Elizabeth. *A Date with a Plate.* Bloomfield, Conn.: Junior Arts and Crafts House, 1981.
234. Dawson, Jean Elizabeth. *It's in the Bag.* Bloomfield, Conn.: Junior Arts and Crafts House, 1981.
235. Deacon, Eileen. *It's Fun to Make Pictures.* New York: Grosset and Dunlap Publishers, 1972.
236. Deacon, Eileen. *Making Jewelry.* Milwaukee, Wisc.: Raintree Childrens Books, 1977.
237. Dean, Audrey Vincente. *Make a Prehistoric Monster.* New York: Taplinger Publishing Co., 1977.
238. Dean, Audrey Vincente. *Wooden Spoon Puppets.* Boston: Plays, 1976.
239. Dean, Bill. *Book of Balsa Models.* New York: Arco Publishing Co., 1970.
240. Dellinger, Annetta. *Creative Games for Young Children.* Elgin, Ill.: The Child's World, 1986.
241. DePaola, Tomie. *Things to Make and Do for Valentine's Day.* New York: Franklin Watts, 1976.
242. Devlin, Wendy. *Cranberry Halloween.* New York: Four Winds Press, 1982.
243. Devlin, Wendy. *Cranberry Thanksgiving.* New York: Four Winds Press, 1980.
244. Devlin, Wendy. *Cranberry Valentine.* New York: Four Winds Press, 1986.
245. Devonshire, Hilary. *Collage.* New York: Franklin Watts, 1988.
246. Dieringer, Beverly. *The Paper Bead Book.* New York: David McKay Co., 1977.

247. Dietrich, Wilson G. *Create with Paper Bags.* Minneapolis, Minn.: T. S. Dennison and Co., 1972.
248. *Dinosaurs and Monsters.* Caroline Pitcher, Consultant. New York: Franklin Watts, 1984.
249. DiNoto, Andrea. *Anytime, Anywhere, Anybody, Games.* Racine, Wisc.: Golden Press, Western Publishing Co., 1977.
250. Disney, Walt. *The Mickey Mouse Make-It Book.* New York: Random House, 1974.
251. *Do a Zoom Do.* Edited by Bernice Chesler. Boston: Little, Brown and Co., 1975.
252. Dobrin, Arnold. *Make a Witch, Make a Goblin, A Book of Halloween Crafts.* New York: Four Winds Press, 1977.
253. Dondiego, Barbara L. *Crafts for Kids. A Month by Month Idea Book.* Blue Ridge Summit, Pa.: Tab Books, 1984.
254. Dondiego, Barbara L. *Year Round Crafts for Kids.* Blue Ridge Summit, Pa.: Tab Books, 1987.
255. Donna, Natalie. *Bead Craft.* New York: Lothrop, Lee and Shepard Co., 1972.
256. Donna, Natalie. *The Peanut Cookbook.* New York: Lothrop, Lee and Shepard Co., 1976.
257. Donna, Natalie. *Peanut Craft.* New York: Lothrop, Lee and Shepard Co., 1974.
258. Donner, Michael. *Bike, Skate and Skateboard Games.* Racine, Wisc.: Golden Press, Western Publishing Co., 1977.
259. *Don't Lick the Spoon Before You Put It in the Pot.* Florissant, Mo.: Ferguson-Florissant School District, 1982.
260. Dowell, Ruth I. *Move Over, Mother Goose.* Mt. Rainier, Md.: Gryphon House, 1987.
261. Downer, Lesley. *Japanese Food and Drink.* New York: The Bookwright Press, 1988.
262. Drucker, Malka. *Hanukkah, Eight Nights, Eight Lights.* New York: Holiday House, 1980.
263. Drucker, Malka. *Passover, A Season of Freedom.* New York: Holiday House, 1981.
264. Drucker, Malka. *Rosh Hashanah and Yom Kippur, Sweet Beginnings.* New York: Holiday House, 1981.
265. Drucker, Malka. *Shabbat, A Peaceful Island.* New York: Holiday House, 1983.
266. Drucker, Malka. *Sukkot, A Time to Rejoice.* New York: Holiday House, 1982.
267. *Easy Crafts Book.* New York: Sterling Publishing Co., 1975.
268. Eaton, Marge. *Flower Pressing.* Minneapolis, Minn.: Lerner Publications, 1973.
269. Einhorn, Barbara. *West German Food and Drink.* New York: The Bookwright Press, 1989.
270. Eisner, Vivienne. *A Boat, A Bat, And a Beanie, Things to Make from Newspaper.* New York: Lothrop, Lee and Shepard Co., 1977.
271. Eisner, Vivienne. *The Newspaper Everything Book.* New York: E. P. Dutton and Co., 1975.
272. Eisner, Vivienne. *Quick and Easy Holiday Costumes.* New York: Lothrop, Lee and Shepard Co., 1977.
273. Elbert, Virginie Fowler. *Christmas Crafts and Customs Around the World.* Englewood Cliffs, N.J.: Prentice-Hall, 1984.

274. Elbert, Virginie Fowler. *Paperworks, Colorful Crafts from Picture Eggs to Fish Kites.* Englewood Cliffs, N.J.: Prentice-Hall, 1982.

275. Ellington, Merlene. *The Fun Collection: Activities for School and Home.* Roswell, Ga.: Blackberry Press, 1986.

276. Ellison, Virginia H. *The Pooh Cook Book.* New York: E. P. Dutton and Co., 1969.

277. Ellison, Virginia H. *The Pooh Party Book.* New York: E. P. Dutton and Co., 1971.

278. Engels, Susan. *Big Oak Busy Book.* Madison, Wisc.: Big Oak Child Care Center, 1988.

279. Englander, Lois. *The Jewish Holiday Do-Book.* New York: Bloch Publishing Co., 1976.

280. Epstein, Sam. *A Year of Japanese Festivals.* Champaign, Ill.: Garrard Publishing Co., 1974.

281. Evans, Mary. *How to Make Historic American Costumes.* Detroit, Mich.: Gale Research Co., 1976.

282. Everix, Nancy. *Windows to the World.* Carthage, Ill.: Good Apple, 1984.

283. Facklam, Margery. *Corn-Husks Crafts.* New York: Sterling Publishing Co., 1973.

284. Faggella, Kathy. *Building on Books.* Bridgeport, Conn.: First Teacher Press, 1987.

285. Faggella, Kathy. *Concept Cookery.* Bridgeport, Conn.: First Teacher Press, 1985.

286. Faggella, Kathy. *Crayons, Crafts and Concepts.* Bridgeport, Conn.: First Teacher Press, 1985.

287. Farnay, Josie. *Egypt: Activities & Projects in Color.* New York: Sterling Publishing Co., 1979.

288. Feelings, Muriel. *Jambo Means Hello, Swahili Alphabet Book.* New York: The Dial Press, 1974.

289. Feelings, Muriel. *Moja Means One, Swahili Counting Book.* New York: The Dial Press, 1971.

290. Feller, Ron. *Fairy Tales.* Seattle, Wa.: The Arts Factory, 1989.

291. Feller, Ron. *Paper Masks and Puppets for Stories, Songs and Plays.* Seattle, Wa.: The Arts Factory, 1985.

292. *Fingerplays and Action Poems for Preschoolers.* Florissant, Mo.: Ferguson-Florissant School District, 1979.

293. Fiarotta, Phyllis. *Be What You Want to Be, The Complete Dress-Up and Pretend Craft Book.* New York: Workman Publishing Co., 1977.

294. Fiarotta, Phyllis. *Confetti, The Kids Make-It-Yourself, Do-It-Yourself Party Book.* New York: Workman Publishing, 1978.

295. Fiarotta, Phyllis. *Pin It, Tack It, Hang It, The Big Book of Kids Bulletin Board Ideas.* New York: Workman Publishing Co., 1975.

296. Fiarotta, Phyllis. *Snips & Snails & Walnut Whales, Nature Crafts for Children.* New York: Workman Publishing Co., 1975.

297. Fiarotta, Phyllis. *Sticks & Stones & Ice Cream Cones.* New York: Workman Publishing Co., 1973.

298. Fiarotta, Phyllis. *The You and Me Heritage Tree, Ethnic Crafts For Children.* New York: Workman Publishing Co., 1976.

299. Fichter, George S. *American Indian Music and Musical Instruments.* New York: David McKay Co., 1978.

300. Fife, Bruce. *Dr. Dropo's Balloon Sculpturing for Beginners.* Colorado Springs, Colo.: Java Publishing Co., 1988.

301. Filstrup, Chris. *Beadazzled, The Story of Beads.* New York: Frederick Warne, 1982.

302. *Finger Frolics.* Liz Cromwell, comp. Pleasant Hills, Calif.: Discovery Toys, Revised Edition, 1983.

303. Fischer, Robert. *Hot Dog.* New York: Julian Messner, 1980.

304. Fletcher, Helen Jill. *String Projects.* Garden City, N.Y.: Doubleday and Co., 1974.

305. Flora, Sherrill. *Holidays and Special Times.* Minneapolis, Minn.: T. S. Denison and Co., 1986.

306. Flores, Anthony. *From the Hands of a Child.* Belmont, Calif.: Fearon Teacher Aids, David S. Lake Publishers, 1987.

307. Fordham, Derek. *Eskimos.* Morristown, N.J.: Silver Burdett, 1979.

308. Forte, Imogene. *Holidays.* Nashville, Tenn.: Incentive Publications, 1983.

309. Forte, Imogene. *Patterns, Projects and Plans.* Nashville, Tenn.: Incentive Publications, 1982.

310. Forte, Imogene. *Puddles and Wings and Grapevine Swings.* Nashville, Tenn.: Incentive Publications, 1982.

311. Forte, Imogene. *Puppets.* Nashville, Tenn.: Incentive Publications, 1985.

312. Foster, Laura Louise. *Keeping the Plants You Pick.* New York: Thomas Y. Crowell Co., 1970.

313. Fox, Lilla M. *Costumes and Customs of the British Isles.* Boston: Plays, 1974.

314. Fressard, M. J. *Creating with Burlap.* New York: Sterling Publishing Co., 1970.

315. Friedrichsen, Carol S. *The Pooh Craft Book.* New York: E. P. Dutton and Co., 1976.

316. Frith, Penelope. *The Stick It, Stitch It and Stuff It Toybook.* New York: M. Evans and Co., 1974.

317. Fronval, George. *Indian Signs and Signals.* New York: Sterling Publishing Co., 1978.

318. Fry-Miller, Kathleen. *Peace Works, Young Peace Makers Project Book II.* Elgin, Ill.: Brethren Press, 1989.

319. Gallagher, Patricia C. *Robin's Play and Learn Book.* Worcester, Pa.: Gallagher, Jordan and Associates, 1987.

320. *Games.* Caroline Pitcher, Consultant. New York: Franklin Watts, 1984.

321. Gaspari, Claudia. *Food in Italy.* Vero Beach, Fla.: Rourke Publications, 1989.

322. Gates, Frieda. *Easy to Make Monster Masks and Disguises.* New York: Harvey House Publishers, 1979.

323. Gates, Frieda. *Easy to Make Puppets.* New York: Harvey House Publishers, 1976.

324. Gates, Frieda. *Easy to Make American Indian Crafts.* New York: Harvey House Publishers, 1981.

325. Gates, Frieda. *Glove, Mitten, and Sock Puppets.* New York: Walker and Co., 1978.

326. Gates, Frieda. *Monsters and Ghouls, Costumes and Lore*. New York. Walker and Co., 1980.

327. Gates, Frieda. *North American Indian Masks, Craft and Legend*. New York: Walker and Co., 1982.

328. Gemming, Elizabeth. *The Cranberry Book*. New York: Coward-McCann, 1983.

329. Ghinger, Judith. *New Year's to Christmas-Hooray Days, Things to Make and Do*. Racine, Wisc.: Western Publishing Co., 1977.

330. Gibbons, Gail. *Things to Make and Do for Columbus Day*. New York: Franklin Watts, 1977.

331. Gibbons, Gail. *Things to Make and Do for Halloween*. New York: Franklin Watts, 1976.

332. Gibbons, Gail. *Things to Make and Do for Your Birthday*. New York: Franklin Watts, 1978.

333. Giblin, James Cross. *Fireworks, Picnics and Flags*. New York: Clarion Books, 1983.

334. Giblin, James. *The Scarecrow Book*. New York: Crown Publishers, 1980.

335. Gibrill, Martin. *African Food and Drink*. New York: The Bookwright Press, 1989.

336. Gilbreath, Alice. *Candles for Beginners to Make*. New York: William Morrow and Co., 1975.

337. Gilbreath, Alice. *Fun with Weaving*. New York: William Morrow and Co., 1976.

338. Gilbreath, Alice. *Making Costumes for Parties, Plays and Holidays*. New York: William Morrow and Co., 1974.

339. Gilbreath, Alice. *Making Toys That Crawl and Slide*. Chicago, Ill.: Follett Publishing Co., 1978.

340. Gilbreath, Alice. *Making Toys That Swim and Float*. Chicago, Ill.: Follett Publishing Co., 1978.

341. Gilbreath, Alice. *Simple Decoupage*. New York: William Morrow and Co., 1978.

342. Gilbreath, Alice. *Spouts, Lids and Cans, Fun with Familiar Metal Objects*. New York: William Morrow and Co., 1973.

343. *Girl Scouts of the U.S. Girl Scout Cookbook*. Chicago, Ill.: Henry Regnery Co., 1971.

344. Glass, Paul. *Songs and Stories of the North American Indians*. New York: Grosset and Dunlap, 1970.

345. Glovach, Linda. *The Little Witch's Black Magic Book of Games*. Englewood Cliffs, N.J.: Prentice-Hall, 1974.

346. Glovach, Linda. *The Little Witch's Book of Toys*. New York: Prentice-Hall Books, 1986.

347. Glovach, Linda. *The Little Witch's Carnival Book*. Englewood Cliffs, N.J.: Prentice-Hall, 1982.

348. Glovach, Linda. *The Little Witch's Cat Book*. Englewood Cliffs, N.J.: Prentice-Hall, 1985.

349. Glovach, Linda. *The Little Witch's Christmas Book*. Englewood Cliffs, N.J.: Prentice-Hall, 1974.

350. Glovach, Linda. *The Little Witch's Dinosaur Book*. Englewood Cliffs, N.J.: Prentice-Hall, 1984.

351. Glovach, Linda. *The Little Witch's Spring Holiday Book*. Englewood Cliffs, N.J.: Prentice-Hall, 1983.

352. Glovach, Linda. *The Little Witch's Summertime Book*. Englewood Cliffs, N.J.: Prentice-Hall, 1986.

353. Glovach, Linda. *The Little Witch's Thanksgiving Book*. Englewood Cliffs, N.J.: Prentice-Hall, 1976.

354. Glovach, Linda. *The Little Witch's Valentine Book*. Englewood Cliffs, N.J.: Prentice-Hall, 1984.

355. Gogniat, Maurice. *Indian Toys You Can Make*. New York: Sterling Publishing Co., 1976.

356. Gogniat, Maurice. *Wild West Toys You Can Make*. New York: Sterling Publishing Co., 1976.

357. Goin, Kenin. *Tools, Readiness Activities for Preschool and Kindergarten*. New York: Chatterbox Press, 1987.

358. Graham, Ada. *Foxtails, Ferns, & Fish Scales*. New York: Four Winds Press, 1976.

359. Grainger, Sylvia. *How to Make Your Own Moccasins*. New York: J. B. Lippincott Co., 1977.

360. Grayson, Marion F. *Let's Do Fingerplays*. Washington, D.C.: Robert B. Luce, 1962.

361. Green, M. C. *Space Age Puppets and Masks*. Boston: Plays, 1969.

362. Greenaway, Kate. *Kate Greenaway's Book of Games*. New York: Viking Press, 1976.

363. Greenberg, Judith E. *Jewish Holidays*. New York: Franklin Watts, 1984.

364. Greene, Ellin. *Clever Cooks, A Concoction of Stories, Charms, Recipes & Riddles*. New York: Lothrop, Lee and Shepard Co., 1973.

365. Greene, Karen. *Once upon a Recipe*. New Hope, Pa.: New Hope Press, 1987.

366. Greenhowe, Jean. *Costumes for Nursery Tale Characters*. Boston: Plays, 1975.

367. Greenhowe, Jean. *Party Costumes for Kids. David and Charles Craft Book*. New York: Sterling Publishing Co., 1988.

368. Greenhowe, Jean. *Stage Costumes for Girls*. Boston: Plays, 1975.

369. Groner, Judyth Saypol. *All About Hanukkah*. Rockville, Md.: Kar-Ben Copies, 1988.

370. Groner, Judyth Saypol. *Miracle Meals, Eight Nights of Food 'N Fun for Chanukah*. Rockville, Md.: Kar-Ben Copies, 1987.

371. Grummer, Arnold E. *The Great Balloon Game Book*. Appleton, Wisc.: Greg Markim, 1987.

372. Gryski, Camilla. *Many Stars and More String Games*. New York: William Morrow and Co., 1985.

373. Gryski, Camilla. *Super String Games*. New York: Morrow Junior Books, 1987.

374. Guth, Phyllis. *Crafts for Kids*. Blue Ridge Summit, Pa.: Tab Books, 1975.

375. Haas, Carolyn. *Backyard Vacation*. Boston: Little, Brown and Co., 1980.

376. Haas, Carolyn B. *Big Book of Fun*. Chicago, Ill.: Chicago Review Press, 1987.

377. Haas, Rudi. *Egg-Carton Zoo*. Toronto, Canada: Oxford University Press, 1986.

378. Haas, Rudi. *Egg-Carton Zoo II*. Toronto, Canada: Oxford University Press, 1989.

379. Haddad, Helen R. *Potato Printing*. New York: Thomas Y. Crowell, 1981.

380. Haldane, Suzanne. *Painting Faces*. New York: E. P. Dutton, 1988.

381. Hall, Carolyn Vosburg. *I Love Popcorn*. Garden City, N.Y.: Doubleday and Co., 1976.

382. Hanauer, Elsie. *The Art of Whittling and Woodcarving.* New York: A. S. Barnes and Co., 1970.

383. Harbin, E. 0. *Games of Many Nations.* New York: Abingdon Press, 1954.

384. Harelson, Randy. *The Kids' Diary of 365 Amazing Days.* New York: Workman Publishing Co., 1979.

385. Hargittai, Magdolna. *Cooking the Hungarian Way.* Minneapolis, Minn.: Lerner Publications, 1986.

386. Harris, Frank W. *Great Games to Play with Groups.* Belmont, Calif.: Fearon Teacher Aids, 1990.

387. Harris, Tom. *Creating with Styrofoam and Related Materials.* Chicago, Ill.: J. G. Ferguson Publishing Co., 1970.

388. Harrison, Supenn. *Cooking the Thai Way.* Minneapolis, Minn.: Lerner Publications, 1986.

389. Harwood, Mark. *Fun with Wood.* New York: Grosset and Dunlap Publishers, 1975.

390. Haskins, Jim. *Count Your Way Through Africa.* Minneapolis, Minn.: Carolrhoda Books, 1989.

391. Haskins, Jim. *Count Your Way Through Canada.* Minneapolis, Minn.: Carolrhoda Books, 1989.

392. Haskins, Jim. *Count Your Way Through China.* Minneapolis, Minn.: Carolrhoda Books, 1987.

393. Haskins, Jim. *Count Your Way Through Germany.* Minneapolis, Minn.: Carolrhoda Books, 1990.

394. Haskins, Jim. *Count Your Way Through Italy.* Minneapolis, Minn.: Carolrhoda Books, 1990.

395. Haskins, Jim. *Count Your Way Through Japan.* Minneapolis, Minn.: Carolrhoda Books, 1987.

396. Haskins, Jim. *Count Your Way Through Korea.* Minneapolis, Minn.: Carolrhoda Books, 1989.

397. Haskins, Jim. *Count Your Way Through Mexico.* Minneapolis, Minn.: Carolrhoda Books, 1989.

398. Haskins, Jim. *Count Your Way Through Russia.* Minneapolis, Minn.: Carolrhoda Books, 1987.

399. Haskins, Jim. *Count Your Way Through the Arab World.* Minneapolis, Minn.: Carolrhoda Books, 1987.

400. Hathaway, Nancy. *Halloween Crafts and Cookbook.* New York: Harvey House, 1979.

401. Hathaway, Nancy. *Thanksgiving Crafts and Cookbook.* New York: Harvey House, 1979.

402. Hautzig, Esther. *Holiday Treats.* New York: Macmillan Publishing Co., 1983.

403. Hautzig, Esther. *Make It Special.* New York: Macmillan Publishing Co., 1986.

404. Hawcock, David. *Making Paper Warplanes.* London, England: David and Charles Publishers, 1989.

405. Hawcock, David. *Paper Dinosaurs.* New York: Sterling Publishing Co., 1988.

406. Hawkesworth, Eric. *Paper Cutting for Storytelling and Entertainment.* New York: S. G. Phillips, 1977.

407. Hawkinson, John. *Music and Instruments for Children to Make.* Chicago, Ill.: Albert Whitman and Co., 1970.

408. Hayes, Phyllis. *Food Fun.* New York: Franklin Watts, 1981.

409. Hayes, Phyllis. *Musical Instruments You Can Make.* New York: Franklin Watts, 1981.

410. Hays, Wilma. *Foods the Indians Gave Us.* New York: Ives Washburn, 1973.

411. Hazell, Bee Gee. *Paper Crafts for the Holidays.* Minneapolis, Minn.: Judy/Instructo, 1981.

412. Hazell, Bee Gee. *Paper Plate Animals.* Minneapolis, Minn.: Judy/Instructo, 1982.

413. Hazell, Bee Gee. *Paper Plate People.* Minneapolis, Minn.: Judy/Instructo, 1985.

414. Hazell, Bee Gee. *Paper Shapes Projects.* Minneapolis, Minn.: Judy/Instructo, 1985.

415. Heady, Eleanor B. *Make Your Own Dolls.* New York: Lothrop, Lee and Shepard Co., 1974.

416. Healey, Tim. *The Life of Monkeys and Apes.* Morristown, N.J.: Silver Burdett Co., 1979.

417. Healy, Daty. *Dress the Show, A Basic Costume Book,* Revised Edition. Rowayton, Conn.: New Plays, 1976.

418. Heinz, Brian J. *Beachcrafts Too!* Shoreham, N.Y.: Ballyhoo Books, 1986.

419. Helfman, Elizabeth S. *Celebrating Nature, Rites and Ceremonies Around the World.* New York: Seabury Press, 1969.

420. Helfman, Harry. *Making Pictures Move.* New York: William Morrow and Co., 1969.

421. Helfman, Harry. *Making Pictures Without Paint.* New York: William Morrow and Co., 1973.

422. Helfman, Harry. *Making Your Own Sculpture.* New York: William Morrow and Co., 1971.

423. Helfman, Harry. *Strings on Your Fingers, How to Make String Figures.* New York: William Morrow and Co., 1965.

424. Henry, Edna. *Native American Cookbook.* New York: Julian Messner, 1983.

425. Herda, D. J. *Christmas.* New York: Franklin Watts, 1983.

426. Herda, D. J. *Halloween.* New York: Franklin Watts, 1983.

427. Hetzer, Linda. *Decorative Crafts.* Milwaukee, Wisc.: Raintree Publishers, 1978.

428. Hetzer, Linda. *Paper Crafts.* Milwaukee, Wisc.: Raintree Publishers, 1978.

429. Hetzer, Linda. *Playtime Crafts.* Milwaukee, Wisc.: Raintree Publishers, 1978.

430. Hetzer, Linda. *Traditional Crafts.* Milwaukee, Wisc.: Raintree Publishers, 1978.

431. Hetzer, Linda. *Workshop Crafts.* Milwaukee, Wisc.: Raintree Publishers, 1978.

432. Hetzer, Linda. *Yarn Crafts.* Milwaukee, Wisc.: Raintree Publishers, 1978.

433. Higgins, Susan Olson. *The Bunny Book.* Shasta, Calif.: Pumpkin Press Publishing House, 1985.

434. Higgins, Susan Olson. *The Elves Christmas Book.* Shasta, Calif.: Pumpkin Press Publishing House, 1986.

435. Higgins, Susan Olson. *The Pumpkin Book.* Shasta, Calif.: Pumpkin Press Publishing House, 1984.

436. Higgins, Susan Olson. *The Thanksgiving Book.* Shasta, Calif.: Pumpkin Press Publishing House, 1984.

437. Hill, Barbara W. *Cooking the English Way.* Minneapolis, Minn.: Lerner Publications, 1982.

438. Hill, Janis. *From Kids with Love.* Belmont, Calif.: David S. Lake Publishers, 1987.

439. Hirsch, S. Carl. *Stilts.* New York: Viking Press, 1972.

440. Hodgson, Harriet. *Artworks.* Palo Alto, Calif.: Monday Morning Books, 1986.

441. Hodgson, Harriet. *Gameworks.* Palo Alto, Calif.: Monday Morning Books, 1986.

442. Hodgson, Harriet. *Toyworks.* Palo Alto, Calif.: Monday Morning Books, 1986.

443. Hoffman, Phyllis. *Happy Halloween.* New York: Charles Scribner's Sons, 1982.

444. Hofsinde, Robert. *Indian Beadwork.* New York: William Morrow and Co., 1958.

445. Hofsinde, Robert. *Indian Games and Crafts.* New York: William Morrow and Co., 1957.

446. *Holiday Cooking Around the World.* Minneapolis, Minn.: Lerner Publications Co., 1988.

447. *Holiday Crafts Kids Can Make.* Better Homes and Gardens. Des Moines, Iowa: Meredith Corp., 1987.

448. *128 Holiday Crafts Kids Can Make.* Editors Highlights. Columbus, Ohio: Highlights for Children, 1981.

449. Hollest, Angela. *Children's Parties.* Loughton, England: Piatkus Publishers Limited, 1983.

450. Holmes, Anita. *Pierced & Pretty.* New York: Lothrop, Lee and Shepard Co., 1984.

451. Holz, Loretta. *The Christmas Spider.* New York: Philomel Books, 1980.

452. Holz, Loretta. *Mobiles You Can Make.* New York: Lothrop, Lee and Shepard Co., 1975.

453. Hoople, Cheryl G. *The Heritage Sampler, A Book of Colonial Arts and Crafts.* New York: The Dial Press, 1975.

454. Hoppe, H. *Whittling and Wood Carving.* New York: Sterling Publishing Co., 1972.

455. *How to Have Fun Making Birdhouses and Birdfeeders.* Mankato, Minn.: Editors of *Creative*, Creative Education, 1974.

456. *How to Have Fun Making Christmas Decorations.* Mankato, Minn.: Editors of *Creative*, Creative Education, 1974.

457. *How to Have Fun Making Kites.* Mankato, Minn.: Editors of *Creative*, Creative Education, 1974.

458. *How to Have Fun Making Mobiles.* Mankato, Minn.: Editors of *Creative*, Creative Educational Society, 1974.

450. *How to Have Fun Making Puppets.* Mankato, Minn.: Editors of *Creative*, Creative Educational Society, 1974.

460. *How to Have Fun with Macrame.* Mankato, Minn.: Editors of *Creative*, Creative Educational Society, 1974.

461. Howard, Lori A. *What to Do with a Squirt of Glue.* Nashville, Tenn.: Incentive Publications, 1987.

462. Hunt, Kari. *Masks and Mask Makers.* New York: Abingdon Press, 1961.

463. Hunt, Tamara. *Pocketful of Puppets.* Austin, Tx.: Nancy Renfro Studios, 1984.

464. Hunt, Tamara. *Pocketful of Puppets: Mother Goose.* Austin, Tx.: Nancy Renfro Studios, 1982.

465. Hunt, W. Ben. *The Complete Book of Indian Crafts and Lore.* Racine, Wisc.: Golden Press, Western Publishing Co., 1954.

466. Hunt, W. Ben. *The Complete How-To-Book of Indiancraft.* New York: Collier Books, Macmillan Publishing Co., 1973.

467. Hunt, W. Ben. *The Golden Book of Crafts and Hobbies.* Racine, Wisc.: Golden Press, Western Publishing Co., 1957.

468. Hunter, Irene. *Simple Folk Instruments to Make and to Play.* New York: Simon and Schuster, 1977.

469. Huntington, Lee Pennock. *Simple Shelters.* New York: Coward, McCann and Geoghegan, 1979.

470. Hutchings, Margaret. *What Shall I Do from Scandinavia.* New York: Taplinger Publishing Co., 1966.

471. *I Saw a Purple Cow, And 100 Other Recipes for Learning.* By Ann Cole. Boston: Little, Brown and Co., 1972.

472. Ichikawa, Satomi. *Happy Birthday.* New York: Philomel Books, 1988.

473. Willson, Robina Beckles. *Merry Christmas.* Illustrated by Satomi Ichikawa. New York: Philomel Books, 1983.

474. Ickis, Marguerite. *The Book of Games and Entertainment the World Over.* New York: Dodd, Mead and Co., 1969.

475. Ickis, Marguerite. *The Book of Religious Holidays and Celebrations.* New York: Dodd, Mead and Co., 1966.

476. Ingram, Victoria. *Animals.* Palo Alto, Calif.: Monday Morning Books, 1987.

477. Ingram, Victoria. *Holidays.* Palo Alto, Calif.: Monday Morning Books, 1987.

478. Ingram, Victoria. *People.* Palo Alto, Calif.: Monday Morning Books, 1987.

479. Irvine, Joan. *How to Make Pop-Ups.* New York: Morrow Junior Books, 1987.

480. Irving, Jan. *Glad Rags.* Littleton, Colo.: Libraries Unlimited, 1987.

481. Jaber, William. *Easy-to-Make Skateboards, Scooters and Racers.* New York: Dover Publications, 1976.

482. Jaeger, Ellsworth. *Easy Crafts.* New York: The Macmillan Co., 1947.

483. Jagendorf, Moritz. *Puppets for Beginners.* Boston: Plays, 1952.

484. Janitch, Valerie. *The Fairy Tale Doll Book, David and Charles Craft Book.* New York: Sterling Publishing Co., 1988.

485. Janvier, Jeannine. *Fabulous Birds You Can Make.* New York: Sterling Publishing Co., 1976.

486. Janvier, Jeannine. *Fantastic Fish You Can Make.* New York: Sterling Publishing Co., 1976.

487. Janvier, Jacqueline. *Felt Crafting.* New York: Sterling Publishing Co., 1970.

488. Johnson, Lois S. *Happy Birthdays Round the World.* New York: Rand McNally and Co., 1963.

489. Johnson, Lois S. *Happy New Year Round the World.* New York: Rand McNally and Co., 1966.

490. Johnson, Pamela. *Let's Celebrate St. Patrick's Day, A Book of Drawing Fun.* Mahwah, N.J.: Watermill Press, 1988.

491. Jones, Iris Sanderson. *Early North American Dollmaking.* San Francisco, Calif.: 101 Productions, 1976.

492. Jones, Judith. *Knead It, Punch It, Bake It.* New York: Thomas Y. Crowell, 1981.

493. Jordan, Nina R. *American Costume Dolls.* New York: Harcourt, Brace and World, 1941.

494. Jordan, Nina R. *Homemade Dolls in Foreign Dress.* New York: Harcourt, Brace and World, 1939.

495. Joseph, Joan. *Folk Toys Around the World, and How to Make Them.* New York: Parents Magazine Press, 1972.

496. Joy, Margaret. *Highdays and Holidays.* London, England: Faber and Faber Limited, 1981.

497. *Joy Through the World.* U.S. Committee for UNICEF. New York: Dodd, Mead and Co., 1985.

498. Judy, Susan. *Gifts of Writing, Creative Projects with Words and Art.* New York: Charles Scribner's Sons, 1980.

499. *Junior Girl Scouts Handbook.* New York: Girl Scouts of the U.S.A., 1986.

500. Kalman, Bobbie. *China, the Culture.* New York: Crabtree Publishing Co., 1989.

501. Kalman, Bobbie. *Food for the Settler.* New York: Crabtree Publishing Co., 1982.

502. Kalman, Bobbie. *We Celebrate Christmas.* New York: Crabtree Publishing Co., 1985.

503. Kalman, Bobbie. *We Celebrate Easter.* New York: Crabtree Publishing Co., 1985.

504. Kalman, Bobbie. *We Celebrate Halloween.* New York: Crabtree Publishing Co., 1985.

505. Kalman, Bobbie. *We Celebrate New Year.* New York: Crabtree Publishing Co., 1985.

506. Kane, Jane A. *Art Through Nature.* Holmes Beach, Fla.: Learning Publications, 1985.

507. Kanitkar, V. P. *Indian Food and Drink.* New York: The Bookwright Press, 1987.

508. Katz, Phyllis. *Exploring Science Through Art.* New York: Franklin Watts, 1990.

509. Katz, Ruth J. *Make It and Wear It.* New York: Walker and Co., 1981.

510. Kaufman, Cheryl Davidson. *Cooking the Caribbean Way.* Minneapolis, Minn.: Lerner Publications Co., 1988.

511. Kaye, Marvin. *The Story of Monopoly, Silly Putty, Bingo, Twister, Frisbee, Scrabble.* New York: Stein and Day, 1973.

512. Keefe, Betty. *Fingerpuppet Tales.* Omaha, Neb.: Special Literature Press, 1986.

513. Keefe, Betty. *Fingerpuppets, Fingerplays and Holidays.* Omaha, Neb.: Special Literature Press, 1984.

514. Keene, Carolyn. *The Nancy Drew Cookbook.* New York: Grosset and Dunlap, 1973.

515. Keene, Francis W. *Fun Around the World.* Pelham, N.Y.: The Seashore Press, 1955.

516. Kelley, Emily. *Christmas Around the World.* Minneapolis, Minn.: Carolrhoda Books, 1986.

517. Kelly, Karin. *Dollhouses.* Minneapolis, Minn.: Lerner Publications Co., 1974.

518. Kelly, Karin. *Soup's On.* Minneapolis, Minn.: Lerner Publications Co., 1974.

519. Kerina, Jane. *African Crafts.* New York: The Lion Press, 1970.

520. Kettelkamp, Larry. *Drums, Rattles and Bells.* New York: William Morrow and Co., 1960.

521. Kettelkamp, Larry. *Flutes, Whistles and Reeds.* New York: William Morrow and Co., 1962.

522. Kettlekamp, Larry. *Singing Strings.* New York: William Morrow and Co., 1958.

523. *Kids Party Cookbook.* Janet M. Stewart, Editor. Milwaukee, Wisc.: Penworthy Publishing Co., 1988.

524. Kinney, Jean. *21 Kinds of American Folk Art and How to Make Each One.* New York: Atheneum, 1972.

525. Kinney, Jean. *Varieties of Ethnic Art and How to Make Each One.* New York: Atheneum, 1976.

526. Kinser, Charleen. *Outdoor Art for Kids.* Chicago, Ill.: Follett Publishing Co., 1975.

527. Kirkman, Will. *Nature Crafts Workshop.* Belmont, Calif.: Fearon Teacher Aids, 1981.

528. *Kitchen Fun.* Editors of *Owl* and *Chicadee* Magazines. Boston: Little, Brown and Co., 1988.

529. Knopf, Mildred O. *Around America, A Cookbook for Young People.* New York: Alfred A. Knopf, 1969.

530. Knopf, Mildred O. *Around the World Cookbook for Young People.* New York: Alfred A. Knopf, 1966.

531. Kohl, Mary Ann F. *Mudworks.* Bellingham, Wash.: Bright Ring Publishing, 1989.

532. Kolba, St. Tamara. *Asian Crafts.* New York: Lion Press, 1970.

533. Kovash, Emily. *How to Have Fun Making Cards.* Mankato, Minn.: Creative Education, 1974.

534. Krisvoy, Jill. *Paper Crafts to Make You Smile.* Carthage, Ill.: Good Apple, 1981.

535. La Croix, Grethe. *Creating with Beads.* New York: Sterling Publishing Co., 1971.

536. Lafargue, Francoise. *French Food and Drink.* New York: The Bookwright Press, 1987.

537. Lancaster, John. *Cardboard.* New York: Franklin Watts, 1989.

538. Lancaster, John. *Paper Sculpture.* New York: Franklin Watts, 1989.

539. Lane, Jane. *How to Make Play Places and Secret Hidy Holes.* Garden City, N.Y.: Doubleday and Co., 1979.

540. Lansky, Vicki. *Vicki Lansky's Kids Cooking.* New York: Scholastic, 1987.

541. Lapenkova, Valentina. *Russian Food and Drink.* New York: The Bookwright Press, 1988.

542. Lapson, Dvora. *Folk Dances for Jewish Festivals.* New York: Board of Jewish Education, 1961.

543. Lazar, Wendy. *The Jewish Holiday Book.* Garden City, N.Y.: Doubleday and Co., 1977.

544. Leedy, Loreen. *A Dragon Christmas, Things to Make and Do.* New York: Holiday House, 1988.

545. Leeming, Joseph. *Fun with Paper.* New York: J. B. Lippincott Co., 1967.

546. Leverich, Kathleen. *Cricket's Expeditions, Outdoor and Indoor Activities.* New York: Random House, 1977.

547. *Life of Sea Mammals.* Morristown, N.J.: Silver Burdett Co., 1979.

548. Lightbody, Donna M. *Braid Craft.* New York: Lothrop, Lee and Shepard Co., 1976.

549. Linderman, C. Emma. *Teachables from Trashables.* St. Paul, Minn.: Toys 'N Things Press, 1979.

550. Linsley, Leslie. *Decoupage for Young Crafters.* New York: E. P. Dutton, 1977.

551. Lofgren, Ulf. *Swedish Toys, Dolls and Gifts You Can Make Yourself.* New York: Collins and World, 1978.

552. Lohf, Sabine. *Building Your Own Toys.* Chicago, Ill.: Childrens Press, 1989.

553. Lohf, Sabine. *Christmas Crafts.* Chicago, Ill.: Childrens Press, 1990.

554. Lohf, Sabine. *I Made It Myself.* Chicago, Ill.: Childrens Press, 1990.

555. Lohf, Sabine. *Making Things for Easter.* Chicago, Ill.: Childrens Press, 1989.

556. Lopshire, Robert. *How to Make Snop Snappers and Other Fine Things.* New York: William Morrow and Co., 1977.

557. Luetje, Carolyn. *Foreign Festivals.* Minneapolis, Minn.: Judy/Instructo, 1986.

558. Luetje, Carolyn. *Hooray for Holidays.* Minneapolis, Minn.: Judy/Instructo, 1986.

559. McCarthy, Colin. *Poisonous Snakes.* New York: Gloucester Press, 1987.

560. McClester, Cedric. *Kwanzaa.* New York: Gumbs and Thomas Publishers, 1985.

561. McClure, Nancee. *Free and Inexpensive Arts and Crafts to Make and Use.* Carthage, Ill.: Good Apple, 1987.

562. McCoy, Elin. *Secret Places, Imaginary Places.* New York: Macmillan Publishing Co., 1986.

563. MacDonald, Kate. *The Anne of Green Gables Cookbook.* Toronto, Canada: Oxford University Press, 1985.

564. MacFarlan, Allan A. *The Boy's Book of Outdoor Discovery.* New York: Galahad Books, 1974.

565. MacFarlan, Allan. *Handbook of American Indian Games.* New York: Dover Publications, 1958.

566. McFarland, Jeanne. *Festivals.* Morristown, N.J.: Silver Burdett, 1981.

567. Maginley, C. J. *Historic Models of Early America.* New York: Harcourt, Brace and World, 1947.

568. Maginley, C. J. *Models of America's Past and How to Make Them.* New York: Harcourt, Brace and World, 1969.

569. MacGregor, Carol. *The Fairy Tale Cookbook.* New York: Macmillan Publishing Co., 1982.

570. MacGregor, Carol. *The Storybook Cookbook.* Garden City, N.Y.: Doubleday and Co., 1967.

571. McLean, Margaret. *Make Your Own Musical Instruments.* Minneapolis, Minn.: Lerner Publications Co., 1988.

572. McLenighan, Valjean. *International Games.* Milwaukee, Wisc.: Raintree Childrens Book, 1978.

573. MacLennan, Jennifer. *Simple Puppets You Can Make.* New York: Sterling Publishing Co., 1988.

574. McNeill, Earldene. *Cultural Awareness for Young Children.* Dallas, Tx.: The Learning Tree, 1981.

575. MacStravic, Suellen. *Print Making.* Minneapolis, Minn.: Lerner Publications Co., 1973.

576. Madavan, Vijay. *Cooking the Indian Way.* Minneapolis, Minn.: Lerner Publications Co., 1985.

578. Mandell, Muriel. *Make Your Own Musical Instruments.* New York: Sterling Publishing Co., 1957.

579. Mann, Shiah. *Paper Lanterns. Two Methods.* New York: A.R.T.S., 1985.

580. Manushkin, Fran. *Latkes and Applesauce.* New York: Scholastic, 1990.

581. Marks, Burton. *Puppet Plays and Puppet-Making.* Boston: Plays, 1982.

582. Marks, Burton. *The Spook Book.* New York: Lothrop, Lee and Shepard Books, 1981.

583. Marks, Mickey Klar. *Sand Sculpturing.* New York: The Dial Press, 1962.

584. Marks, Mickey Klar. *Slate Sculpturing.* New York: The Dial Press, 1963.

585. Martin, Sidney. *Costumes, Puppets and Masks for Dramatic Plays.* Palo Alto, Calif.: Monday Morning Books, 1986.

586. Martin, Sidney. *Calendar Crafts, and Gifts for Each Season.* Palo Alto, Calif.: Monday Morning Books, 1986.

587. Marzollo, Jean. *Superkids.* New York: Harper and Row, Publishers, 1981.

588. *Masks and Puppets.* Caroline Pitcher, Consultant. New York: Franklin Watts, 1984.

589. Mason, Bernard S. *The Book of Indian-Crafts and Costumes.* New York: The Ronald Press Co., 1946.

590. Mason, Bernard S. *The Junior Book of Camping and Woodcraft.* New York: The Ronald Press Co., 1971.

591. Meiczinger, John. *How to Draw Indian Arts and Crafts.* Mahwah, N.J.: Watermill Press, 1989.

592. Meisenheimer, Sharon. *Special Ways with Ordinary Days.* Belmont, Calif.: David S. Lake Publishers, 1988.

593. Metcalfe, Edna. *The Trees of Christmas.* Nashville, Tenn.: Abingdon Press, 1969.

594. Meyer, Carolyn. *The Bread Book, All About Bread and How to Make It.* New York: Harcourt, Brace, Jovanovich, 1971.

595. Meyer, Carolyn. *Christmas Crafts.* New York: Harper and Row, 1974.

596. Meyer, Carolyn. *Mask Magic.* New York: Harcourt Brace Jovanovich, 1978.

597. Meyer, Carolyn. *Milk, Butter and Cheese.* New York: William Morrow and Co., 1974.

598. Meyer, Carolyn. *Miss Patch's Learn-to-Sew Book.* New York: Harcourt, Brace and World, 1969.

599. Meyer, Carolyn. *Rock Tumbling.* New York: William Morrow and Co., 1975.

600. Meyer, Carolyn. *Saw, Hammer, and Paint*. New York: William Morrow and Co., 1973.

601. Millen, Nina. *Children's Festivals from Many Lands*. New York: Friendship Press, 1964.

602. Millen, Nina. *Children's Games from Many Lands*. New York: Friendship Press, 1965.

603. Miller, Donna. *Egg Carton Critters*. New York: Walker and Co., 1978.

604. Miller, Jay. *Nature Crafts*. Minneapolis, Minn.: Lerner Publications Co., 1975.

605. Miller, Marjorie. *Indian Arts and Crafts*. New York: Galahad Books, 1972.

606. Mohr, Carolyn. *Thinking Activities for Books Children Love*. Englewood, Colo.: Libraries Unlimited, 1988.

607. Moncure, Jane Belk. *Our Birthday Book*. Elgin, Ill.: Child's World, 1977.

608. Moncure, Jane Belk. *Our Christmas Book*. Elgin, Ill.: Child's World, 1977.

609. Moncure, Jane Belk. *Our Easter Book*. Elgin, Ill.: Child's World, 1976.

610. Moncure, Jane Belk. *Our Halloween Book*. Elgin, Ill.: Child's World, 1977.

611. Moncure, Jane Belk. *Our Mother's Day Book*. Elgin, Ill.: Child's World, 1977.

612. Moncure, Jane Belk. *Our Thanksgiving Book*. Elgin, Ill.: Child's World, 1976.

613. Moncure, Jane Belk. *Our Valentine Book*. Elgin, Ill.: Child's World, 1976.

614. Moncure, Jane Belk. *What Was It, Before It Was Bread*. Elgin, Ill.: Child's World, 1985.

615. Montanez, Marta. *Games from My Island*. New York: Arts, 1980.

616. Moore, Eva. *The Great Banana Cookbook for Boys and Girls*. New York: Clarion Books, 1983.

617. Mooser, Stephen. *Monster Fun*. New York: Julian Messner, 1979.

618. Morin, Claude. *Braided Cord Animals You Can Make*. New York: Sterling Publishing Co., 1976.

619. Morton, Brenda. *Do-It Yourself Dinosaurs*. New York: Taplinger Publishing Co., 1973.

620. Moss, Joy F. *Focus Units in Literature*. Urbana, Ill.: National Council of Teachers of English, 1984.

621. Munsen, Sylvia. *Cooking the Norwegian Way*. Minneapolis, Minn.: Lerner Publications Co., 1982.

622. Nabwire, Constance. *Cooking the African Way*. Minneapolis, Minn.: Lerner Publications Co., 1988.

623. Nassiet, Claude. *What to Make with Nuts and Grains*. New York: Sterling Publishing Co., 1975.

624. Nelson, Esther L. *Holiday Singing and Dancing Games*. New York: Sterling Publishing Co., 1980.

625. Newsome, Arden J. *Button Collecting and Crafting*. New York: Lothrop, Lee and Shepard Co., 1976.

626. Newsome, Arden J. *Crafts and Toys from Around the World*. New York: Julian Messner, 1972.

627. Newsome, Arden J. *Egg Craft*. New York: Lothrop, Lee and Shepard Co., 1973.

628. Newsome, Arden J. *Make It with Felt*. New York: Lothrop, Lee and Shepard Co., 1972.

629. Newsome, Arden J. *Spoolcraft*. New York: Lothrop, Lee and Shepard Co., 1970.

630. Nguyen, Chi. *Cooking the Vietnamese Way*. Minneapolis, Minn.: Lerner Publications Co., 1985.

631. Nickerson, Betty. *Celebrate the Sun*. New York: J. B. Lippincott Co., 1969.

632. Nicklaus, Carol. *Making Dolls*. New York: Franklin Watts, 1981.

633. Norbeck, Oscar E. *Book of Indian Life Crafts*. New York: Association Press, 1966.

634. Norvell, Flo Ann Hedley. *The Great Big Box Book*. New York: Thomas Y. Crowell Co., 1979.

635. O'Leary, Helen. *Children's Party Book*. North Pomfret, Vt.: David and Charles, 1983.

636. Osborne, Christine. *Australian and New Zealand Food and Drink*. New York: The Bookwright Press, 1989.

637. Osborne, Christine. *Middle Eastern Food and Drink*. New York: The Bookwright Press, 1988.

638. Osborne, Christine. *Southeast Asian Food and Drink*. New York: The Bookwright Press, 1989.

639. Ottenbacher, Joy. *Toot-de-Too Paper People*. Bloomfield, Conn.: Junior Arts and Crafts House, 1982.

640. Ottenbacher, Joy. *Toot-de-Too Paper Pets and Projects*. Bloomfield, Conn.: Junior Arts and Crafts House, 1982.

641. *Papier Mache, Dyeing and Leatherwork*. New York: Franklin Watts, 1972.

642. Paraiso, Aviva. *Caribbean Food and Drink*. New York: The Bookwright Press, 1989.

643. Paraiso, Aviva. *Jewish Food and Drink*. New York: The Bookwright Press, 1989.

644. Parish, Peggy. *Beginning Mobiles*. New York: Macmillan Publishing Co., 1979.

645. Parish, Peggy. *December Decorations*. New York: Macmillan Publishing Co., 1975.

646. Parish, Peggy. *Let's Be Early Settlers with Daniel Boone*. New York: Harper and Row, 1967.

647. Parish, Peggy. *Let's Be Indians*. New York: Harper and Row, 1962.

648. Parish, Peggy. *Let's Celebrate, Holiday Decorations You Can Make*. New York: Greenwillow Books, William Morrow and Co., 1976.

649. Parish, Peggy. *Sheet Magic, Games, Toys and Gifts from Old Sheets*. New York: Macmillan Co., 1971.

650. Parnell, Helga. *Cooking the German Way*. Minneapolis, Minn.: Lerner Publications Co., 1988.

651. *Party Time*. Caroline Pitcher, Consultant. New York: Franklin Watts, 1984.

652. Paul, Aileen. *Kids Cooking, A First Cookbook for Children*. Garden City, N.Y.: Doubleday and Co., 1970.

653. Paul, Aileen. *Kids Cooking Complete Meals*. Garden City, N.Y.: Doubleday and Co., 1975.

654. Paul, Aileen. *The Kids 50-State Cookbook*. New York: Doubleday and Co., 1976.

655. Pearson, Craig. *Make Your Own Games Workshop*. Carthage, Ill.: Fearon Teacher Aids, 1982.

656. Pellicer, Maria Eugenia D. *Spanish Food and Drink*. New York: The Bookwright Press, 1988.

657. Pellowski, Anne. *Hidden Stories in Plants*. New York: Macmillan Publishing Co., 1990.

658. Penner, Lucille Recht. *The Colonial Cookbook.* New York: Hastings House, 1976.

659. Penner, Lucille Recht. *The Thanksgiving Book.* New York: Hastings House, 1986.

660. Perl, Lila. *Candles, Cakes and Donkey Tails.* New York: Houghton Mifflin Co., 1984.

661. Perl, Lila. *Foods and Festivals of the Danube Lands.* New York: World Publishing Co., 1969.

662. Perl, Lila. *The Hamburger Book.* New York: Seabury Press, 1974.

663. Perl, Lila. *Hunter's Stew and Hangtown Fry, What Pioneer America Ate...* New York: Houghton Mifflin/Clarion Books, 1977.

664. Perl, Lila. *Junk Food, Fast Food, Health Food, What America Eats...* New York: Houghton Mifflin/Clarion Books, 1980.

665. Perl, Lila. *Pinatas and Paper Flowers, Holidays of the Americas in English and Spanish.* New York: Houghton Mifflin Co., 1983.

666. Perl, Lila. *Red-Flannel Hash and Shoo-Fly Pie.* New York: The World Publishing Co., 1965.

667. Perl, Lila. *Rice, Spice and Bitter Oranges.* New York: The World Publishing Co., 1967.

668. Perl, Lila. *Slumps, Grunts and Snickerdoodles, What Colonial America Ate and Why.* New York: The Seabury Press, 1975.

669. Perry, Margaret. *Christmas Magic, The Art of Making Decorations and Ornaments.* Garden City, N.Y.: Doubleday and Co., 1964.

670. Perry, Margaret. *Rainy Day Magic, The Art of Making Sunshine on a Stormy Day.* New York: M. Evans and Co., 1970.

671. Peters, Stella. *Bedouin.* Morristown, N.J.: Silver Burdett, 1981.

672. Pettit, Florence H. *Christmas All Around the House.* New York: Thomas Y. Crowell Co., 1976.

673. Pettit, Florence H. *How to Make Whirligigs and Whimmy Diddles, And Other American Folkcraft Objects.* New York: Thomas Y. Crowell Co., 1972.

674. Pettit, Florence H. *The Stamp-Pad Printing Books.* New York: Thomas Y. Crowell Co., 1979.

675. Pettit, Ted S. *Bird Feeders and Shelters You Can Make.* New York: G. P. Putnam's Sons, 1970.

676. Pflug, Betsy. *Boxed-In Doll Houses.* New York: J. B. Lippincott Co., 1971.

677. Pflug, Betsy. *Egg-Speriment, Easy Crafts with Eggs and Egg Cartons.* New York: J. B. Lippincott Co., 1973.

678. Pflug, Betsy. *Funny Bags.* New York: J. B. Lippincott Co., 1974.

679. Pflug, Betsy. *Pint-Size Fun.* New York: J. B. Lippincott Co., 1972.

680. Pflug, Betsy. *You Can.* New York: Van Nostrand Reinhold Co., 1969.

681. Philpott, Violet. *The Know How Book of Puppets.* New York: Sterling Publishing Co., 1975.

682. Pine, Tillie S. *The Incas Knew.* New York: McGraw Hill Book Co., 1968.

683. Pinkerton, Susan. *Concoctions.* Palo Alto, Calif.: Monday Morning Books, 1987.

684. *Planes and Space.* Caroline Pitcher, Consultant. New York: Franklin Watts, 1983.

685. Ploquin, Genevieve. *What to Make with Pine Cones.* New York: Sterling Publishing Co., 1976.

686. Pluckrose, Henry. *Paints.* New York: Franklin Watts, 1987.

687. Pointillart, Marie Blanche. *Costumes from Crepe Paper.* New York: Sterling Publishing Co., 1974.

688. Porteus, Richard. *Early American Crafts You Can Make.* Minneapolis, Minn.: T. S. Denison and Co., 1978.

689. Poulssen, Emilie. *Finger-Plays for Nursery and Kindergarten.* New York: Hart Publishing Co., 1977.

690. Pountney, Kate. *Fun with Wool.* New York: Grosset and Dunlap, 1974.

691. Pountney, Kate. *Make a Mobile.* New York: S. G. Phillips, 1974.

692. Powers, William K. *Here Is Your Hobby, Indian Dancing and Costumes.* New York: G. P. Putnam's Sons, 1966.

693. Prego de Oliver, Victoria. *Airports.* England: Wayland Publishers, Limited, 1976.

694. Price, Christine. *Arts of Clay.* New York: Charles Scribner's Sons, 1977.

695. Price, Christine. *Happy Days.* New York: U.S. Committee for UNICEF, United Nations, 1969.

696. Price, Lowi. *Concoctions.* New York: E. P. Dutton and Co., 1976.

697. Prieto, Mariana. *Play It in Spanish.* New York: John Day Co., 1973.

698. *Pumpkin in a Pear Tree.* Carolyn Haas, et al. Boston: Little, Brown and Co., 1976.

699. Purdy, Susan. *Ancient Egypt, A Civilization Project Book.* New York: Franklin Watts, 1982.

700. Purdy, Susan. *Ancient Greece.* New York: Franklin Watts, 1982.

701. Purdy, Susan. *Ancient Rome.* New York: Franklin Watts, 1982.

702. Purdy, Susan. *Aztecs.* New York: Franklin Watts, 1982.

703. Purdy, Susan. *Christmas Cookbook.* New York: Franklin Watts, 1976.

704. Purdy, Susan. *Christmas Cooking Around the World.* New York: Franklin Watts, 1983.

705. Purdy, Susan. *Christmas Decorations for You to Make.* New York: J. B. Lippincott Co., 1965.

706. Purdy, Susan. *Christmas Gifts for You to Make.* New York: J. B. Lippincott Co., 1976.

707. Purdy, Susan. *Christmas Gifts Good Enough to Eat.* New York: Franklin Watts, 1981.

708. Purdy, Susan. *Eskimos, A Civilization Project Book.* New York: Franklin Watts, 1982.

709. Purdy, Susan. *Festivals for You to Celebrate.* New York: J. B. Lippincott Co., 1969.

710. Purdy, Susan. *Halloween Cookbook.* New York: Franklin Watts, 1977.

711. Purdy, Susan Gold. *Jewish Holiday Cookbook.* New York: Franklin Watts, 1979.

712. Purdy, Susan Gold. *Jewish Holidays, Facts, Activities and Crafts.* New York: J. B. Lippincott Co., 1969.

713. Purdy, Susan. *Let's Give a Party.* New York: Grosset and Dunlap, 1976.

714. Purdy, Susan. *North American Indians.* New York: Franklin Watts, 1982.

715. Quinn, Gardner. *Valentine Crafts and Cookbook.* New York: Harvey House, 1977.

716. Raines, Shirley C. *Story Stretchers.* Mt. Rainier, Md.: Gryphon House, 1989.

717. Raphael, Elaine. *Drawing History: Ancient Egypt.* New York: Franklin Watts, 1989.

718. Rawson, Christopher. *Disguise and Make-Up, The Good Spy Guide.* London, England: Usborn Publishing Ltd., 1978.

719. Razzi, James. *Star-Spangled Fun, Things to Make, Do and See from American History.* New York: Parents' Magazine Press, 1976.

720. *Ready-to-Use Activities for Before and After School Programs.* Verna Stassevitch, et al. West Nyack, N.Y.: Center for Applied Research in Education, 1989.

721. *Recipes for Fun.* By Ann Cole and others. Northfield, Ill.: Par Project, 1970.

722. Reck, Alma Kehoe. *Some Independence Days Around the World.* Los Angeles, Calif.: Elk Grove Press, 1968.

723. Reed, Bob. *Sand Creatures and Castles, How to Build Them.* New York: Holt, Rinehart and Winston, 1976.

724. Reiko, Weston. *Cooking the Japanese Way.* Minneapolis, Minn.: Lerner Publications Co., 1983.

725. Reilly, Mary V. *Seeds of Paradise.* Wilton, Conn.: Morehouse-Barlow Co., 1982.

726. Reilly, Mary V. *Wait in Joyful Hope.* Wilton, Conn.: Morehouse-Barlow Co., 1980.

727. Reis, Mary. *Batik.* Minneapolis, Minn.: Lerner Publications Co., 1973.

728. Renfro, Nancy. *Bags Are Big.* Austin, Tx.: Nancy Renfro Studios, 1986.

729. Renfro, Nancy. *Make Amazing Puppets.* Santa Barbara, Calif.: The Learning Works, 1979.

730. Reyes, Gregg. *Once There Was a House and You Can Make It.* New York: Random House, 1987.

731. Reyes, Gregg. *Once There Was a Knight, And You Can Be One Too.* New York: Random House, 1987.

732. Rice, Wayne. *Play It.* Grand Rapids, Mich.: Zondervan Publishing House, 1986.

733. *Ring a Ring O'Roses.* Flint, Mich.: Flint Public Library, 1981.

734. Roberts, Catherine. *Who's Got the Button?* New York: David McKay Co., 1962.

735. Roberts, Lynda. *Mitt Magic, Fingerplays for Finger Puppets.* Mt. Rainier, Md.: Gryphon House, 1985.

736. Robinson, Jeri. *Activities for Anyone, Anytime, Anywhere.* Boston: Little, Brown and Co., 1983.

737. Rockwell, Anne. *Games (and How to Play Them).* New York: Thomas Y. Crowell Co., 1973.

738. Rockwell, Anne. *Mother Goose Cookie-Candy Book.* New York: Random House, 1983.

739. Rockwell, Harlow. *Printmaking.* Garden City, N.Y.: Doubleday and Co., 1973.

740. Romberg, Jenean. *Let's Discover Crayon.* West Nyack, N.Y.: Center for Applied Research in Education, 1973.

741. Romberg, Jenean. *Let's Discover Mobiles.* West Nyack, N.Y.: Center for Applied Research in Education, 1974.

742. Romberg, Jenean. *Let's Discover Paper.* West Nyack, N.Y.: Center for Applied Research in Education, 1974.

743. Romberg, Jenean. *Let's Discover Papier-Mache.* West Nyack, N.Y.: Center for Applied Research in Education, 1976.

744. Romberg, Jenean. *Let's Discover Printing.* West Nyack, N.Y.: Center for Applied Research in Education, 1974.

745. Romberg, Jenean. *Let's Discover Puppets.* West Nyack, N.Y.: Center for Applied Research in Education, 1976.

746. Romberg, Jenean. *Let's Discover Tempera.* West Nyack, N.Y.: Center for Applied Research in Education, 1974.

747. Romberg, Jenean. *Let's Discover Tissue.* West Nyack, N.Y.: Center for Applied Research in Education, 1973.

748. Romberg, Jenean. *Let's Discover Watercolor.* West Nyack, N.Y.: Center for Applied Research in Education, 1974.

749. Romberg, Jenean. *Let's Discover Weaving.* West Nyack, N.Y.: Center for Applied Research in Education, 1975.

750. Rosen, Clare. *Party Fun.* London, England: Usborne Publishing, Ltd., 1985.

751. Ross, Dave. *Making Robots.* New York: Franklin Watts, 1980.

752. Ross, Dave. *Making Space Puppets.* New York: Franklin Watts, 1980.

753. Ross, Laura. *Finger Puppets.* New York: Lothrop, Lee and Shepard Co., 1971.

754. Ross, Laura. *Holiday Puppets.* New York: Lothrop, Lee and Shepard Co., 1974.

755. Ross, Laura. *Mask-Making with Pantomime and Stories from American History.* New York: Lothrop, Lee and Shepard Co., 1975.

756. Ross, Laura. *Puppet Shows Using Poems and Stories.* New York: Lothrop, Lee and Shepard Co., 1970.

757. Ross, Laura. *Scrap Puppets, How to Make and Move Them.* New York: Holt, Rinehart and Winston, 1978.

758. Rothlein, Liz. *Read It Again: A Guide for Teaching Reading.* Glenview, Ill.: Scott, Foresman and Co., 1989.

759. Rumpf, Betty. *Papier-Mache.* Minneapolis, Minn.: Lerner Publications Co., 1974.

760. Ruppert, Marion C. *Projects and Poems for Early Education.* Atlanta, Ga.: Humanics Learning, 1989.

761. Ruschen, Gaye. *Let's Learn About Arts and Crafts.* Carthage, Ill.: Good Apple, 1987.

762. Russell, Solveig Paulson. *Peanuts, Popcorn, Ice Cream, Candy and Soda Pop, And How They Began.* New York: Abingdon Press, 1970.

763. Sanders, Pete. *Safety Guide on the Road.* New York: Gloucester Press, 1989.

764. Sattler, Helen Roney. *Jar and Bottle Craft.* New York: Lothrop, Lee and Shepard Co., 1974.

765. Sattler, Helen Roney. *Jewelry from Junk.* New York: Lothrop, Lee and Shepard Co., 1973.

766. Sattler, Helen Roney. *Kitchen Carton Crafts.* New York: Lothrop, Lee and Shepard Co., 1970.

767. Sattler, Helen Roney. *Recipes for Art and Craft Materials.* New York: Lothrop, Lee and Shepard Co., 1987.

768. Sattler, Helen Roney. *Sock Craft Toys, Gifts and Other Things to Make.* New York: Lothrop, Lee and Shepard Co., 1972.

769. Saypol, Judyth Robbins. *My Very Own Chanukah Book.* Rockville, Md.: Kar-Ben Copies, 1977.

770. Schal, Hannelore. *Making Things with Yarn.* Chicago, Ill.: Childrens Press, 1990.

771. Schal, Hannelore. *Toys Made of Clay.* Chicago, Ill.: Childrens Press, 1989.

772. Schegger, T. M. *Make Your Own Mobiles.* New York: Sterling Publishing Co., 1965.

773. Schnacke, Dick. *American Folk Toys, How to Make Them.* Baltimore, Md.: Penguin Books, 1973.

774. Schnurnberger, Lynn Edelman. *Kings, Queens, Knights and Jesters, Making Medieval Costumes.* New York: Harper and Row, 1978.

775. Schnurnberger, Lynn Edelman. *A World of Dolls That You Can Make.* New York: Harper and Row, 1982.

776. Scholz-Peters, Ruth. *Indian Bead Stringing and Weaving.* New York: Sterling Publishing Co., 1975.

777. Schultz, Kathleen. *Create Your Own Natural Dyes.* New York: Sterling Publications Co., 1975.

778. Schulz, Charles M. *Charlie Brown's Super Book of Things to Do and Collect.* New York: Random House, 1975.

779. Schwartz, Linda. *The Primary Teacher's Pet.* Santa Barbara, Calif.: The Learning Works, 1984.

780. Scott, Anne. *The Laughing Baby.* Hadley, Mass.: Bergin and Garvey Publishers, 1987.

781. *Seasonal Learning Activities.* Patty Loring, Compiler. Carthage, Ill.: Good Apple, 1988.

782. *Seasonal Piggyback Songs.* Everett, Wash.: Warren Publishing House, 1985.

783. Sechrist, Elizabeth Hough. *It's Time for Thanksgiving.* Philadelphia, Pa.: Macrae Smith Co., 1957.

784. Seidelman, James E. *Creating Mosaics.* New York: Crowell-Collier Press, 1967.

785. Seidelman, James E. *Creating with Clay.* New York: Crowell-Collier Press, 1967.

786. Seidelman, James E. *Creating with Paint.* New York: Crowell-Collier Press, 1967.

787. Seidelman, James E. *Creating with Paper.* New York: Crowell-Collier Press, 1967.

788. Seidelman, James E. *Creating with Papier-Mache.* New York: Macmillan Publishing Co., 1971.

789. Seidelman, James E. *Creating with Wood.* New York: Crowell-Collier Press, 1969.

790. Seidelman, James E. *Shopping Cart Art.* New York: Crowell-Collier Press, Macmillan Co., 1970.

791. Sernaque, Vivienne. *Classic Children's Games.* New York: Dell Publishing Co., 1988.

792. Shalant, Phyllis. *Look What We've Brought You from Vietnam.* New York: Julian Messner, 1988.

793. Shapiro, Rebecca. *A Whole World of Cooking.* Boston: Little, Brown and Co., 1972.

794. Shapiro, Rebecca. *Wide World Cookbook.* Boston: Little, Brown and Co., 1962.

795. Shoemaker, Kathryn E. *Creative Christmas, Simple Crafts from Many Lands.* Minneapolis, Minn.: Winston Press, 1978.

796. Shreckhise, Roseva. *What Was It before It Was My Sweater?* Elgin, Ill.: Child's World, 1985.

797. Shui, Amy. *Chinese Food and Drink.* New York: The Bookwright Press, 1987.

798. Siegel, Alice. *Herb and Spice Book for Kids.* New York: Holt, Rinehart and Winston, 1978.

799. Silverman, Maida. *Festival of Freedom, The Story of Passover.* New York: Simon and Schuster, 1988.

800. Silverstein, Alvin. *Apples, All About Them.* Englewood Cliffs, N.J.: Prentice-Hall, 1976.

801. Silverstein, Alvin. *Potatoes, All About Them.* Englewood Cliffs, N.J.: Prentice-Hall, 1976.

802. Simmonds, Patricia. *Nursery Rhyme Programs for Toddlers.* Piscataway, N.J.: Union Middlesex Regional Library Cooperative, 1988.

803. Simmons, John. *Carpentry Is Easy When You Know How.* New York: Arco Publishing Co., 1974.

804. Simon, Nancy. *American Indian Habitats, How to Make Dwellings and Shelters with Natural Materials.* New York: David McKay Co., 1978.

805. Simons, Robin. *Recyclopedia.* Boston: Houghton Mifflin Co., 1976.

806. Skinner, Michael Kingsley. *How to Make Rubbings.* New York: Van Nostrand Reinhold Co., 1972.

807. Slade, Richard. *Carton Craft.* New York: S. G. Phillips, 1972.

808. Slade, Richard. *Modeling in Clay, Plaster and Papier-Mache.* Lothrop, Lee and Shepard Co., 1967.

809. Smith, Susan. *Happy Birthday.* Lake Oswego, Oreg.: White Pine Press, 1983.

810. Snelling, John. *Buddhist Festivals.* Vero Beach, Fla.: Rourke Enterprises, 1987.

811. Snook, Barbara. *Making Masks for School Plays.* Boston: Plays, 1972.

812. Snowball, Marilyn. *Preschool Pack Rat.* Santa Barbara, Calif.: Learning Works, 1982.

813. Soleillant, Claude. *Activities & Projects: India in Color.* New York: Sterling Publishing Co., 1977.

814. Soleillant, Claude. *Activities & Projects: Japan in Color.* New York: Sterling Publishing Co., 1980.

815. Soleillant, Claude. *Activities & Projects: Mexico in Color.* New York: Sterling Publishing Co., 1977.

816. Sommer, Elyse. *The Bread Dough Craft Book.* New York: Lothrop, Lee and Shepard Co., 1972.

817. Sommer, Elyse. *Designing with Cutouts, The Art of Decoupage.* New York: Lothrop, Lee and Shepard Co., 1973.

818. Sommer, Elyse. *Make It with Burlap.* New York: Lothrop, Lee and Shepard Co., 1973.

819. *Special Holiday Handbook.* Elgin, Ill.: Child's World, 1986.

820. Sproule, Anna. *British Food and Drink.* New York: The Bookwright Press, 1988.

821. Stangl, Jean. *Fingerlings.* Belmont, Calif.: David S. Lake Publishers, 1986.

822. Stangl, Jean. *Flannel Graphs.* Belmont, Calif.: David S. Lake Publishers, 1986.

823. Stangl, Jean. *Hats, Hats and More Hats.* Belmont, Calif.: David S. Lake Publishers, 1989.

824. Stangl, Jean. *Magic Mixtures, Creative Fun for Little Ones.* Belmont, Calif.: David S. Lake Publishers, 1986.

825. Stapleton, Marjorie. *Make Things Sailors Made.* New York: Taplinger Publishing Co., 1975.

826. Steele, Philip. *Festivals Around the World.* Minneapolis, Minn.: Dillon Press, 1986.

827. Stokes, Jack. *Let's Make a Tent.* New York: David McKay Co., 1979.

828. Stone, Anne. *Paper Straw Craft.* New York: Sterling Publishing Co., 1974.

829. Streb, Judith. *Holiday Parties.* New York: Franklin Watts, 1985.

830. *String, Raffia and Materials.* New York: Franklin Watts, 1971.

831. Strobell, Adah Parker. *Like It Was, Bicentennial Games 'N Fun Handbook.* Washington, D.C.: Acropolis Books, Ltd., 1975.

832. Strose, Susanne. *Making Paper Flowers.* New York: Sterling Publishing Co., 1972.

833. Sturner, Fred. *What Did You Do When You Were a Kid?* New York: St. Martin's Press, 1973.

834. Suid, Anna. *Constructions.* Palo Alto, Calif.: Monday Morning Books, 1987.

835. Suid, Anna. *Holiday Crafts.* Palo Alto, Calif.: Monday Morning Books, 1985.

836. Suid, Murray. *Book Factory.* Palo Alto, Calif.: Monday Morning Books, 1988.

837. Suid, Murray. *Greeting Cards.* Palo Alto, Calif.: Monday Morning Books, 1988.

838. Sullivan, Debbie. *Pocketful of Puppets.* Activities for the Special Child. Austin, Tx.: Nancy Renfro Studios, 1982.

839. Sullivan, Dianna J. *Let's Pretend, Career Costumes.* Sunset Beach, Calif.: Teacher Created Materials, 1986.

840. Sullivan, Dianna J. *Let's Pretend, Masks.* Sunset Beach, Calif.: Teacher Created Materials, 1986.

841. Sullivan, Dianna J. *Let's Pretend, Nursery Rhyme Costumes.* Sunset Beach, Calif.: Teacher Created Materials, 1986.

842. Sullivan, Dianna J. *Let's Pretend, Seasonal Costumes.* Sunset Beach, Calif.: Teacher Created Materials, 1986.

843. Sullivan, Emilie P. *Starting with Books!* Englewood, Colo.: Libraries Unlimited, 1990.

844. Supraner, Robyn. *Fun-to-Make Nature Crafts.* Mahwah, N.J.: Troll Associates, 1981.

845. Supraner, Robyn. *Fun with Paper.* Mahwah, N.J.: Troll Associates, 1981.

846. Supraner, Robyn. *Great Masks to Make.* Mahwah, N.J.: Troll Associates, 1981.

847. Supraner, Robyn. *Happy Halloween, Things to Make and Do.* Mahwah, N.J.: Troll Associates, 1981.

848. Supraner, Robyn. *Merry Christmas! Things to Make and Do.* Mahwah, N.J.: Troll Associates, 1981.

849. Supraner, Robyn. *Rainy Day Surprises You Can Make.* Mahwah, N.J.: Troll Associates, 1981.

850. Supraner, Robyn. *Valentine's Day, Things to Make and Do.* Mahwah, N.J.: Troll Associates, 1981.

851. Tabs, Judy. *Matzah Meals.* Rockville, Md.: Kar-Ben Copies, 1985.

852. Takeshita, Jiro. *Food in Japan.* Vero Beach, Fla.: Rourke Publications, 1989.

853. Tan, Jennifer. *Food in China.* Vero Beach, Fla.: Rourke Publications, 1989.

854. Tavlarios, Irene. *Greek Food and Drink.* New York: The Bookwright Press, 1988.

855. Temko, Florence. *The Big Felt Burger.* Garden City, N.Y.: Doubleday and Co., 1977.

856. Temko, Florence. *Folk Crafts for World Friendship.* Garden City, N.Y.: Doubleday and Co., 1976.

857. Temko, Florence. *Paper Cutting.* Garden City, N.Y.: Doubleday and Co., 1973.

858. Tharlet, Eve. *The Little Cooks: Recipes from Around the World.* New York: UNICEF, 1980.

859. *Things You'll Never Have to Draw Again.* Minneapolis, Minn.: Judy/Instructo, 1985.

860. Thomson, Neil. *Fairground Games to Make and Play.* New York: J. B. Lippincott Co., 1977.

861. Thomson, Ruth. *Autumn.* New York: Franklin Watts, 1989.

862. Thomson, Ruth. *Exciting Things to Make with Paper.* New York: J. B. Lippincott Co., 1977.

863. Thomson, Ruth. *Spring.* New York: Franklin Watts, 1990.

864. Thomson, Ruth. *Summer.* New York: Franklin Watts, 1990.

865. Thomson, Ruth. *Winter.* New York: Franklin Watts, 1989.

866. Thorpe, Anne. *Cooking for Fun.* London, England: Tiger Books International, 1980.

867. Tichenor, Tom. *Christmas Tree Crafts.* New York: J. B. Lippincott Co., 1975.

868. Tichenor, Tom. *Folk Plays for Puppets You Can Make.* New York: Abingdon Press, 1959.

869. Tilgner, Linda. *Let's Grow: 72 Gardening Adventures.* Pownal, Vt.: Storey Communications, 1988.

870. Tompkins, Julia. *Easy-to-Make Costumes for Stage and School.* Boston: Plays, 1975.

871. Torre, Betty L. *It's Easy to Cook.* Garden City, N.Y.: Doubleday and Co., 1977.

872. True, Susan. *Nursery Rhyme Crafts.* Palo Alto, Calif.: Monday Morning Books, 1985.

873. Urbanski, Gail. *Lenten Activities for the Family.* Kansas City, Mo.: Sheed and Ward, 1985.

874. Van des Linde, Polly. *Around the World in 80 Dishes.* New York: Scroll Press, 1971.

875. Van Ryzin, Lani. *A Patch of Earth.* New York: Julian Messner, 1981.

876. Vecchione, Glen. *The World's Best Street & Yard Games*. New York: Sterling Publishing Co., 1989.

877. Vermeer, Jackie. *The Little Kid's Americana Craft Book*. New York: Taplinger Publishing Co., 1975.

878. Vermeer, Jackie. *The Little Kid's Craft Book*. New York: Taplinger Publishing Co., 1973.

879. Villiard, Paul. *Jewelry Making*. Garden City, N.Y.: Doubleday and Co., 1973.

880. Villios, Lynne W. *Cooking the Greek Way*. Minneapolis, Minn.: Lerner Publications Co., 1984.

881. Voorst, Dick. *Corrugated Carton Crafting*. New York: Sterling Publishing Co., 1971.

882. Wagner, Lee. *How to Have Fun Making Easter Decorations*. Mankato, Minn.: Creative Education, 1974.

883. Wagner, Lee. *How to Have Fun Making Holiday Decorations*. Mankato, Minn.: Creative Education, 1974.

884. Waldee, Lynne Marie. *Cooking the French Way*. Minneapolis, Minn.: Lerner Publications Co., 1982.

885. Walker, Barbara M. *The Little House Cookbook*. New York: Harper and Row Publishers, 1979.

886. Walker, Lester. *Carpentry for Children*. Woodstock, N.Y.: The Overlook Press, 1982.

887. Walker, Mark. *Creative Costumes for Any Occasion*. Cockeysville, Md.: Liberty Publishing Co., 1984.

888. Walther, Tom. *Make Mine Music*. Boston: Little, Brown and Co., 1981.

889. Waltner, Willard. *Hobbycraft Around the World*. New York: Lantern Press, 1966.

890. Waltner, Willard. *Hobbycraft Toys & Games*. New York: Lantern Press, 1965.

891. Waltner, Willard. *Holiday Hobbycraft*. New York: Lantern Press, 1964.

892. Waltner, Willard. *The New Hobbycraft Book*. New York: Lantern Press, 1963.

893. Waltner, Willard. *A New Look at Old Crafts*. Mt. Vernon, N.Y.: Lantern Press, 1971.

894. Waltner, Willard. *Year Round Hobbycraft*. New York: Lantern Press, 1968.

895. Warner, Margaret Brink. *What's Cooking, Recipes from Around the World*. Boston: Little, Brown and Co., 1981.

896. Warner, Penny. *Happy Birthday Parties*. New York: St. Martins Press, 1985.

897. Warren, Jean. *Crafts*. Palo Alto, Calif.: Monday Morning Books, 1983.

898. Warren, Jean. *"Cut and Tell" Scissor Stories for Fall*. Everett, Wash.: Totline Press, Warren Publishing House, 1984.

899. Warren, Jean. *"Cut and Tell" Scissor Stories for Spring*. Everett, Wash.: Totline Press, Warren Publishing House, 1984.

900. Warren, Jean. *"Cut and Tell" Scissor Stories for Winter*. Everett, Wash.: Totline Press, Warren Publishing House, 1984.

901. Warren, Jean. *Holiday Piggyback Songs*. Everett, Wash.: Warren Publishing House, 1988.

902. Warren, Jean. *More Piggyback Songs*. Everett, Wash.: Warren Publishing House, 1984.

903. Warren, Jean. *1-2-3 Books*. Everett, Wash.: Warren Publishing House, 1989.

904. Warren, Jean. *1-2-3 Colors*. Everett, Wash.: Warren Publishing House, 1988.

905. Warren, Jean. *1-2-3 Games*. Everett, Wash.: Warren Publishing House, 1986.

906. Warren, Jean. *1-2-3 Murals*. Everett, Wash.: Warren Publishing House, 1989.

907. Warren, Jean. *1-2-3 Puppets*. Everett, Wash.: Warren Publishing House, 1989.

908. Warren, Jean. *Piggyback Songs for Infants and Toddlers*. Everett, Wash.: Warren Publishing House, 1985.

909. Warren, Jean. *Small World Celebrations*. Everett, Wash.: Warren Publishing House, 1988.

910. Warren, Jean. *Teeny-Tiny Folktales*. Everett, Wash.: Warren Publishing House, 1987.

911. Warren, Jean. *Theme-a-Saurus*. Everett, Wash.: Warren Publishing House, 1989.

912. Waterfall, Jarie Lee. *Nursery Crafts*. Atlanta, Ga.: Humanics Learning, 1988.

913. Watson, Jane Werner. *India Celebrates*. Champaign, Ill.: Garrard Publishing Co., 1974.

914. Watson, Jane Werner. *A Parade of Soviet Holidays*. Champaign, Ill.: Garrard Publishing Co., 1974.

915. Watson, N. Cameron. *The Little Pigs Puppet Book*. Boston: Little, Brown and Co., 1990.

916. Webster, Harriet. *Winter Book*. New York: Charles Scribner's Sons, 1988.

917. Weil, Lisl. *Santa Claus Around the World*. New York: Holiday House, 1987.

918. Weimer, Tonja Evetts. *Fingerplays and Action Chants, Volume 1, Animals*. Pittsburgh, Pa.: Pearce-Evetts Publishing, 1986.

919. Weiss, Ellen. *Things to Make and Do for Christmas*. New York: Franklin Watts, 1980.

920. Weiss, Harvey. *Carving, How to Carve Wood and Stone*. Reading, Mass.: Addison-Wesley Publishing Co., 1976.

921. Weiss, Harvey. *Games & Puzzles You Can Make*. New York: Thomas Y. Crowell Co., 1976.

922. Weiss, Harvey. *Model Buildings and How to Make Them*. New York: Thomas Y. Crowell, 1979.

923. Weiss, Harvey. *Model Cars and Trucks, And How to Build Them*. New York: Thomas Y. Crowell Co., 1974.

924. Weiss, Harvey. *Sticks, Spools and Feathers*. Reading, Mass.: Young Scott Books, Addison-Wesley Publishing Co., 1962.

925. Weiss, Peter. *Balsa Wood Craft*. New York: Lothrop, Lee and Shepard Co., 1972.

926. Weiss, Peter. *Scrap Wood Craft*. New York: Lothrop, Lee and Shepard Co., 1977.

927. Wendelin, Karla Hawkins, Ph.D. *Storybook Classrooms*. Atlanta, Ga.: Humanics Limited, 1984.

928. West, Robin. *Dinosaur Discoveries*. Minneapolis, Minn.: Carolrhoda Books, 1989.

929. West, Robin. *Far Out, How to Create Your Own Star World*. Minneapolis, Minn.: Carolrhoda Books, 1987.

930. West, Robin. *Paper Circus, How to Create Your Own Circus.* Minneapolis, Minn.: Carolrhoda Books, 1983.

931. White, Alice. *Performing Toys.* New York: Taplinger Publishing Co., 1970.

932. Whitney, Alex. *American Indian Clothes and How to Make Them.* New York: David McKay Co., 1979.

933. Whitney, Alex. *Pads for Pets, How to Make Habitats and Equipment for Small Animals.* New York: David McKay Co., 1977.

934. Whitney, Alex. *Sports and Games the Indians Gave Us.* New York: David McKay Co., 1977.

935. Wiese, Kurt. *You Can Write Chinese.* New York: Viking Press, 1945.

936. Wilkes, Angela. *My First Activity Book.* New York: Alfred A. Knopf, 1989.

937. Wilkins, Marne. *The Long Ago Lake.* New York: Sierra Book Club, Charles Scribner's Sons, 1978.

938. Wilkinson, Elizabeth. *Making Cents.* Boston: Little, Brown and Co., 1989.

939. Williams, Barbara. *Cornzapoppin!* New York: Holt, Rinehart and Winston, 1976.

940. Williams, De Atna M. *More Paper-Bag Puppets.* Belmont, Calif.: David S. Lake Publishers, 1968.

941. Williams, De Atna M. *Paper-Bag Puppets.* Belmont, Calif.: Fearon Teacher Aids, 1966.

942. Williams, J. Alan. *The Kids and Grown-Ups' Toy-Making Book.* New York: William Morrow and Co., 1979.

943. Williams, Vera B. *It's a Gingerbread House.* New York: William Morrow and Co., 1978.

944. Wilmes, Liz. *The Circle Time Book.* Dundee, Ill.: Building Block Publications, 1982.

945. Wilmes, Liz. *Felt Board Fun.* Elgin, Ill.: Building Block Publications, 1984.

946. Wilmes, Liz. *Gifts Cards Wraps.* Elgin, Ill.: Building Block Publications, 1987.

947. Wilson, Sue. *I Can Do It.* Newport Beach, Calif.: Quail Street Publishing Co., 1976.

948. Wilt, Joy. *Game Things.* Waco, Tx.: Creative Resources, 1978.

949. Wilt, Joy. *Puppet Stages and Props with Pizazz.* Waco, Tx.: Creative Resources, 1977.

950. Wilt, Joy. *Puppets with Pizazz.* Waco, Tx.: Creative Resources, 1977.

951. Winer, Yvonne. *Pocketful of Puppets: Three Plump Fish.* Austin, Tx.: Nancy Renfro Studios, 1983.

952. *Wire, Wood and Cork, Color Crafts.* New York: Franklin Watts, 1969.

953. Wiseman, Ann. *Making Musical Things.* New York: Charles Scribner's Sons, 1979.

954. Wiseman, Ann. *Making Things.* Boston: Little, Brown and Co., 1973.

955. Wiseman, Ann. *Making Things, Book 2.* Boston: Little, Brown and Co., 1975.

956. Wiswell, Phil. *Kid's Games.* Garden City, N.Y.: Doubleday and Co., 1987.

957. Wittke, Gloria. *Children's Dressing Up, Ideas to Make in a Day.* London, England: Marshall Cavendish Limited, 1987.

958. Wolff, Diane. *Chinese Writing.* New York: Holt, Rinehart and Winston, 1975.

959. Wolfson, Evelyn. *American Indian Utensils.* New York: David McKay Co., 1979.

960. Wolfson, Evelyn. *American Indian Tools and Ornaments.* New York: David McKay Co., 1981.

961. Wood, Paul W. *Artistry in Stained Glass.* New York: Sterling Publishing Co., 1976.

962. Woodhouse, Kate. *Life of Animals with Hooves.* Morristown, N.J.: Silver Burdett Co., 1975.

963. Woodruff, Marie. *Early America in Miniatures: The 18th Century.* New York: Sterling Publishing Co., 1976.

964. Woodside, Dave. *What Makes Popcorn Pop?* New York: Atheneum, 1980.

965. *Working with Odds and Ends.* New York: Franklin Watts, 1974.

966. *Working with Paper, Color Crafts.* New York: Franklin Watts, 1969.

967. *World Games and Recipes, The World Association of Girl Guides and Girl Scouts.* London, England: The World Bureau, n.d.

968. Wright, Lois A. *Weathered Wood Craft.* New York: Lothrop, Lee and Shepard Co., 1973.

969. Wright, Lyndie. *Masks.* New York: Franklin Watts, 1990.

970. Wright, Lyndie. *Puppets.* New York: Franklin Watts, 1989.

971. Wrigley, Elsie. *Soft Toys.* New York: Frederick Warne, 1977.

972. Wrigley, Elsie. *Wool Toys.* New York: Frederick Warne, 1977.

973. Wyndham, Lee. *Holidays in Scandinavia.* Champaign, Ill.: Garrard Publishing Co., 1975.

974. Yerian, Cameron John. *Easy Tricks and Spooky Games.* Chicago, Ill.: Childrens Press, 1975.

975. Yerian, Cameron John. *For Campers Only.* Chicago, Ill.: Childrens Press, 1975.

976. Yerian, Cameron John. *Fun Time Codes and Mystery Messages.* Chicago, Ill.: Childrens Press, 1975.

977. Yerian, Cameron John. *Fun Time Competitive Games.* Chicago, Ill.: Childrens Press, 1974.

978. Yerian, Cameron John. *Fun Time, Gifts for Everybody.* Chicago, Ill.: Childrens Press, 1975.

979. Yerian, Cameron John. *Fun Time, Group Games.* Chicago, Ill.: Childrens Press, 1974.

980. Yerian, Cameron John. *Fun Time, Jewelry, Candles and Papercraft.* Chicago, Ill.: Childrens Press, 1974.

981. Yerian, Cameron John. *Fun Time, Puppets and Shadow Plays.* Chicago, Ill.: Childrens Press, 1974.

982. Yerian, Cameron John. *Fun Time Sew It! Wear It!* Chicago, Ill.: Childrens Press, 1975.

983. Yerian, Cameron John. *Fun Time, Working with Wood.* Chicago, Ill.: Childrens Press, 1975.

984. Yerian, Cameron John. *Games for 1, 2, or More.* Chicago, Ill.: Childrens Press, 1974.

985. Yerian, Cameron John. *Handmade Toys and Games.* Chicago, Ill.: Childrens Press, 1975.

986. Yu, Ling. *Cooking the Chinese Way.* Minneapolis, Minn.: Lerner Publications Co., 1982.

987. Yue, David. *The Tipi, A Center of Native American Life.* New York: Alfred A. Knopf, 1984.

988. Zaidenburg, Arthur. *How to Draw Costumes and Clothes.* New York; Abelard-Schuman, 1964.

989. Zalben, Jane Breskin. *Beni's First Chanukah.* New York: Henry Holt and Co., 1988.

990. Zamojska-Hutchins, Danuta. *Cooking the Polish Way.* Minneapolis, Minn.: Lerner Publications Co., 1984.

991. Zawadzki, Sandra M. *Creactivities.* Carthage, Ill.: Good Apple, 1979.

992. Zinkgraf, June. *Spring Surprises.* Carthage, Ill.: Good Apple, 1980.

993. Adler, David A. *Malke's Secret Recipe.* Rockville, Md.: Kar-Ben Copies, 1989.

994. Alexandre, Stella V. *Fall Days, Holiday Lingo.* Belmont, Calif.: David. S. Lake Publishers, 1987.

995. Aliki. *Corn Is Maize.* New York: Thomas Y. Crowell Co., 1976.

996. Allison, Linda. *Trash Artists Workshop.* Belmont, Calif.: David S. Lake Publishers, 1981.

997. Amari, Suad. *Cooking the Lebanese Way.* Minneapolis, Minn.: Lerner Publications Co., 1986.

998. Ammon, Richard. *Growing up Amish.* New York: Atheneum, 1989.

999. Andreev, Tania. *Food in Russia.* Vero Beach, Fla.: Rourke Publications, 1989.

1000. Babin, Stanley. *Dance Around the World.* New York: MCA Music, 1969.

1001. Bacon, Josephine. *Cooking the Israeli Way.* Minneapolis, Minn.: Lerner Publications Co., 1986.

1002. Baker, James W. *Arbor Day Magic.* Minneapolis, Minn.: Lerner Publications Co., 1990.

1003. Baker, James W. *Columbus Day Magic.* Minneapolis, Minn.: Lerner Publications Co., 1990.

1004. Baker, James W. *Independence Day Magic.* Minneapolis, Minn.: Lerner Publications Co., 1990.

1005. Baker, James W. *St. Patrick's Day Magic.* Minneapolis, Minn.: Lerner Publications Co., 1990.

1006. Barr, Marilyn. *Patterns for Pinwheels, Pop-Ups, and Puppets.* Belmont, Calif.: David S. Lake Publishers, 1988.

1007. Beaton, Clare. *Costumes.* New York: Warwick Press, 1990.

1008. Berenstain, Stan. *The Berenstain Bears' Make and Do Book.* New York: Random House, 1984.

1009. Bisignano, Alphonse. *Cooking the Italian Way.* Minneapolis, Minn.: Lerner Publications Co., 1982.

1010. Bjork, Christina. *Linnea's Almanac.* New York: R & S Books, Farrar, Straus and Giroux, 1989.

1011. Boechler, Gwenn. *A Piece of Cake.* Garden City, N.Y.: Doubleday and Co., 1989.

1012. Boorer, Michael. *Life of Strange Mammals.* Morristown, N.J.: Silver Burdett Co., 1979.

1013. Bourgeois, Paulette. *The Amazing Apple.* Reading, Mass.: Addison-Wesley Publishing Co., 1987.

1014. Bowden, Marcia. *Nature for the Very Young.* New York: John Wiley and Sons, 1989.

1015. Bresnahan, Michaeline. *The Happiest Birthdays.* Lexington, Mass.: The Stephen Greene Press, 1988.

1016. Bridgewater, Alan. *Holiday Crafts, More Year-Round Crafts Kids Can Make.* Blue Ridge Summit, Pa.: Tab Books, 1990.

1017. Carlson, Laurie. *Kids Create.* Charlotte, Vt.: Williamson Publishing Co., 1990.

1018. Number not used.

1019. Chung, Okwha. *Cooking the Korean Way.* Minneapolis, Minn.: Lerner Publications Co., 1988.

1020. Churchill, E. Richard. *Building with Paper.* New York: Sterling Publishing Co., 1990.

1021. Clark, Elizabeth. *Meat.* Minneapolis, Minn.: Carolrhoda Books, 1990.

1022. Corwin, Judith Hoffman. *African Crafts.* New York: Franklin Watts, 1990.

1023. Coskey, Evelyn. *Christmas Crafts for Everyone.* Nashville, Tenn.: Abingdon, 1976.

1024. *Crazy Creatures.* Better Homes and Gardens. Des Moines, Iowa: Meredith Corporation, 1988.

1025. Devonshire, Hilary. *Christmas Crafts.* New York: Franklin Watts, 1990.

1026. Dyson, John. *Fun with Kites.* Woodbury, N.Y.: Barron's Educational Series, 1978.

1027. Elbert, Virginie Fowler. *Folk Toys Around the World.* Englewood Cliffs, N.J.: Prentice-Hall, 1984.

1028. Ellison, Virginia H. *The Pooh Get-Well Book.* New York: E. P. Dutton and Co., 1973.

1029. Graham, Terry. *Let Loose on Mother Goose.* Nashville, Tenn.: Incentive Publications, 1982.

1030. Hart, Marj. *Pom-Pom Puppets, Stories and Stages.* Belmont, Calif.: David S. Lake Publishers, 1989.

1031. Hughes, Paul. *The Months of the Year.* Ada, Okla.: Garrett Educational Corporation, 1989.

1032. Kenda, Margaret. *Cooking Wizardry for Kids.* Hauppauge, N.Y.: Barron's Educational Series, 1990.

1033. *Let's Pretend.* Better Homes and Gardens. Des Moines, Iowa: Meredith Corporation, 1988.

1034. Levy, Valerie. *Are We Almost There?* New York: Putnam Publishing Group, 1987.

1035. Loeb, Jr. Robert H. *New England Village.* Garden City, N.Y.: Doubleday and Co., 1976.

1036. Maguire, Jack. *Hopscotch, Hangman, Hot Potato, And Ha Ha Ha.* New York: Prentice-Hall Press, 1990.

1037. Oakley, Ruth. *Board and Card Games.* New York: Marshall Cavendish Corp., 1989.

1038. Adams, Faith. *El Salvador, Beauty among the Ashes.* Minneapolis, Minn.: Dillon Press, 1986.

1039. Adams, Faith. *Nicaragua, Struggling with Change.* Minneapolis, Minn.: Dillon Press, 1987.

1040. *At the Zoo.* Des Moines, Iowa: Better Homes and Gardens, Meredith Corporation, 1989.

1041. Baker, Charles F. *The Classical Companion.* Peterborough, N.H.: Cobblestone Publishing, 1988.

1042. Balerdi, Susan. *France: The Crossroads of Europe.* Minneapolis, Minn.: Dillon Press, 1984.

1043. Barchers, Suzanne I. *Cooking Up U.S. History.* Englewood, Colo.: Libraries Unlimited, 1991.

1044. Barry, Sheila Anne. *The World's Best Travel Games.* New York: Sterling Publishing Co., 1987.

1045. Beaton, Clare. *Cards.* New York: Warwick Press, 1990.

1046. Beaton, Clare. *Face Painting.* New York: Warwick Press, 1990.

1047. Beaton, Clare. *T-Shirt Painting.* New York: Warwick Press, 1990.

1048. *Bird Buddies.* Des Moines, Iowa: Better Homes and Gardens, Meredith Corporation, 1989.

1049. Bird, Malcolm. *The Christmas Handbook.* New York: Barron's Educational Series, 1986.

1050. Bresnahan, Michaeline. *The No-Sew Costume Book.* New York: Stephen Greene Press, 1990.

1051. Bridgewater, Alan. *I Made It Myself.* Blue Ridge Summit, Pa.: Tab Books, 1990.

1052. Bryant, Adam. *Canada, Good Neighbor to the World.* Minneapolis, Minn.: Dillon Press, 1987.

1053. *Bugs, Bugs, Bugs.* Des Moines, Iowa: Better Homes and Gardens, Meredith Corporation, 1989.

1054. Burt, Erica. *Natural Materials.* Vero Beach, Fla.: Rourke Enterprises, 1990.

1055. Butzow, Carol M. *Science Through Children's Literature.* Englewood, Colo.: Libraries Unlimited, 1989.

1056. Caballero, Jane A. *Art Projects for Young Children.* Atlanta. Ga.: Humanics Limited, 1979.

1057. Caket, Colin. *Model a Monster, Making Dinosaurs from Everyday Materials.* New York: Blandford Press, 1986.

1058. Carpenter, Mark L. *Brazil, An Awakening Giant.* Minneapolis, Minn.: Dillon Press, 1987.

1059. Carrick, Graham. *Wood.* Vero Beach, Fla.: Rourke Enterprises, 1990.

1060. Chocolate, Deborah M. Newton. *Kwanzaa.* Chicago, Ill.: Childrens Press, 1990.

1061. Clark, Elizabeth. *Fish.* Minneapolis, Minn.: Carolrhoda Books, 1990.

1062. Coleman, Anne. *Fabrics and Yarns.* Vero Beach, Fla.: Rourke Enterprises, 1990.

1063. Collis, Len. *Card Games for Children.* Hauppauge, N.Y.: Barron's Educational Series, 1990.

1064. Davidson, Judith. *Japan, Where East Meets West.* Minneapolis, Minn.: Dillon Press, 1983.

1065. *Day and Night.* Des Moines, Iowa: Better Homes and Gardens, Meredith Corporation, 1989.

1066. Devlin, Wendy. *Cranberry Easter.* New York: Four Winds Press, 1990.

1067. Dondiego, Barbara L. *Crafts for Kids.* Blue Ridge Summit, Pa.: Tab Books, 1991.

1068. Dooley, Norah. *Everybody Cooks Rice.* Minneapolis, Minn.: Carolrhoda Books, 1991.

1069. Eden, Maxwell. *Kiteworks.* New York: Sterling Publishing Co., 1989.

1070. Elbert, Virginie Fowler. *Clayworks, Colorful Crafts Around the World.* New York: Simon and Schuster, 1987.

1071. Farley, Carol. *Korea, A Land Divided.* Minneapolis, Minn.: Dillon Press, 1983.

1072. Filstrup, Chris. *China, From Emperors to Communes.* Minneapolis, Minn.: Dillon Press, 1983.

1073. Ford, Mary. *Party Cakes.* Dorset, England: Mary Ford Cake Artistry Centre Ltd., 1988.

1074. *Games of the World; How to Make Them.* Zurich, Switzerland: Swiss Committee for UNICEF, 1982.

1075. Garland, Sherry. *Vietnam, Rebuilding a Nation.* Minneapolis, Minn.: Dillon Press, 1990.

1076. Germaine, Elizabeth. *Cooking the Australian Way.* Minneapolis, Minn.: Lerner Publications Co., 1990.

1077. Gillies, John. *Soviet Union: The World's Largest Country.* Minneapolis, Minn.: Dillon Press, 1985.

1078. Girl Scouts of the U.S.A. *Games for Girl Scouts.* New York: Girl Scouts of the U.S.A., 1969.

1079. Goldin, Barbara Diamond. *Cakes and Miracles.* New York: Viking Penguin, 1991.

1080. Green, Mary Ann. *Projects for Christmas.* Ada, Okla.: Garrett Educational Corp., 1989.

1081. Griffin, Margaret. *The Amazing Egg Book.* Reading, Mass.: Addison-Wesley Publishing Co., 1990.

1082. Hughes, Helga. *Cooking the Austrian Way.* Minneapolis, Minn.: Lerner Publications Co., 1990.

1083. Hunt, Tamara. *Celebrate! Holidays, Puppets and Creative Drama.* Austin, Tx.: Nancy Renfro Studios, 1987.

1084. *It's a Special Day.* Des Moines, Iowa: Better Homes and Gardens, Meredith Corporation, 1988.

1085. Jacobs, Judy. *Indonesia, A Nation of Islands.* Minneapolis, Minn.: Dillon Press, 1990.

1086. Jarrett, Lauren. *Making and Baking Gingerbread Houses.* New York: Crown Publishers, 1984.

1087. Jenny, Gerri. *Rainy Day Projects for Children.* Nazareth, Pa.: Murdoch Books, 1990.

1088. Jenny, Gerri. *Toys and Games for Children to Make.* Nazareth, Pa.: Murdoch Books, 1990.

1089. Jones, Joan. *Projects for Autumn.* Ada, Okla.: Garrett Educational Corp., 1989.

1090. Kalman, Bobbie. *India, The Culture.* New York: Crabtree Publishing Co., 1990.

1091. Kalman, Bobbie. *Japan, The Culture.* New York: Crabtree Publishing Co., 1989.

1092. Kropa, Susan. *Sky Blue, Grass Green.* Carthage, Ill.: Good Apple, 1986.

1093. Kruise, Carol Sue. *Learning Through Literature.* Englewood, Colo.: Libraries Unlimited, 1990.

1094. Lamarque, Colette. *A World of Models.* New York: Drake Publishers, 1973.

1095. Lancaster, John. *Fabric Art.* New York: Franklin Watts, 1990.

1096. Leedy, Loreen. *The Dragon Halloween Party.* New York: Holiday House, 1986.

1097. Leedy, Loreen. *The Dragon Thanksgiving Feast: Things to Make and Do.* New York: Holiday House, 1990.

1098. Lohf, Sabine. *Things I Can Make with Buttons.* San Francisco, Calif.: Chronicle Books, 1988.

1099. Lohf, Sabine. *Things I Can Make with Cork.* San Francisco, Calif.: Chronicle Books, 1988.

1100. Lohf, Sabine. *Things I Can Make with Paper.* San Francisco, Calif.: Chronicle Books, 1987.

1101. *Look Up, Up, Up.* Des Moines, Iowa: Better Homes and Gardens, Meredith Corporation, 1988.

1102. McCarthy, Kevin. *Saudi Arabia, A Desert Kingdom.* Minneapolis, Minn.: Dillon Press, 1986.

1103. McClure, Vimala. *Bangladesh, Rivers in a Crowded Land.* Minneapolis, Minn.: Dillon Press, 1989.

1104. McKinnon, Elizabeth. *Yankee Doodle Birthday Celebrations.* Everett, Wash.: Warren Publishing House, 1990.

1105. *Make Believe.* Des Moines, Iowa: Better Homes and Gardens, Meredith Corporation, 1989.

1106. Mayberry, Jodine. *Chinese.* New York: Franklin Watts, 1990.

1107. Mehrens, Gloria. *Bagging It with Puppets.* Belmont, Calif.: Fearon Teacher Aids, 1988.

1108. Merrison, Lynne. *Rice.* Minneapolis, Minn.: Carolrhoda Books, 1990.

1109. Miller, Kathy Leichliter. *Sharing Time.* Blue Ridge Summit, Pa.: Tab Books, 1990.

1110. Miller, Susanna. *Beans and Peas.* Minneapolis, Minn.: Carolrhoda Books, 1990.

1111. Moore, Carolyn E., Ph.D. *The Young Chef's Nutrition Guide and Cookbook.* New York: Barron's Educational Series, 1990.

1112. Nathan, Joan. *The Children's Jewish Holiday Kitchen.* New York: Schocken Books, 1987.

1113. *Neat Eats.* New York: Crown Publishers, 1981.

1114. Nelson, Esther L. *Dancing Games for Children of All Ages.* New York: Sterling Publishing Co., 1973.

1115. Nelson, Esther L. *The Great Rounds Song Book.* New York: Sterling Publishing Co., 1985.

1116. Nelson, Esther L. *Musical Games for Children of All Ages.* New York: Sterling Publishing Co., 1976.

1117. Nottridge, Rhoda. *Sugar.* Minneapolis, Minn.: Carolrhoda Books, 1989.

1118. Oakley, Ruth. *Chanting Games.* New York: Marshall Cavendish Corp., 1989.

1119. Oakley, Ruth. *Games with Sticks, Stones and Shells.* New York: Marshall Cavendish Corp., 1989.

1120. *On the Farm.* Des Moines, Iowa: Better Homes and Gardens, Meredith Corporation, 1989.

1121. *Outdoor Fun.* Boston: Little, Brown and Co., 1989.

1122. Parents' Nursery School. *Kids Are Natural Cooks.* Boston: Houghton Mifflin Co., 1974.

1123. Peterson, Marge. *Argentina, A Wild West Heritage.* Minneapolis, Minn.: Dillon Press, 1990.

1124. Pfeiffer, Christine. *Germany: Two Nations, One Heritage.* Minneapolis, Minn.: Dillon Press, 1987.

1125. Pfeiffer, Christine. *Poland: Land of Freedom Fighters.* Minneapolis, Minn.: Dillon Press, 1984.

1126. Playtime Treasury: *A Collection of Playground Rhymes, Games and Action Songs.* New York: Doubleday, 1990.

1127. *Recipes for Fun.* Washington, D.C.: Joseph P. Kennedy, Jr. Foundation, 1986.

1128. Robbins, Maria. *A Christmas Companion, Recipes, Traditions and Customs from Around the World.* New York: Putnam Publishing Group, 1989.

1129. Roussel, Mike. *Clay.* Vero Beach, Fla.: Rourke Enterprises, 1990.

1130. Roussel, Mike. *Scrap Materials.* Vero Beach, Fla.: Rourke Enterprises, 1990.

1131. Rowen, Lawrence. *Beyond Winning: Sports and Games All Kids Want to Play.* Belmont, Calif.: Fearon Teacher Aids, 1990.

1132. Sackson, Sid. *Playing Cards Around the World.* Englewood Cliffs, N.J.: Prentice-Hall, 1981.

1133. Schrepfer, Margaret. *Switzerland, The Summit of Europe.* Minneapolis, Minn.: Dillon Press, 1989.

1134. Schwartz, Linda. *Earth Book for Kids: Activities to Help Heal the Environment.* Santa Barbara, Calif.: The Learning Works, 1990.

1135. *Short-Short Stories.* Jean Warren, comp. Everett, Wash.: Warren Publishing, 1987.

1136. Stark, Al. *Australia: A Lucky Land.* Minneapolis, Minn.: Dillon Press, 1987.

1137. Stark, Al. *Zimbabwe, A Treasure of Africa.* Minneapolis, Minn.: Dillon Press, 1986.

1138. Sullivan, S. Adams. *Bats, Butterflies and Bugs.* Boston: Little, Brown and Co., 1990.

1139. Taitz, Emily. *Israel, A Sacred Land.* Minneapolis, Minn.: Dillon Press, 1987.

1140. Tofts, Hannah. *The Paper Book.* New York: Simon and Schuster, 1989.

1141. Tofts, Hannah. *The 3-D Paper Book.* New York: Simon and Schuster, 1989.

1142. Turner, Dorothy. *Bread.* Minneapolis, Minn.: Carolrhoda Books, 1989.

1143. Turner, Dorothy. *Eggs.* Minneapolis, Minn.: Carolrhoda Books, 1989.

1144. Turner, Dorothy. *Milk.* Minneapolis, Minn.: Carolrhoda Books, 1989.

1145. Turner, Dorothy. *Potatoes.* Minneapolis, Minn.: Carolrhoda Books, 1988.

1146. Van Ryzin, Lani. *Sidewalk Games.* Milwaukee, Wisc.: Raintree Publishers Limited, 1978.

1147. Wake, Susan. *Butter.* Minneapolis, Minn.: Carolrhoda Books, 1989.

1148. Wake, Susan. *Vegetables.* Minneapolis, Minn.: Carolrhoda Books, 1990.

1149. Warren, Jean. *1-2-3 Art.* Everett, Wash.: Warren Publishing House, 1985.

1150. Warren, Jean. *Piggyback Songs.* Everett, Wash.: Warren Publishing House, 1983.

1151. *Water Wonders.* Des Moines, Iowa: Better Homes and Gardens, Meredith Corporation, 1989.

1152. Watrous, Merrill K. *Art and Writing Throughout the Year.* Belmont, Calif.: Fearon Teacher Aids, 1989.

1153. Webster, Harriet. *Going Places.* New York: Charles Scribner's Sons, 1991.

1154. Woods, Geraldine. *Spain, A Shining New Democracy.* Minneapolis, Minn.: Dillon Press, 1987.

1155. Wright, Denise Anton. *One-Person Puppet Plays.* Englewood, Colo.: Libraries Unlimited, 1990.

1156. Yusufali, Jabeen. *Pakistan: An Island Treasury.* Minneapolis, Minn.: Dillon Press, 1990.

1157. Zalben, Jane Breskin. *Goldie's Purim.* New York: Henry Holt and Co., 1991.

1158. Buchwald, Claire. *The Puppet Book: How to Make and Operate Puppets.* Boston: Plays, 1990.

1159. Irving, Jan. *Fanfares: Programs for Classrooms and Libraries.* Englewood, Colo.: Libraries Unlimited, 1990.

1160. Koh, Frances M. *Korean Holidays & Festivals.* Minneapolis, Minn.: East West Press, 1990.

1161. Pellowski, Anne. *The Story Vine.* New York: Macmillan Publishing Co., 1984.

1162. *Addy's Cookbook.* Middleton, Wis.: Pleasant Company Publications, 1994.

1163. *Addy's Craft Book.* Middleton, Wis.: Pleasant Company Publications, 1994.

1164. Adeeb, Hassan. *Nigeria: One Nation, Many Cultures.* Tarrytown, N.Y.: Marshall Cavendish, 1996.

1165. Albyn, Carole Lisa. *The Multicultural Cookbook for Students.* Phoenix, Ariz.: Oryx Press, 1993.

1166. Alden, Laura. *Halloween Safety.* Chicago, Ill.: Childrens Press, 1993.

1167. Alden, Laura. *Thanksgiving.* Chicago, Ill.: Childrens Press, 1993.

1168. Ali, Sharifah Enayat. *Afghanistan.* Tarrytown, N.Y.: Marshall Cavendish, 1995.

1169. *American Heart Association Kids' Cookbook.* New York: Random House, 1992.

1170. *American Indian Activity Book.* Dana Point, Calif.: Edupress, n.d.

1171. Number not used.

1172. Andryszewski, Tricia. *The Seminoles: People of the Southeast.* Brookfield, Conn.: The Millbrook Press, 1995.

1173. Ansary, Mir Tamim. *Afghanistan, Fighting for Freedom.* New York: Dillon Press, 1991.

1174. Asher, Jane. *Jane Asher's Costume Book.* Menlo Park, Calif.: Open Chain Publishing, 1983.

1175. Ayer, Eleanor H. *Germany: In the Heartland of Europe.* Tarrytown, N.Y.: Marshall Cavendish, 1996.

1176. Ayer, Eleanor H. *Poland: A Troubled Past, a New Start.* Tarrytown, N.Y.: Marshall Cavendish, 1996.

1177. Bailey, Vanessa. *Shadow Theater.* New York: Gloucester Press, 1991.

1178. Barrett-Dragon, Patricia. *The Kid's Cookbook: Yum! I Eat It.* Concord, Calif.: Nitty Gritty Productions, 1982. Rev. ed.

1179. Barta, Stacie Hill. *Wacky Cakes and Water Snakes.* New York: Penguin Books, 1995.

1180. Bastyra, Judy. *Hanukkah Fun.* New York: Kingfisher, 1996.

1181. Bawden, Juliet. *101 Things to Make.* New York: Sterling Publishing Co., 1994.

1182. Baxter, Nicola. *Explorations.* New York, Franklin Watts, 1994.

1183. Baxter, Nicola. *Invaders and Settlers.* New York: Franklin Watts, 1994.

1184. Baxter, Nicola. *The Romans: Facts, Things to Make, Activities.* New York: Franklin Watts, 1992.

1185. Beaton, Clare. *The Complete Book of Children's Parties.* New York: Kingfisher Books, 1992.

1186. *Best Kids Cook Book by the Sunset Editors.* Menlo Park, Calif.: Sunset Publishing Corp., 1992.

1187. Bider, Djemma. *A Drop of Honey.* New York: Simon & Schuster, 1988.

1188. Birdseye, Tom. *A Kid's Guide to Building Forts.* Tucson, Ariz.: Harbinger House, 1993.

1189. Bittinger, Gayle. *Exploring Sand and the Desert.* Everett, Wash.: Warren Publishing House, 1993.

1190. Bittinger, Gayle. *Exploring Water and the Ocean.* Everett, Wash.: Warren Publishing House, 1993.

1191. Bond, Carol Taylor. *Marmalade Days: Fall.* Livonia, Mich.: Partner Press, 1987.

1192. Bond, Carol Taylor. *Marmalade Days: Spring.* Mt. Rainier, Md.: Gryphon House, 1988.

1193. Bond, Carol Taylor. *Marmalade Days: Winter.* Livonia, Mich.: Partner Press, 1987.

1194. Bonvillain, Nancy. *The Haidas: People of the Northwest Coast.* Brookfield, Conn.: The Millbrook Press, 1994.

1195. Borlenghi, Patricia. *Italy.* New York: Franklin Watts 1993.

1196. Bourgeois, Paulette. *The Amazing Paper Book.* Reading, Mass.: Addison-Wesley Publishing Co., 1989.

1197. Bourgeois, Paulette. *The Amazing Potato Book.* Reading, Mass.: Addison-Wesley Publishing Co., 1991.

1198. Brady, April A. *Kwanzaa Karamu: Cooking and Crafts for a Kwanzaa Feast.* Minneapolis, Minn.: Carolrhoda Books, 1995.

1199. Braham, Clare Bonfanti. *Happy Birthday, Grandma Moses: Activities for Special Days Throughout the Year.* Chicago, Ill.: Chicago Review Press, 1995.

1200. Brashears, Deya. *Circle Time Activities for Young Children.* Orinda, Calif.: Deya Brashears, 1981.

1201. Briggs, Diane. *Flannel Board Fun.* Metuchen, N.J.: The Scarecrow Press, 1992.

1202. Brokaw, Meredith. *The Penny Whistle Birthday Party Book.* New York: Simon & Schuster, 1992.

1203. Brokaw, Meredith. *The Penny Whistle Christmas Party Book.* New York: Simon & Schuster, 1991.

1204. Brokaw, Meredith. *The Penny Whistle Lunch Box Book.* New York: Weidenfeld & Nicolson, 1989.

1205. Brown, Anne Houlihan. *The Colonial South.* Vero Beach, Fla.: Rourke Publications, 1994.

1206. Brown, Jerome C. *Tales from Many Lands Papercrafts.* Carthage, Ill.: Fearon Teacher Aids, 1991.

1207. Burch, Joann J. *Kenya, Africa's Tamed Wilderness.* New York: Dillon Press, 1992.

1208. Burns, Diane L. *Arbor Day.* Minneapolis, Minn.: Carolrhoda Books, 1989.

1209. Busenberg, Bonnie. *Vanilla, Chocolate and Strawberry: The Story of Your Favorite Flavors.* Minneapolis, Minn.: Lerner Publications Co., 1994.

1210. Campbell, Jeanette R. *Pop-Up Animals.* Monterey, Calif.: Evan-Moor Corp., 1989.

1211. Cappelloni, Nancy. *Ethnic Cooking the Microwave Way.* Minneapolis, Minn.: Lerner Publications Co., 1994.

1212. Carlson, Bernice Wells. *Let's Find the Big Idea.* Nashville, Tenn.: Abingdon Press, 1982.

1213. Carlson, Laurie. *EcoArt!* Charlotte, Vt.: Williamson Publishing Co., 1993.

1214. Carlson, Laurie. *Westward Ho!: An Activity Guide to the Wild West.* Chicago, Ill.: Chicago Review Press, 1996.

1215. Cauley, Lorinda Bryan. *Pease Porridge Hot.* New York: G. P. Putnam's Sons, 1977.

1216. Cefali, Leslie. *Cook-A-Book.* Hagerstown, Md.: Alleyside Press, 1991.

1217. Chambers, Catherine. *Spain.* New York: Franklin Watts, 1993.

1218. Chan, Barbara J. *Kid Pix Around the World: A Multicultural Computer Activity Book.* Reading, Mass.: Addison-Wesley Publishing Co., 1993.

1219. Chapman, Gillian. *Art from Fabric: With Projects Using Rags, Old Clothing and Remnants.* New York: Thomson Learning, 1995.

1220. Chatham-Baker, Odette. *Baby Lore: Ceremonies, Myths and Traditions to Celebrate a Baby's Birth.* New York: Macmillan Publishing Co., 1991.

1221. Cheong-Lum, Roseline Ng. *Haiti.* Tarrytown, N.Y.: Marshall Cavendish Corp., 1994.

1222. Chorzempa, Rosemary A. *My Family Tree Workbook: Genealogy for Beginners.* New York: Dover Publications, 1982.

1223. *Christmas in Brazil.* Chicago, Ill.: World Book, 1991.

1224. *Christmas in Britain.* Chicago, Ill.: World Book, 1988.

1225. *Christmas in Canada.* Chicago, Ill.: World Book, 1994.

1226. *Christmas in Denmark.* Chicago, Ill.: World Book, 1986.

1227. *Christmas in France.* Chicago, Ill.: World Book, 1988.

1228. *Christmas in Germany.* Chicago, Ill.: Passport Books, NTC Publishing Corp., 1991.

1229. *Christmas in Ireland.* Chicago, Ill.: World Book, 1985.

1230. *Christmas in Italy.* Chicago, Ill.: World Book, 1988.

1231. *Christmas in Russia.* Chicago, Ill.: World Book, 1992.

1232. *Christmas in the Holy Land.* Chicago, Ill.: World Book, 1987.

1233. *Christmas in the Philippines.* Chicago, Ill.: World Book, 1990.

1234. *Christmas in Today's Germany.* Chicago, Ill.: World Book, 1993.

1235. *Christmas in Washington, D.C.* Chicago, Ill.: World Book, 1988.

1236. *Christmas Is Coming, Volume 2.* Birmingham, Ala.: Oxmoor House, 1992.

1237. Churchill, E. Richard. *Holiday Paper Projects.* New York: Sterling Publishing Co., 1992.

1238. Churchill, E. Richard. *Terrific Paper Toys.* New York: Sterling Publishing Co., 1991.

1239. Cifarelli, Megan. *India: One Nation, Many Traditions.* Tarrytown, N.Y.: Marshall Cavendish, 1996.

1240. Cobb, Mary. *The Quilt-Block History of Pioneer Days: With Projects Kids Can Make.* Brookfield, Conn.: The Millbrook Press, 1995.

1241. Coleman, South. *Jordan.* Tarrytown, N.Y.: Marshall Cavendish Corp., 1997.

1242. Coleman, South. *Syria.* North Bellmore, N.Y.: Marshall Cavendish Corp., 1995.

1243. Collins, Carolyn Strom. *The World of Little House.* New York: HarperCollins Publishers, 1996.

1244. Cook, Deanna F. *The Kids' Multicultural Cookbook: Food & Fun Around the World.* Charlotte, Vt.: Williamson Publishing Co., 1995.

1245. Cooke, Jean. *Projects for Easter and Holiday Activities.* Ada, Okla.: Garrett Educational Corp., 1989.

1246. Corwin, Judith Hoffman. *Asian Crafts.* New York: Franklin Watts, 1992.

1247. Corwin, Judith Hoffman. *Easter Crafts: A Holiday Craft Book.* New York: Franklin Watts, 1994.

1248. Corwin, Judith Hoffman. *Halloween Crafts: A Holiday Craft Book.* New York: Franklin Watts, 1995.

1249. Corwin, Judith Hoffman. *Harvest Festivals Around the World.* Parsippany, N.J.: Julian Messner, 1995.

1250. Corwin, Judith Hoffman. *Kwanzaa Crafts: A Holiday Craft Book.* New York: Franklin Watts, 1995.

1251. Corwin, Judith Hoffman. *Latin American and Caribbean Crafts.* New York: Franklin Watts, 1991.

1252. Corwin, Judith Hoffman. *Thanksgiving Crafts.* New York: Franklin Watts, 1995.

1253. *Crafts for Celebration.* Caroline Bingham/Karen Foster, editors. Brookfield, Conn.: The Millbrook Press, 1993.

1254. *Crafts for Decoration.* Caroline Bingham/Karen Foster, editors. Brookfield, Conn.: The Millbrook Press, 1993.

1255. *Crafts for Everyday Life.* Caroline Bingham/Karen Foster, editors. Brookfield, Conn.: The Millbrook Press, 1993.

1256. *Crafts for Play.* Caroline Bingham/Karen Foster, editors. Brookfield, Conn.: The Millbrook Press, 1993.

1257. *Crafts in Action: Ideas for Special Occasions.* North Bellmore, N.Y.: Marshall Cavendish Corp., 1991.

1258. *Crafts in Action: Ideas from Nature.* North Bellmore, N.Y.: Marshall Cavendish Corp., 1991.

1259. *Crafts in Action: Making Gifts.* North Bellmore, N.Y.: Marshall Cavendish Corp., 1991.

1260. *Crafts in Action: Making Models & Games.* North Bellmore, N.Y.: Marshall Cavendish Corp., 1991.

1261. *Crafts in Action: Using Paper & Paint.* North Bellmore, N.Y.: Marshall Cavendish Corp., 1991.

1262. *Crafts in Action: Using Yarn, Fabric and Thread.* North Bellmore, N.Y.: Marshall Cavendish Corp., 1991.

1263. Crocker, Betty. *Betty Crocker's Boys and Girls Microwave Cookbook.* New York: Prentice-Hall, 1992.

1264. Dahl, Felicity. *Roald Dahl's Revolting Recipes.* New York: Viking, 1994.

1265. D'Amico, Joan. *The Science Chef Travels Around the World: Fun Food Experiments and Recipes for Kids.* New York: John Wiley & Sons, 1996.

1266. Darling, Kathy. *Holiday Hoopla: Plays, Parades, Parties.* Palo Alto, Calif.: Monday Morning Books, 1990.

1267. Dawson, Imogen. *Food & Feasts in Ancient Greece.* Parsippany, N.J.: New Discovery Books, 1995.

1268. Dawson, Imogen. *Food & Feasts in the Middle Ages.* New York: Macmillan Publishing Co., 1994.

1269. Dawson, Imogen. *Food & Feasts with the Aztecs.* Parsippany, N.J.: New Discovery Books, 1994.

1270. Day, Jon. *Magic.* New York: Thomson Learning, 1994.

1271. Dennee, JoAnne. *In the Three Sisters Garden.* Montpelier, Vt.: Food Works, 1995.

1272. Darling, Abigail. *Teddy Bear's Picnic Cookbook.* New York: Viking Penguin, 1991.

1273. Denny, Roz. *A Taste of Britain.* New York: Thomson Learning, 1994.

1274. Denny, Roz. *A Taste of China.* New York: Thomson Learning, 1994.

1275. Denny, Roz. *A Taste of France.* New York: Thomson Learning, 1994.

1276. Denny, Roz. *A Taste of India.* New York: Thomson Learning, 1994.

1277. Deshpande, Chris. *Festival Crafts.* Milwaukee, Wis.: Gareth Stevens Publishing, 1994.

1278. Deshpande, Chris. *Food Crafts.* Milwaukee, Wis.: Gareth Stevens Publishing, 1994.

1279. Deshpande, Chris. *Silk.* Ada, Okla.: Garrett Educational Corp., 1994.

1280. *Desserts Around the World.* Minneapolis, Minn.: Lerner Publications Co., 1991.

1281. Devonshire, Hilary. *Greeting Cards and Gift Wrap.* New York: Franklin Watts, 1992.

1282. Diamond, Arthur. *Egypt, Gift of the Nile.* New York: Dillon Press, 1992.

1283. Dickinson, Gill. *Children's Costumes.* Secaucus, N.J.: Chartwell Books, 1993.

1284. Diehn, Gwen. *Kid Style Nature Crafts: 50 Terrific Things to Make With Nature's Materials.* New York: Sterling Publishing Co., 1995.

1285. Diehn, Gwen. *Nature Crafts for Kids.* New York: Sterling Publishing Co., 1992.

1286. Dondiego, Barbara L. *After-School Crafts.* Blue Ridge Summit, Pa.: Tab Books, 1992.

1287. Dooley, Norah. *Everybody Bakes Bread.* Minneapolis, Minn.: Carolrhoda Books, 1996.

1288. Drew, Helen. *My First Music Book.* New York: Dorling Kindersley, 1993.

1289. Drucker, Malka. *The Family Treasury of Jewish Holidays.* New York: Little, Brown and Co., 1994.

1290. Drucker, Malka. *Grandma's Latkes.* New York: Harcourt Brace Jovanovich Publishers, 1992.

1291. DuBois, Jill. *Colombia.* Freeport, N.Y.: Marshall Cavendish Corp., 1991.

1292. DuBois, Jill. *Greece.* North Bellmore, N.Y.: Marshall Cavendish Corp., 1992.

1293. DuBois, Jill. *Korea.* North Bellmore, N.Y.: Marshall Cavendish Corp., 1993.

1294. Duch, Mabel. *Easy-to-Make Puppets.* Boston, Mass.: Plays, 1993.

1295. Earl, Amanda. *Masks.* New York: Thomson Learning, 1995.

1296. *Earth Makers Lodge.* Peterborough, N.H.: Cobblestone Publishing, 1994.

1297. Egger-Bovet, Howard. *U.S. Kids History: Book of the American Colonies.* Covelo, Calif.: Yolla Bolly Press, 1996.

1298. Egger-Bovet, Howard. *U.S. Kids History: Book of the American Revolution.* New York: Little, Brown and Co., 1994.

1299. Elliot, Marion. *My Party Book.* New York: Little, Brown and Co., 1994.

1300. Elliot, Marion. *Papier Mache Project Book.* Secaucus, N.J.: Chartwell Books, 1992.

1301. Erickson, Donna. *More Prime Time Activities with Kids.* Minneapolis, Minn.: Augsburg Fortress, 1992.

1302. Erlbach, Arlene. *Peanut Butter.* Minneapolis, Minn.: Lerner Publications Co., 1994.

1303. Esbenshade, Richard S. *Hungary.* North Bellmore, N.Y.: Marshall Cavendish Corp., 1994.

1304. Eshmeyer, R. E. *Ask Any Vegetable.* Englewood Cliffs, N.J.: Prentice-Hall, 1975.

1305. Everix, Nancy. *Ethnic Celebrations Around the World.* Carthage, Ill.: Good Apple, 1991.

1306. *Face Painting.* Palo Alto, Calif.: Klutz Press, 1990.

1307. Falconer, Kieran. *Peru.* Tarrytown, N.Y.: Marshall Cavendish Corp., 1995.

1308. *Felicity's Cookbook.* Middleton, Wis.: Pleasant Company Publications, 1994.

1309. *Felicity's Craft Book.* Middleton, Wis.: Pleasant Company Publications, 1994.

1310. Fiarotta, Noel. *Music Crafts for Kids.* New York: Sterling Publishing Co., 1993.

1311. Fiarotta, Phyllis. *Cups & Cans & Paper Plate Fans.* New York: Sterling Publishing Co., 1992.

1312. Fisher, Timothy. *Hovels and Houses.* Reading, Mass.: Addison-Wesley Publishing Co., 1977.

1313. Fitzjohn, Sue. *Festivals Together.* Gloucestershire, U.K.: Hawthorn Press, 1993.

1314. *Five-Minute Faces by Snazaroo.* New York: Random House, 1992.

1315. Fleischner, Jennifer. *The Aztecs: People of the Southwest.* Brookfield, Conn.: The Millbrook Press, 1994.

1316. Fleischner, Jennifer. *The Inuit: People of the Arctic.* Brookfield, Conn.: The Millbrook Press, 1995.

1317. Foley, Erin L. *Costa Rica.* Tarrytown, N.Y.: Marshall Cavendish Corp., 1997.

1318. Foley, Erin L. *Dominican Republic.* Tarrytown, N.Y.: Marshall Cavendish Corp., 1994.

1319. Foley, Erin L. *Ecuador.* North Bellmore, N.Y.: Marshall Cavendish Corp., 1995.

1320. Ford, Marianne. *Copycats & Artifacts.* Boston, Mass.: David R. Godine, Publisher, 1983.

1321. Fredericks, Anthony D. *Social Studies Through Children's Literature.* Englewood, Colo.: Teacher Ideas Press, Libraries Unlimited, 1991.

1322. Fuller, Barbara. *Britain*. North Bellmore, N.Y.: Marshall Cavendish Corp., 1994.

1323. Gabor, Bob. *Costume of the Iroquois and How to Make It*. Ontario, Canada: Iroqrafts Ltd., 1983.

1324. Galvin, Irene Flum. *Brazil: Many Voices, Many Faces*. Tarrytown, N.Y.: Marshall Cavendish Corp., 1996.

1325. Galvin, Irene Flum. *Japan: A Modern Land with Ancient Roots*. Tarrytown, N.Y.: Marshall Cavendish Corp., 1996.

1326. Ganeri, Anita. *Focus on Romans*. New York: Gloucester Press, 1992.

1327. Ganeri, Anita. *France*. New York: Franklin Watts, 1993.

1328. Ganeri, Anita. *India*. New York: Franklin Watts, 1994.

1329. Ganeri, Anita. *Mexico*. New York: Franklin Watts, 1994.

1330. Ganeri, Anita. *Vikings*. New York: Gloucester Press, 1992.

1331. Garrett, Sandra. *The Pacific Northwest Coast*. Vero Beach, Fla.: Rourke Publications, 1994.

1332. Gaylord, Susan Kapuscinski. *Multicultural Books to Make and Share*. New York: Scholastic, 1994.

1333. Gertz, Susan E. *Teaching Physical Science Through Children's Literature*. Middletown, Ohio: Terrific Science Press, 1996.

1334. Giles, Nancy H. *Creative Milk Carton Crafts*. Carthage, Ill: Good Apple, 1989.

1335. Gillis, Jennifer Storey. *In a Pumpkin Shell: Over 20 Pumpkin Projects for Kids*. Pownal, Vt.: Storey Communications, 1992.

1336. Gish, Steven. *Ethiopia*. Tarrytown, N.Y.: Marshall Cavendish Corp., 1996.

1337. Gold-Vukson, Marji. *Can You Imagine? Creative Drawing Adventures for the Jewish Holidays*. Rockville, Md.: Kar-Ben Copies, 1992.

1338. Gomez, Aurelia. *Crafts of Many Cultures*. New York: Scholastic Professional Books, 1992.

1339. Gomez, Paolo. *Food in Mexico*. Vero Beach, Fla.: Rourke Publications, 1989.

1340. Good, Phyllis Pellman. *Amish Cooking for Kids*. Intercourse, Pa.: Good Books, 1994.

1341. Goodwin, Bob. *A Taste of Spain*. New York: Thomson Learning, 1995.

1342. Gordon, Patricia. *Kids Learn America: Bringing Geography to Life with People, Places and History*. Charlotte, Vt.: Williamson Publishing Co., 1991.

1343. Gordon, Patricia. *Asian Indians*. New York: Franklin Watts, 1990.

1344. Goss, Linda. *It's Kwanzaa Time*. New York: G. P. Putnam's Sons, 1995.

1345. Green, Jen M. *Making Crazy Faces and Masks*. New York: Gloucester Press, 1992.

1346. Green, Jen M. *Making Mad Machines*. New York: Gloucester Press, 1992.

1347. Greenberg, Janet. *California*. Vero Beach, Fla.: Rourke Publications, 1994.

1348. Greene, Peggy R. *Things to Make*. New York: Random House, 1981.

1349. Greenwood, Barbara. *A Pioneer Sampler*. New York: Ticknor & Fields Books for Young Readers, 1995.

1350. Grier, Katherine. *Discover: Investigate the Mysteries of History*. Reading, Mass.: Addison-Wesley Publishing Co., 1989.

1351. Grisewood, Sara. *Models*. New York: Larousse Kingfisher Chambers, 1994.

1352. Gryski, Camilla. *Friendship Bracelets*. New York: William Morrow and Co., 1993.

1353. Gwathmey, Emily Margolin. *Trick or Treat*. New York: Clarkson Potter Publishers, 1992.

1354. Haas, Carolyn. *My Own Fun*. Chicago, Ill.: Chicago Review Press, 1990.

1355. Hall, Godfrey. *Games*. New York: Thomson Learning, 1995.

1356. *Hanukkah Fun*. Honesdale, Pa.: Boyds Mills Press, 1992.

1357. *Hanukkah, Oh, Hanukkah*. Compiled by Wendy Wax. New York: Parachute Press, 1993.

1358. Harlow, Joyce. *Story Play: Costumes, Cooking, Music and More for Young Children*. Englewood, Colo.: Teacher Ideas Press, 1992.

1359. Harris, Colin. *A Taste of West Africa*. New York: Thomson Learning, 1994.

1360. Harry, Cindy Groom. *One-Hour Holiday Crafts*. Lincolnwood, Ill.: Publications International, 1994.

1361. Hart, Avery. *Kids and Weekends: Creative Ways to Make Special Days*. Charlotte, Vt.: Williamson Publishing Co., 1992.

1362. Hart, Avery. *Kids Make Music*. Charlotte, Vt.: Williamson Publishing Co., 1993.

1363. Hart, Rhonda Massingham. *You Can Carve Fantastic Jack-O-Lanterns*. Pownal, Vt.: Storey Communications, 1989.

1364. Hartelius, Margaret A. *Knot Now! The Complete Friendship Bracelet Kit*. New York: Grosset & Dunlap, 1992.

1365. Haskins, Jim. *Count Your Way Through India*. Minneapolis, Minn.: Carolrhoda Books, 1990.

1366. Haskins, Jim. *Count Your Way Through Israel*. Minneapolis, Minn.: Carolrhoda Books, 1990.

1367. Haslam, Andrew. *Ancient Egypt*. New York: Thomson Learning, 1995.

1368. Haslam, Andrew. *North American Indians*. New York: Thomson Learning, 1995.

1369. Hassig, Susan M. *Iraq*. North Bellmore, N.Y.: Marshall Cavendish Corp., 1993.

1370. Hassig, Susan M. *Panama*. Tarrytown, N.Y.: Marshall Cavendish Corp., 1996.

1371. Hassig, Susan M. *Somalia*. Tarrytown, N.Y.: Marshall Cavendish Corp., 1997.

1372. Hauser, Jill Frankel. *Kids' Crazy Concoctions: 50 Mysterious Mixtures for Art and Craft Fun*. Charlotte, Vt.: Williamson Publishing, 1994.

1373. Haycock, Kate. *Pasta*. Minneapolis, Minn.: Carolrhoda Books, 1990.

1374. Heale, Jay. *Poland*. North Bellmore, N.Y.: Marshall Cavendish Corp., 1994.

1375. Heale, Jay. *Portugal*. North Bellmore, N.Y.: Marshall Cavendish Corp., 1995.

1376. Healton, Sarah H. *Baskets, Beads and Black Walnut Owls.* Blue Ridge Summit, Pa.: Tab Books, 1993.

1377. Hebert, Holly. *Super Springtime Crafts.* Los Angeles, Calif.: Lowell House Juvenile, 1996.

1378. Heltshe, Mary Ann. *Multicultural Explorations: Joyous Journeys with Books.* Englewood, Colo.: Teacher Ideas Press, Libraries Unlimited, 1991.

1379. Hershberger, Priscilla. *Make Costumes!: For Creative Play.* Cincinnati, Ohio: North Light Books, 1992.

1380. Hodges, Susan. *Multicultural Snacks.* Everett, Wash.: Warren Publishing House, 1995.

1381. Hodges-Caballero, Jane, Ph.D. *Children Around the World: The Multicultural Journey.* Atlanta, Ga.: Humanics Learning, 1983.

1382. Hoyt-Goldsmith, Diane. *Mardi Gras: A Cajun Country Celebration.* New York: Holiday House, 1995.

1383. Hughes, Helga. *Cooking the Swiss Way.* Minneapolis, Minn.: Lerner Publications Co., 1995.

1384. Hundley, David H. *The Southwest.* Vero Beach, Fla.: Rourke Publications, 1994.

1385. Illsley, Linda. *A Taste of Mexico.* New York: Thomson Learning, 1994.

1386. Irvine, Joan. *Build It With Boxes.* New York: Morrow Junior Books, 1993.

1387. Irvine, Joan. *How to Make Holiday Pop-ups.* New York: Beech Tree Paperback Books, 1996.

1388. Irvine, Joan. *How to Make Super Pop-Ups.* New York: Beech Tree Books, 1992.

1389. Irving, Jan. *Full Speed Ahead.* Englewood, Colo.: Teacher Ideas Press, Libraries Unlimited, 1988.

1390. Irving, Jan. *Raising the Roof: Children's Stories and Activities on Houses.* Englewood, Colo.: Teacher Ideas Press, Libraries Unlimited, 1991.

1391. Irving, Jan. *Second Helpings: Books and Activities About Food.* Englewood Colo.: Teacher Ideas Press, Libraries Unlimited, 1994.

1392. Jaffrey, Madhur. *Market Days.* Mahway, N.J.: Bridgewater Books, 1995.

1393. Jasmine, Julia. *Multicultural Holidays.* Huntington Beach, Calif.: Teacher Created Materials, 1994.

1394. Jennings, Terry. *Beans.* Ada, Okla.: Garrett Educational Corp., 1994.

1395. Kagda, Sakina. *Norway.* Tarrytown, N.Y.: Marshall Cavendish Corp., 1995.

1396. Kalman, Bobbie. *Games from Long Ago.* New York: Crabtree Publishing Co., 1995.

1397. Kalman, Bobbie. *Old-Time Toys.* New York: Crabtree Publishing Co., 1995.

1398. Kalman, Bobbie. *We Celebrate Family Days.* New York: Crabtree Publishing Co., 1993.

1399. Kalman, Bobbie. *We Celebrate Hanukkah.* New York: Crabtree Publishing Co., 1993.

1400. Kalman, Bobbie. *Victorian Christmas.* New York: Crabtree Publishing Co., 1996.

1401. Kalman, Bobbie. *We Celebrate the Harvest.* New York: Crabtree Publishing Co., 1986.

1402. Kalman, Bobbie. *We Celebrate Valentine's Day.* New York: Crabtree Publishing Co., 1986.

1403. Kalman, Bobbie. *We Celebrate Winter.* New York: Crabtree Publishing Co., 1986.

1404. Kalter, Joanmarie. *The World's Best String Games.* New York: Sterling Publishing Co., 1989.

1405. Kaur, Sharon. *Food in India.* Vero Beach, Fla.: Rourke Publications, 1989.

1406. Kendall, Russ. *Eskimo Boy: Life in an Inupiaq Eskimo Village.* New York: Scholastic, 1992.

1407. Kendall, Russ. *Russian Girl: Life in an Old Russian Town.* New York: Scholastic, 1994.

1408. Kennedy, Pamela. *A Christmas Celebration: Traditions and Customs from Around the World.* Nashville, Tenn.: Ideals Publishing Corp., 1992.

1409. Kennedy, Pamela. *An Easter Celebration: Traditions and Customs from Around the World.* Nashville, Tenn.: Ideals Publishing Corp., 1990.

1410. Kent, Deborah. *China: Old Ways Meet New.* Tarrytown, N.Y.: Benchmark Books, Marshall Cavendish Corp., 1996.

1411. Kent, Deborah. *Mexico: Rich in Spirit and Tradition.* Tarrytown, N.Y.: Benchmark Books, Marshall Cavendish Corp., 1996.

1412. Keyworth, Valerie. *New Zealand: Land of the Long White Cloud.* Minneapolis, Minn.: Dillon Press, 1990.

1413. *Kids Cooking.* Palo Alto, Calif.: Klutz Press, 1987.

1414. *Kids Explore America's African-American Heritage.* Santa Fe, N.Mex.: John Muir Publications, 1993.

1415. Kinder, Backbuch. *Let's Bake.* New York: Sterling Publishing Co., 1992.

1416. King, Elizabeth. *Chile Fever: A Celebration of Peppers.* New York: Dutton Children's Books, 1995.

1417. *Kirsten's Cookbook.* Middleton, Wis.: Pleasant Company Publications, 1994.

1418. *Kirsten's Craft Book.* Middleton, Wis.: Pleasant Company Publications, 1994.

1419. Kite, L. Patricia. *Gardening Wizardry for Kids.* Hauppauge, N.Y.: Barron's Educational Series, 1995.

1420. Klettenheimer, Ingrid. *Great Paper Craft Projects.* New York: Sterling Publishing Co., 1992.

1421. Kohl, Mary Ann F. *Good Earth Art: Environmental Art for Kids.* Bellingham, Wash.: Bright Ring Publishing, 1991.

1422. Kraska, Edie. *Toys and Tales from Grandmother's Attic.* Boston, Ma.: Houghton Miflin Co., 1979.

1423. Krensky, Stephen. *The Pizza Book.* New York: Scholastic, 1992.

1424. Krull, Kathleen. *Maria Molina and the Days of the Dead.* New York: Macmillan Publishing Co., 1994.

1425. Lamancusa, Jim. *Dynamite Crafts for Special Occasions.* Blue Ridge Summit, Pa.: Tab Books, 1993.

1426. Lankford, Mary D. *Hopscotch Around the World.* New York: William Morrow and Co., 1992.

1427. Lee, Nancy. *Hands on Heritage.* Los Angeles, Calif.: Children's Book & Music Center, 1978.

1428. Lee, Tan Chung. *Finland.* Tarrytown, N.Y.: Marshall Cavendish Corp., 1996.

1429. Lehne, Judith Logan. *The Never-Be-Bored Book.* New York: Sterling Publishing Co., 1992.

1430. Levy, Patricia. *Ireland.* North Bellmore, N.Y.: Marshall Cavendish Corp., 1994.

1431. Levy, Patricia. *Nigeria.* North Bellmore, N.Y.: Marshall Cavendish Corp., 1993.

1432. Levy, Patricia. *Puerto Rico.* Tarrytown, N.Y.: Marshall Cavendish Corp., 1994.

1433. Levy. Patricia. *Sudan.* Tarrytown, N.Y.: Marshall Cavendish Corp., 1997.

1434. Levy. Patricia. *Switzerland.* North Bellmore, N.Y.: Marshall Cavendish Corp., 1994.

1435. Lipson, Michelle. *The Fantastic Costume Book.* New York: Sterling Publishing Co., 1992.

1436. Littlewood, Valerie. *Scarecrow!* New York: Dutton Children's Books, 1992.

1437. Lizon, Karen Helene. *Colonial American Holidays and Entertainment.* New York: Franklin Watts, 1993.

1438. Loewen, Nancy. *Food in France.* Vero Beach, Fla.: Rourke Publications, 1991.

1439. Loewen, Nancy. *Food in Germany.* Vero Beach, Fla.: Rourke Publications, 1991.

1440. Loewen, Nancy. *Food in Greece.* Vero Beach, Fla.: Rourke Publications, 1991.

1441. Loewen, Nancy. *Food in Israel.* Vero Beach, Fla.: Rourke Publications, 1991.

1442. Loewen, Nancy. *Food in Korea.* Vero Beach, Fla.: Rourke Publications, 1991.

1443. Loewen, Nancy. *Food in Spain.* Vero Beach, Fla.: Rourke Publications, 1991.

1444. Lucas, Eileen. *The Cherokees: People of the Southeast.* Brookfield, Conn.: The Millbrook Press, 1993.

1445. Lucas. Eileen. *The Ojibwas: People of the Northern Forests.* Brookfield, Conn.: The Millbrook Press, 1994.

1446. Lynn, Sara. *Playing with Paint.* New York: Scholastic, 1992.

1447. MacLeod-Brudenell, Iain. *Animal Crafts.* Milwaukee, Wis.: Gareth Stevens Publishing, 1994.

1448. MacLeod-Brudenell, Iain. *Costume Crafts.* Milwaukee, Wis.: Gareth Stevens Publishing, 1994.

1449. Mack-Williams, Kibibi. *Food and Our History.* Vero Beach, Fla.: Rourke Press, 1995.

1450. Malcolm, Peter. *Libya.* North Bellmore, N.Y.: Marshall Cavendish Corp., 1993.

1451. Mandelkern, Nicholas D. *The Jewish Holiday Home Companion.* West Orange, N.J.: Behrman House, 1994.

1452. Marden, Patricia C. *Cooking Up World History.* Englewood, Colo.: Teacher Ideas Press, Libraries Unlimited, 1994.

1453. Markle, Sandra. *Exploring Autumn.* New York: Atheneum, 1991.

1454. Markle, Sandra. *Measuring Up!: Experiments, Puzzles and Games Exploring Measurement.* New York: Aladdin Paperbacks, 1995.

1455. Marks, Diana F. *Glues, Brews and Goos!: Recipes and Formulas for Almost Any Classroom Project.* Englewood, Colo.: Teacher Ideas Press, Libraries Unlimited, 1996.

1456. Marsh, Carole. *New York Kids' Cookbook.* Decatur, Ga.: Gallopade Publishing Group, 1990.

1457. Martell, Hazel Mary. *Food & Feasts with the Vikings.* Parsippany, N.J.: New Discovery Books, 1995.

1458. McCarthy, Tara. *Literature-Based Geography Activities: An Integrated Approach.* New York: Scholastic, 1992.

1459. McDonnell, Janet. *Christmas in Other Lands.* Chicago, Ill.: Childrens Press, 1993.

1460. McDonnell, Janet. *The Easter Surprise.* Chicago, Ill.: Childrens Press, 1993.

1461. McDonnell, Janet. *Martin Luther King Day.* Chicago, Ill.: Childrens Press, 1993.

1462. McDonnell, Janet. *Sharing Hanukkah.* Chicago, Ill.: Childrens Press, 1993.

1463. McGraw, Sheila. *Dolls Kids Can Make.* Buffalo, N.Y.: Firefly Books, 1995.

1464. McGraw, Sheila. *Papier-Mache for Kids.* Buffalo, N.Y.: Firefly Books, 1991.

1465. McGuire, Kevin. *Woodworking for Kids.* New York: Sterling Publishing Co., 1993.

1466. McInnes, Celia. *Projects for Spring and Holiday Activities.* Ada, Okla.: Garrett Educational Corp., 1989.

1467. McInnes, Celia. *Projects for Summer and Holiday Activities.* Ada, Okla.: Garrett Educational Corp., 1989.

1468. McKenley, Yvonne. *A Taste of the Caribbean.* New York: Thomson Learning, 1995.

1469. McKinnon, Elizabeth. *Special Day Celebrations.* Everett, Wash.: Warren Publishing House, 1989.

1470. McLenighan, Valjean. *Christmas in Spain.* Chicago, Ill.: Passport Books, NTC Publishing Group, 1991.

1471. Mellett, Peter. *Food Energy.* New York: Franklin Watts, 1992.

1472. Mellett, Peter. *Hot and Cold.* New York: Franklin Watts, 1993.

1473. Meyer, Carolyn. *Sing and Learn.* Carthage, Ill.: Good Apple, 1989.

1474. Meyer, Kathleen Allan. *Ireland: Land of Mist and Magic.* Minneapolis, Minn.: Dillon Press, 1982.

1475. Michael, David. *Making Kites.* New York: Kingfisher Books, 1993.

1476. Milord, Susan. *Adventures in Art: Art and Craft Experiences for 7-to-14 Year-Olds.* Charlotte, Vt.: Williamson Publishing Co., 1990.

1477. Milord, Susan. *Hands Around the World: 365 Ways to Build Cultural Awareness and Global Respect.* Charlotte, Vt.: Williamson Publishing Co., 1992.

1478. Milord, Susan. *Tales Alive!: Ten Multicultural Folktales with Activities.* Charlotte, Vt.: Williamson Publishing Co., 1995.

1479. Moiz, Azra. *Taiwan.* Tarrytown, N.Y.: Marshall Cavendish Corp., 1995.

1480. *Molly's Cookbook.* Middleton, Wis.: Pleasant Company Publications, 1994.

1481. *Molly's Craft Book.* Middleton, Wis.: Pleasant Company Publications, 1994.

1482. Moncure, Jane Belk. *Step Into Fall: A New Season.* Elgin, Ill.: Child's World, 1990.

1483. Morgan, Paul. *The Ultimate Kite Book.* New York: Simon and Schuster, 1992.

1484. Morris, Ting. *Animals.* New York: Franklin Watts, 1994.

1485. Morris, Ting. *Germany.* New York: Franklin Watts, 1993.

1486. Morris, Ting. *Masks.* New York: Franklin Watts, 1993.

1487. Morris, Ting. *No-Cook Cooking.* New York: Franklin Watts, 1994.

1488. Morris, Ting. *Rain Forest.* New York: Franklin Watts, 1994.

1489. Moss, Miriam. *Eggs.* Ada, Okla.: Garrett Educational Corp., 1991.

1490. Moss, Miriam. *Fruit.* Ada, Okla.: Garrett Educational Corp., 1994.

1491. Munan, Heidi. *Malaysia.* North Bellmore, N.Y.: Marshall Cavendish Corp., 1990.

1492. Murray, Anna. *My Christmas Craft Book for Kids.* Racine, Wis.: Western Publishing Co., 1993.

1493. *Native People of the Northeast Woodland.* New York: Museum of the American Indian, 1990.

1494. Nelson, Wayne E. *International Playtime.* Carthage, Ill.: Fearon Teacher Aids, 1992.

1495. Newmann, Dana. *The Early Childhood Teacher's Almanack: Activities for Every Month of the Year.* West Nyack, N.Y.: Center for Applied Research in Education, 1984.

1496. Norris, Joan Darby. *New England.* Vero Beach, Fla.: Rourke Publications, 1994.

1497. Oakley, Ruth. *Ball Games.* Freeport, N.Y.: Marshall Cavendish Corp., 1989.

1498. Oakley, Ruth. *Chasing Games.* Freeport, N.Y.: Marshall Cavendish Corp., 1989.

1499. Oakley, Ruth. *Games of Strength and Skill.* Freeport, N.Y.: Marshall Cavendish Corp., 1989.

1500. Oakley, Ruth. *Games with Papers and Pencils.* Freeport, N.Y.: Marshall Cavendish Corp., 1989.

1501. Oakley, Ruth. *Games with Rope and String.* Freeport, N.Y.: Marshall Cavendish Corp., 1989.

1502. O'Hare, Jeff. *Hanukkah, Happy Hanukkah.* Honesdale, Pa.: Boyds Mills Press, 1994.

1503. Olsson, Kari. *Sweden, A Good Life for All.* Minneapolis, Minn.: Dillon Press, 1982.

1504. O'Neill, Laurie A. *The Shawnees: People of the Eastern Woodlands.* Brookfield, Conn.: The Millbrook Press, 1995.

1505. O'Reilly, Susie. *Batik and Tie-Dye.* New York: Thomson Learning, 1993.

1506. O'Reilly, Susie. *Weaving.* New York: Thomson Learning, 1993.

1507. Orlando, Louise. *The Multicultural Game Book.* New York: Scholastic Professional Books, 1993.

1508. Osseo-Asare, Fran. *A Good Soup Attracts Chairs: A First African Cookbook for American Kids.* Gretna, La.: Pelican Publishing Co., 1993.

1509. Owen, Cheryl. *My Costume Book.* New York: Little, Brown and Co., 1995.

1510. Owen, Cheryl. *My Nature Craft Book.* New York: Little, Brown and Co., 1993.

1511. Oxlade, Chris. *Everyday Things.* New York: Franklin Watts, 1994.

1512. Oxlade, Chris. *Houses and Homes.* New York: Franklin Watts, 1994.

1513. Paker, Josephine. *Beating the Drum.* Brookfield, Conn.: The Millbrook Press, 1992.

1514. Paker, Josephine. *Music from Strings.* Brookfield, Conn.: The Millbrook Press, 1992.

1515. Cheng, Pang-Guek. *Canada.* North Bellmore, N.Y.: Marshall Cavendish Corp., 1994.

1516. Papi, Liza. *Carnavalia! African-Brazilian Folklore and Crafts.* New York: Rizzoli International Publications, 1994.

1517. Parnell, Helga. *Cooking the South American Way.* Minneapolis, Minn.: Lerner Publications Co., 1991.

1518. Pateman, Robert. *Belgium.* Tarrytown, N.Y.: Marshall Cavendish Corp., 1995.

1519. Pateman, Robert. *Bolivia.* Tarrytown, N.Y.: Marshall Cavendish Corp., 1995.

1520. Pateman, Robert. *Denmark.* North Bellmore, N.Y.: Marshall Cavendish Corp., 1995.

1521. Pateman, Robert. *Kenya.* North Bellmore, N.Y.: Marshall Cavendish Corp., 1993.

1522. Pellowski, Anne. *The Family Storytelling Handbook.* New York: Macmillan Publishing Co., 1987.

1523. Penn, Malka. *The Miracle of the Potato Latkes.* New York: Holiday House, 1994.

1524. Penner, Lucille Recht. *Celebration: The Story of American Holidays.* New York: Macmillan Publishing Co., 1993.

1525. Penner, Lucille Recht. *Eating the Plates.* New York: Macmillan Publishing Co., 1991.

1526. Penner, Lucille Recht. *The Little Women Book: Games, Recipes, Crafts and Other Homemade Pleasures.* New York: Random House, 1995.

1527. Penner, Lucille Recht. *A Native American Feast.* New York: Macmillan Publishing Co., 1994.

1528. Penner, Lucille Recht. *The Tea Party Book.* New York: Random House, 1993.

1529. Pennington, Daniel. *Itse Selu, Cherokee Harvest Festival.* Watertown, Ma.: Charlesbridge Publishing, 1994.

1530. Peterson, Cris. *Extra Cheese, Please! Mozzarella's Journey from Cow to Pizza.* Honesdale, Pa.: Boyds Mills Press, 1994.

1531. Petrash, Carol. *Earthways: Simple Environmental Activities for Young Children.* Mt. Rainier, Md.: Gryphon House, 1992.

1532. Pfeiffer, Christine. *Poland, Land of Freedom Fighters.* Minneapolis, Minn.: Dillon Press, 1991.

1533. Pinsent, Lynsy. *Face Painting.* Secaucus, N.J.: Chartwell Books, 1993.

1534. *Playtime Crafts and Activities.* Honesdale, Pa.: Boyds Mills Press, 1994.

1535. Plotkin, Gregory. *Cooking the Russian Way.* Minneapolis, Minn.: Lerner Publications Co., 1986.

1536. Politi, Leo. *Three Stalks of Corn.* New York: Charles Scribner's Sons, 1976.

1537. Powell, Jillian. *Body Decoration.* New York: Thomson Learning, 1995.

1538. Powell, Jillian. *Food.* New York: Thomson Learning, 1995.

1539. Press, Judy. *The Little Hands Big Fun Craft Book.* Charlotte, Vt.: Williamson Publishing, 1995.

1540. Priceman, Marjorie. *How to Make an Apple Pie and See the World.* New York: Alfred A. Knopf, 1994.

1541. Provenzo, Asterie Baker. *Play It Again.* Englewood Cliffs, N.J.: Prentice-Hall, 1981.

1542. Pulleyn, Micah. *Kids in the Kitchen.* New York: Sterling Publishing Co., 1994.

1543. Raferty, Kevin. *Kids Gardening: A Kids' Guide to Messing Around in the Dirt.* Palo Alto, Calif.: Klutz Press, 1989.

1544. Rajendra, Vijeya. *Australia.* North Bellmore, N.Y.: Marshall Cavendish Corp., 1991.

1545. Ralph, Judy. *The Peanut Butter Cookbook for Kids.* New York: Hyperion Books for Children, 1995.

1546. Randall, Ronne. *Thanksgiving Fun.* New York: Kingfisher, 1994.

1547. Raphael, Elaine. *Drawing America: The Story of the First Thanksgiving.* New York: Scholastic, 1991.

1548. Raphael, Elaine. *Drawing History: Ancient Greece.* New York: Franklin Watts, 1989.

1549. Raphael, Elaine. *Drawing History: Ancient Rome.* New York: Franklin Watts, 1990.

1550. Renfro, Nancy. *Puppets U.S.A., Texas.* Austin, Tex.: Nancy Renfro Studios, 1985.

1551. Ridgwell, Jenny. *A Taste of Italy.* New York: Thomson Learning, 1993.

1552. Ridgwell, Jenny. *A Taste of Japan.* New York: Thomson Learning, 1993.

1553. Riehecky, Janet. *Cinco de Mayo.* Chicago, Ill.: Childrens Press, 1993.

1554. Riehecky, Janet. *Kwanzaa.* Chicago, Ill.: Childrens Press, 1993.

1555. Riordan, James. *Soviet Union.* Morristown, N.J.: Silver Burdett Press, 1987.

1556. Robertson, Linda. *Kwanzaa Fun.* New York: Kingfisher, 1996.

1557. Robins, Deri. *Christmas Fun.* New York: Kingfisher, 1995.

1558. Robins, Deri. *Easter Fun.* New York: Kingfisher, 1996.

1559. Robins, Deri. *The Great Pirate Activity Book.* New York: Kingfisher, 1995.

1560. Robins, Deri. *Kids' Around the World Cookbook.* New York: Kingfisher Chambers, 1994.

1561. Robins, Deri. *Papier-Mache.* New York: Kingfisher, 1993.

1562. Rosin, Arielle. *Eclairs and Brown Bears.* New York: Tichnor & Fields, 1994.

1563. Rosmarin, Ike. *South Africa.* North Bellmore, N.Y.: Marshall Cavendish Corp., 1993.

1564. Ross, Catherine. *The Amazing Milk Book.* Reading, Mass.: Addison-Wesley Publishing Co., 1991.

1565. Ross, Corinne. *Christmas in France.* Chicago, Ill.: Passport Books, NTC Publishing Group, 1991.

1566. Ross, Corinne. *Christmas in Italy.* Chicago, Ill.: Passport Books, NTC Publishing Group, 1991.

1567. Ross, Corinne. *Christmas in Mexico.* Chicago, Ill.: Passport Books, NTC Publishing Group, 1991.

1568. Ross, Kathy. *Crafts for Christmas.* Brookfield, Conn.: The Millbrook Press, 1995.

1569. Ross, Kathy. *Crafts for Halloween.* Brookfield, Conn.: The Millbrook Press, 1994.

1570. Ross, Kathy. *Crafts for Kwanzaa.* Brookfield, Conn.: The Millbrook Press, 1994.

1571. Ross, Kathy. *Crafts for Thanksgiving.* Brookfield, Conn.: The Millbrook Press, 1995.

1572. Ross, Kathy. *Crafts for Valentine's Day.* Brookfield, Conn.: The Millbrook Press, 1995.

1573. Ross, Kathy. *Every Day Is Earth Day.* Brookfield, Conn.: The Millbrook Press, 1995.

1574. Rozakis, Laurie. *Celebrate! Holidays Around the World.* Santa Barbara, Calif.: The Learning Works, 1993.

1575. Sadler, Judy Ann. *Christmas Crafts.* Toronto, Canada: Kids Can Press, 1994.

1576. Sagan, Miriam. *The Middle Atlantic States.* Vero Beach, Fla.: Rourke Publications, 1994.

1577. *Samantha's Cookbook.* Middleton, Wis.: Pleasant Company Publications, 1994.

1578. *Samantha's Craft Book.* Middleton, Wis.: Pleasant Company Publications, 1994.

1579. Sarin, Anita Vohra. *India, An Ancient Land, a New Nation.* Minneapolis, Minn.: Dillon Press, 1985.

1580. Sateren, Shelley Swanson. *Canada: Star of the North.* Tarrytown, N.Y.: Marshall Cavendish Corp., 1996.

1581. Saunders, Richard. *Horrorgami, Spooky Paperfolding Just for Fun.* New York: Sterling Publishing Co., 1991.

1582. Schomp, Virginia. *Russia: New Freedoms, New Challenges.* Tarrytown, N.Y.: Marshall Cavendish Corp., 1996.

1583. Scott, Louise Binder. *Rhymes for Learning Times.* Minneapolis, Minn.: T. S. Denison and Co., 1983.

1584. Seah, Audrey. *Vietnam.* North Bellmore, N.Y.: Marshall Cavendish Corp., 1993.

1585. Seelig, Tina Lynn. *Incredible Edible Science.* New York: W. H. Freeman and Co., 1994.

1586. Sensier, Danielle. *Costumes.* New York: Thomson Learning, 1994.

1587. Seward, Pat. *Morocco.* North Bellmore, N.Y.: Marshall Cavendish Corp., 1995.

1588. Seward, Pat. *Netherlands.* North Bellmore, N.Y.: Marshall Cavendish Corp., 1995.

1589. Shalant, Phyllis. *Look What We've Brought You From Mexico.* New York: Julian Messner, 1992.

1590. Sharman, Rod. *Bookcrafts for Children.* Monroe, N.Y.: Trillium Press, 1988.

1591. Sheehan, Sean. *Cambodia.* Tarrytown, N.Y.: Marshall Cavendish Corp., 1996.

1592. Sheehan, Sean. *Cuba.* Tarrytown, N.Y.: Marshall Cavendish Corp., 1994.

1593. Sheehan, Sean. *Jamaica.* North Bellmore, N.Y.: Marshall Cavendish Corp., 1994.

1594. Sheehan, Sean. *Lebanon.* Tarrytown, N.Y.: Marshall Cavendish Corp., 1997.

1595. Sheehan, Sean. *Pakistan.* North Bellmore, N.Y.: Marshall Cavendish Corp., 1994.

323

1596. Sheehan, Sean. *Romania*. North Bellmore, N.Y.: Marshall Cavendish Corp., 1994.

1597. Sheehan, Sean. *Turkey*. North Bellmore, N.Y.: Marshall Cavendish Corp., 1993.

1598. Sheehan, Sean. *Zimbabwe*. North Bellmore, N.Y.: Marshall Cavendish Corp., 1993.

1599. Sherrow, Victoria. *The Hopis: Pueblo People of the Southwest*. Brookfield, Conn.: The Millbrook Press, 1993.

1600. Sherrow, Victoria. *Huskings, Quiltings, and Barn Raisings: Work-Play Parties in Early America*. New York: Walker Publishing Co., Inc., 1992.

1601. Sherrow, Victoria. *The Nez Perces: People of the Far West*. Brookfield, Conn.: The Millbrook Press, 1994.

1602. Sierra, Judy. *Fantastic Theater*. New York: The H. W. Wilson Co., 1991.

1603. Sierra, Judy. *The Flannel Board Storytelling Book*. New York: The H. W. Wilson Co., 1987.

1604. Sierra, Judy. *Multicultural Folktales*. Phoenix, Ariz.: Oryx Press, 1991.

1605. Silverthorne, Elizabeth. *Fiesta: Mexico's Great Celebrations*. Brookfield, Conn.: The Millbrook Press, 1992.

1606. Sita, Lisa. *The Rattle and the Drum: Native American Rituals and Celebrations*. Brookfield, Conn.: The Millbrook Press, 1994.

1607. *Skip Across the Ocean: Nursery Rhymes from Around the World*. New York: Orchard Books, 1995.

1608. Smith-Baranzini, Marlene. *U.S. Kids History: Book of the American Indians*. New York: Little, Brown and Co., 1994.

1609. Smith-Baranzini, Marlene. *U.S. Kids History: Book of the New American Nation*. New York: Little Brown and Co., 1995.

1610. Smith, Debbie. *Holidays & Festivals Activities*. New York: Crabtree Publishing Co., 1994.

1611. Smoothey, Marion. *Let's Investigate Codes and Sequences*. North Bellmore, N.Y.: Marshall Cavendish Corp., 1995.

1612. Solga, Kim. *Draw*. Cincinnati, Oh.: North Light Books, 1991.

1613. Solga, Kim. *Make Cards*. Cincinnati, Oh.: North Light Books, 1992.

1614. Solga, Kim. *Make Clothes Fun!* Cincinnati, Oh.: North Light Books, 1991.

1615. Solga, Kim. *Make Crafts*. Cincinnati, Oh.: North Light Books, 1993.

1616. Solga, Kim. *Make Gifts*. Cincinnati, Oh.: North Light Books, 1993.

1617. Solga, Kim. *Make Prints*. Cincinnati, Oh.: North Light Books, 1991.

1618. Solga, Kim. *Make Sculptures*. Cincinnati, Oh.: North Light Books, 1992.

1619. Solga, Kim. *Paint*. Cincinnati, Oh.: North Light Books, 1991.

1620. Sproule, Anna. *Great Britain, the Land and Its People*. Morristown, N.J.: Silver Burdett Press, 1987.

1621. Stamper, Judith Bauer. *Thanksgiving Holiday Grab Bag*. Mahway, N.J.: Troll Associates, 1993.

1622. Staples, Danny. *Flutes, Reeds and Trumpets*. Brookfield, Conn.: The Millbrook Press, 1992.

1623. Stavreva, Kirilka. *Bulgaria*. Tarrytown, N.Y.: Marshall Cavendish Corp., 1997.

1624. Steele, Philip. *Food & Feasts Between the Two World Wars*. New York: New Discovery Books, 1994.

1625. Steele, Philip. *Food & Feasts in Ancient Rome*. New York: Macmillan Publishing Co., 1994.

1626. Stoppleman, Monica. *Jewish*. Danbury, Conn.: Childrens Press, 1995.

1627. Sullivan, Margaret. *The Philippines: Pacific Crossroads*. New York: Dillon Press, 1993.

1628. Tames, Richard. *Great Britain*. New York: Franklin Watts, 1994.

1629. Tames, Richard. *Japan*. New York: Franklin Watts, 1994.

1630. Taylor, Barbara. *Create Your Own Magazine*. New York: Sterling Publishing Co., 1993.

1631. Taylor, Barbara. *Sound and Music*. New York: Warwick Press, 1990.

1632. Temko, Florence. *Traditional Crafts from Africa*. Minneapolis, Minn.: Lerner Publications Co., 1996.

1633. Terzian, Alexandra M. *The Kids' Multicultural Art Book: Art & Craft Experiences from Around the World*. Charlotte, Vt.: Williamson Publishing Co., 1993.

1634. Thompson, Helen Davis. *Let's Celebrate Kwanzaa*. New York: Gumbs & Thomas Publishers, 1992.

1635. Thomson, Ruth. *Aztecs*. New York: Franklin Watts, 1993.

1636. Thomson, Ruth. *Indians of the Plains*. New York: Franklin Watts, 1991.

1637. Thomson, Ruth. *Rice*. Ada, Okla.: Garrett Educational Corp., 1990.

1638. Thorne-Thomsen, Kathleen. *Frank Lloyd Wright for Kids: His Life and Ideas*. Chicago, Ill.: Chicago Review Press, 1994.

1639. Thorne-Thomsen, Kathleen. *Shaker Children*. Chicago, Ill.: Chicago Review Press, 1996.

1640. Tofts, Hannah. *The Paint Book*. New York: Simon & Schuster, 1990.

1641. Tofts, Hannah. *The Print Book*. New York: Simon & Schuster, 1990.

1642. Torchinsky, Oleg. *Russia*. North Bellmore, N.Y.: Marshall Cavendish Corp., 1994.

1643. Travers, P. L. *Mary Poppins in the Kitchen: A Cookery Book with a Story*. New York: Harcourt Brace Jovanovich, 1975.

1644. Treat, Rose. *The Seaweed Book: How to Find and Have Fun with Seaweed*. New York: Star Bright Books, 1995.

1645. Tunnacliffe, Chantal. *France*. Morristown, N.J.: Silver Burdett Press, 1987.

1646. Turner, Jessica Baron. *Let's Make Music! Multicultural Songs and Activities*. Milwaukee, Wis.: Hal Leonard Corp., 1994.

1647. Tythacott, Louise. *Dance*. New York: Thomson Learning, 1995.

1648. Tythacott, Louise. *Jewelry*. New York: Thomson Learning, 1995.

1649. Tythacott, Louise. *Musical Instruments*. New York: Thomson Learning, 1995.

1650. Vaughan, Marcia. *How to Cook a Gooseberry Fool*. Minneapolis, Minn.: Lerner Publications Co., 1993.

1651. Vecchione, Glen. *World's Best Outdoor Games*. New York: Sterling Publishing Co., 1992.

1652. *Vegetarian Cooking Around the World*. Minneapolis, Minn.: Lerner Publications Co., 1992.

1653. Veitch, Beverly. *Cook and Learn*. Reading, Mass.: Addison-Wesley Publishing Co., 1981.

1654. *Venture into Cultures: A Resource Book of Multicultural Materials and Programs*. Chicago, Ill.: American Library Association, 1992.

1655. Wake, Susan. *Citrus Fruits*. Minneapolis, Minn.: Carolrhoda Books, 1990.

1656. Walker, Mark. *Creative Costumes for Children (Without Sewing)*. Boca Raton, Fla.: Cool Hand Communications, 1993.

1657. Walter, F. Virginia. *Fun with Paper Bags and Cardboard Tubes*. New York: Sterling Publishing Co., 1992.

1658. Walter, F. Virginia. *Great Newspaper Crafts*. New York: Sterling Publishing Co., 1991.

1659. Walter, Mildred Pitts. *Kwanzaa: A Family Affair*. New York: Lothrop, Lee & Shepard, 1995.

1660. Wanamaker, Nancy. *More Than Graham Crackers*. Washington, D.C.: National Association for Education of Young Children, 1979.

1661. Warner, John F. *Colonial American Home Life*. New York: Franklin Watts, 1993.

1662. Warner, Penny. *Kids' Holiday Fun*. Deephaven, Minn.: Meadowbrook Press, 1994.

1663. Warren, Jean. *Exploring Wood and the Forest*. Everett, Wash.: Warren Publishing House, 1993.

1664. Warren, Jean. *Huff and Puff on Groundhog Day*. Everett, Wash.: Warren Publishing House, 1995.

1665. Waters, Alice. *Fanny at Chez Panisse*. New York: HarperCollins Publishers, 1992.

1666. Webb, Lois Sinaiko. *Holidays of the World Cookbook for Students*. Phoenix, Ariz.: Oryx Press, 1995.

1667. West, Robin. *My Very Own Halloween: A Book of Cooking and Crafts*. Minneapolis, Minn.: Carolrhoda Books, 1993.

1668. West, Robin. *My Very Own Mother's Day: A Book of Cooking and Crafts*. Minneapolis, Minn.: Carolrhoda Books, 1996.

1669. Wilcox, Jonathan. *Iceland*. Tarrytown, N.Y.: Marshall Cavendish Corp., 1996.

1670. Wilder, Laura Ingalls. *My Little House Cookbook*. New York: HarperCollins Publishers, 1996.

1671. Wilkes, Angela. *Dazzling Disguises and Clever Costumes*. New York: Dorling Kindersley Limited, 1996.

1672. Williams, Barbara. *Cookie Crafts*. New York: Holt, Rinehart and Winston, 1977.

1673. Wilsher, Jane. *Spices*. Ada, Okla.: Garrett Educational Corp., 1994.

1674. Wing, Natasha. *Jalapeno Bagels*. New York: Atheneum Books for Young Readers, 1996.

1675. Winter, Jane Kohen. *Venezuela*. North Bellmore, N.Y.: Marshall Cavendish Corp., 1991.

1676. Wolfson, Evelyn. *The Iroquois: People of the Northeast*. Brookfield, Conn.: The Millbrook Press, 1992.

1677. Wolfson, Evelyn. *The Teton Sioux: People of the Plains*. Brookfield, Conn.: The Millbrook Press, 1992.

1678. Wright, Lyndie. *Toy Theaters*. New York: Franklin Watts, 1991.

1679. Wright, Rachel. *Castles*. New York: Franklin Watts, 1992.

1680. Wright, Rachel. *Egyptians*. New York: Franklin Watts, 1992.

1681. Wright, Rachel. *Greeks*. New York: Franklin Watts, 1993.

1682. Wright, Rachel. *Knights*. New York, Franklin Watts, 1992.

1683. Wright, Rachel. *Pirates*. New York: Franklin Watts, 1991.

1684. Wright, Rachel. *Vikings*. New York: Franklin Watts, 1992.

1685. Zalben, Jane Breskin. *Beni's Family Cookbook for the Jewish Holidays*. New York: Henry Holt and Co., 1996.

1686. Zalben, Jane Breskin. *Happy New Year, Beni*. New York: Henry Holt and Co., 1993.

1687. Zalben, Jane Breskin. *Happy Passover, Rosie*. New York: Henry Holt and Co., 1990.

1688. Zaslavsky, Claudia. *Tic Tac Toe*. New York: Thomas Y. Crowell, 1982.

1689. Ziegler, Sandra. *Our St. Patrick's Day Book*. Elgin, Ill.: The Child's World, 1987.

1690. Zurlo. Tony. *China: The Dragon Awakes*. New York: Dillon Press, 1994.

1691. Adler, David A. *The Kids' Catalog of Jewish Holidays*. Philadelphia, Pa.: Jewish Publications Society, 1996.

1692. Burckhardt, Ann L. *Apples*. Mankato, Minn.: Bridgestone Books, 1996.

1693. Burckhardt, Ann L. *Corn*. Mankato, Minn.: Bridgestone Books, 1996.

1694. Burckhardt, Ann L. *The People of Africa and Their Food*. Mankato, Minn.: Capstone Press, 1996.

1695. Burckhardt, Ann L. *The People of China and Their Food*. Mankato, Minn.: Capstone Press, 1996.

1696. Burckhardt, Ann L. *The People of Mexico and Their Food*. Mankato, Minn.: Capstone Press, 1996.

1697. Burckhardt, Ann L. *The People of Russia and Their Food*. Mankato, Minn.: Capstone Press, 1996.

1698. Burckhardt, Ann L. *Pumpkins*. Mankato, Minn.: Bridgestone Books, 1996.

1699. Carlson, Laurie. *More Than Moccasins: A Kid's Activity Guide to Traditional North American Indian Life*. Chicago, Ill.: Chicago Review Press, 1994.

1700. Chambers, Catherine. *Sikh*. New York: Childrens Press, 1996.

1701. Chapman, Gillian. *Art from Rocks and Shells: With Projects Using Pebbles, Feathers, Flotsam and Jetsam.* New York: Thomson Learning, 1995.

1702. Chapman, Gillian. *Art from Wood: With Projects Using Branches, Leaves and Seeds.* New York: Thomson Learning, 1995.

1703. Corwin, Judith Hoffman. *Christmas Crafts.* New York: Franklin Watts, 1996.

1704. Corwin, Judith Hoffman. *Hanukkah Crafts.* New York: Franklin Watts, 1996.

1705. Corwin, Judith Hoffman. *Valentine Crafts.* New York: Franklin Watts, 1996.

1706. Doney, Meryl. *Masks.* New York: Franklin Watts, 1995.

1707. Doney, Meryl. *Puppets.* New York: Franklin Watts, 1995.

1708. Erlbach, Arlene. *Sidewalk Games Around the World.* Brookfield, Conn.: The Millbrook Press, 1997.

1709. Ganeri, Anita. *Hindu.* New York: Childrens Press, 1996.

1710. Hall, Zoe. *The Apple Pie Tree.* New York: The Blue Sky Press, 1996.

1711. Haskins, Jim. *Count Your Way Through Brazil.* Minneapolis, Minn.: Carolrhoda Books, 1996.

1712. Haskins, Jim. *Count Your Way Through France.* Minneapolis, Minn.: Carolrhoda Books, 1996.

1713. Haskins, Jim. *Count Your Way Through Greece.* Minneapolis, Minn.: Carolrhoda Books, 1996.

1714. Haskins, Jim. *Count Your Way Through Ireland.* Minneapolis, Minn.: Carolrhoda Books, 1996.

1715. Hetzer, Linda. *Rainy Days & Saturdays.* New York: Workman Publishing Co., 1995.

1716. Johnson, Dolores. *The Children's Book of Kwanzaa.* New York: Atheneum Books for Young Readers, 1996.

1717. Lankford, Mary D. *Christmas Around the World.* New York: Morrow Junior Books, 1995.

1718. Lankford, Mary D. *Jacks Around the World.* New York: Morrow Junior Books, 1996.

1719. Levine, Shar. *Science Around the World: Travel Through Time and Space with Fun Experiments and Projects.* New York: John Wiley & Sons, 1996.

1720. Saypol, Judyth Robbins. *My Very Own Haggadah.* Rockville, Md.: Kar-Ben Copies, 1983. Rev. ed.

1721. Tames, Richard. *Food: Feasts, Cooks & Kitchens.* New York: Franklin Watts, 1994.

1722. Tames, Richard. *Muslim.* New York: Childrens Press, 1996.

1723. Balkwill, Richard. *Food & Feasts in Ancient Egypt.* New York: New Discovery Books, 1994.

1724. Balkwill, Richard. *Food & Feasts in Tudor Times.* Parsippany, N.J.: New Discovery Books, 1995.

1725. Branigan, Keith. *Stone Age People.* Chicago, Ill.: World Book/Two-Can, 1996.

1726. Hughes, Helga. *Cooking the Irish Way.* Minneapolis, Minn.: Lerner Publications Co., 1996.

1727. Kalman, Bobbie. *Pioneer Projects.* New York: Crabtree Publishing Co., 1997.

1728. Morris, Ting. *Music.* New York: Franklin Watts, 1994.

1729. Skrepcinski, Denice. *Cody Coyote Cooks!: A Southwest Cookbook for Kids.* Berkeley, Calif.: Tricycle Press, 1996.

1730. Temko, Florence. *Traditional Crafts from Mexico and Central America.* Minneapolis, Minn.: Lerner Publications Co., 1996.

1731. Bateson-Hill, Margaret. *Lao Lao of Dragon Mountain.* New York: U.S. Media Holdings, 1996.

1732. Chapman, Gillian. *Art from Paper: With Projects Using Wastepaper and Printed Materials.* New York: Thomson Learning, 1995.

1733. *Christmas in Colonial and Early America.* Chicago, Ill.: World Book, 1996.

1734. Cody, Tod. *The Cowboy's Handbook: How to Become a Hero of the Wild West.* New York: Cobblehill Books, 1996.

1735. Faggella, Kathy. *Hands-On Cooking: Through the Seasons.* Bridgeport, Conn.: First Teacher Press, 1991.

1736. Lincoln, Margarette. *The Pirates Handbook: How to Become a Rogue of the High Seas.* New York: Cobblehill Books, 1995.

Books Indexed by Author

The bold number indicates the book number. See "Books Indexed by Number" for a numerical list of books.

Abisch, Roz. *The Make-It, Play-It Game Book.* New York: Walker and Co., 1975, **1**

Abramson, Lillian S. *Jewish Holiday Party Book.* New York: Bloch Publishing Co., 1966, **2**

Ackley, Edith Flack. *Dolls to Make for Fun and Profit.* New York: J. B. Lippincott Co., 1951, **3**

Adair, Margaret *Weeks. Folk Puppet Plays for the Social Studies.* New York: John Day, 1972, **4**

Adams, Faith. *El Salvador, Beauty Among the Ashes.* Minneapolis, Minn.: Dillon Press, 1986, **1038**

Adams, Faith. *Nicaragua, Struggling with Change.* Minneapolis, Minn.: Dillon Press, 1987, **1039**

Addy's Cookbook. Middleton, Wis.: Pleasant Company Publications, 1994, **1162**

Addy's Craft Book. Middleton, Wis.: Pleasant Company Publications, 1994, **1163**

Adeeb, Hassan. *Nigeria: One Nation, Many Cultures.* Tarrytown, N.Y.: Marshall Cavendish, 1996, **1164**

Adkins, Jan. *The Art and Industry of Sandcastles.* New York: Walker and Co., 1971, **5**

Adkins, Jan. *The Bakers.* New York: Charles Scribner's Sons, 1975, **6**

Adler, David A. *Malke's Secret Recipe.* Rockville, Md.: Kar-Ben Copies, 1989, **993**

Adler, David A. *The Kids' Catalog of Jewish Holidays.* Philadelphia, Pa.: Jewish Publications Society, 1996, **1691**

Albala, Leila. *Easy Halloween Costumes for Children.* Quebec, Canada: Alpel, Chambly, 1987, **7**

Albrechtsen, Lis. *Tepee and Moccasin, Indian Crafts for Young People.* New York: Van Nostrand Reinhold Co., 1970, **8**

Albyn, Carole Lisa. *The Multicultural Cookbook for Students.* Phoenix, Ariz.: Oryx Press, 1993, **1165**

Alden, Laura. *Halloween Safety.* Chicago, Ill.: Childrens Press, 1993, **1166**

Alden, Laura. *Thanksgiving.* Chicago, Ill.: Childrens Press, 1993, **1167**

Alexandre, Stella V. *Fall Days, Holiday Lingo.* Belmont, Calif.: David. S. Lake Publishers, 1987, **994**

Alexandre, Stella V. *Winter Days Holiday Lingo.* Belmont, Calif.: David S.Lake Publishers, 1987, **9**

Ali, Sharifah Enayat. *Afghanistan.* Tarrytown, N.Y.: Marshall Cavendish, 1995, **1168**

Aliki. *Corn Is Maize.* New York: Thomas Y. Crowell Co., 1976, **995**

Alkema, Chester Jay. *Creative Paper Crafts.* New York: Sterling Publishing Co., 1967, **10**

Alkema, Chester Jay. *Masks.* New York: Sterling Publishing Co., 1971, **11**

Alkema, Chester Jay. *Monster Masks.* New York: Sterling Publishing Co., 1973, **12**

Alkema, Chester Jay. *Puppet Making.* New York: Sterling Publishing Co., 1971, **13**

Allen, Judy. *Exciting Things to Do with Nature Materials.* New York: J. B. Lippincott Co., 1977, **14**

Allison, Linda. *Rags: Making a Little Something out of Almost Nothing.* New York: Clarkson N. Porter, 1979, **15**

Allison, Linda. *Trash Artists Workshop.* Belmont, Calif.: David S. Lake Publishers, 1981, **996**

Alton, Walter G. *Making Models from Paper and Card.* New York: Taplinger Publishing Co., 1974, **16**

Alvarado, Manuel. *Mexican Food and Drink.* New York: Bookwright Press, 1988, **17**

Amari, Suad. *Cooking the Lebanese Way.* Minneapolis, Minn.: Lerner Publications Co., 1986, **997**

American Girls Cookbook. Middleton, Wisc.: Pleasant Co., 1990, **18**

American Heart Association Kids' Cookbook. New York: Random House, 1992, **1169**

American Indian Activity Book. Dana Point, Calif.: Edupress, n.d, **1170**

Amery, Heather. *The Knowhow Book of Print and Paint.* New York: Sterling Publishing Co., 1976, **19**

Ammon, Richard. *Growing up Amish.* New York: Atheneum, 1989, **998**

Anderson, Gretchen. *The Louisa May Alcott Cookbook.* Boston: Little, Brown and Co., 1985, **20**

Anderson, Mildred. *Papier Mache and How to Use It.* New York: Sterling Publishing Co., 1971, **21**

Anderson, Mildred. *Papier Mache Crafts.* New York: Sterling Publishing Co., 1975, **22**

Andreev, Tania. *Food in Russia.* Vero Beach, Fla.: Rourke Publications, 1989, **999**

Andryszewski, Tricia. *The Seminoles: People of the Southeast.* Brookfield, Conn.: The Millbrook Press, 1995, **1172**

Animals. Caroline Pitcher, Consultant. New York: Franklin Watts, 1983, **23**

Ansary, Mir Tamim. *Afghanistan, Fighting for Freedom.* New York: Dillon Press, 1991, **1173**

Arnold, Caroline. *Land Masses, Fun, Facts and Activities.* New York: Franklin Watts, 1985, **24**

Arnold, Caroline. *Maps and Globes, Fun, Facts and Activities.* New York: Franklin Watts, 1984, **25**

Arnold, Susan Riser. *Eggshells to Objects, a New Approach to Egg Crafts.* New York: Holt, Rinehart and Winston, 1979, **26**

Artman, John. *Indians: An Activity Book.* Carthage, Ill.: Good Apple, 1987, **27**

Arvois, Edmond. *Making Mosaics.* New York: Sterling Publishing Co., 1964, **28**

Ashe, Rosalind. *Children's Literary Houses.* New York: Facts on File Publications, 1984, **29**

Asher, Jane. *Jane Asher's Costume Book.* Menlo Park, Calif.: Open Chain Publishing, 1983, **1174**

At the Zoo. Des Moines, Iowa: Better Homes and Gardens, Meredith Corporation, 1989, **1040**

Atyeo, Marilyn. *Birthdays, a Celebration.* Atlanta, Ga.: Humanics Limited, 1984, **30**

Ayer, Eleanor H. *Germany: In the Heartland of Europe.* Tarrytown, N.Y.: Marshall Cavendish, 1996, **1175**

Ayer, Eleanor H. *Poland: A Troubled Past, a New Start.* Tarrytown, N.Y.: Marshall Cavendish, 1996, **1176**

Babin, Stanley. *Dance Around the World.* New York: MCA Music, 1969, **1000**

Bacon, Josephine. *Cooking the Israeli Way.* Minneapolis, Minn.: Lerner Publications Co., 1986, **1001**

Bailey, Vanessa. *Shadow Theater.* New York: Gloucester Press, 1991, **1177**

Baker, Charles F. *The Classical Companion.* Peterborough, N.H.: Cobblestone Publishing, 1988, **1041**

Baker, James W. *April Fools' Day Magic.* Minneapolis, Minn.: Lerner Publications Co., 1989, **31**

Baker, James W. *Arbor Day Magic.* Minneapolis, Minn.: Lerner Publications Co., 1990, **1002**

Baker, James W. *Birthday Magic.* Minneapolis, Minn.: Lerner Publications Co., 1988, **32**

Baker, James W. *Christmas Magic.* Minneapolis, Minn.: Lerner Publications Co., 1988, **33**

Baker, James W. *Columbus Day Magic.* Minneapolis, Minn.: Lerner Publications Co., 1990, **1003**

Baker, James W. *Halloween Magic.* Minneapolis, Minn.: Lerner Publications Co., 1988, **34**

Baker, James W. *Independence Day Magic.* Minneapolis, Minn.: Lerner Publications Co., 1990, **1004**

Baker, James W. *New Year's Magic.* Minneapolis, Minn.: Lerner Publications Co., 1989, **35**

Baker, James W. *Presidents' Day Magic.* Minneapolis, Minn.: Lerner Publications Co., 1989, **36**

Baker, James W. *St. Patrick's Day Magic.* Minneapolis, Minn.: Lerner Publications Co., 1990, **1005**

Baker, James W. *Thanksgiving Magic.* Minneapolis, Minn.: Lerner Publications Co., 1989, **37**

Baker, James W. *Valentine Magic.* Minneapolis, Minn.: Lerner Publications Co., 1988, **38**

Baldwin, Margaret. *Thanksgiving.* New York: Franklin Watts, 1983, **39**

Balerdi, Susan. *France: The Crossroads of Europe.* Minneapolis, Minn.: Dillon Press, 1984, **1042**

Balkwill, Richard. *Food & Feasts in Ancient Egypt.* New York: New Discovery Books, 1994, **1723**

Balkwill, Richard. *Food & Feasts in Tudor Times.* Parsippany, N.J.: New Discovery Books, 1995, **1724**

Barchers, Suzanne I. *Cooking Up U.S. History.* Englewood, Colo.: Libraries Unlimited, 1991, **1043**

Barkin, Carol. *Happy Thanksgiving.* New York: Lothrop, Lee and Shepard Books, 1987, **41**

Barkin, Carol. *Happy Valentine's Day.* New York: Lothrop, Lee and Shepard Books, 1988, **40**

Barkin, Carol. *The Scary Halloween Costume Book.* New York: Lothrop, Lee and Shepard Books, 1983, **42**

Barr, Marilyn. *Patterns for Pinwheels, Pop-Ups, and Puppets.* Belmont, Calif.: David S. Lake Publishers, 1988, **1006**

Barrett-Dragon, Patricia. *The Kid's Cookbook: Yum! I Eat It.* Concord, Calif.: Nitty Gritty Productions, 1982. Rev. ed, **1178**

Barron, Cheryl Carter. *Great Parties for Young Children.* New York: Walker and Co., 1981, **43**

Barry, Sheila Anne. *The World's Best Travel Games.* New York: Sterling Publishing Co., 1987, **1044**

Barta, Ginevera. *Metric Cooking for Beginners.* Short Hills, N.J.: Enslow Publishers, 1978, **45**

Barta, Stacie Hill. *Wacky Cakes and Water Snakes.* New York: Penguin Books, 1995, **1179**

Barth, Edna. *Lilies, Rabbits, and Painted Eggs, The Story of the Easter Symbols.* New York: The Seabury Press, 1970, **44**

Barwell, Eve. *Disguises You Can Make.* New York: Lothrop, Lee and Shepard Co., 1977, **46**

Barwell, Eve. *Make Your Pet a Present.* New York: Lothrop, Lee and Shepard Co., 1977, **47**

Bastyra, Judy. *Hanukkah Fun.* New York: Kingfisher, 1996, **1180**

Bateson-Hill, Margaret. *Lao Lao of Dragon Mountain.* New York: U.S. Media Holdings, 1996, **1731**

Batho, Margot. *Sandcasting.* Minneapolis, Minn.: Lerner Publications Co., 1973, **48**

Bauer, Caroline Feller. *Celebrations.* New York: H. W. Wilson Co., 1985, **49**

Bauman, Toni. *Winter Wonders.* Carthage, Ill.: Good Apple, 1986, **50**

Bawden, Juliet. *101 Things to Make.* New York: Sterling Publishing Co., 1994, **1181**

Baxter, Nicola. *Explorations.* New York, Franklin Watts, 1994, **1182**

Baxter, Nicola. *Invaders and Settlers.* New York: Franklin Watts, 1994, **1183**

Baxter, Nicola. *The Romans: Facts, Things to Make, Activities.* New York: Franklin Watts, 1992, **1184**

Beard, Lina. *The American Girls Handy Book.* Boston: David R. Godine, 1987, **51**

Beaton, Clare. *Cards.* New York: Warwick Press, 1990, **1045**

Beaton, Clare. *Costumes.* New York: Warwick Press, 1990, **1007**

Beaton, Clare. *Face Painting.* New York: Warwick Press, 1990, **1046**

Beaton, Clare. *T-Shirt Painting.* New York: Warwick Press, 1990, **1047**

Beaton, Clare. *The Complete Book of Children's Parties.* New York: Kingfisher Books, 1992, **1185**

Becker, Joyce. *Bible Crafts.* New York: Holiday House, 1982, **52**

Becker, Joyce. *Hanukkah Crafts.* New York: Bonim Books, 1978, **53**

Beckman, Carol. *Channels to Children, Early Childhood Activities.* Colorado Springs, Colo.: Channels to Children, 1982, **54**

Beetschen, Louis. *Country Treasures.* New York: Pantheon Books, 1971, **55**

Beetschen, Louis. *Seaside Treasures.* New York: Pantheon Books, 1971, **56**

Beilenson, Evelyn L. *Early American Cooking, Recipes from America's Historic Sites.* White Plains, N.Y.: Peter Pauper Press, 1985, **57**

Benarde, Anita. *Games from Many Lands.* New York: Sayre Publishing, 1970, **58**

Benbow, Mary. *Dolls, Traditional and Topical, and How to Make Them.* Boston: Plays, 1970, **59**

Bender, Lionel. *Crocodiles and Alligators.* New York: Gloucester Press, 1988, **60**

Bender, Lionel. *Lizards and Dragons.* New York: Gloucester Press, 1988, **61**

Berenstain, Michael. *The Castle Book.* New York: David McKay Co., 1977, **62**

Berenstain, Stan. *The Berenstain Bears' Make and Do Book.* New York: Random House, 1984, **1008**

Berger, Gilda. *Easter and Other Spring Holidays.* New York: Franklin Watts, 1983, **64**

Berman, Paul. *Make-Believe Empire, a How-To Book.* New York: Atheneum, 1982, **65**

Bernstein, Bonnie. *Native American Crafts Workshop.* Fearon Teacher Aids. Belmont, Calif.: Pitman Learning, 1982, **63**

Best Kids Cook Book by the Sunset Editors. Menlo Park, Calif.: Sunset Publishing Corp., 1992, **1186**

Bider, Djemma. *A Drop of Honey.* New York: Simon & Schuster, 1988, **1187**

Bird Buddies. Des Moines, Iowa: Better Homes and Gardens, Meredith Corporation, 1989, **1048**

Bird, Malcolm. *The Christmas Handbook.* New York: Barron's Educational Series, 1986, **1049**

Birdseye, Tom. *A Kid's Guide to Building Forts.* Tucson, Ariz.: Harbinger House, 1993, **1188**

Bisignano, Alphonse. *Cooking the Italian Way.* Minneapolis, Minn.: Lerner Publications Co., 1982, **1009**

Bittinger, Gayle. *Exploring Sand and the Desert.* Everett, Wash.: Warren Publishing House, 1993, **1189**

Bittinger, Gayle. *Exploring Water and the Ocean.* Everett, Wash.: Warren Publishing House, 1993, **1190**

Biucchi, Edwina. *Italian Food and Drink.* New York: The Bookwright Press, 1987, **66**

Bjork, Christina. *Linnea's Almanac.* New York: R & S Books, Farrar, Straus and Giroux, 1989, **1010**

Blocksma, Mary. *Action Contraptions.* New York: Prentice Hall Books, Simon and Schuster, 1987, **67**

Blocksma, Mary. *Space-Crafting, Invent Your Own Flying Spaceships.* New York: Simon and Schuster, 1986, **68**

Blood, Charles L. *American Indian Games and Crafts.* New York: Franklin Watts, 1981, **69**

Bodger, Lorraine. *Crafts for All Seasons.* New York: Universe Books, 1980, **70**

Boechler, Gwenn. *A Piece of Cake.* Garden City, N.Y.: Doubleday and Co., 1989, **1011**

Bond, Carol Taylor. *Marmalade Days: Fall.* Livonia, Mich.: Partner Press, 1987, **1191**

Bond, Carol Taylor. *Marmalade Days: Spring.* Mt. Rainier, Md.: Gryphon House, 1988, **1192**

Bond, Carol Taylor. *Marmalade Days: Winter.* Livonia, Mich.: Partner Press, 1987, **1193**

Bonvillain, Nancy. *The Haidas: People of the Northwest Coast.* Brookfield, Conn.: The Millbrook Press, 1994, **1194**

Boorer, Michael. *Life of Strange Mammals.* Morristown, N.J.: Silver Burdett Co., 1979, **1012**

Borghese, Anita. *The Down to Earth Cookbook.* New York: Charles Scribner's Sons, 1973, **71**

Borghese, Anita. *The International Cookie Jar Cookbook.* New York: Charles Scribner's Sons, 1975, **72**

Borlenghi, Patricia. *Italy.* New York: Franklin Watts 1993, **1195**

Bos, Bev. *Don't Move the Muffin Tins.* Roseville, Calif.: Turn the Page Press, 1978, **73**

Boteler, Alison. *The Children's Party Handbook.* Woodbury, N.Y.: Barron's, 1986, **74**

Bottomley, Jim. *Paper Projects for Creative Kids of All Ages.* Boston: Little, Brown and Co., 1983, **75**

Bourgeois, Paulette. *The Amazing Apple.* Reading, Mass.: Addison-Wesley Publishing Co., 1987, **1013**

Bourgeois, Paulette. *The Amazing Paper Book.* Reading, Mass.: Addison-Wesley Publishing Co., 1989, **1196**

Bourgeois, Paulette. *The Amazing Potato Book.* Reading, Mass.: Addison-Wesley Publishing Co., 1991, **1197**

Bowden, Marcia. *Nature for the Very Young.* New York: John Wiley and Sons, 1989, **1014**

Bowman, Bruce. *Toothpick Sculpture & Ice-Cream Stick Art.* New York: Sterling Publishing Co., 1976, **76**

Boxer, Arabella. *The Wind in the Willows Cookbook.* New York: Charles Scribner's Sons, 1983, **77**

Brady, April A. *Kwanzaa Karamu: Cooking and Crafts for a Kwanzaa Feast.* Minneapolis, Minn.: Carolrhoda Books, 1995, **1198**

Braham, Clare Bonfanti. *Happy Birthday, Grandma Moses: Activities for Special Days Throughout the Year.* Chicago, Ill.: Chicago Review Press, 1995, **1199**

Branigan, Keith. *Stone Age People.* Chicago, Ill.: World Book/Two-Can, 1996, **1725**

Brashears, Deya. *Circle Time Activities for Young Children.* Orinda, Calif.: Deya Brashears, 1981, **1200**

Brashears, Deya. *Dribble Drabble, Art Experiences for Young Children.* Fort Collins, Colo.: DMC Publications, 1985, **78**

Bresnahan, Michaeline. *The Happiest Birthdays.* Lexington, Mass.: The Stephen Greene Press, 1988, **1015**

Bresnahan, Michaeline. *The No-Sew Costume Book.* New York: Stephen Greene Press, 1990, **1050**

Breznau, Claudia. *Container Crafts.* Minneapolis, Minn.: Judy/Instructo, 1981., **79**

Bridgewater, Alan. *Holiday Crafts, More Year-Round Crafts Kids Can Make.* Blue Ridge Summit, Pa.: Tab Books, 1990, **1016**

Bridgewater, Alan. *I Made It Myself.* Blue Ridge Summit, Pa.: Tab Books, 1990, **1051**

Briggs, Diane. *Flannel Board Fun.* Metuchen, N.J.: The Scarecrow Press, 1992, **1201**

Brinn, Ruth Esrig. *Let's Celebrate, 57 Jewish Holiday Crafts for Young Children.* Rockville, Md.: Kar-Ben Copies, 1977, **80**

Brinn, Ruth Esrig. *Let's Have a Party.* Rockville, Md.: Kar-Ben Copies, 1981, **81**

Brinn, Ruth Esrig. *More Let's Celebrate, Fifty-Seven All New...* Rockville, Md.: Kar-Ben Copies, 1984, **82**

Brock, Virginia. *Pinatas.* New York: Abingdon Press, 1966, **83**

Brockway, Maureen. *Clay Projects.* Minneapolis, Minn.: Lerner Publications Co., 1973, **85**

Brokamp, Marilyn. *Once upon a Cereal Box.* Minneapolis, Minn.: T. S. Denison and Co., 1982, **84**

Brokaw, Meredith. *The Penny Whistle Birthday Party Book.* New York: Simon & Schuster, 1992, **1202**

Brokaw, Meredith. *The Penny Whistle Christmas Party Book.* New York: Simon & Schuster, 1991, **1203**

Brokaw, Meredith. *The Penny Whistle Lunch Box Book.* New York: Weidenfeld & Nicolson, 1989, **1204**

Brokaw, Meredith. *The Penny Whistle Party Planner.* New York: Weidenfeld and Nicolson, 1987, **86**

Brook, Bonnie. *Let's Celebrate Easter, a Book of Drawing Fun.* Mahwah, N.J. Watermill Press, 1988, **87**

Brown, Anne Houlihan. *The Colonial South.* Vero Beach, Fla.: Rourke Publications, 1994, **1205**

Brown, Elizabeth Burton. *Grains, An Illustrated History with Recipes.* Englewood Cliffs, N.J.: Prentice-Hall, 1977, **88**

Brown, Fern G. *Valentine's Day.* New York: Franklin Watts, 1983, **89**

Brown, Jerome C. *Fables and Tales Papercrafts.* Belmont, Calif.: Fearon Teacher Aids, 1989, **91**

Brown, Jerome C. *Folk Tale Papercrafts.* Belmont, Calif.: David S. Lake Publishers, 1989, **92**

Brown, Jerome C. *Great Gifts for All Occasions.* Belmont, Calif.: Fearon Teacher Aids, 1986, **93**

Brown, Jerome C. *Holiday Art Projects.* Belmont, Calif.: Fearon Teacher Aids, 1984, **94**

Brown, Jerome C. *Holiday Crafts and Greeting Cards.* Belmont, Calif.: Fearon Teacher Aids, 1983, **95**

Brown, Jerome C. *Holiday Gifts and Decorations.* Belmont, Calif.: David S. Lake Publishers, 1986, **96**

Brown, Jerome C. *Paper Designs.* Belmont, Calif.: David S. Lake Publishers, 1983, **97**

Brown, Jerome C. *Paper Menagerie.* Belmont, Calif.: David S. Lake Publishers, 1984, **98**

Brown, Jerome C. *Papercrafts for All Seasons.* Belmont, Calif.: David S. Lake Publishers, 1984, **99**

Brown, Jerome C. *Puppets and Mobiles.* Belmont, Calif.: Fearon Teacher Aids, 1983, **100**

Brown, Jerome C. *Tales from Many Lands Papercrafts.* Carthage, Ill.: Fearon Teacher Aids, 1991, **1206**

Brown, Jerome C. *The Dinosaur Color and Pattern Book.* Belmont, Calif.: David S. Lake Publishers, 1989, **90**

Brown, Marc. *Finger Rhymes.* New York: E. P. Dutton, 1980, **101**

Brown, Marc. *Hand Rhymes.* New York: E. P. Dutton, 1985, **102**

Brown, Marc. *Party Rhymes.* New York: E. P. Dutton, 1988, **103**

Brown, Marc. *Play Rhymes.* New York: E. P. Dutton, 1987, **104**

Brown, Osa. *The Metropolitan Museum of Art Activity Book.* New York: Random House, 1983, **105**

Bruun-Rasmussen, Jens Ole. *Make-Up, Costumes and Masks.* New York: Sterling Publishing Co., 1976, **106**

Bryant, Adam. *Canada, Good Neighbor to the World.* Minneapolis, Minn.: Dillon Press, 1987, **1052**

Buchwald, Claire. *The Puppet Book: How to Make and Operate Puppets.* Boston: Plays, 1990, **1158**

Buell, Hal. *Festivals of Japan.* New York: Dodd, Mead and Co., 1965, **107**

Bugs, Bugs, Bugs. Des Moines, Iowa: Better Homes and Gardens, Meredith Corporation, 1989, **1053**

Build Your Own Airport. Caroline Pitcher, Consultant. New York: Franklin Watts, 1985, **108**

Build Your Own Castle. Caroline Pitcher, Consultant. New York: Franklin Watts, 1985, **110**

Build Your Own Farm Yard. Caroline Pitcher, Consultant. New York: Franklin Watts, 1985, **111**

Build Your Own Space Station. Caroline Pitcher, Consultant. New York: Franklin Watts, 1985, **112**

Burch, Joann J. *Kenya, Africa's Tamed Wilderness.* New York: Dillon Press, 1992, **1207**

Burckhardt, Ann L. *Apples.* Mankato, Minn.: Bridgestone Books, 1996, **1692**

Burckhardt, Ann L. *Corn.* Mankato, Minn.: Bridgestone Books, 1996, **1693**

Burckhardt, Ann L. *Pumpkins.* Mankato, Minn.: Bridgestone Books, 1996, **1698**

Burckhardt, Ann L. *The People of Africa and Their Food.* Mankato, Minn.: Capstone Press, 1996, **1694**

Burckhardt, Ann L. *The People of China and Their Food.* Mankato, Minn.: Capstone Press, 1996, **1695**

Burckhardt, Ann L. *The People of Mexico and Their Food.* Mankato, Minn.: Capstone Press, 1996, **1696**

Burckhardt, Ann L. *The People of Russia and Their Food.* Mankato, Minn.: Capstone Press, 1996, **1697**

Burggraf, Manfred. *Fun with Colored Foil.* New York: Watson-Guptill Publications, 1968, **113**

Burns, Diane L. *Arbor Day.* Minneapolis, Minn.: Carolrhoda Books, 1989, **1208**

Burns, Marilyn. *Good Times. Every Kid's Book of Things to Do.* New York: Bantam Books, 1979, **114**

Burns, Marilyn. *The Hanukkah Book.* New York: Four Winds Press, 1981, **115**

Burstein, Chaya M. *A First Jewish Holiday Cookbook.* New York: Bonim Books, 1979, **116**

Burstein, Chaya M. *A Kid's Catalog of Israel.* New York: Jewish Publications Society, 1988, **117**

Burt, Erica. *Natural Materials.* Vero Beach, Fla.: Rourke Enterprises, 1990, **1054**

Busenberg, Bonnie. *Vanilla, Chocolate and Strawberry: The Story of Your Favorite Flavors.* Minneapolis, Minn.: Lerner Publications Co., 1994, **1209**

Butzow, Carol M. *Science Through Children's Literature.* Englewood, Colo.: Libraries Unlimited, 1989, **1055**

Caballero, Jane A. *Art Projects for Young Children.* Atlanta. Ga.: Humanics Limited, 1979, **1056**

Caket, Colin. *Model a Monster, Making Dinosaurs from Everyday Materials.* New York: Blandford Press, 1986, **1057**

Campbell, Jeanette R. *Pop-Up Animals.* Monterey, Calif.: Evan-Moor Corp., 1989, **1210**

Caney, Steven. *Kids' America.* New York: Workman Publishing, 1978, **118**

Caney, Steven. *Steven Caney's Invention Book.* New York: Workman Publishing Co., 1985, **119**

Caney, Steven. *Steve Caney's Playbook.* New York: Workman Publishing Co., 1975, **120**

Caney, Steven. *Steven Caney's Toy Book.* New York: Workman Publishing Co., 1972, **121**

Cappelloni, Nancy. *Ethnic Cooking the Microwave Way.* Minneapolis, Minn.: Lerner Publications Co., 1994, **1211**

Carlisle, Jody. *Classroom Nursery Rhymes Activity Kit.* West Nyack, N.Y.: The Center for Applied Research in Education, 1983, **122**

Carlson, Bernice Wells. *Let's Find the Big Idea.* Nashville, Tenn.: Abingdon Press, 1982, **1212**

Carlson, Bernice Wells. *Make It Yourself.* New York: Abingdon Press, 1950, **123**

Carlson, Bernice Wells. *Picture That!* Nashville, Tenn.: Abingdon Press, 1977, **125**

Carlson, Bernice Wells. *Quick Wits and Nimble Fingers.* Nashville, Tenn.: Abingdon Press, 1979, **126**

Carlson, Bernice Wells. *The Party Books for Boys and Girls.* New York: Abingdon Press, 1963, **124**

Carlson, Laurie. *EcoArt!* Charlotte, Vt.: Williamson Publishing Co., 1993, **1213**

Carlson, Laurie. *Kids Create.* Charlotte, Vt.: Williamson Publishing Co., 1990, **1017**

Carlson, Laurie. *More Than Moccasins: A Kid's Activity Guide to Traditional North American Indian Life.* Chicago, Ill.: Chicago Review Press, 1994, **1699**

Carlson, Laurie. *Westward Ho!: An Activity Guide to the Wild West.* Chicago, Ill.: Chicago Review Press, 1996, **1214**

Carpenter, Mark L. *Brazil, An Awakening Giant.* Minneapolis, Minn.: Dillon Press, 1987, **1058**

Carrick, Graham. *Wood.* Vero Beach, Fla.: Rourke Enterprises, 1990, **1059**

Carroll, David. *Make Your Own Chess Set.* Englewood Cliffs, N.J.: Prentice-Hall, 1974, **127**

Carroll, Jeri A. *Learning About Spring and Summer Holidays.* Carthage, Ill.: Good Apple, 1988, **128**

Cars and Boats. Caroline Pitcher, Consultant. New York: Franklin Watts, 1983, **129**

Carson, Dale. *Native New England Cooking.* Old Saybrook, Conn.: Peregrine Press, Publishers, 1980, **130**

Cary, Pam. *North American Food and Drink.* New York: The Bookwright Press, 1988, **131**

Cauley, Lorinda Bryan. *Pease Porridge Hot.* New York: G. P. Putnam's Sons, 1977, **1215**

Cauley, Lorinda Bryan. *Things to Make and Do for Thanksgiving.* New York: Franklin Watts, 1977, **132**

Cefali, Leslie. *Cook-A-Book.* Hagerstown, Md.: Alleyside Press, 1991, **1216**

Celebrate Everyday, Hundreds of Celebrations. Edited by Lisa Lyons Durkin. Bridgeport, Conn.: First Teacher Press, 1987, **134**

Celebrate. First United Nursery School. Oak Park, Ill.: Rainbow Publishing Co., 1987, **133**

Chacon, Rick. *Grocery Bag Art, Careers.* Huntington Beach, Calif.: Teacher Created Materials, 1985, **135**

Chacon, Rick. *Grocery Bag Art, Circus.* Huntington Beach, Calif.: Teacher Created Materials, 1985, **136**

Chacon, Rick. *Grocery Bag Art, Farm.* Huntington Beach, Calif.: Teacher Created Materials, 1985, **137**

Chacon, Rick. *Grocery Bag Art, Holidays.* Huntington Beach, Calif.: Teacher Created Materials, 1985, **138**

Chambers, Catherine. *Sikh.* New York: Childrens Press, 1996, **1700**

Chambers, Catherine. *Spain.* New York: Franklin Watts, 1993, **1217**

Chan, Barbara J. *Kid Pix Around the World: A Multicultural Computer Activity Book.* Reading, Mass.: Addison-Wesley Publishing Co., 1993, **1218**

Chapman, Gillian. *Art from Fabric: With Projects Using Rags, Old Clothing and Remnants.* New York: Thomson Learning, 1995, **1219**

Chapman, Gillian. *Art from Paper: With Projects Using Wastepaper and Printed Materials.* New York: Thomson Learning, 1995, **1732**

Chapman, Gillian. *Art from Rocks and Shells: With Projects Using Pebbles, Feathers, Flotsam and Jetsam.* New York: Thomson Learning, 1995, **1701**

Chapman, Gillian. *Art from Wood: With Projects Using Branches, Leaves and Seeds.* New York: Thomson Learning, 1995, **1702**

Chapman, Jean. *Pancakes and Painted Eggs, a Book for Easter and All the Days of...* Chicago, Ill.: Childrens Press, 1983, **139**

Chapman, Jean. *The Sugar-Plum Christmas Book.* Chicago, Ill.: Childrens Press, 1977, **140**

Chatham-Baker, Odette. *Baby Lore: Ceremonies, Myths and Traditions to Celebrate a Baby's Birth.* New York: Macmillan Publishing Co., 1991, **1220**

Cheng, Pang-Guek. *Canada.* North Bellmore, N.Y.: Marshall Cavendish Corp., 1994, **1515**

Cheong-Lum, Roseline Ng. *Haiti.* Tarrytown, N.Y.: Marshall Cavendish Corp., 1994, **1221**

Chernoff, Goldie Taub. *Clay-Dough, Play-Dough.* New York: Walker and Co., 1974, **141**

Chernoff, Goldie Taub. *Easy Costumes You Don't Have to Sew.* New York: Four Winds Press, 1975, **142**

Children Are Children Are Children. Ann Cole et al. Boston: Little, Brown and Co., 1978, **143**

Chivers, David. *Gorillas and Chimpanzees.* New York: Gloucester Press, 1987, **144**

Choate, Judith. *Patchwork.* Garden City, N.Y.: Doubleday and Co., 1976, **145**

Choate, Judith. *Scrapcraft.* Garden City, N.Y.: Doubleday and Co., 1973, **146**

Chocolate, Deborah M. Newton. *Kwanzaa.* Chicago, Ill.: Childrens Press, 1990, **1060**

Chorzempa, Rosemary A. *My Family Tree Workbook: Genealogy for Beginners.* New York: Dover Publications, 1982, **1222**

Christian, Rebecca. *Cooking the Spanish Way.* Minneapolis, Minn.: Lerner Publications Co., 1982, **147**

Christmas. Caroline Pitcher, Consultant. New York: Franklin Watts, 1983, **148**

Christmas Around the World: A Celebration. Dorset, England: New Orchards Editions Ltd., Sterling Publishing Co., 1978, **149**

Christmas in Brazil. Chicago, Ill.: World Book, 1991, **1223**

Christmas in Britain. Chicago, Ill.: World Book, 1988, **1224**

Christmas in Canada. Chicago, Ill.: World Book, 1994, **1225**

Christmas in Colonial and Early America. Chicago, Ill.: World Book, 1996, **1733**

Christmas in Denmark. Chicago, Ill.: World Book, 1986, **1226**

Christmas in France. Chicago, Ill.: World Book, 1988, **1227**

Christmas in Germany. Chicago, Ill.: Passport Books, NTC Publishing Corp., 1991, **1228**

Christmas in Ireland. Chicago, Ill.: World Book, 1985, **1229**

Christmas in Italy. Chicago, Ill.: World Book, 1988, **1230**

Christmas in Russia. Chicago, Ill.: World Book, 1992, **1231**

Christmas in the Holy Land. Chicago, Ill.: World Book, 1987, **1232**

Christmas in the Philippines. Chicago, Ill.: World Book, 1990, **1233**

Christmas in Today's Germany. Chicago, Ill.: World Book, 1993, **1234**

Christmas in Washington, D.C. Chicago, Ill.: World Book, 1988, **1235**

Christmas Is Coming, Volume 2. Birmingham, Ala.: Oxmoor House, 1992, **1236**

Christmas Trims Kids Can Make. Des Moines, Iowa: Meredith Corporation, 1988, **150**

Chung, Okwha. *Cooking the Korean Way.* Minneapolis, Minn.: Lerner Publications Co., 1988, **1019**

Churchill, E. Richard. *Building with Paper.* New York: Sterling Publishing Co., 1990, **1020**

Churchill, E. Richard. *Fast and Funny Paper Toys You Can Make.* New York: Sterling Publishing Co., 1989, **151**

Churchill, E. Richard. *Holiday Paper Projects.* New York: Sterling Publishing Co., 1992, **1237**

Churchill, E. Richard. *Instant Paper Toys.* New York: Sterling Publishing Co., 1986, **152**

Churchill, E. Richard. *Paper Toys That Fly, Soar, Zoom & Whistle.* New York: Sterling Publishing Co., 1989, **153**

Churchill, E. Richard. *Terrific Paper Toys.* New York: Sterling Publishing Co., 1991, **1238**

Cifarelli, Megan. *India: One Nation, Many Traditions.* Tarrytown, N.Y.: Marshall Cavendish, 1996, **1239**

Civardi, Anne. *The Knowhow Book of Action Games.* New York: Sterling Publishing Co., 1976, **154**

Clark, Elizabeth. *Fish.* Minneapolis, Minn.: Carolrhoda Books, 1990, **1061**

Clark, Elizabeth. *Meat.* Minneapolis, Minn.: Carolrhoda Books, 1990, **1021**

Cline, Dallas. *Cornstalk Fiddle and Other Homemade Instruments.* New York: Oak Publications, Div. of Embassy Music Corp., 1976, **156**

Cobb, Mary. *Practical Patterns.* Belmont, Calif.: Fearon Teacher Aids, 1989, **157**

Cobb, Mary. *The Quilt-Block History of Pioneer Days: With Projects Kids Can Make.* Brookfield, Conn.: The Millbrook Press, 1995, **1240**

Cobb, Vicki. *The Secret Life of School Supplies.* New York: J. B. Lippincott Co., 1981, **158**

Cochrane, Louise. *Tabletop Theatres and Plays.* Boston: Plays, 1974, **159**

Cody, Tod. *The Cowboy's Handbook: How to Become a Hero of the Wild West.* New York: Cobblehill Books, 1996, **1734**

Cohen, Lynn. *Fairy Tale World.* Palo Alto, Calif.: Monday Morning Books, 1986, **161**

Colbridge, A. M. *Scale Models in Balsa.* New York: Taplinger Publishing Co., 1971, **162**

Cole, Ann. *Purple Cow to the Rescue.* Boston: Little, Brown and Co., 1982, **163**

Cole, Marion. *Things to Make and Do for Easter.* New York: Franklin Watts, 1979, **164**

Coleman, Anne. *Fabrics and Yarns.* Vero Beach, Fla.: Rourke Enterprises, 1990, **1062**

Coleman, South. *Jordan.* Tarrytown, N.Y.: Marshall Cavendish Corp., 1997, **1241**

Coleman, South. *Syria.* North Bellmore, N.Y.: Marshall Cavendish Corp., 1995, **1242**

Collier, James Lincoln. *Jugbands and Handmade Music.* New York: Grosset and Dunlap, 1973, **165**

Collins, Carolyn Strom. *The World of Little House.* New York: HarperCollins Publishers, 1996, **1243**

Collis, Len. *Card Games for Children.* Hauppauge, N.Y.: Barron's Educational Series, 1990, **1063**

Colonial Holiday Treats. High Point, N.C.: Hutcraft, 1971, **166.**

Comins, Jeremy. *Chinese and Japanese Crafts and Their Cultural Backgrounds.* New York: Lothrop, Lee and Shepard Co., 1978, **167**

Comins, Jeremy. *Eskimo Crafts and Their Cultural Backgrounds.* New York: Lothrop, Lee and Shepard Co., 1975, **168**

Comins, Jeremy. *Latin American Crafts and Their Cultural Backgrounds.* New York: Lothrop, Lee and Shepard Co., 1974, **169**

Comins, Jeremy. *Slotted Sculpture from Cardboard.* New York: Lothrop, Lee and Shepard Co., 1977, **170**

Comins, Jeremy. *Totems, Decoys and Covered Wagons.* New York: Lothrop, Lee and Shepard Co., 1976, **171**

Commins, Elaine. *Lessons from Mother Goose.* Atlanta, Ga.: Humanics Learning, 1989, **172**

Conaway, Judith. *City Crafts from Secret Cities.* Chicago, Ill.: Follett Publishing Co., 1978, **173**

Conaway, Judith. *Dollhouse Fun, Furniture You Can Make.* Mahwah, N.J.: Troll Associates, 1987, **174**

Conaway, Judith. *Easy-to-Make Christmas Crafts.* Mahwah, N.J.: Troll Associates, 1986, **175**

Conaway, Judith. *Great Gifts to Make.* Mahwah, N.J.: Troll Associates, 1986, **176**

Conaway, Judith. *Great Indoor Games from Trash and Other Things.* Milwaukee, Wisc.: Raintree Publishers Limited, 1977, **177**

Conaway, Judith. *Happy Day! Things to Make and Do.* Mahwah, N.J.: Troll Associates, 1987, **178**

Conaway, Judith. *Happy Haunting, Halloween Costumes You Can Make.* Mahwah, N.J.: Troll Associates, 1986, **179**

Conaway, Judith. *Happy Thanksgiving, Things to Make and Do.* Mahwah, N.J.: Troll Associates, 1986, **180**

Conaway, Judith. *Make Your Own Costumes and Disguises.* Mahwah, N.J.: Troll Associates, 1987, **181**

Conaway, Judith. *Manos, South American Crafts for Children.* Chicago, Ill.: Follett Publishing Co., 1978, **182**

Conaway, Judith. *Springtime Surprises! Things to Make and Do.* Mahwah, N.J.: Troll Associates, 1986, **183**

Conaway, Judith. *Things That Go, How to Make Toy Boats, Cars, and Planes.* Mahwah, N.J.: Troll Associates, 1987, **184**

Cook, Deanna F. *The Kids' Multicultural Cookbook: Food & Fun Around the World.* Charlotte, Vt.: Williamson Publishing Co., 1995, **1244**

Cooke, Jean. *Projects for Easter and Holiday Activities.* Ada, Okla.: Garrett Educational Corp., 1989, **1245**

Cooper, Kay. *Where Did You Get Those Eyes.* New York: Walker and Co., 1988, **185**

Cooper, Michael. *Things to Make and Do for George Washington's Birthday.* New York: Franklin Watts, 1979, **186**

Cooper, Terry Touff. *Many Friends Cooking, An International Cookbook for Boys and Girls.* New York: Philomel Books, 1980, **187**

Cooper, Terry Touff. *Many Hands Cooking.* New York: Thomas Y. Crowell Co., 1974, **188**

Coronado, Rosa. *Cooking the Mexican Way.* Minneapolis, Minn.: Lerner Publications Co., 1982, **189**

Corwin, Judith Hoffman. *African Crafts.* New York: Franklin Watts, 1990, **1022**

Corwin, Judith Hoffman. *Asian Crafts.* New York: Franklin Watts, 1992, **1246**

Corwin, Judith Hoffman. *Birthday Fun.* New York: Julian Messner, 1986, **190**

Corwin, Judith Hoffman. *Christmas Crafts.* New York: Franklin Watts, 1996, **1703**

Corwin, Judith Hoffman. *Colonial American Crafts, the Home.* New York: Franklin Watts, 1989, **191**

Corwin, Judith Hoffman. *Colonial American Crafts, the School.* New York: Franklin Watts, 1989, **192**

Corwin, Judith Hoffman. *Colonial American Crafts, The Village.* New York: Franklin Watts, 1989, **193**

Corwin, Judith Hoffman. *Cookie Fun.* New York: Julian Messner, 1985, **194**

Corwin, Judith Hoffman. *Creative Collage.* New York: David McKay Co., 1980, **195**

Corwin, Judith Hoffman. *Easter Crafts: A Holiday Craft Book.* New York: Franklin Watts, 1994, **1247**

Corwin, Judith Hoffman. *Easter Fun.* New York: Julian Messner, 1984, **196**

Corwin, Judith Hoffman. *Halloween Crafts: A Holiday Craft Book.* New York: Franklin Watts, 1995, **1248**

Corwin, Judith Hoffman. *Halloween Fun.* New York: Julian Messner, 1983, **197**

Corwin, Judith Hoffman. *Hanukkah Crafts.* New York: Franklin Watts, 1996, **1704**

Corwin, Judith Hoffman. *Harvest Festivals Around the World.* Parsippany, N.J.: Julian Messner, 1995, **1249**

Corwin, Judith Hoffman. *Kwanzaa Crafts: A Holiday Craft Book.* New York: Franklin Watts, 1995, **1250**

Corwin, Judith Hoffman. *Latin American and Caribbean Crafts.* New York: Franklin Watts, 1991, **1251**

Corwin, Judith Hoffman. *Papercrafts, Origami, Papier-Mache, and Collage.* New York: Franklin Watts, 1988, **198**

Corwin, Judith Hoffman. *Patriotic Fun.* New York: Julian Messner, 1985, **199**

Corwin, Judith Hoffman. *Thanksgiving Crafts.* New York: Franklin Watts, 1995, **1252**

Corwin, Judith Hoffman. *Valentine Crafts.* New York: Franklin Watts, 1996, **1705**

Corwin, Judith Hoffman. *Valentine Fun.* New York: Julian Messner, 1982, **200**

Coskey, Evelyn. *Christmas Crafts for Everyone.* Nashville, Tenn.: Abingdon, 1976, **1023**

Coskey, Evelyn. *Easter Eggs for Everyone.* New York: Abingdon Press, 1973, **201**

Cosman, Madeline Pelner. *Medieval Holidays and Festivals.* New York: Charles Scribner's Sons, 1981, **202**

Cosner, Shaaron. *Masks Around the World and How to Make Them.* New York: David McKay Co., 1979, **204**

Cox, Marcia Lynn. *Creature Costumes.* New York: Grosset and Dunlap, 1977, **205**

Coyle, Rena. *My First Baking Book.* New York: Workman Publishing Co., 1988, **206**

Coyle, Rena. *My First Cookbook.* New York: Workman Publishing Co., 1985, **207**

Cracchiolo, Rachelle. *Calendar Activities.* Sunset Beach, Calif.: Teacher Created Materials, 1980, **208**

Cracchiolo, Rachelle. *Holiday Cards.* Sunset Beach, Calif.: Teacher Created Materials, 1982, **209**

Crafts for Celebration. Caroline Bingham/Karen Foster, editors. Brookfield, Conn.: The Millbrook Press, 1993, **1253**

Crafts for Decoration. Caroline Bingham/Karen Foster, editors. Brookfield, Conn.: The Millbrook Press, 1993, **1254**

Crafts for Everyday Life. Caroline Bingham/Karen Foster, editors. Brookfield, Conn.: The Millbrook Press, 1993, **1255**

Crafts for Play. Caroline Bingham/Karen Foster, editors. Brookfield, Conn.: The Millbrook Press, 1993, **1256**

Crafts in Action: Ideas for Special Occasions. North Bellmore, N.Y.: Marshall Cavendish Corp., 1991, **1257**

Crafts in Action: Ideas from Nature. North Bellmore, N.Y.: Marshall Cavendish Corp., 1991, **1258**

Crafts in Action: Making Gifts. North Bellmore, N.Y.: Marshall Cavendish Corp., 1991, **1259**

Crafts in Action: Making Models & Games. North Bellmore, N.Y.: Marshall Cavendish Corp., 1991, **1260**

Crafts in Action: Using Paper & Paint. North Bellmore, N.Y.: Marshall Cavendish Corp., 1991, **1261**

Crafts in Action: Using Yarn, Fabric and Thread. North Bellmore, N.Y.: Marshall Cavendish Corp., 1991, **1262**

Cramblit, Joella. *Flowers Are for Keeping.* New York: Julian Messner, 1979, **210**

Crazy Creatures. Better Homes and Gardens. Des Moines, Iowa: Meredith Corporation, 1988, **1024**

Crocker, Betty. *Betty Crocker's Boys and Girls Microwave Cookbook.* New York: Prentice-Hall, 1992, **1263**

Cross, Jeanne. *Simple Printing Methods.* New York: S. G. Phillips, 1972, **211**

Cummings, Richard. *Make Your Own Model Forts and Castles.* New York: David McKay Co., 1977, **212**

Cummings, Richard. *101 Costumes for All Ages, All Occasions.* Boston: Plays, 1987, **213**

Curtis, Annabelle. *Knowhow Book of Paper Fun.* New York: Sterling Publishing Co., 1976, **214**

Cutler, Katherine N. *Crafts for Christmas.* New York: Lothrop, Lee and Shepard Co., 1974, **215**

Cutler, Katherine N. *Creative Shellcraft.* New York: Lothrop, Lee and Shepard Co., 1971, **216**

Cutler, Katherine N. *From Petals to Pinecones.* New York: Lothrop, Lee and Shepard Co., 1969, **217**

Cuyler, Margery. *The All-Around Christmas Book.* New York: Holt, Rinehart and Winston, 1982, **218**

Cuyler, Margery. *The All-Around Pumpkin Book.* New York: Holt, Rinehart and Winston, 1980, **219**

Dahl, Felicity. *Roald Dahl's Revolting Recipes.* New York: Viking, 1994, **1264**

D'Alelio, Jane. *I Know That Building.* Washington, D.C.: The Preservation Press, 1989., **220**

D'Amato, Jane Potter. *Who's a Horn? What's an Antler? Crafts of Bone and Horn.* New York: Julian Messner, 1982, **229**

D'Amato, Janet, and Alex D'Amato. *African Crafts for You to Make.* New York: Julian Messner, 1969, **222**

D'Amato, Janet, and Alex D'Amato. *Algonquian and Iroquois, Crafts for You to Make.* New York: Julian Messner, 1979, **223**

D'Amato, Janet, and Alex D'Amato. *American Indian Craft Inspirations.* New York: M. Evans and Co., 1972, **224**

D'Amato, Janet, and Alex D'Amato. *Colonial Crafts for You to Make.* New York: Julian Messner, 1975, **225**

D'Amato, Janet, and Alex D'Amato. *Handicrafts for Holidays.* New York: Lion Press, 1967, **226**

D'Amato, Janet, and Alex D'Amato. *Indian Crafts.* New York: Sayre Publishing, 1968, **227**

D'Amato, Janet, and Alex D'Amato. *More Colonial Crafts for You to Make.* New York: Julian Messner, 1977, **228**

D'Amico, Joan. *The Science Chef Travels Around the World: Fun Food Experiments and Recipes for Kids.* New York: John Wiley & Sons, 1996, **1265**

Dandy Dinosaurs. Better Homes and Gardens. Des Moines, Iowa: Meredith Corporation, 1989, **230**

Darling, Abigail. *Teddy Bear's Picnic Cookbook.* New York: Viking Penguin, 1991, **1272**

Darling, Kathy. *Alphabet Crafts.* Palo Alto, Calif.: Monday Morning Books, 1985, **231**

Darling, Kathy. *Holiday Hoopla: Plays, Parades, Parties.* Palo Alto, Calif.: Monday Morning Books, 1990, **1266**

Davidson, Judith. *Japan, Where East Meets West.* Minneapolis, Minn.: Dillon Press, 1983, **1064**

Dawson, Imogen. *Food & Feasts in Ancient Greece.* Parsippany, N.J.: New Discovery Books, 1995, **1267**

Dawson, Imogen. *Food & Feasts in the Middle Ages.* New York: Macmillan Publishing Co., 1994, **1268**

Dawson, Imogen. *Food & Feasts with the Aztecs.* Parsippany, N.J.: New Discovery Books, 1994, **1269**

Dawson, Jean Elizabeth. *A Date with a Plate.* Bloomfield, Conn.: Junior Arts and Crafts House, 1981, **233**

Dawson, Jean Elizabeth. *Frog's Legs and Scrambled Eggs.* Bloomfield, Conn.: Junior Arts and Crafts House, 1981, **232**

Dawson, Jean Elizabeth. *It's in the Bag.* Bloomfield, Conn.: Junior Arts and Crafts House, 1981, **234**

Day and Night. Des Moines, Iowa: Better Homes and Gardens, Meredith Corporation, 1989, **1065**

Day, Jon. *Magic.* New York: Thomson Learning, 1994, **1270**

Deacon, Eileen. *It's Fun to Make Pictures.* New York: Grosset and Dunlap Publishers, 1972, **235**

Deacon, Eileen. *Making Jewelry.* Milwaukee, Wisc.: Raintree Childrens Books, 1977, **236**

Dean, Audrey Vincente. *Make a Prehistoric Monster.* New York: Taplinger Publishing Co., 1977, **237**

Dean, Audrey Vincente. *Wooden Spoon Puppets.* Boston: Plays, 1976, **238**

Dean, Bill. *Book of Balsa Models.* New York: Arco Publishing Co., 1970, **239**

Dellinger, Annetta. *Creative Games for Young Children.* Elgin, Ill.: The Child's World, 1986, **240**

Dennee, JoAnne. *In the Three Sisters Garden.* Montpelier, Vt.: Food Works, 1995, **1271**

Denny, Roz. *A Taste of Britain.* New York: Thomson Learning, 1994, **1273**

Denny, Roz. *A Taste of China.* New York: Thomson Learning, 1994, **1274**

Denny, Roz. *A Taste of France.* New York: Thomson Learning, 1994, **1275**

Denny, Roz. *A Taste of India.* New York: Thomson Learning, 1994, **1276**

DePaola, Tomie. *Things to Make and Do for Valentine's Day.* New York: Franklin Watts, 1976, **241**

Deshpande, Chris. *Festival Crafts.* Milwaukee, Wis.: Gareth Stevens Publishing, 1994, **1277**

Deshpande, Chris. *Food Crafts. .* Milwaukee, Wis.: Gareth Stevens Publishing, 1994, **1278**

Deshpande, Chris. *Silk.* Ada, Okla.: Garrett Educational Corp., 1994, **1279**

Desserts Around the World. Minneapolis, Minn.: Lerner Publications Co., 1991, **1280**

Devlin, Wendy. *Cranberry Easter.* New York: Four Winds Press, 1990, **1066**

Devlin, Wendy. *Cranberry Halloween.* New York: Four Winds Press, 1982, **242**

Devlin, Wendy. *Cranberry Thanksgiving.* New York: Four Winds Press, 1980, **243**

Devlin, Wendy. *Cranberry Valentine.* New York: Four Winds Press, 1986, **244**

Devonshire, Hilary. *Christmas Crafts.* New York: Franklin Watts, 1990, **1025**

Devonshire, Hilary. *Collage.* New York: Franklin Watts, 1988, **245**

Devonshire, Hilary. *Greeting Cards and Gift Wrap.* New York: Franklin Watts, 1992, **1281**

Diamond, Arthur. *Egypt, Gift of the Nile.* New York: Dillon Press, 1992, **1282**

Dickinson, Gill. *Children's Costumes.* Secaucus, N.J.: Chartwell Books, 1993, **1283**

Diehn, Gwen. *Kid Style Nature Crafts: 50 Terrific Things to Make With Nature's Materials.* New York: Sterling Publishing Co., 1995, **1284**

Diehn, Gwen. *Nature Crafts for Kids.* New York: Sterling Publishing Co., 1992, **1285**

Dieringer, Beverly. *The Paper Bead Book.* New York: David McKay Co., 1977, **246**

Dietrich, Wilson G. *Create with Paper Bags.* Minneapolis, Minn.: T. S. Dennison and Co., 1972, **247**

Dinosaurs and Monsters. Caroline Pitcher, Consultant. New York: Franklin Watts, 1984, **248**

DiNoto, Andrea. *Anytime, Anywhere, Anybody, Games.* Racine, Wisc.: Golden Press, Western Publishing Co., 1977, **249**

Disney, Walt. *The Mickey Mouse Make-It Book.* New York, Random House, 1974, **250**

Do a Zoom Do. Edited by Bernice Chesler. Boston: Little, Brown and Co., 1975, **251**

Dobrin, Arnold. *Make a Witch, Make a Goblin, A Book of Halloween Crafts.* New York: Four Winds Press, 1977, **252**

Dondiego, Barbara L. *After-School Crafts.* Blue Ridge Summit, Pa.: Tab Books, 1992, **1286**

Dondiego, Barbara L. *Crafts for Kids. A Month by Month Idea Book.* Blue Ridge Summit, Pa.: Tab Books, 1984, **253**

Dondiego, Barbara L. *Crafts for Kids.* Blue Ridge Summit, Pa.: Tab Books, 1991, **1067**

Dondiego, Barbara L. *Year Round Crafts for Kids.* Blue Ridge Summit, Pa.: Tab Books, 1987, **254**

Doney, Meryl. *Masks.* New York: Franklin Watts, 1995, **1706**

Doney, Meryl. *Puppets.* New York: Franklin Watts, 1995, **1707**

Donna, Natalie. *Bead Craft.* New York: Lothrop, Lee and Shepard Co., 1972, **255**

Donna, Natalie. *Peanut Craft.* New York: Lothrop, Lee and Shepard Co., 1974, **257**

Donna, Natalie. *The Peanut Cookbook.* New York: Lothrop, Lee and Shepard Co., 1976, **256**

Donner, Michael. *Bike, Skate and Skateboard Games.* Racine, Wisc.: Golden Press, Western Publishing Co., 1977, **258**

Don't Lick the Spoon Before You Put It in the Pot. Florissant, Mo.: Ferguson-Florissant School District, 1982, **259**

Dooley, Norah. *Everybody Bakes Bread.* Minneapolis, Minn.: Carolrhoda Books, 1996, **1287**

Dooley, Norah. *Everybody Cooks Rice.* Minneapolis, Minn.: Carolrhoda Books, 1991, **1068**

Dowell, Ruth I. *Move Over, Mother Goose.* Mt. Rainier, Md.: Gryphon House, 1987, **260**

Downer, Lesley. *Japanese Food and Drink.* New York: The Bookwright Press, 1988, **261**

Drew, Helen. *My First Music Book.* New York: Dorling Kindersley, 1993, **1288**

Drucker, Malka. *Grandma's Latkes.* New York: Harcourt Brace Jovanovich Publishers, 1992, **1290**

Drucker, Malka. *Hanukkah, Eight Nights, Eight Lights.* New York: Holiday House, 1980, **262**

Drucker, Malka. *Passover, A Season of Freedom.* New York: Holiday House, 1981, **263**

Drucker, Malka. *Rosh Hashanah and Yom Kippur, Sweet Beginnings.* New York: Holiday House, 1981, **264**

Drucker, Malka. *Shabbat, A Peaceful Island.* New York: Holiday House, 1983, **265**

Drucker, Malka. *Sukkot, A Time to Rejoice.* New York: Holiday House, 1982, **266**

Drucker, Malka. *The Family Treasury of Jewish Holidays.* New York: Little, Brown and Co., 1994, **1289**

DuBois, Jill. *Colombia.* Freeport, N.Y.: Marshall Cavendish Corp., 1991., **1291**

DuBois, Jill. *Greece.* North Bellmore, N.Y.: Marshall Cavendish Corp., 1992, **1292**

DuBois, Jill. *Korea.* North Bellmore, N.Y.: Marshall Cavendish Corp., 1993, **1293**

Duch, Mabel. *Easy-to-Make Puppets.* Boston, Mass.: Plays, 1993, **1294**

Dyson, John. *Fun with Kites.* Woodbury, N.Y.: Barron's Educational Series, 1978, **1026**

Earl, Amanda. *Masks.* New York: Thomson Learning, 1995, **1295**

Earth Makers Lodge. Peterborough, N.H.: Cobblestone Publishing, 1994, **1296**

Easy Crafts Book. New York: Sterling Publishing Co., 1975, **267**

Eaton, Marge. *Flower Pressing.* Minneapolis, Minn.: Lerner Publications, 1973, **268**

Eden, Maxwell. *Kiteworks.* New York: Sterling Publishing Co., 1989, **1069**

Egger-Bovet, Howard. *U.S. Kids History: Book of the American Colonies.* Covelo, Calif.: Yolla Bolly Press, 1996, **1297**

Egger-Bovet, Howard. *U.S. Kids History: Book of the American Revolution.* Covelo, Calif.: Little, Brown and Co., 1994, **1298**

Einhorn, Barbara. *West German Food and Drink.* New York: The Bookwright Press, 1989, **269**

Eisner, Vivienne. *A Boat, A Bat, And a Beanie, Things to Make from Newspaper.* New York: Lothrop, Lee and Shepard Co., 1977, **270**

Eisner, Vivienne. *Quick and Easy Holiday Costumes.* New York: Lothrop, Lee and Shepard Co., 1977, **272**

Eisner, Vivienne. *The Newspaper Everything Book.* New York: E. P. Dutton and Co., 1975, **271**

Elbert, Virginie Fowler. *Christmas Crafts and Customs Around the World.* Englewood Cliffs, N.J.: Prentice-Hall, 1984, **273**

Elbert, Virginie Fowler. *Clayworks, Colorful Crafts Around the World.* New York: Simon and Schuster, 1987, **1070**

Elbert, Virginie Fowler. *Folk Toys Around the World.* Englewood Cliffs, N.J.: Prentice-Hall, 1984, **1027**

Elbert, Virginie Fowler. *Paperworks, Colorful Crafts from Picture Eggs to Fish Kites.* Englewood Cliffs, N.J.: Prentice-Hall, 1982, **274**

Ellington, Merlene. *The Fun Collection: Activities for School and Home.* Roswell, Ga.: Blackberry Press, 1986, **275**

Elliot, Marion. *My Party Book.* New York: Little, Brown and Co., 1994, **1299**

Elliot, Marion. *Papier Mache Project Book.* Secaucus, N.J.: Chartwell Books, 1992, **1300**

Ellison, Virginia H. *The Pooh Cook Book.* New York: E. P. Dutton and Co., 1969, **276**

Ellison, Virginia H. *The Pooh Get-Well Book.* New York: E. P. Dutton and Co., 1973, **1028**

Ellison, Virginia H. *The Pooh Party Book.* New York: E. P. Dutton and Co., 1971, **277**

Engels, Susan. *Big Oak Busy Book.* Madison, Wisc.: Big Oak Child Care Center, 1988, **278**

Englander, Lois. *The Jewish Holiday Do-Book.* New York: Bloch Publishing Co., 1976, **279**

Epstein, Sam. *A Year of Japanese Festivals.* Champaign, Ill.: Garrard Publishing Co., 1974, **280**

Erickson, Donna. *More Prime Time Activities with Kids.* Minneapolis, Minn.: Augsburg Fortress, 1992, **1301**

Erlbach, Arlene. *Peanut Butter.* Minneapolis, Minn.: Lerner Publications Co., 1994., **1302**

Erlbach, Arlene. *Sidewalk Games Around the World.* Brookfield, Conn.: The Millbrook Press, 1997, **1708**

Esbenshade, Richard S. *Hungary.* North Bellmore, N.Y.: Marshall Cavendish Corp., 1994, **1303**

Eshmeyer, R. E. *Ask Any Vegetable.* Englewood Cliffs, N.J.: Prentice-Hall, 1975, **1304**

Evans, Mary. *How to Make Historic American Costumes.* Detroit, Mich.: Gale Research Co., 1976, **281**

Everix, Nancy. *Ethnic Celebrations Around the World.* Carthage, Ill.: Good Apple, 1991, **1305**

Everix, Nancy. *Windows to the World.* Carthage, Ill.: Good Apple, 1984, **282**

Face Painting. Palo Alto, Calif.: Klutz Press, 1990, **1306**

Facklam, Margery. *Corn-Husks Crafts.* New York: Sterling Publishing Co., 1973, **283**

Faggella, Kathy. *Building on Books.* Bridgeport, Conn.: First Teacher Press, 1987, **284**

Faggella, Kathy. *Concept Cookery.* Bridgeport, Conn.: First Teacher Press, 1985, **285**

Faggella, Kathy. *Crayons, Crafts and Concepts.* Bridgeport, Conn.: First Teacher Press, 1985, **286**

Faggella, Kathy. *Hands-On Cooking: Through the Seasons.* Bridgeport, CT: First Teacher Press, 1991, **1735**

Falconer, Kieran. *Peru.* Tarrytown, N.Y.: Marshall Cavendish Corp., 1995, **1307**

Farley, Carol. *Korea, A Land Divided.* Minneapolis, Minn.: Dillon Press, 1983, **1071**

Farnay, Josie. *Egypt: Activities & Projects in Color.* New York: Sterling Publishing Co., 1979, **287**

Feelings, Muriel. *Jambo Means Hello, Swahili Alphabet Book.* New York: The Dial Press, 1974, **288**

Feelings, Muriel. *Moja Means One, Swahili Counting Book.* New York: The Dial Press, 1971, **289**

Felicity's Cookbook. Middleton, Wis.: Pleasant Company Publications, 1994, **1308**

Felicity's Craft Book. Middleton, Wis.: Pleasant Company Publications, 1994, **1309**

Feller, Ron. *Fairy Tales.* Seattle, Wa.: The Arts Factory, 1989, **290**

Feller, Ron. *Paper Masks and Puppets for Stories, Songs and Plays.* Seattle, Wa.: The Arts Factory, 1985, **291**

Fiarotta, Noel. *Music Crafts for Kids.* New York: Sterling Publishing Co., 1993, **1310**

Fiarotta, Phyllis. *Be What You Want to Be, The Complete Dress-Up and Pretend Craft Book.* New York: Workman Publishing Co., 1977. , **293**

Fiarotta, Phyllis. *Confetti, The Kids Make-It-Yourself, Do-It-Yourself Party Book.* New York: Workman Publishing, 1978, **294**

Fiarotta, Phyllis. *Cups & Cans & Paper Plate Fans.* New York: Sterling Publishing Co., 1992, **1311**

Fiarotta, Phyllis. *Pin It, Tack It, Hang It, The Big Book of Kids Bulletin Board Ideas.* New York: Workman Publishing Co., 1975, **295**

Fiarotta, Phyllis. *Snips & Snails & Walnut Whales, Nature Crafts for Children.* New York: Workman Publishing Co., 1975, **296**

Fiarotta, Phyllis. *Sticks & Stones & Ice Cream Cones.* New York: Workman Publishing Co., 1973, **297**

Fiarotta, Phyllis. *The You and Me Heritage Tree, Ethnic Crafts For Children.* New York: Workman Publishing Co., 1976, **298**

Fichter, George S. *American Indian Music and Musical Instruments.* New York: David McKay Co., 1978, **299**

Fife, Bruce. *Dr. Dropo's Balloon Sculpturing for Beginners.* Colorado Springs, Colo.: Java Publishing Co., 1988, **300**

Filstrup, Chris. *Beadazzled, The Story of Beads.* New York: Frederick Warne, 1982, **301**

Filstrup, Chris. *China, From Emperors to Communes.* Minneapolis, Minn.: Dillon Press, 1983, **1072**

Finger Frolics. Liz Cromwell, comp. Pleasant Hills, Calif.: Discovery Toys, Revised Edition, 1983, **302**

Fingerplays and Action Poems for Preschoolers. Florissant, Mo.: Ferguson-Florissant School District, 1979, **292**

Fischer, Robert. *Hot Dog.* New York: Julian Messner, 1980, **303**

Fisher, Timothy. *Hovels and Houses.* Reading, Mass.: Addison-Wesley Publishing Co., 1977, **1312**

Fitzjohn, Sue. *Festivals Together.* Gloucestershire, U.K.: Hawthorn Press, 1993, **1313**

Five-Minute Faces by Snazaroo. New York: Random House, 1992, **1314**

Fleischner, Jennifer. *The Aztecs: People of the Southwest.* Brookfield, Conn.: The Millbrook Press, 1994, **1315**

Fleischner, Jennifer. *The Inuit: People of the Arctic*. Brookfield, Conn.: The Millbrook Press, 1995, **1316**

Fletcher, Helen Jill. *String Projects*. Garden City, N.Y.: Doubleday and Co., 1974, **304**

Flora, Sherrill. *Holidays and Special Times*. Minneapolis, Minn.: T. S. Denison and Co., 1986, **305**

Flores, Anthony. *From the Hands of a Child*. Belmont, Calif.: Fearon Teacher Aids, David S. Lake Publishers, 1987, **306**

Foley, Erin L. *Costa Rica*. Tarrytown, N.Y.: Marshall Cavendish Corp., 1997, **1317**

Foley, Erin L. *Dominican Republic*. Tarrytown, N.Y.: Marshall Cavendish Corp., 1994, **1318**

Foley, Erin L. *Ecuador*. North Bellmore, N.Y.: Marshall Cavendish Corp., 1995, **1319**

Ford, Marianne. *Copycats & Artifacts*. Boston, Mass.: David R. Godine, Publisher, 1983, **1320**

Ford, Mary. *Party Cakes*. Dorset, England: Mary Ford Cake Artistry Centre Ltd., 1988, **1073**

Fordham, Derek. *Eskimos*. Morristown, N.J.: Silver Burdett, 1979, **307**

Forte, Imogene. *Holidays*. Nashville, Tenn.: Incentive Publications, 1983, **308**

Forte, Imogene. *Patterns, Projects and Plans*. Nashville, Tenn.: Incentive Publications, 1982, **309**

Forte, Imogene. *Puddles and Wings and Grapevine Swings*. Nashville, Tenn.: Incentive Publications, 1982, **310**

Forte, Imogene. *Puppets*. Nashville, Tenn.: Incentive Publications, 1985, **311**

Foster, Laura Louise. *Keeping the Plants You Pick*. New York: Thomas Y. Crowell Co., 1970, **312**

Fox, Lilla M. *Costumes and Customs of the British Isles*. Boston: Plays, 1974, **313**

Fredericks, Anthony D. *Social Studies Through Children's Literature*. Englewood, Colo.: Teacher Ideas Press, Libraries Unlimited, 1991, **1321**

Fressard, M. J. *Creating with Burlap*. New York: Sterling Publishing Co., 1970, **314**

Friedrichsen, Carol S. *The Pooh Craft Book*. New York: E. P. Dutton and Co., 1976, **315**

Frith, Penelope. *The Stick It, Stitch It and Stuff It Toybook*. New York: M. Evans and Co., 1974, **316**

Fronval, George. *Indian Signs and Signals*. New York: Sterling Publishing Co., 1978, **317**

Fry-Miller, Kathleen. *Peace Works, Young Peace Makers Project Book II*. Elgin, Ill.: Brethren Press, 1989, **318**

Fuller, Barbara. *Britain*. North Bellmore, N.Y.: Marshall Cavendish Corp., 1994, **1322**

Gabor, Bob. *Costume of the Iroquois and How to Make It*. Ontario, Canada: Iroqrafts Ltd., 1983, **1323**

Gallagher, Patricia C. *Robin's Play and Learn Book*. Worcester, Pa.: Gallagher, Jordan and Associates, 1987, **319**

Galvin, Irene Flum. *Brazil: Many Voices, Many Faces*. Tarrytown, N.Y.: Marshall Cavendish Corp., 1996, **1324**

Galvin, Irene Flum. *Japan: A Modern Land with Ancient Roots*. Tarrytown, N.Y.: Marshall Cavendish Corp., 1996, **1325**

Games. Caroline Pitcher, Consultant. New York: Franklin Watts, 1984, **320**

Games of the World; How to Make Them. Zurich, Switzerland: Swiss Committee for UNICEF, 1982, **1074**

Ganeri, Anita. *Focus on Romans*. New York: Gloucester Press, 1992, **1326**

Ganeri, Anita. *France*. New York: Franklin Watts, 1993, **1327**

Ganeri, Anita. *Hindu*. New York: Childrens Press, 1996, **1709**

Ganeri, Anita. *India*. New York: Franklin Watts, 1994, **1328**

Ganeri, Anita. *Mexico*. New York: Franklin Watts, 1994, **1329**

Ganeri, Anita. *Vikings*. New York: Gloucester Press, 1992, **1330**

Garland, Sherry. *Vietnam, Rebuilding a Nation*. Minneapolis, Minn.: Dillon Press, 1990, **1075**

Garrett, Sandra. *The Pacific Northwest Coast*. Vero Beach, Fla.: Rourke Publications, 1994, **1331**

Gaspari, Claudia. *Food in Italy*. Vero Beach, Fla.: Rourke Publications, 1989, **321**

Gates, Frieda. *Easy to Make American Indian Crafts*. New York: Harvey House Publishers, 1981, **324**

Gates, Frieda. *Easy to Make Monster Masks and Disguises*. New York: Harvey House Publishers, 1979, **322**

Gates, Frieda. *Easy to Make Puppets*. New York: Harvey House Publishers, 1976, **323**

Gates, Frieda. *Glove, Mitten, And Sock Puppets*. New York: Walker and Co., 1978, **325**

Gates, Frieda. *Monsters and Ghouls, Costumes and Lore*. New York. Walker and Co., 1980, **326**

Gates, Frieda. *North American Indian Masks, Craft and Legend*. New York: Walker and Co., 1982, **327**

Gaylord, Susan Kapuscinski. *Multicultural Books to Make and Share*. New York: Scholastic, 1994, **1332**

Gemming, Elizabeth. *The Cranberry Book*. New York: Coward-McCann, 1983, **328**

Germaine, Elizabeth. *Cooking the Australian Way*. Minneapolis, Minn.: Lerner Publications Co., 1990, **1076**

Gertz, Susan E. *Teaching Physical Science Through Children's Literature*. Middletown, Ohio: Terrific Science Press, 1996, **1333**

Ghinger, Judith. *New Year's to Christmas-Hooray Days, Things to Make and Do*. Racine, Wisc.: Western Publishing Co., 1977, **329**

Gibbons, Gail. *Things to Make and Do for Columbus Day*. New York: Franklin Watts, 1977, **330**

Gibbons, Gail. *Things to Make and Do for Halloween*. New York: Franklin Watts, 1976, **331**

Gibbons, Gail. *Things to Make and Do for Your Birthday*. New York: Franklin Watts, 1978, **332**

Giblin, James Cross. *Fireworks, Picnics and Flags*. New York: Clarion Books, 1983, **333**

Giblin, James. *The Scarecrow Book*. New York: Crown Publishers, 1980, **334**

Gibrill, Martin. *African Food and Drink*. New York: The Bookwright Press, 1989, **335**

Gilbreath, Alice. *Candles for Beginners to Make*. New York: William Morrow and Co., 1975, **336**

Gilbreath, Alice. *Fun with Weaving*. New York: William Morrow and Co., 1976, **337**

Gilbreath, Alice. *Making Costumes for Parties, Plays and Holidays.* New York: William Morrow and Co., 1974, **338**

Gilbreath, Alice. *Making Toys That Crawl and Slide.* Chicago, Ill.: Follett Publishing Co., 1978, **339**

Gilbreath, Alice. *Making Toys That Swim and Float.* Chicago, Ill.: Follett Publishing Co., 1978, **340**

Gilbreath, Alice. *Simple Decoupage.* New York: William Morrow and Co., 1978, **341**

Gilbreath, Alice. *Spouts, Lids and Cans, Fun with Familiar Metal Objects.* New York: William Morrow and Co., 1973, **342**

Giles, Nancy H. *Creative Milk Carton Crafts.* Carthage, Ill: Good Apple, 1989, **1334**

Gillies, John. *Soviet Union: The World's Largest Country.* Minneapolis, Minn.: Dillon Press, 1985, **1077**

Gillis, Jennifer Storey. *In a Pumpkin Shell: Over 20 Pumpkin Projects for Kids.* Pownal, Vt.: Storey Communications, 1992, **1335**

Girl Scouts of the U.S. Girl Scout Cookbook. Chicago, Ill.: Henry Regnery Co., 1971, **343**

Girl Scouts of the U.S.A. *Games for Girl Scouts.* New York: Girl Scouts of the U.S.A., 1969, **1078**

Gish, Steven. *Ethiopia.* Tarrytown, N.Y.: Marshall Cavendish Corp., 1996, **1336**

Glass, Paul. *Songs and Stories of the North American Indians.* New York: Grosset and Dunlap, 1970, **344**

Glovach, Linda. *The Little Witch's Black Magic Book of Games.* Englewood Cliffs, N.J.: Prentice-Hall, 1974, **345**

Glovach, Linda. *The Little Witch's Book of Toys.* New York: Prentice-Hall Books, 1986, **346**

Glovach, Linda. *The Little Witch's Carnival Book.* Englewood Cliffs, N.J.: Prentice-Hall, 1982, **347**

Glovach, Linda. *The Little Witch's Cat Book.* Englewood Cliffs, N.J.: Prentice-Hall, 1985, **348**

Glovach, Linda. *The Little Witch's Christmas Book.* Englewood Cliffs, N.J.: Prentice-Hall, 1974, **349**

Glovach, Linda. *The Little Witch's Dinosaur Book.* Englewood Cliffs, N.J.: Prentice-Hall, 1984, **350**

Glovach, Linda. *The Little Witch's Spring Holiday Book.* Englewood Cliffs, N.J.: Prentice-Hall, 1983, **351**

Glovach, Linda. *The Little Witch's Summertime Book.* Englewood Cliffs, N.J.: Prentice-Hall, 1986, **352**

Glovach, Linda. *The Little Witch's Thanksgiving Book.* Englewood Cliffs, N.J.: Prentice-Hall, 1976, **353**

Glovach, Linda. *The Little Witch's Valentine Book.* Englewood Cliffs, N.J.: Prentice-Hall, 1984, **354**

Gogniat, Maurice. *Indian Toys You Can Make.* New York: Sterling Publishing Co., 1976, **355**

Gogniat, Maurice. *Wild West Toys You Can Make.* New York: Sterling Publishing Co., 1976, **356**

Goin, Kenin. *Tools, Readiness Activities for Preschool and Kindergarten.* New York: Chatterbox Press, 1987, **357**

Gold-Vukson, Marji. *Can You Imagine? Creative Drawing Adventures for the Jewish Holidays.* Rockville, Md.: Kar-Ben Copies, 1992, **1337**

Goldin, Barbara Diamond. *Cakes and Miracles.* New York: Viking Penguin, 1991, **1079**

Gomez, Aurelia. *Crafts of Many Cultures.* New York: Scholastic Professional Books, 1992, **1338**

Gomez, Paolo. *Food in Mexico.* Vero Beach, Fla.: Rourke Publications, 1989, **1339**

Good, Phyllis Pellman. *Amish Cooking for Kids.* Intercourse, Pa.: Good Books, 1994, **1340**

Goodwin, Bob. *A Taste of Spain.* New York: Thomson Learning, 1995, **1341**

Gordon, Patricia. *Asian Indians.* New York: Franklin Watts, 1990, **1343**

Gordon, Patricia. *Kids Learn America: Bringing Geography to Life with People, Places and History.* Charlotte, Vt.: Williamson Publishing Co., 1991, **1342**

Goss, Linda. *It's Kwanzaa Time.* New York: G. P. Putnam's Sons, 1995, **1344**

Graham, Ada. *Foxtails, Ferns, & Fish Scales.* New York: Four Winds Press, 1976, **358**

Graham, Terry. *Let Loose on Mother Goose.* Nashville, Tenn.: Incentive Publications, 1982, **1029**

Grainger, Sylvia. *How to Make Your Own Moccasins.* New York: J. B. Lippincott Co., 1977, **359**

Grayson, Marion F. *Let's Do Fingerplays.* Washington, D.C.: Robert B. Luce, 1962, **360**

Green, Jen M. *Making Crazy Faces and Masks.* New York: Gloucester Press, 1992, **1345**

Green, Jen M. *Making Mad Machines.* New York: Gloucester Press, 1992, **1346**

Green, M. C. *Space Age Puppets and Masks.* Boston: Plays, 1969, **361**

Green, Mary Ann. *Projects for Christmas.* Ada, Okla.: Garrett Educational Corp., 1989, **1080**

Greenaway, Kate. *Kate Greenaway's Book of Games.* New York: Viking Press, 1976, **362**

Greenberg, Janet. *California.* Vero Beach, Fla.: Rourke Publications, 1994, **1347**

Greenberg, Judith E. *Jewish Holidays.* New York: Franklin Watts, 1984, **363**

Greene, Ellin. *Clever Cooks, A Concoction of Stories, Charms, Recipes & Riddles.* New York: Lothrop, Lee and Shepard Co., 1973, **364**

Greene, Karen. *Once upon a Recipe.* New Hope, Pa.: New Hope Press, 1987, **365**

Greene, Peggy R. *Things to Make.* New York: Random House, 1981, **1348**

Greenhowe, Jean. *Costumes for Nursery Tale Characters.* Boston: Plays, 1975, **366**

Greenhowe, Jean. *Party Costumes for Kids. David and Charles Craft Book.* New York: Sterling Publishing Co., 1988, **367**

Greenhowe, Jean. *Stage Costumes for Girls.* Boston: Plays, 1975, **368**

Greenwood, Barbara. *A Pioneer Sampler.* New York: Ticknor & Fields Books for Young Readers, 1995, **1349**

Grier, Katherine. *Discover: Investigate the Mysteries of History.* Reading, Mass.: Addison-Wesley Publishing Co., 1989, **1350**

Griffin, Margaret. *The Amazing Egg Book.* Reading, Mass.: Addison-Wesley Publishing Co., 1990, **1081**

Grisewood, Sara. *Models.* New York: Larousse Kingfisher Chambers, 1994, **1351**

Groner, Judyth Saypol. *All About Hanukkah.* Rockville, Md.: Kar-Ben Copies, 1988, **369**

Groner, Judyth Saypol. *Miracle Meals, Eight Nights of Food 'N Fun for Chanukah.* Rockville, Md.: Kar-Ben Copies, 1987, **370**

Grummer, Arnold E. *The Great Balloon Game Book.* Appleton, Wisc.: Greg Markim, 1987, **371**

Gryski, Camilla. *Friendship Bracelets.* New York: William Morrow and Co., 1993, **1352**

Gryski, Camilla. *Many Stars and More String Games.* New York: William Morrow and Co., 1985, **372**

Gryski, Camilla. *Super String Games.* New York: Morrow Junior Books, 1987, **373**

Guth, Phyllis. *Crafts for Kids.* Blue Ridge Summit, Pa.: Tab Books, 1975, **374**

Gwathmey, Emily Margolin. *Trick or Treat.* New York: Clarkson Potter Publishers, 1992, **1353**

Haas, Carolyn. *Backyard Vacation.* Boston: Little, Brown and Co., 1980, **375**

Haas, Carolyn B. *Big Book of Fun.* Chicago, Ill.: Chicago Review Press, 1987, **376**

Haas, Carolyn. *My Own Fun.* Chicago, Ill.: Chicago Review Press, 1990, **1354**

Haas, Rudi. *Egg-Carton Zoo.* Toronto, Canada: Oxford University Press, 1986, **377**

Haas, Rudi. *Egg-Carton Zoo II.* Toronto, Canada: Oxford University Press, 1989, **378**

Haddad, Helen R. *Potato Printing.* New York: Thomas Y. Crowell, 1981, **379**

Haldane, Suzanne. *Painting Faces.* New York: E. P. Dutton, 1988, **380**

Hall, Carolyn Vosburg. *I Love Popcorn.* Garden City, N.Y.: Doubleday and Co., 1976, **381**

Hall, Godfrey. *Games.* New York: Thomson Learning, 1995, **1355**

Hall, Zoe. *The Apple Pie Tree.* New York: The Blue Sky Press, 1996, **1710**

Hanauer, Elsie. *The Art of Whittling and Woodcarving.* New York: A. S. Barnes and Co., 1970, **382**

Hanukkah Fun. Honesdale, Pa.: Boyds Mills Press, 1992, **1356**

Hanukkah, Oh, Hanukkah. Compiled by Wendy Wax. New York: Parachute Press, 1993, **1357**

Harbin, E. O. *Games of Many Nations.* New York: Abingdon Press, 1954, **383**

Harelson, Randy. *The Kids' Diary of 365 Amazing Days.* New York: Workman Publishing Co., 1979, **384**

Hargittai, Magdolna. *Cooking the Hungarian Way.* Minneapolis, Minn.: Lerner Publications, 1986, **385**

Harlow, Joyce. *Story Play: Costumes, Cooking, Music and More for Young Children.* Englewood, Colo.: Teacher Ideas Press, 1992, **1358**

Harris, Colin. *A Taste of West Africa.* New York: Thomson Learning, 1994, **1359**

Harris, Frank W. *Great Games to Play with Groups.* Belmont, Calif.: Fearon Teacher Aids, 1990, **386**

Harris, Tom. *Creating with Styrofoam and Related Materials.* Chicago, Ill.: J. G. Ferguson Publishing Co., 1970, **387**

Harrison, Supenn. *Cooking the Thai Way.* Minneapolis, Minn.: Lerner Publications, 1986, **388**

Harry, Cindy Groom. *One-Hour Holiday Crafts.* Lincolnwood, Ill.: Publications International, 1994, **1360**

Hart, Avery. *Kids and Weekends: Creative Ways to Make Special Days.* Charlotte, Vt.: Williamson Publishing Co., 1992, **1361**

Hart, Avery. *Kids Make Music.* Charlotte, Vt.: Williamson Publishing Co., 1993, **1362**

Hart, Marj. *Pom-Pom Puppets, Stories and Stages.* Belmont, Calif.: David S. Lake Publishers, 1989, **1030**

Hart, Rhonda Massingham. *You Can Carve Fantastic Jack-O-Lanterns.* Pownal, Vt.: Storey Communications, 1989, **1363**

Hartelius, Margaret A. *Knot Now! The Complete Friendship Bracelet Kit.* New York: Grosset & Dunlap, 1992, **1364**

Harwood, Mark. *Fun with Wood.* New York: Grosset and Dunlap Publishers, 1975, **389**

Haskins, Jim. *Count Your Way Through Africa.* Minneapolis, Minn.: Carolrhoda Books, 1989, **390**

Haskins, Jim. *Count Your Way Through Brazil.* Minneapolis, Minn.: Carolrhoda Books, 1996, **1711**

Haskins, Jim. *Count Your Way Through Canada.* Minneapolis, Minn.: Carolrhoda Books, 1989, **391**

Haskins, Jim. *Count Your Way Through China.* Minneapolis, Minn.: Carolrhoda Books, 1987, **392**

Haskins, Jim. *Count Your Way Through France.* Minneapolis, Minn.: Carolrhoda Books, 1996, **1712**

Haskins, Jim. *Count Your Way Through Germany.* Minneapolis, Minn.: Carolrhoda Books, 1990, **393**

Haskins, Jim. *Count Your Way Through Greece.* Minneapolis, Minn.: Carolrhoda Books, 1996, **1713**

Haskins, Jim. *Count Your Way Through India.* Minneapolis, Minn.: Carolrhoda Books, 1990, **1365**

Haskins, Jim. *Count Your Way Through Ireland.* Minneapolis, Minn.: Carolrhoda Books, 1996, **1714**

Haskins, Jim. *Count Your Way Through Israel.* Minneapolis, Minn.: Carolrhoda Books, 1990, **1366**

Haskins, Jim. *Count Your Way Through Italy.* Minneapolis, Minn.: Carolrhoda Books, 1990, **394**

Haskins, Jim. *Count Your Way Through Japan.* Minneapolis, Minn.: Carolrhoda Books, 1987, **395**

Haskins, Jim. *Count Your Way Through Korea.* Minneapolis, Minn.: Carolrhoda Books, 1989, **396**

Haskins, Jim. *Count Your Way Through Mexico.* Minneapolis, Minn.: Carolrhoda Books, 1989, **397**

Haskins, Jim. *Count Your Way Through Russia.* Minneapolis, Minn.: Carolrhoda Books, 1987, **398**

Haskins, Jim. *Count Your Way Through the Arab World.* Minneapolis, Minn.: Carolrhoda Books, 1987, **399**

Haslam, Andrew. *Ancient Egypt.* New York: Thomson Learning, 1995, **1367**

Haslam, Andrew. *North American Indians.* New York: Thomson Learning, 1995, **1368**

Hassig, Susan M. *Iraq.* North Bellmore, N.Y.: Marshall Cavendish Corp., 1993, **1369**

Hassig, Susan M. *Panama.* Tarrytown, N.Y.: Marshall Cavendish Corp., 1996, **1370**

Hassig, Susan M. *Somalia.* Tarrytown, N.Y.: Marshall Cavendish Corp., 1997, **1371**

Hathaway, Nancy. *Halloween Crafts and Cookbook.* New York: Harvey House, 1979, **400**

Hathaway, Nancy. *Thanksgiving Crafts and Cookbook.* New York: Harvey House, 1979, **401**

Hauser, Jill Frankel. *Kids' Crazy Concoctions: 50 Mysterious Mixtures for Art and Craft Fun.* Charlotte, Vt.: Williamson Publishing, 1994, **1372**

Hautzig, Esther. *Holiday Treats.* New York: Macmillan Publishing Co., 1983, **402**

Hautzig, Esther. *Make It Special.* New York: Macmillan Publishing Co., 1986, **403**

Hawcock, David. *Making Paper Warplanes.* London, England: David and Charles Publishers, 1989, **404**

Hawcock, David. *Paper Dinosaurs.* New York: Sterling Publishing Co., 1988, **405**

Hawkesworth, Eric. *Paper Cutting for Storytelling and Entertainment.* New York: S. G. Phillips, 1977, **406**

Hawkinson, John. *Music and Instruments for Children to Make.* Chicago, Ill.: Albert Whitman and Co., 1970, **407**

Haycock, Kate. *Pasta.* Minneapolis, Minn.: Carolrhoda Books, 1990, **1373**

Hayes, Phyllis. *Food Fun.* New York: Franklin Watts, 1981, **408**

Hayes, Phyllis. *Musical Instruments You Can Make.* New York: Franklin Watts, 1981, **409**

Hays, Wilma. *Foods the Indians Gave Us.* New York: Ives Washburn, 1973, **410**

Hazell, Bee Gee. *Paper Crafts for the Holidays.* Minneapolis, Minn.: Judy/Instructo, 1981, **411**

Hazell, Bee Gee. *Paper Plate Animals.* Minneapolis, Minn.: Judy/Instructo, 1982, **412**

Hazell, Bee Gee. *Paper Plate People.* Minneapolis, Minn.: Judy/Instructo, 1985, **413**

Hazell, Bee Gee. *Paper Shapes Projects.* Minneapolis, Minn.: Judy/Instructo, 1985, **414**

Heady, Eleanor B. *Make Your Own Dolls.* New York: Lothrop, Lee and Shepard Co., 1974, **415**

Heale, Jay. *Poland.* North Bellmore, N.Y.: Marshall Cavendish Corp., 1994, **1374**

Heale, Jay. *Portugal.* North Bellmore, N.Y.: Marshall Cavendish Corp., 1995, **1375**

Healey, Tim. *The Life of Monkeys and Apes.* Morristown, N.J.: Silver Burdett Co., 1979, **416**

Healton, Sarah H. *Baskets, Beads and Black Walnut Owls.* Blue Ridge Summit, Pa.: Tab Books, 1993, **1376**

Healy, Daty. *Dress the Show, A Basic Costume Book,* Revised Edition. Rowayton, Conn.: New Plays, 1976, **417**

Hebert, Holly. *Super Springtime Crafts.* Los Angeles, Calif.: Lowell House Juvenile, 1996, **1377**

Heinz, Brian J. *Beachcrafts Too!* Shoreham, N.Y.: Ballyhoo Books, 1986, **418**

Helfman, Elizabeth S. *Celebrating Nature, Rites and Ceremonies Around the World.* New York: Seabury Press, 1969, **419**

Helfman, Harry. *Making Pictures Move.* New York: William Morrow and Co., 1969, **420**

Helfman, Harry. *Making Pictures Without Paint.* New York: William Morrow and Co., 1973, **421**

Helfman, Harry. *Making Your Own Sculpture.* New York: William Morrow and Co., 1971, **422**

Helfman, Harry. *Strings on Your Fingers, How to Make String Figures.* New York: William Morrow and Co., 1965, **423**

Heltshe, Mary Ann. *Multicultural Explorations: Joyous Journeys with Books.* Englewood, Colo.: Teacher Ideas Press, Libraries Unlimited, 1991, **1378**

Henry, Edna. *Native American Cookbook.* New York: Julian Messner, 1983, **424**

Herda, D. J. *Christmas.* New York: Franklin Watts, 1983, **425**

Herda, D. J. *Halloween.* New York: Franklin Watts, 1983, **426**

Hershberger, Priscilla. *Make Costumes!: For Creative Play.* Cincinnati, Ohio: North Light Books, 1992, **1379**

Hetzer, Linda. *Decorative Crafts.* Milwaukee, Wisc.: Raintree Publishers, 1978, **427**

Hetzer, Linda. *Paper Crafts.* Milwaukee, Wisc.: Raintree Publishers, 1978, **428**

Hetzer, Linda. *Playtime Crafts.* Milwaukee, Wisc.: Raintree Publishers, 1978, **429**

Hetzer, Linda. *Rainy Days & Saturdays.* New York: Workman Publishing Co., 1995, **1715**

Hetzer, Linda. *Traditional Crafts.* Milwaukee, Wisc.: Raintree Publishers, 1978, **430**

Hetzer, Linda. *Workshop Crafts.* Milwaukee, Wisc.: Raintree Publishers, 1978, **431**

Hetzer, Linda. *Yarn Crafts.* Milwaukee, Wisc.: Raintree Publishers, 1978, **432**

Higgins, Susan Olson. *The Bunny Book.* Shasta, Calif.: Pumpkin Press Publishing House, 1985, **433**

Higgins, Susan Olson. *The Elves Christmas Book.* Shasta, Calif.: Pumpkin Press Publishing House, 1986, **434**

Higgins, Susan Olson. *The Pumpkin Book.* Shasta, Calif.: Pumpkin Press Publishing House, 1984, **435**

Higgins, Susan Olson. *The Thanksgiving Book.* Shasta, Calif.: Pumpkin Press Publishing House, 1984, **436**

Hill, Barbara W. *Cooking the English Way.* Minneapolis, Minn.: Lerner Publications, 1982, **437**

Hill, Janis. *From Kids with Love.* Belmont, Calif.: David S. Lake Publishers, 1987, **438**

Hirsch, S. Carl. *Stilts.* New York: Viking Press, 1972, **439**

Hodges, Susan. *Multicultural Snacks.* Everett, Wash.: Warren Publishing House, 1995, **1380**

Hodges-Caballero, Jane, Ph.D. *Children Around the World: The Multicultural Journey.* Atlanta, Ga.: Humanics Learning, 1983, **1381**

Hodgson, Harriet. *Artworks.* Palo Alto, Calif.: Monday Morning Books, 1986, **440**

Hodgson, Harriet. *Gameworks.* Palo Alto, Calif.: Monday Morning Books, 1986, **441**

Hodgson, Harriet. *Toyworks.* Palo Alto, Calif.: Monday Morning Books, 1986, **442**

Hoffman, Phyllis. *Happy Halloween.* New York: Charles Scribner's Sons, 1982, **443**

Hofsinde, Robert. *Indian Beadwork.* New York: William Morrow and Co., 1958, **444**

Hofsinde, Robert. *Indian Games and Crafts.* New York: William Morrow and Co., 1957, **445**

Holiday Cooking Around the World. Minneapolis, Minn.: Lerner Publications Co., 1988, **446**

Holiday Crafts Kids Can Make. Better Homes and Gardens. Des Moines, Iowa: Meredith Corp., 1987, **447**

Hollest, Angela. *Children's Parties.* Loughton, England: Piatkus Publishers Limited, 1983, **449**

Holmes, Anita. *Pierced & Pretty.* New York: Lothrop, Lee and Shepard Co., 1984, **450**

Holz, Loretta. *Mobiles You Can Make.* New York: Lothrop, Lee and Shepard Co., 1975, **452**

Holz, Loretta. *The Christmas Spider.* New York: Philomel Books, 1980, **451**

Hoople, Cheryl G. *The Heritage Sampler, A Book of Colonial Arts and Crafts.* New York: The Dial Press, 1975, **453**

Hoppe, H. *Whittling and Wood Carving.* New York: Sterling Publishing Co., 1972, **454**

How to Have Fun Making Birdhouses and Birdfeeders. Mankato, Minn.: Editors of *Creative,* Creative Education, 1974, **455**

How to Have Fun Making Christmas Decorations. Mankato, Minn.: Editors of *Creative,* Creative Education, 1974, **456**

How to Have Fun Making Kites. Mankato, Minn.: Editors of *Creative,* Creative Education, 1974, **457**

How to Have Fun Making Mobiles. Mankato, Minn.: Editors of *Creative,* Creative Educational Society, 1974, **458**

How to Have Fun Making Puppets. Mankato, Minn.: Editors of *Creative,* Creative Educational Society, 1974, **450**

How to Have Fun with Macrame. Mankato, Minn.: Editors of *Creative,* Creative Educational Society, 1974, **460**

Howard, Lori A. *What to Do with a Squirt of Glue.* Nashville, Tenn.: Incentive Publications, 1987, **461**

Hoyt-Goldsmith, Diane. *Mardi Gras: A Cajun Country Celebration.* New York: Holiday House, 1995, **1382**

Hughes, Helga. *Cooking the Austrian Way.* Minneapolis, Minn.: Lerner Publications Co., 1990, **1082**

Hughes, Helga. *Cooking the Irish Way.* Minneapolis, Minn.: Lerner Publications Co., 1996, **1726**

Hughes, Helga. *Cooking the Swiss Way.* Minneapolis, Minn.: Lerner Publications Co., 1995, **1383**

Hughes, Paul. *The Months of the Year.* Ada, Okla.: Garrett Educational Corporation, 1989, **1031**

Hundley, David H. *The Southwest.* Vero Beach, Fla.: Rourke Publications, 1994, **1384**

Hunt, Kari. *Masks and Mask Makers.* New York: Abingdon Press, 1961, **462**

Hunt, Tamara. *Celebrate! Holidays, Puppets and Creative Drama.* Austin, Tx.: Nancy Renfro Studios, 1987, **1083**

Hunt, Tamara. *Pocketful of Puppets.* Austin, Tx.: Nancy Renfro Studios, 1984, **463**

Hunt, Tamara. *Pocketful of Puppets: Mother Goose.* Austin, Tx.: Nancy Renfro Studios, 1982, **464**

Hunt, W. Ben. *The Complete Book of Indian Crafts and Lore.* Racine, Wisc.: Golden Press, Western Publishing Co., 1954, **465**

Hunt, W. Ben. *The Complete How-To-Book of Indiancraft.* New York: Collier Books, Macmillan Publishing Co., 1973, **466**

Hunt, W. Ben. *The Golden Book of Crafts and Hobbies.* Racine, Wisc.: Golden Press, Western Publishing Co., 1957, **467**

Hunter, Irene. *Simple Folk Instruments to Make and to Play.* New York: Simon and Schuster, 1977, **468**

Huntington, Lee Pennock. *Simple Shelters.* New York: Coward, McCann and Geoghegan, 1979, **469**

Hutchings, Margaret. *What Shall I Do from Scandinavia.* New York: Taplinger Publishing Co., 1966, **470**

I Saw a Purple Cow, And 100 Other Recipes for Learning. By Ann Cole. Boston: Little, Brown and Co., 1972, **471**

Ichikawa, Satomi. *Happy Birthday.* New York: Philomel Books, 1988, **472**

Ickis, Marguerite. *The Book of Games and Entertainment the World Over.* New York: Dodd, Mead and Co., 1969, **474**

Ickis, Marguerite. *The Book of Religious Holidays and Celebrations.* New York: Dodd, Mead and Co., 1966, **475**

Illsley, Linda. *A Taste of Mexico.* New York: Thomson Learning, 1994, **1385**

Ingram, Victoria. *Animals.* Palo Alto, Calif.: Monday Morning Books, 1987, **476**

Ingram, Victoria. *Holidays.* Palo Alto, Calif.: Monday Morning Books, 1987, **477**

Ingram, Victoria. *People.* Palo Alto, Calif.: Monday Morning Books, 1987, **478**

Irvine, Joan. *Build It With Boxes.* New York: Morrow Junior Books, 1993, **1386**

Irvine, Joan. *How to Make Holiday Pop-ups.* New York: Beech Tree Paperback Books, 1996, **1387**

Irvine, Joan. *How to Make Pop-Ups.* New York: Morrow Junior Books, 1987, **479**

Irvine, Joan. *How to Make Super Pop-Ups.* New York: Beech Tree Books, 1992, **1388**

Irving, Jan. *Fanfares: Programs for Classrooms and Libraries.* Englewood, Colo.: Libraries Unlimited, 1990, **1159**

Irving, Jan. *Full Speed Ahead.* Englewood, Colo.: Teacher Ideas Press, Libraries Unlimited, 1988, **1389**

Irving, Jan. *Glad Rags.* Littleton, Colo.: Libraries Unlimited, 1987, **480**

Irving, Jan. *Raising the Roof: Children's Stories and Activities on Houses.* Englewood, Colo.: Teacher Ideas Press, Libraries Unlimited, 1991, **1390**

Irving, Jan. *Second Helpings: Books and Activities About Food.* Englewood Colo.: Teacher Ideas Press, Libraries Unlimited, 1994., **1391**

It's a Special Day. Des Moines, Iowa: Better Homes and Gardens, Meredith Corporation, 1988, **1084**

Jaber, William. *Easy-to-Make Skateboards, Scooters and Racers.* New York: Dover Publications, 1976, **481**

Jacobs, Judy. *Indonesia, A Nation of Islands.* Minneapolis, Minn.: Dillon Press, 1990, **1085**

Jaeger, Ellsworth. *Easy Crafts.* New York: The Macmillan Co., 1947, **482**

Jaffrey, Madhur. *Market Days.* Mahway, N.J.: Bridgewater Books, 1995, **1392**

Jagendorf, Moritz. *Puppets for Beginners.* Boston: Plays, 1952, **483**

Janitch, Valerie. *The Fairy Tale Doll Book, David and Charles Craft Book.* New York: Sterling Publishing Co., 1988, **484**

Janvier, Jacqueline. *Felt Crafting.* New York: Sterling Publishing Co., 1970, **487**

Janvier, Jeannine. *Fabulous Birds You Can Make.* New York: Sterling Publishing Co., 1976, **485**

Janvier, Jeannine. *Fantastic Fish You Can Make.* New York: Sterling Publishing Co., 1976, **486**

Jarrett, Lauren. *Making and Baking Gingerbread Houses.* New York: Crown Publishers, 1984, **1086**

Jasmine, Julia. *Multicultural Holidays.* Huntington Beach, Calif.: Teacher Created Materials, 1994, **1393**

Jennings, Terry. *Beans.* Ada, Okla.: Garrett Educational Corp., 1994, **1394**

Jenny, Gerri. *Rainy Day Projects for Children.* Nazareth, Pa.: Murdoch Books, 1990, **1087**

Jenny, Gerri. *Toys and Games for Children to Make.* Nazareth, Pa.: Murdoch Books, 1990, **1088**

Johnson, Dolores. *The Children's Book of Kwanzaa.* New York: Atheneum Books for Young Readers, 1996, **1716**

Johnson, Lois S. *Happy Birthdays Round the World.* New York: Rand McNally and Co., 1963, **488**

Johnson, Lois S. *Happy New Year Round the World.* New York: Rand McNally and Co., 1966, **489**

Johnson, Pamela. *Let's Celebrate St. Patrick's Day, A Book of Drawing Fun.* Mahwah, N.J.: Watermill Press, 1988, **490**

Jones, Iris Sanderson. *Early North American Dollmaking.* San Francisco, Calif.: 101 Productions, 1976, **491**

Jones, Joan. *Projects for Autumn.* Ada, Okla.: Garrett Educational Corp., 1989, **1089**

Jones, Judith. *Knead It, Punch It, Bake It.* New York: Thomas Y. Crowell, 1981, **492**

Jordan, Nina R. *American Costume Dolls.* New York: Harcourt, Brace and World, 1941, **493**

Jordan, Nina R. *Homemade Dolls in Foreign Dress.* New York: Harcourt, Brace and World, 1939, **494**

Joseph, Joan. *Folk Toys Around the World, And How to Make Them.* New York: Parents Magazine Press, 1972, **495**

Joy Through the World. U.S. Committee for UNICEF. New York: Dodd, Mead and Co., 1985, **497**

Joy, Margaret. *Highdays and Holidays.* London, England: Faber and Faber Limited, 1981, **496**

Judy, Susan. *Gifts of Writing, Creative Projects with Words and Art.* New York: Charles Scribner's Sons, 1980, **498**

Junior Girl Scouts Handbook. New York: Girl Scouts of the U.S.A., 1986, **499**

Kagda, Sakina. *Norway.* Tarrytown, N.Y.: Marshall Cavendish Corp., 1995, **1395**

Kalman, Bobbie. *China, The Culture.* New York: Crabtree Publishing Co., 1989, **500**

Kalman, Bobbie. *Food for the Settler.* New York: Crabtree Publishing Co., 1982, **501**

Kalman, Bobbie. *Games from Long Ago.* New York: Crabtree Publishing Co., 1995, **1396**

Kalman, Bobbie. *India, The Culture.* New York: Crabtree Publishing Co., 1990, **1090**

Kalman, Bobbie. *Japan, The Culture.* New York: Crabtree Publishing Co., 1989, **1091**

Kalman, Bobbie. *Old-Time Toys.* New York: Crabtree Publishing Co., 1995, **1397**

Kalman, Bobbie. *Pioneer Projects.* New York: Crabtree Publishing Co., 1997, **1727**

Kalman, Bobbie. *Victorian Christmas.* New York: Crabtree Publishing Co., 1996, **1400**

Kalman, Bobbie. *We Celebrate Christmas.* New York: Crabtree Publishing Co., 1985, **502**

Kalman, Bobbie. *We Celebrate Easter.* New York: Crabtree Publishing Co., 1985, **503**

Kalman, Bobbie. *We Celebrate Family Days.* New York: Crabtree Publishing Co., 1993, **1398**

Kalman, Bobbie. *We Celebrate Halloween.* New York: Crabtree Publishing Co., 1985, **504**

Kalman, Bobbie. *We Celebrate Hanukkah.* New York: Crabtree Publishing Co., 1993, **1399**

Kalman, Bobbie. *We Celebrate New Year.* New York: Crabtree Publishing Co., 1985, **505**

Kalman, Bobbie. *We Celebrate the Harvest.* New York: Crabtree Publishing Co., 1986, **1401**

Kalman, Bobbie. *We Celebrate Valentine's Day.* New York: Crabtree Publishing Co., 1986, **1402**

Kalman, Bobbie. *We Celebrate Winter.* New York: Crabtree Publishing Co., 1986, **1403**

Kalter, Joanmarie. *The World's Best String Games.* New York: Sterling Publishing Co., 1989, **1404**

Kane, Jane A. *Art Through Nature.* Holmes Beach, Fla.: Learning Publications, 1985, **506**

Kanitkar, V. P. *Indian Food and Drink.* New York: The Bookwright Press, 1987, **507**

Katz, Phyllis. *Exploring Science Through Art.* New York: Franklin Watts, 1990, **508**

Katz, Ruth J. *Make It and Wear It.* New York: Walker and Co., 1981, **509**

Kaufman, Cheryl Davidson. *Cooking the Caribbean Way.* Minneapolis, Minn.: Lerner Publications Co., 1988, **510**

Kaur, Sharon. *Food in India.* Vero Beach, Fla.: Rourke Publications, 1989, **1405**

Kaye, Marvin. *The Story of Monopoly, Silly Putty, Bingo, Twister, Frisbee, Scrabble.* New York: Stein and Day, 1973, **511**

Keefe, Betty. *Fingerpuppet Tales.* Omaha, Neb.: Special Literature Press, 1986, **512**

Keefe, Betty. *Fingerpuppets, Fingerplays and Holidays.* Omaha, Neb.: Special Literature Press, 1984, **513**

Keene, Carolyn. *The Nancy Drew Cookbook.* New York: Grosset and Dunlap, 1973, **514**

Keene, Francis W. *Fun Around the World.* Pelham, N.Y.: The Seashore Press, 1955, **515**

Kelley, Emily. *Christmas Around the World.* Minneapolis, Minn.: Carolrhoda Books, 1986, **516**

Kelly, Karin. *Dollhouses.* Minneapolis, Minn.: Lerner Publications Co., 1974, **517**

Kelly, Karin. *Soup's On.* Minneapolis, Minn.: Lerner Publications Co., 1974, **518**

Kenda, Margaret. *Cooking Wizardry for Kids.* Hauppauge, N.Y.: Barron's Educational Series, 1990, **1032**

Kendall, Russ. *Eskimo Boy: Life in an Inupiaq Eskimo Village.* New York: Scholastic, 1992, **1406**

Kendall, Russ. *Russian Girl: Life in an Old Russian Town.* New York: Scholastic, 1994, **1407**

Kennedy, Pamela. *A Christmas Celebration: Traditions and Customs from Around the World.* Nashville, Tenn.: Ideals Publishing Corp., 1992, **1408**

Kennedy, Pamela. *An Easter Celebration: Traditions and Customs from Around the World.* Nashville, Tenn.: Ideals Publishing Corp., 1990, **1409**

Kent, Deborah. *China: Old Ways Meet New.* Tarrytown, N.Y.: Benchmark Books, Marshall Cavendish Corp., 1996., **1410**

Kent, Deborah. *Mexico: Rich in Spirit and Tradition.* Tarrytown, N.Y.: Benchmark Books, Marshall Cavendish Corp., 1996, **1411**

Kerina, Jane. *African Crafts.* New York: The Lion Press, 1970, **519**

Kettelkamp, Larry. *Drums, Rattles and Bells.* New York: William Morrow and Co., 1960, **520**

Kettelkamp, Larry. *Flutes, Whistles and Reeds.* New York: William Morrow and Co., 1962, **521**

Kettlekamp, Larry. *Singing Strings.* New York: William Morrow and Co., 1958, **522**

Keyworth, Valerie. *New Zealand: Land of the Long White Cloud.* Minneapolis, Minn.: Dillon Press, 1990, **1412**

Kids Cooking. Palo Alto, Calif.: Klutz Press, 1987, **1413**

Kids Explore America's African-American Heritage. Santa Fe, N.Mex.: John Muir Publications, 1993, **1414**

Kids Party Cookbook. Janet M. Stewart, Editor. Milwaukee, Wisc.: Penworthy Publishing Co., 1988, **523**

Kinder, Backbuch. *Let's Bake.* New York: Sterling Publishing Co., 1992, **1415**

King, Elizabeth. *Chile Fever: A Celebration of Peppers.* New York: Dutton Children's Books, 1995, **1416**

Kinney, Jean. *21 Kinds of American Folk Art and How to Make Each One.* New York: Atheneum, 1972, **524**

Kinney, Jean. *Varieties of Ethnic Art and How to Make Each One.* New York: Atheneum, 1976, **525**

Kinser, Charleen. *Outdoor Art for Kids.* Chicago, Ill.: Follett Publishing Co., 1975, **526**

Kirkman, Will. *Nature Crafts Workshop.* Belmont, Calif.: Fearon Teacher Aids, 1981, **527**

Kirsten's Cookbook. Middleton, Wis.: Pleasant Company Publications, 1994, **1417**

Kirsten's Craft Book. Middleton, Wis.: Pleasant Company Publications, 1994, **1418**

Kitchen Fun. Editors of *Owl* and *Chicadee* Magazines. Boston: Little, Brown and Co., 1988, **528**

Kite, L. Patricia. *Gardening Wizardry for Kids.* Hauppauge, N.Y.: Barron's Educational Series, 1995, **1419**

Klettenheimer, Ingrid. *Great Paper Craft Projects.* New York: Sterling Publishing Co., 1992, **1420**

Knopf, Mildred O. *Around America, A Cookbook for Young People.* New York: Alfred A. Knopf, 1969, **529**

Knopf, Mildred O. *Around the World Cookbook for Young People.* New York: Alfred A. Knopf, 1966, **530**

Koh, Frances M. *Korean Holidays & Festivals.* Minneapolis, Minn.: East West Press, 1990, **1160**

Kohl, Mary Ann F. *Good Earth Art: Environmental Art for Kids.* Bellingham, Wash.: Bright Ring Publishing, 1991, **1421**

Kohl, Mary Ann F. *Mudworks.* Bellingham, Wash.: Bright Ring Publishing, 1989, **531**

Kolba, St. Tamara. *Asian Crafts.* New York: Lion Press, 1970, **532**

Kovash, Emily. *How to Have Fun Making Cards.* Mankato, Minn.: Creative Education, 1974, **533**

Kraska, Edie. *Toys and Tales from Grandmother's Attic.* Boston, Ma.: Houghton Miflin Co., 1979, **1422**

Krensky, Stephen. *The Pizza Book.* New York: Scholastic, 1992, **1423**

Krisvoy, Jill. *Paper Crafts to Make You Smile.* Carthage, Ill.: Good Apple, 1981, **534**

Kropa, Susan. *Sky Blue, Grass Green.* Carthage, Ill.: Good Apple, 1986, **1092**

Kruise, Carol Sue. *Learning Through Literature.* Englewood, Colo.: Libraries Unlimited, 1990, **1093**

Krull, Kathleen. *Maria Molina and the Days of the Dead.* New York: Macmillan Publishing Co., 1994, **1424**

La Croix, Grethe. *Creating with Beads.* New York: Sterling Publishing Co., 1971, **535**

Lafargue, Francoise. *French Food and Drink.* New York: The Bookwright Press, 1987, **536**

Lamancusa, Jim. *Dynamite Crafts for Special Occasions.* Blue Ridge Summit, Pa.: Tab Books, 1993, **1425**

Lamarque, Colette. *A World of Models.* New York: Drake Publishers, 1973, **1094**

Lancaster, John. *Cardboard.* New York: Franklin Watts, 1989, **537**

Lancaster, John. *Fabric Art.* New York: Franklin Watts, 1990, **1095**

Lancaster, John. *Paper Sculpture.* New York: Franklin Watts, 1989, **538**

Lane, Jane. *How to Make Play Places and Secret Hidy Holes.* Garden City, N.Y.: Doubleday and Co., 1979, **539**

Lankford, Mary D. *Christmas Around the World.* New York: Morrow Junior Books, 1995, **1717**

Lankford, Mary D. *Hopscotch Around the World.* New York: William Morrow and Co., 1992, **1426**

Lankford, Mary D. *Jacks Around the World.* New York: Morrow Junior Books, 1996, **1718**

Lansky, Vicki. *Vicki Lansky's Kids Cooking.* New York: Scholastic, 1987, **540**

Lapenkova, Valentina. *Russian Food and Drink.* New York: The Bookwright Press, 1988, **541**

Lapson, Dvora. *Folk Dances for Jewish Festivals.* New York: Board of Jewish Education, 1961, **542**

Lazar, Wendy. *The Jewish Holiday Book.* Garden City, N.Y.: Doubleday and Co., 1977, **543**

Lee, Nancy. *Hands on Heritage.* Los Angeles, Calif.: Children's Book & Music Center, 1978, **1427**

Lee, Tan Chung. *Finland.* Tarrytown, N.Y.: Marshall Cavendish Corp., 1996, **1428**

Leedy, Loreen. *A Dragon Christmas, Things to Make and Do.* New York: Holiday House, 1988, **544**

Leedy, Loreen. *The Dragon Halloween Party.* New York: Holiday House, 1986, **1096**

Leedy, Loreen. *The Dragon Thanksgiving Feast: Things to Make and Do.* New York: Holiday House, 1990, **1097**

Leeming, Joseph. *Fun with Paper.* New York: J. B. Lippincott Co., 1967, **545**

Lehne, Judith Logan. *The Never-Be-Bored Book.* New York: Sterling Publishing Co., 1992, **1429**

Let's Pretend. Better Homes and Gardens. Des Moines, Iowa: Meredith Corporation, 1988, **1033**

Leverich, Kathleen. *Cricket's Expeditions, Outdoor and Indoor Activities.* New York: Random House, 1977, **546**

Levine, Shar. *Science Around the World: Travel Through Time and Space with Fun Experiments and Projects.* New York: John Wiley & Sons, 1996, **1719**

Levy, Patricia. *Ireland.* North Bellmore, N.Y.: Marshall Cavendish Corp., 1994, **1430**

Levy, Patricia. *Nigeria.* North Bellmore, N.Y.: Marshall Cavendish Corp., 1993, **1431**

Levy, Patricia. *Puerto Rico.* Tarrytown, N.Y.: Marshall Cavendish Corp., 1994, **1432**

Levy, Patricia. *Sudan.* Tarrytown, N.Y.: Marshall Cavendish Corp., 1997, **1433**

Levy. Patricia. *Switzerland.* North Bellmore, N.Y.: Marshall Cavendish Corp., 1994, **1434**

Levy, Valerie. *Are We Almost There?* New York: Putnam Publishing Group, 1987, **1034**

Life of Sea Mammals. Morristown, N.J.: Silver Burdett Co., 1979, **547**

Lightbody, Donna M. *Braid Craft.* New York: Lothrop, Lee and Shepard Co., 1976, **548**

Lincoln, Margarette. *The Pirates Handbook: How to Become a Rogue of the High Seas.* New York: Cobblehill Books, 1995, **1736**

Linderman, C. Emma. *Teachables from Trashables.* St. Paul, Minn.: Toys 'N Things Press, 1979, **549**

Linsley, Leslie. *Decoupage for Young Crafters.* New York: E. P. Dutton, 1977, **550**

Lipson, Michelle. *The Fantastic Costume Book.* New York: Sterling Publishing Co., 1992, **1435**

Littlewood, Valerie. *Scarecrow!* New York: Dutton Children's Books, 1992, **1436**

Lizon, Karen Helene. *Colonial American Holidays and Entertainment.* New York: Franklin Watts, 1993, **1437**

Loeb, Jr. Robert H. *New England Village.* Garden City, N.Y.: Doubleday and Co., 1976, **1035**

Loewen, Nancy. *Food in France.* Vero Beach, Fla.: Rourke Publications, 1991, **1438**

Loewen, Nancy. *Food in Germany.* Vero Beach, Fla.: Rourke Publications, 1991, **1439**

Loewen, Nancy. *Food in Greece.* Vero Beach, Fla.: Rourke Publications, 1991, **1440**

Loewen, Nancy. *Food in Israel.* Vero Beach, Fla.: Rourke Publications, 1991, **1441**

Loewen, Nancy. *Food in Korea.* Vero Beach, Fla.: Rourke Publications, 1991, **1442**

Loewen, Nancy. *Food in Spain.* Vero Beach, Fla.: Rourke Publications, 1991, **1443**

Lofgren, Ulf. *Swedish Toys, Dolls and Gifts You Can Make Yourself.* New York: Collins and World, 1978, **551**

Lohf, Sabine. *Building Your Own Toys.* Chicago, Ill.: Childrens Press, 1989, **552**

Lohf, Sabine. *Christmas Crafts.* Chicago, Ill.: Childrens Press, 1990, **553**

Lohf, Sabine. *I Made It Myself.* Chicago, Ill.: Childrens Press, 1990, **554**

Lohf, Sabine. *Making Things for Easter.* Chicago, Ill.: Childrens Press, 1989, **555**

Lohf, Sabine. *Things I Can Make with Buttons.* San Francisco, Calif.: Chronicle Books, 1988, **1098**

Lohf, Sabine. *Things I Can Make with Cork.* San Francisco, Calif.: Chronicle Books, 1988, **1099**

Lohf, Sabine. *Things I Can Make with Paper.* San Francisco, Calif.: Chronicle Books, 1987, **1100**

Look Up, Up, Up. Des Moines, Iowa: Better Homes and Gardens, Meredith Corporation, 1988, **1101**

Lopshire, Robert. *How to Make Snop Snappers and Other Fine Things.* New York: William Morrow and Co., 1977, **556**

Lucas, Eileen. *The Cherokees: People of the Southeast.* Brookfield, Conn.: The Millbrook Press, 1993, **1444**

Lucas. Eileen. *The Ojibwas: People of the Northern Forests.* Brookfield, Conn.: The Millbrook Press, 1994, **1445**

Luetje, Carolyn. *Foreign Festivals.* Minneapolis, Minn.: Judy/Instructo, 1986, **557**

Luetje, Carolyn. *Hooray for Holidays.* Minneapolis, Minn.: Judy/Instructo, 1986, **558**

Lynn, Sara. *Playing with Paint.* New York: Scholastic, 1992, **1446**

MacDonald, Kate. *The Anne of Green Gables Cookbook.* Toronto, Canada: Oxford University Press, 1985, **563**

MacFarlan, Allan A. *The Boy's Book of Outdoor Discovery.* New York: Galahad Books, 1974, **564**

MacFarlan, Allan. *Handbook of American Indian Games.* New York: Dover Publications, 1958, **565**

MacGregor, Carol. *The Fairy Tale Cookbook.* New York: Macmillan Publishing Co., 1982, **569**

MacGregor, Carol. *The Storybook Cookbook.* Garden City, N.Y.: Doubleday and Co., 1967, **570**

Mack-Williams, Kibibi. *Food and Our History.* Vero Beach, Fla.: Rourke Press, 1995, **1449**

MacLennan, Jennifer. *Simple Puppets You Can Make.* New York: Sterling Publishing Co., 1988, **573**

MacLeod-Brudenell, Iain. *Animal Crafts.* Milwaukee, Wis.: Gareth Stevens Publishing, 1994, **1447**

MacLeod-Brudenell, Iain. *Costume Crafts.* Milwaukee, Wis.: Gareth Stevens Publishing, 1994, **1448**

MacStravic, Suellen. *Print Making.* Minneapolis, Minn.: Lerner Publications Co., 1973, **575**

Madavan, Vijay. *Cooking the Indian Way.* Minneapolis, Minn.: Lerner Publications Co., 1985, **576**

Maginley, C. J. *Historic Models of Early America.* New York: Harcourt, Brace and World, 1947, **567**

Maginley, C. J. *Models of America's Past and How to Make Them.* New York: Harcourt, Brace and World, 1969, **568**

Maguire, Jack. *Hopscotch, Hangman, Hot Potato, And Ha Ha Ha.* New York: Prentice-Hall Press, 1990, **1036**

Make Believe. Des Moines, Iowa: Better Homes and Gardens, Meredith Corporation, 1989, **1105**

Malcolm, Peter. *Libya.* North Bellmore, N.Y.: Marshall Cavendish Corp., 1993, **1450**

Mandelkern, Nicholas D. *The Jewish Holiday Home Companion.* West Orange, N.J.: Behrman House, 1994, **1451**

Mandell, Muriel. *Make Your Own Musical Instruments.* New York: Sterling Publishing Co., 1957, **578**

Mann, Shiah. *Paper Lanterns. Two Methods.* New York: A.R.T.S., 1985, **579**

Manushkin, Fran. *Latkes and Applesauce.* New York: Scholastic, 1990, **580**

Marden, Patricia C. *Cooking Up World History.* Englewood, Colo.: Teacher Ideas Press, Libraries Unlimited, 1994, **1452**

Markle, Sandra. *Exploring Autumn.* New York: Atheneum, 1991, **1453**

Markle, Sandra. *Measuring Up!: Experiments, Puzzles and Games Exploring Measurement.* New York: Aladdin Paperbacks, 1995, **1454**

Marks, Burton. *Puppet Plays and Puppet-Making.* Boston: Plays, 1982, **581**

Marks, Burton. *The Spook Book.* New York: Lothrop, Lee and Shepard Books, 1981, **582**

Marks, Diana F. *Glues, Brews and Goos!: Recipes and Formulas for Almost Any Classroom Project.* Englewood, Colo.: Teacher Ideas Press, Libraries Unlimited, 1996, **1455**

Marks, Mickey Klar. *Sand Sculpturing.* New York: The Dial Press, 1962, **583**

Marks, Mickey Klar. *Slate Sculpturing.* New York: The Dial Press, 1963, **584**

Marsh, Carole. *New York Kids' Cookbook.* Decatur, Ga.: Gallopade Publishing Group, 1990, **1456**

Martell, Hazel Mary. *Food & Feasts with the Vikings.* Parsippany, N.J.: New Discovery Books, 1995, **1457**

Martin, Sidney. *Calendar Crafts, And Gifts for Each Season.* Palo Alto, Calif.: Monday Morning Books, 1986, **586**

Martin, Sidney. *Costumes, Puppets and Masks for Dramatic Plays.* Palo Alto, Calif.: Monday Morning Books, 1986, **585**

Marzollo, Jean. *Superkids.* New York: Harper and Row, Publishers, 1981, **587**

Masks and Puppets. Caroline Pitcher, Consultant. New York: Franklin Watts, 1984, **588**

Mason, Bernard S. *The Book of Indian-Crafts and Costumes.* New York: The Ronald Press Co., 1946, **589**

Mason, Bernard S. *The Junior Book of Camping and Woodcraft.* New York: The Ronald Press Co., 1971, **590**

Mayberry, Jodine. *Chinese.* New York: Franklin Watts, 1990, **1106**

McCarthy, Colin. *Poisonous Snakes.* New York: Gloucester Press, 1987, **559**

McCarthy, Kevin. *Saudi Arabia, A Desert Kingdom.* Minneapolis, Minn.: Dillon Press, 1986, **1102**

McCarthy, Tara. *Literature-Based Geography Activities: An Integrated Approach.* New York: Scholastic, 1992, **1458**

McClester, Cedric. *Kwanzaa.* New York: Gumbs and Thomas Publishers, 1985, **560**

McClure, Nancee. *Free and Inexpensive Arts and Crafts to Make and Use.* Carthage, Ill.: Good Apple, 1987, **561**

McClure, Vimala. *Bangladesh, Rivers in a Crowded Land.* Minneapolis, Minn.: Dillon Press, 1989, **1103**

McCoy, Elin. *Secret Places, Imaginary Places.* New York: Macmillan Publishing Co., 1986, **562**

McDonnell, Janet. *Christmas in Other Lands.* Chicago, Ill.: Childrens Press, 1993, **1459**

McDonnell, Janet. *Martin Luther King Day.* Chicago, Ill.: Childrens Press, 1993, **1461**

McDonnell, Janet. *Sharing Hanukkah.* Chicago, Ill.: Childrens Press, 1993, **1462**

McDonnell, Janet. *The Easter Surprise.* Chicago, Ill.: Childrens Press, 1993, **1460**

McFarland, Jeanne. *Festivals.* Morristown, N.J.: Silver Burdett, 1981, **566**

McGraw, Sheila. *Dolls Kids Can Make.* Buffalo, N.Y.: Firefly Books, 1995, **1463**

McGraw, Sheila. *Papier-Mache for Kids.* Buffalo, N.Y.: Firefly Books, 1991, **1464**

McGuire, Kevin. *Woodworking for Kids.* New York: Sterling Publishing Co., 1993, **1465**

McInnes, Celia. *Projects for Spring and Holiday Activities.* Ada, Okla.: Garrett Educational Corp., 1989, **1466**

McInnes, Celia. *Projects for Summer and Holiday Activities.* Ada, Okla.: Garrett Educational Corp., 1989, **1467**

McKenley, Yvonne. *A Taste of the Caribbean.* New York: Thomson Learning, 1995, **1468**

McKinnon, Elizabeth. *Special Day Celebrations.* Everett, Wash.: Warren Publishing House, 1989, **1469**

McKinnon, Elizabeth. *Yankee Doodle Birthday Celebrations.* Everett, Wash.: Warren Publishing House, 1990, **1104**

McLean, Margaret. *Make Your Own Musical Instruments.* Minneapolis, Minn.: Lerner Publications Co., 1988, **571**

McLenighan, Valjean. *Christmas in Spain.* Chicago, Ill.: Passport Books, NTC Publishing Group, 1991, **1470**

McLenighan, Valjean. *International Games.* Milwaukee, Wisc.: Raintree Childrens Book, 1978, **572**

McNeill, Earldene. *Cultural Awareness for Young Children.* Dallas, Tx.: The Learning Tree, 1981, **574**

Mehrens, Gloria. *Bagging It with Puppets.* Belmont, Calif.: Fearon Teacher Aids, 1988, **1107**

Meiczinger, John. *How to Draw Indian Arts and Crafts.* Mahwah, N.J.: Watermill Press, 1989, **591**

Meisenheimer, Sharon. *Special Ways with Ordinary Days.* Belmont, Calif.: David S. Lake Publishers, 1988, **592**

Mellett, Peter. *Food Energy.* New York: Franklin Watts, 1992, **1471**

Mellett, Peter. *Hot and Cold.* New York: Franklin Watts, 1993, **1472**

Merrison, Lynne. *Rice.* Minneapolis, Minn.: Carolrhoda Books, 1990, **1108**

Metcalfe, Edna. *The Trees of Christmas.* Nashville, Tenn.: Abingdon Press, 1969, **593**

Meyer, Carolyn. *Christmas Crafts.* New York: Harper and Row, 1974, **595**

Meyer, Carolyn. *Mask Magic.* New York: Harcourt Brace Jovanovich, 1978, **596**

Meyer, Carolyn. *Milk, Butter and Cheese.* New York: William Morrow and Co., 1974, **597**

Meyer, Carolyn. *Miss Patch's Learn-to-Sew Book.* New York: Harcourt, Brace and World, 1969, **598**

Meyer, Carolyn. *Rock Tumbling.* New York: William Morrow and Co., 1975, **599**

Meyer, Carolyn. *Saw, Hammer, And Paint.* New York: William Morrow and Co., 1973, **600**

Meyer, Carolyn. *Sing and Learn.* Carthage, Ill.: Good Apple, 1989, **1473**

Meyer, Carolyn. *The Bread Book, All About Bread and How to Make It.* New York: Harcourt, Brace, Jovanovich, 1971, **594**

Meyer, Kathleen Allan. *Ireland: Land of Mist and Magic.* Minneapolis, Minn.: Dillon Press, 1982, **1474**

Michael, David. *Making Kites.* New York: Kingfisher Books, 1993., **1475**

Millen, Nina. *Children's Festivals from Many Lands.* New York: Friendship Press, 1964, **601**

Millen, Nina. *Children's Games from Many Lands.* New York: Friendship Press, 1965, **602**

Miller, Donna. *Egg Carton Critters.* New York: Walker and Co., 1978, **603**

Miller, Jay. *Nature Crafts.* Minneapolis, Minn.: Lerner Publications Co., 1975, **604**

Miller, Kathy Leichliter. *Sharing Time.* Blue Ridge Summit, Pa.: Tab Books, 1990, **1109**

Miller, Marjorie. *Indian Arts and Crafts.* New York: Galahad Books, 1972, **605**

Miller, Susanna. *Beans and Peas.* Minneapolis, Minn.: Carolrhoda Books, 1990, **1110**

Milord, Susan. *Adventures in Art: Art and Craft Experiences for 7-to-14 Year-Olds.* Charlotte, Vt.: Williamson Publishing Co., 1990, 1476

Milord, Susan. *Hands Around the World: 365 Ways to Build Cultural Awareness and Global Respect.* Charlotte, Vt.: Williamson Publishing Co., 1992, **1477**

Milord, Susan. *Tales Alive!: Ten Multicultural Folktales with Activities.* Charlotte, Vt.: Williamson Publishing Co., 1995, **1478**

Mohr, Carolyn. *Thinking Activities for Books Children Love.* Englewood, Colo.: Libraries Unlimited, 1988, **606**

Moiz, Azra. *Taiwan.* Tarrytown, N.Y.: Marshall Cavendish Corp., 1995, **1479**

Molly's Cookbook. Middleton, Wis.: Pleasant Company Publications, 1994, **1480**

Molly's Craft Book. Middleton, Wis.: Pleasant Company Publications, 1994, **1481**

Moncure, Jane Belk. *Our Birthday Book.* Elgin, Ill.: Child's World, 1977, **607**

Moncure, Jane Belk. *Our Christmas Book.* Elgin, Ill.: Child's World, 1977, **608**

Moncure, Jane Belk. *Our Easter Book.* Elgin, Ill.: Child's World, 1976, **609**

Moncure, Jane Belk. *Our Halloween Book.* Elgin, Ill.: Child's World, 1977, **610**

Moncure, Jane Belk. *Our Mother's Day Book.* Elgin, Ill.: Child's World, 1977, **611**

Moncure, Jane Belk. *Our Thanksgiving Book.* Elgin, Ill.: Child's World, 1976, **612**

Moncure, Jane Belk. *Our Valentine Book.* Elgin, Ill.: Child's World, 1976, **613**

Moncure, Jane Belk. *Step Into Fall: A New Season.* Elgin, Ill.: Child's World, 1990, **1482**

Moncure, Jane Belk. *What Was It, Before It Was Bread.* Elgin, Ill.: Child's World, 1985, **614**

Montanez, Marta. *Games from My Island.* New York: Arts, 1980, **615**

Moore, Carolyn E., Ph.D. *The Young Chef's Nutrition Guide and Cookbook.* New York: Barron's Educational Series, 1990, **1111**

Moore, Eva. *The Great Banana Cookbook for Boys and Girls.* New York: Clarion Books, 1983, **616**

Mooser, Stephen. *Monster Fun.* New York: Julian Messner, 1979, **617**

Morgan, Paul. *The Ultimate Kite Book.* New York: Simon and Schuster, 1992, **1483**

Morin, Claude. *Braided Cord Animals You Can Make.* New York: Sterling Publishing Co., 1976, **618**

Morris, Ting. *Animals.* New York: Franklin Watts, 1994, **1484**

Morris, Ting. *Germany.* New York: Franklin Watts, 1993, **1485**

Morris, Ting. *Masks.* New York: Franklin Watts, 1993, **1486**

Morris, Ting. *Music.* New York: Franklin Watts, 1994, **1728**

Morris, Ting. *No-Cook Cooking.* New York: Franklin Watts, 1994, **1487**

Morris, Ting. *Rain Forest.* New York: Franklin Watts, 1994, **1488**

Morton, Brenda. *Do-It Yourself Dinosaurs.* New York: Taplinger Publishing Co., 1973, **619**

Moss, Joy F. *Focus Units in Literature.* Urbana, Ill.: National Council of Teachers of English, 1984, **620**

Moss, Miriam. *Eggs.* Ada, Okla.: Garrett Educational Corp., 1991, **1489**

Moss, Miriam. *Fruit.* Ada, Okla.: Garrett Educational Corp., 1994, **1490**

Munan, Heidi. *Malaysia.* North Bellmore, N.Y.: Marshall Cavendish Corp., 1990, **1491**

Munsen, Sylvia. *Cooking the Norwegian Way.* Minneapolis, Minn.: Lerner Publications Co., 1982, **621**

Murray, Anna. *My Christmas Craft Book for Kids.* Racine, Wis.: Western Publishing Co., 1993, **1492**

Nabwire, Constance. *Cooking the African Way.* Minneapolis, Minn.: Lerner Publications Co., 1988, **622**

Nassiet, Claude. *What to Make with Nuts and Grains.* New York: Sterling Publishing Co., 1975, **623**

Nathan, Joan. *The Children's Jewish Holiday Kitchen.* New York: Schocken Books, 1987, **1112**

Native People of the Northeast Woodland. New York: Museum of the American Indian, 1990, **1493**

Neat Eats. New York: Crown Publishers, 1981, **1113**

Nelson, Esther L. *Dancing Games for Children of All Ages.* New York: Sterling Publishing Co., 1973, **1114**

Nelson, Esther L. *Holiday Singing and Dancing Games.* New York: Sterling Publishing Co., 1980, **624**

Nelson, Esther L. *Musical Games for Children of All Ages.* New York: Sterling Publishing Co., 1976, **1116**

Nelson, Esther L. *The Great Rounds Song Book.* New York: Sterling Publishing Co., 1985, **1115**

Nelson, Wayne E. *International Playtime.* Carthage, Ill.: Fearon Teacher Aids, 1992, **1494**

Newmann, Dana. *The Early Childhood Teacher's Almanack: Activities for Every Month of the Year.* West Nyack, N.Y.: Center for Applied Research in Education, 1984, **1495**

Newsome, Arden J. *Button Collecting and Crafting.* New York: Lothrop, Lee and Shepard Co., 1976, **625**

Newsome, Arden J. *Crafts and Toys from Around the World.* New York: Julian Messner, 1972, **626**

Newsome, Arden J. *Egg Craft.* New York: Lothrop, Lee and Shepard Co., 1973, **627**

Newsome, Arden J. *Make It with Felt.* New York: Lothrop, Lee and Shepard Co., 1972, **628**

Newsome, Arden J. *Spoolcraft.* New York: Lothrop, Lee and Shepard Co., 1970, **629**

Nguyen, Chi. *Cooking the Vietnamese Way.* Minneapolis, Minn.: Lerner Publications Co., 1985, **630**

Nickerson, Betty. *Celebrate the Sun.* New York: J. B. Lippincott Co., 1969, **631**

Nicklaus, Carol. *Making Dolls.* New York: Franklin Watts, 1981, **632**

Norbeck, Oscar E. *Book of Indian Life Crafts.* New York: Association Press, 1966, **633**

Norris, Joan Darby. *New England.* Vero Beach, Fla.: Rourke Publications, 1994, **1496**

Norvell, Flo Ann Hedley. *The Great Big Box Book.* New York: Thomas Y. Crowell Co., 1979, **634**

Nottridge, Rhoda. *Sugar.* Minneapolis, Minn.: Carolrhoda Books, 1989, **1117**

Oakley, Ruth. *Ball Games.* Freeport, N.Y.: Marshall Cavendish Corp., 1989, **1497**

Oakley, Ruth. *Board and Card Games.* New York: Marshall Cavendish Corp., 1989, **1037**

Oakley, Ruth. *Chanting Games.* New York: Marshall Cavendish Corp., 1989, **1118**

Oakley, Ruth. *Chasing Games.* Freeport, N.Y.: Marshall Cavendish Corp., 1989, **1498**

Oakley, Ruth. *Games of Strength and Skill.* Freeport, N.Y.: Marshall Cavendish Corp., 1989, **1499**

Oakley, Ruth. *Games with Papers and Pencils.* Freeport, N.Y.: Marshall Cavendish Corp., 1989, **1500**

Oakley, Ruth. *Games with Rope and String.* Freeport, N.Y.: Marshall Cavendish Corp., 1989, **1501**

Oakley, Ruth. *Games with Sticks, Stones and Shells.* New York: Marshall Cavendish Corp., 1989, **1119**

O'Hare, Jeff. *Hanukkah, Happy Hanukkah.* Honesdale, Pa.: Boyds Mills Press, 1994, **1502**

O'Leary, Helen. *Children's Party Book.* North Pomfret, Vt.: David and Charles, 1983, **635**

Olsson, Kari. *Sweden, A Good Life for All.* Minneapolis, Minn.: Dillon Press, 1982, **1503**

On the Farm. Des Moines, Iowa: Better Homes and Gardens, Meredith Corporation, 1989, **1120**

128 Holiday Crafts Kids Can Make. Editors Highlights. Columbus, Ohio: Highlights for Children, 1981, **448**

O'Neill, Laurie A. *The Shawnees: People of the Eastern Woodlands.* Brookfield, Conn.: The Millbrook Press, 1995, **1504**

O'Reilly, Susie. *Batik and Tie-Dye.* New York: Thomson Learning, 1993, **1505**

O'Reilly, Susie. *Weaving.* New York: Thomson Learning, 1993, **1506**

Orlando, Louise. *The Multicultural Game Book.* New York: Scholastic Professional Books, 1993, **1507**

Osborne, Christine. *Australian and New Zealand Food and Drink.* New York: The Bookwright Press, 1989, **636**

Osborne, Christine. *Middle Eastern Food and Drink.* New York: The Bookwright Press, 1988, **637**

Osborne, Christine. *Southeast Asian Food and Drink.* New York: The Bookwright Press, 1989, **638**

Osseo-Asare, Fran. *A Good Soup Attracts Chairs: A First African Cookbook for American Kids.* Gretna, La.: Pelican Publishing Co., 1993, **1508**

Ottenbacher, Joy. *Toot-de-Too Paper People.* Bloomfield, Conn.: Junior Arts and Crafts House, 1982, **639**

Ottenbacher, Joy. *Toot-de-Too Paper Pets and Projects.* Bloomfield, Conn.: Junior Arts and Crafts House, 1982, **640**

Outdoor Fun. Boston: Little, Brown and Co., 1989, **1121**

Owen, Cheryl. *My Costume Book.* New York: Little, Brown and Co., 1995, **1509**

Owen, Cheryl. *My Nature Craft Book.* New York: Little, Brown and Co., 1993, **1510**

Oxlade, Chris. *Everyday Things.* New York: Franklin Watts, 1994, **1511**

Oxlade, Chris. *Houses and Homes.* New York: Franklin Watts, 1994, **1512**

Paker, Josephine. *Beating the Drum.* Brookfield, Conn.: The Millbrook Press, 1992, **1513**

Paker, Josephine. *Music from Strings.* Brookfield, Conn.: The Millbrook Press, 1992, **1514**

Papi, Liza. *Carnavalia! African-Brazilian Folklore and Crafts.* New York: Rizzoli International Publications, 1994, **1516**

Papier Mache, Dyeing and Leatherwork. New York: Franklin Watts, 1972, **641**

Paraiso, Aviva. *Caribbean Food and Drink.* New York: The Bookwright Press, 1989, **642**

Paraiso, Aviva. *Jewish Food and Drink.* New York: The Bookwright Press, 1989, **643**

Parents' Nursery School. *Kids Are Natural Cooks.* Boston: Houghton Mifflin Co., 1974, **1122**

Parish, Peggy. *Beginning Mobiles.* New York: Macmillan Publishing Co., 1979, **644**

Parish, Peggy. *December Decorations.* New York: Macmillan Publishing Co., 1975, **645**

Parish, Peggy. *Let's Be Early Settlers with Daniel Boone.* New York: Harper and Row, 1967, **646**

Parish, Peggy. *Let's Be Indians.* New York: Harper and Row, 1962, **647**

Parish, Peggy. *Let's Celebrate, Holiday Decorations You Can Make.* New York: Greenwillow Books, William Morrow and Co., 1976, **648**

Parish, Peggy. *Sheet Magic, Games, Toys and Gifts from Old Sheets.* New York: Macmillan Co., 1971, **649**

Parnell, Helga. *Cooking the German Way.* Minneapolis, Minn.: Lerner Publications Co., 1988, **650**

Parnell, Helga. *Cooking the South American Way.* Minneapolis, Minn.: Lerner Publications Co., 1991, **1517**

Party Time. Caroline Pitcher, Consultant. New York: Franklin Watts, 1984, **651**

Pateman, Robert. *Belgium.* Tarrytown, N.Y.: Marshall Cavendish Corp., 1995, **1518**

Pateman, Robert. *Bolivia.* Tarrytown, N.Y.: Marshall Cavendish Corp., 1995, **1519**

Pateman, Robert. *Denmark.* North Bellmore, N.Y.: Marshall Cavendish Corp., 1995, **1520**

Pateman, Robert. *Kenya.* North Bellmore, N.Y.: Marshall Cavendish Corp., 1993, **1521**

Paul, Aileen. *Kids Cooking Complete Meals.* Garden City, N.Y.: Doubleday and Co., 1975, **653**

Paul, Aileen. *Kids Cooking, A First Cookbook for Children.* Garden City, N.Y.: Doubleday and Co., 1970, **652**

Paul, Aileen. *The Kids 50-State Cookbook.* New York: Doubleday and Co., 1976, **654**

Pearson, Craig. *Make Your Own Games Workshop.* Carthage, Ill.: Fearon Teacher Aids, 1982, **655**

Pellicer, Maria Eugenia D. *Spanish Food and Drink.* New York: The Bookwright Press, 1988, **656**

Pellowski, Anne. *Hidden Stories in Plants.* New York: Macmillan Publishing Co., 1990, **657**

Pellowski, Anne. *The Family Storytelling Handbook.* New York: Macmillan Publishing Co., 1987, **1522**

Pellowski, Anne. *The Story Vine.* New York: Macmillan Publishing Co., 1984, **1161**

Penn, Malka. *The Miracle of the Potato Latkes.* New York: Holiday House, 1994, **1523**

Penner, Lucille Recht. *A Native American Feast.* New York: Macmillan Publishing Co., 1994, **1527**

Penner, Lucille Recht. *Celebration: The Story of American Holidays.* New York: Macmillan Publishing Co., 1993, **1524**

Penner, Lucille Recht. *Eating the Plates.* New York: Macmillan Publishing Co., 1991, **1525**

Penner, Lucille Recht. *The Colonial Cookbook.* New York: Hastings House, 1976, **658**

Penner, Lucille Recht. *The Little Women Book: Games, Recipes, Crafts and Other Homemade Pleasures.* New York: Random House, 1995, **1526**

Penner, Lucille Recht. *The Tea Party Book.* New York: Random House, 1993, **1528**

Penner, Lucille Recht. *The Thanksgiving Book.* New York: Hastings House, 1986, **659**

Pennington, Daniel. *Itse Selu, Cherokee Harvest Festival.* Watertown, Ma.: Charlesbridge Publishing, 1994, **1529**

Perl, Lila. *Candles, Cakes and Donkey Tails.* New York: Houghton Mifflin Co., 1984, **660**

Perl, Lila. *Foods and Festivals of the Danube Lands.* New York: World Publishing Co., 1969, **661**

Perl, Lila. *Hunter's Stew and Hangtown Fry, What Pioneer America Ate...* New York: Houghton Mifflin/Clarion Books, 1977, **663**

Perl, Lila. *Junk Food, Fast Food, Health Food, What America Eats...* New York: Houghton Mifflin/Clarion Books, 1980, **664**

Perl, Lila. *Pinatas and Paper Flowers, Holidays of the Americas in English and Spanish.* New York: Houghton Mifflin Co., 1983, **665**

Perl, Lila. *Red-Flannel Hash and Shoo-Fly Pie.* New York: The World Publishing Co., 1965, **666**

Perl, Lila. *Rice, Spice and Bitter Oranges.* New York: The World Publishing Co., 1967, **667**

Perl, Lila. *Slumps, Grunts and Snickerdoodles, What Colonial America Ate and Why.* New York: The Seabury Press, 1975, **668**

Perl, Lila. *The Hamburger Book.* New York: Seabury Press, 1974, **662**

Perry, Margaret. *Christmas Magic, The Art of Making Decorations and Ornaments.* Garden City, N.Y.: Doubleday and Co., 1964, **669**

Perry, Margaret. *Rainy Day Magic, The Art of Making Sunshine on a Stormy Day.* New York: M. Evans and Co., 1970, **670**

Peters, Stella. *Bedouin.* Morristown, N.J.: Silver Burdett, 1981, **671**

Peterson, Cris. *Extra Cheese, Please! Mozzarella's Journey from Cow to Pizza.* Honesdale, Pa.: Boyds Mills Press, 1994, **1530**

Peterson, Marge. *Argentina, A Wild West Heritage.* Minneapolis, Minn.: Dillon Press, 1990, **1123**

Petrash, Carol. *Earthways: Simple Environmental Activities for Young Children.* Mt. Rainier, Md.: Gryphon House, 1992, **1531**

Pettit, Florence H. *Christmas All Around the House.* New York: Thomas Y. Crowell Co., 1976, **672**

Pettit, Florence H. *How to Make Whirligigs and Whimmy Diddles, and Other American Folkcraft Objects.* New York: Thomas Y. Crowell Co., 1972, **673**

Pettit, Florence H. *The Stamp-Pad Printing Books.* New York: Thomas Y. Crowell Co., 1979, **674**

Pettit, Ted S. *Bird Feeders and Shelters You Can Make.* New York: G. P. Putnam's Sons, 1970, **675**

Pfeiffer, Christine. *Germany: Two Nations, One Heritage.* Minneapolis, Minn.: Dillon Press, 1987, **1124**

Pfeiffer, Christine. *Poland, Land of Freedom Fighters.* Minneapolis, Minn.: Dillon Press, 1991, **1532**

Pfeiffer, Christine. *Poland: Land of Freedom Fighters.* Minneapolis, Minn.: Dillon Press, 1984, **1125**

Pflug, Betsy. *Boxed-In Doll Houses.* New York: J. B. Lippincott Co., 1971, **676**

Pflug, Betsy. *Egg-Speriment, Easy Crafts with Eggs and Egg Cartons.* New York: J. B. Lippincott Co., 1973, **677**

Pflug, Betsy. *Funny Bags.* New York: J. B. Lippincott Co., 1974, **678**

Pflug, Betsy. *Pint-Size Fun.* New York: J. B. Lippincott Co., 1972, **679**

Pflug, Betsy. *You Can.* New York: Van Nostrand Reinhold Co., 1969, **680**

Philpott, Violet. *The Know How Book of Puppets.* New York: Sterling Publishing Co., 1975, **681**

Pine, Tillie S. *The Incas Knew.* New York: McGraw Hill Book Co., 1968, **682**

Pinkerton, Susan. *Concoctions.* Palo Alto, Calif.: Monday Morning Books, 1987, **683**

Pinsent, Lynsy. *Face Painting.* Secaucus, N.J.: Chartwell Books, 1993, **1533**

Planes and Space. Caroline Pitcher, Consultant. New York: Franklin Watts, 1983, **684**

Playtime Crafts and Activities. Honesdale, Pa.: Boyds Mills Press, 1994, **1534**

Playtime Treasury: *A Collection of Playground Rhymes, Games and Action Songs.* New York: Doubleday, 1990, **1126**

Ploquin, Genevieve. *What to Make with Pine Cones.* New York: Sterling Publishing Co., 1976, **685**

Plotkin, Gregory. *Cooking the Russian Way.* Minneapolis, Minn.: Lerner Publications Co., 1986, **1535**

Pluckrose, Henry. *Paints.* New York: Franklin Watts, 1987, **686**

Pointillart, Marie Blanche. *Costumes from Crepe Paper.* New York: Sterling Publishing Co., 1974, **687**

Politi, Leo. *Three Stalks of Corn.* New York: Charles Scribner's Sons, 1976, **1536**

Porteus, Richard. *Early American Crafts You Can Make.* Minneapolis, Minn.: T. S. Denison and Co., 1978, **688**

Poulssen, Emilie. *Finger-Plays for Nursery and Kindergarten.* New York: Hart Publishing Co., 1977, **689**

Pountney, Kate. *Fun with Wool.* New York: Grosset and Dunlap, 1974, **690**

Pountney, Kate. *Make a Mobile.* New York: S. G. Phillips, 1974, **691**

Powell, Jillian. *Body Decoration.* New York: Thomson Learning, 1995, **1537**

Powell, Jillian. *Food.* New York: Thomson Learning, 1995, **1538**

Powers, William K. *Here Is Your Hobby, Indian Dancing and Costumes.* New York: G. P. Putnam's Sons, 1966, **692**

Prego de Oliver, Victoria. *Airports.* England: Wayland Publishers, Limited, 1976, **693**

Press, Judy. *The Little Hands Big Fun Craft Book.* Charlotte, Vt.: Williamson Publishing, 1995, **1539**

Price, Christine. *Arts of Clay.* New York: Charles Scribner's Sons, 1977, **694**

Price, Christine. *Happy Days.* New York: U.S. Committee for UNICEF, United Nations, 1969, **695**

Price, Lowi. *Concoctions.* New York: E. P. Dutton and Co., 1976, **696**

Priceman, Marjorie. *How to Make an Apple Pie and See the World.* New York: Alfred A. Knopf, 1994, **1540**

Prieto, Mariana. *Play It in Spanish.* New York: John Day Co., 1973, **697**

Provenzo, Asterie Baker. *Play It Again.* Englewood Cliffs, N.J.: Prentice-Hall, 1981, **1541**

Pulleyn, Micah. *Kids in the Kitchen.* New York: Sterling Publishing Co., 1994, **1542**

Pumpkin in a Pear Tree. Carolyn Haas, et al. Boston: Little, Brown and Co., 1976, **698**

Purdy, Susan Gold. *Jewish Holiday Cookbook.* New York: Franklin Watts, 1979, **711**

Purdy, Susan Gold. *Jewish Holidays, Facts, Activities and Crafts.* New York: J. B. Lippincott Co., 1969, **712**

Purdy, Susan. *Ancient Egypt, A Civilization Project Book.* New York: Franklin Watts, 1982, **699**

Purdy, Susan. *Ancient Greece.* New York: Franklin Watts, 1982, **700**

Purdy, Susan. *Ancient Rome.* New York: Franklin Watts, 1982, **701**

Purdy, Susan. *Aztecs.* New York: Franklin Watts, 1982, **702**

Purdy, Susan. *Christmas Cookbook.* New York: Franklin Watts, 1976, **703**

Purdy, Susan. *Christmas Cooking Around the World.* New York: Franklin Watts, 1983, **704**

Purdy, Susan. *Christmas Decorations for You to Make.* New York: J. B. Lippincott Co., 1965, **705**

Purdy, Susan. *Christmas Gifts for You to Make.* New York: J. B. Lippincott Co., 1976, **706**

Purdy, Susan. *Christmas Gifts Good Enough to Eat.* New York: Franklin Watts, 1981, **707**

Purdy, Susan. *Eskimos, A Civilization Project Book.* New York: Franklin Watts, 1982, **708**

Purdy, Susan. *Festivals for You to Celebrate.* New York: J. B. Lippincott Co., 1969, **709**

Purdy, Susan. *Halloween Cookbook.* New York: Franklin Watts, 1977, **710**

Purdy, Susan. *Let's Give a Party.* New York: Grosset and Dunlap, 1976, **713**

Purdy, Susan. *North American Indians.* New York: Franklin Watts, 1982, **714**

Quinn, Gardner. *Valentine Crafts and Cookbook.* New York: Harvey House, 1977, **715**

Raferty, Kevin. *Kids Gardening: A Kids' Guide to Messing Around in the Dirt.* Palo Alto, Calif.: Klutz Press, 1989, **1543**

Raines, Shirley C. *Story Stretchers*. Mt. Rainier, Md.: Gryphon House, 1989, **716**

Rajendra, Vijeya. *Australia*. North Bellmore, N.Y.: Marshall Cavendish Corp., 1991, **1544**

Ralph, Judy. *The Peanut Butter Cookbook for Kids*. New York: Hyperion Books for Children, 1995, **1545**

Randall, Ronne. *Thanksgiving Fun*. New York: Kingfisher, 1994, **1546**

Raphael, Elaine. *Drawing America: The Story of the First Thanksgiving*. New York: Scholastic, 1991, **1547**

Raphael, Elaine. *Drawing History: Ancient Egypt*. New York: Franklin Watts, 1989, **717**

Raphael, Elaine. *Drawing History: Ancient Greece*. New York: Franklin Watts, 1989, **1548**

Raphael, Elaine. *Drawing History: Ancient Rome*. New York: Franklin Watts, 1990, **1549**

Rawson, Christopher. *Disguise and Make-Up, The Good Spy Guide*. London, England: Usborn Publishing Ltd., 1978, **718**

Razzi, James. *Star-Spangled Fun, Things to Make, Do and See from American History*. New York: Parents' Magazine Press, 1976, **719**

Ready-to-Use Activities for Before and After School Programs. Verna Stassevitch, et al. West Nyack, N.Y.: Center for Applied Research in Education, 1989, **720**

Recipes for Fun. By Ann Cole and others. Northfield, Ill.: Par Project, 1970, **721**

Recipes for Fun. Washington, D.C.: Joseph P. Kennedy, Jr. Foundation, 1986, **1127**

Reck, Alma Kehoe. *Some Independence Days Around the World*. Los Angeles, Calif.: Elk Grove Press, 1968, **722**

Reed, Bob. *Sand Creatures and Castles, How to Build Them*. New York: Holt, Rinehart and Winston, 1976, **723**

Reiko, Weston. *Cooking the Japanese Way*. Minneapolis, Minn.: Lerner Publications Co., 1983, **724**

Reilly, Mary V. *Seeds of Paradise*. Wilton, Conn.: Morehouse-Barlow Co., 1982, **725**

Reilly, Mary V. *Wait in Joyful Hope*. Wilton, Conn.: Morehouse-Barlow Co., 1980, **726**

Reis, Mary. *Batik*. Minneapolis, Minn.: Lerner Publications Co., 1973, **727**

Renfro, Nancy. *Bags Are Big*. Austin, Tx.: Nancy Renfro Studios, 1986, **728**

Renfro, Nancy. *Make Amazing Puppets*. Santa Barbara, Calif.: The Learning Works, 1979, **729**

Renfro, Nancy. *Puppets U.S.A., Texas*. Austin, Tex.: Nancy Renfro Studios, 1985, **1550**

Reyes, Gregg. *Once There Was a House and You Can Make It*. New York: Random House, 1987, **730**

Reyes, Gregg. *Once There Was a Knight, And You Can Be One Too*. New York: Random House, 1987, **731**

Rice, Wayne. *Play It*. Grand Rapids, Mich.: Zondervan Publishing House, 1986, **732**

Ridgwell, Jenny. *A Taste of Italy*. New York: Thomson Learning, 1993, **1551**

Ridgwell, Jenny. *A Taste of Japan*. New York: Thomson Learning, 1993, **1552**

Riehecky, Janet. *Cinco de Mayo*. Chicago, Ill.: Childrens Press, 1993, **1553**

Riehecky, Janet. *Kwanzaa*. Chicago, Ill.: Childrens Press, 1993, **1554**

Ring a Ring O'Roses. Flint, Mich.: Flint Public Library, 1981, **733**

Riordan, James. *Soviet Union*. Morristown, N.J.: Silver Burdett Press, 1987, **1555**

Robbins, Maria. *A Christmas Companion, Recipes, Traditions and Customs from Around the World*. New York: Putnam Publishing Group, 1989, **1128**

Roberts, Catherine. *Who's Got the Button?* New York: David McKay Co., 1962, **734**

Roberts, Lynda. *Mitt Magic, Fingerplays for Finger Puppets*. Mt. Rainier, Md.: Gryphon House, 1985, **735**

Robertson, Linda. *Kwanzaa Fun*. New York: Kingfisher, 1996, **1556**

Robins, Deri. *Christmas Fun*. New York: Kingfisher, 1995, **1557**

Robins, Deri. *Easter Fun*. New York: Kingfisher, 1996, **1558**

Robins, Deri. *Kids' Around the World Cookbook*. New York: Kingfisher Chambers, 1994, **1560**

Robins, Deri. *Papier-Mache*. New York: Kingfisher, 1993, **1561**

Robins, Deri. *The Great Pirate Activity Book*. New York: Kingfisher, 1995, **1559**

Robinson, Jeri. *Activities for Anyone, Anytime, Anywhere*. Boston: Little, Brown and Co., 1983, **736**

Rockwell, Anne. *Games (and How to Play Them)*. New York: Thomas Y. Crowell Co., 1973, **737**

Rockwell, Anne. *Mother Goose Cookie-Candy Book*. New York: Random House, 1983, **738**

Rockwell, Harlow. *Printmaking*. Garden City, N.Y.: Doubleday and Co., 1973, **739**

Romberg, Jenean. *Let's Discover Crayon*. West Nyack, N.Y.: Center for Applied Research in Education, 1973, **740**

Romberg, Jenean. *Let's Discover Mobiles*. West Nyack, N.Y.: Center for Applied Research in Education, 1974, **741**

Romberg, Jenean. *Let's Discover Paper*. West Nyack, N.Y.: Center for Applied Research in Education, 1974, **742**

Romberg, Jenean. *Let's Discover Papier-Mache*. West Nyack, N.Y.: Center for Applied Research in Education, 1976, **743**

Romberg, Jenean. *Let's Discover Printing*. West Nyack, N.Y.: Center for Applied Research in Education, 1974, **744**

Romberg, Jenean. *Let's Discover Puppets*. West Nyack, N.Y.: Center for Applied Research in Education, 1976, **745**

Romberg, Jenean. *Let's Discover Tempera*. West Nyack, N.Y.: Center for Applied Research in Education, 1974, **746**

Romberg, Jenean. *Let's Discover Tissue*. West Nyack, N.Y.: Center for Applied Research in Education, 1973, **747**

Romberg, Jenean. *Let's Discover Watercolor*. West Nyack, N.Y.: Center for Applied Research in Education, 1974, **748**

Romberg, Jenean. *Let's Discover Weaving*. West Nyack, N.Y.: Center for Applied Research in Education, 1975, **749**

Rosen, Clare. *Party Fun.* London, England: Usborne Publishing, Ltd., 1985, **750**

Rosin, Arielle. *Eclairs and Brown Bears.* New York: Tichnor & Fields, 1994 **1562**

Rosmarin, Ike. *South Africa.* North Bellmore, N.Y.: Marshall Cavendish Corp., 1993 **1563**

Ross, Catherine. *The Amazing Milk Book.* Reading, Mass.: Addison-Wesley Publishing Co., 1991, **1564**

Ross, Corinne. *Christmas in France.* Chicago, Ill.: Passport Books, NTC Publishing Group, 1991, **1565**

Ross, Corinne. *Christmas in Italy.* Chicago, Ill.: Passport Books, NTC Publishing Group, 1991, **1566**

Ross, Corinne. *Christmas in Mexico.* Chicago, Ill.: Passport Books, NTC Publishing Group, 1991, **1567**

Ross, Dave. *Making Robots.* New York: Franklin Watts, 1980, **751**

Ross, Dave. *Making Space Puppets.* New York: Franklin Watts, 1980, **752**

Ross, Kathy. *Crafts for Christmas.* Brookfield, Conn.: The Millbrook Press, 1995, **1568**

Ross, Kathy. *Crafts for Halloween.* Brookfield, Conn.: The Millbrook Press, 1994, **1569**

Ross, Kathy. *Crafts for Kwanzaa.* Brookfield, Conn.: The Millbrook Press, 1994, **1570**

Ross, Kathy. *Crafts for Thanksgiving.* Brookfield, Conn.: The Millbrook Press, 1995, **1571**

Ross, Kathy. *Crafts for Valentine's Day.* Brookfield, Conn.: The Millbrook Press, 1995, **1572**

Ross, Kathy. *Every Day Is Earth Day.* Brookfield, Conn.: The Millbrook Press, 1995, **1573**

Ross, Laura. *Finger Puppets.* New York: Lothrop, Lee and Shepard Co., 1971, **753**

Ross, Laura. *Holiday Puppets.* New York: Lothrop, Lee and Shepard Co., 1974, **754**

Ross, Laura. *Mask-Making with Pantomime and Stories from American History.* New York: Lothrop, Lee and Shepard Co., 1975, **755**

Ross, Laura. *Puppet Shows Using Poems and Stories.* New York: Lothrop, Lee and Shepard Co., 1970, **756**

Ross, Laura. *Scrap Puppets, How to Make and Move Them.* New York: Holt, Rinehart and Winston, 1978, **757**

Rothlein, Liz. *Read It Again: A Guide for Teaching Reading.* Glenview, Ill.: Scott, Foresman and Co., 1989, **758**

Roussel, Mike. *Clay.* Vero Beach, Fla.: Rourke Enterprises, 1990, **1129**

Roussel, Mike. *Scrap Materials.* Vero Beach, Fla.: Rourke Enterprises, 1990, **1130**

Rowen, Lawrence. *Beyond Winning: Sports and Games All Kids Want to Play.* Belmont, Calif.: Fearon Teacher Aids, 1990, **1131**

Rozakis, Laurie. *Celebrate! Holidays Around the World.* Santa Barbara, Calif.: The Learning Works, 1993, **1574**

Rumpf, Betty. *Papier-Mache.* Minneapolis, Minn.: Lerner Publications Co., 1974, **759**

Ruppert, Marion C. *Projects and Poems for Early Education.* Atlanta, Ga.: Humanics Learning, 1989, **760**

Ruschen, Gaye. *Let's Learn About Arts and Crafts.* Carthage, Ill.: Good Apple, 1987, **761**

Russell, Solveig Paulson. *Peanuts, Popcorn, Ice Cream, Candy and Soda Pop, And How They Began.* New York: Abingdon Press, 1970, **762**

Sackson, Sid. *Playing Cards Around the World.* Englewood Cliffs, N.J.: Prentice-Hall, 1981, **1132**

Sadler, Judy Ann. *Christmas Crafts.* Toronto, Canada: Kids Can Press, 1994, **1575**

Sagan, Miriam. *The Middle Atlantic States.* Vero Beach, Fla.: Rourke Publications, 1994, **1576**

Samantha's Cookbook. Middleton, Wis.: Pleasant Company Publications, 1994, **1577**

Samantha's Craft Book. Middleton, Wis.: Pleasant Company Publications, 1994, **1578**

Sanders, Pete. *Safety Guide on the Road.* New York: Gloucester Press, 1989, **763**

Sarin, Anita Vohra. *India, An Ancient Land, a New Nation.* Minneapolis, Minn.: Dillon Press, 1985, **1579**

Sateren, Shelley Swanson. *Canada: Star of the North.* Tarrytown, N.Y.: Marshall Cavendish Corp., 1996, **1580**

Sattler, Helen Roney. *Jar and Bottle Craft.* New York: Lothrop, Lee and Shepard Co., 1974, **764**

Sattler, Helen Roney. *Jewelry from Junk.* New York: Lothrop, Lee and Shepard Co., 1973, **765**

Sattler, Helen Roney. *Kitchen Carton Crafts.* New York: Lothrop, Lee and Shepard Co., 1970, **766**

Sattler, Helen Roney. *Recipes for Art and Craft Materials.* New York: Lothrop, Lee and Shepard Co., 1987, **767**

Sattler, Helen Roney. *Sock Craft Toys, Gifts and Other Things to Make.* New York: Lothrop, Lee and Shepard Co., 1972, **768**

Saunders, Richard. *Horrorgami, Spooky Paperfolding Just for Fun.* New York: Sterling Publishing Co., 1991, **1581**

Saypol, Judyth Robbins. *My Very Own Chanukah Book.* Rockville, Md.: Kar-Ben Copies, 1977, **769**

Saypol, Judyth Robbins. *My Very Own Haggadah.* Rockville, Md.: Kar-Ben Copies, 1983. Rev. ed, **1720**

Schal, Hannelore. *Making Things with Yarn.* Chicago, Ill.: Childrens Press, 1990, **770**

Schal, Hannelore. *Toys Made of Clay.* Chicago, Ill.: Childrens Press, 1989, **771**

Schegger, T. M. *Make Your Own Mobiles.* New York: Sterling Publishing Co., 1965, **772**

Schnacke, Dick. *American Folk Toys, How to Make Them.* Baltimore, Md.: Penguin Books, 1973, **773**

Schnurnberger, Lynn Edelman. *A World of Dolls That You Can Make.* New York: Harper and Row, 1982, **775**

Schnurnberger, Lynn Edelman. *Kings, Queens, Knights and Jesters, Making Medieval Costumes.* New York: Harper and Row, 1978, **774**

Scholz-Peters, Ruth. *Indian Bead Stringing and Weaving.* New York: Sterling Publishing Co., 1975, **776**

Schomp, Virginia. *Russia: New Freedoms, New Challenges.* Tarrytown, N.Y.: Marshall Cavendish Corp., 1996, **1582**

Schrepfer, Margaret. *Switzerland, The Summit of Europe.* Minneapolis, Minn.: Dillon Press, 1989, **1133**

Schultz, Kathleen. *Create Your Own Natural Dyes.* New York: Sterling Publications Co., 1975, **777**

Schulz, Charles M. *Charlie Brown's Super Book of Things to Do and Collect.* New York: Random House, 1975, **778**

Schwartz, Linda. *Earth Book for Kids: Activities to Help Heal the Environment.* Santa Barbara, Calif.: The Learning Works, 1990, **1134**

Schwartz, Linda. *The Primary Teacher's Pet.* Santa Barbara, Calif.: The Learning Works, 1984, **779**

Scott, Anne. *The Laughing Baby.* Hadley, Mass.: Bergin and Garvey Publishers, 1987, **780**

Scott, Louise Binder. *Rhymes for Learning Times.* Minneapolis, Minn.: T. S. Denison and Co., 1983, **1583**

Seah, Audrey. *Vietnam.* North Bellmore, N.Y.: Marshall Cavendish Corp., 1993, **1584**

Seasonal Learning Activities. Patty Loring, Compiler. Carthage, Ill.: Good Apple, 1988, **781**

Seasonal Piggyback Songs. Everett, Wash.: Warren Publishing House, 1985, **782**

Sechrist, Elizabeth Hough. *It's Time for Thanksgiving.* Philadelphia, Pa.: Macrae Smith Co., 1957, **783**

Seelig, Tina Lynn. *Incredible Edible Science.* New York: W. H. Freeman and Co., 1994, **1585**

Seidelman, James E. *Creating Mosaics.* New York: Crowell-Collier Press, 1967, **784**

Seidelman, James E. *Creating with Clay.* New York: Crowell-Collier Press, 1967, **785**

Seidelman, James E. *Creating with Paint.* New York: Crowell-Collier Press, 1967, **786**

Seidelman, James E. *Creating with Paper.* New York: Crowell-Collier Press, 1967, **787**

Seidelman, James E. *Creating with Papier-Mache.* New York: Macmillan Publishing Co., 1971, **788**

Seidelman, James E. *Creating with Wood.* New York: Crowell-Collier Press, 1969, **789**

Seidelman, James E. *Shopping Cart Art.* New York: Crowell-Collier Press, Macmillan Co., 1970, **790**

Sensier, Danielle. *Costumes.* New York: Thomson Learning, 1994, **1586**

Sernaque, Vivienne. *Classic Children's Games.* New York: Dell Publishing Co., 1988, **791**

Seward, Pat. *Morocco.* North Bellmore, N.Y.: Marshall Cavendish Corp., 1995, **1587**

Seward, Pat. *Netherlands.* North Bellmore, N.Y.: Marshall Cavendish Corp., 1995, **1588**

Shalant, Phyllis. *Look What We've Brought You From Mexico.* New York: Julian Messner, 1992, **1589**

Shalant, Phyllis. *Look What We've Brought You from Vietnam.* New York: Julian Messner, 1988, **792**

Shapiro, Rebecca. *A Whole World of Cooking.* Boston: Little, Brown and Co., 1972, **793**

Shapiro, Rebecca. *Wide World Cookbook.* Boston: Little, Brown and Co., 1962, **794**

Sharman, Rod. *Bookcrafts for Children.* Monroe, N.Y.: Trillium Press, 1988, **1590**

Sheehan, Sean. *Cambodia.* Tarrytown, N.Y.: Marshall Cavendish Corp., 1996, **1591**

Sheehan, Sean. *Cuba.* Tarrytown, N.Y.: Marshall Cavendish Corp., 1994, **1592**

Sheehan, Sean. *Jamaica.* North Bellmore, N.Y.: Marshall Cavendish Corp., 1994, **1593**

Sheehan, Sean. *Lebanon.* Tarrytown, N.Y.: Marshall Cavendish Corp., 1997, **1594**

Sheehan, Sean. *Pakistan.* North Bellmore, N.Y.: Marshall Cavendish Corp., 1994, **1595**

Sheehan, Sean. *Romania.* North Bellmore, N.Y.: Marshall Cavendish Corp., 1994, **1596**

Sheehan, Sean. *Turkey.* North Bellmore, N.Y.: Marshall Cavendish Corp., 1993, **1597**

Sheehan, Sean. *Zimbabwe.* North Bellmore, N.Y.: Marshall Cavendish Corp., 1993, **1598**

Sherrow, Victoria. *Huskings, Quiltings, and Barn Raisings: Work-Play Parties in Early America.* New York: Walker Publishing Co., Inc., 1992, **1600**

Sherrow, Victoria. *The Hopis: Pueblo People of the Southwest.* Brookfield, Conn.: The Millbrook Press, 1993, **1599**

Sherrow, Victoria. *The Nez Perces: People of the Far West.* Brookfield, Conn.: The Millbrook Press, 1994, **1601**

Shoemaker, Kathryn E. *Creative Christmas, Simple Crafts from Many Lands.* Minneapolis, Minn.: Winston Press, 1978, **795**

Short-Short Stories. Jean Warren, comp. Everett, Wash.: Warren Publishing, 1987, **1135**

Shreckhise, Roseva. *What Was It before It Was My Sweater?* Elgin, Ill.: Child's World, 1985, **796**

Shui, Amy. *Chinese Food and Drink.* New York: The Bookwright Press, 1987, **797**

Siegel, Alice. *Herb and Spice Book for Kids.* New York: Holt, Rinehart and Winston, 1978, **798**

Sierra, Judy. *Fantastic Theater.* New York: The H. W. Wilson Co., 1991, **1602**

Sierra, Judy. *Multicultural Folktales.* Phoenix, Ariz.: Oryx Press, 1991, **1604**

Sierra, Judy. *The Flannel Board Storytelling Book.* New York: The H. W. Wilson Co., 1987, **1603**

Silverman, Maida. *Festival of Freedom, The Story of Passover.* New York: Simon and Schuster, 1988, **799**

Silverstein, Alvin. *Apples, All About Them.* Englewood Cliffs, N.J.: Prentice-Hall, 1976, **800**

Silverstein, Alvin. *Potatoes, All About Them.* Englewood Cliffs, N.J.: Prentice-Hall, 1976, **801**

Silverthorne, Elizabeth. *Fiesta: Mexico's Great Celebrations.* Brookfield, Conn.: The Millbrook Press, 1992, **1605**

Simmonds, Patricia. *Nursery Rhyme Programs for Toddlers.* Piscataway, N.J.: Union Middlesex Regional Library Cooperative, 1988, **802**

Simmons, John. *Carpentry Is Easy When You Know How.* New York: Arco Publishing Co., 1974, **803**

Simon, Nancy. *American Indian Habitats, How to Make Dwellings and Shelters with Natural Materials.* New York: David McKay Co., 1978, **804**

Simons, Robin. *Recyclopedia.* Boston: Houghton Mifflin Co., 1976, **805**

Sita, Lisa. *The Rattle and the Drum: Native American Rituals and Celebrations.* Brookfield, Conn.: The Millbrook Press, 1994, **1606**

16 Classic American Recipes and the Stories of How They Began. Avery Island, La.: McIlhenny Co., [198-], **155**

Skinner, Michael Kingsley. *How to Make Rubbings.* New York: Van Nostrand Reinhold Co., 1972, **806**

Skip Across the Ocean: Nursery Rhymes from Around the World. New York: Orchard Books, 1995, **1607**

Skrepcinski, Denice. *Cody Coyote Cooks!: A Southwest Cookbook for Kids.* Berkeley, Calif.: Tricycle Press, 1996, **1729**

Slade, Richard. *Carton Craft.* New York: S. G. Phillips, 1972, **807**

Slade, Richard. *Modeling in Clay, Plaster and Papier-Mache.* Lothrop, Lee and Shepard Co., 1967, **808**

Smith, Debbie. *Holidays & Festivals Activities.* New York: Crabtree Publishing Co., 1994, **1610**

Smith, Susan. *Happy Birthday.* Lake Oswego, Oreg.: White Pine Press, 1983, **809**

Smith-Baranzini, Marlene. *U.S. Kids History: Book of the New American Nation.* New York: Little Brown and Co., 1995, **1609**

Smith-Baranzini, Marlene. *U.S. Kids History: Book of the American Indians.* New York: Little, Brown and Co., 1994, **1608**

Smoothey, Marion. *Let's Investigate Codes and Sequences.* North Bellmore, N.Y.: Marshall Cavendish Corp., 1995, **1611**

Snelling, John. *Buddhist Festivals.* Vero Beach, Fla.: Rourke Enterprises, 1987, **810**

Snook, Barbara. *Making Masks for School Plays.* Boston: Plays, 1972, **811**

Snowball, Marilyn. *Preschool Pack Rat.* Santa Barbara, Calif.: Learning Works, 1982, **812**

Soleillant, Claude. *Activities & Projects: India in Color.* New York: Sterling Publishing Co., 1977, **813**

Soleillant, Claude. *Activities & Projects: Japan in Color.* New York: Sterling Publishing Co., 1980, **814**

Soleillant, Claude. *Activities & Projects: Mexico in Color.* New York: Sterling Publishing Co., 1977, **815**

Solga, Kim. *Draw.* Cincinnati, Oh.: North Light Books, 1991, **1612**

Solga, Kim. *Make Cards.* Cincinnati, Oh.: North Light Books, 1992, **1613**

Solga, Kim. *Make Clothes Fun!* Cincinnati, Oh.: North Light Books, 1991, **1614**

Solga, Kim. *Make Crafts.* Cincinnati, Oh.: North Light Books, 1993, **1615**

Solga, Kim. *Make Gifts.* Cincinnati, Oh.: North Light Books, 1991, **1616**

Solga, Kim. *Make Prints.* Cincinnati, Oh.: North Light Books, 1991, **1617**

Solga, Kim. *Make Sculptures.* Cincinnati, Oh.: North Light Books, 1992, **1618**

Solga, Kim. *Paint.* Cincinnati, Oh.: North Light Books, 1991, **1619**

Sommer, Elyse. *Designing with Cutouts, The Art of Decoupage.* New York: Lothrop, Lee and Shepard Co., 1973, **817**

Sommer, Elyse. *Make It with Burlap.* New York: Lothrop, Lee and Shepard Co., 1973, **818**

Sommer, Elyse. *The Bread Dough Craft Book.* New York: Lothrop, Lee and Shepard Co., 1972, **816**

Special Holiday Handbook. Elgin, Ill.: Child's World, 1986, **819**

Sproule, Anna. *British Food and Drink.* New York: The Bookwright Press, 1988, **820**

Sproule, Anna. *Great Britain, the Land and Its People.* Morristown, N.J.: Silver Burdett Press, 1987, **1620**

Stamper, Judith Bauer. *Thanksgiving Holiday Grab Bag.* Mahway, N.J.: Troll Associates, 1993, **1621**

Stangl, Jean. *Fingerlings.* Belmont, Calif.: David S. Lake Publishers, 1986, **821**

Stangl, Jean. *Flannel Graphs.* Belmont, Calif.: David S. Lake Publishers, 1986, **822**

Stangl, Jean. *Hats, Hats and More Hats.* Belmont, Calif.: David S. Lake Publishers, 1989, **823**

Stangl, Jean. *Magic Mixtures, Creative Fun for Little Ones.* Belmont, Calif.: David S. Lake Publishers, 1986, **824**

Staples, Danny. *Flutes, Reeds and Trumpets.* Brookfield, Conn.: The Millbrook Press, 1992, **1622**

Stapleton, Marjorie. *Make Things Sailors Made.* New York: Taplinger Publishing Co., 1975, **825**

Stark, Al. *Australia: A Lucky Land.* Minneapolis, Minn.: Dillon Press, 1987, **1136**

Stark, Al. *Zimbabwe, A Treasure of Africa.* Minneapolis, Minn.: Dillon Press, 1986, **1137**

Stavreva, Kirilka. *Bulgaria.* Tarrytown, N.Y.: Marshall Cavendish Corp., 1997, **1623**

Steele, Philip. *Festivals Around the World.* Minneapolis, Minn.: Dillon Press, 1986, **826**

Steele, Philip. *Food & Feasts Between the Two World Wars.* New York: New Discovery Books, 1994, **1624**

Steele, Philip. *Food & Feasts in Ancient Rome.* New York: Macmillan Publishing Co., 1994, **1625**

Stokes, Jack. *Let's Make a Tent.* New York: David McKay Co., 1979, **827**

Stone, Anne. *Paper Straw Craft.* New York: Sterling Publishing Co., 1974, **828**

Stoppleman, Monica. *Jewish.* Danbury, Conn.: Childrens Press, 1995, **1626**

Streb, Judith. *Holiday Parties.* New York: Franklin Watts, 1985, **829**

String, Raffia and Materials. New York: Franklin Watts, 1971, **830**

Strobell, Adah Parker. *Like It Was, Bicentennial Games 'N Fun Handbook.* Washington, D.C.: Acropolis Books, Ltd., 1975, **831**

Strose, Susanne. *Making Paper Flowers.* New York: Sterling Publishing Co., 1972, **832**

Sturner, Fred. *What Did You Do When You Were a Kid?* New York: St. Martin's Press, 1973, **833**

Suid, Anna. *Constructions.* Palo Alto, Calif.: Monday Morning Books, 1987, **834**

Suid, Anna. *Holiday Crafts.* Palo Alto, Calif.: Monday Morning Books, 1985, **835**

Suid, Murray. *Book Factory.* Palo Alto, Calif.: Monday Morning Books, 1988, **836**

Suid, Murray. *Greeting Cards.* Palo Alto, Calif.: Monday Morning Books, 1988, **837**

Sullivan, Debbie. *Pocketful of Puppets.* Activities for the Special Child. Austin, Tx.: Nancy Renfro Studios, 1982, **838**

Sullivan, Dianna J. *Let's Pretend, Career Costumes.* Sunset Beach, Calif.: Teacher Created Materials, 1986, **839**

Sullivan, Dianna J. *Let's Pretend, Masks.* Sunset Beach, Calif.: Teacher Created Materials, 1986, **840**

Sullivan, Dianna J. *Let's Pretend, Nursery Rhyme Costumes.* Sunset Beach, Calif.: Teacher Created Materials, 1986, **841**

Sullivan, Dianna J. *Let's Pretend, Seasonal Costumes.* Sunset Beach, Calif.: Teacher Created Materials, 1986, **842**

Sullivan, Emilie P. *Starting with Books!* Englewood, Colo.: Libraries Unlimited, 1990, **843**

Sullivan, Margaret. *The Philippines: Pacific Crossroads.* New York: Dillon Press, 1993, **1627**

Sullivan, S. Adams. *Bats, Butterflies and Bugs.* Boston: Little, Brown and Co., 1990, **1138**

Supraner, Robyn. *Fun with Paper.* Mahwah, N.J.: Troll Associates, 1981, **845**

Supraner, Robyn. *Fun-to-Make Nature Crafts.* Mahwah, N.J.: Troll Associates, 1981, **844**

Supraner, Robyn. *Great Masks to Make.* Mahwah, N.J.: Troll Associates, 1981, **846**

Supraner, Robyn. *Happy Halloween, Things to Make and Do.* Mahwah, N.J.: Troll Associates, 1981, **847**

Supraner, Robyn. *Merry Christmas! Things to Make and Do.* Mahwah, N.J.: Troll Associates, 1981, **848**

Supraner, Robyn. *Rainy Day Surprises You Can Make.* Mahwah, N.J.: Troll Associates, 1981, **849**

Supraner, Robyn. *Valentine's Day, Things to Make and Do.* Mahwah, N.J.: Troll Associates, 1981, **850**

Tabs, Judy. *Matzah Meals.* Rockville, Md.: Kar-Ben Copies, 1985, **851**

Taitz, Emily. *Israel, A Sacred Land.* Minneapolis, Minn.: Dillon Press, 1987, **1139**

Takeshita, Jiro. *Food in Japan.* Vero Beach, Fla.: Rourke Publications, 1989, **852**

Tames, Richard. *Food: Feasts, Cooks & Kitchens.* New York: Franklin Watts, 1994, **1721**

Tames, Richard. *Great Britain.* New York: Franklin Watts, 1994, **1628**

Tames, Richard. *Japan.* New York: Franklin Watts, 1994, **1629**

Tames, Richard. *Muslim.* New York: Childrens Press, 1996, **1722**

Tan, Jennifer. *Food in China.* Vero Beach, Fla.: Rourke Publications, 1989, **853**

Tavlarios, Irene. *Greek Food and Drink.* New York: The Bookwright Press, 1988, **854**

Taylor, Barbara. *Create Your Own Magazine.* New York: Sterling Publishing Co., 1993, **1630**

Taylor, Barbara. *Sound and Music.* New York: Warwick Press, 1990, **1631**

Temko, Florence. *Folk Crafts for World Friendship.* Garden City, N.Y.: Doubleday and Co., 1976, **856**

Temko, Florence. *Paper Cutting.* Garden City, N.Y.: Doubleday and Co., 1973, **857**

Temko, Florence. *The Big Felt Burger.* Garden City, N.Y.: Doubleday and Co., 1977, **855**

Temko, Florence. *Traditional Crafts from Africa.* Minneapolis, Minn.: Lerner Publications Co., 1996, **1632**

Temko, Florence. *Traditional Crafts from Mexico and Central America.* Minneapolis, Minn.: Lerner Publications Co., 1996, **1730**

Terzian, Alexandra M. *The Kids' Multicultural Art Book: Art & Craft Experiences from Around the World.* Charlotte, Vt.: Williamson Publishing Co., 1993, **1633**

Tharlet, Eve. *The Little Cooks: Recipes from Around the World.* New York: UNICEF, 1980, **858**

Things You'll Never Have to Draw Again. Minneapolis, Minn.: Judy/Instructo, 1985, **859**

Thompson, Helen Davis. *Let's Celebrate Kwanzaa.* New York: Gumbs & Thomas Publishers, 1992, **1634**

Thomson, Neil. *Fairground Games to Make and Play.* New York: J. B. Lippincott Co., 1977, **860**

Thomson, Ruth. *Autumn.* New York: Franklin Watts, 1989, **861**

Thomson, Ruth. *Aztecs.* New York: Franklin Watts, 1993, **1635**

Thomson, Ruth. *Exciting Things to Make with Paper.* New York: J. B. Lippincott Co., 1977, **862**

Thomson, Ruth. *Indians of the Plains.* New York: Franklin Watts, 1991, **1636**

Thomson, Ruth. *Rice.* Ada, Okla.: Garrett Educational Corp., 1990, **1637**

Thomson, Ruth. *Spring.* New York: Franklin Watts, 1990, **863**

Thomson, Ruth. *Summer.* New York: Franklin Watts, 1990, **864**

Thomson, Ruth. *Winter.* New York: Franklin Watts, 1989, **865**

Thorne-Thomsen, Kathleen. *Frank Lloyd Wright for Kids: His Life and Ideas.* Chicago, Ill.: Chicago Review Press, 1994, **1638**

Thorne-Thomsen, Kathleen. *Shaker Children.* Chicago, Ill.: Chicago Review Press, 1996, **1639**

Thorpe, Anne. *Cooking for Fun.* London, England: Tiger Books International, 1980, **866**

Tichenor, Tom. *Christmas Tree Crafts.* New York: J. B. Lippincott Co., 1975, **867**

Tichenor, Tom. *Folk Plays for Puppets You Can Make.* New York: Abingdon Press, 1959, **868**

Tilgner, Linda. *Let's Grow: 72 Gardening Adventures.* Pownal, Vt.: Storey Communications, 1988, **869**

Tofts, Hannah. *The 3-D Paper Book.* New York: Simon and Schuster, 1989, **1141**

Tofts, Hannah. *The Paint Book.* New York: Simon & Schuster, 1990, **1640**

Tofts, Hannah. *The Paper Book.* New York: Simon and Schuster, 1989, **1140**

Tofts, Hannah. *The Print Book.* New York: Simon & Schuster, 1990, **1641**

Tompkins, Julia. *Easy-to-Make Costumes for Stage and School.* Boston: Plays, 1975, **870**

Torchinsky, Oleg. *Russia.* North Bellmore, N.Y.: Marshall Cavendish Corp., 1994, **1642**

Torre, Betty L. *It's Easy to Cook.* Garden City, N.Y.: Doubleday and Co., 1977, **871**

Travers, P. L. *Mary Poppins in the Kitchen: A Cookery Book with a Story*. New York: Harcourt Brace Jovanovich, 1975, **1643**

Treat, Rose. *The Seaweed Book: How to Find and Have Fun with Seaweed*. New York: Star Bright Books, 1995, **1644**

True, Susan. *Nursery Rhyme Crafts*. Palo Alto, Calif.: Monday Morning Books, 1985, **872**

Tunnacliffe, Chantal. *France*. Morristown, N.J.: Silver Burdett Press, 1987, **1645**

Turner, Dorothy. *Bread*. Minneapolis, Minn.: Carolrhoda Books, 1989, **1142**

Turner, Dorothy. *Eggs*. Minneapolis, Minn.: Carolrhoda Books, 1989, **1143**

Turner, Dorothy. *Milk*. Minneapolis, Minn.: Carolrhoda Books, 1989, **1144**

Turner, Dorothy. *Potatoes*. Minneapolis, Minn.: Carolrhoda Books, 1988, **1145**

Turner, Jessica Baron. *Let's Make Music! Multicultural Songs and Activities*. Milwaukee, Wis.: Hal Leonard Corp., 1994, **1646**

Tythacott, Louise. *Dance*. New York: Thomson Learning, 1995, **1647**

Tythacott, Louise. *Jewelry*. New York: Thomson Learning, 1995, **1648**

Tythacott, Louise. *Musical Instruments*. New York: Thomson Learning, 1995, **1649**

Urbanski, Gail. *Lenten Activities for the Family*. Kansas City, Mo.: Sheed and Ward, 1985, **873**

Van des Linde, Polly. *Around the World in 80 Dishes*. New York: Scroll Press, 1971, **874**

Van Ryzin, Lani. *A Patch of Earth*. New York: Julian Messner, 1981, **875**

Van Ryzin, Lani. *Sidewalk Games*. Milwaukee, Wisc.: Raintree Publishers Limited, 1978, **1146**

Vaughan, Marcia. *How to Cook a Gooseberry Fool*. Minneapolis, Minn.: Lerner Publications Co., 1993, **1650**

Vecchione, Glen. *The World's Best Street & Yard Games*. New York: Sterling Publishing Co., 1989, **876**

Vecchione, Glen. *World's Best Outdoor Games*. New York: Sterling Publishing Co., 1992, **1651**

Vegetarian Cooking Around the World. Minneapolis, Minn.: Lerner Publications Co., 1992, **1652**

Veitch, Beverly. *Cook and Learn*. Reading, Mass.: Addison-Wesley Publishing Co., 1981, **1653**

Venture into Cultures: A Resource Book of Multicultural Materials and Programs. Chicago, Ill.: American Library Association, 1992, **1654**

Vermeer, Jackie. *The Little Kid's Americana Craft Book*. New York: Taplinger Publishing Co., 1975, **877**

Vermeer, Jackie. *The Little Kid's Craft Book*. New York: Taplinger Publishing Co., 1973, **878**

Villiard, Paul. *Jewelry Making*. Garden City, N.Y.: Doubleday and Co., 1973, **879**

Villios, Lynne W. *Cooking the Greek Way*. Minneapolis, Minn.: Lerner Publications Co., 1984, **880**

Voorst, Dick. *Corrugated Carton Crafting*. New York: Sterling Publishing Co., 1971, **881**

Wagner, Lee. *How to Have Fun Making Easter Decorations*. Mankato, Minn.: Creative Education, 1974, **882**

Wagner, Lee. *How to Have Fun Making Holiday Decorations*. Mankato, Minn.: Creative Education, 1974, **883**

Wake, Susan. *Butter*. Minneapolis, Minn.: Carolrhoda Books, 1989, **1147**

Wake, Susan. *Citrus Fruits*. Minneapolis, Minn.: Carolrhoda Books, 1990, **1655**

Wake, Susan. *Vegetables*. Minneapolis, Minn.: Carolrhoda Books, 1990, **1148**

Waldee, Lynne Marie. *Cooking the French Way*. Minneapolis, Minn.: Lerner Publications Co., 1982, **884**

Walker, Barbara M. *The Little House Cookbook*. New York: Harper and Row Publishers, 1979, **885**

Walker, Lester. *Carpentry for Children*. Woodstock, N.Y.: The Overlook Press, 1982, **886**

Walker, Mark. *Creative Costumes for Any Occasion*. Cockeysville, Md.: Liberty Publishing Co., 1984, **887**

Walker, Mark. *Creative Costumes for Children (Without Sewing)*. Boca Raton, Fla.: Cool Hand Communications, 1993, **1656**

Walter, F. Virginia. *Fun with Paper Bags and Cardboard Tubes*. New York: Sterling Publishing Co., 1992, **1657**

Walter, F. Virginia. *Great Newspaper Crafts*. New York: Sterling Publishing Co., 1991, **1658**

Walter, Mildred Pitts. *Kwanzaa: A Family Affair*. New York: Lothrop, Lee & Shepard, 1995, **1659**

Walther, Tom. *Make Mine Music*. Boston: Little, Brown and Co., 1981, **888**

Waltner, Willard. *A New Look at Old Crafts*. Mt. Vernon, N.Y.: Lantern Press, 1971, **893**

Waltner, Willard. *Hobbycraft Around the World*. New York: Lantern Press, 1966, **889**

Waltner, Willard. *Hobbycraft Toys & Games*. New York: Lantern Press, 1965, **890**

Waltner, Willard. *Holiday Hobbycraft*. New York: Lantern Press, 1964, **891**

Waltner, Willard. *The New Hobbycraft Book*. New York: Lantern Press, 1963, **892**

Waltner, Willard. *Year Round Hobbycraft*. New York: Lantern Press, 1968, **894**

Wanamaker, Nancy. *More Than Graham Crackers*. Washington, D.C.: National Association for Education of Young Children, 1979, **1660**

Warner, John F. *Colonial American Home Life*. New York: Franklin Watts, 1993, **1661**

Warner, Margaret Brink. *What's Cooking, Recipes from Around the World*. Boston: Little, Brown and Co., 1981, **895**

Warner, Penny. *Happy Birthday Parties*. New York: St. Martins Press, 1985, **896**

Warner, Penny. *Kids' Holiday Fun*. Deephaven, Minn.: Meadowbrook Press, 1994, **1662**

Warren, Jean. *"Cut and Tell" Scissor Stories for Fall*. Everett, Wash.: Totline Press, Warren Publishing House, 1984, **898**

Warren, Jean. *"Cut and Tell" Scissor Stories for Spring*. Everett, Wash.: Totline Press, Warren Publishing House, 1984, **899**

Warren, Jean. *"Cut and Tell" Scissor Stories for Winter*. Everett, Wash.: Totline Press, Warren Publishing House, 1984, **900**

Warren, Jean. *1-2-3 Art.* Everett, Wash.: Warren Publishing House, 1985, **1149**

Warren, Jean. *1-2-3 Books.* Everett, Wash.: Warren Publishing House, 1989, **903**

Warren, Jean. *1-2-3 Colors.* Everett, Wash.: Warren Publishing House, 1988, **904**

Warren, Jean. *1-2-3 Games.* Everett, Wash.: Warren Publishing House, 1986, **905**

Warren, Jean. *1-2-3 Murals.* Everett, Wash.: Warren Publishing House, 1989, **906**

Warren, Jean. *1-2-3 Puppets.* Everett, Wash.: Warren Publishing House, 1989, **907**

Warren, Jean. *Crafts.* Palo Alto, Calif.: Monday Morning Books, 1983, **897**

Warren, Jean. *Exploring Wood and the Forest.* Everett, Wash.: Warren Publishing House, 1993, **1663**

Warren, Jean. *Holiday Piggyback Songs.* Everett, Wash.: Warren Publishing House, 1988, **901**

Warren, Jean. *Huff and Puff on Groundhog Day.* Everett, Wash.: Warren Publishing House, 1995, **1664**

Warren, Jean. *More Piggyback Songs.* Everett, Wash.: Warren Publishing House, 1984, **902**

Warren, Jean. *Piggyback Songs for Infants and Toddlers.* Everett, Wash.: Warren Publishing House, 1985, **908**

Warren, Jean. *Piggyback Songs.* Everett, Wash.: Warren Publishing House, 1983, **1150**

Warren, Jean. *Small World Celebrations.* Everett, Wash.: Warren Publishing House, 1988, **909**

Warren, Jean. *Teeny-Tiny Folktales.* Everett, Wash.: Warren Publishing House, 1987, **910**

Warren, Jean. *Theme-a-Saurus.* Everett, Wash.: Warren Publishing House, 1989, **911**

Water Wonders. Des Moines, Iowa: Better Homes and Gardens, Meredith Corporation, 1989, **1151**

Waterfall, Jarie Lee. *Nursery Crafts.* Atlanta, Ga.: Humanics Learning, 1988, **912**

Waters, Alice. *Fanny at Chez Panisse.* New York: HarperCollins Publishers, 1992, **1665**

Watrous, Merrill K. *Art and Writing Throughout the Year.* Belmont, Calif.: Fearon Teacher Aids, 1989, **1152**

Watson, Jane Werner. *A Parade of Soviet Holidays.* Champaign, Ill.: Garrard Publishing Co., 1974, **914**

Watson, Jane Werner. *India Celebrates.* Champaign, Ill.: Garrard Publishing Co., 1974, **913**

Watson, N. Cameron. *The Little Pigs Puppet Book.* Boston: Little, Brown and Co., 1990, **915**

Webb, Lois Sinaiko. *Holidays of the World Cookbook for Students.* Phoenix, Ariz.: Oryx Press, 1995, **1666**

Webster, Harriet. *Going Places.* New York: Charles Scribner's Sons, 1991, **1153**

Webster, Harriet. *Winter Book.* New York: Charles Scribner's Sons, 1988, **916**

Weil, Lisl. *Santa Claus Around the World.* New York: Holiday House, 1987, **917**

Weimer, Tonja Evetts. *Fingerplays and Action Chants, Volume 1, Animals.* Pittsburgh, Pa.: Pearce-Evetts Publishing, 1986, **918**

Weiss, Ellen. *Things to Make and Do for Christmas.* New York: Franklin Watts, 1980, **919**

Weiss, Harvey. *Carving, How to Carve Wood and Stone.* Reading, Mass.: Addison-Wesley Publishing Co., 1976, **920**

Weiss, Harvey. *Games & Puzzles You Can Make.* New York: Thomas Y. Crowell Co., 1976, **921**

Weiss, Harvey. *Model Buildings and How to Make Them.* New York: Thomas Y. Crowell, 1979, **922**

Weiss, Harvey. *Model Cars and Trucks, and How to Build Them.* New York: Thomas Y. Crowell Co., 1974, **923**

Weiss, Harvey. *Sticks, Spools and Feathers.* Reading, Mass.: Young Scott Books, Addison-Wesley Publishing Co., 1962, **924**

Weiss, Peter. *Balsa Wood Craft.* New York: Lothrop, Lee and Shepard Co., 1972, **925**

Weiss, Peter. *Scrap Wood Craft.* New York: Lothrop, Lee and Shepard Co., 1977, **926**

Wendelin, Karla Hawkins, Ph.D. *Storybook Classrooms.* Atlanta, Ga.: Humanics Limited, 1984, **927**

West, Robin. *Dinosaur Discoveries.* Minneapolis, Minn.: Carolrhoda Books, 1989, **928**

West, Robin. *Far Out, How to Create Your Own Star World.* Minneapolis, Minn.: Carolrhoda Books, 1987, **929**

West, Robin. *My Very Own Halloween: A Book of Cooking and Crafts.* Minneapolis, Minn.: Carolrhoda Books, 1993, **1667**

West, Robin. *My Very Own Mother's Day: A Book of Cooking and Crafts.* Minneapolis, Minn.: Carolrhoda Books, 1996, **1668**

West, Robin. *Paper Circus, How to Create Your Own Circus.* Minneapolis, Minn.: Carolrhoda Books, 1983, **930**

White, Alice. *Performing Toys.* New York: Taplinger Publishing Co., 1970, **931**

Whitney, Alex. *American Indian Clothes and How to Make Them.* New York: David McKay Co., 1979, **932**

Whitney, Alex. *Pads for Pets, How to Make Habitats and Equipment for Small Animals.* New York: David McKay Co., 1977, **933**

Whitney, Alex. *Sports and Games the Indians Gave Us.* New York: David McKay Co., 1977, **934**

Wiese, Kurt. *You Can Write Chinese.* New York: Viking Press, 1945, **935**

Wilcox, Jonathan. *Iceland.* Tarrytown, N.Y.: Marshall Cavendish Corp., 1996, **1669**

Wilder, Laura Ingalls. *My Little House Cookbook.* New York: HarperCollins Publishers, 1996, **1670**

Wilkes, Angela. *Dazzling Disguises and Clever Costumes.* New York: Dorling Kindersley Limited, 1996, **1671**

Wilkes, Angela. *My First Activity Book.* New York: Alfred A. Knopf, 1989, **936**

Wilkins, Marne. *The Long Ago Lake.* New York: Sierra Book Club, Charles Scribner's Sons, 1978, **937**

Wilkinson, Elizabeth. *Making Cents.* Boston: Little, Brown and Co., 1989, **938**

Williams, Barbara. *Cookie Crafts.* New York: Holt, Rinehart and Winston, 1977, **1672**

Williams, Barbara. *Cornzapoppin!* New York: Holt, Rinehart and Winston, 1976, **939**

Williams, De Atna M. *More Paper-Bag Puppets.* Belmont, Calif.: David S. Lake Publishers, 1968, **940**

Williams, De Atna M. *Paper-Bag Puppets.* Belmont, Calif.: Fearon Teacher Aids, 1966, **941**

Williams, J. Alan. *The Kids and Grown-Ups' Toy-Making Book.* New York: William Morrow and Co., 1979, **942**

Williams, Vera B. *It's a Gingerbread House.* New York: William Morrow and Co., 1978, **943**

Willson, Robina Beckles. *Merry Christmas.* Illustrated by Satomi Ichikawa. New York: Philomel Books, 1983, **473**

Wilmes, Liz. *Felt Board Fun.* Elgin, Ill.: Building Block Publications, 1984, **945**

Wilmes, Liz. *Gifts Cards Wraps.* Elgin, Ill.: Building Block Publications, 1987, **946**

Wilmes, Liz. *The Circle Time Book.* Dundee, Ill.: Building Block Publications, 1982, **944**

Wilsher, Jane. *Spices.* Ada, Okla.: Garrett Educational Corp., 1994, **1673**

Wilson, Sue. *I Can Do It.* Newport Beach, Calif.: Quail Street Publishing Co., 1976, **947**

Wilt, Joy. *Game Things.* Waco, Tx.: Creative Resources, 1978, **948**

Wilt, Joy. *Puppet Stages and Props with Pizazz.* Waco, Tx.: Creative Resources, 1977, **949**

Wilt, Joy. *Puppets with Pizazz.* Waco, Tx.: Creative Resources, 1977, **950**

Winer, Yvonne. *Pocketful of Puppets: Three Plump Fish.* Austin, Tx.: Nancy Renfro Studios, 1983, **951**

Wing, Natasha. *Jalapeno Bagels.* New York: Atheneum Books for Young Readers, 1996, **1674**

Winter, Jane Kohen. *Venezuela.* North Bellmore, N.Y.: Marshall Cavendish Corp., 1991, **1675**

Wire, Wood and Cork, Color Crafts. New York: Franklin Watts, 1969, **952**

Wiseman, Ann. *Making Musical Things.* New York: Charles Scribner's Sons, 1979, **953**

Wiseman, Ann. *Making Things.* Boston: Little, Brown and Co., 1973, **954**

Wiseman, Ann. *Making Things, Book 2.* Boston: Little, Brown and Co., 1975, **955**

Wiswell, Phil. *Kid's Games.* Garden City, N.Y.: Doubleday and Co., 1987, **956**

Wittke, Gloria. *Children's Dressing Up, Ideas to Make in a Day.* London, England: Marshall Cavendish Limited, 1987, **957**

Wolff, Diane. *Chinese Writing.* New York: Holt, Rinehart and Winston, 1975, **958**

Wolfson, Evelyn. *American Indian Tools and Ornaments.* New York: David McKay Co., 1981, **960**

Wolfson, Evelyn. *American Indian Utensils.* New York: David McKay Co., 1979, **959**

Wolfson, Evelyn. *The Iroquois: People of the Northeast.* Brookfield, Conn.: The Millbrook Press, 1992, **1676**

Wolfson, Evelyn. *The Teton Sioux: People of the Plains.* Brookfield, Conn.: The Millbrook Press, 1992, **1677**

Wood, Paul W. *Artistry in Stained Glass.* New York: Sterling Publishing Co., 1976, **961**

Woodhouse, Kate. *Life of Animals with Hooves.* Morristown, N.J.: Silver Burdett Co., 1975, **962**

Woodruff, Marie. *Early America in Miniatures: The 18th Century.* New York: Sterling Publishing Co., 1976, **963**

Woods, Geraldine. *Spain, A Shining New Democracy.* Minneapolis, Minn.: Dillon Press, 1987, **1154**

Woodside, Dave. *What Makes Popcorn Pop?* New York: Atheneum, 1980, **964**

Working with Odds and Ends. New York: Franklin Watts, 1974, **965**

Working with Paper, Color Crafts. New York: Franklin Watts, 1969, **966**

World Games and Recipes, The World Association of Girl Guides and Girl Scouts. London, England: The World Bureau, n.d., **967**

Wright, Denise Anton. *One-Person Puppet Plays.* Englewood, Colo.: Libraries Unlimited, 1990, **1155**

Wright, Lois A. *Weathered Wood Craft.* New York: Lothrop, Lee and Shepard Co., 1973, **968**

Wright, Lyndie. *Masks.* New York: Franklin Watts, 1990, **969**

Wright, Lyndie. *Puppets.* New York: Franklin Watts, 1989, **970**

Wright, Lyndie. *Toy Theaters.* New York: Franklin Watts, 1991, **1678**

Wright, Rachel. *Castles.* New York: Franklin Watts, 1992, **1679**

Wright, Rachel. *Egyptians.* New York: Franklin Watts, 1992, **1680**

Wright, Rachel. *Greeks.* New York: Franklin Watts, 1993, **1681**

Wright, Rachel. *Knights.* New York, Franklin Watts, 1992, **1682**

Wright, Rachel. *Pirates.* New York: Franklin Watts, 1991, **1683**

Wright, Rachel. *Vikings.* New York: Franklin Watts, 1992, **1684**

Wrigley, Elsie. *Soft Toys.* New York: Frederick Warne, 1977, **971**

Wrigley, Elsie. *Wool Toys.* New York: Frederick Warne, 1977, **972**

Wyndham, Lee. *Holidays in Scandinavia.* Champaign, Ill.: Garrard Publishing Co., 1975, **973**

Yerian, Cameron John. *Easy Tricks and Spooky Games.* Chicago, Ill.: Childrens Press, 1975, **974**

Yerian, Cameron John. *For Campers Only.* Chicago, Ill.: Childrens Press, 1975, **975**

Yerian, Cameron John. *Fun Time Codes and Mystery Messages.* Chicago, Ill.: Childrens Press, 1975, **976**

Yerian, Cameron John. *Fun Time Competitive Games.* Chicago, Ill.: Childrens Press, 1974, **977**

Yerian, Cameron John. *Fun Time Sew It! Wear It!* Chicago, Ill.: Childrens Press, 1975, **982**

Yerian, Cameron John. *Fun Time, Gifts for Everybody.* Chicago, Ill.: Childrens Press, 1975, **978**

Yerian, Cameron John. *Fun Time, Group Games.* Chicago, Ill.: Childrens Press, 1974, **979**

Yerian, Cameron John. *Fun Time, Jewelry, Candles and Papercraft.* Chicago, Ill.: Childrens Press, 1974, **980**

Yerian, Cameron John. *Fun Time, Puppets and Shadow Plays.* Chicago, Ill.: Childrens Press, 1974, **981**

Yerian, Cameron John. *Fun Time, Working with Wood.* Chicago, Ill.: Childrens Press, 1975, **983**

Yerian, Cameron John. *Games for 1, 2, or More.* Chicago, Ill.: Childrens Press, 1974, **984**

Yerian, Cameron John. *Handmade Toys and Games.* Chicago, Ill.: Childrens Press, 1975, **985**

Yu, Ling. *Cooking the Chinese Way.* Minneapolis, Minn.: Lerner Publications Co., 1982, **986**

Yue, David. *The Tipi, A Center of Native American Life.* New York: Alfred A. Knopf, 1984, **987**

Yusufali, Jabeen. *Pakistan: An Island Treasury.* Minneapolis, Minn.: Dillon Press, 1990, **1156**

Zaidenburg, Arthur. *How to Draw Costumes and Clothes.* New York; Abelard-Schuman, 1964, **988**

Zalben, Jane Breskin. *Beni's Family Cookbook for the Jewish Holidays.* New York: Henry Holt and Co., 1996, **1685**

Zalben, Jane Breskin. *Beni's First Chanukah.* New York: Henry Holt and Co., 1988, **989**

Zalben, Jane Breskin. *Goldie's Purim.* New York: Henry Holt and Co., 1991, **1157**

Zalben, Jane Breskin. *Happy New Year, Beni.* New York: Henry Holt and Co., 1993, **1686**

Zalben, Jane Breskin. *Happy Passover, Rosie.* New York: Henry Holt and Co., 1990, **1687**

Zamojska-Hutchins, Danuta. *Cooking the Polish Way.* Minneapolis, Minn.: Lerner Publications Co., 1984, **990**

Zaslavsky, Claudia. *Tic Tac Toe.* New York: Thomas Y. Crowell, 1982, **1688**

Zawadzki, Sandra M. *Creactivities.* Carthage, Ill.: Good Apple, 1979, **991**

Ziegler, Sandra. *Our St. Patrick's Day Book.* Elgin, Ill.: The Child's World, 1987, **1689**

Zinkgraf, June. *Spring Surprises.* Carthage, Ill.: Good Apple, 1980, **992**

Zurlo. Tony. *China: The Dragon Awakes.* New York: Dillon Press, 1994, **1690**

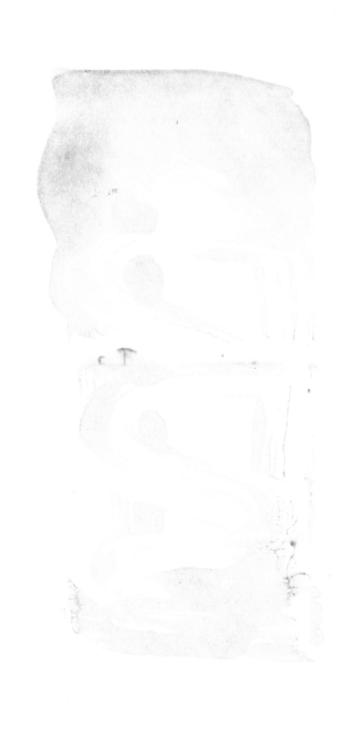